Elementary Statistics
A STEP BY STEP APPROACH

Mc
Graw
Hill

ALLAN G. BLUMAN
PROFESSOR EMERITUS
COMMUNITY COLLEGE OF ALLEGHENY COUNTY

ELEMENTARY STATISTICS: A STEP BY STEP APPROACH, ELEVENTH EDITION

Published by McGraw Hill LLC, 1325 Avenue of the Americas, New York, NY 10019. Copyright ©2023 by McGraw Hill LLC. All rights reserved. Printed in the United States of America. Previous editions ©2018, 2014, 2012. No part of this publication may be reproduced or distributed in any form or by any means, or stored in a database or retrieval system, without the prior written consent of McGraw Hill LLC, including, but not limited to, in any network or other electronic storage or transmission, or broadcast for distance learning.

Some ancillaries, including electronic and print components, may not be available to customers outside the United States.

This book is printed on acid-free paper.

1 2 3 4 5 6 7 8 9 LWI 27 26 25 24 23 22

ISBN 978-1-260-36065-3 (bound edition)
MHID 1-260-36065-2 (bound edition)
ISBN 978-1-260-52503-8 (loose-leaf edition)
MHID 1-260-52503-1 (loose-leaf edition)
ISBN 978-1-260-52514-4 (instructor's edition)
MHID 1-260-52514-7 (instructor's edition)

Product Developer: *Megan Platt*
Marketing Manager: *Emily DiGiovanna*
Content Project Manager: *Jane Mohr*
Buyer: *Sandy Ludovissy*
Content Licensing Specialist: *Lorraine Buczek*
Cover Image: *Design Pics/Alamy Stock Photo*
Compositor: *Aptara®, Inc.*

All credits appearing on page or at the end of the book are considered to be an extension of the copyright page.

Library of Congress Cataloging-in-Publication Data

Names: Bluman, Allan G., author.
Title: Elementary statistics : a step by step approach / Allan G. Bluman,
    Professor Emeritus, Community College of Allegheny County.
Description: Eleventh edition. | New York, NY : McGraw Hill LLC, [2023] |
    Includes index.
Identifiers: LCCN 2022001726 (print) | LCCN 2022001727 (ebook) | ISBN
    9781260360653 (hardcover) | ISBN 9781260525038 (spiral bound) | ISBN
    9781260525144 (hardcover) | ISBN 9781260525281 (ebook)
Subjects: LCSH: Statistics—Textbooks.
Classification: LCC QA276.12 .B585 2023 (print) | LCC QA276.12 (ebook) |
    DDC 519.5—dc23/eng20220521
LC record available at https://lccn.loc.gov/2022001726
LC ebook record available at https://lccn.loc.gov/2022001727

The Internet addresses listed in the text were accurate at the time of publication. The inclusion of a website does not indicate an endorsement by the authors or McGraw Hill LLC, and McGraw Hill LLC does not guarantee the accuracy of the information presented at these sites.

mheducation.com/highered

ABOUT THE AUTHOR

Allan G. Bluman

Allan G. Bluman is a professor emeritus at the Community College of Allegheny County, South Campus, near Pittsburgh, Pennsylvania. He has taught mathematics and statistics for over 35 years. He received an Apple for the Teacher award in recognition of his bringing excellence to the learning environment at South Campus. He has also taught statistics for Penn State University at the Greater Allegheny (McKeesport) Campus and at the Monroeville Center. He received his master's and doctor's degrees from the University of Pittsburgh.

He is also author of *Elementary Statistics: A Brief Version* and he was a coauthor of *Math in Our World*. In addition, he is the author of four mathematics books in the McGraw Hill DeMystified Series. They are *Pre-Algebra, Math Word Problems, Business Math,* and *Probability*.

He is married and has two sons, a granddaughter, and a grandson.

Dedication: *To Betty Bluman, Earl McPeek, and Dr. G. Bradley Seager, Jr.*

CONTENTS

CHAPTER **4**

Probability and
Counting Rules *187*

CHAPTER **5**

Discrete Probability
Distributions *257*

CHAPTER **6**

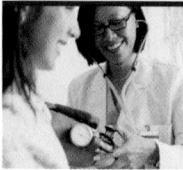

The Normal
Distribution *309*

CHAPTER **7**

Confidence Intervals
and Sample Size *369*

CHAPTER 8

Hypothesis Testing *413*

Photosindia.Com, LLC

CHAPTER 9

Testing the Difference Between Two Means, Two Proportions, and Two Variances *489*

Fuse/Corbis/
Getty Images

CHAPTER 10

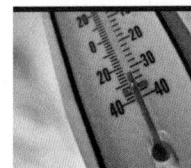

Correlation and Regression *551*

Design Pics Inc./Alamy
Stock Photo

CHAPTER 11

Other Chi-Square Tests *613*

Mitch Hrdlicka/Photodisc/
Getty Images

PREFACE

Approach

Elementary Statistics: A Step by Step Approach was written as an aid in the beginning statistics course to students whose mathematical background is limited to basic algebra. The book follows a nontheoretical approach without formal proofs, explaining concepts intuitively and supporting them with abundant examples. The applications span a broad range of topics certain to appeal to the interests of students of diverse backgrounds, and they include problems in business, sports, health, architecture, education, entertainment, political science, psychology, history, criminal justice, the environment, transportation, physical sciences, demographics, and travel and leisure.

Reflecting the Diverse World Around Us

We believe in unlocking the potential of every learner at every stage of life. To accomplish that, we are dedicated to creating products that reflect, and are accessible to, all the diverse, global customers we serve. Within McGraw Hill, we foster a culture of belonging and we work with partners who share our commitment to equity, inclusion, and diversity in all forms.

The eleventh edition of this text received an extensive and thorough audit to ensure that the examples, applications, and topics referenced throughout support a welcoming and sensitive experience for all learners and uphold McGraw Hill's commitment to equity, inclusion, and diversity.

About This Book

While a number of important changes have been made in the tenth edition, the learning system remains untouched and provides students with a useful framework in which to learn and apply concepts. Some of the retained features include the following:

- Over **1800 exercises** are located at the end of major sections within each chapter.
- **Hypothesis-Testing Summaries** are found at the end of Chapter 9 (z, t, χ^2, and F tests for testing means, proportions, and variances), Chapter 12 (correlation, chi-square, and ANOVA), and Chapter 13 (nonparametric tests) to show students the different types of hypotheses and the types of tests to use.

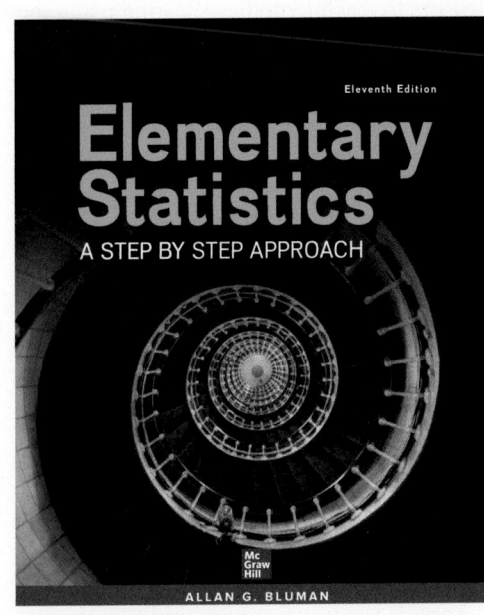

Design Pics/Alamy Stock Photo

- A **Data Bank containing real data** listing various attributes (educational level, cholesterol level, sex, etc.) for 100 people and several additional data sets using real data are included and referenced in various exercises and projects throughout the book.
- An updated **Important Formulas appendix** containing the formulas and the z, t, χ^2, and PPMC tables is included with this textbook.
- End-of-chapter **Summaries, Important Terms,** and **Important Formulas** give students a concise summary of the chapter topics and provide a good source for quiz or test preparation.
- **Review Exercises** are found at the end of each chapter.
- Special sections called **Data Analysis** require students to work with a data set to perform various statistical tests or procedures and then summarize the results. The data are included in the Data Bank in Appendix B.
- **Chapter Quizzes,** found at the end of each chapter, include multiple-choice, true/false, and completion questions along with exercises to test students' knowledge and comprehension of chapter content.
- The **Appendixes** provide students with extensive reference tables, a glossary, and answers to all quiz questions and

odd-numbered exercises. Additional Online Appendixes include algebra review, an outline for report writing, Bayes' theorem, and an alternative method for using the standard normal distribution. These can also be found in the online resources.

- The **Applying the Concepts** feature is included in all sections and gives students an opportunity to think about the new concepts and apply them to examples and scenarios similar to those found in newspapers, magazines, and radio and television news programs.

Changes in the Eleventh Edition

Global Changes

- Replaced over 100 examples with new or updated ones and over 550 new or updated exercises.
- Updated the Technology Tips sections.
- Renumbered statistical tables in the Appendix A.
- Most exercises include the TI answers along with the answers that use the tables in the book.

Chapter Changes

Chapter 1
- New Statistics Today example.
- New statistical examples to introduce how statistics are used today.

Chapter 2
- Updated Statistics Today example.

Chapter 5
- Section 5–3 now includes solving problems using the combination formula in addition to the binomial formula.

Chapters 7, 8, and 9
- These chapters have been revised to allow professors who want to teach proportions before means to do so. They should cover the first sections of these chapters and then skip to the proportions sections, and then do the means sections. For those who prefer to teach means before proportions, just follow the sequence of the book.

Chapters 8, 9, 10, 11, and 12
- These chapters allow professors to teach hypothesis testing using the P-value. It should be noted that some P-values obtained by technology may differ from those in the book since the calculations of P-values depend on the number of decimal places the technology uses to compute the test values.

Chapter 14
- New section on Big Data.

Acknowledgments

It is important to acknowledge the many people whose contributions have gone into the Eleventh Edition of *Elementary Statistics*. Very special thanks are due to Rachel Webb of Portland State University, who updated the Index of Applications, wrote some new exercises, made changes for inclusion and diversity, and updated the technology sections throughout, and to Yolanda Parker of Tarrant County College, who accuracy checked the manuscript.

Finally, at McGraw Hill, thanks to Caroline Celano, Director, Mathematics; Megan Platt, Product Developer; Emily DiGiovanna, Marketing Manager; and Jane Mohr, Lead Content Project Manager.

—Allan G. Bluman

Special thanks for their advice and recommendations for the Eleventh Edition go to:

Luis Beltran, *Miami Dade College, Kendall Campus*
Solomon Willis, *Cleveland Community College*
Nicholas Bianco, *Florida Gulf Coast University*
Larry L. Southard, *Florida Gulf Coast University*
Simon Aman, *Truman College*
Brenda Reed, *Navarro College*
Dr. Toni Kasper, *Bronx Community College (CUNY)*
Adam Molnar, *Oklahoma State University*
H Michael Lueke, *St. Louis Community College*
Shannon Resweber, *Houston Community College*
Stacey Culp, *West Virginia University*
Tracy Leshan, *Baltimore City Community College*
Jose Olivo, *John Jay College*
Christine Davidson, *Suffolk County Community College*
Lisa Crawford, *Piedmont Technical College*
Genesis Alberto, *John Jay College*
Alvin Estrada, *John Jay College*
Petal Sumner, *Baltimore City Community College*
Said Ngobi, *Victor Valley College*
Wesley Anderson, *Northwest Vista College*
Rebecca Head, *Bakersfield College*
Mohamad Ali Salim, *Long Beach City College*

Ryan Kasha, *Valencia College*
Stephen Toner, *Victor Valley College*
Alice Martinez, *El Camino College*
Michael Combs, *Bunker Hill Community College*
Nigie Shi, *Bakersfield College*
Christopher McCarthy, *Borough of Manhattan Community College (CUNY)*
Rachel Repyneck, *Daytona State College*
Benjamin Etgen, *American River College*
Eddie Bishop, *Northwest Vista College*
Jason Samuels, *Borough of Manhattan Community College (CUNY)*
Michael Kaye, *Baltimore City Community College*
Tracy Nguyen, *Citrus College*
Nelson De La Rosa, *Miami Dade College, Kendall Campus*
Robert Fusco, *Broward College*
Bridget Dart, *Suffolk County Community College*
Jae Ki Lee, *Borough of Manhattan Community College (CUNY)*
Kristin Hartford, *Long Beach City College*
Jeffrey Zahnen, *Daytona State College*
Diana Pell, *Riverside City College*

A STEP BY STEP APPROACH

Each chapter begins with an **outline, a list of learning objectives,** and a feature titled **Statistics Today;** in which a real-life problem shows students the relevance of the material. This problem is solved near the end of the chapter using statistical techniques presented in the chapter.

7

Confidence Intervals and Sample Size

Fuse/Getty Images

≡ STATISTICS TODAY

Stress and the College Student

A recent poll conducted by the mtvU/Associated Press found that 85% of college students reported that they experience stress daily. The study said, "It is clear that being stressed is a fact of life on college campuses today."

The study also reports that 74% of students' stress comes from school work, 71% from grades, and 62% from financial woes. The report stated that 2240 undergraduate students were selected and that the poll has a margin of error of ±3.0%.

In this chapter you will learn how to make a true estimate of a parameter, what is meant by the margin of error, and whether or not the sample size was large enough to represent all college students.

See Statistics Today—Revisited at the end of this chapter for more details.

OBJECTIVES

After completing this chapter, you should be able to:

1 Find the confidence interval for the mean when σ is known.

2 Determine the minimum sample size for finding a confidence interval for the mean.

3 Find the confidence interval for the mean when σ is unknown.

4 Find the confidence interval for a proportion.

5 Determine the minimum sample size for finding a confidence interval for a proportion.

6 Find a confidence interval for a variance and a standard deviation.

EXAMPLE 8–6   Cost of College Tuition

A researcher wishes to test the claim that the average cost of tuition and fees at a four-year public college is greater than $5700. She selects a random sample of 36 four-year public colleges and finds the mean to be $5950. The population standard deviation is $659. Is there evidence to support the claim at $\alpha = 0.05$? Use the P-value method.

Source: Based on information from the College Board.

SOLUTION

Step 1   State the hypotheses and identify the claim.

$$H_0: \mu = \$5700 \quad \text{and} \quad H_1: \mu > \$5700 \text{ (claim)}$$

Step 2   Compute the test statistic.

$$z = \frac{\overline{X} - \mu}{\sigma/\sqrt{n}} = \frac{5950 - 5700}{659/\sqrt{36}} = 2.28$$

Step 3   Find the P-value. Using Table A–4 in Appendix A, find the corresponding area under the normal distribution for $z = 2.28$. It is 0.9887. Subtract this value for the area from 1.0000 to find the area in the right tail.

$$1.0000 - 0.9887 = 0.0113$$

Hence, the P-value is 0.0113. (The P-value from the calculator is 0.0114.)

Hundreds of examples with detailed solutions serve as models to help students solve problems on their own. Examples are solved by using a step by step explanation, and illustrations provide a clear display of results.

Procedure Table

Solving Hypothesis-Testing Problems (Traditional Method)

Step 1   State the hypotheses and identify the claim.

Step 2   Find the critical value(s) from the appropriate table in Appendix A.

Step 3   Compute the test statistic.

Step 4   Make the decision to reject or not reject the null hypothesis.

Step 5   Summarize the results.

Numerous **Procedure Tables** summarize processes for students' quick reference.

Critical Thinking sections at the end of each chapter challenge students to apply what they have learned to new situations while deepening conceptual understanding.

Technology Step by Step boxes instruct students how to use Excel, TI-84 Plus graphing calculators, and MINITAB to solve the types of problems covered in the section. Numerous computer or calculator screens are displayed as well as numbered steps.

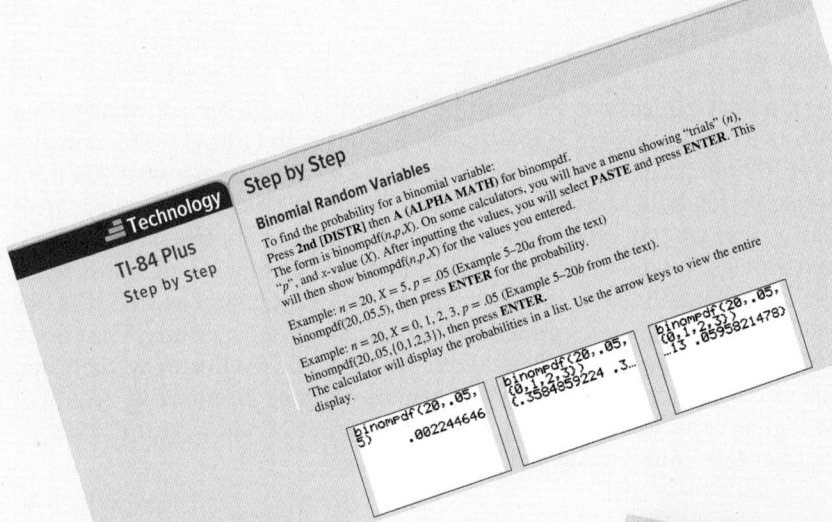

Applying the Concepts are end-of-section exercises that reinforce the concepts explained in the section. They give students an opportunity to think about the concepts and apply them to hypothetical examples similar to real-life ones.

Data Projects, which appear at the end of each chapter, further challenge students' understanding and application of the material presented in the chapter. Many of these require the student to gather, analyze, and report on real data.

SUPPLEMENTS

ALEKS   McGraw Hill ALEKS is a course assistant that helps math and chemistry instructors forge Constructive Learning Paths for their students—blending personalized modules with instructor-driven assignments to ensure every student always has another block to build on their knowledge base. ALEKS gives instructors the flexibility to assign homework, share curated content such as videos, review student progress, and provide student support anytime, anywhere. Instructors can identify what their students know and don't know and, from there, ALEKS will deliver customized practice until they truly get it. In other words, with ALEKS by your side, learning more is a given.

Create
Your Book, Your Way

McGraw Hill's Content Collections Powered by Create® is a self-service website that enables instructors to create custom course materials—print and eBooks—by drawing upon McGraw Hill's comprehensive, cross-disciplinary content. Choose what you want from our high-quality textbooks, articles, and cases. Combine it with your own content quickly and easily, and tap into other rights-secured, third-party content, such as readings, cases, and articles. Content can be arranged in a way that makes the most sense for your course and you can include the course name and information as well. Choose the best format for your course: color print, black-and-white print, or eBook. The eBook can be included in your Connect course and is available on the free ReadAnywhere app for smartphone or tablet access as well. When you are finished customizing, you will receive a free digital copy to review in just minutes! Visit McGraw Hill Create®—**www.mcgrawhillcreate.com**—today and begin building!

TestGen
Computerized Test Bank Online

Among the supplements is a computerized test bank using the algorithm-based testing software TestGen® to create customized exams quickly. Hundreds of text-specific, open-ended, and multiple-choice questions are included in the question bank.

MegaStat®

MegaStat® is a statistical add-in for Microsoft Excel, handcrafted by J. B. Orris of Butler University. When MegaStat is installed, it appears as a menu item on the Excel menu bar and allows you to perform statistical analysis on data in an Excel workbook. The MegaStat plug-in can be purchased at **www.mhhe.com/megastat**.

MINITAB Statistical Software

The student version of MINITAB statistical software is available with copies of the text. Ask your McGraw Hill representative for details.

MINITAB Manual

This manual provides the student with how-to information on data and file management, conducting various statistical analyses, and creating presentation-style graphics while following examples from the text.

TI-84 Plus Graphing Calculator Manual

This friendly, practical manual teaches students to learn about statistics and solve problems by using these calculators while following examples from the text.

Excel Manual

This resource, specially designed to accompany the text, provides additional practice in applying the chapter concepts while using Excel.

Corequisite Workbook

A comprehensive corequisite workbook accompanying this text is available to download in the McGraw Hill resources area of ALEKS.

Guided Student Notes

Guided notes provide instructors with the framework of day-by-day class activities for each section in the book. Each lecture guide can help instructors make more efficient use of class time and can help keep students focused on active learning. Students who use the lecture guides have the framework of well-organized notes that can be completed with the instructor in class.

Lecture and Exercise Videos

Videos address concepts and problem-solving procedures to help students comprehend topics throughout the text. They show students how to work through selected exercises, following methodology employed in the text.

INDEX OF APPLICATIONS

CHAPTER 5
Discrete Probability Distributions

Break down barriers and build student knowledge

Students start your course with varying levels of preparedness. Some will get it quickly. Some won't. ALEKS is a course assistant that helps you meet each student where they are and provide the necessary building blocks to get them where they need to go. You determine the assignments and the content, and ALEKS will deliver customized practice until they truly get it.

Experience The ALEKS Difference

Easily Identify Knowledge Gaps

Gain greater visibility into student performance so you know immediately if your lessons clicked.

- **ALEKS's "Initial Knowledge Check"** helps accurately evaluate student levels and gaps on day one, so you know precisely where students are at and where they need to go when they start your course.

- **You know when students are at risk of falling behind** through ALEKS Insights so, you can remediate – be it through prep modules, practice questions, or written explanations of video tutorials.

- **Students always know where they are**, how they are doing, and can track their own progress easily.

Gain More Flexibility and Engagement

Teach your course your way, with best-in-class content and tools to immerse students and keep them on track.

- **ALEKS gives you flexibility** to assign homework, share a vast library of curated content including videos, review progress and provide student support, anytime anywhere.

- **You save time** otherwise spent performing tedious tasks while having more control over and impact on your students' learning process.

- **Students gain a deeper level of understanding** through interactive and hands-on assignments that go beyond multiple-choice questions.

with ALEKS® Constructive Learning Paths.

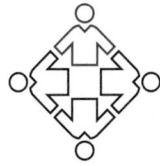

Narrow the Equity Gap

Efficiently and effectively create individual pathways for students without leaving anyone behind.

- **ALEKS creates an equitable experience for all** students, making sure they get the support they need to successfully finish the courses they start.

- **You help reduce attrition,** falling enrollment, and further widening of the learning gap.

- **Student success rates improve** – not just better grades, but better learning.

Count on Hands-on Support

A dedicated Implementation Manager will work with you to build your course exactly the way you want it and your students need it.

- **An ALEKS Implementation Manager** is with you every step of the way through the life of your course.

- **You never have to figure it out on your own** or be your student's customer service. We believe in a consultative approach and take care of all of that for you, so you can focus on your class.

- **Your students benefit** from more meaningful in moments with you, while ALEKS—directed by you—does the rest.

Already benefitting from ALEKS?

Check out our New Enhancements:
mheducation.com/highered/aleks/new-releases.html

The Nature of Probability and Statistics

Monkey Business Images/Shutterstock

≝ STATISTICS TODAY

How Much Do You Owe?

One of the major problems among young people in the United States is that of student loans. Many, many college graduates owe a lot of money that they borrowed to pay for their college educations. Just how big is this problem? In order to examine this problem, we can pose some questions, and then find out the answers.

What is the total amount of loan debt that must be paid back?

How many graduates owe money for college education loans?

How large are student debts?

What is the average debt per graduate?

What is the range of the debts per graduate?

What is the largest concentration in age of the graduates who owe money?

In order to answer these questions and to ascertain how serious the college graduate debt is, we can use statistics. The procedures used to get this information are explained in this chapter. The answers to these questions are found in Statistics Today—Revisited at the end of this chapter.

OUTLINE

OBJECTIVES

After completing this chapter, you should be able to:

❶ Demonstrate knowledge of statistical terms.

❷ Differentiate between the two branches of statistics.

❸ Identify types of data.

❹ Identify the measurement level for each variable.

❺ Identify the four basic sampling techniques.

❻ Explain the difference between an observational and an experimental study.

❼ Explain how statistics can be used and misused.

❽ Explain the importance of computers and calculators in statistics.

Introduction

You may be familiar with probability and statistics through radio, television, newspapers, magazines, and the Internet. For example, you may have read statements like the following found on social media.

> If you work indoors, you need to work out 30 minutes longer to get the same benefits of working outdoors.
>
> *Source: WebMD*

A study by Wayne State University found that older drivers are much worse than younger drivers when texting while driving.

A bipolar disorder results in, on average, 9.2 years' reduction in the expected life span of those who have the disorder as compared to those who do not suffer from this disorder.

A recent study found that people who are in a close relationship may have a lower risk of heart disease than those who are in a negative relationship.

A survey by Cengage found that 43% of college students say that they have skipped meals in order to afford the cost of college course materials.

Forty-nine percent of U.S. adults think that they could become a victim of identity theft.

Source: Experian Identity Works Survey

Statistics is used in almost all fields of human endeavor. In sports, for example, a statistician may keep records of the number of yards a running back gains during a football game, or the number of hits a baseball player gets in a season. In other areas, such as public health, an administrator might be concerned with the number of residents who contract a new strain of flu virus during a certain year. In education, a researcher might want to know if new methods of teaching are better than old ones. These are only a few examples of how statistics can be used in various occupations.

Furthermore, statistics is used to analyze the results of surveys and as a tool in scientific research to make decisions based on controlled experiments. Other uses of statistics include operations research, quality control, estimation, and prediction.

> **Statistics** is the science of conducting studies to collect, organize, summarize, analyze, and draw conclusions from data.

There are several reasons why you should study statistics.

1. Like professional people, you must be able to read and understand the various statistical studies performed in your fields. To have this understanding, you must be knowledgeable about the vocabulary, symbols, concepts, and statistical procedures used in these studies.

2. You may be called on to conduct research in your field, since statistical procedures are basic to research. To accomplish this, you must be able to design experiments; collect, organize, analyze, and summarize data; and possibly make reliable predictions or forecasts for future use. You must also be able to communicate the results of the study in your own words.

3. You can also use the knowledge gained from studying statistics to become better consumers and citizens. For example, you can make intelligent decisions about what products to purchase based on consumer studies, about government spending based on utilization studies, and so on.

It is the purpose of this chapter to introduce the goals for studying statistics by answering questions such as the following:

What are the branches of statistics?

What are data?

How are samples selected?

1–1   Descriptive and Inferential Statistics

To gain knowledge about seemingly haphazard situations, statisticians collect information for *variables*, which describe the situation.

> A **variable** is a characteristic or attribute that can assume different values.

Data are the values (measurements or observations) that the variables can assume. Variables whose values are determined by chance are called **random variables.**

Suppose that an insurance company studies its records over the past several years and determines that, on average, 3 out of every 100 automobiles the company insured were involved in accidents during a 1-year period. Although there is no way to predict the specific automobiles that will be involved in an accident (random occurrence), the company can adjust its rates accordingly, since the company knows the general pattern over the long run. (That is, on average, 3% of the insured automobiles will be involved in an accident each year.)

A collection of data values forms a **data set.** Each value in the data set is called a **data value** or a **datum.**

In statistics it is important to distinguish between a sample and a population.

> A **population** consists of all subjects (human or otherwise) that are being studied.

When data are collected from every subject in the population, it is called a *census*.

For example, every 10 years the United States conducts a census. The primary purpose of this census is to determine the apportionment of the seats in the House of Representatives.

The first census was conducted in 1790 and was mandated by Article 1, Section 2 of the Constitution. As the United States grew, the scope of the census also grew. Today the U.S. Census limits questions to populations, housing, manufacturing, agriculture, and mortality. The U.S. Census is conducted by the Bureau of the Census, which is part of the Department of Commerce.

Most of the time, due to the expense, time, size of population, medical concerns, etc., it is not possible to use the entire population for a statistical study; therefore, researchers use samples.

> A **sample** is a group of subjects selected from a population.

If the subjects of a sample are properly selected, most of the time they should possess the same or similar characteristics as the subjects in the population. See Figure 1–1.

However, the information obtained from a statistical sample is said to be *biased* if the results from the sample of a population are radically different from the results of a census of the population. Also, a sample is said to be biased if it does not represent the population from which it has been selected. The techniques used to properly select a sample are explained in Section 1–3.

The body of knowledge called statistics is sometimes divided into two main areas, depending on how data are used. The two areas are

1. Descriptive statistics

2. Inferential statistics

> **Descriptive statistics** consists of the collection, organization, summarization, and presentation of data.

In *descriptive statistics* the statistician tries to describe a situation. Consider the national census conducted by the U.S. government every 10 years. Results of this census give you the average age, income, and other characteristics of the U.S. population. To obtain this information, the Census Bureau must have some means to collect relevant data. Once data are collected, the bureau must organize and summarize them. Finally, the bureau needs a means of presenting the data in some meaningful form, such as charts, graphs, or tables.

FIGURE 1–1

Population and Sample

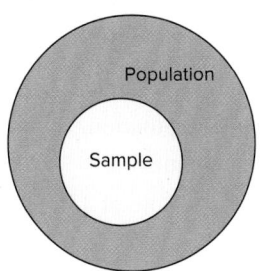

The second area of statistics is called *inferential statistics*.

> **Inferential statistics** consists of generalizing from samples to populations, performing estimations and hypothesis tests, determining relationships among variables, and making predictions.

Historical Note

Inferential statistics originated in the 1600s, when John Graunt published his book on population growth, *Natural and Political Observations Made upon the Bills of Mortality*. About the same time, another mathematician/astronomer, Edmond Halley, published the first complete mortality tables. (Insurance companies use mortality tables to determine life insurance rates.)

Here, the statistician tries to make inferences from *samples* to *populations*. Inferential statistics uses **probability,** i.e., the chance of an event occurring. You may be familiar with the concepts of probability through various forms of gambling. If you play cards, dice, bingo, or lotteries, you win or lose according to the laws of probability. Probability theory is also used in the insurance industry and other areas.

The area of inferential statistics called **hypothesis testing** is a decision-making process for evaluating claims about a population, based on information obtained from samples. For example, a researcher may wish to know if a new drug will reduce the number of heart attacks in men over age 70 years of age. For this study, two groups of men over age 70 would be selected. One group would be given the drug, and the other would be given a placebo (a substance with no medical benefits or harm). Later, the number of heart attacks occurring in each group of men would be counted, a statistical test would be run, and a decision would be made about the effectiveness of the drug.

Statisticians also use statistics to determine *relationships* among variables. For example, relationships were the focus of the most noted study in the 20th century, "Smoking and Health," published by the Surgeon General of the United States in 1964. He stated that after reviewing and evaluating the data, his group found a definite relationship between smoking and lung cancer. He did not say that cigarette smoking actually causes lung cancer, but that there is a relationship between smoking and lung cancer. This conclusion was based on a study done in 1958 by Hammond and Horn. In this study, 187,783 men were observed over a period of 45 months. The death rate from lung cancer in this group of volunteers was 10 times as great for smokers as for nonsmokers.

Finally, by studying past and present data and conditions, statisticians try to make predictions based on this information. For example, a car dealer may look at past sales records for a specific month to decide what types of automobiles and how many of each type to order for that month next year.

Unusual Stat

Twenty-nine percent of Americans want their boss's job.

EXAMPLE 1–1   Descriptive or Inferential Statistics

Determine whether descriptive or inferential statistics were used.

 a. A study of 5000 diners found that people who used a menu printed with calorie counts for meals reduced their caloric consumption by 45 calories per meal.

Source: National Bureau of Economic Research

 b. One person in seven has diabetes and one-third of them don't know that they have the disorder.

Source: WebMD

 c. Twenty million Americans are living with chronic pain that interferes with their daily lives.

Source: CDC

 d. When 1350 children got booster shots or vaccines with unpleasant side effects, only 215 got the same reactions as they did when they got the first injections.

Source: The Pediatric Infectious Disease Journal

SOLUTION

 a. This is a descriptive statistic since it describes the results of a study using 5000 diners.

 b. This is an inferential statistic since it is a generalization about a population.

 c. This is an inferential statistic since it is a generalization about a population.

 d. This is a descriptive statistic since it is based on the results of a sample of 1300 children.

≡ Applying the Concepts 1–1

Attendance and Grades

Read the following on attendance and grades, and answer the questions.

    A study conducted at Manatee Community College revealed that students who attended class 95 to 100% of the time usually received an A in the class. Students who attended class 80 to 90% of the time usually received a B or C in the class. Students who attended class less than 80% of the time usually received a D or an F or eventually withdrew from the class.

    Based on this information, attendance and grades are related. The more you attend class, the more likely it is you will receive a higher grade. If you improve your attendance, your grades will probably improve. Many factors affect your grade in a course. One factor that you have considerable control over is attendance. You can increase your opportunities for learning by attending class more often.

1. What are the variables under study?

2. What are the data in the study?

3. Are descriptive, inferential, or both types of statistics used?

4. What is the population under study?

5. Was a sample collected? If so, from where?

6. From the information given, comment on the relationship between the variables.

See page 38 for the answers.

Answers not appearing on the page can be found in the answers appendix.

≡ Exercises 1–1

1. Define statistics. Statistics is the science of conducting studies to collect, organize, summarize, analyze, and draw conclusions from data.

2. What is a variable? A variable is a characteristic or attribute that can assume different values.

3. What is meant by a census? In a census, the researchers collect data from all subjects in the population.

4. How does a population differ from a sample? A population consists of all subjects under study while a sample is a subgroup of the population.

5. Explain the difference between descriptive and inferential statistics.

6. Name three areas where probability is used. Probability is used in gambling, insurance, and weather forecasting.

7. Why is information obtained from samples used more often than information obtained from populations?

8. What is meant by a biased sample? A biased sample is a sample that is not representative of the population.

For Exercises 9–17, determine whether descriptive or inferential statistics were used.

9. Seventy-seven percent of consumers don't think small businesses should stay open on holidays. This is inferential since consumers think about small businesses staying open on holidays.
Source: Cox Business Consumer Sentiment Survey

10. Sixty-six percent of Americans believe that their communities' drinking water is at risk. This is inferential since it makes a generalization about what Americans believe about their drinking water.
Source: Nestle Waters North American Survey

11. Last year during the week of July 4th, Murrysville Regional Hospital reported that they treated 264 patients for fireworks-related injuries. This is descriptive since it gives the number of patients treated at a specific hospital.

12. In the city of Westbrook, 6 out of the 8 bridges within the city limits were in need of repair. This is descriptive since it gives the specific statistic on the number of bridges that need repair.

13. A survey found that 16.8 days was the average number of vacation days that employees had taken during the year. This is a descriptive statistic since it is the result of a specific survey.
Source: GFK Survey

14. During a recent year, the TSA found 3957 guns at airport security check points. This is descriptive since it is the specific number of guns found at the U.S. airports.

15. In a recent year, 39 people in the United States died from lightning strikes. This is descriptive since it is a specific number of people in the United States who were struck by lightning.
Source: Acosta Survey

16. During a recent year, the average U.S. diners spent a month on food prepared outside the home was $144. This is inferential since it is a generalization made about U.S. diners.
Source: Acosta Survey

17. Fifty-seven percent of Hispanics in the United States have type O blood. This is inferential since it makes an inference to all Hispanics in the United States.
Source: American Red Cross

⬛ Extending the Concepts

18. Find three statistical studies and explain whether they used descriptive or inferential statistics. Answers will vary.

19. Find a gambling game and explain how probability was used to determine the outcome. Answers will vary.

1–2   Variables and Types of Data

OBJECTIVE ❸

Identify types of data.

As stated in Section 1–1, statisticians gain information about a particular situation by collecting data for random variables. This section will explore in greater detail the nature of variables and types of data.

Variables can be classified as qualitative or quantitative.

Qualitative variables are variables that have distinct categories according to some characteristic or attribute.

For example, if subjects are classified according to gender (male or female), then the variable *gender* is qualitative. Other examples of qualitative variables are religious preference and geographic locations.

Quantitative variables are variables that can be counted or measured.

For example, the variable *age* is numerical, and people can be ranked in order according to the value of their ages. Other examples of quantitative variables are heights, weights, and body temperatures.

Quantitative variables can be further classified into two groups: discrete and continuous. *Discrete variables* can be assigned values such as 0, 1, 2, 3 and are said to be *countable*. Examples of discrete variables are the number of children in a family, the number of students in a classroom, and the number of calls received by a call center each day for a month.

Discrete variables assume values that can be counted.

Continuous variables, by comparison, can assume an infinite number of values in an interval between any two specific values. Temperature, for example, is a continuous variable, since the variable can assume an infinite number of values between any two given temperatures.

Continuous variables can assume an infinite number of values between any two specific values. They are obtained by measuring. They often include fractions and decimals.

The classification of variables can be summarized as follows:

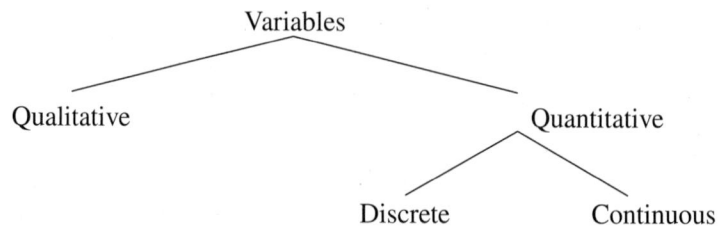

EXAMPLE 1–2   Discrete or Continuous Data

Classify each variable as a discrete or continuous variable.

     a. The number of hours per day that children 6 to 12 years old reported that they played video games

     b. The number of home runs a Major League player made each year of his career

     c. The amount of money drivers spend on gasoline each week

     d. The weights of the players on a hockey team

SOLUTION

     a. Continuous, since the variable time is measured

     b. Discrete, since the number of home runs is counted

     c. Discrete, since the smallest value that money can assume is in cents

     d. Continuous, since the variable weight is measured

Unusual Stat

Fifty-two percent of Americans live within 50 miles of a coastal shoreline.

Since continuous data must be measured, answers must be rounded because of the limits of the measuring device. Usually, answers are rounded to the nearest given unit. For example, heights might be rounded to the nearest inch, weights to the nearest ounce, etc. Hence, a recorded height of 73 inches could mean any measure from 72.5 inches up to but not including 73.5 inches. Thus, the boundary of this measure is given as 72.5–73.5 inches. The **boundary** of a number, then, is defined as a class in which a data value would be placed before the data value was rounded. *Boundaries are written for convenience as 72.5–73.5 but are understood to mean all values up to but not including 73.5.* Actual data values of 73.5 would be rounded to 74 and would be included in a class with boundaries of 73.5 up to but not including 74.5, written as 73.5–74.5. As another example, if a recorded weight is 86 pounds, the exact boundaries are 85.5 up to but not including 86.5, written as 85.5–86.5 pounds. Table 1–1 helps to clarify this concept. The boundaries of a continuous variable are given in one additional decimal place and always end with the digit 5.

TABLE 1–1 Recorded Values and Boundaries		
Variable	**Recorded value**	**Boundaries**
Length	15 centimeters (cm)	14.5–15.5 cm
Temperature	86 degrees Fahrenheit (°F)	85.5–86.5°F
Time	0.43 second (sec)	0.425–0.435 sec
Mass	1.6 grams (g)	1.55–1.65 g

EXAMPLE 1–3   Class Boundaries

Find the boundaries for each measurement.

     a. 32.4 feet

     b. 86° Fahrenheit

     c. 27.54 mg/dl

SOLUTION

     a. 32.35–32.45 feet

     b. 85.5°–86.5° Fahrenheit

     c. 27.535–27.545 mg/dl

Measurement Scales

In addition to being classified as qualitative or quantitative, variables can be classified by how they are categorized, counted, or measured. For example, can the data be organized into specific categories, such as area of residence (rural, suburban, or urban)? Can the data values be ranked, such as first place, second place, etc.? Or are the values obtained from measurement, such as heights, IQs, or temperature? This type of classification—i.e., how variables are categorized, counted, or measured—uses **measurement scales,** and four common types of scales are used: nominal, ordinal, interval, and ratio.

The first level of measurement is called the *nominal level* of measurement. A sample of college instructors classified according to subject taught (e.g., English, history, psychology, or mathematics) is an example of nominal-level measurement. Classifying survey subjects as male or female is another example of nominal-level measurement. No ranking or order can be placed on the data. Classifying residents according to zip codes is also an example of the nominal level of measurement. Even though numbers are assigned as zip codes, there is no meaningful order or ranking. Other examples of nominal-level data are political party (Democratic, Republican, independent, etc.), religion (Christianity, Judaism, Islam, etc.), and marital status (single, married, divorced, widowed, separated).

> The **nominal level of measurement** classifies data into mutually exclusive (nonoverlapping) categories in which no order or ranking can be imposed on the data.

The next level of measurement is called the *ordinal level*. Data measured at this level can be placed into categories, and these categories can be ordered, or ranked. For example, from student evaluations, guest speakers might be ranked as superior, average, or poor. Floats in a homecoming parade might be ranked as first place, second place, etc. *Note that precise measurement of differences in the ordinal level of measurement* does not *exist.* For instance, when people are classified according to their build (small, medium, or large), a large variation exists among the individuals in each class.

Other examples of ordinal data are letter grades (A, B, C, D, F).

> The **ordinal level of measurement** classifies data into categories that can be ranked; however, precise differences between the ranks do not exist.

The third level of measurement is called the *interval level.* This level differs from the ordinal level in that precise differences do exist between units. For example, many standardized psychological tests yield values measured on an interval scale. IQ is an example of such a variable. There is a meaningful difference of 1 point between an IQ of 109 and an IQ of 110. Temperature is another example of interval measurement, since there is a meaningful difference of 1°F between each unit, such as 72 and 73°F. *One property is lacking in the interval scale: There is no true zero.* For example, IQ tests do not measure people who have no intelligence. For temperature, 0°F does not mean no heat at all.

> The **interval level of measurement** ranks data, and precise differences between units of measure do exist; however, there is no meaningful zero.

The final level of measurement is called the *ratio level.* Examples of ratio scales are those used to measure height, weight, area, and number of phone calls received. Ratio scales have differences between units (1 inch, 1 pound, etc.) and a true zero. In addition, the ratio scale contains a true ratio between values. For example, if one person can lift 200 pounds and another can lift 100 pounds, then the ratio between them is 2 to 1. Put another way, the first person can lift twice as much as the second person.

> The **ratio level of measurement** possesses all the characteristics of interval measurement, and there exists a true zero. In addition, true ratios exist when the same variable is measured on two different members of the population.

Unusual Stat

Sixty-three percent of us say we would rather hear the bad news first.

Historical Note

When data were first analyzed statistically by Karl Pearson and Francis Galton, almost all were continuous data. In 1899, Pearson began to analyze discrete data. Pearson found that some data, such as eye color, could not be measured, so he termed such data *nominal data.* Ordinal data were introduced by a German numerologist Frederich Mohs in 1822 when he introduced a hardness scale for minerals. For example, the hardest stone is the diamond, which he assigned a hardness value of 1500. Quartz was assigned a hardness value of 100. This does not mean that a diamond is 15 times harder than quartz. It only means that a diamond is harder than quartz. In 1947, a psychologist named Stanley Smith Stevens made a further division of continuous data into two categories, namely, interval and ratio.

TABLE 1–2 Examples of Measurement Scales			
Nominal-level data	**Ordinal-level data**	**Interval-level data**	**Ratio-level data**
Zip code Gender Eye color (blue, brown, green, hazel) Political affiliation Religious affiliation Major field (mathematics, computers, etc.) Nationality	Grade (A, B, C, D, F) Judging (first place, second place, etc.) Rating scale (poor, good, excellent) Ranking of tennis players	SAT score IQ Temperature	Height Weight Time Salary Age

FIGURE 1–2

Measurement Scales

1. Nominal Level

Blue

White

Red

Black

Automobile color

2. Ordinal Level

Small

Medium

Large

Pizza size

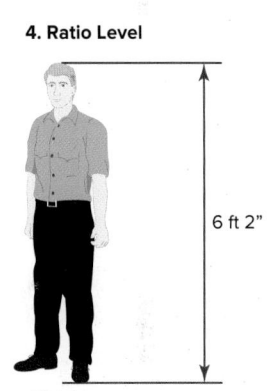

3. Interval Level

Temperature

4. Ratio Level

6 ft 2"

Height

There is not complete agreement among statisticians about the classification of data into one of the four categories. For example, some researchers classify IQ data as ratio data rather than interval. Also, data can be altered so that they fit into a different category. For instance, if the incomes of all professors of a college are classified into the three categories of low, average, and high, then a ratio variable becomes an ordinal variable. Table 1–2 gives some examples of each type of data. See Figure 1–2.

EXAMPLE 1–4   Measurement Levels

What level of measurement would be used to measure each variable?

   a. The ages of the instructors at your college
   b. The occupations of students who work part time after school
   c. The lowest night-time temperatures in December in a large city
   d. The ratings of medical doctors at a hospital

SOLUTION

  a. Ratio

  b. Nominal

  c. Interval

  d. Ordinal

Applying the Concepts 1–2

Fatal Transportation Injuries

Read the following information about the number of fatal accidents for the transportation industry in a specific year, and answer each question.

Industry	Number of fatalities
Highway accidents	968
Railway accidents	44
Water vehicle accidents	52
Aircraft accidents	151

Source: Bureau of Labor Statistics.

1. Name the variables under study.

2. Categorize each variable as quantitative or qualitative.

3. Categorize each quantitative variable as discrete or continuous.

4. Identify the level of measurement for each variable.

5. The railroad had the fewest fatalities for the specific year. Does that mean railroads have fewer accidents than the other industries?

6. What factors other than safety influence a person's choice of transportation?

7. From the information given, comment on the relationship between the variables.

See page 38 for the answers.

Exercises 1–2

1. Explain the difference between qualitative variables and quantitative variables.

2. Explain the difference between discrete and continuous variables.

3. Why are continuous variables rounded when they are used in statistical studies? Continuous variables need to be rounded because of the limits of the measuring device.

4. Name and define the four types of measurement levels used in statistics. There are four types of measurement levels used in statistics: nominal, ordinal, interval, and ratio levels of measurement.

For Exercises 5–10, determine whether the data are qualitative or quantitative.

5. The number of stores a person visits on a shopping trip Quantitative

6. The times spent cleaning each office at a local office building Quantitative

7. The number of toppings on pizzas sold at a local pizza restaurant Qualitative

8. The blood pressure readings of students before taking an exam Quantitative

9. Number of degrees awarded by a college each year for the last 10 years Quantitative

10. Ratings of teachers Qualitative

For Exercises 11–16, determine whether the data are discrete or continuous.

11. The number of hours that students sleep each day Continuous

12. Systolic blood pressure readings Continuous

13. The amount of water, in ounces, an adult consumes during a 24-hour period Continuous

14. The number of physical workouts during the month that an executive completes Discrete

15. The amount of bacteria in raw milk Discrete

16. Temperatures at a seashore resort Continuous

For Exercises 17–22, give the boundaries of each value.

17. 18 inches 17.5–18.5 inches

18. 2.3 kilometers 2.25–2.35 kilometers

19. 76 miles 75.5–76.5 miles

20. 9.67 tons 9.665–9.675 tons

21. 33.2 feet 33.15–33.25 feet

22. 45 pints 44.5–45.5 pints

For Exercises 23–30, classify each as nominal-level, ordinal-level, interval-level, or ratio-level measurement.

23. Social Security numbers Nominal

24. Telephone numbers Nominal

25. Years ending in a double zero Interval

26. Amount of money spent on pet care per year Ratio

27. Debts of college students Ratio

28. Ratings of high schools based on teachers' salaries Ordinal

29. Number of CT scans an imaging center completes Ratio

30. Horsepower of automobile engines Ratio

1–3   Data Collection and Sampling Techniques

OBJECTIVE

Identify the four basic sampling techniques.

In research, statisticians use data in many different ways. As stated previously, data can be used to describe situations or events. For example, a manufacturer might want to know something about the consumers who will be purchasing the manufacturer's product so the manufacturer can plan an effective marketing strategy. In another situation, the management of a company might survey its employees to assess their needs in order to negotiate a new contract with the employees' union. Data can be used to determine whether the educational goals of a school district are being met. Finally, trends in various areas, such as the stock market, can be analyzed, enabling prospective buyers to make more intelligent decisions concerning what stocks to purchase. These examples illustrate a few situations where collecting data will help people make better decisions on courses of action.

Data can be collected in a variety of ways. One of the most common methods is through the use of surveys. Surveys can be done by using a variety of methods. Three of the most common methods are the telephone survey, the mailed questionnaire, and the personal interview.

Telephone surveys have an advantage over personal interview surveys in that they are less costly. Also, people may be more candid in their opinions since there is no face-to-face contact. A major drawback to the telephone survey is that some people in the population will not have phones or will not answer when the calls are made; hence, not all people have a chance of being surveyed. Also, many people now have unlisted numbers and cell phones, so they cannot be surveyed unless the way survey participants are chosen would include unlisted numbers and cell phone numbers. Finally, even the tone of voice of the interviewer might influence the response of the person who is being interviewed.

Mailed questionnaire surveys can be used to cover a wider geographic area than telephone surveys or personal interviews since mailed questionnaire surveys are less expensive to conduct. Also, respondents can remain anonymous if they desire. Disadvantages of mailed questionnaire surveys include a low number of responses and inappropriate answers to questions. Another drawback is that some people may have difficulty reading or understanding the questions.

Wavebreakmedia/iStock/Getty Images

Personal interview surveys have the advantage of obtaining in-depth responses to questions from the person being interviewed. One disadvantage is that interviewers must be trained in asking questions and recording responses, which makes the personal interview survey more costly than the other two survey methods. Another disadvantage is that the interviewer may be biased in the interviewer's selection of respondents.

Data can also be collected in other ways, such as *surveying records* or *direct observation* of situations.

As stated in Section 1–1, researchers use samples to collect data and information about a particular variable from a large population. Using samples saves time and money and in some cases enables the researcher to get more detailed information about a particular subject. Remember, samples cannot be selected in haphazard ways because the information obtained might be biased. For example, interviewing people on a street corner during the day would not include responses from people working in offices at that time or from people attending school; hence, not all subjects in a particular population would have a chance of being selected.

To obtain samples that are unbiased—i.e., that give each subject in the population an equally likely chance of being selected—statisticians use four basic methods of sampling: random, systematic, stratified, and cluster sampling.

Random Sampling

> A **random sample** is a sample in which all members of the population have an equal chance of being selected.

Random samples are selected by using chance methods or random numbers. One such method is to number each subject in the population. Then place numbered cards in a bowl, mix them thoroughly, and select as many cards as needed. The subjects whose numbers are selected constitute the sample. Since it is difficult to mix the cards thoroughly, there is a chance of obtaining a biased sample. For this reason, statisticians use another method of obtaining numbers. They generate random numbers with a computer or calculator. Before the invention of computers, random numbers were obtained from tables.

Some five-digit random numbers are shown in Table A–1 in Appendix A. A section of Table A–1 is shown on page 13. To select a random sample of, say, 15 subjects out of 85 subjects, it is necessary to number each subject from 01 to 85. Then select a starting number by closing your eyes and placing your finger on a number in the table. (Although this may sound somewhat unusual, it enables us to find a starting number at random.) In this case, suppose your finger landed on the number 88948 in the fourth column, the fifth number down from the top. Since you only need two-digit numbers, you can use the last two digits of each of these numbers. The first random number then is 48. Then proceed down until you have selected 15 different numbers between and including 01 and 85. When you reach the bottom of the column, go to the top of the next column. If you select a number 00 or a number greater than 85 or a duplicate number, just omit it.

In our example, we use the numbers (which correspond to the subjects) 48, 43, 44, 19, 07, 27, 57, 24, 68, and so on. Use Table A–1 in the Appendix to get all the random numbers.

Systematic Sampling

> A **systematic sample** is a sample obtained by selecting every *k*th member of the population where *k* is a counting number.

Researchers obtain systematic samples by numbering each subject of the population and then selecting every *k*th subject. For example, suppose there were 2000 subjects in the population and a sample of 50 subjects was needed. Since $2000 \div 50 = 40$, then $k = 40$, and every 40th subject would be selected; however, the first subject (numbered between 1 and 40) would be selected at random. Suppose subject 12 were the first subject selected; then the sample would consist of the subjects whose numbers were 12, 52, 92, etc., until

SPEAKING OF STATISTICS   The Worst Day for Weight Loss

Many overweight people have difficulty losing weight. *Prevention* magazine reported that researchers from Washington University School of Medicine studied the diets of 48 adult weight loss participants. They used food diaries, exercise monitors, and weigh-ins. They found that the participants ate an average of 236 more calories on Saturdays than they did on the other weekdays. This would amount to a weight gain of 9 pounds per year. So if you are watching your diet, be careful on Saturdays.

Are the statistics reported in this study descriptive or inferential in nature? What type of variables are used here?

Jacobs Stock Photography/Getty Images

TABLE A–1 Random Numbers													
51455	02154	06955	88858	02158	76904	28864	95504	68047	41196	88582	99062	21984	67932
06512	07836	88456	36313	30879	51323	76451	25578	15986	50845	57015	53684	57054	93261
71308	35028	28065	74995	03251	27050	31692	12910	14886	85820	42664	68830	57939	34421
60035	97320	62543	61404	94367	07080	66112	56180	15813	15978	63578	13365	60115	99411
64072	76075	91393	88948	99244	60809	10784	36380	5721	24481	86978	74102	49979	28572
14914	85608	96871	74743	73692	53664	67727	21440	13326	98590	93405	63839	65974	05294
93723	60571	17559	96844	88678	89256	75120	62384	77414	24023	82121	01796	03907	35061
86656	43736	62752	53819	81674	43490	07850	61439	52300	55063	50728	54652	63307	83597
31286	27544	44129	51107	53727	65479	09688	57355	20426	44527	36896	09654	63066	92393
95519	78485	20269	64027	53229	59060	99269	12140	97864	31064	73933	37369	94656	57645
78019	75498	79017	22157	22893	88109	57998	02582	34259	11405	97788	37718	64071	66345
45487	22433	62809	98924	96769	24955	60283	16837	02070	22051	91191	40000	36480	07822
64769	25684	33490	25168	34405	58272	90124	92954	43663	39556	40269	69189	68272	60753
00464	62924	83514	97860	98982	84484	18856	35260	22370	22751	89716	33377	97720	78982
73714	36622	04866	00885	34845	26118	47003	28924	98813	45981	82469	84867	50443	00641
84032	71228	72682	40618	69303	58466	03438	67873	87487	33285	19463	02872	36786	28418
70609	51795	47988	49658	29651	93852	27921	16258	28666	41922	33353	38131	64115	39541
37209	94421	49043	11876	43528	93624	55263	29863	67709	39952	50512	93074	66938	09515
80632	65999	34771	06797	02318	74725	10841	96571	12052	41478	50020	59066	30860	96357

50 subjects were obtained. When using systematic sampling, you must be careful about how the subjects in the population are numbered. If subjects were arranged in a manner such as wife, husband, wife, husband, and every 40th subject were selected, the sample would consist of all husbands. Numbering is not always necessary. For example, a researcher may select every 10th item from an assembly line to test for defects.

Systematic sampling has the advantage of selecting subjects throughout an ordered population. This sampling method is fast and convenient if the population can be easily numbered.

Stratified Sampling

A **stratified sample** is a sample obtained by dividing the population into subgroups or strata according to some characteristic relevant to the study. (There can be several subgroups.) Then subjects are selected at random from each subgroup.

Samples within the strata should be randomly selected. For example, suppose the president of a two-year college wants to learn how students feel about a certain issue. Furthermore, the president wishes to see if the opinions of first-year students differ from those of second-year students. The president will randomly select students from each subgroup to use in the sample.

Cluster Sampling

> A **cluster sample** is obtained by dividing the population into sections or clusters and then selecting one or more clusters at random and using all members in the cluster(s) as the members of the sample.

Here the population is divided into groups or clusters by some means such as geographic area or schools in a large school district. Then the researcher randomly selects some of these clusters and uses all members of the selected clusters as the subjects of the samples. Suppose a researcher wishes to survey apartment dwellers in a large city. If there are 10 apartment buildings in the city, the researcher can select at random 2 buildings from the 10 and interview all the residents of these buildings. Cluster sampling is used when the population is large or when it involves subjects residing in a large geographic area. For example, if one wanted to do a study involving the patients in the hospitals in New York City, it would be very costly and time-consuming to try to obtain a random sample of patients since they would be spread over a large area. Instead, a few hospitals could be selected at random, and the patients in these hospitals would be interviewed in a cluster. See Figure 1–3.

The main difference between stratified sampling and cluster sampling is that although in both types of sampling the population is divided into groups, the subjects in the groups for stratified sampling are more or less homogeneous, that is, they have similar characteristics, while the subjects in the clusters form "miniature populations." That is, they vary in characteristics as does the larger population. For example, if a researcher wanted to use the class of first-year students at a university as the population, the researcher might use a class of students in a first-year orientation class as a cluster sample. If using a stratified sample, the researcher would need to divide the first-year students into groups according to their major field, sex, age, etc., or other samples from each group.

Cluster samples save the researcher time and money, but the researcher must be aware that sometimes a cluster does not represent the population.

The four basic sampling methods are summarized in Table 1–3.

Other Sampling Methods

In addition to the four basic sampling methods, researchers use other methods to obtain samples. One such method is called a **convenience sample.** Here a researcher uses subjects who are convenient. For example, the researcher may interview subjects entering a local mall to determine the nature of their visit or perhaps what stores they will be patronizing. This sample is probably not representative of the general customers for several reasons. For one thing, it was probably taken at a specific time of day, so not all customers entering the mall have an equal chance of being selected since they were not there when the survey was being conducted. But convenience samples can be representative of the population. If the researcher investigates the characteristics of the population and determines that the sample is representative, then it can be used.

Another type of sample that is used in statistics is a *volunteer sample* or *self-selected sample.* Here respondents decide for themselves if they wish to be included in the sample. For example, a radio station in Pittsburgh asks a question about a situation and then asks people to call one number if they agree with the action taken or call another number if they disagree with the action. The results are then announced at the end of the day. Note that most often, only people with strong opinions will call. The station does explain that this is not a "scientific poll."

FIGURE 1–3 Sampling Methods

1. Random

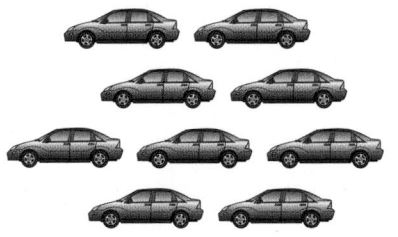

Population

Table D	Random Numbers			
10480	15011	01536	02011	81647
22368	46573	25595	85393	30995
24130	48360	22527	97265	76393
42167	93093	06243	61680	07856
37570	39975	81837	16656	06121
77921	06907	11008	42751	27750
99562	72905	56420	69994	98872
96301	91977	05463	07972	18876
89579	14342	63661	10281	17453
85475	36857	43342	53988	
28918	69578	88321		
63553	40961			

Sample

2. Systematic

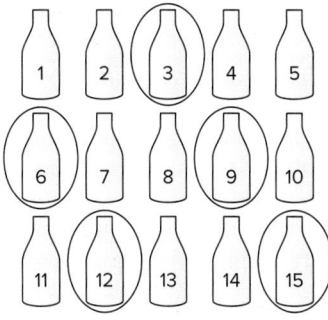

Population

Sample

3. Stratified

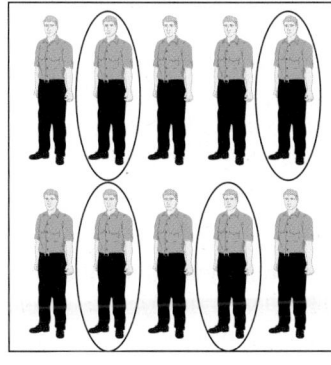

Men

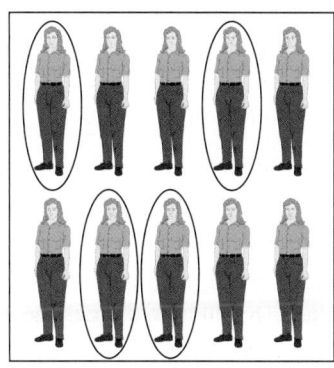

Women

Population

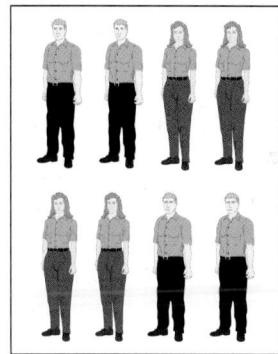

Sample

4. Cluster

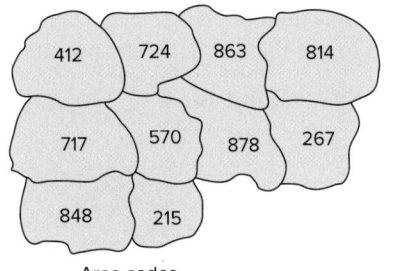

Area codes
Population

Sample

TABLE 1–3	Summary of Sampling Methods
Random	Subjects are selected by random numbers.
Systematic	Subjects are selected by using every *k*th number after the first subject is randomly selected from 1 through *k*.
Stratified	Subjects are selected by dividing up the population into subgroups (strata), and subjects are randomly selected within subgroups.
Cluster	Subjects are selected by using an intact subgroup that is representative of the population.

Since samples are not perfect representatives of the populations from which they are selected, there is always some error in the results. This error is called a *sampling error.*

Sampling error is the difference between the results obtained from a sample and the results obtained from the population from which the sample was selected.

For example, suppose you select a sample of full-time students at your college and find 56% are female. Then you go to the admissions office and get the genders of all full-time students that semester and find that 54% are female. The difference of 2% is said to be due to sampling error.

In most cases, this difference is unknown, but it can be estimated. This process is shown in Chapter 7.

There is another error that occurs in statistics called *nonsampling error.*

A **nonsampling error** occurs when the data are obtained erroneously or the sample is biased, i.e., nonrepresentative.

For example, data could be collected by using a defective scale. Each weight might be off by, say, 2 pounds. Also, recording errors can be made. Perhaps the researcher wrote an incorrect data value.

Caution and vigilance should be used when collecting data.

Other sampling techniques, such as *sequential sampling, double sampling,* and *multistage sampling,* are explained in Chapter 14, along with a more detailed explanation of the four basic sampling techniques.

EXAMPLE 1–5   Sampling Methods

State which sampling method was used.

   a. Out of 14 banks in a city, a researcher selects one bank and records the number of savings deposits made in a one-day period.

   b. A researcher divides a group of students who are majoring in criminal justice as male or female, and then divides the group further as first-years, sophomores, juniors, or seniors. Then 8 students from each group are given a survey to answer questions about the program.

   c. A researcher numbers the subscribers to a movie rental business, selects 1000 subscribers using random numbers, and records the number of movies rented by each for the month of January.

   d. On an assembly line, every 20th automobile is selected and checked for paint defects on the car. The purpose is to insure that the painting apparatus is working properly.

SOLUTION

   a. Cluster

   b. Stratified

   c. Random

   d. Systematic

⬚ Applying the Concepts 1–3

American Culture and Drug Abuse

Assume you are a member of a research team and have become increasingly concerned about drug use by professional sports players as one of several factors affecting people's attitudes toward drug use in general. You set up a plan and conduct a survey on how people believe the American culture (television, movies, magazines, and popular music) influences illegal drug use. Your survey consists of 2250 adults and adolescents from around the country. A consumer group petitions you for more information about your survey. Answer the following questions about your survey.

1. What type of survey did you use (phone, mail, or interview)?
2. What are the advantages and disadvantages of the surveying methods you did not use?
3. What type of scores did you use? Why?
4. Did you use a random method for deciding who would be in your sample?
5. Which of the methods (stratified, systematic, cluster, volunteer, or convenience) did you use?
6. Why was that method more appropriate for this type of data collection?
7. If a convenience sample were obtained consisting of only adolescents, how would the results of the study be affected?

See page 38 for the answers.

⬚ Exercises 1–3

1. Name five ways that data can be collected.

2. What is meant by sampling error and nonsampling error?

3. Why are random numbers used in sampling, and how are random numbers generated?

4. Name and define the four basic sampling methods. The four basic sampling methods are random, systematic, stratified, and cluster methods.

For Exercises 5–10, define a population that may have been used and explain how the sample might have been selected.

5. A survey by McAfee found that 54% of Americans could not last a day without texting while on vacation.

6. A Sallie Mae survey found that the average amount families spent on college expenses was $23,757.

7. The outstanding credit card debt for Americans is $11.02 trillion.
   Source: CreditCards.com

8. Office workers spend, on average, 15 minutes per day on their mobile devices for non-work-related activities in the office.
   Source: OfficeTeam

9. Forty-two percent of pet owners spend at least $1000 in medical expenses a year for their pets.
   Source: AskVet

10. The average January 2012 temperature in Boston was 34.2°F. This was 5.2° higher than the normal January average temperature.
    Source: AccuWeather.com

For Exercises 11–16, indentify the sampling method that was used.

11. A machine fills bags of apple slices for sale to customers who eat at a fast-food restaurant. To check the accuracy of the weight of the bags, every 10th bag is selected and weighed on a scale. Systematic

12. To determine how long people exercise, a researcher interviews 5 people selected from a yoga class, 5 people selected from a weight-lifting class, 5 people selected from an aerobics class, and 5 people from swimming classes. Stratified

13. A fast-food restaurant is selected at random; then the times it takes to fill customers' orders are recorded. These results are used for a commercial for the restaurant chain. Cluster

14. In a medical study, a researcher randomly selects 100 patients that visited the emergency room that week in order to determine the average age of the patients who visited the emergency room. Random

15. On a day selected at random, a researcher selects all food bills for breakfast, lunch, and dinner, and then compares the amounts of the bills for each group. Stratified

16. Ten counties in Pennsylvania are randomly selected to determine the average county real estate tax that the residents pay. Random

1–4   Experimental Design

OBJECTIVE

Explain the difference between an observational and an experimental study.

Observational and Experimental Studies

There are several different ways to classify statistical studies. This section explains two types of studies: *observational studies* and *experimental studies*.

> In an **observational study,** the researcher merely observes what is happening or what has happened in the past and tries to draw conclusions based on these observations.

For example, in August 2015 (*The Verge*) asked "Tons of people are buying Fitbits, but are they actually using them?" Fitbit is a manufacturer of step counting devices. Only 9.5 million registered users out of 19 million are active (50%). The past data showed an active rate of 60% (10.9 million registered, 6.5 million active). Endeavour Partners states that 33% of buyers of step devices continue to use them after 6 months. In this study, the researcher merely observed what had happened to the Fitbit owners over a period of time. There was no type of research intervention.

There are three main types of observational studies. When all the data are collected at one time, the study is called a *cross-sectional study*. When the data are collected using records obtained from the past, the study is called a *retrospective study*. Finally, if the data are collected over a period of time, say, past and present, the study is called a *longitudinal study*.

Observational studies have advantages and disadvantages. One advantage of an observational study is that it usually occurs in a natural setting. For example, researchers can observe people's driving patterns on streets and highways in large cities. Another advantage of an observational study is that it can be done in situations where it would be unethical or downright dangerous to conduct an experiment. Using observational studies, researchers can study suicides, rapes, murders, etc. In addition, observational studies can be done using variables that cannot be manipulated by the researcher, such as drug users versus nondrug users and right-handedness versus left-handedness.

Observational studies have disadvantages, too. As mentioned previously, since the variables are not controlled by the researcher, a definite cause-and-effect situation cannot be shown since other factors may have had an effect on the results. Observational studies can be expensive and time-consuming. For example, if one wanted to study the habitat of lions in Africa, one would need a lot of time and money, and there would be a certain amount of danger involved. Finally, since the researcher may not be using his or her own measurements, the results could be subject to the inaccuracies of those who collected the data. For example, if the researchers were doing a study of events that occurred in the 1800s, they would have to rely on information and records obtained by others from a previous era. There is no way to ensure the accuracy of these records.

The other type of study is called an *experimental study*.

> In an **experimental study,** the researcher manipulates one of the variables and tries to determine how the manipulation influences other variables.

Interesting Fact

The safest day of the week for driving is Tuesday.

For example, a study conducted at Virginia Polytechnic Institute and presented in *Psychology Today* divided female undergraduate students into two groups and had the students perform as many sit-ups as possible in 90 seconds. The first group was told only to "Do your best," while the second group was told to try to increase the actual number of sit-ups done each day by 10%. After four days, the subjects in the group who were given the vague instructions to "Do your best" averaged 43 sit-ups, while the group that was given the more specific instructions to increase the number of sit-ups by 10% averaged 56 sit-ups by the last day's session. The conclusion then was that athletes who were given specific goals performed better than those who were not given specific goals.

This study is an example of a statistical experiment since the researchers intervened in the study by manipulating one of the variables, namely, the type of instructions given to each group.

In a true experimental study, the subjects should be assigned to groups randomly. Also, the treatments should be assigned to the groups at random. In the sit-up study, the article did not mention whether the subjects were randomly assigned to the groups.

Sometimes when random assignment is not possible, researchers use intact groups. These types of studies are done quite often in education where already intact groups are available in the form of existing classrooms. When these groups are used, the study is said to be a **quasi-experimental study.** The treatments, though, should be assigned at random. Most articles do not state whether random assignment of subjects was used.

Statistical studies usually include one or more *independent variables* and one *dependent variable.*

> The **independent variable** in an experimental study is the one that is being manipulated by the researcher. The independent variable is also called the **explanatory variable.** The resultant variable is called the **dependent variable** or the **outcome variable.**

The outcome variable is the variable that is studied to see if it has changed significantly because of the manipulation of the independent variable. For example, in the sit-up study, the researchers gave the groups two different types of instructions, general and specific. Hence, the independent variable is the type of instruction. The dependent variable, then, is the resultant variable, that is, the number of sit-ups each group was able to perform after four days of exercise. If the differences in the dependent or outcome variable are large and other factors are equal, these differences can be attributed to the manipulation of the independent variable. In this case, specific instructions were shown to increase athletic performance.

In the sit-up study, there were two groups. The group that received the special instruction is called the **treatment group** while the other is called the **control group.** The treatment group receives a specific treatment (in this case, instructions for improvement) while the control group does not.

Both types of statistical studies have advantages and disadvantages. Experimental studies have the advantage that the researcher can decide how to select subjects and how to assign them to specific groups. The researcher can also control or manipulate the independent variable. For example, in studies that require the subjects to consume a certain amount of medicine each day, the researcher can determine the precise dosages and, if necessary, vary the dosage for the groups.

There are several disadvantages to experimental studies. First, they may occur in unnatural settings, such as laboratories and special classrooms. This can lead to several problems. One such problem is that the results might not apply to the natural setting. The age-old question then is, "This mouthwash may kill 10,000 germs in a test tube, but how many germs will it kill in my mouth?"

Another disadvantage with an experimental study is the **Hawthorne effect.** This effect was discovered in 1924 in a study of workers at the Hawthorne plant of the Western Electric Company. In this study, researchers found that the subjects who knew they were participating in an experiment actually changed their behavior in ways that affected the results of the study.

Another problem when conducting statistical studies is called *confounding of variables* or *lurking variables.*

> A **confounding variable** is one that influences the dependent or outcome variable but was not separated from the independent variable.

Researchers try to control most variables in a study, but this is not possible in some studies. For example, subjects who are put on an exercise program might also improve their diet unbeknownst to the researcher and perhaps improve their health in other ways not due to exercise alone. Then diet becomes a confounding variable.

When you read the results of statistical studies, decide if the study was observational or experimental. Then see if the conclusion follows logically, based on the nature of these studies.

Another factor that can influence statistical experiments is called the *placebo effect*. Here the subjects used in the study respond favorably or show improvement due to the fact that they had been selected for the study. They could also be reacting to clues given unintentionally by the researchers. For example, in a study on knee pain done at the Houston VA Medical Center, researchers divided 180 patients into three groups. Two groups had surgery to remove damaged cartilage while those in the third group had simulated surgery. After two years, an equal number of patients in each group reported that they felt better after the surgery. Those patients who had simulated surgery were said to be responding to what is called the placebo effect.

To minimize the placebo effect, researchers use what is called *blinding*. In blinding, the subjects do not know whether they are receiving an actual treatment or a placebo. Many times researchers use a sugar pill that looks like a real medical pill. Often *double blinding* is used. Here both the subjects and the researchers are not told which groups are given the placebos.

Researchers use *blocking* to minimize variability when they suspect that there might be a difference between two or more blocks. For example, in the sit-up study mentioned earlier, if we think that men and women would respond differently to "Do your best" versus "Increase by 10% every day," we would divide the subjects into two blocks (men, women) and then randomize which subjects in each block get the treatment.

When subjects are assigned to groups randomly, and the treatments are assigned randomly, the experiment is said to be a *completely randomized design*.

Some experiments use what is called a *matched-pair design*. Here one subject is assigned to a treatment group, and another subject is assigned to a control group. But, before the assignment, subjects are paired according to certain characteristics. In earlier years, studies used identical twins, assigning one twin to one group and the other twin to another group. Subjects can be paired on any characteristics such as ages, heights, and weights.

Another way to validate studies is to use *replication*. Here the same experiment is done in another part of the country or in another laboratory. The same study could also be done using adults who are not going to college instead of using college students. Then the results of the second study are compared to the ones in the original study to see if they are the same.

No matter what type of study is conducted, two studies on the same subject sometimes have conflicting conclusions. Why might this occur? An article titled "Bottom Line: Is It Good for You?" (*USA TODAY Weekend*) states that in the 1960s studies suggested that margarine was better for the heart than butter since margarine contains less saturated fat and users had lower cholesterol levels. In a 1980 study, researchers found that butter was better than margarine since margarine contained trans- fatty acids, which are worse for the heart than butter's saturated fat. Then in a 1998 study, researchers found that margarine was better for a person's health. Now, what is to be believed? Should one use butter or margarine?

The answer here is that you must take a closer look at these studies. Actually, it is not the choice between butter and margarine that counts, but the type of margarine used. In the 1980s, studies showed that solid margarine contains trans- fatty acids, and scientists believe that they are worse for the heart than butter's saturated fat. In the 1998 study, liquid margarine was used. It is very low in trans- fatty acids, and hence it is more healthful than butter because trans- fatty acids have been shown to raise cholesterol. Hence, the conclusion is that it is better to use liquid margarine than solid margarine or butter.

Before decisions based on research studies are made, it is important to get all the facts and examine them in light of the particular situation.

The purpose of a statistical study is to gain and process information obtained from the study in order to answer specific questions about the subject being investigated. Statistical researchers use a specific procedure to do statistical studies to obtain valid results.

The general guidelines for this procedure are as follows:

1. Formulate the purpose of the study.
2. Identify the variables for the study.
3. Define the population.
4. Decide what sampling method you will use to collect the data.
5. Collect the data.
6. Summarize the data and perform any statistical calculations needed.
7. Interpret the results.

There is also a formal way to write up the study procedure and the results obtained. This information is available on the online resources under "Writing the Research Report."

EXAMPLE 1–6   Experimental Design

Researchers randomly assigned 10 people to each of three different groups. Group 1 was instructed to write an essay about the hassles in their lives. Group 2 was instructed to write an essay about circumstances that made them feel thankful. Group 3 was asked to write an essay about events that they felt neutral about. After the exercise, they were given a questionnaire on their outlook on life. The researchers found that those who wrote about circumstances that made them feel thankful had a more optimistic outlook on life. The conclusion is that focusing on the positive makes you more optimistic about life in general. Based on this study, answer the following questions.

  a. Was this an observational or experimental study?
  b. What is the independent variable?
  c. What is the dependent variable?
  d. What may be a confounding variable in this study?
  e. What can you say about the sample size?
  f. Do you agree with the conclusion? Explain your answer.

SOLUTION

  a. This is an experimental study since the variables (types of essays written) were manipulated.
  b. The independent variable was the type of essay the participants wrote.
  c. The dependent variable was the score on the life outlook questionnaire.
  d. Other factors, such as age, upbringing, and income, can affect the results; however, the random assignment of subjects is helpful in eliminating these factors.
  e. In this study, the sample uses 30 participants total.
  f. Answers will vary.

OBJECTIVE

Explain how statistics can be used and misused.

Uses and Misuses of Statistics

As explained previously, statistical techniques can be used to describe data, compare two or more data sets, determine if a relationship exists between variables, test hypotheses, and make estimates about population characteristics. However, there is another aspect of statistics, and that is the misuse of statistical techniques to sell products that don't work properly, to attempt to prove something true that is really not true, or to get our attention by using statistics to evoke fear, shock, and outrage.

Two sayings that have been around for a long time illustrate this point:

"There are three types of lies—lies, damn lies, and statistics."

"Figures don't lie, but liars figure."

Just because we read or hear the results of a research study or an opinion poll in the media, this does not mean that these results are reliable or that they can be applied to any and all situations. For example, reporters sometimes leave out critical details such as the size of the sample used or how the research subjects were selected. Without this information, you cannot properly evaluate the research and properly interpret the conclusions of the study or survey.

It is the purpose of this section to show some ways that statistics can be misused. You should not infer that all research studies and surveys are suspect, but that there are many factors to consider when making decisions based on the results of research studies and surveys. Here are some ways that statistics can be misrepresented.

Suspect Samples   The first thing to consider is the sample that was used in the research study. Sometimes researchers use very small samples to obtain information. Several years ago, advertisements contained such statements as "Three out of four doctors surveyed recommend brand such and such." If only 4 doctors were surveyed, the results could have been obtained by chance alone; however, if 100 doctors were surveyed, the results were probably not due to chance alone.

Not only is it important to have a sample size that is large enough, but also it is necessary to see how the subjects in the sample were selected. As stated previously, studies using volunteers sometimes have a built-in bias. Volunteers generally do not represent the population at large. Sometimes they are recruited from a particular socioeconomic background, and sometimes unemployed people volunteer for research studies to get a stipend. Studies that require the subjects to spend several days or weeks in an environment other than their home or workplace automatically exclude people who are employed and cannot take time away from work. Sometimes only college students or retirees are used in studies. In the past, many studies have used only men, but have attempted to generalize the results to all genders. Opinion polls that require a person to phone or mail in a response most often are not representative of the population in general, since only those with strong feelings for or against the issue usually call or respond by mail.

Another type of sample that may not be representative is the convenience sample. Educational studies sometimes use students in intact classrooms since it is convenient. Quite often, the students in these classrooms do not represent the student population of the entire school district.

When results are interpreted from studies using small samples, convenience samples, or volunteer samples, care should be used in generalizing the results to the entire population.

Ambiguous Averages   In Chapter 3, you will learn that there are four commonly used measures that are loosely called *averages*. They are the *mean, median, mode,* and *midrange.* For the same data set, these averages can differ markedly. People who know this can, without lying, select the one measure of average that lends the most evidence to support their position.

Changing the Subject   Another type of statistical distortion can occur when different values are used to represent the same data. For example, one political candidate who is running for reelection might say, "During my administration, expenditures increased a mere 3%." His opponent, who is trying to unseat him, might say, "During my opponent's administration, expenditures have increased a whopping $6,000,000." Here both figures are correct; however, expressing a 3% increase as $6,000,000 makes it sound like a very large increase. Here again, ask yourself, Which measure better represents the data?

Detached Statistics   A claim that uses a detached statistic is one in which no comparison is made. For example, you may hear a claim such as "Our brand of crackers has one-third fewer calories." Here, no comparison is made. One-third fewer calories than what? Another example is a claim that uses a detached statistic such as "Brand A aspirin works four times faster." Four times faster than what? When you see statements such as this, always ask yourself, Compared to what?

Implied Connections   Many claims attempt to imply connections between variables that may not actually exist. For example, consider the following statement: "Eating fish may help to reduce your cholesterol." Notice the words *may help*. There is no guarantee that eating fish will definitely help you reduce your cholesterol.

"Studies suggest that using our exercise machine will reduce your weight." Here the word *suggest* is used; and again, there is no guarantee that you will lose weight by using the exercise machine advertised.

Another claim might say, "Taking calcium will lower blood pressure in some people." Note the word *some* is used. You may not be included in the group of "some" people. Be careful when you draw conclusions from claims that use words such as *may, in some people,* and *might help*.

Misleading Graphs   Statistical graphs give a visual representation of data that enables viewers to analyze and interpret data more easily than by simply looking at numbers. In Chapter 2, you will see how some graphs are used to represent data. However, if graphs are drawn inappropriately, they can misrepresent the data and lead the reader to draw false conclusions. The misuse of graphs is also explained in Chapter 2.

Faulty Survey Questions   When analyzing the results of a survey using questionnaires, you should be sure that the questions are properly written since the way questions are phrased can often influence the way people answer them. For example, the responses to a question such as "Do you feel that the North Huntingdon School District should build a new football stadium?" might be answered differently than a question such as "Do you favor increasing school taxes so that the North Huntingdon School District can build a new football stadium?" Each question asks something a little different, and the responses could be radically different. When you read and interpret the results obtained from questionnaire surveys, watch out for some of these common mistakes made in the writing of the survey questions.

In Chapter 14, you will find some common ways that survey questions could be misinterpreted by those responding, and could therefore result in incorrect conclusions.

In summary then, statistics, when used properly, can be beneficial in obtaining much information, but when used improperly, can lead to much misinformation. It is like your automobile. If you use your automobile to get to school or work or to go on a vacation, that's good. But if you use it to run over your neighbor's dog because it barks all night long and tears up your flower garden, that's not so good!

Applying the Concepts 1–4

Today's Cigarettes

Vapor or electronic cigarettes have increased dramatically over the past five years. Compared to traditional tobacco products a lot of research has not been performed on alternative smoking devices even though the sales of these devices have double and then tripled. One study conducted at Virginia Commonwealth University considered the following factors: carbon monoxide concentration, heart rate, subjective effects of the user, and plasma nicotine concentration. The study consisted of 32 subjects. The subjects came from four separate groups, traditional cigarettes, 18-mg nicotine cartridge vapor brand, 16-mg nicotine cartridge vapor brand, and a device containing no vapors.

After five minutes of smoking, the smokers of the traditional cigarettes saw increased levels of carbon monoxide, heart rate, and plasma nicotine. The electronic vapor cigarette smokers did not see a significant increase in heart rate or subjective effects to the user. Answer the following questions.

1. What type of study was this (observational, quasi-experimental, or experimental)?
2. What are the independent and dependent variables?
3. Which was the treatment group?
4. Could the subjects' blood pressures be affected by knowing that they are part of a study?
5. List some possible confounding variables.
6. Do you think this is a good way to study the effect of smokeless tobacco?

See pages 38–39 for the answers.

Exercises 1–4

1. Explain the difference between an observational and an experimental study.

2. Name and define the three types of observational studies.

3. List some advantages and disadvantages of an observational study.

4. List some advantages and disadvantages of an experimental study.

5. What is the difference between an experimental study and a quasi-experimental study?

6. What is the difference between independent variables and dependent variables?

7. Why are a treatment group and a control group used in a statistical study?

8. Explain the Hawthorne effect.

9. What is a confounding variable?

10. Define the placebo effect in a statistical study. Sometimes subjects respond favorably when given a placebo rather than the real treatment.

11. What is meant by blinding and double-blinding?

12. Why do researchers use randomization in statistical studies?

13. What is the difference between a completely randomized design and a matched-pair design?

14. Why is replication used in statistical studies?

For Exercises 15–18, determine whether an observational study or an experimental study was used.

15. A group of teachers are asked if they believe that social media and texting are bad for the grammar and spelling of their students. Observational

16. Two groups of college students are randomly selected. One group is shown a promotional video on purchasing life insurance after they graduate. The other group is not shown this video. After this, each group is asked if they are planning to purchase life insurance after they graduate. Experimental

17. A researcher wishes to see if there is a difference between the times that a physician spends on virtual visits and in-person visits with patients. Observational

18. Two groups of students are randomly selected. One group receives a lecture on the importance of mathematics in their lives. The other group does not receive a lecture. Afterward, both groups complete a questionnaire on their attitude towards taking a mathematics course in college and the results are compared. Experimental

In Exercises 19–22, identify the independent variable and the dependent variable.

19. A study was done to see if people who run regularly (at least 3 times a week) are more likely to have lower blood pressure than those who walk regularly (at least 3 times a week). Independent variable—exercise type. Dependent variable—blood pressure.

20. The *Journal of Behavioral Medicine* reported that sharing a hug and holding hands can limit the physical effects of stress such as soaring heart rate and elevated blood pressure. Independent variable—hugs and hand holding. Dependent variable—heart rate and blood pressure.

21. People who have obsessive-compulsive behaviors are likely to be perfectionists. Independent variable—obsessive-compulsive measure. Dependent variable—perfectionist measure.

22. A study was conducted to determine if the marital status of an individual had any effect on the cause of death of the individual. Independent variable—marital status. Dependent variable—cause of death.

For Exercises 23–26, suggest some confounding variables that the researcher might want to consider when doing a study.

23. *Psychology Today* magazine reports that the more intelligent a person is (based on IQ), the more willing the person is to make a cooperative choice rather than a selfish one. Age, income, socioeconomic status. Answers will vary.

24. *The New England Journal of Medicine* reported that when poor women move to better neighborhoods, they lower the risk of developing obesity and diabetes. Age, socioeconomic status, family ties. Answers will vary.

25. *WebMD* reports that you need to run 15% faster on a treadmill as opposed to running outdoors to burn the same number of calories. Answers will vary.

26. York University in Toronto, Canada, stated that people who had suffered from fibromyalgia were able to reduce their pain by participating in twice-weekly yoga sessions. Climate, diet, medicine. Answers will vary.

For Exercises 27–31, give a reason why the statement made might be misleading.

27. Our product will give you the perfect body. How is a perfect body defined statistically?

28. Here is the whole truth about back pain. What is meant by the "whole truth"?

29. Adults have between 50,000 and 70,000 thoughts per day. How are the number of thoughts measured? Answers will vary.

30. By reading this book, you will increase your IQ by 20 points. How can reading a book increase a person's IQ?

31. One in three Americans ate fast-food today. What is the definition of fast-food? What are the ages of the subjects? Answers will vary.

32. List the steps you should perform when conducting a statistical study.

33. **Beneficial Bacteria** According to a pilot study of 20 people conducted at the University of Minnesota, daily doses of a compound called arabinogalactan over a period of 6 months resulted in a significant increase in the beneficial lactobacillus species of bacteria. Why can't it be concluded that the compound is beneficial for the majority of people? Only 20 people were used in the study.

34. Comment on the following statement, taken from a magazine advertisement: "In a recent clinical study, Brand ABC (actual brand will not be named) was proved to be 1950% better than creatine!" The only time claims can be proved is when the entire population is used.

35. In an ad for women, the following statement was made: "For every 100 women, 91 have taken the road less traveled." Comment on this statement.

36. In many ads for weight loss products, under the product claims and in small print, the following statement is made: "These results are not typical." What does this say about the product being advertised?

37. In an ad for moisturizing lotion, the following claim is made: ". . . it's the number 1 dermatologist-recommended brand." What is misleading about this claim? There is no mention of how this conclusion was obtained.

38. An ad for an exercise product stated: "Using this product will burn 74% more calories." What is misleading about this statement? "74% more calories" than what? No comparison group is stated.

39. "Vitamin E is a proven antioxidant and may help in fighting cancer and heart disease." Is there anything ambiguous about this claim? Explain. Since the word *may* is used, there is no guarantee that the product will help fight cancer and heart disease.

40. "Just 1 capsule of Brand X can provide 24 hours of acid control." (Actual brand will not be named.) What needs to be more clearly defined in this statement? What is meant by "24 hours of acid control"? Also *can provide* implies that it might or might not provide control.

41. ". . . Male children born to women who smoke during pregnancy run a risk of violent and criminal behavior that lasts well into adulthood." Can we infer that smoking during pregnancy is responsible for criminal behavior in people? No. There are many other factors that contribute to criminal behavior.

42. **Caffeine and Health** In the 1980s, a study linked coffee to a higher risk of heart disease and pancreatic cancer. In the early 1990s, studies showed that drinking coffee posed minimal health threats. However, in 1994, a study showed that pregnant women who drank 3 or more cups of tea daily may be at risk for miscarriage. In 1998, a study claimed that women who drank more than a half-cup of caffeinated tea every day may actually increase their fertility. In 1998, a study showed that over a lifetime, a few extra cups of coffee a day can raise blood pressure, heart rate, and stress (*Source:* "Bottom Line: Is It Good for You? Or Bad?" by Monika Guttman, *USA TODAY Weekend*). Suggest some reasons why these studies appear to be conflicting. Possible answer: It could be the amount of caffeine in the coffee or tea. It could have been the brewing method.

Extending the Concepts

43. Find an article that describes a statistical study, and identify the study as observational or experimental. Answers will vary.

44. For the article that you used in Exercise 43, identify the independent variable(s) and dependent variable for the study. Answers will vary.

45. For the article that you selected in Exercise 43, suggest some confounding variables that may have an effect on the results of the study. Answers will vary.

46. Select a newspaper or magazine article that involves a statistical study, and write a paper answering these questions. Answers will vary.

  a. Is this study descriptive or inferential? Explain your answer.

  b. What are the variables used in the study? In your opinion, what level of measurement was used to obtain the data from the variables?

  c. Does the article define the population? If so, how is it defined? If not, how could it be defined?

  d. Does the article state the sample size and how the sample was obtained? If so, determine the size of the sample and explain how it was selected. If not, suggest a way it could have been obtained.

  e. Explain *in your own words* what procedure (survey, comparison of groups, etc.) might have been used to determine the study's conclusions.

  f. Do you agree or disagree with the conclusions? State your reasons.

1–5   Computers and Calculators

OBJECTIVE

Explain the importance of computers and calculators in statistics.

In the past, statistical calculations were done with pencil and paper. However, with the advent of calculators, numerical computations became much easier. Computers do all the numerical calculation. All one does is to enter the data into the computer and use the appropriate command; the computer will print the answer or display it on the screen. Now the TI-84 Plus graphing calculator accomplishes the same thing.

There are many statistical packages available. This book uses Microsoft Excel and MINITAB. Instructions for using the TI-84 Plus graphing calculator, Excel, and MINITAB have been placed at the end of each relevant section, in subsections entitled Technology Step by Step.

You should realize that the computer and calculator merely give numerical answers and save the time and effort of doing calculations by hand. You are still responsible for understanding and interpreting each statistical concept. In addition, you should realize that the results come from the data and do not appear magically on the computer. Doing calculations by using the procedure tables will help you reinforce this idea.

The author has left it up to instructors to choose how much technology they will incorporate into the course.

⏚ Technology   Step by Step

TI-84 Plus
Step by Step

The TI-84 Plus graphing calculator can be used for a variety of statistical graphs and tests.

General Information

To turn calculator on:
Press **ON** key.
To turn calculator off:
Press **2nd [OFF]**.

To reset defaults only:

  1. Press **2nd,** then **[MEM]**.

  2. Select **7,** then **2,** then **2.**

Optional. To reset settings on calculator and clear memory (*Note:* this will clear all settings and programs in the calculator's memory):
Press **2nd,** then **[MEM]**. Then press **7,** then **1,** then **2.**
(Also, the contrast may need to be adjusted after this.)
To adjust contrast (if necessary):
Press **2nd.** Then press and hold ▲ to darken or ▼ to lighten contrast.

To clear screen:
Press **CLEAR.**
(*Note:* This will return you to the screen you were using.)
To display a menu:
Press appropriate menu key. Example: **STAT.**
To return to home screen:
Press **2nd,** then **[QUIT].**
To move around on the screens:
Use the arrow keys.
To select items on the menu:
Press the corresponding number or move the cursor to the item, using the arrow keys. Then press **ENTER.**
(*Note:* In some cases, you do not have to press **ENTER,** and in other cases you may need to press **ENTER** twice.)

Entering Data

To enter single-variable data (clear the old list if necessary, see "Editing Data"):

1. Press **STAT** to display the Edit menu.

2. Press **ENTER** to select 1:Edit.

3. Enter the data in L₁ and press **ENTER** after each value.

4. After all data values are entered, press **STAT** to get back to the Edit menu or **2nd [QUIT]** to end.

Example TI1–1

Enter the following data values in L₁: **213, 208, 203, 215, 222.**
To enter multiple-variable data:
The TI-84 Plus will take up to six lists designated
L₁, L₂, L₃, L₄, L₅, and L₆.

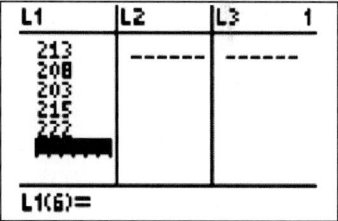

1. To enter more than one set of data values, complete the preceding steps. Then move the cursor to L₂ by pressing the ▶ key.

2. Repeat the steps in the preceding part.

Editing Data

To correct a data value before pressing **ENTER,** use ◀ and retype the value and press **ENTER.**
To correct a data value in a list after pressing **ENTER,** move the cursor to the incorrect value in list and type in the correct value. Then press **ENTER.**
To delete a data value in a list:
Move the cursor to a value and press **DEL.**
To insert a data value in a list:

1. Move cursor to position where data value is to be inserted; then press **2nd [INS].**

2. Type data value; then press **ENTER.**

To clear a list:

1. Press **STAT,** then **4.**

2. Enter list to be cleared. Example: To clear L₁, press **2nd [L₁].** Then press **ENTER.**

   (*Note:* To clear several lists, follow Step 1, but enter each list to be cleared, separating them with commas. To clear all lists at once, follow Step 1; then press **ENTER.**)

Sorting Data

To sort the data in a list:

1. Enter the data in L₁.

2. Press **STAT,** and then **2** to get SortA(to sort the list in ascending order.

3. Then press **2nd [L₁] ENTER.**

The calculator will display Done.

4. Press **STAT** and then **ENTER** to display the sorted list.
(*Note:* The SortD(or **3** sorts the list in descending order.)

Example TI1–2

Sort in ascending order the data values entered in
Example TI1–1.

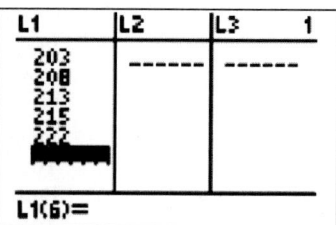

EXCEL
Step by Step

Excel's Analysis
ToolPak Add-In

General Information

Microsoft Excel 2019 has two different ways to solve statistical problems. First, there are built-in functions, such as STDEV and CHITEST, available from the standard toolbar by clicking Formulas, and then selecting the Insert Function icon f_x . Another feature of Excel that is useful for calculating multiple statistical measures and performing statistical tests for a set of data is the Data Analysis command found in the Analysis ToolPak Add-in.

To load the Analysis ToolPak:

Click the File tab in the upper left-hand corner of an Excel workbook, then select Options in the left-hand panel.

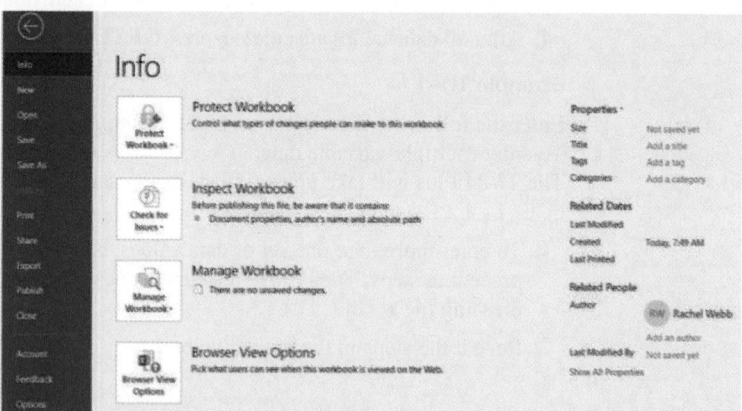

1. Click Add-Ins, and then click the Go button at the bottom of the Excel Options page to the right of the Manage tool.

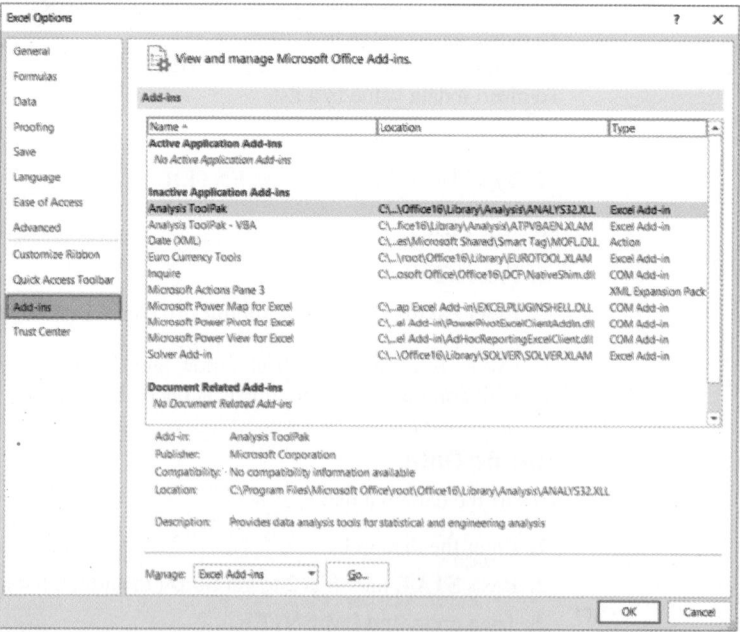

2. Check the Analysis ToolPak Add-in and Analysis ToolPak-VBA, then click OK.

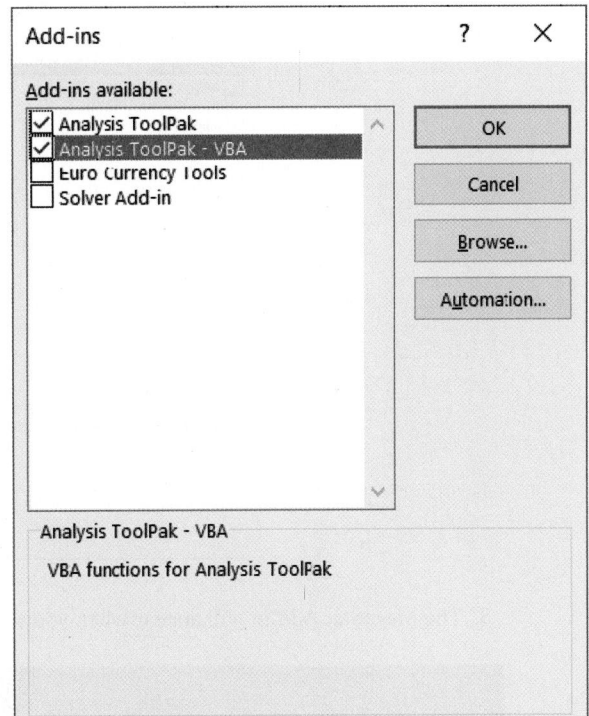

3. Click the Data Tab. The Analysis ToolPak will appear in the Analysis group.

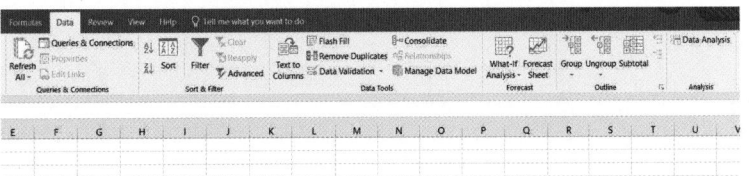

MegaStat

Later in this text you will encounter a few Excel Technology Step by Step operations that will require the use of the MegaStat Add-in for Excel. MegaStat can be purchased from www.mhhe.com/megastat.

1. Save the Zip file containing the MegaStat Excel Add-in file (MegaStat.xla) and the associated help file on your computer's hard drive.

2. Open the Excel software.

3. Click the File tab and select Options (as before with the installation of the Analysis ToolPak).

4. Click the Add-Ins button. MegaStat will not appear as an Application until first installation.

5. Click Go button next to the Manage (Add-Ins) Tool at the bottom of the Excel Options window.

6. Once the Add-Ins Checkbox appears, click Browse to locate the MegaStat.xla file on your computer's hard drive.

7. Select the MegaStat.xla file from the hard drive; click the Checkbox next to it and click OK.

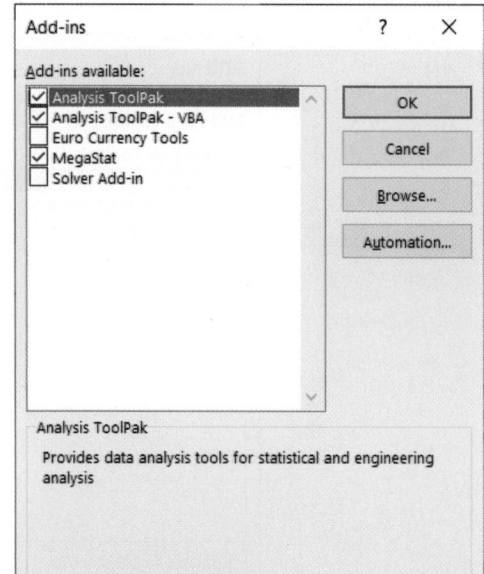

8. The MegaStat Add-in will appear when you select the Add-Ins tab in the Toolbar.

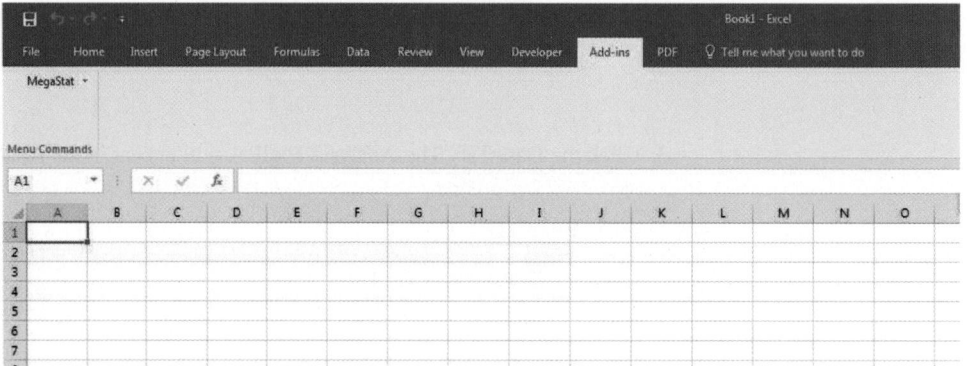

Entering Data

1. Select a cell at the top of a column on an Excel worksheet where you want to enter data. When working with data values for a single variable, you will usually want to enter the values into a single column.

2. Type each data value and press **[Enter]** or **[Tab]** on your keyboard.

You can also add more worksheets to an Excel workbook by clicking the Insert Worksheet icon ⊕ located at the bottom of an open workbook.

Example XL1–1: Opening an existing Excel workbook/worksheet

1. Open the Microsoft Office Excel 2019 program.

2. Click the File tab, then click Open.

3. Click the name of the library that contains the file, such as My documents, and then click Open.

4. Click the name of the Excel file that you want to open and then click Open.

Note: Excel files have the extension .xls or .xlsx.

MINITAB
Step by Step

General Information

MINITAB statistical software provides a wide range of statistical analysis and graphing capabilities.

Take Note

In this text you will see captured MINITAB images from Windows computers running MINITAB Release 17. If you are using an earlier or later release of MINITAB, the screens you see on your computer may bear slight visual differences from the screens pictured in this text.

Start the Program

1. Click the Windows Start Menu, then All Programs.
2. Click the MINITAB folder and then click 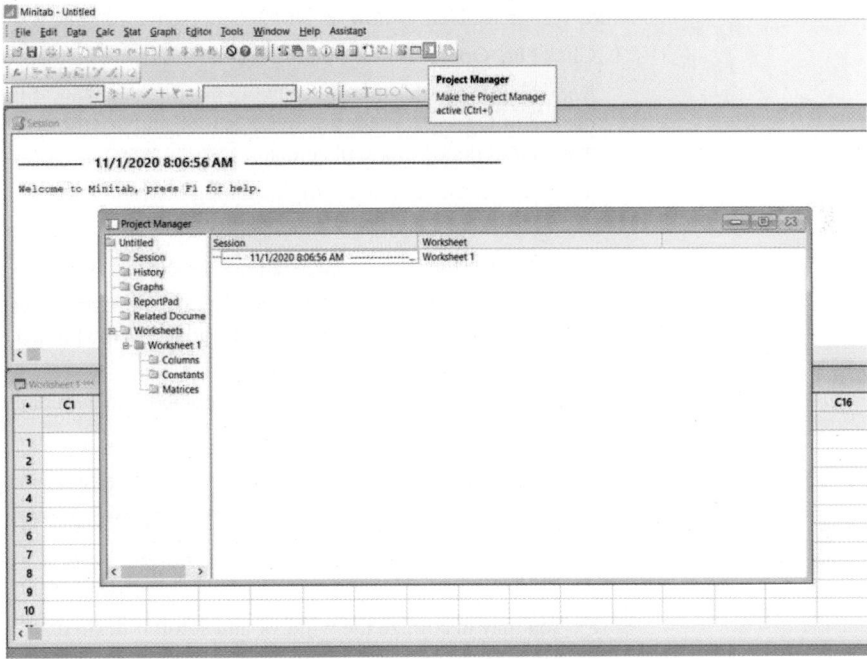 Minitab 17 Statistical Software the program icon. The program screen will look similar to the one shown here. You will see the Session Window, the Worksheet Window, and perhaps the Project Manager Window.
3. Click the Project Manager icon on the toolbar to bring the project manager to the front.

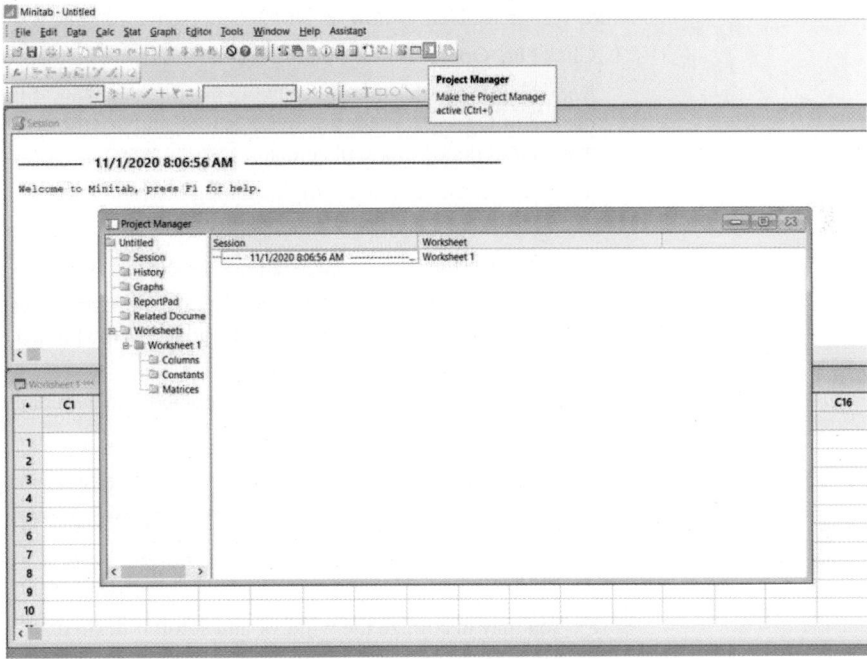

To use the program, data must be entered from the keyboard or from a file.

Entering Data from the Keyboard

In MINITAB, all the data for one variable are stored in a column. Step by step instructions for entering these data follow.

Data

213	208	203	215	222

1. Click in row 1 of Worksheet 1***. This makes the worksheet the active window and puts the cursor in the first cell. The small data entry arrow in the upper left-hand corner of the worksheet should be pointing down. If it is not, click it to change the direction in which the cursor will move when you press the [Enter] key.

2. Type in each number, pressing [Enter] after each entry, including the last number typed.

3. *Optional:* Click in the space above row 1 to type in **Weight,** the column label.

Save a Worksheet File

4. Click on the **File Menu**. *Note:* This is *not* the same as clicking the disk icon 🖫.

5. Click **Save Current Worksheet As . . .**

6. In the dialog box you will need to verify three items:

   a) Save in: Click on or type in the disk drive and directory where you will store your data. This may be a thumb drive such as E:\ or a hard-drive folder such as C:\MinitabData.

   b) File Name: Type in the name of the file, such as **MyData.**

   c) Save as Type: The default here is MINITAB. An extension of mtw is added to the name.

      Click [Save]. The name of the worksheet will change from Worksheet 1*** to MyData. MTW***. The triple asterisks indicate the active worksheet.

Open the Databank File

The raw data are shown in Appendix B. There is a row for each person's data and a column for each variable. MINITAB data files comprised of data sets used in this book are available in the online resources. Here is how to get the data from a file into a worksheet.

1. Click **File>Open Worksheet**. A sequence of menu instructions will be shown this way.

   Note: This is *not* the same as clicking the file icon 📂. If the dialog box says Open Project instead of Open Worksheet, click [Cancel] and use the correct menu item. The Open Worksheet dialog box will be displayed.

2. You must check three items in this dialog box.

   a) The Look In: dialog box should show the directory where the file is located.

   b) Make sure the Files of Type: shows the correct type, MINITAB [*.mtw].

   c) Double-click the file name in the list box Databank.mtw. A dialog box may inform you that a copy of this file is about to be added to the project. Click on the checkbox if you do not want to see this warning again.

3. Click the [OK] button. The data will be copied into a second worksheet. Part of the worksheet is shown here.

	C1	C2	C3	C4	C5	C6	C7	C8	C9	C10	C11-T	C12-T
	ID-NUMBER	AGE	ED-LEVEL	SMOKING STATUS	EXERCISE	WEIGHT	SERUM-CHOL	SYSTOLIC	IQ	SODIUM	GENDER	MARITAL-STATUS
1	1	27	2	1	1	120	193	126	110	136	F	M
2	2	18	1	0	1	145	210	120	105	137	M	S
3	3	32	2	0	0	118	196	128	115	135	F	M
4	4	24	2	0	1	162	208	129	108	142	M	M

   a) You may maximize the window and scroll if desired.

   b) C12-T Marital Status has a T appended to the label to indicate alphanumeric data. MyData.MTW is not erased or overwritten. Multiple worksheets can be available; however, only the active worksheet is available for analysis.

4. To switch between the worksheets, select **Window>MyData.MTW.**

5. Select **File>Exit** to quit. To save the project, click [Yes].

6. Type in the name of the file, **Chapter01.** The Data Window, the Session Window, and settings are all in one file called a project. Projects have an extension of mpj instead of mtw.

   Clicking the disk icon 🖫 on the menu bar is the same as selecting **File>Save Project.**

   Clicking the file icon 📂 is the same as selecting **File>Open Project.**

7. Click [Save]. The mpj extension will be added to the name. The computer will return to the Windows desktop. The two worksheets, the Session Window results, and settings are saved in this project file. When a project file is opened, the program will start up right where you left off.

Summary

- The two major areas of statistics are descriptive and inferential. Descriptive statistics includes the collection, organization, summarization, and presentation of data. Inferential statistics includes making inferences from samples to populations, estimations and hypothesis testing, determining relationships, and making predictions. Inferential statistics is based on *probability theory*. (1–1)*

- Data can be classified as qualitative or quantitative. Quantitative data can be either discrete or continuous, depending on the values they can assume. Data can also be measured by various scales. The four basic levels of measurement are nominal, ordinal, interval, and ratio. (1–2)

- Since in most cases the populations under study are large, statisticians use subgroups called samples to get the necessary data for their studies. There are four basic methods used to obtain samples: random, systematic, stratified, and cluster. (1–3)

- There are two basic types of statistical studies: observational studies and experimental studies. When conducting observational studies, researchers observe what is happening or what has happened and then draw conclusions based on these observations. They do not attempt to manipulate the variables in any way. (1–4)

- When conducting an experimental study, researchers manipulate one or more of the independent or explanatory variables and see how this manipulation influences the dependent or outcome variable. (1–4)

- Finally, the applications of statistics are many and varied. People encounter them in everyday life, such as in reading newspapers or magazines, listening to an MP3 player, or watching television. Since statistics is used in almost every field of endeavor, the educated individual should be knowledgeable about the vocabulary, concepts, and procedures of statistics. Also, everyone should be aware that statistics can be misused. (1–4)

- Today, computers and calculators are used extensively in statistics to facilitate the computations. (1–5)

*The numbers in parentheses indicate the chapter section where the material is explained.

Important Terms

blinding 20	dependent variable 19	measurement scales 8	random variable 3
blocking 20	descriptive statistics 3	nominal level of measurement 8	ratio level of measurement 8
boundary 7	discrete variables 6	nonsampling error 16	replication 20
census 3	double blinding 20	observational study 18	retrospective study 18
cluster sample 14	experimental study 18	ordinal level of measurement 8	sample 3
completely randomized design 20	explanatory variable 19	outcome variable 19	sampling error 16
confounding variable 19	Hawthorne effect 19	placebo effect 20	statistics 2
continuous variables 6	hypothesis testing 4	population 3	stratified sample 13
control group 19	independent variable 19	probability 4	systematic sample 12
convenience sample 14	inferential statistics 4	qualitative variables 6	treatment group 19
cross-sectional study 18	interval level of measurement 8	quantitative variables 6	variable 3
data 3	longitudinal study 18	quasi-experimental study 19	volunteer sample 14
data set 3	lurking variable 19	random sample 12	
data value or datum 3	matched-pair design 20		

Review Exercises

Section 1–1

For Exercises 1–8, state whether descriptive or inferential statistics has been used.

1. By 2040 at least 3.5 billion people will run short of water. Inferential
Source: World Future Society

2. In a sample of 100 individuals, 36% think that watching television is the best way to spend an evening. Descriptive

3. In a survey of 2067 adults ages 50+, 75% said that they posted notes on social media websites. Descriptive
Source: AARP Survey

4. In a poll of 3036 adults, 32% said that they got a flu shot at a retail clinic. Descriptive
Source: Harris Interactive Poll

5. Allergy therapy makes bees go away. Inferential
Source: Prevention

6. Drinking decaffeinated coffee can raise cholesterol levels by 7%. Inferential
Source: American Heart Association

7. In a survey of 1500 people who gave up driving, the average of the ages at which they quit driving was 85. Descriptive
Source: Men's Health

8. Experts say that mortgage rates may soon hit bottom Inferential
Source: USA TODAY

Section 1–2

For Exercises 9–18, classify each as nominal-level, ordinal-level, interval-level, or ratio-level measurement.

9. Pages in the 25 best-selling mystery novels Ratio
10. Rankings of golfers in a tournament Ordinal
11. Temperatures of 10 toasters Interval
12. Weights of selected cell phones Ratio
13. Salaries of the coaches in the NFL Ratio
14. Times required to complete a 6-mile bike ride Ratio
15. Ratings of textbooks (poor, fair, good, excellent) Ordinal
16. Number of amps delivered by battery chargers Ratio
17. Ages of the players on a professional football team Ratio
18. Categories of magazines in a physician's office (sports, women's, health, men's, news) Nominal

For Exercises 19–26, classify each variable as qualitative or quantitative.

19. Marital status of nurses in a hospital Qualitative
20. Time it takes 10 people to complete a *New York Times* crossword puzzle Quantitative
21. Weights of lobsters in a tank in a restaurant Quantitative
22. Colors of automobiles in a shopping center parking lot Qualitative
23. Amount of garbage (in pounds) discarded by residents of a high-rise apartment complex Quantitative
24. Capacity of the NFL football stadiums Quantitative
25. Ages of people living in a personal care home Quantitative
26. The different species of fish sold by a pet shop store Qualitative

For Exercises 27–34, classify each variable as discrete or continuous.

27. Number of street corner mailboxes in the city of Philadelphia Discrete
28. Relative humidity levels in operating rooms at local hospitals Continuous
29. Number of bananas in a bunch at several local supermarkets Discrete
30. Ages of women when they were first married Continuous
31. Weights of the backpacks of first-graders on a school bus Continuous
32. Number of students each day who make appointments with a math tutor at a local college Discrete
33. Duration of marriages in America (in years) Continuous
34. Ages of children in a preschool Continuous

For Exercises 35–38, give the boundaries of each value.

35. 56 yards 55.5–56.5 yards
36. 105.4 miles 105.35–105.45 miles
37. 72.6 tons 72.55–72.65 tons
38. 9.54 millimeters 9.535–9.545 millimeters

Section 1–3

For Exercises 39–44, classify each sample as random, systematic, stratified, cluster, or other.

39. In a large school district, all teachers from two buildings are interviewed to determine whether they believe the students have less homework to do now than in previous years. Cluster
40. All fast-food workers at a randomly selected fast-food restaurant are selected and asked how many hours per week they work. Cluster
41. A group of unmarried men are selected using random numbers and asked how long it has been since their last date. Random
42. Every 100th hamburger manufactured is checked to determine its fat content. Systematic
43. Mail carriers of a large city are divided into groups according to gender and according to whether they walk or ride on their routes. Then 10 are selected from each group and interviewed to determine whether they have been bitten by a dog in the last year. Stratified
44. People are asked to phone in their response to a survey question. Volunteer or other

Section 1–4

For Exercises 45–48, identify each study as being either observational or experimental.

45. Subjects were randomly assigned to two groups, and one group was given an herb and the other group a placebo. After 6 months, the numbers of respiratory tract infections each group had were compared. Experimental

46. A researcher stood at a busy intersection to see if the color of the automobile that a person drives is related to running red lights. Observational

47. A sample of employees were asked if their supervisors (bosses) at work were to hug them, would they consider that a form of sexual harassment? Observational

48. Three groups of gamblers were randomly selected. The first group was given $25 in casino money. The second group was given a $25 coupon for food. The third group was given nothing. After a trip to the casino, each group was surveyed and asked their opinion of their casino experience. Experimental

For Exercises 49–52, identify the independent and dependent variables for each study.

49. A study was conducted to determine if crocodiles raised in captivity (i.e., in a zoo) grew faster than crocodiles living in the wild. Identify the explanatory variable and the outcome variable. Independent variable—habitat. Dependent variable—weight

50. People who walk at least 3 miles a day are randomly selected, and their blood triglyceride levels are measured in order to determine if the number of miles that they walk has any influence on these levels. Independent variable—miles walked Dependent variable—triglyceride level

51. In an article in the *British Journal of Nutrition,* two types of mice were randomly selected. One group received a thyme supplement for a specific time, while another group was used as a control group and received no supplements. The brains of the mice were then analyzed, and it was found that the brains of the group of mice that received the thyme supplements had antioxidant levels similar to those of younger mice. It was concluded that the thyme supplement increased the antioxidants in the brains of the mice. Independent variable—thyme Dependent variable—antioxidants

52. A study was conducted to determine if workers who had a flexible work schedule had greater job satisfaction than those workers who worked a regular nine-to-five work schedule. Independent variable—type of work schedule. Dependent variable—job satisfaction

For Exercises 53–58, explain why the claims of these studies might be suspect. Answers will vary.

53. Based on a recent telephone survey, 72% of those contacted shop online.

54. In High Point County there are 672 raccoons.

55. A survey of a group of people said the thing they dislike most about winter is snow.

56. Only 5% of men surveyed said that they liked romantic comedies.

57. A recent study shows that high school dropouts spend less time on the Internet than those who graduated; therefore, the Internet raises your IQ.

58. Most shark attacks occur in ocean water that is 3 feet deep; therefore, it is safer to swim in deep water.

■ STATISTICS TODAY

How Much Do You Owe? —Revisited

In order to answer the questions posted at the beginning of this chapter, we can use information from the United States Federal Reserve.

The total amount of money owed by college graduates at this writing is over $1.6 trillion.

There are over 45 million graduate borrowers in the United States.

The average college graduate loan is $32,731. The median loan payment is $222 per month. (This means about one-half of the borrowers pay more than $222 and about one-half pay less than $222.)

The largest range of student debt is between $20,000 and $40,000.

The largest concentration of borrowers is between the ages of 25 and 34. (This number accounts for 35 million borrowers.)

More than 3 million graduates who borrowed money to pay for their education owe over $100,000.

Finally, student loan debt is now the second highest consumer debt and is larger than credit card debt and auto loan debt. Only mortgage debt is larger.

As you can see from the statistics, student debt is a serious problem for many people in the United States.

≡ Chapter Quiz

Determine whether each statement is true or false. If the statement is false, explain why.

1. Probability is used as a basis for inferential statistics. True

2. When the sample does not represent the population, it is called a biased sample. True

3. The difference between a sampling measure and a population measure is called a nonsampling error. False

4. When the population of college professors is divided into groups according to their rank (instructor, assistant professor, etc.) and then several are selected from each group to make up a sample, the sample is called a cluster sample. False

5. The variable temperature is an example of a quantitative variable. True

6. The height of basketball players is considered a continuous variable. True

7. The boundary of a value such as 6 inches would be 5.9–6.1 inches. False

Select the best answer.

8. The number of ads on a one-hour television show is what type of data?
   a. Nominal
   b. Qualitative
   c. Discrete
   d. Continuous

9. What are the boundaries of 25.6 ounces?
   a. 25–26 ounces
   b. 25.55–25.65 ounces
   c. 25.5–25.7 ounces
   d. 20–39 ounces

10. A researcher divided subjects into two groups according to gender and then selected members from each group for her sample. What sampling method was the researcher using?
    a. Cluster
    b. Random
    c. Systematic
    d. Stratified

11. Data that can be classified according to color are measured on what scale?
    a. Nominal
    b. Ratio
    c. Ordinal
    d. Interval

12. A study that involves no researcher intervention is called
    a. An experimental study.
    b. A noninvolvement study.
    c. An observational study.
    d. A quasi-experimental study.

13. A variable that interferes with other variables in the study is called
    a. A confounding variable.
    b. An explanatory variable.
    c. An outcome variable.
    d. An interfering variable.

Use the best answer to complete these statements.

14. Two major branches of statistics are _____ and _____. Descriptive, inferential

15. Two uses of probability are _____ and _____. Gambling, insurance Answers may vary.

16. The group of all subjects under study is called a(n) _____. Population

17. A group of subjects selected from the group of all subjects under study is called a(n) _____. Sample

18. Three reasons why samples are used in statistics:
    a. _____ b. _____ c. _____
    a. Saves time b. Saves money c. Use when population is infinite

19. The four basic sampling methods are
    a. _____ b. _____ c. _____ d. _____
    a. Random b. Systematic c. Cluster d. Stratified

20. A study that uses intact groups when it is not possible to randomly assign participants to the groups is called a(n) _____ study. Quasi-experimental

21. In a research study, participants should be assigned to groups using _____ methods, if possible. Random

22. For each statement, decide whether descriptive or inferential statistics is used.
    a. The average life expectancy in New Zealand is 78.49 years. Descriptive
    Source: World Factbook

    b. A diet high in fruits and vegetables will lower blood pressure. Inferential
    Source: Institute of Medicine

    c. The total amount of estimated losses for Hurricane Katrina was $125 billion. Descriptive
    Source: The World Almanac and Book of Facts

    d. Researchers stated that the shape of a person's ears is relative to the person's aggression. Inferential
    Source: American Journal of Human Biology

e. In 2050, it is estimated that there will be 18 million Americans who are age 85 and over. Inferential

Source: U.S. Census Bureau

23. Classify each as nominal-level, ordinal-level, interval-level, or ratio-level of measurement.

a. Rating of movies as G, PG, and R Nominal

b. Number of candy bars sold on a fund drive Ratio

c. Classification of automobiles as subcompact, compact, standard, and luxury Ordinal

d. Temperatures of hair dryers Interval

e. Weights of suitcases on a commercial airliner Ratio

24. Classify each variable as discrete or continuous.

a. Ages of people working in a large factory Continuous

b. Number of cups of coffee served at a restaurant Discrete

c. The amount of drug injected into a guinea pig Continuous

d. The time it takes a student to drive to school Continuous

e. The number of gallons of milk sold each day at a grocery store Discrete

25. Give the boundaries of each.

a. 32 minutes 31.5–32.5 minutes

b. 0.48 millimeter 0.475–0.485 millimeters

c. 6.2 inches 6.15–6.25 inches

d. 19 pounds 18.5–19.5 pounds

e. 12.1 quarts 12.05–12.15 quarts

Critical Thinking Challenges

1. **World's Busiest Airports** A study of the world's busiest airports was conducted by *Airports Council International.* Describe three variables that one could use to determine which airports are the busiest. What *units* would one use to measure these variables? Are these variables categorical, discrete, or continuous?

2. **Smoking and Criminal Behavior** The results of a study published in *Archives of General Psychiatry* stated that male children born to women who smoke during pregnancy run a risk of violent and criminal behavior that lasts into adulthood. The results of this study were challenged by some people in the media. Give several reasons why the results of this study would be challenged.

3. **Piano Lessons Improve Math Ability** The results of a study published in *Neurological Research* stated that

second-graders who took piano lessons and played a computer math game more readily grasped math problems in fractions and proportions than a similar group who took an English class and played the same math game. What type of inferential study was this? Give several reasons why the piano lessons could improve a student's math ability.

4. **ACL Tears in Collegiate Soccer Players** A study of 2958 collegiate soccer players showed that in 46 anterior cruciate ligament (ACL) tears, 36 were in women and 10 were in men. Calculate the percentages of tears for each sex.

a. Can it be concluded that female athletes tear their knees more often than male athletes?

b. Comment on how this study's conclusion might have been reached.

Data Projects

1. **Business and Finance** Investigate the types of data that are collected regarding stock and bonds, for example, price, earnings ratios, and bond ratings. Find as many types of data as possible. For each, identify the level of measurement as nominal, ordinal, interval, or ratio. For any quantitative data, also note if they are discrete or continuous.

2. **Sports and Leisure** Select a professional sport. Investigate the types of data that are collected about that sport, for example, in baseball, the level of play (A, AA, AAA, Major League), batting average, and home runs. For

each, identify the level of measurement as nominal, ordinal, interval, or ratio. For any quantitative data, also note if they are discrete or continuous.

3. **Technology** Music organization programs on computers and music players maintain information about a song, such as the writer, song length, genre, and your personal rating. Investigate the types of data collected about a song. For each, identify the level of measurement as nominal, ordinal, interval, or ratio. For any quantitative data, also note if they are discrete or continuous.

4. **Health and Wellness** Think about the types of data that can be collected about your health and wellness, things such as blood type, cholesterol level, smoking status, and body mass index. Find as many data items as you can. For each, identify the level of measurement as nominal, ordinal, interval, or ratio. For any quantitative data, also note if they are discrete or continuous.

5. **Politics and Economics** Every 10 years since 1790, the federal government has conducted a census of U.S. residents. Investigate the types of data that were collected in the 2020 U.S. Census. For each, identify the level of measurement as nominal, ordinal, interval, or

ratio. For any quantitative data, also note if they are discrete or continuous. Use the library or a genealogy website to find a census form from 1860. What types of data were collected? How do the types of data differ?

6. **Your Class** Your school probably has a database that contains information about each student, such as age, county of residence, credits earned, and ethnicity. Investigate the types of student data that your college collects and reports. For each, identify the level of measurement as nominal, ordinal, interval, or ratio. For any quantitative data, also note if they are discrete or continuous.

Answers to Applying the Concepts

Section 1–1　Attendance and Grades

1. The variables are grades and attendance.

2. The data consist of specific grades and attendance numbers.

3. These are descriptive statistics; however, if an inference were made to all students, then that would be inferential statistics.

4. The population under study is all students at Manatee Community College (MCC).

5. While not specified, we probably have data from a sample of MCC students.

6. Based on the data, it appears that, in general, the better your attendance, the higher your grade.

Section 1–2　Fatal Transportation Injuries

1. The variables are transportation industry and fatal accidents.

2. Transportation industry is a qualitative variable, and the number of fatal accidents is a quantitative variable.

3. The number of fatalities is discrete.

4. The type of industry is nominal, and the number of fatalities is ratio.

5. Even though the number of fatalities for the railroad industry is lowest, you should consider the fact that fewer people use the railroads to travel than the other industries.

6. A person's transportation choice might also be affected by convenience, cost, service, availability, etc.

7. Answers will vary. The railroad industry had the fewest fatalities followed by water vehicle accidents while the aircraft accidents were about three times as many as the water vehicle accidents. Of course, the most fatalities occurred in highway accidents.

Section 1–3　American Culture and Drug Abuse

Answers will vary, so this is one possible answer.

1. I used a telephone survey. The advantage to my survey method is that this was a relatively inexpensive survey method (although more expensive than using the mail) that could get a fairly sizable response. The disadvantage to my survey method is that I have not included anyone without a telephone. (*Note:* My survey used a random dialing method to include unlisted numbers and cell phone exchanges.)

2. A mail survey also would have been fairly inexpensive, but my response rate may have been much lower than what I got with my telephone survey. Interviewing would have allowed me to use follow-up questions and to clarify any questions of the respondents at the time of the interview. However, interviewing is very labor- and cost-intensive.

3. I used ordinal data on a scale of 1 to 5. The scores were 1 = strongly disagree, 2 = disagree, 3 = neutral, 4 = agree, 5 = strongly agree.

4. The random method that I used was a random dialing method.

5. To include people from each state, I used a stratified random sample, collecting data randomly from each of the area codes and telephone exchanges available.

6. This method allowed me to make sure that I had representation from each area of the United States.

7. Convenience samples may not be representative of the population, and a convenience sample of adolescents would probably differ greatly from the general population with regard to the influence of American culture on illegal drug use.

Section 1–4　Today's Cigarettes

1. This was an experiment, since the researchers imposed a treatment on each of the four groups involved in the study.

2. The independent variable was the smoking device. The dependent variables were carbon monoxide, heart rate, and plasma nicotine.

3. The treatment group was the group containing no vapors.

4. A subject's blood pressure might not be affected by knowing that they were part of a study. However, if the subject's blood pressure was affected by this knowledge, all the subjects (in all the groups) would be affected similarly. This might be an example of the Hawthorne effect.

5. Answers will vary. The age of the subjects, gender, previous smoking habits, and their physical fitness could be confounding variables.

6. Answers will vary. One possible answer is that the study design was fine, but that it cannot be generalized beyond the population of backgrounds of the subjects in the study.

2

Frequency Distributions and Graphs

≣ STATISTICS TODAY

How Your Identity Can Be Stolen

Identity fraud is a big business today—more than 9 million people are victims. The total amount of fraud in a recent year was $14.4 million. Identity fraud occurs every 2 seconds. About 1 in 15 people are victims of identity theft. It takes 100–200 hours and six months to correctly identify problems resulting from identity theft. The average amount of theft is $1343 per victim. The percents for the top six types of identity theft for a recent year are shown.

Common Types of Identify Thefts	
Credit Card Fraud	35%
Employment or Tax-Related Fraud	22%
Phone or Utility Fraud	15%
Bank Fraud	13%
Loan or Lease Fraud	8%
Government Documents or Government Benefits Fraud	7%

Looking at a table does not have the impact that presenting numbers in a well-drawn graph does. See Statistics Today—Revisited at the end of this chapter for a graph that can better represent these data. This chapter will show you how to construct appropriate graphs to represent data and help you to get your point across.

OUTLINE

OBJECTIVES

After completing this chapter, you should be able to

1 Organize data using a frequency distribution.

2 Represent data in frequency distributions graphically, using histograms, frequency polygons, and ogives.

3 Represent data using bar graphs, Pareto charts, time series graphs, pie graphs, and dotplots.

4 Draw and interpret a stem and leaf plot.

Introduction

When conducting a statistical study, the researcher must gather data for the particular variable under study. For example, if a researcher wishes to study the number of people who were bitten by poisonous snakes in a specific geographic area over the past several years, the researcher has to gather the data from various doctors, hospitals, or health departments.

To describe situations, draw conclusions, or make inferences about events, the researcher must organize the data in some meaningful way. The most convenient method of organizing data is to construct a *frequency distribution.*

After organizing the data, the researcher must present them so they can be understood by those who will benefit from reading the study. The most useful method of presenting the data is by constructing *statistical charts* and *graphs.* There are many different types of charts and graphs, and each one has a specific purpose.

This chapter explains how to organize data by constructing frequency distributions and how to present the data by constructing charts and graphs. The charts and graphs illustrated here are histograms, frequency polygons, ogives, pie graphs, Pareto charts, and time series graphs. A graph that combines the characteristics of a frequency distribution and a histogram, called a stem and leaf plot, is also explained.

2–1   Organizing Data

OBJECTIVE

Organize data using a frequency distribution.

Suppose a researcher wished to do a study on the ages of the 50 wealthiest people in the world. The researcher first would have to get the data on the ages of the people. In this case, these ages are listed in *Forbes* magazine. When the data are in original form, they are called **raw data** and are listed next.

45	46	64	57	85
92	51	71	54	48
27	66	76	55	69
54	44	54	75	46
61	68	78	61	83
88	45	89	67	56
81	58	55	62	38
55	56	64	81	38
49	68	91	56	68
46	47	83	71	62

Since little information can be obtained from looking at raw data, the researcher organizes the data into what is called a *frequency distribution.*

A **frequency distribution** is the organization of raw data in table form, using classes and frequencies.

Each raw data value is placed into a quantitative or qualitative category called a **class.** The **frequency** of a class then is the number of data values contained in a specific class. A frequency distribution is shown for the preceding data set.

Class limits	Tally	Frequency
27–35	/	1
36–44	///	3
45–53	⟊ ////	9
54–62	⟊ ⟊ ⟊	15
63–71	⟊ ⟊	10
72–80	///	3
81–89	⟊ //	7
90–98	//	2
		50

Now some general observations can be made from looking at the frequency distribution. For example, it can be stated that the majority of the wealthy people in the study are 45 years old or older.

The classes in this distribution are 27–35, 36–44, etc. These values are called *class limits*. The data values 27, 28, 29, 30, 31, 32, 33, 34, 35 can be tallied in the first class; 36, 37, 38, 39, 40, 41, 42, 43, 44 in the second class; and so on.

Two types of frequency distributions that are most often used are the *categorical frequency distribution* and the *grouped frequency distribution*. The procedures for constructing these distributions are shown now.

Categorical Frequency Distributions

The **categorical frequency distribution** is used for data that can be placed in specific categories, such as nominal- or ordinal-level data. For example, data such as political affiliation, religious affiliation, or major field of study would use categorical frequency distributions.

EXAMPLE 2–1   Breakfast Beverages

Forty people were asked what beverage they drink for breakfast. Construct a categorical frequency distribution for the data and summarize the results. Use these classes: W = water, M = milk, J = juice, C = coffee, and T = tea.

W	J	C	C	J	C	T	W	C	T
W	M	M	W	W	M	W	W	M	C
T	W	J	M	M	C	J	C	M	W
W	C	W	W	J	W	W	M	C	J

Source: Based on U.S. Department of Agriculture

SOLUTION

Since the data are categorical, discrete classes are used. They are W, M, J, C, and T.

Step 1   Make a table as shown.

Class	Tally	Frequency	Percent
W			
M			
J			
C			
T			

Step 2   Tally the data and place the results in the second column labeled Tally.

Step 3   Count the tallies and place the results in the third column labeled Frequency.

Step 4   Find the percentage of values in each class by using the formula

$$\% = \frac{f}{n} \cdot 100$$

where f = frequency of the class and n = total number of values. For example, in class W, the percentage is

$$= \frac{14}{40} \cdot 100 = 35\%.$$

Percentages are not normally part of a frequency distribution, but they can be added since they are used in certain types of graphs such as pie graphs. Also, the decimal equivalent of a percent is called a *relative frequency*.

Step 5   Find the totals for the Frequency and Percent columns. The completed table is shown. It is a good idea to add the Percent column to make sure it sums to 100%. This column won't always sum to 100% because of rounding.

Class	Tally	Frequency	Percent
W	𝙽𝙷𝙻 𝙽𝙷𝙻 ////	14	35%
M	𝙽𝙷𝙻 ///	8	20%
J	𝙽𝙷𝙻 /	6	15%
C	𝙽𝙷𝙻 ////	9	22.5%
T	///	3	7.5%
		Total 40	100%

For the sample, most people selected water and the smallest number selected tea.

Grouped Frequency Distributions

When the range of the data is large, the data must be grouped into classes that are more than one unit in width, in what is called a **grouped frequency distribution.** For example, a distribution of the blood glucose levels in milligrams per deciliter (mg/dL) for 50 randomly selected college students is shown.

Class limits	Class boundaries	Tally	Frequency
58–64	57.5–64.5	/	1
65–71	64.5–71.5	𝙽𝙷𝙻 /	6
72–78	71.5–78.5	𝙽𝙷𝙻 𝙽𝙷𝙻	10
79–85	78.5–85.5	𝙽𝙷𝙻 𝙽𝙷𝙻 ////	14
86–92	85.5–92.5	𝙽𝙷𝙻 𝙽𝙷𝙻 //	12
93–99	92.5–99.5	𝙽𝙷𝙻	5
100–106	99.5–106.5	//	2
			Total 50

The procedure for constructing the preceding frequency distribution is given in Example 2–2; however, several things should be noted. In this distribution, the values 58 and 64 of the first class are called *class limits*. The **lower class limit** is 58; it represents the smallest data value that can be included in the class. The **upper class limit** is 64; it represents the largest data value that can be included in the class. The numbers in the second column are called **class boundaries.** These numbers are used to separate the classes so that there are no gaps in the frequency distribution. The gaps are due to the limits; for example, there is a gap between 64 and 65.

Students sometimes have difficulty finding class boundaries when given the class limits. The basic rule of thumb is that *the class limits should have the same decimal place value as the data, but the class boundaries should have one additional place value and end in a 5.* For example, if the values in the data set are whole numbers, such as 59, 68, and 82, the limits for a class might be 58–64, and the boundaries are 57.5–64.5. Find the boundaries by subtracting 0.5 from 58 (the lower class limit) and adding 0.5 to 64 (the upper class limit).

$$\text{Lower limit} - 0.5 = 58 - 0.5 = 57.5 = \text{lower boundary}$$
$$\text{Upper limit} + 0.5 = 64 + 0.5 = 64.5 = \text{upper boundary}$$

If the data are in tenths, such as 6.2, 7.8, and 12.6, the limits for a class hypothetically might be 7.8–8.8, and the boundaries for that class would be 7.75–8.85. Find these values by subtracting 0.05 from 7.8 and adding 0.05 to 8.8.

Class boundaries are not always included in frequency distributions; however, they give a more formal approach to the procedure of organizing data, including the fact that sometimes the data have been rounded. You should be familiar with boundaries since you may encounter them in a statistical study.

Finally, the **class width** for a class in a frequency distribution is found by subtracting the lower (or upper) class limit of one class from the lower (or upper) class limit of the next class. For example, the class width in the preceding distribution on the distribution of blood glucose levels is 7, found from $65 - 58 = 7$.

The class width can also be found by subtracting the lower boundary from the upper boundary for any given class. In this case, $64.5 - 57.5 = 7$.

Note: Do not subtract the limits of a single class. It will result in an incorrect answer.

The researcher must decide how many classes to use and the width of each class. To construct a frequency distribution, follow these rules:

1. *There should be between 5 and 20 classes.* Although there is no hard-and-fast rule for the number of classes contained in a frequency distribution, it is of utmost importance to have enough classes to present a clear description of the collected data.

2. *It is preferable but not absolutely necessary that the class width be an odd number.* This ensures that the midpoint of each class has the same place value as the data. The **class midpoint** X_m is obtained by adding the lower and upper boundaries and dividing by 2, or adding the lower and upper limits and dividing by 2:

$$X_m = \frac{\text{lower boundary} + \text{upper boundary}}{2}$$

or

$$X_m = \frac{\text{lower limit} + \text{upper limit}}{2}$$

For example, the midpoint of the first class in the example with glucose levels is

$$\frac{57.5 + 64.5}{2} = 61 \quad \text{or} \quad \frac{58 + 64}{2} = 61$$

The midpoint is the numeric location of the center of the class. Midpoints are necessary for graphing (see Section 2–2). If the class width is an even number, the midpoint is in tenths. For example, if the class width is 6 and the boundaries are 5.5 and 11.5, the midpoint is

$$\frac{5.5 + 11.5}{2} = \frac{17}{2} = 8.5$$

Rule 2 is only a suggestion, and it is not rigorously followed, especially when a computer is used to group data.

3. *The classes must be mutually exclusive.* Mutually exclusive classes have nonoverlapping class limits so that data cannot be placed into two classes. Many times, frequency distributions such as this

Age
10–20
20–30
30–40
40–50

are found in the literature or in surveys. Into which class should a 40-year-old person be placed? A better way to construct a frequency distribution is to use classes such as

Age
10–20
21–31
32–42
43–53

Recall that boundaries are mutually exclusive. For example, when a class boundary is 5.5 to 10.5, the data values that are included in that class are values from 6 to 10. A data value of 5 goes into the previous class, and a data value of 11 goes into the next-higher class.

4. *The classes must be continuous.* Even if there are no values in a class, the class must be included in the frequency distribution. There should be no gaps in a frequency distribution. The only exception occurs when the class with a zero frequency is the first or last class. A class with a zero frequency at either end can be omitted without affecting the distribution.

5. *The classes must be exhaustive.* There should be enough classes to accommodate all the data.

6. *The classes must be equal in width.* This avoids a distorted view of the data.

One exception occurs when a distribution has a class that is open-ended. That is, the first class has no specific lower limit, or the last class has no specific upper limit. A frequency distribution with an open-ended class is called an **open-ended distribution.** Here are two examples of distributions with open-ended classes.

Age	Frequency
10–20	3
21–31	6
32–42	4
43–53	10
54 and above	8

Minutes	Frequency
Below 110	16
110–114	24
115–119	38
120–124	14
125–129	5

The frequency distribution for age is open-ended for the last class, which means that anybody who is 54 years or older will be tallied in the last class. The distribution for minutes is open-ended for the first class, meaning that any minute values below 110 will be tallied in that class.

The steps for constructing a grouped frequency distribution are summarized in the following Procedure Table.

Procedure Table

Constructing a Grouped Frequency Distribution

Step 1   Determine the classes.

Find the highest and lowest values.

Find the range.

Select the number of classes desired.

Find the width by dividing the range by the number of classes and rounding up.

Select a starting point (usually the lowest value or any convenient number less than the lowest value); add the width to get the lower limits.

Find the upper class limits.

Find the boundaries.

Step 2   Tally the data.

Step 3   Find the numerical frequencies from the tallies, and find the cumulative frequencies.

Example 2–2 shows the procedure for constructing a grouped frequency distribution, i.e., when the classes contain more than one data value.

EXAMPLE 2–2   Record High Temperatures

These data represent the record high temperatures in degrees Fahrenheit (°F) for each of the 50 states. Construct a grouped frequency distribution for the data, using 7 classes.

112	100	127	120	134	118	105	110	109	112
110	118	117	116	118	122	114	114	105	109
107	112	114	115	118	117	118	122	106	110
116	108	110	121	113	120	119	111	104	111
120	113	120	117	105	110	118	112	114	114

Source: The World Almanac and Book of Facts.

SOLUTION

The procedure for constructing a grouped frequency distribution for numerical data follows.

Step 1   Determine the classes.

Find the highest value and lowest value: $H = 134$ and $L = 100$.

Find the range: $R =$ highest value $-$ lowest value $= H - L$, so

$$R = 134 - 100 = 34$$

Select the number of classes desired (usually between 5 and 20). In this case, 7 is arbitrarily chosen.

Find the class width by dividing the range by the number of classes.

$$\text{Width} = \frac{R}{\text{number of classes}} = \frac{34}{7} = 4.9$$

Round the answer up to the nearest whole number if there is a remainder: $4.9 \approx 5$. (Rounding *up* is different from rounding *off*. A number is rounded up if there is any decimal remainder when dividing. For example, $85 \div 6 = 14.167$ and is rounded up to 15. Also, $53 \div 4 = 13.25$ and is rounded up to 14. Also, after dividing, if there is no remainder, you will need to add an extra class to accommodate all the data.)

Select a starting point for the lowest class limit. This can be the smallest data value or any convenient number less than the smallest data value. In this case, 100 is used. Add the width to the lowest score taken as the starting point to get the lower limit of the next class. Keep adding until there are 7 classes, as shown, 100, 105, 110, etc.

Subtract one unit from the lower limit of the second class to get the upper limit of the first class. Then add the width to each upper limit to get all the upper limits.

$$105 - 1 = 104$$

The first class is 100–104, the second class is 105–109, etc.

Find the class boundaries by subtracting 0.5 from each lower class limit and adding 0.5 to each upper class limit:

$$99.5\text{–}104.5, 104.5\text{–}109.5, \text{etc.}$$

Step 2 Tally the data.

Step 3 Find the numerical frequencies from the tallies.

The completed frequency distribution is

Class limits	Class boundaries	Tally	Frequency
100–104	99.5–104.5	//	2
105–109	104.5–109.5	7HL ///	8
110–114	109.5–114.5	7HL 7HL 7HL ///	18
115–119	114.5–119.5	7HL 7HL ///	13
120–124	119.5–124.5	7HL //	7
125–129	124.5–129.5	/	1
130–134	129.5–134.5	/	1
			Total 50

The frequency distribution shows that the class 109.5–114.5 contains the largest number of temperatures (18) followed by the class 114.5–119.5 with 13 temperatures. Hence, most of the temperatures (31) fall between 110 and 119°F.

Sometimes it is necessary to use a *cumulative frequency distribution*. A **cumulative frequency distribution** is a distribution that shows the number of data values less than or equal to a specific value (usually an upper boundary). The values are found by adding the frequencies of the classes less than or equal to the upper class boundary of a specific class. This gives an ascending cumulative frequency. In this example, the cumulative frequency for the first class is $0 + 2 = 2$; for the second class it is $0 + 2 + 8 = 10$; for the third class it is $0 + 2 + 8 + 18 = 28$. Naturally, a shorter way to do this would be to just add the cumulative frequency of the class below to the frequency of the given class. For example, the cumulative frequency for the number of data values less than 114.5 can be found by adding $10 + 18 = 28$. The cumulative frequency distribution for the data in this example is as follows:

	Cumulative frequency
Less than 99.5	0
Less than 104.5	2
Less than 109.5	10
Less than 114.5	28
Less than 119.5	41
Less than 124.5	48
Less than 129.5	49
Less than 134.5	50

Cumulative frequencies are used to show how many data values are accumulated up to and including a specific class. In Example 2–2, of the total record high temperatures 28 are less than or equal to 114°F. Forty-eight of the total record high temperatures are less than or equal to 124°F.

After the raw data have been organized into a frequency distribution, it will be analyzed by looking for peaks and extreme values. The peaks show which class or classes have the most data values compared to the other classes. Extreme values, called *outliers,* show large or small data values that are relative to other data values.

When the range of the data values is relatively small, a frequency distribution can be constructed using single data values for each class. This type of distribution is called an **ungrouped frequency distribution** and is shown next.

EXAMPLE 2–3   Hours Worked by Students

The data show the number of hours 30 students worked part-time on campus for one specific day last week. Construct an ungrouped frequency distribution for the data and analyze the distribution.

```
4   10   4   4   8   9
8    4   9   6   5   5
10   6   5   7   3   4
6    4   5   7   7   4
3   10   9   3   4   6
```

SOLUTION

Step 1   Determine the number of classes. Since the range is small $(10 - 3 = 7)$, classes consisting of a single data value can be used. They are 3, 4, 5, 6, 7, 8, 9, 10.

Note: If the data are continuous, class boundaries can be used. Subtract 0.5 from each class value to get the lower class boundary, and add 0.5 to each class value to get the upper class boundary.

Step 2   Tally the data.

Step 3   From the tallies, find the numerical frequencies and cumulative frequencies. The completed ungrouped frequency distribution is shown.

Class limits	Class boundaries	Tally	Frequency
3	2.5–3.5	///	3
4	3.5–4.5	//// ///	8
5	4.5–5.5	////	4
6	5.5–6.5	////	4
7	6.5–7.5	///	3
8	7.5–8.5	//	2
9	8.5–9.5	///	3
10	9.5–10.5	///	3
			Total 30

In this case, eight students worked 4 hours and this was the largest frequency. The cumulative frequencies are

	Cumulative frequency
Less than 2.5	0
Less than 3.5	3
Less than 4.5	11
Less than 5.5	15
Less than 6.5	19
Less than 7.5	22
Less than 8.5	24
Less than 9.5	27
Less than 10.5	30

When you are constructing a frequency distribution, the guidelines presented in this section should be followed. However, you can construct several different but correct frequency distributions for the same data by using a different class width, a different number of classes, or a different starting point.

Furthermore, the method shown here for constructing a frequency distribution is not unique, and there are other ways of constructing one. Slight variations exist, especially in computer packages. But regardless of what methods are used, classes should be mutually exclusive, continuous, exhaustive, and of equal width.

In summary, the different types of frequency distributions were shown in this section. The first type, shown in Example 2–1, is used when the data are categorical (nominal), such as blood type or political affiliation. This type is called a categorical frequency distribution. The second type of distribution is used when the range is large and classes several units in width are needed. This type is called a grouped frequency distribution and is shown in Example 2–2. Another type of distribution is used for numerical data and when the range of data is small, as shown in Example 2–3. Since each class is only one unit, this distribution is called an ungrouped frequency distribution.

All the different types of distributions are used in statistics and are helpful when one is organizing and presenting data.

The reasons for constructing a frequency distribution are as follows:

1. To organize the data in a meaningful, intelligible way.

2. To enable the reader to determine the nature or shape of the distribution.

3. To facilitate computational procedures for measures of average and spread (shown in Sections 3–1 and 3–2).

4. To enable the researcher to draw charts and graphs for the presentation of data (shown in Section 2–2).

5. To enable the reader to make comparisons among different data sets.

The factors used to analyze a frequency distribution are essentially the same as those used to analyze histograms and frequency polygons, which are shown in Section 2–2.

Interesting Fact

Male dogs bite children more often than female dogs do; however, female cats bite children more often than male cats do.

≡ Applying the Concepts 2–1

Ages of Presidents at Inauguration

The data represent the ages of our Presidents at the time they were first inaugurated.

57	61	57	57	58	57	61	54	68
51	49	64	50	48	65	52	56	46
54	49	51	47	55	55	54	42	51
56	55	51	54	51	60	62	43	55
56	61	52	69	64	46	54	47	70
78								

1. Were the data obtained from a population or a sample? Explain your answer.
2. What was the age of the oldest President?
3. What was the age of the youngest President?
4. Construct a frequency distribution for the data. (Use your own judgment as to the number of classes and class size.)
5. Are there any peaks in the distribution?
6. Identify any possible outliers.
7. Write a brief summary of the nature of the data as shown in the frequency distribution.

See page 109–110 for the answers.

≡ Exercises 2–1

1. List five reasons for organizing data into a frequency distribution.

2. Name the three types of frequency distributions, and explain when each should be used. Categorical, ungrouped, grouped

3. How many classes should frequency distributions have? Why should the class width be an odd number?

4. What are open-ended frequency distributions? Why are they necessary?

For Exercises 5–8, find the class boundaries, midpoints, and widths for each class.

5. 58–62 57.5–62.5; 60; 5

6. 125–131 124.5–131.5, 128, 7

7. 16.35–18.46 16.345–18.465; 17.405; 2.12

8. 16.3–18.5 16.25–18.55, 17.4, 2.3

For Exercises 9–12, show frequency distributions that are incorrectly constructed. State the reasons why they are wrong.

9.
Class	Frequency
10–19	1
20–29	2
30–34	0
35–45	5
46–51	8

Class width is not uniform.

10.
Class	Frequency
5–9	1
9–13	2
13–17	5
17–20	6
20–24	3

Class limits overlap, and class width is not uniform.

11.
Class	Frequency
162–164	3
165–167	7
168–170	18
174–176	0
177–179	5

A class has been omitted

12.
Class	Frequency
9–13	1
14–19	6
20–25	2
26–28	5
29–32	9

Class width is not uniform.

13. **Household Pets** The following data show the household pets that people own: F = fish, D = dog, B = bird, C = cat, and R = reptile. Construct a categorical

frequency distribution for the data and summarize the results.

F	D	F	D	B	C	R	C	D	C
C	F	B	F	C	F	C	F	B	F
F	B	R	C	R	D	C	D	R	C
D	D	B	B	R	F	B	F	B	D
C	C	D	C	F	D	B	C	B	F

Source: Based on information from the National Pet Owners' Society

14. Trust in Internet Information A survey was taken on how much trust people place in the information they read on the Internet. Construct a categorical frequency distribution for the data. A = trust in all that they read, M = trust in most of what they read, H = trust in about one-half of what they read, S = trust in a small portion of what they read. (Based on information from the *UCLA Internet Report.*)

M	M	M	A	H	M	S	M	H	M
S	M	M	M	A	M	M	M	A	M
M	M	H	M	M	M	H	M	H	M
A	M	M	M	H	M	M	M	M	M

15. Eating at Fast Food Restaurants A survey was taken of 50 individuals. They were asked how many days per week they ate at a fast-food restaurant. Construct a frequency distribution using 8 classes (0–7). Based on the distribution, how often did most people eat at a fast-food restaurant?

1	3	4	0	4
5	2	2	3	1
2	2	2	2	2
2	2	2	2	3
2	2	5	2	4
2	4	5	2	1
4	1	3	2	2
2	0	7	2	3
2	2	2	5	2
3	3	4	1	3

16. Ages of Dogs The ages of 20 dogs in a pet shelter are shown. Construct a frequency distribution using 7 classes.

5	8	7	6	3
9	4	4	5	8
7	4	7	5	7
3	5	8	4	9

17. Wind Speed The data show the maximum wind speeds (in miles per hour) at selected cities in the United States. Construct a frequency distribution for the data using eight classes. Summarize the results.

89	83	69	77	70	53	83	87	96	75
71	68	70	78	85	75	67	77	62	72
71	76	68	59	72	103	77	67	66	72
72	75	78	68	77	70	62	70	75	71
72	63	74	48	87	71	78	93	87	101

Source: The World Almanac and Book of Facts

18. Stories in the World's Tallest Buildings The number of stories in each of a sample of the world's 30 tallest buildings follows. Construct a grouped frequency distribution and a cumulative frequency distribution with 7 classes.

88	88	110	88	80	69	102	78	70	55
79	85	80	100	60	90	77	55	75	55
54	60	75	64	105	56	71	70	65	72

Source: New York Times Almanac.

19. Rabies Virus Cases The data show the ages of 22 people who had contracted the rabies virus for a certain year. Construct a frequency distribution for the data and summarize the results. Use five classes.

65	54	77	65	52	28	49
34	63	46	40	20	25	73
70	19	42	55	43	17	55	16

Source: CDC U.S. Government

20. School Districts in States The data show the number of school districts in each state in the United States. Construct a frequency distribution using six classes for the data and summarize the results.

134	54	627	255	1042	178	196	37	136	67
198	1	137	865	369	348	286	174	136	195
24	403	855	519	151	524	410	249	17	161
590	89	695	115	179	1016	520	196	499	49
85	151	1228	125	286	132	295	53	424	48

Source: The World Almanac and Book of Facts

21. World Temperatures The following data show the high temperatures for May 8 in 22 selected cities around the world. Construct a frequency distribution for the data. Use five classes.

81	71	87	102	80	85	70	70	71	78
73	69	73	91	81	79	71	73	91	76
68	61								

Source: USA TODAY

22. Sports-Related Surgery The following data show the ages of 50 patients who had sports-related surgeries. Construct a frequency distribution for the data using five classes and summarize the results.

25	19	16	24	36	38	29	22	27	18
22	27	22	23	25	24	26	26	25	21
17	23	20	22	28	21	27	23	29	27
19	24	16	22	25	28	37	25	23	22
16	26	24	21	33	21	32	23	29	26

23. Days Worked by Medical Doctors A survey of 32 medical doctors shows the number of days that they worked in a recent year. Construct a frequency distribution for the data using six classes. Summarize the results.

240	232	280	261	254	216	224	229
248	246	219	240	220	251	263	218
237	264	210	206	252	265	271	271
209	222	256	214	268	283	229	264

24. **Ranges of Tides** The data show the mean ranges for tides in coastal cities in the United States. The ranges represent the difference of the mean high water mark and the mean low water mark. Construct a frequency distribution using six classes. Summarize the results.

14	18	113	63	110	83	12	15
15	46	30	31	54	42	73	109
111	19	49	49	13	56	90	33

Source: The World Almanac and Book of Facts

25. **Average Wind Speeds** A sample of 40 large cities was selected, and the average of the wind speeds was computed for each city over one year. Construct a frequency distribution, using 7 classes.

12.2	9.1	11.2	9.0
10.5	8.2	8.9	12.2
9.5	10.2	7.1	11.0
6.2	7.9	8.7	8.4
8.9	8.8	7.1	10.1
8.7	10.5	10.2	10.7
7.9	8.3	8.7	8.7
10.4	7.7	12.3	10.7
7.7	7.8	11.8	10.5
9.6	9.6	8.6	10.3

Source: World Almanac and Book of Facts.

26. **Percentage of People Who Completed 4 or More Years of College** Listed by state are the percentages of the population who have completed 4 or more years of a college education. Construct a frequency distribution with 7 classes.

21.4	26.0	25.3	19.3	29.5	35.0	34.7	26.1	25.8	23.4
27.1	29.2	24.5	29.5	22.1	24.3	28.8	20.0	20.4	26.7
35.2	37.9	24.7	31.0	18.9	24.5	27.0	27.5	21.8	32.5
33.9	24.8	31.7	25.6	25.7	24.1	22.8	28.3	25.8	29.8
23.5	25.0	21.8	25.2	28.7	33.6	33.6	30.3	17.3	25.4

Source: New York Times Almanac.

Extending the Concepts

27. **JFK Assassination** A researcher conducted a survey asking people if they believed more than one person was involved in the assassination of John F. Kennedy. The results were as follows: 73% said yes, 19% said no, and 9% had no opinion. Is there anything suspicious about the results?

28. **The Value of Pi** The ratio of the circumference of a circle to its diameter is known as π (pi). The value of π is an irrational number, which means that the decimal part goes on forever and there is no fixed sequence of numbers that repeats. People have found the decimal part of π to over a million places. We can statistically study the number. Shown here is the value of π to 40 decimal places. Construct an ungrouped frequency distribution for the digits. Based on the distribution, do you think each digit appears equally in the number?

   3.1415926535897932384626433832795028841971

29. One hundred randomly selected people were asked, "Do you think our President is doing a good job on foreign policy making?" Forty-two people responded, "Yes," 42 responded, "No," and 16 didn't respond at all. Why should the 16 people be included in the categorical frequency distribution?

30. In making a categorical frequency distribution, why should you always include the total number of subjects in the study at the bottom of the frequency column?

31. In a categorical frequency distribution, sometimes only percents are used. What is one advantage of using percent?

32. Sometimes in a categorical frequency distribution, a category such as "other" is used. For example, on a shelf in a college bookstore there may be 8 algebra books, 3 statistics books, 5 calculus books, and 4 other types of mathematical books. Why must you be cautious when using an "other" category in a categorical frequency distribution?

33. In a survey, 50 college students were asked what color automobile they drive to school. The responses were:

Color	Frequency
White	16
Red	9
Silver	15
Blue	4
Black	7

What is wrong with the distribution? Did the researcher make a mistake or is there some other explanation?

34. A researcher decides to survey 30 college students and asks each one what their favorite pizza topping is. The researcher wants to use a pie chart to summarize the data. The categories are pepperoni, beef, green peppers, olives, tomatoes, mushrooms, pineapple, onions, spinach, and jalapenos. Why might this not be a good idea?

35. A researcher decides to present the results obtained in a frequency distribution by combining the five frequencies of adjacent classes, thus using fewer classes. Why is this *not* a good idea?

⬛ Technology | Step by Step

EXCEL

Step by Step

Categorical Frequency Table (Qualitative or Discrete Data)

1. In an open workbook, select cell A1 and type in all the beverage data from Example 2–1 down column A.

W	J	C	C	J	C	T	W	C	T
W	M	M	W	W	M	W	W	M	C
T	W	J	M	M	C	J	C	M	W
W	C	W	W	J	W	W	M	C	J

2. Type in the variable name **Breakfast Beverage** in cell C1.

3. Select cell C2 and type in the five different beverage types down the column.

4. Type in the name **Count** in cell D1.

5. Select cell D2. From the toolbar, select the Formulas tab on the toolbar.

6. Select the Insert Function icon f_x , then select the Statistical category in the Insert Function dialog box.

7. Select the Countif function from the function name list.

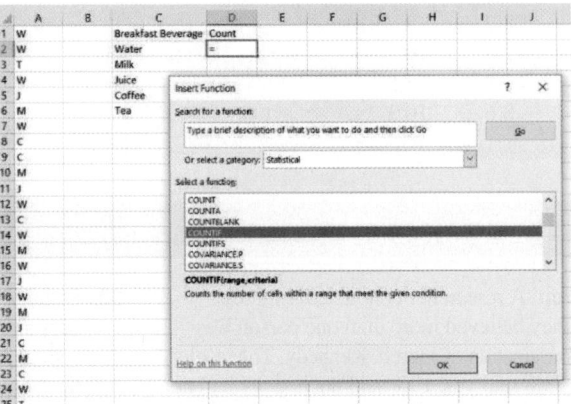

8. In the dialog box, type **A1:A40** in the **Range** box. Type in the beverage type "W" in quotes in the **Criteria** box. The count or frequency of the number of data corresponding to the beverage type should appear in cell D2. Repeat for the remaining beverage types in cells D3-D6.

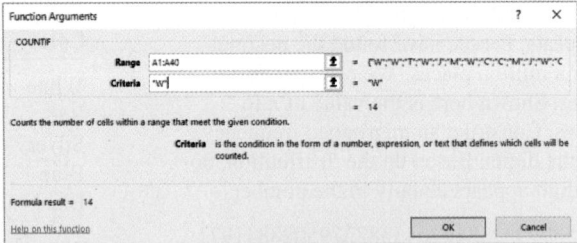

9. After all the data have been counted, select cell D7 in the worksheet.

10. From the toolbar select Formulas, select the dropdown menu All, then select Sum and type in D2:D6 to insert the total of the frequencies into cell D7. If you select each cell, you should see the following formulas.

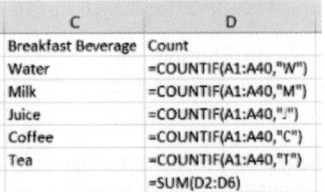

C	D
Breakfast Beverage	Count
Water	=COUNTIF(A1:A40,"W")
Milk	=COUNTIF(A1:A40,"M")
Juice	=COUNTIF(A1:A40,"J")
Coffee	=COUNTIF(A1:A40,"C")
Tea	=COUNTIF(A1:A40,"T")
	=SUM(D2:D6)

After entering data or a heading into a worksheet, you can change the width of a column to fit the input. To automatically change the width of a column to fit the data:

1. Select the column or columns that you want to change.

2. On the Home tab, in the Cells group, select Format.

3. Under Cell Size, click Autofit Column Width.

Making a Grouped Frequency Distribution (Quantitative Data)

1. Press [**Ctrl**]-**N** for a new workbook.

2. Enter the raw data from Example 2–2 in column A, one number per cell. Label the column Temperature.

3. Enter the upper class boundaries in column B. Label the column Bin.

4. From the toolbar select the Data tab, then click Data Analysis.

5. In the Analysis Tools, select Histogram and click [OK].

6. In the Histogram dialog box, type **A1:A51** in the Input Range box and type **B1:B8** in the Bin Range box.

7. Check the Labels box. *Note:* Do not check this box unless your labels are selected in the input range.

8. Select the radio button next to Output range, then type in **D1** to the output range.

9. Check the Cumulative Percentage option. Click [OK]. *Note:* By leaving the Chart Output unchecked, a new worksheet will display the table only.

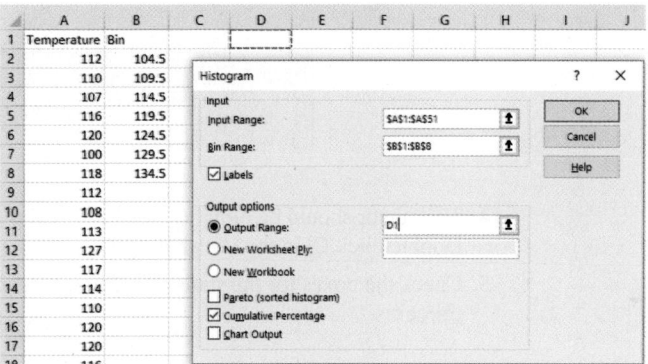

10. You can change the label for the column containing the upper class boundaries and expand the width of the columns automatically after relabeling:

   Select the Home tab from the toolbar.

   Highlight the columns that you want to change.

   Select Format, then AutoFit Column Width.

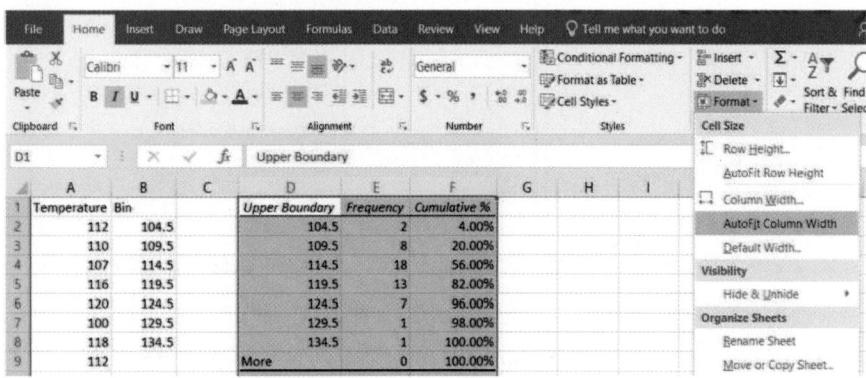

MINITAB
Step by Step

Make a Categorical Frequency Table
(Qualitative or Discrete Data)

1. Type in all the beverage types from Example 2–1 down C1 of the worksheet. Note as you type in text the column header will change to C1-T to signify this column is text instead of numeric.

   W W T W J M W C C M J W C W M M W J W M J C M C W T W J W W
   W C M C M M C T C W J

2. Click above row 1 and name the column **Beverage.**

3. Select **Stat>Tables>Tally Individual Values.**

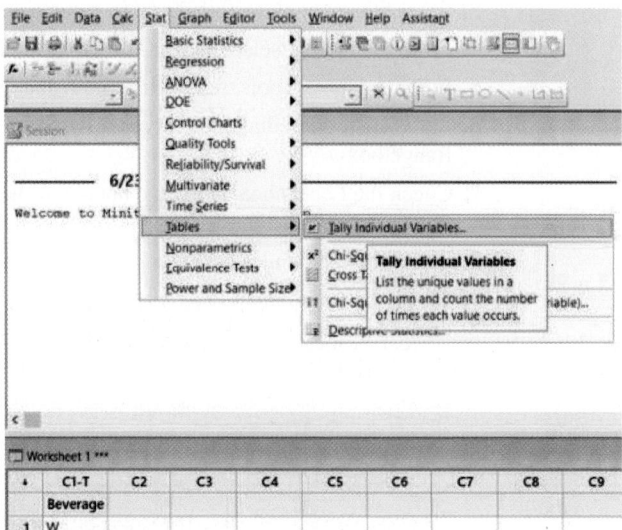

4. The cursor should be blinking in the Variables dialog box. If not, click inside the dialog box. Double-click C1 in the Variables list.

5. Check the boxes for the statistics: Counts, Percents, Cumulative counts, and Cumulative percents.

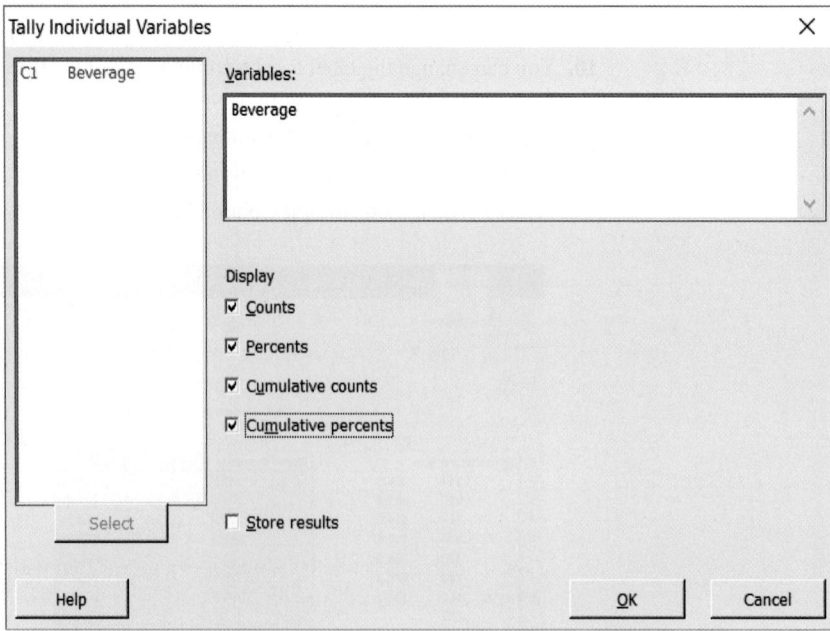

6. Click [OK]. The results will be displayed in the Session Window as shown.

Tally for Discrete Variables: Beverage

Beverage	Count	Percent	CumCnt	CumPct
C	9	22.50	9	22.50
J	6	15.00	15	37.50
M	8	20.00	23	57.50
T	3	7.50	26	65.00
W	14	35.00	40	100.00
N=	40			

Make a Grouped Frequency Distribution (Quantitative Variable)

1. Select **File>New>Minitab Worksheet**. A new worksheet will be added to the project.

2. Type the data used in Example 2–2 into C1. Name the column **Temperatures.**

3. Use the instructions in the textbook to determine the class limits of 100 to 134 in increments of 5.
In the next step you will create a new column of data, converting the numeric variable to text categories that can be tallied.

4. Select **Data>Code>Numeric to Text**.

   a) The cursor should be blinking in Code data from columns. If not, click inside the box, then double-click C1 Temperatures in the list. Only quantitative variables will be shown in this list.

   b) Click inside the Store coded data in columns: box and select type in C2.

   c) Press [Tab] to move to the table.

   d) Type 100:104 in the original values, press [Tab], type 100–104 in the New: column.

   e) Press [Tab] to move to the row, and type the next category **105:109** and **105–109.**

   f) Continue to tab to each dialog box, typing the lower endpoint and upper endpoint and then the category until the last category has been entered.

The dialog box should look like the one shown.

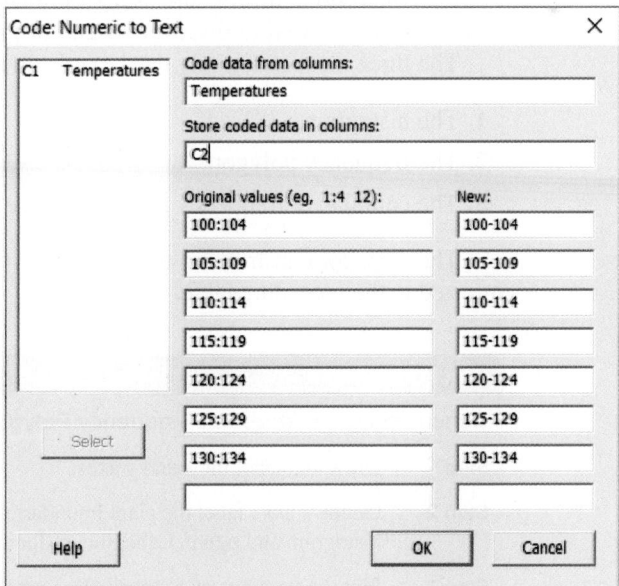

5. Click [OK]. In the worksheet, a new column of data will be created in column C2. This new variable will contain the category for each value in C1. The column C2-T contains alphanumeric data.

6. Click Stat>Tables>Tally Individual Values, then double-click Recoded Temperatures in the Variables list.

   a) Check the boxes for the desired statistics, such as Counts, Percents, Cumulative counts, and Cumulative percents.

   b) Click [OK].

The table will be displayed in the Session Window. Eighteen states have high temperatures between 110 and 114°F. Eighty-two percent of the states have record high temperatures less than or equal to 119°F.

Tally for Discrete Variables: Temperature

Temperature	Count	Percent	CumCnt	CumPct
100–104	2	4.00	2	4.00
105–109	8	16.00	10	20.00
110–114	18	36.00	28	56.00
115–119	13	26.00	41	82.00
120–124	7	14.00	48	96.00
125–129	1	2.00	49	98.00
130–134	1	2.00	50	100.00
N=	50			

7. Click File>Save Project As . . . , and type the name of the project file, **Ch2-1.** This will save the two worksheets and the Session Window.   ▬

2–2   Histograms, Frequency Polygons, and Ogives

OBJECTIVE

Represent data in frequency distributions graphically, using histograms, frequency polygons, and ogives.

After you have organized the data into a frequency distribution, you can present them in graphical form. The purpose of graphs in statistics is to convey the data to the viewers in pictorial form. It is easier for most people to comprehend the meaning of data presented graphically than data presented numerically in tables or frequency distributions. This is especially true if the users have little or no statistical knowledge.

Statistical graphs can be used to describe the data set or to analyze it. Graphs are also useful in getting the audience's attention in a publication or a speaking presentation. They can be used to discuss an issue, reinforce a critical point, or summarize a data set. They can also be used to discover a trend or pattern in a situation over a period of time.

The three most commonly used graphs in research are

1. The histogram.

2. The frequency polygon.

3. The cumulative frequency graph, or ogive (pronounced o-jive).

The steps for constructing the histogram, frequency polygon, and the ogive are summarized in the procedure table.

Procedure Table

Constructing a Histogram, Frequency Polygon, and Ogive

Step 1   Draw and label the x and y axes.

Step 2   On the x axis, label the class boundaries of the frequency distribution for the histogram and ogive. Label the midpoints for the frequency polygon.

Step 3   Plot the frequencies for each class, and draw the vertical bars for the histogram and the lines for the frequency polygon and ogive.

(*Note:* Remember that the lines for the frequency polygon begin and end on the x axis while the lines for the ogive begin on the x axis.)

The Histogram

> The **histogram** is a graph that displays the data by using contiguous vertical bars (unless the frequency of a class is 0) of various heights to represent the frequencies of the classes.

EXAMPLE 2–4   Record High Temperatures

Construct a histogram to represent the data shown for the record high temperatures for each of the 50 states (see Example 2–2).

Class boundaries	Frequency
99.5–104.5	2
104.5–109.5	8
109.5–114.5	18
114.5–119.5	13
119.5–124.5	7
124.5–129.5	1
129.5–134.5	1

SOLUTION

Step 1 Draw and label the x and y axes. The x axis is always the horizontal axis, and the y axis is always the vertical axis.

Step 2 Represent the frequency on the y axis and the class boundaries on the x axis.

Step 3 Using the frequencies as the heights, draw vertical bars for each class. See Figure 2–1.

FIGURE 2–1 Histogram for Example 2–4

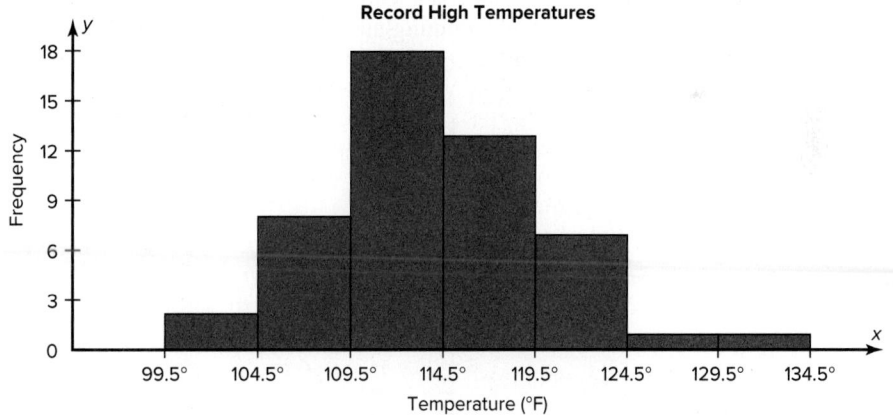

As the histogram shows, the class with the greatest number of data values (18) is 109.5–114.5, followed by 13 for 114.5–119.5. The graph also has one peak with the data clustering around it.

The Frequency Polygon

Another way to represent the same data set is by using a frequency polygon.

> The **frequency polygon** is a graph that displays the data by using lines that connect points plotted for the frequencies at the midpoints of the classes. The frequencies are represented by the heights of the points.

Example 2–5 shows the procedure for constructing a frequency polygon. Be sure to begin and end on the *x* axis.

EXAMPLE 2–5   Record High Temperatures

Using the frequency distribution given in Example 2–4, construct a frequency polygon.

SOLUTION

Step 1   Find the midpoints of each class. Recall that midpoints are found by adding the upper and lower boundaries and dividing by 2:

$$\frac{99.5 + 104.5}{2} = 102 \qquad \frac{104.5 + 109.5}{2} = 107$$

and so on. The midpoints are

Class boundaries	Midpoints	Frequency
99.5–104.5	102	2
104.5–109.5	107	8
109.5–114.5	112	18
114.5–119.5	117	13
119.5–124.5	122	7
124.5–129.5	127	1
129.5–134.5	132	1

Step 2   Draw the *x* and *y* axes. Label the *x* axis with the midpoint of each class, and then use a suitable scale on the *y* axis for the frequencies.

Step 3   Using the midpoints for the *x* values and the frequencies as the *y* values, plot the points.

Step 4   Connect adjacent points with line segments. Draw a line back to the *x* axis at the beginning and end of the graph, at the same distance that the previous and next midpoints would be located, as shown in Figure 2–2.

FIGURE 2–2
Frequency Polygon for Example 2–5

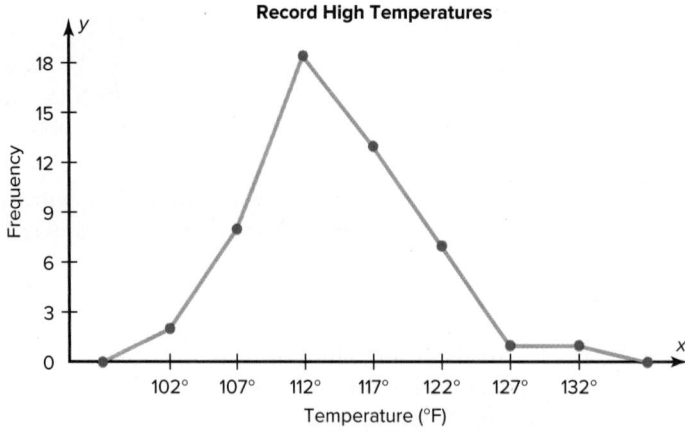

The frequency polygon and the histogram are two different ways to represent the same data set. The choice of which one to use is left to the discretion of the researcher.

The Ogive

The third type of graph that can be used represents the cumulative frequencies for the classes. This type of graph is called the *cumulative frequency graph,* or *ogive.*

The **cumulative frequency** is the sum of the frequencies accumulated up to the upper boundary of a class in the distribution.

> The **ogive** is a graph that represents the cumulative frequencies for the classes in a frequency distribution.

Example 2–6 shows the procedure for constructing an ogive. Be sure to start on the *x* axis.

EXAMPLE 2–6   Record High Temperatures

Construct an ogive for the frequency distribution described in Example 2–4.

SOLUTION

Step 1   Find the cumulative frequency for each class.

	Cumulative frequency
Less than 99.5	0
Less than 104.5	2
Less than 109.5	10
Less than 114.5	28
Less than 119.5	41
Less than 124.5	48
Less than 129.5	49
Less than 134.5	50

Step 2   Draw the *x* and *y* axes. Label the *x* axis with the class boundaries. Use an appropriate scale for the *y* axis to represent the cumulative frequencies. (Depending on the numbers in the cumulative frequency columns, scales such as 0, 1, 2, 3, . . . , or 5, 10, 15, 20, . . . , or 1000, 2000, 3000, . . . can be used. Do *not* label the *y* axis with the numbers in the cumulative frequency column.) In this example, a scale of 0, 5, 10, 15, . . . will be used.

Step 3   Plot the cumulative frequency at each upper class boundary, as shown in Figure 2–3. Upper boundaries are used since the cumulative frequencies represent the number of data values accumulated up to the upper boundary of each class.

Step 4   Starting with the first upper class boundary, 104.5, connect adjacent points with line segments, as shown in Figure 2–4. Then extend the graph to the first lower class boundary, 99.5, on the *x* axis.

FIGURE 2–3

Plotting the Cumulative Frequency for Example 2–6

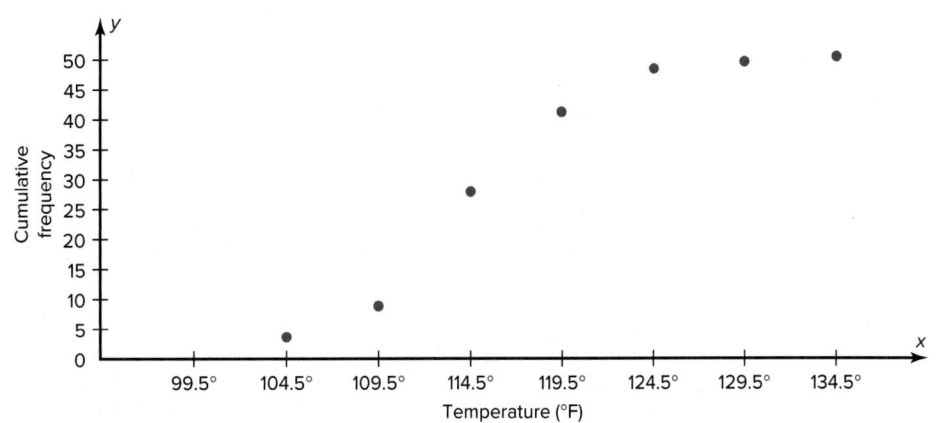

FIGURE 2–4

Ogive for Example 2–6

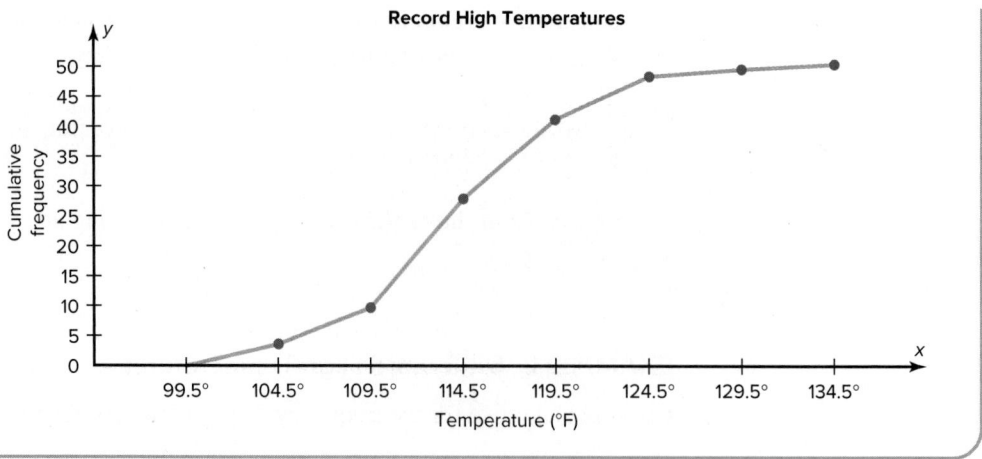

Cumulative frequency graphs are used to visually represent how many values are below a certain upper class boundary. For example, to find out how many record high temperatures are less than 114.5°F, locate 114.5°F on the *x* axis, draw a vertical line up until it intersects the graph, and then draw a horizontal line at that point to the *y* axis. The *y* axis value is 28, as shown in Figure 2–5.

Relative Frequency Graphs

The histogram, the frequency polygon, and the ogive shown previously were constructed by using frequencies in terms of the raw data. These distributions can be converted to distributions using *proportions* instead of raw data as frequencies. These types of graphs are called **relative frequency graphs.**

Graphs of relative frequencies instead of frequencies are used when the proportion of data values that fall into a given class is more important than the actual number of data values that fall into that class. For example, if you wanted to compare the age distribution of adults in Philadelphia, Pennsylvania, with the age distribution of adults of Erie, Pennsylvania, you would use relative frequency distributions. The reason is that since the population of Philadelphia is 1,526,006 and the population of Erie is 101,786, the bars using the actual data values for Philadelphia would be much taller than those for the same classes for Erie.

To convert a frequency into a proportion or relative frequency, divide the frequency for each class by the total of the frequencies. The sum of the relative frequencies will always be 1. These graphs are similar to the ones that use raw data as frequencies, but the values on the *y* axis are in terms of proportions. Example 2–7 shows the three types of relative frequency graphs.

FIGURE 2–5

Finding a Specific Cumulative
Frequency

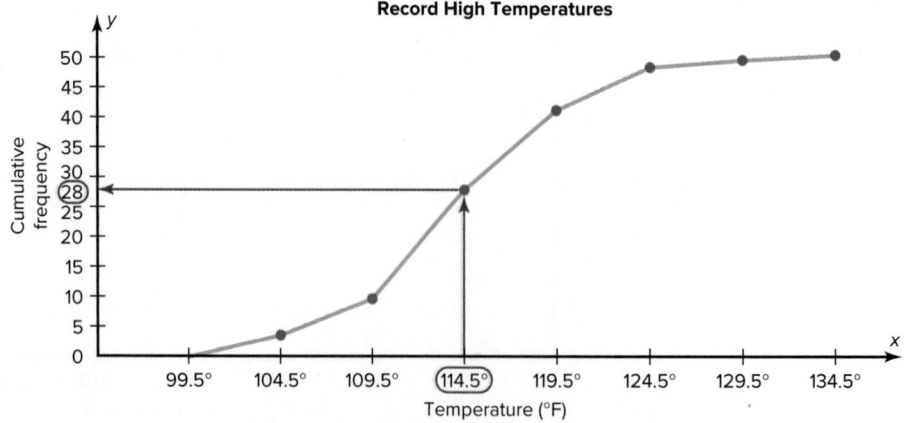

EXAMPLE 2–7 Net Worth of Small Businesses

The following frequency distribution shows the approximate net worth in thousands of dollars of 50 small businesses in a city. Draw a relative histogram, relative frequency polygon, and a relative ogive for the data.

Class boundaries	Frequency
35.5–42.5	8
42.5–49.5	14
49.5–56.5	20
56.5–63.5	5
63.5–70.5	3
	Total 50

SOLUTION

Step 1 Convert each frequency to a proportion or relative frequency by dividing the frequency for each class by the total number of observations.

For the class 35.5–42.5, the relative frequency is $\frac{8}{50} = 0.16$. For the class 42.5–49.5, the relative frequency is $\frac{14}{50} = 0.28$. For the class 49.5–56.5, the relative frequency is $\frac{20}{50} = 0.40$. For the class 56.5–63.5, the relative frequency is $\frac{5}{50} = 0.10$. For the class 63.5–70.5, the relative frequency is $\frac{3}{50} = 0.06$.

Place these values in the column labeled Relative frequency. Also, find the midpoints, as shown in Example 2–5, for each class and place them in the Midpoints column.

Class boundaries	Midpoints	Relative frequency
35.5–42.5	39	0.16
42.5–49.5	46	0.28
49.5–56.5	53	0.40
56.5–63.5	60	0.10
63.5–70.5	67	0.06

Step 2 Find the cumulative relative frequencies. To do this, add the frequency in each class to the total frequency of the preceding class. In this case, $0.00 + 0.16 = 0.16$, $0.16 + 0.28 = 0.44$, $0.44 + 0.40 = 0.84$, $0.84 + 0.10 = 0.94$, and $0.94 + 0.06 = 1.00$. Place these values in a column labeled Cumulative relative frequency.

An alternative method would be to change the cumulative frequencies for the classes to relative frequencies. (Divide each by the total.)

	Cumulative frequency	Cumulative relative frequency
Less than 35.5	0	0.00
Less than 42.5	8	0.16
Less than 49.5	22	0.44
Less than 56.5	42	0.84
Less than 63.5	47	0.94
Less than 70.5	50	1.00

Step 3   Draw each graph as shown in Figure 2–6. For the histogram and ogive, use the class boundaries along the x axis. For the frequency, use the midpoints on the x axis. For the scale on the y axis, use proportions.

FIGURE 2–6

Graphs for Example 2–7

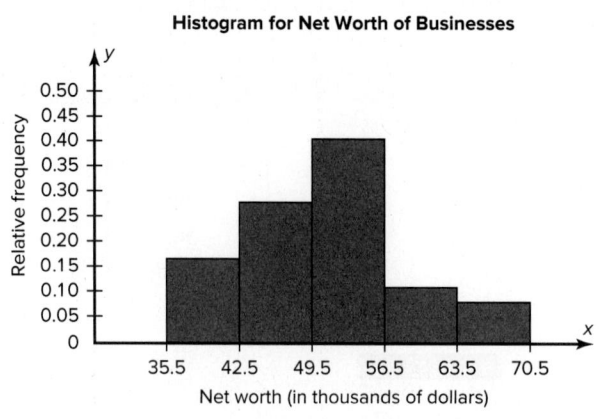

Histogram for Net Worth of Businesses

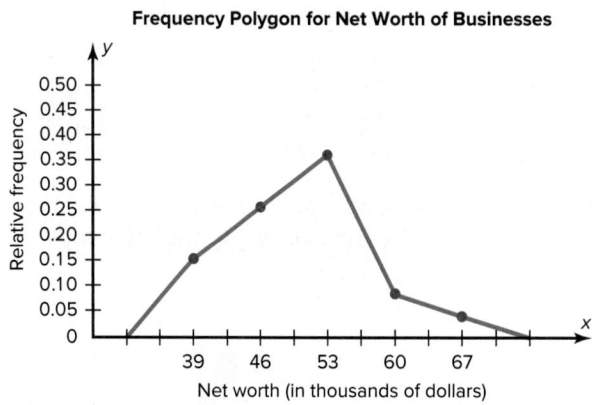

Frequency Polygon for Net Worth of Businesses

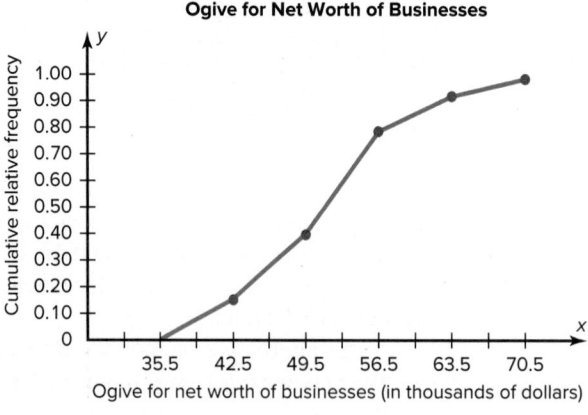

Ogive for Net Worth of Businesses

Distribution Shapes

When one is describing data, it is important to be able to recognize the shapes of the distribution values. In later chapters, you will see that the shape of a distribution also determines the appropriate statistical methods used to analyze the data.

FIGURE 2–7
Distribution Shapes

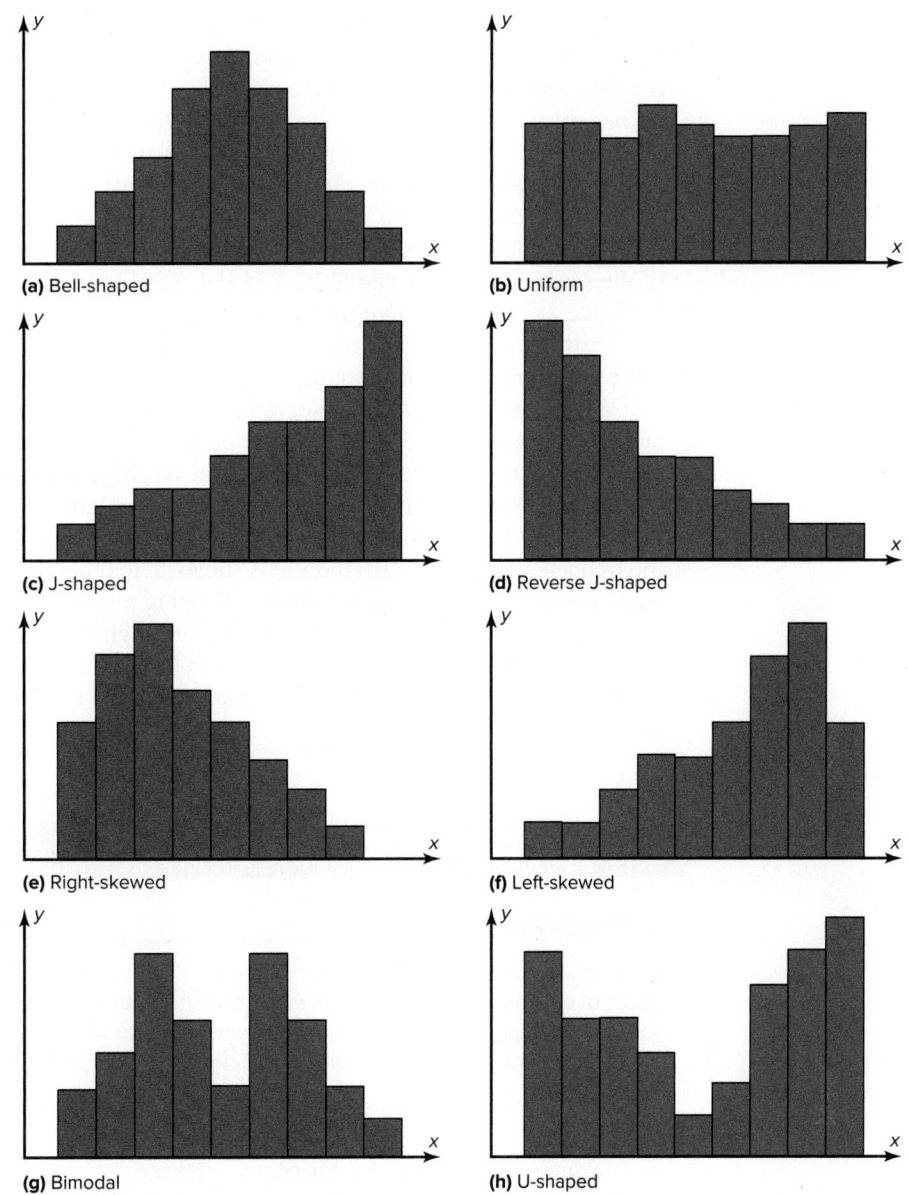

(a) Bell-shaped

(b) Uniform

(c) J-shaped

(d) Reverse J-shaped

(e) Right-skewed

(f) Left-skewed

(g) Bimodal

(h) U-shaped

A distribution can have many shapes, and one method of analyzing a distribution is to draw a histogram or frequency polygon for the distribution. Several of the most common shapes are shown in Figure 2–7: *the bell-shaped or mound-shaped, the uniform-shaped, the J-shaped, the reverse J-shaped, the positively or right-skewed shape, the negatively or left-skewed shape, the bimodal-shaped, and the U-shaped.*

Distributions are most often not perfectly shaped, so it is not necessary to have an exact shape but rather to identify an overall pattern.

A *bell-shaped distribution* shown in Figure 2–7(a) has a single peak and tapers off at either end. It is approximately symmetric; i.e., it is roughly the same on both sides of a line running through the center.

A *uniform distribution* is basically flat or rectangular. See Figure 2–7(b).

A *J-shaped distribution* is shown in Figure 2–7(c), and it has a few data values on the left side and increases as one moves to the right. A *reverse J-shaped distribution* is the opposite of the J-shaped distribution. See Figure 2–7(d).

When the peak of a distribution is to the left and the data values taper off to the right, a distribution is said to be *positively or right-skewed*. See Figure 2–7(e). When the data values are clustered to the right and taper off to the left, a distribution is said to be *negatively or left-skewed*. See Figure 2–7(f). Skewness will be explained in detail in Chapter 3. Distributions with one peak, such as those shown in Figure 2–7(a), (e), and (f), are said to be *unimodal*. (The highest peak of a distribution indicates where the mode of the data values is. The mode is the data value that occurs more often than any other data value. Modes are explained in Chapter 3.) When a distribution has two peaks of the same height, it is said to be *bimodal*. See Figure 2–7(g). Finally, the graph shown in Figure 2–7(h) is a *U-shaped* distribution.

Distributions can have other shapes in addition to the ones shown here; however, these are some of the more common ones that you will encounter in analyzing data.

When you are analyzing histograms and frequency polygons, look at the shape of the curve. For example, does it have one peak or two peaks? Is it relatively flat, or is it U-shaped? Are the data values spread out on the graph, or are they clustered around the center? Are there data values in the extreme ends? These may be *outliers*. (See Section 3–3 for an explanation of outliers.) Are there any gaps in the histogram, or does the frequency polygon touch the x axis somewhere other than at the ends? Finally, are the data clustered at one end or the other, indicating a *skewed distribution*?

For example, the histogram for the record high temperatures in Figure 2–1 shows a single peaked distribution, with the class 109.5–114.5 containing the largest number of temperatures. The distribution has no gaps, and there are fewer temperatures in the highest class than in the lowest class.

▤ Applying the Concepts 2–2

Selling Real Estate

Assume you are a realtor in Bradenton, Florida. You have recently obtained a listing of the selling prices of the homes that have sold in that area in the last 6 months. You wish to organize those data so you will be able to provide potential buyers with useful information. Use the following data to create a histogram, frequency polygon, and cumulative frequency polygon.

395,000	169,000	225,000	1,350,000	239,900	480,000	399,000
199,997	299,900	350,000	285,000	139,900	320,000	359,000
379,900	565,894	339,900	225,000	377,000	244,000	500,000
349,000	299,900	224,900	89,900	289,900	599,000	469,000
210,000	250,000	274,900	375,000	155,000	425,000	499,000
200,000	278,900	194,900	325,000	269,900	299,000	330,000
189,900	369,900	500,000	479,637	269,900	379,000	259,900

Source: https://www.zillow.com/bradenton-fl/

1. What questions could be answered more easily by looking at the histogram rather than the listing of home prices?

2. What different questions could be answered more easily by looking at the frequency polygon rather than the listing of home prices?

3. What different questions could be answered more easily by looking at the cumulative frequency polygon rather than the listing of home prices?

4. Are there any extremely large or extremely small data values compared to the other data values?

5. Which graph displays these extremes the best?

6. Is the distribution skewed?

See page 110 for the answers.

≡ Exercises 2–2

1. Do Students Need Summer Development? For 108 randomly selected college applicants, the following frequency distribution for entrance exam scores was obtained. Construct a histogram, frequency polygon, and ogive for the data. (The data for this exercise will be used for Exercise 13 in this section.)

Class limits	Frequency
90–98	6
99–107	22
108–116	43
117–125	28
126–134	9
	Total 108

Applicants who score above 107 need not enroll in a summer developmental program. In this group, how many students do not have to enroll in the developmental program?

2. Bear Kills The number of bears killed in 2014 for 56 counties in Pennsylvania is shown in the frequency distribution. Construct a histogram, frequency polygon, and ogive for the data. Comment on the skewness of the distribution. How many counties had 75 or fewer bears killed? (The data for this exercise will be used for Exercise 14 of this section.)

Class limits	Frequency
1–25	16
26–50	14
51–75	9
76–100	8
101–125	5
126–150	0
151–175	1
176–200	1
201–225	0
226–250	0
251–275	2
	Total 56

Source: Pennsylvania State Game Commission.

3. Pupils Per Teacher The average number of pupils per teacher in each state is shown. Construct a grouped frequency distribution with 6 classes. Draw a histogram, frequency polygon, and ogive. Analyze the distribution.

16	16	15	12	14
13	16	14	15	14
18	18	18	12	15
15	16	16	15	15
25	19	15	12	22
18	14	13	17	9
13	14	13	16	12
14	16	10	22	20
12	14	18	15	14
16	12	12	13	15

Source: U.S. Department of Education.

4. Number of College Faculty The number of faculty listed for a sample of private colleges that offer only bachelor's degrees is listed below. Use these data to construct a frequency distribution with 7 classes, a histogram, a frequency polygon, and an ogive. Discuss the shape of this distribution. What proportion of schools have 180 or more faculty?

165	221	218	206	138	135	224	204
70	210	207	154	155	82	120	116
176	162	225	214	93	389	77	135
221	161	128	310				

Source: World Almanac and Book of Facts.

5. Railroad Crossing Accidents The data show the number of railroad crossing accidents for the 50 states of the United States for a specific year. Construct a histogram, frequency polygon, and ogive for the data. Comment on the skewness of the distribution. (The data in this exercise will be used for Exercise 15 in this section.)

Class limits	Frequency
1–43	24
44–86	17
87–129	3
130–172	4
173–215	1
216–258	0
259–301	0
302–344	1
	Total 50

Source: Federal Railroad Administration.

6. NFL Salaries The salaries (in millions of dollars) for 31 NFL teams for a specific season are given in this frequency distribution.

Construct a histogram, a frequency polygon, and an ogive for the data; and comment on the shape of the distribution. (The data for this exercise will be used for Exercise 16 of this section.)

Class limits	Frequency
39.9–42.8	2
42.9–45.8	2
45.9–48.8	5
48.9–51.8	5
51.9–54.8	12
54.9–57.8	5
	Total 31

Source: NFL.com

7. Suspension Bridges Spans The following frequency distribution shows the length (in feet) of the main spans of the longest suspension bridges in the United States. Construct a histogram, frequency polygon, and ogive for the distribution. Describe the shape of the distribution.

Class limits	Frequency
1260–1734	12
1735–2209	6
2210–2684	3
2685–3159	1
3160–3634	1
3635–4109	1
4110–4584	2

Source: U.S. Department of Transportation.

8. **Time Spent Looking for a Parking Space** The following frequency distribution shows the amount of time (in hours) that workers in a large city spend each year trying to find a parking space. Draw a histogram, frequency polygon, and ogive for the data. Summarize the results.

Time	Frequency
27–31	23
32–36	28
37–41	19
42–46	15
47–51	11
52–56	4
	Total 100

9. **Debts of Millennials** The following frequency distribution shows the amount of debt (in thousands of dollars) that millennials have for a recent year. Draw a histogram, frequency polygon, and ogive for the data and summarize the results.

Amount	Frequency
7–13	14
14–20	7
21–27	2
28–34	4
35–41	3
	Total 30

10. **Making the Grade** The frequency distributions shown indicate the percentages of public school students in fourth-grade reading and mathematics who performed at or above the required proficiency levels for the 50 states in the United States. Draw histograms for each, and decide if there is any difference in the performance of the students in the subjects.

Class	Reading frequency	Math frequency
17.5–22.5	7	5
22.5–27.5	6	9
27.5–32.5	14	11
32.5–37.5	19	16
37.5–42.5	3	8
42.5–47.5	1	1
	Total 50	Total 50

Source: National Center for Educational Statistics.

11. **Places Visited During a Day** The following frequency distribution shows the number of places (stores, service stations, etc.) a person visits on an average day. Construct a histogram, frequency polygon, and ogive for the data. Comment on the data.

Places Visited	Frequency
1	10
2	12
3	8
4	7
5	6
6	5
7	2
	Total 50

12. **Federal Crime Sentence Lengths** The frequency distribution shows the lengths in months of a random sample of federal racketeering and extortion sentences given to the guilty persons in a U.S. court. Draw a histogram, frequency polygon, and ogive for the data.

Class	Frequency
82–86	18
87–91	24
92–96	43
97–101	10
102–106	4
107–111	4
	Total 103

Source: Based on information in the Sourcebook of Federal Sentencing.

13. Construct a histogram, frequency polygon, and ogive, using relative frequencies for the data in Exercise 1 of this section.

14. Construct a histogram, frequency polygon, and ogive, using relative frequencies for the data in Exercise 2 of this section.

15. Construct a histogram, frequency polygon, and ogive, using relative frequencies for the data in Exercise 5 of this section.

16. Construct a histogram, frequency polygon, and ogive, using relative frequencies for the data in Exercise 6 of this section.

17. **Home Runs** The data show the most number of home runs hit by a batter in the American League over the last 30 seasons. Construct a frequency distribution using 5 classes. Draw a histogram, a frequency polygon, and an ogive for the date, using relative frequencies. Describe the shape of the histogram.

40	43	40
53	47	46
44	57	43
43	52	44
54	47	51
39	48	36
37	56	42
54	56	49
54	52	40
48	50	40

Source: World Almanac and Book of Facts.

18. **Protein Grams in Fast Food** The amount of protein (in grams) for a variety of fast-food sandwiches is reported here. Construct a frequency distribution, using 6 classes. Draw a histogram, a frequency polygon, and an ogive for the data, using relative frequencies. Describe the shape of the histogram.

23	30	20	27	44	26	35	20	29	29
25	15	18	27	19	22	12	26	34	15
27	35	26	43	35	14	24	12	23	31
40	35	38	57	22	42	24	21	27	33

Source: The Doctor's Pocket Calorie, Fat, and Carbohydrate Counter.

Extending the Concepts

19. Using the histogram shown here, do the following.

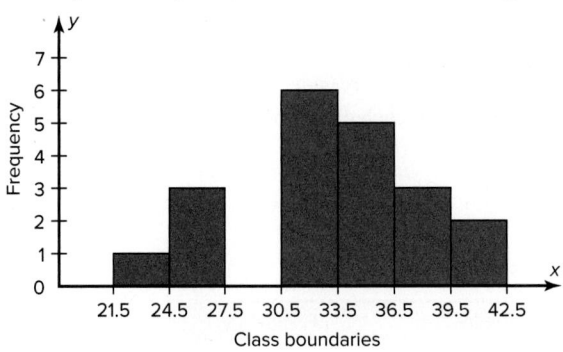

a. Construct a frequency distribution; include class limits, class frequencies, midpoints, and cumulative frequencies.

b. Construct a frequency polygon.

c. Construct an ogive.

20. Using the results from Exercise 19, answer these questions.
   a. How many values are in the class 27.5–30.5? 0
   b. How many values fall between 24.5 and 36.5? 14

c. How many values are below 33.5? 10

d. How many values are above 30.5? 16

21. **Math SAT Scores** Shown is an ogive depicting the cumulative frequency of the average mathematics SAT scores by state. Use it to construct a histogram and a frequency polygon.

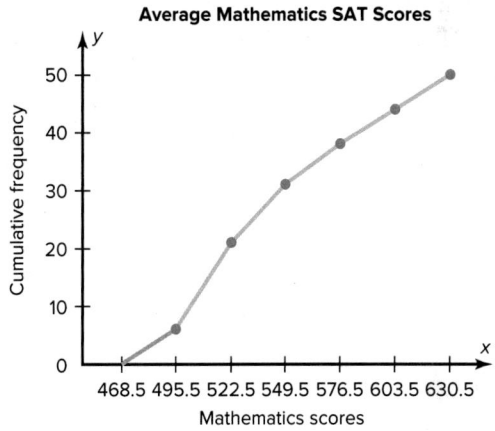

Technology

Step by Step

TI-84 Plus
Step by Step

Constructing a Histogram
To plot the histogram from raw data:

Example TI2–1

Plot a histogram for the following data from Example 2–2.

112	100	127	120	134	118	105	110	109	112
110	118	117	116	118	122	114	114	105	109
107	112	114	115	118	117	118	122	106	110
116	108	110	121	113	120	119	111	104	111
120	113	120	117	105	110	118	112	114	114

1. Enter the data in L_1.
2. Make sure WINDOW values are appropriate for the histogram.

To display the graphs on the screen, enter the appropriate values in the calculator, using the WINDOW menu. The default values are $X_{\min} = -10$, $X_{\max} = 10$, $Y_{\min} = -10$, and $Y_{\max} = 10$.

The X_{scl} changes the distance between the tick marks on the x axis and can be used to change the class width for the histogram.

To change the values in the WINDOW:

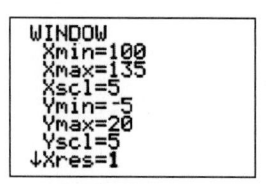

a. Press **WINDOW.**

b. Move the cursor to the value that needs to be changed. Then type in the desired value and press **ENTER.**

c. Continue until all values are appropriate.

d. Press **[2nd] [QUIT]** to leave the WINDOW menu.

3. Press **[2nd] [STAT PLOT] ENTER.**

4. Press **ENTER** to turn the plot 1 on, if necessary.

5. Move cursor to the Histogram symbol and press **ENTER,** if necessary. The histogram is the third option.

6. Make sure Xlist is L_1.

7. Make sure Freq is 1.

8. Press **GRAPH** to display the histogram.

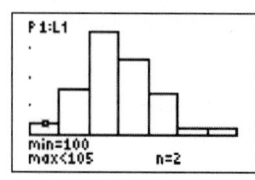

9. To obtain the frequency (number of data values in each class), press the **TRACE** key, followed by ◀ or ▶ keys.

To plot the histogram from grouped data:

Example TI2–2

Plot a histogram for the data from Examples 2–4 and 2–5.

Class boundaries	Midpoints	Frequency
99.5–104.5	102	2
104.5–109.5	107	8
109.5–114.5	112	18
114.5–119.5	117	13
119.5–124.5	122	7
124.5–129.5	127	1
129.5–134.5	132	1

1. Enter the midpoints into L_1.

2. Enter the frequencies into L_2.

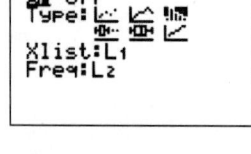

3. Make sure WINDOW values are appropriate for the histogram.

4. Press **[2nd] [STAT PLOT] ENTER.**

5. Press **ENTER** to turn the plot on, if necessary.

6. Move cursor to the histogram symbol, and press **ENTER,** if necessary.

7. Make sure Xlist is L_1.

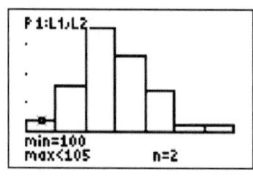

8. Make sure Freq is L_2.

9. Press **GRAPH** to display the histogram.

To plot a frequency polygon from grouped data:

1. Follow the same steps as for the histogram for grouped data, except change the graph type from histogram (third graph) to a line graph (second graph).

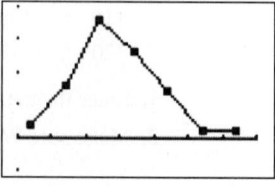

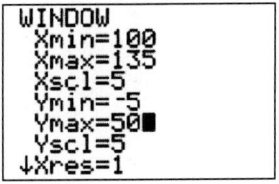

To plot an ogive from grouped data:

1. Enter the first lower class boundary for the first group, followed by all the upper class boundaries into L₁.

2. In L₂, enter 0 for the first value and the rest the cumulative frequencies.

3. Press **[2nd] [STAT PLOT] ENTER.**

4. Change the graph type to line (second graph).

5. Press **WINDOW.** Change the Y_{max} from the WINDOW menu to the sample size.

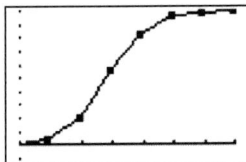

6. Press **GRAPH** to display the ogive.

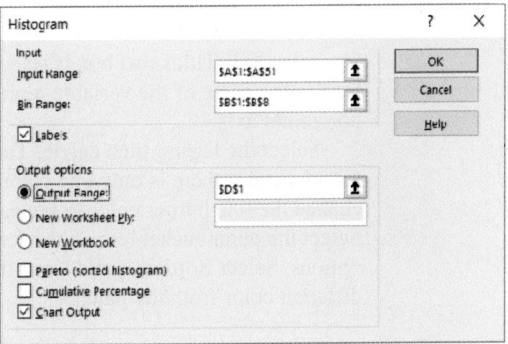

EXCEL
Step by Step

Constructing a Histogram

1. Press **[Ctrl]-N** for a new workbook.

2. Enter the data from Example 2–2 in column A, one number per cell. Label the column Temperature.

3. Enter the upper boundaries into column B. Label the column Bin.

4. From the toolbar, select the Data tab, then select Data Analysis.

5. In Data Analysis, select Histogram and click [OK].

6. In the Histogram dialog box, type **A1:A51** in the Input Range box and type **B1:B8** in the Bin Range box.

7. Check the Labels box. *Note:* Do not check this box unless your labels are selected in the input range.

8. Select the radio button next to Output range, then type in D1 to the output range.

9. Check Chart Output. Click [OK].

Editing the Histogram

To move the vertical bars of the histogram closer together:

1. Right-click one of the bars of the histogram, and select Format Data Series.

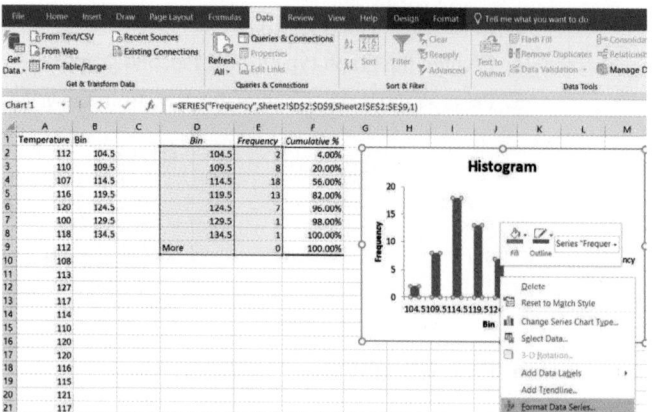

2. Move the Gap Width slider all the way to the left to change the gap width of the bars in the histogram to 0.

3. To change the label for the horizontal axis:

    a. Left-click the mouse over any part of the histogram.

    b. Select the Design tab from the toolbar.

    c. Select the Add Chart Element tab, Axis Titles and Primary Horizontal.

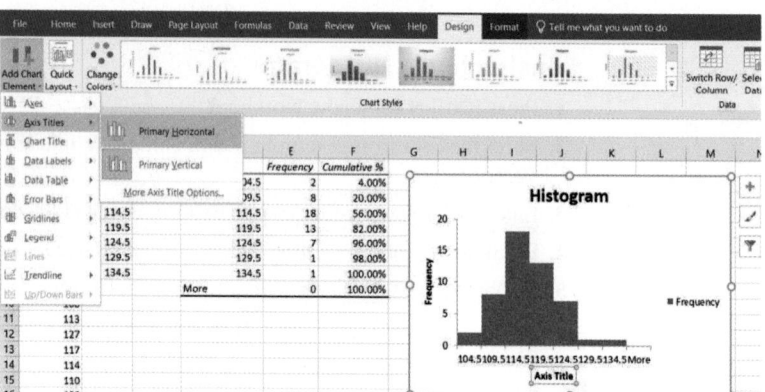

Once the Axis Titles text box is selected, you can type in the name of the variable represented on the horizontal axis.

Select the legend then delete. There is no need for a legend if there is only one color. You can also change the line border color to see each bar better. Select the paint bucket icon in the format data series options. Select Border>Solid Line, then select a different color from the palette.

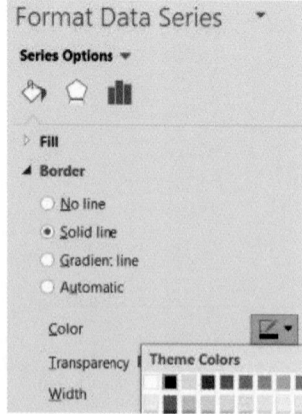

Right-click on the label More on the horizontal axis. Choose the Select Data option. Under the Horizontal Axis Labels, uncheck the More category. Click [OK].

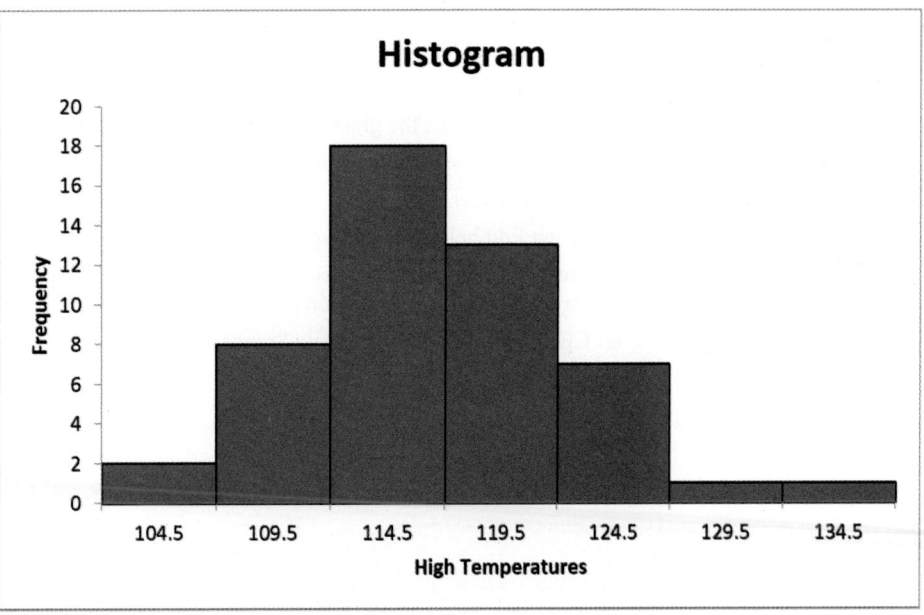

Here is the finished histogram.

Constructing a Frequency Polygon

	A	B
1	Midpoints	Frequency
2	97	0
3	102	2
4	107	8
5	112	18
6	117	13
7	122	7
8	127	1
9	132	1
10	137	0

1. Press [**CTRL**]-**N** for a new notebook.

2. Enter the midpoints of the data from Example 2–2 into column A and the frequencies into column B, including labels.

Note: Classes with frequency 0 have been added at the beginning and the end to "anchor" the frequency polygon to the horizontal axis.

3. Press and hold the left mouse button, and drag over the Frequencies (including the label) from column B.

4. Select the Insert tab from the toolbar and the Line Chart option.

5. Select the 2-D line chart type.

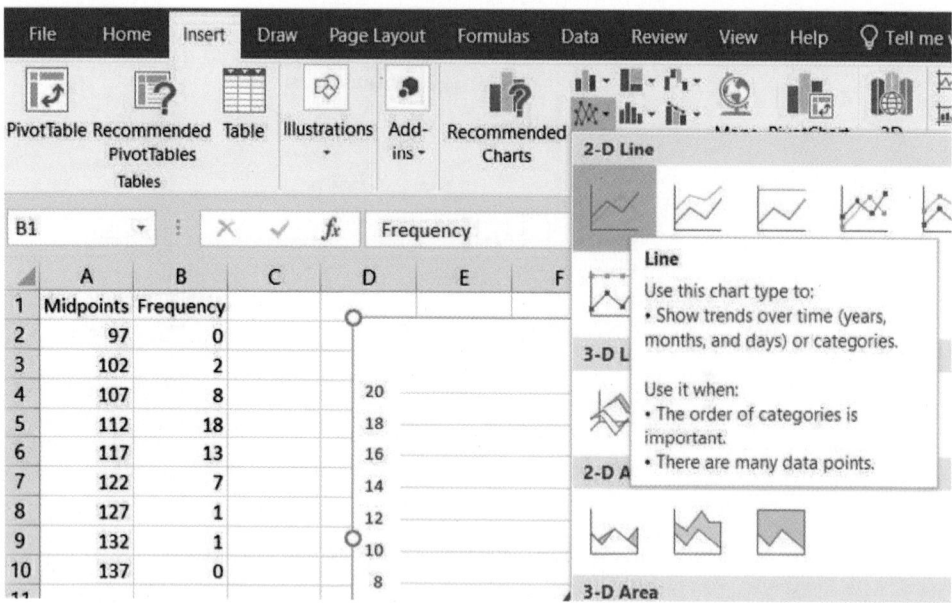

6. We will need to edit the graph so that the midpoints are on the horizontal axis.
   a. Right-click the mouse on any region of the chart.
   b. Choose Select Data.
   c. Select Edit below the Horizontal (Category) Axis Labels panel on the right.
   d. Press and hold the left mouse button, and drag over the midpoints (not including the label) for the Axis label range, then click [OK].
   e. Click [OK] on the Select Data Source box.

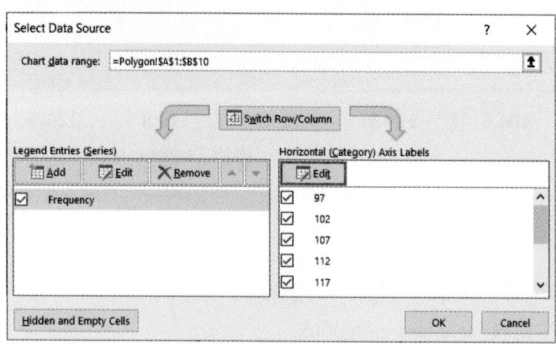
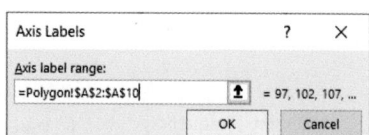

7. Insert labels on both axes.
   a. Click the mouse on any region of the graph.
   b. Select Chart Elements and then Layout on the toolbar.
   c. Select Axis Titles to open the horizontal and vertical axis text boxes. Then manually type in labels for the axes.

8. Change the chart title so that one can easily see what the graph represents.

   a. Select Chart Elements, Layout from the toolbar.

   b. Select Chart Title.

   c. Choose one of the options from the Chart Title menu and edit.

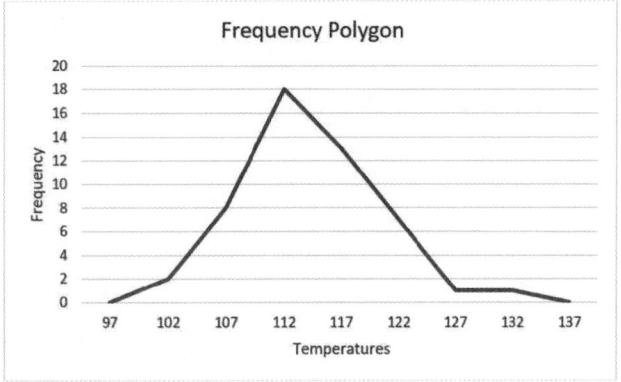

Constructing an Ogive

1. To create an ogive, use the upper class boundaries (horizontal axis) and cumulative frequencies (vertical axis) from the frequency distribution.

2. Type the upper class boundaries (including a class with frequency 0 before the lowest class to anchor the graph to the horizontal axis) and corresponding cumulative frequencies into adjacent columns of an Excel worksheet.

3. Press and hold the left mouse button, and drag over the Cumulative Frequencies from column B. Select Line Chart, then the 2-D Line option.

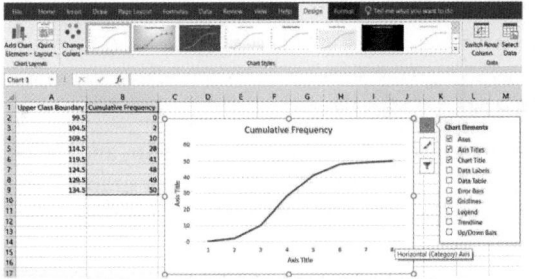 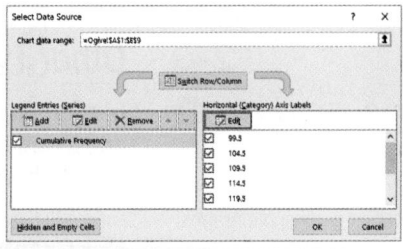

As with the frequency polygon, you can insert labels on the axes and a chart title for the ogive.

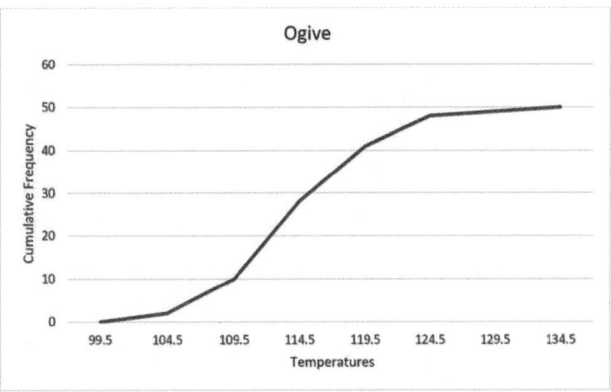

MINITAB

Step by Step

Construct a Histogram

1. Enter the data from Example 2–2, the high temperatures for the 50 states, into C1.
2. Select **Graph>Histogram**.
3. Select [Simple], then click [OK].
4. Click C1 Temperatures in the Graph variables dialog box, and label the graph.
5. Click [OK]. A new graph window containing the histogram will open.
6. Click the **File** menu to print or save the graph.

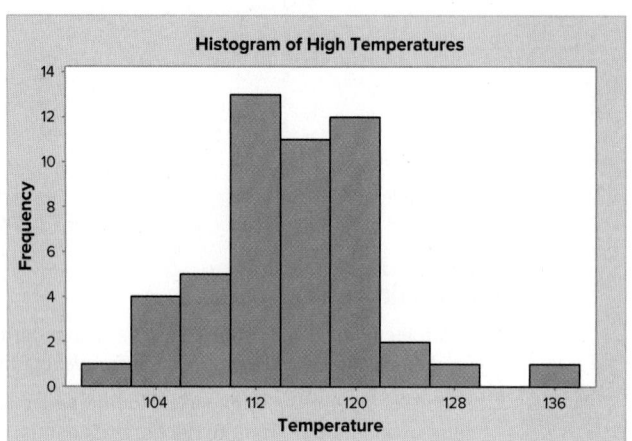

7. Click **File>Exit**.
8. Save the project as **Example 2-2.mpj.**

2–3   Other Types of Graphs

OBJECTIVE

Represent data using bar graphs, Pareto charts, time series graphs, pie graphs, and dotplots.

In addition to the histogram, the frequency polygon, and the ogive, several other types of graphs are often used in statistics. They are the bar graph, Pareto chart, time series graph, pie graph, and the dotplot. Figure 2–8 shows an example of each type of graph.

Bar Graphs

When the data are qualitative or categorical, bar graphs can be used to represent the data. A bar graph can be drawn using either horizontal or vertical bars.

> A **bar graph** represents the data by using vertical or horizontal bars whose heights or lengths represent the frequencies of the data.

EXAMPLE 2–8   College Spending for First-Year Students

The table shows the average money spent by first-year college students. Draw a horizontal and vertical bar graph for the data.

Electronics	$728
Dorm decor	344
Clothing	141
Shoes	72

Source: The National Retail Federation.

FIGURE 2–8   Other Types of Graphs Used in Statistics

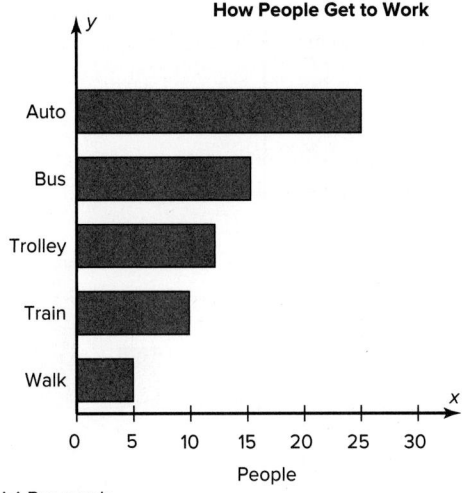

(a) Bar graph

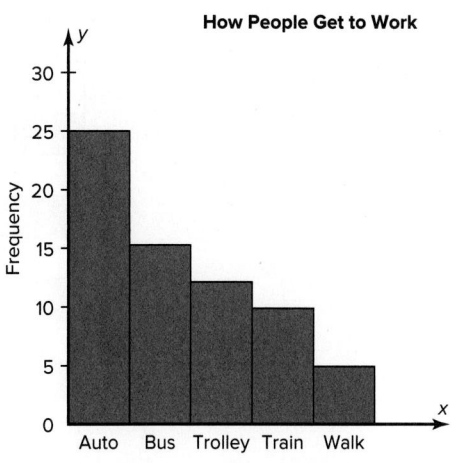

(b) Pareto chart

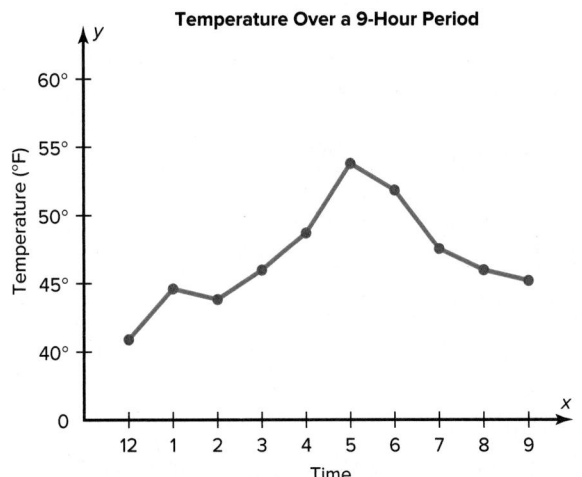

(c) Time series graph

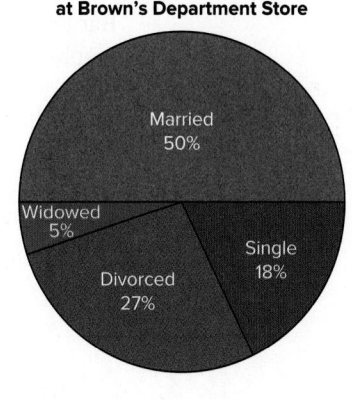

(d) Pie graph

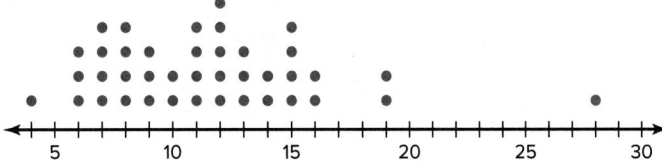

(e) Dotplot

SOLUTION

Step 1   Draw and label the x and y axes. For the horizontal bar graph place the frequency scale on the x axis, and for the vertical bar graph place the frequency scale on the y axis.

Step 2   Draw the bars corresponding to the frequencies. See Figure 2–9.

FIGURE 2–9 Bar Graphs for Example 2–8

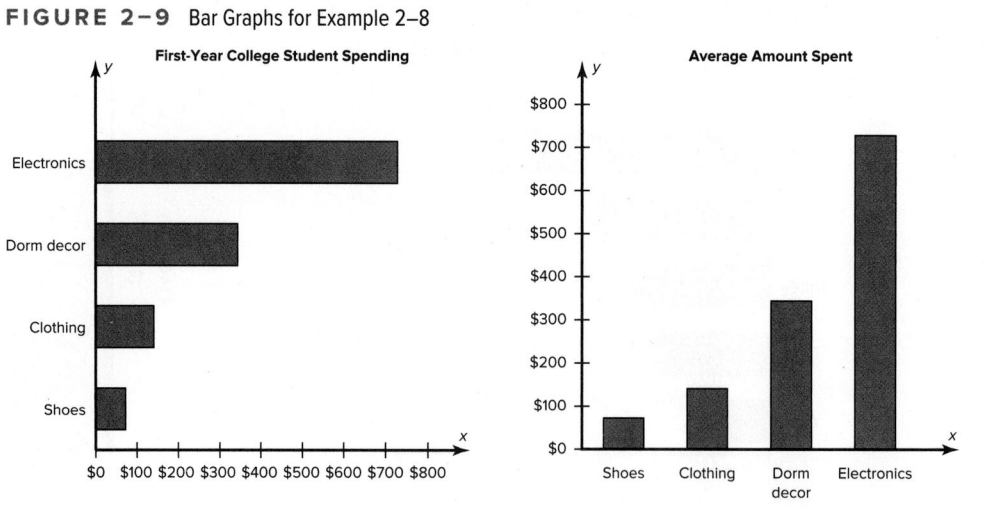

The graphs show that first-year college students spend the most on electronic equipment.

Bar graphs can also be used to compare data for two or more groups. These types of bar graphs are called **compound bar graphs.** Consider the following data for the average times (in hours) that adults in the United States spend viewing television each week. (*Note:* It is not necessary to have equal class sizes in these types of graphs.)

Total Number of Hours Per Week		
Age	**Men**	**Women**
18–24	14	16
25–54	27	31
55+	46	50

Source: Nielson Media Research

Figure 2–10 shows a bar graph that compares the average time (in hours) that men and women watch television each week. The comparison is made by placing the bars for each gender next to each other; then the heights of the bars can be compared.

The graph shows that people spend more time watching television as they grow older. Also, it shows that for each age group, women watch slightly more television than men.

FIGURE 2–10

Example of a Compound Bar Graph

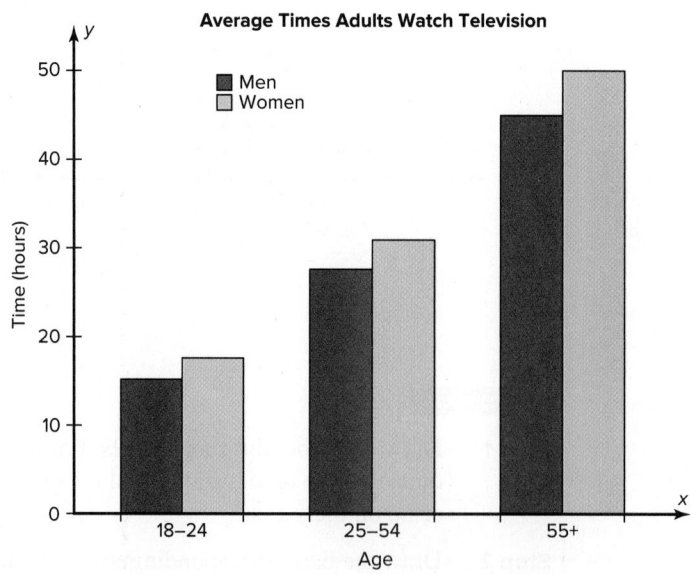

Pareto Charts

When the variable displayed on the horizontal axis is qualitative or categorical, a *Pareto chart* can also be used to represent the data.

> A **Pareto chart** is used to represent a frequency distribution for a categorical variable, and the frequencies are displayed by the heights of vertical bars, which are arranged in order from highest to lowest.

EXAMPLE 2–9   Organic Foods

A study found that people are willing to pay at least 20% more for organic food than they do for regular food. The excess amount spent for organic foods is shown. Draw a Pareto chart for the data.

Type	Excess Amount
Milk	32%
Cereal bars	27%
Fresh vegetables	44%
Beef	36%
Pork	30%

Source: Hartman Group

SOLUTION

Step 1   Arrange the data from largest value to smallest value.

Type	Excess Amount
Fresh vegetables	44%
Beef	36%
Milk	32%
Pork	30%
Cereal bars	27%

Step 2   Draw and label the *x* and *y* axes.

Step 3   Draw vertical bars to represent the percents. See Figure 2–11.

FIGURE 2–11   Pareto Chart for Example 2–9

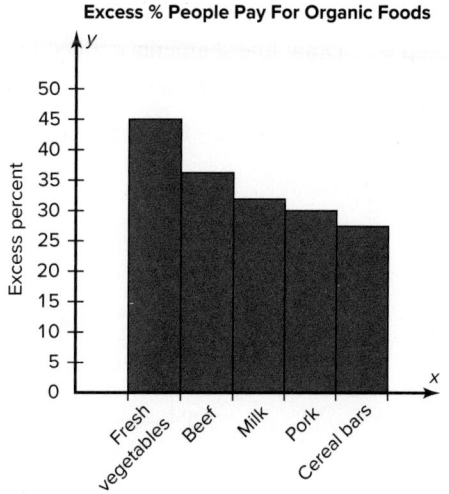

The graph shows that people will pay as much as 44% more for fresh vegetables and as much as 27% for cereal bars.

Historical Note

Vilfredo Pareto (1848–1923) was an Italian scholar who developed theories in economics, statistics, and the social sciences. His contributions to statistics include the development of a mathematical function used in economics. This function has many statistical applications and is called the Pareto distribution. In addition, he researched income distribution, and his findings became known as Pareto's law.

> **Suggestions for Drawing Pareto Charts**
>
> 1. Make the bars the same width.
> 2. Arrange the data from largest to smallest according to frequency.
> 3. Make the units that are used for the frequency equal in size.

When you analyze a Pareto chart, make comparisons by looking at the heights of the bars.

The Time Series Graph

When data are collected over a period of time, they can be represented by a time series graph.

> A **time series graph** represents data that occur over a specific period of time.

Example 2–10 shows the procedure for constructing a time series graph.

EXAMPLE 2–10   Water Consumption

The data show the average water consumption in a specific city in millions of cubic meters for a one-year period. Draw a time series graph for the data and describe the results.

Jan 15.5	May 17.6	Sept 25.4
Feb 14.3	June 20.6	Oct 18.0
Mar 14.1	July 26.1	Nov 15.1
Apr 15.3	Aug 28.7	Dec 14.2

SOLUTION

Step 1   Draw and label the x and y axes.

Step 2   Label the x axis for months and the y axis for millions of cubic meters.

Step 3   Plot each point for the values shown.

Step 4   Draw line segments connecting adjacent points. Do not draw a smooth curve through the points. See Figure 2–12.

FIGURE 2–12 Water Consumption for Example 2–10

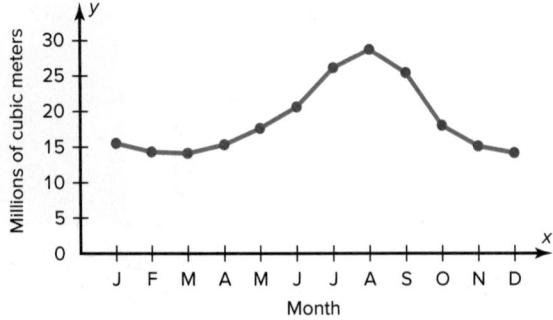

Water consumption was highest in July, August, and September, and then returned to values close to those in January through April.

Historical Note

Time series graphs are over 1000 years old. The first ones were used to chart the movements of the planets and the sun.

FIGURE 2-13

Two Time Series Graphs for Comparison

Elderly in the U.S. Labor Force

*Estimated

Source: Bureau of Census, U.S. Department of Commerce.

When you analyze a time series graph, look for a trend or pattern that occurs over the time period. For example, is the line ascending (indicating an increase over time) or descending (indicating a decrease over time)? Another thing to look for is the slope, or steepness, of the line. A line that is steep over a specific time period indicates a rapid increase or decrease over that period.

Two or more data sets can be compared on the same graph called a *compound time series graph* if two or more lines are used, as shown in Figure 2-13. This graph shows the percentage of elderly men and women in the U.S. labor force from 1960 to 2020. It shows that the percentage of elderly men decreased significantly from 1960 to 1990 and then increased slightly after that. For the elderly females, the percentage decreased slightly from 1960 to 1980 and then increased from 1980 to 2020.

The Pie Graph

Pie graphs are used extensively in statistics. The purpose of the pie graph is to show the relationship of the parts to the whole by visually comparing the sizes of the sections. Percentages or proportions can be used. The variable is nominal or categorical.

> A **pie graph** is a circle that is divided into sections or wedges according to the percentage of frequencies in each category of the distribution.

Example 2-11 shows the procedure for constructing a pie graph.

EXAMPLE 2-11 Super Bowl Snack Foods

This frequency distribution shows the number of pounds of each snack food eaten during the Super Bowl. Construct a pie graph for the data.

Snack	Pounds (frequency)
Potato chips	11.2 million
Tortilla chips	8.2 million
Pretzels	4.3 million
Popcorn	3.8 million
Snack nuts	2.5 million
	Total $n = 30.0$ million

Source: USA TODAY Weekend.

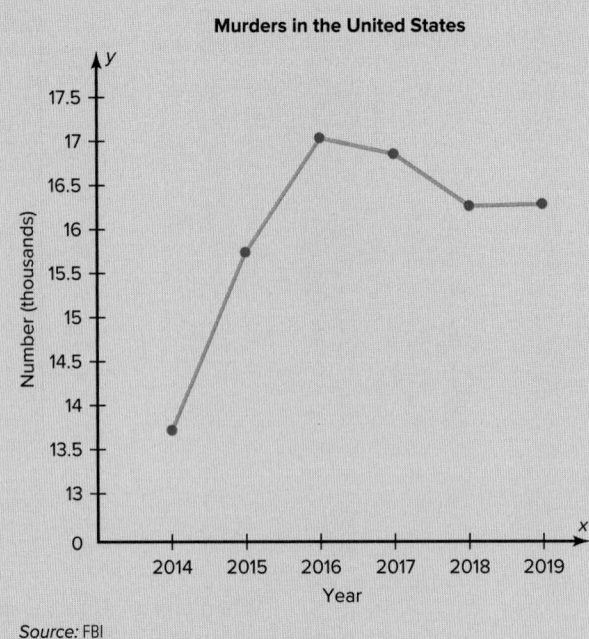

◢ SPEAKING OF STATISTICS   Murders in the United States

The graph shows the number of murders (in thousands) that have occurred in the United States since 2014. Based on the graph, do you think the number of murders is increasing, decreasing, or remaining the same?

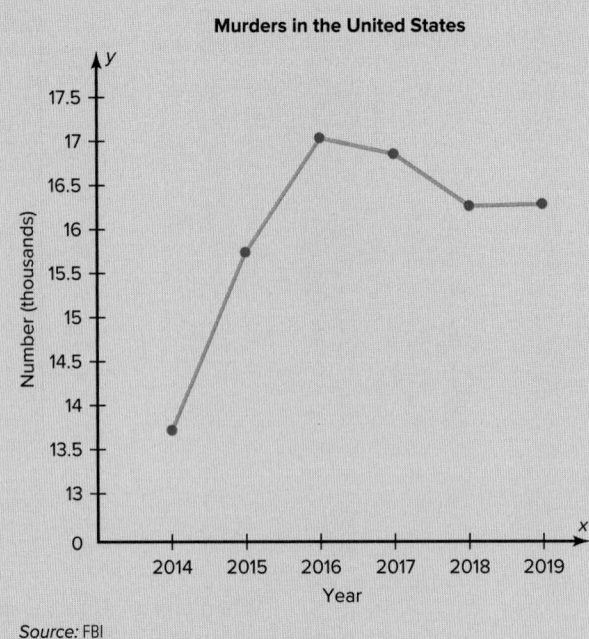

Murders in the United States

Source: FBI

SOLUTION

Step 1   Since there are 360° in a circle, the frequency for each class must be converted to a proportional part of the circle. This conversion is done by using the formula

$$\text{Degrees} = \frac{f}{n} \cdot 360°$$

where f = frequency for each class and n = sum of the frequencies. Hence, the following conversions are obtained. The degrees should sum to 360°.[1]

Potato chips	$\frac{11.2}{30} \cdot 360° = 134°$	
Tortilla chips	$\frac{8.2}{30} \cdot 360° = 98°$	
Pretzels	$\frac{4.3}{30} \cdot 360° = 52°$	
Popcorn	$\frac{3.8}{30} \cdot 360° = 46°$	
Snack nuts	$\frac{2.5}{30} \cdot 360° = 30°$	
Total		$\overline{360°}$

Step 2   Each frequency must also be converted to a percentage. Recall from Example 2–1 that this conversion is done by using the formula

$$\% = \frac{f}{n} \cdot 100$$

[1]*Note:* The degrees column does not always sum to 360° due to rounding.

Hence, the following percentages are obtained. The percentages should sum to 100%.[2]

Potato chips $\frac{11.2}{30} \cdot 100 = 37.3\%$

Tortilla chips $\frac{8.2}{30} \cdot 100 = 27.3\%$

FIGURE 2–14 Pie Graph for Example 2–11

Pretzels $\frac{4.3}{30} \cdot 100 = 14.3\%$

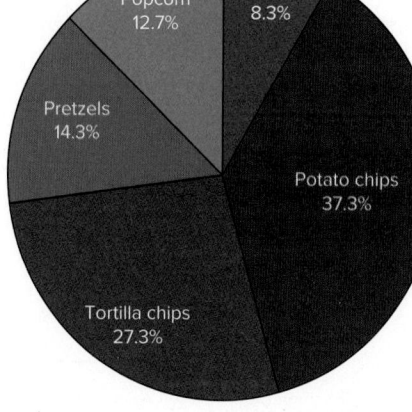

Super Bowl Snacks

Popcorn $\frac{3.8}{30} \cdot 100 = 12.7\%$

Snack nuts $\frac{2.5}{30} \cdot 100 = 8.3\%$

Total $\overline{}$
99.9%

Step 3   Next, using a protractor and a compass, draw the graph, using the appropriate degree measures found in Step 1, and label each section with the name and percentages, as shown in Figure 2–14.

[2]*Note:* The percent column does not always sum to 100% due to rounding.

EXAMPLE 2–12   Police Calls

Construct and analyze a pie graph for the calls received each shift by a local municipality for a recent year. (Data obtained by author.)

Shift	Frequency
1. Day	2594
2. Evening	2800
3. Night	2436
	7830

SOLUTION

Step 1   Find the number of degrees for each shift, using the formula:

$$\text{Degrees} = \frac{f}{n} \cdot 360°$$

For each shift, the following results are obtained:

Day: $\frac{2594}{7830} \cdot 360° = 119°$

Evening: $\frac{2800}{7830} \cdot 360° = 129°$

Night: $\frac{2436}{7830} \cdot 360° = 112°$

Step 2   Find the percentages:

Day: $\frac{2594}{7830} \cdot 100 = 33\%$

Evening: $\frac{2800}{7830} \cdot 100 = 36\%$

Night: $\frac{2436}{7830} \cdot 100 = 31\%$

Step 3   Using a protractor, graph each section and write its name and corresponding percentage as shown in Figure 2–15.

FIGURE 2–15 Figure for Example 2–12

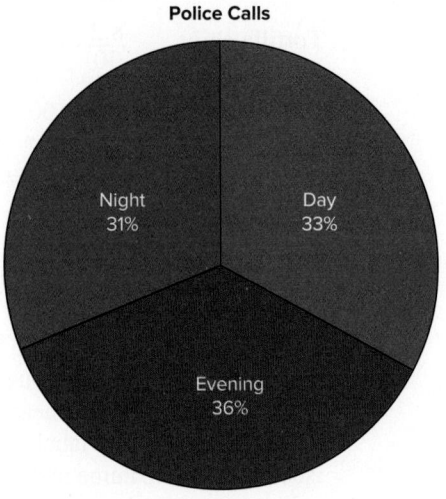

Police Calls

Night 31%

Day 33%

Evening 36%

To analyze the nature of the data shown in the pie graph, look at the size of the sections in the pie graph. For example, are any sections relatively large compared to the rest? Figure 2–15 shows that the number of calls for the three shifts are about equal, although slightly more calls were received on the evening shift.

Note: Computer programs can construct pie graphs easily, so the mathematics shown here would only be used if those programs were not available.

Dotplots

A dotplot uses points or dots to represent the data values. If the data values occur more than once, the corresponding points are plotted above one another.

> A **dotplot** is a statistical graph in which each data value is plotted as a point (dot) above the horizontal axis.

Dotplots are used to show how the data values are distributed and to see if there are any extremely high or low data values.

EXAMPLE 2–13   Federal Waste Sites

The data show the number of federal waste sites in each of the 50 states. Draw a dot plot for the data and summarize the results.

3	5	2	0	13	3	1	1	2	6
2	1	2	2	4	0	1	1	1	1
3	10	6	0	2	6	3	0	1	0
1	6	1	4	2	0	3	1	2	6
1	2	2	1	3	4	5	0	0	11

Step 1   Find the lowest and highest data values, and decide what scale to use on the horizontal axis. The lowest data value is 0 and the highest data value is 13, so a scale from 0 to 13 is needed.

Step 2   Draw a horizontal line, and draw the scale on the line.

Step 3 Plot each data value above the line. If the value occurs more than once, plot the other point above the first point. See Figure 2–16.

FIGURE 2–16 Figure for Example 2–13

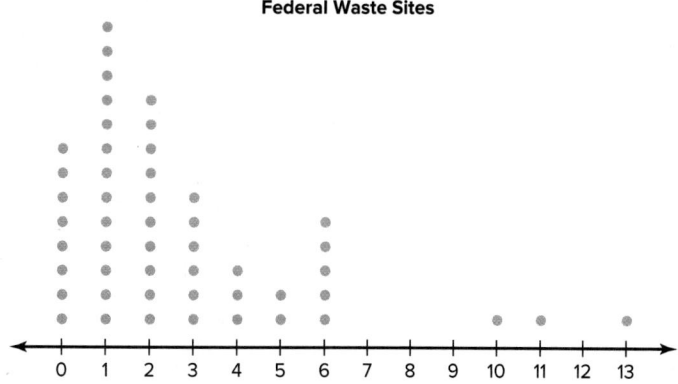

The graph shows that most of the states have between zero and three waste sites, with 13 states having one waste site. This is the largest frequency.

Stem and Leaf Plots

The stem and leaf plot is a method of organizing data and is a combination of sorting and graphing. It has the advantage over a grouped frequency distribution of retaining the actual data while showing them in graphical form.

OBJECTIVE **4**

Draw and interpret a stem and leaf plot.

> A **stem and leaf plot** is a data plot that uses part of the data value as the stem and part of the data value as the leaf to form groups or classes.

For example, a data value of 34 would have 3 as the stem and 4 as the leaf. A data value of 356 would have 35 as the stem and 6 as the leaf.

Example 2–14 shows the procedure for constructing a stem and leaf plot.

EXAMPLE 2–14   Out Patient Cardiograms

At an outpatient testing center, the number of cardiograms performed each day for 20 days is shown. Construct a stem and leaf plot for the data.

25	31	20	32	13
14	43	02	57	23
36	32	33	32	44
32	52	44	51	45

SOLUTION

Step 1 Arrange the data in order:

02, 13, 14, 20, 23, 25, 31, 32, 32, 32,
32, 33, 36, 43, 44, 44, 45, 51, 52, 57

Note: Arranging the data in order is not essential and can be cumbersome when the data set is large; however, it is helpful in constructing a stem and leaf plot. The leaves in the final stem and leaf plot should be arranged in order.

Step 2   Separate the data according to the first digit, as shown.

02   13, 14   20, 23, 25   31, 32, 32, 32, 32, 33, 36
43, 44, 44, 45   51, 52, 57

Step 3   A display can be made by using the leading digit as the *stem* and the trail-ing digit as the *leaf*. For example, for the value 32, the leading digit, 3, is the stem and the trailing digit, 2, is the leaf. For the value 14, the 1 is the stem and the 4 is the leaf. Now a plot can be constructed as shown in Figure 2–17.

FIGURE 2–17

Stem and Leaf Plot for Example 2–14

0	2
1	3 4
2	0 3 5
3	1 2 2 2 2 3 6
4	3 4 4 5
5	1 2 7

Leading digit (stem)	Trailing digit (leaf)
0	2
1	3 4
2	0 3 5
3	1 2 2 2 2 3 6
4	3 4 4 5
5	1 2 7

Figure 2–17 shows that the distribution peaks in the center and that there are no gaps in the data. For 7 of the 20 days, the number of patients receiving cardiograms was between 31 and 36. The plot also shows that the testing center treated from a minimum of 2 patients to a maximum of 57 patients in any one day.

If there are no data values in a class, you should write the stem number and leave the leaf row blank. Do not put a zero in the leaf row.

EXAMPLE 2–15   Number of Car Thefts in a Large City

An insurance company researcher conducted a survey on the number of car thefts in a large city for a period of 30 days last summer. The raw data are shown. Construct a stem and leaf plot by using classes 50–54, 55–59, 60–64, 65–69, 70–74, and 75–79.

52	62	51	50	69
58	77	66	53	57
75	56	55	67	73
79	59	68	65	72
57	51	63	69	75
65	53	78	66	55

SOLUTION

Step 1   Arrange the data in order.

50, 51, 51, 52, 53, 53, 55, 55, 56, 57, 57, 58, 59, 62, 63, 65, 65, 66, 66, 67, 68, 69, 69, 72, 73, 75, 75, 77, 78, 79

Step 2   Separate the data according to the classes.

50, 51, 51, 52, 53, 53   55, 55, 56, 57, 57, 58, 59
62, 63   65, 65, 66, 66, 67, 68, 69, 69   72, 73
75, 75, 77, 78, 79

FIGURE 2–18

Stem and Leaf Plot for Example 2–15

5	0 1 1 2 3 3
5	5 5 6 7 7 8 9
6	2 3
6	5 5 6 6 7 8 9 9
7	2 3
7	5 5 7 8 9

Step 3   Plot the data as shown here.

Leading digit (stem)	Trailing digit (leaf)
5	0 1 1 2 3 3
5	5 5 6 7 7 8 9
6	2 3
6	5 5 6 6 7 8 9 9
7	2 3
7	5 5 7 8 9

The graph for this plot is shown in Figure 2–18.

When you analyze a stem and leaf plot, look for peaks and gaps in the distribution. See if the distribution is symmetric or skewed. Check the variability of the data by looking at the spread.

Related distributions can be compared by using a back-to-back stem and leaf plot. The back-to-back stem and leaf plot uses the same digits for the stems of both distributions, but the digits that are used for the leaves are arranged in order out from the stems on both sides. Example 2–16 shows a back-to-back stem and leaf plot.

EXAMPLE 2–16   Number of Stories in Tall Buildings

The number of stories in two randomly selected samples of tall buildings in Miami and Houston are shown. Construct a back-to-back stem and leaf plot for the data and compare the distributions.

Miami					Houston				
64	57	52	45	60	71	53	55	47	46
55	47	51	56	52	64	55	40	36	36
60	50	49	48	56	54	34	52	45	35
63	43	41	53	49	49	41	40	37	33
58	34	45	44	46	50	42	40	37	33

Source: World Almanac and Book of Facts

2–47

SOLUTION

Step 1   Arrange the data for both data sets in order.

Step 2   Construct a stem and leaf plot, using the same digits as stems. Place the digits for the leaves for Miami on the left side of the stem and the digits for the leaves for Houston on the right side, as shown. See Figure 2–19.

FIGURE 2–19   Back-to-Back Stem and Leaf Plot for Example 2–16

Miami		Houston
4	3	3 3 4 5 6 6 7 7
9 9 8 7 6 5 5 4 3 1	4	0 0 0 1 2 5 6 7 9
8 7 6 6 5 3 2 2 1 0	5	0 2 3 4 5 5
4 3 0 0	6	4
	7	1

Step 3   Compare the distributions. Miami's buildings are somewhat higher than those in Houston. The distribution for the buildings in Miami peak at 40 to 49 stories and 50 to 59 stories, while those in Houston peak at 40 to 49 stories.

Stem and leaf plots are part of the techniques called *exploratory data analysis.* More information on this topic is presented in Chapter 3.

Misleading Graphs

Graphs give a visual representation that enables readers to analyze and interpret data more easily than they could simply by looking at numbers. However, inappropriately drawn graphs can misrepresent the data and lead the reader to false conclusions. For example, a car manufacturer's ad stated that 98% of the vehicles it had sold in the past 10 years were still on the road. The ad then showed a graph similar to the one in Figure 2–20. The graph shows the percentage of the manufacturer's automobiles still on

FIGURE 2–20
Graph of Automaker's Claim Using a Scale from 95 to 100%

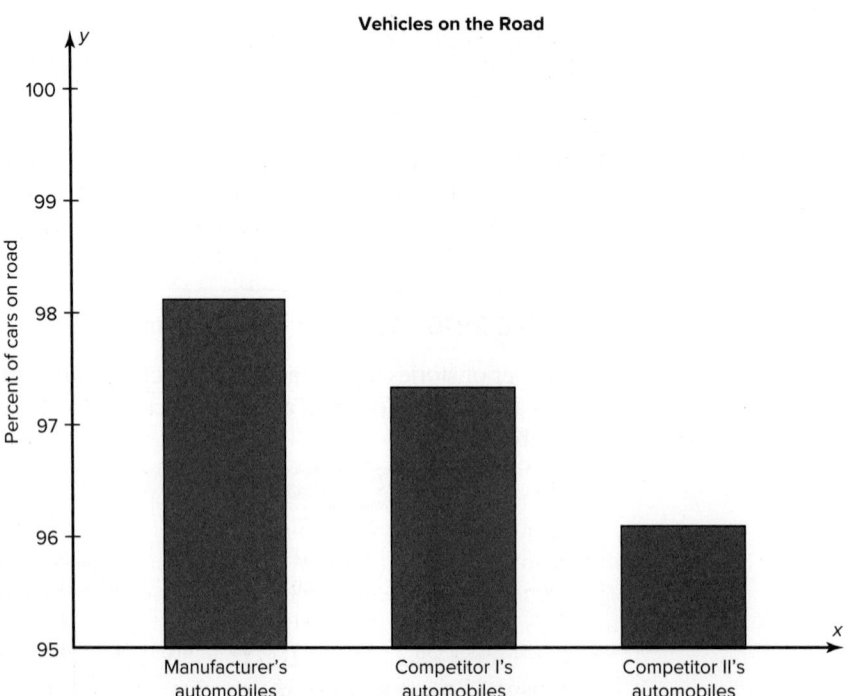

FIGURE 2–21

Graph in Figure 2–20 Redrawn Using a Scale from 0 to 100%

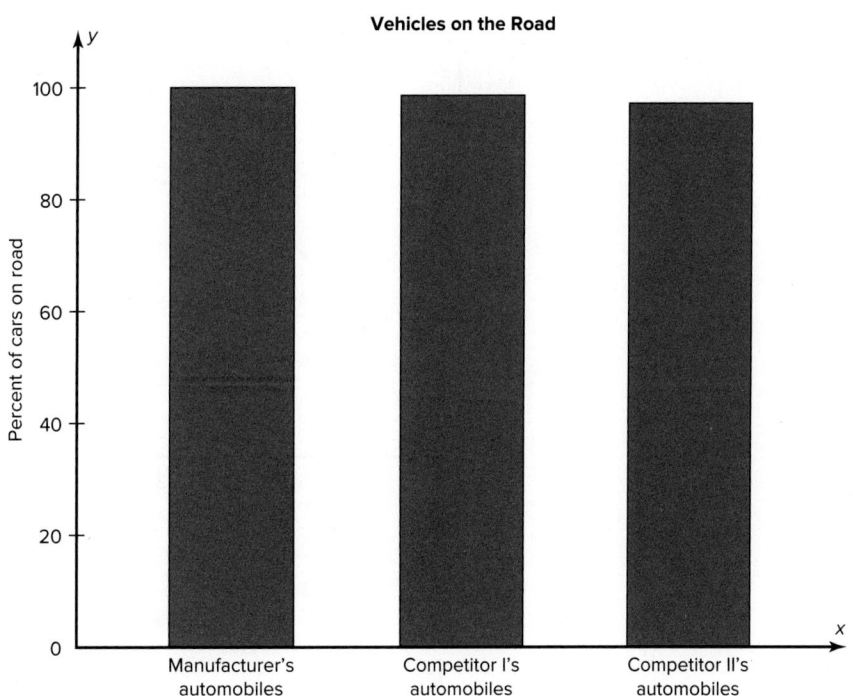

the road and the percentage of its competitors' automobiles still on the road. Is there a large difference? Not necessarily.

Notice the scale on the vertical axis in Figure 2–20. It has been cut off (or truncated) and starts at 95%. When the graph is redrawn using a scale that goes from 0 to 100%, as in Figure 2–21, there is hardly a noticeable difference in the percentages. Thus, changing the units at the starting point on the y axis can convey a very different visual representation of the data.

It is not wrong to truncate an axis of the graph; many times it is necessary to do so. However, the reader should be aware of this fact and interpret the graph accordingly. Do not be misled if an inappropriate impression is given.

Let us consider another example. The projected required fuel economy in miles per gallon for vehicles is shown. In this case, an increase from 14.1 to 16 miles per gallon is projected.

Year	2011	2012	2013	2014	2015	2016
MPG	14.1	15.0	15.5	15.5	15.8	16

Source: National Highway Traffic Safety Administration.

When you examine the graph shown in Figure 2–22(a), you see a slight increase from 14.1 to 16, but when you spread out the scale as shown in Figure 2–22(b), you see a much larger increase for the same data values. Again, by manipulating the scale, you can change the visual presentation.

Another misleading graphing technique sometimes used involves exaggerating a one-dimensional increase by showing it in two dimensions. For example, the average cost of a 30-second Super Bowl commercial has increased from $42,000 in 1967 to $5.6 million in 2020.

The increase shown by the graph in Figure 2–23(a) represents the change by a comparison of the heights of the two bars in one dimension. The same data are shown

FIGURE 2–22

Projected Miles per Gallon

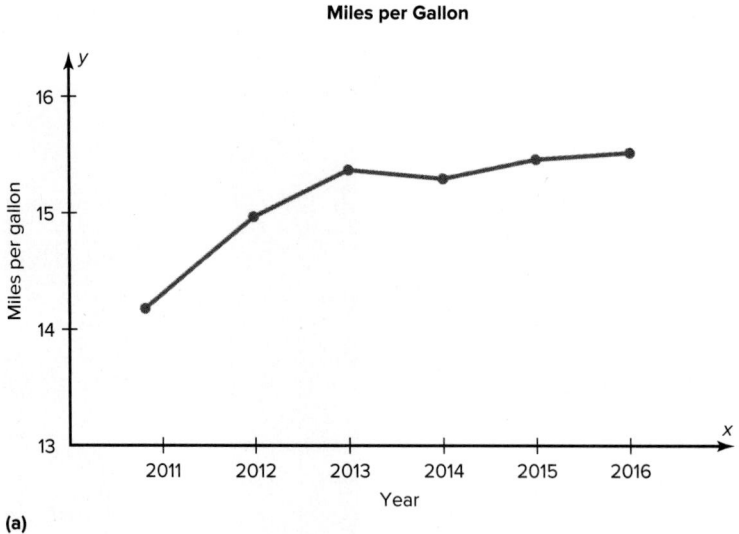

(a)

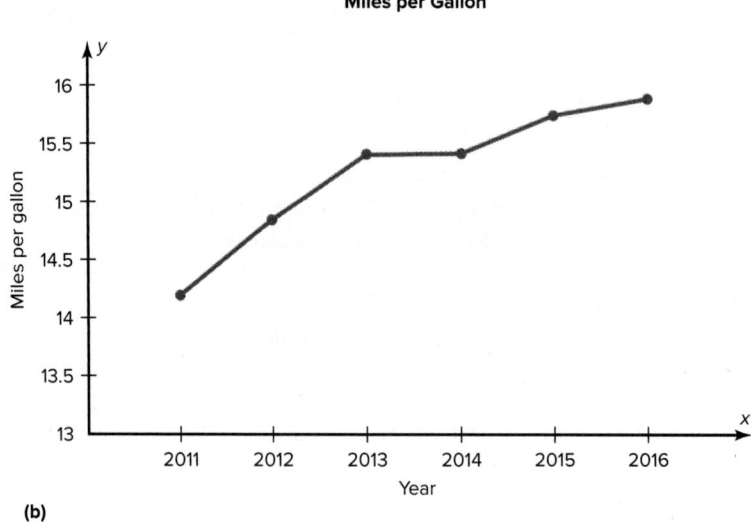

(b)

two-dimensionally with circles in Figure 2–23(b). Notice that the difference seems much larger because the eye is comparing the areas of the circles rather than the lengths of the diameters.

Note that it is not wrong to use the graphing techniques of truncating the scales or representing data by two-dimensional pictures. But when these techniques are used, the reader should be cautious of the conclusion drawn on the basis of the graphs.

Another way to misrepresent data on a graph is by omitting labels or units on the axes of the graph. The graph shown in Figure 2–24 compares the cost of living, economic growth, population growth, etc., of four main geographic areas in the United States. However, since there are no numbers on the y axis, very little information can be gained from this graph, except a crude ranking of each factor. There is no way to decide the actual magnitude of the differences.

Finally, all graphs should contain a source for the information presented. The inclusion of a source for the data will enable you to check the reliability of the organization presenting the data.

FIGURE 2–23

Comparison of Costs for a 30-Second Super Bowl Commercial

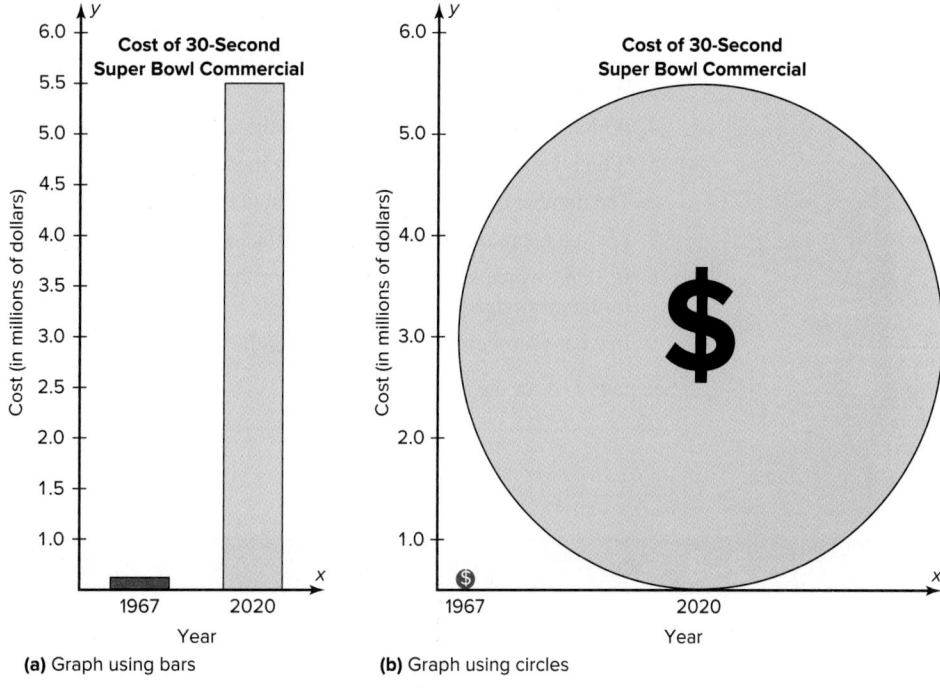

(a) Graph using bars   **(b)** Graph using circles

FIGURE 2–24

A Graph with No Units on the *y* Axis

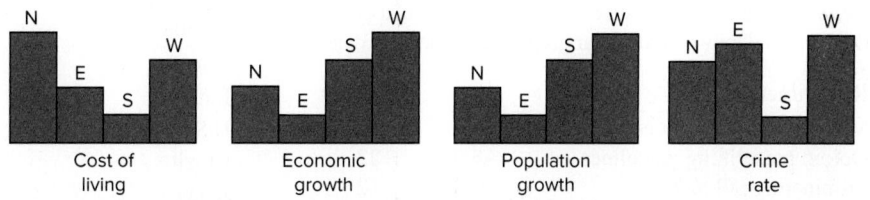

Cost of living   Economic growth   Population growth   Crime rate

⬛ Applying the Concepts 2–3

Causes of Accidental Deaths in the United States, 1999–2009

The graph shows the number of deaths in the United States due to accidents. Answer the following questions about the graph.

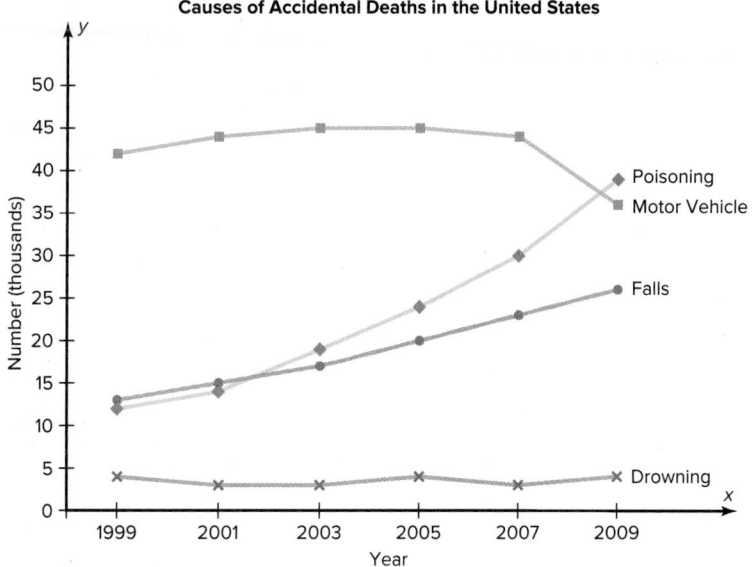

Source: National Safety Council.

1. Name the variables used in the graph.
2. Are the variables qualitative or quantitative?
3. What type of graph is used here?
4. Which variable shows a decrease in the number of deaths over the years?
5. Which variable or variables show an increase in the number of deaths over the years?
6. The number of deaths in which variable remains about the same over the years?
7. List the approximate number of deaths for each category for the year 2001.
8. In 1999, which variable accounted for the most deaths? In 2009, which variable accounted for the most deaths?
9. In what year were the numbers of deaths from poisoning and falls about the same?

See page 110 for the answers.

≡ Exercises 2–3

1. Controlled Substances Prescription Guidelines The National Safety Council has set 6 recommendations for states to follow in prescribing controlled substances. The data show the number of states that have laws in that particular area. Draw a vertical bar graph to illustrate the data.

Recommendation	Number
Mandating prescriber education	17
Opioid prescribing guidelines	22
Eliminating pill mills	12
Prescription drug monitoring programs	42
Increase access to naloxone	35
Availability of opioid user disorder treatment	3

Source: National Safety Council

2. Paying Off a College Debt The following data show the ages at which millennials (20–29) expect to pay off their college debt. Draw a horizontal bar graph to represent the data.

Age	Percent
20–29	32%
30–39	40%
40–49	14%
50+	14%

Source: TD Ameritrade Survey

3. Snack Food The following data represent the amount of money in billions of dollars spent by United States residents on snack foods for a recent year. Draw a Pareto chart for the data.

Snack	Amount spent
Salty snacks	27.72
Candy	20.96
Cheese	17.3
Cookies	7.36
Ice Cream	6.64

Source: Consumer Goods and FMCG

4. Internet Users The data show the top five nations with the most Internet users in millions. Draw a Pareto chart for the data.

Nation	Internet users
China	658
India	326
U.S.	290
Brazil	123
Japan	112

Source: Computer Industry Almanac

5. Online Ad Spending The amount spent (in billions of dollars) for ads online is shown. (The numbers for 2016 through 2019 were projected numbers.) Draw a time series graph and comment on the trend.

Year	2014	2015	2016	2017	2018	2019
Amount	$19.72	$31.53	$43.83	$53.29	$61.14	$69.04

Source: eMarketer.

6. Medical Prescriptions The number of medical prescriptions dispensed over the years from 2015 to 2019 is shown. Draw a time series graph and comment on the nature of the situation.

Year	Amount in millions
2015	4368
2016	4453
2017	4237
2018	4213
2019	4218

7. World Population The data (in millions) for the population of the world for the specific years is shown. Draw a time series graph for the data.

Year	1995	2000	2005	2010	2015	2020
Population	5327	6143	6541	6956	7379	7794

8. **Automobile Sales** The data show the number of automobiles sold by an automobile dealership. Draw a time series graph for the data and analyze the results.

Year	Number
2014	3851
2015	3461
2016	2827
2017	2076
2018	1717
2019	1278
2020	1078

9. **What's Cooking?** A study of 1063 U.S. adults found that 24% used a microwave oven to prepare a meal, 44% use the stove-top, 25% used the oven, and 7% used another method. Draw a pie graph for the data and analyze the graph.

Source: Pieapod Survey

10. **FEMA Help for Hurricane Victims** The following survey by Morning Consult/Politico asked whether or not the Federal Emergency Management Agency (FEMA) had done enough for Texas and Louisiana residents after Hurricane Harvey made landfall. Assume that they surveyed 1000 people. Draw a pie graph for the information.

	Number
Did enough	560
Did not do enough	240
Don't know	200

11. **Lottery Winners** A survey by BMO Harris asked 304 small business owners if they would sell their businesses if they won the lottery. The results are shown. Draw a pie graph for the data.

	Number
Yes	118
No	162
Don't know	24

12. **Children's Living Arrangements** The following data represent the living arrangement for children with single parents. Draw two pie graphs and compare the results.

Ages of children	Single mothers	Single fathers
0–5 years	35%	43%
6–11 years	35%	30%
12–17 years	30%	27%

Source: U.S. Census Bureau

13. **Prior Prison Sentences** The following data show the number of prior prison sentences that persons have after being convicted of a crime. Construct a dot plot for the data.

0	2	5	6	1	3	0	2	1	5
1	3	0	1	2	1	2	1	3	2
0	2	4	0	3	0	3	5	6	4
1	4	3	3	4	3	5	0	4	0
2	0	2	1	0	1	2	1	3	1

14. **Teacher Strikes** In Pennsylvania the numbers of teacher strikes for the last 14 years are shown. Construct a dotplot for the data. Comment on the graph.

9	13	15	7	7	14	9
10	14	18	7	8	8	3

Source: School Leader News.

15. **Years of Experience** The data show the number of years of experience the players on the Pittsburgh Steelers football team have at the beginning of the season. Draw and analyze a dot plot for the data.

4	4	2	9	7	3	7	12	6
5	1	4	5	2	7	6	12	3
12	4	0	4	0	0	0	2	9
2	6	7	13	4	2	6	9	4
4	0	3	5	4	2	6	9	4
4	0	3	5	3	11	1	4	2
3	15	1	6	0	11	3	10	3

16. **Commuting Times** Fifty off-campus students were asked how long it takes them to get to school. The times (in minutes) are shown. Construct a dotplot and analyze the data.

23	22	29	19	12
18	17	30	11	27
11	18	26	25	20
25	15	24	21	31
29	14	22	25	29
24	12	30	27	21
27	25	21	14	28
17	17	24	20	26
13	20	27	26	17
18	25	21	33	29

17. **50 Home Run Club** There are 43 Major League baseball players (as of 2015) who have hit 50 or more home runs in one season. Construct a stem and leaf plot and analyze the data.

50	51	52	54	59	51	53
54	50	58	51	54	53	
56	58	56	70	54	52	
58	54	64	52	73	57	
50	60	56	50	66	54	
52	51	58	63	57	52	
51	50	61	52	65	50	

Source: The World Almanac and Book of Facts.

18. **Terrorist Attacks** The data show the number of terrorist attacks against the United States over a recent 16-year period. Draw a stem and leaf plot for the data.

32	41	33	32	9	20	6	9
18	10	17	10	17	19	26	38

Source: Global Terrorism Data Base

19. Length of Major Rivers The data show the lengths (in hundreds of miles) of major rivers in South America and Europe. Construct a back-to-back stem and leaf plot, and compare the distributions.

South America				Europe				
39	21	10	10	5	12	7	6	8
11	10	2	10	5	5	4	6	
10	14	10	12	18	5	13	9	
17	15	10		14	6	6	11	
15	25	16		8	6	3	4	

Source: The World Almanac and Book of Facts.

20. Math and Reading Achievement Scores The math and reading achievement scores from the National Assessment of Educational Progress for selected states are listed below. Construct a back-to-back stem and leaf plot with the data, and compare the distributions.

Math					Reading				
52	66	69	62	61	65	76	76	66	67
63	57	59	59	55	71	70	70	66	61
55	59	74	72	73	61	69	78	76	77
68	76	73			77	77	80		

Source: World Almanac.

21. State which type of graph (Pareto chart, time series graph, or pie graph) would most appropriately represent the data.

   a. Situations that distract automobile drivers

   b. Number of persons in an automobile used for getting to and from work each day

   c. Amount of money spent for textbooks and supplies for one semester

   d. Number of people killed by tornados in the United States each year for the last 10 years

   e. The number of pets (dogs, cats, birds, fish, etc.) in the United States this year

   f. The average amount of money that a person spent for a significant other for Christmas for the last 6 years

22. State which graph (Pareto chart, time series graph, or pie graph) would most appropriately represent the given situation.

   a. The number of students enrolled at a local college for each year during the last 5 years

   b. The budget for the student activities department at a certain college for a specific year

   c. The means of transportation the students use to get to school

   d. The percentage of votes each of the four candidates received in the last election

   e. The record temperatures of a city for the last 30 years

   f. The frequency of each type of crime committed in a city during the year

23. Credit Scores The following factors contribute to a FICO credit score. Draw a pie chart and vertical bar graph for the data. Which graph is a better representation of the data?

Factor	Percent
Payment history	35%
Amount owed	30%
Length of credit history	15%
Credit mix	10%
New credit	10%

Source: Experian

24. Alcohol Poisoning The following data show the ages and the percents of individuals who have died from alcohol poisoning for a specific year. Draw a pie chart and a vertical bar graph for the data. Which graph do you think better illustrates the significance of the data? Explain.

Age	Percent
15–24	5%
25–34	13%
35–44	21%
45–54	34%
55–64	21%
65+	6%

Source: Addictionresource.com
(*Note:* Class width here is 10 and was already decided by the researchers, so it can be used here.)

25. Cost of Milk The graph shows the increase in the price of a quart of milk. Why might the increase appear to be larger than it really is?

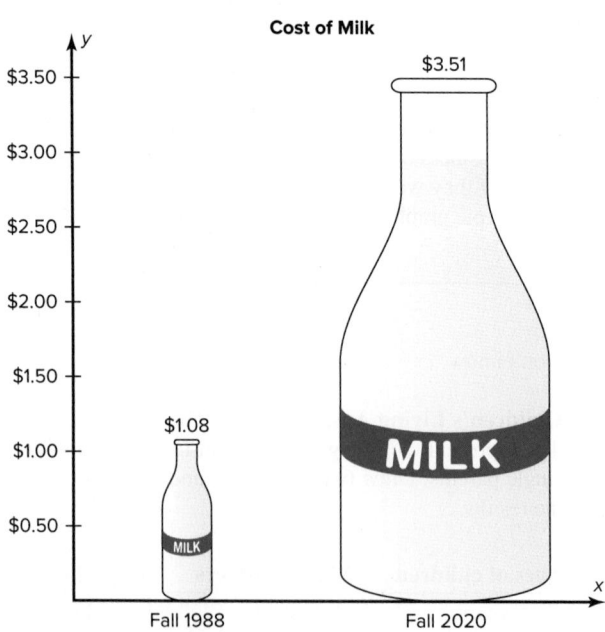

26. Websites The data show the number (in millions) of websites in the United States from 2012 to 2020. Draw a time series graph for the data.

Year	2012	2013	2014	2015	2016	2017	2018	2019	2020
Number of websites	697	672	968	863	1045	1767	1630	1711	1811

27. Chicago Homicides The data represent the number of homicides that occurred in Chicago from 2013 to 2020. Draw a time series graph for the data.

Year	2013	2014	2015	2016	2017	2018	2019	2020
Number of deaths	370	365	422	632	590	483	451	643

28. Trip Reimbursements The average amount requested for business trip reimbursement is itemized below.

Illustrate the data with an appropriate graph. Do you have any questions regarding the data?

Flight	$440
Hotel stay	323
Entertainment	139
Phone usage	95
Transportation	65
Meal	38
Parking	34

Source: USA TODAY.

Technology — Step by Step

TI-84 Plus
Step by Step

To graph a time series, follow the procedure for a frequency polygon from Section 2–2, using the following data for the number of outdoor drive-in theaters

Year	1988	1990	1992	1994	1996	1998	2000
Number	1497	910	870	859	826	750	637

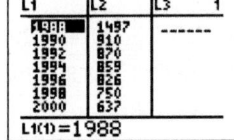 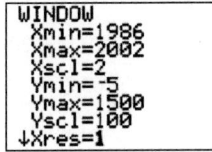  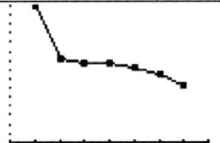

EXCEL
Step by Step

Constructing a Pareto Chart

To make a Pareto chart:

1. Enter the snack food categories from Example 2–11 into column A of a new worksheet.
2. Enter the corresponding frequencies in column B. The data should be entered in descending order according to frequency.
3. Highlight the data from columns A and B, and select the Insert tab from the toolbar.
4. Select the Column Chart type.

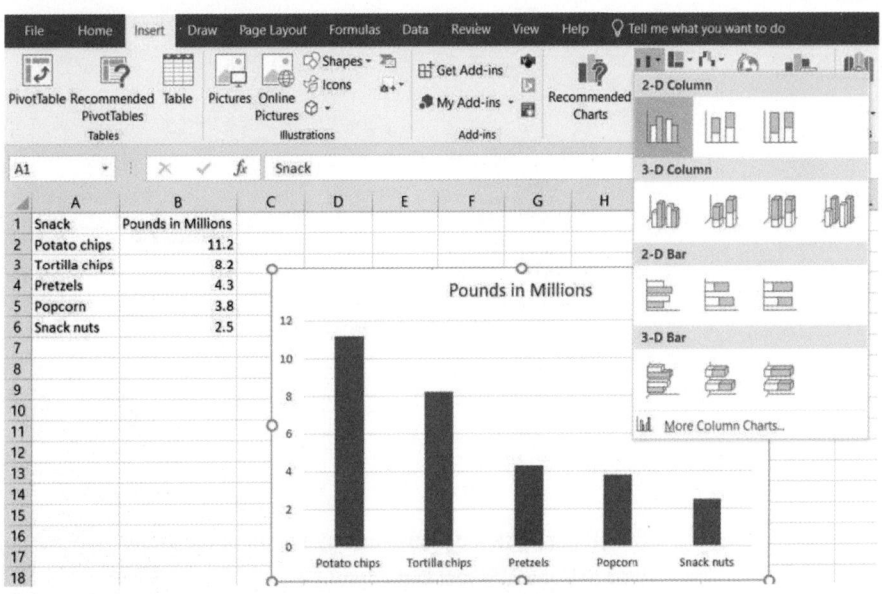

5. To change the title of the chart, click on the current title of the chart.

6. When the text box containing the title is highlighted, click the mouse in the text box and change the title.

7. Right-click on any bar and select Format Data Series. Change the gap width to zero.

8. Add labels to the axes and delete the legend.

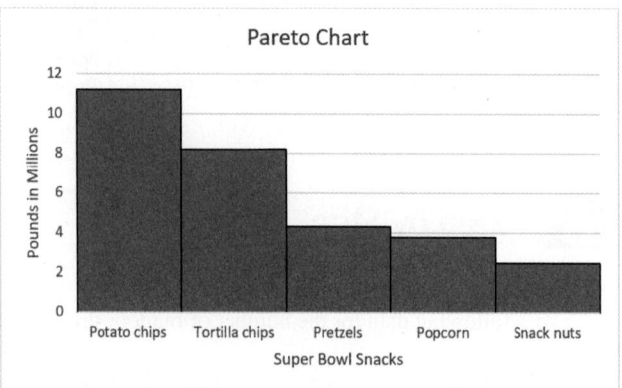

Constructing a Time Series Chart

Example

Year	2009	2010	2011	2012	2013	2014	2015	2016	2017	2018
Vehicles*	162.6	163.6	165.2	165	163.7	163.8	166.2	171.6	172.6	172.5

*Vehicles (in millions) that used the Pennsylvania Turnpike.
Source: https://www.paturnpike.com/pdfs/business/finance/AuditorGeneralsPeformanceAuditMar2019.pdf

To make a time series chart:

1. Enter the years 2009 through 2018 from the example in column A of a new Excel worksheet.

2. Enter the corresponding frequencies in column B.

3. Highlight the data from column B and select the Insert tab from the toolbar.

4. Select the Line chart type.

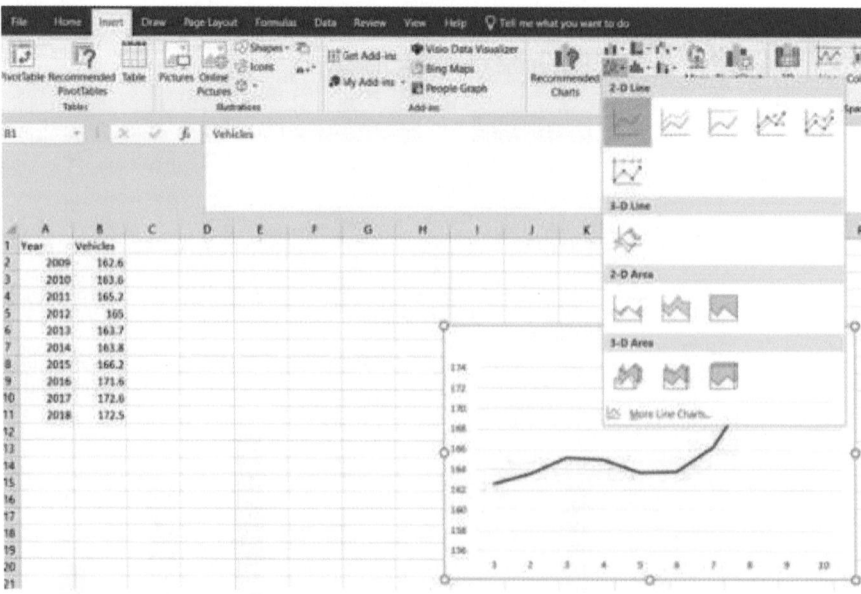

5. Right-click the mouse on any region of the graph.

6. Select the Select Data option.

7. Select Edit from the Horizontal Axis Labels and highlight the years from column A, then click [OK].

8. Click [OK] on the Select Data Source box.

9. Create a title for your chart, such as Vehicles Using the Pennsylvania Turnpike. Right-click the mouse on any region of the chart. Select the Chart Tools tab from the toolbar, then Layout.

10. Select Chart Title and highlight the current title to change the title.

11. Select Axis Titles to change the horizontal and vertical axis labels.

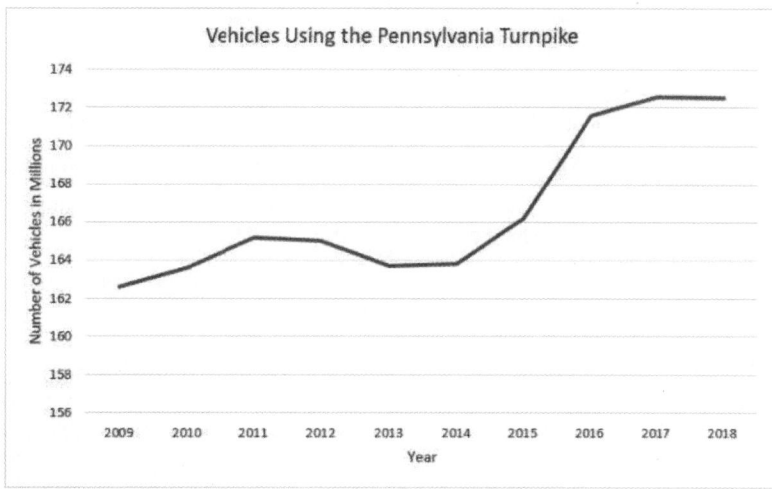

Constructing a Pie Chart

To make a pie chart:

1. Enter the shifts from Example 2–12 into column A of a new worksheet.

2. Enter the frequencies corresponding to each shift in column B.

3. Highlight the data in columns A and B and select Insert from the toolbar; then select the Pie chart type.

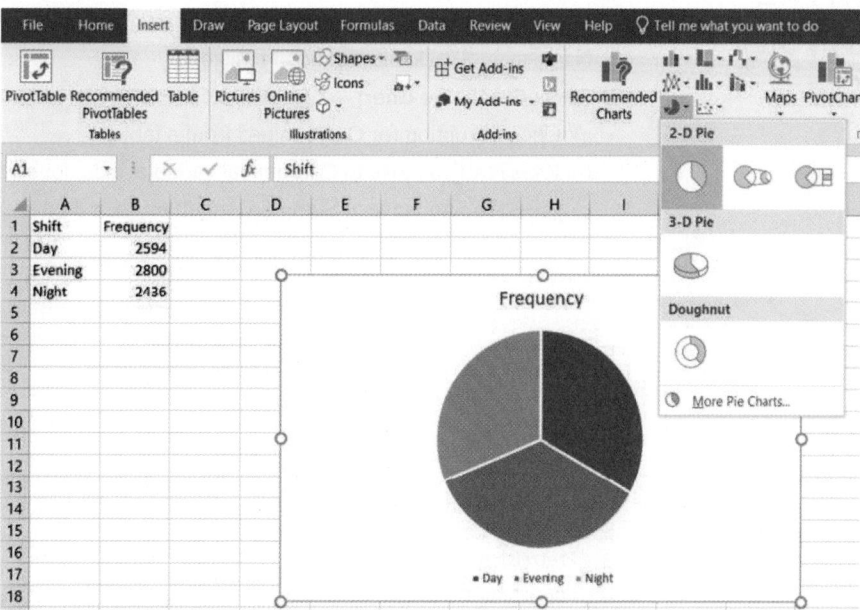

4. Click on any region of the chart. Then select Design from the Chart Tools tab on the toolbar.

5. Select Add Chart Elements from the chart Layouts tab on the toolbar. Under Format Data Labels, check Category Name and Percentage; uncheck legend.

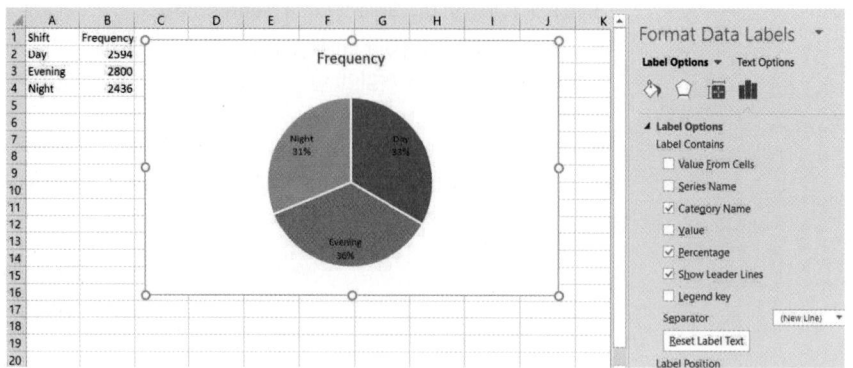

6. To change the title of the chart, click on the current title of the chart.

7. When the text box containing the title is highlighted, click the mouse in the text box and change the title.

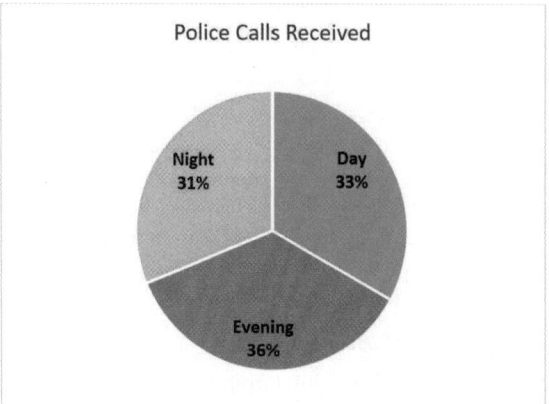

MINITAB

Step by Step

Construct a Pie Chart

1. Enter the summary data for snack foods and frequencies from Example 2–11 into C1 and C2.
2. Name them **Snack** and **Pounds in Millions**.
3. Select **Graph>Pie Chart.**
   a) Click the option for Chart values from a table.
   b) Press [Tab] to move to Categorical variable, then double-click C1 to select it.
   c) Press [Tab] to move to Summary variables, then double-click C2 to select it.

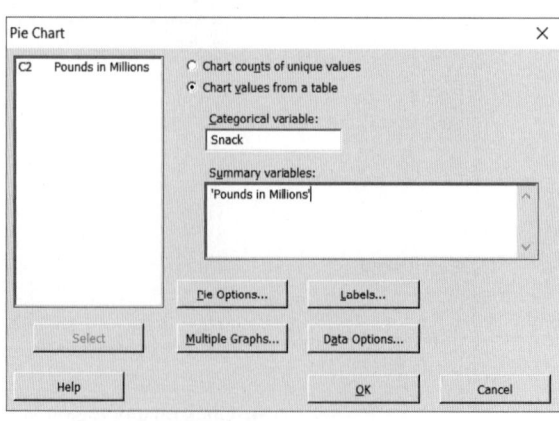

4. Click the [Labels] tab, then Titles/Footnotes.

   a) Type in the title: **Super Bowl Snacks in Millions of Pounds.**

   b) Click the Slice Labels tab, then the options for Category name and Percent.

   c) Click the option to Draw a line from label to slice.

   d) Click [OK] twice to create the chart.

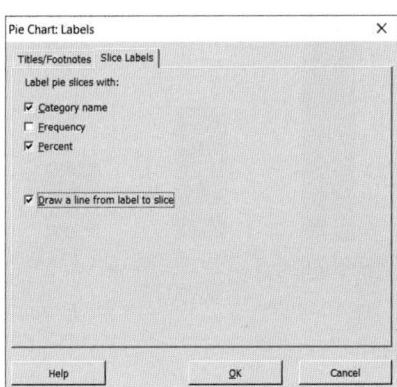
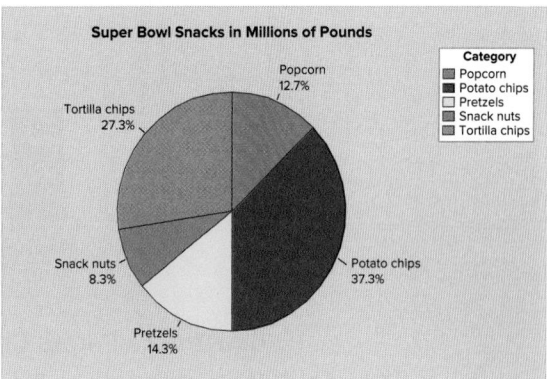

Construct a Bar Chart

The procedure for constructing a bar chart is similar to that for the pie chart.

1. Select **Graph>Bar Chart.**

   a) Click on the drop-down list in Bars Represent: and then select values from a table.

   b) Click on the Simple chart, then click [OK]. The dialog box will be similar to the Pie Chart Dialog Box.

2. Select the frequency column C2 Pounds in Millions for Graph variables: and C1 Snack for the Categorical variable.

3. Click on [Labels], then type the title in the Titles/Footnote tab: **Super Bowl Snacks in Millions of Pounds.**

4. Click the tab for Data Labels, then click the option to Use labels from column: and select C1 Snacks.

5. Click [OK] twice.

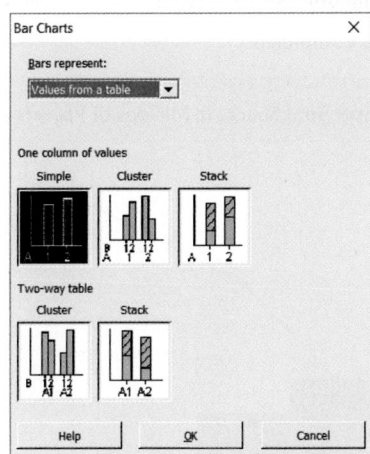
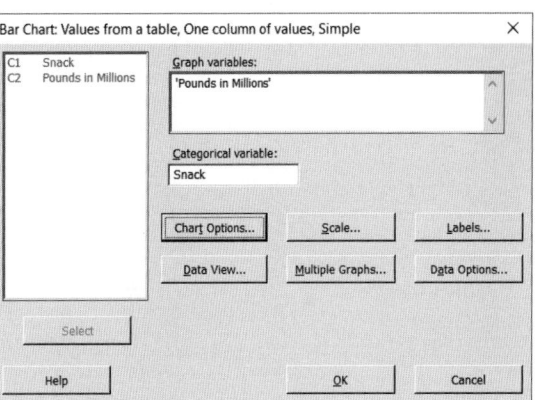

After the graph is made, right-click over any bar to change the appearance such as the color of the bars. To change the gap between them, right-click on the horizontal axis and then choose Edit X scale. To change the *y* Scale to percents, right-click on the vertical axis and then choose Graph options and Show Y as a Percent.

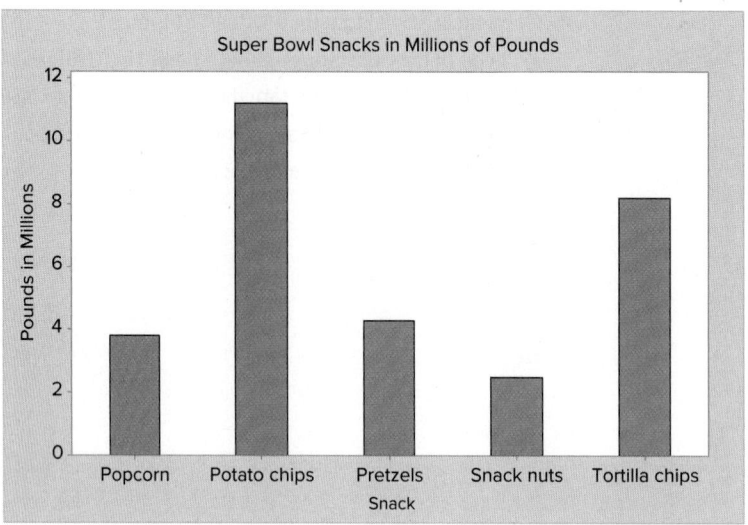

Construct a Pareto Chart

Pareto charts are a quality control tool. They are similar to a bar chart with no gaps between the bars, and the bars are arranged by frequency.

1. Select **Stat>Quality Tools>Pareto**.

2. Click in the box for Defects or attribute in: and select C1 Snack.

3. Click in the box Frequencies in: and select C2 Pounds in Millions.

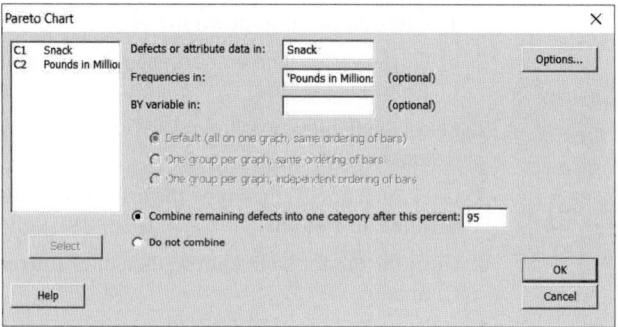

4. Click on [Options]. Type in the title, Super Bowl Snacks in Millions of Pounds.

5. Click [OK] twice. The chart is completed.

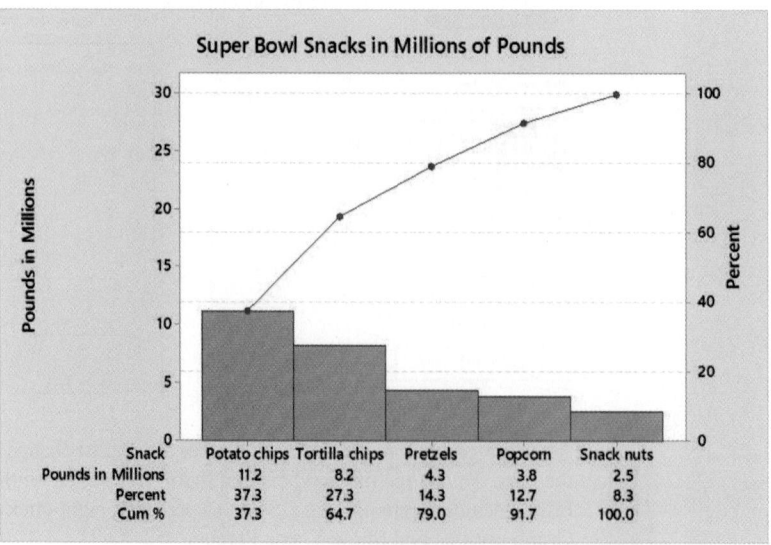

Construct a Time Series Plot

The data show the average water consumption in a specific city in millions of cubic meters for a one-year period (Example 2–10).

Month	J	F	M	A	M	J	J	A	S	O	N	D
Water consumption	15.5	14.3	14.1	15.3	17.6	20.6	26.1	28.7	25.4	18	15.1	14.2

1. Add a blank worksheet to the project by selecting **File>New>New-Minitab Worksheet.**
2. Type the months from January to December in C1; label the column **Month.**
3. Type water consumption numbers in column C2. Label the column **Water Consumption.**
4. To make the graph, select **Graph>Time series plot,** then Simple, and press [OK].
   a) For Series select Water Consumption.
   b) Click [Time/scale], select the Stamp option and select Month for the Stamp column.
   c) Click the Gridlines tab and select all three boxes, Y major, Y minor, and X major.
   d) Click [OK] twice. A new window will open that contains the graph.
   e) To change the title, double-click the title in the graph window. A dialog box will open, allowing you to change the text to Average Water Consumption in Millions of Cubic Meters.

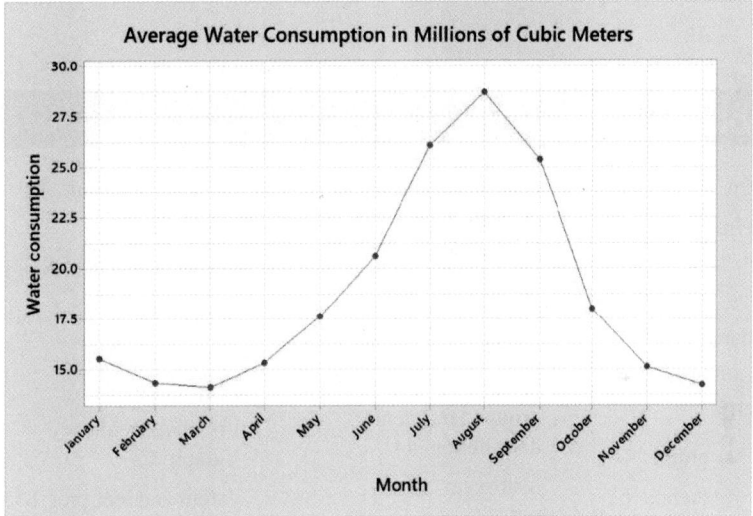

Construct a Stem and Leaf Plot

1. Type in the data for Example 2–15. Label the column **Car Thefts.**
2. Select **Graph>Stem-and-Leaf.**
3. Double-click on C1 Car Thefts in the column list.
4. Click in the Increment text box, and enter the class width of 5.
5. Click [OK]. This character graph will be displayed in the session window.

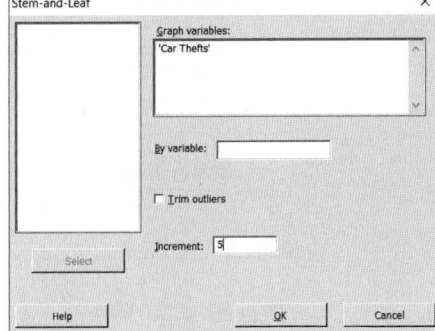

```
Stem-and-leaf of Car Thefts   N   = 30
Leaf Unit = 1.0


  6    5    011233
 13    5    5567789
 15    6    23
 15    6    55667899
  7    7    23
  5    7    55789
```

⬛ Summary

- When data are collected, the values are called raw data. Since very little knowledge can be obtained from raw data, they must be organized in some meaningful way. A frequency distribution using classes is the common method that is used. (2–1)

- Once a frequency distribution is constructed, graphs can be drawn to give a visual representation of the data. The most commonly used graphs in statistics are the histogram, frequency polygon, and ogive. (2–2)

- Other graphs such as the bar graph, Pareto chart, time series graph, pie graph and dotplot can also be used. Some of these graphs are frequently seen in newspapers, magazines, and various statistical reports. (2–3)

- A stem and leaf plot uses part of the data values as stems and part of the data values as leaves. This graph has the advantage of a frequency distribution and a histogram. (2–3)

- Finally, graphs can be misleading if they are drawn improperly. For example, increases and decreases over time in time series graphs can be exaggerated by truncating the scale on the *y* axis. One-dimensional increases or decreases can be exaggerated by using two-dimensional figures. Finally, when labels or units are purposely omitted, there is no actual way to decide the magnitude of the differences between the categories. (2–3)

⬛ Important Terms

bar graph 76

categorical frequency distribution 43

class 42

class boundaries 45

class midpoint 45

class width 45

compound bar graphs 78

cumulative frequency 61

cumulative frequency distribution 48

dotplot 84

frequency 42

frequency distribution 42

frequency polygon 59

grouped frequency distribution 44

histogram 59

lower class limit 44

ogive 61

open-ended distribution 46

Pareto chart 79

pie graph 81

raw data 42

relative frequency graph 62

stem and leaf plot 85

time series graph 80

ungrouped frequency distribution 49

upper class limit 44

⬛ Important Formulas

Formula for the percentage of values in each class:

$$\% = \frac{f}{n} \cdot 100$$

where

f = **frequency of class**

n = **total number of values**

Formula for the range:

R = **highest value − lowest value**

Formula for the class width:

Class width = upper boundary − lower boundary

Formula for the class midpoint:

$$X_m = \frac{\textbf{lower boundary + upper boundary}}{\textbf{2}}$$

or

$$X_m = \frac{\textbf{lower limit + upper limit}}{\textbf{2}}$$

Formula for the degrees for each section of a pie graph:

$$\textbf{Degrees} = \frac{f}{n} \cdot \textbf{360°}$$

Review Exercises

Section 2–1

1. **Alcohol Consumption** A survey shows the type of alcoholic beverages that a person consumes. Construct a categorical frequency distribution for the data: B = beer, W = wine, and S = spirits.

B	W	S	B	B	S	W	S	B	S
S	B	B	B	W	S	B	B	W	S
S	B	S	B	W	S	S	S	B	B
B	B	W	B	B	B	B	B	S	B
B	B	B	S	B	S	W	B	S	W

2. **Takeout Food** A survey of 30 people were asked what type of takeout food they usually ordered. The responses were hot dogs (D), hamburgers (H), pizza (P), hoagies (G), and salads (S). Construct a frequency distribution for the data.

D	P	P	S	H	P	H	H	S	G
H	P	G	H	P	S	S	G	P	S
G	H	D	D	S	H	G	S	P	H

3. **BUN Count** The blood urea nitrogen (BUN) count of 20 randomly selected patients is given here in milligrams per deciliter (mg/dl). Construct an ungrouped frequency distribution for the data.

17	18	13	14
12	17	11	20
13	18	19	17
14	16	17	12
16	15	19	22

4. **Wind Speed** The data show the average wind speed for 36 days in a large city. Construct an ungrouped frequency distribution for the data.

8	15	9	8	9	10
8	10	14	9	8	8
12	9	8	8	14	9
9	13	13	10	12	9
13	8	11	11	9	8
9	13	9	8	8	10

5. **Waterfall Heights** The data show the heights (in feet) of notable waterfalls in North America. Organize the data into a grouped frequency distribution using 6 classes. This data will be used for Exercises 7, 9, and 11.

90	420	300	194
640	68	268	276
620	76	165	833
370	53	132	600
594	70	308	
574	215	109	
317	850	212	
300	256	187	

Source: National Geographic Society

6. **Ages of the Vice Presidents at the Time of Their Death** The ages at the time of death of those Vice Presidents of the United States who have passed away are listed below. Use the data to construct a frequency distribution. Use 6 classes. The data for this exercise will be used for Exercises 8, 10, and 12.

90	83	80	73	70	51	68	79	70	71	
72	74	67	54	81	66	62	63	68	57	
66	96	78	55	60	66	57	71	60	85	
76	98	77	88	78	81	64	66	77	93	70

Source: World Almanac and Book of Facts.

Section 2–2

7. Find the relative frequency for the frequency distribution for the data in Exercise 5.

8. Find the relative frequency for the frequency distribution for the data in Exercise 6.

9. Construct a histogram, frequency polygon, and ogive for the data in Exercise 5.

10. Construct a histogram, frequency polygon, and ogive for the data in Exercise 6.

11. Construct a histogram, frequency polygon, and ogive, using relative frequencies for the data in Exercise 5.

12. Construct a histogram, frequency polygon, and ogive, using relative frequencies for the data in Exercise 6.

Section 2–3

13. **Non-Alcoholic Beverages** The data show the yearly consumption (in gallons) of popular non-alcoholic beverages. Draw a vertical and horizontal bar graph to represent the data.

Soft drinks	52
Water	34
Milk	26
Coffee	21

Source: U.S. Department of Agriculture

14. **Family Size** The following data represent the percents of family sizes of residents in the United States. Draw a vertical bar graph for the data and summarize the results.

1 person	28%
2 people	34%
3 people	15%
4 people	12%
5 or more people	11%

Source: U.S. Census Bureau

15. Crime The data show the percentage of the types of crimes commonly committed in the United States. Construct a Pareto chart for the data.

Theft	55%
Burglary	20%
Motor Vehicle Theft	11%
Assault	8%
Rape & Homicide	1%

Source: FBI

16. Hours of Sleep The following data show the recommended number of hours per night that people need for sleep. Draw a Pareto graph for the data and summarize the results.

Age	Number of hours
0–2 months	15
3–11 months	14.5
1–3 years	13
4–5 years	12
6–10 years	10.5
11–17 years	9
18+ years	8

Source: SleepFoundation.org

17. Broadway Stage Engagements The data represent the number of new shows on Broadway from 2014 to 2020. Draw a time series graph for the data.

Year	2014	2015	2016	2017	2018	2019	2020
Number of shows	42	42	37	41	38	40	22

18. Internet Users The data (in hundred millions) show the number of Internet users worldwide from 2010 to 2019. Draw a time series graph for the data.

Year	2010	2011	2012	2013	2014	2015	2016	2017	2018	2019
Number of users	20	22	24	27	28	30	33	37	39	41

19. Spending of First-Year College Students The average amounts spent by first-year college students for school items are shown. Construct a pie graph for the data.

Electronics/computers	$728
Dorm items	344
Clothing	153
Shoes	83
Personal care	79

Source: National Retail Federation.

20. Smart Phone Insurance Construct and analyze a pie graph for the people who did or did not buy insurance for their smart phones at the time of purchase.

Response	Frequency
Yes	573
No	557
Don't Remember	166
Not offered any	211

Source: Based on information from Anderson Analytics

21. Peyton Manning's Colts Career Peyton Manning played for the Indianapolis Colts for 14 years. (He did not play in 2011.) The data show the number of touchdowns he scored for the years 1998–2010. Construct a dotplot for the data and comment on the graph.

26	33	27	49	31	27	33
26	26	29	28	31	33	

Source: NFL.com

22. Songs on CDs The data show the number of songs on each of 40 CDs from the author's collection. Construct a dotplot for the data and comment on the graph.

10	14	18	11
11	15	16	10
10	17	10	15
22	9	14	12
18	12	12	15
21	22	20	15
10	19	20	21
17	9	13	15
11	12	12	9
14	20	12	10

23. Weights of Football Players A local football team has 30 players; the weight of each player is shown. Construct a stem and leaf plot for the data. Use stems 20__, 21__, 22__, etc.

213	202	232	206	219
246	248	239	215	221
223	220	203	233	249
238	254	223	218	224
258	227	230	256	254
219	235	262	233	263

24. Public Libraries The numbers of public libraries in operation for selected states are listed below. Organize the data with a stem and leaf plot.

102	176	210	142	189	176	108	113	205
209	184	144	108	192	176			

Source: World Almanac.

25. Pain Relief The graph below shows the time it takes Quick Pain Relief to relieve a person's pain. The graph below that shows the time a competitor's product takes to relieve pain. Why might these graphs be misleading?

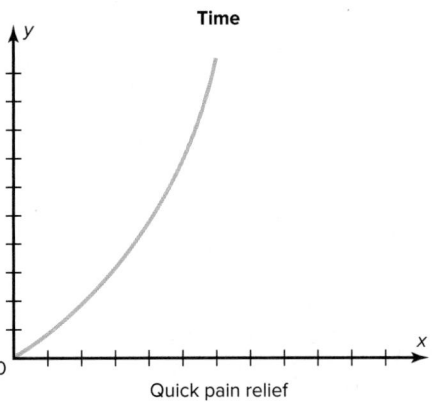

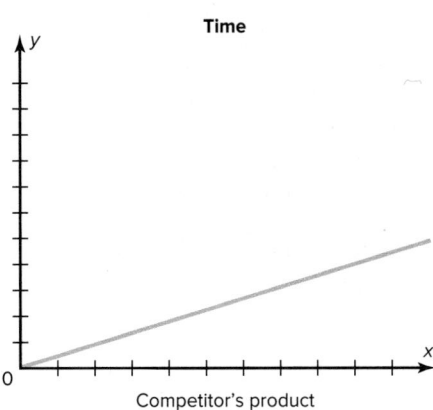

26. Casino Payoffs The graph shows the payoffs obtained from the White Oak Casino compared to the nearest competitor's casino. Why is this graph misleading?

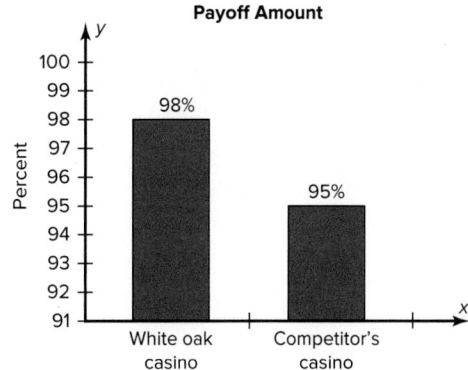

Data Analysis

A Data Bank is found in Appendix B.

1. From the Data Bank located in Appendix B, choose one of the following variables: age, weight, cholesterol level, systolic pressure, IQ, or sodium level. Select at least 30 values. For these values, construct a grouped frequency distribution. Draw a histogram, frequency polygon, and ogive for the distribution. Describe briefly the shape of the distribution.

2. From the Data Bank, choose one of the following variables: educational level, smoking status, or exercise. Select at least 20 values. Construct an ungrouped frequency distribution for the data. For the distribution, draw a Pareto chart and describe briefly the nature of the chart.

3. From the Data Bank, select at least 30 subjects and construct a categorical distribution for their marital status. Draw a pie graph and describe briefly the findings.

4. Using the data from Data Set IV in Appendix B, construct a frequency distribution and draw a histogram. Describe briefly the shape of the distribution of the tallest buildings in New York City.

5. Using the data from Data Set XI in Appendix B, construct a frequency distribution and draw a frequency polygon. Describe briefly the shape of the distribution for the number of pages in statistics books.

6. Using the data from Data Set IX in Appendix B, divide the United States into four regions, as follows:

Northeast   CT ME MA NH NJ NY PA RI VT

Midwest   IL IN IA KS MI MN MD MS NE ND OH SD WI

South   AL AR DE DC FL GA KY LA MD NC OK SC TN TX VA WV

West   AK AZ CA CO HI ID MT NV NM OR UT WA WY

Find the total population for each region, and draw a Pareto chart and a pie graph for the data. Analyze the results. Explain which chart might be a better representation for the data.

7. Using the data from Data Set I in Appendix B, make a stem and leaf plot for the record low temperatures in the United States. Describe the nature of the plot.

STATISTICS TODAY

How Your Identity Can Be Stolen —Revisited

Data presented in numerical form do not convey an easy-to-interpret conclusion; however, when data are presented in graphical form, readers can see the visual impact of the numbers. In the case of identity fraud, the reader can see that most of the identity fraud is credit card fraud followed by employment of tax-related fraud. These two types of fraud account for over half (57%) of the identity frauds.

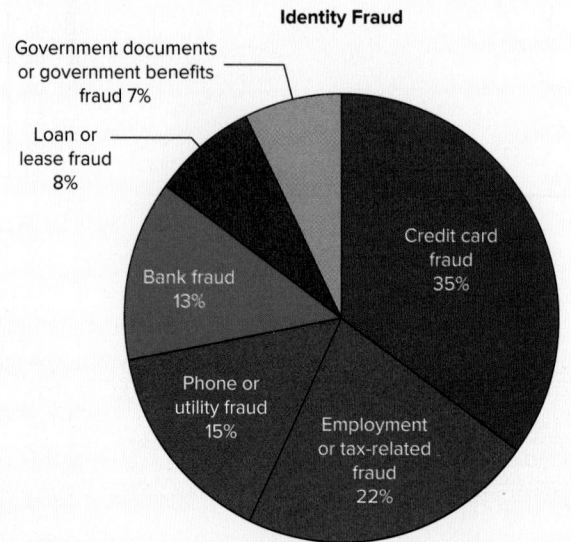

Identity Fraud

The Federal Trade Commission suggests some ways to protect your identity:

1. Shred all financial documents no longer needed.
2. Protect your Social Security number.
3. Don't give out personal information on the phone, through the mail, or over the Internet.
4. Never click on links sent in unsolicited emails.
5. Don't use an obvious password for your computer documents.
6. Keep your personal information in a secure place at home.

Chapter Quiz

Determine whether each statement is true or false. If the statement is false, explain why.

1. In the construction of a frequency distribution, it is a good idea to have overlapping class limits, such as 10–20, 20–30, 30–40. False. Classes should not be overlapping.

2. Bar graphs can be drawn by using vertical or horizontal bars. True

3. It is not important to keep the width of each class the same in a frequency distribution. False. The class width should be the same for all classes.

4. Frequency distributions can aid the researcher in drawing charts and graphs. True

5. The type of graph used to represent data is determined by the type of data collected and by the researcher's purpose. True

6. In construction of a frequency polygon, the class limits are used for the x axis. False. Class midpoints should be used for the points on the x axis.

7. Data collected over a period of time can be graphed by using a pie graph. False. You should use the time series graph.

Select the best answer.

8. What is another name for the ogive?
   a. Histogram
   b. Frequency polygon
   c. Cumulative frequency graph
   d. Pareto chart

9. What are the boundaries for 8.6–8.8?
   a. 8–9
   b. 8.5–8.9
   c. 8.55–8.85 ⟵(circled)
   d. 8.65–8.75

10. What graph should be used to show the relationship between the parts and the whole?
   a. Histogram
   b. Pie graph ⟵(circled)
   c. Pareto chart
   d. Ogive

11. Except for rounding errors, relative frequencies should add up to what sum?
   a. 0
   b. 1 ⟵(circled)
   c. 50
   d. 100

Complete these statements with the best answers.

12. The three types of frequency distributions are _____, _____, and _____. Categorical, ungrouped, grouped

13. In a frequency distribution, the number of classes should be between _____ and _____. 5, 20

14. Data such as blood types (A, B, AB, O) can be organized into a(n) _____ frequency distribution. Categorical

15. Data collected over a period of time can be graphed using a(n) _____ graph. Time series

16. A statistical device used in exploratory data analysis that is a combination of a frequency distribution and a histogram is called a(n) _____. Stem and leaf plot

17. On a Pareto chart, the frequencies should be represented on the _____ axis. Vertical or y

18. **Housing Arrangements** A questionnaire on housing arrangements showed this information obtained from 25 respondents. Construct a frequency distribution for the data (H = house, A = apartment, M = mobile home, C = condominium). These data will be used in Exercise 19.

H	C	H	M	H	A	C	A	M
C	M	C	A	M	A	C	C	M
C	C	H	A	H	H	M		

19. Construct a pie graph for the data in Exercise 18.

20. **Items Purchased at a Convenience Store** When 30 randomly selected customers left a convenience store, they were asked the number of items they had purchased. Construct an ungrouped frequency distribution for the data. These data will be used in Exercise 21.

2	9	4	3	6
6	2	8	6	5
7	5	3	8	6
6	2	3	2	4
6	9	9	8	9
4	2	1	7	4

21. Construct a histogram, a frequency polygon, and an ogive for the data in Exercise 20.

22. **Coal Consumption** The following data represent the energy consumption of coal (in billions of Btu) by each of the 50 states and the District of Columbia. Use the data to construct a frequency distribution and a relative frequency distribution with 7 classes.

631	723	267	60	372	15	19	92	306	38
413	8	736	156	478	264	1015	329	679	1498
52	1365	142	423	365	350	445	776	1267	0
26	356	173	373	335	34	937	250	33	84
0	253	84	1224	743	582	2	33	0	426
474									

   Source: Time Almanac.

23. Construct a histogram, frequency polygon, and ogive for the data in Exercise 22. Analyze the histogram.

24. **Recycled Trash** Construct a Pareto chart and a horizontal bar graph for the number of tons (in millions) of trash recycled per year by Americans based on an Environmental Protection Agency study.

Type	Amount
Paper	320.0
Iron/steel	292.0
Aluminum	276.0
Yard waste	242.4
Glass	196.0
Plastics	41.6

   Source: USA TODAY.

25. **Identity Thefts** The results of a survey of 84 people whose identities were stolen using various methods are shown. Draw a pie chart for the information.

Lost or stolen wallet, checkbook, or credit card	38
Retail purchases or telephone transactions	15
Stolen mail	9
Computer viruses or hackers	8
Phishing	4
Other	10
	84

   Source: Javelin Strategy and Research.

26. Needless Deaths of Children *The New England Journal of Medicine* predicted the number of needless deaths due to childhood obesity. Draw a time series graph for the data.

Year	2020	2025	2030	2035
Deaths	130	550	1500	3700

27. Museum Visitors The number of visitors to the Historic Museum for 25 randomly selected hours is shown. Construct a stem and leaf plot for the data.

15	53	48	19	38
86	63	98	79	38
62	89	67	39	26
28	35	54	88	76
31	47	53	41	68

28. Parking Meter Revenue In a small city the number of quarters collected from the parking meters is shown. Construct a dotplot for the data.

13	12	11	7	16
10	16	15	7	11
3	5	14	3	6
8	3	10	9	3
5	7	8	9	9
9	2.	6	4	11
7	4	2	8	10
7	17	4	11	8
2	5	5	14	6
3	9	3	12	3

29. Water Usage The graph shows the average number of gallons of water a person uses for various activities. Can you see anything misleading about the way the graph is drawn? The bottles have different diameters, so your eyes will compare areas instead of heights.

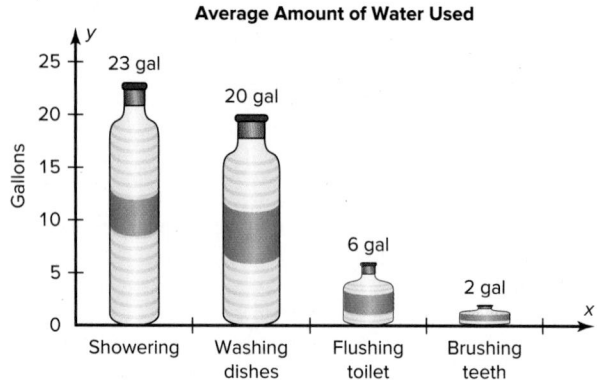

Average Amount of Water Used

▤ Critical Thinking Challenges

1. The Great Lakes Shown are various statistics about the Great Lakes.

Answer the following questions and decide which graph would best illustrate the answers.

a. What is the volume of the largest of the Great Lakes?

b. What is the total U.S. shoreline of the Great Lakes?

c. Which is the widest lake?

d. What percentage of the total area of the Great Lakes are Lake Superior and Lake Michigan combined?

e. Which is the deepest of the Great Lakes? Which is the shallowest?

f. What is the relationship between the areas of Lake Ontario and Lake Superior?

g. Which is the smallest of the Great Lakes? What did you use to reach this conclusion?

	Superior	Michigan	Huron	Erie	Ontario
Length (miles)	350	307	206	241	193
Breadth (miles)	160	118	183	57	53
Depth (feet)	1,330	923	750	210	802
Volume (cubic miles)	2,900	1,180	850	116	393
Area (square miles)	31,700	22,300	23,000	9,910	7,550
Shoreline (U.S., miles)	863	1,400	580	431	300

Source: The World Almanac and Book of Facts.

2. Road Rage Here are some statistics on road rage. If you are giving a presentation on this subject, what type of graph could you use to emphasize the given statistics? Draw the graph.

Road rage is a serious and dangerous problem that today's drivers have to deal with almost daily. Road rage can lead to serious consequences and even death.

A recent study by the American Automobile Association (AAA) reported the following information based on the responses of millions of drivers. The most common responses of drivers who exhibit road rage are

Tailgating (104 million or 51%)
Yelling at another driver (95 million or 47%)
Honking the horn (91 million or 45%)
Making angry gestures (67 million or 33%)
Blocking another vehicle on purpose (49 million or 24%)

Cutting off another vehicle (24 million or 12%)
Getting out of the automobile and confronting the other driver (7.6 million or 4%)
Deliberately ramming another vehicle (5.7 million or 3%)

Some causes for road rage are

Ignoring other drivers because of cell phone use
Keeping high beams on regardless of traffic conditions
Failing to use turn signals when changing lanes
Forgetting to check the blind spot when changing lanes
Causing other drivers to change their speed or use their brakes

The AAA suggests that drivers be tolerant and forgiving of other drivers and never respond to other drivers' road rage actions.

Data Projects

Where appropriate, use the TI-84 Plus, Excel, MINITAB, or a computer program of your choice to complete the following exercises.

1. **Business and Finance** Consider the 30 stocks listed as the Dow Jones Industrials. For each, find its earnings per share. Randomly select 30 stocks traded on the NASDAQ. For each, find its earnings per share. Create a frequency table with 5 categories for each data set. Sketch a histogram for each. How do the two data sets compare?

2. **Sports and Leisure** Use systematic sampling to create a sample of 25 National League and 25 American League baseball players from the most recently completed season. Find the number of home runs for each player. Create a frequency table with 5 categories for each data set. Sketch a histogram for each. How do the two leagues compare?

3. **Technology** Randomly select 50 songs from your music player or music organization program. Find the length (in seconds) for each song. Use these data to create a frequency table with 6 categories. Sketch a frequency polygon for the frequency table. Is the shape of the distribution of times uniform, skewed, or bell-shaped? Also note the genre of each song.

Create a Pareto chart showing the frequencies of the various categories. Finally, note the year each song was released. Create a pie chart organized by decade to show the percentage of songs from various time periods.

4. **Health and Wellness** Use information from the Red Cross to create a pie chart depicting the percentages of Americans with various blood types. Also find information about blood donations and the percentage of each type donated. How do the charts compare? Why is the collection of type O blood so important?

5. **Politics and Economics** Consider the U.S. Electoral College System. For each of the 50 states, determine the number of delegates received. Create a frequency table with 8 classes. Is this distribution uniform, skewed, or bell-shaped?

6. **Your Class** Have each person in class take their pulse and determine the heart rate (beats in 1 minute). Use the data to create a frequency table with 6 classes. Then have everyone in the class do 25 jumping jacks and immediately take the pulse again after the activity. Create a frequency table for those data as well. Compare the two results. Are they similarly distributed? How does the range of scores compare?

Answers to Applying the Concepts

Section 2–1   Ages of Presidents at Inauguration

1. The data were obtained from the population of all Presidents at the time this text was written.

2. The oldest inauguration age was 78 years old.

3. The youngest inauguration age was 42 years old.

4. Answers will vary. One possible answer is

Class	Frequency
42–48	7
49–55	19
56–62	13
63–69	5
70–76	1
77–83	1
	46

5. Answers will vary. For the distribution shown, there is a peak at the 49–55 class.

6. The age 78 could be an outlier.

7. The distribution is unimodal with 49–55 being the modal class. It is somewhat positively skewed.

Section 2–2   Selling Real Estate

1. A histogram of the data gives price ranges and the counts of homes in each price range. We can also talk about how the data are distributed by looking at a histogram.

2. A frequency polygon shows increases or decreases in the number of home prices around values.

3. A cumulative frequency polygon shows the number of homes sold at or below a given price.

4. The house that sold for $1,350,000 is an extreme value in this data set.

5. Answers will vary. One possible answer is that the histogram displays the outlier well since there is a gap in the prices of the homes sold.

6. The distribution of the data is skewed to the right.

Section 2–3   Causes of Accidental Deaths in the United States

1. The variables in the graph are the year, cause of death, and number of deaths in thousands.

2. The cause of death is qualitative, while the year and number of deaths are quantitative.

3. A time series graph is used here.

4. The motor vehicle accidents showed a slight increase from 1999 to 2007, and then a decrease.

5. The number of deaths due to poisoning and falls is increasing.

6. The number of deaths due to drowning remains about the same over the years.

7. For 2001, about 44,000 people died in motor vehicle accidents, about 15,000 people died from falls, about 14,000 people died from poisoning, and about 3000 people died from drowning.

8. In 1999, motor vehicle accidents claimed the most lives, while in 2009, poisoning claimed the most lives.

9. Around 2002, the number of deaths from falls and poisoning were about the same.

Data Description

©Alan Schein/Alamy Stock Photo

How Long Are You Delayed by Road Congestion?

No matter where you live, at one time or another, you have been stuck in traffic. To see whether there are more traffic delays in some cities than in others, statisticians make comparisons using descriptive statistics. A statistical study by the Texas Transportation Institute found that a driver is delayed by road congestion an average of 36 hours per year. To see how selected cities compare to this average, see Statistics Today—Revisited at the end of the chapter.

This chapter will show you how to obtain and interpret descriptive statistics such as measures of average, measures of variation, and measures of position.

OUTLINE

OBJECTIVES

After completing this chapter, you should be able to:

1   Summarize data, using measures of central tendency, such as the mean, median, mode, and midrange.

2   Describe data, using measures of variation, such as the range, variance, and standard deviation.

3   Identify the position of a data value in a data set, using various measures of position, such as percentiles, deciles, and quartiles.

4   Use the techniques of exploratory data analysis, including boxplots and five-number summaries, to discover various aspects of data.

Introduction

Chapter 2 showed how you can gain useful information from raw data by organizing them into a frequency distribution and then presenting the data by using various graphs. This chapter shows the statistical methods that can be used to summarize data. The most familiar of these methods is the finding of averages.

For example, you may read that the average speed of a car crossing midtown Manhattan during the day is 5.3 miles per hour or that the average number of hours an American father spends on child care each week is 8.[1]

An author once described the word "average" as:

Average when you think about it is a funny concept. Even though it describes all of us, it describes none of us. We don't want to be the average person, but we all want to know about the average person.

Some unusual averages are:

A cow produces on average 40 glasses of milk a day.
The lifespan of a mosquito is on average two weeks.
On average a bank teller loses $250 every year.
A person has on average 1460 dreams per year.

In these examples, the word *average* is ambiguous, since several different methods can be used to obtain an average. Loosely stated, the average means the center of the distribution or the most typical case. Measures of average are also called *measures of central tendency* and include the *mean, median, mode,* and *midrange.*

Knowing the average of a data set is not enough to describe the data set entirely. Even though a shoe store owner knows that the average size of a man's shoe is size 10, she would not be in business very long if she ordered only size 10 shoes.

fotog/Getty Images

---

[1]https://www.pewresearch.org/fact-tank/2019/06/12/fathers-day-facts/#:~:text=In%202016%2C%20fathers%20reported%20spending,time%20they%20provided%20in%201965.

As this example shows, in addition to knowing the average, you must know how the data values are dispersed. That is, do the data values cluster around the average, or are they spread more evenly throughout the distribution? The measures that determine the spread of the data values are called *measures of variation,* or *measures of dispersion.* These measures include the *range, variance,* and *standard deviation.*

Finally, another set of measures is necessary to describe data. These measures are called *measures of position.* They tell where a specific data value falls within the data set or its relative position in comparison with other data values. The most common position measures are *percentiles, deciles,* and *quartiles.* These measures are used extensively in psychology and education. Sometimes they are referred to as *norms.*

The measures of central tendency, variation, and position explained in this chapter are part of what is called *traditional statistics.*

Section 3–4 shows the techniques of what is called *exploratory data analysis.* These techniques include the *boxplot* and the *five-number summary.* They can be used to explore data to see what they show (as opposed to the traditional techniques, which are used to confirm conjectures about the data).

3–1   Measures of Central Tendency

OBJECTIVE

Summarize data, using measures of central tendency, such as the mean, median, mode, and midrange.

Chapter 1 stated that statisticians use samples taken from populations; however, when populations are small, it is not necessary to use samples since the entire population can be used to gain information. For example, suppose an insurance manager wanted to know the average weekly sales of all the company's representatives. If the company employed a large number of salespeople, say, nationwide, he would have to use a sample and make an inference to the entire sales force. But if the company had only a few salespeople, say, only 87 agents, he would be able to use all representatives' sales for a randomly chosen week and thus use the entire population.

Measures found by using all the data values in the population are called *parameters.* Measures obtained by using the data values from samples are called *statistics;* hence, the average of the sales from a sample of representatives is a *statistic,* and the average of sales obtained from the entire population is a *parameter.*

> A **statistic** is a characteristic or measure obtained by using the data values from a sample.
>
> A **parameter** is a characteristic or measure obtained by using all the data values from a specific population.

These concepts as well as the symbols used to represent them will be explained in detail in this chapter.

General Rounding Rule   In statistics the basic rounding rule is that when computations are done in the calculation, rounding should not be done until the final answer is calculated. When rounding is done in the intermediate steps, it tends to increase the difference between that answer and the exact one. But in the textbook and solutions manual, it is not practical to show long decimals in the intermediate calculations; hence, the values in the examples are carried out to enough places (usually three or four) to obtain the same answer that a calculator would give after rounding on the last step.

There are specific rounding rules for many statistics, and they will be given in the appropriate sections.

The Mean

The *mean,* also known as the *arithmetic average,* is found by adding the values of the data and dividing by the total number of values. For example, the mean of 3, 2, 6, 5, and 4 is found by adding $3 + 2 + 6 + 5 + 4 = 20$ and dividing by 5; hence, the mean of the data is $20 \div 5 = 4$. The values of the data are represented by X's. In this data set, $X_1 = 3$, $X_2 = 2$, $X_3 = 6$,

$X_4 = 5$, and $X_5 = 4$. To show a sum of the total X values, the symbol Σ (the capital Greek letter sigma) is used, and ΣX means to find the sum of the X values in the data set. The summation notation is explained in the online resource section under "Algebra Review."

> The **mean** is the sum of the values, divided by the total number of values.
>
> The **sample mean,** denoted by $\overline{X}$ (pronounced "X bar"), is calculated by using sample data. The sample mean is a statistic.
>
> $$\overline{X} = \frac{X_1 + X_2 + X_3 + \cdots + X_n}{n} = \frac{\Sigma X}{n}$$
>
> where n represents the total number of values in the sample.
>
> The **population mean,** denoted by μ (pronounced "mew"), is calculated by using all the values in the population. The population mean is a parameter.
>
> $$\mu = \frac{X_1 + X_2 + X_3 + \cdots + X_N}{N} = \frac{\Sigma X}{N}$$
>
> where N represents the total number of values in the population.

In statistics, Greek letters are used to denote parameters, and Roman letters are used to denote statistics. Assume that the data are obtained from samples unless otherwise specified.

Rounding Rule for the Mean   The mean should be rounded to one more decimal place than occurs in the raw data. For example, if the raw data are given in whole numbers, the mean should be rounded to the nearest tenth. If the data are given in tenths, the mean should be rounded to the nearest hundredth, and so on.

EXAMPLE 3–1 Internet Users

The nine nations show the number of Internet users (in millions) for a recent year. Find the mean.

> 54.9,   326.4,   123.0,   90.0,   111.9,   70.7,   87.3,   657.6,   289.5

Source: Computer Industry Almanac

SOLUTION

$$\overline{X} = \frac{\Sigma X}{n} = \frac{54.9 + 326.4 + 123.0 + 90.0 + 111.9 + 70.7 + 87.3 + 657.6 + 289.5}{9}$$

$$= \frac{1811.3}{9} = 201.26$$

Hence, the mean number of Internet users for the nine nations is 201.26 million users.

EXAMPLE 3–2 Store Sales

The data show the systemwide sales (in millions) for U.S. franchises of a well-known donut store for a 5-year period. Find the mean.

> $221 $239 $262 $281 $318

Source: Krispy Kreme.

SOLUTION

$$\overline{X} = \frac{\Sigma X}{n} = \frac{221 + 239 + 262 + 281 + 318}{5} = \frac{1321}{5} = 264.2$$

The mean amount of sales for the stores over the 5-year period is $264.2 million.

The mean, in most cases, is not an actual data value.

The procedure for finding the mean for grouped data assumes that the mean of all the raw data values in each class is equal to the midpoint of the class. In reality, this is not true, since the average of the raw data values in each class usually will not be exactly equal to the midpoint. However, using this procedure will give an acceptable approximation of the mean, since some values fall above the midpoint and other values fall below the midpoint for each class, and the midpoint represents an estimate of all values in the class.

The steps for finding the mean for grouped data are shown in the next Procedure Table.

Procedure Table

Finding the Mean for Grouped Data

Step 1 Make a table as shown.

A Class	B Frequency f	C Midpoint X_m	D $f \cdot X_m$

Step 2 Find the midpoints of each class and place them in column C.

Step 3 Multiply the frequency by the midpoint for each class, and place the product in column D.

Step 4 Find the sum of column D.

Step 5 Divide the sum obtained in column D by the sum of the frequencies obtained in column B.

The formula for the mean is

$$\bar{X} = \frac{\Sigma f \cdot X_m}{n}$$

[*Note:* The symbols $\Sigma f \cdot X_m$ mean to find the sum of the product of the frequency (f) and the midpoint (X_m) for each class.]

EXAMPLE 3–3 Salaries of CEOs

The frequency distribution shows the salaries (in million dollars) for a specific year of the top 25 CEOs in the United States. Find the mean.

Source: S & P Capital.

Class boundaries	Frequency
15.5–20.5	13
20.5–25.5	6
25.5–30.5	4
30.5–35.5	1
35.5–40.5	1
	Total 25

SOLUTION

A Class	B Frequency	C Midpoint X_m	D $f \cdot X_m$
15.5–20.5	13		
20.5–25.5	6		
25.5–30.5	4		
30.5–35.5	1		
35.5–40.5	1		
	$n = 25$		

Interesting Fact

The average time it takes a person to find a new job is 5.9 months.

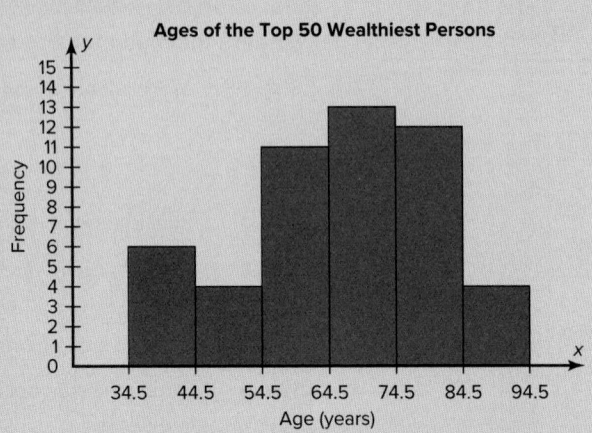
$$X_m = \frac{15.5 + 20.5}{2} = 18 \qquad \frac{20.5 + 25.5}{2} = 23 \quad \text{etc.}$$

$$13 \cdot 18 = 234 \qquad 6 \cdot 23 = 138 \quad \text{etc.}$$

A Class	B Frequency	C Midpoint X_m	D $f \cdot X_m$
15.5–20.5	13	18	234
20.5–25.5	6	23	138
25.5–30.5	4	28	112
30.5–35.5	1	33	33
35.5–40.5	1	38	38
	$n = 25$		$\Sigma f \cdot X_m = 555$

$$\overline{X} = \frac{\Sigma f \cdot X_m}{n} = \frac{555}{25} = \$22.2 \text{ million}$$

The mean salary is \$22.2 million.

The Median

An article recently reported that the median income for college professors was \$82,974. This measure of central tendency means that one-half of all the professors surveyed earned more than \$82,974, and one-half earned less than \$82,974.

The *median* is the halfway point in a data set. Before you can find this point, the data must be arranged in ascending or increasing order. When the data set is ordered, it is called a **data array.** The median either will be a specific value in the data set or will fall between two values, as shown in the next examples.

> The **median** is the midpoint of the data array. The symbol for the median is MD.

The Procedure Table for finding the median is shown next.

Procedure Table

Finding the Median

Step 1   Arrange the data values in ascending order.

Step 2   Determine the number of values in the data set.

Step 3   *a*. If *n* is odd, select the middle data value as the median.

   b. If *n* is even, find the mean of the two middle values. That is, add them and divide the sum by 2.

EXAMPLE 3–4   Visitors to Websites

For a recent year, the number of visitors (in millions) to the top seven websites is shown. Find the median for the data.

$$148, \quad 155, \quad 241, \quad 203, \quad 180, \quad 184, \quad 186$$

Source: ComScore Inc.

SOLUTION

Step 1   Arrange the data values in ascending order.

$$148, \quad 155, \quad 180, \quad 184, \quad 186, \quad 203, \quad 241$$
$$\uparrow$$

Step 2   There are an odd number of data values, namely 7, so find the middle data value.

$$MD = 184$$

The median number of visitors (in millions) is 184.

EXAMPLE 3–5   Tornadoes in the United States

The number of tornadoes that have occurred in the United States over an 8-year period is as follows. Find the median.

$$684, \quad 764, \quad 656, \quad 702, \quad 856, \quad 1133, \quad 1132, \quad 1303$$

Source: The Universal Almanac.

SOLUTION

Step 1   Arrange the data values in ascending order.

$$656, \quad 684, \quad 702, \quad 764, \quad 856, \quad 1132, \quad 1133, \quad 1303$$

Step 2   There are an even number of data values, namely, 8.

Step 3   The middle two data values are 764 and 856.

$$656, 684, 702, 764, 856, 1132, 1133, 1303$$
$$\uparrow$$
$$\text{Median}$$

Since the middle point falls halfway between 764 and 856, find the median MD by adding the two values and dividing by 2.

$$\text{MD} = \frac{764 + 856}{2} = \frac{1620}{2} = 810$$

The median number of tornadoes is 810.

The Mode

The third measure of average is called the *mode.* The mode is the value that occurs most often in the data set. It is sometimes said to be the most typical case.

> The value that occurs most often in a data set is called the **mode.**

A data set that has only one value that occurs with the greatest frequency is said to be **unimodal.**

If a data set has two values that occur with the same greatest frequency, both values are considered to be the mode and the data set is said to be **bimodal.** If a data set has more than two values that occur with the same greatest frequency, each value is used as the mode, and the data set is said to be **multimodal.** When no data value occurs more than once, the data set is said to have *no mode. Note: Do not say that the mode is zero.* That would be incorrect, because in some data, such as temperature, zero can be an actual value. A data set can have more than one mode or no mode at all. These situations will be shown in some of the examples that follow.

EXAMPLE 3–6   Wind Speed

The maximum wind speeds in miles per hour for seven randomly selected areas are shown. Find the mode.

$$72, \quad 68, \quad 70, \quad 74, \quad 77, \quad 68, \quad 53$$

SOLUTION

It is helpful to arrange the data in order, although it is not necessary.

$$53, \quad 68, \quad 68, \quad 70, \quad 72, \quad 74, \quad 77$$

The mode is 68 because it occurs twice, which is more than any other value.

EXAMPLE 3–7   Licensed Nuclear Reactors

The data show the number of licensed nuclear reactors in the United States for a recent 15-year period. Find the mode.

Source: The World Almanac and Book of Facts.

104	104	104	104	104
107	109	109	109	110
109	111	112	111	109

SOLUTION

Since the values 104 and 109 both occur 5 times, the modes are 104 and 109. The data set is said to be bimodal.

EXAMPLE 3–8   Major Earthquakes

The data show the sizes of 8 major earthquakes in the world. Find the mode.

7.3,   6.6,   6.1,   7.6,   9.1,   8.6,   6.3,   7.0

Source: Global Volcanism Network

SOLUTION

Since each value occurs only once, there is no mode.

The mode for grouped data is the modal class. The **modal class** is the class with the largest frequency.

EXAMPLE 3–9   Salaries of CEOs

Find the modal class for the frequency distribution for the salaries of the top CEOs in the United States, shown in Example 3–3.

SOLUTION

Class	Frequency
15.5–20.5	13 ←Modal class
20.5–25.5	6
25.5–30.5	4
30.5–35.5	1
35.5–40.5	1

Since the class 15.5–20.5 has the largest frequency, 13, it is the modal class. Sometimes the midpoint of the class is used. In this case, it is 18.

The mode is the only measure of central tendency that can be used in finding the most typical case when the data are nominal or categorical.

EXAMPLE 3–10   Sentences for Crimes

The data show the number of people who were sentenced for various crimes in a specific city. Find the mode.

Crime	Number
Drugs	127
Kidnapping	43
Robbery	57
Arson	16
Firearms	5

SOLUTION

Since the category of drugs has the largest frequency, 127, we can say that the most typical crime committed was for drugs.

An extremely high or extremely low data value in a data set can have a striking effect on the mean of the data set. These extreme values are called *outliers*. This is one reason why, when analyzing a frequency distribution, you should be aware of any of these values. For the data set shown in Example 3–11, the mean, median, and mode can be quite different because of extreme values. A method for identifying outliers is given in Section 3–3.

EXAMPLE 3–11   Salaries of Personnel

A small company consists of the owner, the manager, the salesperson, and two technicians, all of whose annual salaries are listed here. (Assume that this is the entire population.)

Staff	Salary
Owner	$100,000
Manager	40,000
Salesperson	24,000
Technician	18,000
Technician	18,000

Find the mean, median, and mode.

SOLUTION

$$\mu = \frac{\Sigma X}{N} = \frac{\$100,000 + 40,000 + 24,000 + 18,000 + 18,000}{5} = \frac{\$200,000}{5} = \$40,000$$

Hence, the mean is $40,000, the median is $24,000, and the mode is $18,000.

In Example 3–11, the mean is much higher than the median or the mode. This is so because the extremely high salary of the owner tends to raise the value of the mean. In this and similar situations, the median should be used as the measure of central tendency.

The Midrange

The *midrange* is a rough estimate of the middle. It is found by adding the lowest and highest values in the data set and dividing by 2. It is a very rough estimate of the average and can be affected by one extremely high or low value.

> The **midrange** is defined as the sum of the lowest and highest values in the data set, divided by 2. The symbol MR is used for the midrange.
>
> $$MR = \frac{\text{lowest value} + \text{highest value}}{2}$$

EXAMPLE 3–12   Bank Failures

The number of bank failures for a recent 5-year period is shown. Find the midrange.

$$3, 30, 148, 157, 71$$

Source: Federal Deposit Insurance Corporation.

SOLUTION

The lowest data value is 3, and the highest data value is 157.

$$MR = \frac{3 + 157}{2} = \frac{160}{2} = 80$$

The midrange for the number of bank failures is 80.

EXAMPLE 3–13 Successful Space Launches

The number of successful space launches in five 10-year periods in Russia is shown. Find the midrange.

$$399, 1028, 1132, 542, 246$$

Source: The World Almanac

SOLUTION

Add the lowest value, 246, and the highest value, 1132, and divide the sum by 2.

$$\text{MR} = \frac{246 + 1132}{2} = \frac{1378}{2} = 689$$

The midrange is 689.

In statistics, several measures can be used for an average. The most common measures are the mean, median, mode, and midrange. Each has its own specific purpose and use. Exercises 36 through 38 show examples of other averages, such as the harmonic mean, the geometric mean, and the quadratic mean. Their applications are limited to specific areas, as shown in the exercises.

The Weighted Mean

Sometimes, you must find the mean of a data set in which not all values are equally represented. Consider the case of finding the average cost of a gallon of gasoline for three taxis. Suppose the drivers buy gasoline at three different service stations at a cost of $3.22, $3.53, and $3.63 per gallon. You might try to find the average by using the formula

$$\overline{X} = \frac{\Sigma X}{n}$$
$$= \frac{3.22 + 3.53 + 3.63}{3} = \frac{10.38}{3} = \$3.46$$

But not all drivers purchased the same number of gallons. Hence, to find the true average cost per gallon, you must take into consideration the number of gallons each driver purchased.

The type of mean that considers an additional factor is called the *weighted mean,* and it is used when the values are not all equally represented.

Find the **weighted mean** of a variable X by multiplying each value by its corresponding weight and dividing the sum of the products by the sum of the weights.

$$\overline{X} = \frac{w_1 X_1 + w_2 X_2 + \cdots + w_n X_n}{w_1 + w_2 + \cdots + w_n} = \frac{\Sigma w X}{\Sigma w}$$

where $w_1, w_2, \ldots, w_n$ are the weights and $X_1, X_2, \ldots, X_n$ are the values.

Example 3–14 shows how the weighted mean is used to compute a grade point average. Since courses vary in their credit value, the number of credits must be used as weights.

EXAMPLE 3–14 Grade Point Average

A student received an A in English Composition I (3 credits), a C in Introduction to Psychology (3 credits), a B in Biology I (4 credits), and a D in Physical Education (2 credits). Assuming A = 4 grade points, B = 3 grade points, C = 2 grade points, D = 1 grade point, and F = 0 grade points, find the student's grade point average.

SOLUTION

Course	Credits (w)	Grade (X)
English Composition I	3	A (4 points)
Introduction to Psychology	3	C (2 points)
Biology I	4	B (3 points)
Physical Education	2	D (1 point)

$$\bar{X} = \frac{\Sigma wX}{\Sigma w} = \frac{3 \cdot 4 + 3 \cdot 2 + 4 \cdot 3 + 2 \cdot 1}{3 + 3 + 4 + 2} = \frac{32}{12} \approx 2.7$$

The grade point average is 2.7.

TABLE 3–1 Summary of Measures of Central Tendency		
Measure	**Definition**	**Symbol(s)**
Mean	Sum of values, divided by total number of values	$\mu, \bar{X}$
Median	Middle point in data set that has been ordered	MD
Mode	Most frequent data value	None
Midrange	Lowest value plus highest value, divided by 2	MR

Table 3–1 summarizes the measures of central tendency.

Researchers and statisticians must know which measure of central tendency is being used and when to use each measure of central tendency. The properties and uses of the four measures of central tendency are summarized next.

Properties and Uses of Central Tendency

The Mean

1. The mean is found by using all the values of the data.
2. The mean varies less than the median or mode when samples are taken from the same population and all three measures are computed for these samples.
3. The mean is used in computing other statistics, such as the variance.
4. The mean for the data set is unique and not necessarily one of the data values.
5. The mean cannot be computed for the data in a frequency distribution that has an open-ended class.
6. The mean is affected by extremely high or low values, called outliers, and may not be the appropriate average to use in these situations.

The Median

1. The median is used to find the center or middle value of a data set.
2. The median is used when it is necessary to find out whether the data values fall into the upper half or lower half of the distribution.
3. The median is used for an open-ended distribution.
4. The median is affected less than the mean by extremely high or extremely low values.

The Mode

1. The mode is used when the most typical case is desired.
2. The mode is the easiest average to compute.
3. The mode can be used when the data are nominal or categorical, such as religious preference, gender, or political affiliation.

4. The mode is not always unique. A data set can have more than one mode, or the mode may not exist for a data set.

The Midrange

1. The midrange is easy to compute.
2. The midrange gives the midpoint.
3. The midrange is affected by extremely high or low values in a data set.

Distribution Shapes

Frequency distributions can assume many shapes. The three most important shapes are positively skewed, symmetric, and negatively skewed. Figure 3–1 shows histograms of each.

In a **positively skewed** or **right-skewed distribution,** the majority of the data values fall to the left of the mean and cluster at the lower end of the distribution; the "tail" is to the right. Also, the mean is to the right of the median, and the mode is to the left of the median.

For example, if an instructor gave an examination and most of the students did poorly, their scores would tend to cluster on the left side of the distribution. A few high scores would constitute the tail of the distribution, which would be on the right side. Another example of a positively skewed distribution is the incomes of the population of the United States. Most of the incomes cluster about the low end of the distribution; those with high incomes are in the minority and are in the tail at the right of the distribution.

In a **symmetric distribution,** the data values are evenly distributed on both sides of the mean. In addition, when the distribution is unimodal, the mean, median, and mode are the same and are at the center of the distribution. Examples of symmetric distributions are IQ scores and heights of adult males.

FIGURE 3–1

Types of Distributions

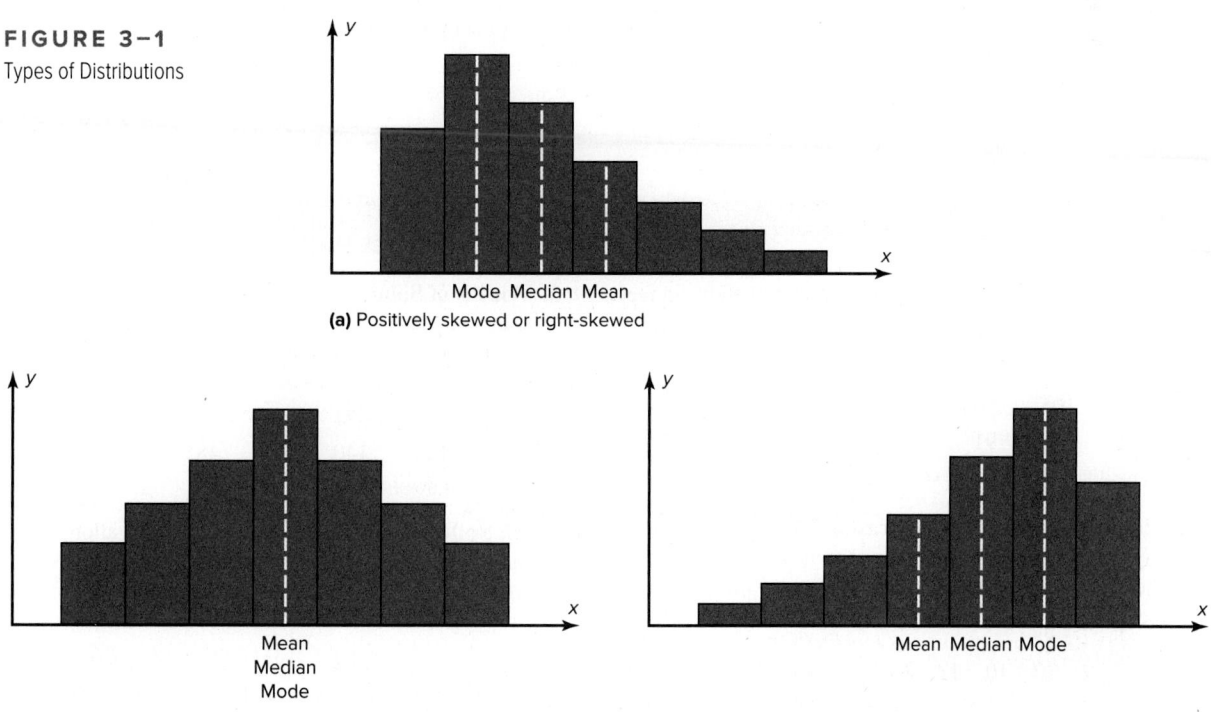

(a) Positively skewed or right-skewed

(b) Symmetric

(c) Negatively skewed or left-skewed

When the majority of the data values fall to the right of the mean and cluster at the upper end of the distribution, with the tail to the left, the distribution is said to be **negatively skewed** or **left-skewed.** Also, the mean is to the left of the median, and the mode is to the right of the median. As an example, a negatively skewed distribution results if the majority of students score very high on an instructor's examination. These scores will tend to cluster to the right of the distribution.

When a distribution is extremely skewed, the value of the mean will be pulled toward the tail, but the majority of the data values will be greater than the mean or less than the mean (depending on which way the data are skewed); hence, the median rather than the mean is a more appropriate measure of central tendency. An extremely skewed distribution can also affect other statistics.

A measure of skewness for a distribution is discussed in Exercise 48 in Section 3–2.

≡ Applying the Concepts 3–1

Teacher Salaries

The following data represent salaries (in dollars) from a school district in Greenwood, South Carolina.

| 50,000 | 51,000 | 51,000 | 52,500 | 54,300 | 57,500 |
| 58,000 | 56,600 | 59,200 | 61,560 | 56,400 | 147,000 |

1. First, assume you work for the school board in Greenwood and do not wish to raise taxes to increase salaries. Compute the mean, median, and mode, and decide which one would best support your position to not raise salaries.

2. Second, assume you work for the teachers' union and want a raise for the teachers. Use the best measure of central tendency to support your position.

3. Explain how outliers can be used to support one or the other position.

4. If the salaries represented every teacher in the school district, would the averages be parameters or statistics?

5. Which measure of central tendency can be misleading when a data set contains outliers?

6. When you are comparing the measures of central tendency, does the distribution display any skewness? Explain.

See page 186 for the answers

≡ Exercises 3–1

1. **Roller Coaster Speeds** The data show the heights in feet of 14 roller coasters. Find the mean, median, midrange, and mode for the data. 104.1; 102; 105; 50, 95 and 102

| 95 | 105 | 50 | 125 | 102 | 120 | 160 |
| 102 | 118 | 91 | 160 | 95 | 50 | 84 |

Source: UltimateRollerCoaster.com.

2. **Clear Days in Omaha, Nebraska** The number of clear days in Omaha, Nebraska, per year over 12 months is shown. Find the mean, median, mode, and midrange for the data. 9.5; 9.5; 10; 10.5

7 7 9 10 10 13 15 12 10 9 6 6

3. **Widths of Solar Eclipses** The widths in miles of 14 solar eclipses in the United States are shown. Find the mean, median, mode, and midrange for the data.
162.9; 124; no mode; 270.5

| 304 | 96 | 71 | 125 | 56 | 260 | 123 |
| 183 | 160 | 140 | 105 | 485 | 100 | 72 |

Source: The World Almanac

4. **Oil Spills** The data show the number of gallons in millions of some notable oil spills that occurred in the world since 1950. Find the mean, median, mode, and midrange for the data. 28.9; 18; no mode; 66.5

17 3 21 10 13 22 18 26 130

Which measure seems to be the best measure of average?

Source: The World Almanac

5. Top Video Games The following represent XBOX One Top Selling Games and units sold: 6,190,000; 5,600,000; no mode; 6,860,000

Grand Theft Auto V	8,720,000
PlayerUnknown's Battlegrounds	8,000,000
Call of Duty: Black Ops III	7,370,000
Call of Duty: WWII	6,230,000
Red Dead Redemption 2	5,770,000
Minecraft: Xbox One Edition	5,430,000
Call of Duty: Advanced Warfare	5,220,000
Battlefield 1	5,130,000
Fallout 4	5,030,000
Halo 5: Guardians	5,000,000

Find the mean, median, mode, and midrange.

Source: https://en.wikipedia.org/wiki/List_of_best-selling_Xbox_One_video_games

6. Earnings of Nonliving Celebrities *Forbes* magazine prints an annual Top-Earning Nonliving Celebrities list (based on royalties and estate earnings). Find the mean, median, mode, and midrange for the data. Comment on the skewness. Figures represent millions of dollars. 19; 10; 7; 28.5 (Isn't it cool that Albert Einstein is on this list?) The data are positively skewed.

Kurt Cobain	50	Ray Charles	10
Elvis Presley	42	Marilyn Monroe	8
Charles M. Schulz	35	Johnny Cash	8
John Lennon	24	J.R.R. Tolkien	7
Albert Einstein	20	George Harrison	7
Andy Warhol	19	Bob Marley	7
Theodore Geisel (Dr. Seuss)	10		

Source: articles.moneycentral.msn.com

7. Super Bowl Commercials The number of television commercials for the Super Bowls over the past several years is given. Find the mean, median, mode, and midrange for the data. 89.2; 88; 84 and 92; 91

92 92 84 84 104 96 78 97 83 82

Source: National Retail Federation

8. Top-Paid CEOs The data shown are the total compensation (in millions of dollars) for the 50 top-paid CEOs for a recent year. Compare the averages, and state which one you think is the best measure.

17.5	18.0	36.8	31.7	31.7
17.3	24.3	47.7	38.5	17.0
23.7	16.5	25.1	17.4	18.0
37.6	19.7	21.4	28.6	21.6
19.3	20.0	16.9	25.2	19.8
25.0	17.2	20.4	20.1	29.1
19.1	25.2	23.2	25.9	24.0
41.7	24.0	16.8	26.8	31.4
16.9	17.2	24.1	35.2	19.1
22.9	18.2	25.4	35.4	25.5

Source: USA TODAY. 24.42; 23.45; 16.9, 17.2, 18, 19.1, 24, 25.2, 31.7; 32.1. The mean and the median are close, and the midrange is higher than both. There are many modes. It appears that the mean and median are good measures of the average.

9. Airplane Seats The maximum number of seats in various models of passenger airplanes is shown. Find the mean, median, mode, and midrange for the data.

132 156 180 220 380 440 375 440 475 853

Source: The World Almanac 365.1; 377.5; 440; 492.5

10. Elephants' Speeds The data show the running speeds in miles per hour for elephants over a quarter-mile distance. Find the mean, median, mode, and midrange for the data. Which measure seems most representative of the data? 25.3; 25; 25; 26.5

27 24 25 25 26 20 22 33

11. Distances of Stars Of the 25 brightest stars, the distances from earth (in light-years) for those with distances less than 100 light-years are found below. Find the mean, median, mode, and midrange for the data.

8.6	36.7	42.2	16.8	33.7	77.5	87.9
4.4	25.3	11.4	65.1	25.1	51.5	

Source: New York Times Almanac 2010. 37.4; 33.7; none; 46.15

12. Mean Range of Tides The mean range of tides in selected cities in the United States is shown. The mean range of tides is the difference between the mean highest water mark minus the mean lowest water mark. Find the mean, median, mode, and midrange of the data.

14	18	114	63	220	83	12	15	15	46	30	31	54
42	73	109	111	19	49	13	56	90	33	49		

Source: The World Almanac 56.6; 47.5; 15 and 49; 116

13. Wind Speeds The data show the maximum wind speeds for a sample of 40 states. Find the mean and modal class for the data.

Class boundaries	Frequency
47.5–54.5	3
54.5–61.5	2
61.5–68.5	9
68.5–75.5	13
75.5–82.5	8
82.5–89.5	3
89.5–96.5	2 71.65; 68.5–75.5

Source: NOAA

14. Hourly Compensation for Production Workers The hourly compensation costs (in U.S. dollars) for production workers in selected countries are represented below. Find the mean and modal class for the data.

Class	Frequency
2.48–7.48	7
7.49–12.49	3
12.50–17.50	1
17.51–22.51	7 17.684; 2.48–7.48 and
22.52–27.52	5 17.51–22.51. Group mean
27.53–32.53	5 is less.

Compare the mean of these grouped data to the U.S. mean of $21.97.

Source: New York Times Almanac.

15. **Calls Received By a 911 Operator** The data show the number of calls received by a 911 operator over a period of 30 days. Find the mean and modal class.

Class	Frequency
19–21	3
22–24	5
25–27	17
28–30	3
31–33	2 26.5; 25–27

16. **Doctor Visits** The frequency distribution shows the number of visits adults ages 18 to 24 made to medical doctors last year. Find the mean and modal class for the data.

Class	Frequency
0–2	9
3–5	15
6–8	8
9–11	7
12–14	5 5.9; 3–5

17. **Percentage of College-Educated Population over 25** Below are the percentages of the population over 25 years of age who have completed 4 years of college or more for the 50 states and the District of Columbia. Find the mean and modal class. 26.66; 24.2–28.6

Percentage	Frequency
15.2–19.6	3
19.7–24.1	15
24.2–28.6	19
28.7–33.1	6
33.2–37.6	7
37.7–42.1	0
42.2–46.6	1

Source: New York Times Almanac.

18. **Months Served by Military Personnel** The data show the number of months that retired military veterans served before retiring. Find the mean and modal class for the data. 72; 71–79

Class	Frequency
44–52	15
53–61	22
62–70	26
71–79	38
80–88	29
89–97	18

19. **Specialty Coffee Shops** A random sample of 30 states shows the number of specialty coffee shops for a specific company. Find the mean and modal class for the data. 34.1; 0.5–19.5

Class boundaries	Frequency
0.5–19.5	12
19.5–38.5	7
38.5–57.5	5
57.5–76.5	3
76.5–95.5	3

20. **Ages of Hospital Patients** The frequency distribution shows the ages of patients who are staying overnight at a local hospital. Find the mean and modal class of the data. 46.4; 46–54

Class	Frequency
10–18	9
19–27	15
28–36	24
37–45	36
46–54	42
55–63	27
64–72	16
73–81	11

21. **Children of U.S. Presidents** The data show the number of children U.S. Presidents through Obama, had. Construct an ungrouped frequency distribution and find the mean and modal class. 3.2; 2

```
0 5 6 0 3 4 1 4 10 8
7 0 6 1 0 3 4 5 4 8
7 3 5 2 1 2 1 5 3 3
0 0 2 2 6 1 2 3 2 2
4 4 2 6 1 2 2
```

Source: World Almanac and Book of Facts.

22. **Enrollments for Selected Independent Religiously Controlled 4-Year Colleges** Listed below are the enrollments for selected independent religiously controlled 4-year colleges that offer bachelor's degrees only. Construct a grouped frequency distribution with six classes and find the mean and modal class. 1804.6; 1013–1345

```
1013 1867 1268 1666 2309 1231 3005 2895 2166 1136
1532 1461 1750 1069 1723 1827 1155 1714 2391 2155
1412 1688 2471 1759 3008 2511 2577 1082 1067 1062
1319 1037 2400
```

Source: World Almanac.

23. **Automobile Selling Prices** Find the weighted mean price of three models of automobiles sold. The number and price of each model sold are shown in this list. $9866.67

Model	Number	Price
A	8	$10,000
B	10	12,000
C	12	8,000

24. **Fat Grams** Using the weighted mean, find the average number of grams of fat per ounce of meat or fish that a person would consume over a 5-day period if he ate these:

Meat or fish	Fat (g/oz)
3 oz fried shrimp	3.33
3 oz veal cutlet (broiled)	3.00
2 oz roast beef (lean)	2.50
2.5 oz fried chicken drumstick	4.40
4 oz tuna (canned in oil)	1.75

Source: The World Almanac and Book of Facts. 2.896

25. Diet Cola Preference A recent survey of a new diet cola reported the following percentages of people who liked the taste. Find the weighted mean of the percentages. 35.4%

Area	% Favored	Number surveyed
1	40	1000
2	30	3000
3	50	800

26. Number of Eclipses There are between 4 and 7 eclipses per year in the world each year. The number of eclipses from 2000 B.C. to 3000 A.D. is shown. Find the weighted mean for the data. 4.8

Number	Number of years
4	2401
5	1391
6	1053
7	155

Source: moonblink.info

27. Final Grade An instructor grades exams, 20%; term paper, 30%; final exam, 50%. A student had grades of 83, 72, and 90, respectively, for exams, term paper, and final exam. Find the student's final average. Use the weighted mean. 83.2

28. Final Grade Another instructor gives four 1-hour exams and one final exam, which counts as two 1-hour exams. Find a student's grade if she received 62, 83, 97, and 90 on the 1-hour exams and 82 on the final exam. 82.7

29. For these situations, state which measure of central tendency—mean, median, or mode—should be used.

 a. The most typical case is desired. Mode

 b. The distribution is open-ended. Median

 c. There is an extreme value in the data set. Median

 d. The data are categorical. Mode

 e. Further statistical computations will be needed. Mean

 f. The values are to be divided into two approximately equal groups, one group containing the larger values and one containing the smaller values. Median

30. Describe which measure of central tendency—mean, median, or mode—was probably used in each situation.

 a. One-half of the factory workers make more than $5.37 per hour, and one-half make less than $5.37 per hour. Median

 b. The average number of children per family in the Plaza Heights Complex is 1.8. Mean

 c. Most people preferred convertibles over any other color. Mode

 d. The average person cuts the lawn once a week. Mode

 e. The most common fear today is fear of speaking in public. Mode

 f. The average age of college professors is 42.3 years. Mean

31. What types of symbols are used to represent sample statistics? Give an example. What types of symbols are used to represent population parameters? Give an example. Roman letters, $\overline{X}$; Greek letters, μ

32. A local fast-food company claims that the average salary of its employees is $13.23 per hour. An employee states that most employees make minimum wage. If both are being truthful, how could both be correct? Both could be true since one may be using the mean for the average salary and the other may be using the mode for the average.

33. Could the mean be one of the numbers in the data set? Explain your answer. Yes. It depends on the numbers in the data set. For example, if the data were 3, 4, and 5, the mean would be (3 + 4 + 5)/3 = 12/3 = 4.

34. When would the median be one of the numbers in the data set? If the data set contains an odd number of data values, the median would be one of the numbers in the data set.

35. When would the mean or the median be the largest data value in the data set? If all the data values were the same, then the mean and median would be the largest (or smallest) data value.

36. When the mean of the salaries of a company is $34,000 and all employees are given a $2500 raise, what happens to the mean and median of the salaries? The mean and median of the salaries will increase by $2500.

37. When the mean and median of the salaries of the employees of a company are both $34,000 and all employees are given a 5% raise, what happens to the mean and median of the salaries? The mean and median will increase by 5%.

38. Is the median always the exact value between the lowest and highest data value? No. That value is called the midrange.

Extending the Concepts

39. If the mean of five values is 64, find the sum of the values. 320

40. If the mean of five values is 8.2 and four of the values are 6, 10, 7, and 12, find the fifth value. 6

41. Find the mean of 10, 20, 30, 40, and 50.

 a. Add 10 to each value and find the mean. 40

 b. Subtract 10 from each value and find the mean. 20

 c. Multiply each value by 10 and find the mean. 300

d. Divide each value by 10 and find the mean. 3

e. Make a general statement about each situation.
The results will be the same as if you add, subtract, multiply, and divide the mean by 10.

42. Harmonic Mean The *harmonic mean* (HM) is defined as the number of values divided by the sum of the reciprocals of each value. The formula is

$$HM = \frac{n}{\Sigma(1/X)}$$

For example, the harmonic mean of 1, 4, 5, and 2 is

$$HM = \frac{4}{1/1 + 1/4 + 1/5 + 1/2} \approx 2.051$$

This mean is useful for finding the average speed. Suppose a person drove 100 miles at 40 miles per hour and returned driving 50 miles per hour. The average miles per hour is *not* 45 miles per hour, which is found by adding 40 and 50 and dividing by 2. The average is found as shown.
Since

$$\text{Time} = \text{distance} \div \text{rate}$$

then

$$\text{Time } 1 = \frac{100}{40} = 2.5 \text{ hours to make the trip}$$

$$\text{Time } 2 = \frac{100}{50} = 2 \text{ hours to return}$$

Hence, the total time is 4.5 hours, and the total miles driven are 200. Now, the average speed is

$$\text{Rate} = \frac{\text{distance}}{\text{time}} = \frac{200}{4.5} \approx 44.444 \text{ miles per hour}$$

This value can also be found by using the harmonic mean formula

$$HM = \frac{2}{1/40 + 1/50} \approx 44.444$$

Using the harmonic mean, find each of these.

a. A salesperson drives 300 miles round trip at 30 miles per hour going to Chicago and 45 miles per hour returning home. Find the average miles per hour. 36 mph

b. A bus driver drives the 50 miles to West Chester at 40 miles per hour and returns driving 25 miles per hour. Find the average miles per hour. 30.8 mph

c. A carpenter buys $500 worth of nails at $50 per pound and $500 worth of nails at $10 per pound. Find the average cost of 1 pound of nails. $16.67

43. Geometric Mean The *geometric mean* (GM) is defined as the *n*th root of the product of *n* values. The formula is

$$GM = \sqrt[n]{(X_1)(X_2)(X_3) \cdots (X_n)}$$

The geometric mean of 4 and 16 is

$$GM = \sqrt{(4)(16)} = \sqrt{64} = 8$$

The geometric mean of 1, 3, and 9 is

$$GM = \sqrt[3]{(1)(3)(9)} = \sqrt[3]{27} = 3$$

The geometric mean is useful in finding the average of percentages, ratios, indexes, or growth rates. For example, if a person receives a 20% raise after 1 year of service and a 10% raise after the second year of service, the average percentage raise per year is not 15 but 14.89%, as shown.

$$GM = \sqrt{(1.2)(1.1)} \approx 1.1489$$

or

$$GM = \sqrt{(120)(110)} \approx 114.89\%$$

The salary is 120% at the end of the first year and 110% at the end of the second year. This is equivalent to an average of 14.89%, since 114.89% − 100% = 14.89%.
This answer can also be shown by assuming that the person makes $10,000 to start and receives two raises of 20% and 10%.

$$\text{Raise } 1 = 10{,}000 \cdot 20\% = \$2000$$
$$\text{Raise } 2 = 12{,}000 \cdot 10\% = \$1200$$

The total salary raise is $3200. This total is equivalent to

$$\$10{,}000 \cdot 14.89\% = \$1489.00$$
$$\underline{\$11{,}489 \cdot 14.89\% = \$1710.71}$$
$$\$3199.71 \approx \$3200$$

Find the geometric mean of each of these.

a. The growth rates of the Living Life Insurance Corporation for the past 3 years were 35, 24, and 18%. 25.5%

b. A person received these percentage raises in salary over a 4-year period: 8, 6, 4, and 5%. 5.7%

c. A stock increased each year for 5 years at these percentages: 10, 8, 12, 9, and 3%. 8.4%

d. The price increases, in percentages, for the cost of food in a specific geographic region for the past 3 years were 1, 3, and 5.5%. 3.2%

44. Quadratic Mean A useful mean in the physical sciences (such as voltage) is the *quadratic mean* (QM), which is found by taking the square root of the average of the squares of each value. The formula is

$$QM = \sqrt{\frac{\Sigma X^2}{n}}$$

The quadratic mean of 3, 5, 6, and 10 is

$$QM = \sqrt{\frac{3^2 + 5^2 + 6^2 + 10^2}{4}}$$
$$= \sqrt{42.5} \approx 6.519$$

Find the quadratic mean of 8, 6, 3, 5, and 4. 5.5

45. Median for Grouped Data An approximate median can be found for data that have been grouped into a frequency distribution. First it is necessary to find the median class. This is the class that contains the median value. That is the *n*/2 data value. Then it is assumed that the data values are evenly distributed throughout the median class. The formula is

$$MD = \frac{n/2 - cf}{f}(w) + L_m$$

where n = sum of frequencies
         cf = cumulative frequency of class immediately preceding the median class

w = width of median class
f = frequency of median class
L_m = lower boundary of median class

Using this formula, find the median for data in the frequency distribution of Exercise 16. 5.1

≡ Technology   Step by Step

EXCEL
Step by Step

Finding Measures of Central Tendency

Example XL3–1

Find the mean, mode, and median of the data from Example 3–7. The data represent the population of licensed nuclear reactors in the United States for a recent 15-year period.

104	104	104	104	104
107	109	109	109	110
109	111	112	111	109

1. On an Excel worksheet enter the numbers in cells A2–A16. Enter a label for the variable in cell A1.

On the same worksheet as the data:

2. Compute the mean of the data: key in **=AVERAGE(A2:A16)** in a blank cell.

3. Compute the mode of the data: key in **=MODE(A2:A16)** in a blank cell.

4. Compute the median of the data: key in **=MEDIAN(A2:A16)** in a blank cell.

These and other statistical functions can also be accessed without typing them into the worksheet directly.

1. Select the Formulas tab from the toolbar and select the Insert Function Icon f_x .

2. Select the Statistical category for statistical functions.

3. Scroll to find the appropriate function and click [OK].

	A	B	C
1	Number of Reactors		
2	104	107.73333	Mean
3	107	104	Mode
4	109	109	Median
5	104		
6	109		
7	111		
8	104		
9	109		
10	112		
11	104		
12	109		
13	111		
14	104		
15	110		
16	109		
17			

(Excel reports only the first mode in a bimodal or multimodal distribution.)

3–2   Measures of Variation

In statistics, to describe the data set accurately, statisticians must know more than the measures of central tendency. Consider Example 3–15.

OBJECTIVE

Describe data, using measures of variation, such as the range, variance, and standard deviation.

EXAMPLE 3–15   Comparison of Outdoor Paint

A testing lab wishes to test two experimental brands of outdoor paint to see how long each will last before fading. The testing lab makes 6 gallons of each paint to test. Since different chemical agents are added to each group and only six cans are involved, these two groups constitute two small populations. The results (in months) are shown. Find the mean of each group.

Brand A	Brand B
10	35
60	45
50	30
30	35
40	40
20	25

SOLUTION

The mean for brand A is

$$\mu = \frac{\Sigma X}{N} = \frac{210}{6} = 35 \text{ months}$$

The mean for brand B is

$$\mu = \frac{\Sigma X}{N} = \frac{210}{6} = 35 \text{ months}$$

Since the means are equal in Example 3–15, you might conclude that both brands of paint last equally well. However, when the data sets are examined graphically, a somewhat different conclusion might be drawn. See Figure 3–2.

As Figure 3–2 shows, even though the means are the same for both brands, the spread, or variation, is quite different. Figure 3–2 shows that brand B performs more consistently; it is less variable. For the spread or variability of a data set, three measures are commonly used: *range, variance,* and *standard deviation.* Each measure will be discussed in this section.

FIGURE 3–2
Examining Data Sets
Graphically

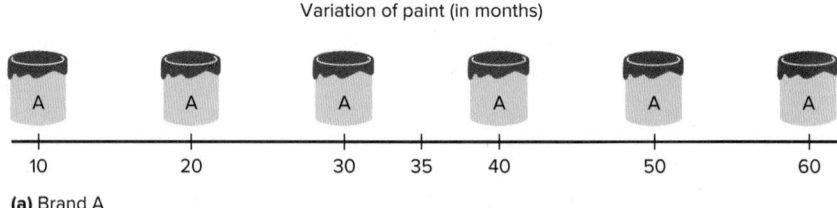

(a) Brand A

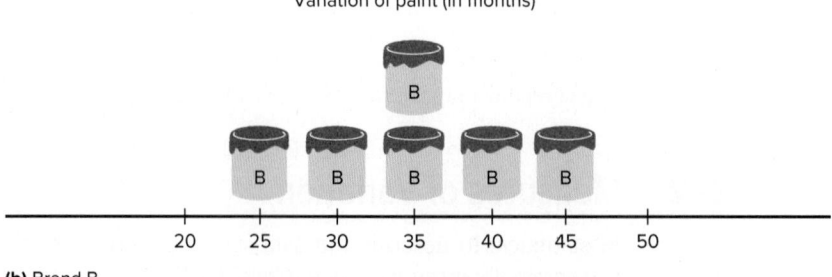

(b) Brand B

Range

The range is the simplest of the three measures and is defined now.

> The **range** is the highest value minus the lowest value. The symbol R is used for the range.
>
> $$R = \text{highest value} - \text{lowest value}$$

EXAMPLE 3–16   Comparison of Outdoor Paint

Find the ranges for the paints in Example 3–15.

SOLUTION

For brand A, the range is

$$R = 60 - 10 = 50 \text{ months}$$

For brand B, the range is

$$R = 45 - 25 = 20 \text{ months}$$

Make sure the range is given as a single number.

The range for brand A shows that 50 months separate the largest data value from the smallest data value. For brand B, 20 months separate the largest data value from the smallest data value, which is less than one-half of brand A's range.

One extremely high or one extremely low data value can affect the range markedly, as shown in Example 3–17.

EXAMPLE 3–17   Internet Connections

The number of cable modem connections in millions for a select 6-year period are shown. Find the range.

$$55, \quad 38, \quad 14, \quad 46, \quad 60, \quad 51$$

Source: Federal Communications Commission

SOLUTION

Range $R = 60 - 14 = 46$ million connections.

The range for these data is quite large since it depends on the highest data value and the lowest data value. To have a more meaningful statistic to measure the variability, statisticians use measures called the *variance* and *standard deviation.*

Population Variance and Standard Deviation

Before these measures can be defined, it is necessary to know what *data variation* means. It is based on the difference or distance each data value is from the mean. This difference or distance is called a *deviation.* In the outdoor paint example, the mean for brand A paint is $\mu = 35$ months, and for a specific can, say, the can that lasted for 50 months, the deviation is $X - \mu$ or $50 - 35 = 15$. Hence, the deviation for that data value is 15 months. If you find the sum of the deviations for all data values about the mean (without rounding), this sum will always be zero. That is, $\Sigma(X - \mu) = 0$. (You can see this if you sum all the deviations for the paint example.)

To eliminate this problem, we sum the squares, that is, $\Sigma(X - \mu)^2$ and find the mean of these squares by dividing by N (the total number of data values), symbolically $\Sigma(X - \mu)^2/N$. This measure is called the *population variance* and is symbolized by σ^2, where σ is the symbol for Greek lowercase letter sigma.

Since this measure (σ^2) is in square units and the data are in regular units, statisticians take the square root of the variance and call it the *standard deviation*.

Formally defined,

The **population variance** is the average of the squares of the distance each value is from the mean. The symbol for the population variance is σ^2 (σ is the Greek lowercase letter sigma).

The formula for the population variance is

$$\sigma^2 = \frac{\Sigma(X - \mu)^2}{N}$$

where X = individual value
μ = population mean
N = population size

The **population standard deviation** is the square root of the variance. The symbol for the population standard deviation is σ.

The corresponding formula for the population standard deviation is

$$\sigma = \sqrt{\sigma^2} = \sqrt{\frac{\Sigma(X - \mu)^2}{N}}$$

To find the variance and standard deviation for a data set, the following Procedure Table can be used.

Procedure Table

Finding the Population Variance and Population Standard Deviation

Step 1   Find the mean for the data.

$$\mu = \frac{\Sigma X}{N}$$

Step 2   Find the deviation for each data value.

$$X - \mu$$

Step 3   Square each of the deviations.

$$(X - \mu)^2$$

Step 4   Find the sum of the squares.

$$\Sigma(X - \mu)^2$$

Step 5   Divide by N to get the variance.

$$\sigma^2 = \frac{\Sigma(X - \mu)^2}{N}$$

Step 6   Take the square root of the variance to get the standard deviation.

$$\sigma = \sqrt{\frac{\Sigma(X - \mu)^2}{N}}$$

Interesting Fact

The average American drives about 10,000 miles a year.

Rounding Rule for the Standard Deviation   The rounding rule for the standard deviation is the same as that for the mean. The final answer should be rounded to one more decimal place than that of the original data.

EXAMPLE 3–18   Comparison of Outdoor Paint

Find the variance and standard deviation for the data set for brand A paint in Example 3–15. The number of months brand A lasted before fading was

$$10, 60, 50, 30, 40, 20$$

SOLUTION

Step 1   Find the mean for the data.

$$\mu = \frac{\Sigma X}{N} = \frac{10 + 60 + 50 + 30 + 40 + 20}{6} = \frac{210}{6} = 35$$

Step 2   Subtract the mean from each data value $(X - \mu)$.

$$10 - 35 = -25 \qquad 50 - 35 = 15 \qquad 40 - 35 = 5$$
$$60 - 35 = 25 \qquad 30 - 35 = -5 \qquad 20 - 35 = -15$$

Step 3   Square each result $(X - \mu)^2$.

$$(-25)^2 = 625 \qquad (15)^2 = 225 \qquad (5)^2 = 25$$
$$(25)^2 = 625 \qquad (-5)^2 = 25 \qquad (-15)^2 = 225$$

Step 4   Find the sum of the squares $\Sigma(X - \mu)^2$.

$$625 + 625 + 225 + 25 + 25 + 225 = 1750$$

Step 5   Divide the sum by N to get the variance $\dfrac{\Sigma(X - \mu)^2}{N}$.

$$\text{Variance} = 1750 \div 6 \approx 291.7$$

Step 6   Take the square root of the variance to get the standard deviation. Hence, the standard deviation equals $\sqrt{291.7}$, or 17.1. It is helpful to make a table.

A Values X	B $X - \mu$	C $(X - \mu)^2$
10	−25	625
60	25	625
50	15	225
30	−5	25
40	5	25
20	−15	225
		1750

Column A contains the raw data X. Column B contains the differences $X - \mu$ obtained in step 2. Column C contains the squares of the differences obtained in step 3.

The preceding computational procedure reveals several things. First, the square root of the variance gives the standard deviation; and vice versa, squaring the standard deviation gives the variance. Second, the variance is actually the average of the square of the distance that each value is from the mean. Therefore, if the values are near the mean, the variance will be small. In contrast, if the values are far from the mean, the variance will be large.

You might wonder why the squared distances are used instead of the actual distances. As previously stated, the reason is that the sum of the distances will always be zero. To verify this result for a specific case, add the values in column B of the table in Example 3–18. When each value is squared, the negative signs are eliminated.

Finally, why is it necessary to take the square root? Again, the reason is that since the distances were squared, the units of the resultant numbers are the squares of the units of

Historical Note

Karl Pearson in 1892 and 1893 introduced the statistical concepts of the range and standard deviation.

the original raw data. Finding the square root of the variance puts the standard deviation in the same units as the raw data.

When you are finding the square root, always use its positive value, since the variance and standard deviation of a data set can never be negative.

EXAMPLE 3–19   Comparison of Outdoor Paint

Find the variance and standard deviation for brand B paint data in Example 3–15. The months brand B lasted before fading were

$$35, 45, 30, 35, 40, 25$$

SOLUTION

Step 1   Find the mean.

$$\mu = \frac{\Sigma X}{N} = \frac{35 + 45 + 30 + 35 + 40 + 25}{6} = \frac{210}{6} = 35$$

Step 2   Subtract the mean from each value, and place the result in column B of the table.

$$35 - 35 = 0 \qquad 45 - 35 = 10 \qquad 30 - 35 = -5$$
$$35 - 35 = 0 \qquad 40 - 35 = 5 \qquad 25 - 35 = -10$$

Step 3   Square each result and place the squares in column C of the table.

A X	B $X - \mu$	C $(X - \mu)^2$
35	0	0
45	10	100
30	−5	25
35	0	0
40	5	25
25	−10	100

Step 4   Find the sum of the squares in column C.

$$\Sigma(X - \mu)^2 = 0 + 100 + 25 + 0 + 25 + 100 = 250$$

Step 5   Divide the sum by N to get the variance.

$$\sigma^2 = \frac{\Sigma(X - \mu)^2}{N} = \frac{250}{6} = 41.7$$

Step 6   Take the square root to get the standard deviation.

$$\sigma = \sqrt{\frac{\Sigma(X - \mu)^2}{N}} = \sqrt{41.7} \approx 6.5$$

Hence, the standard deviation is 6.5.

Since the standard deviation of brand A is 17.1 (see Example 3–18) and the standard deviation of brand B is 6.5, the data are more variable for brand A. *In summary, when the means are equal, the larger the variance or standard deviation is, the more variable the data are.*

Sample Variance and Standard Deviation

When computing the variance for a sample, one might expect the following expression to be used:

$$\frac{\Sigma(X - \overline{X})^2}{n}$$

where $\overline{X}$ is the sample mean and n is the sample size. *This formula is not usually used, however, since in most cases the purpose of calculating the statistic is to estimate the corresponding parameter.* For example, the sample mean $\overline{X}$ is used to estimate the population mean μ. The expression

$$\frac{\Sigma(X - \overline{X})^2}{n}$$

does not give the best estimate of the population variance because when the population is large and the sample is small (usually less than 30), the variance computed by this formula usually underestimates the population variance. Therefore, instead of dividing by n, find the variance of the sample by dividing by $n - 1$, giving a slightly larger value and an *unbiased* estimate of the population variance.

Formula for the Sample Variance

The formula for the sample variance (denoted by s^2) is

$$s^2 = \frac{\Sigma(X - \overline{X})^2}{n - 1}$$

where X = individual value
$\overline{X}$ = sample mean
n = sample size

To find the standard deviation of a sample, you must take the square root of the sample variance, which was found by using the preceding formula.

Formula for the Sample Standard Deviation

The formula for the sample standard deviation, denoted by s, is

$$s = \sqrt{s^2} = \sqrt{\frac{\Sigma(X - \overline{X})^2}{n - 1}}$$

where X = individual value
$\overline{X}$ = sample mean
n = sample size

The procedure for finding the sample variance and the sample standard deviation is the same as the procedure for finding the population variance and the population standard deviation *except* the sum of the squares is divided by $n - 1$ (sample size minus 1) instead of N (population size). Refer to the previous Procedure Table if necessary. The next example shows these steps.

EXAMPLE 3–20   Air Pollution

The sulfur dioxide content of air pollution in millions of tons of five randomly selected cities is shown. Find the variance and standard deviation for the data.

$$11 \quad 90 \quad 33 \quad 49 \quad 27$$

Source: World Health Organization

SOLUTION

Step 1 Find the mean of the data values.

$$\overline{X} = \frac{\Sigma X}{n} = \frac{11 + 90 + 33 + 49 + 27}{5} = \frac{210}{5} = 42$$

Step 2 Find the deviation for each data value $(X - \overline{X})$.

$$11 - 42 = -31 \qquad 33 - 42 = -9 \qquad 27 - 42 = -15$$
$$90 - 42 = 48 \qquad 49 - 42 = 7$$

Step 3   Square each of the deviations $(X - \overline{X})^2$.

$$(-31)^2 = 961 \qquad (-9)^2 = 81 \qquad (-15)^2 = 225$$
$$48^2 = 2304 \qquad 7^2 = 49$$

Step 4   Find the sum of the squares.

$$\Sigma(X - \overline{X})^2 = 961 + 2304 + 81 + 49 + 225 = 3620$$

Step 5   Divide the sum by $n - 1$ to get the variance.

$$s^2 = \frac{\Sigma(X - \overline{X})^2}{n - 1} = \frac{3620}{5 - 1} = \frac{3620}{4} = 905$$

Step 6   Find the square root of the variance to get the standard deviation.

$$s = \sqrt{\frac{\Sigma(X - \overline{X})^2}{n - 1}} = \sqrt{905} \approx 30.1 \text{ rounded}$$

The variance is 905 and the standard deviation is 30.1.

Shortcut formulas for computing the variance and standard deviation are presented next and will be used in the remainder of the chapter and in the exercises. These formulas are mathematically equivalent to the preceding formulas and do not involve using the mean. They save time when repeated subtracting and squaring occur in the original formulas. They are also more accurate when the mean has been rounded.

Shortcut or Computational Formulas for s^2 and s

The shortcut formulas for computing the variance and standard deviation for data obtained from samples are as follows.

Variance	Standard deviation
$s^2 = \dfrac{n(\Sigma X^2) - (\Sigma X)^2}{n(n - 1)}$	$s = \sqrt{\dfrac{n(\Sigma X^2) - (\Sigma X)^2}{n(n - 1)}}$

Note that ΣX^2 is not the same as $(\Sigma X)^2$. The notation ΣX^2 means to square the values first, then sum; $(\Sigma X)^2$ means to sum the values first, then square the sum.

Example 3–21 explains how to use the shortcut formulas.

EXAMPLE 3–21   Air Pollution

The sulfur dioxide content of the air in millions of tons in five randomly selected cities is shown. Find the variance and standard deviation for the data.

$$11 \quad 90 \quad 33 \quad 49 \quad 27$$

Source: World Health Organization

SOLUTION

Step 1   Find the sum of the data values.

$$\Sigma X = 11 + 90 + 33 + 49 + 27 = 210$$

Step 2   Square each value and find the sum.

$$\Sigma X^2 = 11^2 + 90^2 + 33^2 + 49^2 + 27^2 = 12,440$$

Step 3   Substitute in the formula and solve.

$$s^2 = \frac{n(\Sigma X^2) - (\Sigma X)^2}{n(n - 1)}$$

$$= \frac{5(12,440) - 210^2}{5(5 - 1)}$$

$$= \frac{62{,}200 - 44{,}100}{5(4)}$$

$$= \frac{18{,}100}{20}$$

$$= 905$$

The variance is 905.

$$s = \sqrt{905} \approx 30.1$$

The standard deviation is 30.1.

These values are the same as those found in Example 3–20.

Variance and Standard Deviation for Grouped Data

The procedure for finding the variance and standard deviation for grouped data is similar to that for finding the mean for grouped data, and it uses the midpoints of each class.

This procedure uses the shortcut formula, and X_m is the symbol for the class midpoint.

Shortcut or Computational Formula for s^2 and s for Grouped Data

Sample variance:

$$s^2 = \frac{n(\Sigma f \cdot X_m^2) - (\Sigma f \cdot X_m)^2}{n(n-1)}$$

Sample standard deviation

$$s = \sqrt{\frac{n(\Sigma f \cdot X_m^2) - (\Sigma f \cdot X_m)^2}{n(n-1)}}$$

where X_m is the midpoint of each class and f is the frequency of each class.

The steps for finding the sample variance and sample standard deviation for grouped data are summarized in this Procedure Table.

Procedure Table

Finding the Sample Variance and Standard Deviation for Grouped Data

Step 1 Make a table as shown, and find the midpoint of each class.

A Class	B Frequency	C Midpoint	D $f \cdot X_m$	E $f \cdot X_m^2$

Step 2 Multiply the frequency by the midpoint for each class, and place the products in column D.

Step 3 Multiply the frequency by the square of the midpoint, and place the products in column E.

Step 4 Find the sums of columns B, D, and E. (The sum of column B is n. The sum of column D is $\Sigma f \cdot X_m$. The sum of column E is $\Sigma f \cdot X_m^2$.)

Step 5 Substitute in the formula and solve to get the variance.

$$s^2 = \frac{n(\Sigma f \cdot X_m^2) - (\Sigma f \cdot X_m)^2}{n(n-1)}$$

Step 6 Take the square root to get the standard deviation.

EXAMPLE 3-22   Miles Run per Week

Find the sample variance and the sample standard deviation for the frequency distribution of the data shown. The data represent the number of miles that 20 runners ran during one week.

Class	Frequency	Midpoint
5.5–10.5	1	8
10.5–15.5	2	13
15.5–20.5	3	18
20.5–25.5	5	23
25.5–30.5	4	28
30.5–35.5	3	33
35.5–40.5	2	38

SOLUTION

Step 1   Make a table as shown, and find the midpoint of each class.

A Class	B Frequency f	C Midpoint X_m	D $f \cdot X_m$	E $f \cdot X_m^2$
5.5–10.5	1	8		
10.5–15.5	2	13		
15.5–20.5	3	18		
20.5–25.5	5	23		
25.5–30.5	4	28		
30.5–35.5	3	33		
35.5–40.5	2	38		

Step 2   Multiply the frequency by the midpoint for each class, and place the products in column D.

$$1 \cdot 8 = 8 \qquad 2 \cdot 13 = 26 \qquad \ldots \qquad 2 \cdot 38 = 76$$

Step 3   Multiply the frequency by the square of the midpoint, and place the products in column E.

$$1 \cdot 8^2 = 64 \qquad 2 \cdot 13^2 = 338 \qquad \ldots \qquad 2 \cdot 38^2 = 2888$$

Step 4   Find the sums of columns B, D, and E. The sum of column B is n, the sum of column D is $\Sigma f \cdot X_m$, and the sum of column E is $\Sigma f \cdot X_m^2$. The completed table is shown.

A Class	B Frequency	C Midpoint	D $f \cdot X_m$	E $f \cdot X_m^2$
5.5–10.5	1	8	8	64
10.5–15.5	2	13	26	338
15.5–20.5	3	18	54	972
20.5–25.5	5	23	115	2,645
25.5–30.5	4	28	112	3,136
30.5–35.5	3	33	99	3,267
35.5–40.5	2	38	76	2,888
	$n = 20$		$\Sigma f \cdot X_m = 490$	$\Sigma f \cdot X_m^2 = 13{,}310$

Step 5   Substitute in the formula and solve for s^2 to get the variance.

$$s^2 = \frac{n(\Sigma f \cdot X_m^2) - (\Sigma f \cdot X_m)^2}{n(n-1)}$$

$$= \frac{20(13{,}310) - 490^2}{20(20-1)}$$

$$= \frac{266{,}200 - 240{,}100}{20(19)}$$

$$= \frac{26{,}100}{380}$$

$$\approx 68.7$$

Step 6   Take the square root to get the standard deviation.

$$s \approx \sqrt{68.7} \approx 8.3$$

Be sure to use the number found in the sum of column B (i.e., the sum of the frequencies) for n. Do not use the number of classes.

The three measures of variation are summarized in Table 3–2.

TABLE 3–2 Summary of Measures of Variation

Measure	Definition	Symbol(s)
Range	Distance between highest value and lowest value	R
Variance	Average of the squares of the distance that each value is from the mean	σ^2, s^2
Standard deviation	Square root of the variance	σ, s

Uses of the Variance and Standard Deviation

1. As previously stated, variances and standard deviations can be used to determine the spread of the data. If the variance or standard deviation is large, the data are more dispersed. This information is useful in comparing two (or more) data sets to determine which is more (most) variable.

2. The measures of variance and standard deviation are used to determine the consistency of a variable. For example, in the manufacture of fittings, such as nuts and bolts, the variation in the diameters must be small, or else the parts will not fit together.

3. The variance and standard deviation are used to determine the number of data values that fall within a specified interval in a distribution. For example, Chebyshev's theorem (explained later) shows that, for any distribution, at least 75% of the data values will fall within 2 standard deviations of the mean.

4. Finally, the variance and standard deviation are used quite often in inferential statistics. These uses will be shown in later chapters of this textbook.

Coefficient of Variation

Whenever two samples have the same units of measure, the variance and standard deviation for each can be compared directly. For example, suppose an automobile dealer wanted to compare the standard deviation of miles driven for the cars she received as trade-ins on new cars. She found that for a specific year, the standard deviation for Buicks was 422 miles and the standard deviation for Cadillacs was 350 miles. She could say that the variation in mileage was greater in the Buicks. But what if a manager wanted to compare the standard deviations of two different variables, such as the number of sales per salesperson over a 3-month period and the commissions made by these salespeople?

A statistic that allows you to compare standard deviations when the units are different, as in this example, is called the *coefficient of variation.*

> The **coefficient of variation,** denoted by CVar, is the standard deviation divided by the mean. The result is expressed as a percentage.
>
> | For samples, | For populations, |
> |---|---|
> | $\text{CVar} = \dfrac{s}{\overline{X}} \cdot 100\%$ | $\text{CVar} = \dfrac{\sigma}{\mu} \cdot 100\%$ |

EXAMPLE 3–23   Space Launches

The mean number of successful space launches for six 10-year periods for the United States is 311.6. The standard deviation is 174.2. The mean number of successful space launches for six 10-year periods for Russia is 669.4. The standard deviation is 390.9. Compute the coefficient of variation for the two. Which data set is more variable?

SOLUTION

The coefficients of variation are

$$\text{U.S.:}\quad \text{CVar} = \frac{174.2}{311.6} \cdot 100\% \approx 0.56 = 56\%$$

$$\text{Russia:}\quad \text{CVar} = \frac{390.9}{669.4} \cdot 100\% \approx 0.58 = 58\%$$

The variation of the space launches for Russia is only slightly larger than the variation for the U.S. space launches since the coefficient of variation for Russia is larger than the coefficient for the United States.

EXAMPLE 3–24   Roller Coasters

The mean speed for the five fastest wooden roller coasters is 69.16 miles per hour, and the variance is 2.76. The mean height for the five tallest roller coasters is 177.80 feet, and the variance is 157.70. Compare the variations of the two data sets.

Source: Ultimate RollerCoaster.com

SOLUTION

$$\text{CVar} = \frac{\sqrt{2.76}}{69.16} \cdot 100\% \approx 2.4\%$$

$$\text{CVar} = \frac{\sqrt{157.70}}{177.80} \cdot 100\% \approx 7.1\%$$

The variation in the heights is slightly larger than the variation in the speeds of the roller coasters.

Range Rule of Thumb

The range can be used to approximate the standard deviation. The approximation is called the **range rule of thumb.**

> **The Range Rule of Thumb**
>
> A rough estimate of the standard deviation is
>
> $$s \approx \frac{\text{range}}{4}$$

In other words, if the range is divided by 4, an approximate value for the standard deviation is obtained. For example, the standard deviation for the data set 5, 8, 8, 9, 10, 12, and 13 is 2.7, and the range is $13 - 5 = 8$. The range rule of thumb is $s \approx 2$. The range rule of thumb in this case underestimates the standard deviation somewhat; however, it is in the ballpark.

A note of caution should be mentioned here. The range rule of thumb is only an *approximation* and should be used when the distribution of data values is unimodal and roughly symmetric.

The range rule of thumb can be used to estimate the largest and smallest data values of a data set. The smallest data value will be approximately 2 standard deviations below the mean, and the largest data value will be approximately 2 standard deviations above the mean of the data set. The mean for the previous data set is 9.3; hence,

$$\text{Smallest data value} = \overline{X} - 2s = 9.3 - 2(2.7) = 3.9$$

$$\text{Largest data value} = \overline{X} + 2s = 9.3 + 2(2.7) = 14.7$$

Notice that the smallest data value was 5, and the largest data value was 13. Again, these are rough approximations. For many data sets, almost all data values will fall within 2 standard deviations of the mean. Better approximations can be obtained by using Chebyshev's theorem and the empirical rule. These are explained next.

Chebyshev's Theorem

As stated previously, the variance and standard deviation of a variable can be used to determine the spread, or dispersion, of a variable. That is, the larger the variance or standard deviation, the more the data values are dispersed. For example, if two variables measured in the same units have the same mean, say, 70, and the first variable has a standard deviation of 1.5 while the second variable has a standard deviation of 10, then the data for the second variable will be more spread out than the data for the first variable. *Chebyshev's theorem,* developed by the Russian mathematician Chebyshev (1821–1894), specifies the proportions of the spread in terms of the standard deviation.

Chebyshev's theorem The proportion of values from a data set that will fall within k standard deviations of the mean will be at least $1 - 1/k^2$, where k is a number greater than 1 (k is not necessarily an integer).

This theorem states that at least three-fourths, or 75%, of the data values will fall within 2 standard deviations of the mean of the data set. This result is found by substituting $k = 2$ in the expression

$$1 - \frac{1}{k^2} \quad \text{or} \quad 1 - \frac{1}{2^2} = 1 - \frac{1}{4} = \frac{3}{4} = 75\%$$

For the example in which variable 1 has a mean of 70 and a standard deviation of 1.5, at least three-fourths, or 75%, of the data values fall between 67 and 73. These values are found by adding 2 standard deviations to the mean and subtracting 2 standard deviations from the mean, as shown:

$$70 + 2(1.5) = 70 + 3 = 73$$

and

$$70 - 2(1.5) = 70 - 3 = 67$$

For variable 2, at least three-fourths, or 75%, of the data values fall between 50 and 90. Again, these values are found by adding and subtracting, respectively, 2 standard deviations to and from the mean.

$$70 + 2(10) = 70 + 20 = 90$$

and

$$70 - 2(10) = 70 - 20 = 50$$

FIGURE 3–3

Chebyshev's Theorem

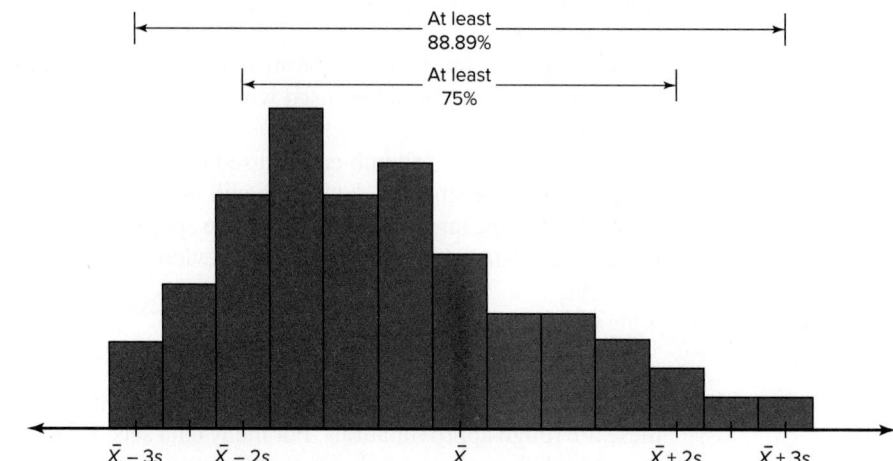

Furthermore, the theorem states that at least eight-ninths, or 88.89%, of the data values will fall within 3 standard deviations of the mean. This result is found by letting $k = 3$ and substituting in the expression.

$$1 - \frac{1}{k^2} \quad \text{or} \quad 1 - \frac{1}{3^2} = 1 - \frac{1}{9} = \frac{8}{9} = 88.89\%$$

For variable 1, at least eight-ninths, or 88.89%, of the data values fall between 65.5 and 74.5, since

$$70 + 3(1.5) = 70 + 4.5 = 74.5$$

and

$$70 - 3(1.5) = 70 - 4.5 = 65.5$$

For variable 2, at least eight-ninths, or 88.89%, of the data values fall between 40 and 100. In summary, then, Chebyshev's theorem states

- At least three-fourths, or 75%, of all data values fall within 2 standard deviations of the mean.

- At least eight-ninths, or 89%, of all data values fall within 3 standard deviations of the mean.

This theorem can be applied to any distribution regardless of its shape (see Figure 3–3). Examples 3–25 and 3–26 illustrate the application of Chebyshev's theorem.

EXAMPLE 3–25 Prices of Homes

The mean price of houses in a certain neighborhood is $50,000, and the standard deviation is $10,000. Find the price range for which at least 75% of the houses will sell.

SOLUTION

Chebyshev's theorem states that three-fourths, or 75%, of the data values will fall within 2 standard deviations of the mean. Thus,

$$\$50,000 + 2(\$10,000) = \$50,000 + \$20,000 = \$70,000$$

and

$$\$50,000 - 2(\$10,000) = \$50,000 - \$20,000 = \$30,000$$

Hence, at least 75% of all homes sold in the area will have a price range from $30,000 to $70,000.

Chebyshev's theorem can be used to find the minimum percentage of data values that will fall between any two given values. The procedure is shown in Example 3–26.

EXAMPLE 3–26   Travel Allowances

A survey of local companies found that the mean amount of travel allowance for couriers was $0.25 per mile. The standard deviation was $0.02. Using Chebyshev's theorem, find the minimum percentage of the data values that will fall between $0.20 and $0.30.

SOLUTION

Step 1   Subtract the mean from the larger value.
$$\$0.30 - \$0.25 = \$0.05$$

Step 2   Divide the difference by the standard deviation to get k.
$$k = \frac{0.05}{0.02} = 2.5$$

Step 3   Use Chebyshev's theorem to find the percentage.
$$1 - \frac{1}{k^2} = 1 - \frac{1}{2.5^2} = 1 - \frac{1}{6.25} = 1 - 0.16 = 0.84 \quad \text{or} \quad 84\%$$

Hence, at least 84% of the data values will fall between $0.20 and $0.30.

The Empirical (Normal) Rule

Chebyshev's theorem applies to any distribution regardless of its shape. However, when a distribution is *bell-shaped* (or what is called *normal*), the following statements, which make up the **empirical rule,** are true.

- Approximately 68% of the data values will fall within 1 standard deviation of the mean.

- Approximately 95% of the data values will fall within 2 standard deviations of the mean.

- Approximately 99.7% of the data values will fall within 3 standard deviations of the mean.

For example, suppose that the scores on a national achievement exam have a mean of 480 and a standard deviation of 90. If these scores are normally distributed, then approximately 68% will fall between 390 and 570 (480 + 90 = 570 and 480 − 90 = 390). Approximately 95% of the scores will fall between 300 and 660 (480 + 2 · 90 = 660 and 480 − 2 · 90 = 300). Approximately 99.7% will fall between 210 and 750 (480 + 3 · 90 = 750 and 480 − 3 · 90 = 210). See Figure 3–4. (The empirical rule is explained in greater detail in Chapter 6.)

FIGURE 3–4
The Empirical Rule

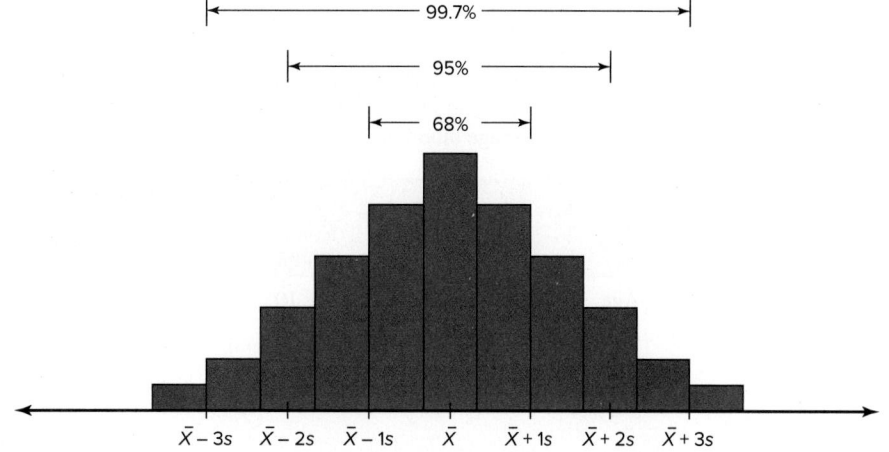

Because the empirical rule requires that the distribution be approximately bell-shaped, the results are more accurate than those of Chebyshev's theorem, which applies to all distributions.

Linear Transformation of Data

In statistics, sometimes it is necessary to transform the data values into other data values. For example, if you are using temperature values collected from Canada, these values will be given using the Celsius temperature scale. If the study is to be used in the United States, you might want to change the data values to the Fahrenheit temperature scale. This change is called the *linear transformation of the data.* The question then arises, How does a linear transformation of the data values affect the mean and standard deviation of the data values?

Let's look at an example. Suppose you own a small store with five employees. Their hourly salaries are

$$\$10 \qquad \$13 \qquad \$10 \qquad \$11 \qquad \$16$$

The mean of the salaries is $\overline{X} = \$12$, and the standard deviation is 2.550. Suppose you decide after a profitable year to give each employee a raise of $1.00 per hour. The new salaries would be

$$\$11 \qquad \$14 \qquad \$11 \qquad \$12 \qquad \$17$$

The mean of the new salaries is $\overline{X} = \$13$, and the standard deviation of the new salaries is 2.550. Notice that the value of the mean increases by the amount that was added to each data value, and the standard deviation does not change.

Suppose that the five employees worked the number of hours per week shown here.

$$15 \qquad 12 \qquad 18 \qquad 20 \qquad 10$$

The mean for the number of hours for the original data is $\overline{X} = 15$, and the standard deviation for the number of hours is 4.123. You next decide to double the amount of each employee's hours for December. How does this affect the mean and standard deviation of the variable?

If each data value is multiplied by 2, the new data set is

$$30 \qquad 24 \qquad 36 \qquad 40 \qquad 20$$

The mean of the new data set is $\overline{X} = 30$, and the standard deviation is 8.246. The values of the mean and standard deviation double.

Hence, when each data value is multiplied by a constant, the mean of the new data set will be equal to the constant times the mean of the original set, and the standard deviation of the new data set will be equal to the absolute value (positive value) of the constant times the standard deviation of the original data set.

Applying the Concepts 3–2

Blood Pressure

The table lists means and standard deviations. The mean is the number before the plus/minus, and the standard deviation is the number after the plus/minus. The results are from a study attempting to find the average blood pressure of older adults. Use the results to answer the questions.

	Normotensive		Hypertensive	
	Men (*n* = 1200)	**Women** (*n* = 1400)	**Men** (*n* = 1100)	**Women** (*n* = 1300)
Age	55 ± 10	55 ± 10	60 ± 10	64 ± 10
Blood pressure (mm Hg)				
Systolic	123 ± 9	121 ± 11	153 ± 17	156 ± 20
Diastolic	78 ± 7	76 ± 7	91 ± 10	88 ± 10

1. Apply Chebyshev's theorem to the systolic blood pressure of normotensive men. At least how many of the men in the study fall within 1 standard deviation of the mean?

2. At least how many of those men in the study fall within 2 standard deviations of the mean?

Assume that blood pressure is normally distributed among older adults. Answer the following questions, using the empirical rule instead of Chebyshev's theorem.

3. What are the ranges for the diastolic blood pressure (normotensive and hypertensive) of older women?

4. Do the normotensive, male, systolic blood pressure ranges overlap with the hypertensive, male, systolic blood pressure ranges?

See page 186 for the answers.

Exercises 3–2

1. What is the relationship between the variance and the standard deviation? The square root of the variance is the standard deviation.

2. Why might the range *not* be the best estimate of variability? One extremely high or one extremely low data value will influence the range.

3. What are the symbols used to represent the population variance and standard deviation? σ^2; σ

4. What are the symbols used to represent the sample variance and standard deviation? s^2; s

5. Why is the unbiased estimator of variance used?

6. The three data sets have the same mean and range, but is the variation the same? Prove your answer by computing the standard deviation. Assume the data were obtained from samples.
   a. 5, 7, 9, 11, 13, 15, 17
   b. 5, 6, 7, 11, 15, 16, 17
   c. 5, 5, 5, 11, 17, 17, 17 No, the standard deviations are $s = 4.3$, $s = 5.1$, and $s = 6$. So *a* has the smallest variation and *c* has the biggest variation.

7. **Traveler Spending** The data show the traveler spending in billions of dollars for a recent year for a sample of the states. Find the range, variance, and standard deviation for the data. 90.7; 891.88; 29.86

20.1	33.5	21.7	58.4	23.2	110.8	30.9
24.0	74.8	60.0				

   Source: U.S. Travel Agency.

8. **Cigarette Taxes** The increases (in cents) in cigarette taxes for 17 states in a 6-month period are

   60, 20, 40, 40, 45, 12, 34, 51, 30, 70, 42, 31, 69, 32, 8, 18, 50

   Find the range, variance, and standard deviation for the data. Use the range rule of thumb to estimate the standard deviation. Compare the estimate to the actual standard deviation. 62; 332.4; 18.2; using the range rule of thumb, $s \approx 15.5$. This is close to the actual standard deviation of 18.2.

   Source: Federation of Tax Administrators.

9. **Sugar Bowl Winner Scores** The data show the scores of the winning teams of the Sugar Bowls for a recent 20-year period. Find the range, variance, and standard deviation for the data. 35; 98.8; 9.9

35	48	42	45	33	23	31	51	31	41	41	38	16
21	26	47	37	46	24	31						

   Source: The World Almanac

10. **Size of U.S. States** The total surface area (in square miles) for each of six selected eastern states is listed here.

28,995	PA	37,534	FL
31,361	NY	27,087	VA
20,966	ME	37,741	GA

    The total surface area for each of six selected western states is listed (in square miles).

72,964	AZ	70,763	NV
101,510	CA	62,161	OR
66,625	CO	54,339	UT

    Find the standard deviation for each data set. Which set is more variable?

    Source: New York Times Almanac.

11. **Multiple Births** The numbers of various multiple births in the United States for the past 10 years are listed. Find the range, variance, and standard deviation of the data sets. Which set of data is the most variable?

Triplets			Quadruplets			Quintuplets		
5877	7110	5937	345	468	369	46	85	91
6898	6118	6885	434	355	501	69	67	85
6208	6742	6750	418	506	439	68	77	86
	6742			512			67	

    Source: World Almanac 2012.

12. **Marathon Winners** The data show the times of a random sample of local marathon winners in hours. Find the range, variance, and standard deviation for the data.

3.2	2.6	2.4	2.4	2.3	2.4

    0.9; 0.111; 0.333

13. Ages of U.S. Astronaut Candidates The average age of U.S. astronaut candidates in the past has been 34, but candidates have ranged in age from 26 to 46. Use the range rule of thumb to estimate the standard deviation of the applicants' ages. $s \approx R/4$ so $s \approx 5$ years.

Source: www.nasa.gov

14. SAT Scores The means over several years of the math and reading and writing SAT scores are given. Find the range, variance, and standard deviation of the data. Compare the results. Math 19, 30.6, 5.53
Reading and writing 108, 900, 30
The reading and writing scores are more variable.

Math

515	514	514	514	513	511	508	527

Reading and writing

500	497	494	496	497	425	494	533

Source: The College Board

15. Space Launches The number of successful space launches by Russia and the United States over each 10-year period from 1966 is shown. Find the range, variance, and standard deviation for each data set and compare the results. Russia 933; 187,489; 433
United States 491; 30,276; 174
The Russian launches are more variable.

Russia

399	1028	1132	542	246	199

United States

614	247	191	300	206	123

Source: The World Almanac

16. Passenger Vehicle Deaths The number of people killed in each state from passenger vehicle crashes for a specific year is shown. Find the range, variance, and standard deviation for the data. 2721; 355,427.6; 596.2

778	309	1110	324	705
1067	826	76	205	152
218	492	65	186	712
193	262	452	875	82
730	1185	2707	1279	390
305	123	948	343	602
69	451	951	104	985
155	450	2080	565	875
414	981	2786	82	793
214	130	396	620	797

Source: National Highway Traffic Safety Administration.

17. Annual Precipitation Days The number of annual precipitation days for one-half of the 50 largest U.S. cities is listed below. Find the range, variance, and standard deviation of the data. 130; 1156.7; 34.0

135	128	136	78	116	77	111	79	44	97
116	123	88	102	26	82	156	133	107	35
112	98	45	122	125					

18. Use the data from Exercises 7, 15, and 17 (travelers' spending, space launches, and precipitation) and compare the standard deviation with that obtained by the range rule of thumb (R/4.) Comment on the results.

19. Road Service Times A recent survey of 60 randomly selected drivers found the following frequency distribution it took in minutes to get road side service. Find the variance and standard deviation for the data. 74.4; 8.6

Time	Frequency
22–28	7
29–35	5
36–42	28
43–49	12
50–56	5
57–63	3
	60

20. Speeds of the Daytona 500 Winners The frequency distribution shows the average speeds in miles per hour of the recent Daytona 500 winners. Find the variance and standard deviation for the data. 98.8; 9.94

Class	Frequency
130–138	5
139–147	6
148–156	11
157–165	7
166–174	1

Source: The World Almanac

21. Fire Calls The frequency distribution shows the number of fire calls per month a volunteer fire department received over a 2-year period. Find the variance and standard deviation for the data. 11.3; 3.4

Class	Frequency
3–5	2
6–8	6
9–11	10
12–14	3
15–17	3

22. Texts Sent Daily A survey by Experian Marketing found that people age 18–24 receive on average 72 texts per day. A survey of 50 randomly selected people age 18–24 found the following data. Find the variance and standard deviation of the data. 88.9; 9.4

Class	Frequency
50–58	8
59–67	14
68–76	19
77–85	7
86–94	2
	50

23. Miles Traveled to Work A recent survey found the following distribution in miles that people travel to work. Find the mean, variance, and standard deviation of the data. 8.8; 32.6; 5.7

Miles	Frequency
1–5	30
6–10	21
11–15	17
16–20	10
21–25	2
	80

Source: Based on information from the Department of Transportation

24. Driving to Work The following distribution shows the number of minutes 30 randomly selected drivers take to get to work. Find the mean, variance, and standard deviation of the data. 16.7; 29.2; 5.4

Class	Frequency
5–9	3
10–14	5
15–19	16
20–24	4
25–29	1
30–34	1

25. Time It Takes to Find a Job A statistic on *Jobrite* found that it takes on average 43 days for a person to find a high-level job. A study of 40 randomly selected individuals found the following frequency distribution for the time in days it took each person to find a job. Find the variance and standard deviation for the data. 29.1; 5.4

Days	Frequency
31–35	7
36–40	10
41–45	16
46–50	5
51–55	2
	40

26. Weight Gain of First-Year College Students It has been hypothesized that the average weight gain by first-year college students is 15 pounds. The frequency distribution shows the weight gain in pounds for 20 first-year college students. Find the variance and standard deviation for the data. Those who lost weight were not included in the data. 12.7; 3.6

Class	Frequency
0–2	2
3–5	12
6–8	16
9–11	5
12–14	3
15–17	2
	40

27. Missing Work The average number of days that construction workers miss per year is 11. The standard deviation is 2.3. The average number of days that factory workers miss per year is 8 with a standard deviation of 1.8. Which class is more variable in terms of days missed? CVar = 20.9%; CVar = 22.5%. The factory workers' data are more variable.

28. Suspension Bridges The lengths (in feet) of the main span of the longest suspension bridges in the United States and the rest of the world are shown below. Which set of data is more variable?

United States 4205, 4200, 3800, 3500, 3478, 2800, 2800, 2310
World   6570, 5538, 5328, 4888, 4626, 4544, 4518, 3970

Source: World Almanac.

29. Hospital Emergency Waiting Times The mean of the waiting times in an emergency room is 80.2 minutes with a standard deviation of 10.5 minutes for people who are admitted for additional treatment. The mean waiting time for patients who are discharged after receiving treatment is 120.6 minutes with a standard deviation of 18.3 minutes. Which times are more variable?

30. Ages of Accountants The average age of the accountants at Three Rivers Corp. is 26 years, with a standard deviation of 6 years; the average salary of the accountants is $31,000, with a standard deviation of $4000. Compare the variations of age and income. CVar = 23.1%; CVar = 12.9%; age is more variable.

31. Using Chebyshev's theorem, solve these problems for a distribution with a mean of 80 and a standard deviation of 10.

a. At least what percentage of values will fall between 60 and 100? 75%

b. At least what percentage of values will fall between 65 and 95? 56%

32. The mean of a distribution is 20 and the standard deviation is 2. Use Chebyshev's theorem.

a. At least what percentage of the values will fall between 10 and 30? 96%

b. At least what percentage of the values will fall between 12 and 28? 93.75%

33. In a distribution of 160 values with a mean of 72, at least 120 fall within the interval 67–77. Approximately what percentage of values should fall in the interval 62–82? Use Chebyshev's theorem. At least 93.75%

34. Calories in Bagels The average number of calories in a regular-size bagel is 240. If the standard deviation is 38 calories, find the range in which at least 75% of the data will lie. Use Chebyshev's theorem. Between 164 and 316 calories

35. Time Spent Online Americans spend an average of 3 hours per day online. If the standard deviation is 32 minutes, find the range in which at least 88.89% of the data will lie. Use Chebyshev's theorem.

Source: www.cs.cmu.edu Between 84 and 276 minutes

36. Solid Waste Production The average college student produces 640 pounds of solid waste each year. If the standard deviation is approximately 85 pounds, within what weight limits will at least 88.89% of all students' garbage lie? Between 385 and 895 pounds

Source: Environmental Sustainability Committee, www.esc.mtu.edu

37. Sale Price of Homes The average sale price of one-family houses in the United States for January 2016 was $258,100. Find the range of values in which at least 75% of the sale prices will lie if the standard deviation is $48,500. Between $161,100 and $355,100.

Source: YCharts.com

38. Trials to Learn a Maze The average of the number of trials it took a sample of mice to learn to traverse a maze was 12. The standard deviation was 3. Using Chebyshev's theorem, find the minimum percentage of data values that will fall in the range of 4–20 trials. At least 86%

39. Farm Sizes The average farm in the United States in 2014 contained 504 acres. The standard deviation is 55.7 acres. Use Chebyshev's theorem to find the minimum percentage of data values that will fall in the range of 364.75 and 643.25 acres. At least 84%

Source: World Almanac.

40. Citrus Fruit Consumption The average U.S. yearly per capita consumption of citrus fruit is 26.8 pounds. Suppose that the distribution of fruit amounts consumed is bell-shaped with a standard deviation equal to 4.2 pounds. What percentage of Americans would you expect to consume more than 31 pounds of citrus fruit per year? About 16%

Source: USDA/Economic Research Service.

41. SAT Scores The national average for mathematics SATs in 2014 was 538. Suppose that the distribution of scores was approximately bell-shaped and that the standard deviation was approximately 48. Within what boundaries would you expect 68% of the scores to fall? What percentage of scores would be above 634? 490–586; About 2.5%

42. Work Hours for College Faculty The average full-time faculty member in a postsecondary degree-granting institution works an average of 53 hours per week.

a. If we assume the standard deviation is 2.8 hours, what percentage of faculty members work more than 58.6 hours a week? 25%

b. If we assume a bell-shaped distribution, what percentage of faculty members work more than 58.6 hours a week? About 2.5%

Source: National Center for Education Statistics.

43. Prices of Musical Instruments The average price of an instrument at a small music store is $325. The standard deviation of the price is $52. If the owner decides to raise the price of all the instruments by $20, what will be the new mean and standard deviation of the prices? $345; $52

44. Hours of Employment The mean and standard deviation of the number of hours the employees work in the music store per week are, respectively, 18.6 and 3.2 hours. If the owner increases the number of hours each employee works per week by 4 hours, what will be the new mean and standard deviation of the number of hours worked by the employees?

45. Price of Pet Fish The mean price of the fish in a pet shop is $2.17, and the standard deviation of the price is $0.55. If the owner decides to triple the prices, what will be the mean and standard deviation of the new prices?

46. Bonuses The mean and standard deviation of the bonuses that the employees of a company received 10 years ago were, respectively, $2000 and $325. Today the amount of the bonuses is 5 times what it was 10 years ago. Find the mean and standard deviation of the new bonuses.

≡ Extending the Concepts

47. Serum Cholesterol Levels For this data set, find the mean and standard deviation of the variable. The data represent the serum cholesterol levels of 30 individuals. Count the number of data values that fall within 2 standard deviations of the mean. Compare this with the number obtained from Chebyshev's theorem. Comment on the answer.

211	240	255	219	204
200	212	193	187	205
256	203	210	221	249
231	212	236	204	187
201	247	206	187	200
237	227	221	192	196

$\bar{X} = 215.0$, $s = 20.8$. All the data values fall within 2 standard deviations of the mean. This agrees with Chebyshev's theorem, which states that at least 75% of the data values will fall within 2 standard deviations of the mean.

48. Ages of Consumers For this data set, find the mean and standard deviation of the variable. The data represent the ages of 30 customers who ordered a product advertised on television. Count the number of data values that fall within 2 standard deviations of the mean. Compare this with the number obtained from Chebyshev's theorem. Comment on the answer. $\bar{X} = 34.5$, $s = 13.3$; 28 of the values (93.3%). All but two data values fall within 2 standard deviations of the mean. This agrees with Chebyshev's theorem, which states that at least 75% of the data values will fall within 2 standard deviations of the mean.

42	44	62	35	20
30	56	20	23	41
55	22	31	27	66
21	18	24	42	25
32	50	31	26	36
39	40	18	36	22

49. Using Chebyshev's theorem, complete the table to find the minimum percentage of data values that fall within k standard deviations of the mean.

k	1.5	2	2.5	3	3.5
Percent	56	75	84	89	92

50. Use this data set: 10, 20, 30, 40, 50

    a. Find the standard deviation. 15.8

    b. Add 5 to each value, and then find the standard deviation. 15.8

    c. Subtract 5 from each value and find the standard deviation. 15.8

    d. Multiply each value by 5 and find the standard deviation. 79.1

    e. Divide each value by 5 and find the standard deviation. 3.2

    f. Generalize the results of parts *b* through *e*.

    g. Compare these results with those in Exercise 35 of Exercises 3–1.

51. Mean Deviation The mean deviation is found by using this formula:

$$\text{Mean deviation} = \frac{\Sigma |X - \overline{X}|}{n}$$

where X = value

    $\overline{X}$ = mean

    n = number of values

    $||$ = absolute value

Find the mean deviation for these data.

5, 9, 10, 11, 11, 12, 15, 18, 20, 22 4.36

52. Pearson Coefficient of Skewness A measure to determine the skewness of a distribution is called the *Pearson coefficient (PC) of skewness*. The formula is

$$PC = \frac{3(\overline{X} - MD)}{s}$$

The values of the coefficient usually range from -3 to $+3$. When the distribution is symmetric, the coefficient is zero; when the distribution is positively skewed, it is positive; and when the distribution is negatively skewed, it is negative.

Using the formula, find the coefficient of skewness for each distribution, and describe the shape of the distribution.

    a. Mean = 10, median = 8, standard deviation = 3.

    b. Mean = 42, median = 45, standard deviation = 4.

    c. Mean = 18.6, median = 18.6, standard deviation = 1.5.

    d. Mean = 98, median = 97.6, standard deviation = 4.

53. All values of a data set must be within $s\sqrt{n-1}$ of the mean. If a person collected 25 data values that had a mean of 50 and a standard deviation of 3 and you saw that one data value was 67, what would you conclude?

Technology Step by Step

EXCEL
Step by Step

Finding Measures of Variation

Example XL3–2

Find the sample variance, sample standard deviation, and range of the data from Example 3–20.

    11   90   33   49   27

1. On an Excel worksheet enter the data in cells A2–A7. Enter a label for the variable in cell A1.
2. In a blank cell enter = **VAR.S(A2:A6)** for the sample variance.
3. In a blank cell enter = **STDEV.S(A2:A6)** for the sample standard deviation.
4. For the range, compute the difference between the maximum and the minimum values by entering = **Max(A2:A6)-Min(A2:A6)**.

Note: The command for computing the population variance is VAR.P and for the population standard deviation is STDEV.P

These and other statistical functions can also be accessed without typing them into the worksheet directly.

1. Select the Formulas tab from the Toolbar and select the Insert Function Icon, f_x .
2. Select the Statistical category for statistical functions.
3. Scroll to find the appropriate function and click [OK].

	A	B	C	D
1	Sulfur Dioxide in Millions of Tons			
2	11			
3	90		Variance	905
4	33		Standard Deviation	30.08322
5	49		Range	79
6	27			

3–3   Measures of Position

OBJECTIVE ③

Identify the position of a data value in a data set, using various measures of position, such as percentiles, deciles, and quartiles.

In addition to measures of central tendency and measures of variation, there are measures of position or location. These measures include standard scores, percentiles, deciles, and quartiles. They are used to locate the relative position of a data value in the data set. For example, if a value is located at the 80th percentile, it means that 80% of the values fall below it in the distribution and 20% of the values fall above it. The *median* is the value that corresponds to the 50th percentile, since one-half of the values fall below it and one-half of the values fall above it. This section discusses these measures of position.

Standard Scores

There is an old saying, "You can't compare apples and oranges." But with the use of statistics, it can be done to some extent. Suppose that a student scored 90 on a music test and 45 on an English exam. Direct comparison of raw scores is impossible, since the exams might not be equivalent in terms of number of questions, value of each question, and so on. However, a comparison of a relative standard similar to both can be made. This comparison uses the mean and standard deviation and is called a *standard score* or *z* score. (We also use *z* scores in later chapters.)

A standard score or *z* score tells how many standard deviations a data value is above or below the mean for a specific distribution of values. If a standard score is zero, then the data value is the same as the mean.

A **z score** or **standard score** for a value is obtained by subtracting the mean from the value and dividing the result by the standard deviation. The symbol for a standard score is *z*. The formula is

$$z = \frac{\text{value} - \text{mean}}{\text{standard deviation}}$$

For samples, the formula is

$$z = \frac{X - \overline{X}}{s}$$

For populations, the formula is

$$z = \frac{X - \mu}{\sigma}$$

The *z* score represents the number of standard deviations that a data value falls above or below the mean.

For the purpose of this section, it will be assumed that when we find *z* scores, the data were obtained from samples.

EXAMPLE 3–27   Chloride Levels

A man's blood level of chloride was 104 mEq/L and the mean level for men is 102 mEq/L with a standard deviation of 2.8 mEq/L. The chloride level in a woman is 107 mEq/L. The mean level of chloride for women is 104 mEq/L with a standard deviation of 3.2 mEq/L. Compare the relative positions of the chloride levels for men and women.

SOLUTION

Find the *z* scores for both subjects.

For the man $z = \dfrac{X - \mu}{\sigma} = \dfrac{104 - 102}{2.8} = 0.71$

For the woman $z = \dfrac{X - \mu}{\sigma} = \dfrac{107 - 104}{3.2} = 0.94$

Since the z score for the women is higher than the z score for the man, her relative position for the chloride levels is higher than the man's relative level.

Note that if the z score is positive, the score is above the mean. If the z score is 0, the score is the same as the mean. And if the z score is negative, the score is below the mean.

EXAMPLE 3–28   Marriage Ages

In a recent study, the mean age at which men get married is said to be 26.4 years with a standard deviation of 2 years. The mean age at which women marry is 23.5 years with a standard deviation of 2.3 years. Find the relative positions for a man who marries at age 24 and a woman who marries at age 22.

SOLUTION

$$\text{Man } z = \frac{X - \overline{X}}{s} = \frac{24 - 26.4}{2} = -1.2$$

$$\text{Woman } z = \frac{X - \overline{X}}{s} = \frac{22 - 23.5}{2.3} \approx -0.65$$

In this case, the woman's age at marriage is relatively higher than the man's age at marriage.

When all data for a variable are transformed into z scores, the resulting distribution will have a mean of 0 and a standard deviation of 1. A z score, then, is actually the number of standard deviations each value is from the mean for a specific distribution. In Example 3–27, the woman's chloride level was 0.94 standard deviations above the mean, while the man's chloride level was 0.71 standard deviations above the mean. This will be explained in greater detail in Chapter 6.

Percentiles

Percentiles are position measures used in educational and health-related fields to indicate the position of an individual in a group.

Percentiles divide the data set into 100 equal groups.

Percentiles are symbolized by

$$P_1, P_2, P_3, \ldots, P_{99}$$

and divide the distribution into 100 groups.

TABLE 3–3 Percentile Ranks and Scaled Scores on the Test of English as a Foreign Language*

Scaled score	Section 1: Listening comprehension	Section 2: Structure and written expression	Section 3: Vocabulary and reading comprehension	Total scaled score	Percentile rank
68	99	98			
66	98	96	98	660	99
64	96	94	96	640	97
62	92	90	93	620	94
60	87	84	88	600	89
→58	81	76	81	580	82
56	73	68	72	560	73
54	64	58	61	540	62
52	54	48	50	520	50
50	42	38	40	500	39
48	32	29	30	480	29
46	22	21	23	460	20
44	14	15	16	440	13
42	9	10	11	420	9
40	5	7	8	400	5
38	3	4	5	380	3
36	2	3	3	360	1
34	1	2	2	340	1
32		1	1	320	
30		1	1	300	
Mean	51.5	52.2	51.4	517	Mean
S.D.	7.1	7.9	7.5	68	S.D.

*Based on the total group of 1,178,193 examinees.

Source: Data from Educational Testing Service.

In many situations, the graphs and tables showing the percentiles for various measures such as test scores, heights, or weights have already been completed. Table 3–3 shows the percentile ranks for scaled scores on the Test of English as a Foreign Language. If a student had a scaled score of 58 for section 1 (listening and comprehension), that student would have a percentile rank of 81. Hence, that student did better than 81% of the students who took section 1 of the exam.

Figure 3–5 shows percentiles in graphical form of weights of girls from ages 2 to 18. To find the percentile rank of an 11-year-old who weighs 82 pounds, start at the 82-pound weight on the left axis and move horizontally to the right. Find 11 on the horizontal axis and move up vertically. The two lines meet at the 50th percentile curved line; hence, an 11-year-old girl who weighs 82 pounds is in the 50th percentile for her age group. If the lines do not meet exactly on one of the curved percentile lines, then the percentile rank must be approximated.

Percentiles are also used to compare an individual's test score with the national norm. For example, tests such as the National Educational Development Test (NEDT) are taken by students in ninth or tenth grade. A student's scores are compared with those of other

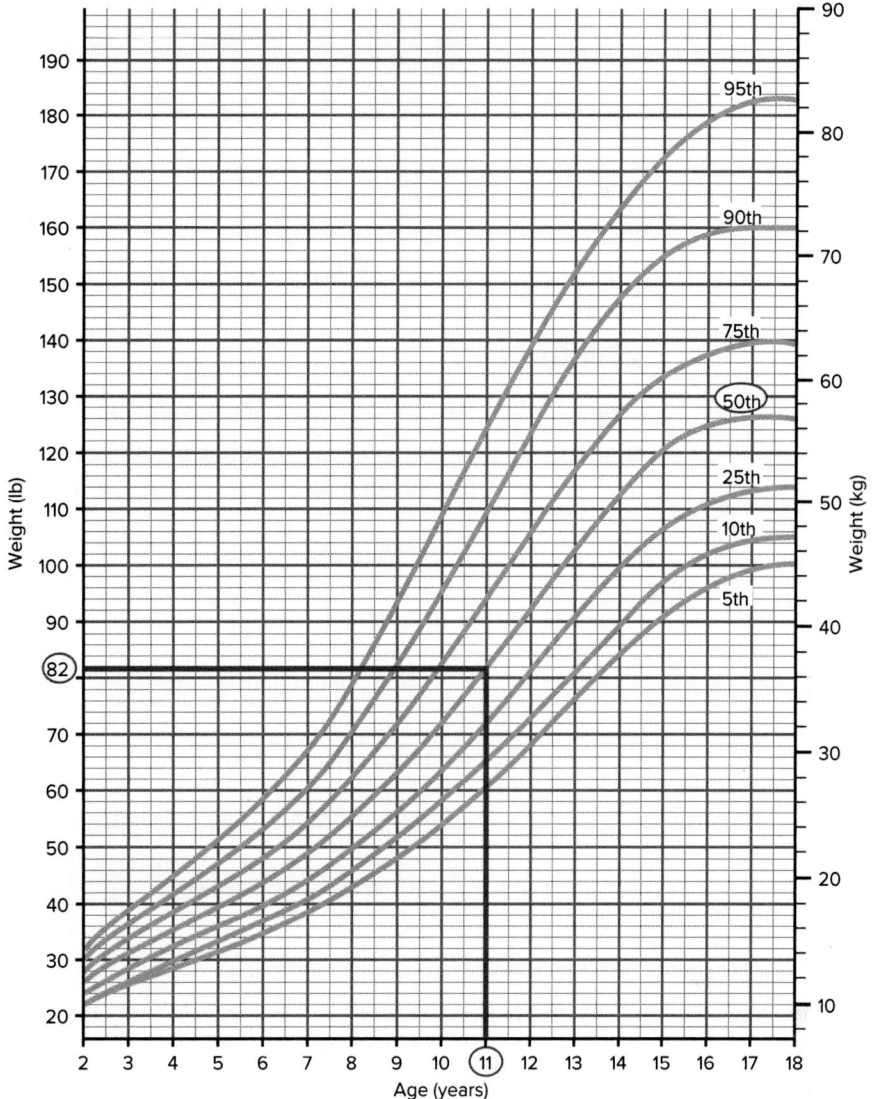

FIGURE 3–5

Weights of Girls by Age and Percentile Rankings

Source: Centers for Disease Control and Prevention

students locally and nationally by using percentile ranks. A similar test for elementary school students is called the California Achievement Test.

Percentiles are not the same as percentages. That is, if a student gets 72 correct answers out of a possible 100, she obtains a percentage score of 72. There is no indication of her position with respect to the rest of the class. She could have scored the highest, the lowest, or somewhere in between. On the other hand, if a raw score of 72 corresponds to the 64th percentile, then she did better than 64% of the students in her class.

Percentile graphs can be constructed as shown in Example 3–29 and Figure 3–6. Percentile graphs use the same values as the cumulative relative frequency graphs described in Section 2–2, except that the proportions have been converted to percents.

EXAMPLE 3–29   Systolic Blood Pressure

The frequency distribution for the systolic blood pressure readings (in millimeters of mercury, mm Hg) of 200 randomly selected college students is shown here. Construct a percentile graph.

A Class boundaries	B Frequency	C Cumulative frequency	D Cumulative percent
89.5–104.5	24		
104.5–119.5	62		
119.5–134.5	72		
134.5–149.5	26		
149.5–164.5	12		
164.5–179.5	$\underline{4}$		
	200		

SOLUTION

Step 1   Find the cumulative frequencies and place them in column C.

Step 2   Find the cumulative percentages and place them in column D. To do this step, use the formula

$$\text{Cumulative \%} = \frac{\text{cumulative frequency}}{n} \cdot 100$$

For the first class,

$$\text{Cumulative \%} = \frac{24}{200} \cdot 100 = 12\%$$

The completed table is shown here.

A Class boundaries	B Frequency	C Cumulative frequency	D Cumulative percent
89.5–104.5	24	24	12
104.5–119.5	62	86	43
119.5–134.5	72	158	79
134.5–149.5	26	184	92
149.5–164.5	12	196	98
164.5–179.5	$\underline{4}$	200	100
	200		

Step 3   Graph the data, using class boundaries for the x axis and the percentages for the y axis, as shown in Figure 3–6.

Once a percentile graph has been constructed, one can find the approximate corresponding percentile ranks for given blood pressure values and find approximate blood pressure values for given percentile ranks.

For example, to find the percentile rank of a blood pressure reading of 130, find 130 on the x axis of Figure 3–6 and draw a vertical line to the graph. Then move horizontally to the value on the y axis. Note that a blood pressure of 130 corresponds to approximately the 70th percentile.

If the value that corresponds to the 40th percentile is desired, start on the y axis at 40 and draw a horizontal line to the graph. Then draw a vertical line to the x axis and read the value. In Figure 3–6, the 40th percentile corresponds to a value of approximately 118. Thus, if a person has a blood pressure of 118, that person is at the 40th percentile.

Finding values and the corresponding percentile ranks by using a graph yields only approximate answers. Several mathematical methods exist for computing percentiles for data. These methods can be used to find the approximate percentile rank of a data value

FIGURE 3-6

Percentile Graph for
Example 3-29

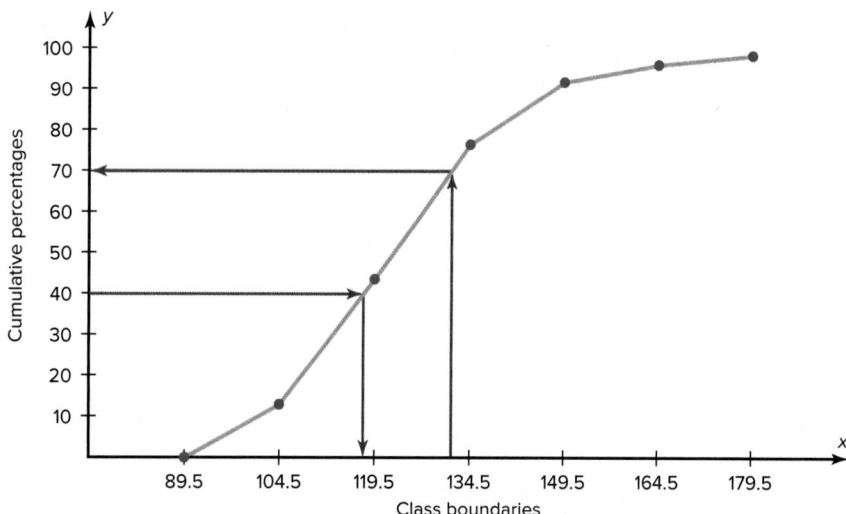

or to find a data value corresponding to a given percentile. When the data set is large (100 or more), these methods yield better results. Examples 3–30 and 3–31 show these methods.

Percentile Formula

The percentile corresponding to a given value X is computed by using the following formula:

$$\text{Percentile} = \frac{(\text{number of values below } X) + 0.5}{\text{total number of values}} \cdot 100$$

EXAMPLE 3-30   Traffic Violations

The number of traffic violations recorded by a police department for a 10-day period is shown. Find the percentile rank of 16.

$$22 \quad 19 \quad 25 \quad 24 \quad 18 \quad 15 \quad 9 \quad 12 \quad 16 \quad 20$$

SOLUTION

Arrange the data in order from lowest to highest.

$$9 \quad 12 \quad 15 \quad 16 \quad 18 \quad 19 \quad 20 \quad 22 \quad 24 \quad 25$$

Then substitute into the formula.

$$\text{Percentile} = \frac{(\text{number of values below } X) + 0.5}{\text{total number of values}} \cdot 100$$

Since there are 3 numbers below the value of 16, the solution is

$$\text{Percentile} = \frac{3 + 0.5}{10} \cdot 100 = 35\text{th percentile}$$

Hence, the value of 16 is higher than 35% of the data values.

Note: One assumes that a value of 16, for instance, means theoretically any value between 15.5 and 16.5.

EXAMPLE 3–31   Traffic Violations

Using the data in Example 3–30, find the percentile rank of 24.

SOLUTION

There are 8 values below 24; thus,

$$\text{Percentile} = \frac{8 + 0.5}{10} \cdot 100 = 85\text{th percentile}$$

Therefore, the data value 24 is higher than 85% of the values in the data set.

The steps for finding a value corresponding to a given percentile are summarized in this Procedure Table.

Procedure Table

Finding a Data Value Corresponding to a Given Percentile

Step 1   Arrange the data in order from lowest to highest.

Step 2   Substitute into the formula

$$c = \frac{n \cdot p}{100}$$

where n = total number of values
p = percentile

Step 3A   If c is not a whole number, round up to the next whole number. Starting at the lowest value, count over to the number that corresponds to the rounded-up value.

Step 3B   If c is a whole number, use the value halfway between the cth and $(c + 1)$st values when counting up from the lowest value.

Examples 3–32 and 3–33 show a procedure for finding a value corresponding to a given percentile.

EXAMPLE 3–32   Traffic Violations

Using the data in Example 3–30, find the value corresponding to the 65th percentile.

SOLUTION

Step 1   Arrange the data in order from lowest to highest.

$$9 \quad 12 \quad 15 \quad 16 \quad 18 \quad 19 \quad 20 \quad 22 \quad 24 \quad 25$$

Step 2   Compute

$$c = \frac{n \cdot p}{100}$$

where n = total number of values
p = percentile
Thus,

$$c = \frac{10 \cdot 65}{100} = 6.5$$

Since c is not a whole number, round it up to the next whole number; in this case, it is $c = 7$.

Start at the lowest value and count over to the 7th value, which is 20. Hence, the value of 20 corresponds to the 65th percentile.

EXAMPLE 3–33   Traffic Violations

Using the data in Example 3–30, find the data value corresponding to the 30th percentile.

SOLUTION

Step 1   Arrange the data in order from lowest to highest.

$$9 \;\; 12 \;\; 15 \;\; 16 \;\; 18 \;\; 19 \;\; 20 \;\; 22 \;\; 24 \;\; 25$$

Step 2   Substitute in the formula.

$$c = \frac{n \cdot p}{100} \qquad c = \frac{10 \cdot 30}{100} = 3$$

In this case, it is the 3rd and 4th values.

Step 3   Since c is a whole number, use the value halfway between the c and $c + 1$ values when counting up from the lowest. In this case, it is the third and fourth values.

$$9 \;\; 12 \;\; 15 \qquad 16 \;\; 18 \;\; 19 \;\; 20 \;\; 22 \;\; 24 \;\; 25$$
$$\uparrow \qquad \uparrow$$
$$\text{3rd} \qquad \text{4th}$$
$$\text{value} \quad \text{value}$$

The halfway value is between 15 and 16. It is 15.5. Hence, 15.5 corresponds to the 30th percentile.

Quartiles and Deciles

Quartiles divide the distribution into four equal groups, denoted by Q_1, Q_2, Q_3.

Note that Q_1 is the same as the 25th percentile; Q_2 is the same as the 50th percentile, or the median; Q_3 corresponds to the 75th percentile, as shown:

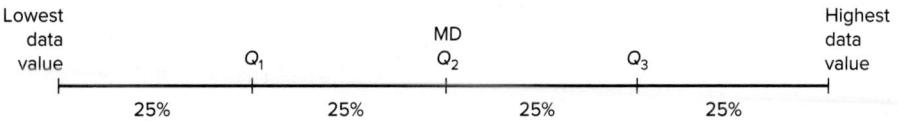

Quartiles can be computed by using the formula given for computing percentiles on page 155. For Q_1 use $p = 25$. For Q_2 use $p = 50$. For Q_3 use $p = 75$. However, an easier method for finding quartiles is found in this Procedure Table.

Procedure Table
Finding Data Values Corresponding to Q_1, Q_2, and Q_3
Step 1   Arrange the data in order from lowest to highest.
Step 2   Find the median of the data values. This is the value for Q_2.
Step 3   Find the median of the data values that fall below Q_2. This is the value for Q_1.
Step 4   Find the median of the data values that fall above Q_2. This is the value for Q_3.

Example 3–34 shows how to find the values of Q_1, Q_2, and Q_3.

EXAMPLE 3–34   Sodium Levels

The sodium levels in mEq/L for 9 students is shown. Find Q_1, Q_2, and Q_3.

136, 142, 148, 138, 136, 144, 139, 141, 143

SOLUTION

Step 1   Arrange the data in order from lowest value to highest value.

136, 136, 138, 139, 141, 142, 143, 144, 148

Step 2   Find the median or Q_2 for the data.

136, 136, 138, 139, 141, 142, 143, 144, 148

↑

Median = 141

Step 3   Find the median of the data values below 141 to get Q_1.

136, 136, 138, 139

↑

$$Q_1 = \frac{136 + 138}{2} = 137$$

Step 4   Find the median of the data values above 141.

$$Q_3 = \frac{143 + 144}{2} = 143.5$$

Hence, $Q_1 = 137$, $Q_2 = 141$, and $Q_3 = 143.5$.

In addition to dividing the data set into four groups, quartiles can be used as a rough measure of variability. This measure of variability which uses quartiles is called the *interquartile range* and is the range of the middle 50% of the data values.

> The **interquartile range (IQR)** is the difference between the third and first quartiles.
>
> $$IQR = Q_3 - Q_1$$

EXAMPLE 3–35   Sodium Levels

Find the interquartile range for the data in Example 3–34.

SOLUTION

Find the values for Q_1 and Q_3. This was done in Example 3–34. $Q_1 = 137$ and $Q_3 = 143.5$.

Next find $Q_3 - Q_1$. IQR = $Q_3 - Q_1 = 143.5 - 137 = 6.5$.

The interquartile range is 6.5.

Like the standard deviation, the more variable the data set is, the larger the value of the interquartile range will be.

Deciles divide the distribution into 10 groups, as shown. They are denoted by D_1, D_2, etc.

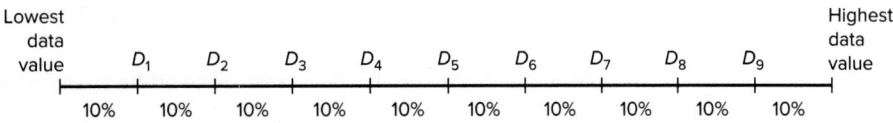

Note that D_1 corresponds to P_{10}; D_2 corresponds to P_{20}; etc. Deciles can be found by using the formulas given for percentiles. Taken altogether then, these are the relationships among percentiles, deciles, and quartiles.

Deciles are denoted by $D_1, D_2, D_3, \ldots, D_9$, and they correspond to $P_{10}, P_{20}, P_{30}, \ldots, P_{90}$.

Quartiles are denoted by Q_1, Q_2, Q_3 and they correspond to P_{25}, P_{50}, P_{75}.

The median is the same as P_{50} or Q_2 or D_5.

The position measures are summarized in Table 3–4.

TABLE 3–4 Summary of Position Measures		
Measure	**Definition**	**Symbol(s)**
Standard score or z score	Number of standard deviations that a data value is above or below the mean	z
Percentile	Position in hundredths that a data value holds in the distribution	P_n
Decile	Position in tenths that a data value holds in the distribution	D_n
Quartile	Position in fourths that a data value holds in the distribution	Q_n

Outliers

A data set should be checked for extremely high or extremely low values. These values are called *outliers*.

> An **outlier** is an extremely high or an extremely low data value when compared with the rest of the data values.

An outlier can strongly affect the mean and standard deviation of a variable. For example, suppose a researcher mistakenly recorded an extremely high data value. This value would then make the mean and standard deviation of the variable much larger than they really were.

Since these measures (mean and standard deviation) are affected by outliers, they are called *nonresistant statistics*. The median and interquartile range are less affected by outliers, so they are called *resistant* statistics. Sometimes when a distribution is skewed or contains outliers, the median and interquartile range can be used to more accurately describe the data than the mean and standard deviation. Outliers can have an effect on other statistics as well.

There are several ways to check a data set for outliers. One method is shown in this Procedure Table.

Procedure Table

Procedure for Identifying Outliers

Step 1   Arrange the data in order from lowest to highest and find Q_1 and Q_3.

Step 2   Find the interquartile range: IQR $= Q_3 - Q_1$.

Step 3   Multiply the IQR by 1.5.

Step 4   Subtract the value obtained in step 3 from Q_1 and add the value obtained in step 3 to Q_3.

Step 5   Check the data set for any data value that is smaller than $Q_1 - 1.5(\text{IQR})$ or larger than $Q_3 + 1.5(\text{IQR})$.

This procedure is shown in Example 3–36.

EXAMPLE 3–36   Outliers

Check the following set for outliers: 2, 3, 9, 16, 19, 24, 26, 62.

SOLUTION

The data value 62 is an extreme value and could be an outlier.

Step 1   Find Q_1 and Q_3.

$$Q_1 = \frac{3+9}{2} = 6 \qquad Q_3 = \frac{24+26}{2} = 25$$

Step 2   Find the interquartile range (IQR).

$$\text{IQR} = Q_3 - Q_1 = 25 - 6 = 19$$

Step 3   Multiply the IQR by 1.5.

$$1.5(19) = 28.5$$

Step 4   Subtract the value obtained in Step 3 from Q_1 and add it to Q_3.

$$6 - 28.5 = -22.5 \text{ and } 25 + 28.5 = 53.5$$

Step 5   Check the data set for any values less than -22.5 or greater than 53.5. The data value 62 is greater than 53.5; hence, it can be considered an outlier.

There are several reasons why outliers may occur. First, the data value may have resulted from a measurement or observational error. Perhaps the researcher measured the variable incorrectly. Second, the data value may have resulted from a recording error. That is, it may have been written or typed incorrectly. Third, the data value may have been obtained from a subject that is not in the defined population. For example, suppose test scores were obtained from a seventh-grade class, but a student in that class was actually in the sixth grade and had special permission to attend the class. This student might have scored extremely low on that particular exam on that day. Fourth, the data value might be a legitimate value that occurred by chance (although the probability is extremely small).

There are no hard-and-fast rules on what to do with outliers, nor is there complete agreement among statisticians on ways to identify them. Obviously, if they occurred as a result of an error, an attempt should be made to correct the error or else the data value should be omitted entirely. When they occur naturally by chance, the statistician must make a decision about whether to include them in the data set.

When a distribution is normal or bell-shaped, data values that are beyond 3 standard deviations of the mean can be considered suspected outliers.

Applying the Concepts 3–3

Determining Dosages

In an attempt to determine necessary dosages of a new drug (HDL) used to control sepsis, assume you administer varying amounts of HDL to 40 mice. You create four groups and label them *low dosage, moderate dosage, large dosage,* and *very large dosage.* The dosages also vary within each group. After the mice are injected with the HDL and the sepsis bacteria, the time until the onset of sepsis is recorded. Your job as a statistician is to effectively communicate the results of the study.

1. Which measures of position could be used to help describe the data results?
2. If 40% of the mice in the top quartile survived after the injection, how many mice would that be?
3. What information can be given from using percentiles?
4. What information can be given from using quartiles?
5. What information can be given from using standard scores?

See page 186 for the answers.

Exercises 3–3

1. **What is a z score?** A z score tells how many standard deviations a data value is above or below the mean.

2. **Define *percentile rank*.** A percentile rank indicates the percentage of data values that fall below the specific rank.

3. **What is the difference between a percentage and a percentile?** A percentile is a relative measurement of position; a percentage is an absolute measure of the part to the total.

4. **Define *quartile*.** A quartile is a relative measure of position obtained by dividing the data set into quarters.

5. **What is the relationship between quartiles and percentiles?** $Q_1 = P_{25}$; $Q_2 = P_{50}$; $Q_3 = P_{75}$

6. **What is a decile?** A decile is a relative measure of position obtained by dividing the data set into tenths.

7. **How are deciles related to percentiles?** $D_1 = P_{10}$; $D_2 = P_{20}$; $D_3 = P_{30}$; etc.

8. **To which percentile, quartile, and decile does the median correspond?** P_{50}; Q_2; D_5

9. **Daily Caloric Intake** According to www.dailymail.com.uk, people eat on average 3770 calories per day. If the standard deviation is 325 calories, find the z score for each raw score.

   a. 3250 calories −1.6
   b. 4160 calories 1.2
   c. 3490 calories −0.86
   d. 4320 calories 1.69
   e. 3615 calories −0.48

10. **Fast-Food Expenditures** The average person spends $151 per year on fast-foods (Gallup). If the standard

deviation is $12, find the corresponding z score for each raw score.

   a. $138 −1.08
   b. $172 1.75
   c. $160 0.75
   d. $144 −0.58
   e. $180 2.42

11. **Pizza Delivery** The average time it takes to get a pizza delivered to a home is 30 minutes. If the standard deviation is 4 minutes, find the corresponding z score for each raw score.

   a. 32 minutes 0.5
   b. 24 minutes −1.5
   c. 21 minutes −2.25
   d. 28.5 minutes −0.375
   e. 36 minutes 1.5

12. **eBooks** A person reads on average 28 eBooks per year. Assume the standard deviation is 3. Find the corresponding z score for each raw score.

   a. 25 books −1
   b. 36 books 2.67
   c. 22 books −2
   d. 24 books −1.33
   e. 32 books 1.33

13. **Test Scores** Which is a better relative position, a score of 83 on a geography test that has a mean of 72 and a standard deviation of 6, or a score of 61 on an accounting test that has a mean of 55 and a standard deviation of 3.5? Geography test $z = 1.83$. Accounting test $z = 1.71$. The geography test score is relatively higher than the accounting test score.

14. **College and University Debt** A student graduated from a 4-year college with an outstanding loan of $9650 where the average debt is $8455 with a standard deviation of $1865. Another student graduated from a

university with an outstanding loan of $12,360 where the average of the outstanding loans was $10,326 with a standard deviation of $2143. Which student had a higher debt determined by z scores? 0.64; 0.95. The student from the university has a higher relative debt.

15. **Annual Miles Driven** The average miles driven annually per licensed driver in the United States is approximately 14,090 miles. If we assume a fairly mound-shaped distribution with a standard deviation of approximately 3500 miles, find the following:

   a. z score for 16,000 miles 0.55

   b. z score for 10,000 miles −1.17

   c. Number of miles corresponding to z scores of 1.6, −0.5, and 0. 19,690; 12,340; 14,090

   Source: World Almanac 2012.

16. Which score indicates the highest relative position?

   a. A score of 3.2 on a test with $\overline{X} = 4.6$ and $s = 1.5$ −0.93

   b. A score of 630 on a test with $\overline{X} = 800$ and $s = 200$ −0.85

   c. A score of 43 on a test with $\overline{X} = 50$ and $s = 5$
   −1.4; score in part *b* has the highest relative position.

17. The data show the population (in thousands) for a recent year of a sample of cities in South Carolina.

29	26	15	13	17	58
14	25	37	19	40	67
23	10	97	12	129	
27	20	18	120	35	
66	21	11	43	22	

   Source: U.S. Census Bureau.

   Find the data value that corresponds to each percentile.

   a. 40th percentile 21   *c.* 90th percentile 97

   b. 75th percentile 43   *d.* 30th percentile 19

   Using the same data, find the percentile corresponding to the given data value.

   e. 27 57   *g.* 58 80

   f. 40 72   *h.* 67 87

18. **Costs of Automobile Repairs** A random selection of 100 automobile repairs at an auto repair shop is summarized in this frequency distribution. Find the repair cost associated with the following percentiles by constructing a percentile graph.

   a. 30th percentile 437   *c.* 75th percentile 722

   b. 50th percentile 578

Cost (in dollars)	Frequency
100–248	9
249–397	16
398–546	19
547–695	28
696–844	17
845–993	7
994–1142	4
	100

Using the same frequency distribution, find the approximate percentile rank of each.

   d. 415 27th

   e. 680 69th

   f. 873 90th

19. **Achievement Test Scores** The data shown represent the scores on a national achievement test for a group of 10th-grade students. Find the approximate percentile ranks of these scores by constructing a percentile graph.

   a. 220 6   *d.* 280 76

   b. 245 24   *e.* 300 94

   c. 276 68

Score	Frequency
196.5–217.5	5
217.5–238.5	17
238.5–259.5	22
259.5–280.5	48
280.5–301.5	22
301.5–322.5	6

   For the same data, find the approximate scores that correspond to these percentiles.

   f. 15th 234   *i.* 65th 274

   g. 29th 251   *j.* 80th 284

   h. 43rd 263

20. **Airplane Speeds** The airborne speeds in miles per hour of 21 planes are shown. Find the approximate values that correspond to the given percentiles by constructing a percentile graph.

Class	Frequency
366–386	4
387–407	2
408–428	3
429–449	2
450–470	1
471–491	2
492–512	3
513–533	4
	21

   Source: The World Almanac and Book of Facts.

   a. 9th 375   *d.* 60th 477

   b. 20th 389   *e.* 75th 504

   c. 45th 433

   Using the same data, find the approximate percentile ranks of the following speeds in miles per hour (mph).

   f. 380 mph 13th   *i.* 505 mph 76th

   g. 425 mph 40th   *j.* 525 mph 92nd

   h. 455 mph 54th

21. **Average Weekly Earnings** The average weekly earnings in dollars for various industries are listed below. Find the percentile rank of each value.

804 736 659 489 777 623 597 524 228
94th; 72nd; 61st; 17th; 83rd; 50th; 39th; 28th; 6th

For the same data, what value corresponds to the 40th percentile? 597

Source: New York Times Almanac.

22. **Test Scores** Find the percentile rank for each test score in the data set. 7th; 21st; 36th; 50th; 64th; 79th; 93rd

12, 28, 35, 42, 47, 49, 50

What value corresponds to the 60th percentile? 47

23. **Hurricane Damage** Find the percentile rank for each value in the data set. The data represent the values in billions of dollars of the damage of 10 hurricanes. 5th; 15th; 25th; 35th; 45th; 55th; 65th; 75th; 85th; 95th

1.1, 1.7, 1.9, 2.1, 2.2, 2.5, 3.3, 6.2, 6.8, 20.3

What value corresponds to the 40th percentile? 2.2

Source: Insurance Services Office.

24. **Test Scores** Find the percentile rank for each test score in the data set. 8th; 25th; 42nd; 58th; 75th; 92nd

5, 12, 15, 16, 20, 21

What test score corresponds to the 33rd percentile? 12

25. **Taxes** The data for a recent year show the taxes (in millions of dollars) received from a random sample of 10 states. Find the first and third quartiles and the IQR. $Q_1 = 11$; $Q_3 = 32$; IQR = 21

13 15 32 36 11 24 6 25 11 71

Source: U.S. Census Bureau.

26. **Medical Marijuana 2015 Sales Tax** The data show the amount of sales tax paid in Denver County,

Colorado. Find the first and third quartiles for the data. $Q_1 = 353,617$; $Q_3 = 512,838.5$

Month	Sales Tax	Month	Sales Tax
Jan	363,061	July	518,868
Feb	358,208	August	554,013
March	418,500	September	506,809
April	266,771	October	341,421
May	399,814	November	349,026
June	453,698	December	532,545

Source: Colorado Department of Revenue

27. **Populations** For a recent year, the data in millions show the population of the 10 largest cities in the United States. Find the first and third quartiles and the IQR. $Q_1 = 1.4$, $Q_3 = 2.7$, IQR = 1.3

8.5 2.3 2.7 1.6 1.3 3.9 1.4 1.4 1.5 1.9

Source: The World Almanac

28. **Presidential Vetoes** The number of vetoes issued by 10 selected Presidents is shown. Find the first and third quartiles and find the IQR for the data set. $Q_1 = 4$, $Q_3 = 25$, IQR = 21

2 7 1 4 5 8 48 110 25 12

Source: The World Almanac

29. Check each data set for outliers.
    a. 46, 28, 32, 21, 25, 29, 34, 19 None
    b. 82, 100, 97, 93, 89, 90, 65, 94, 101 65
    c. 527, 1007, 489, 371, 175 None

30. Check each data set for outliers.
    a. 88, 72, 97, 84, 86, 85, 100 None
    b. 145, 119, 122, 118, 125, 116 145
    c. 14, 16, 27, 18, 13, 19, 36, 15, 20 None

Extending the Concepts

31. Another measure of the average is called the *midquartile;* it is the numerical value halfway between Q_1 and Q_3, and the formula is

$$\text{Midquartile} = \frac{Q_1 + Q_3}{2}$$

   Using this formula and other formulas, find Q_1, Q_2, Q_3, the midquartile, and the interquartile range for each data set.
    a. 5, 12, 16, 25, 32, 38 12; 20.5; 32; 22; 20
    b. 53, 62, 78, 94, 96, 99, 103 62; 94; 99; 80.5; 37

32. An employment evaluation exam has a variance of 250. Two particular exams with raw scores of 142 and 165 have z scores of -0.5 and 0.955, respectively. Find the mean of the distribution. About 149.9

33. A particular standardized test has scores that have a mound-shaped distribution with mean equal to 125 and

standard deviation equal to 18. Tom had a raw score of 158, Dick scored at the 98th percentile, and Harry had a z score of 2.00. Arrange these three students in order of their scores from lowest to highest. Explain your reasoning.

34. In a game such as golf, the lower your score is, the better player you are. Suppose a person has a z score of $+1.5$ and another player has a z score of -1.5. Which player is the better player? Explain your answer.
   The player with a z score of -1.5 is a better player since it indicates a regular score below the mean, and in golf the lower the score, the better it is.

35. What does it mean when a z score is 0? A z score of zero means the data value is exactly at the mean.

36. If the data values of a data set are graphed, then they are converted to z values and these values are graphed, how will the graphs compare to each other? The graphs have the same shapes.

⊴Technology   Step by Step

TI-84 Plus
Step by Step

Calculating Descriptive Statistics

To calculate various descriptive statistics:

1. Enter data into L1.
2. Press **STAT** to get the menu.
3. Press → to move cursor to CALC; then press 1 for 1-Var Stats.
4. Under List, press **2nd [L1],** then **ENTER**.
5. Leave FreqList blank, then press **ENTER**.
6. While highlighting Calculate, press **ENTER**.

The calculator will display

$\bar{x}$	sample mean
Σx	sum of the data values
Σx^2	sum of the squares of the data values
S_x	sample standard deviation
σ_x	population standard deviation
n	number of data values
$minX$	smallest data value
Q_1	lower quartile
Med	median
Q_3	upper quartile
$maxX$	largest data value

Example TI3–1

Compute descriptive statistics for the data in Example 3–20: 11, 90, 33, 49, 27.

Following the steps just shown, we obtain these results, as shown on the screen:

The mean is 42.

The sum of x is 210.

The sum of x^2 is 12440.

The sample standard deviation S_x is 30.08321791.

The population standard deviation σ_x is 26.90724809. (*Note:* This is a sample, so you would not use in this example.)

The sample size n is 5.

The smallest data value is 11.

The first quartile Q_1 is 19.

The median is 33.

The third quartile Q_3 is 69.5.

The largest data value is 90.

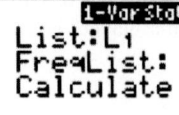
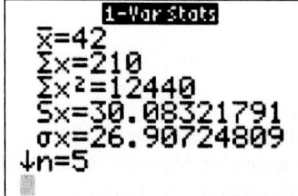

To calculate the mean and standard deviation from grouped data:

1. Enter the midpoints into **L1**.
2. Enter the frequencies into **L2**.

3. Press **STAT** to get the menu.

4. Use the arrow keys to move the cursor to CALC; then press 1 for 1-Var Stats.

5. Under List, press **2nd [L1]**, then **ENTER**.

6. Under Freqlist press **2nd [L2]**, then **ENTER**.

7. While highlighting Calculate, press **ENTER**.

Example TI3–2

Calculate the mean and standard deviation for the data given in Example 3–22.

Class	Frequency	Midpoint
5.5–10.5	1	8
10.5–15.5	2	13
15.5–20.5	3	18
20.5–25.5	5	23
25.5–30.5	4	28
30.5–35.5	3	33
35.5–40.5	2	38

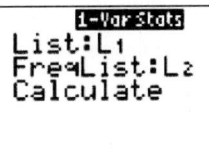 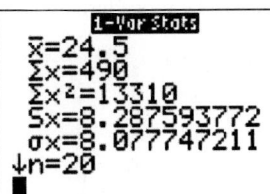 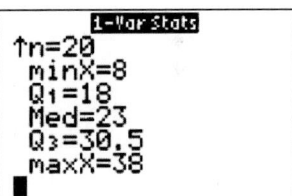

The sample mean is 24.5, and the sample standard deviation is 8.287593772.

Example TI3–3

Use the data from Example 3–29 to graph a percentile graph. Follow the procedure for an ogive (Section 2–2).

Class Boundaries	Cumulative Percent
89.5	0
104.5	12
119.5	43
134.5	79
149.5	92
164.5	98
179.5	100

1. Type in the first left-hand class boundary followed by all the right-hand class boundaries into L1.

2. Type the cumulative percent in L2, but add a "for the first class".

3. Press **WINDOW**. Change the $X_{min} = 89$, $X_{max} = 180$, $Y_{min} = -5$, and $Y_{max} = 100$.

 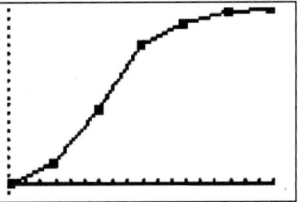

EXCEL
Step by Step

Measures of Position

Example XL3–3

Find the z scores for each value of the data shown.

$$5 \quad 6 \quad 12 \quad 13 \quad 15 \quad 18 \quad 22 \quad 50$$

1. On an Excel worksheet enter the data in cells A2–A9. Enter a label for the variable in cell A1.
2. Label cell B1 as z score.
3. Select cell B2.
4. Select the Formulas tab from the toolbar and Insert Function f_x .
5. Select the Statistical category for statistical functions and scroll in the function list to STANDARDIZE and click [OK].

In the STANDARDIZE dialog box:

6. Type A2 for the X value.
7. Type AVERAGE(A2:A9) for the mean.
8. Type STDEV.S(A2:A9) for the sample standard deviation. Then click [OK].
9. Repeat the procedure above for each data value in column A.

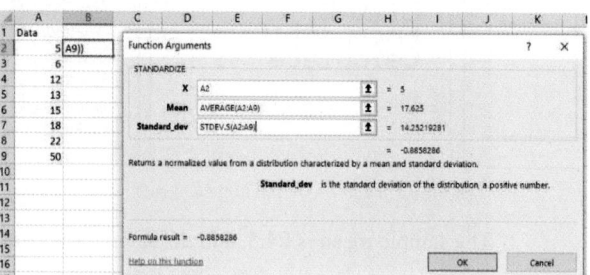

Example XL3–4

Excel has two built-in functions to find the Percentile Rank corresponding to a value in a set of data.

PERCENTRANK.INC calculates the Percentile Rank corresponding to a data value in the range 0 to 1 inclusively.

PERCENTRANK.EXC calculates the Percentile Rank corresponding to a data value in the range 0 to 1 exclusively.

We will compute Percentile Ranks for the data shown, using both PERCENTRANK.INC and PERCENTRANK.EXC to demonstrate the difference between the two functions.

$$5 \quad 6 \quad 12 \quad 13 \quad 15 \quad 18 \quad 22 \quad 50$$

1. On an Excel worksheet enter the data in cells A2–A9. Enter the label **Data** in cell A1.
2. Label cell B1 as **Percent Rank INC** and cell C1 as **Percent Rank EXC.**
3. Select cell B2.
4. Select the Formulas tab from the toolbar and Insert Function f_x .
5. Select the Statistical category for statistical functions and scroll in the function list to PERCENTRANK.INC (PERCENTRANK.EXC) and click [OK].

In the PERCENTRANK.INC (PERCENTRANK.EXC) dialog boxes:

6. Type A2:A9 for the Array.
7. Type A2 for X, then click [OK]. You can leave the Significance box blank unless you want to change the number of significant digits of the output (the default is 3 significant digits).
8. Repeat the procedure above for each data value in the set.

The function results for both PERCENTRANK.INC and PERCENTRANK.EXC are shown below.

Note: Both functions return the Percentile Ranks as a number between 0 and 1. You may convert these to numbers between 0 and 100 by multiplying each function value by 100.

	A	B	C
1	Data	Percent Rank INC	Percent Rank EXC
2	5	0	0.111
3	6	0.142	0.222
4	12	0.285	0.333
5	13	0.428	0.444
6	15	0.571	0.555
7	18	0.714	0.666
8	22	0.857	0.777
9	50	1	0.888

Descriptive Statistics in Excel

Example XL3–5

Excel Analysis Tool-Pak Add-in Data Analysis includes an item called Descriptive Statistics that reports many useful measures for a set of data.

1. Enter the data set shown in cells A1 to A9 of a new worksheet.

12   17   15   16   16   14   18   13   10

See the Excel Step by Step in Chapter 1 for the instructions on loading the Analysis Tool-Pak Add-in.

2. Select the Data tab on the toolbar and select Data Analysis.
3. In the Analysis Tools dialog box, scroll to Descriptive Statistics, then click [OK].
4. Type A1:A9 in the Input Range box and check the Grouped by Columns option.
5. Select the Output Range option and type in cell C1.
6. Check the Summary statistics option and click [OK].

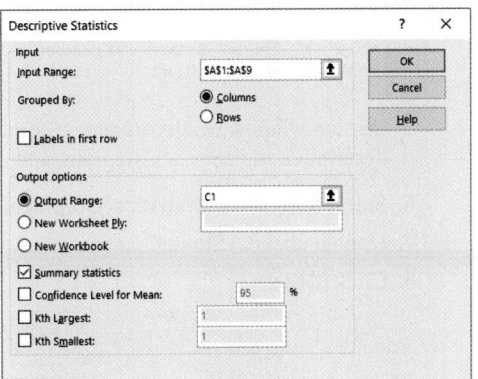

Below is the summary output for this data set.

	A	B	C	D
1	12		*Column1*	
2	17			
3	15		Mean	14.55556
4	16		Standard Error	0.851651
5	16		Median	15
6	14		Mode	16
7	18		Standard Deviation	2.554952
8	13		Sample Variance	6.527778
9	10		Kurtosis	-0.39439
10			Skewness	-0.51631
11			Range	8
12			Minimum	10
13			Maximum	18
14			Sum	131
15			Count	9

MINITAB

Step by Step

Calculate Descriptive Statistics from Data

Example MT3–1

1. Enter the data on teacher strikes shown into C1 of MINITAB. Name the column **Strikes.**

9,   10,   14,   7,   8,   3

2. Select **Stat>Basic Statistics>Display Descriptive Statistics.**

3. The cursor will be blinking in the Variables text box. Double-click C1 Strikes.

4. Click [Statistics] to view the statistics that can be calculated with this command.

   a) Check the boxes for Mean, Standard deviation, Variance, Coefficient of variation, First Quartile, Median, Third Quartile, Minimum, Maximum, and N nonmissing.

   b) Remove the checks from other options.

5. Click [OK] twice.

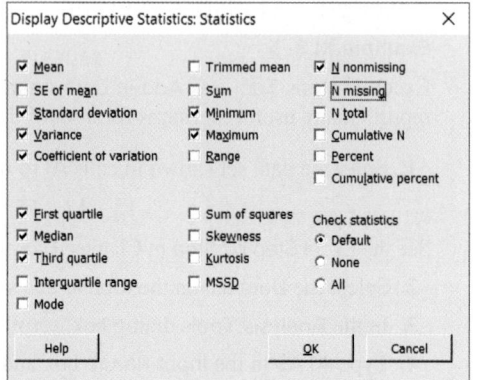

The results will be displayed in the session window as shown.

Descriptive Statistics: Strikes

Variable	N	Mean	StDev	Variance	CoefVar	Minimum	Q1	Median	Q3	Maximum
Strikes	6	8.50	3.62	13.10	42.58	3.00	6.00	8.50	11.00	14.00

Session window results are in text format. A high-resolution graphical window displays the descriptive statistics, a histogram, and a boxplot.

6. Select **Stat>Basic Statistics>Graphical Summary.**

7. Double-click C1 Strikes.

8. Click [OK].

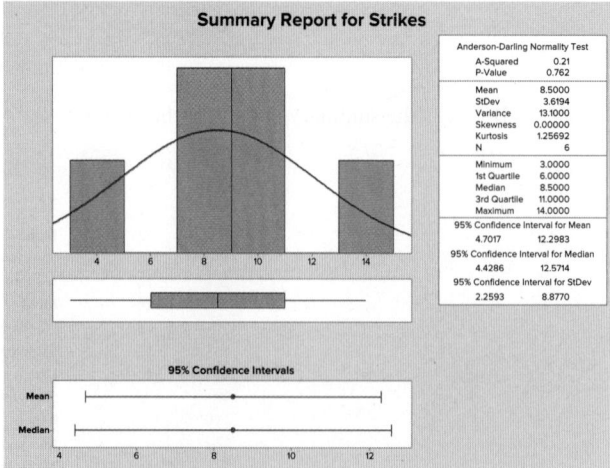

The graphical summary will be displayed in a separate window as shown.

Calculate Descriptive Statistics from a Frequency Distribution

Multiple menu selections must be used to calculate the statistics from a table. We will use data given in Example 3–22 on miles run per week.

Enter Midpoints and Frequencies

1. Select **File>New>New Worksheet** to open an empty worksheet.

2. To enter the midpoints into C1, select **Calc>Make Patterned Data>Simple Set of Numbers.**

   a) Type **X** in Store Patterned data in: to name the column.

   b) Type in **8** for the From first value, **38** for the To last value, and **5** for In steps of.

   c) Click [OK].

3. Enter the frequencies 1, 2, 3, 5, 4, 3, 2 in C2. Name the column **f.**

Calculate Columns for $f \cdot X$ and $f \cdot X^2$

4. Select **Calc>Calculator.**

   a) Type in **fX** for the Store results in variable and **'f' * 'X'** in the Expression dialog box. Click [OK].

   b) Select **Edit>Edit Last Dialog** and type in **fX2** for 'Store Result in Variable' and **'f' * 'X'^2** for the expression. If you double-click the constants instead of typing them, single quotes will surround the names. The quotes are not required unless the column name has spaces.

   c) Click [OK]. There are now four columns in the worksheet.

Calculate the Column Sums

5. Select **Calc>Column Statistics.**

   This command stores results in constants, not columns.

   Click [OK] after each step.

   a) Click the option for Sum; then select C2 f for the Input variable, and type **n** for Store result in.

   b) Select **Edit>Edit Last Dialog**; then select C3 fX for the input variable and type **sumX** for Store result in.

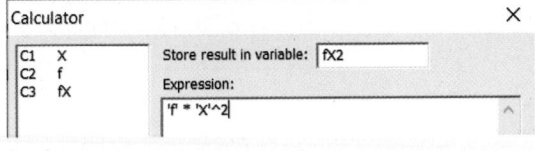

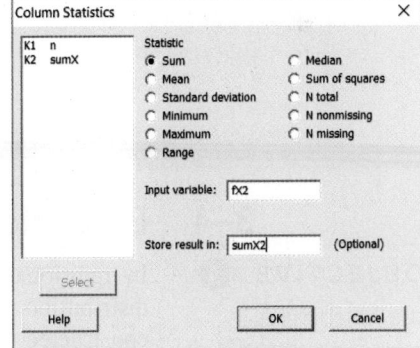

   c) Edit the last dialog box again. This time select C4 fX2 for the Input variable, then type **sumX2** for Store result in.

To verify the results, navigate to the Project Manager window, then the constants folder of the worksheet. The sums are 20, 490, and 13,310.

Calculate the Mean, Variance, and Standard Deviation

6. Select **Calc>Calculator.**

   a) Type **Mean** for the Store results in variable, then click in the box for the Expression and type **'sumX' / 'n'.** Click [OK].

   b) Click the **EditLast Dialog** icon and type **Variance** for the variable.

   c) In the expression box type in

   ('sumX2' - 'sumX'^2 / 'n') / ('n' - 1)

   d) Edit the last dialog box and type **S** for the variable. In the expression box, drag the mouse over the previous expression to highlight it.

e) Click the button in the keypad for parentheses. Type **SQRT** at the beginning of the line, upper- or lowercase will work. The expression should be SQRT((sumX2-sumX**2/n)/(n-1)).

f) Click [OK].

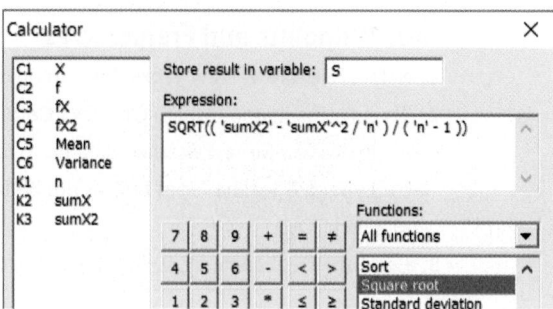

Display Results

g) Select **Data>Display Data**, then highlight all columns and constants in the list.

h) Click [Select] then [OK].

The session window will display all our work! Create the histogram with instructions from Chapter 2, but follow the instructions for bar chart, values from a table, and adjust bars to touch.

Data Display

```
n          20.0000
sumX      490.000
sumX2    13310.0
```

Row	X	f	fX	fX2	Mean	Variance	S
1	8	1	8	64	24.5	68.6842	8.28759
2	13	2	26	338			
3	18	3	54	972			
4	23	5	115	2645			
5	28	4	112	3136			
6	33	3	99	3267			
7	38	2	76	2888			

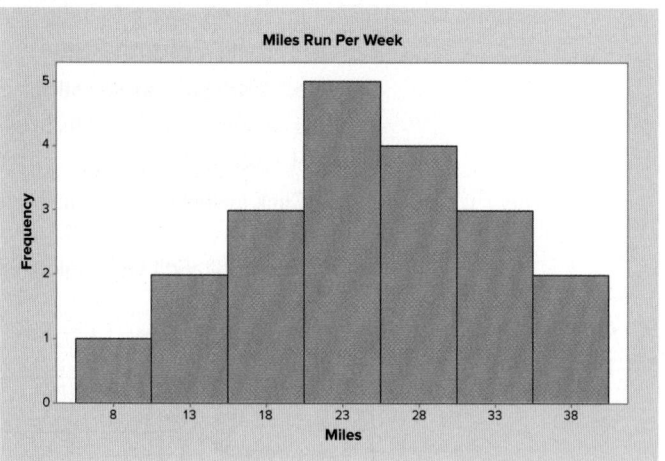

3–4   Exploratory Data Analysis

OBJECTIVE

Use the techniques of exploratory data analysis, including boxplots and five-number summaries, to discover various aspects of data.

In traditional statistics, data are organized by using a frequency distribution. From this distribution various graphs such as the histogram, frequency polygon, and ogive can be constructed to determine the shape or nature of the distribution. In addition, various statistics such as the mean and standard deviation can be computed to summarize the data.

The purpose of traditional analysis is to confirm various conjectures about the nature of the data. For example, from a carefully designed study, a researcher might want to know if the proportion of Americans who are exercising today has increased from 10 years ago. This study would contain various assumptions about the population, various definitions such as the definition of exercise, and so on.

In **exploratory data analysis (EDA),** data can be organized using a *stem and leaf plot*. (See Chapter 2.) The measure of central tendency used in EDA is the *median*. The measure of variation used in EDA is the *interquartile range* Q_3–Q_1. In EDA the data are represented graphically using a *boxplot* (sometimes called a box and whisker plot). The purpose of exploratory data analysis is to examine data to find out what information can be discovered about the data, such as the center and the spread. Exploratory data analysis was developed by John Tukey and presented in his book *Exploratory Data Analysis* (Addison-Wesley, 1977).

The Five-Number Summary and Boxplots

A **boxplot** can be used to graphically represent the data set. These plots involve five specific values:

1. The lowest value of the data set (i.e., minimum)

2. Q_1

3. The median

4. Q_3

5. The highest value of the data set (i.e., maximum)

These values are called a **five-number summary** of the data set.

A **boxplot** is a graph of a data set obtained by drawing a horizontal line from the minimum data value to Q_1, drawing a horizontal line from Q_3 to the maximum data value, and drawing a box whose vertical sides pass through Q_1 and Q_3 with a vertical line inside the box passing through the median or Q_2.

Procedure Table

Constructing a Boxplot

Step 1   Find the five-number summary for the data.

Step 2   Draw a horizontal axis and place the scale on the axis. The scale should start on or below the minimum data value and end on or above the maximum data value.

Step 3   Locate the lowest data value, Q_1, the median, Q_3, and the highest data value; then draw a box whose vertical sides go through Q_1 and Q_3. Draw a vertical line through the median. Finally, draw a line from the minimum data value to the left side of the box, and draw a line from the maximum data value to the right side of the box.

EXAMPLE 3–37   Hidden Chemicals in Beer

The amount of weed killer glyphosate, in parts per billion, found in a random sample of 10 beers is 49.7, 31.1, 25.1, 20.9, 14.5, 18.7, 11.8, 29.8, 5.7, 9.1. Construct a box plot for the data.

Source: U.S. Public Interest Research Group

SOLUTION

Step 1   Find the five-number summary for the data. Arrange the data in order:

$$5.7, 9.1, 11.8, 14.5, 18.7, 20.9, 25.1, 29.8, 31.1, 49.7$$
$$\uparrow$$
$$\text{Median}$$

$$\text{Median} = \frac{18.7 + 20.9}{2} = 19.8$$

Find Q_1.

$$5.7, 9.1, 11.8, 14.5, 18.7$$
$$\uparrow$$
$$Q_1$$
$$Q_1 \text{ is } 11.8.$$

Find Q_3.

$$20.9, 25.1, 29.8, 31.1, 49.7$$
$$\uparrow$$
$$Q_3$$
$$Q_3 = 29.8$$

The minimum value is 5.7 and the maximum value is 49.7.

Step 2   Draw a horizontal axis.

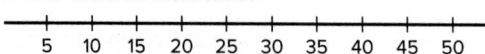

Step 3   Draw a box plot above the scale using the lowest and highest values, Q_1 and Q_3, and the median. See Figure 3–7.

FIGURE 3–7   Boxplot for Example 3–37

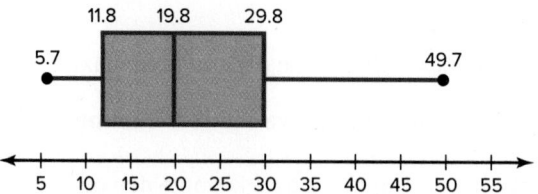

The box plot in Figure 3–7 is positively skewed with a high value of 49.7 and a low value of 5.7 in parts per billion.

Information Obtained from a Boxplot

1. *a.* If the median is near the center of the box, the distribution is approximately symmetric.
   b. If the median falls to the left of the center of the box, the distribution is positively skewed.
   c. If the median falls to the right of the center, the distribution is negatively skewed.
2. *a.* If the lines are about the same length, the distribution is approximately symmetric.
   b. If the right line is larger than the left line, the distribution is positively skewed.
   c. If the left line is larger than the right line, the distribution is negatively skewed.

The boxplot in Figure 3–7 indicates that the distribution is slightly positively skewed.

If the boxplots for two or more data sets are graphed on the same axis, the distributions can be compared. To compare the averages, use the location of the medians. To compare the variability, use the interquartile range, i.e., the length of the boxes. Example 3–38 shows this procedure.

EXAMPLE 3–38   Speeds of Roller Coasters

The data shown are the speeds in miles per hour of a sample of wooden roller coasters and a sample of steel roller coasters. Compare the distributions by using boxplots.

Wood				Steel			
50	56	60	48	55	70	48	28
35	67	72	68	100	106	102	120

Source: UltimateRollerCoaster.com

SOLUTION

Step 1   For the wooden coasters,

$$35 \quad 48 \quad 50 \quad 56 \quad 60 \quad 67 \quad 68 \quad 72$$

$$\qquad \uparrow \qquad\quad \uparrow \qquad\quad \uparrow$$

$$\qquad Q_1 \qquad\ \ MD \qquad\ Q_3$$

$$Q_1 = \frac{48 + 50}{2} = 49 \qquad MD = \frac{56 + 60}{2} = 58 \qquad Q_3 = \frac{67 + 68}{2} = 67.5$$

Step 2   For the steel coasters,

$$28 \;\; 48 \;\; 55 \;\; 70 \;\; 100 \;\; 102 \;\; 106 \;\; 120$$

$$\qquad\qquad \uparrow \qquad\quad \uparrow \qquad\quad \uparrow$$
$$\qquad\qquad Q_1 \qquad MD \qquad Q_3$$

$$Q_1 = \frac{48 + 55}{2} = 51.5 \qquad MD = \frac{70 + 100}{2} = 85 \qquad Q_3 = \frac{102 + 106}{2} = 104$$

Step 3   Draw the boxplots. See Figure 3–8.

FIGURE 3–8   Boxplots for Example 3–38

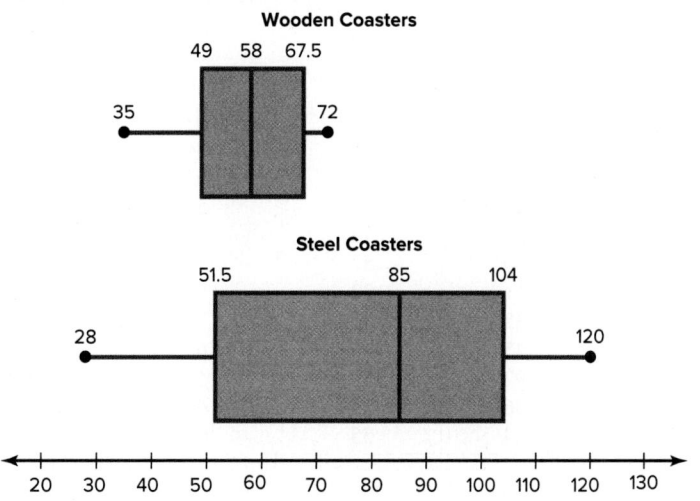

The boxplots show that the median of the speeds of the steel coasters is much higher than the median speeds of the wooden coasters. The interquartile range (spread) of the steel coasters is much larger than that of the wooden coasters. Finally, the range of the speeds of the steel coasters is larger than that of the wooden coasters.

A *modified boxplot* can be drawn and used to check for outliers. See Exercise 19 in Extending the Concepts in this section.

In exploratory data analysis, *hinges* are used instead of quartiles to construct boxplots. When the data set consists of an even number of values, hinges are the same as quartiles. Hinges for a data set with an odd number of values differ somewhat from quartiles. However, since most calculators and computer programs use quartiles, they will be used in this textbook.

Table 3–5 shows the correspondence between the traditional and the exploratory data analysis approach.

TABLE 3–5 Traditional versus EDA Techniques	
Traditional	**Exploratory data analysis**
Frequency distribution	Stem and leaf plot
Histogram	Boxplot
Mean	Median
Standard deviation	Interquartile range

Applying the Concepts 3–4

The Noisy Workplace

Assume you work for OSHA (Occupational Safety and Health Administration) and have complaints about noise levels from some of the workers at a state power plant. You charge the power plant with taking decibel readings at six different areas of the plant at different times of the day and week. The results of the data collection are listed. Use boxplots to initially explore the data and make recommendations about which plant areas workers must be provided with protective ear wear. The safe hearing level is approximately 120 decibels.

Area 1	Area 2	Area 3	Area 4	Area 5	Area 6
30	64	100	25	59	67
12	99	59	15	63	80
35	87	78	30	81	99
65	59	97	20	110	49
24	23	84	61	65	67
59	16	64	56	112	56
68	94	53	34	132	80
57	78	59	22	145	125
100	57	89	24	163	100
61	32	88	21	120	93
32	52	94	32	84	56
45	78	66	52	99	45
92	59	57	14	105	80
56	55	62	10	68	34
44	55	64	33	75	21

See page 186 for the answers.

Exercises 3–4

For Exercises 1–6, identify the five-number summary and find the interquartile range.

1. 9, 3, 15, 18, 8, 7, 20 3, 7, 9, 10, 20; 11

2. 19, 16, 48, 22, 7 7, 11.5, 19, 35, 48; 23.5

3. 43, 21, 32, 29, 38 21, 25, 40.5, 43; 15.5

4. 487, 391, 625, 462, 586, 603 391, 462, 536.5, 603, 625; 141

5. 19.7, 13.6, 12.8, 15.2, 16.3, 11.2, 20.1, 22.2, 10.6 10.6, 12, 15.2, 19.9, 22.2; 7.9

6. 9.7, 4.6, 2.2, 3.7, 6.2, 9.4, 3.8 2.2, 3.7, 4.6, 9.4, 9.7; 5.7

For Exercises 7–10, use each boxplot to identify the maximum value, minimum value, median, first quartile, third quartile, and interquartile range.

7. 27.3, 3, 18, 9, 21, 12

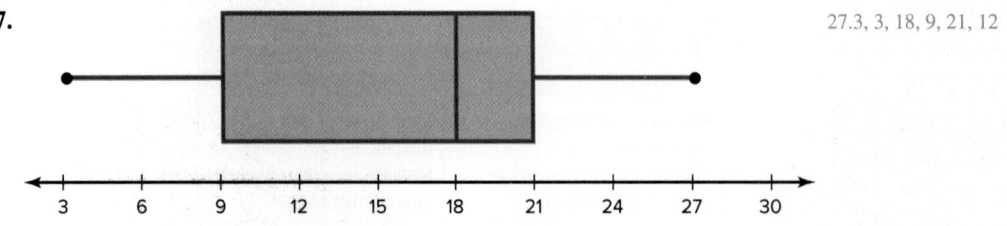

8.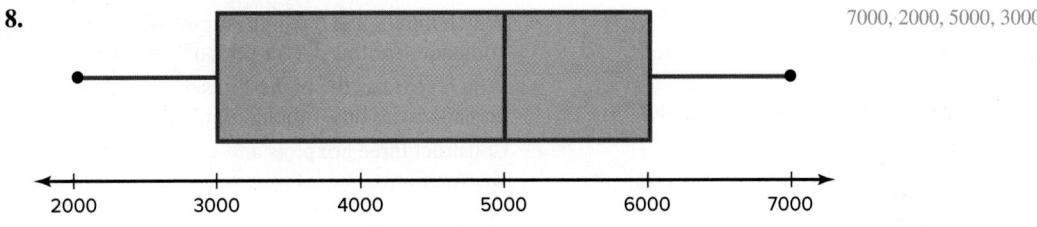

7000, 2000, 5000, 3000, 6000, 3000

9.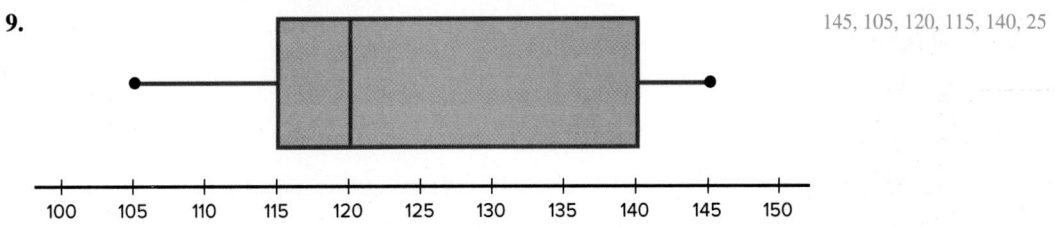

145, 105, 120, 115, 140, 25

10.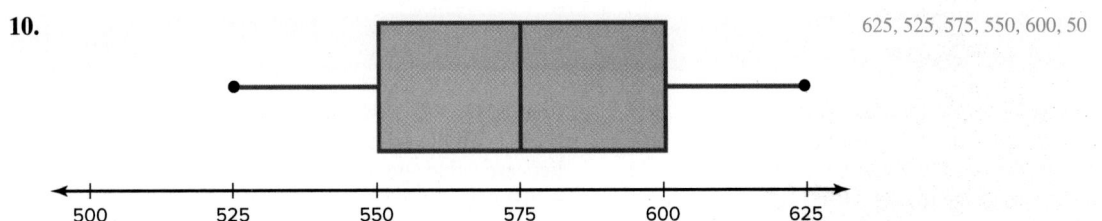

625, 525, 575, 550, 600, 50

11. SAT Scores Construct a box plot for the average SAT scores for 10 local school districts in Westmoreland County.

992 1137 996 1045 1095 1153 1066 1135 1128 1114

Source: Pennsylvania Department of Education

12. School District Enrollments For a recent year, the number of students enrolled in 12 school districts in Westmoreland County is shown. Identify the five-number summary, interquartile range, and draw a box plot for the data. Is the distribution skewed?

1873 2482 5744 8186 956 3359 2107
2100 2915 3719 5229 3481

Source: Pennsylvania Department of Education

13. Congested Urban Areas The data show the average number of hours per year that people spend in traffic for the top 10 urban areas in the United States. Find the five-number summary, interquartile range, and draw a box plot for the data.

Seattle 65	San Francisco 79
Boston 60	Dallas 54
New York 91	Atlanta 70
Chicago 57	Miami 64
Washington, DC 63	Los Angeles 102

Source: INRIX

14. Hurricane Damages The data show the damages in billions of dollars of nine hurricanes in the United States. Construct a box plot and comment on the skewness of the distribution.

Ivan 8.9	Harvey 22.5
Ike 14.0	Charley 9.3
Katrina 49.8	Wilma 12.5
Sandy 19.9	
Irma 50.0	
Andrew 24.5	

Source: Insurance Information Institute

15. Areas of Islands The data show the sizes in square miles of notable islands in the Baltic Sea and the Aleutian Islands. Construct a boxplot for each data set and compare the distributions.

Baltic Sea	Aleutian Islands
610	275
228	1051
1154	571
1159	686
2772	350

16. Size of Dams These data represent the volumes in cubic yards of the largest dams in the United States and in South America. Construct a boxplot of the data for each region and compare the distributions.

United States	South America
125,628	311,539
92,000	274,026
78,008	105,944
77,700	102,014
66,500	56,242
62,850	46,563
52,435	
50,000	

Source: New York Times Almanac.

17. Congressional Travel Expenses The data show the travel expenses in millions of dollars for U.S. senators and representatives for a recent ten-year span. Find the five-number summary, interquartile range, and draw a box plot for the data. Comment on the nature of data values.

13.9   13.1   19.3   17.6   9.9   10.9   11.7   9.7   12.5   11.0

Source: Annual Report of the Treasury Department

18. Number of Tornadoes A four-month record for the number of tornadoes in 2013–2015 is given here.

	2013	2014	2015
April	80	130	170
May	227	133	382
June	126	280	184
July	69	90	116

a. Which month had the highest mean number of tornadoes for this 3-year period? May: 247.3

b. Which year has the highest mean number of tornadoes for this 4-month period? 2015: 213

c. Construct three boxplots and compare the distributions.

Extending the Concepts

19. Unhealthy Smog Days A *modified boxplot* can be drawn by placing a box around Q_1 and Q_3 and then extending the whiskers to the highest and/or lowest values within 1.5 times the interquartile range (that is, $Q_3 - Q_1$). *Mild outliers* are values greater than $Q_3 + 1.5(IQR)$ or less than $Q_1 - 1.5(IQR)$. Extreme outliers are values greater than $Q_3 + 3(IQR)$ or less than $Q_1 - 3(IQR)$.

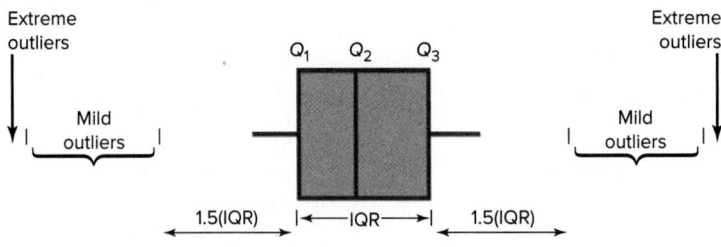

For the data shown here, draw a modified boxplot and identify any mild or extreme outliers. The data represent the number of unhealthy smog days for a specific year for the highest 10 locations.

97   39   43   66   91
43   54   42   53   39

Source: U.S. Public Interest Research Group and Clean Air Network.

Technology   Step by Step

TI-84 Plus

Step by Step

Constructing a Boxplot

To draw a boxplot:

1. Enter data into L_1.
2. Press **[2nd] [STAT PLOT]**, then **1** for Plot **1**.
3. Press **ENTER** to turn on Plot 1.
4. Move cursor to Boxplot symbol (fourth graph) on the Type: line, then press **ENTER**.
5. Make sure Xlist is L_1.
6. Make sure Freq is 1.
7. Press **ZOOM**, move cursor down to option 9: ZoomStat, press **ENTER** to display the boxplot.
8. Press **TRACE** followed by ← or → to obtain the values from the five-number summary on the boxplot.

To display two boxplots on the same screen, follow the above steps and use the 2: Plot 2 and L_2 symbols.

Example TI3–3

Construct a boxplot for the data values:

$$33, 38, 43, 30, 29, 40, 51, 27, 42, 23, 31$$

  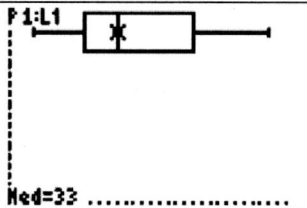

Using the **TRACE** key along with the ← and → keys, we obtain the five-number summary. The minimum value is 23; Q_1 is 29; the median is 33; Q_3 is 42; the maximum value is 51.

EXCEL
Step by Step

Constructing a Stem and Leaf Plot and a Boxplot

Example XL3–6

Excel does not have procedures to produce stem and leaf plots or boxplots. However, you may construct these plots by using the MegaStat Add-in available from the online resources. If you have not installed this add-in, refer to the instructions in the Excel Step by Step section of Chapter 1.

To obtain a boxplot and stem and leaf plot:

1. Enter the data values 33, 38, 43, 30, 29, 40, 51, 27, 42, 23, 31 into column A of a new Excel worksheet.

2. Select the Add-Ins tab, then MegaStat from the toolbar.

3. Select Descriptive Statistics from the MegaStat menu.

4. Enter the cell range A1:A11 in the Input range.

5. Check both Boxplot and Stem and Leaf Plot. *Note:* You may leave the other output options unchecked for this example. Click [OK].

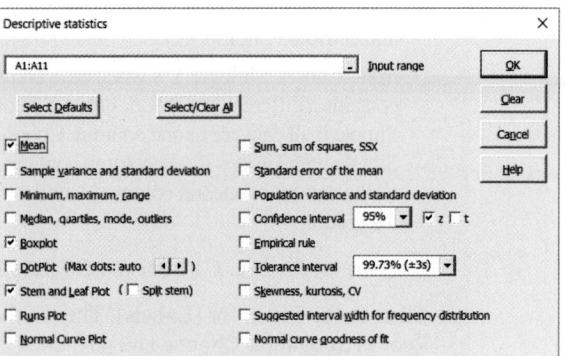

The stem and leaf plot and the boxplot are shown below.

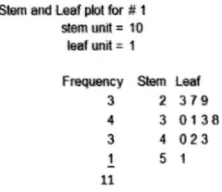

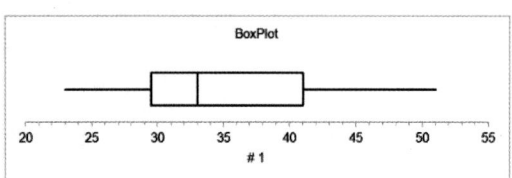

MINITAB
Step by Step

Construct a Boxplot

1. Type in the data 89, 47,164, 296, 30, 215, 138, 78, 48, 39. Label the column **Meteorites.**
2. Select **Graph>Boxplot.**

Note: Choose simple Y if all data is in one column.

3. Double-click **Meteorites** to select it for the graph variable.
4. Click on [Labels]. In the Title of the Title/Footnotes folder, type **Number of Meteorites.**
5. Click [OK] twice. The graph will be displayed in a graph window.

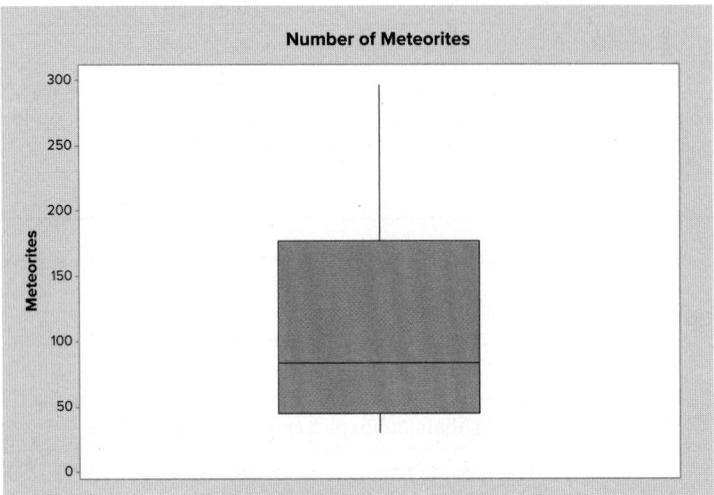

Compare Two Distributions Using Boxplots

A sample of real cheese and another sample of a cheese substitute are tested for their sodium levels in milligrams. The data are used are shown.

1. Type the data into C1 and C2 of a Minitab worksheet as shown.

    a. Select **Graph>Boxplot** then **Multiple Y's** and **Simple.** Click [OK].

    Note: Choose Multiple Y's when each column contains a different variable or group. Choose Simple if all data are in one column. Choose Simple with Groups if one column contains all the data and a second column identifies the group.

	C1	C2
	Real	Substitute
1	310	270
2	420	180
3	45	250
4	40	290
5	220	130
6	240	260
7	180	340
8	90	310

2. Drag the mouse over C1 Real and C2 Substitute, and then click the button for [**Select**].

3. Click on the button for [**Labels**]. Then in the Title dialog box type **Comparison of Sodium in Real vs Substitute Cheese** and next click [**OK**].

4. Click the button for [**Scale**].

    a. Click the tab for **Gridlines** as shown.

    b. Check the box for **Y major ticks**.

5. Click [**OK**] twice. Hover the mouse over the box to see the details. The quartiles may not be the same as those calculated in the text. The method varies by technology. The values will be similar.

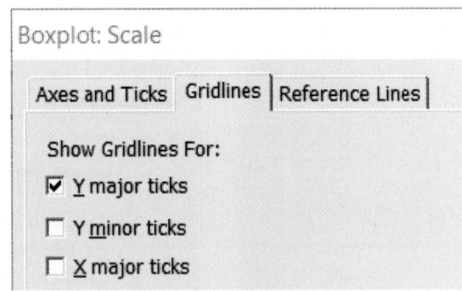

The boxplots show there is greater variation in the sodium levels for the real cheese. The median level is lower for the real cheese than the median for the sodium in the cheese substitute. The longer whisker for the real cheese indicates the distribution is skewed right. The sodium levels for the substitutes are more symmetrical and not as spread out.

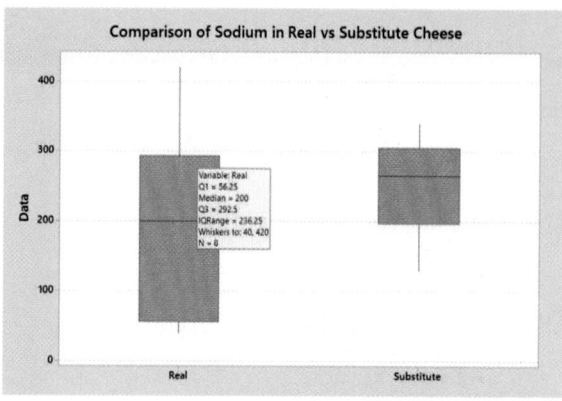

6. Select Stat>Basic Statistics>Display Descriptive Statistics. The Session window will contain the descriptive statistics for sodium for each cheese type as shown. The mean amount of sodium for real cheese is 193.1 milligrams compared to 253.8 for the substitute. Even though the mean is smaller for the real group, the standard deviation is almost double, indicating greater variation in the sodium levels for the real cheese.

Descriptive Statistics: Real, Substitute

Variable	N	Mean	StDev	Minimum	Q1	Median	Q3	Maximum	IQR
Real	8	193.1	133.2	40.0	56.3	200.0	292.5	420.0	236.3
Substitute	8	253.8	68.6	130.0	197.5	265.0	305.0	340.0	107.5

Summary

- This chapter explains the basic ways to summarize data. These include measures of central tendency. They are the mean, median, mode, and midrange. The weighted mean can also be used. (3–1)

- To summarize the variation of data, statisticians use measures of variation or dispersion. The three most common measures of variation are the range, variance, and standard deviation. The coefficient of variation can be used to compare the variation of two data sets. The data values are distributed according to Chebyshev's theorem or the empirical rule. (3–2)

- There are several measures of the position of data values in the set. There are standard scores or z scores, percentiles, quartiles, and deciles. Sometimes a data set contains an extremely high or extremely low data value, called an outlier. (3–3)

- Other methods can be used to describe a data set. These methods are the five-number summary and boxplots. These methods are called exploratory data analysis. (3–4)

The techniques explained in Chapter 2 and this chapter are the basic techniques used in descriptive statistics.

Important Terms

Important Formulas

Formula for the mean for individual data:

Sample	Population

$$\overline{X} = \frac{\Sigma X}{n} \qquad \mu = \frac{\Sigma X}{N}$$

Formula for the mean for grouped data:

$$\overline{X} = \frac{\Sigma f \cdot X_m}{n}$$

Formula for the weighted mean:

$$\overline{X} = \frac{\Sigma wX}{\Sigma w}$$

Formula for the midrange:

$$\text{MR} = \frac{\text{lowest value} + \text{highest value}}{2}$$

Formula for the range:

$$R = \text{highest value} - \text{lowest value}$$

Formula for the variance for population data:

$$\sigma^2 = \frac{\Sigma(X - \mu)^2}{N}$$

Formula for the variance for sample data (shortcut formula for the unbiased estimator):

$$s^2 = \frac{n(\Sigma X^2) - (\Sigma X)^2}{n(n - 1)}$$

Formula for the variance for grouped data:

$$s^2 = \frac{n(\Sigma f \cdot X_m^2) - (\Sigma f \cdot X_m)^2}{n(n - 1)}$$

Formula for the standard deviation for population data:

$$\sigma = \sqrt{\frac{\Sigma(X - \mu)^2}{N}}$$

Formula for the standard deviation for sample data (shortcut formula):

$$s = \sqrt{\frac{n(\Sigma X^2) - (\Sigma X)^2}{n(n - 1)}}$$

Formula for the standard deviation for grouped data:

$$s = \sqrt{\frac{n(\Sigma f \cdot X_m^2) - (\Sigma f \cdot X_m)^2}{n(n - 1)}}$$

Formula for the coefficient of variation:

$$\text{CVar} = \frac{s}{\overline{X}} \cdot 100 \qquad \text{or} \qquad \text{CVar} = \frac{\sigma}{\mu} \cdot 100$$

Range rule of thumb:

$$s \approx \frac{\text{range}}{4}$$

Expression for Chebyshev's theorem: The proportion of values from a data set that will fall within k standard deviations of the mean will be at least

$$1 - \frac{1}{k^2}$$

where k is a number greater than 1.

Formula for the z score (standard score):

Sample	Population

$$z = \frac{X - \overline{X}}{s} \qquad \text{or} \qquad z = \frac{X - \mu}{\sigma}$$

Formula for the cumulative percentage:

$$\text{Cumulative \%} = \frac{\text{cumulative frequency}}{n} \cdot 100$$

Formula for the percentile rank of a value X:

$$\text{Percentile} = \frac{\text{number of values below } X + 0.5}{\text{total number of values}} \cdot 100$$

Formula for finding a value corresponding to a given percentile:

$$c = \frac{n \cdot p}{100}$$

Formula for interquartile range:

$$\text{IQR} = Q_3 - Q_1$$

Review Exercises

SECTION 3–1

1. **Bank Failures** The data show the number of bank failures over a 15-year period. Find the mean, median, midrange, and mode for the data. 36.5; 11; 78.5; 0, 3, and 4.

14	24	51	92	157	148	30	3
0	0	4	3	11	4	7	

Source: Federal Deposit Insurance Corporation.

2. **Shark Attacks** The number of shark attacks and deaths over a recent 5-year period is shown. Find the mean, median, mode, and midrange for the data.

Attacks: 63.6; 64; no mode; 64

Deaths: 4; 4; 4; 4

Attacks	71	64	61	65	57
Deaths	1	4	4	7	4

3. Systolic Blood Pressure The data show the systolic blood pressure of 30 college students. Find the mean and modal class. 120; 120–124; and 125–129

Class	Frequency
105–109	2
110–114	5
115–119	6
120–124	8
125–129	8
130–134	1

4. SAT Scores The mean SAT math scores for selected states are represented. Find the mean and modal class. $\bar{X} = 531.5$; modal class 505–531

Score	Frequency
478–504	4
505–531	6
532–558	2
559–585	2
586–612	2

Source: World Almanac.

5. Households of Four Television Networks A survey showed the number of viewers and number of households of four television networks. Find the average number of viewers, using the weighted mean. 1.43 viewers

Households	1.4	0.8	0.3	1.6
Viewers (in millions)	1.6	0.8	0.4	1.8

Source: Nielsen Media Research.

6. Investment Earnings An investor calculated these percentages of each of three stock investments with payoffs as shown. Find the average payoff. Use the weighted mean. $4700.00

Stock	Percent	Payoff
A	30	$10,000
B	50	3,000
C	20	1,000

SECTION 3–2

7. Confirmed Measles Cases The data show a sample of the number of confirmed measles cases over a recent 12-year period. Find the range, variance, and standard deviation for the data. 175; 2597.0; 51.0

212   63   71   140   43   55   66   37   56
44   116   86

Source: Centers for Disease Control and Prevention.

8. Tallest Buildings The number of stories in the 13 tallest buildings in Houston are shown. Find the range, variance, and standard deviation for the data. 28; 78.9; 8.9

75   71   64   56   53   55   47   55   52   50
50   50   47

Source: World Almanac.

9. Playing Video Games The frequency distribution shows the number of hours per week that 40 college students spent online playing video games. Find the mean, modal class, variance, and standard deviation for the data. 7.1; 6–8; 12.7; 3.6

Class	Frequency
0–2	2
3–5	12
6–8	16
9–11	5
12–14	3
15–17	2
	40

10. Driving to Work The data in the frequency distribution show the time in minutes it takes 50 randomly selected people to drive to work. Find the mean, modal class, variance, and standard deviation. 19; 15–19; 52.0; 7.2

Class	Frequency
5–9	7
10–14	3
15–19	19
20–24	10
25–29	6
30–34	5
	50

11. If the range of a data set is 24, find the approximate value of the standard deviation, using the range rule of thumb. 6

12. If the range of a data set is 56, find the approximate value of the standard deviation, using the range rule of thumb. 14

13. Textbooks in Professors' Offices If the average number of textbooks in professors' offices is 16, the standard deviation is 5, and the average age of the professors is 43, with a standard deviation of 8, which data set is more variable? Books CVar = 31.25%; Ages CVar = 18.6%; the number of books is more variable

14. Magazines in Bookstores A survey of bookstores showed that the average number of magazines carried is 56, with a standard deviation of 12. The same survey showed that the average length of time each store had been in business was 6 years, with a standard deviation of 2.5 years. Which is more variable, the number of magazines or the number of years? Magazine CVar = 21.4%; Years CVar = 41.7%; years are more variable

15. Cost of Car Rentals A survey of car rental agencies shows that the average cost of a car rental is $0.32 per mile. The standard deviation is $0.03. Using Chebyshev's theorem, find the range in which at least 75% of the data values will fall. $0.26–$0.38

16. **Average Earnings of Workers** The average earnings of year-round full-time workers 25–34 years old with a bachelor's degree or higher were $58,500 in 2003. If the standard deviation is $11,200, what can you say about the percentage of these workers who earn.

    a. Between $47,300 and $69,700? Nothing because $k = 1$
    b. More than $80,900? At most ¼ or 25%
    c. How likely is it that someone earns more than $100,000? At most 7.3%

    Source: New York Times Almanac.

17. **Labor Charges** The average labor charge for automobile mechanics is $54 per hour. The standard deviation is $4. Find the minimum percentage of data values that will fall within the range of $48 to $60. Use Chebyshev's theorem. 56%

18. **Costs to Train Employees** For a certain type of job, it costs a company an average of $231 to train an employee to perform the task. The standard deviation is $5. Find the minimum percentage of data values that will fall in the range of $219 to $243. Use Chebyshev's theorem. 83%

19. **Cost of a Man's Haircut** The average cost of a man's haircut is $21. The standard deviation is $4. If the variable is approximately bell-shaped, within what limits would 68% of the haircut cost? $17–$25

20. **Exam Completion Time** The mean time it takes a group of students to complete a statistics final exam is 44 minutes, and the standard deviation is 9 minutes. Within what limits would you expect approximately 95% of the students to complete the exam? Assume the variable is approximately normally distributed. 26–62

21. **Cases of Meningitis** The data show the number of specific recorded cases of meningitis for 14 specific states.

10	1	1	28	15	41	4	4	8	2	3
53	34	1								

    Source: Centers for Disease Control and Prevention

    Find the z values for each

    a. 10 −0.27
    b. 28 0.77
    c. 41 1.53

SECTION 3–3

22. **Exam Grades** Which of these exam grades has a better relative position?

    a. A grade of 82 on a test with $\overline{X} = 85$ and $s = 6$ −0.5
    b. A grade of 56 on a test with $\overline{X} = 60$ and $s = 5$ −0.8
       The grade in part a has better position.

23. The number of police calls a small police department received each month is shown in the frequency distribution.

Class limits	Frequency
39.9–42.8	2
42.9–45.8	2
45.9–48.8	5
48.9–51.8	5
51.9–54.8	12
54.9–57.8	3

    a. Construct a percentile graph.
    b. Find the values that correspond to the 35th, 65th, and 85th percentiles. 50, 53, 55
    c. Find the percentile of values 44, 48, and 54. 10th; 26th; 78th

24. **Printer Repairs** The frequency distribution shows the number of days it took to fix each of 80 computer's printers.

Class limits	Frequency
1–3	7
4–6	9
7–9	32
10–12	20
13–15	12
	80

    a. Construct a percentile graph.
    b. Find the 20th, 50th, and 70th percentiles. 6.5; 8.75; 10.7.
    c. Find the percentile values of 5, 10, and 14. 14th; 64th; 93rd

25. Check each data set for outliers.

    a. 506, 511, 517, 514, 400, 521 400
    b. 3, 7, 9, 6, 8, 10, 14, 16, 20, 12 None

26. Check each data set for outliers.

    a. 14, 18, 27, 26, 19, 13, 5, 25 None
    b. 112, 157, 192, 116, 153, 129, 131 None

SECTION 3–4

27. **Named Storms** The data show the number of named storms for the years 1851–1860 and 1941 and 1950. Construct a boxplot for each data set and compare the distributions.

1851–1860	6	5	8	5	5	6	4	6	8	7
1941–1950	6	10	10	11	11	6	9	9	13	13

    Source: National Hurricane Center

28. **Hours Worked** The data shown here represent the number of hours that 12 part-time employees at a toy store worked during the weeks before and after Christmas. Construct two boxplots and compare the distributions.

Before	38	16	18	24	12	30	35	32	31	30	24	35
After	26	15	12	18	24	32	14	18	16	18	22	12

STATISTICS TODAY

How Long Are You Delayed by Road Congestion? —Revisited

The average number of hours per year that a driver is delayed by road congestion is listed here.

City	Hours
Los Angeles	56
Atlanta	53
Seattle	53
Houston	50
Dallas	46
Washington	46
Austin	45
Denver	45
St. Louis	44
Orlando	42
U.S. average	36

Source: Texas Transportation Institute.

By making comparisons using averages, you can see that drivers in these 10 cities are delayed by road congestion more than the national average.

Data Analysis

A Data Bank is found in Appendix B.

1. From the Data Bank, choose one of the following variables: age, weight, cholesterol level, systolic pressure, IQ, or sodium level. Select at least 30 values, and find the mean, median, mode, and midrange. State which measurement of central tendency best describes the average and why.

2. Find the range, variance, and standard deviation for the data selected in Exercise 1.

3. From the Data Bank, choose 10 values from any variable, construct a boxplot, and interpret the results.

4. Randomly select 10 values from the number of suspensions in the local school districts in southwestern Pennsylvania in Data Set V in Appendix B. Find the mean, median, mode, range, variance, and standard deviation of the number of suspensions by using the Pearson coefficient of skewness.

5. Using the data from Data Set VII in Appendix B, find the mean, median, mode, range, variance, and standard deviation of the acreage owned by the municipalities. Comment on the skewness of the data, using the Pearson coefficient of skewness.

Chapter Quiz

Determine whether each statement is true or false. If the statement is false, explain why.

1. When the mean is computed for individual data, all values in the data set are used. True

2. The mean cannot be found for grouped data when there is an open class. True

3. A single, extremely large value can affect the median more than the mean. False

4. One-half of all the data values will fall above the mode, and one-half will fall below the mode. False

5. In a data set, the mode will always be unique. False

6. The range and midrange are both measures of variation. False

7. One disadvantage of the median is that it is not unique. False

8. The mode and midrange are both measures of variation. False

9. If a person's score on an exam corresponds to the 75th percentile, then that person obtained 75 correct answers out of 100 questions. False

Select the best answer.

10. What is the value of the mode when all values in the data set are different?

a. 0   c. There is no mode.

b. 1   d. It cannot be determined unless the data values are given.

11. When data are categorized as, for example, places of residence (rural, suburban, urban), the most appropriate measure of central tendency is the

a. Mean   c. Mode

b. Median   d. Midrange

12. P_{50} corresponds to *a and b*

a. Q_2 c. IQR

b. D_5 d. Midrange

13. Which is not part of the five-number summary?

a. Q_1 and Q_3 c. The median

b. The mean   d. The smallest and the largest data values

14. A statistic that tells the number of standard deviations a data value is above or below the mean is called

a. A quartile   c. A coefficient of variation

b. A percentile   d. A z score

15. When a distribution is bell-shaped, approximately what percentage of data values will fall within 1 standard deviation of the mean?

a. 50%   c. 95%

b. 68%   d. 99.7%

Complete these statements with the best answer.

16. A measure obtained from sample data is called a(n) _____. Statistic

17. Generally, Greek letters are used to represent _____, and Roman letters are used to represent _____. Parameters, statistics

18. The positive square root of the variance is called the _____. Standard deviation

19. The symbol for the population standard deviation is _____. σ

20. When the sum of the lowest data value and the highest data value is divided by 2, the measure is called the _____. Midrange

21. If the mode is to the left of the median and the mean is to the right of the median, then the distribution is _____ skewed. Positively

22. An extremely high or extremely low data value is called a(n) _____. Outlier

23. Miles per Gallon The number of highway miles per gallon of the 10 worst vehicles is shown.

12   15   13   14   15   16   17   16   17   18

Source: Pittsburgh Post Gazette.

Find each of these.

a. Mean 15.3   e. Range 6

b. Median 15.5   f. Variance 3.6

c. Mode 15, 16, and 17   g. Standard deviation 1.9

d. Midrange 15

24. Errors on a Typing Test The distribution of the number of errors that 10 students made on a typing test is shown.

Errors	Frequency
0–2	1
3–5	3
6–8	4
9–11	1
12–14	1

Find each of these.

a. Mean 6.4   c. Variance 11.6

b. Modal class 6–8   d. Standard deviation 3.4

25. Employee Years of Service In an advertisement, a retail store stated that its employees averaged 9 years of service. The distribution is shown here. 4.5

Number of employees	Years of service
8	2
2	6
3	10

Using the weighted mean, calculate the correct average.

26. Newspapers for Sale The average number of newspapers for sale in an airport newsstand is 56 with a standard deviation of 6. The average number of newspapers for sale in a convenience store is 44 with a standard deviation of 5. Which data set is more variable? The number of newspapers sold in a convenience store is more variable.

27. Delivery Charges The average delivery charge for a refrigerator is $32. The standard deviation is $4. Find the minimum percentage of data values that will fall in the range of $20 to $44. Use Chebyshev's theorem. 88.89%

28. SAT Scores The average national SAT score is 1019. If we assume a bell-shaped distribution and a standard deviation equal to 110, what percentage of scores will you expect to fall above 1129? Above 799? 16%; 97.5%

Source: New York Times Almanac.

29. If the range of a data set is 18, estimate the standard deviation of the data. 4.5

30. Test Scores A student scored 76 on a general science test where the class mean and standard deviation were 82 and 8, respectively; the student also scored 53 on a psychology test where the class mean and standard deviation were 58 and 3, respectively. In which class was the student's relative position higher? −0.75; −1.67; science

31. Exam Scores On a philosophy comprehensive exam, this distribution was obtained from 25 students.

Score	Frequency
40.5–45.5	3
45.5–50.5	8
50.5–55.5	10
55.5–60.5	3
60.5–65.5	1

a. Construct a percentile graph.

b. Find the values that correspond to the 22nd, 78th, and 99th percentiles. 47; 55; 64

c. Find the percentiles of the values 52, 43, and 64. 56th, 6th, 99th percentiles

32. **Gas Prices for Rental Cars** The first column of these data represents the prebuy gas price of a rental car, and the second column represents the price charged if the car is returned without refilling the gas tank for a selected car rental company. Draw two boxplots for the data and compare the distributions. (*Note:* The data were collected several years ago.)

Prebuy cost	No prebuy cost
$1.55	$3.80
1.54	3.99
1.62	3.99
1.65	3.85
1.72	3.99
1.63	3.95
1.65	3.94
1.72	4.19
1.45	3.84
1.52	3.94

Source: USA TODAY.

Critical Thinking Challenges

1. **Average Cost of Weddings** Averages give us information to help us see where we stand and enable us to make comparisons. Here is a study on the average cost of a wedding. What type of average—mean, median, mode, or midrange—might have been used for each category?

Wedding Costs

The average cost of a wedding varies each year. The average cost of a wedding for a specific year was $26,444. The average cost of the reception venue, catering, and rentals were $11,784. The cost for wedding flowers was $1579. The cost of the wedding invitations was $896. The cost of a wedding planner was $1646. The cost of photography and videography was $1646.

2. **Average Cost of Smoking** The average yearly cost of smoking a pack of cigarettes a day is $1190. Find the average cost of a pack of cigarettes in your area, and compute the cost per day for 1 year. Compare your answer with the one in the article.

3. **Ages of U.S. Residents** The table shows the median ages of residents for the 10 oldest states and the 10 youngest states of the United States including Washington, DC. Explain why the median is used instead of the mean.

10 Oldest			10 Youngest		
Rank	State	Median age	Rank	State	Median age
1	West Virginia	38.9	51	Utah	27.1
2	Florida	38.7	50	Texas	32.3
3	Maine	38.6	49	Alaska	32.4
4	Pennsylvania	38.0	48	Idaho	33.2
5	Vermont	37.7	47	California	33.3
6	Montana	37.5	46	Georgia	33.4
7	Connecticut	37.4	45	Mississippi	33.8
8	New Hampshire	37.1	44	Louisiana	34.0
9	New Jersey	36.7	43	Arizona	34.2
10	Rhode Island	36.7	42	Colorado	34.3

Source: U.S. Census Bureau.

Data Projects

Where appropriate, use MINITAB, the TI-84 Plus, Excel, or a computer program of your choice to complete the following exercises.

1. **Business and Finance** Use the data collected in data project 1 of Chapter 2 regarding earnings per share. Determine the mean, mode, median, and midrange for the two data sets. Is one measure of center more appropriate than the other for these data? Do the measures of center appear similar? What does this say about the symmetry of the distribution?

2. **Sports and Leisure** Use the data collected in data project 2 of Chapter 2 regarding home runs. Determine the mean, mode, median, and midrange for the two data sets. Is one measure of center more appropriate than the other for these data? Do the measures of center appear similar? What does this say about the symmetry of the distribution?

3. **Technology** Use the data collected in data project 3 of Chapter 2. Determine the mean for the frequency table created in that project. Find the actual mean length of all 50 songs. How does the grouped mean compare to the actual mean?

4. **Health and Wellness** Use the data collected in data project 6 of Chapter 2 regarding heart rates. Determine

the mean and standard deviation for each set of data. Do the means seem very different from one another? Do the standard deviations appear very different from one another?

5. **Politics and Economics** Use the data collected in data project 5 of Chapter 2 regarding delegates. Use the formulas for population mean and standard deviation to compute the parameters for all 50 states. What is the *z* score associated with California? Delaware? Ohio?

Which states are more than 2 standard deviations from the mean?

6. **Your Class** Use your class as a sample. Determine the mean, median, and standard deviation for the age of students in your class. What *z* score would a 40-year-old have? Would it be unusual to have an age of 40? Determine the skew of the data, using the Pearson coefficient of skewness. (See Exercise 48 in Exercise 3–2.)

Answers to Applying the Concepts

Section 3–1   Teacher Salaries

1. The sample mean is $62,921.67, the sample median is $56,500, and the sample mode is $51,000. If you work for the school board and do not want to raise salaries, you could say that the average teacher salary is $62,921.67.

2. If you work for the teachers' union and want a raise for the teachers, the sample mode of $51,000 would be a good measure of center to report.

3. The outlier is $147,000. With the outlier removed, the sample mean is $55,278.18, the sample median is $56,400, and the sample mode is still $51,000. The mean is greatly affected by the outlier and allows the school board to report an average teacher salary that is not representative of a "typical" teacher salary.

4. If the salaries represented every teacher in the school district, the averages would be parameters, since we have data from the entire population.

5. The mean and midrange can be misleading in the presence of outliers, since they are greatly affected by these extreme values.

6. Since the mean is greater than both the median and the mode, the distribution is skewed to the right (positively skewed).

Section 3–2   Blood Pressure

1. Chebyshev's theorem does not work for scores within 1 standard deviation of the mean.

2. At least 75% (900) of the normotensive men have systolic blood pressures that fall between 105 and 141 mm Hg.

3. About 68% (952) of the normotensive women have diastolic blood pressures between 69 and 83 mm Hg. About 95% (1330) of the normotensive women have diastolic blood pressures between 62 and 90 mm Hg. About 99.7% (1396) of the normotensive women have diastolic blood pressures between 55 and 97 mm Hg.

   About 68% (884) of the hypertensive women have diastolic blood pressures between 78 and 98 mm Hg. About 95% (1235) of the hypertensive women have diastolic blood pressures between 68 and 108 mm Hg. About 99.7% (1296) of the hypertensive women have diastolic blood pressures between 58 and 118 mm Hg.

4. About 68% (816) of the normotensive men have systolic blood pressures between 114 and 132 mm Hg. About 95% (1140) of the normotensive men have systolic blood pressures between 105 and 141 mm Hg. About

99.7% (1196) of the normotensive men have systolic blood pressures between 96 and 150 mm Hg.

   About 68% (748) of the hypertensive men have systolic blood pressures between 136 and 170 mm Hg. About 95% (1045) of the hypertensive men have systolic blood pressures between 119 and 187 mm Hg. About 99.7% (1097) of the hypertensive men have systolic blood pressures between 102 and 204 mm Hg.

   The "68%" ranges do not overlap. The "95%" and "99.7%" ranges overlap.

Section 3–3   Determining Dosages

1. Standard scores (*z* scores), percentiles, deciles, and quartiles can be used to describe the data results.

2. Since there are 10 mice in the upper quartile, this would mean that 4 of them survived.

3. The percentiles would give us the position of a single mouse with respect to all other mice.

4. The quartiles divide the data into four groups of equal size.

5. Standard scores would give us the position of a single mouse with respect to the mean time until the onset of sepsis.

Section 3–4   The Noisy Workplace

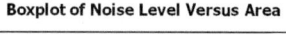
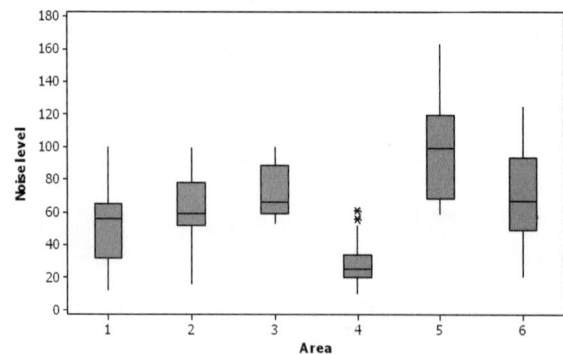

Boxplot of Noise Level Versus Area

From this boxplot, we see that about 25% of the readings in area 5 are above the safe hearing level of 120 decibels. Those workers in area 5 should definitely have protective ear wear. One of the readings in area 6 is above the safe hearing level. It might be a good idea to provide protective ear wear to those workers in area 6 as well. Areas 1–4 appear to be "safe" with respect to hearing level, with area 4 being the safest.

Probability and Counting Rules

askhamdesign/E+/Getty Images

━ STATISTICS TODAY

Would You Bet Your Life?

Humans not only bet money when they gamble, but also bet their lives by engaging in unhealthy activities such as smoking, drinking, using drugs, and exceeding the speed limit when driving. Many people don't care about the risks involved in these activities since they do not understand the concepts of probability. On the other hand, people may fear activities that involve little risk to health or life because these activities have been sensationalized by the press and media.

In his book *Probabilities in Everyday Life* (Ivy Books, p. 191), John D. McGervey states

> *When people have been asked to estimate the frequency of death from various causes, the most overestimated categories are those involving pregnancy, tornadoes, floods, fire, and homicide. The most underestimated categories include deaths from diseases such as diabetes, strokes, tuberculosis, asthma, and stomach cancer (although cancer in general is overestimated).*

The question then is, Would you feel safer if you flew across the United States on a commercial airline or if you drove? How much greater is the risk of one way to travel over the other? See Statistics Today—Revisited at the end of the chapter for the answer.

In this chapter, you will learn about probability—its meaning, how it is computed, and how to evaluate it in terms of the likelihood of an event actually happening.

OUTLINE

OBJECTIVES

After completing this chapter, you should be able to:

1   Determine sample spaces and find the probability of an event, using classical probability or empirical probability.

2   Find the probability of compound events, using the addition rules.

3   Find the probability of compound events, using the multiplication rules.

4   Find the conditional probability of an event.

5   Find the total number of outcomes in a sequence of events, using the fundamental counting rule.

6   Find the number of ways that *r* objects can be selected from *n* objects, using the permutation rule.

7   Find the number of ways that *r* objects can be selected from *n* objects without regard to order, using the combination rule.

8   Find the probability of an event, using the counting rules.

Introduction

A cynical person once said, "The only two sure things are death and taxes." This philosophy no doubt arose because so much in people's lives is affected by chance. From the time you awake until you go to bed, you make decisions regarding the possible events that are governed at least in part by chance. For example, should you carry an umbrella to work today? Will your car battery last until spring? Should you accept that new job?

Probability as a general concept can be defined as the chance of an event occurring. Many people are familiar with probability from observing or playing games of chance, such as card games, slot machines, or lotteries. In addition to being used in games of chance, probability theory is used in the fields of insurance, investments, and weather forecasting and in various other areas. Finally, as stated in Chapter 1, probability is the basis of inferential statistics. For example, predictions are based on probability, and hypotheses are tested by using probability.

The basic concepts of probability are explained in this chapter. These concepts include *probability experiments, sample spaces,* the *addition* and *multiplication rules,* and the *probabilities of complementary events.* Also in this chapter, you will learn the rule for counting, the differences between permutations and combinations, and how to figure out how many different combinations for specific situations exist. Finally, Section 4–5 explains how the counting rules and the probability rules can be used together to solve a wide variety of problems.

4–1   Sample Spaces and Probability

The theory of probability grew out of the study of various games of chance using coins, dice, and cards. Since these devices lend themselves well to the application of concepts of probability, they will be used in this chapter as examples. This section begins by explaining some basic concepts of probability. Then the types of probability and probability rules are discussed.

Basic Concepts

Processes such as flipping a coin, rolling a die, or drawing a card from a deck are called *probability experiments.*

OBJECTIVE

Determine sample spaces and find the probability of an event, using classical probability or empirical probability.

> A **probability experiment** is a chance process that leads to well-defined results called outcomes.
>
> An **outcome** is the result of a single trial of a probability experiment.

A trial means flipping a coin once, rolling one die once, or the like. When a coin is tossed, there are two possible outcomes: head or tail. (*Note:* We exclude the possibility of a coin landing on its edge.) In the roll of a single die, there are six possible outcomes: 1, 2, 3, 4, 5, or 6. In any experiment, the set of all possible outcomes is called the *sample space.*

> A **sample space** is the set of all possible outcomes of a probability experiment.

Some sample spaces for various probability experiments are shown here.

Experiment	Sample space
Toss one coin	Head, tail
Roll a die	1, 2, 3, 4, 5, 6
Answer a true/false question	True, false
Toss two coins	Head-head, tail-tail, head-tail, tail-head

It is important to realize that when two coins are tossed, there are *four* possible outcomes, as shown in the fourth experiment above. Both coins could fall heads up. Both coins could fall tails up. Coin 1 could fall heads up and coin 2 tails up. Or coin 1 could fall tails up and coin 2 heads up. Heads and tails will be abbreviated as H and T throughout this chapter.

Another assumption commonly made in probability theory is that the number of male births is equal to the number of female births and that the probability of a boy being born is ½ and the probability of a girl being born is ½. We know this is not exactly true since biological sex is not necessarily binary: it exists on a spectrum, and the exact split of males and females varies from location to location.

EXAMPLE 4–1   Rolling Dice

Find the sample space for rolling two dice.

SOLUTION

Since each die can land in six different ways, and two dice are rolled, the sample space can be presented by a rectangular array, as shown in Figure 4–1. The sample space is the list of pairs of numbers in the chart.

FIGURE 4–1

Sample Space for Rolling Two Dice (Example 4–1)

Die 1	Die 2					
	1	2	3	4	5	6
1	(1, 1)	(1, 2)	(1, 3)	(1, 4)	(1, 5)	(1, 6)
2	(2, 1)	(2, 2)	(2, 3)	(2, 4)	(2, 5)	(2, 6)
3	(3, 1)	(3, 2)	(3, 3)	(3, 4)	(3, 5)	(3, 6)
4	(4, 1)	(4, 2)	(4, 3)	(4, 4)	(4, 5)	(4, 6)
5	(5, 1)	(5, 2)	(5, 3)	(5, 4)	(5, 5)	(5, 6)
6	(6, 1)	(6, 2)	(6, 3)	(6, 4)	(6, 5)	(6, 6)

EXAMPLE 4–2   Drawing Cards

Find the sample space for drawing one card from an ordinary deck of cards.

SOLUTION

Since there are 4 suits (hearts, clubs, diamonds, and spades) and 13 cards for each suit (ace through king), there are 52 outcomes in the sample space. See Figure 4–2.

FIGURE 4–2 Sample Space for Drawing a Card (Example 4–2)

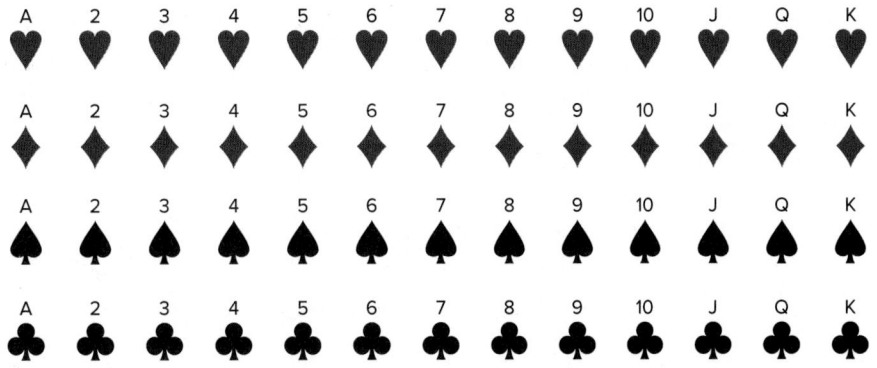

EXAMPLE 4–3   Rolling a Die

A die is rolled three times and the number of spots obtained is noted as either odd (1, 3, or 5) or even (2, 4, or 6). Find the sample space for the experiment.

SOLUTION

Use O for an odd number and E for an even number. Here there are eight possibilities since there are two ways the die could land, namely, an odd number or an even number. The sample space is shown:

OOO   OOE   OEO   EOO   EEO   EOE   OEE   EEE

In Examples 4–1 through 4–3, the sample spaces were found by observation and reasoning; however, another way to find all possible outcomes of a probability experiment is to use a *tree diagram.*

A **tree diagram** is a device consisting of line segments emanating from a starting point and also from the outcome point. It is used to determine all possible outcomes of a probability experiment.

EXAMPLE 4–4   Gender of Children

Use a tree diagram to find the sample space for the gender of three children in a family.

SOLUTION

Since there are two possibilities (boy or girl) for the first child, draw two branches from a starting point and label one B and the other G. Then if the first child is a boy, there are two possibilities for the second child (boy or girl), so draw two branches from B and label one B and the other G. Do the same if the first child is a girl. Follow the same procedure for the third child. The completed tree diagram is shown in Figure 4–3. To find the outcomes for the sample space, trace through all the possible branches, beginning at the starting point for each one.

FIGURE 4–3   Tree Diagram for Example 4–4

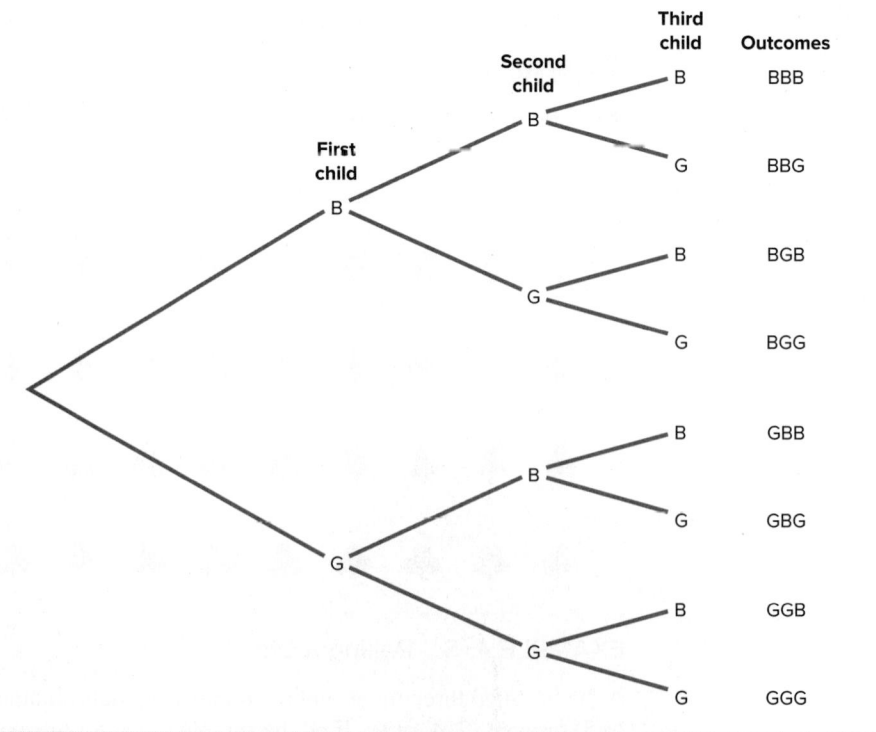

An outcome was defined previously as the result of a single trial of a probability experiment. In many problems, one must find the probability of two or more outcomes. For this reason, it is necessary to distinguish between an outcome and an event.

> An **event** consists of a set of outcomes of a probability experiment.

Historical Note

During the mid-1600s, a professional gambler named Chevalier de Méré made a considerable amount of money on a gambling game. He would bet unsuspecting patrons that in four rolls of a die, he could get at least one 6. He was so successful at the game that some people refused to play. He decided that a new game was necessary to continue his winnings. By reasoning, he figured he could roll at least one double 6 in 24 rolls of two dice, but his reasoning was incorrect and he lost systematically. Unable to figure out why, he contacted a mathematician named Blaise Pascal (1623–1662) to find out why.

Pascal became interested and began studying probability theory. He corresponded with a French government official, Pierre de Fermat (1601–1665), whose hobby was mathematics. Together the two formulated the beginnings of probability theory.

An event can be one outcome or more than one outcome. For example, if a die is rolled and a 6 shows, this result is called an *outcome,* since it is a result of a single trial. An event with one outcome is called a **simple event.** The event of getting an odd number when a die is rolled is called a **compound event,** since it consists of three outcomes or three simple events. In general, a compound event consists of two or more outcomes or simple events.

There are three basic interpretations of probability:

1. Classical probability
2. Empirical or relative frequency probability
3. Subjective probability

Classical Probability

Classical probability uses sample spaces to determine the numerical probability that an event will happen. You do not actually have to perform the experiment to determine that probability. Classical probability is so named because it was the first type of probability studied formally by mathematicians in the 17th and 18th centuries.

Classical probability assumes that all outcomes in the sample space are equally likely to occur. For example, when a single die is rolled, each outcome has the same probability of occurring. Since there are six outcomes, each outcome has a probability of $\frac{1}{6}$. When a card is selected from an ordinary deck of 52 cards, you assume that the deck has been shuffled, and each card has the same probability of being selected. In this case, it is $\frac{1}{52}$.

> **Equally likely events** are events that have the same probability of occurring.

> **Formula for Classical Probability**
>
> The probability of any event E is
>
> $$\frac{\text{Number of outcomes in } E}{\text{Total number of outcomes in the sample space}}$$
>
> This probability is denoted by
>
> $$P(E) = \frac{n(E)}{n(S)}$$
>
> where $n(E)$ is the number of outcomes in E and $n(S)$ is the number of outcomes in the sample space S.

Probabilities can be expressed as fractions, decimals, or—where appropriate—percentages. If you ask, "What is the probability of getting a head when a coin is tossed?" typical responses can be any of the following three.

"One-half."

"Point five."

"Fifty percent."[1]

---

[1]Strictly speaking, a percent is not a probability. However, in everyday language, probabilities are often expressed as percents (i.e., there is a 60% chance of rain tomorrow). For this reason, some probabilities will be expressed as percents throughout this book.

These answers are all equivalent. In most cases, the answers to examples and exercises given in this chapter are expressed as fractions or decimals, but percentages are used where appropriate.

Rounding Rule for Probabilities Probabilities should be expressed as reduced fractions or rounded to three decimal places. When the probability of an event is an extremely small decimal, it is permissible to round the decimal to the first nonzero digit after the point. For example, 0.0000587 would be 0.00006. When obtaining probabilities from one of the tables in Appendix A, use the number of decimal places given in the table. If decimals are converted to percentages to express probabilities, move the decimal point two places to the right and add a percent sign.

EXAMPLE 4–5   Rolling Dice

When two dice are rolled, find the probability that one die will show a three and the other die will show a six.

SOLUTION

There are 36 outcomes when two dice are rolled. See Example 4–1 for the sample space. There are two ways to get a three on one die and a six on the other die. That is, (3, 6) and (6, 3). Hence, the probability is

$$\frac{2}{36} = \frac{1}{18} \approx 0.056$$

EXAMPLE 4–6   Gender of Children

If a family has three children, find the probability that exactly two of the three children are boys.

SOLUTION

The sample space for the gender of three children has eight outcomes BBB, BBG, BGB, GBB, GGG, GGB, GBG, and BGG. Since there are three ways to get two boys and one girl, that is BBG, BGB, and GBB, the probability of having exactly two boys is $\frac{3}{8}$.

Historical Note

Ancient Greeks and Romans made crude dice from animal bones, various stones, minerals, and ivory. When the dice were tested mathematically, some were found to be quite accurate.

In probability theory, it is important to understand the meaning of the words *and* and *or*. For example, if you were asked to find the probability of getting a queen *and* a heart when you were drawing a single card from a deck, you would be looking for the queen of hearts. Here the word *and* means "at the same time." The word *or* has two meanings. For example, if you were asked to find the probability of selecting a queen *or* a heart when one card is selected from a deck, you would be looking for one of the 4 queens or one of the 13 hearts. In this case, the queen of hearts would be included in both cases and counted twice. So there would be 4 + 13 − 1 = 16 possibilities.

On the other hand, if you were asked to find the probability of getting a queen *or* a king, you would be looking for one of the 4 queens or one of the 4 kings. In this case, there would be 4 + 4 = 8 possibilities. In the first case, both events can occur at the same time; we say that this is an example of the *inclusive or*. In the second case, both events cannot occur at the same time, and we say that this is an example of the *exclusive or*.

EXAMPLE 4–7   Drawing Cards

A card is drawn from an ordinary well-shuffled deck. Find the probability of getting

a. A club.
b. A red card.
c. The 7 of spades.
d. A king.
e. A face card.

SOLUTION

a. Refer to the sample space shown in Figure 4–2. There are 13 clubs in the deck of 52 cards; hence,

$$P(\clubsuit) = \frac{13}{52} = \frac{1}{4} = 0.25$$

b. Since there are 26 red cards in the deck, 13 hearts and 13 diamonds, the probability of getting a red card is

$$P(\text{red card}) = \frac{26}{52} = \frac{1}{2}$$

c. Since there is only one seven of spades in the deck, the probability is

$$P(7\spadesuit) = \frac{1}{52} \approx 0.019$$

d. There are 4 kings in a deck of 52 cards, so the probability is

$$P(\text{king}) = \frac{4}{52} = \frac{1}{13} \approx 0.077$$

e. There are 12 face cards in an ordinary deck of cards, that is, 4 suits (diamonds, hearts, spades, and clubs) and 3 face cards of each suit (jack, queen, and king), so

$$P(\text{face card}) = \frac{12}{52} = \frac{3}{13} \approx 0.231$$

There are four basic probability rules. These rules are helpful in solving probability problems, in understanding the nature of probability, and in deciding if your answers to the problems are correct.

Probability Rules

1. The probability of any event E is a number (either a fraction or decimal) between and including 0 and 1. This is denoted by $0 \leq P(E) \leq 1$.
2. The sum of the probabilities of all the outcomes in a sample space is 1.
3. If an event E cannot occur (i.e., the event contains no members in the sample space), its probability is 0.
4. If an event E is certain, then the probability of E is 1.

Rule 1 states that probability values range from 0 to 1. When the probability of an event is close to 0, its occurrence is highly unlikely. When the probability of an event is near 0.5, there is about a 50-50 chance that the event will occur; and when the probability of an event is close to 1, the event is highly likely to occur. See Figure 4–4.

FIGURE 4–4

Range of Probability

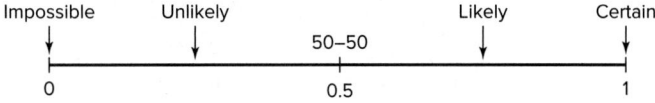

Rule 2 can be illustrated by the example of rolling a single die. Each outcome in the sample space has a probability of $\frac{1}{6}$, and the sum of the probabilities of all the outcomes is 1, as shown.

Outcome	1	2	3	4	5	6
Probability	$\frac{1}{6}$	$\frac{1}{6}$	$\frac{1}{6}$	$\frac{1}{6}$	$\frac{1}{6}$	$\frac{1}{6}$
Sum	$\frac{1}{6}$ +	$\frac{1}{6}$ +	$\frac{1}{6}$ +	$\frac{1}{6}$ +	$\frac{1}{6}$ +	$\frac{1}{6} = \frac{6}{6} = 1$

Rule 3 states if an event cannot occur then $P(E) = 0$.
Rule 3 is illustrated in Example 4–8.

EXAMPLE 4–8   Drawing a Card

The black cards in an ordinary deck are removed; then the 26 red cards are well shuffled. One card is selected. Find the probability of getting a black card.

SOLUTION

Since there are no black cards in the 26 red cards, it is impossible to get a black card, so

$$P(\text{black card}) = \frac{0}{26} = 0$$

Rule 4 states that if $P(E) = 1$, then the event E is certain to occur. This rule is illustrated in Example 4–9.

EXAMPLE 4–9   Drawing a Card

The black cards are removed from an ordinary deck of cards. The 26 red cards are well shuffled, and one card in selected. Find the probability that it is a red card.

SOLUTION

Since there are 26 ways to get a red card, the probability of getting a red card is

$$P(\text{red card}) = \frac{26}{26} = 1$$

Complementary Events

Another important concept in probability theory is that of *complementary events*. When a die is rolled, for instance, the sample space consists of the outcomes 1, 2, 3, 4, 5, and 6. The event E of getting odd numbers consists of the outcomes 1, 3, and 5. The event of not getting an odd number is called the *complement* of event E, and it consists of the outcomes 2, 4, and 6.

> The **complement of an event** E is the set of outcomes in the sample space that are not included in the outcomes of event E. The complement of E is denoted by $\bar{E}$ (read "E bar").

Example 4–10 further illustrates the concept of complementary events.

EXAMPLE 4–10   Finding Complements

Find the complement of each event:

  a. Selecting a month that has 30 days
  b. Selecting a day of the week that begins with the letter S
  c. Rolling two dice and getting a number whose sum is 7
  d. Selecting a letter of the alphabet (excluding y) that is a vowel

SOLUTION

  a. Selecting a month that has 28 or 31 days, that is, January, February, March, May, July, August, October, or December
  b. Selecting a day of the week that does not begin with S, that is, Monday, Tuesday, Wednesday, Thursday, or Friday
  c. Rolling two dice and getting a sum of 2, 3, 4, 5, 6, 8, 9, 10, 11, or 12
  d. Selecting a letter of the alphabet that is a consonant

The outcomes of an event and the outcomes of the complement make up the entire sample space. For example, if two coins are tossed, the sample space is HH, HT, TH, and TT. The complement of "getting all heads" is not "getting all tails," since the event "all heads" is HH, and the complement of HH is HT, TH, and TT. Hence, the complement of the event "all heads" is the event "getting at least one tail."

Since the event and its complement make up the entire sample space, it follows that the sum of the probability of the event and the probability of its complement will equal 1. That is, $P(E) + P(\overline{E}) = 1$. For example, let E = all heads, or HH, and let $\overline{E}$ = at least one tail, or HT, TH, TT. Then $P(E) = \frac{1}{4}$ and $P(\overline{E}) = \frac{3}{4}$; hence, $P(E) + P(\overline{E}) = \frac{1}{4} + \frac{3}{4} = 1$.

The rule for complementary events can be stated algebraically in three ways.

Rule for Complementary Events

$$P(\overline{E}) = 1 - P(E) \qquad \text{or} \qquad P(E) = 1 - P(\overline{E}) \qquad \text{or} \qquad P(E) + P(\overline{E}) = 1$$

Stated in words, the rule is: *If the probability of an event or the probability of its complement is known, then the other can be found by subtracting the probability from 1.* This rule is important in probability theory because at times the best solution to a problem is to find the probability of the complement of an event and then subtract from 1 to get the probability of the event itself.

Probabilities can be represented pictorially by **Venn diagrams.** Figure 4–5(a) shows the probability of a simple event E. The area inside the circle represents the probability of event E, that is, $P(E)$. The area inside the rectangle represents the probability of all the events in the sample space $P(S)$.

The Venn diagram that represents the probability of the complement of an event $P(\overline{E})$ is shown in Figure 4–5(b). In this case, $P(\overline{E}) = 1 - P(E)$, which is the area inside the rectangle but outside the circle representing $P(E)$. Recall that $P(S) = 1$ and $P(E) = 1 - P(\overline{E})$. The reasoning is that $P(E)$ is represented by the area of the circle and $P(\overline{E})$ is the probability of the events that are outside the circle.

FIGURE 4–5

Venn Diagram for the Probability and Complement

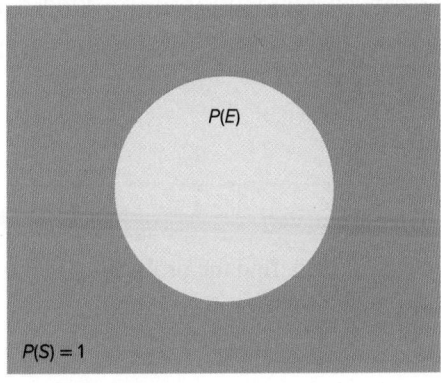

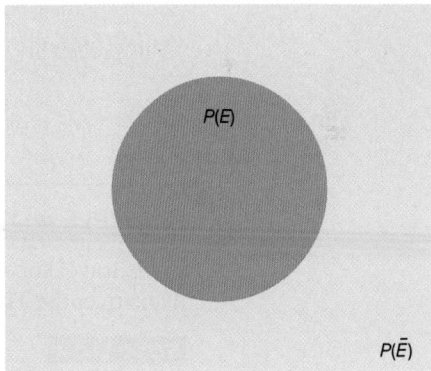

(a) Simple probability

(b) $P(\overline{E}) = 1 - P(E)$

EXAMPLE 4–11   Driving Time

A study found that 51% of workers drove 10 miles or less to work, 27% drove 11 to 20 miles to work, and 22% drove 21 or more miles to work. If a person is selected at random, find the probability that the person drives 11 or more miles to work.

Source: U.S. Department of Transportation

SOLUTION

$$P(\text{does not drive 11 or more miles to work})$$
$$= 1 - P(\text{drives 10 or less miles to work})$$
$$= 1 - 0.51 = 0.49 = 49\%$$

Empirical Probability

The difference between classical and **empirical probability** is that classical probability assumes that certain outcomes are equally likely (such as the outcomes when a die is rolled), while empirical probability relies on actual experience to determine the likelihood of outcomes. In empirical probability, one might actually roll a given die 6000 times, observe the various frequencies, and use these frequencies to determine the probability of an outcome.

Suppose, for example, that a researcher for the American Automobile Association (AAA) asked 50 people who plan to travel over the Thanksgiving holiday how they will get to their destination. The results can be categorized in a frequency distribution as shown.

Method	Frequency
Drive	41
Fly	6
Train or bus	3
	50

Now probabilities can be computed for various categories. For example, the probability of selecting a person who is driving is $\frac{41}{50}$, since 41 out of the 50 people said that they were driving.

Formula for Empirical Probability

Given a frequency distribution, the probability of an event being in a given class is

$$P(E) = \frac{\text{frequency for the class}}{\text{total frequencies in the distribution}} = \frac{f}{n}$$

This probability is called *empirical probability* and is based on observation.

EXAMPLE 4–12   Travel Survey

In the travel survey just described, find the probability that the person will travel by plane over the Thanksgiving holiday.

SOLUTION

$$P(\text{plane}) = \frac{6}{50} = 0.12$$

EXAMPLE 4–13   Distribution of Blood Types

In a sample of 50 people, 21 had type O blood, 22 had type A blood, 5 had type B blood, and 2 had type AB blood. Set up a frequency distribution and find the following probabilities.

 a. A person has type O blood.

 b. A person has type A or type B blood.

 c. A person has neither type A nor type O blood.

 d. A person does not have type AB blood.

Source: The American Red Cross.

SOLUTION

Type	Frequency
A	22
B	5
AB	2
O	21
	Total 50

a. $P(O) = \dfrac{f}{n} = \dfrac{21}{50}$

b. $P(A \text{ or } B) = \dfrac{22}{50} + \dfrac{5}{50} = \dfrac{27}{50}$

(Add the frequencies of the two classes.)

c. $P(\text{neither A nor O}) = \dfrac{5}{50} + \dfrac{2}{50} = \dfrac{7}{50}$

(Neither A nor O means that a person has either type B or type AB blood.)

d. $P(\text{not AB}) = 1 - P(AB) = 1 - \dfrac{2}{50} = \dfrac{48}{50} = \dfrac{24}{25}$

(Find the probability of not AB by subtracting the probability of type AB from 1.)

EXAMPLE 4–14   Family Size

A recent random survey found the following distribution for the sizes of families of students in a junior college.

Size	Frequency
1 person	14
2 persons	18
3 persons	27
4 persons	35
5 or more persons	6
	100

If a student is selected at random from the sample, find each of the following probabilities:

a. The student has a family size of 2 persons.

b. The student has a family size of fewer than 3 persons.

c. The student has a family size of at most 3 persons.

d. The student has a family size of at least 4 persons.

SOLUTION

a. $P(2 \text{ persons}) = \dfrac{18}{100} = \dfrac{9}{50} = 0.18$

b. $P(\text{fewer than 3 persons}) = \dfrac{14}{100} + \dfrac{18}{100} = \dfrac{32}{100} = \dfrac{8}{25} = 0.32$

c. $P(\text{at most 3 persons}) = \dfrac{14}{100} + \dfrac{18}{100} + \dfrac{27}{100} = \dfrac{59}{100} = 0.59$

d. $P(\text{at least 4 persons}) = \dfrac{35}{100} + \dfrac{6}{100} = \dfrac{41}{100} = 0.41$

Empirical probabilities can also be found by using a relative frequency distribution, as shown in Section 2–2. For example, the relative frequency distribution of the travel survey shown previously is

Method	Frequency	Relative frequency
Drive	41	0.82
Fly	6	0.12
Train or bus	3	0.06
	50	1.00

These frequencies are the same as the relative frequencies explained in Chapter 2.

Law of Large Numbers

When a coin is tossed one time, it is common knowledge that the probability of getting a head is $\frac{1}{2}$. But what happens when the coin is tossed 50 times? Will it come up heads 25 times? Not all the time. You should expect about 25 heads if the coin is fair. But due to chance variation, 25 heads will not occur most of the time.

If the empirical probability of getting a head is computed by using a small number of trials, it is usually not exactly $\frac{1}{2}$. However, as the number of trials increases, the empirical probability of getting a head will approach the theoretical probability of $\frac{1}{2}$, if in fact the coin is fair (i.e., balanced). This phenomenon is an example of the **law of large numbers.**

You should be careful to not think that the number of heads and number of tails tend to "even out." As the number of trials increases, the proportion of heads to the total number of trials will approach $\frac{1}{2}$. This law holds for any type of gambling game—tossing dice, playing roulette, and so on.

It should be pointed out that the probabilities that the proportions steadily approach may or may not agree with those theorized in the classical model. If not, it can have important implications, such as "the die is not fair." Pit bosses in Las Vegas watch for empirical trends that do not agree with classical theories, and they will sometimes take a set of dice out of play if observed frequencies are too far out of line with classical expected frequencies.

Subjective Probability

The third type of probability is called *subjective probability.* **Subjective probability** uses a probability value based on an educated guess or estimate, employing opinions and inexact information.

In subjective probability, a person or group makes an educated guess at the chance that an event will occur. This guess is based on the person's experience and evaluation of a solution. For example, a sportswriter may say that there is a 70% probability that the Pirates will win the pennant next year. A physician might say that, on the basis of her diagnosis, there is a 30% chance the patient will need an operation. A seismologist might say there is an 80% probability that an earthquake will occur in a certain area. These are only a few examples of how subjective probability is used in everyday life.

All three types of probability (classical, empirical, and subjective) are used to solve a variety of problems in business, engineering, and other fields.

Probability and Risk Taking

An area in which people fail to understand probability is risk taking. Actually, people fear situations or events that have a relatively small probability of happening rather than those events that have a greater likelihood of occurring. For example, many people think that the crime rate is increasing every year. However, in his book entitled *How Risk Affects Your Everyday Life,* author James Walsh states: "Despite widespread concern about the number of crimes committed in the United States, FBI and Justice Department statistics show that the national crime rate has remained fairly level for 20 years. It even dropped slightly in the early 1990s."

He further states, "Today most media coverage of risk to health and well-being focuses on shock and outrage." Shock and outrage make good stories and can scare us about the wrong dangers. For example, the author states that if a person is 20% over-weight, the loss of life expectancy is 900 days (about 3 years), but loss of life expectancy from exposure to radiation emitted by nuclear power plants is 0.02 day. As you can see, being overweight is much more of a threat than being exposed to radioactive emission.

Many people gamble daily with their lives, for example, by using tobacco, drinking and driving, and riding motorcycles. When people are asked to estimate the probabilities or frequencies of death from various causes, they tend to overestimate causes such as accidents, fires, and floods and to underestimate the probabilities of death from diseases (other than cancer), strokes, etc. For example, most people think that their chances of dying of a heart attack are 1 in 20, when in fact they are almost 1 in 3; the chances of dying by pesticide poisoning are 1 in 200,000 (*True Odds* by James Walsh). The reason people think this way is that the news media sensationalize deaths resulting from cata-strophic events and rarely mention deaths from disease.

When you are dealing with life-threatening catastrophes such as hurricanes, floods, automobile accidents, or texting while driving, it is important to get the facts. That is, get the actual numbers from accredited statistical agencies or reliable statistical studies, and then compute the probabilities and make decisions based on your knowledge of probability and statistics.

In summary, then, when you make a decision or plan a course of action based on probability, make sure that you understand the true probability of the event occurring. Also, find out how the information was obtained (i.e., from a reliable source). Weigh the cost of the action and decide if it is worth it. Finally, look for other alternatives or courses of action with less risk involved.

Applying the Concepts 4–1

Tossing a Coin

Assume you are at a carnival and decide to play one of the games. You spot a table where a person is flipping a coin, and since you have an understanding of basic probability, you believe that the odds of winning are in your favor. When you get to the table, you find out that all you have to do is to guess which side of the coin will be facing up after it is tossed. You are assured that the coin is fair, meaning that each of the two sides has an equally likely chance of occurring. You think back about what you learned in your statistics class about probability before you decide what to bet on. Answer the following questions about the coin-tossing game.

1. What is the sample space?
2. What are the possible outcomes?
3. What does the classical approach to probability say about computing probabilities for this type of problem?

You decide to bet on heads, believing that it has a 50% chance of coming up. A friend of yours, who had been playing the game for awhile before you got there, tells you that heads has come up the last 9 times in a row. You remember the law of large numbers.

4. What is the law of large numbers, and does it change your thoughts about what will occur on the next toss?
5. What does the empirical approach to probability say about this problem, and could you use it to solve this problem?
6. Can subjective probabilities be used to help solve this problem? Explain.
7. Assume you could win $1 million if you could guess what the results of the next toss will be. What would you bet on? Why?

See page 255 for the answers.

≡ Exercises 4–1

1. What is a probability experiment? A probability experiment is a chance process that leads to well-defined outcomes.

2. Define *sample space*. The set of all possible outcomes of a probability experiment is called a *sample space*.

3. What is the difference between an outcome and an event? An outcome is the result of a single trial of a probability experiment, but an event can consist of more than one outcome.

4. What are equally likely events? Equally likely events have the same probability of occurring.

5. What is the range of the values of the probability of an event? The range of values is 0 to 1 inclusive.

6. When an event is certain to occur, what is its probability? 1

7. If an event cannot happen, what value is assigned to its probability? 0

8. What is the sum of the probabilities of all the outcomes in a sample space? 1

9. If the probability that it will rain tomorrow is 0.20, what is the probability that it won't rain tomorrow? Would you recommend taking an umbrella? 0.80   Since the probability that it won't rain is 80%, you could leave your umbrella at home and be fairly safe.

10. A probability experiment is conducted. Which of these cannot be considered a probability outcome? c, d, e, h

    a. $\frac{5}{8}$ *d.* 2.14   *g.* 1

    b. 0.29   *e.* −0.63   *h.* 153%

    c. $-\frac{1}{3}$ *f.* 0   *i.* 87%

11. Classify each statement as an example of classical probability, empirical probability, or subjective probability.

    a. The probability that a person will watch the 6 o'clock evening news is 0.15. Empirical

    b. The probability of winning at a Chuck-a-Luck game is $\frac{5}{36}$. Classical

    c. The probability that a bus will be in an accident on a specific run is about 6%. Empirical

    d. The probability of getting a royal flush when five cards are selected at random is $\frac{1}{649,740}$. Classical

12. Classify each statement as an example of classical probability, empirical probability, or subjective probability.

    a. The probability that a student will get a C or better in a statistics course is about 70%. Empirical

    b. The probability that a new fast-food restaurant will be a success in Chicago is 35%. Empirical

    c. The probability that interest rates will rise in the next 6 months is 0.50. Subjective

    d. The probability that the unemployment rate will fall next month is 0.03. Subjective

13. **Rolling a Die** If a die is rolled one time, find these probabilities:

    a. Getting a 9 0

    b. Getting a number greater than 2 $\frac{2}{3}$

    c. Getting a number less than 7 1

    d. Getting a prime number $\frac{1}{2}$

14. **Rolling a Die** If a die is rolled one time, find these probabilities:

    a. Getting a number less than 7. 1

    b. Getting a number greater than or equal to 3 $\frac{2}{3}$

    c. Getting a number greater than 2 and an even number $\frac{1}{3}$

    d. Getting a number less than 1 0

15. **Rolling Two Dice** If two dice are rolled at one time, find the probability of getting these results:

    a. A sum of 9 $\frac{1}{9}$

    b. A sum of 4 or 5 $\frac{7}{36}$

    c. A 5 on one die or both dice $\frac{11}{36}$

16. **Rolling Two Dice** If two dice are rolled one time, find the probability of getting these results:

    a. A sum less than 9 $\frac{13}{18}$

    b. A sum greater than or equal to 10 $\frac{1}{6}$

    c. A 3 on one die or on both dice. $\frac{11}{36}$

17. **Drawing a Card** If one card is drawn from a deck, find the probability of getting these results:

    a. A 3 or a diamond $\frac{4}{13}$

    b. A red six $\frac{1}{26}$

    c. A black card higher than a 10 (don't count aces) $\frac{3}{26}$

    d. A spade $\frac{1}{4}$

    e. A red card $\frac{1}{2}$

18. **Drawing a Card** If a card is drawn from a deck, find the probability of getting these results:

    a. A 6 and a spade $\frac{1}{52}$

    b. A black king $\frac{1}{26}$

    c. A red card and a 7 $\frac{1}{26}$

    d. A diamond or a heart $\frac{1}{2}$

    e. A black card $\frac{1}{2}$

19. **Children's Obesity** The following information shows the percentage of children who are obese for 3 age groups:

Age	Percent
3–5	8.9
6–11	17.5
12–19	20.5

If a person is selected at random, find each probability.

    a. If you select a 3–5 year old person, the person is obese. 8.9%

    b. If you select a 12–19 year old person, the person is not obese. 79.5%

Source: U.S. Department of Health and Human Services

20. Selecting a State Randomly choose one of the 50 states in the United States.

a. What is the probability that it begins with the letter "O"? $\frac{3}{50}$

b. What is the probability that it is in New England? $\frac{3}{25}$

21. Human Blood Types Human blood is grouped into four types. The percentages of Americans with each type are listed below.

    O 43%   A 40%   B 12%   AB 5%

Choose one American at random. Find the probability that this person

a. Has type B blood. 0.12

b. Has type AB or O blood. 0.48

c. Does not have type O blood. 0.57

22. Prescription Drugs The data show where the money spent on prescription drugs comes from.

Personal funds	Private insurance	Medicaid	Other
58%	24%	14%	4%

If a person is selected

a. Find the probability that a person's prescription drug is paid for by private insurance. 24%

b. Find the probability that the prescription drug in not paid by Medicaid. 86%

c. Find the probability that the prescription drug is paid by personal funds or Medicaid. 72%

Source: U.S. Health Care Financing

23. Oil Spill Locations The following survey consists of the percent of common oil spill locations and where they occur.

Factories/ buildings	Roads	Pipelines	Railroads	Other
75%	8%	3%	6%	8%

If an oil spill is selected at random, find the probability that

a. It occurred in an oil pipeline. 3%

b. It occurred in a factory or railroad. 81%

c. It did not occur in a road accident. 92%

24. Rural Speed Limits Rural speed limits for all 50 states are indicated below.

55 mph	60 mph	65 mph	70 mph	75 mph
12	4	19	12	3

Choose one state at random. Find the probability that its speed limit is

a. 60 or 70 miles per hour. 0.32

b. Greater than 65 miles per hour. 0.30

c. 70 miles per hour or less. 0.94

Source: https://en.wikipedia.org/wiki/Speed_limits_in_the_United_States

25. Gender of Children A couple has four children. Find each probability that they are

a. All boys. $\frac{1}{16}$

b. Exactly 3 boys and one girl. $\frac{1}{4}$

c. At least one child who is a boy. $\frac{15}{16}$

d. At least one child of each gender. $\frac{7}{8}$

26. Sources of Energy Uses in the United States A breakdown of the sources of energy used in the United States is shown below. Choose one energy source at random.

Oil 39%	Natural gas 24%	Coal 23%
Nuclear 8%	Hydropower 3%	Other 3%

Find the probability that it is

a. Not natural gas. 76%

b. Oil or nuclear. 47%

c. Coal. 23%

Source: www.infoplease.com

27. Game of Craps In a game of craps, a player wins on the first roll if the player rolls a sum of 7 or 11, and the player loses if the player rolls a 2, 3, or 12. Find the probability that the game will last only one roll. $\frac{1}{3}$

28. Computers in Elementary Schools Elementary schools were classified by the number of computers they had.

Computers	1–10	11–20	21–50	51–100	100+
Schools	3170	4590	16,741	23,753	34,803

Choose one school at random. Find the probability that it has

a. Between 11 and 20 computers. 0.055

b. More than 20 computers. 0.907

c. Fewer than 51 computers. 0.295

Source: World Almanac.

29. College Debt The following information shows the amount of debt students who graduated from college incur for a specific year.

$1 to $5000	$5001 to $20,000	$20,001 to $50,000	$50,000+
27%	40%	19%	14%

If a person who graduates has some debt, find the probability that

a. It is less than $5001. 27%

b. It is more than $20,000. 33%

c. It is between $1 and $20,000. 67%

d. It is more than $50,000. 14%

Source: USA TODAY.

30. Color of Automobiles According to *CarMax,* 22.25% of preowned automobiles sold are black, 19.34% are white, 17.63% are gray, and 14.64% are silver. If a preowned automobile is selected at random, find the probability that it is either gray or silver. 0.3227

31. Crimes Committed The numbers show the number of crimes committed in a large city. If a crime is selected at random, find the probability that it is a motor vehicle theft. What is the probability that it is not an assault?

Theft	1375
Burglary of home or office	500
Motor vehicle theft	275
Assault	200
Robbery	125
Rape or homicide	25 0.11; 0.92

Source: Based on FBI statistics.

32. Living Arrangements for Children Here are the living arrangements of children under 18 years old living in the United States in a recent year. Numbers are in thousands.

Both parents	51,823
Mother only	17,283
Father only	2,572
Neither parent	3,041

Choose one child at random; what is the probability that the child lives with both parents? With the mother present? 0.694; 0.925

Source: Time Almanac.

33. Motor Vehicle Accidents During a recent year, there were 13.5 million automobile accidents, 5.2 million truck accidents, and 178,000 motorcycle accidents. If one accident is selected at random, find the probability that it is either a truck or motorcycle accident. What is the probability that it is not a truck accident? 0.285, 0.725

Source: Based on data from the National Safety Council.

34. Federal Government Revenue The source of federal government revenue for a specific year is

50% from individual income taxes
32% from social insurance payroll taxes
10% from corporate income taxes
3% from excise taxes
5% other

If a revenue source is selected at random, what is the probability that it comes from individual or corporate income taxes? 0.6

Source: New York Times Almanac.

35. Selecting a Bill A box contains a $1 bill, a $5 bill, a $10 bill, and a $20 bill. A bill is selected at random, and it is not replaced; then a second bill is selected at random. Draw a tree diagram and determine the sample space.

36. Tossing Coins Draw a tree diagram and determine the sample space for tossing four coins.

37. Selecting Numbered Balls Four balls numbered 1 through 4 are placed in a box. A ball is selected at random, and its number is noted; then it is replaced. A second ball is selected at random, and its number is noted. Draw a tree diagram and determine the sample space.

38. Family Dinner Combinations A family special at a neighborhood restaurant offers dinner for four for $39.99. There are 3 appetizers available, 4 entrees, and 3 desserts from which to choose. The special includes one of each. Represent the possible dinner combinations with a tree diagram.

39. Required First-Year College Courses First-year students at a particular college must take one English class, one class in mathematics, a first-year seminar, and an elective. There are 2 English classes to choose from, 3 mathematics classes, 5 electives, and everyone takes the same first-year seminar. Represent the possible schedules, using a tree diagram.

40. Tossing a Coin and Rolling a Die A coin is tossed; if it falls heads up, it is tossed again. If it falls tails up, a die is rolled. Draw a tree diagram and determine the outcomes.

≡ Extending the Concepts

41. Distribution of CEO Ages The distribution of ages of CEOs is as follows:

Age	Frequency
21–30	1
31–40	8
41–50	27
51–60	29
61–70	24
71–up	11

Source: Information based on *USA TODAY* Snapshot.

If a CEO is selected at random, find the probability that the CEO's age is

a. Between 31 and 40. 0.08

b. Under 31. 0.01

c. Over 30 and under 51. 0.35

d. Under 31 or over 60. 0.36

42. Tossing a Coin A person flipped a coin 100 times and obtained 73 heads. Can the person conclude that the coin was unbalanced? Probably

43. Medical Treatment A medical doctor stated that with a certain treatment, a patient has a 50% chance of recovering without surgery. That is, "Either he will get well or he won't get well." Comment on this statement. The statement is probably not based on empirical probability, and is probably not true.

44. Wheel Spinner The wheel spinner shown here is spun twice. Find the sample space, and then determine the probability of the following events.

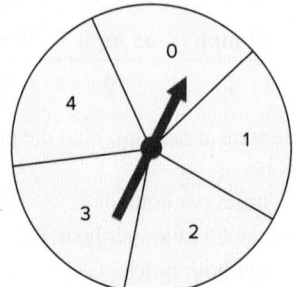

a. An odd number on the first spin and an even number on the second spin (*Note:* 0 is considered even.) $\frac{6}{25}$

b. A sum greater than 4 $\frac{2}{5}$

c. Even numbers on both spins $\frac{9}{25}$

d. A sum that is odd $\frac{12}{25}$

e. The same number on both spins $\frac{1}{5}$

45. Tossing Coins Toss three coins 128 times and record the number of heads (0, 1, 2, or 3); then record your results with the theoretical probabilities. Compute the empirical probabilities of each. Answers will vary. However they should be approximately $\frac{1}{8}, \frac{3}{8}, \frac{3}{8}, \frac{1}{8}$

46. Tossing Coins Toss two coins 100 times and record the number of heads (0, 1, 2). Compute the probabilities of each outcome, and compare these probabilities with the theoretical results. Approximately $\frac{1}{4}, \frac{1}{2}$, and $\frac{1}{4}$, respectively

47. Odds Odds are used in gambling games to make them fair. For example, if you rolled a die and won every time you rolled a 6, then you would win on average once every 6 times. So that the game is fair, the odds of 5 to 1 are given. This means that if you bet \$1 and won, you could win \$5. On average, you would win \$5 once in 6 rolls and lose \$1 on the other 5 rolls—hence the term *fair game.*

In most gambling games, the odds given are not fair. For example, if the odds of winning are really 20 to 1, the house might offer 15 to 1 in order to make a profit.

Odds can be expressed as a fraction or as a ratio, such as $\frac{5}{1}$, 5:1, or 5 to 1. Odds are computed in favor of the event or against the event. The formulas for odds are

$$\text{Odds in favor} = \frac{P(E)}{1 - P(E)}$$

$$\text{Odds against} = \frac{P(\overline{E})}{1 - P(\overline{E})}$$

In the die example,

$$\text{Odds in favor of a } 6 = \frac{\frac{1}{6}}{\frac{5}{6}} = \frac{1}{5} \text{ or } 1{:}5$$

$$\text{Odds against a } 6 = \frac{\frac{5}{6}}{\frac{1}{6}} = \frac{5}{1} \text{ or } 5{:}1$$

Find the odds in favor of and against each event.

a. Rolling a die and getting a 2 1:5, 5:1

b. Rolling a die and getting an even number 1:1, 1:1

c. Drawing a card from a deck and getting a spade 1:3, 3:1

d. Drawing a card and getting a red card 1:1, 1:1

e. Drawing a card and getting a queen 1:12, 12:1

f. Tossing two coins and getting two tails 1:3, 3:1

g. Tossing two coins and getting exactly one tail 1:1, 1:1

48. When you take an exam that uses multiple-choice questions with 5 answer selections for each question, is the probability of guessing a correct answer $\frac{1}{2}$ since either the answer is correct or incorrect? No. The probability of guessing the correct answer is $\frac{1}{5}$ since you have a total of 5 choices and only one choice is correct!

49. In a state lottery you need to select 5 numbers from 1 to 50. Which choice would give you a better chance to win, 5, 19, 26, 34, 42 or 1, 2, 3, 4, or 5? Both selections have the same probability of winning.

50. You are playing roulette and you have selected the red space and won three times in a row. Which would be a better choice for the next selection, red or black? Either choice has the same probability of winning. There is no such thing as a "run" when each outcome is independent.

51. When you flip a coin five times, the probability of getting 5 heads is $1 \div 2^5$ or $\frac{1}{32}$. Does this mean that if I perform this experiment 32 times then I will get 5 heads one of the 32 times? No. In the long run, 5 heads will occur on average once in 32 times, but there is no guarantee that 5 heads will occur when you repeat the experiment 32 times.

52. Which is a better bet when flipping a coin 4 times: getting 2 heads (the mean) or getting either one or three heads? The probability of getting 2 heads is $\frac{6}{16}$, while the probability of getting one or three heads is $\frac{8}{16}$. So, getting one or three heads is a better bet.

4–2   The Addition Rules for Probability

OBJECTIVE ❷

Find the probability of compound events, using the addition rules.

Many problems involve finding the probability of two or more events. For example, at a large political gathering, you might wish to know, for a person selected at random, the probability that the person is a female or is a Republican. In this case, there are three possibilities to consider:

1. The person is a female.

2. The person is a Republican.

3. The person is both a female and a Republican.

Consider another example. At the same gathering there are Republicans, Democrats, and Independents. If a person is selected at random, what is the probability that the person is a Democrat or an Independent? In this case, there are only two possibilities:

1. The person is a Democrat.

2. The person is an Independent.

The difference between the two examples is that in the first case, the person selected can be a female and a Republican at the same time. In the second case, the person selected cannot be both a Democrat and an Independent at the same time. In the second case, the two events are said to be *mutually exclusive;* in the first case, they are not mutually exclusive.

> Two events are **mutually exclusive events** or **disjoint events** if they cannot occur at the same time (i.e., they have no outcomes in common).

In another situation, the events of getting a 4 and getting a 6 when a single card is drawn from a deck are mutually exclusive events, since a single card cannot be both a 4 and a 6. On the other hand, the events of getting a 4 and getting a heart on a single draw are not mutually exclusive, since you can select the 4 of hearts when drawing a single card from an ordinary deck.

EXAMPLE 4–15   Determining Mutually Exclusive Events

Determine whether the two events are mutually exclusive. Explain your answer.

   a. Randomly selecting a female student
   Randomly selecting a student who is a junior

   b. Randomly selecting a person with type A blood
   Randomly selecting a person with type O blood

   c. Rolling a die and getting an odd number
   Rolling a die and getting a number less than 3

   d. Randomly selecting a person who is under 21 years of age
   Randomly selecting a person who is over 30 years of age

SOLUTION

   a. These events are not mutually exclusive since a student can be both female and a junior.

   b. These events are mutually exclusive since a person cannot have type A blood and type O blood at the same time.

   c. These events are not mutually exclusive since the number 1 is both an odd number and a number less than 3.

   d. These events are mutually exclusive since a person cannot be both under 21 and over 30 years of age at the same time.

EXAMPLE 4–16   Drawing a Card

Determine which events are mutually exclusive when a single card is drawn at random from a deck of cards.

   a. Getting an ace and getting a queen

   b. Getting a jack and getting a club

   c. Getting a face card and getting a four

   d. Getting a diamond and getting a red card

SOLUTION

   a. These events are mutually exclusive since you cannot get an ace and a queen at the same time when only one card is selected.

   b. These events are *not* mutually exclusive since you can get the jack of clubs when one card is drawn.

   c. These events are mutually exclusive since you cannot get a face card and a four at the same time when one card is selected.

   d. These events are not mutually exclusive since you can get a diamond and a red card at the same time.

FIGURE 4–6

Venn Diagram for Addition Rule 1 When the Events Are Mutually Exclusive

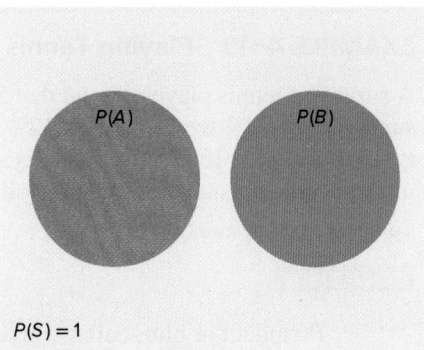

$P(S) = 1$

Mutually exclusive events
$P(A \text{ or } B) = P(A) + P(B)$

The probability of two or more events can be determined by the *addition rules*. The first addition rule is used when the events are mutually exclusive.

Addition Rule 1

When two events A and B are mutually exclusive, the probability that A or B will occur is

$$P(A \text{ or } B) = P(A) + P(B)$$

Figure 4–6 shows a Venn diagram that represents two mutually exclusive events A and B. In this case, $P(A \text{ or } B) = P(A) + P(B)$, since these events are mutually exclusive and do not overlap. In other words, the probability of occurrence of event A or event B is the sum of the areas of the two circles.

EXAMPLE 4–17   Endangered Species

In the United States there are 59 different species of mammals that are endangered, 75 different species of birds that are endangered, and 68 species of fish that are endangered. If one animal is selected at random, find the probability that it is either a mammal or a fish.

Source: Based on information from the U.S. Fish and Wildlife Service.

SOLUTION

Since there are 59 species of mammals and 68 species of fish that are endangered and a total of 202 endangered species, $P(\text{mammal or fish}) = P(\text{mammal}) + P(\text{fish}) = \frac{59}{202} + \frac{68}{202} = \frac{127}{202} = 0.629$. The events are mutually exclusive.

EXAMPLE 4–18   Research and Development Employees

The corporate research and development centers for three local companies have the following numbers of employees:

U.S. Steel	110
Alcoa	750
Bayer Material Science	250

If a research employee is selected at random, find the probability that the employee is employed by U.S. Steel or Alcoa.

Source: Pittsburgh Tribune Review.

SOLUTION

$$P(\text{U.S. Steel or Alcoa}) = P(\text{U.S. Steel}) + P(\text{Alcoa})$$
$$= \frac{110}{1110} + \frac{750}{1110} = \frac{860}{1110} = \frac{86}{111} = 0.775$$

EXAMPLE 4–19   Playing Tennis

A survey of tennis players found that 53% were white-collar workers (managers or supervisors), 24% were students, 12% were blue-collar workers, and 11% were other types of workers. If a tennis player is selected at random, find the probability that the player is either a student or a blue-collar worker.

Source: Tennis Industry Association

SOLUTION

$$P(\text{student or blue-collar worker}) = P(\text{student}) + P(\text{blue-collar worker})$$
$$= 0.24 + 0.12 = 0.36 = 36\%$$

These events are mutually exclusive.

Historical Note

Venn diagrams were developed by mathematician John Venn (1834–1923) and are used in set theory and symbolic logic. They have been adapted to probability theory also. In set theory, the symbol ∪ represents the *union* of two sets, and $A \cup B$ corresponds to *A or B*. The symbol ∩ represents the *intersection* of two sets, and $A \cap B$ corresponds to *A and B*. Venn diagrams show only a general picture of the probability rules and do not portray all situations, such as $P(A) = 0$, accurately.

The probability rules can be extended to three or more events. For three mutually exclusive events *A*, *B*, and *C*,

$$P(A \text{ or } B \text{ or } C) = P(A) + P(B) + P(C)$$

When events are not mutually exclusive, addition rule 2 can be used to find the probability of the events.

Addition Rule 2

If *A* and *B* are *not* mutually exclusive, then

$$P(A \text{ or } B) = P(A) + P(B) - P(A \text{ and } B)$$

Note: This rule can also be used when the events are mutually exclusive, since $P(A \text{ and } B)$ will always equal 0. However, it is important to make a distinction between the two situations.

Figure 4–7 represents the probability of two events that are *not* mutually exclusive. In this case, $P(A \text{ or } B) = P(A) + P(B) - P(A \text{ and } B)$. The area in the intersection or overlapping part of both circles corresponds to $P(A \text{ and } B)$; and when the area of circle *A* is added to the area of circle *B*, the overlapping part is counted twice. It must therefore be subtracted once to get the correct area or probability.

FIGURE 4–7

Venn Diagram for Addition Rule 2 When Events Are Not Mutually Exclusive

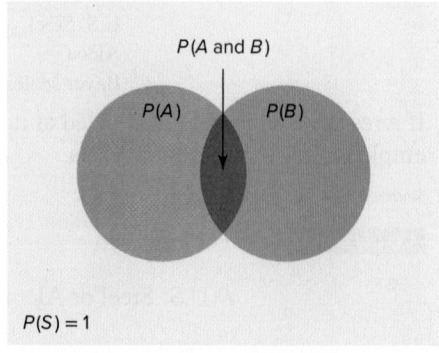

Nonmutually exclusive events
$P(A \text{ or } B) = P(A) + P(B) - P(A \text{ and } B)$

EXAMPLE 4–20   Drawing a Card

A single card is drawn at random from an ordinary deck of cards. Find the probability that it is a seven or a black card.

SOLUTION

There are 4 sevens and 26 black cards in a deck; however, there are two sevens that are black cards, the seven of clubs and the seven of spades. Hence,

$$P(7 \text{ or a black card}) = P(7) + P(\text{black card}) - P(7\clubsuit \text{ or } 7\spadesuit)$$

$$= \frac{4}{52} + \frac{26}{52} - \frac{2}{52} = \frac{28}{52} = \frac{7}{13} \approx 0.538$$

EXAMPLE 4–21   Selecting a Dog or Cat

In an animal shelter, there are 8 dogs and 10 cats that are available for adoption. Six of the dogs are females and 3 of the cats are females. If a dog or cat is adopted today, find the probability that it is a cat or a male.

SOLUTION

The sample space is shown here.

Animal	Females	Males	Total
Dog	6	2	8
Cat	3	7	10
Total	9	9	18

Then the probability is

$$P(\text{cat or male}) = P(\text{cat}) + P(\text{male}) - P(\text{male cat})$$

$$= \frac{10}{18} + \frac{9}{18} - \frac{7}{18} = \frac{12}{18} = \frac{2}{3} \approx 0.67$$

EXAMPLE 4–22   Driving While Intoxicated

On New Year's Eve, the probability of a person driving while intoxicated is 0.32, the probability of a person having a driving accident is 0.09, and the probability of a person having a driving accident while intoxicated is 0.06. What is the probability of a person driving while intoxicated or having a driving accident?

SOLUTION

$$P(\text{intoxicated or accident}) = P(\text{intoxicated}) + P(\text{accident})$$
$$- P(\text{intoxicated and accident})$$
$$= 0.32 + 0.09 - 0.06 = 0.35$$

For three events that are *not* mutually exclusive,

$$P(A \text{ or } B \text{ or } C) = P(A) + P(B) + P(C) - P(A \text{ and } B) - P(A \text{ and } C)$$
$$- P(B \text{ and } C) + P(A \text{ and } B \text{ and } C)$$

See Exercises 23 and 24 in this section.

In summary, then, when the two events are mutually exclusive, use addition rule 1. When the events are not mutually exclusive, use addition rule 2.

Applying the Concepts 4–2

Which Pain Reliever Is Best?

Assume that following an injury you received from playing your favorite sport, you obtain and read information on new pain medications. In that information you read of a study that was conducted to test the side effects of two new pain medications. Use the following table to answer the questions and decide which, if any, of the two new pain medications you will use.

Side effect	Number of side effects in 12-week clinical trial		
	Placebo $n = 192$	Drug A $n = 186$	Drug B $n = 188$
Upper respiratory congestion	10	32	19
Sinus headache	11	25	32
Stomachache	2	46	12
Neurological headache	34	55	72
Cough	22	18	31
Lower respiratory congestion	2	5	1

1. How many subjects were in the study?

2. How long was the study?

3. What were the variables under study?

4. What type of variables are they, and what level of measurement are they on?

5. Are the numbers in the table exact figures?

6. What is the probability that a randomly selected person was receiving a placebo?

7. What is the probability that a person was receiving a placebo or drug A? Are these mutually exclusive events? What is the complement to this event?

8. What is the probability that a randomly selected person was receiving a placebo or experienced a neurological headache?

9. What is the probability that a randomly selected person was not receiving a placebo or experienced a sinus headache?

See page 255 for the answers.

Exercises 4–2

1. Define mutually exclusive events, and give an example of two events that are mutually exclusive and two events that are not mutually exclusive. Two events are mutually exclusive if they cannot occur at the same time (i.e., they have no outcomes in common). Examples will vary.

2. Explain briefly why addition rule 2 can be used when two events are mutually exclusive. Addition rule 2 can be used because $P(A$ and $B) = 0$ when the events are mutually exclusive.

3. Cards, Dice, and Students Determine whether or not these events are mutually exclusive:

   a. Draw a card: get a club or get a six. Not mutually exclusive since you can get the 6 of clubs

   b. Roll a die: get a prime number (2, 3, 5) or get an even number. Not mutually exclusive since 2 is both an even number and a prime number

   c. Roll two dice: get a sum of 9 or get a sum of 12. Mutually exclusive

   d. Select a student at random: get a commuter student or a business major. Not mutually exclusive since a commuter student can also be a business major

4. Determine whether these events are mutually exclusive.

   a. Roll two dice: Get a sum of 7 or get doubles. Yes

   b. Select a student in your college: The student is a sophomore and the student is a business major. No

   c. Select any course: It is a calculus course and it is an English course. Yes

   d. Select a registered voter: The voter is a Republican and the voter is a Democrat. Yes

5. College Degrees Awarded The table below represents the college degrees awarded in a recent academic year by gender.

	Bachelor's	Master's	Doctorate
Men	573,079	211,381	24,341
Women	775,424	301,264	21,683

Choose a degree at random. Find the probability that it is

a. A bachelor's degree. 0.707

b. A doctorate or a degree awarded to a woman. 0.589

c. A doctorate awarded to a woman. 0.011

d. Not a master's degree. 0.731

Source: www.nces.ed.gov

6. **Riding to School** The probability that John will drive to school is 0.37, the probability that he will ride with friends is 0.23, and the probability that his parents will take him is 0.4. He is not allowed to have passengers in the car when he is driving. What is the probability that John will have company on the way to school? 0.63

7. **Medical Specialities** The following doctors were observed on staff at a local hospital.

	MD	Doctor of Osteopathy
Pathology	6	1
Pediatrics	7	2
Orthopedics	20	2

Choose one doctor at random; what is the probability that

a. The doctor is a pathologist? $\frac{7}{38} = 0.184$

b. The doctor is an orthopedist or an MD? $\frac{35}{38} = 0.921$

8. **Children's Role Models** A survey of 60 randomly selected children asking what type of role model they admired showed the following results:

Person	Number
Actors	22
Musicians	16
Athletes	11
Comedians	8
Politicians	3

If one child is selected at random, find each probability:

a. The child selected an athlete or a musician. 0.45

b. The child selected a comedian or politician. 0.183

c. The child did not select an actor. 0.633

9. **Snack Foods** In a meeting room in a dormitory there are 8 bags of potato chips, 5 bags of popcorn, 2 bags of pretzels, and 1 bag of cheese puffs. If a student selects 1 bag at random, find the probability that it is a bag of potato chips or a bag of pretzels. $\frac{5}{8}$

10. **Returning Workers** A survey of 100 retired workers who returned to their jobs gave the following reasons for returning:

Reason	Number
Job satisfaction	53
Avoid boredom	26
Make a contribution to society	14
Other	7

If one worker is selected at random, find each probability:

a. They returned to work for job satisfaction. 0.53

b. They returned to work to avoid boredom or to make a contribution to society. 0.4

c. They did not state that they wanted to make a contribution to society. 0.86

11. **Pizza Sales** A pizza restaurant sold 24 cheese pizzas and 16 pizzas with one or more toppings. Twelve of the cheese pizzas were eaten at work, and 10 of the pizzas with one or more toppings were eaten at work. If a pizza was selected at random, find the probability of each:

a. It was a cheese pizza eaten at work. $\frac{3}{10} = 0.3$

b. It was a pizza with either one or more toppings, and it was not eaten at work. $\frac{6}{40} = 0.15$

c. It was a cheese pizza, or it was a pizza eaten at work. $\frac{17}{20} = 0.85$

12. **Selecting a Book** At a used-book sale, 100 books are adult books and 160 are children's books. Of the adult books, 70 are nonfiction while 60 of the children's books are nonfiction. If a book is selected at random, find the probability that it is

a. Fiction. 0.5

b. Not a children's nonfiction book. 0.769 or $\frac{10}{13}$

c. An adult book or a children's nonfiction book. 0.615 or $\frac{8}{13}$

13. Following are the ages of 250 randomly selected adults who participated in a sweepstakes contest.

Age	Republicans	Democrats
21 to 34	27	18
35 to 44	19	23
45 to 54	32	41
55+	41	49

If one participant is selected at random, find each probability:

a. The participant is a Democrat 45 to 54 years old. 0.164

b. The participant is from 35 to 54 years old. 0.168

c. The participant is a Republican age 45 or older. 0.292

14. **Endangered Species** The chart below shows the numbers of endangered and threatened species both here in the United States and abroad.

	Endangered		Threatened	
	United States	Foreign	United States	Foreign
Mammals	68	251	10	20
Birds	77	175	13	6
Reptiles	14	64	22	16
Amphibians	11	8	10	1

Source: www.infoplease.com

Choose one species at random. Find the probability that it is

a. Threatened and in the United States. 0.072

b. An endangered foreign bird. 0.228

c. A mammal or a threatened foreign species. 0.486

15. People Who Did Not Show Up for Their Trials A survey of 50 randomly selected men and 50 randomly selected women found that 18 men and 7 women did not show up for their trials. If one person from the group is randomly selected, find the probability that

a. The person was a man who did not show up for the trial. 0.18

b. The person was a woman who showed up for her trial or the person was a man. 0.93

c. The person did not show up for the trial. 0.25

d. The person did show up for trial or the person was a woman. 0.82

16. Licensed Drivers in the United States In a recent year there were the following numbers (in thousands) of licensed drivers in the United States.

	Male	Female
Age 19 and under	4746	4517
Age 20	1625	1553
Age 21	1679	1627

Source: World Almanac.

Choose one driver at random. Find the probability that the driver is

a. Male and 19 years or under. 0.301

b. Age 20 or female. 0.592

c. At least 20 years old. 0.412

17. Prison Education In a federal prison, inmates can select to complete high school, take college courses, or do neither. The following survey results were obtained using ages of the inmates.

Age	High School Courses	College Courses	Neither
Under 30	53	107	450
30 and over	27	32	367

If a prisoner is selected at random, find these probabilities:

a. The prisoner does not take classes. 0.789

b. The prisoner is under 30 and is taking either a high school class or a college class. 0.154

c. The prisoner is over 30 and is taking either a high school class or a college class. 0.057

18. Mail Delivery A local postal carrier distributes first-class letters, advertisements, and magazines. For a certain day, she distributed the following numbers of each type of item.

Delivered to	First-class letters	Ads	Magazines
Home	325	406	203
Business	732	1021	97

If an item of mail is selected at random, find these probabilities.

a. The item went to a home. $\frac{467}{1392}$

b. The item was an ad, or it went to a business. $\frac{47}{58}$

c. The item was a first-class letter, or it went to a home. $\frac{833}{1392}$

19. Medical Tests on Emergency Patients The frequency distribution shown here illustrates the number of medical tests conducted on 30 randomly selected emergency patients.

Number of tests performed	Number of patients
0	12
1	8
2	2
3	3
4 or more	5

If a patient is selected at random, find these probabilities.

a. The patient has had exactly 2 tests done. $\frac{1}{15}$

b. The patient has had at least 2 tests done. $\frac{1}{3}$

c. The patient has had at most 3 tests done. $\frac{5}{6}$

d. The patient has had 3 or fewer tests done. $\frac{5}{6}$

e. The patient has had 1 or 2 tests done. $\frac{1}{3}$

20. Population of Midwestern States For a recent year the population for a group of Midwestern states in millions was distributed as follows:

Age group	Number
Under 5 years old	5.1
5–17 years	12.2
18–24 years	6.8
25–44 years	20.1
45–64 years	14.2
65+ years	9.1

Source: Based on the U.S. Census

If a person is selected at random from a Midwestern state, find the probability that the person is

a. Either 5–17 years old or 25–44 years old. 0.479

b. Either 5–24 years old or 45–64 years old. 0.492

c. Either under 5 years old or over 64 years old. 0.21

21. Emergency Room Tests The frequency distribution shows the number of medical tests conducted on 30 randomly selected emergency room patients.

Number of tests performed	Number of patients
0	11
1	9
2	5
3	4
4 or more	1

If a patient is selected at random, find these probabilities:

a. The patient had exactly 3 tests done. $\frac{2}{15}$

b. The patient had at most 2 tests done. $\frac{5}{6}$

c. The patient has 1 or 2 tests done. $\frac{7}{15}$

d. The patient had fewer than 3 tests done. $\frac{5}{6}$

e. The patient had at least 3 tests done. $\frac{1}{6}$

22. **Medical Patients** A recent study of 300 patients found that of 100 alcoholic patients, 87 had elevated cholesterol levels, and of 200 nonalcoholic patients, 43 had elevated cholesterol levels. If a patient is selected at random, find the probability that the patient is the following.

a. An alcoholic with elevated cholesterol level $\frac{29}{100}$

b. A nonalcoholic $\frac{2}{3}$

c. A nonalcoholic with nonelevated cholesterol level $\frac{157}{300}$

23. **Selecting a Card** If one card is drawn at random from an ordinary deck of shuffled cards, find the probability of getting

a. A 2, 3, 4, or 5. $\frac{4}{13}$

b. A club or an ace of diamonds. $\frac{7}{26}$

c. A diamond or a 6. $\frac{4}{13}$

24. **Rolling Dice** Two dice are rolled. Find the probability of getting

a. A sum of 2, 3, or 5. $\frac{7}{36}$

b. Doubles or a sum of 8. $\frac{5}{18}$

c. A sum greater than 10 or less than 4. $\frac{1}{6}$

d. Based on the answers to *a, b, c,* which event is least likely to occur? c

25. **Apple Production** For a recent year, about 11 billion pounds of apples were harvested. About 4.4 billion pounds of apples were made into apple juice, about 1 billion pounds of apples were made into apple sauce, and 1 billion pounds of apples were used for other commercial purposes. If 1 billion pounds of apples were selected at random, what is the probability that the apples were used for apple juice or applesauce? 0.491

Source: International Apple Institute.

26. **Rolling Dice** Three dice are rolled. Find the probability of getting

a. Doubles (do not count triples). $\frac{5}{12}$

b. A sum of 4. $\frac{1}{72}$

Extending the Concepts

27. **Purchasing a Pizza** The probability that a customer selects a pizza with mushrooms or pepperoni is 0.55, and the probability that the customer selects only mushrooms is 0.32. If the probability that the customer selects only pepperoni is 0.17, find the probability of the customer selecting both items. 0.06

28. **Building a New Home** In building new homes, a contractor finds that the probability of a home buyer selecting a two-car garage is 0.70 and of selecting a one-car garage is 0.20. Find the probability that the buyer will select no garage. The builder does not build houses with three-car or more garages. 0.10

29. In Exercise 28, find the probability that the buyer will not want a two-car garage. 0.30

30. Suppose that $P(A) = 0.42$, $P(B) = 0.38$, and $P(A \text{ or } B) = 0.70$. Are A and B mutually exclusive? Explain. No. $P(A \text{ and } B) \neq 0$

31. The probability of event A occurring is $m/(2m + n)$, and the probability of event B occurring is $n/(2m + n)$. Find the probability of A or B occurring if the events are mutually exclusive. $(m + n)/(2m + n)$

32. Events A and B are mutually exclusive with $P(A)$ equal to 0.392 and $P(A \text{ or } B)$ equal to 0.653. Find

a. $P(B)$. 0.261

b. $P(\text{not } A)$. 0.608

c. $P(A \text{ and } B)$. 0

Technology Step by Step

TI-84 Plus

Step by Step

Days	Frequency
3	15
4	32
5	56
6	19
7	5

To construct a relative frequency table:

1. Enter the data values in L_1 and the frequencies in L_2.
2. Move the cursor to the top of the L_3 column so that L_3 is highlighted.
3. Type L_2 divided by the sample size, then press **ENTER**.

Example TI4–1

Construct a relative frequency table for the following data that represent the number of days patients stayed in the hospital following a knee replacement.

EXCEL
Step by Step

Days	Frequency
3	15
4	32
5	56
6	19
7	5

Constructing a Relative Frequency Distribution

Use the knee replacement data.

1. In a new worksheet, type the label **DAYS** in cell A1. Beginning in cell A2, type in the data for the variable representing the number of days knee replacement patients stayed in the hospital.

2. In cell B1, type the label for the frequency, **COUNT.** Beginning in cell B2, type in the frequencies.

3. In cell B7, compute the total frequency by selecting the sum icon Σ from the toolbar and press **Enter**.

4. In cell C1, type a label for the relative frequencies, **RF.** In cell C2, type = **(B2)/(B7)** and **Enter**. Copy and paste the formula from cell C2 to cells C3 through C6. In cell C3, you should now see the formula = **(B3)/(B7)**. By typing in the $ signs you are anchoring the cell with the total when you copy and paste for each of the remaining frequencies.

5. To find the total relative frequency, select the sum icon Σ from the toolbar and **Enter**. This sum should be 1.

	A	B	C
1	Days	Count	RF
2	3	15	0.11811
3	4	32	0.25197
4	5	56	0.44094
5	6	19	0.14961
6	7	5	0.03937
7		127	1
8			

Constructing a Contingency Table

Example XL4–1

For this example, you will need to have the MegaStat Add-In installed on Excel (refer to Chapter 1, Excel Step by Step section for instructions on installing MegaStat).

1. Open the Databank.xls file from the text website. To do this:

    Copy the files to your Desktop by choosing "Save Target As ..." or "Save Link As ..."

    Double-click the datasets folder. Then double-click the all_data-sets folder.

    Double-click the bluman_es_data-sets_excel-windows folder. In this folder double-click the Databank.xls file. The Excel program will open automatically once you open this file.

2. Highlight the column labeled SMOKING STATUS to copy these data onto a new Excel worksheet.

3. Select File, New, Blank Workbook, then Create.

4. With cell A1 selected, click the Paste icon on the toolbar to paste the data into the new workbook.

5. Return to the Databank.xls file. Highlight the column labeled Gender. Copy and paste these data into column B of the worksheet containing the SMOKING STATUS data.

6. Type in the categories for SMOKING STATUS, **0, 1,** and **2** into cells C2–C4. In cell D2, type M for male and in cell D3, type F for female.

	A	B	C	D
1	SMOKING	GENDER		
2	1	F	0	M
3	0	M	1	F
4	0	F	2	
5	0	M		
6	2	F		
7	0	F		
8	2	M		
9	1	M		
10	0	F		

7. On the toolbar, select Add-Ins. Then select MegaStat. *Note:* You may need to open MegaStat from the file MegaStat.xls saved on your computer's hard drive.

8. Select **Chi-Square/Crosstab>Crosstabulation.**

9. In the Row variable Data range box, type A1:A101. In the Row variable Specification range box, type C2:C4. In the Column variable Data range box, type B1:B101. In the Column variable Specification range box, type D2:D3. Remove any checks from the Output Options. Then click [OK].

Crosstabulation

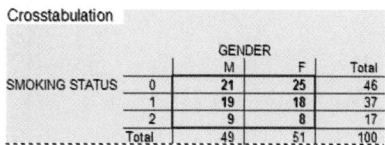

		GENDER M	F	Total
SMOKING STATUS	0	21	25	46
	1	19	18	37
	2	9	8	17
Total		49	51	100

MINITAB
Step by Step

Days	Frequency
3	15
4	32
5	56
6	19
7	5

Calculate Relative Frequency Probabilities

The random variable X represents the number of days patients stayed in the hospital.

1. In C1 of a worksheet, type in the values of X. Name the column **X.**

2. In C2 enter the frequencies. Name the column **f.**

3. To calculate the relative frequencies and store them in a new column named Px:

   a) Select **Calc>Calculator.**

   b) Type **Px** in the box for Store result in variable:.

   c) Click in the Expression box, then double-click C2 f.

   d) Type or click the division operator.

   e) Scroll down the function list to Sum, then click [Select].

   f) Double-click C2 f to select it.

   g) Click [OK].

The dialog box and completed worksheet are shown.

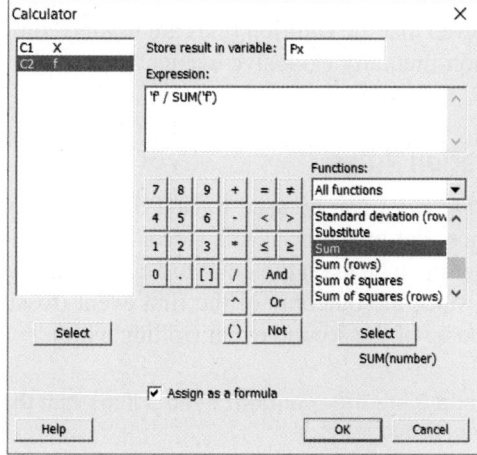

↓	C1	C2	C3
	X	f	Px
1	3	15	0.118110
2	4	32	0.251969
3	5	56	0.440945
4	6	19	0.149606
5	7	5	0.039370

If the original data, rather than the table, are in a worksheet, use **Stat>Tables>Tally** to make the tables with percents (Section 2–1).

MINITAB can also make a two-way classification table.

Construct a Contingency Table

1. Select **File>Open Worksheet** to open the Databank.mtw file.
2. Select **Stat>Tables>Crosstabulation . . .**
   a) Press [TAB] and then double-click C4 SMOKING STATUS to select it for the Rows: Field.
   b) Press [TAB] and then select C11 GENDER for the Columns: Field.
   c) Click on option for Counts and then [OK].

The session window and completed dialog box are shown.

Tabulated statistics: SMOKING STATUS, GENDER

Rows: SMOKING STATUS   Columns: GENDER

	F	M	All
0	25	22	47
1	18	19	37
2	7	9	16
All	50	50	100

Cell Contents: Count

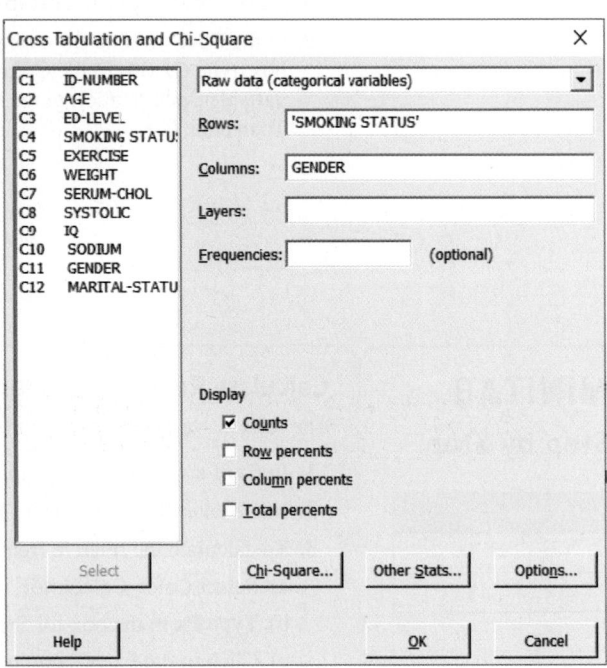

In this sample of 100 there are 25 females who do not smoke compared to 22 men. Sixteen individuals smoke 1 pack or more per day.

4–3   The Multiplication Rules and Conditional Probability

Section 4–2 showed that the addition rules are used to compute probabilities for mutually exclusive and non-mutually exclusive events. This section introduces the multiplication rules.

The Multiplication Rules

OBJECTIVE

Find the probability of compound events, using the multiplication rules.

The *multiplication rules* can be used to find the probability of two or more events that occur in sequence. For example, if you toss a coin and then roll a die, you can find the probability of getting a head on the coin *and* a 4 on the die. These two events are said to be *independent* since the outcome of the first event (tossing a coin) does not affect the probability outcome of the second event (rolling a die).

> Two events *A* and *B* are **independent events** if the fact that *A* occurs does not affect the probability of *B* occurring.

Here are other examples of independent events:

Rolling a die and getting a 6, and then rolling a second die and getting a 3.

Drawing a card from a deck and getting a queen, replacing it, and drawing a second card and getting a queen.

To find the probability of two independent events that occur in sequence, you must find the probability of each event occurring separately and then multiply the answers. For example, if a coin is tossed twice, the probability of getting two heads is $\frac{1}{2} \cdot \frac{1}{2} = \frac{1}{4}$. This result can be verified by looking at the sample space HH, HT, TH, TT. Then $P(\text{HH}) = \frac{1}{4}$.

Multiplication Rule 1

When two events are independent, the probability of both occurring is

$$P(A \text{ and } B) = P(A) \cdot P(B)$$

EXAMPLE 4–23   Tossing a Coin and Rolling a Die

A coin is flipped and a die is rolled. Find the probability of getting a tail on the coin and a prime number (2, 3, or 5) on the die.

SOLUTION

The sample space for the coin is H, T, and the sample space for the die is 1, 2, 3, 4, 5, 6. The probability of a tail is $\frac{1}{2}$ and the probability of a prime number is $\frac{3}{6}$, so

$$P(\text{tail and prime number}) = P(\text{tail}) \cdot P(\text{prime number})$$
$$= \frac{1}{2} \cdot \frac{3}{6} = \frac{3}{12} = \frac{1}{4}$$

The problem in Example 4–23 can also be solved by using the sample space

H1   H2   H3   H4   H5   H6   T1   T2   T3   T4   T5   T6

The solution is $\frac{1}{4}$ since there are 3 ways to get a tail and a prime number. They are T2, T3, and T5, and $\frac{3}{12} = \frac{1}{4}$.

EXAMPLE 4–24   Drawing a Card

A card is drawn from a deck and replaced, and then a second card is drawn. Find the probability of getting a club and then a queen.

SOLUTION

The probability of getting a club is $\frac{13}{52} = \frac{1}{4}$. The probability of getting a queen is $\frac{4}{52} = \frac{1}{13}$, then $P(\text{club and a queen}) = \frac{1}{4} \cdot \frac{1}{13} = \frac{1}{52}$.

EXAMPLE 4–25   Selecting a Colored Ball

An urn contains 2 red balls, 5 blue balls, and 3 white balls. A ball is selected and its color is noted. Then it is replaced. A second ball is selected and its color is noted. Find the probability of each of these events.

    a. Selecting 3 blue balls

    b. Selecting 1 white ball and then a red ball

    c. Selecting 2 blue balls and then one white ball

SOLUTION

a. $P(\text{blue and blue and blue}) = P(\text{blue}) \cdot P(\text{blue}) \cdot P(\text{blue}) = \frac{5}{10} \cdot \frac{5}{10} \cdot \frac{5}{10} = \frac{125}{1000} = \frac{1}{8} = 0.125$

b. $P(\text{white and red}) = P(\text{white}) \cdot P(\text{red}) = \frac{3}{10} \cdot \frac{2}{10} = \frac{6}{100} = \frac{3}{50} = 0.06$

c. $P(\text{blue and blue and white}) = P(\text{blue}) \cdot P(\text{blue}) \cdot P(\text{white}) = \frac{5}{10} \cdot \frac{5}{10} \cdot \frac{3}{10} = \frac{75}{1000} = \frac{3}{40} = 0.075$

Multiplication rule 1 can be extended to three or more independent events by using the formula

$$P(A \text{ and } B \text{ and } C \text{ and } \ldots \text{ and } K) = P(A) \cdot P(B) \cdot P(C) \cdots P(K)$$

When a small sample is selected from a large population and the subjects are not replaced, the probability of the event occurring changes so slightly that for the most part, it is considered to remain the same. Examples 4–26 and 4–27 illustrate this concept.

EXAMPLE 4–26   Obesity

For a recent year, it is estimated that 36% of adults are overweight. If three adults are randomly selected, find the probability that all three will be overweight.

SOLUTION

Let O be the probability that a person is overweight; then

$P(O \text{ and } O \text{ and } O) = P(O) \cdot P(O) \cdot P(O) = (0.36)(0.36)(0.36) \approx 0.047$. There is a 4.7% chance that all three people will be overweight.

EXAMPLE 4–27   Male Color Blindness

Approximately 9% of men have a type of color blindness that prevents them from distinguishing between red and green. If 3 men are selected at random, find the probability that all of them will have this type of red-green color blindness.
Source: USA TODAY.

SOLUTION

Let C denote red-green color blindness. Then

$$P(C \text{ and } C \text{ and } C) = P(C) \cdot P(C) \cdot P(C)$$
$$= (0.09)(0.09)(0.09)$$
$$= 0.000729$$

Hence, the rounded probability is 0.0007.

There is a 0.07% chance that all three men selected will have this type of red-green color blindness.

In Examples 4–23 through 4–27, the events were independent of one another, since the occurrence of the first event in no way affected the outcome of the second event. On the other hand, when the occurrence of the first event changes the probability of the occurrence of the second event, the two events are said to be *dependent*. For example, suppose a card is drawn from a deck and *not* replaced, and then a second card is drawn. What is the probability of selecting an ace on the first card and a king on the second card?

Before an answer to the question can be given, you must realize that the events are dependent. The probability of selecting an ace on the first draw is $\frac{4}{52}$. If that card is *not* replaced, the probability of selecting a king on the second card is $\frac{4}{51}$, since there are 4 kings and 51 cards remaining. The outcome of the first draw has affected the outcome of the second draw.

Dependent events are formally defined now.

> When the outcome or occurrence of the first event affects the outcome or occurrence of the second event in such a way that the probability is changed, the events are said to be **dependent events.**

Here are some examples of dependent events:

Drawing a card from a deck, not replacing it, and then drawing a second card

Selecting a ball from an urn, not replacing it, and then selecting a second ball

Being a lifeguard and getting a suntan

Having high grades and getting a scholarship

Parking in a no-parking zone and getting a parking ticket

To find probabilities when events are dependent, use the multiplication rule with a modification in notation. For the problem just discussed, the probability of getting an ace on the first draw is $\frac{4}{52}$, and the probability of getting a king on the second draw is $\frac{4}{51}$. By the multiplication rule, the probability of both events occurring is

$$\frac{4}{52} \cdot \frac{4}{51} = \frac{16}{2652} = \frac{4}{663} \approx 0.006$$

The event of getting a king on the second draw *given* that an ace was drawn the first time is called a *conditional probability.*

The **conditional probability** of an event B in relationship to an event A is the probability that event B occurs after event A has already occurred. The notation for conditional probability is $P(B|A)$. This notation does not mean that B is divided by A; rather, it means the probability that event B occurs given that event A has already occurred. In the card example, $P(B|A)$ is the probability that the second card is a king given that the first card is an ace, and it is equal to $\frac{4}{51}$ since the first card was *not* replaced.

Multiplication Rule 2

When two events are dependent, the probability of both occurring is

$$P(A \text{ and } B) = P(A) \cdot P(B|A)$$

EXAMPLE 4–28   Unemployed Workers

For a specific year, 5.2% of U.S. workers were unemployed. During that time, 33% of those who were unemployed received unemployment benefits. If a person is selected at random, find the probability that the person received unemployment benefits if the person is unemployed.

Source: Bureau of Labor Statistics

SOLUTION

$P(\text{unemployed benefits and unemployed}) = P(U) \cdot P(B|U) = (0.052)(0.33) = 0.017$

There is a 0.017 probability that a person is unemployed and receiving unemployment benefits.

EXAMPLE 4–29   Age and Smoking

A recent survey found that 30% of the randomly selected adults smoke; of those, 75% smoked their first cigarette before the age of 18. If an adult is selected at random, find the probability that the adult smoked their first cigarette before 18 years of age.

SOLUTION

S = smoker and B = first cigarette before 18.

$$P(S \text{ and } B) = P(S) \cdot P(B|S) = (0.30)(0.75) = 0.225$$

There is a 22.5% probability that the adult smoker had their first cigarette before the age of 18.

This multiplication rule can be extended to three or more events, as shown in Example 4–30.

EXAMPLE 4–30   Drawing Cards

Three cards are drawn from an ordinary deck and not replaced. Find the probability of these events.

    a. Getting 3 jacks

    b. Getting an ace, a king, and a queen in order

    c. Getting a club, a spade, and a heart in order

    d. Getting 3 clubs

SOLUTION

    a. $P(3 \text{ jacks}) = \dfrac{4}{52} \cdot \dfrac{3}{51} \cdot \dfrac{2}{50} = \dfrac{24}{132{,}600} = \dfrac{1}{5525} \approx 0.0002$

    b. $P(\text{ace and king and queen}) = \dfrac{4}{52} \cdot \dfrac{4}{51} \cdot \dfrac{4}{50} = \dfrac{64}{132{,}600} = \dfrac{8}{16{,}575} \approx 0.0005$

    c. $P(\text{club and spade and heart}) = \dfrac{13}{52} \cdot \dfrac{13}{51} \cdot \dfrac{13}{50} = \dfrac{2197}{132{,}600} = \dfrac{169}{10{,}200} \approx 0.017$

    d. $P(3 \text{ clubs}) = \dfrac{13}{52} \cdot \dfrac{12}{51} \cdot \dfrac{11}{50} = \dfrac{1716}{132{,}600} = \dfrac{11}{850} \approx 0.013$

Tree diagrams can be used as an aid to finding the solution to probability problems when the events are sequential. Example 4–31 illustrates the use of tree diagrams.

EXAMPLE 4–31   Selecting Colored Balls

Box 1 contains 2 red balls and 1 blue ball. Box 2 contains 3 blue balls and 1 red ball. A coin is tossed. If it falls heads up, box 1 is selected and a ball is drawn. If it falls tails up, box 2 is selected and a ball is drawn. Find the probability of selecting a red ball.

SOLUTION

The first two branches designate the selection of either box 1 or box 2. Then from box 1, either a red ball or a blue ball can be selected. Likewise, a red ball or blue ball can be selected from box 2. Hence, a tree diagram of the example is shown in Figure 4–8.

    Next determine the probabilities for each branch. Since a coin is being tossed for the box selection, each branch has a probability of $\frac{1}{2}$, that is, heads for box 1 or tails for box 2. The probabilities for the second branches are found by using the basic probability rule. For example, if box 1 is selected and there are 2 red balls and 1 blue ball, the probability of selecting a red ball is $\frac{2}{3}$ and the probability of selecting a blue ball is $\frac{1}{3}$. If box 2 is selected and it contains 3 blue balls and 1 red ball, then the probability of selecting a red ball is $\frac{1}{4}$ and the probability of selecting a blue ball is $\frac{3}{4}$.

Next multiply the probability for each outcome, using the rule $P(A \text{ and } B) = P(A) \cdot P(B|A)$. For example, the probability of selecting box 1 and selecting a red ball is $\frac{1}{2} \cdot \frac{2}{3} = \frac{2}{6}$. The probability of selecting box 1 and a blue ball is $\frac{1}{2} \cdot \frac{1}{3} = \frac{1}{6}$. The probability of selecting box 2 and selecting a red ball is $\frac{1}{2} \cdot \frac{1}{4} = \frac{1}{8}$. The probability of selecting box 2 and a blue ball is $\frac{1}{2} \cdot \frac{3}{4} = \frac{3}{8}$. (Note that the sum of these probabilities is 1.)

Finally, a red ball can be selected from either box 1 or box 2 so $P(\text{red}) = \frac{2}{6} + \frac{1}{8} = \frac{8}{24} + \frac{3}{24} = \frac{11}{24}$.

FIGURE 4–8 Tree Diagram for Example 4–31

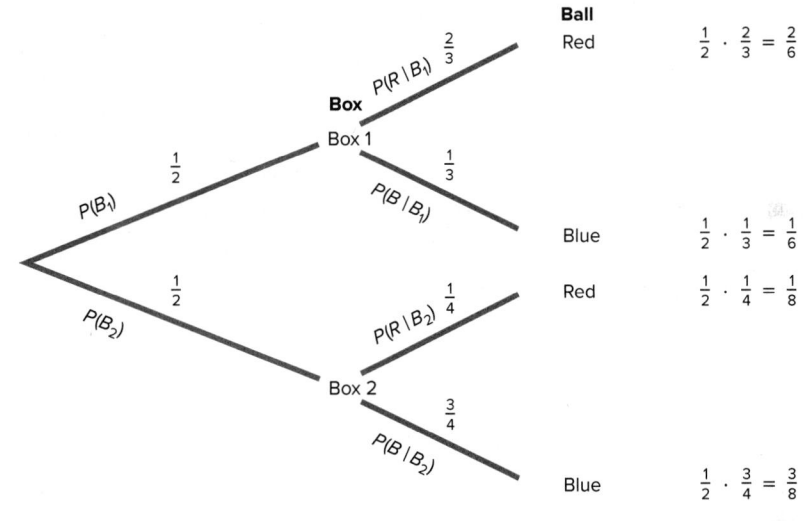

Tree diagrams can be used when the events are independent or dependent, and they can also be used for sequences of three or more events.

<table>
<tr><td>OBJECTIVE </td></tr>
<tr><td>Find the conditional probability of an event.</td></tr>
</table>

Conditional Probability

The conditional probability of an event B in relationship to an event A was defined as the probability that event B occurs after event A has already occurred.

The conditional probability of an event can be found by dividing both sides of the equation for multiplication rule 2 by $P(A)$, as shown:

$$P(A \text{ and } B) = P(A) \cdot P(B|A)$$

$$\frac{P(A \text{ and } B)}{P(A)} = \frac{P(A) \cdot P(B|A)}{P(A)}$$

$$\frac{P(A \text{ and } B)}{P(A)} = P(B|A)$$

Formula for Conditional Probability

The probability that the second event B occurs given that the first event A has occurred can be found by dividing the probability that both events occurred by the probability that the first event has occurred. The formula is

$$P(B|A) = \frac{P(A \text{ and } B)}{P(A)}$$

The Venn diagram for conditional probability is shown in Figure 4–9. In this case,

$$P(B|A) = \frac{P(A \text{ and } B)}{P(A)}$$

which is represented by the area in the intersection or overlapping part of the circles A and B, divided by the area of circle A. The reasoning here is that if you assume A has occurred, then A becomes the sample space for the next calculation and is the denominator of the probability fraction $P(A \text{ and } B)/P(A)$. The numerator $P(A \text{ and } B)$ represents the probability of the part of B that is contained in A. Hence, $P(A \text{ and } B)$ becomes the numerator of the probability fraction $P(A \text{ and } B)/P(A)$. Imposing a condition reduces the sample space.

FIGURE 4–9

Venn Diagram for Conditional Probability

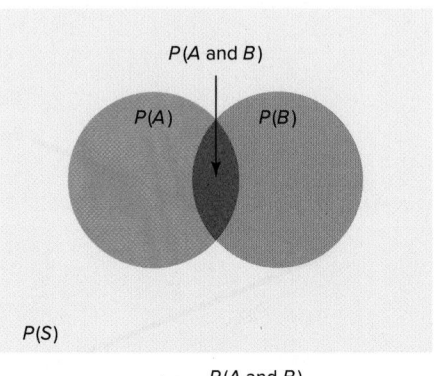

$$P(B|A) = \frac{P(A \text{ and } B)}{P(A)}$$

Examples 4–32, 4–33, and 4–34 illustrate the use of this rule.

EXAMPLE 4–32   Selecting Colored Chips

A box contains black chips and white chips. A person selects two chips without replacement. If the probability of selecting a black chip *and* a white chip is $\frac{15}{56}$ and the probability of selecting a black chip on the first draw is $\frac{3}{8}$, find the probability of selecting the white chip on the second draw, *given* that the first chip selected was a black chip.

SOLUTION

Let

$$B = \text{selecting a black chip} \qquad W = \text{selecting a white chip}$$

Then

$$P(W|B) = \frac{P(B \text{ and } W)}{P(B)} = \frac{15/56}{3/8}$$

$$= \frac{15}{56} \div \frac{3}{8} = \frac{15}{56} \cdot \frac{8}{3} = \frac{\overset{5}{\cancel{15}}}{\underset{7}{\cancel{56}}} \cdot \frac{\overset{1}{\cancel{8}}}{\underset{1}{\cancel{3}}} = \frac{5}{7} \approx 0.714$$

Hence, the probability of selecting a white chip on the second draw given that the first chip selected was black is $\frac{5}{7} \approx 0.714$.

EXAMPLE 4–33   Parking Tickets

The probability that Sam parks in a no-parking zone *and* gets a parking ticket is 0.06, and the probability that Sam cannot find a legal parking space and has to park in the no-parking zone is 0.20. On Tuesday, Sam arrives at school and has to park in a no-parking zone. Find the probability that he will get a parking ticket.

SOLUTION

Let

$$N = \text{parking in a no-parking zone} \qquad T = \text{getting a ticket}$$

Then

$$P(T|N) = \frac{P(N \text{ and } T)}{P(N)} = \frac{0.06}{0.20} = 0.30$$

Hence, Sam has a 0.30 probability or 30% chance of getting a parking ticket, given that he parked in a no-parking zone.

The conditional probability of events occurring can also be computed when the data are given in table form, as shown in Example 4–34.

EXAMPLE 4–34   Survey on Women and Household Tasks

A recent survey asked 100 people if they thought women should handle household tasks. The results of the survey are shown.

Gender	Yes	No	Total
Male	32	18	50
Female	8	42	50
Total	40	60	100

Find these probabilities.

    a. The respondent answered yes, given that the respondent was a female.

    b. The respondent was a male, given that the respondent answered no.

SOLUTION

Let

$$M = \text{respondent was a male} \qquad Y = \text{respondent answered yes}$$

$$F = \text{respondent was a female} \qquad N = \text{respondent answered no}$$

    a. The problem is to find $P(Y|F)$. The rule states

$$P(Y|F) = \frac{P(F \text{ and } Y)}{P(F)}$$

The probability $P(F \text{ and } Y)$ is the number of females who responded yes, divided by the total number of respondents:

$$P(F \text{ and } Y) = \frac{8}{100}$$

The probability $P(F)$ is the probability of selecting a female:

$$P(F) = \frac{50}{100}$$

Then

$$P(Y|F) = \frac{P(F \text{ and } Y)}{P(F)} = \frac{8/100}{50/100}$$

$$= \frac{8}{100} \div \frac{50}{100} = \frac{\overset{4}{\cancel{8}}}{\cancel{100}} \cdot \frac{\overset{1}{\cancel{100}}}{\underset{25}{\cancel{50}}} = \frac{4}{25} = 0.16$$

b. The problem is to find $P(M|N)$.

$$P(M|N) = \frac{P(N \text{ and } M)}{P(N)} = \frac{18/100}{60/100}$$

$$= \frac{18}{100} \div \frac{60}{100} = \frac{\overset{3}{\cancel{18}}}{\cancel{100}} \cdot \frac{\overset{1}{\cancel{100}}}{\underset{10}{\cancel{60}}} = \frac{3}{10} = 0.3$$

Probabilities for "At Least"

The multiplication rules can be used with the complementary event rule (Section 4–1) to simplify solving probability problems involving "at least." Examples 4–35, 4–36, and 4–37 illustrate how this is done.

EXAMPLE 4–35   Drawing Cards

A person selects 3 cards from an ordinary deck and replaces each card after it is drawn. Find the probability that the person will get at least one heart.

SOLUTION

It is much easier to find the probability that the person will not select a heart in three draws and subtract this value from 1. To do the problem directly, you would have to find the probability of selecting 1 heart, 2 hearts, and 3 hearts and then add the results.

Let

$$E = \text{at least 1 heart is drawn} \quad \text{and} \quad \overline{E} = \text{no hearts are drawn}$$

$$P(\overline{E}) = \frac{39}{52} \cdot \frac{39}{52} \cdot \frac{39}{52} = \frac{3}{4} \cdot \frac{3}{4} \cdot \frac{3}{4} = \frac{27}{64}$$

$$P(E) = 1 - P(\overline{E})$$

$$= 1 - \frac{27}{64} = \frac{37}{64} \approx 0.578 = 57.8\%$$

Hence, a person will select at least one heart about 57.8% of the time.

EXAMPLE 4–36   Rolling a Die

A single die is rolled 5 times; find the probability of getting at least one 3.

SOLUTION

It is easier to find the probability of getting the complement of the event, which is getting no threes. Then subtract this probability from one to get the probability of getting at least one 3.

$$P(\text{at least one 3}) = 1 - P(\text{no 3's})$$

$$= 1 - \left(\frac{5}{6}\right)^5 = 1 - \frac{3125}{7776} = \frac{4651}{7776} \approx 0.598$$

There is a 59.8% of getting at least one 3 when a die is rolled 5 times.

EXAMPLE 4–37   Ties

The Neckware Association of America reported that 3% of ties sold in the United States are bow ties. If 4 customers who purchased a tie are randomly selected, find the probability that at least 1 purchased a bow tie.

SOLUTION

Let E = at least 1 bow tie is purchased and $\overline{E}$ = no bow ties are purchased. Then

$$P(E) = 0.03 \quad \text{and} \quad P(\overline{E}) = 1 - 0.03 = 0.97$$

$P(\text{no bow ties are purchased}) = (0.97)(0.97)(0.97)(0.97) \approx 0.885$; hence,
$P(\text{at least one bow tie is purchased}) = 1 - 0.885 = 0.115$.

There is an 11.5% chance of a person purchasing at least one bow tie.

Applying the Concepts 4–3

Guilty or Innocent?

In July 1964, an elderly woman was mugged in Costa Mesa, California. In the vicinity of the crime a tall, bearded man sat waiting in a yellow car. Shortly after the crime was committed, a young, tall woman, wearing her blond hair in a ponytail, was seen running from the scene of the crime and getting into the car, which sped off. The police broadcast a description of the suspected muggers. Soon afterward, a couple fitting the description was arrested and convicted of the crime. Although the evidence in the case was largely circumstantial, the two people arrested were nonetheless convicted of the crime. The prosecutor based his entire case on basic probability theory, showing the unlikeness of another couple being in that area while having all the same characteristics that the elderly woman described. The following probabilities were used.

Characteristic	Assumed probability
Drives yellow car	1 out of 12
Man over 6 feet tall	1 out of 10
Man wearing tennis shoes	1 out of 4
Man with beard	1 out of 11
Woman with blond hair	1 out of 3
Woman with hair in a ponytail	1 out of 13
Woman over 6 feet tall	1 out of 100

1. Compute the probability of another couple being in that area with the same characteristics.

2. Would you use the addition or multiplication rule? Why?

3. Are the characteristics independent or dependent?

4. How are the computations affected by the assumption of independence or dependence?

5. Should any court case be based solely on probabilities?

6. Would you convict the couple who was arrested even if there were no eyewitnesses?

7. Comment on why in today's justice system no person can be convicted solely on the results of probabilities.

8. In actuality, aren't most court cases based on uncalculated probabilities?

See page 255 for the answers.

Exercises 4–3

1. State which events are independent and which are dependent.
   a. Tossing a coin and drawing a card from a deck Independent
   b. Drawing a ball from an urn, not replacing it, and then drawing a second ball Dependent
   c. Getting a raise in salary and purchasing a new car Dependent
   d. Driving on ice and having an accident Dependent

2. State which events are independent and which are dependent.
   a. Having a large shoe size and having a high IQ Independent
   b. A father being left-handed and a daughter being left-handed Dependent
   c. Smoking excessively and having lung cancer Dependent
   d. Eating an excessive amount of ice cream and smoking an excessive amount of cigarettes Independent

3. **Wild Fires** Sixteen percent of wildfires are caused by lightning. Select 4 wildfires at random and find the probability that
   a. None is caused by lightning. 0.500
   b. All four are caused by lightning. 0.00066
   Source: National Academy of Sciences

4. **Seat Belt Use** The Gallup Poll reported that 90.7% of Americans used a seat belt the last time they got into a car. If 4 people are selected at random, find the probability that they all used a seat belt the last time they got into a car. 67.7%

5. **Promotions** Sixty-three percent of professionals prefer a promotion without a raise rather than a raise with no promotion. If 3 professionals are selected at random, find the probability that all will select a promotion with no raise. Is this a likely or unlikely event? 0.25, unlikely
   Source: Korn Ferry Survey

6. **Prison Populations** If 16.8% of U.S. federal prison inmates are not U.S. citizens, find the probability that 2 randomly selected federal prison inmates will not be U.S. citizens. 2.8%

7. **Doctorate Degrees and Counselors** In a sample of 100 counselors, 60% are female and 40% are male. Of the female counselors, 25% have a doctorate degree. Of the male counselors, 10% have a doctorate degree. If a counselor is selected at random, find each probability.
   a. The probability that a female had a doctorate degree 15%
   b. The probability that the counselor is a male without a doctorate degree 36%
   c. The probability that a counselor does not have a doctorate degree 81%

8. **Debt Free** Twenty-four percent of adults say that they are debt-free, while 12% say that they will pass away in debt. If 5 adults are randomly selected, find the probability that at least one is debt-free. Find the probability that all 5 believe that they will pass away in debt. 0.746, 0.0000249
   Source: Credit Cards.com

9. **Smiling People** Sixty percent of adults say that a smile from a stranger improves their day. If 6 people are randomly selected, find the probability that none will improve their day when smiled at by a stranger. 0.0041
   Source: Dignity Health/Qualtrics Survey

10. **Selecting Marbles** A bag contains 9 red marbles, 8 white marbles, and 6 blue marbles. Randomly choose two marbles, one at a time, and without replacement. Find the following.
    a. The probability that the first marble is red and the second is white 0.142
    b. The probability that both are the same color 0.312
    c. The probability that the second marble is blue 0.261

11. **Healthy Eating** Fifty-nine percent of adults believe that the best way to achieve the ideal body type is to eat healthy as opposed to exercising. Randomly select 3 adults and find the probability that
    a. None of the 3 believe that healthy eating will achieve the ideal body type. 0.0689
    b. All of the 3 believe that healthy eating will achieve the ideal body type. 0.205
    c. At least one of the 3 will believe that healthy eating will achieve the ideal body type. 0.931
    Source: Harris Poll

12. **Flashlight Batteries** A flashlight has 6 batteries, 2 of which are defective. If 2 are selected at random without replacement, find the probability that both are defective. $\frac{1}{15}$

13. **Drawing Cards** Four cards are drawn from an ordinary deck of cards without replacement. Find these probabilities.
    a. All cards are kings. 0.00000369
    b. All cards are red cards. 0.0552
    c. All cards are spades. 0.00264

14. **Scientific Study** In a scientific study there are 8 guinea pigs, 5 of which are pregnant. If 3 are selected at random without replacement, find the probability that all are pregnant. $\frac{5}{28}$

15. **Drawing Cards** If two cards are drawn from a deck without replacement, find these probabilities.
    a. Both cards are diamonds. $\frac{1}{17}$
    b. Both cards are red cards. $\frac{25}{102}$
    c. Both cards are of the same suit. $\frac{4}{17}$

16. **Winning a Door Prize** At a gathering consisting of 10 men and 20 women, two door prizes are awarded. Find the probability that both prizes are won by men. The winning ticket is not replaced. Would you consider this event likely or unlikely to occur? $\frac{3}{29}$, unlikely

17. **Defective Batteries** In a box of 12 batteries, 2 are dead. If 2 batteries are selected at random for a flashlight, find the probability that both are dead. Would you consider this event likely or unlikely? $\frac{1}{66}$, highly unlikely

18. **Sales** A manufacturer makes two models of an item: model I, which accounts for 80% of unit sales, and model II, which accounts for 20% of unit sales. Because of defects, the manufacturer has to replace (or exchange) 10% of its model I and 18% of its model II. If a model is selected at random, find the probability that it will be defective. 0.116

19. **Student Financial Aid** In a recent year 8,073,000 male students and 10,980,000 female students were enrolled as undergraduates. Receiving aid were 60.6% of the male students and 65.2% of the female students. Of those receiving aid, 44.8% of the males got federal aid and 50.4% of the females got federal aid. Choose 1 student at random. (*Hint:* Make a tree diagram.) Find the probability that the student is
    a. A male student without aid. 0.167
    b. A male student, given that the student has aid. 0.406
    c. A female student or a student who receives federal aid. 0.691
    Source: www.nces.gov

20. **Selecting Colored Balls** Urn 1 contains 4 red balls and 2 black balls. Urn 2 contains 1 red ball and 3 black balls. Urn 3 contains 3 red balls and 3 black balls. If an urn is selected at random and a ball is drawn, find the probability that it will be a black ball. $\frac{19}{36}$

21. **Automobile Insurance** An insurance company classifies drivers as low-risk, medium-risk, and high-risk. Of those insured, 60% are low-risk, 30% are medium-risk, and 10% are high-risk. After a study, the company finds that during a 1-year period, 1% of the low-risk drivers had an accident, 5% of the medium-risk drivers had an accident, and 9% of the high-risk drivers had an accident. If a driver is selected at random, find the probability that the driver will have had an accident during the year. 0.03

22. **Defective Items** A production process produces an item. On average, 15% of all items produced are defective. Each item is inspected before being shipped, and the inspector misclassifies an item 10% of the time. What proportion of the items will be "classified as good"? What is the probability that an item is defective given that it was classified as good? 0.78; 0.018

23. **Prison Populations** For a recent year, 0.99 of the incarcerated population is adults and 0.07 of the incarcerated are adult females. If an incarcerated person is selected at random, find the probability that the person is a female given that the person is an adult. 0.071
    Source: Bureau of Justice.

24. **Rolling Dice** Roll two standard dice and add the numbers. What is the probability of getting a number larger than 9 for the first time on the third roll? 0.116

25. **Heart Disease** Twenty-five percent of all deaths (all ages) are caused by diseases of the heart. Ischemic heart disease accounts for 16.4% of all deaths and heart failure for 2.3%. Choose one death at random. What is the probability that it is from ischemic heart disease given that it was from heart disease? Choose two deaths at random; what is the probability that at least one is from heart disease? 0.656; 0.438
    Source: Time Almanac.

26. **Country Club Activities** At the Avonlea Country Club, 73% of the members play bridge and swim, and 82% play bridge. If a member is selected at random, find the probability that the member swims, given that the member plays bridge. 89%

27. **College Courses** At a large university, the probability that a student takes calculus and is on the dean's list is 0.042. The probability that a student is on the dean's list is 0.21. Find the probability that the student is taking calculus, given that the student is on the dean's list. 0.2

28. **Terms of Office** In a large organization, there is a governing board which consists of elected officers. Their terms expire in the following years: 2020, 2022, and 2024.

	2020	2022	2024
Male	6	4	8
Female	1	10	11

If an elected officer is selected at random, find each.

a. P(female and term expires in 2022) $\frac{1}{4}$

b. P(male or term expires in 2024) $\frac{29}{40}$

c. P(female or term expires in 2024) $\frac{3}{4}$

29. **Pizza and Salads** In a pizza restaurant, 95% of the customers order pizza. If 65% of the customers order pizza and a salad, find the probability that a customer who orders pizza will also order a salad. 68.4%

30. **Gift Baskets** The Gift Basket Store had the following premade gift baskets containing the following combinations in stock.

	Cookies	Mugs	Candy
Coffee	20	13	10
Tea	12	10	12

Choose 1 basket at random. Find the probability that it contains

a. Coffee or candy. 0.714

b. Tea given that it contains mugs. 0.435

c. Tea and cookies. 0.156

Source: www.infoplease.com

31. **Blood Types and Rh Factors** In addition to being grouped into four types, human blood is grouped by its Rhesus (Rh) factor. Consider the figures below which show the distributions of these groups for Americans.

	O	A	B	AB
Rh+	37%	34%	10%	4%
Rh−	6%	6%	2%	1%

Choose one American at random. Find the probability that the person

a. Is a universal donor, i.e., has O-negative blood. 0.06

b. Has type O blood given that the person is Rh+. 0.435

c. Has A+ or AB− blood. 0.35

d. Has Rh− given that the person has type B. 0.167

Source: www.infoplease.com

32. **Doctor Specialties** Below are listed the numbers of doctors in various specialties by gender.

	Pathology	Pediatrics	Psychiatry
Male	12,575	33,020	27,803
Female	5,604	33,351	12,292

Choose one doctor at random.

a. Find P(male|pediatrician). 0.498

b. Find P(pathologist|female). 0.109

c. Are the characteristics "female" and "pathologist" independent? Explain. No. P(path|female) ≠ P(path)

Source: World Almanac.

33. **Reasons for Quitting a Job** The results of a survey of 70 randomly selected adults who gave the following reasons for quitting a job is shown.

Reason	Males	Females
High anxiety	13	16
Loss of job due to a merger	9	8
Burnout	7	5
Failure to get promoted	5	4
Being fired	2	1

If a person is selected at random, find the probability that the person is

a. A male given that he was fired. $\frac{2}{3}$

b. The person was a female given that she suffered from burnout. $\frac{5}{12}$

c. Someone who lost their job due to a merger given that the person was a male. $\frac{1}{4}$

34. **Reasons for Being Fired** A survey of 100 randomly selected people who were recently fired from a job showed the following results.

Reason	Age: Under 30	Age: 30 and over
Incompetence	24	16
Inability to get along with others	20	13
Dishonesty	5	3
Lack of motivation	7	9
Other	2	1

If a person is randomly selected, find each probability.

a. The person was fired for incompetence given that the person is 30 or over. $\frac{8}{21}$

b. The person was under 30 given that the person was fired for being dishonest. $\frac{5}{8}$

c. The person was fired for lack of motivation and is under 30 years old. $\frac{7}{100}$

35. **Leisure Time Exercise** Only 27% of U.S. adults get enough leisure time exercise to achieve cardiovascular fitness. Choose 3 adults at random. Find the probability that

a. All 3 get enough daily exercise. 0.020

b. At least 1 of the 3 gets enough exercise. 0.611

Source: www.infoplease.com

36. **Customer Purchases** In a department store there are 120 customers, 90 of whom will buy at least 1 item. If 5 customers are selected at random, one by one, find the probability that all will buy at least 1 item. 0.237

37. **Marital Status of Women** According to the *Statistical Abstract of the United States,* 70.3% of females ages 20 to 24 have never been married. Choose 5 young women in this age category at random. Find the probability that
    a. None has ever been married. 0.172
    b. At least 1 has been married. 0.828
    Source: New York Times Almanac.

38. **Fatal Accidents** The American Automobile Association (AAA) reports that of the fatal car and truck accidents, 54% are caused by car driver error. If 3 accidents are chosen at random, find the probability that
    a. All are caused by car driver error. 0.157
    b. None is caused by car driver error. 0.097
    c. At least 1 is caused by car driver error. 0.903
    Source: AAA quoted on CNN.

39. **On-Time Arrivals** At the dentist's office, 93% of the patients arrive on time. If 5 patients are selected at random, find the probability that at least one patient was not on time. 0.304

40. **On-Time Flights** A flight from Pittsburgh to Charlotte has a 90% on-time record. From Charlotte to Jacksonville, North Carolina, the flight is on time 80% of the time. The return flight from Jacksonville to Charlotte is on time 50% of the time and from Charlotte to Pittsburgh, 90% of the time. Consider a round trip from Pittsburgh to Jacksonville on these flights. Assume the flights are independent.
    a. What is the probability that all 4 flights are on time? 0.324
    b. What is the probability that at least 1 flight is not on time? 0.676
    c. What is the probability that at least 1 flight is on time? 0.999
    d. Which events are complementary? *a* and *b*

41. **Reading to Children** Fifty-eight percent of American children (ages 3 to 5) are read to every day by someone at home. Suppose 5 children are randomly selected. What is the probability that at least 1 is read to every day by someone at home? 0.987
    Source: Federal Interagency Forum on Child and Family Statistics.

42. **Doctoral Assistantships** Of Ph.D. students, 60% have paid assistantships. If 3 students are selected at random, find the probabilities that
    a. All have assistantships. 0.216
    b. None has an assistantship. 0.064
    c. At least 1 has an assistantship. 0.936
    Source: U.S. Department of Education, Chronicle of Higher Education.

43. **Drawing Cards** If 5 cards are drawn at random from a deck of 52 cards and are not replaced, find the probability of getting at least one diamond. $\frac{7411}{9520}$

44. **Autism** In recent years it was thought that approximately 1 in 110 children exhibited some form of autism. The most recent CDC study concluded that the proportion may be as high as 1 in 88. If indeed these new figures are correct, choose 3 children at random and find these probabilities.
    a. What is the probability that none have autism? 0.966
    b. What is the probability that at least 1 has autism? 0.034
    c. Choose 10 children at random. What is the probability that at least 1 has autism? 0.108
    Source: cdc.gov

45. **Video Games** Video games are rated according to content. Twenty-eight percent of the games are rated as violent. If 6 games are selected at random, find the probability that
    a. None of the six was rated violent. 0.139
    b. At least one of the six games is rated violent. 0.861

46. **Medication Effectiveness** A medication is 75% effective against a bacterial infection. Find the probability that if 12 people take the medication, at least 1 person's infection will not improve. 96.8%

47. **Selecting Digits** If 3 digits are selected at random with replacement, find the probability of getting at least one odd number. Would you consider this event likely or unlikely? Why? 0.875, likely

48. **Selecting a Letter of the Alphabet** If 3 letters of the alphabet are selected at random, find the probability of getting at least 1 letter x. Letters can be used more than once. Would you consider this event likely to happen? Explain your answer. 0.111; the event is unlikely to occur since the probability is only about 11%.

49. **Rolling a Die** A die is rolled twice. Find the probability of getting at least one 6. 0.306

50. **Child Care** A recent survey found that 35% of child care is done in the child's home, 51% at a day care center, and 14% in other places. If 5 children are randomly selected, find the probability that
    a. All were cared for in a day care center. 0.0345
    b. None was cared for in a day care center. 0.028
    c. At least one was cared for in a day care center. 0.972

51. **Lucky People** Twelve percent of people in Western countries consider themselves lucky. If 3 people are selected at random, what is the probability that at least one will consider themselves lucky? 0.319
    Source: San Diego-Tribune.

52. **Selecting a Flower** In a large vase, there are 8 roses, 5 daisies, 12 lilies, and 9 orchids. If 4 flowers are selected at random, and not replaced, find the probability that at least 1 of the flowers is a rose. Would you consider this event likely to occur? Explain your answer. 0.678; yes the event is more likely to occur than not since the probability is about 68%.

≡ Extending the Concepts

53. Let A and B be two mutually exclusive events. Are A and B independent events? Explain your answer. No, since $P(A \text{ and } B) = 0$ and does not equal $P(A) \cdot P(B)$.

54. Types of Vehicles The Bargain Auto Mall has the following cars in stock.

	SUV	Compact	Mid-sized
Foreign	20	50	20
Domestic	65	100	45

Are the events "compact" and "domestic" independent? Explain. No, since $P(C|D) \neq P(C)$.

55. College Enrollment An admissions director knows that the probability a student will enroll after a campus visit is 0.55, or $P(E) = 0.55$. While students are on campus visits, interviews with professors are arranged. The admissions director computes these conditional probabilities for students enrolling after visiting three professors, DW, LP, and MH.

$P(E|\text{DW}) = 0.95 \qquad P(E|\text{LP}) = 0.55 \qquad P(E|\text{MH}) = 0.15$

What do you observe about the results?

56. Commercials Event A is the event that a person remembers a certain product commercial. Event B is the event that a person buys the product. If $P(B) = 0.35$, comment on each of these conditional probabilities if you were vice president for sales.

a. $P(B|A) = 0.20$

b. $P(B|A) = 0.35$

c. $P(B|A) = 0.55$

57. Given a sample space with events A and B such that $P(A) = 0.342$, $P(B) = 0.279$, and $P(A \text{ or } B) = 0.601$. Are A and B mutually exclusive? Are A and B independent? Find $P(A|B)$, $P(\text{not } B)$, and $P(A \text{ and } B)$. No; no; 0.072; 0.721; 0.02

58. Child's Board Game In a child's board game of the tortoise and the hare, the hare moves by roll of a standard die and the tortoise by a six-sided die with the numbers 1, 1, 1, 2, 2, and 3. Roll each die once. What is the probability that the tortoise moves ahead of the hare? $\frac{1}{9}$

59. Bags Containing Marbles Two bags contain marbles. Bag 1 contains 1 black marble and 9 white marbles. Bag 2 contains 1 black marble and x white marbles. If you choose a bag at random, then choose a marble at random, the probability of getting a black marble is $\frac{2}{15}$. How many white marbles are in bag 2? 5

4–4   Counting Rules

Many times a person must know the number of all possible outcomes for a sequence of events. To determine this number, three rules can be used: the *fundamental counting rule,* the *permutation rule,* and the *combination rule.* These rules are explained here, and they will be used in Section 4–5 to find probabilities of events.

The first rule is called the **fundamental counting rule.**

The Fundamental Counting Rule

OBJECTIVE ⑤

Find the total number of outcomes in a sequence of events, using the fundamental counting rule.

Fundamental Counting Rule

In a sequence of n events in which the first one has k_1 possibilities and the second event has k_2 and the third has k_3, and so forth, the total number of possibilities of the sequence will be

$$k_1 \cdot k_2 \cdot k_3 \cdots k_n$$

Note: In this case *and* means to multiply.

Examples 4–38 through 4–41 illustrate the fundamental counting rule.

EXAMPLE 4–38   Tossing a Coin and Rolling a Die

A coin is tossed and a die is rolled. Find the number of outcomes for the sequence of events.

SOLUTION

Since the coin can land either heads up or tails up and since the die can land with any one of six numbers showing face up, there are $2 \cdot 6 = 12$ possibilities. A tree diagram can also be drawn for the sequence of events. See Figure 4–10.

FIGURE 4–10

Complete Tree Diagram for Example 4–38

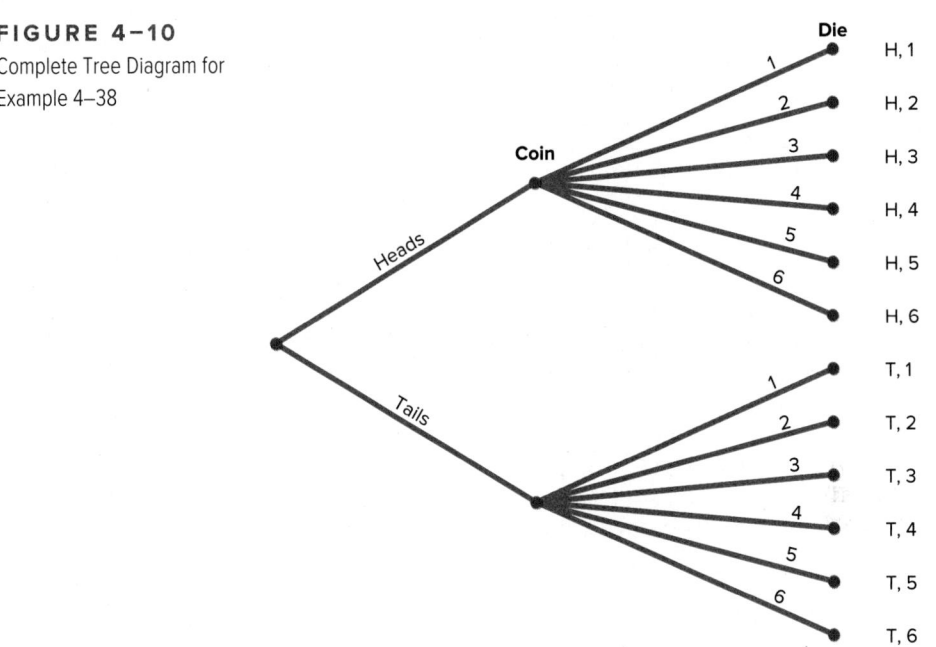

EXAMPLE 4–39   Higher Education

Students wishing to plan their education after high school can select from these categories:

    Type of school: University, four-year college, two-year college
    Major field: Business, education, psychology, health care, computer science
    Living accommodations: On-campus, off-campus
    Work: Full-time, part-time, not working

How many different situations can students select for their educational experience?

SOLUTION

The person can choose one selection from each category. Using the fundamental counting rule, the person has $3 \cdot 5 \cdot 2 \cdot 3 = 90$ ways to select their higher education experience.

EXAMPLE 4–40   Distribution of Blood Types

There are four blood types, A, B, AB, and O. Blood can also be Rh+ and Rh−. Finally, a blood donor can be classified as either male or female. How many different ways can a donor's blood be labeled?

SOLUTION

Since there are 4 possibilities for blood type, 2 possibilities for Rh factor, and 2 possibilities for the gender of the donor, there are $4 \cdot 2 \cdot 2$, or 16, different classification categories.

A tree diagram for the events is shown in Figure 4–11.

FIGURE 4–11

Complete Tree Diagram
for Example 4–40

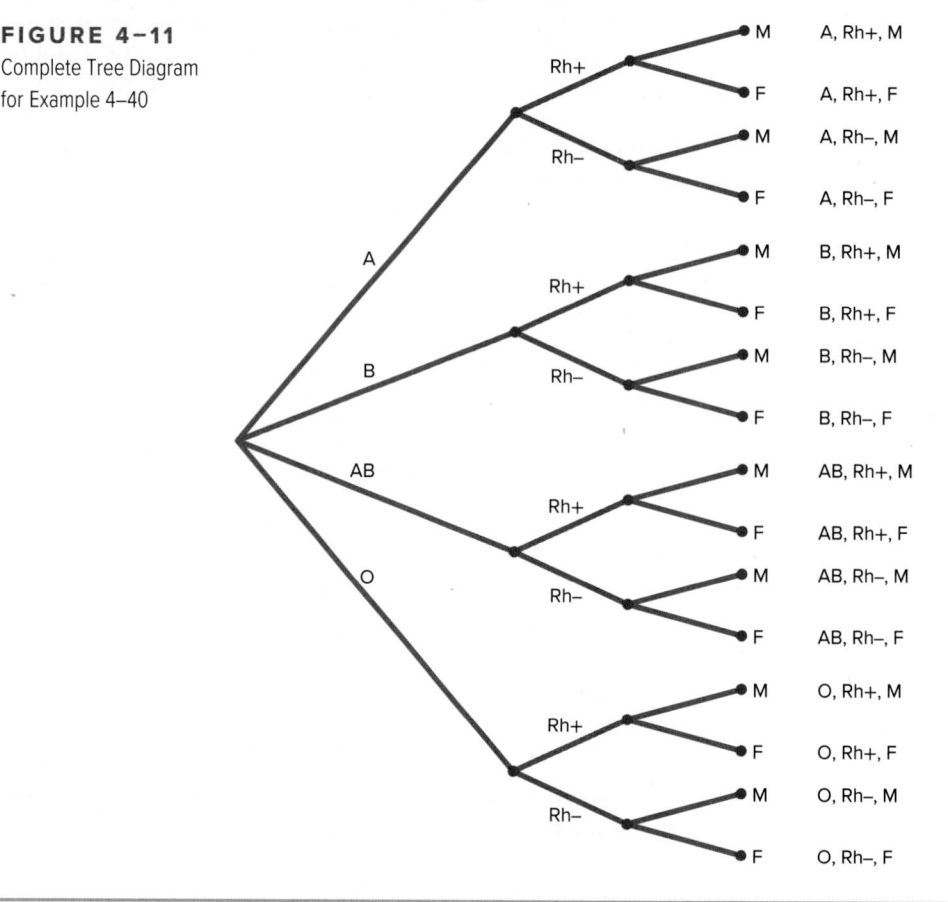

When determining the number of different possibilities of a sequence of events, you must know whether repetitions are permissible.

EXAMPLE 4–41   Railroad Memorial License Plates

The first year the state of Pennsylvania issued railroad memorial license plates, the plates had a picture of a steam engine followed by four digits. Assuming that repetitions are allowed, how many railroad memorial plates could be issued?

SOLUTION

Since there are four spaces to fill for each space, the total number of plates that can be issued is $10 \cdot 10 \cdot 10 \cdot 10 = 10{,}000$. *Note:* Actually there was such a demand for the plates, Pennsylvania had to use letters also.

Now if repetitions are not permitted, the first digit in the plate in Example 4–41 could be selected in 10 ways, the second digit in 9 ways, etc. So the total number of plates that could be issued is $10 \cdot 9 \cdot 8 \cdot 7 = 5040$.

The same situation occurs when one is drawing balls from an urn or cards from a deck. If the ball or card is replaced before the next one is selected, then repetitions are permitted, since the same one can be selected again. But if the selected ball or card is not replaced, then repetitions are not permitted, since the same ball or card cannot be selected the second time.

These examples illustrate the fundamental counting rule. In summary: *If repetitions are permitted, then the numbers stay the same going from left to right. If repetitions are not permitted, then the numbers decrease by 1 for each place left to right.*

Two other rules that can be used to determine the total number of possibilities of a sequence of events are the permutation rule and the combination rule.

Factorial Notation

These rules use *factorial notation.* The factorial notation uses the exclamation point.

$$5! = 5 \cdot 4 \cdot 3 \cdot 2 \cdot 1$$
$$9! = 9 \cdot 8 \cdot 7 \cdot 6 \cdot 5 \cdot 4 \cdot 3 \cdot 2 \cdot 1$$

To use the formulas in the permutation and combination rules, a special definition of 0! is needed: $0! = 1$.

> **Factorial Formulas**
>
> For any counting number n
> $$n! = n(n-1)(n-2) \cdots 1$$
> $$0! = 1$$

Permutations

> A **permutation** is an arrangement of n objects in a specific order.

Examples 4–42 and 4–43 illustrate permutations.

EXAMPLE 4–42   Family Photograph

A family has 4 children. How many different ways can they line up in a row for a photograph?

SOLUTION

There are 4 choices for the first person, 3 choices for the second person, 2 choices for the third person, and one way to select for the fourth person. Hence, $4! = 4 \cdot 3 \cdot 2 \cdot 1 = 24$. There are 24 different ways for four children to line up for a photograph.

In Example 4–42 all objects were used up. But what happens when not all objects are used up? The answer to this question is given in Example 4–43.

EXAMPLE 4–43   Business Location

A business owner wishes to rank the top 3 locations selected from 5 locations for a business. How many different ways can she rank them?

SOLUTION

Using the fundamental counting rule, she can select any one of the 5 for first choice, then any one of the remaining 4 locations for her second choice, and finally, any one of the remaining locations for her third choice, as shown.

$$5 \cdot 4 \cdot 3 = 60$$

The solutions in Examples 4–42 and 4–43 are permutations.

OBJECTIVE

Find the number of ways that *r* objects can be selected from *n* objects, using the permutation rule.

Permutation Rule 1

The arrangement of *n* objects in a specific order using *r* objects at a time is called a *permutation of n objects taking r objects at a time*. It is written as $_nP_r$, and the formula is

$$_nP_r = \frac{n!}{(n-r)!}$$

The notation $_nP_r$ is used for permutations.

$$_6P_4 \text{ means} \qquad \frac{6!}{(6-4)!} \qquad or \qquad \frac{6!}{2!} = \frac{6 \cdot 5 \cdot 4 \cdot 3 \cdot \cancel{2} \cdot \cancel{1}}{\cancel{2} \cdot \cancel{1}} = 360$$

Although Examples 4–42 and 4–43 were solved by the multiplication rule, they can now be solved by the permutation rule.

In Example 4–42, five locations were taken and then arranged in order; hence,

$$_5P_5 = \frac{5!}{(5-5)!} = \frac{5!}{0!} = \frac{5 \cdot 4 \cdot 3 \cdot 2 \cdot 1}{1} = 120$$

(Recall that $0! = 1$.)

In Example 4–43, three locations were selected from 5 locations, so $n = 5$ and $r = 3$; hence,

$$_5P_3 = \frac{5!}{(5-3)!} = \frac{5!}{2!} = \frac{5 \cdot 4 \cdot 3 \cdot \cancel{2} \cdot \cancel{1}}{\cancel{2} \cdot \cancel{1}} = 60$$

Examples 4–44 and 4–45 illustrate the permutation rule.

EXAMPLE 4–44   Radio Show Guests

A radio talk show host can select 3 of 6 special guests for the program. The order of appearance of the guests is important. How many different ways can the guests be selected?

SOLUTION

Since the order of appearance on the show is important, there are $_6P_3$ ways to select the guests.

$$_6P_3 = \frac{6!}{(6-3)!} = \frac{6!}{3!} = \frac{6 \cdot 5 \cdot 4 \cdot 3!}{3!} = 120$$

Hence, there can be 120 different ways to select 3 guests and present them on the program in a specific order.

EXAMPLE 4–45   School Musical Plays

A school musical director can select 2 musical plays to present next year. One play will be presented in the fall, and one play will be presented in the spring. If the music director has 9 plays to pick from, how many different possibilities are there?

SOLUTION

Order is important since one play can be presented in the fall and the other play in the spring.

$$_9P_2 = \frac{9!}{(9-2)!} = \frac{9!}{7!} = \frac{9 \cdot 8 \cdot 7!}{7!} = 72$$

There are 72 different possibilities.

In the previous examples, all items involving permutations were different, but when some of the items are identical, a second permutation rule can be used.

Permutation Rule 2

The number of permutations of n objects when r_1 objects are identical, r_2 objects are identical, . . . , r_p objects are identical, etc., is

$$\frac{n!}{r_1! r_2! \cdots r_p!}$$

where $r_1 + r_2 + \cdots + r_p = n$.

EXAMPLE 4–46 Letter Permutations

How many permutations of the letters can be made from the word *STATISTICS*?

SOLUTION

In the word *STATISTICS*, there are 3 S's, 3 T's, 2 I's, 1 A, and 1 C.

$$\frac{10!}{3!3!2!1!1!} = \frac{10 \cdot 9 \cdot 8 \cdot 7 \cdot 6 \cdot 5 \cdot 4 \cdot 3 \cdot 2 \cdot 1}{3 \cdot 2 \cdot 1 \cdot 3 \cdot 2 \cdot 1 \cdot 2 \cdot 1 \cdot 1 \cdot 1} = 50{,}400$$

There are 50,400 permutations that can be made from the word *STATISTICS*.

Combinations

Suppose a dress designer wishes to select two colors of material to design a new dress. The designer has on hand four colors to choose from. How many different possibilities can there be in this situation?

OBJECTIVE 7

Find the number of ways that *r* objects can be selected from *n* objects without regard to order, using the combination rule.

This type of problem differs from previous ones in that the order of selection is not important. That is, if the designer selects yellow and red, this selection is the same as the selection red and yellow. This type of selection is called a *combination*. The difference between a permutation and a combination is that in a combination, the order or arrangement of the objects is not important; by contrast, order *is* important in a permutation. Example 4–46 illustrates this difference.

A selection of distinct objects without regard to order is called a **combination.**

The McGraw Hill Companies, Inc./Evelyn Jo Hebert, photographer

The difference between a combination and a permutation can be shown using the letters A, B, C, and D. The permutations for the letters A, B, C, and D are

AB	BA	CA	DA
AC	BC	CB	DB
AD	BD	CD	DC

In permutations, AB is different from BA. But in combinations, AB is the same as BA since the order of the objects does not matter in combinations. Therefore, if duplicates are removed from a list of permutations, what is left is a list of combinations, as shown.

AB	B̸A̸	C̸A̸	D̸A̸
AC	BC	C̸B̸	D̸B̸
AD	BD	CD	D̸C̸

Hence, the combinations of A, B, C, and D are AB, AC, AD, BC, BD, and CD. (Alternatively, BA could be listed and AB crossed out, etc.) The combinations have been listed alphabetically for convenience, but this is not a requirement.

Combinations are used when the order or arrangement is not important, as in the selecting process. Suppose a committee of 5 students is to be selected from 25 students. The 5 selected students represent a combination, since it does not matter who is selected first, second, etc.

Combination Rule

The number of combinations of r objects selected from n objects is denoted by $_nC_r$ and is given by the formula

$$_nC_r = \frac{n!}{(n-r)!r!}$$

EXAMPLE 4–47 Combinations

How many combinations of 4 objects are there, taken 2 at a time?

SOLUTION

Since this is a combination problem, the answer is

$$_4C_2 = \frac{4!}{(4-2)!2!} = \frac{4!}{2!2!} = \frac{\overset{2}{\cancel{4}} \cdot 3 \cdot \cancel{2!}}{\cancel{2} \cdot 1 \cdot \cancel{2!}} = 6$$

This is the same result as shown previously.

Notice that the expression for $_nC_r$ is

$$\frac{n!}{(n-r)!r!}$$

which is the formula for permutations with $r!$ in the denominator. In other words,

$$_nC_r = \frac{_nP_r}{r!}$$

This $r!$ divides out the duplicates from the number of permutations. For each two letters, there are two permutations but only one combination. Hence, dividing the number of permutations by $r!$ eliminates the duplicates. This result can be verified for other values of n and r. *Note:* $_nC_n = 1$.

EXAMPLE 4–48   Movies at the Park

The director of Movies at the Park must select 4 movies from a total of 10 movies to show on Movie Night at the Park. How many different ways can the selections be made?

SOLUTION

$$_{10}C_4 = \frac{10!}{(10-4)!4!} = \frac{10!}{6!4!} = \frac{10 \cdot 9 \cdot 8 \cdot 7}{4 \cdot 3 \cdot 2 \cdot 1} = 210$$

The director has 210 different ways to select four movies from 10 movies. In this case, the order in which the movies are shown is not important.

EXAMPLE 4–49   Committee Selection

In a club there are 7 women and 5 men. A committee of 3 women and 2 men is to be chosen. How many different possibilities are there?

SOLUTION

Here, you must select 3 women from 7 women, which can be done in $_7C_3$, or 35, ways. Next, 2 men must be selected from 5 men, which can be done in $_5C_2$, or 10, ways. Finally, by the fundamental counting rule, the total number of different ways is $35 \cdot 10 = 350$, since you are choosing both men and women. Using the formula gives

$$_7C_3 \cdot _5C_2 = \frac{7!}{(7-3)!3!} \cdot \frac{5!}{(5-2)!2!} = 350$$

Table 4–1 summarizes the counting rules.

TABLE 4–1 Summary of Counting Rules		
Rule	**Definition**	**Formula**
Fundamental counting rule	The number of ways a sequence of n events can occur if the first event can occur in k_1 ways, the second event can occur in k_2 ways, etc.	$k_1 \cdot k_2 \cdot k_3 \cdots k_n$
Permutation rule 1	The number of permutations of n objects taking r objects at a time (order is important)	$_nP_r = \frac{n!}{(n-r)!}$
Permutation rule 2	The number of permutations of n objects when r_1 objects are identical, r_2 objects are identical, . . . , r_p objects are identical	$\frac{n!}{r_1! r_2! \cdots r_p!}$
Combination rule	The number of combinations of r objects taken from n objects (order is not important)	$_nC_r = \frac{n!}{(n-r)!r!}$

≡ Applying the Concepts 4–4

Garage Door Openers

Garage door openers originally had a series of four on/off switches so that homeowners could personalize the frequencies that opened their garage doors. If all garage door openers were set at the same frequency, anyone with a garage door opener could open anyone else's garage door.

1. Use a tree diagram to show how many different positions 4 consecutive on/off switches could be in.

After garage door openers became more popular, another set of 4 on/off switches was added to the systems.

2. Find a pattern of how many different positions are possible with the addition of each on/off switch.

3. How many different positions are possible with 8 consecutive on/off switches?

4. Is it reasonable to assume, if you owned a garage door opener with 8 switches, that someone could use your garage door opener to open your garage door by trying all the different possible positions?

For a specific year it was reported that the ignition keys for Dodge Caravans were made from a single blank that had five cuts on it. Each cut was made at one out of five possible levels. For that year assume there were 420,000 Dodge Caravans sold in the United States.

5. How many different possible keys can be made from the same key blank?

6. How many different Dodge Caravans could any one key start?

Look at the ignition key for your car and count the number of cuts on it. Assume that the cuts are made at one of any of five possible levels. Most car companies use one key blank for all their makes and models of cars.

7. Conjecture how many cars your car company sold over recent years, and then figure out how many other cars your car key could start. What could you do to decrease the odds of someone being able to open another vehicle with their own key?

See page 256 for the answers.

≡ Exercises 4–4

1. **Zip Codes** How many 5-digit zip codes are possible if digits can be repeated? If there cannot be repetitions? 100,000; 30,240

2. **Letter Permutations** List all the permutations of the letters in the word *MATH*.

3. **Speaking Order** Seven elementary students are selected to give a 3-minute presentation on what they did during summer vacation. How many different ways can the speakers be arranged? 5040

4. **Movie Marquee** A movie theater plans to show 7 different movies, one per night, over 7 days. How many different ways could the manager select the order of the films the theater will show? 5040

5. **Magazine Articles** A magazine editor has six articles to be put in the magazine. How many different ways can the articles appear in the magazine? 720

6. **Claims Adjuster** An insurance adjuster must see 9 people with 9 automobile claims on Thursday. How many different ways can the adjuster visit the claimants? 362,880

7. **Eight-Sided Dice** Four eight-sided dice are rolled. How many different outcomes are there? 4096

8. **Radio Station Call Letters** The call letters of a radio station must have 4 letters. The first letter must be a K or a W. How many different station call letters can be made if repetitions are not allowed? If repetitions are allowed? 27,600; 35,152

9. **Batting Order** A baseball team has nine players. How many different batting orders are there? If the pitcher always bats last, how many different batting orders are there? 362,880; 40,320

10. **High School Library** A high school librarian received a grant to purchase one book from each of these categories.

There are 5 biographies, 8 mysteries, and 3 science fiction. How many different ways can a book be selected? 120

11. **Rolling Dice** If 5 regular dice are rolled, how many different outcomes are possible? 7776

12. **Automobile and Truck Repairs** How many ways can 4 automobiles and 2 trucks be repaired if *a.* there are no restrictions and *b.* the trucks must be repaired first? *a.* 720; *b.* 48

13. Evaluate each expression.
    a. 0! 1   *e.* $_7P_3$ 210   *i.* $_9P_5$ 15,120
    b. 8! 40,320   *f.* $_{11}P_9$ 19,958,400 *j.* $_{11}P_6$ 332,640
    c. 1! 1   *g.* $_5P_5$ 120
    d. 5! 120   *h.* $_6P_0$ 1

14. Evaluate each expression.
    a. 4! 24   *e.* $_{10}P_9$ 3,628,800   *i.* $_8P_1$ 8
    b. 2! 2   *f.* $_7P_5$ 2520   *j.* $_4P_4$ 24
    c. 3! 6   *g.* $_9P_0$ 1
    d. 7! 5040   *h.* $_{10}P_4$ 5040

15. **Background Color** An artist can select 4 colors for a sign. If the artist has 6 colors to choose from, how many different ways can the artist paint the sign? 360

16. **Manufacturing Tests** An inspector must select 3 tests to perform in a certain order on a manufactured part. He has a choice of 7 tests. How many ways can he perform 3 different tests? 210

17. **Endangered Amphibians** There are 9 endangered amphibian species in the United States. How many ways can a student select 3 of these species to write a report about them? The order of selection is important. 504

18. **Inspecting Restaurants** How many different ways can a city health department inspector visit 5 restaurants in a city with 10 restaurants? 30,240

19. **Word Permutation** How many different 4-letter permutations can be written from the word *hexagon*? 840

20. **Cell Phone Models** A particular cell phone company offers 4 models of phones, each in 6 different colors and each available with any one of 5 calling plans. How many combinations are possible? 120

21. **ID Cards** How many different ID cards can be made if there are 6 digits on a card and no digit can be used more than once? 151,200

22. **Free-Sample Requests** An online coupon service has 13 offers for free samples. How many different requests are possible if a customer must request exactly 3 free samples? How many are possible if the customer may request up to 3 free samples? 286; 378 (count 0)

23. **Ticket Selection** How many different ways can 4 tickets be selected from 50 tickets if each ticket wins a different prize? 5,527,200

24. **Movie Selections** The Foreign Language Club is showing a four-movie marathon of subtitled movies. How many ways can they choose 4 from the 11 available? 330

25. **Task Assignments** How many ways can an adviser choose 4 students from a class of 12 if they are all assigned the same task? How many ways can the students be chosen if they are each given a different task? 495; 11,880

26. **Agency Cases** An investigative agency has 7 cases and 5 agents. How many different ways can the cases be assigned if only 1 case is assigned to each agent? 2520

27. **Signal Flags** How many different flag signals, each consisting of 7 flags hung vertically, can be made when there are 3 indistinguishable red flags, 2 blue flags, and 2 white flags? 210

28. **Word Permutations** How many permutations can be made using all the letters in the word *MASSACHUSETTS*? 64,864,800

29. **Code Words** How many different 9-letter code words can be made using the symbols %, %, %, %, &, &, &, +, +? 1260

30. **Toothpaste Display** How many different ways can 5 identical tubes of tartar control toothpaste, 3 identical tubes of bright white toothpaste, and 4 identical tubes of mint toothpaste be arranged in a grocery store counter display? 27,720

31. **Book Arrangements** How many different ways can 6 identical hardback books, 3 identical paperback books, and 3 identical boxed books be arranged on a shelf in a bookstore? 18,480

32. **Letter Permutations** How many different permutations of the letters in the word *CINCINNATI* are there? 50,400

33. Evaluate each expression.
    a. $_{10}C_5$ 252   *d.* $_{10}C_9$ 10
    b. $_4C_4$ 1   *e.* $_5C_4$ 5
    c. $_6C_0$ 1

34. Evaluate each expression.
    a. $_7C_3$ 35   *d.* $_8C_6$ 28
    b. $_4C_0$ 1   *e.* $_9C_6$ 84
    c. $_5C_1$ 5

35. **Medications for Depression** A researcher wishes her patients to try a new medicine for depression. How many different ways can she select 5 patients from 50 patients? 2,118,760

36. **Sports Teams** How many ways can 5 soccer players and 7 football players be selected from 10 soccer players and 10 football players? 30,240

37. **True/False Quiz** An instructor wants to program a test correction machine to correct a 10-question true/false test. How many different ways are possible for the answer sheet? If the instructor decides to have 5 questions with answers that are true and five questions with answers that are false, how many different answer sheets are possible? 1024; 252

38. **Snack Selections** In how many ways can you choose 3 kinds of cheese and 5 kinds of crackers from an appetizer tray containing 6 kinds of cheese and 8 kinds of crackers? 1120

39. **Buffet Desserts** In how many ways can you choose 3 kinds of ice cream and 2 toppings from a dessert buffet with 10 kinds of ice cream and 6 kinds of toppings? 1800

40. **Bridge Foursomes** How many different tables of 4 can you make from 16 potential bridge players? How many different tables if 4 of the players insist on playing together? 1820; 496

41. **Music Recital** Six students are performing one song each in a jazz vocal recital. Two students have repertoires of five numbers, and the others have four songs each prepared. How many different programs are possible without regard to order? Assume that the repertory selections are all unique. 6400

42. **Freight Train Cars** In a train yard there are 4 tank cars, 12 boxcars, and 7 flatcars. How many ways can a train be made up consisting of 2 tank cars, 5 boxcars, and 3 flatcars? (In this case, order is not important.) 166,320

43. **Selecting a Committee** There are 7 women and 5 men in a department. How many ways can a committee of 4 people be selected? How many ways can this committee be selected if there must be 2 men and 2 women on the committee? How many ways can this committee be selected if there must be at least 2 women on the committee? 495; 210; 420

44. **Shirt Package Inspection** A quality inspector must ex- amine 6 men's dress shirts to determine if the garments are properly packaged. If the inspector has 9 solid color shirts and 10 striped shirts, how many ways can he select 3 of each to examine? 10,080

45. **Hawaiian Words** The Hawaiian alphabet consists of 7 consonants and 5 vowels. How many three-letter "words" are possible if there are never two consonants together and if a word must always end in a vowel? 475

46. **Selecting a Jury** How many ways can a jury of 6 women and 6 men be selected from 10 women and 12 men? 194,040

47. **Selecting Students** How many ways can you pick 4 students from 10 students (6 men, 4 women) if you must have an equal number of each gender or all of the same gender? 106

48. **Investigative Team** The state narcotics bureau must form a 5-member investigative team. If it has 25 agents from which to choose, how many different possible teams can be formed? 53,130

49. **Dominoes** A domino is a flat rectangular block whose face is divided into two square parts, each part showing from zero to six pips (or dots). Playing a game consists of playing dominoes with a matching number of pips. Explain why there are 28 dominoes in a complete set. $_7C_2$ is 21 combinations + 7 double tiles = 28

50. **Charity Event Participants** There are 16 seniors and 15 juniors in a particular social organization. In how many ways can 4 seniors and 2 juniors be chosen to participate in a charity event? 191,100

51. **Automobile Selection** An automobile dealer has 12 small automobiles, 8 mid-size automobiles, and 6 large automobiles on his lot. How many ways can two of each type of automobile be selected from his inventory? 27,720

52. **DVD Selection** How many ways can a person select 8 DVDs from a display of 13 DVDs? 1287

53. **Railroad Accidents** A researcher wishes to study railroad accidents. He wishes to select 3 railroads from 10 Class I railroads, 2 railroads from 6 Class II railroads, and 1 railroad from 5 Class III railroads. How many different possibilities are there for his study? 9,000

54. **Selecting a Location** An advertising manager decides to have an ad campaign in which 8 special calculators will be hidden at various locations in a shopping mall. If he has 17 locations from which to pick, how many different possible combinations can he choose? 24,310

Permutations and Combinations

55. **Selecting Posters** A buyer decides to stock 8 different posters. How many ways can she select these 8 if there are 20 from which to choose? 125,970

56. **Test Marketing Products** Anderson Research Company decides to test-market a product in 6 areas. How many different ways can 3 areas be selected in a certain order for the first test? 120

57. **Nuclear Power Plants** How many different ways can a government researcher select 5 nuclear power plants from 9 nuclear power plants in Pennsylvania? 126

58. **Selecting Musicals** How many different ways can a theatrical group select 2 musicals and 3 dramas from 11 musicals and 8 dramas to be presented during the year? 3080

59. **Textbook Selection** How many different ways can an instructor select 2 textbooks from a possible 17? 136

60. **Coded Cards** How many different 3-color code stripes can be made on an identification card if each code con- sists of the colors black, orange, and white? All colors are used only once. 6

61. **Flight Attendants** How many different ways can 3 flight attendants be selected from 11 flight attendants for a routine flight? 165

62. **Signal Flags** How many different signals can be made by using at least 3 different flags if there are 5 different flags from which to select? 300

63. **Dinner Selections** How many ways can a dinner patron select 3 appetizers and 2 vegetables if there are 6 appetizers and 5 vegetables on the menu? 200

64. **Air Pollution** The Environmental Protection Agency must investigate 9 mills for complaints of air pollution. How many different ways can a representative select 5 of these to investigate this week? 126

65. Construction Site Inspections How many different ways can a building inspector visit 4 new construction sites in an area where there are 10 new construction sites? 210

66. Selecting Council Members The presidents, vice presidents, and secretary-treasurers from each of four classes are eligible for an all-school council. How many ways can four officers be chosen from these representatives? How many ways can they be chosen if the president must be selected from the sitting presidents, the vice president from the sitting vice presidents, the secretary from the sitting secretary-treasurers, and the treasurer from everybody who's left? 11,880; 576

Extending the Concepts

67. Selecting Coins How many different ways can you select one or more coins if you have 2 nickels, 1 dime, and 1 half-dollar? 15

68. People Seated in a Circle In how many ways can 3 people be seated in a circle? 4? n? (*Hint:* Think of them standing in a line before they sit down and/or draw diagrams.) 2; 6; $(n - 1)!$

69. Seating in a Movie Theater How many different ways can 5 people—A, B, C, D, and E—sit in a row at a movie theater if (*a*) A and B must sit together; (*b*) C must sit to the right of, but not necessarily next to, B; (*c*) D and E will not sit next to each other? *a.* 48   *b.* 60   *c.* 72

70. Poker Hands Using combinations, calculate the number of each type of poker hand in a deck of cards. (A poker hand consists of 5 cards dealt in any order.)
   a. Royal flush 4
   b. Straight flush (not including a royal flush) 36
   c. Four of a kind 624
   d. Full house 3744

71. How many different combinations can be made from $(x + 2)$ things taken x at a time? $(x + 2)(x + 1)/2$

72. A game of concentration (memory) is played with a standard 52-card deck. How many potential two-card matches are there (e.g., one jack "matches" any other jack)? 78 ∎

Technology | Step by Step

TI-84 Plus Step by Step

Factorials, Permutations, and Combinations

Factorials *n*!
   1. Type the value of n.
   2. Press **MATH** and move the cursor to PRB, then press **4** for !.
   3. Press **ENTER**.

Permutations $_nP_r$
   1. Type the value of n.
   2. Press **MATH** and move the cursor to PRB, then press **2** for $_nP_r$.
   3. Type the value of r.
   4. Press **ENTER**.

Combinations $_nC_r$
   1. Type the value of n.
   2. Press **MATH** and move the cursor to PRB, then press **3** for $_nC_r$.
   3. Type the value of r.
   4. Press **ENTER**.

Example TI 4–2

Calculate 5!

 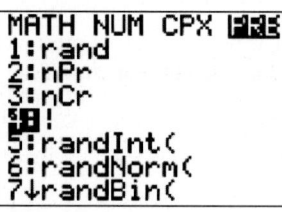 

Calculate $_6P_3$

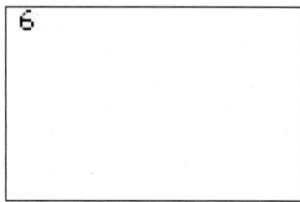 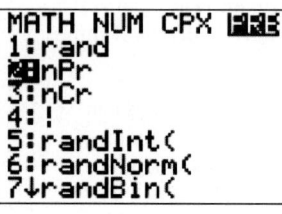 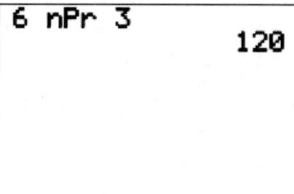

Calculate $_{10}C_3$

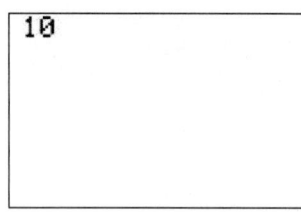 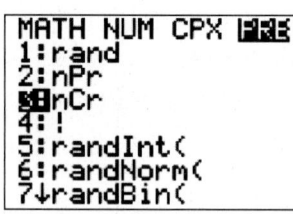 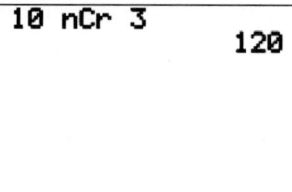

EXCEL

Step by Step

Permutations, Combinations, and Factorials

To find a value of a permutation, for example, $_5P_3$:

1. In an open cell in an Excel worksheet, select the Formulas tab on the toolbar. Then click the Insert function icon f_x .

2. Select the Statistical function category, then the PERMUT function, and click [OK].

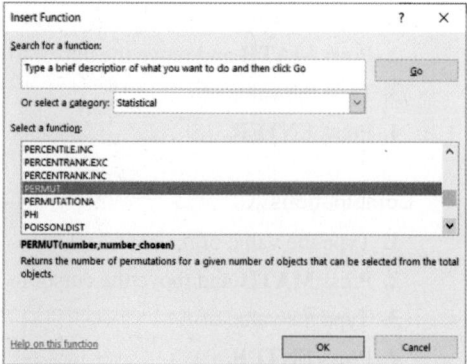

3. Type **5** in the Number box.

4. Type **3** in the Number_chosen box and click [OK].

The selected cell will display the answer: 60.

To find a value of a combination, for example, $_5C_3$:

1. In an open cell, select the Formulas tab on the toolbar. Click the Insert function icon.

2. Select the All function category, then the COMBIN function, and click [OK].

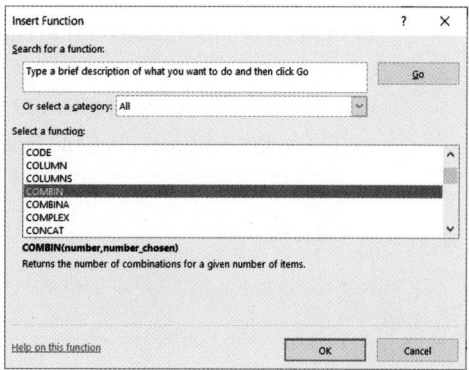

3. Type **5** in the Number box.

4. Type **3** in the Number_chosen box and click [OK].

The selected cell will display the answer: 10.

To find a factorial of a number, for example, 7!:

1. In an open cell, select the Formulas tab on the toolbar. Click the Insert function icon.

2. Select the Math & Trig function category, then the FACT function, and click [OK].

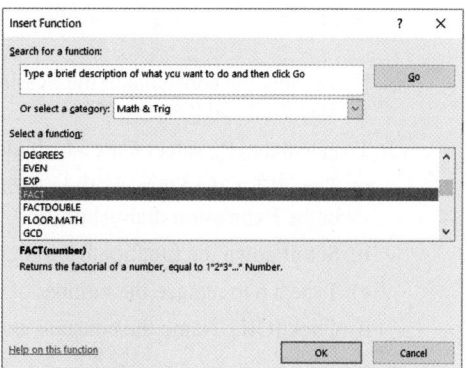

3. Type **7** in the Number box and click [OK].

The selected cell will display the answer: 5040.

MINITAB
Step by Step

Factorials, Permutations, and Combinations

We will use Minitab to calculate $5!$, $_6P_3$, and $_{10}C_3$

The results are stored in a constant; MINITAB has 1000 of them available in each worksheet. They are numbered from K1 to K1000. By default, MINITAB assigns the values of missing constants, e, and pi to the last three stored constants: K998 = *; K999 = 2.71828; and K1000 = 3.14159. To reduce clutter, MINITAB does not list these in the Constants subfolder.

1. To calculate $5!$, select **Calc>Calculator.**

   a) Type K1 in the Store result in variable, then press the Tab key on your keyboard or click in the Expression dialog box.

   b) Scroll down the function list to Factorial, then click [Select].

   c) Type a 5 to replace the number of items that is highlighted.

   d) Click [OK]. The value of $5! = 120$ will be stored in a constant that is not visible.

   e) To see the constant, click the icon for Project Manager, then the Constants item in the worksheet folder. Right-click on the Untitled name, then choose Rename and type 5Factorial. Storing the constant makes it available to be used in future calculations.

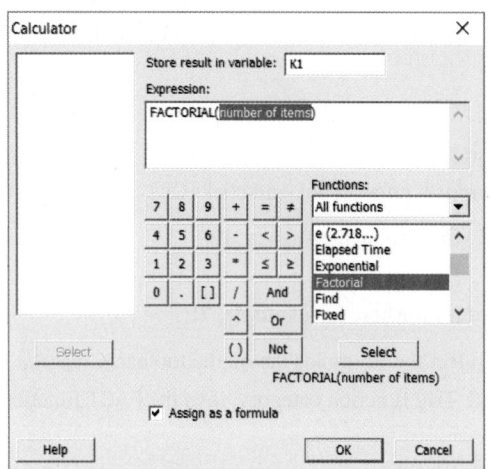
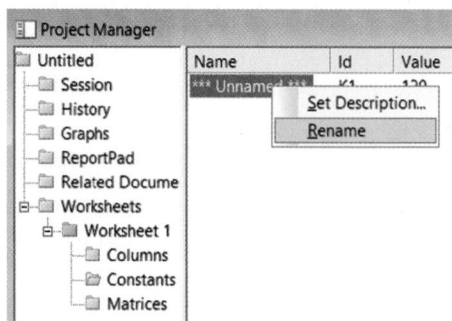

   f) To view the constants in the Session window, select **Data>Display Data** then choose K1 5factorial and [OK].

2. To calculate $_6P_3$, select **Calc>Calculator.**

   a) Type K2 in the Store result in variable, then press the Tab key on your keyboard or click in the Expression dialog box.

   b) Scroll down the function list to Permutations, then click [Select].

   c) Type a 6 to replace the number of items, then 3 to replace number to choose.

   d) Click [OK]. Name the constant and display it, using the instructions in steps 1e and 1f.

3. To calculate $_{10}C_3$, select **Calc>Calculator.**

   a) Type K3 in the Store result in variable, then press the Tab key on your keyboard or click in the Expression dialog box.

   b) Scroll down the function list to Combinations, then click [Select].

   c) Type a 10 to replace the number of items, then 3 to replace number to choose.

   d) Click [OK]. Name the constant and display it, using the instructions in steps 1e and 1f.

The Project Manager is shown. Coincidence! The values are all 120. These values can be very large and exceed the storage capability for constants. Values larger in absolute value than 1.001000E+18 in K1 are converted to missing. In scientific notation that is 1.001000×10^{18}.

Untitled	Name	Id	Value
⌐ Session	5Factorial	K1	120
⌐ History	6P3	K2	120
⌐ Graphs	10C3	K3	120
⌐ ReportPad			
⌐ Related Docume			
⌐ Worksheets			
⌐ Worksheet 1			
⌐ Columns			
⌐ Constants			
⌐ Matrices			

4–5   Probability and Counting Rules

OBJECTIVE 8

Find the probability of an event, using the counting rules.

The counting rules can be combined with the probability rules in this chapter to solve many types of probability problems. By using the fundamental counting rule, the permutation rules, and the combination rule, you can compute the probability of outcomes of many experiments, such as getting a full house when 5 cards are dealt or selecting a committee of 3 women and 2 men from a club consisting of 10 women and 10 men.

©Fuse/Corbis/Getty Images RF

EXAMPLE 4–50   Four Aces

Find the probability of getting 4 aces when 5 cards are drawn from an ordinary deck of cards.

SOLUTION

There are $_{52}C_5$ ways to draw 5 cards from a deck. There is only 1 way to get 4 aces (that is, $_4C_4$), but there are 48 possibilities to get the fifth card. Therefore, there are 48 ways to get 4 aces and 1 other card. Hence,

$$P(4 \text{ aces}) = \frac{_4C_4 \cdot 48}{_{52}C_5} = \frac{1 \cdot 48}{2{,}598{,}960} = \frac{48}{2{,}598{,}960} = \frac{1}{54{,}145}$$

EXAMPLE 4–51   Defective Integrated Circuits

A box contains 24 integrated circuits, 4 of which are defective. If 4 are sold at random, find the following probabilities.

    a. Exactly 2 are defective.   *c.* All are defective.

    b. None is defective.   *d.* At least 1 is defective.

SOLUTION

There are $_{24}C_4$ ways to sell 4 integrated circuits, so the denominator in each case will be 10,626.

    a. Two defective integrated circuits can be selected as $_4C_2$ and two nondefective ones as $_{20}C_2$. Hence,

$$P(\text{exactly 2 defectives}) = \frac{_4C_2 \cdot {}_{20}C_2}{_{24}C_4} = \frac{1140}{10{,}626} = \frac{190}{1771}$$

    b. The number of ways to choose no defectives is $_{20}C_4$. Hence,

$$P(\text{no defectives}) = \frac{_{20}C_4}{_{24}C_4} = \frac{4845}{10{,}626} = \frac{1615}{3542}$$

    c. The number of ways to choose 4 defectives from 4 is $_4C_4$, or 1. Hence,

$$P(\text{all defective}) = \frac{1}{_{24}C_4} = \frac{1}{10{,}626}$$

    d. To find the probability of at least 1 defective transistor, find the probability that there are no defective integrated circuits, and then subtract that probability from 1.

$$P(\text{at least 1 defective}) = 1 - P\,(\text{no defectives})$$

$$= 1 - \frac{_{20}C_4}{_{24}C_4} = 1 - \frac{1615}{3542} = \frac{1927}{3542}$$

EXAMPLE 4–52   Term Paper Selection

A student needs to select two topics to write two term papers for a course. There are 8 topics in economics and 11 topics in science. Find the probability that the student selects one topic in economics and one topic in science to complete the assignment.

SOLUTION

$$P(\text{economics and science}) = \frac{_8C_1 \cdot {}_{11}C_1}{_{19}C_2}$$

$$= \frac{8 \cdot 11}{19 \cdot 18}$$

$$= \frac{88}{171} = 0.515 \approx 51.5\%$$

Hence, there is about a 51.5% probability that a person will select one topic from economics and one topic from science.

EXAMPLE 4–53   State Lottery Number

In the Pennsylvania State Lottery, a person selects a three-digit number and repetitions are permitted. If a winning number is selected, find the probability that it will have all three digits the same.

SOLUTION

Since there are 10 different digits, there are $10 \cdot 10 \cdot 10 = 1000$ ways to select a winning number. When all of the digits are the same, that is, 000, 111, 222, . . . , 999, there are 10 possibilities, so the probability of selecting a winning number which has 3 identical digits is $\frac{10}{1000} = \frac{1}{100}$.

Gambling is big business. There are state lotteries, casinos, sports betting, and church bingos. It seems that today everybody is either watching or playing Texas Hold 'Em Poker.

Using permutations, combinations, and the probability rules, mathematicians can find the probabilities of various gambling games. Here are the probabilities of the various 5-card poker hands.

Hand	Number of ways	Probability
Straight flush (Including a Royal Flush)	40	0.000015
Four of a kind	624	0.000240
Full house	3,744	0.001441
Flush	5,108	0.001965
Straight	10,200	0.003925
Three of a kind	54,912	0.021129
Two pairs	123,552	0.047539
One pair	1,098,240	0.422569
Less than one pair	1,302,540	0.501177
Total	2,598,960	1.000000

Randall Fung/Corbis/Getty Images

The chance of winning at gambling games can be compared by using what is called the house advantage, house edge, or house percentage. For example, the house advantage for roulette is about 5.26%, which means in the long run, the house wins 5.26 cents on every $1 bet; or you will lose, on average, 5.26 cents on every $1 you bet. The lower the house advantage, the more favorable the game is to you.

For the game of craps, the house advantage is anywhere between 1.4 and 15%, depending on what you bet on. For the game called Keno, the house advantage is 29.5%. The house advantage for Chuck-a-Luck is 7.87%, and for Baccarat, it is either 1.36 or 1.17%, depending on your bet.

Slot machines have a house advantage anywhere from about 4 to 10% depending on the geographic location, such as Atlantic City, Las Vegas, and Mississippi, and the amount put in the machine, such as 5 cents, 25 cents, and $1.

Actually, gamblers found winning strategies for the game blackjack or 21, such as card counting. However, the casinos retaliated by using multiple decks and by banning card counters.

EXAMPLE 4–54 Tennis Tournament

There are 8 married couples in a tennis club. If two people are selected at random to plan the summer tournament, find the probability that they are married to each other.

SOLUTION

Since there are 8 ways to select the first person and 8 ways to select the partner, there are $8 \cdot 8$, or 64, ways to select the couple. Since there are 8 married couples, the solution is $\frac{8}{64} = \frac{1}{8}$.

As indicated at the beginning of this section, the counting rules and the probability rules can be used to solve a large variety of probability problems found in business, gambling, economics, biology, and other fields.

Applying the Concepts 4–5

Counting Rules and Probability

One of the biggest problems for students when doing probability problems is to decide which formula or formulas to use. Another problem is to decide whether two events are independent or dependent. Use the following problem to help develop a better understanding of these concepts.

Assume you are given a five-question multiple-choice quiz. Each question has 5 possible answers: A, B, C, D, and E.

1. How many events are there?
2. Are the events independent or dependent?
3. If you guess at each question, what is the probability that you get all of them correct?
4. What is the probability that a person guesses answer A for each question?

Assume that you are given a five-question matching test in which you are to match the correct answers in the right column with the questions in the left column. You can use each answer only once.

5. How many events are there?
6. Are the events independent or dependent?
7. What is the probability of getting them all correct if you are guessing?
8. What is the difference between the two problems?

See page 256 for the answers.

Exercises 4–5

1. **Selecting Cards** Find the probability of getting 2 face cards (king, queen, or jack) when 2 cards are drawn from a deck without replacement. $\frac{11}{221}$

2. **Selecting Cards** Cards numbered 1–10 are shuffled and dealt face down. What is the probability that they are in order? 0.0000005

3. **Scholarship Applicants** A university received 10 applications for 4 scholarships. If 5 applicants are men and 5 applicants are women, find these probabilities.
   a. All applicants selected are women. $\frac{1}{42}$
   b. Two men and two women are selected. $\frac{10}{21}$
   c. No women are selected. $\frac{1}{42}$
   d. Three women and one man are selected. $\frac{5}{21}$

4. **Municipality Partisanship** A large city has 10 elected council persons to run the city. The council presently has 5 Democrats, 4 Republicans, and 1 Independent. A new committee of 5 council members is being selected to study the traffic patterns in the city. Find each of these probabilities.
   a. All members are Democrats. $\frac{1}{252}$
   b. Two members are Democrats, 2 members are Republicans, and 1 member is an Independent. $\frac{5}{21}$

5. **Job Applications** Six men and seven women apply for two identical jobs. If the jobs are filled at random, find the following:
   a. The probability that both are filled by men. 0.192
   b. The probability that both are filled by women. 0.269
   c. The probability that one man and one woman are hired. 0.538
   d. The probability that the one man and one woman who are twins are hired. 0.013

6. **Defective Resistors** A package contains 12 resistors, 3 of which are defective. If 4 are selected, find the probability of getting
   a. 0 defective resistors. $\frac{14}{55}$
   b. 1 defective resistor. $\frac{28}{55}$
   c. 3 defective resistors. $\frac{1}{55}$

7. **Winning Tickets** At a meeting of 10 executives (7 women and 3 men), two door prizes are awarded. Find the probability that both prizes are won by men. $\frac{1}{15}$

8. **Getting a Full House** Find the probability of getting a full house (3 cards of one denomination and 2 of another) when 5 cards are dealt from an ordinary deck. $\frac{18}{12,495} = \frac{6}{4165}$

9. **Automobiles Sold** A small car dealer has 4 white automobiles, 3 red automobiles, and 2 gray automobiles on the lot. If dealer sells 3 automobiles over the weekend, find these probabilities.

   a. All three automobiles sold are white. $\frac{1}{21}$

   b. Two automobiles sold are red and 1 is gray. $\frac{1}{14}$

   c. At least 1 automobile sold is white. $\frac{37}{42}$

   d. No automobile sold is red. $\frac{10}{84}$

10. **Selecting Cards** The red face cards and the black cards numbered 2–9 are put into a bag. Four cards are drawn at random without replacement. Find the following probabilities.

    a. All 4 cards are red. 0.002

    b. 2 cards are red and 2 cards are black. 0.246

    c. At least 1 of the cards is red. 0.751

    d. All 4 cards are black. 0.249

11. **Socks in a Drawer** A drawer contains 11 identical red socks and 8 identical black socks. Suppose that you choose 2 socks at random in the dark.

    a. What is the probability that you get a pair of red socks? 0.322

    b. What is the probability that you get a pair of black socks? 0.164

    c. What is the probability that you get 2 unmatched socks? 0.515

    d. Where did the other red sock go? It probably got lost in the wash!

12. **Selecting Books** Find the probability of selecting 3 science books and 4 math books from 8 science

books and 9 math books. The books are selected at random. $\frac{882}{2431}$

13. **Rolling Dice** If three dice are rolled, find the probability of getting a sum of 5. $\frac{1}{72}$

14. **Football Team Selection** A football team consists of 20 first-year students, 20 sophomores, 15 juniors, and 10 seniors. Four players are selected at random to serve as captains. Find the probability that

    a. All 4 are seniors. 0.0003

    b. There is 1 each: first-year student, sophomore, junior, and senior. 0.089

    c. There are 2 sophomores and 2 first-year students. 0.053

    d. At least 1 of the students is a senior. 0.496

15. **Arrangement of Washers** Find the probability that if 5 different-sized washers are arranged in a row, they will be arranged in order of size. $\frac{1}{60}$

16. **Poker Hands** Using the information in Exercise 70 in Section 4–4, find the probability of each poker hand.

    a. Royal flush $\frac{4}{2,598,960}$

    b. Straight flush $\frac{36}{2,598,960}$

    c. Four of a kind $\frac{624}{2,598,960}$

17. **Plant Selection** All holly plants are dioecious—a male plant must be planted within 30 to 40 feet of the female plants in order to yield berries. A home improvement store has 12 unmarked holly plants for sale, 8 of which are female. If a homeowner buys 3 plants at random, what is the probability that berries will be produced? 0.727

Summary

In this chapter, the basic concepts of probability are explained.

- There are three basic types of probability: classical probability, empirical probability, and subjective probability. Classical probability uses sample spaces. Empirical probability uses frequency distributions, and subjective probability uses an educated guess to determine the probability of an event. The probability of any event is a number from 0 to 1. If an event cannot occur, the probability is 0. If an event is certain, the probability is 1. The sum of the probability of all the events in the sample space is 1. To find the probability of the complement of an event, subtract the probability of the event from 1. (4–1)

- Two events are mutually exclusive if they cannot occur at the same time; otherwise, the events are not mutually exclusive. To find the probability of two mutually exclusive events occurring, add the probability of each event. To find the probability of two events when they are not mutually exclusive, add the possibilities of the individual events and then subtract the probability that both events occur at the same time. These types of probability problems can be solved by using the addition rules. (4–2)

- Two events are independent if the occurrence of the first event does not change the probability of the second event occurring. Otherwise, the events are dependent. To find the probability of two independent events occurring, multiply the probabilities of each event. To find the probability that two dependent events occur, multiply the probability that the first event occurs by the probability that the second event occurs, given that the first event has already occurred. The complement of an event is found by selecting the outcomes in the sample space that are not involved in the outcomes of the event. These types of problems can be solved by using the multiplication rules and the complementary event rules. (4–3)

- Finally, when a large number of events can occur, the fundamental counting rule, the permutation rules, and the combination rule can be used to determine the number of ways that these events can occur. (4–4)

- The counting rules and the probability rules can be used to solve more-complex probability problems. (4–5)

≣ Important Terms

classical probability 191

combination 233

complement of an event 194

compound event 191

conditional probability 217

dependent events 217

disjoint events 204

empirical probability 196

equally likely events 191

event 191

fundamental counting rule 228

independent events 214

law of large numbers 198

mutually exclusive events 204

outcome 188

permutation 231

probability 188

probability experiment 188

sample space 188

simple event 191

subjective probability 198

tree diagram 190

Venn diagrams 195

≣ Important Formulas

Formula for classical probability:

$$P(E) = \frac{\text{number of outcomes in } E}{\text{total number of outcomes in sample space}} = \frac{n(E)}{n(S)}$$

Formula for empirical probability:

$$P(E) = \frac{\text{frequency for class}}{\text{total frequencies in distribution}} = \frac{f}{n}$$

Addition rule 1, for two mutually exclusive events:

$$P(A \text{ or } B) = P(A) + P(B)$$

Addition rule 2, for events that are not mutually exclusive:

$$P(A \text{ or } B) = P(A) + P(B) - P(A \text{ and } B)$$

Multiplication rule 1, for independent events:

$$P(A \text{ and } B) = P(A) \cdot P(B)$$

Multiplication rule 2, for dependent events:

$$P(A \text{ and } B) = P(A) \cdot P(B|A)$$

Formula for conditional probability:

$$P(B|A) = \frac{P(A \text{ and } B)}{P(A)}$$

Formula for complementary events:

$$P(\overline{E}) = 1 - P(E) \quad \text{or} \quad P(E) = 1 - P(\overline{E})$$
$$\text{or} \quad P(E) + P(\overline{E}) = 1$$

Fundamental counting rule: In a sequence of n events in which the first one has k_1 possibilities, the second event has k_2 possibilities, the third has k_3 possibilities, etc., the total number of possibilities of the sequence will be

$$k_1 \cdot k_2 \cdot k_3 \cdots k_n$$

Permutation rule 1: The number of permutations of n objects taking r objects at a time when order is important is

$$_nP_r = \frac{n!}{(n-r)!}$$

Permutation rule 2: The number of permutations of n objects when r_1 objects are identical, r_2 objects are identical, ..., r_p objects are identical is

$$\frac{n!}{r_1! \, r_2! \cdots r_p!}$$

Combination rule: The number of combinations of r objects selected from n objects when order is not important is

$$_nC_r = \frac{n!}{(n-r)!r!}$$

≣ Review Exercises

Section 4–1

1. **Rolling a Die** An eight-sided die is rolled. Find the probability of each.

   a. Getting a 6 0.125

   b. Getting a number larger than 5 0.375

   c. Getting an odd number 0.50

2. **Selecting a Card** When a card is selected from a deck, find the probability of getting

   a. A club. $\frac{1}{4}$

   b. A face card or a heart. $\frac{11}{26}$

   c. A 6 and a spade. $\frac{1}{52}$

   d. A king. $\frac{1}{13}$

   e. A red card. $\frac{1}{2}$

3. **Software Selection** The top-10 selling computer software titles in a recent year consisted of 3 for doing taxes, 5 antivirus or security programs, and 2 "other." Choose one title at random.

   a. What is the probability that it is not used for doing taxes? 0.7

   b. What is the probability that it is used for taxes or is one of the "other" programs? 0.5

   Source: www.infoplease.com

4. **Motor Vehicle Producers** The top five motor vehicle producers in the world are listed below with the number of vehicles produced in 2010 (in thousands of vehicles).

China	16,144
Japan	9,197
United States	7,632
Germany	5,700
South Korea	4,184

   Choose one vehicle at random.

   a. What is the probability that it was produced in the United States? 0.178

   b. What is the probability that it was not produced in Asia? 0.311

   c. What is the probability that it was produced in Germany or Japan? 0.348

   Source: World Almanac 2012.

5. **Exercise Preference** In a local fitness club, 32% of the members lifted weights to exercise, 41% preferred aerobics, and 6% preferred both. If a member is selected at random, find the probability that the member prefers another method (neither weights nor aerobics) to exercise. 0.33

6. **Rolling Two Dice** When two dice are rolled, find the probability of getting

   a. A sum of 5 or 6. $\frac{1}{4}$

   b. A sum greater than 9. $\frac{1}{6}$

   c. A sum less than 4 or greater than 9. $\frac{1}{4}$

   d. A sum that is divisible by 4. $\frac{1}{4}$

   e. A sum of 14. 0

   f. A sum less than 13. 1

Section 4–2

7. **New Cars** The probability that a new automobile has a backup camera is 0.6. The probability that a new automobile has a GPS system is 0.4. The probability that a new automobile has both a backup camera and a GPS is 0.2. If a new automobile is selected at random, find the probability that it has neither a backup camera nor a GPS. 0.2

8. **Breakfast Drink** In a recent survey, 18 people preferred milk, 29 people preferred coffee, and 13 people preferred juice as their primary drink for breakfast. If a person is selected at random, find the probability that the person preferred juice as their primary drink. $\frac{13}{60}$

9. **Lawnmower and Weed Wacker Ownership** The probability that a homeowner owns a lawnmower is 0.7. The probability that a homeowner owns a weed wacker is 0.5. The probability that a home owner owns both a lawnmower and a weed wacker is 0.3. If a homeowner is selected at random, find the probability that the homeowner owns either a lawnmower or a weed wacker. 0.9

10. **Casino Gambling** The probability that a gambler plays table games is 0.32. The probability that a person plays the slot machines is 0.85. The probability that a person plays both is 0.15. A gambler can play more than one type of game. Find the probability that a gambler plays table games given that this person plays the slot machines. 0.176

11. **Online Course Selection** Roughly 1 in 6 students enrolled in higher education took at least one online course last fall. Choose 5 enrolled students at random. Find the probability that

    a. All 5 took online courses. 0.0001

    b. None of the 5 took a course online. 0.402

    c. At least 1 took an online course. 0.598

    Source: www.encarta.msn.com

12. **Purchasing Sweaters** During a sale at a men's store, 16 white sweaters, 3 red sweaters, 9 blue sweaters, and 7 yellow sweaters were purchased. If a customer is selected at random, find the probability that he bought

    a. A blue sweater. $\frac{9}{35}$

    b. A yellow or a white sweater. $\frac{23}{35}$

    c. A red, a blue, or a yellow sweater. $\frac{19}{35}$

    d. A sweater that was not white. $\frac{19}{35}$

Section 4–3

13. **Drawing Cards** Three cards are drawn from an ordinary deck *without* replacement. Find the probability of getting

    a. All black cards. $\frac{2}{17}$

    b. All spades. $\frac{11}{850}$

    c. All queens. $\frac{1}{5525}$

14. **Coin Toss and Card Drawn** A coin is tossed and a card is drawn from a deck. Find the probability of getting

    a. A head and a 6. $\frac{1}{26}$

    b. A tail and a red card. $\frac{1}{4}$

    c. A head and a club. $\frac{1}{8}$

15. **Movie Releases** The top five countries for movie releases for a specific year are the United States with 471 releases, United Kingdom with 386, Japan with 79, Germany with 316, and France with 132. Choose 1 new release at random. Find the probability that it is

    a. European. 0.603

    b. From the United States. 0.340

    c. German or French. 0.324

    d. German given that it is European. 0.379

    Source: www.showbizdata.com

16. **Factory Output** A manufacturing company has three factories: X, Y, and Z. The daily output of each is shown here.

Product	Factory X	Factory Y	Factory Z
TVs	18	32	15
Stereos	6	20	13

If 1 item is selected at random, find these probabilities.

   a. It was manufactured at factory X or is a stereo. $\frac{57}{104}$

   b. It was manufactured at factory Y or factory Z. $\frac{10}{13}$

   c. It is a TV or was manufactured at factory Z. $\frac{3}{4}$

17. **Effectiveness of Vaccine** A vaccine has a 90% probability of being effective in preventing a certain disease. The probability of getting the disease if a person is not vaccinated is 50%. In a certain geographic region, 25% of the people get vaccinated. If a person is selected at random, find the probability that the person will contract the disease. 0.4

18. **T-shirt Factories** Two T-shirt printing factories produce T-shirts for a local sports team. Factory A produces 60% of the shirts and factory B produces 40%. Five percent of the shirts from factory A are defective, and 6% of the shirts from factory B are defective. Choose 1 shirt at random. Given that the shirt is defective, what is the probability that it came from factory A? 0.556

19. **Car Purchase** The probability that Kiara will live on campus and buy a new car is 0.37. If the probability that she will live on campus is 0.73, find the probability that she will buy a new car, given that she lives on campus. 0.507

20. **Applying Shipping Labels** Four unmarked packages have lost their shipping labels, and you must reapply them. What is the probability that you apply the labels and get all 4 of them correct? Exactly 3 correct? Exactly 2? At least 1 correct? 0.042; impossible; 0.25; 0.625

21. **Health Club Membership** Of the members of the Blue River Health Club, 43% have a lifetime membership and exercise regularly (three or more times a week). If 75% of the club members exercise regularly, find the probability that a randomly selected member is a life member, given that the person exercises regularly. 57.3%

22. **Bad Weather** The probability that it snows and the bus arrives late is 0.023. José hears the weather forecast, and there is a 40% chance of snow tomorrow. Find the probability that the bus will be late, given that it snows. 0.058

23. **Education Level and Smoking** At a large factory, the employees were surveyed and classified according to their level of education and whether they smoked. The data are shown in the table.

| | Educational level | | |
Smoking habit	Not high school graduate	High school graduate	College graduate
Smoke	6	14	19
Do not smoke	18	7	25

If an employee is selected at random, find these probabilities.

   a. The employee smokes, given that the employee graduated from college. $\frac{19}{44}$

   b. Given that the employee did not graduate from high school, the employee is a smoker. $\frac{1}{4}$

24. **War Veterans** Approximately 8% of the civilian population are veterans. Choose 5 civilians at random. What is the probability that none are veterans? What is the probability that at least 1 is a veteran? 0.659; 0.341

25. **Television Sets** If 98% of households have at least one television set and 4 households are selected, find the probability that at least one household has a television set. 0.99999984

26. **Chronic Sinusitis** The U.S. Department of Health and Human Services reports that 15% of Americans have chronic sinusitis. If 5 people are selected at random, find the probability that at least 1 has chronic sinusitis. 55.6%

   Source: 100% American.

Section 4–4

27. **Motorcycle License Plates** If a motorcycle license plate consists of two letters followed by three digits, how many different license plates can be made if repetitions are allowed? How many different license plates can be made if repetitions are not allowed? How many license plates can be made if repetitions are allowed in the digits but not in the letters? 676,000; 468,000; 650,000

28. **Types of Copy Paper** White copy paper is offered in 5 different strengths and 11 different degrees of brightness, recycled or not, and acid-free or not. How many different types of paper are available for order? 220

29. **Baseball Players** How many ways can 3 outfielders and 4 infielders be chosen from 5 outfielders and 7 infielders? 350

30. **Carry-on Items** The following items are allowed as airline carry-on items: (1) safety razors, (2) eyedrops and saline, (3) nail clippers and tweezers, (4) blunt-tipped scissors, (5) cell phones, (6) umbrellas, (7) common lighters, (8) beverages purchased after security screening, and (9) musical instruments. Suppose that your airline allows only 6 of these items. In how many ways can you pick 3 not to take? 84

31. Names for Boys The top 10 names for boys in America in 2015 were Liam, Noah, Ethan, Mason, Lucas, Logan, Oliver, Jackson, Aiden, and Jacob. The top 10 names for 2020 are Liam, Noah, William, James, Oliver, Benjamin, Elijah, Lucas, Mason, and Logan. In how many ways can you choose 5 names from the 2020 list? 252

32. Committee Representation There are 6 Republican, 5 Democrat, and 4 Independent candidates. How many different ways can a committee of 3 Republicans, 2 Democrats, and 1 Independent be selected? 800

33. Song Selections A promotional flash drive is available with the capacity to store 100 songs, which can be reordered at the push of a button. How many different arrangements of these songs are possible? (*Note:* Factorials get very big, very fast! How large a factorial will your calculator calculate?) 100! (Answers may vary regarding calculator.)

34. Employee Health Care Plans A new employee has a choice of 5 health care plans, 3 retirement plans, and 2 different expense accounts. If a person selects 1 of each option, how many different options does the person have? 30

35. Course Enrollment There are 12 students who wish to enroll in a particular course. There are only 4 seats left in the classroom. How many different ways can 4 students be selected to attend the class? 495

36. Candy Selection A candy store allows customers to select 3 different candies to be packaged and mailed. If there are 13 varieties available, how many possible selections can be made? 286

37. House Numbers A home improvement store has the following house numbers: 335666 left after a sale. How many different six-digit house numbers can be made from those numbers? 60

38. Word Permutations From which word can you make more permutations, *MATHEMATICS* or *PROBABILITY*? How many more? Probability—4,989,600 more permutations

39. Movie Selections If a person can select one movie for each week night except Saturday, how many different ways can the selection be made if the person can select from 16 movies? 8008

40. Course Selection If a student can select one of 3 language courses, one of 5 mathematics courses, and one of 4 history courses, how many different schedules can be made? 60

Section 4–5

41. Catalog ID Numbers In a catalog, movies are identified by an ID number—2 letters followed by 3 digits. Repetitions are permitted. How many catalog numbers can be made? What is the probability that the ID number is divisible by 5? (Include the 2 letters in the ID number.) 676,000; 0.2

42. License Plates A certain state's license plate has 3 letters followed by 4 numbers. Repeats are not allowed for the letters, but they are for the numbers. How many such license plates are possible? If they are issued at random, what is the probability that the 3 letters are 3 consecutive letters in alphabetical order? 156,000,000; 0.002

43. Territorial Selection Several territories and colonies today are still under the jurisdiction of another country. France holds the most with 16 territories, the United Kingdom has 15, the United States has 14, and several other countries have territories as well. Choose 3 territories at random from those held by France, the United Kingdom, and the United States. What is the probability that all 3 belong to the same country? 0.097
Source: www.infoplease.com

44. Yahtzee Yahtzee is a game played with 5 dice. Players attempt to score points by rolling various combinations. When all 5 dice show the same number, it is called a *Yahtzee* and scores 50 points for the first one and 100 points for each subsequent Yahtzee in the same game. What is the probability that a person throws a Yahtzee on the very first roll? What is the probability that a person throws two Yahtzees on two successive turns? 0.0008; 0.0000006

45. Personnel Classification For a survey, a subject can be classified as follows:

    Gender: male or female
    Marital status: single, married, widowed, divorced
    Occupation: administration, faculty, staff
Draw a tree diagram for the different ways a person can be classified.

⊟ STATISTICS TODAY

Would You Bet Your Life?—Revisited

In his book *Probabilities in Everyday Life*, John D. McGervey states that the chance of being killed on any given commercial airline flight is almost 1 in 1 million and that the chance of being killed during a transcontinental auto trip is about 1 in 8000. The corresponding probabilities are 1/1,000,000 = 0.000001 as compared to 1/8000 = 0.000125. Since the second number is 125 times greater than the first number, you have a much higher risk driving than flying across the United States.

⚏ Chapter Quiz

Determine whether each statement is true or false. If the statement is false, explain why.

1. Subjective probability has little use in the real world. False

2. Classical probability uses a frequency distribution to compute probabilities. False

3. In classical probability, all outcomes in the sample space are equally likely. True

4. When two events are not mutually exclusive, $P(A \text{ or } B) = P(A) + P(B)$. False

5. If two events are dependent, they must have the same probability of occurring. False

6. An event and its complement can occur at the same time. False

7. The arrangement ABC is the same as BAC for combinations. True

8. When objects are arranged in a specific order, the arrangement is called a combination. False

Select the best answer.

9. The probability that an event happens is 0.42. What is the probability that the event won't happen?
   a. −0.42   c. 0
   b. 0.58   d. 1

10. When a meteorologist says that there is a 30% chance of showers, what type of probability is the person using?
    a. Classical   c. Relative
    b. Empirical   d. Subjective

11. The sample space for tossing 3 coins consists of how many outcomes?
    a. 2   c. 6
    b. 4   d. 8

12. The complement of guessing 5 correct answers on a 5-question true/false exam is
    a. Guessing 5 incorrect answers.
    b. Guessing at least 1 incorrect answer.
    c. Guessing at least 1 correct answer.
    d. Guessing no incorrect answers.

13. When two dice are rolled, the sample space consists of how many events?
    a. 6   c. 36
    b. 12   d. 54

14. What is $_nP_0$?
    a. 0   c. n
    b. 1   d. It cannot be determined.

15. What is the number of permutations of 6 different objects taken all together?
    a. 0   c. 36
    b. 1   d. 720

16. What is 0!?
    a. 0   c. Undefined
    b. 1   d. 10

17. What is $_nC_n$?
    a. 0   c. n
    b. 1   d. It cannot be determined.

Complete the following statements with the best answer.

18. The set of all possible outcomes of a probability experiment is called the _____. Sample space

19. The probability of an event can be any number between and including _____ and _____. 0, 1

20. If an event cannot occur, its probability is _____. 0

21. The sum of the probabilities of the events in the sample space is _____. 1

22. When two events cannot occur at the same time, they are said to be _____. Mutually exclusive

23. When a card is drawn, find the probability of getting
    a. A jack. $\frac{1}{13}$ b. A 4. $\frac{1}{13}$
    c. A card less than 6 (an ace is considered above 6). $\frac{4}{13}$

24. **Selecting a Card** When a card is drawn from a deck, find the probability of getting
    a. A diamond. $\frac{1}{4}$ b. A 5 or a heart. $\frac{4}{13}$
    c. A 5 and a heart. $\frac{1}{52}$ d. A king. $\frac{1}{13}$
    e. A red card. $\frac{1}{2}$

25. **Selecting a Sweater** At a men's clothing store, 12 men purchased blue golf sweaters, 8 purchased green sweaters, 4 purchased gray sweaters, and 7 bought black sweaters. If a customer is selected at random, find the probability that he purchased
    a. A blue sweater. $\frac{12}{31}$
    b. A green or gray sweater. $\frac{12}{31}$
    c. A green or black or blue sweater. $\frac{27}{31}$
    d. A sweater that was not black. $\frac{24}{31}$

26. **Rolling Dice** When 2 dice are rolled, find the probability of getting
    a. A sum of 6 or 7. $\frac{11}{36}$
    b. A sum greater than 8. $\frac{5}{18}$
    c. A sum less than 3 or greater than 8. $\frac{11}{36}$
    d. A sum that is divisible by 3. $\frac{1}{3}$
    e. A sum of 16. 0
    f. A sum less than 11. $\frac{11}{12}$

27. **Appliance Ownership** The probability that a person owns a microwave oven is 0.75, that a person owns a compact disk player is 0.25, and that a person owns both a microwave and a CD player is 0.16. Find the probability that a person owns either a microwave or a CD player, but not both. 0.68

28. **Starting Salaries** Of the physics graduates of a university, 30% received a starting salary of $30,000 or more. If 5 of the graduates are selected at random, find the probability that all had a starting salary of $30,000 or more. 0.002

29. **Selecting Cards** Five cards are drawn from an ordinary deck *without* replacement. Find the probability of getting

    a. All red cards. $\frac{253}{9996}$

    b. All diamonds. $\frac{33}{66,640}$

    c. All aces. 0

30. **Scholarships** The probability that Samantha will be accepted by the college of her choice and obtain a scholarship is 0.35. If the probability that she is accepted by the college is 0.65, find the probability that she will obtain a scholarship given that she is accepted by the college. 0.538

31. **New-Car Warranty** The probability that a customer will buy a new car and an extended warranty is 0.16. If the probability that a customer will purchase a new car is 0.30, find the probability that the customer will also purchase the extended warranty. 0.533

32. **Bowling and Club Membership** Of the members of the Spring Lake Bowling Lanes, 57% have a lifetime membership and bowl regularly (three or more times a week). If 70% of the club members bowl regularly, find the probability that a randomly selected member is a lifetime member, given that the member bowls regularly. 0.814

33. **Work and Weather** The probability that Mike has to work overtime and it rains is 0.028. Mike hears the weather forecast, and there is a 50% chance of rain. Find the probability that he will have to work overtime, given that it rains. 0.056

34. **Education of Factory Employees** At a large factory, the employees were surveyed and classified according to their level of education and whether they attend a sports event at least once a month. The data are shown in the table.

Educational level

Sports event	High school graduate	Two-year college degree	Four-year college degree
Attend	16	20	24
Do not attend	12	19	25

If an employee is selected at random, find the probability that

   a. The employee attends sports events regularly, given that the employee graduated from college (2- or 4-year degree) $\frac{1}{2}$

   b. Given that the employee is a high school graduate, the employee does not attend sports events regularly $\frac{3}{7}$

35. **Heart Attacks** In a certain high-risk group, the chances of a person having suffered a heart attack are 55%. If 6 people are chosen, find the probability that at least 1 will have had a heart attack. 0.992

36. **Rolling a Die** A single die is rolled 4 times. Find the probability of getting at least one 5. 0.518

37. **Eye Color** If 85% of all people have brown eyes and 6 people are selected at random, find the probability that at least 1 of them has brown eyes. 0.9999886

38. **Singer Selection** How many ways can 5 sopranos and 4 altos be selected from 7 sopranos and 9 altos? 2646

39. **Speaker Selection** How many different ways can 8 speakers be seated on a stage? 40,320

40. **Stocking Machines** A soda machine servicer must restock and collect money from 15 machines, each one at a different location. How many ways can she select 4 machines to service in 1 day? 1365

41. **ID Cards** One company's ID cards consist of 5 letters followed by 2 digits. How many cards can be made if repetitions are allowed? If repetitions are not allowed? 1,188,137,600; 710,424,000

42. **Word Permutation** How many different arrangements of the letters in the word *number* can be made? 720

43. **Physics Test** A physics test consists of 25 true/false questions. How many different possible answer keys can be made? 33,554,432

44. **Cell Phones** How many different ways can 5 cellular telephones be selected from 8 cell phones? 56

45. **Fruit Selection** On a lunch counter, there are 3 oranges, 5 apples, and 2 bananas. If 3 pieces of fruit are selected, find the probability that 1 orange, 1 apple, and 1 banana are selected. $\frac{1}{4}$

46. **Cruise Ship Activities** A cruise director schedules 4 different movies, 2 bridge games, and 3 tennis games for a two-day period. If a couple selects 3 activities, find the probability that they attend 2 movies and 1 tennis game. $\frac{3}{14}$

47. **Committee Selection** At a sorority meeting, there are 6 seniors, 4 juniors, and 2 sophomores. If a committee of 3 is to be formed, find the probability that 1 of each will be selected. $\frac{12}{55}$

48. **Banquet Meal Choices** For a banquet, a committee can select beef, pork, chicken, or veal; baked potatoes or mashed potatoes; and peas or green beans for a vegetable. Draw a tree diagram for all possible choices of a meat, a potato, and a vegetable.

49. **Toy Display** A toy store manager wants to display 7 identical stuffed dogs, 4 identical stuffed cats, and 3 identical stuffed teddy bears on a shelf. How many different arrangements can be made? 120,120

50. **Commercial Order** A local television station must show commercial X twice, commercial Y twice, and commercial Z three times during a 2-hour show. How many different ways can this be done? 210

▤ Critical Thinking Challenges

1. **Con Man Game** Consider this problem: A con man has 3 coins. One coin has been specially made and has a head on each side. A second coin has been specially made, and on each side it has a tail. Finally, a third coin has a head and a tail on it. All coins are of the same denomination. The con man places the 3 coins in his pocket, selects one, and shows you one side. It is heads. He is willing to bet you even money that it is the two-headed coin. His reasoning is that it can't be the two-tailed coin since a head is showing; therefore, there is a 50-50 chance of it being the two-headed coin. Would you take the bet?

2. **de Méré Dice Game** Chevalier de Méré won money when he bet unsuspecting patrons that in 4 rolls of 1 die, he could get at least one 6; but he lost money when he bet that in 24 rolls of 2 dice, he could get at least a double 6. Using the probability rules, find the probability of each event and explain why he won the majority of the time on the first game but lost the majority of the time when playing the second game. (*Hint:* Find the probabilities of losing each game and subtract from 1.)

3. **Classical Birthday Problem** How many people do you think need to be in a room so that 2 people will have the same birthday (month and day)? You might think it is 366. This would, of course, guarantee it (excluding leap year), but how many people would need to be in a room so that there would be a 90% probability that 2 people would be born on the same day? What about a 50% probability?

    Actually, the number is much smaller than you may think. For example, if you have 50 people in a room, the probability that 2 people will have the same birthday is 97%. If you have 23 people in a room, there is a 50% probability that 2 people were born on the same day!

    The problem can be solved by using the probability rules. It must be assumed that all birthdays are equally likely, but this assumption will have little effect on the answers. The way to find the answer is by using the complementary event rule as $P(2$ people having the same birthday$) = 1 - P($all have different birthdays$)$.

For example, suppose there were 3 people in the room. The probability that each had a different birthday would be

$$\frac{365}{365} \cdot \frac{364}{365} \cdot \frac{363}{365} = \frac{_{365}P_3}{365^3} = 0.992$$

Hence, the probability that at least 2 of the 3 people will have the same birthday will be

$$1 - 0.992 = 0.008$$

Hence, for k people, the formula is

$P($at least 2 people have the same birthday$)$

$$= 1 - \frac{_{365}P_k}{365^k}$$

Using your calculator, complete the table and verify that for at least a 50% chance of 2 people having the same birthday, 23 or more people will be needed.

Number of people	Probability that at least 2 have the same birthday
1	0.000
2	0.003
5	0.027
10	
15	
20	
21	
22	
23	

4. **Contracting a Disease** We know that if the probability of an event happening is 100%, then the event is a certainty. Can it be concluded that if there is a 50% chance of contracting a communicable disease through contact with an infected person, there would be a 100% chance of contracting the disease if 2 contacts were made with the infected person? Explain your answer.

▤ Data Projects

1. **Business and Finance** Select a pizza restaurant and a sandwich shop. For the pizza restaurant look at the menu to determine how many sizes, crust types, and toppings are available. How many different pizza types are possible? For the sandwich shop determine how many breads, meats, veggies, cheeses, sauces, and condiments are available. How many different sandwich choices are possible?

2. **Sports and Leisure** When poker games are shown on television, there are often percentages displayed that show how likely it is that a certain hand will win.

Investigate how these percentages are determined. Show an example with two competing hands in a Texas Hold 'Em game. Include the percentages that each hand will win after the deal, the flop, the turn, and the river.

3. **Technology** A music player or music organization program can keep track of how many different artists are in a library. First note how many different artists are in your music library. Then find the probability that if 25 songs are selected at random, none will have the same artist.

4. **Health and Wellness** Assume that the gender distribution of babies is such that one-half the time females are born and one-half the time males are born. In a family of 3 children, what is the probability that all are girls? In a family of 4? Is it unusual that in a family with 4 children all would be girls? In a family of 5?

5. **Politics and Economics** Consider the U.S. Senate. Find out about the composition of any three of the Senate's standing committees. How many different committees of Senators are possible, knowing the party composition of the Senate and the number of committee members from each party for each committee?

6. **Your Class** Research the famous Monty Hall probability problem. Conduct a simulation of the Monty Hall problem online using a simulation program or in class using live "contestants." After 50 simulations compare your results to those stated in the research you did. Did your simulation support the conclusions?

Answers to Applying the Concepts

Section 4–1   Tossing a Coin

1. The sample space is the listing of all possible outcomes of the coin toss.

2. The possible outcomes are heads or tails.

3. Classical probability says that a fair coin has a 50% chance of coming up heads and a 50% chance of coming up tails.

4. The law of large numbers says that as you increase the number of trials, the overall results will approach the theoretical probability. However, since the coin has no "memory," it still has a 50% chance of coming up heads and a 50% chance of coming up tails on the next toss. Knowing what has already happened should not change your opinion on what will happen on the next toss.

5. The empirical approach to probability is based on running an experiment and looking at the results. You cannot do that at this time.

6. Subjective probabilities could be used if you believe the coin is biased.

7. Answers will vary; however, they should address that a fair coin has a 50% chance of coming up heads and a 50% chance of coming up tails on the next flip.

Section 4–2   Which Pain Reliever Is Best?

1. There were $192 + 186 + 188 = 566$ subjects in the study.

2. The study lasted for 12 weeks.

3. The variables are the type of pain reliever and the side effects.

4. Both variables are qualitative and nominal.

5. The numbers in the table are exact figures.

6. The probability that a randomly selected person was receiving a placebo is $192/566 = 0.339$ (about 34%).

7. The probability that a randomly selected person was receiving a placebo or drug A is $(192 + 186)/566 = 378/566 = 0.668$ (about 67%). These are mutually exclusive events. The complement is that a randomly selected person was receiving drug B.

8. The probability that a randomly selected person was receiving a placebo or experienced a neurological headache is $(192 + 55 + 72)/566 = 319/566 = 0.564$ (about 56%).

9. The probability that a randomly selected person was not receiving a placebo or experienced a sinus headache is $(186 + 188)/566 + 11/566 = 385/566 = 0.680$ (about 68%).

Section 4–3   Guilty or Innocent?

1. The probability of another couple with the same characteristics being in that area is $\frac{1}{12} \cdot \frac{1}{10} \cdot \frac{1}{4} \cdot \frac{1}{11} \cdot \frac{1}{3} \cdot \frac{1}{13} \cdot \frac{1}{100} = \frac{1}{20,592,000}$, assuming the characteristics are independent of one another.

2. You would use the multiplication rule, since you are looking for the probability of multiple events happening together.

3. We do not know if the characteristics are dependent or independent, but we assumed independence for the calculation in question 1.

4. The probabilities would change if there were dependence among two or more events.

5. Answers will vary. One possible answer is that probabilities can be used to explain how unlikely it is to have a set of events occur at the same time (in this case, how unlikely it is to have another couple with the same characteristics in that area).

6. Answers will vary. One possible answer is that if the only eyewitness was the woman who was mugged and the probabilities are accurate, it seems very unlikely that a couple matching these characteristics would be in that area at that time. This might cause you to convict the couple.

7. Answers will vary. One possible answer is that our probabilities are theoretical and serve a purpose when appropriate, but that court cases are based on much more than impersonal chance.

8. Answers will vary. One possible answer is that juries decide whether to convict a defendant if they find evidence "beyond a reasonable doubt" that the person is guilty. In probability terms, this means that if the defendant was actually innocent, then the chance of seeing the events that occurred is so unlikely as to have occurred by chance. Therefore, the jury concludes that the defendant is guilty.

Section 4–4   Garage Door Openers

1. Four on/off switches lead to 16 different settings.

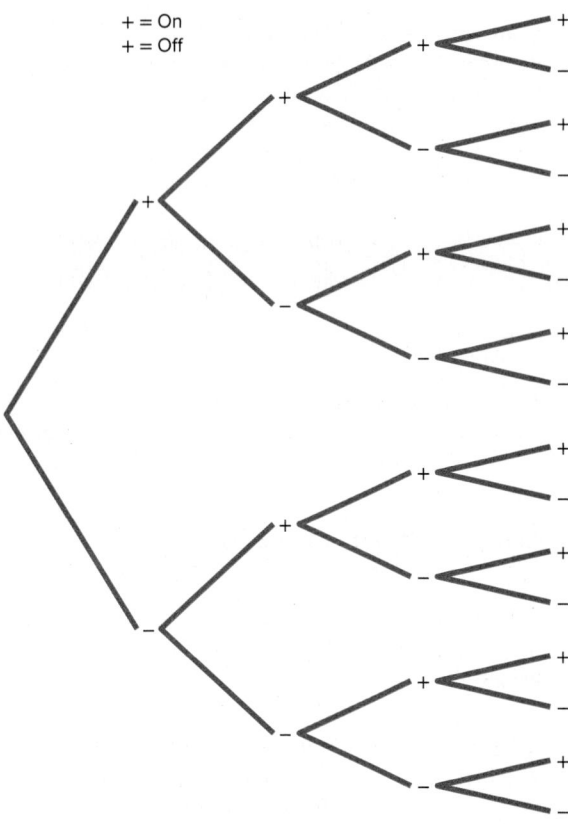

+ = On
+ = Off

2. With 5 on/off switches, there are $2^5 = 32$ different settings. With 6 on/off switches, there are $2^6 = 64$ different settings. In general, if there are k on/off switches, there are 2^k different settings.

3. With 8 consecutive on/off switches, there are $2^8 = 256$ different settings.

4. It is less likely for someone to be able to open your garage door if you have 8 on/off settings (probability about 0.4%) than if you have 4 on/off switches (probability about 6.0%). Having 8 on/off switches in the opener seems pretty safe.

5. Each key blank could be made into $5^5 = 3125$ possible keys.

6. If there were 420,000 Dodge Caravans sold in the United States, then any one key could start about $420,000/3125 = 134.4$, or about 134, different Caravans.

7. Answers will vary.

Section 4–5   Counting Rules and Probability

1. There are five different events: each multiple-choice question is an event.

2. These events are independent.

3. If you guess on 1 question, the probability of getting it correct is 0.20. Thus, if you guess on all 5 questions, the probability of getting all of them correct is $(0.20)^5 = 0.00032$.

4. The probability that a person would guess answer A for a question is 0.20, so the probability that a person would guess answer A for each question is $(0.20)^5 = 0.00032$.

5. There are five different events: each matching question is an event.

6. These are dependent events.

7. The probability of getting them all correct if you are guessing is $\frac{1}{5} \cdot \frac{1}{4} \cdot \frac{1}{3} \cdot \frac{1}{2} \cdot \frac{1}{1} = \frac{1}{120} = 0.008$.

8. The difference between the two problems is that we are sampling without replacement in the second problem, so the denominator changes in the event probabilities.

Discrete Probability Distributions

Suwit Rattiwan/Shutterstock

≡ STATISTICS TODAY

Is Pooling Worthwhile?

Blood samples are used to screen people for certain diseases. When the disease is rare, health care workers sometimes combine or pool the blood samples of a group of individuals into one batch and then test it. If the test result of the batch is negative, no further testing is needed since none of the individuals in the group has the disease. However, if the test result of the batch is positive, each individual in the group must be tested.

Consider this hypothetical example: Suppose the probability of a person having the disease is 0.05, and a pooled sample of 15 individuals is tested. What is the probability that no further testing will be needed for the individuals in the sample? The answer to this question can be found by using what is called the *binomial distribution*. See Statistics Today—Revisited at the end of the chapter.

This chapter explains probability distributions in general and a specific, often used distribution called the binomial distribution. The Poisson, hypergeometric, geometric, and multinomial distributions are also explained.

OUTLINE

OBJECTIVES

After completing this chapter, you should be able to

1   Construct a probability distribution for a random variable.

2   Find the mean, variance, standard deviation, and expected value for a discrete random variable.

3   Find the exact probability for X successes in n trials of a binomial experiment.

4   Find the mean, variance, and standard deviation for the variable of a binomial distribution.

5   Find probabilities for outcomes of variables, using the Poisson, hypergeometric, geometric, and multinomial distributions.

Introduction

Many decisions in business, insurance, and other real-life situations are made by assigning probabilities to all possible outcomes pertaining to the situation and then evaluating the results. For example, a salesperson can compute the probability that she will make 0, 1, 2, or 3 or more sales in a single day. An insurance company might be able to assign probabilities to the number of vehicles a family owns. A self-employed speaker might be able to compute the probabilities for giving 0, 1, 2, 3, or 4 or more speeches each week. Once these probabilities are assigned, statistics such as the mean, variance, and standard deviation can be computed for these events. With these statistics, various decisions can be made. The salesperson will be able to compute the average number of sales made per week, and if working on commission, will be able to approximate weekly income over a period of time, say, monthly. The public speaker will be able to plan ahead and approximate his average income and expenses. The insurance company can use its information to design special computer forms and programs to accommodate its customers' future needs.

This chapter explains the concepts and applications of what is called a *probability distribution*. In addition, special probability distributions, such as the *binomial, multinomial, Poisson, hypergeometric,* and *geometric* distributions, are explained.

5–1   Probability Distributions

OBJECTIVE

Construct a probability distribution for a random variable.

Before probability distribution is defined formally, the definition of a variable is reviewed. In Chapter 1, a *variable* was defined as a characteristic or attribute that can assume different values. Various letters of the alphabet, such as X, Y, or Z, are used to represent variables. Since the variables in this chapter are associated with probability, they are called *random variables*.

For example, if a die is rolled, a letter such as X can be used to represent the outcomes. Then the value that X can assume is 1, 2, 3, 4, 5, or 6, corresponding to the outcomes of rolling a single die. If two coins are tossed, a letter, say Y, can be used to represent the number of heads, in this case 0, 1, or 2. As another example, if the temperature at 8:00 A.M. is 43° and at noon it is 53°, then the values T that the temperature assumes are said to be random, since they are due to various atmospheric conditions at the time the temperature was taken.

> A **random variable** is a variable whose values are determined by chance.

Also recall from Chapter 1 that you can classify variables as discrete or continuous by observing the values the variable can assume. If a variable can assume only a specific number of values, such as the outcomes for the roll of a die or the outcomes for the toss of a coin, then the variable is called a *discrete variable*.

Discrete variables have a finite number of possible values or an infinite number of values that can be counted. The word *counted* means that they can be enumerated using the numbers 1, 2, 3, etc. For example, the number of joggers on a trail each day and the number of phone calls received after a TV commercial airs are examples of discrete variables, since they can be counted.

Variables that can assume all values in the interval between any two given values are called *continuous variables*. For example, if the temperature goes from 62° to 78° in a 24-hour period, it has passed through every possible number from 62 to 78. *Continuous random variables are obtained from data that can be measured rather than counted.* Continuous random variables can assume an infinite number of values and can be decimal and fractional values. On a continuous scale, a person's weight might be exactly 183.426 pounds if a scale could measure weight to the thousandths place; however, on a digital scale that measures only to tenths of a pound, the weight would be 183.4 pounds. Examples of continuous variables are heights, weights, temperatures, and time. In this chapter only discrete random variables are used; Chapter 6 explains continuous random variables.

The procedure shown here for constructing a probability distribution for a discrete random variable uses the probability experiment of tossing three coins. Recall that when three coins are tossed, the sample space is represented as TTT, TTH, THT, HTT, HHT, HTH, THH, HHH; and if X is the random variable for the number of heads, then X assumes the value 0, 1, 2, or 3.

Probabilities for the values of X can be determined as follows:

No heads	One head			Two heads			Three heads
TTT	TTH	THT	HTT	HHT	HTH	THH	HHH
$\frac{1}{8}$	$\frac{1}{8}$	$\frac{1}{8}$	$\frac{1}{8}$	$\frac{1}{8}$	$\frac{1}{8}$	$\frac{1}{8}$	$\frac{1}{8}$
$\frac{1}{8}$	$\frac{3}{8}$			$\frac{3}{8}$			$\frac{1}{8}$

Hence, the probability of getting no heads is $\frac{1}{8}$, one head is $\frac{3}{8}$, two heads is $\frac{3}{8}$, and three heads is $\frac{1}{8}$. From these values, a probability distribution can be constructed by listing the outcomes and assigning the probability of each outcome, as shown here.

Number of heads X	0	1	2	3
Probability $P(X)$	$\frac{1}{8}$	$\frac{3}{8}$	$\frac{3}{8}$	$\frac{1}{8}$

A **discrete probability distribution** consists of the values a random variable can assume and the corresponding probabilities of the values. The probabilities are determined theoretically or by observation.

Procedure Table

Constructing a Probability Distribution

Step 1 Make a frequency distribution for the outcomes of the variable.

Step 2 Find the probability for each outcome by dividing the frequency of the outcome by the sum of the frequencies.

Step 3 If a graph is required, place the outcomes on the x axis and the probabilities on the y axis, and draw vertical bars for each outcome and its corresponding probability.

Discrete probability distributions can be shown by using a graph or a table. Probability distributions can also be represented by a formula. See Exercises 31–36 at the end of this section for examples.

EXAMPLE 5–1   Rolling a Die

Construct a probability distribution for rolling a single die.

SOLUTION

Since the sample space is 1, 2, 3, 4, 5, 6 and each outcome has a probability of $\frac{1}{6}$, the distribution is as shown.

Outcome X	1	2	3	4	5	6
Probability $P(X)$	$\frac{1}{6}$	$\frac{1}{6}$	$\frac{1}{6}$	$\frac{1}{6}$	$\frac{1}{6}$	$\frac{1}{6}$

When probability distributions are shown graphically, the values of X are placed on the x axis and the probabilities $P(X)$ on the y axis. These graphs are helpful in determining the shape of the distribution (right-skewed, left-skewed, or symmetric).

EXAMPLE 5–2   Tossing Coins

Represent graphically the probability distribution for the sample space for tossing three coins.

Number of heads X	0	1	2	3
Probability $P(X)$	$\frac{1}{8}$	$\frac{3}{8}$	$\frac{3}{8}$	$\frac{1}{8}$

SOLUTION

The values that X assumes are located on the x axis, and the values for $P(X)$ are located on the y axis. The graph is shown in Figure 5–1.

FIGURE 5–1   Probability Distribution for Example 5–2

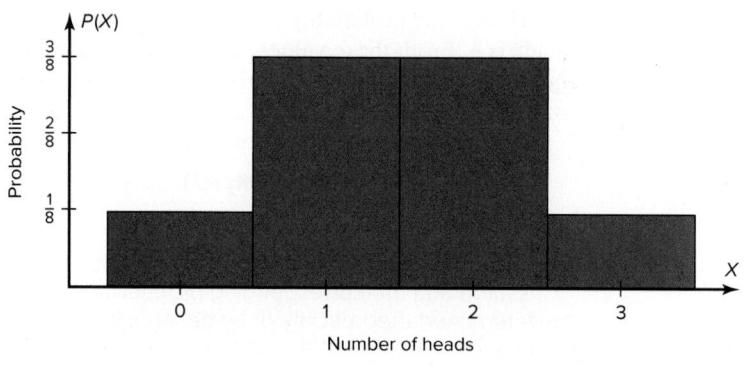

Note that for visual appearances, it is not necessary to start with 0 at the origin.

Examples 5–1 and 5–2 are illustrations of *theoretical* probability distributions. You did not need to actually perform the experiments to compute the probabilities. In contrast, to construct actual probability distributions, you must observe the variable over a period of time. They are empirical, as shown in Example 5–3.

EXAMPLE 5–3   Successful Sales

A company employs 25 salespeople. During a randomly selected week, 5 people made 2 sales, 11 people made 3 sales, 6 people made 4 sales, and 3 people made 5 sales. Construct a probability distribution for the number of sales employees made for the week.

SOLUTION

Step 1   Make a frequency distribution for the variable.

Sales	2	3	4	5
Frequency	5	11	6	3

Step 2   Find the probability for each outcome. Hence,

$$P(2) = \frac{5}{25} = 0.20 \qquad P(3) = \frac{11}{25} = 0.44$$

$$P(4) = \frac{6}{25} = 0.24 \qquad P(5) = \frac{3}{25} = 0.12$$

The probability distribution is

Sales *X*	2	3	4	5
Frequency *P(X)*	0.20	0.44	0.24	0.12

Step 3   Draw the graph using the *x* axis for the outcome and the *y* axis for the probabilities. See Figure 5–2.

FIGURE 5–2

Probability Distribution for Example 5–3

Two Requirements for a Probability Distribution

1. The sum of the probabilities of all the events in the sample space must equal 1; that is, $\Sigma P(X) = 1$.
2. The probability of each event in the sample space must be between or equal to 0 and 1. That is, $0 \leq P(X) \leq 1$.

The first requirement states that the sum of the probabilities of all the events must be equal to 1. This sum cannot be less than 1 or greater than 1 since the sample space includes *all* possible outcomes of the probability experiment. The second requirement states that the probability of any individual event must be a value from 0 to 1. The reason (as stated in Chapter 4) is that the range of the probability of any individual value can be 0, 1, or any value between 0 and 1. A probability cannot be a negative number or greater than 1.

EXAMPLE 5–4   Probability Distributions

Determine whether each distribution is a probability distribution.

a.
X	1	3	5	7	9
P(X)	0.4	0.2	0.1	0.3	0.1

b.
X	−$5	$0	$5	$10
P(X)	$\frac{1}{4}$	$\frac{1}{2}$	$\frac{1}{8}$	$\frac{1}{8}$

c.
X	0	1	2	3
P(X)	$\frac{1}{4}$	$\frac{1}{4}$	$\frac{1}{4}$	$\frac{1}{4}$

d.
X	5	10	15	20	25
P(X)	−0.5	0.2	0.3	0.6	0.4

SOLUTION

a. No. The sum of the probabilities is greater than 1.

b. Yes. The sum of the probabilities of all the events is equal to 1. Each probability is greater than or equal to 0 and less than or equal to 1.

c. Yes. The sum of the probabilities of all the events is equal to 1. Each probability is greater than or equal to 0 and less than or equal to 1.

d. No. One of the probabilities is less than 0.

Examples of random events such as tossing coins are used in almost all books on probability. But is flipping a coin really a random event?

Tossing coins dates back to ancient Roman times when the coins usually consisted of the Emperor's head on one side (i.e., heads) and another icon such as a ship on the other side (i.e., tails). Tossing coins was used in both fortune telling and ancient Roman games.

A Chinese form of divination called the *I-Ching* (pronounced E-Ching) is thought to be at least 4000 years old. It consists of 64 hexagrams made up of six horizontal lines. Each line is either broken or unbroken, representing the yin and the yang. These 64 hexagrams are supposed to represent all possible situations in life. To consult the *I-Ching,* a question is asked and then three coins are tossed six times. The way the coins fall, either heads up or heads down, determines whether the line is broken (yin) or unbroken (yang). Once the hexagram is determined, its meaning is consulted and interpreted to get the answer to the question. (*Note:* Another method used to determine the hexagram employs yarrow sticks.)

In the 16th century, a mathematician named Abraham DeMoivre used the outcomes of tossing coins to study what later became known as the normal distribution; however, his work at that time was not widely known.

Mathematicians usually consider the outcomes of a coin toss to be a random event. That is, each probability of getting a head is $\frac{1}{2}$, and the probability of getting a tail is $\frac{1}{2}$. Also, it is not possible to predict with 100% certainty which outcome will occur. But new studies question this theory. During World War II a South African mathematician named John Kerrich tossed a coin 10,000 times while he was interned in a German prison camp. Although the results of his experiment were never officially recorded, most references indicate that out of his 10,000 tosses, 5067 were heads.

Several studies have shown that when a coin-tossing device is used, the probability that a coin will land on the same side on which it is placed on the coin-tossing

PNC/Stockbyte/Getty Images

device is about 51%. It would take about 10,000 tosses to become aware of this bias. Furthermore, researchers showed that when a coin is spun on its edge, the coin falls tails up about 80% of the time since there is more metal on the heads side of a coin. This makes the coin slightly heavier on the heads side than on the tails side.

Another assumption commonly made in probability theory is that the number of male births is equal to the number of female births and that the probability of a male being born is $\frac{1}{2}$ and the probability of a female being born is $\frac{1}{2}$. We know this is not exactly true since biological sex is not necessarily binary: It exists on a spectrum, and the exact split of males and females varies from location to location.

Fengqing Chao et al. showed in a 2019 study of 10,835 observations that the sex ratio at birth (the ratio of male to female live births) was about 1.031. This means that, on average, there are 103 males born (about 50.7%) to every 100 females (about 49.3%), not including nonbinary individuals. Even though there are discrepancies, we generally consider the outcomes to be 50-50 since these discrepancies are relatively small.

Based on this article, would you consider the coin toss at the beginning of a football game fair?

Many variables in business, education, engineering, and other areas can be analyzed by using probability distributions. Section 5–2 shows methods for finding the mean and standard deviation for a probability distribution.

Applying the Concepts 5–1

Dropping College Courses

Use the following table to answer the questions.

Reason for dropping a college course	Frequency	Percentage
Too difficult	45	
Illness	40	
Change in work schedule	20	
Change of major	14	
Family-related problems	9	
Money	7	
Miscellaneous	6	
No meaningful reason	3	

1. What is the variable under study? Is it a random variable?

2. How many people were in the study?

3. Complete the table.

4. From the information given, what is the probability that a student will drop a class because of illness? Money? Change of major?

5. Would you consider the information in the table to be a probability distribution?

6. Are the categories mutually exclusive?

7. Are the categories independent?

8. Are the categories exhaustive?

9. Are the two requirements for a discrete probability distribution met?

See page 308 for the answers.

Exercises 5–1

1. Define and give three examples of a random variable. *A random variable is a variable whose values are determined by chance. Examples will vary.*

2. Explain the difference between a discrete and a continuous random variable.

3. Give three examples of a discrete random variable.

4. Give three examples of a continuous random variable.

5. List three continuous random variables and three discrete random variables associated with a major league baseball game.

6. What is a probability distribution? Give an example.

For Exercises 7 through 12, determine whether the distribution represents a probability distribution. If it does not, state why.

7.

X	3	5	8	10
P(X)	0.3	0.2	0.5	−0.7

No. Probabilities cannot be negative.

8.

X	15	20	25
P(X)	0.4	−0.2	0.6

No. Probabilities cannot be negative.

9.

X	$\frac{1}{2}$	$\frac{1}{3}$	$\frac{1}{4}$	$\frac{1}{5}$	$\frac{1}{6}$
P(X)	0.2	0.4	0.1	0.1	0.2

Yes

10.

X	7	14	21	28
P(X)	0.03	0.52	0.40	0.05

Yes

11.

X	1	3	5	7
P(X)	0.2	0.1	0.7	0.1

No. The sum of the probabilities is greater than one.

12.

X	−3	−5	2	7
P(X)	$\frac{1}{9}$	$\frac{4}{9}$	$\frac{2}{9}$	$\frac{2}{9}$

Yes

For Exercises 13 through 18, state whether the variable is discrete or continuous.

13. The number of bees in a hive Discrete

14. The number of boats on Lake Erie on any specific day Discrete

15. The time it takes a person to drive to school Continuous

16. The temperatures on New Year's Day in the United States Continuous

17. The number of police officers in each of 10 communities Discrete

18. The sugar content in grams in 10 cookies Continuous

For Exercises 19 through 26, construct a probability distribution for the data and draw a graph for the distribution.

19. Pizza Sales The probability that a pizza shop sells 0, 1, 2, or 3 pizzas to one person is $\frac{1}{8}, \frac{1}{2}, \frac{1}{4}, \frac{1}{8}$, respectively.

20. Tornados The probability that there will be 0, 1, 2, 3, 4, or 5 tornados in a specific year is 0.3, 0.2, 0.1, 0.2, 0.1, 0.1, respectively.

21. Automobile Sales The probability that a person sells 1, 2, 3, or 4 automobiles on a Saturday is 0.45, 0.27, 0.18, and 0.10, respectively

22. Song Downloads The probabilities that a customer will download 0, 1, 2, 3, or 4 songs on a single visit to the website are 0.15, 0.25, 0.3, 0.25, and 0.05, respectively.

23. Loaded Die A die is loaded in such a way that the probabilities of getting 1, 2, 3, 4, 5, and 6 are $\frac{1}{2}, \frac{1}{6}, \frac{1}{12}, \frac{1}{12}, \frac{1}{12}$, and $\frac{1}{12}$, respectively.

24. Item Selection The probabilities that a customer selects 1, 2, 3, 4, and 5 items at a convenience store are 0.32, 0.12, 0.23, 0.18, and 0.15, respectively.

25. Student Classes The probabilities that a student is registered for 2, 3, 4, or 5 classes are 0.01, 0.34, 0.62, and 0.03, respectively.

26. Garage Space The probabilities that a randomly selected home has garage space for 0, 1, 2, or 3 cars are 0.22, 0.33, 0.37, and 0.08, respectively.

27. Cards There are cards with the numbers 1, 3, 6, 10, 15, and 21 printed on them. The cards are placed face down and mixed. Choose two cards at random, and let X be the sum of the two numbers. Construct the probability distribution for this random variable X.

28. Child Play in Day Care In a popular day care center, the probability that a child will play with the computer is 0.45; the probability that a child will play dress-up is 0.27; play with blocks, 0.18; and paint, 0.1. Construct the probability distribution for this discrete random variable.

29. Goals in Hockey The probability that a hockey team scores a total of 1 goal in a game is 0.124; 2 goals, 0.297; 3 goals, 0.402; 4 goals, 0.094; and 5 goals, 0.083. Construct the probability distribution for this discrete random variable and draw the graph.

30. Mathematics Tutoring Center At a drop-in mathematics tutoring center, each teacher sees 4 to 8 students per hour. The probability that a tutor sees 4 students in an hour is 0.117; 5 students, 0.123; 6 students, 0.295; and 7 students, 0.328. Find the probability that a tutor sees 8 students in an hour, construct the probability distribution, and draw the graph.

Extending the Concepts

A probability distribution can be written in formula notation such as $P(X) = 1/X$, where $X = 2, 3, 6$. The distribution is shown as follows:

X	2	3	6
P(X)	$\frac{1}{2}$	$\frac{1}{3}$	$\frac{1}{6}$

For Exercises 31 through 36, write the distribution for the formula and determine whether it is a probability distribution.

31. $P(X) = X/6$ for $X = 1, 2, 3$

32. $P(X) = X/2$ for $X = 6, 4, 2$

33. $P(X) = X + 0.2$ for $X = 0.05, 0.10, 0.25$

34. $P(X) = X + 0.1$ for $X = 0.1, 0.02, 0.04$

35. $P(X) = X/7$ for $X = 1, 2, 4$

36. $P(X) = X/(X + 2)$ for $X = 0, 1, 2$

37. Computer Games The probability that a child plays one computer game is one-half as likely as that of playing two computer games. The probability of playing three games is twice as likely as that of playing two games, and the probability of playing four games is the average of the other three. Let X be the number of computer games played. Construct the probability distribution for this random variable and draw the graph.

5–2   Mean, Variance, Standard Deviation, and Expectation

OBJECTIVE ❷

Find the mean, variance, standard deviation, and expected value for a discrete random variable.

The mean, variance, and standard deviation for a probability distribution are computed differently from the mean, variance, and standard deviation for samples. This section explains how these measures—as well as a new measure called the *expectation*—are calculated for probability distributions.

Mean

In Chapter 3, the mean for a sample or population was computed by adding the values and dividing by the total number of values, as shown in these formulas:

$$\text{Sample mean:} \quad \overline{X} = \frac{\Sigma X}{n} \qquad \text{Population mean:} \quad \mu = \frac{\Sigma X}{N}$$

> **Historical Note**
>
> A professor, Augustin Louis Cauchy (1789–1857), wrote a book on probability. While he was teaching at the Military School of Paris, one of his students was Napoleon Bonaparte.

But how would you compute the mean of the number of spots that show on top when a die is rolled? You could try rolling the die, say, 10 times, recording the number of spots, and finding the mean; however, this answer would only approximate the true mean. What about 50 rolls or 100 rolls? Actually, the more times the die is rolled, the better the approximation. You might ask, then, How many times must the die be rolled to get the exact answer? *It must be rolled an infinite number of times.* Since this task is impossible, the previous formulas cannot be used because the denominators would be infinity. Hence, a new method of computing the mean is necessary. This method gives the exact theoretical value of the mean as if it were possible to roll the die an infinite number of times.

Before the formula is stated, an example will be used to explain the concept. Suppose two coins are tossed repeatedly, and the number of heads that occurred is recorded. What will be the mean of the number of heads? The sample space is

HH, HT, TH, TT

and each outcome has a probability of $\frac{1}{4}$. Now, in the long run, you would *expect* two heads (HH) to occur approximately $\frac{1}{4}$ of the time, one head to occur approximately $\frac{1}{2}$ of the time (HT or TH), and no heads (TT) to occur approximately $\frac{1}{4}$ of the time. Hence, on average, you would expect the number of heads to be

$$2 \cdot \tfrac{1}{4} + 1 \cdot \tfrac{1}{2} + 0 \cdot \tfrac{1}{4} = 1$$

That is, if it were possible to toss the coins many times or an infinite number of times, the *average* of the number of heads would be 1.

Hence, to find the mean for a probability distribution, you must multiply each possible outcome by its corresponding probability and find the sum of the products.

Formula for the Mean of a Probability Distribution

The mean of a random variable with a discrete probability distribution is

$$\mu = X_1 \cdot P(X_1) + X_2 \cdot P(X_2) + X_3 \cdot P(X_3) + \cdots + X_n \cdot P(X_n)$$

$$= \Sigma X \cdot P(X)$$

where $X_1, X_2, X_3, \ldots, X_n$ are the outcomes and $P(X_1), P(X_2), P(X_3), \ldots, P(X_n)$ are the corresponding probabilities.

Note: $\Sigma X \cdot P(X)$ means to sum the products.

Rounding Rule for the Mean, Variance, and Standard Deviation for a Probability Distribution   The rounding rule for the mean, variance, and standard deviation for variables of a probability distribution is this: The mean, variance, and standard deviation should be rounded to one more decimal place than the outcome X. When fractions are used, they should be reduced to lowest terms.

Examples 5–5 through 5–8 illustrate the use of the formula.

EXAMPLE 5–5   Rolling a Die

Find the mean of the number of spots that appear when a die is tossed.

SOLUTION

In the toss of a die, the mean can be computed thus.

Outcome X	1	2	3	4	5	6
Probability P(X)	$\frac{1}{6}$	$\frac{1}{6}$	$\frac{1}{6}$	$\frac{1}{6}$	$\frac{1}{6}$	$\frac{1}{6}$

$$\mu = \Sigma X \cdot P(X) = 1 \cdot \tfrac{1}{6} + 2 \cdot \tfrac{1}{6} + 3 \cdot \tfrac{1}{6} + 4 \cdot \tfrac{1}{6} + 5 \cdot \tfrac{1}{6} + 6 \cdot \tfrac{1}{6}$$
$$= \tfrac{21}{6} = 3\tfrac{1}{2} \text{ or } 3.5$$

That is, when a die is tossed many times, the theoretical mean will be 3.5. Note that even though the die cannot show a 3.5, the theoretical average is 3.5.

The reason why this formula gives the theoretical mean is that in the long run, each outcome would occur approximately $\frac{1}{6}$ of the time. Hence, multiplying the outcome by its corresponding probability and finding the sum would yield the theoretical mean. In other words, outcome 1 would occur approximately $\frac{1}{6}$ of the time, outcome 2 would occur approximately $\frac{1}{6}$ of the time, etc.

EXAMPLE 5–6   Water System Valves

A very old water system in a manufacturing plant has 4 independent valves that have a 50% chance of working correctly over a year. The valves are checked yearly to make sure a valve is either bad (B) or good (G). Find the mean number of good valves in the system.

SOLUTION

First, it is necessary to find the sample space. There are 16 outcomes, as shown.

BBBB	BGBB	GBBB	GGBB
BBBG	BGBG	GBBG	GGBG
BBGB	BGGB	GBGB	GGGB
BBGG	BGGG	GBGG	GGGG

(A tree diagram may help.)
Next, make a probability distribution.

Number of Good Valves X	0	1	2	3	4
Probability P(X)	$\frac{1}{16}$	$\frac{4}{16}$	$\frac{6}{16}$	$\frac{4}{16}$	$\frac{1}{16}$

Then multiply X and P(X) for each outcome and find the sum.

$$\mu = \Sigma X \cdot P(X) = 0 \cdot \left(\frac{1}{16}\right) + 1 \cdot \left(\frac{4}{16}\right) + 2 \cdot \left(\frac{6}{16}\right) + 3 \cdot \left(\frac{4}{16}\right) + 4 \cdot \left(\frac{1}{16}\right) = 2$$

Hence, the mean of the number of good water valves is 2.

EXAMPLE 5–7   Tossing Coins

If three coins are tossed, find the mean of the number of heads that occur. (See the table preceding Example 5–1.)

SOLUTION

The probability distribution is

Number of heads X	0	1	2	3
Probability P(X)	$\frac{1}{8}$	$\frac{3}{8}$	$\frac{3}{8}$	$\frac{1}{8}$

The mean is

$$\mu = \Sigma X \cdot P(X) = 0 \cdot \tfrac{1}{8} + 1 \cdot \tfrac{3}{8} + 2 \cdot \tfrac{3}{8} + 3 \cdot \tfrac{1}{8} = \tfrac{12}{8} = 1\tfrac{1}{2} \text{ or } 1.5$$

The value 1.5 cannot occur as an outcome. Nevertheless, it is the long-run or theoretical average.

EXAMPLE 5–8   Successful Sales

Find the mean for the number of successful sales per person per week using the data in Example 5–3.

SOLUTION

The probability distribution is

Outcome X	2	3	4	5
Probability $P(X)$	0.20	0.44	0.24	0.12

$$\mu = \Sigma X \cdot P(X) = 2(0.20) + 3(0.44) + 4(0.24) + 5(0.12) = 3.28$$

Hence, the mean number of successful sales per week is 3.28.

Variance and Standard Deviation

For a probability distribution, the mean of the random variable describes the measure of the so-called long-run or theoretical average, but it does not tell anything about the spread of the distribution. Recall from Chapter 3 that to measure this spread or variability, statisticians use the variance and standard deviation. These formulas were used:

$$\sigma^2 = \frac{\Sigma(X - \mu)^2}{N} \qquad \text{or} \qquad \sigma = \sqrt{\frac{\Sigma(X - \mu)^2}{N}}$$

These formulas cannot be used for a random variable of a probability distribution since N is infinite, so the variance and standard deviation must be computed differently.

To find the variance for the random variable of a probability distribution, subtract the theoretical mean of the random variable from each outcome and square the difference. Then multiply each difference by its corresponding probability and add the products. The formula is

$$\sigma^2 = \Sigma[(X - \mu)^2 \cdot P(X)]$$

Finding the variance by using this formula is somewhat tedious. So for simplified computations, a shortcut formula can be used. This formula is algebraically equivalent to the longer one and is used in the examples that follow.

> **Formula for the Variance of a Probability Distribution**
>
> Find the variance of a probability distribution by multiplying the square of each outcome by its corresponding probability, summing those products, and subtracting the square of the mean. The formula for the variance of a probability distribution is
>
> $$\sigma^2 = \Sigma[X^2 \cdot P(X)] - \mu^2$$
>
> The standard deviation of a probability distribution is
>
> $$\sigma = \sqrt{\sigma^2} \qquad \text{or} \qquad \sigma = \sqrt{\Sigma[X^2 \cdot P(X)] - \mu^2}$$

Remember that the variance and standard deviation cannot be negative.

EXAMPLE 5–9   Rolling a Die

Compute the variance and standard deviation for the probability distribution in Example 5–5.

SOLUTION

Recall that the mean is $\mu = 3.5$, as computed in Example 5–5. Square each outcome and multiply by the corresponding probability, sum those products, and then subtract the square of the mean.

$$\sigma^2 = (1^2 \cdot \tfrac{1}{6} + 2^2 \cdot \tfrac{1}{6} + 3^2 \cdot \tfrac{1}{6} + 4^2 \cdot \tfrac{1}{6} + 5^2 \cdot \tfrac{1}{6} + 6^2 \cdot \tfrac{1}{6}) - (3.5)^2 = 2.917$$

To get the standard deviation, find the square root of the variance.

$$\sigma = \sqrt{2.917} \approx 1.708$$

Hence, the standard deviation for rolling a die is 1.708.

EXAMPLE 5–10   Selecting Numbered Balls

A box contains 5 balls. Two are numbered 3, one is numbered 4, and two are numbered 5. The balls are mixed and one is selected at random. After a ball is selected, its number is recorded. Then it is replaced. If the experiment is repeated many times, find the variance and standard deviation of the numbers on the balls.

SOLUTION

Let X be the number on each ball. The probability distribution is

Number of ball X	3	4	5
Probability $P(X)$	$\tfrac{2}{5}$	$\tfrac{1}{5}$	$\tfrac{2}{5}$

The mean is

$$\mu = \Sigma X \cdot P(X) = 3 \cdot \tfrac{2}{5} + 4 \cdot \tfrac{1}{5} + 5 \cdot \tfrac{2}{5} = 4$$

The variance is

$$\sigma^2 = \Sigma[X^2 \cdot P(X)] - \mu^2$$

$$= 3^2 \cdot \tfrac{2}{5} + 4^2 \cdot \tfrac{1}{5} + 5^2 \cdot \tfrac{2}{5} - 4^2$$

$$= 16\tfrac{4}{5} - 16$$

$$= \tfrac{4}{5} \text{ or } 0.8$$

The standard deviation is

$$\sigma = \sqrt{\tfrac{4}{5}} = \sqrt{0.8} \approx 0.894$$

The mean, variance, and standard deviation can also be found by using vertical columns, as shown.

X	$P(X)$	$X \cdot P(X)$	$X^2 \cdot P(X)$
3	0.4	1.2	3.6
4	0.2	0.8	3.2
5	0.4	2.0	10
		$\Sigma X \cdot P(X) = 4.0$	16.8

Find the mean by summing the $X \cdot P(X)$ column, and find the variance by summing the $X^2 \cdot P(X)$ column and subtracting the square of the mean.

$$\sigma^2 = 16.8 - 4^2 = 16.8 - 16 = 0.8$$

and

$$\sigma = \sqrt{0.8} \approx 0.894$$

EXAMPLE 5–11   Prior Sentences

On a randomly selected day, 25 people were found guilty of illegally selling various drugs. Nine had no prior sentences. Six had one prior sentence. Five had two prior sentences. Three had three prior sentences, and two had four prior sentences. Find the variance and standard deviation of the number of prior sentences the convicted people had.

SOLUTION

Make a probability distribution for the data.

$$P(0) = \tfrac{9}{25} = 0.36$$

$$P(1) = \tfrac{6}{25} = 0.24$$

$$P(2) = \tfrac{5}{25} = 0.20$$

$$P(3) = \tfrac{3}{25} = 0.12$$

$$P(4) = \tfrac{2}{25} = 0.08$$

X	0	1	2	3	4
P(X)	0.36	0.24	0.20	0.12	0.08

The mean is

$$\mu = \Sigma XP(X)$$
$$= 0(0.36) + 1(0.24) + 2(0.20) + 3(0.12) + 4(0.08)$$
$$= 1.32$$

The variance is

$$\sigma^2 = \Sigma[X^2 \cdot P(X)] - \mu^2$$
$$= 0^2(0.36) + 1^2(0.24) + 2^2(0.2) + 3^2(0.12) + 4^2(0.08) - 1.32^2$$
$$= 0 + 0.24 + 0.8 + 1.08 + 1.28 - 1.7424$$
$$= 3.4 - 1.7424$$
$$= 1.6576$$

The standard deviation is $\sigma = \sqrt{\sigma^2} = \sqrt{1.6576} \approx 1.287$.

Expectation

Another concept related to the mean for a probability distribution is that of expected value or expectation. Expected value is used in various types of games of chance, in insurance, and in other areas, such as decision theory.

> The **expected value** of a discrete random variable of a probability distribution is the theoretical average of the variable. The formula is
>
> $$\mu = E(X) = \Sigma X \cdot P(X)$$
>
> The symbol $E(X)$ is used for the expected value.

The formula for the expected value is the same as the formula for the theoretical mean. The expected value, then, is the theoretical mean of the probability distribution. That is, $E(X) = \mu$.

When expected value problems involve money, it is customary to round the answer to the nearest cent.

EXAMPLE 5–12   Winning Tickets

One thousand tickets are sold at $1 each for a smart television valued at $750. What is the expected value of the gain if you purchase one ticket?

SOLUTION

The problem can be set up as follows:

	Win	Lose
Gain X	$749	−$1
Probability P(X)	$\dfrac{1}{1000}$	$\dfrac{999}{1000}$

Two things should be noted. First, for a win, the net gain is $749, since you do not get the cost of the ticket ($1) back. Second, for a loss, the gain is represented by a negative number, in this case −$1. The solution, then, is

$$E(X) = \$749 \cdot \frac{1}{1000} + (-\$1) \cdot \frac{999}{1000} = -\$0.25$$

Hence, a person would lose, on average, −$0.25 on each ticket purchased.

Expected value problems of this type can also be solved by finding the overall gain (i.e., the value of the prize won or the amount of money won, not considering the cost of the ticket for the prize or the cost to play the game) and subtracting the cost of the tickets or the cost to play the game, as shown:

$$E(X) = \$750 \cdot \frac{1}{1000} - \$1 = -\$0.25$$

Here, the overall gain ($750) must be used.

Note that the expectation is −$0.25. This does not mean that you lose $0.25, since you can only win a television set valued at $750 or lose $1 on the ticket. What this expectation means is that the average of the losses is $0.25 for each of the 1000 ticket holders. Here is another way of looking at this situation: If you purchased one ticket each week over a long time, the average loss would be $0.25 per ticket, since theoretically, on average, you would win the television set once for each 1000 tickets purchased.

EXAMPLE 5–13   Poker Chips

Poker chips are numbered $1, $5, $10, $20, and $50. Four chips are numbered $1. Two chips are numbered $5. Two chips are numbered $10. One chip is numbered $20. One chip is numbered $50. If one chip is selected at random, find the expected value of the chip.

SOLUTION

The probability distribution for the chips is

Value X	$1	$5	$10	$20	$50
Probability $P(X)$	$\frac{4}{10}$	$\frac{2}{10}$	$\frac{2}{10}$	$\frac{1}{10}$	$\frac{1}{10}$

The expected value is

$$\mu = \Sigma X \cdot P(X) = 1 \cdot \frac{4}{10} + 5 \cdot \frac{2}{10} + 10 \cdot \frac{2}{10} + 20 \cdot \frac{1}{10} + 50 \cdot \frac{1}{10} = \$10.40$$

EXAMPLE 5–14   Bond Investment

A financial adviser suggests that his client select one of two types of bonds in which to invest $5000. Bond X pays a return of 4% and has a default rate of 2%. Bond Y has a $2\frac{1}{2}$% return and a default rate of 1%. Find the expected rate of return and decide which bond would be a better investment. When the bond defaults, the investor loses all the investment.

SOLUTION

The return on bond X is $5000 \cdot 4\% = \$200$. The expected return then is

$$E(X) = \$200(0.98) - \$5000(0.02) = \$96$$

The return on bond Y is $5000 \cdot 2\frac{1}{2}\% = \$125$. The expected return then is

$$E(Y) = \$125(0.99) - \$5000(0.01) = \$73.75$$

Hence, bond X would be a better investment since the expected return is higher.

In gambling games, if the expected value of the game is zero, the game is said to be fair. If the expected value of a game is positive, then the game is in favor of the player. That is, the player has a better than even chance of winning. If the expected value of the game is negative, then the game is said to be in favor of the house. That is, in the long run, the players will lose money.

In his book *Probabilities in Everyday Life* (Ivy Books, 1986), author John D. McGervy gives the expectations for various casino games. For keno, the house wins $0.27 on every $1.00 bet. For Chuck-a-Luck, the house wins about $0.52 on every $1.00 bet. For roulette, the house wins about $0.90 on every $1.00 bet. For craps, the house wins about $0.88 on every $1.00 bet. The bottom line here is that if you gamble long enough, sooner or later you will end up losing money.

Applying the Concepts 5–2

Radiation Exposure

On March 28, 1979, the nuclear generating facility at Three Mile Island, Pennsylvania, began discharging radiation into the atmosphere. People exposed to even low levels of radiation can experience health problems ranging from very mild to severe, even causing death. A local newspaper reported that 11 babies were born with kidney problems in the three-county area surrounding the Three Mile Island nuclear power plant. The expected value for that problem in infants in that area was 3. Answer the following questions.

1. What does *expected value* mean?
2. Would you expect the exact value of 3 all the time?

3. If a news reporter stated that the number of cases of kidney problems in newborns was nearly four times as many as was usually expected, do you think pregnant mothers living in that area would be overly concerned?

4. Is it unlikely that 11 occurred by chance?

5. Are there any other statistics that could better inform the public?

6. Assume that 3 out of 2500 babies were born with kidney problems in that three-county area the year before the accident. Also assume that 11 out of 2500 babies were born with kidney problems in that three-county area the year after the accident. What is the real percentage increase in that abnormality?

7. Do you think that pregnant mothers living in that area should be overly concerned after looking at the results in terms of rates?

See page 308 for the answers.

Exercises 5–2

1. Coffee with Meals A researcher wishes to determine the number of cups of coffee a customer drinks with an evening meal at a restaurant. Find the mean, variance, and standard deviation for the distribution. 1.04; 0.858; 0.926

X	0	1	2	3	4
P(X)	0.31	0.42	0.21	0.04	0.02

2. Catching Fish The number of fish anglers catch per day at Ye Olde Fishing Hole is shown. Find the mean, variance, and standard deviation for the distribution. 1.36; 1.29; 1.14

Number of Fish Caught, X	0	1	2	3	4	5
Probability P(X)	0.24	0.36	0.27	0.08	0.03	0.02

3. Sports Utility Vehicles The probability that an automotive dealer sells 0, 1, 2, or 3 sports utility vehicles in one day is $\frac{2}{9}$, $\frac{4}{9}$, $\frac{2}{9}$, and $\frac{1}{9}$, respectively. Find the mean, variance, and standard deviation for the distribution. 1.222; 0.8395; 0.916

4. Garbage Disposal The number of pounds of garbage (not including recycled products) thrown away by Americans each day is shown. Find the mean, variance, and standard deviation for the distribution. 1.88; 0.986; 0.993

X	0	1	2	3	4
P(X)	0.03	0.4	0.3	0.2	0.07

5. Extracurricular Activities The probability that a student participates in 0, 1, 2, 3, or 4 extracurricular activities is 0.1, 0.3, 0.2, 0.2, and 0.2. Find the mean, variance, and standard deviation for the distribution. 2.1; 1.69; 1.3

6. Traffic Accidents The county highway department recorded the following probabilities for the number of accidents per day on a certain freeway for one month.

The number of accidents per day and their corresponding probabilities are shown. Find the mean, variance, and standard deviation. 1.3; 1.8; 1.3

Number of accidents X	0	1	2	3	4
Probability P(X)	0.4	0.2	0.2	0.1	0.1

7. Scoring Touchdowns The probability that a football team scores 0, 1, 2, 3, 4, or 5 touchdowns in a game is 0.30, 0.40, 0.2, 0.05, 0.025, and 0.025, respectively. Find the mean, variance, and standard deviation for the distribution. 1.175; 1.294; 1.138

8. Benford's Law The leading digits in actual data, such as stock prices, population numbers, death rates, and lengths of rivers, do not occur randomly as one might suppose, but instead follow a distribution according to Benford's law. Below is the probability distribution for the leading digits in real-life lists of data. Calculate the mean for the distribution. $\mu = 3.441$

X	1	2	3	4	5	6	7	8	9
P(X)	0.301	0.176	0.125	0.097	0.079	0.067	0.058	0.051	0.046

9. Bicycle Sales The probability that a bicycle shop sells 0, 1, 2, or 3 bicycles in a week is $\frac{3}{8}$, $\frac{1}{4}$, $\frac{1}{4}$, and $\frac{1}{8}$, respectively. Find the mean, variance, and standard deviation for the distribution. 1.125; 1.109; 1.053

10. Treadmill Mileage The number of miles a person runs on a treadmill in a typical workout is shown. Find the mean, variance, and standard deviation for the data. 1.95; 3.25; 1.80

Miles, X	1	2	3	5	10
Probability, P(X)	0.6	0.2	0.1	0.07	0.03

11. Grab Bags At a party, the hostess made 20 grab bags. Ten bags contain $2.00 each, six bags contain $5.00 each, three bags contain $10.00 each, and one bag contains $20.00. Find the expected value if one bag is selected. $5.00

12. **Family Farming** A family owns a large farm. The probability that they plant 5, 6, 7, or 8 field sections in a season is 0.25, 0.31, 0.42, and 0.02, respectively. Find the expected value for the field sections planted. 6.21

13. **Rolling Dice** If a person rolls doubles when tossing two dice, the person wins $5. For the game to be fair, how much should the person pay to play the game? $0.83

14. **Dice Game** A person pays $2 to play a certain game by rolling a single die once. If a 1 or a 2 comes up, the person wins nothing. If, however, the player rolls a 3, 4, 5, or 6, the person wins the difference between the number rolled and $2. Find the expectation for this game. Is the game fair? −33.3 cents; no

15. **Lottery Prizes** A lottery offers one $1000 prize, one $500 prize, and five $100 prizes. One thousand tickets are sold at $3 each. Find the expectation if a person buys one ticket. −$1.00

16. **Lottery Prizes** In Exercise 15, find the expectation if a person buys two tickets. Assume that the player's ticket is replaced after each draw and that the same ticket can win more than one prize. −$2.00

17. **Winning the Lottery** For a daily lottery, a person selects a three-digit number. If the person plays for $1, that person can win $500. Find the expectation. In the same daily lottery, if a person boxes a number, that person will win $80. Find the expectation if the number 123 is played for $1 and boxed. (When a number is "boxed," it can win when the digits occur in any order.) −$0.50; −$0.52

18. **Life Insurance** A 35-year-old woman purchases a $100,000 term life insurance policy for an annual payment of $360. Based on a period life table for the U.S. government, the probability that she will survive the year is 0.999057. Find the expected value of the policy for the insurance company. $265.36

19. **Roulette** A roulette wheel has 38 numbers, 1 through 36, 0, and 00. One-half of the numbers from 1 through 36 are red, and the other half are black; 0 and 00 are green. A ball is rolled, and it falls into one of the 38 slots, giving a number and a color. The payoffs (winnings) for a $1 bet are as follows:

Red or black	$1	0	$35
Odd or even	$1	00	$35
1–18	$1	Any single number	$35
9–36	$1	0 or 00	$17

If a person bets $1, find the expected value for each.

a. Red −5.26 cents   *d.* Any single number −5.26 cents

b. Even −5.26 cents   *e.* 0 or 00 −5.26 cents

c. 00 −5.26 cents

≣ Extending the Concepts

20. **Rolling Dice** Construct a probability distribution for the sum shown on the faces when two dice are rolled. Find the mean, variance, and standard deviation of the distribution. 7; 5.8; 2.4

21. **Rolling a Die** When one die is rolled, the expected value of the number of dots is 3.5. In Exercise 20, the mean number of dots was found for rolling two dice. What is the mean number of dots if three dice are rolled? 10.5

22. The formula for finding the variance for a probability distribution is

$$\sigma^2 = \Sigma[(X - \mu)^2 \cdot P(X)]$$

Verify algebraically that this formula gives the same result as the shortcut formula shown in this section.

23. Complete the following probability distribution if $P(6)$ equals two-thirds of $P(4)$. Then find μ, σ^2, and σ for the distribution.

X	1	2	4	6	9
$P(X)$	0.23	0.18	?	?	0.015

24. **Rolling Two Dice** Roll two dice 100 times and find the mean, variance, and standard deviation of the sum of the dots. Compare the result with the theoretical results obtained in Exercise 20. Answers will vary.

25. **Extracurricular Activities** Conduct a survey of the number of extracurricular activities your classmates are enrolled in. Construct a probability distribution and find the mean, variance, and standard deviation. Answers will vary.

26. **Promotional Campaign** In a recent promotional campaign, a company offered these prizes and the corresponding probabilities. Find the expected value of winning. The tickets are free.

Number of prizes	Amount	Probability
1	$100,000	$\frac{1}{1,000,000}$
2	10,000	$\frac{1}{50,000}$
5	1,000	$\frac{1}{10,000}$
10	100	$\frac{1}{1000}$

If the winner has to mail in the winning ticket to claim the prize, what will be the expectation if the cost of the stamp is considered? Use the current cost of a stamp for a first-class letter. $2.00, $1.42 with a stamp price of $0.58

27. **Probability Distribution** A bag contains five balls numbered 1, 2, 4, 7, and *. Choose two balls at random without replacement and add the numbers. If one ball has the *, double the amount on the other ball. Construct the probability distribution for this random variable X and calculate μ, σ^2, and σ.

☰ Technology   Step by Step

TI-84 Plus
Step by Step

Calculating the Mean, Variance, and Standard Deviation of a Discrete Random Variable

Example TI5–1

Number on ball X	0	2	4	6	8
Probability $P(X)$	$\frac{1}{5}$	$\frac{1}{5}$	$\frac{1}{5}$	$\frac{1}{5}$	$\frac{1}{5}$

Calculate the mean, variance, and standard deviation for the discrete random variable:

1. Enter the x values into L_1 and the probabilities into L_2.
2. Move the cursor to the top of the L_3 column so that L_3 is highlighted.
3. Type L_1 multiplied by L_2, then press **ENTER.**

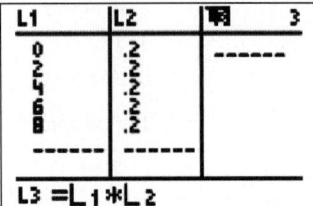

4. Move the cursor to the top of the L_4 column so that L_4 is highlighted.
5. Type L_1 followed by the square x^2 key multiplied by L_2, then press **ENTER.**

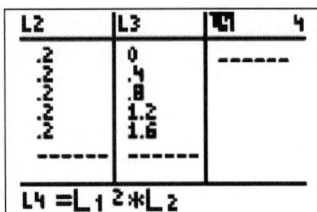

6. Type **2nd QUIT** to return to the home screen.
7. Type **2nd LIST,** move the cursor to MATH, type 5 for sum, then type L_3, then press **ENTER.** (This is the mean.)
8. Type **2nd ENTER,** move the cursor to L_3, type L_4, then press **ENTER.**

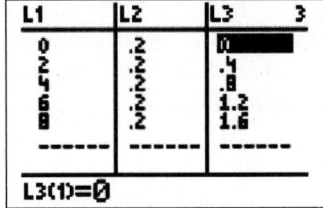

The mean is 4 and the variance is 8. Take the square root of 8 to find the standard deviation of 2.83.

 To calculate the mean, variance, and standard deviation for a discrete random variable without using the formulas, modify the procedure to calculate the mean, variance, and standard deviation from grouped data (Chapter 3) by entering the x values into L_1 and the probabilities into L_2.

1-Var Stats	**1-Var Stats**	σx^2
List:L₁ FreqList:L₂ Calculate	x̄=4 Σx=4 Σx²=24 Sx= σx=2.828427125 ↓n=1	8

The mean is 4 and the standard deviation is 2.828427125. To calculate the variance, square the standard deviation. Select Vars, select 5: Statistics, select 4: σx, select the square x^2 key. ▄

5–3   The Binomial Distribution

OBJECTIVE 3

Find the exact probability for X successes in n trials of a binomial experiment.

Many types of probability problems have only two outcomes or can be reduced to two outcomes. For example, when a coin is tossed, it can land heads or tails. When a 6-sided die is tossed, it will land on an odd or even number. In a basketball game, a team either wins or loses. A true/false item can be answered in only two ways, true or false. Other situations can be reduced to two outcomes. For example, a medical treatment can be classified as effective or ineffective, depending on the results. A person can be classified as having normal or abnormal blood pressure, depending on the measure of the blood pressure gauge. A multiple-choice question, even though there are four or five answer choices, can be classified as correct or incorrect. Situations like these are called *binomial experiments*.

U.S. Navy photo

Each repetition of the experiment is called a *trial*.

| Historical Note

In 1653, Blaise Pascal created a triangle of numbers called *Pascal's triangle* that can be used in the binomial distribution.

A **binomial experiment** is a probability experiment that satisfies the following four requirements:

1. There must be a fixed number of trials.
2. Each trial can have only two outcomes or outcomes that can be reduced to two outcomes. These outcomes can be considered as either success or failure.
3. The outcomes of each trial must be independent of one another.
4. The probability of a success must remain the same for each trial.

The word *success* does not imply that something good or positive has occurred. For example, in a probability experiment, we might want to select 10 people and let *S* represent the number of people who were in an automobile accident in the last six months. In this case, a success would not be a positive or good thing.

EXAMPLE 5–15

Decide whether each experiment is a binomial experiment. If not, state the reason why.

 a. Selecting 20 university students and recording their class rank
 b. Selecting 20 students from a university and recording if they live on campus
 c. Drawing five cards from a deck without replacement and recording whether they are red or black cards
 d. Selecting five students from a large school and asking them if they are on the dean's list
 e. Recording the number of children in 50 randomly selected families

SOLUTION

 a. No. There are five possible outcomes: freshman, sophomore, junior, senior, and graduate student.
 b. Yes. All four requirements are met.
 c. No. Since the cards are not replaced, the events are not independent.
 d. Yes. All four requirements are met.
 e. No. There can be more than two categories for the answers.

A binomial experiment and its results give rise to a special probability distribution called the *binomial distribution.*

> The outcomes of a binomial experiment and the corresponding probabilities of these outcomes are called a **binomial distribution.**

In binomial experiments, the outcomes are usually classified as successes or failures. For example, the correct answer to a multiple-choice item can be classified as a success, but any of the other choices would be incorrect and hence classified as a failure. The notation that is commonly used for binomial experiments and the binomial distribution is defined now.

Notation for the Binomial Distribution

$P(S)$	The symbol for the probability of success
$P(F)$	The symbol for the probability of failure
p	The numerical probability of a success
q	The numerical probability of a failure

$$P(S) = p \quad \text{and} \quad P(F) = 1 - p = q$$

n	The number of trials
X	The number of successes in n trials

Note that $0 \leq X \leq n$ and $X = 0, 1, 2, 3, \ldots, n$.

The probability of a success in a binomial experiment can be computed with this formula.

Binomial Probability Formula

In a binomial experiment, the probability of exactly X successes in n trials is

$$P(X) = \frac{n!}{(n-X)!X!} \cdot p^X \cdot q^{n-X} \text{ or } P(X) = {}_nC_X \cdot p^X \cdot q^{n-X}.$$

An explanation of why the formula works is given following Example 5–16.

EXAMPLE 5–16   Tossing Coins

A coin is tossed 3 times. Find the probability of getting exactly two heads.

SOLUTION

This problem can be solved by looking at the sample space. There are three ways to get two heads.

$$\text{HHH, } \underline{\text{HHT, HTH, THH,}} \text{ TTH, THT, HTT, TTT}$$

The answer is $\frac{3}{8}$, or 0.375.

Looking at the problem in Example 5–16 from the standpoint of a binomial experiment, one can show that it meets the four requirements.

1. There are a fixed number of trials (three).
2. There are only two outcomes for each trial, heads or tails.
3. The outcomes are independent of one another (the outcome of one toss in no way affects the outcome of another toss).
4. The probability of a success (heads) is $\frac{1}{2}$ in each case.

In this case, $n = 3$, $X = 2$, $p = \frac{1}{2}$, and $q = \frac{1}{2}$. Hence, substituting in the formula gives

$$P(2 \text{ heads}) = {}_3C_2 \cdot \left(\tfrac{1}{2}\right)^2\left(\tfrac{1}{2}\right)^1 = \frac{3!}{((3-2)! \cdot 2!)} \cdot \left(\tfrac{1}{2}\right)^2\left(\tfrac{1}{2}\right)^1 = 0.375$$

which is the same answer obtained by using the sample space.

The same example can be used to explain the formula. First, note that there are three ways to get exactly two heads and one tail from a possible eight ways. They are HHT, HTH, and THH. In this case, then, the number of ways of obtaining two heads from three coin tosses is ${}_3C_2$, or 3, as shown in Chapter 4. In general, the number of ways to get X successes from n trials without regard to order is

$$ {}_nC_X = \frac{n!}{(n-X)!X!} $$

This is the first part of the binomial formula. (Some calculators can be used for this.)

Next, each success has a probability of $\frac{1}{2}$ and can occur twice. Likewise, each failure has a probability of $\frac{1}{2}$ and can occur once, giving the $\left(\frac{1}{2}\right)^2\left(\frac{1}{2}\right)^1$ part of the formula. To generalize, then, each success has a probability of p and can occur X times, and each failure has a probability of q and can occur $n - X$ times. Putting it all together yields the binomial probability formula.

When sampling is done without replacement, such as in surveys, the events are dependent events; however, the events can be considered independent if the size of the sample is no more than 5% of the size of the population. That is, $n \leq 0.05N$. The reason is that when one item is selected from a large number of items and is not replaced before the second item is selected, the change in the probability of the second item being selected is so small that it can be ignored.

EXAMPLE 5–17   Pet Ownership

A survey found that 2 out of 5 households own a dog. If 10 households are selected at random, find the probability that exactly two households will own a dog.

Source: Based on American Veterinary Medical Association

SOLUTION

In this case, $n = 10$, $X = 2$, $p = \frac{2}{5}$, and $q = \frac{3}{5}$. Hence,

$$P(2) = \frac{10!}{(10-2)!2!} \left(\frac{2}{5}\right)^2 \left(\frac{3}{5}\right)^8 = 45(0.16)(0.01679616) \approx 0.121$$

So, there is about a 0.121 probability that in a random sample of 10 households exactly 2 will own a dog.

Alternate Solution: Using the combination formula

$$P(2) = {}_{10}C_2 \left(\frac{2}{5}\right)^2 \left(\frac{3}{5}\right)^8 = 0.121$$

EXAMPLE 5–18   Survey on Employment

A survey from Teenage Research Unlimited (Northbrook, Illinois) found that 30% of teenage consumers receive their spending money from part-time jobs. If 5 teenagers are selected at random, find the probability that at least 3 of them will have part-time jobs.

SOLUTION

To find the probability that at least 3 have part-time jobs, it is necessary to find the individual probabilities for 3, or 4, or 5 and then add them to get the total probability.

$$P(3) = \frac{5!}{(5-3)!3!}(0.3)^3(0.7)^2 \approx 0.132$$

$$P(4) = \frac{5!}{(5-4)!4!}(0.3)^4(0.7)^1 \approx 0.028$$

$$P(5) = \frac{5!}{(5-5)!5!}(0.3)^5(0.7)^0 \approx 0.002$$

Hence,

$$P(\text{at least three teenagers have part-time jobs})$$
$$= 0.132 + 0.028 + 0.002 = 0.162$$

Alternate Solution: Using the combination formula

$$P(3) = {}_5C_3 \cdot (0.3)^3 \cdot (0.7)^2 \approx 0.132$$
$$P(4) = {}_5C_4 \cdot (0.3)^4 \cdot (0.7)^1 \approx 0.028$$
$$P(5) = {}_5C_5 \cdot (0.3)^5 \cdot (0.7)^0 \approx 0.002$$

Hence,

$$P(\text{at least three teenagers have part-time jobs})$$
$$= 0.132 + 0.028 + 0.002 = 0.162$$

Computing probabilities by using the binomial probability formula can be quite tedious at times, so tables have been developed for selected values of n and p. Table A–2 in Appendix A gives the probabilities for individual events. Example 5–19 shows how to use Table A–2 to compute probabilities for binomial experiments.

EXAMPLE 5–19   Tossing Coins

Solve the problem in Example 5–16 by using Table A–2.

SOLUTION

Since $n = 3$, $X = 2$, and $p = 0.5$, the value 0.375 is found as shown in Figure 5–3.

FIGURE 5–3   Using Table A–2 for Example 5–16

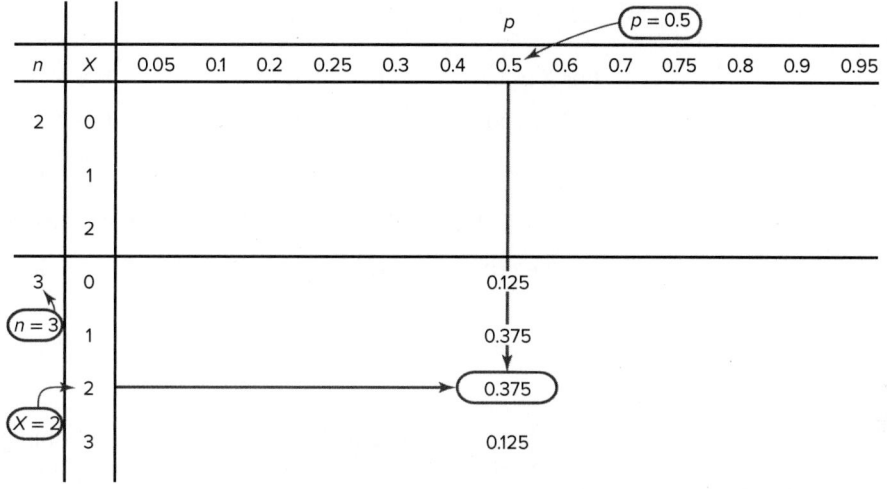

EXAMPLE 5–20   Survey on Fear of Being Home Alone at Night

Public Opinion reported that 5% of Americans are afraid of being alone in a house at night. If a random sample of 20 Americans is selected, find these probabilities by using the binomial table in Appendix A.

    a. There are exactly 5 people in the sample who are afraid of being alone at night.

    b. There are at most 3 people in the sample who are afraid of being alone at night.

    c. There are at least 3 people in the sample who are afraid of being alone at night.

Source: 100% American by Daniel Evan Weiss.

SOLUTION

    a. $n = 20$, $p = 0.05$, and $X = 5$. From the table, we get 0.002.

    b. $n = 20$ and $p = 0.05$. "At most 3 people" means 0, or 1, or 2, or 3.

    Hence, the solution is

$$P(X \leq 3) = P(0) + P(1) + P(2) + P(3) = 0.358 + 0.377 + 0.189 + 0.060$$

$$= 0.984$$

    c. $n = 20$ and $p = 0.05$. "At least 3 people" means 3, 4, 5, . . . , 20. This problem can best be solved by finding $P(X \leq 2) = P(0) + P(1) + P(2)$ and subtracting from 1.

$$P(0) + P(1) + P(2) = 0.358 + 0.377 + 0.189 = 0.924$$

$$P(X \geq 3) = 1 - 0.924 = 0.076$$

EXAMPLE 5–21   Driving While Intoxicated

A report from the Secretary of Health and Human Services stated that 70% of single-vehicle traffic fatalities that occur on weekend nights involve an intoxicated driver. If a random sample of 20 drivers is selected, find the probability that between 10 and 15, inclusive, accidents involve drivers who are intoxicated.

SOLUTION

$n = 20$, $p = 0.70$, and $X = 10, 11, 12, 13, 14$, or 15

For $X = 10$,	$P(10) = 0.031$	For $X = 13$,	$P(13) = 0.164$
For $X = 11$,	$P(11) = 0.065$	For $X = 14$,	$P(14) = 0.192$
For $X = 12$,	$P(12) = 0.114$	For $X = 15$,	$P(15) = 0.179$

$$P(10 \leq X \leq 15) = 0.031 + 0.065 + 0.114 + 0.164 + 0.192 + 0.179 = 0.745.$$

Hence, the probability that between 10 and 15 drivers, inclusive, were intoxicated is 0.745.

The mean, variance, and standard deviation for a binomial variable can be found by using the formulas in Section 5–2; however, shorter but mathematically equivalent formulas for the mean, variance, and standard deviation are used.

OBJECTIVE **4**

Find the mean, variance, and standard deviation for the variable of a binomial distribution.

Mean, Variance, and Standard Deviation for the Binomial Distribution

The mean, variance, and standard deviation of a variable that has the *binomial distribution* can be found by using the following formulas.

  Mean: $\mu = n \cdot p$ Variance: $\sigma^2 = n \cdot p \cdot q$ Standard deviation: $\sigma = \sqrt{n \cdot p \cdot q}$

EXAMPLE 5–22   Tossing a Coin

A coin is tossed 4 times. Find the mean, variance, and standard deviation of the number of heads that will be obtained.

SOLUTION

With the formulas for the binomial distribution and $n = 4$, $p = \frac{1}{2}$, and $q = \frac{1}{2}$, the results are

$$\mu = n \cdot p = 4 \cdot \tfrac{1}{2} = 2$$

$$\sigma^2 = n \cdot p \cdot q = 4 \cdot \tfrac{1}{2} \cdot \tfrac{1}{2} = 1$$

$$\sigma = \sqrt{1} = 1$$

In this case, the mean is two heads. The variance is 1 and the standard deviation is 1.

From Example 5–22, when four coins are tossed many, many times, the average of the number of heads that appear is 2, and the standard deviation of the number of heads is 1. Note that these are theoretical values.

As stated previously, this problem can be solved by using the formulas for expected value. The distribution is shown.

No. of heads X	0	1	2	3	4
Probability $P(X)$	$\frac{1}{16}$	$\frac{4}{16}$	$\frac{6}{16}$	$\frac{4}{16}$	$\frac{1}{16}$

$$\mu = E(X) = \Sigma X \cdot P(X) = 0 \cdot \tfrac{1}{16} + 1 \cdot \tfrac{4}{16} + 2 \cdot \tfrac{6}{16} + 3 \cdot \tfrac{4}{16} + 4 \cdot \tfrac{1}{16} = \tfrac{32}{16} = 2$$

$$\sigma^2 = \Sigma X^2 \cdot P(X) - \mu^2$$

$$= 0^2 \cdot \tfrac{1}{16} + 1^2 \cdot \tfrac{4}{16} + 2^2 \cdot \tfrac{6}{16} + 3^2 \cdot \tfrac{4}{16} + 4^2 \cdot \tfrac{1}{16} - 2^2 = \tfrac{80}{16} - 4 = 1$$

$$\sigma = \sqrt{1} = 1$$

Hence, the simplified binomial formulas give the same results.

EXAMPLE 5–23   Rolling a Die

An 8-sided die (with numbers 1 through 8 on the faces) is rolled 480 times. Find the mean, variance, and standard deviation of the number of 3s that will be rolled.

SOLUTION

This is a binomial experiment with $n = 480$, $p = \tfrac{1}{8}$, and $q = \tfrac{7}{8}$. Then

$$\mu = n \cdot p = 480 \cdot \tfrac{1}{8} = 60$$

$$\sigma^2 = n \cdot p \cdot q = 480 \cdot \tfrac{1}{8} \cdot \tfrac{7}{8} = 52.5$$

$$\sigma = \sqrt{52.5} = 7.25$$

In this case, the mean number of 3s obtained is 60. The variance is 52.5, and the standard deviation is 7.25.

EXAMPLE 5–24   Intoxicated Drivers

The *Sourcebook of Criminal Justice Statistics* states that 65% of Americans favor sentencing drunk drivers to jail even if they have not caused an accident. If a random number of 1000 individuals is selected, find the mean, variance, and standard deviation of the people who feel this way.

SOLUTION

This is a binomial situation since either people feel that drunk drivers should be sentenced or they feel that they should not.

$$\mu = n \cdot p = (1000)(0.65) = 650$$

$$\sigma^2 = n \cdot p \cdot q = (1000)(0.65)(0.35) = 227.5$$

$$\sigma = \sqrt{n \cdot p \cdot q} = \sqrt{227.5} = 15.083$$

For the sample, the mean is 650, the variance is 277.5, and the standard deviation is 15.083.

⊒ Applying the Concepts **5–3**

Unsanitary Restaurants

Health officials routinely check the sanitary condition of restaurants. Assume you visit a popular tourist spot and read on social media that in 3 out of every 7 restaurants checked, unsatisfactory health conditions were found. Assuming you are planning to eat out 10 times while you are there on vacation, answer the following questions.

1. How likely is it that you will eat at three restaurants with unsanitary conditions?

2. How likely is it that you will eat at four or five restaurants with unsanitary conditions?

3. Explain how you would compute the probability of eating in at least one restaurant with unsanitary conditions. Could you use the complement to solve this problem?

4. What is the most likely number to occur in this experiment?

5. How variable will the data be around the most likely number?

6. How do you know that this is a binomial distribution?

7. If it is a binomial distribution, does that mean that the likelihood of a success is always 50% since there are only two possible outcomes?

Check your answers by using the following computer-generated table.

Mean = 4.29   Std. dev. = 1.56492

X	P(X)	Cum. prob.
0	0.00371	0.00371
1	0.02784	0.03155
2	0.09396	0.12552
3	0.18792	0.31344
4	0.24665	0.56009
5	0.22199	0.78208
6	0.13874	0.92082
7	0.05946	0.98028
8	0.01672	0.99700
9	0.00279	0.99979
10	0.00021	1.00000

See page 308 for the answers.

⊒ Exercises **5–3**

1. Which of the following are binomial experiments or can be reduced to binomial experiments?

   a. Surveying 100 people to determine if they like Sudsy Soap Yes

   b. Tossing a coin 100 times to see how many heads occur Yes

   c. Drawing a card with replacement from a deck and getting a heart Yes

   d. Asking 1000 people which brand of jeans they wear No

   e. Testing four different brands of aspirin to see which brands are effective No

2. Which of the following are binomial experiments or can be reduced to binomial experiments?

   a. Testing one brand of aspirin by using 10 people to determine whether it is effective Yes

   b. Asking 100 people if they take public transportation Yes

   c. Checking 1000 applicants to see whether they were admitted to White Oak College Yes

   d. Surveying 300 prisoners to see how many different crimes they were convicted of No

   e. Surveying 300 prisoners to see whether this is their first offense Yes

3. Compute the probability of *X* successes, using Table A–2 in Appendix A.

   a. $n = 3, p = 0.40, X = 3$ 0.064
   b. $n = 5, p = 0.90, X = 4$ 0.328
   c. $n = 6, p = 0.60, X = 2$ 0.138
   d. $n = 10, p = 0.50, X = 4$ 0.205
   e. $n = 12, p = 0.30, X = 1$ 0.071

4. Compute the probability of *X* successes, using Table A–2 in Appendix A.

   a. $n = 15, p = 0.80, X = 12$ 0.250
   b. $n = 17, p = 0.05, X = 0$ 0.418
   c. $n = 20, p = 0.50, X = 10$ 0.176
   d. $n = 16, p = 0.20, X = 3$ 0.246

5. Compute the probability of *X* successes, using the binomial formula.

   a. $n = 5, X = 4, p = 0.4$ 0.0768
   b. $n = 3, X = 1, p = 0.25$ 0.422
   c. $n = 6, X = 2, p = 0.71$ 0.0535

6. Compute the probability of *X* successes, using the binomial formula.

   a. $n = 9, X = 0, p = 0.42$ 0.007
   b. $n = 10, X = 5, p = 0.37$ 0.173

For Exercises 7 through 16, assume all variables are binomial. (Note: If values are not found in Table A–2 of Appendix A, use the binomial formula.)

7. **Sleep Disorders** A survey finds that 20% of Americans suffer from a sleep disorder. For a randomly selected sample of 20 people, find each probability:

   a. That at least 2 people have a sleep disorder 0.93
   b. That one or 2 people have a sleep disorder 0.195
   c. That exactly 3 people have a sleep disorder 0.205

   Source: NIH

8. **Multiple-Choice Exam** A student takes a 20-question, multiple-choice exam with five choices for each question and guesses on each question. Find the probability of guessing at least 15 out of 20 correctly. Would you consider this event likely or unlikely to occur? Explain your answer. 0.000; the probability is extremely small; this event is unlikely to occur

9. **High Blood Pressure** Twenty percent of Americans ages 25 to 74 have high blood pressure. If 16 randomly selected Americans ages 25 to 74 are selected, find each probability.

   a. None will have high blood pressure. 0.028
   b. One-half will have high blood pressure. 0.006
   c. Exactly 4 will have high blood pressure. 0.200

   Source: www.factfinder.census.gov

10. **Travel Opportunities** A survey found that 25% of people who work globally accepted their jobs because of the travel opportunities that the job offered. If a randomly selected sample of 10 people who work globally was selected, find each probability:

    a. No more than 2 people accepted their jobs because of the travel opportunities. 0.526
    b. At least 3 people selected their jobs because of the travel opportunities. 0.474
    c. Exactly one person selected the job because of the travel opportunities. 0.188

11. **Advertising** Three out of four people think most advertising seeks to persuade people to buy things they don't need or can't afford. Find the probability that exactly 5 out of 9 randomly selected people will agree with this statement. 0.117

    Source: Opinion Research Corporation.

12. **Language Spoken at Home by the U.S. Population** In a recent year the percentage of the U.S. population that speak English only in the home is 78.1%. Choose 15 U.S. people at random. What is the probability that exactly one-third of them speak English only? At least one-third? What is the probability that at least 9 do not speak English in the home? 0.000, 1.000, 0.002

    Source: World Almanac

13. **Prison Inmates** Forty percent of prison inmates were unemployed when they entered prison. If 5 inmates are randomly selected, find these probabilities:

    a. Exactly 3 were unemployed. 0.230
    b. At most 4 were unemployed. 0.990
    c. At least 3 were unemployed. 0.317
    d. Fewer than 2 were unemployed. 0.337

    Source: U.S. Department of Justice.

14. **Swimming Pool Services** A survey found that 4 in 10 private swimming pool owners employ a pool service to care for their swimming pools. Find each probability for a sample of ten people:

    a. Exactly 6 homeowners employ a pool service. 0.198
    b. At least 8 homeowners employ a pool service. 0.285
    c. Fewer than 4 homeowners employ a pool service. 0.065

15. **People Who Have Some College Education** Fifty-three percent of all persons in the U.S. population have at least some college education. Choose 10 persons at random. Find the probability that

    a. Exactly one-half have some college education. 0.242
    b. At least 5 do not have any college education. 0.547
    c. Fewer than 5 have some college education. 0.306

    Source: New York Times Almanac.

16. **School Violence** A survey found that 10% of problems in schools were caused by violent actions of students. If

a randomly selected sample of 9 school problems were selected, find the probability that

a. Exactly 5 were problems caused by violent actions 0.001

b. At least 3 were problems caused by violent actions 0.053

c. More than 2 were caused by violent actions 0.225

17. Find the mean, variance, and standard deviation for each of the values of n and p when the conditions for the binomial distribution are met.

a. $n = 200, p = 0.6$ 120; 48; 6.928

b. $n = 40, p = 0.2$ 8; 6.4; 2.53

c. $n = 24, p = 0.4$ 9.6; 5.76; 2.4

d. $n = 50, p = 0.5$ 25; 12.5; 3.54

18. Find the mean, variance, and standard deviation for each of the values of n and p when the conditions for the binomial distributions are met.

a. $n = 36, p = 0.5$ 18; 9; 3

b. $n = 500, p = 0.7$ 350; 105; 10.247

c. $n = 60, p = 0.3$ 18; 12.6; 3.55

d. $n = 10, p = 0.8$ 8; 1.6; 1.265

19. **Prison Inmates** A survey found that 24% of inmates in state prisons live in units with 50 or more inmates. If a sample of 500 inmates is randomly selected, find the mean, variance, and standard deviation of the distribution of inmates who live in units with 50 or more inmates. 120; 91.2; 9.55

Source: U.S. Department of Justice

20. **Tossing Coins** Find the mean, variance, and standard deviation for the number of heads when 20 coins are tossed. 10; 5; 2.236

21. **American and Foreign-Born Citizens** In a recent year the percentage of the U.S. population who was foreign-born was 13.5. Choose 60 U.S. residents at random. How many would you expect to be American-born? Find the mean, variance, and standard deviation for the number who are foreign-born. 51.9; 8.1; 7.0; 2.6

Source: World Almanac 2012.

22. **Vacation Planning** About $\frac{1}{3}$ of potential vacationers have delayed or cancelled a trip because of the stress of planning. If 200 potential vacation planners are randomly selected, find the mean, variance, and standard deviation of those who have delayed or cancelled a trip because of the stress of planning. 66.67; 44.444; 6.667

23. **Watching Fireworks** A survey found that 21% of Americans watch fireworks on television on July 4. Find the mean, variance, and standard deviation of the number of individuals who watch fireworks on television on July 4 if a random sample of 1000 Americans is selected.

Source: USA Snapshot, USA TODAY. 210; 165.9; 12.9

24. **Alternate Sources of Fuel** Eighty-five percent of Americans favor spending government money to develop alternative sources of fuel for automobiles. For

a random sample of 120 Americans, find the mean, variance, and standard deviation for the number who favor government spending for alternative fuels.

Source: www.pollingreport.com 102; 15.3; 3.9

25. **Survey on Bathing Pets** A survey found that 25% of pet owners had their pets bathed professionally rather than do it themselves. If 18 pet owners are randomly selected, find the probability that exactly 5 people have their pets bathed professionally. 0.199

Source: USA Snapshot, USA TODAY.

26. **Children's Behavior** A survey of teachers found that 81% of U.S. teachers stated that children's behaviors change positively after recess. If 10 teachers are selected at random, find the probability that exactly 6 will feel that children's behaviors change positively after recess. 0.077

Source: International Play Equipment Manufacturers Association Survey

27. **Poverty and the Federal Government** One out of every three Americans believes that the U.S. government should take "primary responsibility" for eliminating poverty in the United States. If 10 Americans are selected, find the probability that at most 3 will believe that the U.S. government should take primary responsibility for eliminating poverty. 0.559

Source: Harper's Index.

28. **Internet Purchases** Thirty-two percent of all computer purchases are online. For a random sample of 200 computer purchases, find the mean, variance, and standard deviation for the number who have purchased a computer online. 64; 43.5; 6.6

Source: www.infoplease.com

29. **Runaways** Fifty-eight percent of runaways in the United States are female. In 20 runaways are selected at random, find the probability that exactly 14 are female. 0.104

Source: U.S. Department of Justice.

30. **Job Elimination** In a recent year, 13% of businesses have eliminated jobs. If 5 businesses are selected at random, find the probability that at least 3 have eliminated jobs during that year. 0.018

Source: USA TODAY.

31. **Popping Bubble Wrap** A survey of randomly selected Americans by Clorox found that 44% of them found popping bubble wrap a satisfying behavior. If 8 adults are randomly selected, find the probability that 4 or 5 adults will find popping bubble wrap a satisfying behavior. 0.42

32. Is this a binomial distribution? Explain.

X	0	1	2	3
$P(X)$	0.064	0.288	0.432	0.216

Extending the Concepts

33. Children in a Family The graph shown here represents the probability distribution for the number of girls in a family of three children. From this graph, construct a probability distribution.

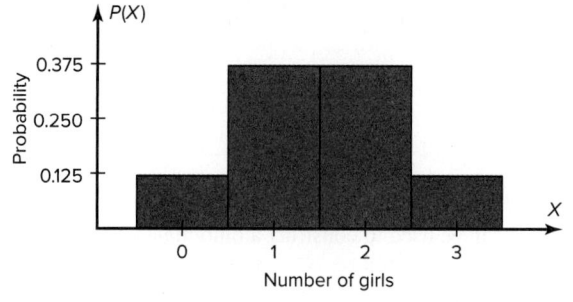

34. Construct a binomial distribution graph for the number of defective computer chips in a lot of 4 if $p = 0.3$.

35. Show that the mean for a binomial random variable X with $n = 3$ is $3p$.

Technology | Step by Step

TI-84 Plus

Step by Step

Binomial Random Variables

To find the probability for a binomial variable:
Press **2nd [DISTR]** then **A (ALPHA MATH)** for binompdf.
The form is binompdf(n,p,X). On some calculators, you will have a menu showing "trials" (n), "p", and x-value (X). After inputting the values, you will select **PASTE** and press **ENTER**. This will then show binompdf(n,p,X) for the values you entered.

Example: $n = 20$, $X = 5$, $p = .05$ (Example 5–20a from the text)
binompdf(20,.05,5), then press **ENTER** for the probability.

Example: $n = 20$, $X = 0, 1, 2, 3$, $p = .05$ (Example 5–20b from the text).
binompdf(20,.05,{0,1,2,3}), then press **ENTER.**
The calculator will display the probabilities in a list. Use the arrow keys to view the entire display.

```
binompdf(20,.05,
5)
      .002244646
```

```
binompdf(20,.05,
{0,1,2,3})
{.3584859224 .3…
```

```
binompdf(20,.05,
{0,1,2,3})
…13 .05958221478}
```

```
binomcdf(20,.05,
3)
      .984098474
```

To find the cumulative probability for a binomial random variable:
Press **2nd [DISTR]** then **B (ALPHA APPS)** for binomcdf
The form is binomcdf(n,p,X). This will calculate the cumulative probability for values from 0 to X.

Example: $n = 20$, $X = 0, 1, 2, 3$, $p = .05$ (Example 5–20b from the text)
binomcdf(20,.05,3), then press **ENTER.**

To construct a binomial probability table:

1. Enter the X values (0 through n) into L_1.

2. Move the cursor to the top of the L_2 column so that L_2 is highlighted.

3. Type the command binompdf(n,p,L_1), then press **ENTER.**

Example: $n = 20$, $p = .05$ (Example 5–20 from the text)

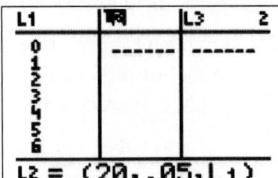
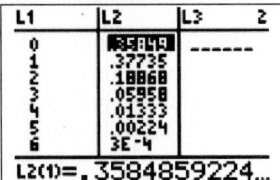

EXCEL
Step by Step

Creating a Binomial Distribution and Graph

These instructions will demonstrate how Excel can be used to construct a binomial distribution table for $n = 20$ and $p = 0.35$.

1. Type **X** for the binomial variable label in cell A1 of an Excel worksheet.

2. Type **P(X)** for the corresponding probabilities in cell B1.

3. Enter the integers from 0 to 20 in column A, starting at cell A2. A fast way to autofill the numbers is to type in 0 to cell A2, type 1 into cell A3, and with your mouse highlight the 0 and 1. Move the cursor to the bottom right corner of cell A3 while the cells are highlighted. The cursor will turn to a black plus sign. Drag with your mouse down to cell A22 and you will see the numbers 2-20 autofill in each cell.

4. To determine the probability corresponding to the first value of the binomial random variable, select cell B2 and type: **=BINOM.DIST(A1,20,.35,FALSE)**. This will give the probability of obtaining 0 successes in 20 trials of a binomial experiment for which the probability of success is 0.35.

5. Repeat step **4,** changing the first parameter, for each of the values of the random variable from column A. Since the cell reference number A1 was used where the $X = 0$ value was stored, you can copy and paste the formula from cell B2 down to cells B3 through B20 and Excel will automatically change the cell reference number to the next row each time. The last few numbers are very small and may appear in scientific notation. You can widen the column or select the comma style under the number menu on the Home tab.

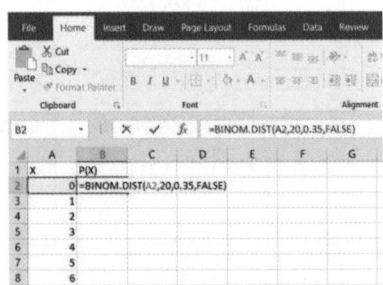

Note: If you wish to obtain the cumulative probabilities for each of the values in column A, you can type: **=BINOM.DIST(A1,20,.35,TRUE)** and repeat for each of the values in column A.

To create the graph:

1. Highlight the probabilities by clicking cell B2 and dragging the mouse down to cell B22. All the cells with probabilities should now be highlighted.

2. Click the *insert* tab from the toolbar and then the button *insert column or bar chart.* (This is the first button on the top row next to recommended charts.)

3. Select the *clustered column* chart (the first column chart under the 2-D Column selections).

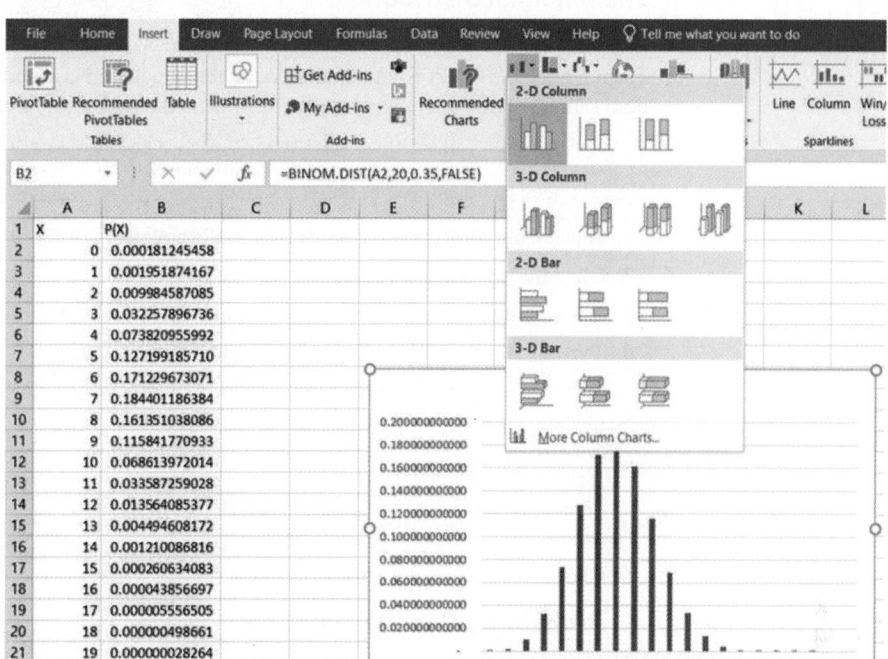

4. You will need to edit the horizontal labels to represent the values of X.

   a) Right click anywhere in the chart and choose *select data*.

   b) Click *Edit* under Horizontal (Category) Axis Labels.

   c) Select the values of X by clicking cell A2 and dragging the mouse down to cell A22. All cells with X values should now be highlighted. Click OK.

   d) Click OK to verify these changes overall.

5. To change the title of the chart:

   a) Left-click once on the current title.

   b) Type a new title for the chart, for example, Binomial Distribution (20, .35, .65).

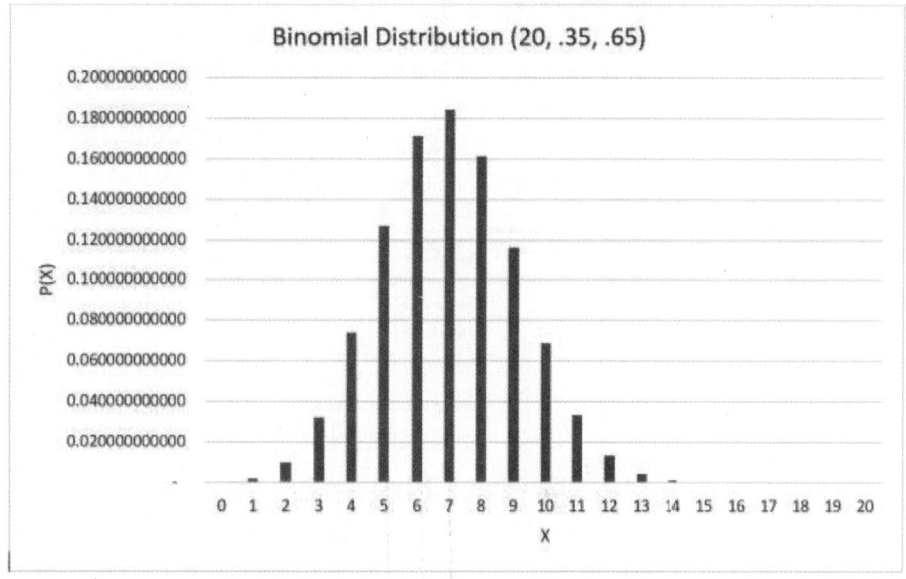

MINITAB

Step by Step

The Binomial Distribution

Calculate a Binomial Probability

From Example 5–20, it is known that 5% of the population is afraid of being alone at night. If a random sample of 20 Americans is selected, what is the probability that exactly 5 of them are afraid?

$$n = 20 \qquad p = 0.05 \ (5\%) \qquad \text{and} \qquad X = 5 \ (5 \text{ out of } 20)$$

No data need to be entered in the worksheet.

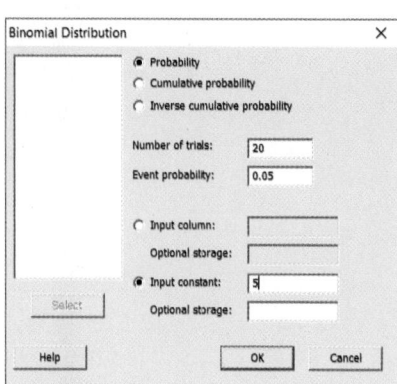

1. Select **Calc>Probability Distributions>Binomial.**
2. Click the option for Probability.
3. Click in the text box for Number of trials:.
4. Type in **20,** then Tab to Event Probability, then type **.05.**
5. Click the option for Input constant, then type in **5.** Leave the text box for Optional storage empty. If the name of a constant such as K1 is entered here, the results are stored but not displayed in the session window.
6. Click [OK]. The results are visible in the session window.

Probability Density Function

```
Binomial with n = 20 and p = 0.05

x   P( X = x )
5   0.0022446
```

Construct a Binomial Distribution

These instructions will use $n = 20$ and $p = 0.05$.

1. Select **Calc>Make Patterned Data>Simple Set of Numbers.**
2. You must enter three items:
    a) Enter **X** in the box for Store patterned data in:. MINITAB will use the first empty column of the active worksheet and name it X.
    b) Press Tab. Enter the value of **0** for the first value. Press Tab.
    c) Enter **20** for the last value. This value should be n. In steps of:, the value should be 1.
3. Click [OK].
4. Select **Calc>Probability Distributions>Binomial.**
5. In the dialog box you must enter five items.
    a) Click the button for Probability.
    b) In the box for Number of trials enter **20.**
    c) Enter **.05** in the Event Probability.

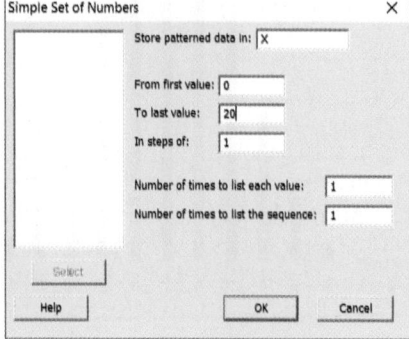
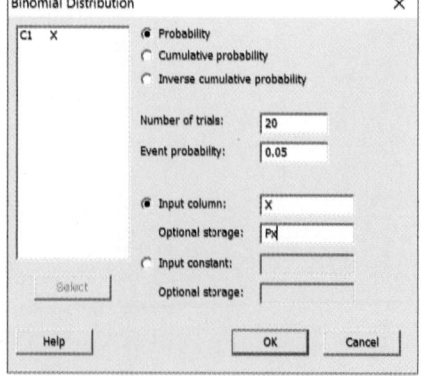

↓	C1	C2
	X	Px
1	0	0.358486
2	1	0.377354
3	2	0.188677
4	3	0.059582
5	4	0.013328
6	5	0.002245
7	6	0.000295
8	7	0.000031
9	8	0.000003
10	9	0.000000
11	10	0.000000
12	11	0.000000
13	12	0.000000
14	13	0.000000
15	14	0.000000
16	15	0.000000
17	16	0.000000
18	17	0.000000
19	18	0.000000
20	19	0.000000
21	20	0.000000

d) Check the button for Input columns, then type the column name, **X,** in the text box.

e) Click in the box for Optional storage, then type **Px.**

6. Click [OK]. The first available column will be named Px, and the calculated probabilities will be stored in it.

To view the completed table, click the worksheet icon on the toolbar .

Graph a Binomial Distribution

The table must be available in the worksheet.

Select **Graph>Scatterplot,** then Simple.

a) Double-click on C2 Px for the Y variable and C1 X for the X variable.

b) Click [Data view], then Project lines, then [OK]. Deselect any other type of display that may be selected in this list.

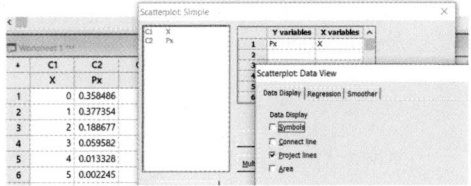

c) Click on [Labels], then Title/Footnotes. Type an appropriate title, such as **Binomial Distribution n = 20, p = .05.**

d) Optional: Click [Scales] then [Gridlines], then check the box for Y major ticks.

e) Click [OK] twice.

The graph will be displayed in a window. Right-click the control box to save, print, or close the graph.

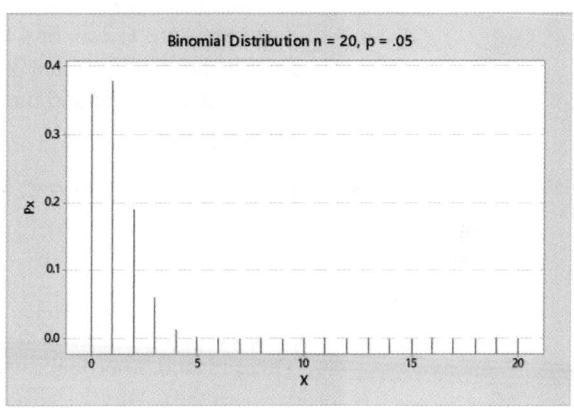

5–4   Other Types of Distributions

In addition to the binomial distribution, other types of distributions are used in statistics. Four of the most commonly used distributions are the multinomial distribution, the Poisson distribution, the hypergeometric distribution, and the geometric distribution. They are described next.

The Multinomial Distribution

Recall that for an experiment to be binomial, two outcomes are required for each trial. But if each trial in an experiment has more than two outcomes, a distribution called the **multinomial distribution** must be used. For example, a survey might require the responses of "approve," "disapprove," or "no opinion." In another situation, a person may have a choice of one of five activities for Friday night, such as a movie, dinner, baseball game, play, or party. Since these situations have more than two possible outcomes for each trial, the binomial distribution cannot be used to compute probabilities.

The multinomial distribution can be used for such situations.

A **multinomial experiment** is a probability experiment that satisfies the following four requirements:

1. There must be a fixed number of trials.
2. Each trial has a specific—but not necessarily the same—number of outcomes.
3. The trials are independent.
4. The probability of a particular outcome remains the same.

Formula for the Multinomial Distribution

If X consists of events $E_1, E_2, E_3, \ldots, E_k$, which have corresponding probabilities $p_1, p_2, p_3, \ldots, p_k$ of occurring, and X_1 is the number of times E_1 will occur, X_2 is the number of times E_2 will occur, X_3 is the number of times E_3 will occur, etc., then the probability that X will occur is

$$P(X) = \frac{n!}{X_1! \cdot X_2! \cdot X_3! \cdots X_k!} \cdot p_1^{X_1} \cdot p_2^{X_2} \cdots p_k^{X_k}$$

where $X_1 + X_2 + X_3 + \cdots + X_k = n$ and $p_1 + p_2 + p_3 + \cdots + p_k = 1$.

EXAMPLE 5–25   Facebook Visits

A random survey of Facebook users found that the probability a user visits the site on a daily basis are 1, 2, 3, or 4 times are 0.4, 0.3, 0.25, and 0.05. If 8 customers are selected, find the probabilities that 3 will visit the site once, 2 will the site two times, 2 will visit the site three times, and one person will visit the site 4 times.

SOLUTION

Let $n = 8$, $X_1 = 3$, $X_2 = 2$, $X_3 = 2$, and $X_4 = 1$; $p_1 = 0.4$, $p_2 = 0.3$, $p_3 = 0.25$, and $p_4 = 0.05$.

$$P(X) = \frac{8!}{3! \cdot 2! \cdot 1! \cdot 1!} \times (0.4)^3 (0.3)^2 (0.25)^2 (0.05)^1 = 3360(0.000018) \approx 0.06.$$

There is an 0.06 probability that the results will occur as described.

Again, note that the multinomial distribution can be used even though replacement is not done, provided that the sample is small in comparison with the population.

EXAMPLE 5–26   Coffee Shop Customers

A small airport coffee shop manager found that the probabilities a customer buys 0, 1, 2, or 3 cups of coffee are 0.3, 0.5, 0.15, and 0.05, respectively. If 8 customers enter the shop, find the probability that 2 will purchase something other than coffee, 4 will purchase 1 cup of coffee, 1 will purchase 2 cups, and 1 will purchase 3 cups.

SOLUTION

Let $n = 8$, $X_1 = 2$, $X_2 = 4$, $X_3 = 1$, and $X_4 = 1$.

$$p_1 = 0.3 \qquad p_2 = 0.5 \qquad p_3 = 0.15 \qquad \text{and} \qquad p_4 = 0.05$$

Then

$$P(X) = \frac{8!}{2!4!1!1!} \cdot (0.3)^2(0.5)^4(0.15)^1(0.05)^1 \approx 0.0354$$

There is a 0.0354 probability that the results will occur as described.

EXAMPLE 5–27 Selecting Colored Balls

A box contains 4 white balls, 3 red balls, and 3 blue balls. A ball is selected at random, and its color is written down. It is replaced each time. Find the probability that if 5 balls are selected, 2 are white, 2 are red, and 1 is blue.

SOLUTION

We know that $n = 5$, $X_1 = 2$, $X_2 = 2$, $X_3 = 1$; $p_1 = \frac{4}{10}$, $p_2 = \frac{3}{10}$, and $p_3 = \frac{3}{10}$; hence,

$$P(X) = \frac{5!}{2!2!1!} \cdot \left(\frac{4}{10}\right)^2\left(\frac{3}{10}\right)^2\left(\frac{3}{10}\right)^1 = \frac{81}{625} = 0.1296$$

There is a 0.1296 probability that the results will occur as described.

Historical Notes

Simeon D. Poisson (1781–1840) formulated the distribution that bears his name. It appears only once in his writings and is only one page long. Mathematicians paid little attention to it until 1907, when a statistician named W. S. Gosset found real applications for it.

Thus, the multinomial distribution is similar to the binomial distribution but has the advantage of allowing you to compute probabilities when there are more than two outcomes for each trial in the experiment. That is, the multinomial distribution is a general distribution, and the binomial distribution is a special case of the multinomial distribution.

The Poisson Distribution

A discrete probability distribution that is useful when n is large and p is small and when the independent variables occur over a period of time is called the **Poisson distribution.** In addition to being used for the stated conditions (that is, n is large, p is small, and the variables occur over a period of time), the Poisson distribution can be used when a density of items is distributed over a given area or volume, such as the number of plants growing per acre or the number of defects in a given length of videotape.

A **Poisson experiment** is a probability experiment that satisfies the following requirements:

1. The random variable X is the number of occurrences of an event over some interval (i.e., length, area, volume, period of time, etc.).
2. The occurrences occur randomly.
3. The occurrences are independent of one another.
4. The average number of occurrences over an interval is known.

Formula for the Poisson Distribution

The probability of X occurrences in an interval of time, volume, area, etc., for a variable where λ (Greek letter lambda) is the mean number of occurrences per unit (time, volume, area, etc.) is

$$P(X; \lambda) = \frac{e^{-\lambda}\lambda^X}{X!} \qquad \text{where } X = 0, 1, 2, \ldots$$

The letter e is a constant approximately equal to 2.7183.

FIGURE 5–4

Using Table A–3

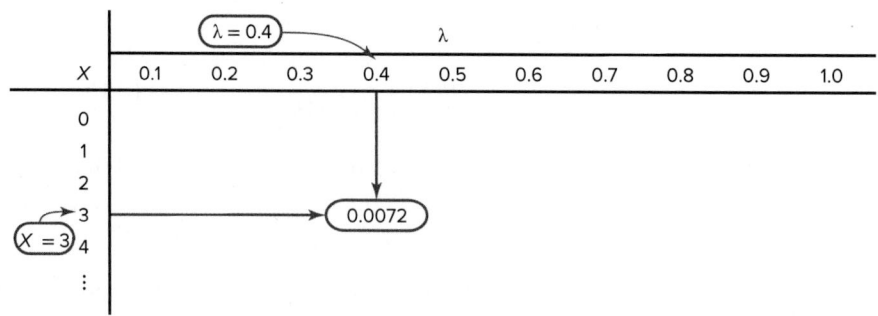

Round the answers to four decimal places.

EXAMPLE 5–28   Typographical Errors

If there are 200 typographical errors randomly distributed in a 500-page manuscript, find the probability that a given page contains exactly 3 errors.

SOLUTION

First, find the mean number λ of errors. Since there are 200 errors distributed over 500 pages, each page has an average of

$$\lambda = \frac{200}{500} = \frac{2}{5} = 0.4$$

or 0.4 error per page. Since $X = 3$, substituting into the formula yields

$$P(X; \lambda) = \frac{e^{-\lambda}\lambda^{X}}{X!} = \frac{(2.7183)^{-0.4}(0.4)^{3}}{3!} \approx 0.0072$$

Thus, there is less than a 1% chance that any given page will contain exactly 3 errors.

Since the mathematics involved in computing Poisson probabilities is somewhat complicated, tables have been compiled for these probabilities. Table A–3 in Appendix A gives P for various values for λ and X.

In Example 5–28, where X is 3 and λ is 0.4, the table gives the value 0.0072 for the probability. See Figure 5–4.

EXAMPLE 5–29   Toll-Free Telephone Calls

A sales firm receives, on average, 3 calls per hour on its toll-free number. For any given hour, find the probability that it will receive the following.

    a. At most 3 calls   *b.* At least 3 calls   *c.* 5 or more calls

SOLUTION

    a. "At most 3 calls" means 0, 1, 2, or 3 calls. Hence,

$$P(0; 3) + P(1; 3) + P(2; 3) + P(3; 3)$$
$$= 0.0498 + 0.1494 + 0.2240 + 0.2240$$
$$= 0.6472$$

b. "At least 3 calls" means 3 or more calls. It is easier to find the probability of 0, 1, and 2 calls and then subtract this answer from 1 to get the probability of at least 3 calls.

$$P(0; 3) + P(1; 3) + P(2; 3) = 0.0498 + 0.1494 + 0.2240 = 0.4232$$

and

$$1 - 0.4232 = 0.5768$$

c. For the probability of 5 or more calls, it is easier to find the probability of getting 0, 1, 2, 3, or 4 calls and subtract this answer from 1. Hence,

$$P(0; 3) + P(1; 3) + P(2; 3) + P(3; 3) + P(4; 3)$$
$$= 0.0498 + 0.1494 + 0.2240 + 0.2240 + 0.1680$$
$$= 0.8152$$

and

$$1 - 0.8152 = 0.1848$$

Thus, for the events described, the part *a* event is most likely to occur, and the part *c* event is least likely to occur.

The Poisson distribution can also be used to approximate the binomial distribution when the expected value $\lambda = n \cdot p$ is less than 5, as shown in Example 5–30. (The same is true when $n \cdot q < 5$.)

EXAMPLE 5–30   Left-Handed People

If approximately 2% of the people in a room of 200 people are left-handed, find the probability that exactly 5 people there are left-handed.

SOLUTION

Since $\lambda = n \cdot p$, then $\lambda = (200)(0.02) = 4$. Hence,

$$P(X; \lambda) = \frac{(2.7183)^{-4}(4)^5}{5!} \approx 0.1563$$

which is verified by the formula $_{200}C_5(0.02)^5(0.98)^{195} \approx 0.1579$. The difference between the two answers is based on the fact that the Poisson distribution is an approximation and rounding has been used.

The Hypergeometric Distribution

When sampling is done *without* replacement, the binomial distribution does not give exact probabilities, since the trials are not independent. The smaller the size of the population, the less accurate the binomial probabilities will be.

For example, suppose a committee of 4 people is to be selected from 7 women and 5 men. What is the probability that the committee will consist of 3 women and 1 man?

To solve this problem, you must find the number of ways a committee of 3 women and 1 man can be selected from 7 women and 5 men. This answer can be found by using combinations; it is

$$_7C_3 \cdot {_5C_1} = 35 \cdot 5 = 175$$

Next, find the total number of ways a committee of 4 people can be selected from 12 people. Again, by the use of combinations, the answer is

$$_{12}C_4 = 495$$

Finally, the probability of getting a committee of 3 women and 1 man from 7 women and 5 men is

$$P(X) = \frac{175}{495} = \frac{35}{99}$$

The results of the problem can be generalized by using a special probability distribution called the hypergeometric distribution. The **hypergeometric distribution** is a distribution of a variable that has two outcomes when sampling is done without replacement.

A **hypergeometric experiment** is a probability experiment that satisfies the following requirements:

1. There are a fixed number of trials.
2. There are two outcomes, and they can be classified as success or failure.
3. The sample is selected without replacement.

The probabilities for the hypergeometric distribution can be calculated by using the formula given next.

Formula for the Hypergeometric Distribution

Given a population with only two types of objects (defective and nondefective, successes and failures, etc.), such that there are a items of one kind and b items of another kind and $a + b$ equals the total population, the probability $P(X)$ of selecting without replacement a sample of size n with X items of type a and $n - X$ items of type b is

$$P(X) = \frac{{}_aC_X \cdot {}_bC_{n-X}}{{}_{a+b}C_n}$$

The basis of the formula is that there are ${}_aC_X$ ways of selecting the first type of items, ${}_bC_{n-X}$ ways of selecting the second type of items, and ${}_{a+b}C_n$ ways of selecting n items from the entire population.

EXAMPLE 5–31   Assistant Manager Applicants

Ten people apply for a job as assistant manager of a restaurant. Five have completed college and five have not. If the manager selects 3 applicants at random, find the probability that all 3 are college graduates.

SOLUTION

Assigning the values to the variables gives

$$a = 5 \text{ college graduates} \qquad n = 3$$
$$b = 5 \text{ nongraduates} \qquad X = 3$$

and $n - X = 0$. Substituting in the formula gives

$$P(X) = \frac{{}_5C_3 \cdot {}_5C_0}{{}_{10}C_3} = \frac{10}{120} = \frac{1}{12} \approx 0.083$$

There is a 0.083 probability that all 3 applicants will be college graduates.

EXAMPLE 5–32   Pudgy Dogs

A recent survey found that 3 out of 10 dog owners said that their dogs were pudgy. If 5 dog owners are randomly selected, find the probability that exactly 2 will say that their dog is pudgy.

SOLUTION

In this example, $a = 3$, $b = 7$, $n = 5$, and $X = 2$.

$$P(X) = \frac{{}_3C_2 \cdot {}_7C_3}{{}_{10}C_5} = \frac{3 \cdot 35}{252} \approx 0.417.$$

There is a 0.417 probability that out of 5 subjects, exactly 2 will say that their dog is pudgy.

In many situations where objects are manufactured and shipped to a company, the company selects a few items and tests them to see whether they are satisfactory or defective. If a certain percentage is defective, the company then can refuse the whole shipment. This procedure saves the time and cost of testing every single item. To make the judgment about whether to accept or reject the whole shipment based on a small sample of tests, the company must know the probability of getting a specific number of defective items. To calculate the probability, the company uses the hypergeometric distribution.

EXAMPLE 5–33   Defective Compressor Tanks

A lot of 12 compressor tanks is checked to see whether there are any defective tanks. Three tanks are checked for leaks. If 1 or more of the 3 is defective, the lot is rejected. Find the probability that the lot will be rejected if there are actually 3 defective tanks in the lot.

SOLUTION

Since the lot is rejected if at least 1 tank is found to be defective, it is necessary to find the probability that none are defective and subtract this probability from 1.

Here, $a = 3$, $b = 9$, $n = 3$, and $X = 0$; so

$$P(X) = \frac{{}_3C_0 \cdot {}_9C_3}{{}_{12}C_3} = \frac{1 \cdot 84}{220} \approx 0.382$$

Hence,

$$P(\text{at least 1 defective}) = 1 - P(\text{no defectives}) = 1 - 0.382 = 0.618$$

There is a 0.618 or 61.8%, probability that the lot will be rejected when 3 of the 12 tanks are defective.

The Geometric Distribution

Another useful distribution is called the *geometric distribution*. This distribution can be used when we have an experiment that has two outcomes and is repeated until a successful outcome is obtained. For example, we could flip a coin until a head is obtained, or we could roll a die until we get a 6. In these cases, our successes would come on the nth trial. The geometric probability distribution tells us when the success is likely to occur.

A **geometric experiment** is a probability experiment if it satisfies the following requirements:

1. Each trial has two outcomes that can be either success or failure.
2. The outcomes are independent of each other.
3. The probability of a success is the same for each trial.
4. The experiment continues until a success is obtained.

Formula for the Geometric Distribution

If p is the probability of a success on each trial of a binomial experiment and n is the number of the trial at which the first success occurs, then the probability of getting the first success on the nth trial is

$$P(n) = p(1 - p)^{n-1}$$

where $n = 1, 2, 3, \ldots$.

EXAMPLE 5–34   Rolling a Die

A die is rolled repeatedly. Find the probability of getting a 6 on the fourth roll.

SOLUTION

To get a 6 on the fourth roll, the first three rolls must be any other number than a 6; hence, the probability is $P(\text{not } 6, \text{not } 6, \text{not } 6, 6)$:

$$\frac{5}{6} \cdot \frac{5}{6} \cdot \frac{5}{6} \cdot \frac{1}{6} = \frac{125}{1296} \approx .096.$$

Next, by using the formula, you get the same results:

$$P(n) = p(1 - p)^{n-1}$$
$$= \frac{1}{6}\left(1 - \frac{1}{6}\right)^{4-1}$$
$$= \frac{1}{6}\left(\frac{5}{6}\right)^3$$
$$= \frac{125}{1296} \approx .096.$$

Hence, the probability of getting the first 6 on the fourth roll is $\frac{125}{1296} \approx .096$.

EXAMPLE 5–35   Blood Types

In the United States, approximately 42% of people have type A blood. If 4 people are selected at random, find the probability that the fourth person is the first one selected with type A blood.

SOLUTION

Let $p = 0.42$ and $n = 4$.

$$P(n) = p(1 - p)^{n-1}$$
$$P(4) = (0.42)(1 - 0.42)^{4-1}$$
$$= (0.42)(0.58)^3$$
$$\approx 0.0819 \approx 0.082$$

There is a 0.082 probability that the fourth person selected will be the first one to have type A blood.

A summary of the discrete distributions used in this chapter is shown in Table 5–1.

TABLE 5–1 Summary of Discrete Distributions

1. Binomial distribution

$$P(X) = {}_nC_X \cdot p^X q^{n-X}$$

$$\mu = n \cdot p \qquad \sigma = \sqrt{n \cdot p \cdot q}$$

It is used when there are only two outcomes for a fixed number of independent trials and the probability for each success remains the same for each trial.

2. Multinomial distribution

$$P(X) = \frac{n!}{X_1! \cdot X_2! \cdot X_3! \cdots X_k!} \cdot p_1^{X_1} \cdot p_2^{X_2} \cdots p_k^{X_k}$$

where

$$X_1 + X_2 + X_3 + \cdots + X_k = n \quad \text{and} \quad p_1 + p_2 + p_3 + \cdots + p_k = 1$$

It is used when the distribution has more than two outcomes, the probabilities for each trial remain constant, outcomes are independent, and there are a fixed number of trials.

3. Poisson distribution

$$P(X; \lambda) = \frac{e^{-\lambda}\lambda^X}{X!} \qquad \text{where } X = 0, 1, 2, \ldots$$

It is used when n is large and p is small, and the independent variable occurs over a period of time, or a density of items is distributed over a given area or volume.

4. Hypergeometric distribution

$$P(X) = \frac{{}_aC_X \cdot {}_bC_{n-X}}{{}_{a+b}C_n}$$

It is used when there are two outcomes and sampling is done without replacement.

5. Geometric distribution

$$P(n) = p(1-p)^{n-1} \qquad \text{where } n = 1, 2, 3, \ldots$$

It is used when there are two outcomes and we are interested in the probability that the first success occurs on the nth trial.

Applying the Concepts 5–4

Rockets and Targets

During the latter days of World War II, the Germans developed flying rocket bombs. These bombs were used to attack London. Allied military intelligence didn't know whether these bombs were fired at random or had a sophisticated aiming device. To determine the answer, they used the Poisson distribution.

To assess the accuracy of these bombs, London was divided into 576 square regions. Each region was $\frac{1}{4}$ square kilometer in area. They then compared the number of actual hits with the theoretical number of hits by using the Poisson distribution. If the values in both distributions were close, then they would conclude that the rockets were fired at random. The actual distribution is as follows:

Hits	0	1	2	3	4	5
Regions	229	211	93	35	7	1

1. Using the Poisson distribution, find the theoretical values for each number of hits. In this case, the number of bombs was 535, and the number of regions was 576. So

$$\lambda = \frac{535}{576} \approx 0.929$$

For 3 hits,

$$P(X) = \frac{e^{-\lambda} \cdot \lambda^X}{X!}$$

$$= \frac{(2.7183)^{-0.929}(0.929)^3}{3!} \approx 0.0528$$

Hence, the number of hits is $(0.0528)(576) = 30.4128$. Complete the table for the other number of hits.

Hits	0	1	2	3	4	5
Regions				30.4		

2. Write a brief statement comparing the two distributions.

3. Based on your answer to question 2, can you conclude that the rockets were fired at random?

See page 308 for the answer.

Exercises 5–4

1. Use the multinomial formula and find the probabilities for each.
   a. $n = 8$, $X_1 = 4$, $X_2 = 3$, $X_3 = 1$, $p_1 = 0.4$, $p_2 = 0.5$, $p_3 = 0.1$ 0.0896
   b. $n = 10$, $X_1 = 3$, $X_2 = 3$, $X_3 = 4$, $p_1 = 0.2$, $p_2 = 0.2$, $p_3 = 0.6$ 0.0348
   c. $n = 7$, $X_1 = 1$, $X_2 = 2$, $X_3 = 4$, $p_1 = 0.3$, $p_2 = 0.2$, $p_3 = 0.5$ 0.0788

2. Use the multinomial formula and find the probabilities for each.
   a. $n = 9$, $X_1 = 4$, $X_2 = 3$, $X_3 = 2$, $p_1 = 0.6$, $p_2 = 0.2$, $p_3 = 0.2$ 0.0523
   b. $n = 6$, $X_1 = 2$, $X_2 = 2$, $X_3 = 2$, $p_1 = 0.4$, $p_2 = 0.2$, $p_3 = 0.4$ 0.09216
   c. $n = 5$, $X_1 = 1$, $X_2 = 1$, $X_3 = 3$, $p_1 = 0.2$, $p_2 = 0.5$, $p_3 = 0.3$ 0.054

3. **M&M's Color Distribution** According to the manufacturer, M&M's are produced and distributed in the following proportions: 13% brown, 13% red, 14% yellow, 16% green, 20% orange, and 24% blue. In a random sample of 12 M&M's, what is the probability of having 2 of each color? 0.0025

4. **Dinner Beverage** According to a leading restaurant, 40% of patrons drink coffee with their dinner, 23% drink tea, 18% drink milk, and 19% drink water. In a random sample of 10 individuals, what is the probability that 6 will drink coffee, 2 will drink tea, 1 will drink milk, and 1 will drink water? 0.0187

5. **Drug Prescriptions** The probability that a person has 1, 2, 3, or 4 prescriptions when they enter a pharmacy is 0.5, 0.3, 0.15, or 0.05. For a sample of 10 people who enter the pharmacy, find the probability that 3 will have one prescription filled, 3 will have two prescriptions filled, 2 will have three prescriptions filled, and 2 will have four prescriptions filled. 0.0048

6. **Mendel's Theory** According to Mendel's theory, if tall and colorful plants are crossed with short and colorless plants, the corresponding probabilities are $\frac{9}{16}$, $\frac{3}{16}$, $\frac{3}{16}$, and $\frac{1}{16}$ for tall and colorful, tall and colorless, short and colorful, and short and colorless, respectively. If 8 plants are selected, find the probability that 1 will be tall and colorful, 3 will be tall and colorless, 3 will be short and colorful, and 1 will be short and colorless. 0.002

7. Find each probability $P(X; \lambda)$, using Table A–3 in Appendix A.
   a. $P(6; 4)$ 0.1042
   b. $P(3; 5)$ 0.1404
   c. $P(4; 2)$ 0.0902

8. Find each probability $P(X; \lambda)$ using Table A–3 in Appendix A.
   a. $P(9; 7)$ 0.1014
   b. $P(10; 6)$ 0.0413
   c. $P(2; 5)$ 0.0842

9. **Study of Robberies** A recent study of robberies for a certain geographic region showed an average of 1 robbery per 20,000 people. In a city of 80,000 people, find the probability of the following.
   a. 0 robberies 0.0183
   b. 1 robbery 0.0733
   c. 2 robberies 0.1465
   d. 3 or more robberies 0.7619

10. Households Touched by Crime Twenty percent of households are touched by crime each year. In a random sample of 100 households, find the probability that 15 were touched by crime in the last year. Use the Poisson approximation. 0.0516

Source: U.S. Department of Justice

11. A real estate agency sells, on average, 4 homes a day. Find the probability that the agency will sell exactly 19 homes in a 7-day week. 0.0178

12. Online Ordering A company receives an average of 5 orders per 500 solicitations. If the company sends out 100 advertisements, find the probability that the company receives at least 2 orders. 0.2642

13. Company Mailing Of a company's mailings, an average of 3 items are returned because of incorrect or incomplete addresses. In a mailing of 200 pieces, find the probability that none will be returned. 0.0498

14. Emission Inspection Failures On average, 2.7 cars fail the emissions inspection every day. Find the probability that exactly 3 will fail in a day. 0.2205

15. Phone Inquiries The average number of phone inquiries per day at the poison control center is 4. Find the probability it will receive 5 calls on a given day. Use the Poisson distribution. 0.1563

16. Defective Calculators In a batch of 2000 calculators, there are, on average, 8 defective ones. If a random sample of 150 is selected, find the probability of 5 defective ones. 0.0004

17. School Newspaper Staff A school newspaper staff is comprised of 5 seniors and 4 juniors. If 2 staff members are chosen at random for a publicity photo, what is the probability that there will be 1 student from each class? 0.556

18. Missing Pages from Books A bookstore owner examines 5 books from each lot of 25 to check for missing pages. If he finds at least 2 books with missing pages, the entire lot is returned. If, indeed, there are 5 books with missing pages, find the probability that the lot will be returned. 0.252

19. Job Applicants Twelve people apply for a teaching position in mathematics at a local college. Six have a Ph.D. and six have a master's degree. If the department chairperson selects three applicants at random for an interview, find the probability that all three have a Ph.D. 0.0909

20. Defective Computer Keyboards A shipment of 24 computer keyboards is rejected if 4 are checked for defects and at least 1 is found to be defective. Find the probability that the shipment will be returned if there are actually 6 defective keyboards. 0.712

21. Defective Electronics A shipment of 24 smartphones is rejected if 3 are checked for defects and at least 1 is found to be defective. Find the probability that the shipment will be returned if there are actually 6 smartphones that are defective. 0.597

22. Job Applications Ten people apply for a job at Computer Warehouse. Five are college graduates and five are not. If the manager selects 3 applicants at random, find the probability that all 3 are college graduates. $\frac{1}{12} \approx 0.083$

23. Auto Repair Insurance A dealership calls people to ask if they would like to extend their automobile insurance beyond the normal 3 years. The probability that the respondent says yes is about 33%. If the dealership calls 12 people, find the probability that the first person to say yes will occur with the fourth customer. 0.099

24. Winning a Prize A soda pop manufacturer runs a contest and places a winning bottle cap on every sixth bottle. If a person buys the soda pop, find the probability that the person will (*a*) win on the first purchase, (*b*) win on the third purchase, or (*c*) not win on any of the first five purchases. $\frac{1}{6}$; $\frac{25}{216}$; $\left(\frac{5}{6}\right)^5 \approx 0.402$

25. Throwing Darts A person throws darts at a target and hits the bull's eye center circle 30% of the time. Find the probability that the person will hit the bull's eye on the second throw. 0.21

26. Amusement Park Game At an amusement park basketball game, the player gets 3 throws for $1. If a player makes a basket, the player wins a prize. One person makes about 80% of the shots. Find the probability that this person wins a prize on the third shot. 0.032

Extending the Concepts

Another type of problem that can be solved uses what is called the *negative binomial distribution,* which is a generalization of the binomial distribution. In this case, it tells the average number of trials needed to get k successes of a binomial experiment. The formula is

$$\mu = \frac{k}{p}$$

where k = the number of successes

p = the probability of a success

Use this formula for Exercises 27–30.

27. Drawing Cards A card is randomly drawn from a deck of cards and then replaced. The process continues until 3 clubs are obtained. Find the average number of trials needed to get 3 clubs. 12

28. Rolling an 8-Sided Die An 8-sided die is rolled. The sides are numbered 1 through 8. Find the average number of rolls it takes to get two 5s. 16

29. Drawing Cards Cards are drawn at random from a deck and replaced after each draw. Find the average number of cards that would be drawn to get 4 face cards. 17.33 or 18

30. Blood Type About 4% of the citizens of the United States have type AB blood. If an agency needed type AB blood and donors came in at random, find the average number of donors that would be needed to get a person with type AB blood. 25

The mean of a geometric distribution is $\mu = 1/p$, and the standard deviation is $\sigma = \sqrt{q/p^2}$, where $p =$ the probability of the outcome and $q = 1 - p$. Use these formulas for Exercises 31–34.

31. Shower or Bath Preferences It is estimated that 4 out of 5 men prefer showers to baths. Find the mean and standard deviation for the distribution of men who prefer showers to baths. 1.25; 0.559

32. Lessons Outside of School About 2 out of every 3 children take some kind of lessons outside of school. These lessons include music, art, and sports. Find the mean and standard deviation of the distribution of the number of children who take lessons outside of school. 1.5; 0.866

33. Teachers and Summer Vacations One in five teachers stated that they became a teacher because of the long summer vacations. Find the mean and standard deviation for the distribution of teachers who say they became teachers because of the long summer vacation. 5; 4.472

34. Work versus Conscience One in four American workers admit they do some things at work that go against their consciences. Find the mean and standard deviation for the distribution of workers who admit to having to do some things at work that go against their consciences. 4; 3.464

≡ Technology | Step by Step

TI-84 Plus

Step by Step

Poisson Distribution

To find the probability for a Poisson random variable:
Press **2nd [DISTR]** then arrow down to **poissonpdf**, select **ENTER**.

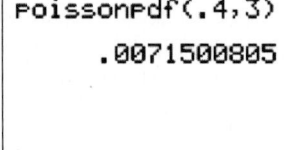

Note the form is different from that used in text, $P(X; \lambda)$. And on some calculators (as with binomial cdf and pdf) you will be presented with a menu for inputting X and λ.

Example: $\lambda = 0.4$, $X = 3$ (Example 5–28 from the text)
poissonpdf(.4, 3)

Example: $\lambda = 3$, $X = 0, 1, 2, 3$ (Example 5–29a from the text)
poissonpdf (3, {0, 1, 2, 3})

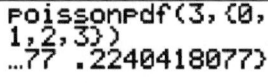

The calculator will display the probabilities in a list. Use the arrow keys to view the entire display.

To find the cumulative probability for a Poisson random variable:
Press **2nd [DISTR]** then arrow down to **poissoncdf**, select **ENTER**.
The form is poissoncdf(λ, X). This will calculate the cumulative probability for values from 0 to X.

Example: $\lambda = 3$, $X = 0, 1, 2, 3$ (Example 5–29a from the text)
poissoncdf(3, 3)

To construct a Poisson probability table:

1. Enter the X values 0 through a large possible value of X into L₁.

2. Move the cursor to the top of the L₂ column so that L₂ is highlighted.

3. Enter the command poissonpdf (λ, L₁) then press **ENTER**.

Example: $\lambda = 3$, $X = 0, 1, 2, 3, \ldots, 10$ (Example 5–29 from the text)

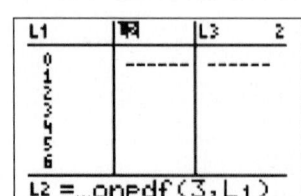

EXCEL

Step by Step

Excel can be used to calculate probabilities (and cumulative probabilities). The built-in discrete probability distribution functions available in Excel include the hypergeometric, Poisson, and geometric.

Calculating a Hypergeometric Probability

We will use Excel to calculate the probability from Example 5–32.

In this example, $a = 2$, $b = 7$, $n = 5$, and $X = 2$.

1. Select the Insert Function icon fx from the Toolbar.
2. Select the Statistical function category from the list of available categories.
3. Select the HYPGEOM.DIST function from the function list. The Function Arguments dialog box will appear.
4. Type 2 for Sample_s, the number of successes in the sample.
5. Type 5 for Number_sample, the size of the sample.
6. Type 3 for Population_s, the number of successes in the population.
7. Type 10 for Number_pop, the size of the population.
8. Type 0 or FALSE for Cumulative, since the probability to be calculated is for a single event.
9. Click OK.

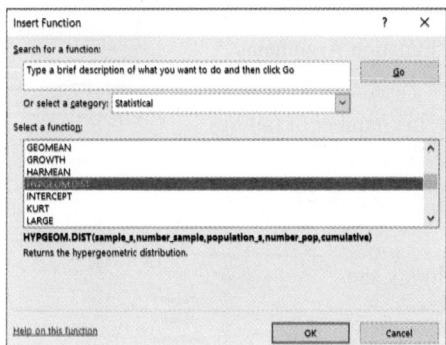
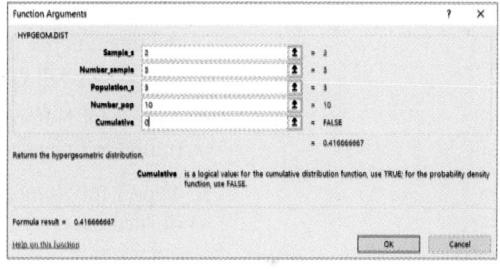

Note: If you are calculating a cumulative probability, you should type 1 or TRUE for Cumulative.

Calculating a Poisson Probability

We will use Excel to calculate the probability from Example 5–28, where X is 3 and λ is 0.4.

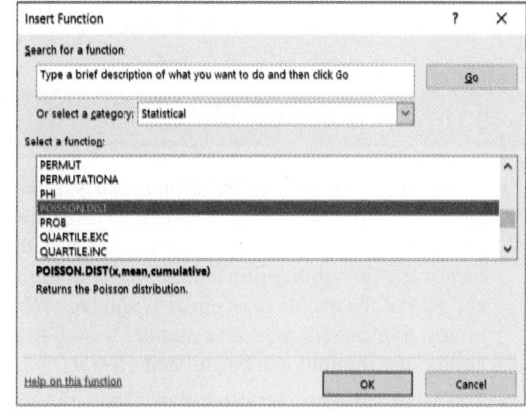

1. Select the Insert Function Icon fx from the Toolbar.
2. Select the Statistical function category from the list of available categories.
3. Select the POISSON.DIST function from the function list. The Function Arguments dialog box will appear.
4. Type 3 for X, the number of occurrences.
5. Type 0.4 for the Mean.
6. Type FALSE for Cumulative, since the probability to be calculated is for a single event.

7. Click OK.

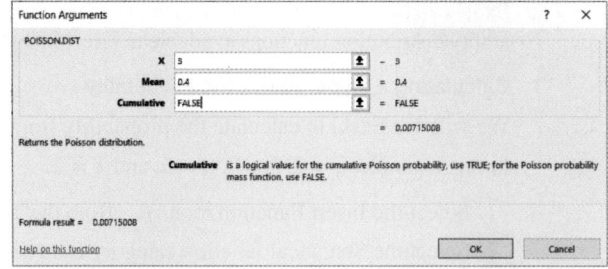

Calculating a Geometric Probability

We will use Excel to calculate the probability from Example 5–35, where *X* is 3 and *p* is 0.42.

Note: Excel does not have a built-in Geometric Probability Distribution function. We must use the built-in Negative Binomial Distribution function—which gives the probability that there will be a certain number of failures until a certain number of successes occur—to calculate probabilities for the Geometric Distribution. The Geometric Distribution is a special case of the Negative Binomial for which the threshold number of successes is 1.

1. Select the Insert Function Icon fx from the Toolbar.

2. Select the Statistical function category from the list of available categories.

3. Select the NEGBINOM.DIST function from the function list. The Function Arguments dialog box will appear.

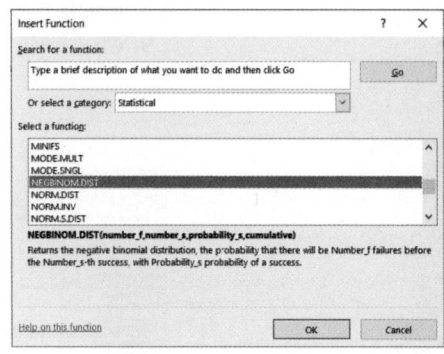

4. Type 3 for Number_f, the number of failures (until the first success).

5. Type 1 for Number_s, the threshold number of successes.

6. Type .42 for Probability_s, the probability of a success.

7. Type FALSE for cumulative.

8. Click OK.

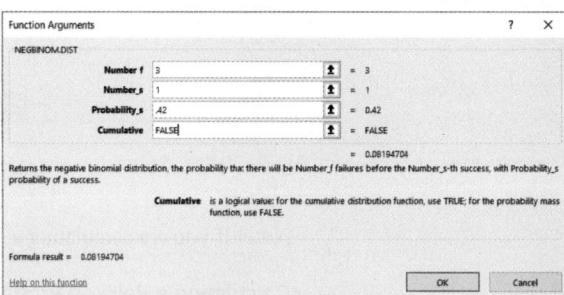

Summary

- A discrete probability distribution consists of the values a random variable can assume and the corresponding probabilities of these values. There are two requirements of a probability distribution: the sum of the probabilities of the events must equal 1, and the probability of any single event must be a number from 0 to 1. Probability distributions can be graphed. (5–1)

- The mean, variance, and standard deviation of a probability distribution can be found. The expected value of a discrete random variable of a probability distribution can also be found. This is basically a measure of the average. (5–2)

- A binomial experiment has four requirements. There must be a fixed number of trials. Each trial can have only two outcomes. The outcomes are independent of each other, and the probability of a success must remain the same for each trial. The probabilities of the outcomes can be found by using the binomial formula or the binomial table. (5–3)

- In addition to the binomial distribution, there are some other commonly used probability distributions. They are the multinomial distribution, the Poisson distribution, the hypergeometric distribution, and the geometric distribution. (5–4)

≣ Important Terms

binomial distribution 276	geometric distribution 295	hypergeometric experiment 294	Poisson distribution 291
binomial experiment 275	geometric experiment 296	multinomial distribution 289	Poisson experiment 291
discrete probability distribution 259	hypergeometric distribution 294	multinomial experiment 290	random variable 258
expected value 269			

≣ Important Formulas

Formula for the mean of a probability distribution:

$$\mu = \Sigma X \cdot P(X)$$

Formulas for the variance and standard deviation of a probability distribution:

$$\sigma^2 = \Sigma[X^2 \cdot P(X)] - \mu^2$$

$$\sigma = \sqrt{\Sigma[X^2 \cdot P(X)] - \mu^2}$$

Formula for expected value:

$$E(X) = \Sigma X \cdot P(X)$$

Binomial probability formula:

$$P(X) = \frac{n!}{(n-X)!X!} \cdot p^X \cdot q^{n-X} \text{ where } X = 0, 1, 2, 3, \ldots, n$$

Formula for the mean of the binomial distribution:

$$\mu = n \cdot p$$

Formulas for the variance and standard deviation of the binomial distribution:

$$\sigma^2 = n \cdot p \cdot q \qquad \sigma = \sqrt{n \cdot p \cdot q}$$

Formula for the multinomial distribution:

$$P(X) = \frac{n!}{X_1! \cdot X_2! \cdot X_3! \cdots X_k!} \cdot p_1^{X_1} \cdot p_2^{X_2} \cdots p_k^{X_k}$$

(The X's sum to n and the p's sum to 1.)

Formula for the Poisson distribution:

$$P(X; \lambda) = \frac{e^{-\lambda}\lambda^X}{X!} \qquad \text{where } X = 0, 1, 2, \ldots$$

Formula for the hypergeometric distribution:

$$P(X) = \frac{{}_aC_X \cdot {}_bC_{n-X}}{{}_{a+b}C_n}$$

Formula for the geometric distribution:

$$P(n) = p(1-p)^{n-1} \qquad \text{where } n = 1, 2, 3, \ldots$$

≣ Review Exercises

Section 5–1

For Exercises 1 through 3, determine whether the distribution represents a probability distribution. If it does not, state why.

1.

X	1	2	3	4	5	
P(X)	$\frac{1}{10}$	$\frac{3}{10}$	$\frac{1}{10}$	$\frac{2}{10}$	$\frac{3}{10}$	Yes

2.

X	5	10	15	No. The sum of the
P(X)	0.3	0.4	0.1	probabilities does not equal 1.

3.

X	1	4	9	16	No. The sum of the
P(X)	$\frac{3}{8}$	$\frac{1}{4}$	$\frac{1}{8}$	$\frac{1}{2}$	probabilities is greater than 1.

4. Emergency Calls The number of emergency calls that a local police department receives per 24-hour period is distributed as shown here. Construct a graph for the data.

Number of calls X	10	11	12	13	14
Probability P(X)	0.02	0.12	0.40	0.31	0.15

5. Credit Cards A large retail company encourages its employees to get customers to apply for the store credit card.

Below is the distribution for the number of credit card applications received per employee for an 8-hour shift.

X	0	1	2	3	4	5
P(X)	0.27	0.28	0.20	0.15	0.08	0.02

a. What is the probability that an employee will get 2 or 3 applications during any given shift? 0.35

b. Find the mean, variance, and standard deviation for this probability distribution. 1.55; 1.808; 1.344

6. Coins in a Box A box contains 5 pennies, 3 dimes, 1 quarter, and 1 half-dollar. A coin is drawn at random. Construct a probability distribution and draw a graph for the data.

7. Shoe Purchases At Shoe World, the manager finds the probability that a woman will buy 1, 2, 3, or 4 pairs of shoes is shown. Construct a graph for the distribution.

Number X	1	2	3	4
Probability P(X)	0.63	0.27	0.08	0.02

Section 5–2

8. Customers in a Bank A bank has a drive-through service. The number of customers arriving during a 15-minute period is distributed as shown. Find the mean, variance, and standard deviation for the distribution. 2.1; 1.4; 1.2

Number of customers X	0	1	2	3	4
Probability $P(X)$	0.12	0.20	0.31	0.25	0.12

9. Arrivals at an Airport At a small rural airport, the number of arrivals per hour during the day has the distribution shown. Find the mean, variance, and standard deviation for the data. 7.2; 2.2; 1.5

Number X	5	6	7	8	9	10
Probability $P(X)$	0.14	0.21	0.24	0.18	0.16	0.07

10. Cans of Paint Purchased During a recent paint sale at Corner Hardware, the number of cans of paint purchased was distributed as shown. Find the mean, variance, and standard deviation of the distribution. 2.1; 1.5; 1.2

Number of cans X	1	2	3	4	5
Probability $P(X)$	0.42	0.27	0.15	0.10	0.06

11. Phone Customers A phone service center keeps track of the number of customers it services for a random 1-hour period during the day. The distribution is shown.

Number of calls X	0	1	2	3	4
$P(X)$	0.15	0.43	0.32	0.06	0.04

Find the mean, variance, and standard deviation for the data. Based on the results of the data, how many service representatives should the store employ? 1.4; 0.9; 0.95. Two people at most should be employed.

12. Outdoor Regatta A producer plans an outdoor regatta for May 3. The cost of the regatta is $8000. This includes advertising, security, printing tickets, entertainment, etc. The producer plans to make $15,000 profit if all goes well. However, if it rains, the regatta will have to be canceled. According to the weather report, the probability of rain is 0.3. Find the producer's expected profit. $8100

13. Card Game A game is set up as follows: All the diamonds are removed from a deck of cards, and these 13 cards are placed in a bag. The cards are mixed up, and then one card is chosen at random (and then replaced). The player wins according to the following rules.

If the ace is drawn, the player loses $20.
If a face card is drawn, the player wins $10.
If any other card (2–10) is drawn, the player wins $2.

How much should be charged to play this game in order for it to be fair? $2.15

14. Card Game Using Exercise 13, how much should be charged if instead of winning $2 for drawing a 2–10, the player wins the amount shown on the card in dollars? $4.92

Section 5–3

15. Let x be a binomial random variable with $n = 12$ and $p = 0.3$. Find the following:

a. $P(X = 8)$ 0.008
b. $P(X < 5)$ 0.724
c. $P(X \geq 10)$ 0.0002
d. $P(4 < X \leq 9)$ 0.276

16. Internet Access via Cell Phone In a retirement community, 14% of cell phone users use their cell phones to access the Internet. In a random sample of 10 cell phone users, what is the probability that exactly 2 have used their phones to access the Internet? More than 2? 0.264; 0.155

17. Self-Driving Automobile Fifty-eight percent of people surveyed said that they would take a ride in a fully self-driving automobile. Find the mean, variance, and standard deviation of the number of people who would agree to ride in the self-driving automobile if 250 people were asked. 145; 60.9; 7.8

Source: World Economic Forum and Boston Consulting Group Survey.

18. Flu Shots It has been reported that 63% of adults aged 65 and over got their flu shots last year. In a random sample of 300 adults aged 65 and over, find the mean, variance, and standard deviation for the number who got their flu shots. 189; 69.9; 8.4

Source: U.S. Centers for Disease Control and Prevention.

19. U.S. Police Chiefs and the Death Penalty The chance that a U.S. police chief believes the death penalty "significantly reduces the number of homicides" is 1 in 4. If a random sample of 8 police chiefs is selected, find the probability that at most 3 believe that the death penalty significantly reduces the number of homicides. 0.886

Source: Harper's Index.

20. Household Wood Burning *American Energy Review* reported that 27% of American households burn wood. If a random sample of 500 American households is selected, find the mean, variance, and standard deviation of the number of households that burn wood. 135; 98.6; 9.9

Source: 100% American by Daniel Evan Weiss.

21. Pizza for Breakfast Three out of four American adults under age 35 have eaten pizza for breakfast. If a random sample of 20 adults under age 35 is selected, find the probability that exactly 16 have eaten pizza for breakfast. 0.190

Source: Harper's Index.

22. Unmarried Women According to survey records, 75.4% of women aged 20–24 have never been married. In a random sample of 250 young women aged 20–24, find the mean, variance, and standard deviation for the number who are or who have been married. 61.5; 46.4; 6.8

Source: www.infoplease.com

Section 5–4

23. Accuracy Count of Votes After a recent national election, voters were asked how confident they were that votes in their state would be counted accurately. The results are shown below.

46% Very confident   41% Somewhat confident
9% Not very confident   4% Not at all confident

If 10 voters are selected at random, find the probability that 5 would be very confident, 3 somewhat confident, 1 not very confident, and 1 not at all confident. 0.026

Source: New York Times.

24. Defective USB Flash Drives Before a USB flash drive leaves the factory, it is given a quality control check. The probabilities that a USB flash drive contains 0, 1, or 2 defects are 0.90, 0.06, and 0.04, respectively. In a sample of 12 USB flash drives, find the probability that 8 have 0 defects, 3 have 1 defect, and 1 has 2 defects. 0.007

25. Accounting Errors The probability that an accounting company will make 0, 1, 2, or 3 errors in preparing a yearly budget for a small company is 0.50, 0.28, 0.15, and 0.07 respectively. If 20 companies have the firm prepare their budgets, find the probability that 9 will contain 0 errors, 6 will contain one error, 3 will contain 2 errors, and 2 will contain 3 errors. 0.012

26. Lost Luggage in Airlines Transportation officials reported that on average 8.25 out of every 1000 airline passengers lost luggage during their travels last year. If we randomly select 400 airline passengers, what is the probability that 5 lost some luggage? 0.120

Source: U.S. Department of Transportation.

27. Computer Assistance Computer Help Hot Line receives, on average, 6 calls per hour asking for assistance. The distribution is Poisson. For any randomly selected hour, find the probability that the company will receive

a. At least 6 calls 0.5543
b. 4 or more calls 0.8488
c. At most 5 calls 0.4457

28. Boating Accidents The number of boating accidents on Lake Emilie follows a Poisson distribution. The average number of boating accidents per week is 3. Find the probability that there will be 6 accidents on the lake in a week. 0.0504

29. Drawing Cards If 5 cards are drawn from a deck, find the probability that 2 will be hearts. 0.274

30. Car Sales Of the 50 automobiles in a used-car lot, 10 are white. If 5 automobiles are selected to be sold at an auction, find the probability that exactly 2 will be white. 0.21

31. Items Donated to a Food Bank At a food bank a case of donated items contains 8 cans of vegetables and 8 cans of fruit. If 3 cans are selected at random to distribute, find the probability of getting 1 can of vegetables and 2 cans of fruit. 0.4

32. Tossing a Die A die is rolled until a 3 is obtained. Find the probability that the first 3 will be obtained on the fourth roll. $\frac{125}{1296}$

33. Selecting a Card A card is selected at random from an ordinary deck and replaced. Find the probability that the first face card will be selected on the fourth draw. 0.105

STATISTICS TODAY

Is Pooling Worthwhile?— **Revisited**

In the case of the pooled sample, the probability that only one test will be needed can be determined by using the binomial distribution. The question being asked is, In a sample of 15 individuals, what is the probability that no individual will have the disease? Hence, $n = 15$, $p = 0.05$, and $X = 0$. The probability is 0.463, or 46% of the time, only one test will be needed. For screening purposes, then, pooling samples in this case would save considerable time, money, and effort as opposed to testing every individual in the population.

Chapter Quiz

Determine whether each statement is true or false. If the statement is false, explain why.

1. The expected value of a random variable can be thought of as a long-run average. True

2. The number of courses a student is taking this semester is an example of a continuous random variable. False

3. When the binomial distribution is used, the outcomes must be dependent. False

4. A binomial experiment has a fixed number of trials. True

Complete these statements with the best answer.

5. Random variable values are determined by __chance__.

6. The mean for a binomial variable can be found by using the expression __$n \cdot p$__.

7. One requirement for a probability distribution is that the sum of all the events in the sample space equals __1__.

Select the best answer.

8. What is the sum of the probabilities of all outcomes in a probability distribution?

   a. 0

   b. $\frac{1}{2}$

   c. 1

   d. It cannot be determined.

9. How many outcomes are there in a binomial experiment?

   a. 0

   b. 1

   c. 2

   d. It varies.

10. The number of trials for a binomial experiment

   a. Can be infinite.

   b. Is unchanged.

   c. Is unlimited.

   d. Must be fixed.

For exercises 11 through 14, determine if the distribution represents a probability distribution. If not, state why.

11.

X	1	2	3	4	5
P(X)	$\frac{1}{7}$	$\frac{2}{7}$	$\frac{2}{7}$	$\frac{3}{7}$	$\frac{2}{7}$

No, since $\Sigma P(X) > 1$

12.

X	3	6	9	12	15
P(X)	0.3	0.5	0.1	0.08	0.02

Yes

13.

X	50	75	100
P(X)	0.5	0.2	0.3

Yes

14.

X	4	8	12	16
P(X)	$\frac{1}{6}$	$\frac{3}{12}$	$\frac{1}{2}$	$\frac{1}{12}$

Yes

15. **Calls for a Fire Company** The number of fire calls the Conestoga Valley Fire Company receives per day is distributed as follows:

Number X	5	6	7	8	9
Probability P(X)	0.28	0.32	0.09	0.21	0.10

Construct a graph for the data.

16. **Cell phones per Household** A study was conducted to determine the number of cell phones each household has. The data are shown here.

Number of cell phones	0	1	2	3	4
Frequency	2	30	48	13	7

Construct a probability distribution and draw a graph for the data.

17. **Music Purchases** During a recent sale of vinyl records at Matt's Music Store, the number of vinyl records customers purchased was distributed as follows:

Number X	0	1	2	3	4
Probability P(X)	0.10	0.23	0.31	0.27	0.09

Find the mean, variance, and standard deviation of the distribution. 2.0; 1.3; 1.1

18. **Calls for a Crisis Hot Line** The number of calls received per day at a crisis hot line is distributed as follows:

Number X	30	31	32	33	34
Probability P(X)	0.05	0.21	0.38	0.25	0.11

Find the mean, variance, and standard deviation of the distribution. 32.2; 1.1; 1.0

19. **Selecting a Card** There are 6 playing cards placed face down in a box. They are the 4 of diamonds, the 5 of hearts, the 2 of clubs, the 10 of spades, the 3 of diamonds, and the 7 of hearts. A person selects a card. Find the expected value of the draw. 5.2

20. **Selecting a Card** A person selects a card from an ordinary deck of cards. If it is a black card, she wins $2. If it is a red card between or including 3 and 7, she wins $10. If it is a red face card, she wins $25; and if it is a black jack, she wins an extra $100. Find the expectation of the game. $9.65

21. **Carpooling** If 40% of all commuters ride to work in carpools, find the probability that if 8 workers are selected, 5 will ride in carpools. 0.124

22. **Employed College Students** If 60% of all college students are employed, find the probability that in a sample of 20 college students

   a. Exactly 15 are employed 0.075

   b. At least 10 are employed 0.872

   c. At most 5 are not employed 0.126

23. **Driver's Exam** If 80% of the applicants are able to pass a driver's proficiency road test, find the mean, variance, and standard deviation of the number of people who pass the test in a sample of 300 applicants. 240; 48; 6.9

24. **Meeting Attendance** A history class has 75 members. If there is a 12% absentee rate per class meeting, find the mean, variance, and standard deviation of the number of students who will be absent from each class. 9; 7.9; 2.8

25. **Income Tax Errors** The probability that a person will make 0, 1, 2, or 3 errors on their income tax return is 0.50, 0.30, 0.15, and 0.05, respectively. If 30 claims are selected, find the probability that 15 will contain 0 errors, 8 will contain 1 error, 5 will contain 2 errors, and 2 will contain 3 errors. 0.008

26. **Quality Control Check** Before a television set leaves the factory, it is given a quality control check. The probability that a television contains 0, 1, or 2 defects is 0.88, 0.08, and 0.04, respectively. In a sample of 16 televisions, find the probability that 9 will have 0 defects, 4 will have 1 defect, and 3 will have 2 defects. 0.0003

27. **Bowling Team Uniforms** Among the teams in a bowling league, the probability that the uniforms are all 1 color is 0.45, that 2 colors are used is 0.35, and that 3 or more colors are used is 0.20. If a sample of 12 uniforms is selected, find the probability that 5 contain only 1 color, 4 contain 2 colors, and 3 contain 3 or more colors. 0.061

28. Elm Trees There are on average 8 elm trees every square block in Portland's Park Blocks. Find the probability that there are exactly 6 elm trees in one park block. Assume the distribution is approximately Poisson. 0.122

29. Sports Score Hot Line Calls Sports Scores Hot Line receives, on the average, 8 calls per hour requesting the latest sports scores. The distribution is Poisson in nature. For any randomly selected hour, find the probability that the company will receive

    a. At least 8 calls   0.5470

    b. 3 or more calls   0.9862

    c. At most 7 calls   0.453

30. Color of Raincoats There are 48 raincoats for sale at a local men's clothing store. Twelve are black. If 6 raincoats are selected to be marked down, find the probability that exactly 3 will be black.   0.128

31. Roadside Emergency For roadside emergencies, a police officer or a deputy sheriff may arrive first to the scene. If there are 8 police officers and 6 deputy sheriffs on shift when 4 roadside emergencies are called in, find the probability that exactly

    a. 3 are deputy sheriffs   0.160

    b. 2 are deputy sheriffs   0.42

    c. 4 are police officers   0.07

32. Blood Types About 4% of the citizens of the United States have type AB blood. If an agency needs type AB blood and donors come in at random, find the probability that the sixth person is the first person with type AB blood.   0.033

33. Alcohol Abstainers About 35% of Americans abstain from the consumption of alcohol. If Americans are selected at random, find the probability that the 10th person selected will be the first one who doesn't drink alcohol.   0.007

Critical Thinking Challenges

1. Lottery Numbers Pennsylvania has a lottery entitled "Big 4." To win, a player must correctly match four digits from a daily lottery in which four digits are selected. Find the probability of winning.

2. Lottery Numbers In the Big 4 lottery, for a bet of $100, the payoff is $5000. What is the expected value of winning? Is it worth it?

3. Lottery Numbers If you played the same four-digit number every day (or any four-digit number for that matter) in the Big 4, how often (in years) would you win, assuming you have average luck?

4. Chuck-a-Luck In the game Chuck-a-Luck, three dice are rolled. A player bets a certain amount (say $1.00) on a number from 1 to 6. If the number appears on 1 die, the person wins $1.00. If it appears on 2 dice, the person wins $2.00, and if it appears on all 3 dice, the person wins $3.00. What are the chances of winning $1.00? $2.00? $3.00?

5. Chuck-a-Luck What is the expected value of the game of Chuck-a-Luck if a player bets $1.00 on one number?

Data Projects

1. Business and Finance Assume that a life insurance company would like to make a profit of $250 on a $100,000 policy sold to a person whose probability of surviving the year is 0.9985. What premium should the company charge the customer? If the company would like to make a $250 profit on a $100,000 policy at a premium of $500, what is the lowest life expectancy it should accept for a customer?

2. Sports and Leisure Baseball, hockey, and basketball all use a seven-game series to determine their championship. Find the probability that with two evenly matched teams a champion will be found in 4 games. Repeat for 5, 6, and 7 games. Look at the historical results for the three sports. How do the actual results compare to the theoretical?

3. Technology Use your most recent itemized phone bill for the data in this problem. Assume that incoming and outgoing calls are equal in the population (why is this a reasonable assumption?). This means assume $p = 0.5$. For the number of calls you made last month, what would be the mean number of outgoing calls in a random selection of calls? Also, compute the standard deviation. Was the number of outgoing calls you made an unusual

amount given the above? In a selection of 12 calls, what is the probability that less than 3 were outgoing?

4. Health and Wellness Use Red Cross data to determine the percentage of the population with an Rh factor that is positive (A+, B+, AB+, or O+ blood types). Use that value for p. How many students in your class have a positive Rh factor? Is this an unusual amount?

5. Politics and Economics Find out what percentage of citizens in your state is registered to vote. Assuming that this is a binomial variable, what would be the mean number of registered voters in a random group of citizens with a sample size equal to the number of students in your class? Also determine the standard deviation. How many students in your class are registered to vote? Is this an unusual number, given the above?

6. Your Class Have each student in class toss 4 coins, and note how many heads are showing. Create a frequency table displaying the results. Compare the frequency table to the theoretical probability distribution for the outcome when 4 coins are tossed. Find the mean for the frequency table. How does it compare with the mean for the probability distribution?

≣ Answers to Applying the Concepts

Section 5–1   Dropping College Courses

1. The random variable under study is the reason for dropping a college course.

2. There were a total of 144 people in the study.

3. The complete table is as follows:

Reason for dropping a college course	Frequency	Percentage
Too difficult	45	31.25
Illness	40	27.78
Change in work schedule	20	13.89
Change of major	14	9.72
Family-related problems	9	6.25
Money	7	4.86
Miscellaneous	6	4.17
No meaningful reason	3	2.08

4. The probability that a student will drop a class because of illness is about 28%. The probability that a student will drop a class because of money is about 5%. The probability that a student will drop a class because of a change of major is about 10%.

5. The information is not itself a probability distribution, but it can be used as one.

6. The categories are not necessarily mutually exclusive, but we treated them as such in computing the probabilities.

7. The categories are not independent.

8. The categories are exhaustive.

9. Since all the probabilities are between 0 and 1, inclusive, and the probabilities sum to 1, the requirements for a discrete probability distribution are met.

Section 5–2   Radiation Exposure

1. The expected value is the mean of a random variable associated with a probability distribution.

2. We would expect variation from the expected value of 3.

3. Answers will vary. One possible answer is that pregnant mothers in that area might be overly concerned upon hearing that the number of cases of kidney problems in newborns was nearly 4 times what was usually expected. Other mothers (particularly those who had taken a statistics course!) might ask for more information about the claim.

4. Answers will vary. One possible answer is that it does seem unlikely to have 11 newborns with kidney problems when we expect only 3 newborns to have kidney problems.

5. The public might be better informed by percentages or rates (e.g. number of newborns with kidney problems per 1000 newborns).

6. The increase of 8 babies born with kidney problems represents a 0.32% increase (less than $\frac{1}{2}$%).

7. Answers will vary. One possible answer is that the percentage increase does not seem to be something to be overly concerned about.

Section 5–3   Unsanitary Restaurants

1. The probability of eating at 3 restaurants with unsanitary conditions out of the 10 restaurants is 0.18792.

2. The probability of eating at 4 or 5 restaurants with unsanitary conditions out of the 10 restaurants is 0.24665 + 0.22199 = 0.46864 ≈ 0.469.

3. To find this probability, you could add the probabilities for eating at 1, 2, . . . , 10 unsanitary restaurants. An easier way to compute the probability is to subtract the probability of eating at no unsanitary restaurants from 1 (using the complement rule).

4. The highest probability for this distribution is 4, but the expected number of unsanitary restaurants that you would eat at is $10 \cdot \frac{3}{7} = 4.29$.

5. The standard deviation for this distribution is $\sqrt{(10)(\frac{3}{7})(\frac{4}{7})} \approx 1.565$.

6. We have two possible outcomes: "success" is eating in an unsanitary restaurant; "failure" is eating in a sanitary restaurant. The probability that one restaurant is unsanitary is independent of the probability that any other restaurant is unsanitary. The probability that a restaurant is unsanitary remains constant at $\frac{3}{7}$. And we are looking at the number of unsanitary restaurants that we eat at out of 10 "trials."

7. The likelihood of success will vary from situation to situation. Just because we have two possible outcomes, this does not mean that each outcome occurs with probability 0.50.

Section 5–4   Rockets and Targets

1. The theoretical values for the number of hits are as follows:

Hits	0	1	2	3	4	5
Regions	227.5	211.3	98.2	30.4	7.1	1.3

2. The actual values are very close to the theoretical values.

3. Since the actual values are close to the theoretical values, it does appear that the rockets were fired at random.

6

The Normal Distribution

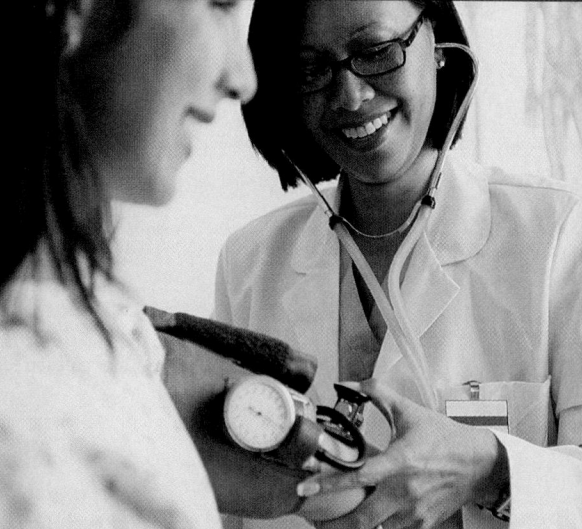

Fuse/Getty Images

≡ STATISTICS TODAY

What Is Normal?

Medical researchers have determined so-called normal intervals for a person's blood pressure, cholesterol, triglycerides, and the like. For example, the normal range of systolic blood pressure is 110 to 140. The normal interval for a person's triglycerides is from 30 to 200 milligrams per deciliter (mg/dl). By measuring these variables, a physician can determine if a patient's vital statistics are within the normal interval or if some type of treatment is needed to correct a condition and avoid future illnesses. The question then is, How does one determine the so-called normal intervals? See Statistics Today—Revisited at the end of the chapter.

In this chapter, you will learn how researchers determine normal intervals for specific medical tests by using a normal distribution. You will see how the same methods are used to determine the lifetimes of batteries, the strength of ropes, and many other traits.

OUTLINE

OBJECTIVES

After completing this chapter, you should be able to:

1. Identify the properties of a normal distribution.

2. Identify distributions as symmetric or skewed.

3. Find the area under the standard normal distribution, given various z values.

4. Find probabilities for a normally distributed variable by transforming it into a standard normal variable.

5. Find specific data values for given percentages, using the standard normal distribution.

6. Use the central limit theorem to solve problems involving sample means for large samples.

7. Use the normal approximation to compute probabilities for a binomial variable.

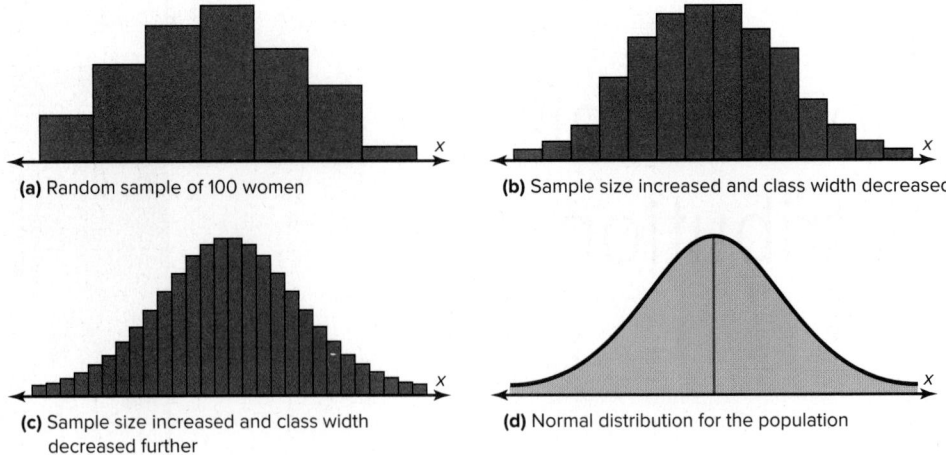

(a) Random sample of 100 women

(b) Sample size increased and class width decreased

(c) Sample size increased and class width decreased further

(d) Normal distribution for the population

Introduction

Random variables can be either discrete or continuous. Discrete variables and their distributions were explained in Chapter 5. Recall that a discrete variable cannot assume all values between any two given values of the variables. On the other hand, a continuous variable can assume all values between any two given values of the variables. Examples of continuous variables are the height of adult men, body temperature of rats, and cholesterol level of adults. Many continuous variables, such as the examples just mentioned, have distributions that are bell-shaped, and these are called *approximately normally distributed variables.* For example, if a researcher selects a random sample of 100 adult women, measures their heights, and constructs a histogram, the researcher gets a graph similar to the one shown in Figure 6–1(a). Now, if the researcher increases the sample size and decreases the width of the classes, the histograms will look like the ones shown in Figure 6–1(b) and (c). Finally, if it were possible to measure exactly the heights of all adult females in the United States and plot them, the histogram would approach what is called a *normal distribution curve,* as shown in Figure 6–1(d). This distribution is also known as a *bell curve* or a *Gaussian distribution curve,* named for the German mathematician Carl Friedrich Gauss (1777–1855), who derived its equation.

No variable fits a normal distribution perfectly, since a normal distribution is a theoretical distribution. However, a normal distribution can be used to describe many variables, because the deviations from a normal distribution are very small. This concept will be explained further in Section 6–1.

This chapter will also present the properties of a normal distribution and discuss its applications. Then a very important fact about a normal distribution called the *central limit theorem* will be explained. Finally, the chapter will explain how a normal distribution curve can be used as an approximation to other distributions, such as the binomial distribution. Since a binomial distribution is a discrete distribution, a correction for continuity may be employed when a normal distribution is used for its approximation.

6–1   Normal Distributions

In mathematics, curves can be represented by equations. For example, the equation of the circle shown in Figure 6–2 is $x^2 + y^2 = r^2$, where r is the radius. A circle can be used to represent many physical objects, such as a wheel or a gear. Even though it is not possible to manufacture a wheel that is perfectly round, the equation and the properties of a circle can be used to study many aspects of the wheel, such as area, velocity, and acceleration. In a similar manner, the theoretical curve, called a *normal distribution curve,* can be used to study many variables that are not perfectly normally distributed but are nevertheless approximately normal.

> If a random variable has a probability distribution whose graph is continuous, bell-shaped, and symmetric, it is called a **normal distribution**. The graph is called a *normal distribution* curve.

The mathematical equation for a normal distribution is

$$y = \frac{e^{-(X-\mu)^2/(2\sigma^2)}}{\sigma\sqrt{2\pi}}$$

where $e \approx 2.718$ ($\approx$ means "is approximately equal to")

$\pi \approx 3.14$

μ = population mean

σ = population standard deviation

This equation may look formidable, but in applied statistics, tables or technology is used for specific problems instead of the equation.

Another important consideration in applied statistics is that the area under a normal distribution curve is used more often than the values on the y axis. Therefore, when a normal distribution is pictured, the y axis is sometimes omitted.

Circles can be different sizes, depending on their diameters (or radii), and can be used to represent wheels of different sizes. Likewise, normal curves have different shapes and can be used to represent different variables.

The shape and position of a normal distribution curve depend on two parameters, the *mean* and the *standard deviation.* Each normally distributed variable has its own normal distribution curve, which depends on the values of the variable's mean and standard deviation.

Suppose one normally distributed variable has $\mu = 0$ and $\sigma = 1$, and another normally distributed variable has $\mu = 0$ and $\sigma = 2$. As you can see in Figure 6–3(a), when the value

FIGURE 6–2

Graph of a Circle and an Application

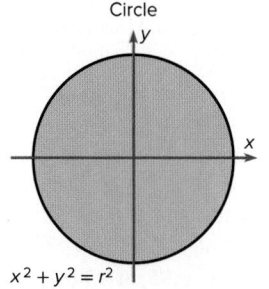
Circle

$x^2 + y^2 = r^2$

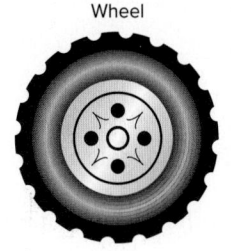
Wheel

FIGURE 6–3

Shapes of Normal Distributions

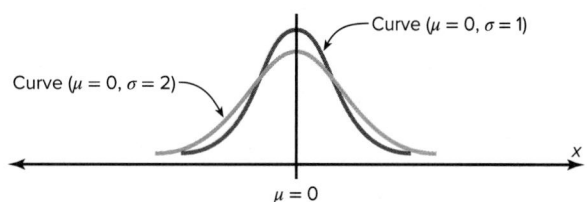

(a) Same means but different standard deviations

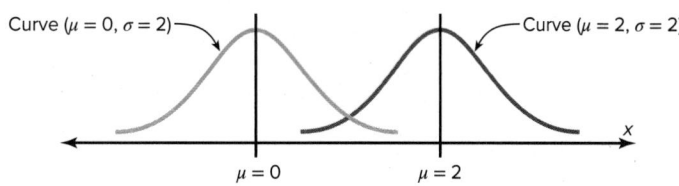

(b) Different means but same standard deviations

OBJECTIVE **1**

Identify the properties of a normal distribution.

of the standard deviation increases, the shape of the curve spreads out. If one normally distributed variable has $\mu = 0$ and $\sigma = 2$ and another normally distributed variable has $\mu = 2$, and $\sigma = 2$, then the shapes of the curve are the same, but the curve with $\mu = 2$ moves 2 units to the right. See Figure 6–3(b).

The properties of a normal distribution, including those mentioned in the definition, are explained next.

Historical Notes

The discovery of the equation for a normal distribution can be traced to three mathematicians. In 1733, the French mathematician Abraham DeMoivre derived an equation for a normal distribution based on the random variation of the number of heads appearing when a large number of coins were tossed. Not realizing any connection with the naturally occurring variables, he showed this formula to only a few friends. About 100 years later, two mathematicians, Pierre Laplace in France and Carl Gauss in Germany, derived the equation of the normal curve independently and without any knowledge of DeMoivre's work. In 1924, Karl Pearson found that DeMoivre had discovered the formula before Laplace or Gauss.

Summary of the Properties of the Theoretical Normal Distribution

1. A normal distribution curve is bell-shaped.
2. The mean, median, and mode are equal and are located at the center of the distribution.
3. A normal distribution curve is unimodal (i.e., it has only one mode).
4. The curve is symmetric about the mean, which is equivalent to saying that its shape is the same on both sides of a vertical line passing through the center.
5. The curve is continuous; that is, there are no gaps or holes. For each value of X, there is a corresponding value of Y.
6. The curve never touches the x axis. Theoretically, no matter how far in either direction the curve extends, it never meets the x axis—but it gets increasingly close.
7. The total area under a normal distribution curve is equal to 1.00, or 100%. This fact may seem unusual, since the curve never touches the x axis, but one can prove it mathematically by using calculus. (The proof is beyond the scope of this text.)
8. The area under the part of a normal curve that lies within 1 standard deviation of the mean is approximately 0.68, or 68%; within 2 standard deviations, about 0.95, or 95%; and within 3 standard deviations, about 0.997, or 99.7%. See Figure 6–4, which also shows the area in each region.

The values given in item 8 of the summary follow the *empirical rule* for data given in Section 3–2.

You must know these properties in order to solve problems involving distributions that are approximately normal.

Recall from Chapter 2 that the graphs of distributions can have many shapes. When the data values are evenly distributed about the mean, a distribution is said to be a **symmetric distribution.** (A normal distribution is symmetric.) Figure 6–5(a) shows a symmetric distribution. When the majority of the data values fall to the left or right of the mean, the distribution is said to be *skewed*. When the majority of the data values fall to

FIGURE 6–4

Areas Under a Normal Distribution Curve

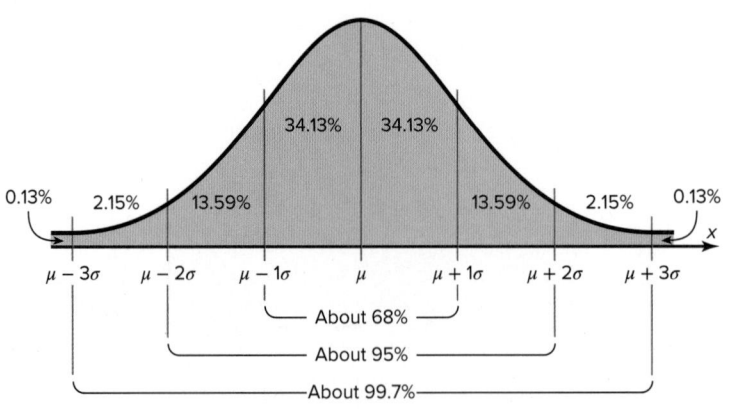

FIGURE 6–5
Normal and Skewed
Distributions

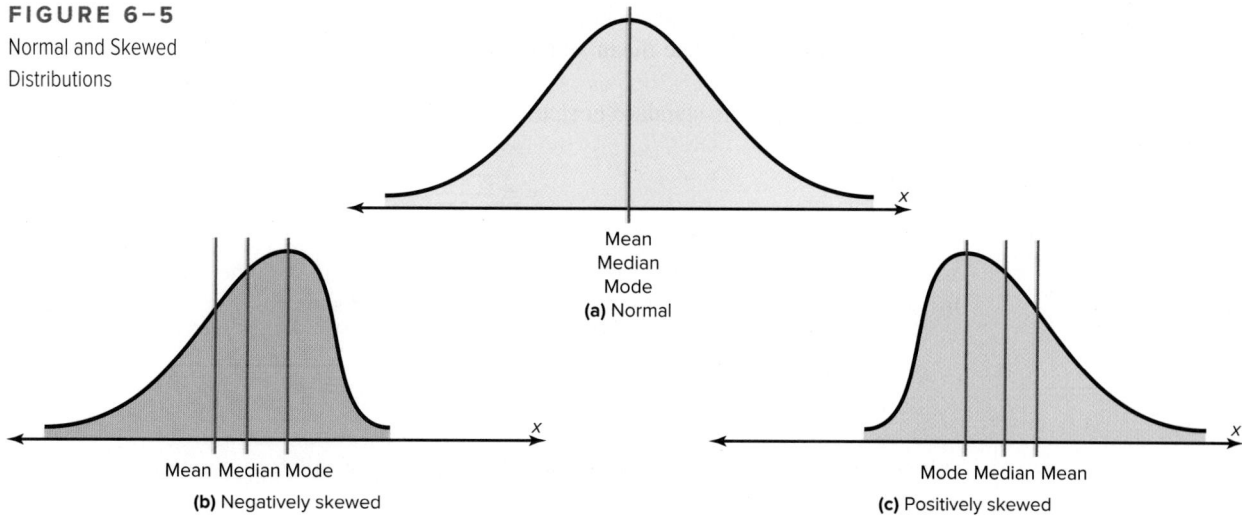

Mean
Median
Mode
(a) Normal

Mean Median Mode
(b) Negatively skewed

Mode Median Mean
(c) Positively skewed

OBJECTIVE **2**

Identify distributions as
symmetric or skewed.

the right of the mean, the distribution is said to be a **negatively or left-skewed distribution.** The mean is to the left of the median, and the mean and the median are to the left of the mode. See Figure 6–5(b). When the majority of the data values fall to the left of the mean, a distribution is said to be a **positively or right-skewed distribution.** The mean falls to the right of the median, and both the mean and the median fall to the right of the mode. See Figure 6–5(c).

The "tail" of the curve indicates the direction of skewness (right is positive, left is negative). These distributions can be compared with the ones shown in Figure 3–1. Both types follow the same principles.

The Standard Normal Distribution

Since each normally distributed variable has its own mean and standard deviation, as stated earlier, the shape and location of these curves will vary. In practical applications, then, you would have to have a table of areas under the curve for each variable. To simplify this situation, statisticians use what is called the *standard normal distribution.*

OBJECTIVE **3**

Find the area under the
standard normal distribu-
tion, given various *z* values.

> The **standard normal distribution** is a normal distribution with a mean of 0 and a standard deviation of 1.

The standard normal distribution is shown in Figure 6–6.

FIGURE 6–6
Standard Normal Distribution

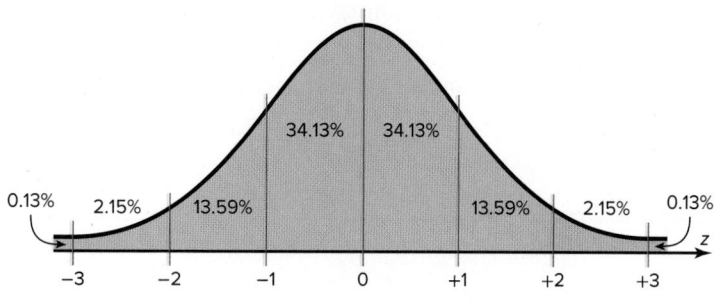

The values under the curve indicate the proportion of area in each section. For example, the area between the mean and 1 standard deviation above or below the mean is about 0.3413, or 34.13%.

The formula for the standard normal distribution is

$$y = \frac{e^{-z^2/2}}{\sqrt{2\pi}}$$

All normally distributed variables can be transformed into the standard normally distributed variable by using the formula for the standard score:

$$z = \frac{\text{value} - \text{mean}}{\text{standard deviation}} \qquad \text{or} \qquad z = \frac{X - \mu}{\sigma}$$

This is the same formula used in Section 3–3. The use of this formula will be explained in Section 6–3.

As stated earlier, the area under a normal distribution curve is used to solve practical application problems, such as finding the percentage of adult women whose height is between 5 feet 4 inches and 5 feet 7 inches, or finding the probability that a new battery will last longer than 4 years. Hence, the major emphasis of this section will be to show the procedure for finding the area under the standard normal distribution curve for any z value. The applications will be shown in Section 6–2. Once the X values are transformed by using the preceding formula, they are called z values. The **z value** or **z score** is actually the number of standard deviations that a particular X value is away from the mean. Table A–4 in Appendix A gives the area (to four decimal places) under the standard normal curve for any z value from -3.49 to 3.49.

Finding Areas Under the Standard Normal Distribution Curve

For the solution of problems using the standard normal distribution, a two-step process is recommended with the use of the Procedure Table shown.

The two steps are as follows:

Step 1   Draw the normal distribution curve and shade the area.

Step 2   Find the appropriate figure in the Procedure Table and follow the directions given.

There are three basic types of problems, and all three are summarized in the Procedure Table. Note that this table is presented as an aid in understanding how to use the standard normal distribution table and in visualizing the problems. After learning the procedures, you should not find it necessary to refer to the Procedure Table for every problem.

Procedure Table

Finding the Area Under the Standard Normal Distribution Curve

1. To the left of any z value:
    Look up the z value in the table and use the area given.

2. To the right of any z value:
    Look up the z value and subtract the area from 1.

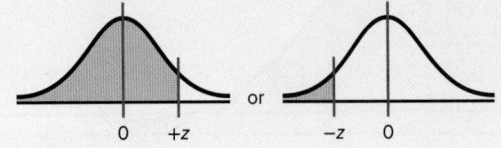

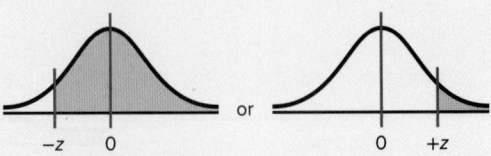

3. Between any two *z* values:
Look up both *z* values and subtract the corresponding areas.

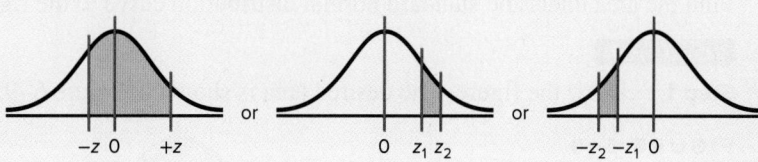

FIGURE 6–7
Table A–4 Area Value for
z = 1.39

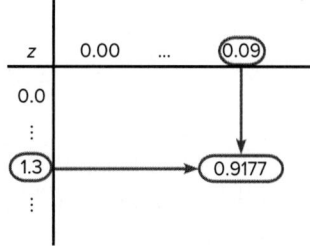

Table A–4 in Appendix A gives the area under the normal distribution curve to the left of any *z* value given in two decimal places. For example, the area to the left of a *z* value of 1.39 is found by looking up 1.3 in the left column and 0.09 in the top row. Where the row and column lines meet gives an area of 0.9177. See Figure 6–7.

EXAMPLE 6–1

Find the area under the standard normal distribution curve to the left of $z = 2.16$.

SOLUTION

Step 1   Draw the figure. The desired area is shown in Figure 6–8.

FIGURE 6–8
Area Under the Standard
Normal Distribution Curve for
Example 6–1

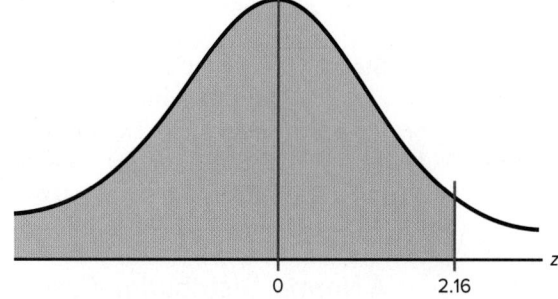

Step 2   We are looking for the area under the standard distribution curve to the left of $z = 2.16$. Since this is an example of the first case, look up the answer in the table. It is 0.9846. Hence, 98.46% of the area is to the left of $z = 2.16$.

EXAMPLE 6–2

Find the area under the standard normal distribution curve to the right of $z = -1.09$.

SOLUTION

Step 1   Draw the figure. The desired area is shown in Figure 6–9.

FIGURE 6–9
Area Under the Standard Normal Distribution Curve for Example 6–2

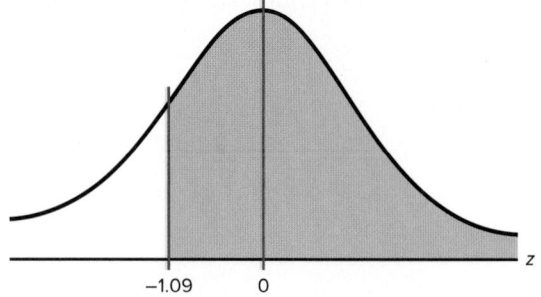

-1.09 0 z

Step 2   We are looking for the area to the right of $z = -1.09$. This is an example of the second case. Look up the area for $z = -1.09$. It is 0.1379. Subtract the area from 1.000: $1.000 - 0.1379 = 0.8621$. Hence, 86.21% of the area under the standard normal distribution is to the right of $z = -1.09$.

Note: In this situation, we subtract the area 0.1379 from 1.000 because the table gives the area up to -1.09. So to get the area under the curve to the right of -1.09, subtract the area 0.1379 from 1.000, the total area under the standard normal distribution curve.

EXAMPLE 6–3

Find the area under the standard normal distribution curve between $z = 1.43$ and $z = -1.87$.

SOLUTION

Step 1   Draw the figure as shown in Figure 6–10. The desired area is between the two z values of 1.43 and -1.87.

FIGURE 6–10
Area Under the Standard Normal Distribution Curve for Example 6–3

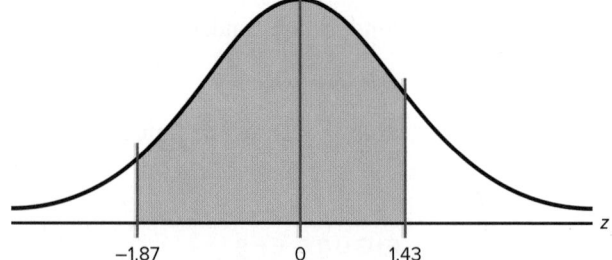

-1.87 0 1.43 z

Step 2   Since the area desired is between two given z values, look up the areas corresponding to the two z values and subtract the smaller area from the larger area. (Do not subtract the z values.) The area for $z = 1.43$ is 0.9236. The area for $z = -1.87$ is 0.0307. The area between the two z values is $0.9236 - 0.0307 = 0.8929$ or 89.29%.

A Normal Distribution Curve as a Probability Distribution Curve

A normal distribution curve can be used as a probability distribution curve for normally distributed variables. Recall that a normal distribution is a *continuous distribution,* as opposed to a discrete probability distribution, as explained in Chapter 5. The fact that it is continuous means that there are no gaps in the curve. In other words, for every z value on the x axis, there is a corresponding height, or frequency, value.

The area under the standard normal distribution curve can also be thought of as a probability or as the proportion of the population with a given characteristic. That is, if it were possible to select a z value at random, the probability of choosing one, say, between 0 and 2.00 would be the same as the area under the curve between 0 and 2.00. In this case, the area is 0.4772. Therefore, the probability of randomly selecting a z value between 0 and 2.00 is 0.4772. The problems involving probability are solved in the same manner as the previous examples involving areas in this section. For example, if the problem is to find the probability of selecting a z value between 2.25 and 2.94, solve it by using the method shown in case 3 of the Procedure Table.

For probabilities, a special notation is used to denote the probability of a standard normal variable z. For example, if the problem is to find the probability of any z value between 0 and 2.32, this probability is written as $P(0 < z < 2.32)$.

Note: In a continuous distribution, the probability of any exact z value is 0 since the area would be represented by a vertical line above the value. But vertical lines in theory have no area. So $P(a \leq z \leq b) = P(a < z < b)$.

EXAMPLE 6–4

Find the probability for each. (Assume this is a standard normal distribution.)

    a. $P(0 < z < 2.53)$ *b.* $P(z < 1.73)$ *c.* $P(z > 1.98)$

SOLUTION

    a. $P(0 < z < 2.53)$ is used to find the area under the standard normal distribution curve between $z = 0$ and $z = 2.53$. First, draw the curve and shade the desired area. This is shown in Figure 6–11. Second, find the area in Table A–4 corresponding to $z = 2.53$. It is 0.9943. Third, find the area in Table A–4 corresponding to $z = 0$. It is 0.5000. Finally, subtract the two areas: $0.9943 - 0.5000 = 0.4943$. Hence, the probability is 0.4943, or 49.43%.

FIGURE 6–11

Area Under the Standard
Normal Distribution Curve for
Part *a* of Example 6–4

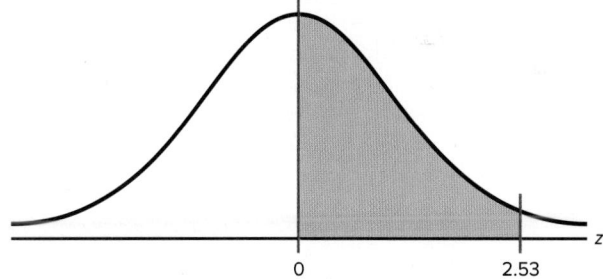

    b. $P(z < 1.73)$ is used to find the area under the standard normal distribution curve to the left of $z = 1.73$. First, draw the curve and shade the desired area. This is shown in Figure 6–12. Second, find the area in Table A–4 corresponding to 1.73. It is 0.9582. Hence, the probability of obtaining a z value less than 1.73 is 0.9582, or 95.82%.

FIGURE 6–12

Area Under the Standard
Normal Distribution Curve
for Part *b* of Example 6–4

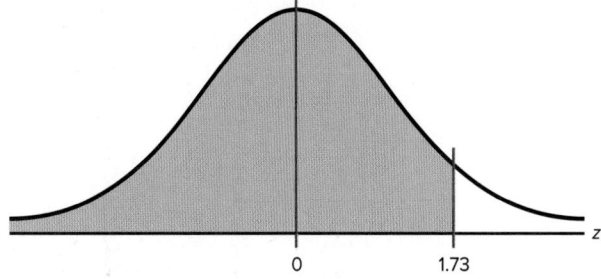

    c. $P(z > 1.98)$ is used to find the area under the standard normal distribution curve to the right of $z = 1.98$. First, draw the curve and shade the desired area.

See Figure 6–13. Second, find the area corresponding to $z = 1.98$ in Table A–4. It is 0.9761. Finally, subtract this area from 1.0000. It is $1.0000 - 0.9761 = 0.0239$. Hence, the probability of obtaining a z value greater than 1.98 is 0.0239, or 2.39%.

FIGURE 6–13

Area Under the Standard
Normal Distribution Curve for
Part c of Example 6–4

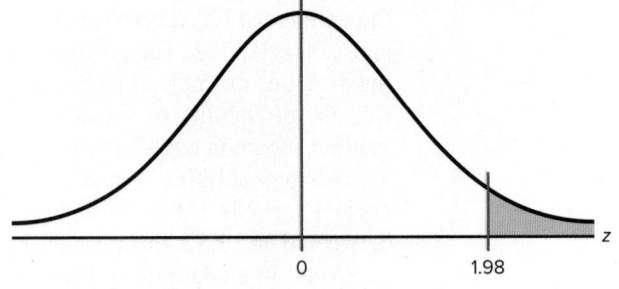

Sometimes, one must find a specific z value for a given area under the standard normal distribution curve. The procedure is to work backward, using Table A–4.

Since Table A–4 is cumulative, it is necessary to locate the cumulative area up to a given z value. Example 6–5 shows this.

EXAMPLE 6–5

Find the z value such that the area under the standard normal distribution curve between 0 and the z value is 0.2123.

SOLUTION

Draw the figure. The area is shown in Figure 6–14.

FIGURE 6–14

Area Under the Standard
Normal Distribution Curve for
Example 6–5

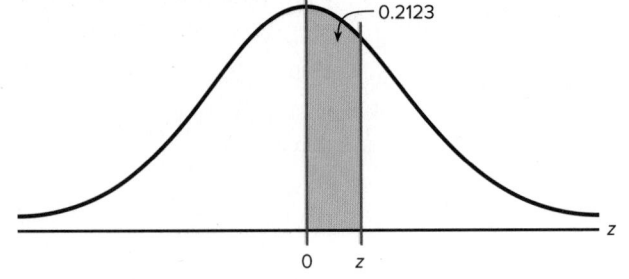

In this case it is necessary to add 0.5000 to the given area of 0.2123 to get the cumulative area of 0.7123. Look up the area in Table A–4. The value in the left column is 0.5, and the top value is 0.06. Add these two values to get $z = 0.56$. See Figure 6–15.

FIGURE 6–15

Finding the z Value
from Table A–4 for
Example 6–5

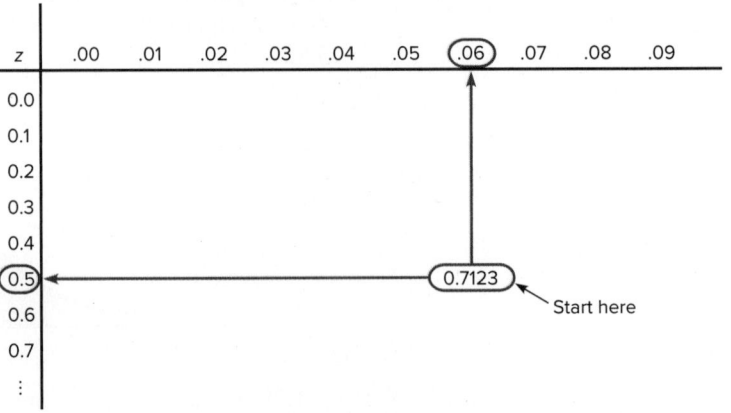

FIGURE 6–16

The Relationship Between
Area and Probability

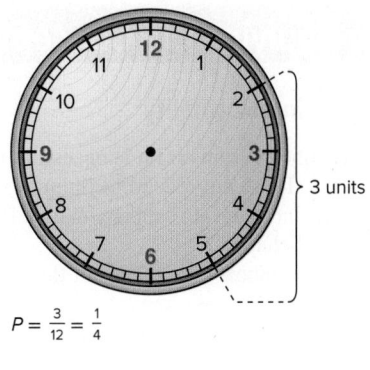

$$P = \frac{3}{12} = \frac{1}{4}$$

(a) Clock

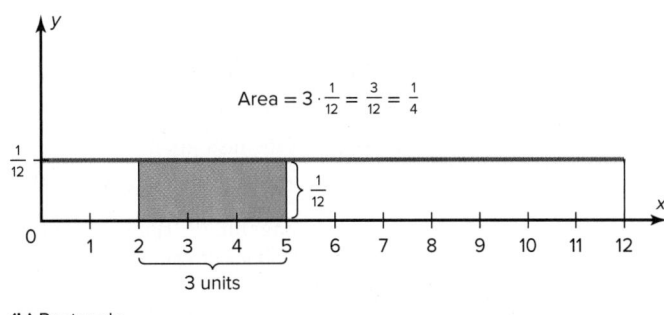

(b) Rectangle

If the exact area cannot be found, use the closest value. For example, if you wanted to find the z value for an area 0.9241, the closest area is 0.9236, which gives a z value of 1.43. See Table A–4 in Appendix A.

The rationale for using an area under a continuous curve to determine a probability can be understood by considering the example of a watch that is powered by a battery. When the battery goes dead, what is the probability that the minute hand will stop somewhere between the numbers 2 and 5 on the face of the watch? In this case, the values of the variable constitute a continuous variable since the hour hand can stop anywhere on the dial's face between 0 and 12 (one revolution of the minute hand). Hence, the sample space can be considered to be 12 units long, and the distance between the numbers 2 and 5 is $5 - 2$, or 3 units. Hence, the probability that the minute hand stops on a number between 2 and 5 is $\frac{3}{12} = \frac{1}{4}$. See Figure 6–16(a).

The problem could also be solved by using a graph of a continuous variable. Let us assume that since the watch can stop anytime at random, the values where the minute hand would land are spread evenly over the range of 0 through 12. The graph would then consist of a *continuous uniform distribution* with a range of 12 units. Now if we required the area under the curve to be 1 (like the area under the standard normal distribution), the height of the rectangle formed by the curve and the x axis would need to be $\frac{1}{12}$. The reason is that the area of a rectangle is equal to the base times the height. If the base is 12 units long, then the height has to be $\frac{1}{12}$ since $12 \cdot \frac{1}{12} = 1$.

The area of the rectangle with a base from 2 through 5 would be $3 \cdot \frac{1}{12}$, or $\frac{1}{4}$. See Figure 6–16(b). Notice that the area of the small rectangle is the same as the probability found previously. Hence, the area of this rectangle corresponds to the probability of this event. The same reasoning can be applied to the standard normal distribution curve shown in Example 6–5.

Finding the area under the standard normal distribution curve is the first step in solving a wide variety of practical applications in which the variables are normally distributed. Some of these applications will be presented in Section 6–2.

Applying the Concepts 6–1

Assessing Normality

Many times in statistics it is necessary to see if a set of data values is approximately normally distributed. There are special techniques that can be used. One technique is to draw a histogram for the data and see if it is approximately bell-shaped. (*Note:* It does not have to be exactly symmetric to be bell-shaped.)

The numbers of branches of the 50 top banks are shown.

67	84	80	77	97	59	62	37	33	42
36	54	18	12	19	33	49	24	25	22
24	29	9	21	21	24	31	17	15	21
13	19	19	22	22	30	41	22	18	20
26	33	14	14	16	22	26	10	16	24

1. Construct a frequency distribution for the data.

2. Construct a histogram for the data.

3. Describe the shape of the histogram.

4. Based on your answer to question 3, do you feel that the distribution is approximately normal?

In addition to the histogram, distributions that are approximately normal have about 68% of the values fall within 1 standard deviation of the mean, about 95% of the data values fall within 2 standard deviations of the mean, and almost 100% of the data values fall within 3 standard deviations of the mean. (See Figure 6–5.)

5. Find the mean and standard deviation for the data.

6. What percent of the data values fall within 1 standard deviation of the mean?

7. What percent of the data values fall within 2 standard deviations of the mean?

8. What percent of the data values fall within 3 standard deviations of the mean?

9. How do your answers to questions 6, 7, and 8 compare to 68, 95, and 100%, respectively?

10. Does your answer help support the conclusion you reached in question 4? Explain.

(More techniques for assessing normality are explained in Section 6–2.)
See pages 366–367 for the answers.

Exercises 6–1

1. What are the characteristics of a normal distribution?

2. Why is the standard normal distribution important in statistical analysis? Many variables are normally distributed, and the distribution can be used to describe these variables.

3. What is the total area under the standard normal distribution curve? 1 or 100%

4. What percentage of the area falls below the mean? Above the mean? 50% of the area lies below the mean, and 50% of the area lies above the mean.

5. About what percentage of the area under the normal distribution curve falls within 1 standard deviation above and below the mean? 2 standard deviations? 3 standard deviations? 68%; 95%; 99.7%

6. What are two other names for a normal distribution? Gaussian distribution and bell curve

For Exercises 7 through 26, find the area under the standard normal distribution curve.

7. To the left of $z = -1.77$ 0.0384

8. To the left of $z = -0.75$ 0.2266

9. To the right of $z = 0.24$ 0.4052

10. To the right of $z = 2.09$ 0.0183

11. Between $z = 0$ and $z = 1.02$ 0.3461

12. Between $z = 0$ and $z = 0.87$ 0.3078

13. Between $z = 0$ and $z = -2.19$ 0.4857

14. Between $z = 0$ and $z = -0.45$ 0.1736

15. Between $z = 1.03$ and $z = -1.79$ 0.8118

16. Between $z = 1.23$ and $z = 1.90$ 0.0806

17. Between $z = -1.63$ and $z = -1.92$ 0.0242

18. Between $z = -0.96$ and $z = -0.36$ 0.1909

19. Between $z = -1.28$ and $z = -1.81$ 0.0652

20. Between $z = 0.24$ and $z = -1.12$ 0.4634

21. To the left of $z = 2.11$ 0.9826

22. To the left of $z = 1.31$ 0.9049

23. To the right of $z = -0.16$ 0.5636

24. To the right of $z = -1.92$ 0.9726

25. To the right of $z = 1.92$ and to the left of $z = -0.44$ 0.3574

26. To the left of $z = -2.15$ and to the right of $z = 1.62$ 0.0684

In Exercises 27 through 40, find the probabilities for each, using the standard normal distribution.

27. $P(0 < z < 0.73)$ 0.2673

28. $P(0 < z < 1.96)$ 0.4750

29. $P(-1.38 < z < 0)$ 0.4162

30. $P(-1.23 < z < 0)$ 0.3907

31. $P(z > 2.27)$ 0.0116

32. $P(z > 0.82)$ 0.2061

33. $P(z < -1.59)$ 0.0559

34. $P(z < -1.77)$ 0.0384

35. $P(-2.07 < z < 1.88)$ 0.9507

36. $P(-0.20 < z < 1.56)$ 0.5199

37. $P(1.47 < z < 2.25)$ 0.0586

38. $P(1.12 < z < 1.43)$ 0.0550

39. $P(z < 1.33)$ 0.9082

40. $P(z > -1.43)$ 0.9236

For Exercises 41 through 46, find the z value that corresponds to the given area.

41.
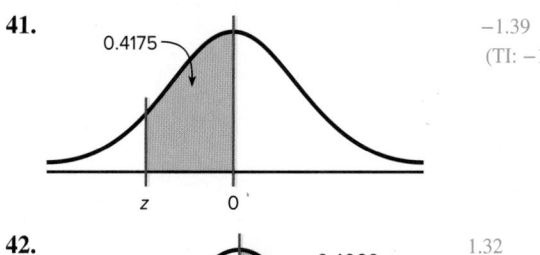
−1.39 (TI: −1.3885)

42.
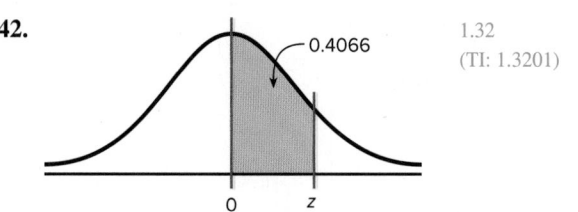
1.32 (TI: 1.3201)

43.
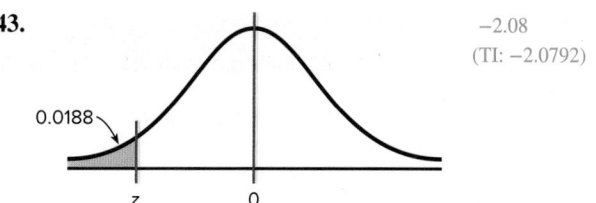
−2.08 (TI: −2.0792)

44.
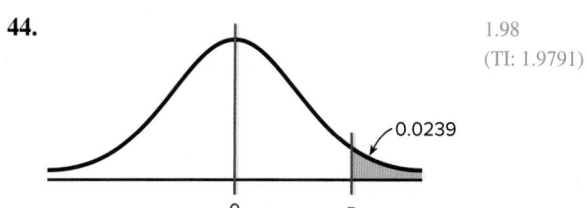
1.98 (TI: 1.9791)

45.
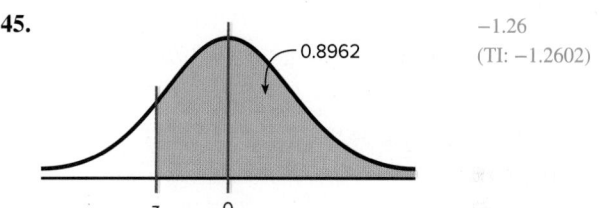
−1.26 (TI: −1.2602)

46.
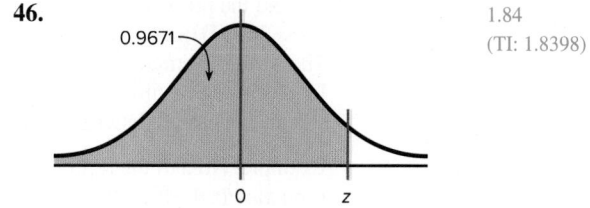
1.84 (TI: 1.8398)

47. Find the z value to the left of the mean so that
   a. 98.87% of the area under the distribution curve lies to the right of it. −2.28 (TI: −2.2801)
   b. 82.12% of the area under the distribution curve lies to the right of it. −0.92 (TI: −0.91995)
   c. 60.64% of the area under the distribution curve lies to the right of it. −0.27 (TI: −0.26995)

48. Find the z value to the right of the mean so that
   a. 54.78% of the area under the distribution curve lies to the left of it. 0.12 (TI: 0.1201)
   b. 69.85% of the area under the distribution curve lies to the left of it. 0.52 (TI: 0.5201)
   c. 88.10% of the area under the distribution curve lies to the left of it. 1.18

49. Find two z values, one positive and one negative, that are equidistant from the mean so that the areas in the two tails add to the following values.
   a. 5% $z = +1.96$ and $z = -1.96$ (TI: ±1.95996)
   b. 10% $z = +1.65$ and $z = -1.65$, approximately (TI: ±1.64485)
   c. 1% $z = +2.58$ and $z = -2.58$, approximately (TI: ±2.57583)

50. Find two z values so that 48% of the middle area is bounded by them. $z = \pm0.64$ (TI: ±0.64335)

Extending the Concepts

51. Find $P(-1<z<1)$, $P(-2<z<2)$, and $P(-3<z<3)$. How do these values compare with the empirical rule? 0.6827; 0.9545; 0.9973; they are very close.

52. In the standard normal distribution, find the values of z for the 75th, 80th, and 92nd percentiles. 0.6745; 0.8416; 1.41

For Exercises 53–56, z_0 is the statistical notation for an unknown z value. It serves that same function as x does in an algebraic equation.

53. Find z_0 such that $P(-1.2<z<z_0)=0.8671$. 2.10

54. Find z_0 such that $P(z_0<z<2.5)=0.7672$. −0.75

55. Find z_0 such that the area between z_0 and $z=-0.5$ is 0.2345 (two answers). −1.45 and 0.11

56. Find z_0 such that $P(-z_0<z<z_0)=0.76$. 1.175

57. Find the equation for the standard normal distribution by substituting 0 for μ and 1 for σ in the equation

$$y=\frac{e^{-(X-\mu)^2/(2\sigma^2)}}{\sigma\sqrt{2\pi}} \quad y=\frac{e^{-X^2/2}}{\sqrt{2\pi}}$$

58. Graph by hand the standard normal distribution by using the formula derived in Exercise 57. Let $\pi\approx3.14$ and $e\approx2.718$. Use X values of −2, −1.5, −1, −0.5, 0, 0.5, 1, 1.5, and 2. (Use a calculator to compute the y values.)

59. Find $P(z<2.3 \text{ or } z>-1.2)$. 1.00

60. Find $P(z>2.3 \text{ and } z<-1.2)$. 0

Technology Step by Step

TI–84 Plus
Step by Step

Standard Normal Random Variables

To find the probability for a standard normal random variable:
Press **2nd [DISTR]**, then **2** for normalcdf(
The form is normalcdf(lower z score, upper z score, μ, σ).
Use E99 for ∞ (infinity) and −E99 for −∞ (negative infinity). Press **2nd [EE]** to get E. Make sure to not use the letter E or number e keys.

Example: Area to the right of $z=1.11$
normalcdf(1.11,E99)

```
normalcdf(1.11,E
99,0,1)
        .1334995565
```

Example: Area to the left of $z=-1.93$
normalcdf(−E99,−1.93)

```
normalcdf(-E99,-
1.93,0,1)
        .0268033499
```

Example: Area between $z=2.00$ and $z=2.47$
normalcdf(2.00,2.47)

```
normalcdf(2,2.47
,0,1)
        .0159944012
```

To find the percentile for a standard normal random variable:
Press **2nd [DISTR],** then **3** for the invNorm(

The form is invNorm(area to the left of z score, μ, σ)

Example: Find the z score such that the area under the standard normal curve to the left of it is 0.7123.
invNorm(.7123,0,1)

```
invNorm(.7123,0,
1)
           .560116461
```

EXCEL
Step by Step

The Standard Normal Distribution

Finding Areas under the Standard Normal Distribution Curve

Example XL6–1

Find the area to the left of $z = 1.99$.
In a blank cell type: =NORM.S.DIST(1.99,TRUE)
Answer: 0.976705

Example XL6–2

Find the area to the right of $z = -2.04$.
In a blank cell type: = 1-NORM.S.DIST(−2.04,TRUE)
Answer: 0.979325

Example XL6–3

Find the area between $z = -2.04$ and $z = 1.99$.
In a blank cell type: =NORM.S.DIST(1.99,TRUE) − NORM.S.DIST(−2.04,TRUE)
Answer: 0.956029

Finding a _z_ Value Given an Area Under the Standard Normal Distribution Curve

Example XL6–4

Find a z score given the cumulative area (area to the left of z) is 0.0250.
In a blank cell type: =NORM.S.INV(.025)
Answer: −1.95996

Example XL6–5

Find a z score, given the area to the right of z is 0.4567.
We must find the z score corresponding to a cumulative area $1 - 0.4567$.
In a blank cell type: =NORM.S.INV(1 − .4567)
Answer: 0.108751

Example XL6–6

Find a (positive) z score given the area between $-z$ and z is 0.98.
We must find the z score corresponding to a cumulative area $0.98 + 0.01$ or 0.99
In a blank cell type: =NORM.S.INV(.99)
Answer: 2.326348

Note: We could also type: = −NORM.S.INV(.01) to find the z score for Example XL6–6.

MINITAB

Step by Step

Normal Distributions with MINITAB

Finding the area above an interval for a normal distribution is synonymous with finding a probability. We never find the probability that X or Z is exactly equal to a value. We always find the probability that the value is some interval, some range of values. These MINITAB instructions will show you how to get the same results that you would by using Table A–4, Standard Normal Distribution. Five cases follow.

Open MINITAB. It doesn't matter if something is in the worksheet or not.

Case 1: Find the Probability That z Is to the Left of a Given Value

Find the area to the left of $z = -1.96$. This is the same as saying $z < -1.96$, represented by the number line to the left of -1.96.

1. Select **Graph>Probability Distribution Plot>View Probability,** then click [OK].

   a) The distribution should be Normal with the Mean set to **0.0** and the Standard deviation set to **1.0.**

   b) Choose the tab for Shaded Area, then select the radio button for X Value.

   c) Click the picture for Left Tail.

   d) Type in the X value of -1.96 and click [OK].

$$P(Z < -1.96) = 0.02500.$$

You can copy and paste the graph into a document if you like. To copy, select Edit, Copy Graph.

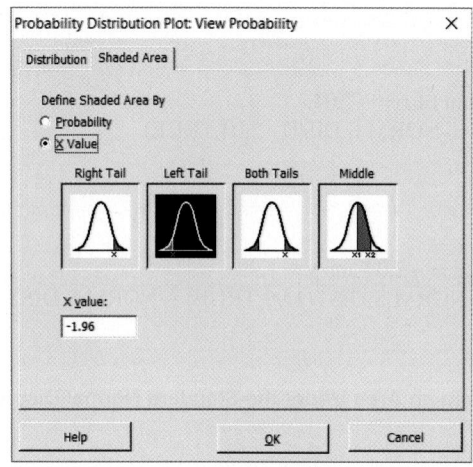

Case 1 Dialogue Box   **Case 1 Graph**

Case 2: Find the Probability That z Is to the Right of a Given Value

Use these instructions for positive or negative values of z.
Find the area **to the right of** $z = +2.33$. This is the same as $Z > 2.33$.

2. Select **Edit, Edit Last Dialog** box or select **Graph>Probability Distribution Plot>View Probability** and click [OK].

   a) The distribution should be normal with the mean set to 0.0 and the standard deviation set to 1.0.

   b) Choose the tab for Shaded Area, then select the radio button for X Value.

   c) Click the picture for Right Tail.

   d) Type in the X value of 2.33 and click [OK].

$$P(Z > 2.33) = 0.009903.$$

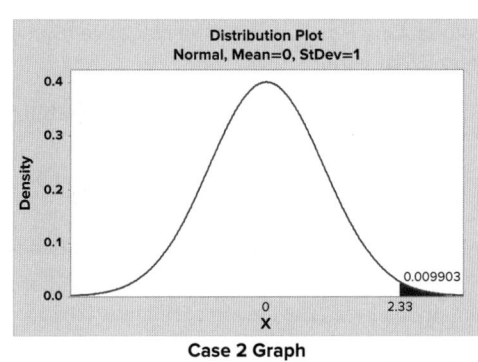

Case 2 Graph

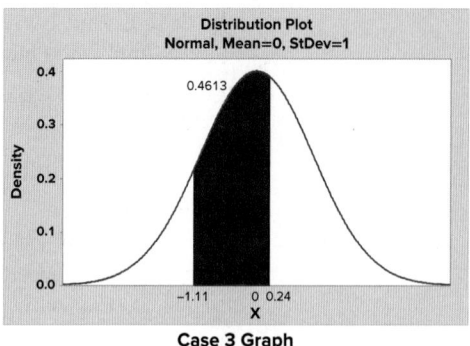

Case 3 Graph

Case 3: Find the Probability That *Z* Is between Two Values

Find the area if z is between -1.11 and 0.24.

3. Select **Edit, Edit Last Dialog** box or select **Graph>Probability Distribution Plot>View Probability** and click [OK].

    a) The distribution should be Normal with the Mean set to **0.0** and the Standard deviation set to **1.0.**

    b) Choose the tab for Shaded Area, then select the radio button for *X* Value.

    c) Click the picture for Middle.

    d) Type in the smaller value -1.11 for *X* value 1 and then the larger value 0.24 for the *X* value 2. Click [OK]. Remember that smaller values are to the left on the number line.

$$P(-1.11 < Z < 0.24) = 0.4613.$$

Case 4: Find *z* if the Area Is Given

If the area to the left of some z value is 0.0188, find the z value.

4. Select **Graph>Probability Distribution Plot>View Probability** and click [OK].

    a) The distribution should be Normal with the Mean set to 0.0 and the Standard deviation set to 1.0.

    b) Choose the tab for Shaded Area and then the radio button for Probability.

    c) Select Left Tail.

    d) Type in 0.0188 for probability and then click [OK]. The z value is -2.079.

$$P(Z < -2.079) = 0.0188.$$

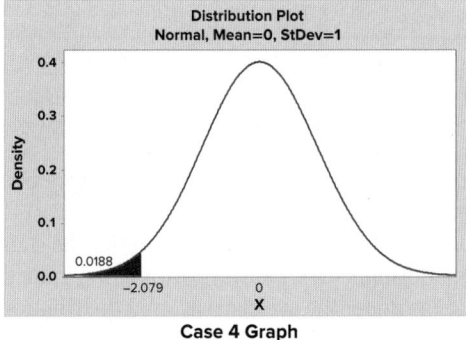

Case 4 Graph

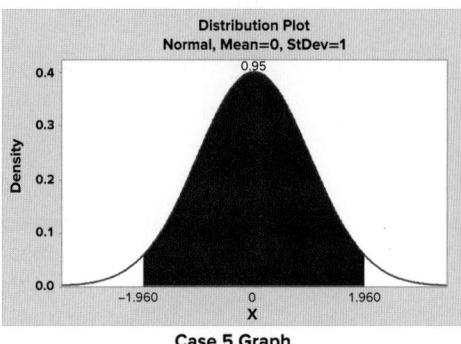

Case 5 Graph

Case 5: Find Two *z* Values, One Positive and One Negative (Same Absolute Value), so That the Area in the Middle is 0.95

5. Select **Graph>Probability Distribution Plot>View Probability** or click the **Edit Last Dialog** icon.

   a) The distribution should be Normal with the Mean set to **0.0** and the Standard deviation set to **1.0.**

   b) Choose the tab for Shaded Area, then select the radio button for Probability.

   c) Select Middle. You will need to know the area in each tail of the distribution. Subtract 0.95 from 1, then divide by 2. The area in each tail is 0.025.

   d) Type in the first probability of **0.025** and the same for the second probability. Click [OK].

$$P(-1.960 < Z < 1.96) = 0.9500.$$

6–2 Applications of the Normal Distribution

The standard normal distribution curve can be used to solve a wide variety of practical problems. The only requirement is that the variable be normally or approximately normally distributed. There are several mathematical tests to determine whether a variable is normally distributed. See the Critical Thinking Challenges on page 365. For all the problems presented in this chapter, you can assume that the variable is normally or approximately normally distributed.

To solve problems by using the standard normal distribution, transform the original variable to a standard normal distribution variable by using the formula

$$z = \frac{\text{value} - \text{mean}}{\text{standard deviation}} \qquad \text{or} \qquad z = \frac{X - \mu}{\sigma}$$

This is the same formula presented in Section 3–3. This formula transforms the values of the variable into standard units or *z* values. Once the variable is transformed, then the Procedure Table and Table A–4 in Appendix A can be used to solve problems.

For example, suppose that the scores for a standardized test are normally distributed, have a mean of 100, and have a standard deviation of 15. When the scores are transformed to *z* values, the two distributions coincide, as shown in Figure 6–17. (Recall that the *z* distribution has a mean of 0 and a standard deviation of 1.)

FIGURE 6–17
Test Scores and Their Corresponding *z* Values

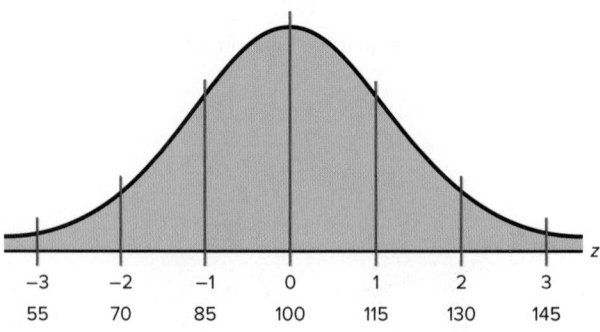

Note: The *z* values are rounded to two decimal places because Table A–4 gives the *z* values to two decimal places.

Since we now have the ability to find the area under the standard normal curve, we can find the area under any normal curve by transforming the values of the variable to *z* values, and then we find the areas under the standard normal distribution, as shown in Section 6–1.

This procedure is summarized next.

Procedure Table

Finding the Area Under Any Normal Curve

Step 1   Draw a normal curve and shade the desired area.

Step 2   Convert the values of X to z values, using the formula $z = \dfrac{X - \mu}{\sigma}$.

Step 3   Find the corresponding area, using a table, calculator, or software.

EXAMPLE 6–6   Liters of Blood

An adult has on average 5.2 liters of blood. Assume the variable is normally distributed and has a standard deviation of 0.3. Find the percentage of people who have less than 5.4 liters of blood in their system.

SOLUTION

Step 1   Draw a normal curve and shade the desired area. See Figure 6–18.

FIGURE 6–18
Area Under a
Normal Curve for
Example 6–6

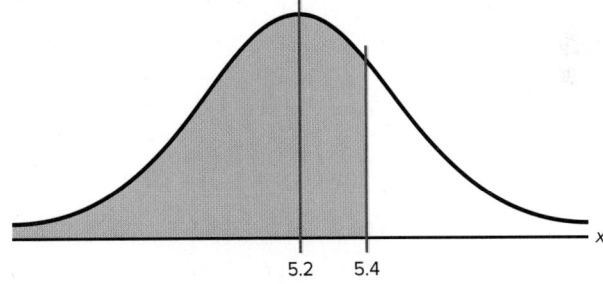

Step 2   Find the z value corresponding to 5.4.

$$z = \frac{X - \mu}{\sigma} = \frac{5.4 - 5.2}{0.3} = \frac{0.2}{0.3} = 0.67$$

Hence, 5.4 is 0.67 of a standard deviation above the mean, as shown in Figure 6–19.

FIGURE 6–19
Area and z Values for
Example 6–6

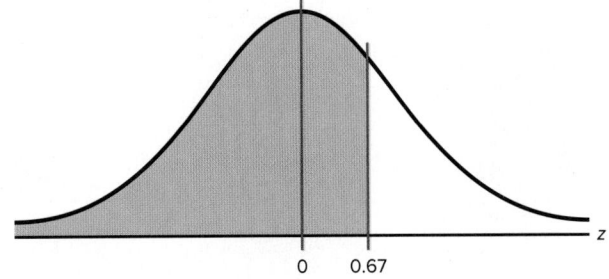

Step 3   Find the corresponding area in Table A–4. The area under the standard normal curve to the left of $z = 0.67$ is 0.7486.

Therefore, 0.7486, or 74.86%, of adults have less than 5.4 liters of blood in their system.

EXAMPLE 6–7   Monthly Recycling

Each month, an American household generates an average of 28 pounds of recyclable paper waste. Assume the variable is approximately normally distributed and the standard deviation is 2 pounds. If a household is selected at random, find the probability of its generating

> *a.* Between 27 and 31 pounds per month.
>
> *b.* More than 30.2 pounds per month.

Source: Michael D. Shook and Robert L. Shook, *The Book of Odds.*

SOLUTION *a*

Step 1   Draw a normal curve and shade the desired area. See Figure 6–20.

FIGURE 6–20

Area Under a Normal Curve for Part *a* of Example 6–7

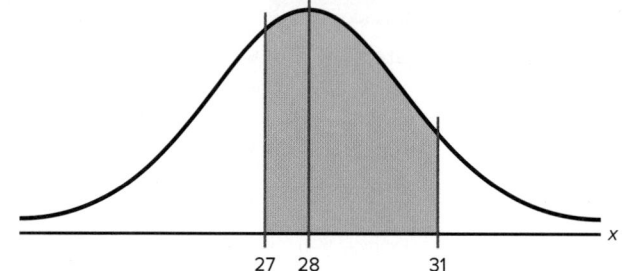

Step 2   Find the two z values.

$$z_1 = \frac{X - \mu}{\sigma} = \frac{27 - 28}{2} = -\frac{1}{2} = -0.5$$

$$z_2 = \frac{X - \mu}{\sigma} = \frac{31 - 28}{2} = \frac{3}{2} = 1.5$$

Step 3   Find the appropriate area, using Table A–4. The area to the left of z_2 is 0.9332, and the area to the left of z_1 is 0.3085. Hence, the area between z_1 and z_2 is $0.9332 - 0.3085 = 0.6247$. See Figure 6–21.

Nathan Mead/Age Fotostock

FIGURE 6–21

Area and z Values for Part *a* of Example 6–7

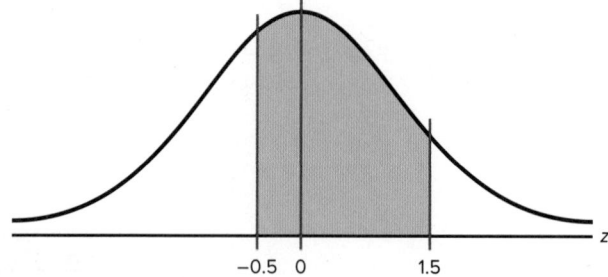

Hence, the probability that a randomly selected household generates between 27 and 31 pounds of newspapers per month is 62.47%.

SOLUTION *b*

Step 1   Draw a normal curve and shade the desired area, as shown in Figure 6–22.

FIGURE 6–22

Area Under a Normal
Curve for Part *b* of
Example 6–7

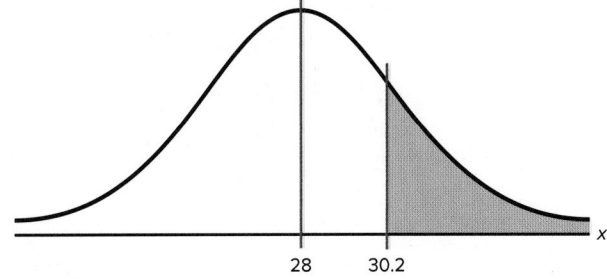

Step 2 Find the *z* value for 30.2.

$$z = \frac{X - \mu}{\sigma} = \frac{30.2 - 28}{2} = \frac{2.2}{2} = 1.1$$

Step 3 Find the appropriate area. The area to the left of $z = 1.1$ is 0.8643. Hence, the area to the right of $z = 1.1$ is $1.0000 - 0.8643 = 0.1357$. See Figure 6–23.

FIGURE 6–23

Area and *z* Values for
Part *b* of Example 6–7

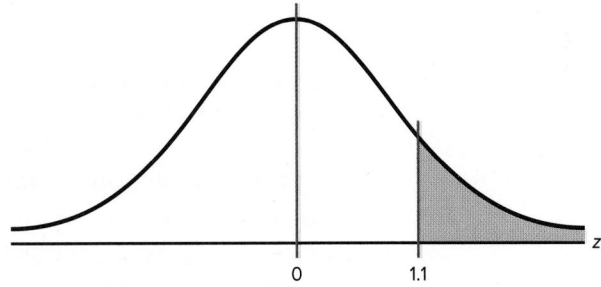

Hence, the probability that a randomly selected household will accumulate more than 30.2 pounds of recyclable paper waste is 0.1357, or 13.57%.

A normal distribution can also be used to answer questions of "How many?" This application is shown in Example 6–8.

EXAMPLE 6–8   Weight of a Male Brain

The average weight of the human male brain is 3.08 pounds. Assume the variable is approximately normally distributed, and the population standard deviation is 0.3 pounds. If 50 males are randomly selected, approximately how many will weigh less than 2.96 pounds?

SOLUTION

Step 1 Draw a normal curve and shade in the desired area. See Figure 6–24.

FIGURE 6–24

Area Under a Normal
Curve for Example 6–8

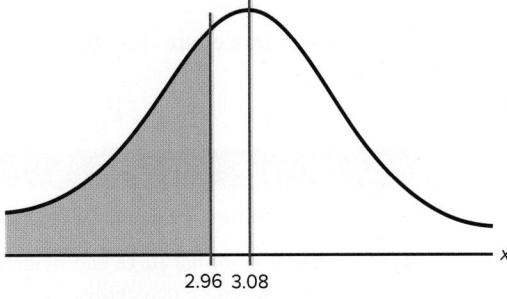

Step 2 Find the *z* value corresponding to 2.96.

$$z = \frac{X - \mu}{\sigma} = \frac{2.96 - 3.08}{0.3} = -0.4$$

Step 3   Find the area in Table A–4 corresponding to $z = -0.4$. It is 0.3446. See Figure 6–25.

FIGURE 6–25
Area and z Value for Example 6–8

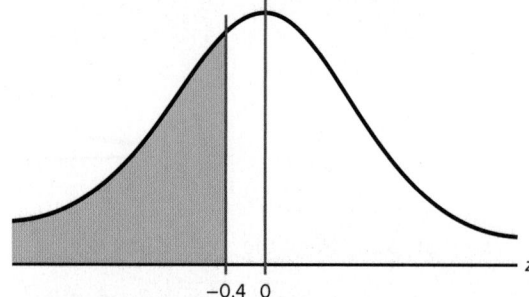

To find the number of males whose brain weight is less than 2.96 pounds, multiply $50 \times 0.3446 = 17.23$. Round this to 17. Hence, approximately 17 out of 50 randomly selected males have a brain weight of less than 2.96 pounds.

Note: For problems using percentages, be sure to write the percentage as a decimal before multiplying. Also round the answer to the nearest whole number, if necessary.

Finding Data Values Given Specific Probabilities

A normal distribution can also be used to find specific data values for given percentages. In this case, you are given a probability or percentage and need to find the corresponding data value X. You can use the formula $z = \frac{X-\mu}{\sigma}$. Substitute the values for z, μ, and σ; then solve for X. However, you can transform the formula and solve for X as shown.

$$z = \frac{X - \mu}{\sigma}$$

$z \cdot \sigma = X - \mu$ Multiply both sides by σ.

$z \cdot \sigma + \mu = X - \mu + \mu$ Add μ to both sides.

$X = z \cdot \sigma + \mu$ Exchange both sides of the equation.

Now you can use this new formula and find the value for X.

Formula for Finding the Value of a Normal Variable X

$$X = z \cdot \sigma + \mu$$

The complete procedure for finding an X value is summarized in the Procedure Table shown.

Procedure Table

Finding Data Values for Specific Probabilities

Step 1   Draw a normal curve and shade the desired area that represents the probability, proportion, or percentile.

Step 2   Find the z value from the table that corresponds to the desired area.

Step 3   Calculate the X value by using the formula $X = z\sigma + \mu$.

OBJECTIVE ❺

Find specific data values for given percentages, using the standard normal distribution.

EXAMPLE 6–9   Police Academy Qualifications

To qualify for a police academy, candidates must score in the top 10% on a general abilities test. Assume the test scores are normally distributed and the test has a mean of 200 and a standard deviation of 20. Find the lowest possible score to qualify.

SOLUTION

Step 1   Draw a normal distribution curve and shade the desired area that represents the probability.

Since the test scores are normally distributed, the test value X that cuts off the upper 10% of the area under a normal distribution curve is desired. This area is shown in Figure 6–26.

FIGURE 6–26
Area Under a Normal Curve for Example 6–9

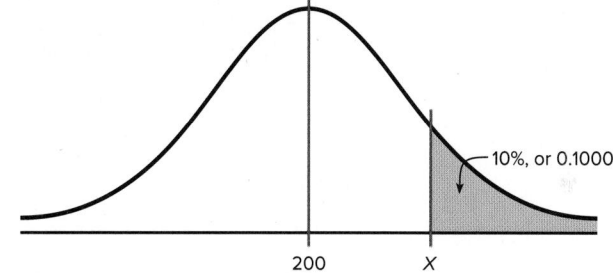

Work backward to solve this problem.

Subtract 0.1000 from 1.0000 to get the area under the normal distribution to the left of x: $1.0000 - 0.1000 = 0.9000$.

Step 2   Find the z value from Table A–4 that corresponds to the desired area.

Find the z value that corresponds to an area of 0.9000 by looking up 0.9000 in the area portion of Table A–4. If the specific value cannot be found, use the closest value—in this case 0.8997, as shown in Figure 6–27. The corresponding z value is 1.28. (If the area falls exactly halfway between two z values, use the larger of the two z values. For example, the area 0.9500 falls halfway between 0.9495 and 0.9505. In this case use 1.65 rather than 1.64 for the z value.)

FIGURE 6–27
Finding the z Value from Table A–4 (Example 6–9)

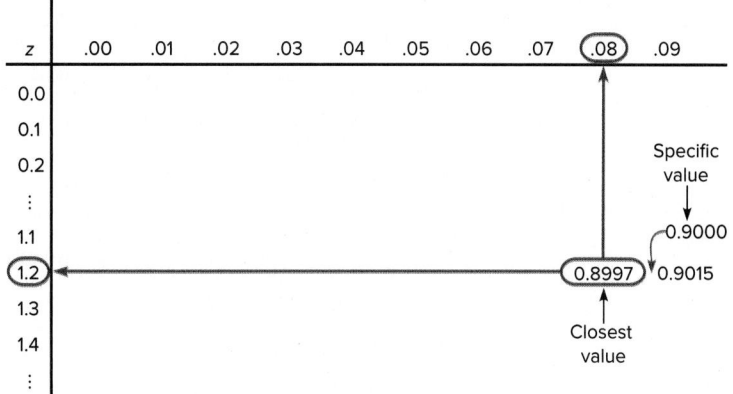

Interesting Fact

Americans are the largest consumers of chocolate. We spend $16.6 billion annually.

Step 3   Find the X value.

$$X = z \cdot \sigma + \mu = 1.28(20) + 200 = 25.6 + 200$$
$$= 225.6 = 226 \text{ (rounded)}$$

A score of 226 should be used as a cutoff. Anybody scoring 226 or higher qualifies for the academy.

EXAMPLE 6–10   Systolic Blood Pressure

For a medical study, a researcher wishes to select people in the middle 60% of the population based on blood pressure. Assuming that blood pressure readings are normally distributed and the mean systolic blood pressure is 120 and the standard deviation is 8.

   a. What is the blood pressure for the lowest 20% of the population?
   b. Find the lower and upper blood pressure readings for the middle 60% of the population.

SOLUTION *a*

Step 1   Draw a normal distribution curve and shade the desired area that represents the probability. Since the test scores are normally distributed, the test value *X* that cuts off the lower 20% of the area under a normal distribution curve is desired. This area is shown in Figure 6–28.

FIGURE 6–28
Area Under a
Normal Curve for
Example 6–10

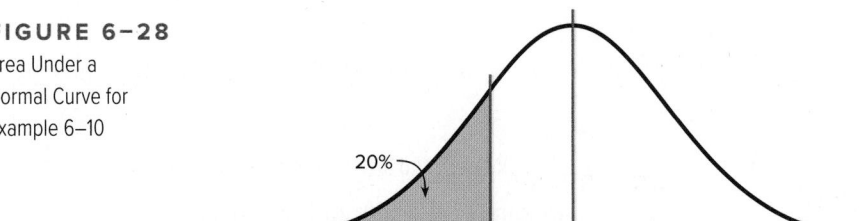

Step 2   Find the *z* value.

The *z* value with area to the left closest to 0.2000 is −0.84.

Step 3   Calculate the *X* value.

Substituting in the formula $X = z\sigma + \mu$ gives

$$X = (-0.84)(8) + 120 = 113.28$$

Therefore, the lower 20% will have blood pressure readings of $X < 113.28$.

SOLUTION *b*

Step 1   Draw a normal distribution curve and shade the desired area. The cutoff points are shown in Figure 6–29.

Two values are needed, one above the mean and one below the mean.

FIGURE 6–29
Area Under a
Normal Curve for
Example 6–10

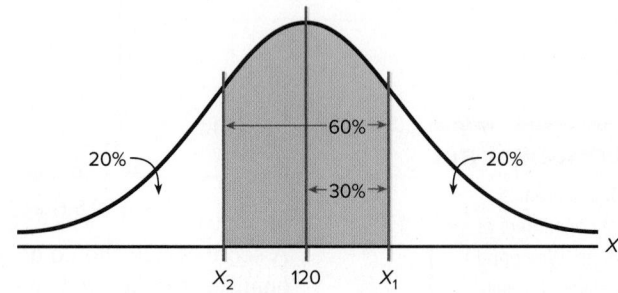

Step 2   Find the *z* values.

To get the area to the left of the positive *z* value, add 0.5000 + 0.3000 = 0.8000 (30% = 0.3000). The *z* value with area to the left closest to 0.8000 is 0.84.

Step 3   Calculate the *X* values.

Substituting in the formula $X = z\sigma + \mu$ gives

$$X_1 = z\sigma + \mu = (0.84)(8) + 120 = 126.72$$

The area to the left of the negative *z* value is 20%, or 0.2000. The area closest to 0.2000 is −0.84.

$$X_2 = (-0.84)(8) + 120 = 113.28$$

Therefore, the middle 60% will have blood pressure readings of $113.28 < X < 126.72$.

As shown in this section, a normal distribution is a useful tool in answering many questions about variables that are normally or approximately normally distributed.

Determining Normality

A normally shaped or bell-shaped distribution is only one of many shapes that a distribution can assume; however, it is very important since many statistical methods require that the distribution of values (shown in subsequent chapters) be normally or approximately normally shaped.

There are several ways statisticians check for normality. The easiest way is to draw a histogram for the data and check its shape. If the histogram is not approximately bell-shaped, then the data are not normally distributed.

Skewness can be checked by using the Pearson coefficient (PC) of skewness also called Pearson's index of skewness. The formula is

$$PC = \frac{3(\overline{X} - \text{median})}{s}$$

If the index is greater than or equal to +1 or less than or equal to −1, it can be concluded that the data are significantly skewed.

In addition, the data should be checked for outliers by using the method shown in Chapter 3. Even one or two outliers can have a big effect on normality.

Examples 6–11 and 6–12 show how to check for normality.

EXAMPLE 6–11 Technology Inventories

A survey of 18 high-tech firms showed the number of days' inventory they had on hand. Determine if the data are approximately normally distributed.

5	29	34	44	45	63	68	74	74
81	88	91	97	98	113	118	151	158

Source: USA TODAY.

SOLUTION

Step 1   Construct a frequency distribution and draw a histogram for the data, as shown in Figure 6–30.

Class	Frequency
5–29	2
30–54	3
55–79	4
80–104	5
105–129	2
130–154	1
155–179	1

FIGURE 6–30

Histogram for Example 6–11

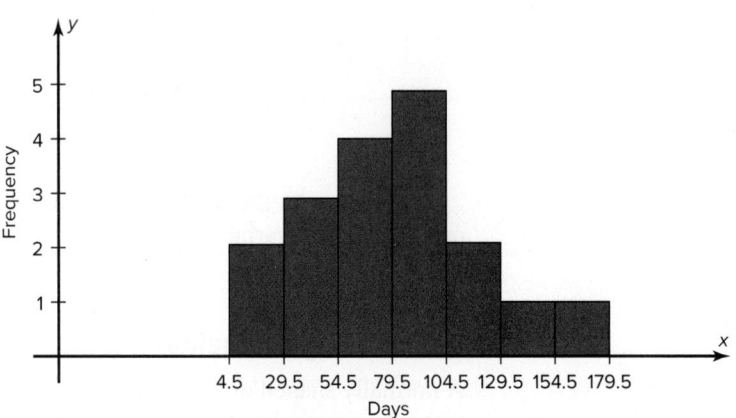

Since the histogram is approximately bell-shaped, we can say that the distribution is approximately normal.

Step 2   Check for skewness. For these data, $\overline{X} = 79.5$, median $= 77.5$, and $s = 40.5$. Using the Pearson coefficient of skewness gives

$$PC = \frac{3(79.5 - 77.5)}{40.5}$$

$$= 0.148$$

In this case, PC is not greater than $+1$ or less than -1, so it can be concluded that the distribution is not significantly skewed.

Step 3   Check for outliers. Recall that an outlier is a data value that lies more than $1.5(\text{IQR})$ units below Q_1 or $1.5(\text{IQR})$ units above Q_3. In this case, $Q_1 = 45$ and $Q_3 = 98$; hence, $\text{IQR} = Q_3 - Q_1 = 98 - 45 = 53$. An outlier would be a data value less than $45 - 1.5(53) = -34.5$ or a data value larger than $98 + 1.5(53) = 177.5$. In this case, there are no outliers.

Since the histogram is approximately bell-shaped, the data are not significantly skewed, and there are no outliers, it can be concluded that the distribution is approximately normally distributed.

EXAMPLE 6–12   Number of Baseball Games Played

The data shown consist of the number of games played each year in the career of Baseball Hall of Famer Bill Mazeroski. Determine if the data are approximately normally distributed.

81	148	152	135	151	152
159	142	34	162	130	162
163	143	67	112	70	

Source: Greensburg Tribune Review.

SOLUTION

Step 1   Construct a frequency distribution and draw a histogram for the data. See Figure 6–31.

FIGURE 6–31   Histogram for Example 6–12

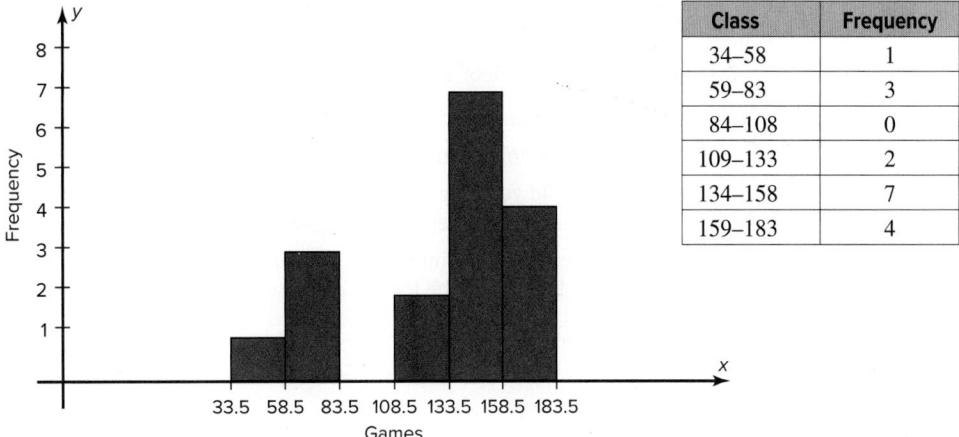

Class	Frequency
34–58	1
59–83	3
84–108	0
109–133	2
134–158	7
159–183	4

The histogram shows that the frequency distribution is somewhat negatively skewed.

Step 2   Check for skewness; $\overline{X} = 127.24$, median $= 143$, and $s = 39.87$.

$$PC = \frac{3(\overline{X} - \text{median})}{s}$$

$$= \frac{3(127.24 - 143)}{39.87}$$

$$\approx -1.19$$

Since the PC is less than -1, it can be concluded that the distribution is significantly skewed to the left.

Step 3   Check for outliers. In this case, $Q_1 = 96.5$ and $Q_3 = 155.5$. IQR $=$ $Q_3 - Q_1 = 155.5 - 96.5 = 59$. Any value less than $96.5 - 1.5(59) = 8$ or above $155.5 + 1.5(59) = 244$ is considered an outlier. There are no outliers.

In summary, the distribution is somewhat negatively skewed.

Another method that is used to check normality is to draw a *normal quantile plot.* *Quantiles,* sometimes called *fractiles,* are values that separate the data set into approximately equal groups. Recall that quartiles separate the data set into four approximately equal groups, and deciles separate the data set into 10 approximately equal groups. A normal quantile plot consists of a graph of points using the data values for the *x* coordinates and the *z* values of the quantiles corresponding to the *x* values for the *y* coordinates. (*Note:* The calculations of the *z* values are somewhat complicated, and technology is usually used to draw the graph. The Technology Step by Step section shows how to draw a normal quantile plot.) If the points of the quantile plot do not lie in an approximately straight line, then normality can be rejected.

There are several other methods used to check for normality. A method using normal probability graph paper is shown in the Critical Thinking Challenge section at the end of this chapter, and the chi-square goodness-of-fit test is shown in Chapter 11. Two other tests sometimes used to check normality are the Kolmogorov-Smirnov test and the Lilliefors test. An explanation of these tests can be found in advanced texts.

≡ Applying the Concepts **6–2**

Smart People

Assume you are thinking about starting a Mensa chapter in your hometown, which has a population of about 10,000 people. You need to know how many people would qualify for Mensa, which requires an IQ of at least 130. You realize that IQ is normally distributed with a mean of 100 and a standard deviation of 15. Complete the following.

1. Find the approximate number of people in your hometown who are eligible for Mensa.
2. Is it reasonable to continue your quest for a Mensa chapter in your hometown?
3. How could you proceed to find out how many of the eligible people would actually join the new chapter? Be specific about your methods of gathering data.
4. What would be the minimum IQ score needed if you wanted to start an Ultra-Mensa club that included only the top 1% of IQ scores?

See page 367 for the answers.

≡ Exercises **6–2**

1. **Credit Card Debt** The average credit card debt for households that have credit cards is $16,061. If the distribution is approximately normal and the standard deviation is $2011, what is the probability that a randomly selected household has one or more credit cards with the debt of each card less than $13,500? 0.1014
   Source: Nerd Wallet

2. **Uber Rides** In a large city, the average number of rides an Uber driver makes in a week is 36. Assume the distribution is approximately normally distributed and the standard deviation is 5. Find the probability that a randomly selected Uber driver makes
   a. Between 30 and 45 rides per week. 0.8490
   b. More than 40 rides per week. 0.2119
   c. Less than 46 rides per week. 0.9772

3. **Population in U.S. Jails** The average daily jail population in the United States is 706,242. If the distribution is normal and the standard deviation is 52,145, find the probability that on a randomly selected day, the jail population is
   a. Greater than 750,000 0.2005 (TI: 0.2007)
   b. Between 600,000 and 700,000 0.4315 (TI: 0.4316)
   Source: New York Times Almanac.

4. **SAT Scores** The national average SAT score (for Verbal and Math) is 1028. If we assume a normal distribution with $\sigma = 92$, what is the 90th percentile score? What is the probability that a randomly selected score exceeds 1200? 1146; 0.0307 (TI: 1146; 0.0308)
   Source: New York Times Almanac.

5. **Chocolate Bar Calories** The average number of calories in a 1.5-ounce chocolate bar is 225. Suppose that the distribution of calories is approximately normal with $\sigma = 10$. Find the probability that a randomly selected chocolate bar will have
   a. Between 200 and 220 calories. 0.3023
   b. Less than 200 calories. 0.0062
   Source: The Doctor's Pocket Calorie, Fat, and Carbohydrate Counter.

6. **Monthly Mortgage Payments** The average monthly mortgage payment including principal and interest is $1275 in the United States. If the standard deviation is approximately $180 and the mortgage payments are approximately normally distributed, find the probability that a randomly selected monthly payment is
   a. More than $1293. 0.4602
   b. More than $1768. 0.0031
   c. Between $1093 and $1443. 0.6676 (TI: 0.6687)

7. **Netflix Decisions** A recent survey found that Americans spend 23 minutes choosing what to watch on Netflix. If the times are approximately normally distributed with a standard deviation of 4 minutes and a person who watches Netflix is randomly selected, find these probabilities.
   a. The person spends more than 30 minutes deciding what to watch. 0.0401
   b. The person spends less than 18 minutes deciding what to watch. 0.1056
   Source: orgain.com

8. **College Graduates' Starting Salaries** A recent survey found that the average starting salaries for college graduates was $49,785. Assume that the distribution of starting salaries is approximately normal and the standard deviation is $4503. Find these probabilities for randomly selected graduates.

   a. The graduate makes more than $55,000.
   0.1230 (TI: 0.1234)

   b. The graduate makes between $40,000 and $50,000.
   0.0549 (TI: 0.5042)

   c. The graduate makes less than $42,000.
   0.0418 (TI: 0.0419)

   Source: Hay Group

9. **Miles Driven Annually** The mean number of miles driven per vehicle annually in the United States is 12,494 miles. Choose a randomly selected vehicle, and assume the annual mileage is normally distributed with a standard deviation of 1290 miles. What is the probability that the vehicle was driven more than 15,000 miles? Less than 8000 miles? Would you buy a vehicle if you had been told that it had been driven less than 6000 miles in the past year? 0.0262 and 0.0003; would want to know why it had only been driven less than 6000 miles (TI: 0.0260; 0.0002)

   Source: World Almanac.

10. **Commute Time to Work** The average commute to work (one way) is 25 minutes according to the 2005 American Community Survey. If we assume that commuting times are normally distributed and that the standard deviation is 6.1 minutes, what is the probability that a randomly selected commuter spends more than 30 minutes commuting one way? Less than 18 minutes? 0.2061; 0.1251 (TI: 0.1256)

    Source: www.census.gov

11. **Credit Card Debt** The average credit card debt for college seniors is $3262. If the debt is normally distributed with a standard deviation of $1100, find these probabilities.

    a. The senior owes at least $1000. 0.9803 (TI: 0.9801)

    b. The senior owes more than $4000.

    c. The senior owes between $3000 and $4000.

    Source: USA TODAY. b. 0.2514 (TI: 0.2511)   *c.* 0.3434 (TI: 0.3430)

12. **Financial Burden for a Divorce** The average amount of financial losses in a divorce is $19,922. Assume that the variable is approximately normally distributed and the standard deviation is $3000. If a randomly selected divorced person is chosen, find the probability that

    a. The person has spent at least $10,000. 0.9995

    b. The person has spent between $20,000 and $23,000.
    0.3365 (TI: 0.3372)

    c. The person has spent less than $25,000. 0.9545
    (TI: 0.9547)

    Source: Experian Survey

13. **Potholes** The average number of potholes per 10 miles of paved U.S. roads is 130. Assume this variable is

approximately normally distributed and has a standard deviation of 5. Find the probability that a randomly selected road has

   a. More than 142 potholes per 10 miles. 0.0082

   b. Less than 125 potholes per 10 miles. 0.1587

   c. Between 128 and 136 potholes per 10 miles.
   0.5403 (TI: 0.5404)

   Source: Infrastructure Technology Institute.

14. **Newborn Elephant Weights** Newborn elephant calves usually weigh between 200 and 250 pounds—until October 2006, that is. An Asian elephant at the Houston (Texas) Zoo gave birth to a male calf weighing in at a whopping 384 pounds! Mac (like the truck) is believed to be the heaviest elephant calf ever born at a facility accredited by the Association of Zoos and Aquariums. If, indeed, the mean weight for newborn elephant calves is 225 pounds with a standard deviation of 45 pounds, what is the probability of a newborn weighing at least 384 pounds? Assume that the weights of newborn elephants are normally distributed.
   Less than 0.0002

   Source: www.houstonzoo.org

15. **Heart Rates** For a certain group of individuals, the average heart rate is 72 beats per minute. Assume the variable is normally distributed and the standard deviation is 3 beats per minute. If a subject is selected at random, find the probability that the person has the following heart rate.

    a. Between 68 and 74 beats per minute 0.6568 (TI: 0.6563)

    b. Higher than 70 beats per minute 0.7475 (TI: 0.7486)

    c. Less than 75 beats per minute 0.8413

16. **Salary of Full Professors** The average salary of a male full professor at a public four-year institution offering classes at the doctoral level is $99,685. For a female full professor at the same kind of institution, the salary is $90,330. If the standard deviation for the salaries of both genders is approximately $5200 and the salaries are normally distributed, find the 80th percentile salary for male professors and for female professors. Men: $104,053 (TI: men: $104,241)   Women: $94,698 (TI: women: $94,706)

    Source: World Almanac.

17. **Cat Behavior** A report stated that the average number of times a cat returns to its food bowl during the day is 36. Assuming the variable is normally distributed with a standard deviation of 5, what is the probability that a cat would return to its dish between 32 and 38 times a day? 0.4435

18. **Screen Time** Americans spend an average of 7 hours a day looking at a screen. Assume the variable is approximately normally distributed and the standard deviation is 1.3 hours. Find the time limits for the middle 50% of screen viewers. 6.129 and 7.871 (TI: 6.123; 7.877)

    Source: American Optometric Association

19. **Eyeball Measurement** The average width of a human eyeball is normally distributed with a mean of 22.822 mm and a standard deviation of 1.7 mm.

    a. What is the probability that the width of a person's eyeball is less than 23 mm? 0.54

    b. In a group of 40 patients, how many patients would have eyeball widths less than 23 mm? 22 people

    Source: Variations in Eyeball Diameters of the Healthy Adults
    https://www.hindawi.com/journals/joph/2014/503645/

20. **Weights of Florida Manatees** The weight of the adult male Florida manatees is normally distributed with a mean weight of 450 kg with a standard deviation of 45.3 kg. The U.S. Fish and Wildlife Service wildlife research permit allowed for the capture and release to measure 120 adult manatees in the Crystal River. How many of these adult manatees would have a weight of over 500 kg? 16 manatees

21. **New-Home Sizes** A contractor decided to build homes that will include the middle 80% of the market. If the average size of homes built is 1810 square feet, find the maximum and minimum sizes of the homes the contractor should build. Assume that the standard deviation is 92 square feet and the variable is normally distributed. 1692.24–1927.76 (TI: 1692.10–1927.90)

    Source: Michael D. Shook and Robert L. Shook, *The Book of Odds.*

22. **New-Home Prices** If the average price of a new one-family home is $246,300 with a standard deviation of $15,000, find the minimum and maximum prices of the houses that a contractor will build to satisfy the middle 80% of the market. Assume that the variable is normally distributed. $227,100 to $265,500 (TI: $227,077 to $265,523)

    Source: New York Times Almanac.

23. **Cost of Personal Computers** The average price of a personal computer (PC) is $949. If the computer prices are approximately normally distributed and $\sigma = \$100$, what is the probability that a randomly selected PC costs more than $1200? The least expensive 10% of personal computers cost less than what amount? 0.006; $821

    Source: New York Times Almanac.

24. **Reading Improvement Program** To help students improve their reading, a school district decides to implement a reading program. It is to be administered to the bottom 5% of the students in the district, based on the scores on a reading achievement exam. If the average score for the students in the district is 122.6, find the cutoff score that will make a student eligible for the program. The standard deviation is 18. Assume the variable is normally distributed. 92.99 or 93

25. **Qualifying Blood Pressure** To qualify for a medical study, an applicant must have a systolic blood pressure in the 50% of the middle range. If the systolic blood pressure is normally distributed with a mean of 120 and a standard deviation of 4, find the upper and lower limits of blood pressure a person must have to qualify for the study. 117.3–122.7

    Source: Charleston Post and Courier.

26. **Ages of Amtrak Passenger Cars** The average age of Amtrak passenger train cars is 19.4 years. If the distribution of ages is normal and 20% of the cars are older than 22.8 years, find the standard deviation. 4.05

    Source: New York Times Almanac.

27. **Lengths of Hospital Stays** The average length of a hospital stay for all diagnoses is 4.8 days. If we assume that the lengths of hospital stays are normally distributed with a variance of 2.1, then 10% of hospital stays are longer than how many days? Thirty percent of stays are less than how many days?

    Source: www.cdc.gov 6.7; 4.05 (TI: for 10%, 6.657; for 30%, 4.040)

28. **High School Competency Test** A mandatory competency test for high school sophomores has a normal distribution with a mean of 400 and a standard deviation of 100.

    a. The top 3% of students receive $500. What is the minimum score you would need to receive this award? 588

    b. The bottom 1.5% of students must go to summer school. What is the minimum score you would need to stay out of this group? You would need a score of 184 to stay out of the group since a score of 183 is exactly 1.5%, and you would be included in the group with that score.

29. **Risky Driving Habits** A study found that a randomly selected driver uses the phone on average of 135 seconds before an accident. Assume that the times are approximately normally distributed and the standard deviation is 32 seconds. Find the time which would include the lower 30% of the accidents. 118.22

    Source: EverQuote and Cambridge Mobile Telematics

30. **Bottled Drinking Water** Americans drank an average of 34 gallons of bottled water per capita in 2014. If the standard deviation is 2.7 gallons and the variable is normally distributed, find the probability that a randomly selected American drank more than 25 gallons of bottled water. What is the probability that the selected person drank between 28 and 30 gallons? 0.9996; 0.0562

    Source: Beverage Marketing Corporation

31. **Wristwatch Lifetimes** The mean lifetime of a wristwatch is 25 months, with a standard deviation of 5 months. If the distribution is normal, for how many months should a guarantee be made if the manufacturer does not want to exchange more than 10% of the watches? Assume the variable is normally distributed. 18.6 months

32. **Dangerous Drinking** A study of breathalyzer tests of people who use alcohol found that the average blood alcohol content reading for a large city was 0.251. Assume that the standard deviation was 0.05 and that the readings are approximately normally distributed. If the top 20% of people in this study are selected for alcohol counseling, find the blood alcohol content reading cutoff point. 0.293

    Source: AlcoMate

33. In the distributions shown, state the mean and standard deviation for each. *Hint:* See Figures 6–4 and 6–6.

Also the vertical lines are 1 standard deviation apart.
a. $\mu = 120$, $\sigma = 20$; *b.* $\mu = 15$, $\sigma = 2.5$; *c.* $\mu = 30$, $\sigma = 5$

a.

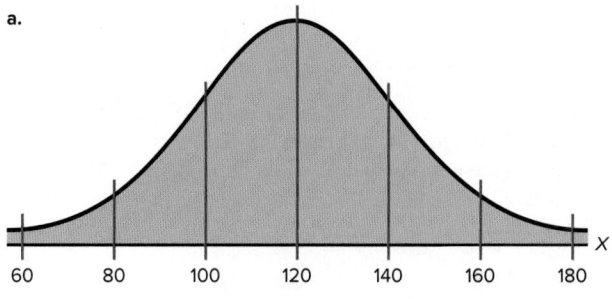

b.

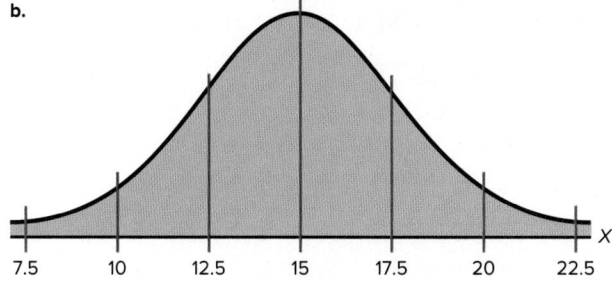

c.

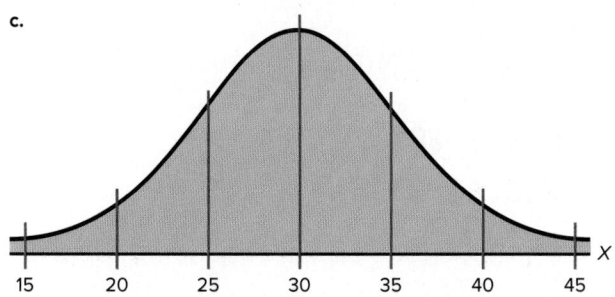

34. SAT Scores Suppose that the mathematics SAT scores for high school seniors for a specific year have a mean of 456 and a standard deviation of 100 and are approximately normally distributed. If a subgroup of these high school seniors, those who are in the National Honor Society, is selected, would you expect the distribution of scores to have the same mean and standard deviation? Explain your answer.

35. Sleep Time The mean sleep time for people is 55.4 hours per week. Assuming an approximately normal distribution, what would the standard deviation have to be if 10% of the times would be higher than 60 hours? 3.59

36. Standardizing If a distribution of raw scores were plotted and then the scores were transformed to *z* scores, would the shape of the distribution change? Explain your answer. No. The shape of the distribution would be the same.

37. Social Security Payments Consider the distribution of monthly Social Security (OASDI) payments. Assume a normal distribution with a standard deviation of $120. If one-fourth of the payments are above $1255.94, what is the mean monthly payment? $1175.54

Source: World Almanac 2012.

38. Find the Mean In a normal distribution, find μ when σ is 6 and 3.75% of the area lies to the left of 85. 95.68

39. Internet Users U.S. Internet users spend an average of 18.3 hours a week online. If 95% of users spend between 13.1 and 23.5 hours a week, what is the probability that a randomly selected user is online less than 15 hours a week? 0.1075

Source: World Almanac 2012.

40. Exam Scores An instructor gives a 100-point examination in which the grades are normally distributed. The mean is 60 and the standard deviation is 10. If there are 5% A's and 5% F's, 15% B's and 15% D's, and 60% C's, find the scores that divide the distribution into those categories.

41. Drive-in Movies The data shown represent the number of outdoor drive-in movies in the United States for a 14-year period. Check for normality. Somewhat positively skewed

2084	1497	1014	910	899	870	837	859
848	826	815	750	637	737		

Source: National Association of Theater Owners.

42. Cigarette Taxes The data shown represent the cigarette tax (in cents) for the 50 U.S. states. Check for normality. Not significantly skewed

200	160	156	200	30	300	224	346	170	55
160	170	270	60	57	80	37	153	200	60
100	178	302	84	251	125	44	435	79	166
68	37	153	252	300	141	57	42	134	136
200	98	45	118	200	87	103	250	17	62

Source: http://www.tobaccofreekids.org

43. Box Office Revenues The data shown represent the box office total revenue (in millions of dollars) for a randomly selected sample of the top-grossing films in 2009. Check for normality. Not normal

37	32	155	277
146	80	66	113
71	29	166	36
28	72	32	32
30	32	52	84
37	402	42	109

Source: http://boxofficemojo.com

44. Number of Runs Made The data shown represent the number of runs made each year during Bill Mazeroski's career. Check for normality. Somewhat negatively skewed

30	59	69	50	58	71	55	43	66	52	56	62
36	13	29	17	3							

Source: Greensburg Tribune Review.

45. Use your calculator to generate 20 random integers from 1–100, and check the set of data for normality. Would you expect these data to be normal? Explain. Answers will vary.

⚏ Technology | Step by Step

TI-84 Plus

Step by Step

Normal Random Variables

To find the probability for a normal random variable:

Press **2nd [DISTR]**, then **2** for normalcdf(

The form is normalcdf(lower x value, upper x value, μ, σ)

Use E99 for ∞ (infinity) and −E99 for $-\infty$ (negative infinity). Press **2nd [EE]** to get E. Make sure to not use the letter E or number e keys.

Example: Find the probability that x is between 27 and 31 when $\mu = 28$ and $\sigma = 2$. (Example 6–7a from the text).

normalcdf(27,31,28,2)

```
normalcdf(27,31,
28,2)
          .6246552391
```

To find the percentile for a normal random variable:

Press **2nd [DISTR]**, then **3** for invNorm(

The form is invNorm(area to the left of x value, μ, σ)

Example: Find the 90th percentile when $\mu = 200$ and $\sigma = 20$ (Example 6–9 from text).

invNorm(.9,200,20)

```
invNorm(.9,200,2
0)
          225.6310313
```

To construct a normal quantile plot:

1. Enter the data values into L_1.

2. Press **2nd [STAT PLOT]** to get the STAT PLOT menu.

3. Press **1** for Plot 1.

4. Turn on the plot by pressing **ENTER** while the cursor is flashing over ON.

5. Move the cursor to the normal quantile plot (6th graph).

6. Make sure L_1 is entered for the Data List and X is highlighted for the Data Axis.

7. Press **ZOOM**, select option 9: ZoomStat to view the graph.

Example: A data set is given below. Check for normality by constructing a normal quantile plot.

5	29	34	44	45	63	68	74	74
81	88	91	97	98	113	118	151	158

  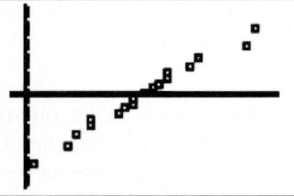

Since the points in the normal quantile plot lie close to a straight line, the distribution is approximately normal.

EXCEL

Step by Step

Data

5	29	34	44	45
63	68	74	74	81
88	91	97	98	113
118	151	158		

Sort &
Filter ▾

Normal Quantile Plot

Excel can be used to construct a normal quantile plot in order to examine if a set of data is approximately normally distributed.

1. Enter the data from Example 6–11 into column A of a new worksheet. The data should be sorted in ascending order. If the data are not already sorted in ascending order, highlight the data to be sorted and select the Sort & Filter icon from the toolbar. Then select Sort Smallest to Largest.

2. After all the data are entered and sorted in column A, select cell B1. Type: =NORM.S.INV(1/(2*18)). Since the sample size is 18, each score represents $\frac{1}{18}$, or approximately 5.6%, of the sample. Each data value is assumed to subdivide the data into equal intervals. Each data value corresponds to the midpoint of a particular subinterval. Thus, this procedure will standardize the data by assuming each data value represents the midpoint of a subinterval of width $\frac{1}{18}$.

3. Repeat the procedure from step 2 for each data value in column A. However, for each subsequent value in column A, enter the next odd multiple of $\frac{1}{36}$ in the argument for the NORM.S.INV function. For example, in cell B2, type: =NORM.S.INV(3/(2*18)). In cell B3, type: =NORM.S.INV(5/(2*18)), and so on until all the data values have corresponding z scores.

4. Highlight the data from columns A and B, and select Insert, then Scatter chart. Select the Scatter with only markers (the first Scatter chart).

5. To insert a title to the chart: Left-click on any region of the chart. Select Chart Tools and Layout from the toolbar. Then select Chart Title. Title the chart Normal Quantile Plot.

6. To insert a label for the variable on the horizontal axis: Left-click on any region of the chart. Select Chart Tools and Layout from the toolbar. Then select Axis Titles>Primary Horizontal Axis Title. Title the horizontal axis Number of Days' Inventory.

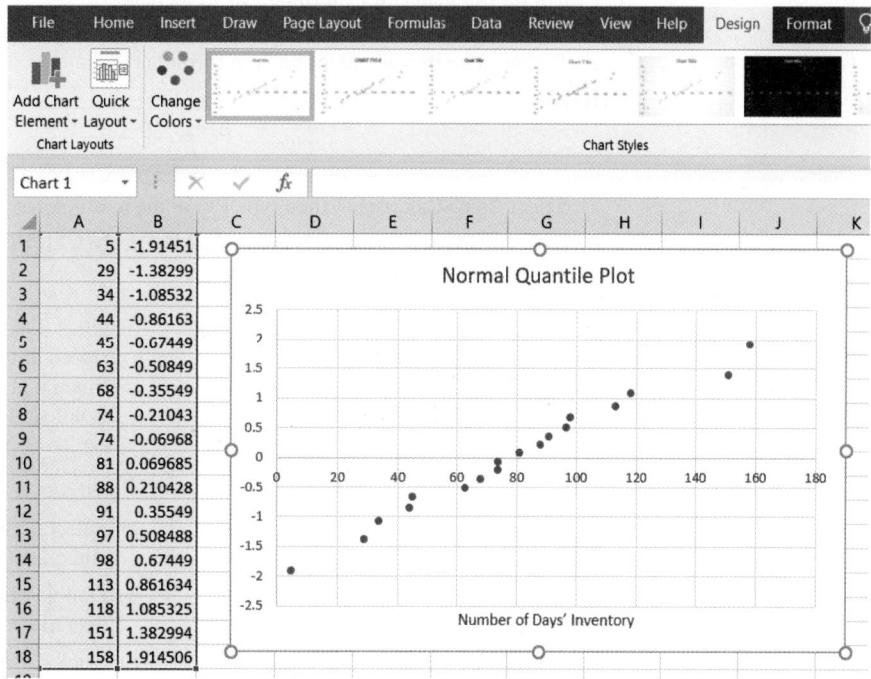

The points on the chart appear to lie close to a straight line. Thus, we deduce that the data are approximately normally distributed.

MINITAB
Step by Step

Determining Normality

There are several ways in which statisticians test a data set for normality. Four are shown here.

Data

5	29	34	44	45
63	68	74	74	81
88	91	97	98	113
118	151	158		

1. **Construct a Histogram**

   Inspect the histogram for shape.

   a) Enter the data in the first column of a new worksheet. Name the column Inventory.

   b) Use Stat>Basic Statistics>Graphical Summary to create the histogram. Is it symmetric? Is there a single peak? The instructions in Section 2–2 can be used to change the X scale to match the histogram.

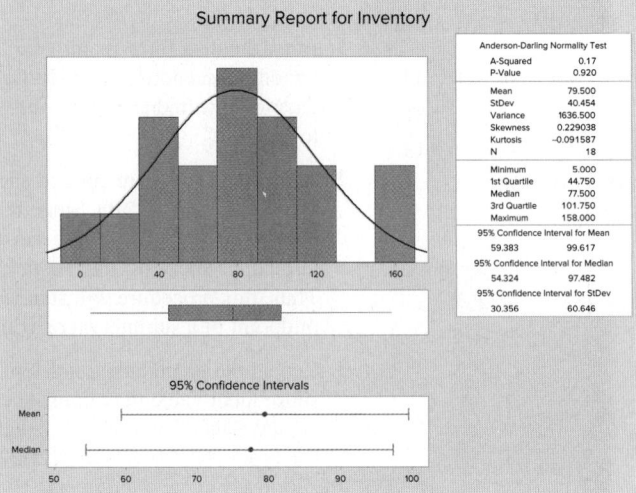

2. **Construct a Boxplot**

   a) Inspect the boxplot for outliers. Use the boxplot in the graphical summary. There are no outliers in this graph.

   b) Inspect the boxplot for symmetry. The box is approximately in the middle of the range, and the median is close to the middle of the box. Most likely this is not a skewed distribution.

3. **Calculate the Pearson Coefficient of Skewness**

   The measure of skewness in the graphical summary is not the same as the Pearson coefficient. Use the calculator and the formula.

   $$PC = \frac{3(\overline{X} - \text{median})}{s}$$

   a) Select **Calc>Calculator,** then type **PC** in the text box for Store result in:.

   b) Enter the expression: **3*(MEAN(C1)-MEDIAN(C1))/(STDEV(C1)).** Make sure you get all the parentheses in the right place!

   c) Click [OK]. The result, 0.148318, will be stored in the first row of C2 named PC. Since it is smaller than +1, the distribution is not skewed.

4. **Construct a Normal Probability Plot**

   a) Select **Graph>Probability Plot,** then Single and click [OK].

   b) Double-click C1 Inventory to select the data to be graphed.

   c) Click [Distribution] and make sure that Normal is selected. Click [OK].

   d) Click [Labels] and enter the title for the graph: **Quantile Plot for Inventory.**

   e) Click [OK] twice. Inspect the graph to see if the graph of the points is linear.

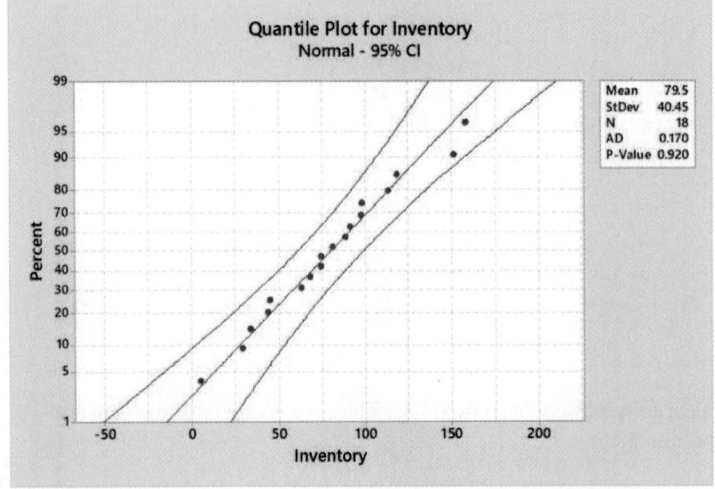

These data are nearly normal.

What do you look for in the plot?

- An "S curve" indicates a distribution that is too thick in the tails, a uniform distribution, for example.
- Concave plots indicate a skewed distribution.
- If one end has a point that is extremely high or low, there may be outliers.

This data set appears to be nearly normal by every one of the four criteria! ▬

6–3   The Central Limit Theorem

OBJECTIVE

Use the central limit theorem to solve problems involving sample means for large samples.

In addition to knowing how individual data values vary about the mean for a population, statisticians are interested in knowing how the means of samples of the same size taken from the same population vary about the population mean.

Distribution of Sample Means

Suppose a researcher selects a sample of 30 adult males and finds the mean of the measure of the triglyceride levels for the sample subjects to be 187 milligrams/deciliter. Then suppose a second sample is selected, and the mean of that sample is found to be 192 milligrams/deciliter. Continue the process for 100 samples. What happens then is that the mean becomes a random variable, and the sample means 187, 192, 184, . . . , 196 constitute a *sampling distribution of sample means.*

> A **sampling distribution of sample means** is a distribution using the means computed from all possible random samples of a specific size taken from a population.

If the samples are randomly selected with replacement, the sample means, for the most part, will be somewhat different from the population mean μ. These differences are caused by sampling error.

> **Sampling error** is the difference between the sample measure and the corresponding population measure due to the fact that the sample is not a perfect representation of the population.

When all possible samples of a specific size are selected with replacement from a population, the distribution of the sample means for a variable has two important properties, which are explained next.

Properties of the Distribution of Sample Means

1. The mean of the sample means will be the same as the population mean.
2. The standard deviation of the sample means will be smaller than the standard deviation of the population, and it will be equal to the population standard deviation divided by the square root of the sample size.

The following example illustrates these two properties. Suppose a professor gave an 8-point quiz to a small class of four students. The results of the quiz were 2, 6, 4, and 8. For the sake of discussion, assume that the four students constitute the population. The mean of the population is

$$\mu = \frac{2 + 6 + 4 + 8}{4} = 5$$

FIGURE 6–32
Distribution of Quiz Scores

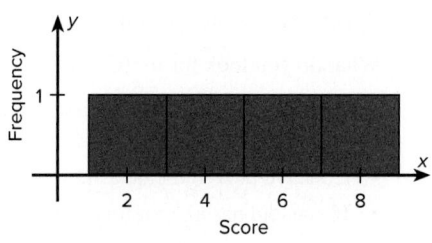

The standard deviation of the population is

$$\sigma = \sqrt{\frac{(2-5)^2 + (6-5)^2 + (4-5)^2 + (8-5)^2}{4}} \approx 2.236$$

The graph of the original distribution is shown in Figure 6–32. This is called a *uniform distribution.*

Now, if all samples of size 2 are taken with replacement and the mean of each sample is found, the distribution is as shown.

Sample	Mean	Sample	Mean
2, 2	2	6, 2	4
2, 4	3	6, 4	5
2, 6	4	6, 6	6
2, 8	5	6, 8	7
4, 2	3	8, 2	5
4, 4	4	8, 4	6
4, 6	5	8, 6	7
4, 8	6	8, 8	8

A frequency distribution of sample means is as follows.

$\bar{X}$	f
2	1
3	2
4	3
5	4
6	3
7	2
8	1

For the data from the example just discussed, Figure 6–33 shows the graph of the sample means. The histogram appears to be approximately normal.

The mean of the sample means, denoted by $\mu_{\bar{X}}$, is

$$\mu_{\bar{X}} = \frac{2 + 3 + \cdots + 8}{16} = \frac{80}{16} = 5$$

FIGURE 6–33
Distribution of Sample Means

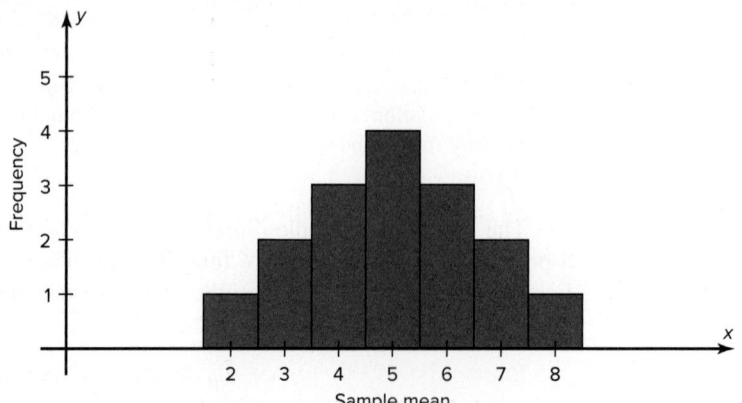

which is the same as the population mean. Hence,

$$\mu_{\overline{X}} = \mu$$

The standard deviation of sample means, denoted by $\sigma_{\overline{X}}$, is

$$\sigma_{\overline{X}} = \sqrt{\frac{(2-5)^2 + (3-5)^2 + \cdots + (8-5)^2}{16}} \approx 1.581$$

which is the same as the population standard deviation, divided by $\sqrt{2}$:

$$\sigma_{\overline{X}} = \frac{2.236}{\sqrt{2}} \approx 1.581$$

Unusual Stats

Each year a person living in the United States consumes on average 1400 pounds of food.

(*Note:* Rounding rules were not used here in order to show that the answers coincide.)

In summary, if all possible samples of size n are taken with replacement from the same population, the mean of the sample means, denoted by $\mu_{\overline{X}}$, equals the population mean μ; and the standard deviation of the sample means, denoted by $\sigma_{\overline{X}}$, equals $\sigma/\sqrt{n}$. The standard deviation of the sample means is called the **standard error of the mean.** Hence,

$$\sigma_{\overline{X}} = \frac{\sigma}{\sqrt{n}}$$

A third property of the sampling distribution of sample means pertains to the shape of the distribution and is explained by the **central limit theorem.**

The Central Limit Theorem

As the sample size n increases without limit, the shape of the distribution of the sample means taken with replacement from a population with mean μ and standard deviation σ will approach a normal distribution. As previously shown, this distribution will have a mean μ and a standard deviation $\sigma/\sqrt{n}$.

If the sample size is sufficiently large, the central limit theorem can be used to answer questions about sample means in the same manner that a normal distribution can be used to answer questions about individual values. The only difference is that a new formula must be used for the z values. It is

$$z = \frac{\overline{X} - \mu}{\sigma/\sqrt{n}}$$

Notice that $\overline{X}$ is the sample mean, and the denominator must be adjusted since means are being used instead of individual data values. The denominator is the standard deviation of the sample means.

If a large number of samples of a given size are selected from a normally distributed population, or if a large number of samples of a given size that is greater than or equal to 30 are selected from a population that is not normally distributed, and the sample means are computed, then the distribution of sample means will look like the one shown in Figure 6–34. Their percentages indicate the areas of the regions.

It's important to remember two things when you use the central limit theorem:

1. When the original variable is normally distributed, the distribution of the sample means will be normally distributed, for any sample size n.

2. When the distribution of the original variable is not normal, a sample size of 30 or more is needed to use a normal distribution to approximate the distribution of the sample means. The larger the sample, the better the approximation will be.

Examples 6–13 through 6–15 show how the standard normal distribution can be used to answer questions about sample means.

FIGURE 6–34

Distribution of Sample Means for a Large Number of Samples

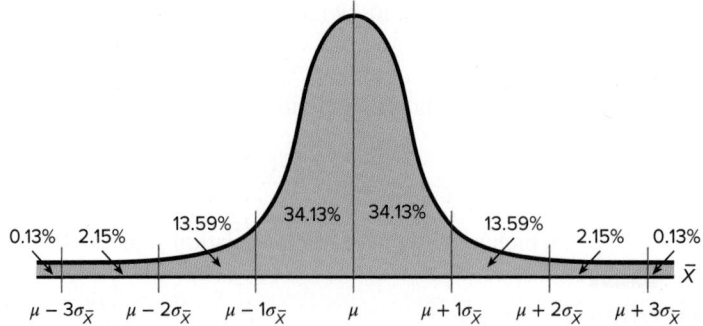

0.13% 2.15% 13.59% 34.13% 34.13% 13.59% 2.15% 0.13%

$\mu - 3\sigma_{\overline{X}}$ $\mu - 2\sigma_{\overline{X}}$ $\mu - 1\sigma_{\overline{X}}$ μ $\mu + 1\sigma_{\overline{X}}$ $\mu + 2\sigma_{\overline{X}}$ $\mu + 3\sigma_{\overline{X}}$

EXAMPLE 6–13   Hours That Children Watch Television

A. C. Neilsen reported that children between the ages of 2 and 5 watch an average of 25 hours of television per week. Assume the variable is normally distributed and the standard deviation is 3 hours. If 20 children between the ages of 2 and 5 are randomly selected, find the probability that the mean of the number of hours they watch television will be greater than 26.3 hours.

Source: Michael D. Shook and Robert L. Shook, *The Book of Odds.*

SOLUTION

Since the variable is approximately normally distributed, the distribution of sample means will be approximately normal, with a mean of 25. The standard deviation of the sample means is

$$\sigma_{\overline{X}} = \frac{\sigma}{\sqrt{n}} = \frac{3}{\sqrt{20}} = 0.671$$

Step 1   Draw a normal curve and shade the desired area.

The distribution of the means is shown in Figure 6–35, with the appropriate area shaded.

FIGURE 6–35

Distribution of the Means for Example 6–13

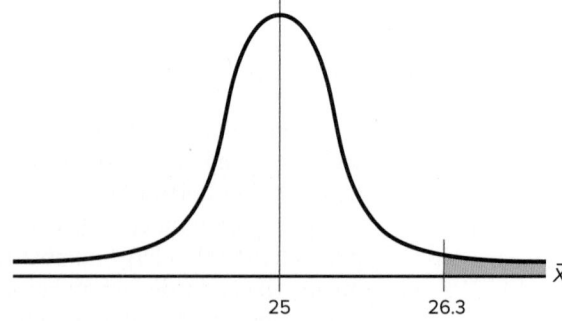

25   26.3

Step 2   Convert the $\overline{X}$ value to a z value.

The z value is

$$z = \frac{\overline{X} - \mu}{\sigma/\sqrt{n}} = \frac{26.3 - 25}{3/\sqrt{20}} = \frac{1.3}{0.671} = 1.94$$

Step 3   Find the corresponding area for the z value.

The area to the right of 1.94 is $1.000 - 0.9738 = 0.0262$, or 2.62%.

One can conclude that the probability of obtaining a sample mean larger than 26.3 hours is 2.62% [that is, $P(\overline{X} > 26.3) = 0.0262$]. Specifically, the probability that the 20 children selected between the ages of 2 and 5 watch more than 26.3 hours of television per week is 2.62%.

EXAMPLE 6–14   Skipping Breakfast

A recent study found that an American skips breakfast on average 50 times a year. Assume the standard deviation is 4. If a random sample of 36 Americans is selected, find the probability that the mean of the sample is between 48 and 51 times.

SOLUTION

Step 1   Draw a normal curve and shade the desired area. Since the sample is larger than 30 or more, the normality assumption is not necessary. The desired area is shown in Figure 6–36.

FIGURE 6–36
Area Under a
Normal Curve for
Example 6–14

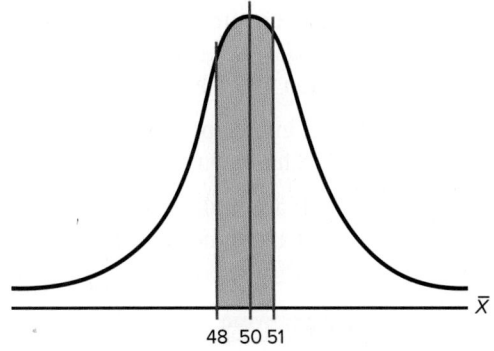

48 50 51

Step 2   Convert the $\overline{X}$ values to z values. The two z values are

$$z_1 = \frac{48 - 50}{4/\sqrt{36}} = -3$$

$$z_2 = \frac{51 - 50}{4/\sqrt{36}} = 1.5$$

Step 3   Find the area corresponding to each z value. To find the area between the two z values of -3 and 1.5, look up the corresponding area in Table A–4, and then subtract the smaller area value from the larger area value. The area for $z = -3$ is 0.0013, and the area for $z = 1.5$ is 0.9332. Hence, the area between $z = -3$ and $z = 1.5$ is $0.9332 - 0.0013 = 0.9319$ or 93.19%.

So, the probability of obtaining a sample mean between 48 and 51 for a sample size of 36 is 93.19%.

Students sometimes have difficulty deciding whether to use

$$z = \frac{\overline{X} - \mu}{\sigma/\sqrt{n}} \quad \text{or} \quad z = \frac{X - \mu}{\sigma}$$

The formula

$$z = \frac{\overline{X} - \mu}{\sigma / \sqrt{n}}$$

should be used to gain information about a sample mean, as shown in this section. The formula

$$z = \frac{X - \mu}{\sigma}$$

is used to gain information about an individual data value obtained from the population. Notice that the first formula contains $\overline{X}$, the symbol for the sample mean, while the second formula contains X, the symbol for an individual data value. Example 6–15 illustrates the uses of the two formulas.

EXAMPLE 6–15   Working Weekends

The average time spent by construction workers who work on weekends is 7.93 hours (over 2 days). Assume the distribution is approximately normal and has a standard deviation of 0.8 hour.

  a. Find the probability that an individual who works at that trade works fewer than 8 hours on the weekend.

  b. If a sample of 40 construction workers is randomly selected, find the probability that the mean of the sample will be less than 8 hours.

Source: Bureau of Labor Statistics.

SOLUTION *a*

Step 1   Draw a normal distribution and shade the desired area.

Since the question concerns an individual person, the formula $z = (X - \mu)/\sigma$ is used. The distribution is shown in Figure 6–37.

FIGURE 6–37
Area Under a Normal
Curve for Part *a* of
Example 6–15

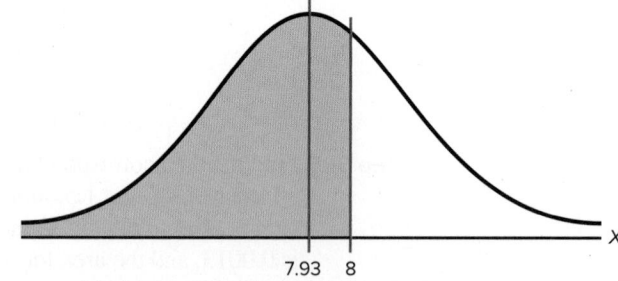

7.93   8
Distribution of individual data values for the population

Step 2   Find the z value.

$$Z = \frac{X - \mu}{\sigma} = \frac{8 - 7.93}{0.8} \approx 0.09$$

Step 3   Find the area to the left of $z = 0.09$.
         It is 0.5359.

Hence, the probability of selecting a construction worker who works less than 8 hours on a weekend is 0.5359, or 53.59%.

SOLUTION b

Step 1 Draw a normal curve and shade the desired area.

Since the question concerns the mean of a sample with a size of 40, the central limit theorem formula $z = (\overline{X} - \mu)/(\sigma/\sqrt{n})$ is used. The area is shown in Figure 6–38.

FIGURE 6–38
Area Under a Normal
Curve for Part *b* of
Example 6–15

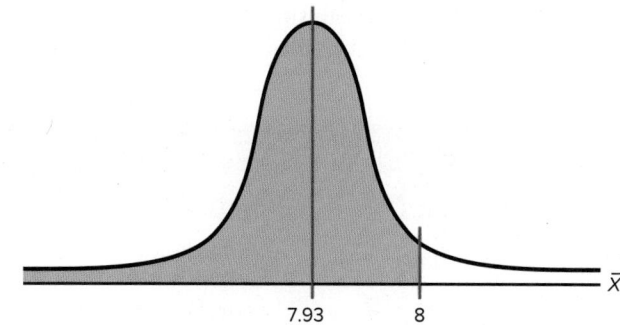

7.93   8

Distribution of means for all samples of size 40 taken from the population

Step 2 Find the z value for a mean of 8 hours and a sample size of 40.

$$z = \frac{\overline{X} - \mu}{\sigma/\sqrt{n}} = \frac{8 - 7.93}{0.8/\sqrt{40}} \approx 0.55$$

Step 3 Find the area corresponding to $z = 0.55$. The area is 0.7088.

Hence, the probability of getting a sample mean of less than 8 hours when the sample size is 40 is 0.7088, or 70.88%.

Comparing the two probabilities, you can see the probability of selecting an individual construction worker who works less than 8 hours on a weekend is 53.59%. The probability of selecting a random sample of 40 construction workers with a mean of less than 8 hours per week is 70.88%. This difference of 17.29% is due to the fact that the distribution of sample means is much less variable than the distribution of individual data values. The reason is that as the sample size increases, the standard deviation of the means decreases.

Finite Population Correction Factor (Optional)

The formula for the standard error of the mean $\sigma/\sqrt{n}$ is accurate when the samples are drawn with replacement or are drawn without replacement from a very large or infinite population. Since sampling with replacement is for the most part unrealistic, a *correction factor* is necessary for computing the standard error of the mean for samples drawn without replacement from a finite population. Compute the correction factor by using the expression

$$\sqrt{\frac{N - n}{N - 1}}$$

where N is the population size and n is the sample size.

This correction factor is necessary if relatively large samples (usually greater than 5% of the population) are taken from a small population, because the sample mean will then more accurately estimate the population mean and there will be less error in the estimation. Therefore, the standard error of the mean must be multiplied by the correction factor to adjust for large samples taken from a small population. That is,

$$\sigma_{\overline{X}} = \frac{\sigma}{\sqrt{n}} \cdot \sqrt{\frac{N - n}{N - 1}}$$

Interesting Fact

The bubonic plague killed more than 25 million people in Europe between 1347 and 1351.

Finally, the formula for the z value becomes

$$z = \frac{\overline{X} - \mu}{\dfrac{\sigma}{\sqrt{n}} \cdot \sqrt{\dfrac{N-n}{N-1}}}$$

When the population is large and the sample is small, the correction factor is generally not used, since it will be very close to 1.00.

The formulas and their uses are summarized in Table 6–1.

TABLE 6–1 Summary of Formulas and Their Uses

Formula	Use
1. $z = \dfrac{X - \mu}{\sigma}$	Used to gain information about an individual data value when the variable is normally distributed
2. $z = \dfrac{\overline{X} - \mu}{\sigma/\sqrt{n}}$	Used to gain information when applying the central limit theorem about a sample mean when the variable is normally distributed or when the sample size is 30 or more

Applying the Concepts 6–3

Times To Travel to School

Twenty students from a statistics class each collected a random sample of times on how long it took students to get to class from their homes. All the sample sizes were 30. The resulting means are listed.

Student	Mean	Std. Dev.	Student	Mean	Std. Dev.
1	22	3.7	11	27	1.4
2	31	4.6	12	24	2.2
3	18	2.4	13	14	3.1
4	27	1.9	14	29	2.4
5	20	3.0	15	37	2.8
6	17	2.8	16	23	2.7
7	26	1.9	17	26	1.8
8	34	4.2	18	21	2.0
9	23	2.6	19	30	2.2
10	29	2.1	20	29	2.8

1. The students noticed that everyone had different answers. If you randomly sample over and over from any population, with the same sample size, will the results ever be the same?
2. The students wondered whose results were right. How can they find out what the population mean and standard deviation are?
3. Input the means into the computer and check if the distribution is normal.
4. Check the mean and standard deviation of the means. How do these values compare to the students' individual scores?
5. Is the distribution of the means a sampling distribution?
6. Check the sampling error for students 3, 7, and 14.
7. Compare the standard deviation of the sample of the 20 means. Is that equal to the standard deviation from student 3 divided by the square root of the sample size? How about for student 7, or 14?

See page 367 for the answers.

Exercises 6–3

1. If samples of a specific size are selected from a population and the means are computed, what is this distribution of means called? The distribution is called the sampling distribution of sample means.

2. Why do most of the sample means differ somewhat from the population mean? What is this difference called? A sample is not a perfect representation of the population. The difference is due to what is called sampling error.

3. What is the mean of the sample means? The mean of the sample means is equal to the population mean.

4. What is the standard deviation of the sample means called? What is the formula for this standard deviation? The standard error of the mean: $\sigma_{\bar{X}} = \sigma / \sqrt{n}$

5. What does the central limit theorem say about the shape of the distribution of sample means? The distribution will be approximately normal when the sample size is large.

6. What formula is used to gain information about an individual data value when the variable is normally distributed? $z = \dfrac{X - \mu}{\sigma}$

For Exercises 7 through 25, assume that the sample is taken from a large population and the correction factor can be ignored.

7. **Life of Smoke Detectors** The average lifetime of smoke detectors that a company manufactures is 5 years, or 60 months, and the standard deviation is 8 months. Find the probability that a random sample of 30 smoke detectors will have a mean lifetime between 58 and 63 months. 0.8945 (TI: 0.8946)

8. **Email Times Spent by Americans** A survey found that the average time per weekday Americans spend checking their email is 5.4 hours. Assume the variable is approximately normally distributed and the standard deviation is 1.8 hours. If a random sample of 32 people is selected, find the probability that the mean of the sample will be between 5.1 hours and 5.3 hours. 0.2047 (TI: 0.2038)
Source: Adobe Campaign

9. **New Residences** The average number of moves a person makes in the person's lifetime is 12. If the standard deviation is 3.2, find the probability that the mean of a sample of 36 people is
   a. Less than 13. 0.9699 (TI: 0.9696)
   b. Greater than 13. 0.0301 (TI: 0.0304)
   c. Between 11 and 12. 0.4699 (TI: 0.4696)

10. **Delivery Costs** A survey found that the average cost of delivering a baby in a U.S. hospital is $11,543. Assume the variable is approximately normally distributed and the standard deviation is $2165. If a random sample of 20 deliveries is selected, find the probability that the mean of the sample is between $11,000 and $12,000. 0.695 (TI: 0.6964)
Source: IBM Watson Health MarketScan

11. **Automobile Insurance** A recent survey found that the average amount a person pays for automobile insurance is $1427 per year. Assume the variable is approximately normally distributed and that the standard deviation is $210. If a random sample of 35 people is selected, find the probability that the mean amount of insurance paid is between $1400 and $1410. 0.092 (TI: 0.0926)
Source: The Zebra's Auto Insurance Report

12. **Teachers' Salaries in North Dakota** The average teacher's salary in North Dakota is $37,764. Assume a normal distribution with $\sigma = \$5100$.
   a. What is the probability that a randomly selected teacher's salary is greater than $45,000? 0.0778 (TI: 0.0780)
   b. For a sample of 75 teachers, what is the probability that the sample mean is greater than $38,000? 0.3446 (TI: 0.3443)
Source: New York Times Almanac.

13. **Movie Ticket Prices** In the second quarter of 2015, the average movie ticket cost $8.61. In a random sample of 50 movie tickets from various areas, what is the probability that the mean cost exceeds $8.00, given that the population standard deviation is $1.39? 0.9990
Source: Variety.

14. **SAT Scores** The national average SAT score (for Verbal and Math) is 1028. Suppose that nothing is known about the shape of the distribution and that the standard deviation is 100. If a random sample of 200 scores were selected and the sample mean were calculated to be 1050, would you be surprised? Explain. Yes—the probability of such is less than 0.001.
Source: New York Times Almanac.

15. **Catching Up on Sleep** It was found that Americans take on average 4.3 days per year to catch up on sleep. Assume the variable is approximately normally distributed and the standard deviation is 0.8 days. If a random sample of 25 individuals is selected, find the probability that the mean of the sample is less than 4 days per year. 0.0301 (TI: 0.0304)

16. **Pet Valentine's Gifts** A survey found that the mean amount customers spend for a Valentine's gift for their pets is $4.44. Assume the distribution of the amount spent is approximately normal and the standard deviation is $0.56. If a random sample of 33 pet owners is selected, find the probability that the mean amount spent of the sample will be less than $4.75. 0.9993
Source: National Retail Federation

17. **Water Use** The *Old Farmer's Almanac* reports that the average person uses 123 gallons of water daily. If the standard deviation is 21 gallons, find the probability that the mean of a randomly selected sample of 15 people will be between 120 and 126 gallons. Assume the variable is normally distributed. 0.4177 (TI: 0.4199)

18. **Medicare Hospital Insurance** The average yearly Medicare Hospital Insurance benefit per person was $4064 in a recent year. If the benefits are normally distributed with a standard deviation of $460, find the probability that the mean benefit for a random sample of 20 patients is

    a. Less than $3800. 0.0051

    b. More than $4100. 0.3632

    Source: New York Times Almanac.

19. **Migraine Headaches** A study done by Eli Lilly and Company found that the mean number of days per month that people who suffer from migraine headaches is 15.4 days. Assume that the variable is approximately normally distributed and the standard deviation is 2 days. Find the probability that if a random sample of 50 people who suffer from migraine headaches is selected, the mean of the sample will be between 15 and 16 days. 0.9037 (TI: 0.9044)

    Source: Eli Lilly and Co.

20. **Digital Content Viewing** A survey found that the mean amount that U.S. consumers spend a day viewing digital content is 7.8 hours. Assume the variable is normally distributed and the standard deviation is 0.9 hours. If a random sample of 40 consumers is selected, find the probability that the mean of the sample will be greater than 7.5 hours. Find the probability that the mean will be greater than 8.1 hours. 0.9826 (TI: 0.9825); 0.0174

    Source: Adobe Consumer Content Survey

21. **Monthly Precipitation for Miami** The mean precipitation for Miami in August is 8.9 inches. Assume that the standard deviation is 1.6 inches and the variable is normally distributed.

    a. Find the probability that a randomly selected August month will have precipitation of less than 8.2 inches. (This month is selected from August months over the last 10 years.) 0.3300 (TI: 0.3309)

    b. Find the probability that a sample of 10 August months will have a mean of less than 8.2 inches. 0.0838 (TI: 0.0833)

    c. Does it seem reasonable that a randomly selected August month will have less than 8.2 inches of rain? yes

    d. Does it seem reasonable that a sample of 10 months will have a mean of less than 8.2 months? yes, but not as likely.

    Source: National Climatic Data Center.

22. **Cost of Parking** A survey found that the mean amount of time a driver in Boston spends to find a

parking space is 53 hours per year. Assume the variable is normally distributed and the standard deviation is 6 hours.

    a. If an individual driver from Boston is randomly selected, find the probability they will spend between 52 and 55 hours per year trying to find a parking space. 0.5818

    b. If a sample of 30 drivers is randomly selected, find the probability that the mean of the sample will be between 52 and 55 hours. 0.785

    c. Why is the answer to part *a* smaller than the answer to part *b*? Part *a* uses individual data, whereas part *b* uses a mean of sample size 30.

    Source: INRIX

23. **Cholesterol Content** The average cholesterol content of a certain brand of eggs is 215 milligrams, and the standard deviation is 15 milligrams. Assume the variable is normally distributed.

    a. If a single egg is selected, find the probability that the cholesterol content will be greater than 220 milligrams. 0.3707 (TI: 0.3694)

    b. If a sample of 25 eggs is selected, find the probability that the mean of the sample will be larger than 220 milligrams. 0.0475 (TI: 0.04779)

    Source: Living Fit.

24. **Ages of Proofreaders** At a large publishing company, the mean age of proofreaders is 36.2 years, and the standard deviation is 3.7 years. Assume the variable is normally distributed.

    a. If a proofreader from the company is randomly selected, find the probability that the proofreader's age will be between 36 and 37.5 years. 0.1567 (TI: 0.1589)

    b. If a random sample of 15 proofreaders is selected, find the probability that the mean age of the proofreaders in the sample will be between 36 and 37.5 years. 0.4963 (TI: 0.4961)

25. **TIMSS Test** On the Trends in International Mathematics and Science Study (TIMSS) test in a recent year, the United States scored an average of 508 (well below South Korea, 597; Singapore, 593; Hong Kong, 572; and Japan, 570). Suppose that we take a random sample of n United States scores and that the population standard deviation is 72. If the probability that the mean of the sample exceeds 520 is 0.0985, what was the sample size? Approximately 60

    Source: World Almanac.

Extending the Concepts

For Exercises 26 and 27, check to see whether the correction factor should be used. If so, be sure to include it in the calculations.

26. **Life Expectancies** In a study of the life expectancy of 500 people in a certain geographic region, the mean age

at death was 72.0 years, and the standard deviation was 5.3 years. If a sample of 50 people from this region is selected, find the probability that the mean life expectancy will be less than 70 years. 0.0025

27. Back to College Expenses Based on a survey, it was found that the mean cost people spend for back to college expenses is $969.88. Assume the variable is approximately normally distributed and the standard deviation is $120. If a random sample of 16 people is selected, find the probability that the mean of the sample is greater than $950. 0.7454 (TI: 0.7462)

Source: National Retail Federation

28. Breaking Strength of Steel Cable The average breaking strength of a certain brand of steel cable is 2000 pounds, with a standard deviation of 100 pounds.

A sample of 20 cables is selected and tested. Find the sample mean that will cut off the upper 95% of all samples of size 20 taken from the population. Assume the variable is normally distributed. 1963.10 pounds (TI: 1963.33)

29. The standard deviation of a variable is 15. If a sample of 100 individuals is selected, compute the standard error of the mean. What size sample is necessary to double the standard error of the mean? $\sigma_{\bar{X}} = 1.5$, $n = 25$

30. In Exercise 29, what size sample is needed to cut the standard error of the mean in half? 400

6–4 The Normal Approximation to the Binomial Distribution

OBJECTIVE

Use the normal approximation to compute probabilities for a binomial variable.

A normal distribution is often used to solve problems that involve the binomial distribution since when n is large (say, 100), the calculations are too difficult to do by hand using the binomial distribution. Recall from Chapter 5 that a binomial distribution has the following characteristics:

1. There must be a fixed number of trials.

2. The outcome of each trial must be independent.

3. Each experiment can have only two outcomes or outcomes that can be reduced to two outcomes.

4. The probability of a success must remain the same for each trial.

Also, recall that a binomial distribution is determined by n (the number of trials) and p (the probability of a success). When p is approximately 0.5, and as n increases, the shape of the binomial distribution becomes similar to that of a normal distribution. The larger n is and the closer p is to 0.5, the more similar the shape of the binomial distribution is to that of a normal distribution.

But when p is close to 0 or 1 and n is relatively small, a normal approximation is inaccurate. As a rule of thumb, statisticians generally agree that a normal approximation should be used only when $n \cdot p$ and $n \cdot q$ are both greater than or equal to 5. (*Note:* $q = 1 - p$.) For example, if p is 0.3 and n is 10, then $np = (10)(0.3) = 3$, and a normal distribution should not be used as an approximation. On the other hand, if $p = 0.5$ and $n = 10$, then $np = (10)(0.5) = 5$ and $nq = (10)(0.5) = 5$, and a normal distribution can be used as an approximation. See Figure 6–39.

In addition to the previous condition of $np \geq 5$ and $nq \geq 5$, a correction for continuity may be used in the normal approximation.

> A **correction for continuity** is a correction employed when a continuous distribution is used to approximate a discrete distribution.

The continuity correction means that for any specific value of X, say 8, the boundaries of X in the binomial distribution (in this case, 7.5 to 8.5) must be used. (See Section 1–2.) Hence, when you employ a normal distribution to approximate the binomial, you must use the boundaries of any specific value X as they are shown in the binomial distribution. For example, for $P(X = 8)$, the correction is $P(7.5 < X < 8.5)$. For $P(X \leq 7)$, the correction is $P(X < 7.5)$. For $P(X \geq 3)$, the correction is $P(X > 2.5)$.

Students sometimes have difficulty deciding whether to add 0.5 or subtract 0.5 from the data value for the correction factor. Table 6–2 summarizes the different situations.

Interesting Fact

Of the 12 months, August ranks first in the number of births for Americans.

The formulas for the mean and standard deviation for the binomial distribution are necessary for calculations. They are

$$\mu = n \cdot p \qquad \text{and} \qquad \sigma = \sqrt{n \cdot p \cdot q}$$

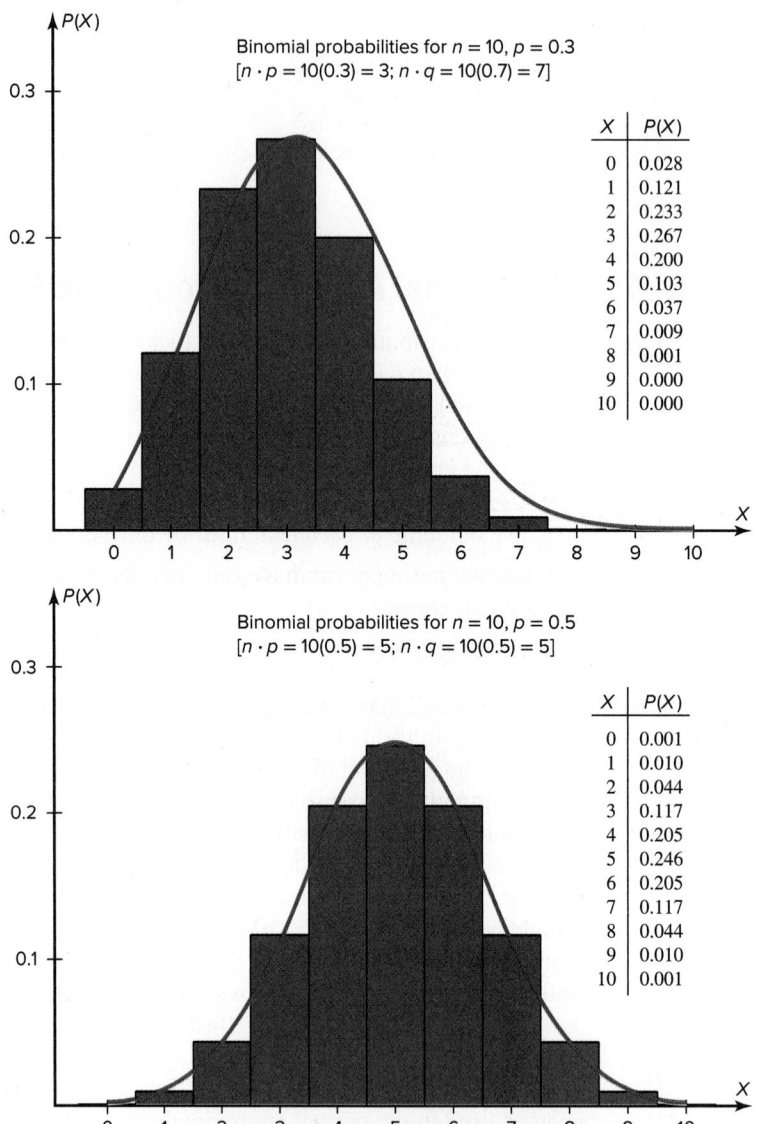

TABLE 6–2 Summary of the Normal Approximation to the Binomial Distribution

Binomial	Normal
When finding:	Use:
1. $P(X = a)$	$P(a - 0.5 < X < a + 0.5)$
2. $P(X \geq a)$	$P(X > a - 0.5)$
3. $P(X > a)$	$P(X > a + 0.5)$
4. $P(X \leq a)$	$P(X < a + 0.5)$
5. $P(X < a)$	$P(X < a - 0.5)$

For all cases, $\mu = n \cdot p$, $\sigma = \sqrt{n \cdot p \cdot q}$, $n \cdot p \geq 5$, and $n \cdot q \geq 5$.

The steps for using the normal distribution to approximate the binomial distribution are shown in this Procedure Table.

Procedure Table

Procedure for the Normal Approximation to the Binomial Distribution

Step 1 Check to see whether the normal approximation can be used.

Step 2 Find the mean μ and the standard deviation σ.

Step 3 Write the problem in probability notation, using X.

Step 4 Rewrite the problem by using the continuity correction factor, and show the corresponding area under the normal distribution.

Step 5 Find the corresponding z values.

Step 6 Find the solution.

EXAMPLE 6–16   Falling Asleep While Driving

It has been reported that last year 25% of drivers have fallen asleep at the wheel. If 200 drivers are selected at random, find the probability that 62 will say that they have fallen asleep while driving.

Source: National Sleep Foundation.

SOLUTION

Here $p = 0.25$, $q = 0.75$, and $n = 200$.

Step 1 Check to see whether a normal approximation can be used.

$$np = (200)(0.25) = 50 \qquad nq = (200)(0.75) = 150$$

Since $nq \geq 5$ and $nq \geq 5$, the normal distribution can be used.

Step 2 Find the mean and standard deviation.

$$\mu = np = (200)(0.25) = 50$$

$$\sigma = \sqrt{npq} = \sqrt{(200)(0.25)(0.75)} = \sqrt{37.5} \approx 6.12$$

Step 3 Write the problem in probability notation: $P(X = 62)$.

Step 4 Rewrite the problem by using the continuity connection factor. See approximation 1 in Table 6–2: $P(62 - 0.5 < X < 62 + 0.5) = P(61.5 < X < 62.5)$. Show the corresponding area under the normal distribution curve. See Figure 6–40.

FIGURE 6–40

Area Under a Normal Curve and X Values for Example 6–16

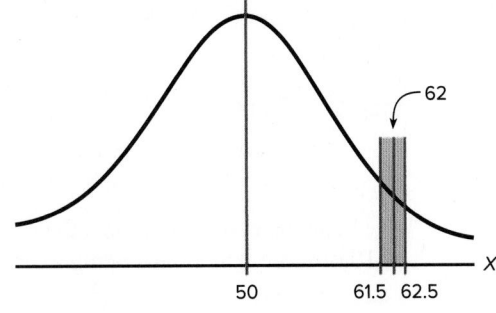

Step 5   Find the corresponding z values. Since 72 represents any value between 71.5 and 72.5, find both z values.

$$z_1 = \frac{61.5 - 50}{6.12} \approx 1.88$$

$$z_2 = \frac{62.5 - 50}{6.12} \approx 2.04$$

Step 6   The area to the left of $z = 1.88$ is 0.9699, and the area to the left of $z = 2.04$ is 0.9793. The area between the two z values is $0.9793 - 0.9699 = 0.0094$, or about 0.94%. (It is close to 1%.) Hence, the probability that exactly 62 people say that they fell asleep at the wheel while driving is 0.94%.

EXAMPLE 6–17   Ragweed Allergies

Ten percent of Americans are allergic to ragweed. If a random sample of 200 people is selected, find the probability that 10 or more will be allergic to ragweed.

SOLUTION

Step 1   Check to see whether the normal approximate can be used.

Here $p = 0.10$, $q = 0.90$, and $n = 200$. Since $np = (200)(0.10) = 20$ and $nq = (200)(0.90) = 180$, the normal approximation can be used.

Step 2   Find the mean and the standard deviation.

$$\mu = np = (200)(0.10) = 20$$

$$\sigma = \sqrt{npq} = \sqrt{(200)(0.10)(0.90)} = \sqrt{18} \approx 4.24$$

Step 3   Write the problem in probability notation, using X.

$$P(X \geq 10)$$

Step 4   Rewrite the problem, using the continuity correction factor, and show the corresponding area under the normal distribution.

See approximation number 2 in Table 6–2: $P(X > 10 - 0.5) = P(X > 9.5)$. The desired area is shown in Figure 6–41.

FIGURE 6–41

Area Under a Normal
Curve and X Value for
Example 6–17

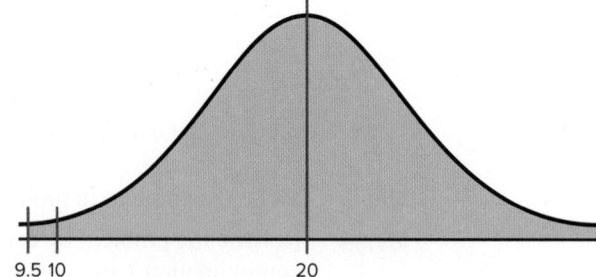

9.5 10   20

Step 5   Find the corresponding z values.

Since the problem is to find the probability of 10 or more positive responses, a normal distribution graph is as shown in Figure 6–41.

The z value is

$$z = \frac{9.5 - 20}{4.24} = -2.48$$

Step 6   Find the solution.

The area to the left of $z = -2.48$ is 0.0066. Hence, the area to the right of $z = -2.48$ is $1.0000 - 0.0066 = 0.9934$, or 99.34%.

It can be concluded, then, that in a random sample of 200 Americans the probability of 10 or more Americans being allergic to ragweed is 99.34%.

EXAMPLE 6–18   Changing Majors

A recent survey found that 40% of students in college change their major field at least once in their college careers. Find the probability that in a random sample of 100 college students, at most 36 will change their major in their careers.

SOLUTION

Step 1   Check to see whether or not the normal approximate can be used. Here $p = 0.4$, $q = 0.6$, and $n = 100$. So, $np = (100)(0.4) = 40$ and $nq = (100)(0.6) = 60$. Since both values are greater than or equal to 5, the normal approximation to the binomial distribution can be used.

Step 2   Find the mean and standard deviation.

$$\mu = np = (100)(0.4) = 40$$

$$\sigma = \sqrt{npq} = \sqrt{(100)(0.4)(0.6)} \approx 4.90$$

Step 3   Write the exercise in probability notation using X, then use the correction factor $P(X \leq 36)$.

$$P(X < 36 + 0.5) = P(X < 36.5)$$

The desired area is shown in Figure 6–42.

FIGURE 6–42

Area Under a
Normal Curve for
Example 6–18

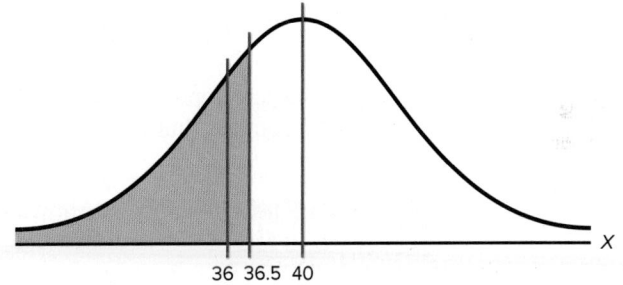

36 36.5 40

Step 4   Find the corresponding z value.

$$z = \frac{36.5 - 40}{4.90} = -0.71$$

Step 5   Use Table A–4 in Appendix A to get the corresponding area.

The area to the left of $z = -0.71$ is 0.2389 or 23.89%.

It can be concluded that the probability that at most 36 students out of 100 changed their majors is 23.89%.

The closeness of the normal approximation is shown in Example 6–19.

EXAMPLE 6–19   Binomial versus Normal Approximation

When $n = 10$ and $p = 0.5$, use the binomial distribution table (Table A–2 in Appendix A) to find the probability that $X = 6$. Then use the normal approximation to find the probability that $X = 6$.

SOLUTION

From Table A–2 in Appendix A, for $n = 10$, $p = 0.5$, and $X = 6$, the probability is 0.205. For a normal approximation,

$$\mu = np = (10)(0.5) = 5$$

$$\sigma = \sqrt{npq} = \sqrt{(10)(0.5)(0.5)} \approx 1.58$$

Now, $X = 6$ is represented by the boundaries 5.5 and 6.5. So the z values are

$$z_1 = \frac{6.5 - 5}{1.58} \approx 0.95 \qquad z_2 = \frac{5.5 - 5}{1.58} \approx 0.32$$

The corresponding area for 0.95 is 0.8289, and the corresponding area for 0.32 is 0.6255. The area between the two z values of 0.95 and 0.32 is $0.8289 - 0.6255 = 0.2034$, which is very close to the binomial table value of 0.205. See Figure 6–43.

FIGURE 6–43

Area Under a Normal Curve for Example 6–19

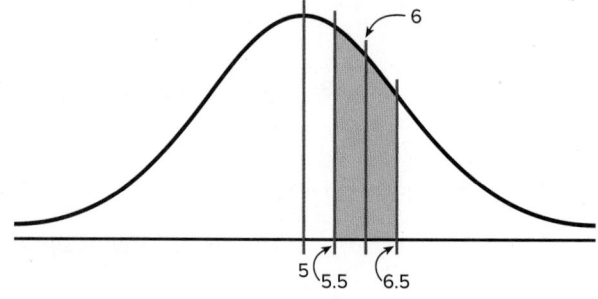

The normal approximation also can be used to approximate other distributions, such as the Poisson distribution (see Table A–3 in Appendix A).

≣ Applying the Concepts **6–4**

Mountain Climbing Safety

Assume one of your favorite activities is mountain climbing. When you go mountain climbing, you have several safety devices to keep you from falling. You notice that attached to one of your safety hooks is a reliability rating of 97%. You estimate that throughout the next year you will be using this device about 100 times. Answer the following questions.

1. Does a reliability rating of 97% mean that there is a 97% chance that the device will not fail any of the 100 times?
2. What is the probability of at least one failure?
3. What is the complement of this event?
4. Can this be considered a binomial experiment?
5. Can you use the binomial probability formula? Why or why not?
6. Find the probability of at least two failures.
7. Can you use a normal distribution to accurately approximate the binomial distribution? Explain why or why not.
8. Is correction for continuity needed?
9. How much safer would it be to use a second safety hook independent of the first?

See page 367 for the answers.

Exercises 6–4

1. Explain why a normal distribution can be used as an approximation to a binomial distribution.

2. What conditions must be met to use the normal distribution to approximate the binomial distribution?
   The conditions are that $n \cdot p$ and $n \cdot q$ are both ≥ 5.

3. Why is a correction for continuity necessary?

4. When is the normal distribution not a good approximation for the binomial distribution?

5. Use the normal approximation to the binomial to find the probabilities for the specific value(s) of X.
   a. $n = 30, p = 0.3, X = 11$ 0.1156
   b. $n = 50, p = 0.7, X = 36$ 0.1176
   c. $n = 100, p = 0.9, X = 85$ 0.0332

6. Use the normal approximation to find the probabilities for the specific value(s) of X.
   a. $n = 30, p = 0.2, X \geq 5$ 0.7517
   b. $n = 10, p = 0.5, X < 7$ 0.8289
   c. $n = 60, p = 0.8, X \leq 50$ 0.7910

7. Check each binomial distribution to see whether it can be approximated by a normal distribution (i.e., are $np \geq 5$ and $nq \geq 5$?).
   a. $n = 30, p = 0.3$ Yes
   b. $n = 10, p = 0.7$ No
   c. $n = 20, p = 0.8$ No

8. Check each binomial distribution to see whether it can be approximated by a normal distribution (i.e., are $np \geq 5$ and $nq \geq 5$?).
   a. $n = 25, p = 0.2$ Yes
   b. $n = 50, p = 0.4$ Yes
   c. $n = 30, p = 0.9$ No

9. **Reducing Heart Disease** In a recent survey only 11% of women said that reducing heart disease is a top priority for them. What is the probability that in a random sample of 120 women, more than 20 would say that reducing heart disease is a top priority for them? 0.0166
   Source: Quaker Oats Company

10. **School Enrollment** Of all 3- to 5-year-old children, 56% are enrolled in school. If a sample of 500 such children is randomly selected, find the probability that at least 250 will be enrolled in school. 0.9965 (TI: 0.9970)
   Source: Statistical Abstract of the United States.

11. **Home Robots** Seventy-seven percent of Americans think that in 20 years it will be normal to have a robot in their homes. If a random sample of 50 people is selected, what is the probability that at least 35 will agree that it will be normal to have a robot in their houses within 20 years? 0.9099
   Source: Finn Partners Survey

12. **Mail Order** A mail order company has an 8% success rate. If it mails advertisements to 600 people, find the probability of getting fewer than 40 sales. 0.1003

13. **Unpleasant Shopping** A recent survey found that 46% of Americans found that shopping is an unpleasant experience. If a random sample of 50 people is selected, what is the probability that at least 24 will consider shopping an unpleasant experience? 0.4443 (TI: 0.4435)
   Source: R H Bruskin Associates

14. **Selected Technologies** According to the World Almanac, 72% of households own smartphones. If a random sample of 180 households is selected, what is the probability that more than 115 but fewer than 125 have a smartphone? 0.1880 (TI: 0.1889)
   Source: World Almanac.

15. **Back Injuries** Twenty-two percent of work injuries are back injuries. If 400 work-injured people are selected at random, find the probability that 92 or fewer have back injuries. 0.7054 (TI: 0.7066)
   Source: The World Almanac

16. **Population of College Cities** College students often make up a substantial portion of the population of college cities and towns. State College, Pennsylvania, ranks first with 71.1% of its population made up of college students. What is the probability that in a random sample of 150 people from State College, more than 50 are not college students? 0.0985 (TI: 0.0988)
   Source: www.infoplease.com

17. **Mistakes in Restaurant Bills** About 12.5% of restaurant bills are incorrect. If 200 bills are selected at random, find the probability that at least 22 will contain an error. Is this likely or unlikely to occur? 0.7734 (TI: 0.7727); likely
   Source: Harper's Index.

18. **Internet Browsers** The top web browser in 2015 was Chrome with 51.74% of the market. In a random sample of 250 people, what is the probability that fewer than 110 did not use Chrome? 0.0793 (TI: 0.0791)
   Source: New York Times Almanac.

19. **Prescription Drug Abuse** Eight in ten Americans don't recognize that prescription drug abuse is a treatable problem. If a sample of 400 people is randomly selected, what is the probability that 300 or less will recognize that prescription drug abuse is a treatable problem?
   Source: Michigan State University Survey 0.0073 (TI: 0.0074)

20. **Residences of U.S. Citizens** According to the U.S. Census, 67.5% of the U.S. population were born in their state of residence. In a random sample of 200 Americans, what is the probability that fewer than 125 were born in their state of residence? 0.0559 (TI: 0.0564)

    Source: www.census.gov

21. **Driving to Work** Sixty-four percent of American workers drive to work alone each day. If a random sample of 80 workers is selected, what is the probability

    that 60 workers drive alone to work each day? 0.0118 (TI: 0.0114)

    Source: U.S. Census Bureau

22. **Parking Lot Construction** The mayor of a small town estimates that 35% of the residents in the town favor the construction of a municipal parking lot. If there are 350 people at a town meeting, find the probability that at least 100 favor construction of the parking lot. Based on your answer, is it likely that 100 or more people would favor the parking lot? 0.9951; yes (TI: 0.9950)

Extending the Concepts

23. Recall that for use of a normal distribution as an approximation to the binomial distribution, the conditions $np \geq 5$ and $nq \geq 5$ must be met. For each given probability, compute the minimum sample size needed for use of the normal approximation.

    a. $p = 0.1$ $n \geq 50$ d. $p = 0.8$ $n \geq 25$
    b. $p = 0.3$ $n \geq 17$ e. $p = 0.9$ $n \geq 50$
    c. $p = 0.5$ $n \geq 10$

Summary

- A normal distribution can be used to describe a variety of variables, such as heights, weights, and temperatures. A normal distribution is bell-shaped, unimodal, symmetric, and continuous; its mean, median, and mode are equal. Since each normally distributed variable has its own distribution with mean μ and standard deviation σ, mathematicians use the standard normal distribution, which has a mean of 0 and a standard deviation of 1. Other approximately normally distributed variables can be transformed to the standard normal distribution with the formula $z = (X - \mu)/\sigma$. (6–1)

- A normal distribution can be used to solve a variety of problems in which the variables are approximately normally distributed. (6–2)

- A sampling distribution of sample means is a distribution using the means computed from all possible random samples of a specific size taken from a

  population. The difference between a sample measure and the corresponding population measure is due to what is called *sampling error*. The mean of the sample means will be the same as the population mean. The standard deviation of the sample means will be equal to the population standard deviation divided by the square root of the sample size. The central limit theorem states that as the sample size increases without limit, the shape of the distribution of the sample means taken with replacement from a population will approach that of a normal distribution. (6–3)

- A normal distribution can be used to approximate other distributions, such as a binomial distribution. For a normal distribution to be used as an approximation, the conditions $np \geq 5$ and $nq \geq 5$ must be met. Also, a correction for continuity may be used for more accurate results. (6–4)

Important Terms

central limit theorem 345	normal distribution 311	sampling error 343	symmetric distribution 312
correction for continuity 353	positively or right-skewed distribution 313	standard error of the mean 345	z value (z score) 314
negatively or left-skewed distribution 313	sampling distribution of sample means 343	standard normal distribution 313	

Important Formulas

Formula for the z score (or standard score):

$$z = \frac{X - \mu}{\sigma}$$

Formula for finding a specific data value:

$$X = z \cdot \sigma + \mu$$

Formula for the mean of the sample means:

$$\mu_{\overline{X}} = \mu$$

Formula for the standard error of the mean:

$$\sigma_{\overline{X}} = \frac{\sigma}{\sqrt{n}}$$

Formula for the z value for the central limit theorem:

$$z = \frac{\overline{X} - \mu}{\sigma/\sqrt{n}}$$

Formulas for the mean and standard deviation for the binomial distribution:

$$\mu = n \cdot p \qquad \sigma = \sqrt{n \cdot p \cdot q}$$

Review Exercises

Section 6–1

1. Find the area under the standard normal distribution curve for each.
   a. Between $z = 0$ and $z = 2.06$ 0.4803
   b. Between $z = 0$ and $z = 0.53$ 0.2019
   c. Between $z = 1.26$ and 1.74 0.0629
   d. Between $z = -1.02$ and $z = 1.63$ 0.7945
   e. Between $z = -0.07$ and $z = 0.49$ 0.2158

2. Find the area under the standard normal distribution for each.
   a. Between $z = 1.10$ and $z = -1.80$ 0.8284
   b. To the right of $z = 1.99$ 0.0233
   c. To the right of $z = -1.36$ 0.9131
   d. To the left of $z = -2.09$ 0.0183
   e. To the left of $z = 1.68$ 0.9535

3. Using the standard normal distribution, find each probability.
   a. $P(0 < z < 2.23)$ 0.4871
   b. $P(-1.75 < z < 0)$ 0.4599
   c. $P(-1.48 < z < 1.68)$ 0.8841
   d. $P(1.22 < z < 1.77)$ 0.0728
   e. $P(-2.31 < z < 0.32)$ 0.6151

4. Using the standard normal distribution, find each probability.
   a. $P(z > 1.66)$ 0.0485
   b. $P(z < -2.03)$ 0.0212
   c. $P(z > -1.19)$ 0.8830
   d. $P(z < 1.93)$ 0.9732
   e. $P(z > -1.77)$ 0.9616

Section 6–2

5. Per Capita Spending on Health Care The average per capita spending on health care in the United States is $5274. If the standard deviation is $600 and the distribution of health care spending is approximately normal, what is the probability that a randomly selected person spends more than $6000? Find the limits of the middle 50% of individual health care expenditures.
Source: World Almanac. 0.1131; $4872 and $5676 (TI: $4869.31 minimum, $5678.69 maximum)

6. Salaries for Actuaries The average salary for graduates entering the actuarial field is $63,000. If the salaries are normally distributed with a standard deviation of $5000, find the probability that
   a. An individual graduate will have a salary over $68,000. 0.1587
   b. A group of nine graduates will have a group average over $68,000. 0.0013
Source: www.payscale.com

7. Commuter Train Passengers On a certain run of a commuter train, the average number of passengers is 476 and the standard deviation is 22. Assume the variable is normally distributed. If the train makes the run, find the probability that the number of passengers will be
   a. Between 476 and 500 passengers. 0.3621 or 36.21% (TI: 0.3623 or 36.23%)
   b. Fewer than 450 passengers. 0.1190 or 11.9% (TI: 0.1186 or 11.86%)
   c. More than 510 passengers. 0.0606 or 6.06% (TI: 0.611 or 6.11%)

8. Monthly Spending for Paging and Messaging Services The average individual monthly spending in the United States for paging and messaging services is $10.15. If the standard deviation is $2.45 and the amounts are normally distributed, what is the probability that a randomly selected user of these services pays more than $15.00 per month? Between $12.00 and $14.00 per month? 0.0239; 0.1654 (TI: 0.1671)
Source: New York Times Almanac.

9. Cost of Smartphone Repair The average cost of repairing a smartphone is $120 with a standard deviation of $10.50. The costs are normally distributed. If 15% of the costs are considered excessive, find the cost in dollars that would be considered excessive. $130.92 (TI: 130.88)

10. Slot Machine Earnings The average amount a slot machine makes per month is $8000. This is after payouts. Assume the earnings are normally distributed with a standard deviation of $750. Find the amount of earnings if 15% is considered too low. $7220 (TI: 7222.67)

11. **Private Four-Year College Enrollment** A random sample of enrollments in Pennsylvania's private four-year colleges is listed here. Check for normality. Not normal

1350	1886	1743	1290	1767
2067	1118	3980	1773	4605
1445	3883	1486	980	1217
3587				

Source: New York Times Almanac.

12. **Heights of Active Volcanoes** The heights (in feet above sea level) of a random sample of the world's active volcanoes are shown here. Check for normality. Not normal

13,435	5,135	11,339	12,224	7,470
9,482	12,381	7,674	5,223	5,631
3,566	7,113	5,850	5,679	15,584
5,587	8,077	9,550	8,064	2,686
5,250	6,351	4,594	2,621	9,348
6,013	2,398	5,658	2,145	3,038

Source: New York Times Almanac.

Section 6–3

13. **Confectionary Products** Americans ate an average of 25.7 pounds of confectionary products each last year and spent an average of $61.50 per person doing so. If the standard deviation for consumption is 3.75 pounds and the standard deviation for the amount spent is $5.89, find the following:

    a. The probability that the sample mean confectionary consumption for a random sample of 40 American consumers was greater than 27 pounds

    b. The probability that for a random sample of 50, the sample mean for confectionary spending exceeded $60.00

    Source: www.census.gov a. 0.0143 (TI: 0.0142) b. 0.9641

14. **Average Precipitation** For the first 7 months of the year, the average precipitation in Toledo, Ohio, is 19.32 inches. If the average precipitation is normally distributed with a standard deviation of 2.44 inches, find these probabilities.

    a. A randomly selected year will have precipitation greater than 18 inches for the first 7 months.

    b. Five randomly selected years will have an average precipitation greater than 18 inches for the first 7 months.

    Source: Toledo Blade. a. 0.7054 (TI: 0.7057) b. 0.8869 (TI: 0.8868)

15. **Sodium in Frozen Food** The average number of milligrams (mg) of sodium in a certain brand of low-salt microwave frozen dinners is 660 mg, and the standard deviation is 35 mg. Assume the variable is normally distributed.

    a. If a single dinner is selected, find the probability that the sodium content will be more than 670 mg.

    a. 0.3859 (TI: 0.3875)

    b. If a sample of 10 dinners is selected, find the probability that the mean of the sample will be larger than 670 mg. 0.1841 (TI: 0.1831)

    c. Why is the probability for part a greater than that for part b? Individual values are more variable than means.

16. **Wireless Sound System Lifetimes** A recent study of the life span of wireless sound systems found the average to be 3.7 years with a standard deviation of 0.6 year. If a random sample of 32 people who own wireless sound systems is selected, find the probability that the mean lifetime of the sample will be less than 3.4 years. If the sample mean is less than 3.4 years, would you consider that 3.7 years might be incorrect? 0.0023; yes, since the probability is less than 1%.

Section 6–4

17. **Retirement Income** Of the total population of American households, including older Americans and perhaps some not so old, 17.3% receive retirement income. In a random sample of 120 households, what is the probability that more than 20 households but fewer than 35 households receive a retirement income? *Source: www.bls.gov* 0.5234 (TI: 0.5246)

18. **Slot Machines** The probability of winning on a slot machine is 5%. If a person plays the machine 500 times, find the probability of winning 30 times. Use the normal approximation to the binomial distribution. 0.0496 (TI: 0.0484)

19. **Multiple-Job Holders** According to the government, 5.3% of those employed are multiple-job holders. In a random sample of 150 people who are employed, what is the probability that fewer than 10 hold multiple jobs? What is the probability that more than 50 are not multiple-job holders? *Source: www.bls.gov* 0.7157; 0.9999 (TI: 0.7142)

20. **Enrollment in Personal Finance Course** In a large university, 30% of the incoming first-year students elect to enroll in a personal finance course offered by the university. Find the probability that of 800 randomly selected incoming first-year students, at least 260 have elected to enroll in the course. 0.0668 (TI: 0.0662)

21. **U.S. Population** Of the total U.S. population, 37% live in the South. If 200 U.S. residents are selected at random, find the probability that at least 80 live in the South. 0.2090 (TI: 0.2103)
    Source: Statistical Abstract of the United States.

22. **Larceny-Thefts** Excluding motor vehicle thefts, 26% of all larceny-thefts involved items taken from motor vehicles. Local police forces are trying to help the situation with their "Put your junk in the trunk!" campaign. Consider a random sample of 60 larceny-thefts. What is the probability that 20 or more were items stolen from motor vehicles? 0.1251 (TI: 0.1257)
    Source: World Almanac.

≣ STATISTICS TODAY

What Is Normal?— **Revisited**

Many of the variables measured in medical tests—blood pressure, triglyceride level, etc.—are approximately normally distributed for the majority of the population in the United States. Thus, researchers can find the mean and standard deviation of these variables. Then, using these two measures along with the **z** values, they can find normal intervals for healthy individuals. For example, 95% of the systolic blood pressures of healthy individuals fall within 2 standard deviations of the mean. If an individual's pressure is outside the determined normal range (either above or below), the physician will look for a possible cause and prescribe treatment if necessary.

≣ Chapter Quiz

Determine whether each statement is true or false. If the statement is false, explain why.

1. The total area under a normal distribution is infinite. False

2. The standard normal distribution is a continuous distribution. True

3. All variables that are approximately normally distributed can be transformed to standard normal variables. True

4. The z value corresponding to a number below the mean is always negative. True

5. The area under the standard normal distribution to the left of $z = 0$ is negative. False

6. The central limit theorem applies to means of samples selected from different populations. False

Select the best answer.

7. The mean of the standard normal distribution is
   - a. 0.
   - b. 1.
   - c. 100.
   - d. Variable.

8. Approximately what percentage of normally distributed data values will fall within 1 standard deviation above or below the mean?
   - a. 68%
   - b. 95%
   - c. 99.7%
   - d. Variable

9. Which is not a property of the standard normal distribution?
   - a. It's symmetric about the mean.
   - b. It's uniform.
   - c. It's bell-shaped.
   - d. It's unimodal.

10. When a distribution is positively skewed, the relationship of the mean, median, and mode from left to right will be
    - a. Mean, median, mode.
    - b. Mode, median, mean.
    - c. Median, mode, mean.
    - d. Mean, mode, median.

11. The standard deviation of all possible sample means equals
    - a. The population standard deviation.
    - b. The population standard deviation divided by the population mean.
    - c. The population standard deviation divided by the square root of the sample size.
    - d. The square root of the population standard deviation.

Complete the following statements with the best answer.

12. When one is using the standard normal distribution, $P(z < 0) =$ _____. 0.5

13. The difference between a sample mean and a population mean is due to _____. sampling error

14. The mean of the sample means equals the population mean.

15. The standard deviation of all possible sample means is called the _____. standard error of the mean

16. The normal distribution can be used to approximate the binomial distribution when $n \cdot p$ and $n \cdot q$ are both greater than or equal to _____. 5

17. The correction factor for the central limit theorem should be used when the sample size is greater than _____ of the size of the population. 5%

18. Find the area under the standard normal distribution for each.
    - a. Between 0 and 1.50 0.4332
    - b. Between 0 and −1.25 0.3944
    - c. Between 1.56 and 1.96 0.0344
    - d. Between −1.20 and −2.25 0.1029
    - e. Between −0.06 and 0.73 0.2912
    - f. Between 1.10 and −1.80 0.8284
    - g. To the right of $z = 1.75$ 0.0401
    - h. To the right of $z = -1.28$ 0.8997
    - i. To the left of $z = -2.12$ 0.017
    - j. To the left of $z = 1.36$ 0.9131

19. Using the standard normal distribution, find each probability.

    a. $P(0 < z < 2.16)$ 0.4846

    b. $P(-1.87 < z < 0)$ 0.4693

    c. $P(-1.63 < z < 2.17)$ 0.9334

    d. $P(1.72 < z < 1.98)$ 0.0188

    e. $P(-2.17 < z < 0.71)$ 0.7461

    f. $P(z > 1.77)$ 0.0384

    g. $P(z < -2.37)$ 0.0089

    h. $P(z > -1.73)$ 0.9582

    i. $P(z < 2.03)$ 0.9788

    j. $P(z > -1.02)$ 0.8461

20. **Amount of Rain in a City** The average amount of rain per year in Greenville is 49 inches. The standard deviation is 8 inches. Find the probability that next year Greenville will receive the following amount of rainfall. Assume the variable is normally distributed.

    a. At most 55 inches of rain 0.7734

    b. At least 62 inches of rain 0.0516 (TI: 0.0521)

    c. Between 46 and 54 inches of rain 0.3837 (TI: 0.3802)

    d. How many inches of rain would you consider to be an extremely wet year?

21. **Heights of People** The average height of a certain age group of people is 53 inches. The standard deviation is 4 inches. If the variable is normally distributed, find the probability that a selected individual's height will be

    a. Greater than 59 inches. 0.0668

    b. Less than 45 inches. 0.0228

    c. Between 50 and 55 inches. 0.4649

    d. Between 58 and 62 inches. 0.0934

22. **Sports Drink Consumption** The average number of gallons of sports drinks consumed by the football team during a game is 20, with a standard deviation of 3 gallons. Assume the variable is normally distributed. When a game is played, find the probability of using

    a. Between 20 and 25 gallons. 0.4525 (TI: 0.4522)

    b. Less than 19 gallons. 0.3707 (TI: 0.3694)

    c. More than 21 gallons. 0.3707 (TI: 0.3694)

    d. Between 26 and 28 gallons. 0.019 (TI: 0.0189)

23. **Years to Complete a Graduate Program** The average number of years a person takes to complete a graduate degree program is 3. The standard deviation is 4 months. Assume the variable is normally distributed. If an individual enrolls in the program, find the probability that it will take

    a. More than 4 years to complete the program. 0.0013

    b. Less than 3 years to complete the program. 0.5

    c. Between 3.8 and 4.5 years to complete the program. 0.0082

    d. Between 2.5 and 3.1 years to complete the program. 0.5511

24. **Passengers on a Bus** On the daily run of an express bus, the average number of passengers is 48. The standard deviation is 3. Assume the variable is normally distributed. Find the probability that the bus will have

    a. Between 36 and 40 passengers. 0.0038

    b. Fewer than 42 passengers. 0.0228

    c. More than 48 passengers. 0.5

    d. Between 43 and 47 passengers. 0.3232 (TI: 0.3217)

25. **Thickness of Library Books** The average thickness of books on a library shelf is 8.3 centimeters. The standard deviation is 0.6 centimeter. If 20% of the books are oversized, find the minimum thickness of the oversized books on the library shelf. Assume the variable is normally distributed. 8.804 centimeters (TI: 8.805)

26. **Membership in an Organization** Membership in an elite organization requires a test score in the upper 30% range. If $\mu = 115$ and $\sigma = 12$, find the lowest acceptable score that would enable a candidate to apply for membership. Assume the variable is normally distributed. 121.24 is the lowest acceptable score. (TI: 121.29)

27. **Repair Cost for Microwave Ovens** The average repair cost of a microwave oven is $55, with a standard deviation of $8. The costs are normally distributed. If 12 ovens are repaired, find the probability that the mean of the repair bills will be greater than $60. 0.015 (TI: 0.0152)

28. **Electric Bills** The average electric bill in a residential area is $72 for the month of April. The standard deviation is $6. If the amounts of the electric bills are normally distributed, find the probability that the mean of the bill for 15 residents will be less than $75. 0.9738 (TI: 0.9736)

29. **Sleep Survey** According to a recent survey, 38% of Americans get 6 hours or less of sleep each night. If 25 people are selected, find the probability that 14 or more people will get 6 hours or less of sleep each night. Does this number seem likely? 0.0495 (TI: 0.0499); no

    Source: Amazing Almanac.

30. **Unemployment** If 8% of all people in a certain geographic region are unemployed, find the probability that in a sample of 200 people, fewer than 10 people are unemployed. 0.0455 or 4.55% (TI: 0.0453 or 4.53%)

31. **Household Online Connection** The percentage of U.S. households that have online connections is 78%. In a random sample of 420 households, what is the probability that fewer than 315 have online connections? 0.618 (TI: 0.0614)

    Source: World Almanac.

32. **Computer Ownership** Eighty-nine percent of U.S. households have a personal computer. In a random sample of 250 households, what is the probability that fewer than 215 have a PC? 0.0526 (TI: 0.530)

33. Calories in Fast-Food Sandwiches The number of calories contained in a selection of fast-food sandwiches is shown here. Check for normality. Approximately normal

390	405	580	300	320
540	225	720	470	560
535	660	530	290	440
390	675	530	1010	450
320	460	290	340	610
430	530			

Source: The Doctor's Pocket Calorie, Fat, and Carbohydrate Counter.

34. GMAT Scores The average GMAT scores for the top-30 ranked graduate schools of business are listed here. Check for normality. Approximately normal

718	703	703	703	700	690	695	705	690	688
676	681	689	686	691	669	674	652	680	670
651	651	637	662	641	645	645	642	660	636

Source: U.S. News & World Report Best Graduate Schools.

Critical Thinking Challenges

Sometimes a researcher must decide whether a variable is normally distributed. There are several ways to do this. One simple but very subjective method uses special graph paper, which is called *normal probability paper*. For the distribution of systolic blood pressure readings given in Chapter 3 of the text, the following method can be used:

1. Make a table, as shown.

Boundaries	Frequency	Cumulative frequency	Cumulative percent frequency
89.5–104.5	24		
104.5–119.5	62		
119.5–134.5	72		
134.5–149.5	26		
149.5–164.5	12		
164.5–179.5	4		
	200		

2. Find the cumulative frequencies for each class, and place the results in the third column.

3. Find the cumulative percents for each class by dividing each cumulative frequency by 200 (the total frequencies) and multiplying by 100%. (For the first class, it would be $24/200 \times 100\% = 12\%$.) Place these values in the last column.

4. Using the normal probability paper shown in Table 6–3, label the *x* axis with the class boundaries as shown and plot the percents.

5. If the points fall approximately in a straight line, it can be concluded that the distribution is normal. Do you feel that this distribution is approximately normal? Explain your answer.

6. To find an approximation of the mean or median, draw a horizontal line from the 50% point on the *y* axis over

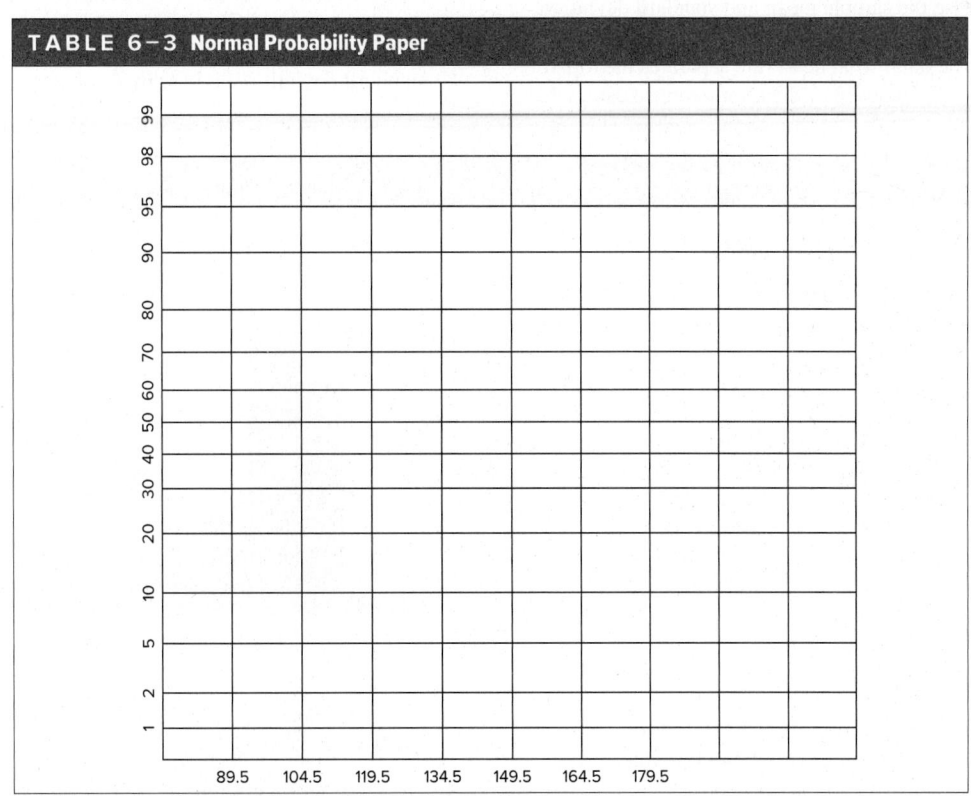

TABLE 6–3 Normal Probability Paper

to the curve and then a vertical line down to the *x* axis. Compare this approximation of the mean with the computed mean.

7. To find an approximation of the standard deviation, locate the values on the *x* axis that correspond to the

16 and 84% values on the *y* axis. Subtract these two values and divide the result by 2. Compare this approximate standard deviation to the computed standard deviation.

8. Explain why the method used in step 7 works.

Data Projects

1. **Business and Finance** Use the data collected in data project 1 of Chapter 2 regarding earnings per share to complete this problem. Use the mean and standard deviation computed in data project 1 of Chapter 3 as estimates for the population parameters. What value separates the top 5% of stocks from the others?

2. **Sports and Leisure** Find the mean and standard deviation for the batting average for a player in the most recently completed MLB season. What batting average would separate the top 5% of all hitters from the rest? What is the probability that a randomly selected player bats over 0.300? What is the probability that a team of 25 players has a mean that is above 0.275?

3. **Technology** Use the data collected in data project 3 of Chapter 2 regarding song lengths. If the sample estimates for mean and standard deviation are used as replacements for the population parameters for this data set, what song length separates the bottom 5% and top 5% from the other values?

4. **Health and Wellness** Use the data regarding heart rates collected in data project 6 of Chapter 2 for this problem. Use the sample mean and standard deviation as estimates of the population parameters. For the before-exercise data, what heart rate separates the top 10% from the other values? For the after-exercise data, what

heart rate separates the bottom 10% from the other values? If a student were selected at random, what would be the probability of the student's mean heart rate before exercise being less than 72? If 25 students were selected at random, what would be the probability that their mean heart rate before exercise was less than 72?

5. **Politics and Economics** Collect data regarding Math SAT scores to complete this problem. What are the mean and standard deviation for statewide Math SAT scores? What SAT score separates the bottom 10% of states from the others? What is the probability that a randomly selected state has a statewide SAT score above 500?

6. **Formulas** Confirm the two formulas hold true for the central limit theorem for the population containing the elements {1, 5, 10}. First, compute the population mean and standard deviation for the data set. Next, create a list of all 9 of the possible two-element samples that can be created with replacement: {1, 1}, {1, 5}, etc. For each of the 9 compute the sample mean. Now find the mean of the sample means. Does it equal the population mean? Compute the standard deviation of the sample means. Does it equal the population standard deviation, divided by the square root of *n*?

Answers to Applying the Concepts

Section 6–1   Assessing Normality

1. Answers will vary. One possible frequency distribution is the following:

Limits	Frequency
0–9	1
10–19	14
20–29	17
30–39	7
40–49	3
50–59	2
60–69	2
70–79	1
80–89	2
90–99	1

2. Answers will vary according to the frequency distribution in question 1. This histogram matches the frequency distribution in question 1.

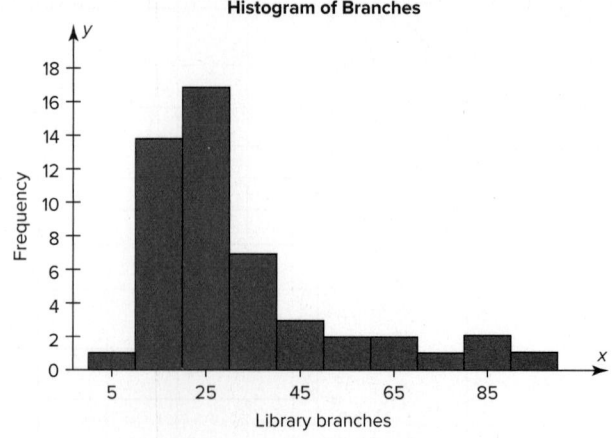

Histogram of Branches

3. The histogram is unimodal and skewed to the right (positively skewed).

4. The distribution does not appear to be normal.

5. The mean number of branches is $\overline{X} = 31.4$, and the standard deviation is $s = 20.6$.

6. Of the data values, 80% fall within 1 standard deviation of the mean (between 10.8 and 52).

7. Of the data values, 92% fall within 2 standard deviations of the mean (between 0 and 72.6).

8. Of the data values, 98% fall within 3 standard deviations of the mean (between 0 and 93.2).

9. My values in questions 6–8 differ from the 68, 95, and 100% that we would see in a normal distribution.

10. These values support the conclusion that the distribution of the variable is not normal.

Section 6–2   Smart People

1. $z = \frac{130 - 100}{15} = 2$. The area to the right of 2 in the standard normal table is about 0.0228, so I would expect about $10{,}000(0.0228) = 228$ people in my hometown to qualify for Mensa.

2. It does seem reasonable to continue my quest to start a Mensa chapter in my hometown.

3. Answers will vary. One possible answer would be to randomly call telephone numbers (both home and cell phones) in my hometown, ask to speak to an adult, and ask whether the person would be interested in joining Mensa.

4. To have an Ultra-Mensa club, I would need to find the people in my hometown who have IQs that are at least 2.326 standard deviations above average. This means that I would need to recruit those with IQs that are at least 135:

$$2.326 = \frac{x - 100}{15} \Rightarrow x = 100 + 2.326(15) = 134.89$$

Section 6–3   Times To Travel to School

1. It is very unlikely that we would ever get the same results for any of our random samples. While it is a remote possibility, it is highly unlikely.

2. A good estimate for the population mean would be to find the average of the students' sample means. Similarly, a good estimate for the population standard deviation would be to find the average of the students' sample standard deviations.

3. The distribution appears to be somewhat left-skewed (negatively skewed).

Histogram of Central Limit Theorem Means

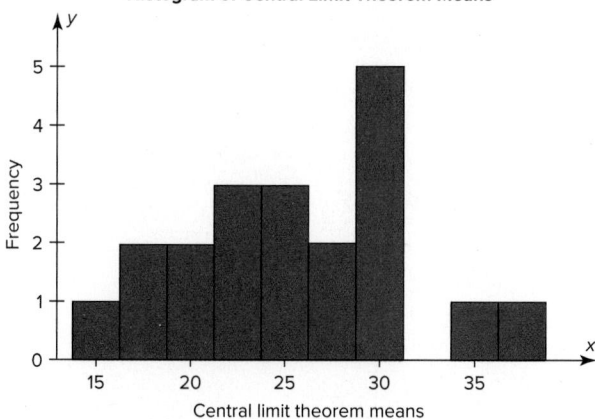

4. The mean of the students' means is 25.4, and the standard deviation is 5.8.

5. The distribution of the means is not a sampling distribution, since it represents just 20 of all possible samples of size 30 from the population.

6. The sampling error for student 3 is $18 - 25.4 = -7.4$; the sampling error for student 7 is $26 - 25.4 = +0.6$; the sampling error for student 14 is $29 - 25.4 = +3.6$.

7. The standard deviation for the sample of the 20 means is greater than the standard deviations for each of the individual students. So it is not equal to the standard deviation divided by the square root of the sample size.

Section 6–4   Mountain Climbing Safety

1. A reliability rating of 97% means that, on average, the device will not fail 97% of the time. We do not know how many times it will fail for any particular set of 100 climbs.

2. The probability of at least 1 failure in 100 climbs is $1 - (0.97)^{100} = 1 - 0.0476 = 0.9524$ (about 95%).

3. The complement of the event in question 2 is the event of "no failures in 100 climbs."

4. This can be considered a binomial experiment. We have two outcomes: success and failure. The probability of the equipment working (success) remains constant at 97%. We have 100 independent climbs. And we are counting the number of times the equipment works in these 100 climbs.

5. We could use the binomial probability formula, but it would be very messy computationally.

6. The probability of at least two failures *cannot* be estimated with the normal distribution (see below). So the probability is $1 - [(0.97)^{100} + 100(0.97)^{99}(0.03)] = 1 - 0.1946 = 0.8054$ (about 80.5%).

7. We *should not* use the normal approximation to the binomial since $nq < 5$.

8. If we had used the normal approximation, we would have needed a correction for continuity, since we would have been approximating a discrete distribution with a continuous distribution.

9. Since a second safety hook will be successful or will fail independently of the first safety hook, the probability of failure drops from 3% to $(0.03)(0.03) = 0.0009$, or 0.09%.

7

Confidence Intervals and Sample Size

Fuse/Getty Images

STATISTICS TODAY

Stress and the College Student

A recent poll conducted by the mtvU/Associated Press found that 85% of college students reported that they experience stress daily. The study said, "It is clear that being stressed is a fact of life on college campuses today."

The study also reports that 74% of students' stress comes from school work, 71% from grades, and 62% from financial woes. The report stated that 2240 undergraduate students were selected and that the poll has a margin of error of ±3.0%.

In this chapter you will learn how to make a true estimate of a parameter, what is meant by the margin of error, and whether or not the sample size was large enough to represent all college students.

See Statistics Today—Revisited at the end of this chapter for more details.

OUTLINE

OBJECTIVES

After completing this chapter, you should be able to:

1   Find the confidence interval for the mean when σ is known.

2   Determine the minimum sample size for finding a confidence interval for the mean.

3   Find the confidence interval for the mean when σ is unknown.

4   Find the confidence interval for a proportion.

5   Determine the minimum sample size for finding a confidence interval for a proportion.

6   Find a confidence interval for a variance and a standard deviation.

Introduction

One aspect of inferential statistics is **estimation,** which is the process of estimating the value of a parameter from information obtained from a sample. For example, consider the following statements:

> "For each dollar you pay in county property tax, 22 cents covers the cost of incarcerating prisoners." (*Pittsburgh City Paper*)
>
> "The average amount employees and employers pay for health insurance is $11,664 per year." (*USA TODAY*)
>
> "For people who were asked if they won $5,000 tomorrow, 54% of them said that they would use it to pay off their debts." (ING U.S. Survey)
>
> "The average amount spent by a TV Super Bowl viewer is $63.87." (Retail Advertising and Marketing Association)
>
> "Eight percent of the people surveyed in the United States said that they participate in skiing in the winter time." (IMRE sports)
>
> "Consumers spent an average of $126 for Valentine's Day this year." (National Retail Federation)

Since the populations from which these values were obtained are large, these values are only *estimates* of the true parameters and are derived from data collected from samples.

The statistical procedures for estimating the population mean, proportion, variance, and standard deviation will be explained in this chapter.

An important question in estimation is that of sample size. How large should the sample be in order to make an accurate estimate? This question is not easy to answer since the size of the sample depends on several factors, such as the accuracy desired and the probability of making a correct estimate. The question of sample size will be explained in this chapter also.

Inferential statistical techniques have various **assumptions** that must be met before valid conclusions can be obtained. One common assumption is that the samples must be randomly selected. Chapter 1 explains how to obtain a random sample. The other common assumption is that either the sample size must be greater than or equal to 30 or the population must be normally or approximately normally distributed if the sample size is less than 30.

To check this assumption, you can use the methods explained in Chapter 6. Just for review, the methods are to check the histogram to see if it is approximately bell-shaped, check for outliers, and if possible, generate a normal quantile plot and see whether the points fall close to a straight line. (*Note:* An area of statistics called nonparametric statistics does not require the variable to be normally distributed.)

7–1   Confidence Intervals

OBJECTIVE

Find the confidence interval for the mean when σ is known.

The main objective of this section is to explain the basics of estimating a parameter such as a mean, proportion, or variance.

Sample measures (i.e., statistics) are used to estimate population measures (i.e., parameters). For example, a sample mean is used to estimate a population mean. A sample proportion is used to estimate a population proportion. These statistics are called **estimators.**

Suppose a college president wishes to estimate the average age of students attending classes this semester. The president could select a random sample of 100 students and find the average age of these students, say, 22.3 years. From the sample mean, the president could infer that the average age of all the students is 22.3 years. This type of estimate is called a *point estimate.*

Another example might be that a restaurant owner wishes to see what proportion of Americans purchase take-out food every day. A random sample of 1000 individuals shows that 0.11 or 11% of the people in the sample purchase take-out food every day. The same is true of other statistics. These types of estimates are called **point estimates.**

> A **point estimate** is a specific numerical value estimate of a parameter. The best point estimate of the population mean μ is the sample mean $\overline{X}$.

A good estimator should satisfy the three properties described next.

Three Properties of a Good Estimator

1. The estimator should be an **unbiased estimator.** That is, the expected value or the mean of the estimates obtained from samples of a given size is equal to the parameter being estimated.
2. The estimator should be consistent. For a **consistent estimator,** as sample size increases, the value of the estimator approaches the value of the parameter estimated.
3. The estimator should be a **relatively efficient estimator.** That is, of all the statistics that can be used to estimate a parameter, the relatively efficient estimator has the smallest variance.

As stated in Chapter 6, the sample mean will be, for the most part, somewhat different from the population mean due to sampling error. Therefore, you might ask a second question: How good is a point estimate? The answer is that there is no way of knowing how close a particular point estimate is to the population mean.

This answer creates some doubt about the accuracy of point estimates. For this reason, statisticians prefer another type of estimate, called an *interval estimate.*

> An **interval estimate** of a parameter is an interval or a range of values used to estimate the parameter. This estimate may or may not contain the value of the parameter being estimated.

In an interval estimate, the parameter is specified as being between two values. For example, an interval estimate for the average age of all students might be $21.9 < \mu < 22.7$, or 22.3 ± 0.4 years.

Also, an interval estimate for a proportion is the proportion of adults who purchase fast-food every day is between 0.107 and 0.113 or between 10.7% and 11.3% or $11\% \pm 0.3\%$.

Either the interval contains the parameter or it does not. A degree of confidence (usually a percent) must be assigned before an interval estimate is made. For instance, you may wish to be 95% confident that the interval contains the true population mean. Another question then arises. Why 95%? Why not 99 or 99.5%?

If you desire to be more confident, such as 99 or 99.5% confident, then you must make the interval larger. For example, a 99% confidence interval for the mean age of college students might be $21.7 < \mu < 22.9$, or 22.3 ± 0.6. Hence, a tradeoff occurs. To be more confident that the interval contains the true population mean, you must make the interval wider.

Historical Notes

Point and interval estimates were known as long ago as the late 1700s. However, it wasn't until 1937 that a mathematician, J. Neyman, formulated practical applications for them.

> The **confidence level** of an interval estimate of a parameter is the probability that the interval estimate will contain the parameter, assuming that a large number of samples are selected and that the estimation process on the same parameter is repeated.
>
> A **confidence interval** is a specific interval estimate of a parameter determined by using data obtained from a sample and by using the specific confidence level of the estimate.

Intervals constructed in this way are called *confidence intervals.* Three common confidence intervals are used: the 90%, the 95%, and the 99% confidence intervals.

A population has a fixed value for the mean or proportion and when a confidence interval is constructed from a sample, it either includes these parameters or it won't. If it were possible to construct 95% confidence intervals for a statistic such as a mean or proportion for all possible samples of a specific size, we can conclude that 95% of them would contain the population parameter. See Figure 7–1.

You can be 95% confident that the population mean is contained within that interval when the values of the variable are normally distributed in the population.

FIGURE 7–1

95% Confidence Intervals for Each Sample Mean

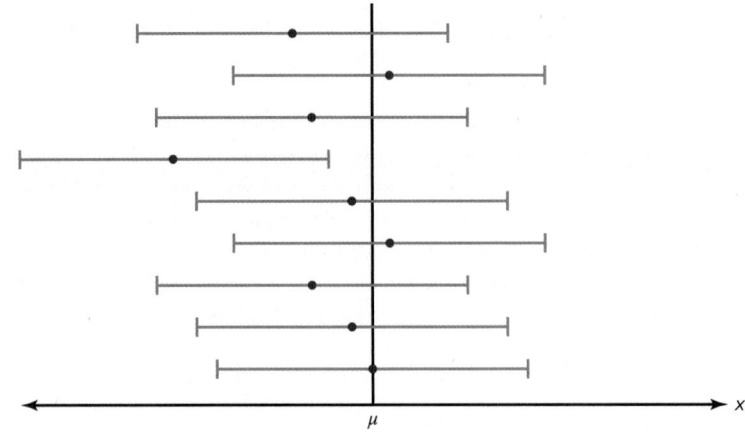

Each • represents a sample mean.

Each ⊢——⊣ represents a 95% confidence interval.

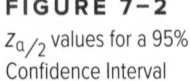

Interesting Fact

A postal worker who delivers mail walks on average 5.2 miles per day.

The value used for the 95% confidence interval, 1.96, is obtained from Table A–4 in Appendix A. For a 99% confidence interval, the value 2.58 is used instead of 1.96 in the formula. This value is also obtained from Table A–4 and is based on the standard normal distribution. Since other confidence intervals are used in statistics, the symbol $z_{\alpha/2}$ (read "zee sub alpha over two") is used in the general formula for confidence intervals. The Greek letter α (alpha) represents the total area in both tails of the standard normal distribution curve, and $\alpha/2$ represents the area in each one of the tails. The value $z_{\alpha/2}$ is called a *critical value*.

The relationship between α and the confidence level is that the stated confidence level is the percentage equivalent to the decimal value of $1 - \alpha$, and vice versa. When the 95% confidence interval is to be found, $\alpha = 0.05$, since $1 - 0.05 = 0.95$, or 95%. When $\alpha = 0.01$, then $1 - \alpha = 1 - 0.01 = 0.99$, and the 99% confidence interval is being calculated.

For a specific value, say $\alpha = 0.05$, 95% of the sample means or proportions will fall within this error value on either side of the population mean or proportion. See Figure 7–2.

> The **margin of error**, also called the *maximum error of the estimate*, is the maximum likely difference between the point estimate of a parameter and the actual value of the parameter.

In the age of students example, where the confidence interval is $21.9 < \mu < 22.7$ or 22.3 ± 0.4, 0.4 is the margin of error. In the proportion of the example where the confidence interval is $10.7\% < p < 11.3\%$ or $11\% + 0.3\%$, 0.003 or 0.3% is the margin of error. The formulas for confidence intervals and margins of errors are shown in the next section.

Confidence intervals can also be represented using parentheses. For example, the confidence interval for the age of students is (21.9, 22.7). For the proportion, the confidence interval is (10.7%, 11.3%).

FIGURE 7–2

$z_{\alpha/2}$ values for a 95% Confidence Interval

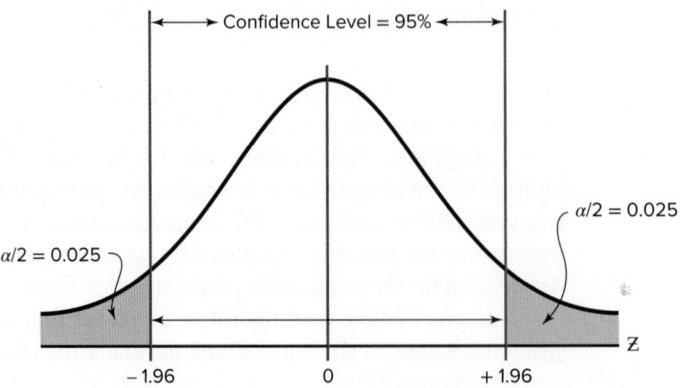

A more detailed explanation of the margin of error follows Examples 7–1 and 7–2, which illustrate the computation of confidence intervals.

Applying the Concepts **7–1**

Sick Leave

1. Do you feel that your population should be limited to a select group of workers such as government employees, hospital workers, teachers, fast-food workers, etc.?
2. What type of sample would you use?
3. How large a sample do you think you should have?
4. Would you use a point estimate or an interval estimate?
5. If you decide to use an interval estimate, would you use a 90%, 95%, or 99% confidence interval?
6. Would your estimate meet the three properties of a good estimator?

See page 412 for the answers.

Exercises **7–1**

1. What is the difference between a point estimate and an interval estimate of a parameter? Which is better? Why?

2. What information is necessary to calculate a confidence interval?

3. What is the margin of error?

4. What is meant by the 95% confidence interval of the mean?

5. What are three properties of a good estimator? A good estimator should be unbiased, consistent, and relatively efficient.

6. What is meant by the 99% confidence interval for a proportion?

For Exercises 7–12, determine the margin of error for each confidence interval.

7. The confidence interval for the mean is $47 < \mu < 54$.
   3.5

8. The confidence interval for the proportion is $0.571 < p < 0.623$. 0.026

9. The confidence interval for the mean is 23 ± 0.5. 0.5

10. The confidence interval for the proportion is 0.29 ± 0.004. 0.004

11. The confidence interval for the proportion is $0.623 < p < 0.629$. 0.003

12. The confidence interval for the mean is $94 < \mu < 104$. 5

Extending the Concepts

13. If in a sample of adults, it was found that 15% of the adults were left-handed. The margin of error is 2 percentage points at the 95% level of confidence. Can it be concluded that the percentage of all adults who are left-handed is between 13% and 17%? No

14. In the previous example, can it be concluded that there is a 95% probability that the true population percentage is between 13% and 17%? No

15. Which is better, a wide confidence interval or a narrow confidence interval? Narrow

7–2   Confidence Intervals for the Mean When σ Is Known

In order to compute the confidence interval for the mean when σ is known, there are two assumptions that must be met.

Assumptions for Finding a Confidence Interval for a Mean When σ Is Known

1. The sample is a random sample.
2. Either $n \geq 30$ or the population is normally distributed when $n < 30$.

In this book, the assumptions will be stated in the exercises; however, when encountering statistics in other situations, you must check to see that these assumptions have been met before proceeding.

Some statistical techniques are called **robust.** This means that the distribution of the variable can depart somewhat from normality, and valid conclusions can still be obtained.

When you estimate a population mean, you should use the sample mean.

You might ask why other measures of central tendency, such as the median and mode, are not used to estimate the population mean. The reason is that the means of samples vary less than other statistics (such as medians and modes) when many samples are selected from the same population. Therefore, the sample mean is the best estimate of the population mean.

> **Formula for the Confidence Interval of the Mean for a Specific α When σ Is Known**
>
> $$\overline{X} - z_{\alpha/2}\left(\frac{\sigma}{\sqrt{n}}\right) < \mu < \overline{X} + z_{\alpha/2}\left(\frac{\sigma}{\sqrt{n}}\right)$$
>
> For a 90% confidence interval, $z_{\alpha/2} = 1.65$; for a 95% confidence interval, $z_{\alpha/2} = 1.96$; and for a 99% confidence interval, $z_{\alpha/2} = 2.58$.

The term $z_{\alpha/2}(\sigma/\sqrt{n})$ is called the *margin of error* (also called the *maximum error of the estimate*). For a specific value, say, $\alpha = 0.05$, 95% of the sample means will fall within this error value on either side of the population mean, as previously explained.

Rounding Rule for a Confidence Interval for a Mean   When you are computing a confidence interval for a population mean by using *raw data,* round off to one more decimal place than the number of decimal places in the original data. When you are computing a confidence interval for a population mean by using a sample mean and a standard deviation, round off to the same number of decimal places as given for the mean.

EXAMPLE 7–1   Skipping Breakfast

A researcher wishes to estimate the number of times a person skips breakfast during the year. A random sample of 49 people had a mean of 50. Assume the population standard deviation is 2.6. Find the best point estimate of the mean and the 95% confidence interval for the population mean.

Source: USA TODAY

SOLUTION

The best point estimate of the mean is 50 times. For the 95% confidence interval, use $z = 1.96$.

$$\overline{X} - z_{\alpha/2}\left(\frac{\sigma}{\sqrt{n}}\right) < \mu < \overline{X} + z_{\alpha/2}\left(\frac{\sigma}{\sqrt{n}}\right)$$

$$50 - 1.96\left(\frac{2.6}{\sqrt{49}}\right) < \mu < 50 + 1.96\left(\frac{2.6}{\sqrt{49}}\right)$$

$$50 - 0.7 < \mu < 50 + 0.7$$

$$49.3 < \mu < 50.7$$

Hence, one can say with 95% confidence that the interval between 49.3 and 50.7 does contain the population mean based on a sample of 49 people.

EXAMPLE 7–2   Amount of Candy Consumed

A nutritionist wanted to find the average amount of candy consumed per year by adult Americans. The nutritionist selected a random sample of 60 adults to study. The sample mean was 23.9 pounds of candy consumed per year. Assume the population standard deviation is 4.8. Find the best point estimate of the mean and the 99% confidence interval of the population mean.

Source: National Confectioners Association

SOLUTION

The best point estimate of the population mean is 23.9 pounds. Use $z = 2.58$ to find the 99% confidence interval of the population mean.

$$\overline{X} - z_{\alpha/2}\left(\frac{\sigma}{\sqrt{n}}\right) < \mu < \overline{X} + z_{\alpha/2}\left(\frac{\sigma}{\sqrt{n}}\right)$$

$$23.9 - 2.58\left(\frac{4.8}{\sqrt{60}}\right) < \mu < 23.9 + 2.58\left(\frac{4.8}{\sqrt{60}}\right)$$

$$23.9 - 1.6 < \mu < 23.9 + 1.6$$

$$22.3 < \mu < 25.5$$

Hence, one can be 99% confident that the mean number of pounds of candy that a person consumes is between 22.3 and 25.5 pounds.

According to the central limit theorem, approximately 95% of the sample means fall within 1.96 standard deviations of the population mean if the sample size is 30 or more, or if σ is known when n is less than 30 and the population is normally distributed. If it were possible to build a confidence interval about each sample mean, as was done in Examples 7–1 and 7–2 for μ, then 95% of these intervals would contain the population mean, as shown in Figure 7–3. Hence, you can be 95% confident that an interval built around a specific sample mean would contain the population mean. If you desire to be 99% confident, you must enlarge the confidence intervals so that 99 out of every 100 intervals contain the population mean.

Since other confidence intervals (besides 90, 95, and 99%) are sometimes used in statistics, an explanation of how to find the values for $z_{\alpha/2}$ is necessary. As stated previously, the Greek letter α represents the total of the areas in both tails of the normal distribution. The value for α is found by subtracting the decimal equivalent for the desired confidence level from 1. For example, if you wanted to find the 98% confidence interval, you would change 98% to 0.98 and find $\alpha = 1 - 0.98$, or 0.02. Then $\alpha/2$ is obtained by dividing α by 2. So $\alpha/2$ is 0.02/2, or 0.01. Finally, $z_{0.01}$ is the z score that will give an area of 0.01 in the right tail of the standard normal distribution curve. See Figure 7–4.

Once $\alpha/2$ is determined, the corresponding $z_{\alpha/2}$ value can be found by using the procedure shown in Chapter 6, which is reviewed here. To get the $z_{\alpha/2}$ value for a 98% confidence interval, subtract 0.01 from 1.0000 to get 0.9900. Next, locate the area that is closest to 0.9900 (in this case, 0.9901) in Table A–4, and then find the corresponding z score. In this example, it is 2.33. See Figure 7–5.

For confidence intervals, only the positive z score is used in the formula.

When the original variable is normally distributed and σ is known, the standard normal distribution can be used to find confidence intervals regardless of the size of the sample. When $n \geq 30$, the distribution of means will be approximately normal even if the original distribution of the variable departs from normality.

FIGURE 7–3
95% Interval for Sample Means

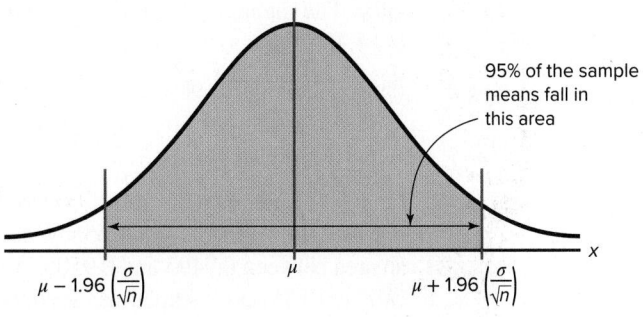

95% of the sample means fall in this area

$\mu - 1.96\left(\frac{\sigma}{\sqrt{n}}\right)$ μ $\mu + 1.96\left(\frac{\sigma}{\sqrt{n}}\right)$

FIGURE 7–4

Finding $\alpha/2$ for a 98%
Confidence Interval

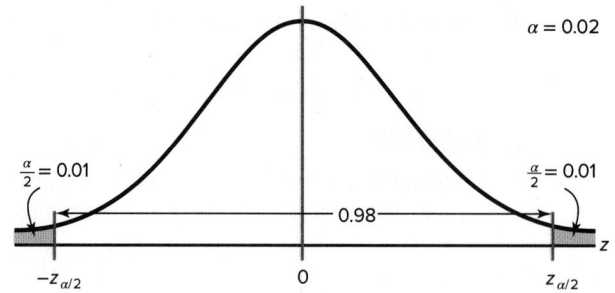

$\alpha = 0.02$

$\frac{\alpha}{2} = 0.01$ $\frac{\alpha}{2} = 0.01$

0.98

$-z_{\alpha/2}$ 0 $z_{\alpha/2}$ z

FIGURE 7–5

Finding $z_{\alpha/2}$ for a 98%
Confidence Interval

			Table A–4			
		The Standard Normal Distribution				
z	.00	.01	.02	.03	...	.09
0.0						
0.1						
⋮						
2.3				0.9901		

EXAMPLE 7–3   Credit Union Assets

The following data represent a random sample of the assets (in millions of dollars) of 30 credit unions in southwestern Pennsylvania. Assume the population standard deviation is 14.405. Find the 90% confidence interval of the mean.

12.23	16.56	4.39
2.89	1.24	2.17
13.19	9.16	1.42
73.25	1.91	14.64
11.59	6.69	1.06
8.74	3.17	18.13
7.92	4.78	16.85
40.22	2.42	21.58
5.01	1.47	12.24
2.27	12.77	2.76

Source: Pittsburgh Post Gazette.

SOLUTION

Step 1   Find the mean for the data. Use the formula shown in Chapter 3 or your calculator. The mean $\overline{X} = 11.091$. Assume the standard deviation of the population is 14.405.

Step 2   Find $\alpha/2$. Since the 90% confidence interval is to be used, $\alpha = 1 - 0.90 = 0.10$, and

$$\frac{\alpha}{2} = \frac{0.10}{2} = 0.05$$

Step 3   Find $z_{\alpha/2}$. Subtract 0.05 from 1.000 to get 0.9500. The corresponding z score obtained from Table A–4 is 1.65. (*Note:* This value is found by using the z score for an area between 0.9495 and 0.9505. A more precise z score obtained mathematically is 1.645 and is sometimes used; however, 1.65 will be used in this text.)

Step 4 Substitute in the formula

$$\overline{X} - z_{\alpha/2}\left(\frac{\sigma}{\sqrt{n}}\right) < \mu < \overline{X} + z_{\alpha/2}\left(\frac{\sigma}{\sqrt{n}}\right)$$

$$11.091 - 1.65\left(\frac{14.405}{\sqrt{30}}\right) < \mu < 11.091 + 1.65\left(\frac{14.405}{\sqrt{30}}\right)$$

$$11.091 - 4.339 < \mu < 11.091 + 4.339$$

$$6.752 < \mu < 15.430$$

Hence, one can be 90% confident that the population mean of the assets of all credit unions is between $6.752 million and $15.430 million, based on a sample of 30 credit unions.

When σ is unknown, s can be used as an estimate of σ, but a different distribution is used for the critical values. This method is explained in Section 7–3.

Comment to Computer and Statistical Calculator Users

This chapter and subsequent chapters include examples using raw data. If you are using computer or calculator programs to find the solutions, the answers you get may vary somewhat from the ones given in the text. This is so because computers and calculators do not round the answers in the intermediate steps and can use 12 or more decimal places for computation. Also, they use more-exact critical values than those given in the tables in the back of this book.

When you are calculating other statistics, such as the z, t, χ^2, or F values (shown in this chapter and later chapters), it is permissible to carry out the values of means, variances, and standard deviations to more decimal places than specified by the rounding rules in Chapter 3. This will give answers that are closer to the calculator or computer values. These small discrepancies are part of statistics.

Sample Size

OBJECTIVE 2

Determine the minimum sample size for finding a confidence interval for the mean.

Sample size determination is closely related to statistical estimation. Quite often you ask, How large a sample is necessary to make an accurate estimate? The answer is not simple, since it depends on three things: the margin of error, the population standard deviation, and the degree of confidence. For example, how close to the true mean do you want to be (2 units, 5 units, etc.), and how confident do you wish to be (90, 95, 99%, etc.)? For the purposes of this chapter, it will be assumed that the population standard deviation of the variable is known or has been estimated from a previous study.

The formula for sample size is derived from the margin of error formula

$$E = z_{\alpha/2}\left(\frac{\sigma}{\sqrt{n}}\right)$$

and this formula is solved for n as follows:

$$E\sqrt{n} = z_{\alpha/2}(\sigma)$$

$$\sqrt{n} = \frac{z_{\alpha/2} \cdot \sigma}{E}$$

Hence,
$$n = \left(\frac{z_{\alpha/2} \cdot \sigma}{E}\right)^2$$

Formula for the Minimum Sample Size Needed for an Interval Estimate of the Population Mean

$$n = \left(\frac{z_{\alpha/2} \cdot \sigma}{E}\right)^2$$

where E is the margin of error. If necessary, round the answer up to obtain a whole number. That is, if there is any fraction or decimal portion in the answer, use the next whole number for sample size n.

EXAMPLE 7–4   Automobile Thefts

A sociologist wishes to estimate the average number of automobile thefts in a large city per day within 2 automobiles. He wishes to be 99% confident, and from a previous study the standard deviation was found to be 4.2. How many days should he select to survey?

SOLUTION

Since $\alpha = 0.01$ (or $1 - 0.99$), $z_{\alpha/2} = 2.58$ and $E = 2$. Substitute in the formula

$$n = \left(\frac{z_{\alpha/2} \cdot \sigma}{E}\right)^2 = \left[\frac{(2.58)(4.2)}{2}\right]^2 = 29.35$$

Round the value up to 30. Therefore, to be 99% confident that the estimate is within 2 automobiles of the true mean, the sociologist needs to sample the thefts for at least 30 days.

In most cases in statistics, we round off; however, when determining sample size, we always round up to the next whole number.

Interesting Fact

It has been estimated that the amount of pizza consumed every day in the United States would cover a farm consisting of 75 acres.

Notice that when you are finding the sample size, the size of the population is irrelevant when the population is large or infinite or when sampling is done with replacement. In other cases, an adjustment is made in the formula for computing sample size. This adjustment is beyond the scope of this book.

The formula for determining sample size requires the use of the population standard deviation. What happens when σ is unknown? In this case, an attempt is made to estimate σ. One such way is to use the standard deviation s obtained from a sample taken previously as an estimate for σ. The standard deviation can also be estimated by dividing the range by 4.

Sometimes, interval estimates rather than point estimates are reported. For instance, you may read a statement: "On the basis of a sample of 200 families, the survey estimates that an American family of two spends an average of $84 per week for groceries. One can be 95% confident that this estimate is accurate within $3 of the true mean." This statement means that the 95% confidence interval of the true mean is

$$\$84 - \$3 < \mu < \$84 + \$3$$
$$\$81 < \mu < \$87$$

The algebraic derivation of the formula for a confidence interval is shown next. As explained in Chapter 6, the sampling distribution of the mean is approximately normal when large samples ($n \geq 30$) are taken from a population. Also,

$$z = \frac{\overline{X} - \mu}{\sigma/\sqrt{n}}$$

Furthermore, there is a probability of $1 - \alpha$ that a z will have a value between $-z_{\alpha/2}$ and $+z_{\alpha/2}$. Hence,

$$-z_{\alpha/2} < \frac{\overline{X} - \mu}{\sigma/\sqrt{n}} < z_{\alpha/2}$$

By using algebra, the formula can be rewritten as

$$-z_{\alpha/2} \cdot \frac{\sigma}{\sqrt{n}} < \overline{X} - \mu < z_{\alpha/2} \cdot \frac{\sigma}{\sqrt{n}}$$

Subtracting $\overline{X}$ from both sides and from the middle gives

$$-\overline{X} - z_{\alpha/2} \cdot \frac{\sigma}{\sqrt{n}} < -\mu < -\overline{X} + z_{\alpha/2} \cdot \frac{\sigma}{\sqrt{n}}$$

Multiplying by -1 gives

$$\overline{X} + z_{\alpha/2} \cdot \frac{\sigma}{\sqrt{n}} > \mu > \overline{X} - z_{\alpha/2} \cdot \frac{\sigma}{\sqrt{n}}$$

Reversing the inequality yields the formula for the confidence interval:

$$\overline{X} - z_{\alpha/2} \cdot \frac{\sigma}{\sqrt{n}} < \mu < \overline{X} + z_{\alpha/2} \cdot \frac{\sigma}{\sqrt{n}}$$

▤ Applying the Concepts 7–2

How Many Tissues Should Be in a Box?

Assume you work for a corporation that makes facial tissues. The job you are presently working on requires you to decide how many tissues are to be put in the new automobile glove compartment boxes. Complete the following.

1. How will you decide on a reasonable number of tissues to put in the boxes?
2. When do people usually need tissues?
3. What type of data collection technique would you use?
4. Assume you found out that from your sample of 85 people, an average of about 57 tissues are used throughout the duration of a cold, with a population standard deviation of 15. Use a confidence interval to help you decide how many tissues will go in the boxes.
5. Explain how you decided how many tissues will go in the boxes.

See page 412 for the answers.

▤ Exercises 7–2

1. What statistic best estimates μ? $\overline{X}$

2. What two assumptions must be met when you find a confidence interval for a mean when σ is known?

For Exercises 3 to 7, find each.

3. $z_{\alpha/2}$ for the 99% confidence interval 2.58

4. $z_{\alpha/2}$ for the 98% confidence interval 2.33

5. $z_{\alpha/2}$ for the 95% confidence interval 1.96

6. $z_{\alpha/2}$ for the 90% confidence interval 1.65

7. $z_{\alpha/2}$ for the 94% confidence interval 1.88

8. What is necessary to determine the sample size?

9. **Stealing Automobiles** A random sample of 32 months has a mean of 54 automobiles stolen per month. The population standard deviation was 4 automobiles obtained from a long-term study. Find the 95% confidence interval for the mean. $53 < \mu < 55$

10. **Motorcycle Noise** A recent study of 44 motorcycles found that the average noise pollution in decibels is 90. If the population standard deviation is 4.2 decibels, find the 90% confidence interval for the mean. $89 < \mu < 91$

11. **Overweight Men** For a random sample of 60 overweight men, the mean of the number of pounds that they were overweight was 30. The standard deviation of the population is 4.2 pounds.

    a. Find the best point estimate of the average number of excess pounds that they weighed. 30 pounds
    b. Find the 95% confidence interval of the mean of these pounds. $28.9 < \mu < 31.1$
    c. Find the 99% confidence interval of these pounds. $28.6 < \mu < 31.4$
    d. Which interval is larger? Why? The 99% confidence interval is larger.

12. **Number of Jobs** A sociologist found that in a random sample of 50 retired men, the average number of jobs they had during their lifetimes was 7.2. The population standard deviation is 2.1.

    a. Find the best point estimate of the population mean. 12.5 jobs
    b. Find the 95% confidence interval of the mean number of jobs. $11.9 < \mu < 13.1$
    c. Find the 99% confidence interval of the mean number of jobs. $11.7 < \mu < 13.3$
    d. Which is smaller? Explain why.

13. **Divorce Rates** The number of years that first-time married couples stay together before they divorce is shown. If the sample is random and σ is 2.1, find the 99% confidence interval for the mean. $5.0 < \mu < 7.0$

10	6	2	3	3	5	8	11	4	5
3	1	4	11	8	9	3	12	6	10
5	3	2	7	9	11	6	3	5	5

14. **Freshmen GPAs** First-semester GPAs for a random selection of freshmen at a large university are shown. Estimate the true mean GPA of the freshman class with 99% confidence. Assume $\sigma = 0.62$. $2.55 < \mu < 3.09$

1.9	3.2	2.0	2.9	2.7	3.3
2.8	3.0	3.8	2.7	2.0	1.9
2.5	2.7	2.8	3.2	3.0	3.8
3.1	2.7	3.5	3.8	3.9	2.7
2.0	2.8	1.9	4.0	2.2	2.8
2.1	2.4	3.0	3.4	2.9	2.1

15. **Student Discipline Problems** The data for a random sample of 32 months for the number of discipline problems that occurred each month at a large high school are

shown. Find the 98% confidence interval for the mean when $\sigma = 3$. 18.7 < μ < 21.2

15	24	19	16	15	17	21	18
11	16	14	23	21	19	26	23
12	19	22	28	27	23	17	16
16	14	21	26	23	25	22	29

16. **Number of Farms** A random sample of the number of farms (in thousands) in various states follows. Estimate the mean number of farms per state with 90% confidence. Assume $\sigma = 31.0$. 34.3 < μ < 52.6

47	95	54	33	64	4	8	57	9	80
8	90	3	49	4	44	79	80	48	16
68	7	15	21	52	6	78	109	40	50
29

Source: New York Times Almanac.

17. **Miles Driven Per Day** A random sample of 36 drivers found that they had driven on average 22 miles per day. Find the 95% confidence interval of the mean if the population standard deviation is 5.2. Find the 90% confidence interval of the mean. Which interval would you consider more appropriate? 20.3 < μ < 23.7
20.6 < μ < 23.4   Both, since they are close

18. **Day Care Tuition** A random sample of 50 four-year-olds attending day care centers provided a yearly tuition average of $10,158 and the population standard deviation of $630. Find the 90% confidence interval of the true mean. If a day care center were starting up and wanted to keep tuition low, what would be a reasonable amount to charge? $10,011 < μ < $10,305; $10,011

19. **Hospital Noise Levels** Noise levels at various area urban hospitals were measured in decibels. The mean of the noise levels in 84 randomly selected corridors was 61.2 decibels, and the standard deviation of the population was 7.9. Find the 95% confidence interval of the true mean. 59.5 < μ < 62.9

Source: M. Bayo, A. Garcia, and A. Garcia, "Noise Levels in an Urban Hospital and Workers' Subjective Responses," Archives of Environmental Health 50(3): 247-51 (May-June 1995).

20. **Length of Growing Seasons** The growing seasons for a random sample of 35 U.S. cities were recorded, yielding a sample mean of 190.7 days and the population standard deviation of 54.2 days. Estimate for all U.S. cities the true mean of the growing season with 95% confidence. 172.7 < μ < 208.7

Source: The Old Farmer's Almanac.

21. **Christmas Presents** How large a sample is needed to estimate the population mean for the amount of money a person spends on Christmas presents within $2 and be 95% confident? The standard deviation of the population is $7.50. 55

22. **Hospital Noise Levels** In the hospital study cited in Exercise 19, the mean noise level in 171 randomly selected ward areas was 58.0 decibels, and the population standard deviation was 4.8. Find the 90% confidence interval of the true mean. 57.4 < μ < 58.6

Source: M. Bayo, A. Garcia, and A. Garcia, "Noise Levels in an Urban Hospital and Workers' Subjective Responses," Archives of Environmental Health 50(3): 247-51 (May-June 1995).

23. **Internet Viewing** A researcher wishes to estimate the average number of minutes per day a person spends on the Internet. How large a sample must she select if she wishes to be 90% confident that the population mean is within 10 minutes of the sample mean? Assume the population standard deviation is 42 minutes. 49

24. **Cost of Pizzas** A pizza shop owner wishes to find the 95% confidence interval of the true mean cost of a large cheese pizza. How large should the sample be if she wishes to be accurate to within $0.15? A previous study showed that the standard deviation of the price was $0.26. 12

25. **Water Temperature** If the variance of the water temperature in a lake is 28°, how many days should the researcher select to measure the temperature to estimate the true mean within 3° with 99% confidence? 21

26. **Undergraduate GPAs** It is desired to estimate the mean GPA of each undergraduate class at a large university. How large a sample is necessary to estimate the GPA within 0.25 at the 99% confidence level? The population standard deviation is 1.2. 154

Extending the Concepts

27. When the sample size is increased and the confidence level remains the same, what happens to the margin of error? It decreases.

28. When the confidence level is increased and the sample size remains the same, what happens to the margin of error? It increases.

29. What do you need to do to increase the confidence level and keep the margin of error small? Increase sample size, if possible.

30. When you add or subtract the margin of error to the mean value, does this guarantee that the interval will contain the population mean? No. You can only expect the interval to contain the population mean with the value of the confidence level.

31. Does the margin of error have anything to do with the errors made in collecting data? No. It only involves errors due to the sampling process.

32. What happens to a 95% confidence interval when you increase the sample size? As you increase sample size, the width of the interval gets smaller.

33. Pollsters try to predict the winners of elections by using the results of samples. However, sometimes one candidate will lead the other candidate by a few percentage points, but the statisticians will say, "The winner is too close to call because both percents fall within the margin of error." (However, they will very seldom tell you what the margin of error is.) Explain how they arrive at this conclusion. When you use the margin of error and compute the confidence intervals for both results, they will overlap. Thus, you cannot say one candidate will win over the other candidate.

≡ Technology   Step by Step

TI-84 Plus
Step by Step

Finding a *z* Confidence Interval for the Mean (Data)

1. Enter the data into L₁.
2. Press **STAT** and move the cursor to TESTS.
3. Press **7** for ZInterval.
4. Move the cursor to Data and press **ENTER**.
5. Type in the appropriate values.
6. Move the cursor to Calculate and press **ENTER**.

Example TI7–1

For Example 7–3 from the text, find the 90% confidence interval for the population mean, given the data values.

12.23	2.89	13.19	73.25	11.59	8.74	7.92	40.22	5.01	2.27
16.56	1.24	9.16	1.91	6.69	3.17	4.78	2.42	1.47	12.77
4.39	2.17	1.42	14.64	1.06	18.13	16.85	21.58	12.24	2.76

In the example, the population standard deviation σ is assumed to be 14.405. After the data values are entered in L₁ (step 1 above), press **STAT** and move cursor to TESTS. Press 7 for ZInterval. Move the cursor to Data and press **ENTER**. Type in the given population's standard deviation enter 14.405 on the line for σ. Make sure your list name has L₁ and that frequency is set as 1. Change the confidence interval level to 0.90. Move the cursor to Calculate and press **ENTER**.

The 90% confidence interval is $6.765 < \mu < 15.417$. The difference between these limits and the ones in Example 7–3 is due to rounding.

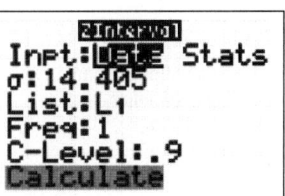

Finding a *z* Confidence Interval for the Mean (Statistics)

1. Press **STAT** and move the cursor to TESTS.
2. Press **7** for ZInterval.
3. Move the cursor to Stats and press **ENTER**.
4. Type in the appropriate values.
5. Move the cursor to Calculate and press **ENTER**.

Example TI7–2

Find the 95% confidence interval for the population mean, given $\sigma = 2$, $\overline{X} = 23.2$, and $n = 50$.

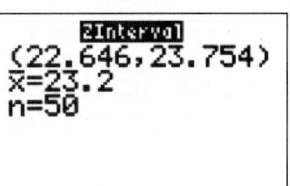

The 95% confidence interval is $22.646 < \mu < 23.754$.

EXCEL
Step by Step

Finding a z Confidence Interval for the Mean

Excel has a procedure to compute the margin of error. But it does not compute confidence intervals. However, you may determine confidence intervals for the mean by using the MegaStat Add-in available in your online resources. If you have not installed this add-in, do so, following the instructions from the Chapter 1 Excel Step by Step.

Example XL7–1

Find the 95% confidence interval for the mean if $\sigma = 11$, using this sample:

43	52	18	20	25	45	43	21	42	32	24	32	19	25	26
44	42	41	41	53	22	25	23	21	27	33	36	47	19	20

1. Enter the data into an Excel worksheet.
2. Calculate the mean of your data using **=AVERAGE()**. Your result should be approximately 32.03.
3. From the toolbar, select Add-Ins, **MegaStat>Confidence Intervals/Sample Size**.
   Note: You may need to open **MegaStat** from the **MegaStat.xls** file on your computer's hard drive.
4. Enter the mean of the data, **32.03.**
5. Select *z* for the standard normal distribution.
6. Enter **11** for the standard deviation and **30** for *n*, the sample size.
7. Either type in or scroll to 95% for the Confidence Level, then click [OK].

The result of the procedure is shown next.

Confidence Interval—Mean

95%	Confidence level
32.03	Mean
11	Standard deviation
30	*n*
1.960	*z*
3.936	Half-width
35.966	Upper confidence limit
28.094	Lower confidence limit

MINITAB
Step by Step

Finding a z Confidence Interval for the Mean

For Example 7–3, find the 90% confidence interval estimate for the mean amount of assets for credit unions in southwestern Pennsylvania.

1. Enter the data into C1 of a MINITAB worksheet. Label the column Assets.
2. Select **Stat>Basic Statistics>1-Sample Z.** Sigma is given as 14.405.
   a) Select One or more samples, each in a column from the menu.
   b) Select C1 Assets by clicking the open space below this menu and double-clicking the column name.
   c) Click on the box for Known standard deviation and type 14.405.

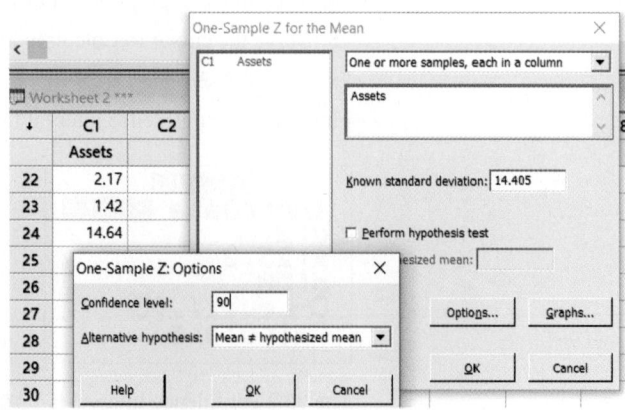

3. Click the [Options] button. In the dialog box make sure the Confidence Level is 90 and the alternative hypothesis is mean ≠ hypothesized mean. Click [OK].

4. Optional: Click [Graphs], then select Boxplot of data. The boxplot of these data will show possible outliers!

5. Click [OK] twice. The results will be displayed in the session window and boxplot.

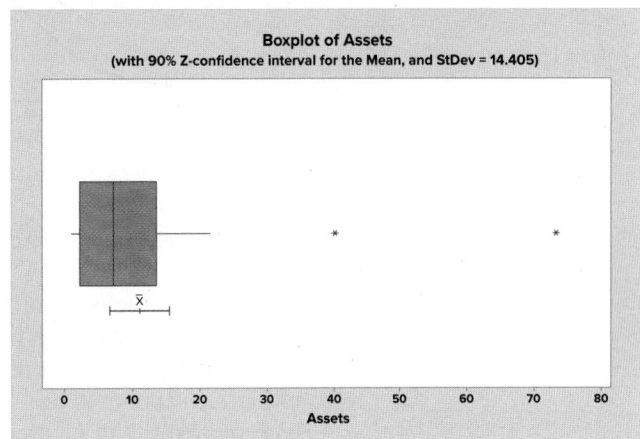

One-Sample Z: Assets

```
The assumed standard deviation = 14.405


Variable   N   Mean  StDev  SE Mean     90% CI
Assets    30  11.09  14.41     2.63  (6.76, 15.42)
```

7–3 Confidence Intervals for the Mean When σ Is Unknown

OBJECTIVE **3**

Find the confidence interval for the mean when σ is unknown.

When σ is known and the sample size is 30 or more, or the population is normally distributed if the sample size is less than 30, the confidence interval for the mean can be found by using the z distribution, as shown in Section 7–1. However, most of the time, the value of σ is not known, so it must be estimated by using s, namely, the standard deviation of the sample. When s is used, especially when the sample size is small, critical values greater than the values for $z_{\alpha/2}$ are used in confidence intervals in order to keep the interval at a given confidence level, such as 95%. These values are taken from the *Student's t distribution,* most often called the ***t* distribution.**

To use this method, the samples must be simple random samples, and the population from which the samples were taken must be normally or approximately normally distributed, or the sample size must be 30 or more.

Some important characteristics of the t distribution are described now.

Historical Notes

The t distribution was formulated in 1908 by an Irish brewing employee named W. S. Gosset. Gosset was involved in researching new methods of manufacturing ale. Because brewing employees were not allowed to publish results, Gosset published his finding using the pseudonym *Student;* hence, the t distribution is sometimes called *Student's t distribution.*

Characteristics of the *t* Distribution

The t distribution shares some characteristics of the standard normal distribution and differs from it in others. The t distribution is similar to the standard normal distribution in these ways:

1. It is bell-shaped.
2. It is symmetric about the mean.
3. The mean, median, and mode are equal to 0 and are located at the center of the distribution.
4. The curve approaches but never touches the x axis.

The t distribution differs from the standard normal distribution in the following ways:

1. The variance is greater than 1.
2. The t distribution is actually a family of curves based on the concept of *degrees of freedom*, which is related to sample size.
3. As the sample size increases, the t distribution approaches the standard normal distribution. See Figure 7–6.

Many statistical distributions use the concept of degrees of freedom, and the formulas for finding the degrees of freedom vary for different statistical tests. The **degrees of freedom** are the number of values that are free to vary after a sample statistic has been computed,

FIGURE 7-6

The *t* Family of Curves

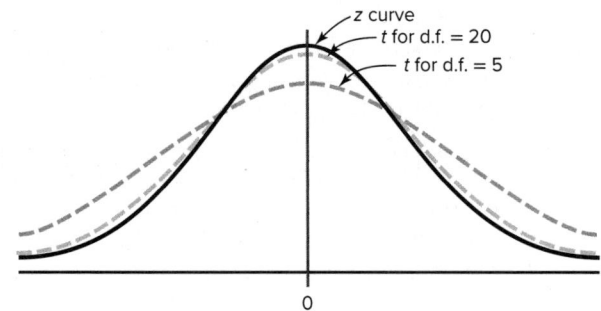

and they tell the researcher which specific curve to use when a distribution consists of a family of curves.

For example, if the mean of 5 values is 10, then 4 of the 5 values are free to vary. But once 4 values are selected, the fifth value must be a specific number to get a sum of 50, since $50 \div 5 = 10$. Hence, the degrees of freedom are $5 - 1 = 4$, and this value tells the researcher which *t* curve to use.

The symbol d.f. will be used for degrees of freedom. The degrees of freedom for a confidence interval for the mean are found by subtracting 1 from the sample size. That is, d.f. $= n - 1$. *Note:* For some statistical tests used later in this book, the degrees of freedom are not equal to $n - 1$.

The formula for finding the confidence interval using the *t* distribution has a critical value $t_{\alpha/2}$.

The values for $t_{\alpha/2}$ are found in Table A–5 in Appendix A. The top row of Table A–5, labeled Confidence Intervals, is used to get these values. The other two rows, labeled One tail and Two tails, will be explained in Chapter 8 and should not be used here.

Example 7–5 shows how to find the value in Table A–5 for $t_{\alpha/2}$.

EXAMPLE 7-5

Find the $t_{\alpha/2}$ value for a 95% confidence interval when the sample size is 22.

SOLUTION

The d.f. $= 22 - 1$, or 21. Find 21 in the left column and 95% in the row labeled Confidence Intervals. The intersection where the two meet gives the value for $t_{\alpha/2}$, which is 2.080. See Figure 7–7.

FIGURE 7-7 Finding $t_{\alpha/2}$ for Example 7–5

Table A–5						
The *t* Distribution						
	Confidence Intervals	80%	90%	95%	98%	99%
d.f.	One tail α	0.10	0.05	0.025	0.01	0.005
	Two tails α	0.20	0.10	0.05	0.02	0.01
1						
2						
3						
$\vdots$						
21				2.080	2.518	2.831
$\vdots$						
$(z)\infty$			1.282^{a}	1.645^{b}	1.960	2.326^{c}	2.576^{d}

When d.f. is greater than 30, it may fall between two table values. For example, if d.f. = 68, it falls between 65 and 70. Many texts say to use the closest value, for example, 68 is closer to 70 than 65; however, in this text a conservative approach is used. In this case, always round down to the nearest table value. In this case, 68 rounds down to 65.

Note: At the bottom of Table A–5, where d.f. is large or ∞, the $z_{\alpha/2}$ values can be found for specific confidence intervals. The reason is that as the degrees of freedom increase, the t distribution approaches the standard normal distribution.

Examples 7–6 and 7–7 show how to find the confidence interval when you are using the t distribution.

The formula for finding a confidence interval for the mean by using the t distribution is given next.

Formula for a Specific Confidence Interval for the Mean When σ Is Unknown

$$\overline{X} - t_{\alpha/2}\left(\frac{s}{\sqrt{n}}\right) < \mu < \overline{X} + t_{\alpha/2}\left(\frac{s}{\sqrt{n}}\right)$$

The degrees of freedom are $n - 1$.

The assumptions for finding a confidence interval for a mean when σ is unknown are given next.

Assumptions for Finding a Confidence Interval for a Mean When σ Is Unknown

1. The sample is a random sample.
2. Either $n \geq 30$ or the population is normally distributed when $n < 30$.

In this text, the assumptions will be stated in the exercises; however, when encountering statistics in other situations, you must check to see that these assumptions have been met before proceeding.

EXAMPLE 7–6   Life Expectancy of Cats

A random sample of 16 cats had a mean life expectancy of 15.3 years. The standard deviation of the sample was 2.3 years. Assume the variable is normally distributed. Find the 95% confidence interval of the population mean life expectancy of cats.

SOLUTION

$$\overline{X} = 15.3 \quad s = 2.3 \quad n = 16$$

Since σ is unknown and s must replace it, the t distribution (Table A–5) must be used for the confidence interval. Hence, with 15 degrees of freedom, $t_{\alpha/2} = 2.131$. The 95% confidence interval can be found by substituting in the following formula.

$$\overline{X} - t_{\alpha/2}\left(\frac{s}{\sqrt{n}}\right) < \mu < \overline{X} + t_{\alpha/2}\left(\frac{s}{\sqrt{n}}\right)$$

$$15.3 - 2.131\left(\frac{2.3}{\sqrt{16}}\right) < \mu < 15.3 + 2.131\left(\frac{2.3}{\sqrt{16}}\right)$$

$$15.3 - 1.2 < \mu < 15.3 + 1.2$$

$$14.1 < \mu < 16.5$$

Therefore, one can be 95% confident that the population mean for the life expectancy in years for cats is between 14.1 and 16.5 years.

EXAMPLE 7–7   Home Fires Started by Candles

The data represent a random sample of the number of home fires started by candles for the past several years. (Data are from the National Fire Protection Association.) Find the 99% confidence interval for the mean number of home fires started by candles each year.

5460	5900	6090	6310	7160	8440	9930

SOLUTION

Step 1   Find the mean and standard deviation for the data. Use the formulas in Chapter 3 or your calculator. The mean $\overline{X} = 7041.4$. The standard deviation $s = 1610.3$.

Step 2   Find $t_{\alpha/2}$ in Table A–5. Use the 99% confidence interval with d.f. = 6. It is 3.707.

Step 3   Substitute in the formula and solve.

$$\overline{X} - t_{\alpha/2}\left(\tfrac{s}{\sqrt{n}}\right) < \mu < \overline{X} + t_{\alpha/2}\left(\tfrac{s}{\sqrt{n}}\right)$$

$$7041.4 - 3.707\left(\frac{1610.3}{\sqrt{7}}\right) < \mu < 7041.4 + 3.707\left(\frac{1610.3}{\sqrt{7}}\right)$$

$$7041.4 - 2256.2 < \mu < 7041.4 + 2256.2$$

$$4785.2 < \mu < 9297.6$$

One can be 99% confident that the population mean number of home fires started by candles each year is between 4785.2 and 9297.6, based on a sample of home fires occurring over a period of 7 years.

Students sometimes have difficulty deciding whether to use $z_{\alpha/2}$ or $t_{\alpha/2}$ values when finding confidence intervals for the mean. As stated previously, when σ is known, $z_{\alpha/2}$ values can be used *no matter what the sample size is,* as long as the variable is normally distributed or $n \geq 30$. When σ is unknown and $n \geq 30$, then s can be used in the formula and $t_{\alpha/2}$ values can be used. Finally, when σ is unknown and $n < 30$, s is used in the formula and $t_{\alpha/2}$ values are used, as long as the variable is approximately normally distributed. These rules are summarized in Figure 7–8.

FIGURE 7–8

When to Use the *z* or *t* Distribution

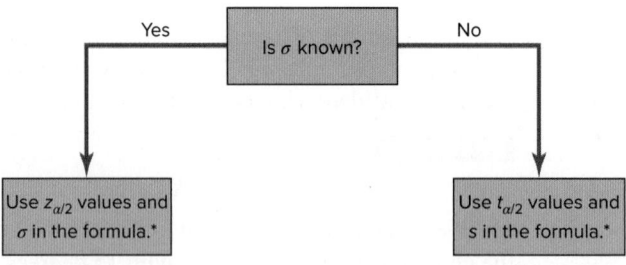

*If $n < 30$, the variable must be normally distributed.

☰ Applying the Concepts 7–3

Sport Drink Decision

Assume you get a new job as a coach for a sports team, and one of your first decisions is to choose the sports drink that the team will use during practices and games. You obtain a *Sports Report* magazine so you can use your statistical background to help you make the best decision. The following table lists the most popular sports drinks and some important information about each. Answer the following questions about the table.

Drink	Calories	Sodium (mg)	Potassium (mg)	Cost ($)
Gatorade	200	400	112.5	1.49
POWERADE	200	375	87.5	1.29
Sqwincher	280	220	180	2.40
BODYARMOR	210	30	1240	2.49
Monster Hydro	159	95	127	2.29
Xtend	0	500	400	2.50
Propel	0	320	80	1.29

1. Would this be considered a small sample?

2. Compute the mean cost per container, and create a 90% confidence interval about that mean. Do all the costs per container fall inside the confidence interval? If not, which ones do not?

3. Are there any you would consider outliers?

4. How many degrees of freedom are there?

5. If cost is a major factor influencing your decision, would you consider cost per container or cost per serving?

6. List which drink you would recommend and why.

See page 412 for the answers.

Exercises 7–3

1. What are the properties of the t distribution?

2. What is meant by *degrees of freedom?*

3. Find the values for each.

   a. $t_{\alpha/2}$ and $n = 18$ for the 99% confidence interval for the mean 2.898

   b. $t_{\alpha/2}$ and $n = 23$ for the 95% confidence interval for the mean 2.074

   c. $t_{\alpha/2}$ and $n = 15$ for the 98% confidence interval for the mean 2.624

   d. $t_{\alpha/2}$ and $n = 10$ for the 90% confidence interval for the mean 1.833

   e. $t_{\alpha/2}$ and $n = 20$ for the 95% confidence interval for the mean 2.093

4. When should the t distribution be used to find a confidence interval for the mean? The t distribution should be used when σ is unknown.

For Exercises 5 through 20, assume that all variables are approximately normally distributed.

5. **High School Graduation Gifts** A random survey of 24 couples who had children graduating from high school found that they spent an average of $98.52 on graduation gifts. The standard deviation of the sample is $5.60. Find the 95% confidence interval for the mean amount of money couples spent for graduation gifts. $96 < \mu < 101$

6. **Monthly Income of D.C. Workers** A survey of 15 randomly selected employed people in Washington, DC, found that the mean monthly income was $5050.

The standard deviation for the sample is $843. Find the 99% confidence interval for the mean monthly income of the workers in Washington, DC. $4402 < \mu < 5698$

7. **Women Representatives in State Legislature** A state representative wishes to estimate the mean number of women representatives per state legislature. A random sample of 17 states is selected, and the number of women representatives is shown. Based on the sample, what is the point estimate of the mean? Find the 90% confidence interval of the mean population. (*Note:* The population mean is actually 147.66, or about 148.) Compare this value to the point estimate and the confidence interval. There is something unusual about the data. Describe it and state how it would affect the confidence interval. $153.3 < \mu < 215.5$

132	213	197	253	141
177	236	174	120	170
140	149	112	150	424
200	147			

8. **State Gasoline Taxes** A random sample of state gasoline taxes (in cents) is shown here for 12 states. Use the data to estimate the true population mean gasoline tax with 90% confidence. Does your interval contain the national average of 44.7 cents? $38.70 < \mu < 48.28$; yes

38.4	40.9	67	32.5	51.5	43.4
38	43.4	50.7	35.4	39.3	41.4

Source: http://www.api.org/statistics/fueltaxes/

9. **Calories in Candy Bars** The number of calories per candy bar for a random sample of standard-size candy

bars is shown below. Estimate the mean number of calories per candy bar with 98% confidence.

$226.3 < \mu < 260.1$

220	220	210	230	275
260	240	260	220	240
240	280	230	280	

10. **Dance Company Students** The number of students who belong to the dance company at each of several randomly selected small universities is shown here. Estimate the true population mean size of a university dance company with 99% confidence.

$25.8 < \mu < 33.9$

21	25	32	22	28	30	29	30
47	26	35	26	35	26	28	28
32	27	40					

11. **Vacation Days** During a recent year, working Americans took on average 17.2 vacation days. This survey was based on a random survey of 18 workers. The standard deviation of the sample was 2.3 days. Find the 90% confidence interval for the mean number of vacation days workers took per year. $16 < \mu < 18$

12. **Thunderstorm Speeds** A meteorologist who sampled 13 randomly selected thunderstorms found that the average speed at which they traveled across a certain state was 15.0 miles per hour. The standard deviation of the sample was 1.7 miles per hour. Find the 99% confidence interval of the mean. If a meteorologist wanted to use the highest speed to predict the times it would take storms to travel across the state in order to issue warnings, what figure would she likely use? $13.6 < \mu < 16.4$; 16.4 miles per hour

13. **Insomnia Sufferers** A random survey of 27 individuals who suffered from insomnia found that the average yearly medical cost for their treatment was $3676. The standard deviation of the sample was $476. Find the 95% confidence interval of the yearly mean medical cost for people who suffer from insomnia.

$3488 < \mu < 3864$

14. **Social Networking Sites** A recent survey of 8 randomly selected social networking sites has a mean of 13.1 million visitors for a specific month. The sample standard deviation is 4.1 million. Find the 95% confidence interval of the true mean.
Source: ComScore Media Matrix. 9.7 million $< \mu < 16.5$

15. **Parking Costs in Dallas** A survey of 10 randomly selected workers in Dallas found that the average cost for parking was $14.00 per hour. The sample standard deviation of the sample was $1.92. Find the 90% confidence interval of the mean hourly parking cost for workers in that city. $12.89 < \mu < 15.11$

16. **Hospital Noise Levels** For a random sample of 24 operating rooms, the mean noise level was 41.6 decibels, and the standard deviation was 7.5. Find the 95% confidence interval of the true mean of the noise levels in the operating rooms. $38.4 < \mu < 44.8$
Source: M. Bayo, A. Garcia, and A. Garcia, "Noise Levels in an Urban Hospital and Workers' Subjective Responses," *Archives of Environmental Health* 50(3): 247–51 (May–June 1995).

17. **Costs for a 30-Second Spot on Cable Television** The approximate costs in thousands of dollars for 30-second randomly selected spots for various cable networks in a random selection of cities are shown. Estimate the true population mean cost for a 30-second advertisement on cable network with 90% confidence. $32.0 < \mu < 70.9$

14	55	165	9	15	66	23	30	150
22	12	13	54	73	55	41	78	

18. **Indy 500 Qualifier Speeds** The speeds in miles per hour of eight randomly selected qualifiers for the Indianapolis 500 (in 2020) are listed below. Estimate the mean qualifying speed with 95% confidence.
$229.1229 < \mu < 230.9129$

230.539	230.775	227.758	230.296
229.234	231.051	229.924	230.566

19. **NYSE Stock Prices** An investing club randomly selects 15 NYSE stocks for consideration, and the prices per share are listed here. Estimate the mean price in dollars of all stocks with 95% confidence.
$22.828 < \mu < 58.160$

41.53	19.83	15.18	50.40	29.97
58.42	21.63	121.17	5.49	54.87
13.10	87.78	19.32	54.83	13.89

20. **Unhealthy Days in Cities** The number of unhealthy days based on the AQI (Air Quality Index) for a random sample of metropolitan areas is shown. Construct a 98% confidence interval based on the data.
$8.8 < \mu < 58.2$

61	12	6	40	27	38	93	5	13	40

Source: New York Times Almanac.

Extending the Concepts

21. **Parking Meter Revenue** A *one-sided confidence* interval can be found for a mean by using

$$\mu > \overline{X} - t_\alpha \frac{s}{\sqrt{n}} \quad \text{or} \quad \mu < \overline{X} + t_\alpha \frac{s}{\sqrt{n}}$$

where t_α is the value found under the row labeled One tail. Find two one-sided 95% confidence intervals of the population mean for the data shown, and interpret the answers. The data represent the daily revenues in dollars from 20 parking meters in a small municipality.

2.60	1.05	2.45	2.90
1.30	3.10	2.35	2.00
2.40	2.35	2.40	1.95
2.80	2.50	2.10	1.75
1.00	2.75	1.80	1.95

≡ Technology | Step by Step

TI-84 Plus
Step by Step

Finding a *t* Confidence Interval for the Mean (Data)

1. Enter the data into L₁.
2. Press **STAT** and move the cursor to TESTS.
3. Press **8** for TInterval.
4. Move the cursor to Data and press **ENTER**.
5. Type in the appropriate values.
6. Move the cursor to Calculate and press **ENTER**.

Finding a *t* Confidence Interval for the Mean (Statistics)

1. Press **STAT** and move the cursor to TESTS.
2. Press **8** for TInterval.
3. Move the cursor to Stats and press **ENTER**.
4. Type in the appropriate values.
5. Move the cursor to Calculate and press **ENTER**.

Example TI7–3

For Example 7–6, find the 95% confidence interval for the mean life expectancy of cats.

  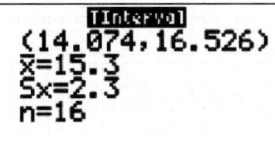

The 95% confidence interval is $14.074 < \mu < 16.526$.

EXCEL
Step by Step

Finding a *t* Confidence Interval for the Mean

Excel has a procedure to compute the margin of error. But it does not compute confidence intervals. However, you may determine confidence intervals for the mean by using the MegaStat Add-in available in your online resources. If you have not installed this add-in, do so, following the instructions from the Chapter 1 Excel Step by Step.

Example XL7–2

Find the 95% confidence interval, using these sample data:

625	675	535	406	512	680	483	522	619	575

1. Enter the data into an Excel worksheet.
2. Calculate the mean of your data using **=AVERAGE()**. Your result should be approximately 563.2.
3. Calculate the sample standard deviation using **=STDEV.S()**. Your result should be approximately 87.9.
4. From the toolbar, select Add-Ins, **MegaStat>Confidence Intervals/Sample Size**. *Note:* You may need to open **MegaStat** from the **MegaStat.xls** file on your computer's hard drive.
5. Enter the mean of the data, **563.2**.
6. Select *t* for the *t* distribution.
7. Enter **87.9** for the standard deviation and **10** for *n*, the sample size.

8. Either type in or scroll to 95% for the Confidence Level, then click [OK].

The result of the procedure is shown next.

Confidence Interval—Mean

95%	Confidence level
563.2	Mean
87.9	Standard deviation
10	n
2.262	t (d.f. = 9)
62.880	Half-width
626.080	Upper confidence limit
500.320	Lower confidence limit

MINITAB
Step by Step

Find a *t* Interval for the Mean

For Example 7–7, find the 99% confidence interval for the mean number of home fires started by candles each year.

1. Type the data into C1 of a MINITAB worksheet. Label the column **Home Fires.**

2. Select Stat>Basic Statistics>1-Sample

    a) Select One or more samples, each in a column from the menu.

    b) Select C1 Home Fires by clicking the open space below this menu and double-clicking the column name.

3. Click the [Options] button. In the dialog box, make sure the confidence level is 99 and the alternative hypothesis is mean ≠ hypothesized mean.

4. Click [OK] twice.

5. Check for normality:

    a) Select **Graph>Probability Plot**, then Single.

    b) Select C1 Home Fires for the **Graph** variable.

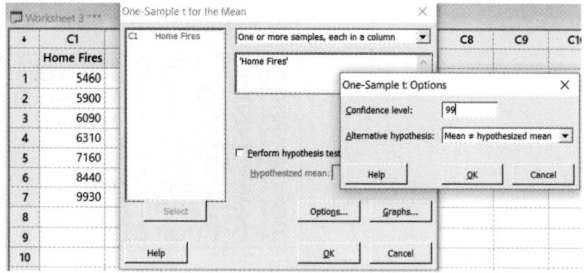

6. Click [OK]. The normal plot is concave, a skewed distribution.

In the session window you will see the results. The 99% confidence interval estimate for μ is between 4785 and 9298. The sample size, mean, standard deviation, and standard error of the mean are also shown.

    However, this small sample appears to have a non-normal population. The interval is less likely to contain the true mean.

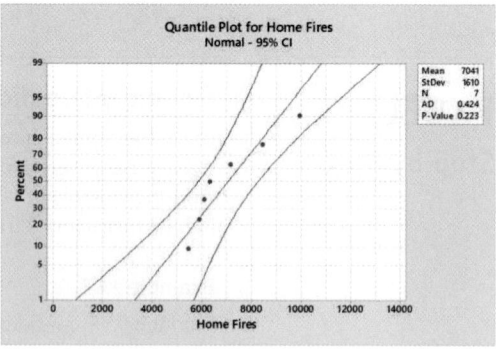

One-Sample T: Home Fires

```
Variable     N  Mean  StDev  SE Mean     99% CI
Home Fires   7  7041   1610      609  (4785, 9298)
```

7–4   Confidence Intervals and Sample Size for Proportions

OBJECTIVE ❹

Find the confidence interval for a proportion.

One of the most common types of confidence intervals is one that uses proportions. Many statistical studies involve finding a proportion of the population that has a certain characteristic. In this section, you will learn how to find the confidence interval for a population.

A *USA TODAY* Snapshots feature stated that 12% of the pleasure boats in the United States were named *Serenity*. The parameter 12% is called a **proportion.** It means that of all the pleasure boats in the United States, 12 out of every 100 are named *Serenity*. A proportion represents a part of a whole. It can be expressed as a fraction, decimal, or percentage. In this case, $12\% = 0.12 = \frac{12}{100}$ or $\frac{3}{25}$. Proportions can also represent probabilities. In this case, if a pleasure boat is selected at random, the probability that it is called *Serenity* is 0.12.

Proportions can be obtained from samples or populations. The following symbols will be used.

Symbols Used in Proportion Notation

$$p = \text{population proportion}$$

$$\hat{p} \text{ (read "} p \text{ hat")} = \text{sample proportion}$$

For a sample proportion,

$$\hat{p} = \frac{X}{n} \quad \text{and} \quad \hat{q} = \frac{n - X}{n} \quad \text{or} \quad \hat{q} = 1 - \hat{p}$$

where X = number of sample units that possess the characteristics of interest and n = sample size.

For example, in a study, 200 people were asked if they were satisfied with their jobs or professions; 162 said that they were. In this case, $n = 200$, $X = 162$, and $\hat{p} = X/n = 162/200 = 0.81$. It can be said that for this sample, 0.81, or 81%, of those surveyed were satisfied with their jobs or professions. The sample proportion is $\hat{p} = 0.81$.

The proportion of people who did not respond favorably when asked if they were satisfied with their jobs or professions constituted $\hat{q}$, where $\hat{q} = (n - X)/n$. For this survey, $\hat{q} = (200 - 162)/200 = 38/200$, or 0.19, or 19%.

When $\hat{p}$ and $\hat{q}$ are given in decimals or fractions, $\hat{p} + \hat{q} = 1$. When $\hat{p}$ and $\hat{q}$ are given in percentages, $\hat{p} + \hat{q} = 100\%$. It follows, then, that $\hat{q} = 1 - \hat{p}$, or $\hat{p} = 1 - \hat{q}$, when $\hat{p}$ and $\hat{q}$ are in decimal or fraction form. For the sample survey on job satisfaction, $\hat{q}$ can also be found by using $\hat{q} = 1 - \hat{p}$, or $1 - 0.81 = 0.19$.

Similar reasoning applies to population proportions; that is, $p = 1 - q$, $q = 1 - p$, and $p + q = 1$, when p and q are expressed in decimal or fraction form. When p and q are expressed as percentages, $p + q = 100\%$, $p = 100\% - q$, and $q = 100\% - p$.

EXAMPLE 7–8   Assault Victims

A random sample of 150 assault victims in a large city found that 45 took no self-protection actions against the criminal. Find $\hat{p}$ and $\hat{q}$, where $\hat{p}$ is the proportion of victims who took no self-protection action against the criminal.

SOLUTION

In this case, $X = 45$ and $n = 150$.

$$\hat{p} = \frac{X}{n} = \frac{45}{150} = 0.30 = 30\%$$

$$\hat{q} = \frac{n - X}{n} = \frac{150 - 45}{150} = \frac{105}{150} = 0.70 = 70\%$$

Also $\hat{q}$ can be found by using the formula $\hat{q} = 1 - \hat{p}$. In this case, $\hat{q} = 1 - 0.30 = 0.70$. So 70% of the victims used some self-protection action against the criminal.

As with means, the statistician, given the sample proportion, tries to estimate the population proportion. Point and interval estimates for a population proportion can be made by using the sample proportion. For a point estimate of p (the population proportion), $\hat{p}$ (the sample proportion) is used. On the basis of the three properties of a good estimator, $\hat{p}$ is unbiased, consistent, and relatively efficient. But as with means, one is not able to decide how good the point estimate of p is. Therefore, statisticians also use an interval estimate for a proportion, and they can assign a probability that the interval will contain the population proportion.

The confidence interval for a particular p is based on the sampling distribution of $\hat{p}$. When the sample size n is no more than 5% of the population size, the sampling distribution of $\hat{p}$ is approximately normal with a mean of p and a standard deviation of $\sqrt{pq/n}$, where $q = 1 - p$.

Confidence Intervals

To construct a confidence interval about a proportion, you must use the margin of error, which is

$$E = z_{\alpha/2} \sqrt{\frac{\hat{p}\hat{q}}{n}}$$

Confidence intervals about proportions must meet the criteria that $n\hat{p} \geq 5$ and $n\hat{q} \geq 5$.

Formula for a Specific Confidence Interval for a Proportion

$$\hat{p} - z_{\alpha/2} \sqrt{\frac{\hat{p}\hat{q}}{n}} < p < \hat{p} + z_{\alpha/2} \sqrt{\frac{\hat{p}\hat{q}}{n}}$$

when $n\hat{p}$ and $n\hat{q}$ are each greater than or equal to 5.

Assumptions for Finding a Confidence Interval for a Population Proportion

1. The sample is a random sample.
2. The conditions for a binomial experiment are satisfied (see Chapter 5).

In this book, the assumptions will be stated in the exercises; however, when encountering statistics in other situations, you must check to see that these assumptions have been met before proceeding.

Rounding Rule for a Confidence Interval for a Proportion   Round off to three decimal places.

EXAMPLE 7–9   Covering College Costs

A survey conducted by Sallie Mae and Gallup of 1404 respondents found that 323 students paid for their education by student loans. Find the 90% confidence interval of the true proportion of students who paid for their education by student loans.

SOLUTION

Step 1   Determine $\hat{p}$ and $\hat{q}$.

$$\hat{p} = \frac{X}{n} = \frac{323}{1404} = 0.23$$
$$\hat{q} = 1 - \hat{p} = 1.00 - 0.23 = 0.77$$

Step 2   Determine the critical value.

$$\alpha = 1 - 0.90 = 0.10$$

$$\frac{\alpha}{2} = \frac{0.10}{2} = 0.05$$

$$z_{\alpha/2} = 1.65$$

Step 3   Substitute in the formula

$$\hat{p} - z_{\alpha/2}\sqrt{\frac{\hat{p}\hat{q}}{n}} < p < \hat{p} + z_{\alpha/2}\sqrt{\frac{\hat{p}\hat{q}}{n}}$$

$$0.23 - 1.65\sqrt{\frac{(0.23)(0.77)}{1404}} < p < 0.23 + 1.65\sqrt{\frac{(0.23)(0.77)}{1404}}$$

$$0.23 - 0.019 < p < 0.23 + 0.019$$
$$0.211 < p < 0.249$$

or
$$21.1\% < p < 24.9\%$$

Hence, you can be 90% confident that the percentage of students who pay for their college education by student loans is between 21.1 and 24.9%.

When a specific percentage is given, the percentage becomes $\hat{p}$ when it is changed to a decimal. For example, if the problem states that 12% of the applicants were men, then $\hat{p} = 0.12$.

EXAMPLE 7–10   Self-Driving Cars

A survey of 6000 adults found that 58% say that they would take a ride in a fully self-driving car. Find the 90% confidence interval of the true proportion who said that they would take a ride in a self-driving car.

Source: World Economic Forum and Boston Consulting Group.

SOLUTION

Step 1   Determine $\hat{p}$ and $\hat{q}$.

In this case, $\hat{p}$ is already given. It is 58%, or 0.58. Then $\hat{q}$ is $1 - \hat{p}$, or $1 - 0.58 = 0.42$.

Step 2   Determine the critical value.

$$\alpha = 1 - 0.90 = 0.10$$
$$\frac{\alpha}{2} = \frac{0.10}{2} = 0.05$$
$$z_{\alpha/2} = 1.65$$

Step 3   Substitute in the formula

$$\hat{p} - z_{\alpha/2}\sqrt{\frac{\hat{p}\hat{q}}{n}} < p < \hat{p} + z_{\alpha/2}\sqrt{\frac{\hat{p}\hat{q}}{n}}$$

$$0.58 - 1.65\sqrt{\frac{(0.58)(0.42)}{6000}} < p < 0.58 + 1.65\sqrt{\frac{(0.58)(0.42)}{6000}}$$

$$0.58 - 0.0105 < p < 0.58 + 0.0105$$
$$0.570 < p < 0.591$$
$$57.0\% < p < 59.1\%$$

Hence, you can say with 90% confidence that the true percentage of people who would take a ride in a self-driving car is between 57.0% and 59.1%.

Sample Size for Proportions

To find the sample size needed to determine a confidence interval about a proportion, use this formula:

OBJECTIVE

Determine the minimum sample size for finding a confidence interval for a proportion.

> **Formula for Minimum Sample Size Needed for Interval Estimate of a Population Proportion**
>
> $$n = \hat{p}\hat{q}\left(\frac{z_{\alpha/2}}{E}\right)^2$$
>
> If necessary, round up to obtain a whole number.

This formula can be found by solving the margin of error value for n in the formula

$$E = z_{\alpha/2}\sqrt{\frac{\hat{p}\hat{q}}{n}}$$

There are two situations to consider. First, if some approximation of $\hat{p}$ is known (e.g., from a previous study), that value can be used in the formula.

Second, if no approximation of $\hat{p}$ is known, you should use $\hat{p} = 0.5$. This value will give a sample size sufficiently large to guarantee an accurate prediction, given the confidence interval and the error of estimate. The reason is that when $\hat{p}$ and $\hat{q}$ are each 0.5, the product $\hat{p}\hat{q}$ is at maximum, as shown here.

$\hat{p}$	$\hat{q}$	$\hat{p}\hat{q}$
0.1	0.9	0.09
0.2	0.8	0.16
0.3	0.7	0.21
0.4	0.6	0.24
0.5	**0.5**	**0.25**
0.6	0.4	0.24
0.7	0.3	0.21
0.8	0.2	0.16
0.9	0.1	0.09

Using the maximum value yields the largest possible value of n for a given margin of error and for a given confidence interval.

The disadvantage of this method is that it can lead to a larger sample size than is necessary.

EXAMPLE 7–11   Land Line Phones

A researcher wishes to estimate, with 95% confidence, the proportion of people who did not have a land line phone. A previous study shows that 40% of those interviewed did not have a land line phone. The researcher wishes to be accurate within 2% of the true proportion. Find the minimum sample size necessary.

SOLUTION

Since $z_{\alpha/2} = 1.96, E = 0.02, \hat{p} = 0.40,$ and $\hat{q} = 0.60,$ then

$$n = \hat{p}\hat{q}\left(\frac{z_{\alpha/2}}{E}\right)^2 = (0.40)(0.60)\left(\frac{1.96}{0.02}\right)^2 = 2304.96$$

which, when rounded up, is 2305 people to interview. So the researcher must interview 2305 people.

W. C. Fields said, "Start every day off with a smile and get it over with."

Do you think people are happy because they are successful, or are they successful because they are happy people? A recent survey conducted by *Money* magazine showed that 34% of the people surveyed said that they were happy because they were successful; however, 63% said that they were successful because they were happy individuals. The people surveyed had an average household income of $75,000 or more. The margin of error was ±2.5%. Based on the information in this article, what would be the confidence interval for each percent?

Pixtal/Age Fotostock

EXAMPLE 7–12   Home Computers

In Example 7–11 assume that no previous study was done. Find the minimum sample size necessary to be accurate within 2% of the true population.

SOLUTION

Here we do not know the values of $\hat{p}$ and $\hat{q}$. So we use $\hat{p} = 0.5$ and $\hat{q} = 0.5$.

$$E = 0.02 \qquad \text{and} \qquad z_{\alpha/2} = 1.96$$

$$n = \hat{p}\hat{q}\left(\frac{z_{\alpha/2}}{E}\right)^2$$

$$= (0.5)(0.5)\left(\frac{1.96}{0.02}\right)^2$$

$$= 2401$$

Hence, 2401 people must be interviewed when $\hat{p}$ is unknown. This is 96 more people than needed if $\hat{p}$ is known.

In determining the sample size, the size of the population is irrelevant. Only the degree of confidence and the margin of error are necessary to make the determination.

Applying the Concepts 7–4

College Dropout Rates

A researcher wishes to see if there is a difference between the dropout rate of students who attend two-year colleges and the dropout rate of students who attend four-year colleges. The researcher randomly selects 1000 students, ages 20–23, from each type of college and finds that the dropout rate for students who attend two-year colleges is 51% and the dropout rate for students who attend four-year colleges is 47%.* Although it looks like there is a difference in the percents, the researcher decides to use confidence intervals to be more certain. The 95% confidence interval for the percent of dropouts for the two-year college students is 47.9%–54.1%, and the 95% percent confidence interval for the dropouts for four-year colleges is 43.9%–50.1%.

*Based on information from EDUCATIONALDATA.ORG.

1. What are the point estimates for the dropout rates?

2. What is the margin of error for the dropout rate for the two-year college students?

3. How does the sample size affect the size of the confidence intervals?

4. Comparing the two confidence intervals, can the researcher conclude that there is a difference in the percents of dropouts for the two-year colleges and the four-year colleges?

See page 412 for the answers.

Exercises 7–4

1. In each case, find $\hat{p}$ and $\hat{q}$.
   a. $n = 40, X = 30$ 0.75, 0.25
   b. $n = 60, X = 55$ 0.92, 0.08
   c. $n = 150, X = 120$ 0.8, 0.2
   d. 35% 0.35, 0.65
   e. 48% 0.48, 0.52

2. Find $\hat{p}$ and $\hat{q}$ for each situation.
   a. $n = 50, X = 35$ 0.7, 0.3
   b. $n = 75, X = 60$ 0.8, 0.2
   c. $n = 90, X = 52$ 0.58, 0.42
   d. 28% 0.28, 0.72
   e. 62% 0.62, 0.38

3. **Employee Pay** Forty-four percent of employers said that their employees are fairly paid, while only 20% of the employees agreed. If 50 employers and 200 employees were surveyed, find the 95% confidence level of the proportions for each group. $0.302 < p < 0.578; 0.145 < p < 0.255$
   Source: Pay Scale Survey

4. **Manual Transmission Automobiles** In 2019, 1.1% of the cars sold had a manual transmission. A random sample of college students who owned cars revealed the following: out of 128 cars, 8 had manual transmissions. Estimate the proportion of college students who drive cars with manual transmissions with 90% confidence. $0.027 < p < 0.098$

5. **Graduation Gifts** Eighty-eight percent of students said that cash is their top choice for a graduation gift. If 125 students were surveyed, find the 90% confidence interval for the proportion. $0.832 < p < 0.928$

6. **Belief in Haunted Places** A random sample of 205 college students was asked if they believed that places could be haunted, and 65 responded yes. Estimate the true proportion of college students who believe in the possibility of haunted places with 99% confidence. According to *Time* magazine, 37% of all Americans believe that places can be haunted. $0.233 < p < 0.401$
   Source: Time magazine, Oct. 2006.

7. **Microwave Cooking** A survey of 60 households found that 45% use the microwave to prepare their meals. Find the 95% confidence interval for the proportion. $0.324 < p < 0.576$
   Source: Peapod Survey

8. **Travel to Outer Space** A CBS News/*New York Times* poll found that 329 out of 763 randomly selected adults said they would travel to outer space in their lifetime, given the chance. Estimate the true proportion of adults who would like to travel to outer space with 92% confidence. $0.400 < p < 0.462$
   Source: www.pollingreport.com

9. **High School Graduates Who Take the SAT** The national average for the percentage of high school graduates taking the SAT is 49%, but the state averages vary from a low of 4% to a high of 92%. A random sample of 300 graduating high school seniors was polled across a particular tristate area, and it was found that 195 had taken the SAT. Estimate the true proportion of high school graduates in this region who take the SAT with 95% confidence. $0.596 < p < 0.704$
   Source: World Almanac.

10. **Emergency Escape Plan** A random sample of 180 residents of the Southeastern United States found 114 had no emergency escape plan for severe weather. Find the 90% confidence interval of the true proportion of individuals living in the Southeastern United States who do not have an emergency escape plan for severe weather. $0.574 < p < 0.692$

11. **Inflating Job Skills** A survey of 260 post-graduate students found that 52 said that they have inflated their job skills on their resumes when looking for a job. Estimate the true proportion of post-graduate students who have inflated their job skills on their resumes at the 95% confidence level. $0.151 < p < 0.249$
    Source: Jobuit Survey

12. **Checking on a Pet** A pet supply company claims that one in five employed individuals said that they go home at lunchtime to check on their pets. If 120 pet owners are surveyed, estimate the true proportion of individuals who go home at lunchtime to check on their pets. Use a 95% confidence interval. $0.128 < p < 0.272$
    Source: Wellness Natural Pet Food Survey

13. **Smartphone Ownership** A recent survey of 349 people ages 18 to 29 found that 86% of them own a smartphone. Find the 99% confidence interval of the population proportion. $0.812 < p < 0.908$
    Source: Pew Research Center.

14. Home Internet Access According to a study, 96% of adults ages 18–29 had Internet access at home in 2015. A researcher wanted to estimate the proportion of undergraduate college students (18 to 29 years) with access, so she randomly sampled 180 undergraduates and found that 157 had access. Estimate the true proportion with 90% confidence. $0.831 < p < 0.913$

15. Overseas Travel A researcher wishes to be 95% confident that her estimate of the true proportion of individuals who travel overseas is within 4% of the true proportion. Find the sample necessary if, in a prior study, a sample of 200 people showed that 40 traveled overseas last year. If no estimate of the sample proportion is available, how large should the sample be? 385; 601

16. Widows A recent study indicated that 29% of the 100 women over age 55 in the study were widows.

   a. How large a sample must you take to be 90% confident that the estimate is within 0.05 of the true proportion of women over age 55 who are widows? 225

   b. If no estimate of the sample proportion is available, how large should the sample be? 273

17. Female Executives A pilot study found that 16% of female executives stated that supporting their families is their primary motivation for their careers.

How large a sample is necessary to estimate the true percentage of female executives who feel this way with a 95% confidence and within 3 percentage points of the true value? How large a sample is necessary if nothing is known about the proportion?
Source: Russel Reynolds Associated Survey   574; 1068

18. Sick Co-workers A manager claims that 67% of workers feel that a sick co-worker should stay home instead of coming to work. How large a sample should be taken to estimate within 2% the true proportion of workers that feel this way with 95% confidence? 2124

19. U.S. Fitness Guidelines According to the World Almanac, 35.2% of men ages 18 to 44 meets the U.S. Fitness Guidelines. How large a sample is necessary to estimate the true proportion of men that are fit in this age group within 2 ½ percentage points with 90% confidence? 994
Source: World Almanac 2016.

20. Diet Habits A federal report indicated that 27% of children ages 2 to 5 years had a good diet—an increase over previous years. How large a sample is needed to estimate the true proportion of children with good diets within 2% with 95% confidence? 1893
Source: Federal Interagency Forum on Child and Family Statistics, Washington Observer-Reporter.

Extending the Concepts

21. Gun Control If a random sample of 600 people is selected and the researcher decides to have a margin of error of 4% on the specific proportion who favor gun control, find the degree of confidence. A recent study showed that 50% were in favor of some form of gun control. 95%

22. Survey on Politics In a study, 68% of 1015 randomly selected adults said that they believe the Republicans favor the rich. If the margin of error was 3 percentage points, what was the confidence level used for the proportion? 96%
Source: USA TODAY.

Technology Step by Step

TI-84 Plus
Step by Step

Finding a Confidence Interval for a Proportion

1. Press **STAT** and move the cursor to TESTS.

2. Press **A (ALPHA, MATH)** for 1-PropZInt.

3. Type in the appropriate values.

4. Move the cursor to Calculate and press **ENTER.**

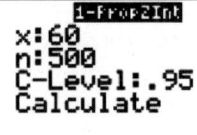

Example TI7–3

Find the 95% confidence interval of *p* when *X* = 60 and *n* = 500.
   The 95% confidence level for *p* is $0.09152 < p < 0.14848$.
Also $\hat{p}$ is given.

EXCEL
Step by Step

Finding a Confidence Interval for a Proportion

Excel has a procedure to compute the margin of error. But it does not compute confidence intervals. However, you may determine confidence intervals for a proportion by using the MegaStat Add-in available in your online resources. If you have not installed this add-in, do so, following the instructions from the Chapter 1 Excel Step by Step.

Example XL7–3

There were 500 nursing applications in a sample, including 60 from men. Find the 90% confidence interval for the true proportion of male applicants.

1. From the toolbar, select Add-Ins, **MegaStat>Confidence Intervals/Sample Size.**
   Note: You may need to open **MegaStat** from the **MegaStat.xls** file on your computer's hard drive.

2. In the dialog box, select Confidence interval—*p*.

3. Enter **60** in the box labeled *p*; *p* will automatically change to *x*.

4. Enter **500** in the box labeled *n*.

5. Either type in or scroll to 90% for the Confidence Level, then click [OK].

The result of the procedure is shown next.

Confidence Interval—Proportion

90%   Confidence level
0.12   Proportion
500   *n*
1.645   *z*
0.024   Half-width
0.144   Upper confidence limit
0.096   Lower confidence limit

MINITAB
Step by Step

Find a Confidence Interval for a Proportion

MINITAB will calculate a confidence interval, given the statistics from a sample *or* given the raw data. From Example 7–9 covering college costs, 323 out of 1404 respondents paid for their education by student loans. Find the 90% confidence interval of the true proportion of students who paid for their education by student loans.

1. Select **Stat>Basic Statistics>1 Proportion.**

2. In the drop-down menu, select Summarized data. No data will be entered in the worksheet.

3. In the Number of events: box, enter 323.

4. Click in the box for Number of trials and enter 1404.

5. Click the [Options] button. In the dialog box, make sure the confidence level is 90 and the alternative hypothesis is Proportion ≠ hypothesized proportion.

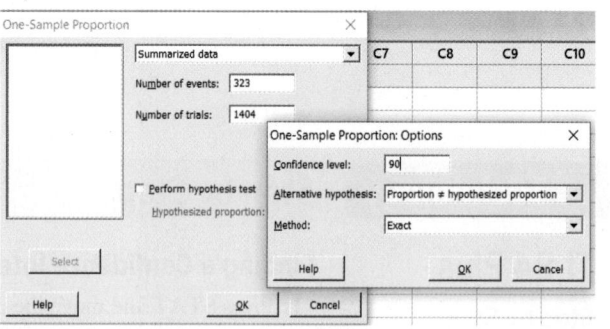

6. Select Normal Approximation for method.

7. Click [OK] twice.

The results for the confidence interval will be displayed in the session window.

Test and CI for One Proportion

```
Sample    X    N    Sample p        90% CI
1        323  1404  0.230057  (0.211656, 0.249299)
```

Using the normal approximation.

7–5   Confidence Intervals for Variances and Standard Deviations

OBJECTIVE ⑥

Find a confidence interval for a variance and a standard deviation.

In Sections 7–1 through 7–3 confidence intervals were calculated for means and proportions. This section will explain how to find confidence intervals for variances and standard deviations. In statistics, the variance and standard deviation of a variable are as important as the mean. For example, when products that fit together (such as pipes) are manufactured, it is important to keep the variations of the diameters of the products as small as possible; otherwise, they will not fit together properly and will have to be scrapped. In the manufacture of medicines, the variance and standard deviation of the medication in the pills play an important role in making sure patients receive the proper dosage. For these reasons, confidence intervals for variances and standard deviations are necessary.

To calculate these confidence intervals, a new statistical distribution is needed. It is called the **chi-square distribution.**

The chi-square variable is similar to the t variable in that its distribution is a family of curves based on the number of degrees of freedom. The symbol for chi-square is χ^2 (Greek letter chi, pronounced "ki"). Several of the distributions are shown in Figure 7–9, along with the corresponding degrees of freedom. The chi-square distribution is obtained from the values of $(n-1)s^2/\sigma^2$ when random samples are selected from a normally distributed population whose variance is σ^2.

A chi-square variable cannot be negative, and the distributions are skewed to the right. At about 100 degrees of freedom, the chi-square distribution becomes somewhat symmetric. The area under each chi-square distribution is equal to 1.00, or 100%.

Historical Note

The χ^2 distribution with 2 degrees of freedom was formulated by a mathematician named Hershel in 1869 while he was studying the accuracy of shooting arrows at a target. Many other mathematicians have since contributed to its development.

Guy Cali/Corbis/Getty Images

FIGURE 7–9

The Chi-Square Family of Curves

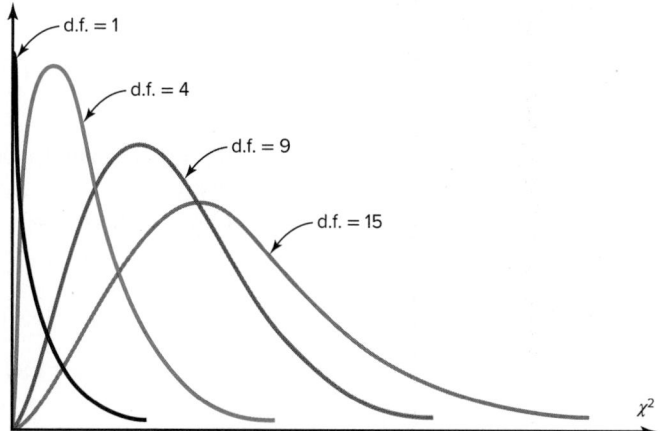

FIGURE 7–10

Chi-Square Distribution for
d.f. $= n - 1$

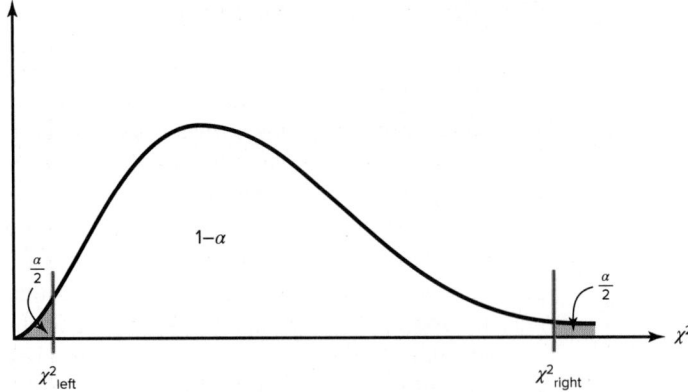

A summary of the characteristics of the chi-square distribution is given next.

Characteristics of the Chi-Square Distribution

1. All chi-square values are greater than or equal to 0.
2. The chi-square distribution is a family of curves based on the degrees of freedom.
3. The area under each chi-square distribution curve is equal to 1.
4. The chi-square distributions are positively skewed.

Table A–6 in Appendix A gives the values for the chi-square distribution. These values are used in the denominators of the formulas for confidence intervals. Two different values are used in the formula because the distribution is not symmetric. One value is found on the left side of the table, and the other is on the right. See Figure 7–10.

Table A–6 is set up similarly to the table used for the t distribution. The left column denotes the degrees of freedom, and the top row represents the area to the *right* of the critical value. For example, to find the table values corresponding to the 95% confidence interval, you must first change 95% to a decimal and subtract it from 1 $(1 - 0.95 = 0.05)$. Then divide the answer by 2 $(\alpha/2 = 0.05/2 = 0.025)$. This is the column on the right side of the table, used to get the values for χ^2_{right}. To get the value for χ^2_{left}, subtract the value of $\alpha/2$ from 1 $(1 - 0.05/2 = 0.975)$. Finally, find the appropriate row corresponding to the degrees of freedom $n - 1$. A similar procedure is used to find the values for a 90 or 99% confidence interval.

EXAMPLE 7–13

Find the values for χ^2_{right} and χ^2_{left} for a 90% confidence interval when $n = 25$.

SOLUTION

To find χ^2_{right}, subtract $1 - 0.90 = 0.10$; then divide 0.10 by 2 to get 0.05.
To find χ^2_{left}, subtract $1 - 0.05 = 0.95$.
Then use the 0.95 and 0.05 columns with d.f. $= n - 1 = 25 - 1 = 24$. See Figure 7–11.

The values are

$$\chi^2_{\text{right}} = 36.415$$

$$\chi^2_{\text{left}} = 13.848$$

See Figure 7–12.

FIGURE 7–11 χ^2 Table for Example 7–13

Degrees of freedom	α									
	0.995	0.99	0.975	0.95	0.90	0.10	0.05	0.025	0.01	0.005
1										
2										
⋮										
24				13.848			36.415			

Table A–6
The Chi-square Distribution

χ^2_{left} χ^2_{right}

FIGURE 7–12 χ^2 Distribution for Example 7–13

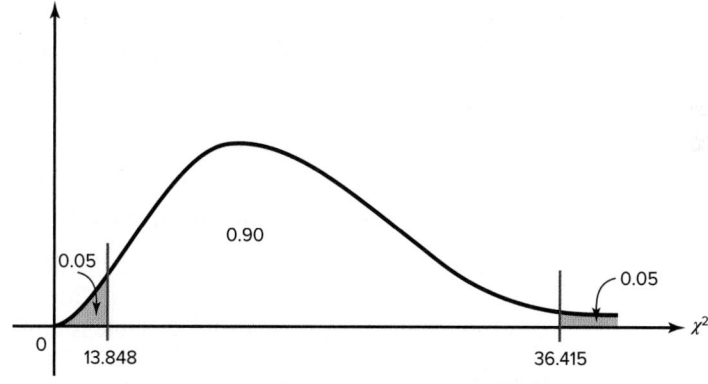

0.05

0.90

0.05

0

13.848

36.415

χ^2

If the number for the degrees of freedom is not given in the table, use the closest lower value in the table. For example, for d.f. = 53, use d.f. = 50. This is a conservative approach.

Useful estimates for σ^2 and σ are s^2 and s, respectively.

To find confidence intervals for variances and standard deviations, you must assume that the variable is normally distributed.

The formulas for the confidence intervals are shown here.

Formula for the Confidence Interval for a Variance

$$\frac{(n-1)s^2}{\chi^2_{\text{right}}} < \sigma^2 < \frac{(n-1)s^2}{\chi^2_{\text{left}}}$$

$$\text{d.f.} = n - 1$$

Formula for the Confidence Interval for a Standard Deviation

$$\sqrt{\frac{(n-1)s^2}{\chi^2_{\text{right}}}} < \sigma < \sqrt{\frac{(n-1)s^2}{\chi^2_{\text{left}}}}$$

$$\text{d.f.} = n - 1$$

Recall that s^2 is the symbol for the sample variance and s is the symbol for the sample standard deviation. If the problem gives the sample standard deviation s, be sure to *square* it when you are using the formula. But if the problem gives the sample variance s^2, *do not square it* when you are using the formula, since the variance is already in square units.

> **Assumptions for Finding a Confidence Interval for a Variance or Standard Deviation**
>
> 1. The sample is a random sample.
> 2. The population must be normally distributed.

In this text, the assumptions will be stated in the exercises; however, when encountering statistics in other situations, you must check to see that these assumptions have been met before proceeding.

Rounding Rule for a Confidence Interval for a Variance or Standard Deviation
When you are computing a confidence interval for a population variance or standard deviation by using raw data, round off to one more decimal place than the number of decimal places in the original data.

When you are computing a confidence interval for a population variance or standard deviation by using a sample variance or standard deviation, round off to the same number of decimal places as given for the sample variance or standard deviation.

Example 7–14 shows how to find a confidence interval for a variance and standard deviation.

EXAMPLE 7–14   Ages of Automobiles

A study of 30 automobile owners found that the standard deviation of the ages of their automobiles is 1.7 years. Find the 95% confidence interval of the variance and standard deviation of the ages. Assume the variable is normally distributed.

SOLUTION

Since $\alpha = 0.05$, and the degrees of freedom is 29, the two critical values are 16.047 and 45.722. Substitute in the following formula.

$$\frac{(n-1)s^2}{\chi^2_{\text{right}}} < \sigma^2 < \frac{(n-1)s^2}{\chi^2_{\text{left}}}$$

$$\frac{(30-1)(1.7)^2}{45.722} < \sigma^2 < \frac{(30-1)(1.7)^2}{16.047}$$

$$1.83 < \sigma^2 < 5.22$$

Hence, you can be 95% confident that the true variance for the ages is between 1.83 and 5.22 years. For the standard deviation, the confidence interval is

$$\sqrt{1.83} < \sigma < \sqrt{5.22}$$

$$1.35 < \sigma < 2.28$$

Hence, you can be 95% confident that the true standard deviation is between 1.35 and 2.28 years based on a sample of 30 automobiles.

EXAMPLE 7–15   Named Storms

Find the 90% confidence interval for the variance and standard deviation for the number of named storms per year in the Atlantic basin. A random sample of 10 years has been used. Assume the distribution is approximately normal.

10	5	12	11	13
15	19	18	14	16

Source: Atlantic Oceanographic and Meteorological Laboratory.

SOLUTION

Step 1   Find the variance for the data. Use the formulas in Chapter 3 or your calculator. The variance $s^2 = 16.9$.

Step 2   Find χ^2_{right} and χ^2_{left} from Table A–6 in Appendix A, using $10 - 1 = 9$ degrees of freedom.

In this case, use $\alpha = 0.05$ and 0.95; $\chi^2_{\text{right}} = 3.325$; $\chi^2_{\text{left}} = 16.919$.

Step 3   Substitute in the formula.

$$\frac{(n-1)s^2}{\chi^2_{\text{right}}} < \sigma^2 < \frac{(n-1)s^2}{\chi^2_{\text{left}}}$$

$$\frac{(10-1)(16.9)}{16.919} < \sigma^2 < \frac{(10-1)(16.9)}{3.325}$$

$$8.99 < \sigma^2 < 45.74$$

$$\sqrt{8.99} < \sigma < \sqrt{45.74}$$

$$3.0 < \sigma < 6.8$$

Hence, you can be 90% confident that the standard deviation for the number of named storms is between 3.0 and 6.8 based on a random sample of 10 years.

Note: If you are using the standard deviation instead (as in Example 7–14) of the variance, be sure to square the standard deviation when substituting in the formula.

≡ Applying the Concepts 7–5

Ages of Presidents at the Time of Their Deaths

Shown are the ages (in years) of the Presidents at the times of their deaths.

67	90	83	85	73	80	78	79
68	71	53	65	74	64	77	56
66	63	70	49	57	71	67	71
58	60	72	67	57	60	90	63
88	78	46	64	81	93	93	

1. Do the data represent a population or a sample?
2. Select a random sample of 12 ages and find the variance and standard deviation.
3. Find the 95% confidence interval of the standard deviation.
4. Find the standard deviation of all the data values.
5. Does the confidence interval calculated in question 3 contain the standard deviation?
6. If it does not, give a reason why.
7. What assumption(s) must be considered for constructing the confidence interval in step 3?

See page 412 for the answers.

≡ Exercises 7–5

1. What distribution must be used when computing confidence intervals for variances and standard deviations? Chi-square

2. What assumption must be made when computing confidence intervals for variances and standard deviations? The variable must be normally distributed.

3. Using Table A–6, find the values for χ^2_{left} and χ^2_{right}.
   a. $\alpha = 0.10, n = 15$ 6.571, 23.685
   b. $\alpha = 0.05, n = 22$ 10.283, 35.479
   c. $\alpha = 0.01, n = 8$ 0.989, 20.278
   d. $\alpha = 0.05, n = 29$ 15.308, 44.461
   e. $\alpha = 0.10, n = 12$ 4.575, 19.675

4. Retail Thefts Find the 90% confidence interval for the variance and standard deviation of the number of retail thefts per week at 22 convenience stores if the standard deviation of the sample is 6.3. Assume the variable is approximately normally distributed.
$25.5 < \sigma^2 < 71.9$; $5.1 < \sigma < 8.5$

5. Carbohydrates in Yogurt The number of carbohydrates (in grams) per 8-ounce serving of yogurt for each of a random selection of brands is listed below. Estimate the true population variance and standard deviation for the number of carbohydrates per 8-ounce serving of yogurt with 95% confidence. Assume the variable is normally distributed.
$56.6 < \sigma^2 < 236.3$; $7.5 < \sigma < 15.4$

| 17 | 42 | 41 | 20 | 39 | 41 | 35 | 15 | 43 |
| 25 | 38 | 33 | 42 | 23 | 17 | 25 | 34 | |

6. Best-selling Books For a sample of 18 best-selling paperback books, the standard deviation for the number of pages in the books is 14.6. Find the 99% confidence interval for the true variance and standard deviation if the variable is normally distributed.
$101.5 < \sigma^2 < 636.1$; $10.1 < \sigma < 25.2$

7. Eating Times Find the 95% confidence interval of the standard deviation for the number of minutes a person takes to eat lunch at a specific restaurant. The standard deviation of a sample of 16 people was 12 minutes. Assume the variable is normally distributed.
$9 < \sigma < 19$

8. Football Kicks For a sample of 22 professional football team kicks, the average number of yards per kick was 45.3 and the standard deviation was 4.8 yards. Find the 95% confidence interval of the variance and standard deviation of the length of the kicks if the variable is normally distributed. $13.6 < \sigma^2 < 47.1$; $3.7 < \sigma < 6.9$

9. Salaries for Web Designers The average starting salary for a sample of 9 Web designers was $5300 per month and the standard deviation of the sample was $300. Find the 90% confidence interval for the variance and standard deviation assuming the salaries are approximately normally distributed.
$46430.64 < \sigma^2 < 263446.76$; $215.48 < \sigma < 513.27$

10. Stock Prices A random sample of stock prices per share (in dollars) is shown. Find the 90% confidence interval for the variance and standard deviation for the prices. Assume the variable is normally distributed.

26.69	13.88	28.37	12.00
75.37	7.50	47.50	43.00
3.81	53.81	13.62	45.12
6.94	28.25	28.00	60.50
40.25	10.87	46.12	14.75

Source: Pittsburgh Tribune-Review.
$259.334 < \sigma^2 < 772.724$; $16.104 < \sigma < 27.798$

11. Holiday Credit Card Bills A recent survey of 23 individuals found that the mean time it took the individuals to pay off their holiday credit card debt was 10 months. The standard deviation of the sample was 2.6 months. Find the 95% confidence interval of the variance and standard deviation assuming the variable is normally distributed. $4.0 < \sigma^2 < 13.5$; $2.0 < \sigma < 3.7$

12. Home Ownership Rates The percentage rates of home ownership for 8 randomly selected states are listed below. Estimate the population variance and standard deviation for the percentage rate of home ownership with 99% confidence. Assume the variable is normally distributed.

| 66.0 | 75.8 | 70.9 | 73.9 | 63.4 | 68.5 | 73.3 | 65.9 |

Source: World Almanac. $6.83 < \sigma^2 < 140.05$; $2.61 < \sigma < 11.83$

13. Calories in a Standard Size Candy Bar Estimate the standard deviation in calories for these randomly selected standard-size candy bars with 95% confidence. (The number of calories is listed for each.) Assume the variable is normally distributed.
$17.3 < \sigma < 38.4$

| 220 | 220 | 210 | 230 | 275 | 260 | 240 |
| 220 | 240 | 240 | 280 | 230 | 280 | 260 |

14. SAT Scores Estimate the variance in mean mathematics SAT scores by state, using the randomly selected scores listed below. Estimate with 99% confidence. Assume the variable is normally distributed.

| 490 | 502 | 211 | 209 | 499 | 565 |
| 469 | 543 | 572 | 550 | 515 | 500 |

Source: World Almanac 2012. $6410.7 < \sigma^2 < 65,897.9$

15. Daily Cholesterol Intake The American Heart Association recommends a daily cholesterol intake of less than 300 mg. Here are the cholesterol amounts in a random sample of single servings of grilled meats. Estimate the standard deviation in cholesterol with 95% confidence. Assume the variable is normally distributed. $31.5 < \sigma < 67.9$

90	200	80	105	95
85	70	105	115	110
100	225	125	130	145

Extending the Concepts

16. Calculator Battery Lifetimes A confidence interval for a standard deviation for large samples taken from a normally distributed population can be approximated by

$$s - z_{\alpha/2}\frac{s}{\sqrt{2n}} < \sigma < s + z_{\alpha/2}\frac{s}{\sqrt{2n}}$$

Find the 95% confidence interval for the population standard deviation of calculator batteries. A random sample of 200 calculator batteries has a standard deviation of 18 months. $16.2 < \sigma < 19.8$

≡ Technology   Step by Step

TI-84 Plus
Step by Step

The TI-84 Plus does not have a built-in confidence interval for the variance or standard deviation. However, the downloadable program named SDINT is available in your online resources. Follow the instructions online for downloading the program.

Finding a Confidence Interval for the Variance and Standard Deviation (Data)

1. Enter the data values into L_1.
2. Press **PRGM,** move the cursor to the program named SDINT, and press **ENTER** twice.
3. Press **1** for Data.
4. Type L_1 (Press [2nd] [1]) for the list and press **ENTER.**
5. Type the confidence level and press **ENTER.**
6. Press **ENTER** to clear the screen.

Example TI7–4

Find the 90% confidence interval for the variance and standard deviation for the data:

59   54   53   52   51   39   49   46   49   48

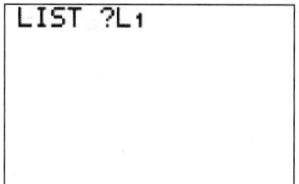

Finding a Confidence Interval for the Variance and Standard Deviation (Statistics)

1. Press **PRGM,** move the cursor to the program named SDINT, and press **ENTER** twice.
2. Press **2** for Stats.
3. Type the sample standard deviation and press **ENTER.**
4. Type the sample size and press **ENTER.**
5. Type the confidence level and press **ENTER.**
6. Press **ENTER** to clear the screen.

Example TI7–5

This refers to Example 7–14 in the text. Find the 95% confidence interval for the variance and standard deviation, given $n = 30$ and $s = 1.7$.

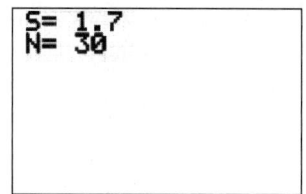

MINITAB

Step by Step

Find a Confidence Interval for a Variance and Standard Deviation

MINITAB will calculate a confidence interval, given the statistics from a sample or given the raw data. For Example 7–15, find the 90% confidence interval for the variance and standard deviation of the number of named storms per year in the Atlantic basin.

1. Type the data into C1 of a MINITAB worksheet. Label the column Storms.

2. Select **Stat>Basic Statistics>1-Variance.**

   a) Select One or more samples, each in a column from the menu.

   b) Select C1 Storms by clicking the open space below this menu and double-clicking the column name.

3. Click the [Options] button. In the dialog box, make sure the confidence level is 90 and the alternative hypothesis is standard deviation ≠ hypothesized standard deviation.

4. Click [OK] twice.

In the session window you will see the results. The 90% confidence interval estimate for σ is between 3 and 6.76. The 90% confidence interval estimate for σ is between 9 and 45.7. The sample size, standard deviation, and variance are also shown.

Test and CI for One Variance: Storms

Method

The chi-square method is only for the normal distribution.
The Bonett method is for any continuous distribution.

Statistics

Variable	N	StDev	Variance
Storms	10	4.11	16.9

90% Confidence Intervals

Variable	Method	CI for StDev	CI for Variance
Storms	Chi-Square	(3.00, 6.76)	(9.0, 45.7)
	Bonett	(2.75, 7.34)	(7.6, 53.9)

Summary

- An important aspect of inferential statistics is estimation. Estimations of parameters of populations are accomplished by selecting a random sample from that population and choosing and computing a statistic that is the best estimator of the parameter. A good estimator must be unbiased, consistent, and relatively efficient. The best estimate of μ is $\overline{X}$. (7–1)

- There are two types of estimates of a parameter: point estimates and interval estimates. A point estimate is a specific value. For example, if a researcher wishes to estimate the average length of a certain adult fish, a

sample of the fish is selected and measured. The mean of this sample is computed, for example, 3.2 centimeters. From this sample mean, the researcher estimates the population mean to be 3.2 centimeters. The problem with point estimates is that the accuracy of the estimate cannot be determined. For this reason, statisticians prefer to use the interval estimate. By computing an interval about the sample value, statisticians can be 95 or 99% (or some other percentage) confident that their estimate contains the true parameter. The confidence level is determined by the researcher. The higher the confidence level, the wider the interval of the estimate must be. For example, a 95% confidence interval of the true mean length of a certain species of fish might be

$$3.17 < \mu < 3.23$$

whereas the 99% confidence interval might be

$$3.15 < \mu < 3.25 \quad (7\text{--}1)$$

- When the population standard deviation is known, the z score is used to compute the confidence interval. (7–2)

- Closely related to computing confidence intervals is the determination of the sample size to make an estimate of the mean. This information is needed to determine the minimum sample size necessary.

1. The degree of confidence must be stated.
2. The population standard deviation must be known or be able to be estimated.
3. The margin of error must be stated. (7–1)

- If the population standard deviation is unknown, the t value is used. When the sample size is less than 30, the population must be normally distributed. (7–3)

- Confidence intervals and sample sizes can also be computed for proportions by using the normal distribution. (7–4)

- Finally, confidence intervals for variances and standard deviations can be computed by using the chi-square distribution. (7–5)

Important Terms

assumptions 370	degrees of freedom 383	point estimate 370	t distribution 383
chi-square distribution 399	estimation 370	proportion 391	unbiased estimator 371
confidence interval 371	estimator 370	relatively efficient estimator 371	
confidence level 371	interval estimate 371		
consistent estimator 371	margin of error 372	robust 374	

Important Formulas

Formula for the confidence interval of the mean when σ is known (when $n \geq 30$, s can be used if σ is unknown):

$$\overline{X} - z_{\alpha/2}\left(\frac{\sigma}{\sqrt{n}}\right) < \mu < \overline{X} + z_{\alpha/2}\left(\frac{\sigma}{\sqrt{n}}\right)$$

Formula for the sample size for means:

$$n = \left(\frac{z_{\alpha/2} \cdot \sigma}{E}\right)^2$$

where E is the margin of error.

Formula for the confidence interval of the mean when σ is unknown:

$$\overline{X} - t_{\alpha/2}\left(\frac{s}{\sqrt{n}}\right) < \mu < \overline{X} + t_{\alpha/2}\left(\frac{s}{\sqrt{n}}\right)$$

Formula for the confidence interval for a proportion:

$$\hat{p} - z_{\alpha/2}\sqrt{\frac{\hat{p}\hat{q}}{n}} < p < \hat{p} + z_{\alpha/2}\sqrt{\frac{\hat{p}\hat{q}}{n}}$$

where $\hat{p} = X/n$ and $\hat{q} = 1 - \hat{p}$.

Formula for the sample size for proportions:

$$n = \hat{p}\hat{q}\left(\frac{z_{\alpha/2}}{E}\right)^2$$

Formula for the confidence interval for a variance:

$$\frac{(n-1)s^2}{\chi^2_{\text{right}}} < \sigma^2 < \frac{(n-1)s^2}{\chi^2_{\text{left}}}$$

Formula for the confidence interval for a standard deviation:

$$\sqrt{\frac{(n-1)s^2}{\chi^2_{\text{right}}}} < \sigma < \sqrt{\frac{(n-1)s^2}{\chi^2_{\text{left}}}}$$

≡ Review Exercises

Section 7–2

1. **Eye Blinks** A survey of 49 individuals found that the average number of times people blink their eyes is 25 times per minute. Based on this survey, find the 90% confidence of the population mean number of eye blinks per minute. The population standard deviation is 4. $24 < \mu < 26$

2. **Vacation Days** A U.S. Travel Data Center survey reported that Americans stayed an average of 7.5 nights when they went on vacation. The sample size was 1500. Find a point estimate of the population mean. Find the 95% confidence interval of the true mean. Assume the population standard deviation was 0.8.

   Source: USA TODAY. $7.5; 7.46 < \mu < 7.54$

3. **Blood Pressure** A researcher wishes to estimate within 2 points the average systolic blood pressure of female college students. If she wishes to be 90% confident, how large a sample should she select if the population standard deviation of female systolic blood pressure is 4.8? 16

4. **Shopping Survey** A random sample of 49 shoppers showed that they spend an average of $23.45 per visit at the Saturday Mornings Bookstore. The standard deviation of the population is $2.80. Find a point estimate of the population mean. Find the 90% confidence interval of the true mean. $23.45; $22.79 < \mu < 24.11

Section 7–3

5. **Lengths of Children's Animated Films** The lengths (in minutes) of a random selection of popular children's animated films are listed below. Estimate the true mean length of all children's animated films with 95% confidence. Assume the variable is normally distributed.
   $76.9 < \mu < 88.3$

   | 93 | 83 | 76 | 92 | 77 | 81 | 78 | 100 | 78 | 76 | 75 |

6. **Dog Bites to Postal Workers** For a certain urban area, in a random sample of 5 months, an average of 28 mail carriers were bitten by dogs each month. The standard deviation of the sample was 3. Find the 90% confidence interval of the true mean number of mail carriers who are bitten by dogs each month. Assume the variable is normally distributed. $25 < \mu < 31$

Section 7–4

7. **Number of Credit Cards** In a recent survey of 1000 adults ages 18 to 40, 34% said they had no credit cards. Find the 95% confidence interval of the population proportion. $0.311 < p < 0.369$

   Source: CRC International.

8. **Vacation Sites** A U.S. Travel Data Center's survey of 1500 randomly selected adults found that 42% of respondents stated that they favor historical sites as vacations. Find the 95% confidence interval of the true proportion of all adults who favor visiting historical sites for vacations.

   Source: USA TODAY. $0.395 < p < 0.445$

9. **Marriages in the United States** In 1960, 67.6% of the U.S. population (aged 14 and over) was married. A random sample of 600 Americans in 2014 indicated that 316 were married. Estimate the true proportion of married Americans with 99% confidence. Assume the variable is normally distributed. $0.474 < p < 0.579$

   Source: World Almanac 2016.

10. **Adult Educational Activities** A local county has a very active adult education venue. A random sample of the population showed that 189 out of 400 persons 16 years old or older participated in some type of formal adult education activities, such as basic skills training, apprenticeships, personal interest courses, and part-time college or university degree programs. Estimate the true proportion of adults participating in some kind of formal education program with 98% confidence. Assume the variable is normally distributed. $0.414 < p < 0.531$

11. **Cat Owners** A person recently read that 53% of cat owners are women. How large a sample should the person take if they want to be 90% confident that the proportion is within 3% of the true population proportion? 754 (TI: 749)

12. **Child Care Programs** A study found that 73% of randomly selected prekindergarten children ages 3 to 5 whose mothers had a bachelor's degree or higher were enrolled in center-based early childhood care and education programs. How large a sample is needed to estimate the true proportion within 3 percentage points with 95% confidence? How large a sample is needed if you had no prior knowledge of the proportion?
    842 children; 1068 children

Section 7–5

13. **Baseball Diameters** The standard deviation of the diameter of 18 randomly selected baseballs was 0.29 cm. Find the 95% confidence interval of the true standard deviation of the diameters of the baseballs. Do you think the manufacturing process should be checked for inconsistency? Assume the variable is normally distributed. $0.22 < \sigma < 0.43$. Yes.
    It seems that there is a large standard deviation.

14. **MPG for Lawn Mowers** A random sample of 22 lawn mowers was selected, and the motors were tested to see how many miles per gallon of gasoline each one obtained. The variance of the measurements was 2.6. Find the 95% confidence interval of the true variance. Assume the variable is normally distributed. $1.5 < \sigma^2 < 5.3$

15. Lifetimes of Snowmobiles A random sample of 15 snowmobiles was selected, and the lifetime (in months) of the batteries was measured. The variance of the sample was 8.6. Find the 90% confidence interval of the true variance. Assume the variable is normally distributed. $5.1 < \sigma^2 < 18.3$

16. Length of Children's Animated Films Use the data from Exercise 5 to estimate the population variance and standard deviation in length of children's animated films with 99% confidence. Assume the variable is normally distributed. $28.6 < \sigma^2 < 334.2; 5.3 < \sigma < 18.3$

≡ STATISTICS TODAY

Stress and the College Student —Revisited

The estimates given in the survey were point estimates; however, since the margin of error was 3 percentage points, a confidence interval can be constructed. For example, a confidence interval for the 85% figure would be $82% < p < 88%$. We don't know whether this is a 90%, 95%, 99%, or some other confidence level because this was not specified in the report.

Using the formula in Section 7–4, a minimum sample size could be found. We can take $\hat{p}$ and $\hat{q}$ as 0.5 since no value for $\hat{p}$ is known, and $z_{\alpha/2} = 1.96$ for a 95% confidence interval.

$$n = \hat{p}\hat{q}\left(\frac{z_{\alpha/2}}{E}\right)^2$$

$$= (0.5)(0.5)\left(\frac{1.96}{0.03}\right)^2 = 1067.1$$

For a 95% confidence interval, then, the minimum sample size would be 1068 people (rounded up). Since the survey used 2240 students, it can be said that we are at least 95% confident that the true proportion of students who experience stress in college is somewhere between 82 and 88%.

≡ Data Analysis

The Data Bank is found in Appendix B.

1. From the Data Bank choose a variable, find the mean, and construct the 95 and 99% confidence intervals of the population mean. Use a sample of at least 30 subjects. Find the mean of the population, and determine whether it falls within the confidence interval.

2. Repeat Exercise 1, using a different variable and a sample of 15.

3. Repeat Exercise 1, using a proportion. For example, construct a confidence interval for the proportion of individuals who did not complete high school.

4. From Data Set III in Appendix B, select a sample of 30 values and construct the 95 and 99% confidence intervals of the mean length in miles of major North American rivers. Find the mean of all the values, and determine if the confidence intervals contain the mean.

5. From Data Set VI in Appendix B, select a sample of 20 values and find the 90% confidence interval of the mean of the number of acres. Find the mean of all the values, and determine if the confidence interval contains the mean.

6. Select a random sample of 20 of the record high temperatures in the United States, found in Data Set I in Appendix B. Find the proportion of temperatures below 110°. Construct a 95% confidence interval for this proportion. Then find the true proportion of temperatures below 110°, using all the data. Is the true proportion contained in the confidence interval? Explain.

Chapter Quiz

Determine whether each statement is true or false. If the statement is false, explain why.

1. Interval estimates are preferred over point estimates since a confidence level can be specified. True

2. For a specific confidence interval, the larger the sample size, the smaller the margin of error will be. True

3. An estimator is consistent if as the sample size decreases, the value of the estimator approaches the value of the parameter estimated. False

4. To determine the sample size needed to estimate a parameter, you must know the margin of error. True

Select the best answer.

5. When a 99% confidence interval is calculated instead of a 95% confidence interval with n being the same, the margin of error will be
   a. Smaller   c. The same
   b. Larger   d. It cannot be determined.

6. The best point estimate of the population mean is
   a. The sample mean
   b. The sample median
   c. The sample mode
   d. The sample midrange

7. When the population standard deviation is unknown and the sample size is less than 30, what table value should be used in computing a confidence interval for a mean?
   a. z
   b. t
   c. Chi-square
   d. None of the above

Complete the following statements with the best answer.

8. A good estimator should be _____, _____, and _____. Unbiased, consistent, relatively efficient

9. The maximum likely difference between the point estimate of a parameter and the actual value of the parameter is called the _____. Margin of error

10. The statement "The average height of an adult male is 5 feet 10 inches" is an example of a(n) _____ estimate. Point

11. The three confidence levels used most often are the _____%, _____%, and _____%. 90; 95; 99

12. **Cost of Texts** An irate student complained that the cost of textbooks was too high. The student randomly surveyed 36 other students and found that the mean amount of money spent for texts was $121.60. If the standard deviation of the population was $6.36, find the best point estimate and the 90% confidence interval of the true mean. $121.60; $119.85 < μ < $123.35

13. **Doctor Visit Costs** An irate patient complained that the cost of a doctor's visit was too high. The patient randomly surveyed 20 other patients and found that the mean amount of money they spent on each doctor's visit was $244.80. The standard deviation of the sample was $3.53. Find a point estimate of the population mean. Find the 95% confidence interval of the population mean. Assume the variable is normally distributed. $244.80; $243.15 < μ < $246.45

14. **Weights of Minivans** The average weight of 40 randomly selected minivans was 4150 pounds. The population standard deviation was 480 pounds. Find a point estimate of the population mean. Find the 99% confidence interval of the true mean weight of the minivans. 4150; 3954 < μ < 4346

15. **Ages of Insurance Representatives** In a study of 10 randomly selected insurance sales representatives from a certain large city, the average age of the group was 48.6 years and the standard deviation was 4.1 years. Assume the variable is normally distributed. Find the 95% confidence interval of the population mean age of all insurance sales representatives in that city. 45.7 < μ < 51.5

16. **Patients Treated in Hospital Emergency Rooms** In a hospital, a random sample of 8 weeks was selected, and it was found that an average of 438 patients were treated in the emergency room each week. The standard deviation was 16. Find the 99% confidence interval of the true mean. Assume the variable is normally distributed. 418 < μ < 458

17. **Burglaries** For a certain urban area, it was found that in a random sample of 4 months, an average of 31 burglaries occurred each month. The standard deviation was 4. Assume the variable is normally distributed. Find the 90% confidence interval of the true mean number of burglaries each month. 26 < μ < 36

18. **Hours Spent Studying** A university dean wishes to estimate the average number of hours that freshmen study each week. The standard deviation from a previous study is 2.6 hours. How large a sample must be selected if he wants to be 99% confident of finding whether the true mean differs from the sample mean by 0.5 hour? 180

19. **Money Spent on Road Repairs** A researcher wishes to estimate within $300 the true average amount of money a county spends on road repairs each year. If she wants to be 90% confident, how large a sample is necessary? The standard deviation is known to be $900. 25

20. **Political Survey** A political analyst found that 43% of 300 randomly selected Republican voters feel that the federal government has too much power. Find the 95% confidence interval of the population proportion of Republican voters who feel this way. 0.374 < p < 0.486

21. **Emergency Room Accidents** In a study of 150 randomly selected accidents that required treatment in an emergency room, 36% involved children under 6 years of age. Find the 90% confidence interval of the true proportion of accidents that involve children under the age of 6. $0.295 < p < 0.425$

22. **Television Set Ownership** A survey of 90 randomly selected families showed that 40 owned at least one television set. Find the 95% confidence interval of the true proportion of families who own at least one television set. $0.342 < p < 0.547$

23. **Skipping Lunch** A nutritionist wishes to determine, within 3%, the true proportion of adults who do not eat any lunch. If he wishes to be 95% confident that his estimate contains the population proportion, how large a sample will be necessary? A previous study found that 15% of the 125 people surveyed said they did not eat lunch. 545

24. **Novel Pages** A random sample of 25 novels has a standard deviation of 9 pages. Find the 95% confidence interval of the population standard deviation. Assume the variable is normally distributed. $7 < \sigma < 13$

25. **Truck Safety Check** Find the 90% confidence interval for the variance and standard deviation for the time it takes a state police inspector to check a truck for safety if a random sample of 27 trucks has a standard deviation of 6.8 minutes. Assume the variable is normally distributed. $30.9 < \sigma^2 < 78.2; 5.6 < \sigma < 8.8$

26. **Automobile Pollution** A random sample of 20 automobiles has a pollution by-product release standard deviation of 2.3 ounces when 1 gallon of gasoline is used. Find the 90% confidence interval of the population standard deviation. Assume the variable is normally distributed. $1.8 < \sigma < 3.2$

Critical Thinking Challenges

A confidence interval for a median can be found by using these formulas

$$U = \frac{n+1}{2} + \frac{z_{\alpha/2}\sqrt{n}}{2} \qquad \text{(round up)}$$

$$L = n - U + 1$$

to define positions in the set of ordered data values.

Suppose a data set has 30 values, and you want to find the 95% confidence interval for the median. Substituting in the formulas, you get

$$U = \frac{30+1}{2} + \frac{1.96\sqrt{30}}{2} = 21 \qquad \text{(rounded up)}$$

$$L = 30 - 21 + 1 = 10$$

when $n = 30$ and $z_{\alpha/2} = 1.96$.

Arrange the data in order from smallest to largest, and then select the 10th and 21st values of the data array; hence, $X_{10} < \text{median} < X_{21}$.

Using the previous information, find the 90% confidence interval for the median for the given data.

84	49	3	133	85	4340	461	60	28	97
14	252	18	16	24	346	254	29	254	6
31	104	72	29	391	19	125	10	6	17
72	31	23	225	72	5	61	366	77	8
26	8	55	138	158	846	123	47	21	82

Data Projects

1. **Business and Finance** Use 30 stocks classified as the Dow Jones industrials as the sample. Note the amount each stock has gained or lost in the last quarter. Compute the mean and standard deviation for the data set. Compute the 95% confidence interval for the mean and the 95% confidence interval for the standard deviation. Compute the percentage of stocks that had a gain in the last quarter. Find a 95% confidence interval for the percentage of stocks with a gain.

2. **Sports and Leisure** Use the top home run hitter from each major league baseball team as the data set. Find the mean and the standard deviation for the number of home runs hit by the top hitter on each team. Find a 95% confidence interval for the mean number of home runs hit.

3. **Technology** Use the data collected in data project 3 of Chapter 2 regarding song lengths. Select a specific genre, and compute the percentage of songs in the sample that are of that genre. Create a 95% confidence

interval for the true percentage. Use the entire music library, and find the population percentage of the library with that genre. Does the population percentage fall within the confidence interval?

4. **Health and Wellness** Use your class as the sample. Have the students take their temperatures on a day when they are healthy. Compute the mean and standard deviation for the sample. Create a 95% confidence interval for the mean temperature. Does the confidence interval obtained support the long-held belief that the average body temperature is 98.6°F?

5. **Politics and Economics** Select five political polls and note the margin of error, sample size, and percentage favoring the candidate for each. For each poll, determine the level of confidence that must have been used to obtain the margin of error given, knowing the percentage favoring the candidate and number of participants. Is there a pattern that emerges?

6. **Your Class** Have the students compute their body mass index (BMI) (703 times weight in pounds, divided by the square of the height in inches). Find the mean and standard deviation for the data set. Compute a 95% con-fidence interval for the mean BMI of a student. A BMI score over 30 is considered obese. Does the confidence interval indicate that the mean for BMI could be in the obese range?

Answers to Applying the Concepts

Section 7–1   Sick Leave

1. The population should be limited to a specific group of workers since a general estimate could not meet all assumptions.

2. Answers will vary. It would depend on the size of the population.

3. The larger the sample the better, since a large sample would have a smaller margin of error than a smaller sample.

4. Interval estimates are generally better, but it would depend on the situation.

5. Answer will vary.

6. Answers will vary depending on the methods used.

Section 7–2   How Many Tissues Should Be in a Box?

1. Answers will vary. One possible answer is to find out the average number of tissues that a group of randomly selected individuals use in a 2-week period.

2. People usually need tissues when they have colds or when their allergies are acting up.

3. If we want to concentrate on the number of tissues used when people have colds, we select a random sample of people with colds and have them keep a record of how many tissues they use during their colds.

4. Answers may vary. I will use a 95% confidence interval:

$$\bar{x} \pm 1.96\frac{\sigma}{\sqrt{n}} = 57 \pm 1.96\frac{15}{\sqrt{85}} = 57 \pm 3$$

I am 95% confident that the interval 54–60 contains the true mean number of tissues used by people when they have colds. It seems reasonable to put 60 tissues in the new automobile glove compartment boxes.

5. Answers will vary. Since I am 95% confident that the interval contains the true average, any number of tissues between 54 and 60 would be reasonable. Sixty seemed to be the most reasonable answer, since it is close to 2 standard deviations above the sample mean.

Section 7–3   Sport Drink Decision

1. Answers vary. One possible answer is that this is a small sample since I am only looking at seven popular sport drinks.

2. The mean cost per container is $1.964, with standard deviation of $0.5764. The 90% confidence interval is

$$\bar{x} \pm t_{\alpha/2}\frac{s}{\sqrt{n}} = 1.964 \pm 1.943\frac{0.5764}{\sqrt{7}}$$

or $1.54 < \mu < $2.39

Gatorade, POWERADE, Sqwincher, BODYARMOR, Xtend, and Propel all fall outside of the confidence interval.

3. Answers will vary. $1.29 is far enough outside the interval that it may affect its results.

4. There are $7 - 1 = 6$ degrees of freedom.

5. Cost per serving would impact my decision on purchasing a sport drink, since this would allow me to compare the costs on an equal scale.

6. Answers will vary.

Section 7–4   College Dropout Rates

1. The point estimates for the two-year colleges is 51% and for the four-year college is 47%.

2. The margin of error for the two-year colleges is 3.1%.

3. Larger sample sizes would result in smaller confidence intervals.

4. Since the confidence intervals overlap, it cannot be concluded that there is a difference in the percents. Another way to see if there is a difference in the percents is shown in Chapter 9.

Section 7–5   Ages of Presidents at the Time of Their Deaths

1. The data represent a population, since we have the age at death for all deceased Presidents (at the time of the writing of this book).

2. Answers will vary. One possible sample is 56, 67, 53, 46, 63, 77, 63, 57, 71, 57, 80, 65, which results in a standard deviation of 9.9 years and a variance of 98.1.

3. Answers will vary. The 95% confidence interval for the standard deviation is $\sqrt{\frac{(n-1)s^2}{\chi^2_{\text{right}}}}$ to $\sqrt{\frac{(n-1)s^2}{\chi^2_{\text{left}}}}$. In this case we have $\sqrt{\frac{(12-1)9.9^2}{21.920}} = \sqrt{49.1839} = 7.0$ to $\sqrt{\frac{(12-1)9.9^2}{3.816}} = \sqrt{282.524} = 16.8$, or 7.0 to 16.8 years.

4. The standard deviation for all the data values is 11.9 years.

5. Answers will vary. Yes, the confidence interval does contain the population standard deviation.

6. Answers will vary.

7. We need to assume that the distribution of ages at death is normal.

Hypothesis Testing

Photosindia.Com, Llc

≡ STATISTICS TODAY

How Much Better Is Better?

Suppose a school superintendent reads an article which states that the overall mean score for the SAT is 910. Furthermore, suppose that, for a sample of students, the average of the SAT scores in the superintendent's school district is 960. Can it be concluded that the students in the superintendent's school district scored higher on average? At first glance, you might be inclined to say yes, since 960 is higher than 910. But recall that the means of samples vary about the population mean when samples are selected from a specific population. So the question arises, is there a real difference in the means, or is the difference simply due to chance (i.e., sampling error)? In this chapter, you will learn how to answer that question by using statistics that explain hypothesis testing. See Statistics Today—Revisited at the end of the chapter for the answer. In this chapter, you will learn how to answer many questions of this type by using statistics that are explained in the theory of hypothesis testing.

OUTLINE

OBJECTIVES

After completing this chapter, you should be able to:

1. Understand the definitions used in hypothesis testing.

2. State the null and alternative hypotheses.

3. Find critical values for the *z* test.

4. State the five steps used in hypothesis testing.

5. Test means when σ is known, using the *z* test.

6. Test means when σ is unknown, using the *t* test.

7. Test proportions, using the *z* test.

8. Test variances or standard deviations, using the chi-square test.

9. Test hypotheses, using confidence intervals.

10. Explain the relationship between type I and type II errors and the power of a test.

Introduction

Researchers are interested in answering many types of questions. For example, a scientist might want to know whether there is evidence of global warming. A physician might want to know whether a new medication will lower a person's blood pressure. An educator might wish to see whether a new teaching technique is better than a traditional one. A retail merchant might want to know whether the public prefers a certain color in a new line of fashion. Automobile manufacturers are interested in determining whether a new type of seat belt will reduce the severity of injuries caused by accidents. These types of questions can be addressed through statistical **hypothesis testing,** which is a decision-making process for evaluating claims about a population. In hypothesis testing, the researcher must define the population under study, state the particular hypotheses that will be investigated, give the significance level, select a sample from the population, collect the data, perform the calculations required for the statistical test, and reach a conclusion.

Hypotheses concerning parameters such as means and proportions can be investigated. There are two specific statistical tests used for hypotheses concerning means: the *z test* and the *t test*. This chapter will explain in detail the hypothesis-testing procedure along with the *z* test and the *t* test. In addition, a hypothesis-testing procedure for testing a single variance or standard deviation using the chi-square distribution is explained in Section 8–5.

The three methods used to test hypotheses are

1. The traditional method
2. The *P*-value method
3. The confidence interval method

The *traditional method* will be explained first. It has been used since the hypothesis-testing method was formulated. A newer method, called the *P-value method,* has become popular with the advent of modern computers and high-powered statistical calculators. The third method, the *confidence interval method,* is explained in Section 8–6 and illustrates the relationship between hypothesis testing and confidence intervals.

8–1   Steps in Hypothesis Testing—Traditional Method

Every hypothesis-testing situation begins with the statement of a hypothesis.

> A **statistical hypothesis** is a conjecture about a population parameter. This conjecture may or may not be true.

OBJECTIVE ❶

Understand the definitions used in hypothesis testing.

There are two types of statistical hypotheses for each situation: the null hypothesis and the alternative hypothesis.

> The **null hypothesis,** symbolized by H_0, is a statistical hypothesis that states that there is no difference between a parameter and a specific value, or that there is no difference between two parameters.
>
> The **alternative hypothesis,** symbolized by H_1, is a statistical hypothesis that states the existence of a difference between a parameter and a specific value, or states that there is a difference between two parameters.

(*Note:* Although the definitions of null and alternative hypotheses given here use the word *parameter,* these definitions can be extended to include other terms such as *distributions* and *randomness.* This is explained in later chapters.)

As an illustration of how hypotheses should be stated, three different statistical studies will be used as examples.

OBJECTIVE 2

State the null and alternative hypotheses.

Situation A A medical researcher is interested in finding out whether a new medication will have any undesirable side effects. The researcher is particularly concerned with the pulse rate of the patients who take the medication. Will the pulse rate increase, decrease, or remain unchanged after a patient takes the medication?

Since the researcher knows that the mean pulse rate for the population under study is 82 beats per minute, the hypotheses for this situation are

$$H_0: \mu = 82 \qquad \text{and} \qquad H_1: \mu \neq 82$$

The null hypothesis specifies that the mean will remain unchanged, and the alternative hypothesis states that it will be different. This test is called a *two-tailed test* (a term that will be formally defined later in this section), since the possible side effects of the medicine could be to raise or lower the pulse rate.

If you are testing a proportion and you feel that 60% of people watch television every night, you could state the hypotheses as

$$H_0: p = 0.60 \qquad \text{and} \qquad H_1: p \neq 60$$

Situation B A chemist invents an additive to increase the life of an automobile battery. If the mean lifetime of the automobile battery without the additive is 36 months, then the hypotheses are

$$H_0: \mu = 36 \qquad \text{and} \qquad H_1: \mu > 36$$

In this situation, the chemist is interested only in increasing the lifetime of the batteries, so the alternative hypothesis is that the mean is greater than 36 months. The null hypothesis is that the mean is equal to 36 months. This test is called *right-tailed,* since the interest is in an increase only.

If you feel that more than 85% of assaults are committed by men, you could state the hypotheses as

$$H_0: p = 0.85 \qquad \text{and} \qquad H_1: p > 0.85$$

Unusual Stat

Sixty-three percent of people would rather hear bad news before hearing the good news.

Situation C A contractor wishes to lower heating bills by using a special type of insulation in houses. If the average of the monthly heating bills is $78, the hypotheses about heating costs with the use of insulation are

$$H_0: \mu = \$78 \qquad \text{and} \qquad H_1: \mu < \$78$$

This test is a *left-tailed test,* since the contractor is interested only in lowering heating costs.

If you feel that less than 24% of people will open a sales email, then you could state the hypotheses as

$$H_0: p = 0.24 \qquad \text{and} \qquad H_1: p < 0.24$$

To state hypotheses correctly, researchers must translate the *conjecture* or *claim* from words into mathematical symbols. The basic symbols used are as follows:

Equal to	=	Greater than	>
Not equal to	≠	Less than	<

The null and alternative hypotheses are stated together, and the null hypothesis contains the equals sign, as shown (where k represents a specified number).

Also notice that in a right-tailed test, the inequality sign points to the right; and in a left-tailed test, the inequality sign points to the left. Right- and left-tailed tests are also called one-tailed tests.

Two-tailed test	**Right-tailed test**	**Left-tailed test**
$H_0: \mu = k$	$H_0: \mu = k$	$H_0: \mu = k$
$H_1: \mu \neq k$	$H_1: \mu > k$	$H_1: \mu < k$
$H_0: p = k$	$H_0: p = k$	$H_0: p = k$
$H_1: p \neq k$	$H_1: p > k$	$H_1: p < k$

The formal definitions of the different types of tests are given later in this section.

In this book, the null hypothesis is always stated using the equals sign. This is done because in most professional journals, and when we test the null hypothesis, the assumption is that the mean, proportion, or standard deviation is equal to a given specific value. Also, when a researcher conducts a study, the researcher is generally looking for evidence to support a claim. Therefore, the claim should be stated as the alternative hypothesis, i.e., using < or > or ≠. Because of this, the alternative hypothesis is sometimes called the **research hypothesis.**

A claim, however, can be stated as either the null hypothesis or the alternative hypothesis; but the statistical evidence can only *support* the claim if it is the alternative hypothesis. Statistical evidence can be used to *reject* the claim if the claim is the null hypothesis. These facts are important when you are stating the conclusion of a statistical study.

Table 8–1 shows some common phrases that are used in hypotheses and conjectures, and the corresponding symbols. This table should be helpful in translating verbal conjectures into mathematical symbols.

TABLE 8–1 Hypothesis-Testing Common Phrases	
>	<
Is greater than	Is less than
Is above	Is below
Is higher than	Is lower than
Is longer than	Is shorter than
Is bigger than	Is smaller than
Is increased	Is decreased or reduced from
=	≠
Is equal to	Is not equal to
Is no different from	Is different from
Has not changed from	Has changed from
Is the same as	Is not the same as

Note: Sometimes a claim can be stated using the words "at least" or "at most." In these cases, the claims are null hypotheses. For example, "In order to purchase cigarettes in some states, you must be at least 21 years of age," means that you have to be 21 years of age or older. If this was a claim about a sample mean, it would be written as $\mu \geq 21$ (written as $\mu = 21$): then the alternative hypothesis would be written as $\mu < 21$.

The same reasoning applies to the phrase "at most." For example, the statement "A theater can seat at most 115 persons" means 115 or less persons. If this was used as the mean of a sample, it would be written as $\mu \leq 115$ (written as $\mu = 115$), which is the null hypothesis. Hence, the alternative hypothesis would be $\mu > 115$.

EXAMPLE 8–1

State the null and alternative hypotheses for each conjecture.

    a. A researcher thinks that the average amount of sugar consumed by an adult is less than 147 pounds per year.

    b. A researcher feels that the average age a person gives up driving an automobile is greater than 85 years old.

    c. A researcher thinks that the average time it takes a person to fall asleep is less than 15 minutes.

    d. Fifty-four percent of car accidents are caused by sleep deprivation.

    e. More than 40% of Americans have a "lucky number."

    f. Less than 62% of spouses keep some money hidden from their significant other.

SOLUTION

a. H_0: $\mu = 147$ and H_1: $\mu < 147$

b. H_0: $\mu = 85$ and H_1: $\mu > 85$

c. H_0: $\mu = 15$ and H_1: $\mu < 15$

d. H_0: $p = 0.54$ and H_1: $p \neq 0.54$

e. H_0: $p = 0.40$ and H_1: $p > 0.40$

f. H_0: $p = 0.62$ and H_1: $p < 0.62$

After stating the hypothesis, the researcher designs the study. The researcher selects the correct *statistical test,* chooses an appropriate *level of significance,* and formulates a plan for conducting the study. In situation A, for instance, the researcher will select a sample of patients who will be given the drug. After allowing a suitable time for the drug to be absorbed, the researcher will measure each person's pulse rate.

Recall that when samples of a specific size are selected from a population, the means of these samples will vary about the population mean, and the distribution of the sample means will be approximately normal when the sample size is 30 or more. (See Section 6–3.) So even if the null hypothesis is true, the mean of the pulse rates of the sample of patients will not, in most cases, be exactly equal to the population mean of 82 beats per minute. There are two possibilities. Either the null hypothesis is true, and the difference between the sample mean and the population mean is due to chance; *or* the null hypothesis is false, and the sample came from a population whose mean is not 82 beats per minute but is some other value that is not known. These situations are shown in Figure 8–1.

The farther away the sample mean is from the population mean, the more evidence there would be for rejecting the null hypothesis. The probability that the sample came from a population whose mean is 82 decreases as the distance or absolute value of the difference between the means increases.

If the mean pulse rate of the sample were, say, 83, the researcher would probably conclude that this difference was due to chance and would not reject the null hypothesis. But if the sample mean were, say, 90, then in all likelihood the researcher would conclude that the medication increased the pulse rate of the users and would reject the null hypothesis. The same reasoning applies when testing other parameters such as proportions. The question is,

FIGURE 8–1

Situations in
Hypothesis Testing

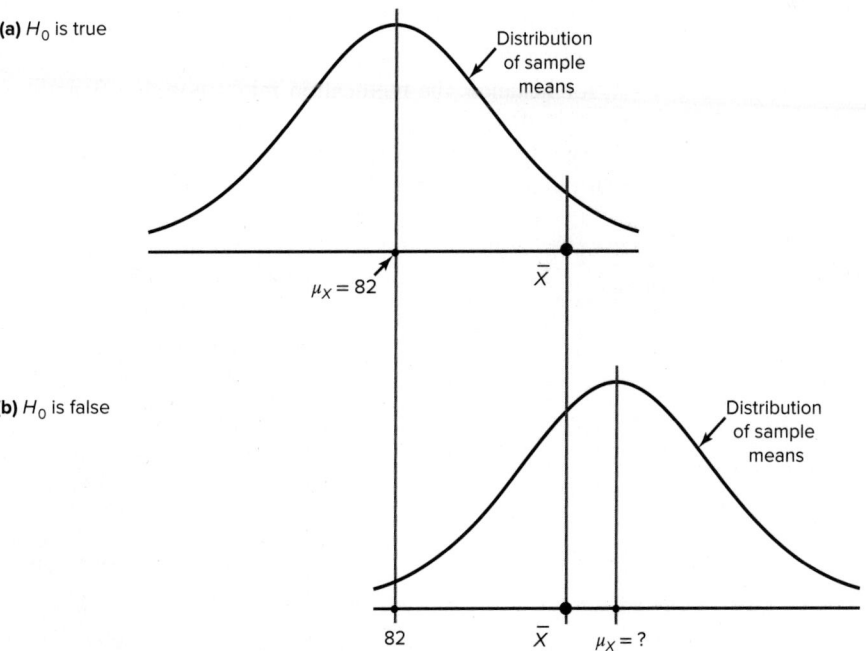

Where does the researcher draw the line? This decision is not made on feelings or intuition; it is made statistically. That is, the difference must be significant and in all likelihood not due to chance. Here is where the concepts of statistical test and level of significance are used.

> A **statistical test** uses the data obtained from a sample to make a decision about whether the null hypothesis should be rejected.
>
> The numerical value obtained from a statistical test is called the **test statistic.**

In this type of statistical test, the mean is computed for the data obtained from the sample and is compared with the population mean. Then a decision is made to reject or not reject the null hypothesis on the basis of the value obtained from the statistical test. If the difference is significant, the null hypothesis is rejected. If it is not, then the null hypothesis is not rejected.

As previously stated, sample data are used to determine if a null hypothesis should be rejected. Because this decision is based on sample data, there is a possibility that an incorrect decision can be made.

In the hypothesis-testing situation, there are four possible outcomes. In reality, the null hypothesis may or may not be true, and a decision is made to reject or not reject it on the basis of the data obtained from a sample. The four possible outcomes are shown in Figure 8–2. Notice that there are two possibilities for a correct decision and two possibilities for an incorrect decision.

The four possibilities are as follows:

1. We reject the null hypothesis when it is true. This would be an incorrect decision and would result in a **type I error.**

2. We reject the null hypothesis when it is false. This would be a correct decision.

3. We do not reject the null hypothesis when it is true. This would be a correct decision.

4. We do not reject the null hypothesis when it is false. This would be an incorrect decision and would result in a **type II error.**

> A **type I error** occurs if you reject the null hypothesis when it is true.
>
> A **type II error** occurs if you do not reject the null hypothesis when it is false.

If a null hypothesis is true and it is rejected, then a *type I error* is made. In situation A, for instance, the medication might not significantly change the pulse rate of all the users in the population; but it might change the rate, by chance, of the subjects in the sample. In this case, the researcher will reject the null hypothesis when it is really true, thus committing a type I error.

FIGURE 8–2

Possible Outcomes of a Hypothesis Test

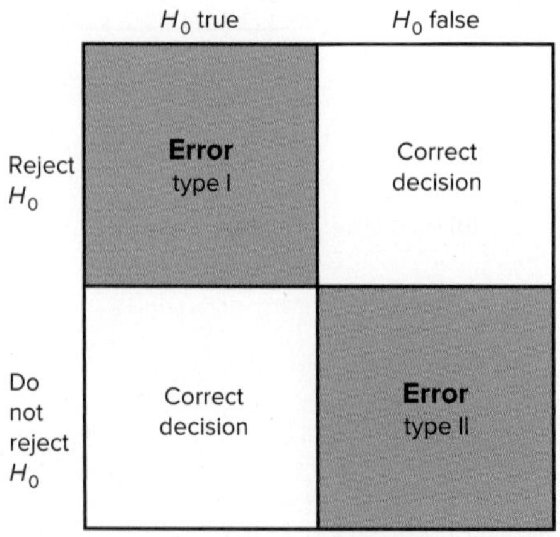

On the other hand, the medication might not change the pulse rate of the subjects in the sample; but when it is given to the general population, it might cause a significant increase or decrease in the pulse rate of users. The researcher, on the basis of the data obtained from the sample, will not reject the null hypothesis, thus committing a *type II error*.

In situation B, the additive might not significantly increase the lifetimes of automobile batteries in the population, but it might increase the lifetimes of the batteries in the sample. In this case, the null hypothesis would be rejected when it was really true. This would be a type I error. On the other hand, the additive might not work on the batteries selected for the sample, but if it were to be used in the general population of batteries, it might significantly increase their lifetimes. The researcher, on the basis of information obtained from the sample, would not reject the null hypothesis, thus committing a type II error.

The hypothesis-testing situation can be likened to a jury trial. In a jury trial, there are four possible outcomes. The defendant is either guilty or innocent, and will be convicted or acquitted. See Figure 8–3.

Now the hypotheses are

H_0: The defendant is innocent.

H_1: The defendant is not innocent (i.e., guilty).

Next, the evidence is presented in court by the prosecutor, and based on this evidence, the jury decides the verdict, guilty or not guilty.

If the defendant is convicted but did not commit the crime, then a type I error has been committed. See block 1 of Figure 8–3. In other words, a type I error means an innocent person is put in jail. On the other hand, if the defendant is convicted and has committed the crime, then a correct decision has been made. See block 2.

If the defendant is acquitted and did not commit the crime, a correct decision has been made by the jury. See block 3. However, if the defendant is acquitted and did commit the crime, then a type II error has been made. See block 4. In other words, a type II error is letting a guilty person go free.

The decision of the jury does not prove that the defendant did or did not commit the crime. The decision is based on the evidence presented. If the evidence is strong enough, the defendant will be convicted in most cases. If the evidence is weak, the defendant will be acquitted in most cases. Nothing is proved absolutely. Likewise, the decision to reject or not reject the null hypothesis does not prove anything. *The only way to prove anything statistically is to use the entire population,* which, in most cases, is not possible. The decision, then, is made on the basis of probabilities. That is, when there is a large difference between the mean obtained from the sample and the hypothesized mean, the null hypothesis is probably not true. The question is, How large a difference is necessary to reject the null hypothesis? Here is where the level of significance is used.

FIGURE 8–3

Hypothesis Testing and a Jury Trial

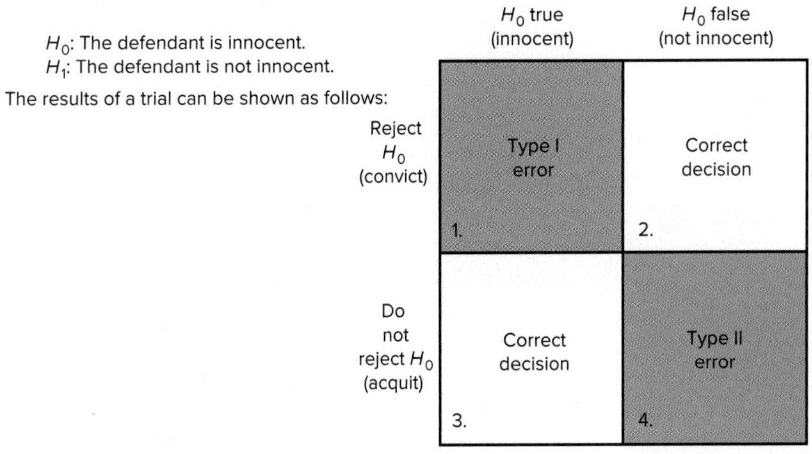

H_0: The defendant is innocent.
H_1: The defendant is not innocent.

The results of a trial can be shown as follows:

The **level of significance** is the maximum probability of committing a type I error. This probability is symbolized by α (Greek letter **alpha**). That is, P(type I error) = α.

The probability of a type II error is symbolized by β, the Greek letter **beta.** That is, P(type II error) = β. In most hypothesis-testing situations, β cannot be easily computed; however, α and β are related in that decreasing one increases the other.

Statisticians generally agree on using three arbitrary significance levels: the 0.10, 0.05, and 0.01 levels. That is, if the null hypothesis is rejected, the probability of a type I error will be 10, 5, or 1%, depending on which level of significance is used. Here is another way of putting it: When $\alpha = 0.10$, there is a 10% chance of rejecting a true null hypothesis; when $\alpha = 0.05$, there is a 5% chance of rejecting a true null hypothesis; and when $\alpha = 0.01$, there is a 1% chance of rejecting a true null hypothesis.

In a hypothesis-testing situation, the researcher decides what level of significance to use. It does not have to be the 0.10, 0.05, or 0.01 level. It can be any level, depending on the seriousness of the type I error. After a significance level is chosen, a *critical value* is selected from a table for the appropriate test. If a z test is used, for example, the z table (Table A–4 in Appendix A) is consulted to find the critical value. The critical value determines the critical and noncritical regions.

The **critical** or **rejection region** is the range of test statistics that indicates that there is a significant difference and that the null hypothesis should be rejected.

The **noncritical** or **nonrejection region** is the range of test statistics that indicates that the difference was probably due to chance and that the null hypothesis should not be rejected.

The **critical value** separates the critical region from the noncritical region. The symbol for critical value is C.V.

The critical value can be on the right side of the mean or on the left side of the mean for a one-tailed test. Its location depends on the inequality sign of the alternative hypothesis. For example, in situation B, where the chemist is interested in increasing the average lifetime of automobile batteries, the alternative hypothesis is H_1: $\mu > 36$. Since the inequality sign is >, the null hypothesis will be rejected only when the sample mean is significantly greater than 36. Hence, the critical value must be on the right side of the mean. Therefore, this test is called a right-tailed test.

A **one-tailed test** indicates that the null hypothesis should be rejected when the test statistic is in the critical region on one side of the mean. A one-tailed test is either a **right-tailed test** or a **left-tailed test,** depending on the direction of the inequality of the alternative hypothesis.

To obtain the critical value, the researcher must choose an alpha level. In situation B, suppose the researcher chose $\alpha = 0.01$. Then the researcher must find a z score such that 1% of the area falls to the right of the z score and 99% falls to the left of the z score, as shown in Figure 8–4(a).

OBJECTIVE ❸

Find critical values for the z test.

Next, the researcher must find the area value in Table A–4 closest to 0.9900. The critical z score is 2.33, since that z score gives the area closest to 0.9900 (that is, 0.9901), as shown in Figure 8–4(b).

The critical and noncritical regions and the critical value are shown in Figure 8–5.

Now, move on to situation C, where the contractor is interested in lowering the heating bills. The alternative hypothesis is H_1: $\mu < \$78$. Hence, the critical value falls to the left of the mean. This test is thus a left-tailed test. At $\alpha = 0.01$, the critical value is -2.33, since 0.0099 is the closest z score to 0.01. This is shown in Figure 8–6.

FIGURE 8–4 Finding the Critical Value for $\alpha = 0.01$ (Right-Tailed Test)

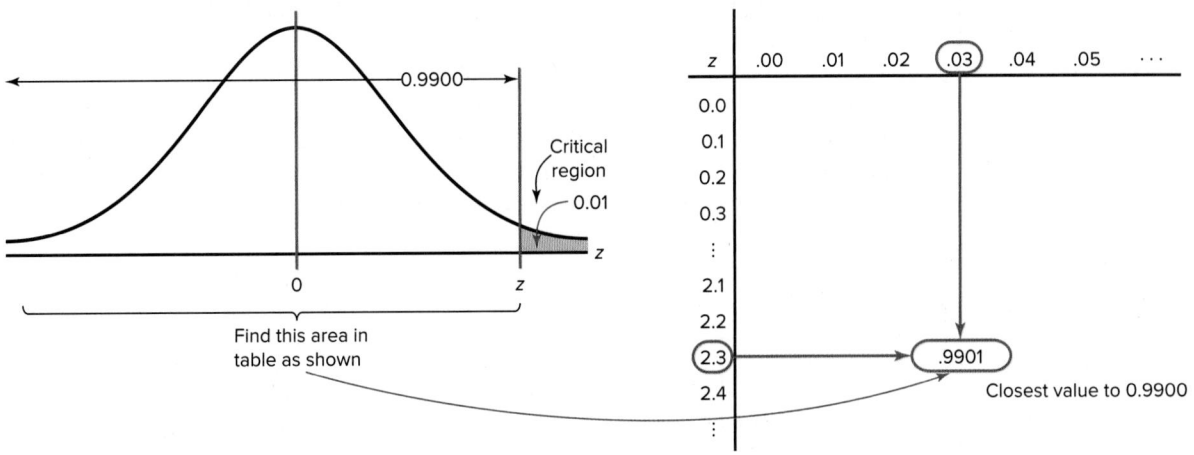

(a) The critical region

(b) The critical value from Table A–4

FIGURE 8–5
Critical and Noncritical
Regions for $\alpha = 0.01$
(Right-Tailed Test)

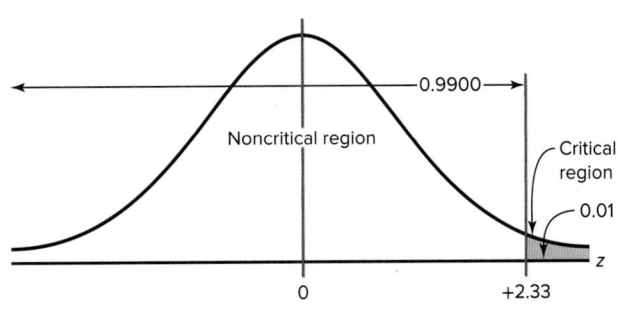

FIGURE 8–6
Critical and Noncritical
Regions for $\alpha = 0.01$
(Left-Tailed Test)

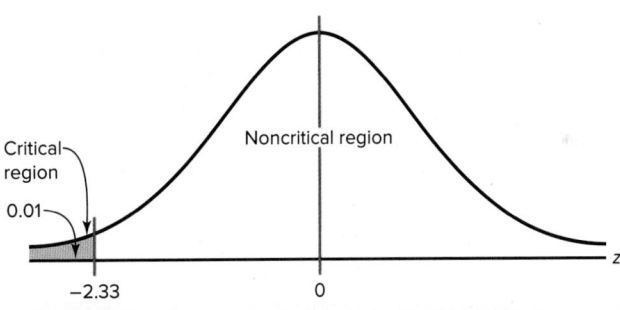

When a researcher conducts a two-tailed test, as in situation A, the null hypothesis can be rejected when there is a significant difference in either direction, above or below the mean.

> In a **two-tailed test,** the null hypothesis should be rejected when the test statistic is in either of the two critical regions.

For a two-tailed test, then, the critical region must be split into two equal parts. If $\alpha = 0.01$, then one-half of the area, or 0.005, must be to the right of the mean and one-half must be to the left of the mean, as shown in Figure 8–7.

In this case, the z score on the left side is found by looking up the z score corresponding to an area of 0.0050. The z score falls about halfway between -2.57 and -2.58 corresponding to the areas 0.0051 and 0.0049. The average of -2.57 and -2.58 is $[(-2.57) + (-2.58)] \div 2 = -2.575$ so if the z score is needed to three decimal places, -2.575 is used; however, if the z score is rounded to two decimal places, -2.58 is used.

On the right side, it is necessary to find the z score corresponding to $0.99 + 0.005$, or 0.9950. Again, the value falls between 0.9949 and 0.9951, so $+2.575$ or 2.58 can be used. See Figure 8–7.

The critical values are $+2.58$ and -2.58, as shown in Figure 8–8.

Similar procedures are used to find other values of α.

Figure 8–9 with rejection regions shaded shows the critical values (C.V.) for the three situations discussed in this section for $\alpha = 0.10$, $\alpha = 0.05$, and $\alpha = 0.01$. The procedure for finding critical values is outlined next (where k is a specified number).

FIGURE 8–7

Finding the Critical Values for $\alpha = 0.01$ (Two-Tailed Test)

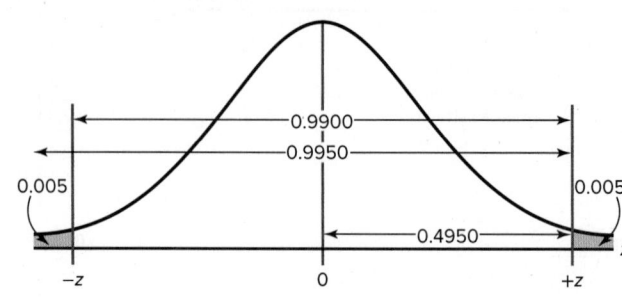

FIGURE 8–8

Critical and Noncritical Regions for $\alpha = 0.01$ (Two-Tailed Test)

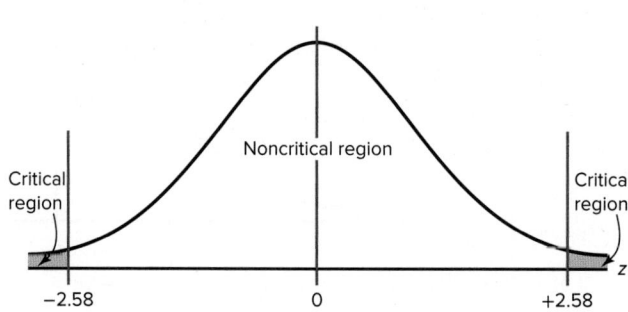

FIGURE 8–9

Summary of Hypothesis Testing and Critical Values

$H_0: \mu = k$
$H_1: \mu < k$
$\begin{cases} \alpha = 0.10, \text{C.V.} = -1.28 \\ \alpha = 0.05, \text{C.V.} = -1.65 \\ \alpha = 0.01, \text{C.V.} = -2.33 \end{cases}$

(a) Left-tailed

$H_0: \mu = k$
$H_1: \mu > k$
$\begin{cases} \alpha = 0.10, \text{C.V.} = +1.28 \\ \alpha = 0.05, \text{C.V.} = +1.65 \\ \alpha = 0.01, \text{C.V.} = +2.33 \end{cases}$

(b) Right-tailed

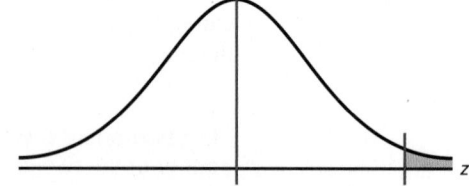

$H_0: \mu = k$
$H_1: \mu \neq k$
$\begin{cases} \alpha = 0.10, \text{C.V.} = \pm1.65 \\ \alpha = 0.05, \text{C.V.} = \pm1.96 \\ \alpha = 0.01, \text{C.V.} = \pm2.58 \end{cases}$

(c) Two-tailed

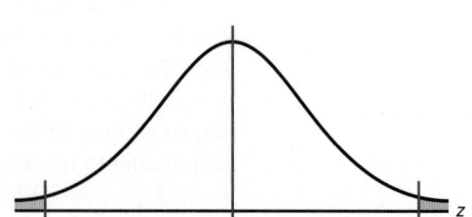

Procedure Table

Finding the Critical Values for Specific α Values, Using Table A–4

Step 1   Draw the figure and indicate the appropriate area.

      a. If the test is left-tailed, the critical region, with an area equal to α, will be on the left side of the mean.

      b. If the test is right-tailed, the critical region, with an area equal to α, will be on the right side of the mean.

      c. If the test is two-tailed, α must be divided by 2; one-half of the area will be to the right of the mean, and one-half will be to the left of the mean.

Step 2   *a.* For a left-tailed test, use the z score that corresponds to the area equivalent to α in Table A–4.

      b. For a right-tailed test, use the z score that corresponds to the area equivalent to $1 - \alpha$.

      c. For a two-tailed test, use the z score that corresponds to $\alpha/2$ for the left value. It will be negative. For the right value, use the z score that corresponds to the area equivalent to $1 - \alpha/2$. It will be positive.

EXAMPLE 8–2

Using Table A–4 in Appendix A, find the critical value(s) for each situation and draw the appropriate figure, showing the critical region.

     a. A left-tailed test with $\alpha = 0.10$.

     b. A two-tailed test with $\alpha = 0.02$.

     c. A right-tailed test with $\alpha = 0.005$.

SOLUTION *a*

Step 1   Draw the figure and indicate the appropriate area. Since this is a left-tailed test, the area of 0.10 is located in the left tail, as shown in Figure 8–10.

Step 2   Find the area closest to 0.1000 in Table A–4. In this case, it is 0.1003. Find the z score that corresponds to the area 0.1003. It is -1.28. See Figure 8–10.

FIGURE 8–10

Critical Value and Critical Region for part *a* of Example 8–2

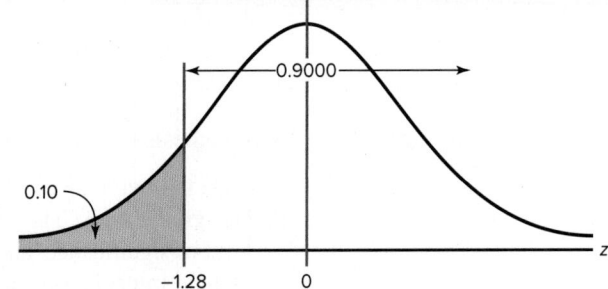

SOLUTION *b*

Step 1   Draw the figure and indicate the appropriate area. In this case, there are two areas equivalent to $\alpha/2$, or $0.02/2 = 0.01$.

Step 2   For the left z critical value, find the z score that corresponds to the area closest to $\alpha/2$, or $0.02/2 = 0.01$. In this case, it is 0.0099.

      For the right z critical value, find the z score that corresponds to the area closest to $1 - \alpha/2$, or $1 - 0.02/2 = 0.9900$. In this case, it is 0.9901.

For 0.0099, $z = -2.33$. For the area of 0.9901, $z = +2.33$. See Figure 8–11.

FIGURE 8–11
Critical Values and Critical
Regions for Part *b* of
Example 8–2

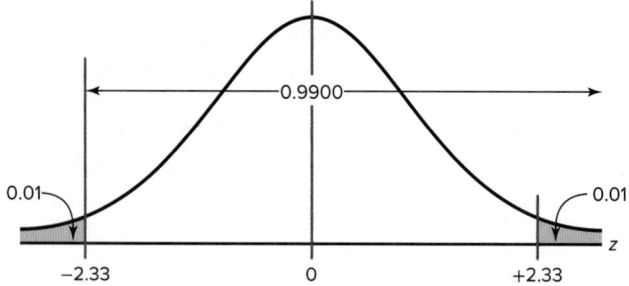

SOLUTION c

Step 1   Draw the figure and indicate the appropriate area. Since this is a right-tailed test, the area 0.005 is located in the right tail, as shown in Figure 8–12.

FIGURE 8–12
Critical Value and Critical
Region for Part *c* of
Example 8–2

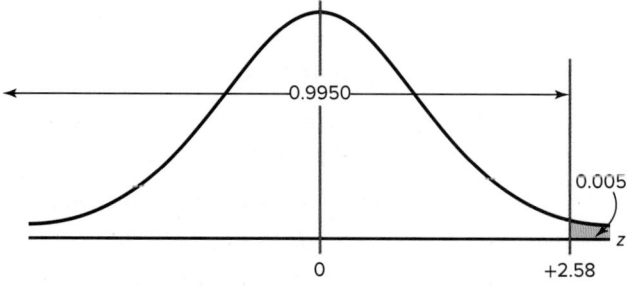

Step 2   Find the area closest to $1 - \alpha$, or $1 - 0.005 = 0.9950$. In this case, it is 0.9949 or 0.9951.

The two z scores corresponding to areas 0.9949 and 0.9951 are +2.57 and +2.58 respectively. Since 0.9500 is halfway between these two z scores, find the average of the two z scores $(+2.57 + 2.58) \div 2 = +2.575$. However, 2.58 is most often used. See Figure 8–12.

OBJECTIVE

State the five steps used in hypothesis testing.

In hypothesis testing, the following steps are recommended.

a. State the hypotheses. Be sure to state both the null and alternative hypotheses.
b. Design the study. This step includes selecting the correct statistical test, choosing a level of significance, and formulating a plan to carry out the study. The plan should include information such as the definition of the population, the way the sample will be selected, and the methods that will be used to collect the data.
c. Conduct the study and collect the data.
d. Evaluate the data. The data should be tabulated in this step, and the statistical test should be conducted. Finally, decide whether to reject or not reject the null hypothesis.
e. Summarize the results.

For the purposes of this chapter, a simplified version of the hypothesis-testing procedure will be used, since designing the study and collecting the data will be omitted. The steps are summarized in the Procedure Table.

Procedure Table

Solving Hypothesis-Testing Problems (Traditional Method)

Step 1   State the hypotheses and identify the claim.

Step 2   Find the critical value(s) from the appropriate table in Appendix A.

Step 3   Compute the test statistic.

Step 4   Make the decision to reject or not reject the null hypothesis.

Step 5   Summarize the results.

It is important to summarize the results of a statistical study correctly. The following table will help you when you summarize the results.

	Claim	
Decision	**Claim is H_0**	**Claim is H_1**
Reject H_0	There is enough evidence to reject the claim.	There is enough evidence to support the claim.
Do not reject H_0	There is not enough evidence to reject the claim.	There is not enough evidence to support the claim.

To further illustrate, the claim can be either the null or alternative hypothesis, and one should identify which it is. After the study is completed, the null hypothesis is either rejected or not rejected. From these two facts, the decision can be identified in the appropriate block.

For example, suppose a researcher claims that the mean weight of an adult animal of a particular species is 42 pounds. In this case, the claim would be the null hypothesis, H_0: $\mu = 42$, since the researcher is asserting that the parameter is a specific value. If the null hypothesis is rejected, the conclusion would be that there is enough evidence to reject the claim that the mean weight of the adult animal is 42 pounds.

On the other hand, suppose the researcher claims that the mean weight of the adult animals is not 42 pounds. The claim would be the alternative hypothesis H_1: $\mu \neq 42$. Furthermore, suppose that the null hypothesis is not rejected. The conclusion, then, would be that there is not enough evidence to support the claim that the mean weight of the adult animals is not 42 pounds.

Again, remember that nothing is being proved true or false. The statistician is only stating that there is or is not enough evidence to say that a claim is *probably* true or false. As noted previously, the only way to prove something would be to use the entire population under study, and usually this cannot be done, especially when the population is large.

P-Value Method for Hypothesis Testing

Statisticians usually test hypotheses at the common α levels of 0.05 or 0.01 and sometimes at 0.10. Recall that the choice of the level depends on the seriousness of the type I error. Besides listing an α value, many computer statistical packages give a *P*-value for hypothesis tests.

The ***P*-value** (or probability value) is the probability of getting a sample statistic (such as the sample mean) or a more extreme sample statistic in the direction of the alternative hypothesis when the null hypothesis is true.

In other words, the *P*-value is the actual area under the standard normal distribution curve (or other curve, depending on what statistical test is being used) representing the

FIGURE 8–13

Comparison of α Values and P-Values

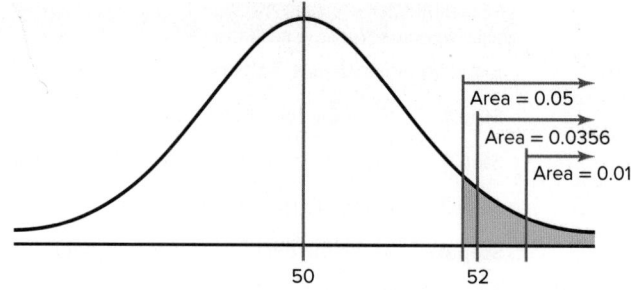

probability of a particular sample statistic or a more extreme sample statistic occurring if the null hypothesis is true.

For example, suppose that an alternative hypothesis is H_1: $\mu > 50$ and the mean of a sample is $\overline{X} = 52$. If the computer printed a P-value of 0.0356 for a statistical test, then the probability of getting a sample mean of 52 or greater is 0.0356 if the true population mean is 50 (for the given sample size and standard deviation). The relationship between the P-value and the α value can be explained in this manner. For $P = 0.0356$, the null hypothesis would be rejected at $\alpha = 0.05$ but not at $\alpha = 0.01$. See Figure 8–13.

When the hypothesis test is two-tailed, the area in one tail must be doubled. For a two-tailed test, if α is 0.05 and the area in one tail is 0.0356, the P-value will be $2(0.0356) = 0.0712$. That is, the null hypothesis should not be rejected at $\alpha = 0.05$, since 0.0712 is greater than 0.05. In summary, then, if the P-value is less than α, reject the null hypothesis. If the P-value is greater than α, do not reject the null hypothesis.

P-values for hypothesis tests are usually given on statistical software packages and calculators such as Excel, MINITAB, and TI-84 Plus. Different technologies may give slightly different P-values depending on the number of digits these technologies use for the calculations. Calculated P-values can also be found using the tables in the Appendix. Finding these values are shown in later sections of this chapter.

Applying the Concepts 8–1

Eggs and Your Health

The Incredible Edible Egg company recently found that eating eggs does not increase a person's blood serum cholesterol. Five hundred subjects participated in a study that lasted for 2 years. The participants were randomly assigned to either a no-egg group or a moderate-egg group. The blood serum cholesterol levels were checked at the beginning and at the end of the study. Overall, the groups' levels were not significantly different. The company reminds us that eating eggs is healthy if done in moderation. Many of the previous studies relating eggs and high blood serum cholesterol jumped to improper conclusions.

Using this information, answer these questions.

1. What prompted the study?

2. What is the population under study?

3. Was a sample collected?

4. What was the hypothesis?

5. Were data collected?

6. Were any statistical tests run?

7. What was the conclusion?

See page 487 for the answers.

≡ Exercises 8–1

1. Define *null* and *alternative hypotheses,* and give an example of each.

2. What is meant by a type I error? A type II error? How are they related?

3. What is meant by a statistical test?

4. Explain the difference between a one-tailed and a two-tailed test.

5. What is meant by the critical region? The *noncritical* region?

6. What symbols are used to represent the null hypothesis and the alternative hypothesis? H_0 represents the null hypothesis; H_1 represents the alternative hypothesis.

7. What symbols are used to represent the probabilities of type I and type II errors? α, β

8. Explain what is meant by a significant difference.

9. When should a one-tailed test be used? A two-tailed test?

10. In hypothesis testing, why can't the hypothesis be proved true?

11. Using the z table (Table A–4), find the critical value (or values) for each.
    a. $\alpha = 0.01$, left-tailed test -2.33
    b. $\alpha = 0.005$, right-tailed test 2.58
    c. $\alpha = 0.10$, two-tailed test ± 1.65
    d. $\alpha = 0.05$, right-tailed test 1.65
    e. $\alpha = 0.01$, two-tailed test ± 2.58

12. Using the z table (Table A–4), find the critical value (or values) for each.
    a. $\alpha = 0.05$, two-tailed test ± 1.96
    b. $\alpha = 0.02$, right-tailed test 2.05
    c. $\alpha = 0.10$, left-tailed test -1.28
    d. $\alpha = 0.02$, two-tailed test ± 2.33
    e. $\alpha = 0.04$, right-tailed test 1.75

13. For each conjecture, state the null and alternative hypotheses.
    a. The average age for a new automobile buyer is 46.7 years. $H_0: \mu = 46.7$ and $H_1: \mu \neq 46.7$
    b. The average number of motor vehicles an American family owns is less than 2.8 vehicles. $H_0: \mu = 2.8$ and $H_1: \mu < 2.8$
    c. The average cost of books on Amazon is more than $15.28. $H_0: \mu = \$15.28$ and $H_1: \mu > \$15.28$
    d. The average number of dogs an American family who owns is 1.6. $H_0: \mu = 1.6$ and $H_1: \mu \neq 1.6$
    e. The average amount of candy consumed by Americans per year is more than 23.9 pounds. $H_0: \mu = 23.9$ and $H_1: \mu > 23.9$

14. For each conjecture, state the null and alternative hypotheses.
    a. The average amount of money spent on a significant other for Valentine's Day is $88.98. $H_0: \mu = \$88.98$ and $H_1: \mu \neq \$88.98$
    b. The average annual income for a cashier is $27,923. $H_0: \mu = \$27,923$ and $H_1: \mu \neq \$27,923$
    c. The average number of minutes retail shoppers spend reading food labels is less than 4 minutes. $H_0: \mu = 4$ and $H_1: \mu < 4$
    d. The average number of pounds of beef that Americans ate in a specific year is greater than 54.8 pounds. $H_0: \mu = 54.8$ and $H_1: \mu > 54.8$
    e. The average amount of money spent by companies to ransom software piracy in a specific year is greater than $2543. $H_0: \mu = \$2543$ and $H_1: \mu > \$2543$

15. For each conjecture, state the null and alternative hypotheses.
    a. More than 84% of cat owners are women. $H_0: p = 0.84$ and $H_1: p > 0.84$
    b. Less than 60% of books sold in a book store are hardback books. $H_0: p = 0.6$ and $H_1: p < 0.6$
    c. Eighty-five percent of people arrested for gambling are men. $H_0: p = 0.85$ and $H_1: p \neq 0.85$

16. For each conjecture, state the null and alternative hypotheses.
    a. Ninety percent of people who commit vandalism are male. $H_0: p = 0.90$ and $H_1: p \neq 0.90$
    b. More than 45% of people who are committed to psychiatric institutions are schizophrenics. $H_0: p = 0.45$ and $H_1: p > 0.45$
    c. Less than 25% of households are touched by crime each year. $H_0: p = 0.25$ and $H_1: p < 0.25$

17. For each situation, decide whether the null hypothesis should be rejected.
    a. $\alpha = 0.05$, P-value $= 0.033$ Reject H_0.
    b. $\alpha = 0.01$, P-value $= 0.011$ Do not reject H_0.
    c. $\alpha = 0.10$, P-value $= 0.136$ Do not reject H_0.
    d. $\alpha = 0.05$, P-value $= 0.043$ Reject H_0.

18. For each situation, decide whether the null hypothesis should be rejected.
    a. $\alpha = 0.01$, P-value $= 0.042$ Do not reject H_0.
    b. $\alpha = 0.10$, P-value $= 0.086$ Reject H_0.
    c. $\alpha = 0.05$, P-value $= 0.035$ Reject H_0.
    d. $\alpha = 0.01$, P-value $= 0.017$ Do not reject H_0.

8–2   *z* Test for a Mean

In this chapter, two statistical tests will be explained: the *z* test is used when σ is known, and the *t* test is used when σ is unknown. This section explains the *z* test, and Section 8–3 explains the *t* test.

Many hypotheses are tested using a statistical test based on the following general formula:

$$\text{Test statistic} = \frac{(\text{observed value}) - (\text{expected value})}{\text{standard error}}$$

The observed value is the statistic (such as the sample mean) that is computed from the sample data. The expected value is the parameter (such as the population mean) that you would expect to obtain if the null hypothesis were true—in other words, the hypothesized value. The denominator is the standard error of the statistic being tested (in this case, the standard error of the mean).

The *z* test is defined formally as follows.

The **z test** is a statistical test for the mean of a population. It can be used either when $n \geq 30$ or when the population is normally distributed and σ is known.
  The formula for the *z* test statistic is

$$z = \frac{\overline{X} - \mu}{\sigma/\sqrt{n}}$$

where $\overline{X}$ = sample mean
    μ = hypothesized population mean
    σ = population standard deviation
    n = sample size

For the *z* test, the observed value is the value of the sample mean. The expected value is the value of the population mean, assuming that the null hypothesis is true. The denominator $\sigma/\sqrt{n}$ is the standard error of the mean.

The formula for the *z* test statistic is the same formula shown in Chapter 6 for the situation where you are using a distribution of sample means. Recall that the central limit theorem allows you to use the standard normal distribution to approximate the distribution of sample means when $n \geq 30$.

The assumptions for the *z* test when σ is known are given next.

Assumptions for the *z* Test for a Mean When σ Is Known

1. The sample is a random sample.
2. Either $n \geq 30$ or the population is normally distributed when $n < 30$.

In this text, the assumptions will be stated in the exercises; however, when encountering statistics in other situations, you must check to see that these assumptions have been met before proceeding.

As stated in Section 8–1, there are five steps for solving *hypothesis-testing* problems:

Step 1   State the hypotheses and identify the claim.

Step 2   Find the critical value(s).

Step 3   Compute the test statistic.

Step 4   Make the decision to reject or not reject the null hypothesis.

Step 5   Summarize the results.

Note: Your first encounter with hypothesis testing can be somewhat challenging and confusing, since there are many new concepts being introduced at the same time. *To understand all the concepts, you must carefully follow each step in the examples and try each exercise that is assigned.* Only after careful study and patience will these concepts become clear.

Again, *z* scores are rounded to two decimal places because they are given to two decimal places in Table A–4.

EXAMPLE 8–3   Hours in Traffic

A researcher believes that the average number of hours a person spends in traffic each year is more than the national average of 46 (*Texas Transportation Institute*). Assume the population standard deviation is 3.6 years. A random sample of 30 subjects is selected and the mean time of the sample is 47.8 hours. Test the claim at $\alpha = 0.05$.

SOLUTION

Step 1   State the hypotheses and identify the claim.

H_0: $\mu = 46$ and H_1: $\mu > 46$ (claim)

Step 2   Find the critical value. Since $\alpha = 0.05$ and the test is right-tailed, the critical value is $z = +1.65$.

Step 3   Compute the test statistic.

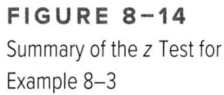

$$z = \frac{\overline{X} - \mu}{\sigma/\sqrt{n}} = \frac{47.8 - 46}{3.6/\sqrt{30}} = 2.74$$

Step 4   Make the decision. Since 2.74 is greater than the critical value 1.65, the decision is to reject the null hypothesis. This is shown in Figure 8–14.

FIGURE 8–14

Summary of the *z* Test for Example 8–3

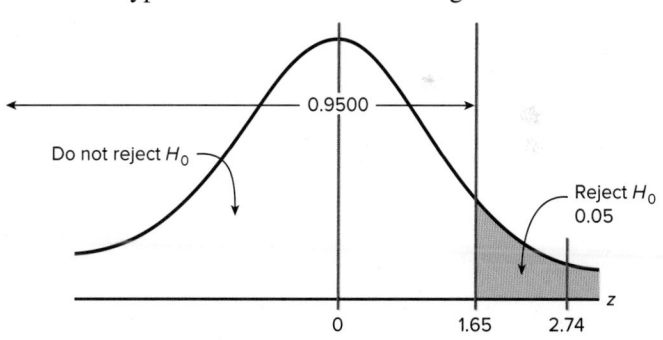

Step 5   Summarize the results. There is enough evidence to support the claim that the average amount of time a person spends in traffic each year is greater than 46 hours.

Comment: In Example 8–3, the difference is said to be statistically significant. However, when the null hypothesis is rejected, there is always a chance of a type I error. In this case, the probability of a type I error is at most 0.05, or 5%.

EXAMPLE 8–4   SAT Tests

For a specific year, the average score on the SAT Math test was 515.* The variable is normally distributed, and the population standard deviation is 100. A school superintendent wishes to see if her students scored significantly below the national average

Source: www.chacha.com

on the test. She randomly selected 36 student scores, as shown. At $\alpha = 0.10$, is there enough evidence to support the claim?

496	506	507	505	438	499
505	522	531	762	513	493
522	668	543	519	349	506
519	516	714	517	511	551
287	523	576	516	515	500
243	509	523	503	414	504

SOLUTION

Step 1   State the hypotheses and identify the claim.

$$H_0: \mu = 515 \quad \text{and} \quad H_1: \mu < 515 \text{ (claim)}$$

Step 2   Find the critical value. Since $\alpha = 0.10$ and the test is a left-tailed test, the critical value is -1.28.

Step 3   Compute the test statistic. Since the exercise gives raw data, it is necessary to find the mean of the data.

$$\overline{X} = \frac{496 + 505 + 522 + \cdots + 504}{36} = \frac{18,325}{36} = 509.028$$

$$z = \frac{\overline{X} - \mu}{\sigma/\sqrt{n}} = \frac{509.028 - 515}{100/\sqrt{36}} = -0.36$$

Step 4   Make the decision. Since the test statistic, -0.36, falls in the noncritical region, the decision is to not reject the null hypothesis. See Figure 8–15.

FIGURE 8–15
Critical Values and Test
Statistic for Example 8–4

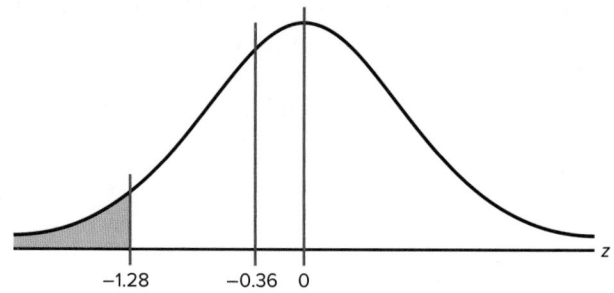

Step 5   Summarize the results. There is not enough evidence to support the claim that the students scored below the national average.

Comment: Even though in Example 8–4 the sample mean of 509.028 is lower than the hypothesized population mean of 515, it is not *significantly* lower. Hence, the difference may be due to chance. When the null hypothesis is not rejected, there is still a probability of a type II error, i.e., of not rejecting the null hypothesis when it is false.

The probability of a type II error is not easily ascertained. Further explanation about the type II error is given in Section 8–6. For now, it is only necessary to realize that the probability of type II error exists when the decision is to not reject the null hypothesis.

Also note that when the null hypothesis is not rejected, it cannot be accepted as true. There is merely not enough evidence to say that it is false. This guideline may sound a little confusing, but the situation is analogous to a jury trial. The verdict is either guilty or not guilty and is based on the evidence presented. If a person is judged not guilty, it does not mean that the person is proved innocent; it only means that there was not enough evidence to reach the guilty verdict.

EXAMPLE 8–5   Not Eating Breakfast

It was reported in *USA TODAY* that American adults skip breakfast on average 50 times per year. A researcher selects a random sample of 40 adults and finds that the mean number of times a person skipped breakfast over one period was not equal to 51.2 times. Assume that the population standard deviation is 3.1. At $\alpha = 0.01$, can it be concluded that the mean is not equal to 50?

SOLUTION

Step 1   State the hypotheses and identify the claim.

$H_0\colon \mu = 50$ and $H_1\colon \mu \neq 50$ (claim)

Step 2   Find the critical values. Since $\alpha = 0.01$ and the test is a two-tailed test, the critical values are $+2.58$ and -2.58.

Step 3   Compute the test statistic.

$$z = \frac{\overline{X} - \mu}{\sigma/\sqrt{n}} = \frac{51.2 - 50}{3.1/\sqrt{40}} = 2.45$$

Step 4   Make the decision. Do not reject the null hypothesis since the test statistic falls in the noncritical region, as shown in Figure 8–16.

FIGURE 8–16
Critical Values and Test
Statistic for Example 8–5

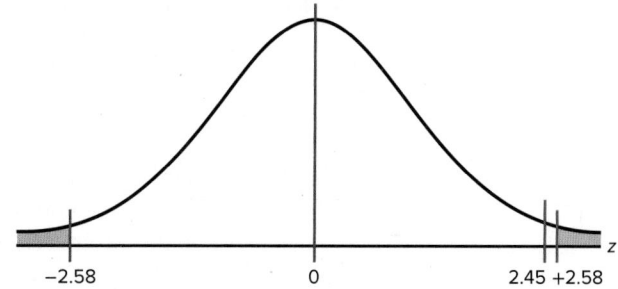

Step 5   Summarize the results. There is not enough evidence to support the claim that the average number of times a person skips breakfast per year is not equal to 50.

P-values are usually found in statistical software programs or on statistical calculators. Approximate *P*-values for test statistics can also be found by using the areas in the tables in Appendix A. These methods are shown in the examples for the statistical tests.

Recall from Section 8–1 that the steps for testing hypotheses were shown in the procedure table. For review, it is included here.

Procedure Table
Solving Hypothesis-Testing Problems (*P*-Value Method)
Step 1   State the hypotheses and identify the claim.
Step 2   Compute the test statistic.
Step 3   Find the *P*-value.
Step 4   Make the decision.
Step 5   Summarize the results.

The decision rule stated in Section 8–1 is shown here.

> **Decision Rule When Using a *P*-Value**
>
> If *P*-value ≤ α, reject the null hypothesis.
> If *P*-value > α, do not reject the null hypothesis.

EXAMPLE 8–6   Cost of College Tuition

A researcher wishes to test the claim that the average cost of tuition and fees at a four-year public college is greater than $5700. She selects a random sample of 36 four-year public colleges and finds the mean to be $5950. The population standard deviation is $659. Is there evidence to support the claim at α = 0.05? Use the *P*-value method.

Source: Based on information from the College Board.

SOLUTION

Step 1   State the hypotheses and identify the claim.

$$H_0: \mu = \$5700 \qquad \text{and} \qquad H_1: \mu > \$5700 \text{ (claim)}$$

Step 2   Compute the test statistic.

$$z = \frac{\overline{X} - \mu}{\sigma/\sqrt{n}} = \frac{5950 - 5700}{659/\sqrt{36}} = 2.28$$

Step 3   Find the *P*-value. Using Table A–4 in Appendix A, find the corresponding area under the normal distribution for z = 2.28. It is 0.9887. Subtract this value for the area from 1.0000 to find the area in the right tail.

$$1.0000 - 0.9887 = 0.0113$$

Hence, the *P*-value is 0.0113. (The *P*-value from the calculator is 0.0114.)

Step 4   Make the decision. Since the *P*-value is less than 0.05, the decision is to reject the null hypothesis. See Figure 8–17.

FIGURE 8–17
P-Value and α Value for
Example 8–6

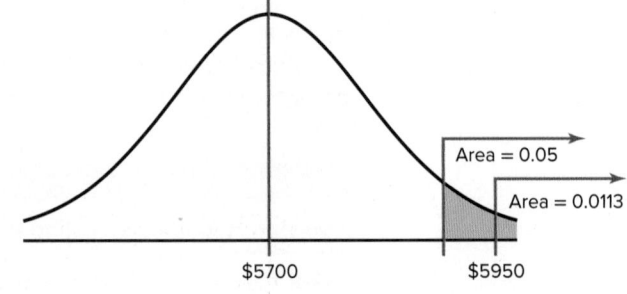

$5700 $5950

Area = 0.05
Area = 0.0113

Step 5   Summarize the results. There is enough evidence to support the claim that the tuition and fees at four-year public colleges are greater than $5700.
Note: Had the researcher chosen α = 0.01, the null hypothesis would not have been rejected since the *P*-value (0.0113) is greater than 0.01.

EXAMPLE 8–7   Wind Speed

A researcher claims that the average wind speed in a certain city is 8 miles per hour. A sample of 32 days has an average wind speed of 8.2 miles per hour. The standard deviation of the population is 0.6 mile per hour. At $\alpha = 0.05$, is there enough evidence to reject the claim? Use the *P*-value method.

SOLUTION

Step 1 State the hypotheses and identify the claim.

$$H_0: \mu = 8 \text{ (claim)} \qquad \text{and} \qquad H_1: \mu \neq 8$$

Step 2 Compute the test statistic.

$$z = \frac{8.2 - 8}{0.6/\sqrt{32}} = 1.89$$

Step 3 Find the *P*-value. Using Table A–4, find the corresponding area for $z = 1.89$. It is 0.9706. Subtract the value from 1.0000.

$$1.0000 - 0.9706 = 0.0294$$

Since this is a two-tailed test, the area of 0.0294 must be doubled to get the *P*-value.

$$2(0.0294) = 0.0588 \text{ (The } P\text{-value from the calculator is 0.0593.)}$$

Step 4 Make the decision. The decision is to not reject the null hypothesis, since the *P*-value is greater than 0.05. See Figure 8–18.

FIGURE 8–18
P-Values and α Values for Example 8–7

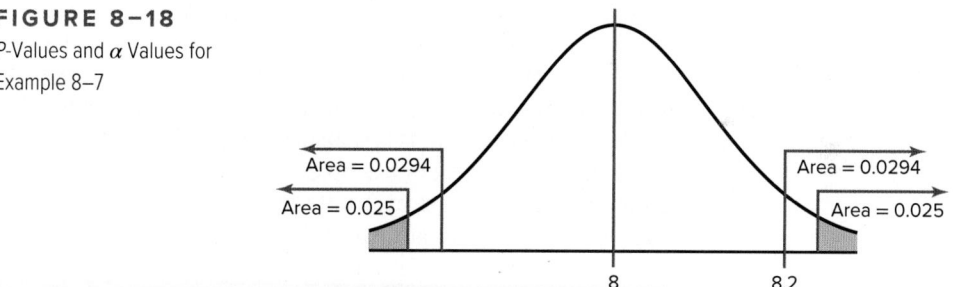

Step 5 Summarize the results. There is not enough evidence to reject the claim that the average wind speed is 8 miles per hour.

In Examples 8–6 and 8–7, the *P*-value and the α value were shown on a normal distribution curve to illustrate the relationship between the two values; however, it is not necessary to draw the normal distribution curve to make the decision whether to reject the null hypothesis. You can use the following rule:

Decision Rule When Using a *P*-Value

If *P*-value $\leq \alpha$, reject the null hypothesis.
If *P*-value $> \alpha$, do not reject the null hypothesis.

In Example 8–6, *P*-value = 0.0113 and $\alpha = 0.05$. Since *P*-value $\leq \alpha$, the null hypothesis was rejected. In Example 8–7, *P*-value = 0.0588 and $\alpha = 0.05$. Since *P*-value $> \alpha$, the null hypothesis was not rejected.

The *P*-values given on calculators and computers are slightly different from those found with Table A–4. This is so because *z* scores and the values in Table A–4 have been rounded. *Also, most calculators and computers give the exact P-value for two-tailed tests, so it should not be doubled (as it should when the area found in Table A–4 is used).*

A clear distinction between the α value and the *P*-value should be made. The α value is chosen by the researcher *before* the statistical test is conducted. The *P*-value is computed after the sample mean has been found.

There are two schools of thought on *P*-values. Some researchers do not choose an α value but report the *P*-value and allow the reader to decide whether the null hypothesis should be rejected.

In this case, the following guidelines can be used, but be advised that these guidelines are not written in stone, and some statisticians may have other opinions.

Guidelines for *P*-Values

If *P*-value ≤ 0.01, reject the null hypothesis. The difference is highly significant.

If *P*-value > 0.01 but *P*-value ≤ 0.05, reject the null hypothesis. The difference is significant.

If *P*-value > 0.05 but *P*-value ≤ 0.10, consider the consequences of type I error before rejecting the null hypothesis.

If *P*-value > 0.10, do not reject the null hypothesis. The difference is not significant.

Others decide on the α value in advance and use the *P*-value to make the decision, as shown in Examples 8–6 and 8–7. A note of caution is needed here: If a researcher selects $\alpha = 0.01$ and the *P*-value is 0.03, the researcher may decide to change the α value from 0.01 to 0.05 so that the null hypothesis will be rejected. This, of course, should not be done. If the α level is selected in advance, it should be used in making the decision.

One additional note on hypothesis testing is that the researcher should distinguish between *statistical significance* and *practical significance*. When the null hypothesis is rejected at a specific significance level, it can be concluded that the difference is probably not due to chance and thus is statistically significant. However, the results may not have any practical significance. For example, suppose that a new fuel additive increases the miles per gallon that a car can get by $\frac{1}{4}$ mile for a sample of 1000 automobiles. The results may be statistically significant at the 0.05 level, but it would hardly be worthwhile to market the product for such a small increase. Hence, there is no practical significance to the results. It is up to the researcher to use common sense when interpreting the results of a statistical test.

≡ Applying the Concepts 8–2

Car Thefts

You recently received a job with a company that manufactures an automobile antitheft device. To conduct an advertising campaign for the product, you need to make a claim about the number of automobile thefts per year. Since the population of various cities in the United States varies, you decide to use rates per 10,000 people. (The rates are based on the number of people living in the cities.) Your boss said that last year the theft rate per 10,000 people was 44 vehicles. You want to see if it has changed. The following are rates per 10,000 people for 36 randomly selected locations in the United States. Assume $\sigma = 30.3$.

55	42	125	62	134	73
39	69	23	94	73	24
51	55	26	66	41	67
15	53	56	91	20	78
70	25	62	115	17	36
58	56	33	75	20	16

Source: Based on information from the National Insurance Crime Bureau.

Using this information, answer these questions.

1. What hypotheses would you use?

2. Is the sample considered small or large?

3. What assumption must be met before the hypothesis test can be conducted?

4. Which probability distribution would you use?

5. Would you select a one- or two-tailed test? Why?

6. What critical value(s) would you use?

7. Conduct a hypothesis test.

8. What is your decision?

9. What is your conclusion?

10. Write a brief statement summarizing your conclusion.

11. If you lived in a city whose population was about 50,000, how many automobile thefts per year would you expect to occur?

See page 487 for the answers.

Exercises 8–2

For Exercises 1 through 25, perform each of the following steps.

   a. State the hypotheses and identify the claim.

   b. Find the critical value(s) or use the *P*-value method.

   c. Compute the test statistic.

   d. Make the decision.

   e. Summarize the results.

Use diagrams to show the critical region (or regions), and use the traditional method of hypothesis testing unless the P-value method is specified by your instructor.

1. **Warming and Ice Melt** The average depth of the Hudson Bay is 305 feet. Climatologists were interested in seeing if warming and ice melt were affecting the water level. Fifty-five measurements over a period of randomly selected weeks yielded a sample mean of 306.2 feet. The population variance is known to be 3.6. Can it be concluded at the 0.05 level of significance that the average depth has increased? Is there evidence of what caused this to happen?

   Source: World Almanac and Book of Facts 2010.

2. **Facebook Friends** Many people believe that the average number of Facebook friends is 338. The population standard deviation is 43.2. A random sample of 50 college students in a particular county revealed that the average number of Facebook friends was 350. At $\alpha = 0.05$, is there sufficient evidence to conclude that the mean number of friends is greater than 338?

3. **Cost of Rolex Watches** The average cost of a Rolex watch is $7521. A researcher selected a random sample of 40 jewelry stores and found the average cost of Rolex watches was $7496. If $\sigma = \$86$ and $\alpha = 0.05$, can it be concluded that the average cost of a Rolex watch in that area is less than $7521?

4. **Moviegoers** The average "moviegoer" sees 8.5 movies a year. A *moviegoer* is defined as a person who sees at least one movie in a theater in a 12-month period. A random sample of 40 moviegoers from a large university revealed that the average number of movies seen per person was 9.6. The population standard deviation is 3.2 movies. At the 0.05 level of significance, can it be concluded that this represents a difference from the national average?

   Source: MPAA Study.

5. **Caffeine in Tea Bags** In a recent study, researchers found that the average amount of caffeine in tea bags is 26 mg. The standard deviation of the population is 3 mg. If a random sample of 32 newly manufactured tea bags has a mean of 24.8 mg of caffeine, can it be concluded that the new brand of tea bags contain less caffeine than the average found in the recent study? Use $\alpha = 0.10$.

6. **Cost of Building a Home** According to the National Association of Home Builders, the average cost of building a home in the Northeast is $117.91 per square foot. A random sample of 36 new homes indicated that the mean cost was $122.57 per square foot and the population standard deviation was $20. Can it be concluded that the mean cost differs from $117.91, using the 0.10 level of significance?

7. **Heights of 1-Year-Olds** The average 1-year-old is 29 inches tall. A random sample of 30 1-year-olds in a large day care franchise resulted in the following heights. At $\alpha = 0.05$, can it be concluded that the average height differs from 29 inches? Assume $\sigma = 2.61$.

25	32	35	25	30	26.5	26	25.5	29.5	32
30	28.5	30	32	28	31.5	29	29.5	30	34
29	32	27	28	33	28	27	32	29	29.5

Source: www.healthepic.com

8. **New Automobile Ownership** According to an R.L. Polk survey, the average length of time a person keeps a new automobile is 71.4 months. The average time 30 randomly selected automobile owners kept their new automobiles was 70.8 months with $\sigma = 4.1$ months. At the 0.01 level of significance, can it be concluded that for this type of automobile, the owners kept their new automobile less than 71.4 months?

9. **Telephone Calls** A researcher knew that before cell phones, a person made on average 2.8 calls per day. He believes that the number of calls made per day today is higher. The researcher selects a random sample of 30 individuals who use a cell phone and asks them to keep track of the number of calls that they made on a certain day. The mean was 3.1. At $\alpha = 0.01$ is there enough evidence to support the researcher's claim? The standard deviation for the population found by a previous study is 0.8. Would the null hypothesis be rejected at $\alpha = 0.05$?

10. **Daily Driving** The average number of miles a person drives per day is 24. A researcher wishes to see if people over age 60 drive less than 24 miles per day on average. She selects a random sample of 49 drivers over the age of 60 and finds that the mean number of miles driven is 22.8. The population standard deviation is 3.5 miles. At $\alpha = 0.05$ is there sufficient evidence that those drivers over 60 years old drive less on average than 24 miles per day?

11. **Costs of College Textbooks** Based on the research of the National Association of College Bookstores, the average amount spent on textbooks for one semester at this writing was $655. A random sample of 45 college students who used a local college bookstore found that they spent on average $663. Assume $\sigma = \$19$. At $\alpha = 0.05$, can it be concluded that the average amount they spent at the bookstore was not equal to $655?

12. **Student Expenditures** The average expenditure per student (based on average daily attendance) for a certain school year was $10,337 with a population standard deviation of $1560. A survey for the next school year of 150 randomly selected students resulted in a sample mean of $10,798. Do these results indicate that the average expenditure has changed? Choose your own level of significance.

Source: World Almanac.

13. **Cost of a Movie Ticket** The average cost of a movie ticket is $10.50. A random sample in a specific city of 36 movie theaters found that the average cost of a movie ticket was $10.59. If $\sigma = \$0.38$ and $\alpha = 0.10$, can it be concluded that the average cost of movie tickets in that city is not $10.50?

14. **Prison Sentences** The average length of prison term in the United States for white collar crime is 34.9 months. A random sample of 40 prison terms indicated a mean stay of 28.5 months. The standard deviation of the population is 8.9 months. At $\alpha = 0.04$, is there sufficient evidence to conclude that the average stay differs from 34.9 months?

Source: californiawatch.org

15. **Reject or Not** State whether the null hypothesis should be rejected on the basis of the given *P*-value.

   a. *P*-value = 0.258, $\alpha = 0.05$, one-tailed test   Do not reject.

   b. *P*-value = 0.0684, $\alpha = 0.10$, two-tailed test Reject.

   c. *P*-value = 0.0153, $\alpha = 0.01$, one-tailed test   Do not reject.

   d. *P*-value = 0.0232, $\alpha = 0.05$, two-tailed test Reject.

   e. *P*-value = 0.002, $\alpha = 0.01$, one-tailed test Reject.

16. **Soft Drink Consumption** A researcher claims that the yearly consumption of soft drinks per person is 52 gallons. In a sample of 50 randomly selected people, the mean of the yearly consumption was 56.3 gallons. The standard deviation of the population is 3.5 gallons. Find the *P*-value for the test. On the basis of the *P*-value, is the researcher's claim valid?

Source: U.S. Department of Agriculture.

17. **Stopping Distances** A study found that the average stopping distance of a school bus traveling 50 miles per hour was 264 feet. A group of automotive engineers decided to conduct a study of its school buses and found that for 20 randomly selected buses, the average stopping distance of buses traveling 50 miles per hour was 262.3 feet. The standard deviation of the population was 3 feet. Test the claim that the average stopping distance of the company's buses is actually less than 264 feet. Find the *P*-value. On the basis of the *P*-value, should the null hypothesis be rejected at $\alpha = 0.01$? Assume that the variable is normally distributed.

Source: Snapshot, USA TODAY.

18. **Copy Machine Use** A store manager hypothesizes that the average number of pages a person copies on the store's copy machine is less than 40. A random sample of 50 customers' orders is selected. At $\alpha = 0.01$, is there enough evidence to support the claim? Use the *P*-value hypothesis-testing method. Assume $\sigma = 30.9$.

2	2	2	5	32
5	29	8	2	49
21	1	24	72	70
21	85	61	8	42
3	15	27	113	36
37	5	3	58	82
9	2	1	6	9
80	9	51	2	122
21	49	36	43	61
3	17	17	4	1

19. Hours Dogs Sleep The Canadian Press reported that dogs sleep on average 14 hours per day. A veterinarian studied a random sample of 25 dogs and found that they sleep on average 13.1 hours. The standard deviation of the population, which was 1.7 hours, was found from previous studies. At $\alpha = 0.05$, can it be concluded that on average dogs do not sleep 14 hours per day? Assume the variable is normally distributed.

20. Breaking Strength of Cable A special cable has a breaking strength of 800 pounds. The standard deviation of the population is 12 pounds. A researcher selects a random sample of 20 cables and finds that the average breaking strength is 793 pounds. Can he reject the claim that the breaking strength is 800 pounds? Find the P-value. Should the null hypothesis be rejected at $\alpha = 0.01$? Assume that the variable is normally distributed.

21. Farm Sizes The average farm size in the United States is 444 acres. A random sample of 40 farms in Oregon indicated a mean size of 430 acres, and the population standard deviation is 52 acres. At $\alpha = 0.05$, can it be concluded that the average farm in Oregon differs from the national mean? Use the P-value method.

Source: New York Times Almanac.

22. Farm Sizes Ten years ago, the average acreage of farms in a certain geographic region was 65 acres. The standard deviation of the population was 7 acres. A recent study consisting of 22 randomly selected farms showed that the average was 63.2 acres per farm. Test the claim, at $\alpha = 0.10$, that the average has not changed by finding the P-value for the test. Assume that σ has not changed and the variable is normally distributed.

23. Transmission Service A car dealer recommends that transmissions be serviced at 30,000 miles. To see whether her customers are adhering to this recommendation, the dealer selects a random sample of 40 customers and finds that the average mileage of the automobiles serviced is 30,456. The standard deviation of the population is 1684 miles. By finding the P-value, determine whether the owners are having their transmissions serviced at 30,000 miles. Use $\alpha = 0.10$. Do you think the α value of 0.10 is an appropriate significance level?

24. Speeding Tickets A motorist claims that the South Boro Police issue an average of 60 speeding tickets per day. These data show the number of speeding tickets issued each day for a randomly selected period of 30 days. Assume σ is 13.42. Is there enough evidence to reject the motorist's claim at $\alpha = 0.05$? Use the P-value method.

72	45	36	68	69	71	57	60
83	26	60	72	58	87	48	59
60	56	64	68	42	57	57	
58	63	49	73	75	42	63	

25. Sick Days A manager states that in his factory, the average number of days per year missed by the employees due to illness is less than the national average of 10. The following data show the number of days missed by 40 randomly selected employees last year. Is there sufficient evidence to believe the manager's statement at $\alpha = 0.05$? $\sigma = 3.63$. Use the P-value method.

0	6	12	3	3	5	4	1
3	9	6	0	7	6	3	4
7	4	7	1	0	8	12	3
2	5	10	5	15	3	2	5
3	11	8	2	2	4	1	9

Extending the Concepts

26. Significance Levels Suppose a statistician chose to test a hypothesis at $\alpha = 0.01$. The critical value for a right-tailed test is $+2.33$. If the test statistic is 1.97, what would the decision be? What would happen if, after seeing the test statistic, the statistician decided to choose $\alpha = 0.05$? What would the decision be? Explain the contradiction, if there is one.

27. Hourly Wage The president of a company states that the average hourly wage of her employees is $8.65. A random sample of 50 employees has the distribution shown. At $\alpha = 0.05$, is the president's statement believable? Assume $\sigma = 0.105$.

Class	Frequency
8.35–8.43	2
8.44–8.52	6
8.53–8.61	12
8.62–8.70	18
8.71–8.79	10
8.80–8.88	2

Technology   Step by Step

TI-84 Plus

Step by Step

Hypothesis Test for the Mean and the z Distribution (Data)

1. Enter the data values into L_1.
2. Press **STAT** and move the cursor to TESTS.
3. Press **l** for ZTest.

4. Move the cursor to Data and press **ENTER.**

5. Type in the appropriate values.

6. Move the cursor to the appropriate alternative hypothesis and press **ENTER.**

7. Move the cursor to Calculate and press **ENTER.**

Example TI8–1

This relates to Example 8–4 from the text. At the 10% significance level, test the claim that $\mu < 515$, given the data values.

496	506	507	505	438	499	505	522	531	762	513	493
522	668	543	519	349	506	519	516	714	517	511	551
287	523	576	516	515	500	243	509	523	503	414	504

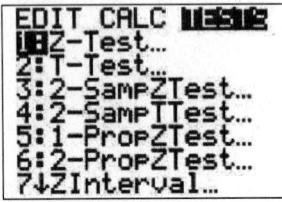  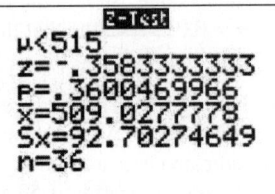

The test statistic is $z = -0.3583333333$, and the *P*-value is 0.3600469966.

Hypothesis Test for the Mean and the *z* Distribution (Statistics)

1. Press **STAT** and move the cursor to TESTS.

2. Press **1** for ZTest.

3. Move the cursor to Stats and press **ENTER.**

4. Type in the appropriate values.

5. Move the cursor to the appropriate alternative hypothesis and press **ENTER.**

6. Move the cursor to Calculate and press **ENTER.**

Example TI8–2

At the 5% significance level, test the claim that $\mu > 42,000$ given $\sigma = 5230$, $\overline{X} = 43,260$, and $n = 30$.

The test statistic is $z = 1.319561037$, and the *P*-value is 0.0934908728.

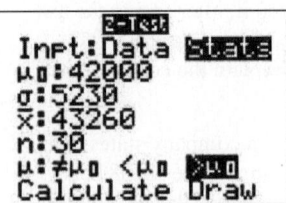 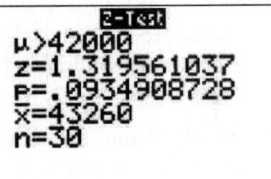

EXCEL

Step by Step

Hypothesis Test for the Mean: *z* Test

Excel does not have a procedure to conduct a hypothesis test for a single population mean. However, you may conduct the test of the mean by using the MegaStat Add-in available in your online resources. If you have not installed this add-in, do so, following the instructions from the Chapter 1 Excel Step by Step.

Example XL8–1

This example relates to Example 8–4 from the text. At the 10% level of significance, test the claim that $\mu < 515$. The MegaStat *z* test uses the *P*-value method. Therefore, it is not necessary to enter a significance level.

1. Enter the data from Example 8–4 into column A of a new Excel worksheet. Label the column SAT.

2. From the Toolbar, select Data, **MegaStat>Hypothesis Tests>Mean vs. Hypothesized Value.** *Note:* You may need to open MegaStat from the MegaStat.xls file on your computer's hard drive.

3. Select data input and type **A1:A37** as the Input Range.

4. Type **515** for the Hypothesized mean and select the Alternative "less than."

5. Select *z* test, change the confidence interval level to 90%, and click [OK].

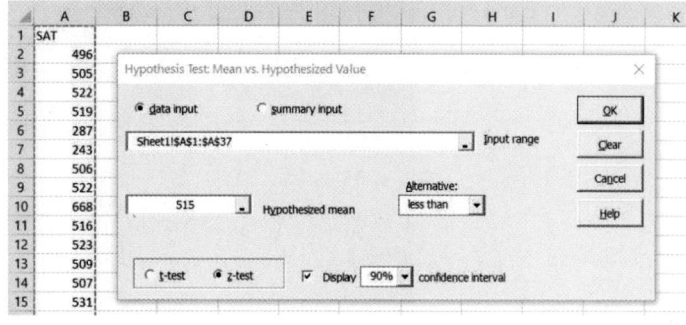

The result of the procedure is shown next.

Hypothesis Test: Mean vs. Hypothesized Value

515.000	Hypothesized value
509.028	Mean data
92.703	Std. dev.
15.450	Std. error
36	*n*
−0.39	*z*
0.3495	*P*-value (one-tailed, lower)

MINITAB
Step by Step

Hypothesis Test for the Mean: *z* Test

MINITAB can be used to calculate the test statistic and the *P*-value. Although the *P*-value approach does not require a critical value from the table, MINITAB can also calculate a critical value as in Example 8–2.

Example 8–2

Find the critical value(s) for each situation and draw the appropriate figure.

Step 1 To find the critical value of *z* for a left-tailed test with $\alpha = 0.10$, select **Graph>Probability Distribution Plot,** then **View Probability,** and then click **[OK].**

Step 2 The Distribution should be set for Normal with a mean of 0 and a standard deviation of 1.

Step 3 Click the tab for **Shaded Area.**

a) Select **Left Tail.**

b) Select the radio button for **Probability.**

c) Type in the value of alpha for probability, **0.10.**

d) Click **[OK].** The critical value of *z* to three decimal places is −1.282.

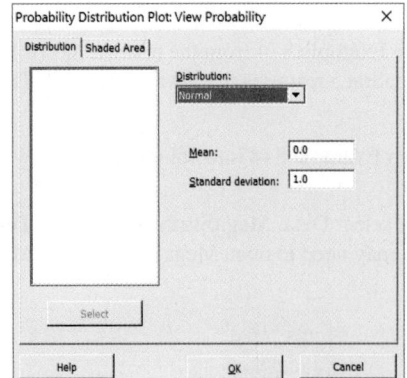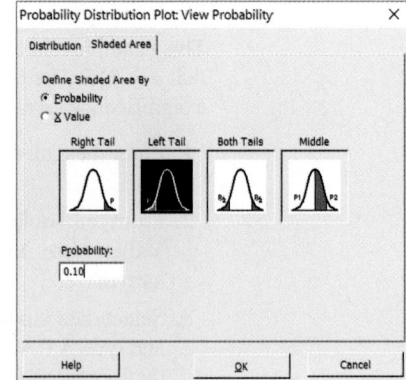

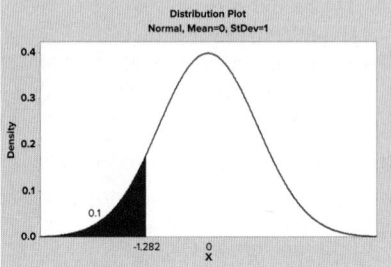

You may click the Edit Last Dialog button and then change the settings for additional critical values.

Example 8–3 Hours in Traffic

MINITAB will calculate the test statistic and *P*-value from the summary statistics. There are no data for this example.

Step 1 Select **Stat>Basic Statistics> 1-sample z.** This is the same menu item used to obtain a *z* interval in Chapter 7.

Step 2 Select **Summarized Data** from the drop-down menu.
   a) Type in the sample size of **30.**
   b) Type in the sample mean of **47.8.**
   c) Type in the population standard deviation of **3.6.**

Step 3 Check the box for Perform hypothesis test, then type in the Hypothesized value of **46.**

Step 4 Click the button for [**Options**].
   a) Type the percentage for the Confidence level, **95.**
   b) Click the drop-down menu for the Alternative hypothesis, "Mean > hypothesized mean."

Step 5 Click [**OK**] twice.

In the session window you will see the results including a confidence interval estimate. The test statistic $z = 2.74$ with a *P*-value of 0.003. Since the *P*-value is smaller than α, the null hypothesis is rejected.

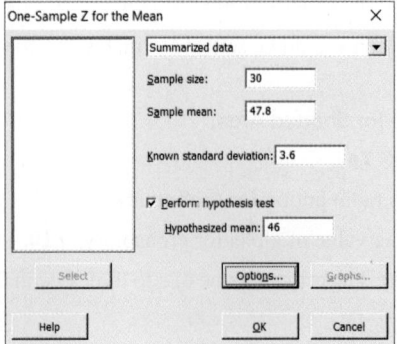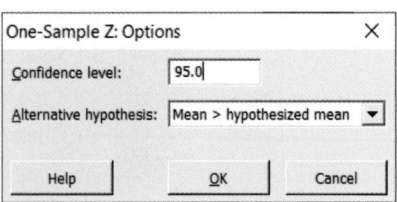

One-Sample Z

```
Test of µ = 46 vs > 46
The assumed standard deviation = 3.6


 N    Mean   SE Mean   95% Lower Bound    Z      P
30   47.800   0.657             46.719  2.74  0.003
```

Example 8–4 SAT Tests

MINITAB will calculate the test statistic and *P*-value.

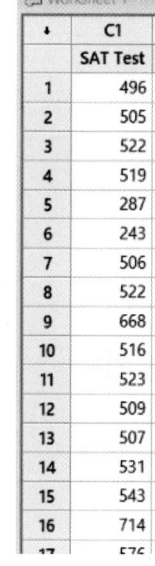

Step 1   Type the data into column C1. Label the column SAT Test.

Step 2   Select **Stat>Basic Statistics> 1-sample z.**

Step 3   Select **One or more samples, each in a column.** To select the data, click inside the next dialog box; then select C1 SAT Test from the list.

Step 4   Type in the population standard deviation of **100.**

Step 5   Select the box for Perform hypothesis test, then type in the Hypothesized value of **515.**

Step 6   Click the button for [**Options**].

     a) Type the confidence level **90.**

     b) Click the drop-down menu for the Alternative hypothesis, Mean < hypothesized mean.

Step 7   Click [**OK**] twice.

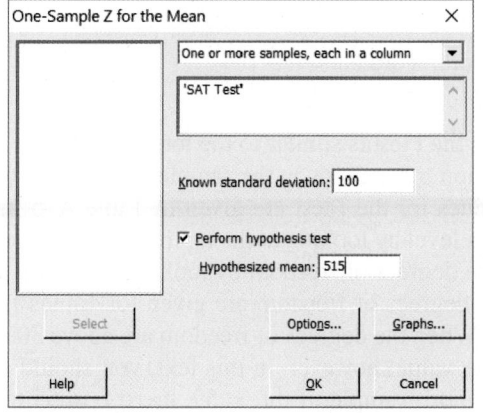

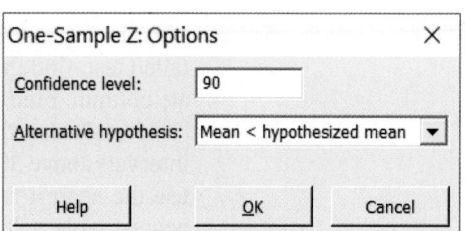

One-Sample Z: SAT Test

```
Test of µ = 515 vs < 515
The assumed standard deviation = 100


Variable   N    Mean   StDev   SE Mean   90% Upper Bound    Z      P
SAT Test  36   509.0   92.7     16.7              530.4  -0.36  0.360
```

The test statistic *z* is equal to −0.36. The null hypothesis cannot be rejected since the *P*-value of 0.360 is larger than 0.10.

8–3   *t* Test for a Mean

When the population standard deviation is unknown, the *z* test is not typically used for testing hypotheses involving means. A different test, called the *t test,* is used. The distribution of the variable should be approximately normal.

As stated in Chapter 7, the *t* distribution is similar to the standard normal distribution in the following ways.

1. It is bell-shaped.

2. It is symmetric about the mean.

3. The mean, median, and mode are equal to 0 and are located at the center of the distribution.

4. The curve approaches but never touches the *x* axis.

The *t* distribution differs from the standard normal distribution in the following ways.

1. The variance is greater than 1.

2. The *t* distribution is a family of curves based on the *degrees of freedom,* which is a number related to sample size. (Recall that the symbol for degrees of freedom is d.f. See Section 7–2 for an explanation of degrees of freedom.)

3. As the sample size increases, the *t* distribution approaches the normal distribution.

The *t* test is defined next.

The **t test** is a statistical test for the mean of a population and is used when the population is normally or approximately normally distributed and σ is unknown. The formula for the *t* test statistic is

$$t = \frac{\overline{X} - \mu}{s/\sqrt{n}}$$

The degrees of freedom are d.f. $= n - 1$.

The formula for the *t* test is similar to the formula for the *z* test. But since the population standard deviation σ is unknown, the sample standard deviation *s* is used instead.

The critical values for the *t* test are given in Table A–5 in Appendix A. For a one-tailed test, find the α level by looking at the top row of the table and finding the appropriate column. Find the degrees of freedom by looking down the left-hand column.

Notice that the degrees of freedom are given for values from 1 through 30, then at intervals above 30. When the degrees of freedom are above 30, some texts will tell you to use the nearest table value; however, in this text, you should always round down to the nearest table value. For example, if d.f. = 59, use d.f. = 55 to find the critical value or values. This is a conservative approach.

As the degrees of freedom get larger, the critical values approach the *z* scores. Hence, the bottom values (large sample size) are the same as the *z* scores that were used in the last section.

EXAMPLE 8–8

Find the critical *t* value for $\alpha = 0.05$ with d.f. = 16 for a right-tailed *t* test.

SOLUTION

Find the 0.05 column in the top row labeled One tail and 16 in the left-hand column. Where the row and column meet, the appropriate critical value is found; it is +1.746. See Figure 8–19.

FIGURE 8–19

Finding the Critical Value
for the *t* Test in Table A–5
(Example 8–8)

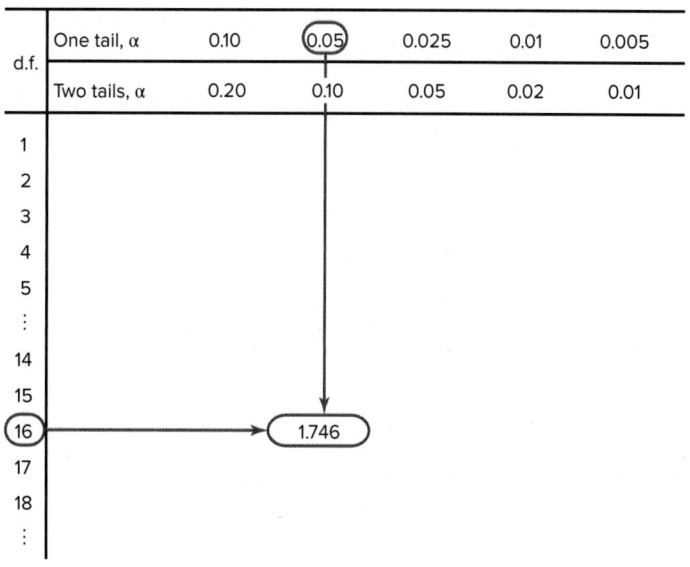

d.f.	One tail, α	0.10	0.05	0.025	0.01	0.005
	Two tails, α	0.20	0.10	0.05	0.02	0.01
1						
2						
3						
4						
5						
⋮						
14						
15						
16		1.746				
17						
18						
⋮						

EXAMPLE 8–9

Find the critical *t* value for $\alpha = 0.05$ with d.f. = 21 for a left-tailed *t* test.

SOLUTION

Find the critical value in the 0.05 column in the row labeled One tail, and find 21 in the left column (d.f.). The critical value is -1.721.

EXAMPLE 8–10

Find the critical values for $\alpha = 0.01$ with d.f. = 14 for a two-tailed test.

SOLUTION

Find the 0.01 column in the row labeled Two tails, and find 18 in the column labeled d.f. The critical values are -2.977 and $+2.977$.

EXAMPLE 8–11

Find the critical value for $\alpha = 0.10$ with d.f. = 8 for a right-tailed test.

SOLUTION

Find the critical value in the 0.10 column in the One tail row and 8 in the d.f. column. The critical value is 1.397.

In order to test hypotheses regarding the population mean when the standard deviation is unknown, these assumptions should be verified first.

Assumptions for the *t* Test for a Mean When σ Is Unknown

1. The sample is a random sample.
2. Either $n \geq 30$ or the population is normally distributed when $n < 30$.

In this text, the assumptions will be stated in the exercises; however, when encountering statistics in other situations, you must check to see that these assumptions have been met before proceeding.

When you test hypotheses by using the *t* test (traditional method), follow the same procedure as for the *z* test, except use Table A–5.

Step 1 State the hypotheses and identify the claim.

Step 2 Find the critical value(s) from Table A–5.

Step 3 Compute the test statistic.

Step 4 Make the decision to reject or not reject the null hypothesis.

Step 5 Summarize the results.

Remember that the t test should be used when the population is approximately normally distributed and the population standard deviation is unknown.

Examples 8–12 and 8–13 illustrate the application of the *t* test, using the traditional approach.

EXAMPLE 8–12   Hospital Infections

A medical investigation claims that the average number of infections per week at a hospital in southwestern Pennsylvania is 16.3. A random sample of 10 weeks had a mean number of 17.7 infections. The sample standard deviation is 1.8. Is there enough evidence to reject the investigator's claim at $\alpha = 0.05$? Assume the variable is normally distributed.

Source: Based on information obtained from Pennsylvania Health Care Cost Containment Council.

SOLUTION

Step 1 State the hypotheses and identify the claim. H_0: $\mu = 16.3$ (claim) and H_1: $\mu \neq 16.3$.

Step 2 Find the critical values. The critical values are $+2.262$ and -2.262 for $\alpha = 0.05$ and d.f. = 9.

Step 3 Compute the test statistic.

$$t = \frac{\overline{X} - \mu}{s/\sqrt{n}} = \frac{17.7 - 16.3}{1.8/\sqrt{10}} = 2.460$$

Step 4 Make the decision. Reject the null hypothesis since $2.460 > 2.262$. See Figure 8–20.

FIGURE 8–20

Summary of the *t* Test of Example 8–12

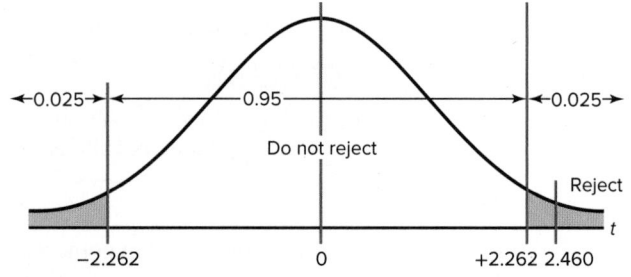

Step 5 Summarize the results. There is enough evidence to reject the claim that the average number of infections is 16.3.

EXAMPLE 8–13   Age of Automobiles

A study found that people keep an automobile on average for 6.5 years. A researcher believes that the average time a person keeps their vehicle is less than 6.5 years. A random sample of 10 automobile owners was selected and the number of years that they kept their last automobile is shown:

| 4.3 | 5.1 | 7.6 | 3.3 | 8.2 | 6.4 | 3.9 | 6.3 | 5.9 | 2.1 |

Test the claim at $\alpha = 0.10$. Assume the variable is normally distributed.

SOLUTION

Step 1   State the hypotheses and identify the claim.

$$H_0: \mu = 6.5 \quad \text{and} \quad H_1: \mu < 6.5 \text{ (claim)}$$

Step 2   Find the critical value. At $\alpha = 0.10$ and d.f. $= 9$, the critical value is -1.383.

Step 3   Compute the test statistic. In this case you must find the mean and standard deviation for the data. Use the formulas in Chapter 3 or your calculator.

$$\overline{X} = 5.31, \qquad s = 1.93$$

$$t = \frac{\overline{X} - \mu}{s/\sqrt{n}} = \frac{5.31 - 6.5}{1.93/\sqrt{10}} = -1.95$$

Step 4   Make the decision. Reject the null hypothesis since -1.95 falls in the critical region. See Figure 8–21.

FIGURE 8–21
Critical Value and Test Statistic
for Example 8–13

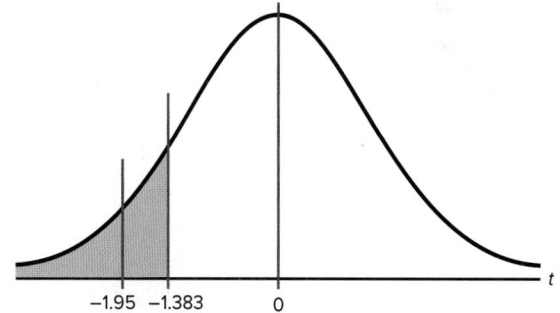

$-1.95 \quad -1.383 \qquad 0$

t

Step 5   Summarize the results. There is enough evidence to support the claim that the number of years a person keeps their car is less than 6.5 years.

The *P*-values for the *t* test can be found by using Table A–5; however, specific *P*-values for *t* tests cannot be obtained from the table since only selected values of α (for example, 0.01, 0.05) are given. To find specific *P*-values for *t* tests, you would need a table similar to Table A–4 for each degree of freedom. Since this is not practical, only *intervals* can be found for *P*-values. Examples 8–14 to 8–16 show how to use Table A–5 to determine intervals for *P*-values for the *t* test.

EXAMPLE 8–14

Find the *P*-value when the *t* test statistic is 2.056, the sample size is 11, and the test is right-tailed.

SOLUTION

To get the *P*-value, look across the row with 10 degrees of freedom (d.f. $= n - 1$) in Table A–5 and find the two values that 2.056 falls between. They are 1.812 and 2.228. Since this is a right-tailed test, look up to the row labeled One tail, α and find the two α values corresponding to 1.812 and 2.228. They are 0.05 and 0.025, respectively. See Figure 8–22.

Confidence intervals	80%	90%	95%	98%	99%
One tail, α	0.10	(0.05)	(0.025)	0.01	0.005
d.f. Two tails, α	0.20	0.10	0.05	0.02	0.01
1	3.078	6.314	12.706	31.821	63.657
2	1.886	2.920	4.303	6.965	9.925
3	1.638	2.353	3.182	4.541	5.841
4	1.533	2.132	2.776	3.747	4.604
5	1.476	2.015	2.571	3.365	4.032
6	1.440	1.943	2.447	3.143	3.707
7	1.415	1.895	2.365	2.998	3.499
8	1.397	1.860	2.306	2.896	3.355
9	1.383	1.833	2.262	2.821	3.250
(10)	1.372 →	(1.812) *	(2.228)	2.764	3.169
11	1.363	1.796	2.201	2.718	3.106
12	1.356	1.782	2.179	2.681	3.055
13	1.350	1.771	2.160	2.650	3.012
14	1.345	1.761	2.145	2.624	2.977
15	1.341	1.753	2.131	2.602	2.947
⋮	⋮	⋮	⋮	⋮	⋮
(z) ∞	1.282	1.645	1.960	2.326	2.576

*2.056 falls between 1.812 and 2.228.

Hence, the *P*-value would be contained in the interval $0.025 <$ *P*-value < 0.05. This means that the *P*-value is between 0.025 and 0.05. If α were 0.05, you would reject the null hypothesis since the *P*-value is less than 0.05. But if α were 0.01, you would not reject the null hypothesis since the *P*-value is greater than 0.01. (Actually, it is greater than 0.025.)

EXAMPLE 8–15

Find the *P*-value when the *t* test statistic is 2.983, the sample size is 6, and the test is two-tailed.

SOLUTION

To get the *P*-value, look across the row with d.f. = 5 in Table A–5 and find the two values that 2.983 falls between. They are 2.571 and 3.365. Then look up the row labeled Two tails, α to find the corresponding α values.

In this case, they are 0.05 and 0.02. Hence, the *P*-value is contained in the interval $0.02 <$ *P*-value < 0.05. This means that the *P*-value is between 0.02 and 0.05. In this case, if $\alpha = 0.05$, the null hypothesis can be rejected since *P*-value < 0.05; but if $\alpha = 0.01$, the null hypothesis cannot be rejected since *P*-value > 0.01 (actually *P*-value > 0.02).

Note: **Since many of you will be using calculators or computer programs that give the specific *P*-value for the *t* test and other tests presented later in this textbook, these specific values, in addition to the intervals, will be given for the answers to the examples and exercises.**

The *P*-value obtained from a calculator for Example 8–14 is 0.033. The *P*-value obtained from a calculator for Example 8–15 is 0.031.

To test hypotheses using the *P*-value method, follow the same steps as explained in Section 8–2. These steps are repeated here.

Step 1   State the hypotheses and identify the claim.

Step 2   Compute the test statistic.

Step 3   Find the *P*-value.

Step 4   Make the decision.

Step 5   Summarize the results.

This method is shown in Example 8–16.

EXAMPLE 8–16   Jogger's Oxygen Uptake

A physician claims that joggers' maximal volume oxygen uptake is greater than the average of all adults. A random sample of 15 joggers has a mean of 40.6 milliliters per kilogram (ml/kg) and a standard deviation of 6 ml/kg. If the average of all adults is 36.7 ml/kg, is there enough evidence to support the physician's claim at $\alpha = 0.05$? Assume the variable is normally distributed.

SOLUTION

Step 1   State the hypotheses and identify the claim.

$$H_0: \mu = 36.7 \quad \text{and} \quad H_1: \mu > 36.7 \text{ (claim)}$$

Step 2   Compute the test statistic. The test statistic is

$$t = \frac{\overline{X} - \mu}{s/\sqrt{n}} = \frac{40.6 - 36.7}{6/\sqrt{15}} = 2.517$$

Step 3   Find the *P*-value. Looking across the row with d.f. = 14 in Table A–5, you see that 2.517 falls between 2.145 and 2.624, corresponding to $\alpha = 0.025$ and $\alpha = 0.01$ since this is a right-tailed test. Hence, *P*-value > 0.01 and *P*-value < 0.025, or 0.01 < *P*-value < 0.025. That is, the *P*-value is somewhere between 0.01 and 0.025. (The *P*-value obtained from a calculator is 0.012.)

Step 4   Reject the null hypothesis since *P*-value < 0.05 (that is, *P*-value < α).

Step 5   There is enough evidence to support the claim that the joggers' maximal volume oxygen uptake is greater than 36.7 ml/kg.

Interesting Fact

The area of Alaska contains $\frac{1}{6}$ of the total area of the United States.

Students sometimes have difficulty deciding whether to use the *z* test or *t* test. The rules are the same as those pertaining to confidence intervals.

1. If σ is known, use the *z* test. The variable must be normally distributed if $n < 30$.

2. If σ is unknown but $n \geq 30$, use the *t* test.

3. If σ is unknown and $n < 30$, use the *t* test. (The population must be approximately normally distributed.)

These rules are summarized in Figure 8–23.

A study conducted at the University of Pittsburgh showed that hospital patients in rooms with lots of sunlight required less pain medication the day after surgery and during their total stay in the hospital than patients who were in darker rooms.

Patients in the sunny rooms averaged 3.2 milligrams of pain reliever per hour for their total stay as opposed to 4.1 milligrams per hour for those in darker rooms. This study compared two groups of patients. Although no statistical tests were mentioned in the article, what statistical test do you think the researchers used to compare the groups?

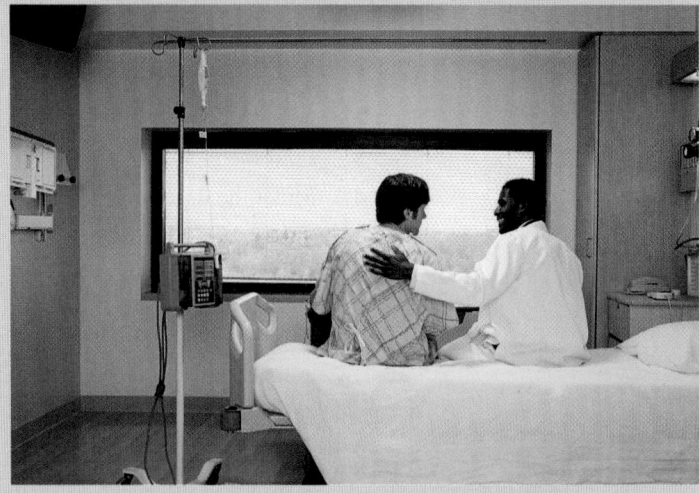

© Jupiterimages/Imagesource

FIGURE 8–23

Using the *z* or *t* Test

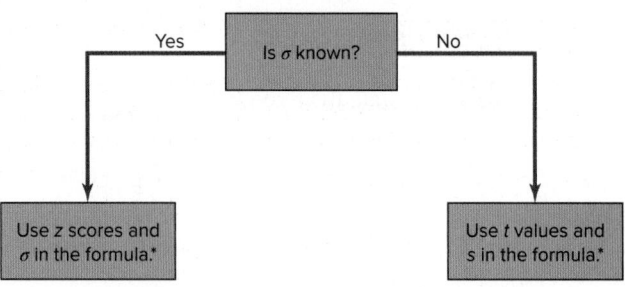

*If *n* < 30, the variable must be normally distributed.

≜ Applying the Concepts 8–3

How Much Nicotine Is in Those Cigarettes?

A tobacco company claims that its best-selling cigarettes contain at most 40 mg of nicotine. This claim is tested at the 1% significance level by using the results of 15 randomly selected cigarettes. The mean is 42.6 mg and the standard deviation is 3.7 mg. Evidence suggests that nicotine is normally distributed. Information from a computer output of the hypothesis test is listed.

Sample mean = 42.6   *P*-value = 0.008
Sample standard deviation = 3.7   Significance level = 0.01
Sample size = 15   Test statistic $t = 2.72155$
Degrees of freedom = 14   Critical value $t = 2.62449$

1. What are the degrees of freedom?
2. Is this a *z* or *t* test?
3. Is this a comparison of one or two samples?
4. Is this a right-tailed, left-tailed, or two-tailed test?
5. From observing the *P*-value, what would you conclude?
6. By comparing the test statistic to the critical value, what would you conclude?
7. Is there a conflict in this output? Explain.
8. What has been proved in this study?

See page 487 for the answers.

⬛ Exercises 8–3

1. In what ways is the *t* distribution similar to the standard normal distribution? In what ways is the *t* distribution different from the standard normal distribution?

2. What are the degrees of freedom for the *t* test?

3. Find the critical value (or values) for the *t* test for each.
   a. $n = 12$, $\alpha = 0.05$, two-tailed ±2.201
   b. $n = 22$, $\alpha = 0.01$, right-tailed 2.518
   c. $n = 9$, $\alpha = 0.025$, right-tailed 2.306
   d. $n = 5$, $\alpha = 0.005$, left-tailed −4.604

4. Find the critical value (or values) for the *t* test for each.
   a. $n = 16$, $\alpha = 0.02$, two-tailed ±2.602
   b. $n = 27$, $\alpha = 0.01$, right-tailed 2.479
   c. $n = 24$, $\alpha = 0.005$, left-tailed −2.807
   d. $n = 8$, $\alpha = 0.05$, two-tailed ±2.365

5. Using Table A–5, find the *P*-value interval for each test statistic.
   a. $t = 2.321$, $n = 15$, right-tailed $0.01 < P\text{-value} < 0.025$ (0.018)
   b. $t = 1.945$, $n = 28$, two-tailed $0.05 < P\text{-value} < 0.10$ (0.062)
   c. $t = -1.267$, $n = 8$, left-tailed $0.10 < P\text{-value} < 0.25$ (0.123)
   d. $t = 1.562$, $n = 17$, two-tailed $0.10 < P\text{-value} < 0.20$ (0.138)

6. Using Table A–5, find the *P*-value interval for each test statistic.
   a. $t = 3.025$, $n = 24$, right-tailed $P\text{-value} < 0.005$ (0.003)
   b. $t = -1.145$, $n = 5$, left-tailed $0.10 < P\text{-value} < 0.25$ (0.158)
   c. $t = 2.179$, $n = 13$, two-tailed $P\text{-value} = 0.05$ (0.05)
   d. $t = 0.665$, $n = 10$, right-tailed $P\text{-value} > 0.25$ (0.261)

For Exercises 7 through 23, perform each of the following steps.
   a. State the hypotheses and identify the claim.
   b. Find the critical value(s) or use the *P*-value method.
   c. Find the test statistic.
   d. Make the decision.
   e. Summarize the results.

Use the traditional method of hypothesis testing unless the P-value method is specified by your instructor.

Assume that the population is approximately normally distributed.

7. **Cigarette Smoking** A researcher found that a cigarette smoker smokes on average 31 cigarettes a day. A smoker feels that this average is too high and selects a random sample of 10 smokers and found that the mean number of cigarettes they smoked per day was 28. The sample standard deviation was 2.7. At $\alpha = 0.05$ is there enough evidence to support the smoker's claim?

8. **Cost of Braces** The average cost for teeth straightening with metal braces is approximately $5400. A nationwide franchise thinks that its cost is below that figure. A random sample of 28 patients across the country had an average cost of $5250 with a standard deviation of $629. At $\alpha = 0.025$, can it be concluded that the mean is less than $5400?

9. **Waiting Times for Family Physicians** A researcher selected a random sample of 10 patients of a family physician and found the waiting times shown. At $\alpha = 0.05$, can it be concluded that the waiting times are less than the national average of 19 minutes?

21.2	18.6	16.2	19.3	14.7
17.1	16.8	15.9	19.5	17.6

10. **Number of Words in a Novel** The National Novel Writing Association states that the average novel is at least 50,000 words. A particularly ambitious writing club at a college-preparatory high school had randomly selected members with works of the following lengths. At $\alpha = 0.10$, is there sufficient evidence to conclude that the mean length is greater than 50,000 words?

48,972	50,100	51,560
49,800	50,020	49,900
52,193		

11. **Television Viewing by Teens** Teens are reported to watch the fewest total hours of television per week of all the demographic groups. The average television viewing for teens on Sunday from 1:00 to 7:00 P.M. is 58 minutes. A random sample of local teens disclosed the following times for Sunday afternoon television viewing. At $\alpha = 0.01$, can it be concluded that the average is greater than the national viewing time? (*Note:* Change all times to minutes.)

2:30	2:00	1:30	3:20
1:00	2:15	1:50	2:10
1:30	2:30		

Source: World Almanac.

12. **Chocolate Chip Cookie Calories** The average 1-ounce chocolate chip cookie contains 110 calories. A random sample of 15 different brands of 1-ounce chocolate chip cookies resulted in the following calorie amounts. At the $\alpha = 0.01$ level, is there sufficient evidence that the average calorie content is greater than 110 calories?

100	125	150	160	185	125	155	145	160
100	150	140	135	120	110			

Source: The Doctor's Pocket Calorie, Fat, and Carbohydrate Counter.

13. **Times for a Bicycle Commute to Work** The average time for a bicycle commute to work is 26.4 minutes. A researcher randomly surveyed 12 bicycle commuters in a large city and found the times for the commutes shown. At $\alpha = 0.10$, are the times for these commuters not equal to 26.4 minutes?

30.1	29.4	27.3	23.7	26.8	24.3
27.0	30.1	28.3	24.6	31.8	25.9

14. **Internet Visits** A U.S. Web Usage Snapshot indicated a monthly average of 36 Internet visits a particular website per user from home. A random sample of 24 Internet users yielded a sample mean of 42.1 visits with a standard deviation of 5.3. At the 0.01 level of significance, can it be concluded that this differs from the national average?

Source: New York Times Almanac.

15. Cell Phone Bills The average monthly cell phone bill was reported to be $50.07 by the U.S. Wireless Industry. Random sampling of a large cell phone company found the following monthly cell phone charges (in dollars):

55.83	49.88	62.98	70.42
60.47	52.45	49.20	50.02
58.60	51.29		

At the 0.05 level of significance, can it be concluded that the average phone bill has increased?

Source: World Almanac.

16. Teaching Assistants' Stipends A random sample of stipends of teaching assistants in economics is listed. Is there sufficient evidence at the $\alpha = 0.05$ level to conclude that the average stipend differs from $15,000? The stipends listed (in dollars) are for the academic year.

14,000	18,000	12,000	14,356	13,185
13,419	14,000	11,981	17,604	12,283
16,338	15,000			

Source: Chronicle of Higher Education.

17. Response Times for EMS Vehicles The average response time for Emergency Medical Services (EMS) vehicles is 19.3 minutes. A researcher randomly selects 15 EMS response times for a specific facility and found that the sample has a mean of 18.4 minutes and a standard deviation of 2.6 minutes. At $\alpha = 0.05$, can it be concluded that the response times for the EMS at this facility is less than 19.3 minutes?

18. Cell Phone Call Lengths The average local cell phone call length was reported to be 2.27 minutes. A random sample of 20 phone calls showed an average of 2.98 minutes in length with a standard deviation of 0.98 minute. At $\alpha = 0.05$, can it be concluded that the average differs from the population average?

Source: World Almanac.

19. Computer Repair Costs A recent survey found that the average computer repair cost for a computer is $148.27. A random sample of 16 randomly selected computer costs at a computer repair store had a mean of $150.06 with a standard deviation of $5.26. At $\alpha = 0.10$, can it be concluded that the average computer repair cost at this store is greater than $148.27?

20. Average Family Size The average family size was reported as 3.18. A random sample of families in a particular school district resulted in the following family sizes:

5	4	5	4	4	3	6	4	3	3	5
6	3	3	2	7	4	5	2	2	2	3
5	2									

At $\alpha = 0.05$, does the average family size differ from the national average?

Source: New York Times Almanac.

21. Doctor Visits A report by the Gallup Poll stated that on average a woman visits her physician 5.8 times a year. A researcher randomly selects 20 women and obtained these data.

3	2	1	3	7	2	9	4	6	6
8	0	5	6	4	2	1	3	4	1

At $\alpha = 0.05$, can it be concluded that the average is still 5.8 visits per year? Use the P-value method.

22. Number of Jobs The U.S. Bureau of Labor and Statistics reported that a person between the ages of 18 and 34 has had an average of 9.2 jobs. To see if this average is correct, a researcher selected a random sample of 8 workers between the ages of 18 and 34 and asked how many different places they had worked. The results were as follows:

8	12	15	6	1	9	13	2

At $\alpha = 0.05$, can it be concluded that the mean is 9.2? Use the P-value method. Give one reason why the respondents might not have given the exact number of jobs that they have worked.

23. Police Officer Salaries At this writing the average salary of a police officer is $61,470. A researcher randomly selects 28 police officers in a large city and found that the mean salary of the officers is $61,543. The sample standard deviation is $210.53. At $\alpha = 0.10$, can it be concluded that the average salary of police officers in this city is greater than $61,470?

≡ Technology   Step by Step

TI-84 Plus

Step by Step

Hypothesis Test for the Mean and the t Distribution (Data)

1. Enter the data values into L_1.

2. Press **STAT** and move the cursor to TESTS.

3. Press **2** for T-Test.

4. Move the cursor to Data and press **ENTER.**

5. Type in the appropriate values.

6. Move the cursor to the appropriate alternative hypothesis and press **ENTER.**

7. Move the cursor to Calculate and press **ENTER.**

Hypothesis Test for the Mean and the *t* Distribution (Statistics)

1. Press **STAT** and move the cursor to TESTS.
2. Press **2** for T-Test.
3. Move the cursor to Stats and press **ENTER**.
4. Type in the appropriate values.
5. Move the cursor to the appropriate alternative hypothesis and press **ENTER**.
6. Move the cursor to Calculate and press **ENTER**.

Example TI8–3

For Example 8–16, test the claim that the joggers' maximal volume oxygen uptake is greater than 36.7 ml/kg.

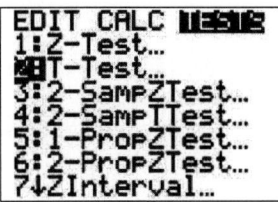  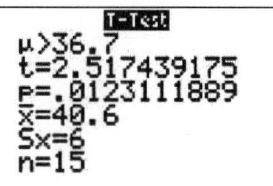

Reject the null hypothesis since the *P*-value of 0.0123 is less than $\alpha = 0.05$.

EXCEL
Step by Step

Hypothesis Test for the Mean: *t* Test

Excel does not have a procedure to conduct a hypothesis test for the mean. However, you may conduct the test of the mean using the MegaStat Add-in available in your online resources. If you have not installed this add-in, do so, following the instructions from the Chapter 1 Excel Step by Step.

Substitute Teachers' Salaries

An educator claims that the average salary of substitute teachers in school districts in Allegheny County, Pennsylvania, is less than $60 per day. A random sample of eight school districts is selected, and the daily salaries (in dollars) are shown. Is there enough evidence to support the educator's claim at $\alpha = 0.10$? Assume the variable is normally distributed.

$$60 \quad 56 \quad 60 \quad 55 \quad 70 \quad 55 \quad 60 \quad 55$$

Source: Pittsburgh Tribune-Review.

     The MegaStat *t* test uses the *P*-value method. Therefore, it is not necessary to enter a significance level.

1. Enter the data into column A of a new worksheet.
2. From the toolbar, select Add-Ins, **MegaStat>Hypothesis Tests>Mean vs. Hypothesized Value**. *Note:* You may need to open MegaStat from the MegaStat.xls file on your computer's hard drive.
3. Select data input and type **A1:A8** as the Input Range.
4. Type **60** for the Hypothesized mean and select the "less than" Alternative.
5. Select *t* test and click [OK].

The result of the procedure is shown next.

Hypothesis Test: Mean vs. Hypothesized Value

60.000	Hypothesized value
58.875	Mean data
5.083	Standard deviation
1.797	Standard error
8	*n*
7	d.f.

−0.63	*t*
0.2756	*P*-value (one-tailed, lower)

MINITAB

Step by Step

Hypothesis Test for the Mean and the *t* Distribution

MINITAB can be used to look up a critical value of *t*.

Example 8–8

Find the critical *t* value for $\alpha = 0.05$ with d.f. = 16 for a right-tailed *t* test.

Step 1 To find the critical value of *t* for a right-tailed test, select **Graph>Probability Distribution Plot,** then **View Probability,** and then click **[OK].**

Step 2 Change the Distribution to a *t* distribution with Degrees of freedom equal to **16.**

Step 3 Click the tab for **Shaded Area.**

   a) Select the radio button for **Probability.**

   b) Select **Right Tail.**

   c) Type in the value of alpha for Probability, **0.05.**

   d) Click **[OK].**

The critical value of *t* to three decimal places is 1.746.

   You may click the Edit Last Dialog button and then change the settings for additional critical values.

Example 8–13 Aspirin Tablets

MINITAB will calculate the test statistic and *P*-value from the data.

Step 1 Type the data into column C1. Label the column Tablets.

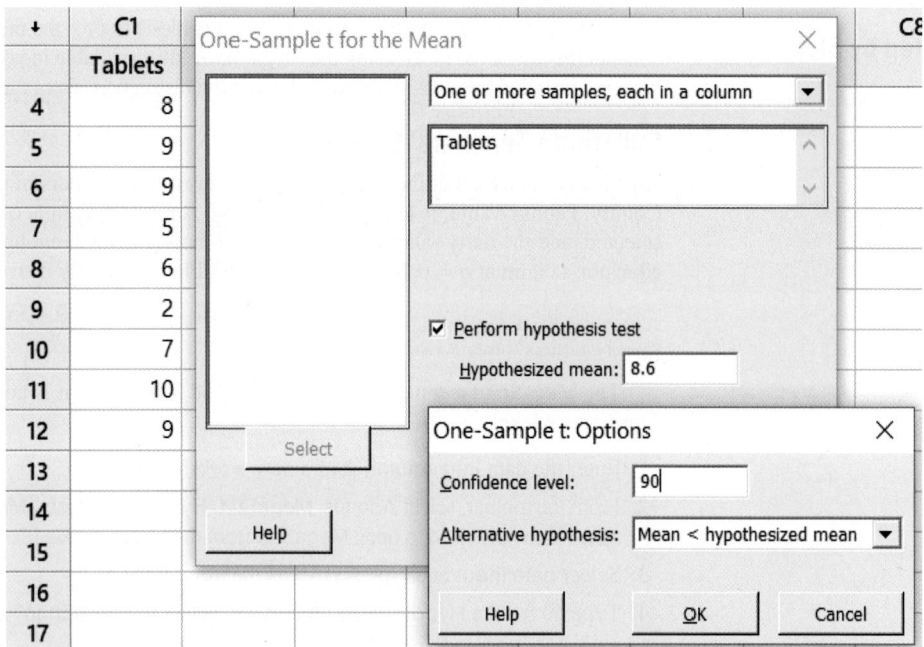

Step 2 Select **Stat>Basic Statistics> 1-sample t.**

Step 3 Select **One or more samples, each in a column,** if not already selected.

   To select the data, click inside the next dialog box; then select C1 Tablets from the list.

Step 4 Select the box for Perform hypothesis test, and then type in the Hypothesized value of **8.6.**

Step 5 Click the button for **[Options].**

   a) Type the default confidence level 90.

   b) Click the drop-down menu for the Alternative hypothesis, **"Mean < hypothesized mean."**

Step 6   Click [OK] twice.

The test statistic is −2.58. Since the *P*-value of 0.013 is less than alpha, the null hypothesis is rejected.

One-Sample T: Tablets

```
Test of μ = 8.6 vs < 8.6


Variable   N   Mean   StDev   SE Mean   90% Upper Bound     T      P
Tablets    12  6.833  2.368   0.683                7.765  -2.58  0.013
```

8–4   *z* Test for a Proportion

OBJECTIVE 7

Test proportions, using the *z* test.

Many hypothesis-testing situations involve proportions. Recall from Chapter 7 that a *proportion* is the same as a percentage of the population.

These data were obtained from *The Book of Odds* by Michael D. Shook and Robert L. Shook (New York: Penguin Putnam, Inc.):

- 59% of consumers purchase gifts for their fathers.
- 85% of people over 21 said they have entered a sweepstakes.
- 51% of Americans buy generic products.
- 35% of Americans go out for dinner once a week.

A hypothesis test involving a population proportion can be considered as a binomial experiment when there are only two outcomes and the probability of a success does not change from trial to trial. Recall from Section 5–3 that the mean is $\mu = np$ and the standard deviation is $\sigma = \sqrt{npq}$ for the binomial distribution.

Since a normal distribution can be used to approximate the binomial distribution when $np \geq 5$ and $nq \geq 5$, the standard normal distribution can be used to test hypotheses for proportions.

Formula for the *z* Test for Proportions

$$z = \frac{\hat{p} - p}{\sqrt{pq/n}}$$

where $\hat{p} = \frac{X}{n}$ sample proportion

p = population proportion
n = sample size

The formula is derived from the normal approximation to the binomial and follows the general formula

$$\text{Test statistic} = \frac{(\text{observed value}) - (\text{expected value})}{\text{standard error}}$$

We obtain $\hat{p}$ from the sample (i.e., observed value), p is the expected value (i.e., hypothesized population proportion), and $\sqrt{pq/n}$ is the standard error.

The formula $z = \dfrac{\hat{p} - p}{\sqrt{pq/n}}$ can be derived from the formula $z = \dfrac{X - \mu}{\sigma}$ by substituting $\mu = np$ and $\sigma = \sqrt{npq}$ and then dividing both numerator and denominator by n. Some algebra is used. See Exercise 23 in this section.

The assumptions for testing a proportion are given next.

> **Assumptions for Testing a Proportion**
>
> 1. The sample is a random sample.
> 2. The conditions for a binomial experiment are satisfied. (See Chapter 5.)
> 3. $np \geq 5$ and $nq \geq 5$.

In this book, the assumptions will be stated in the exercises; however, when encountering statistics in other situations, you must check to see that these assumptions have been met before proceeding.

The steps for hypothesis testing are the same as those shown in Section 8–3. Table A–4 is used to find critical values and *P*-values.

Examples 8–17 to 8–19 show the traditional method of hypothesis testing. Example 8–20 shows the *P*-value method.

Sometimes it is necessary to find $\hat{p}$, as shown in Examples 8–17, 8–19, and 8–20, and sometimes $\hat{p}$ is given in the exercise. See Example 8–18.

EXAMPLE 8–17   Black and White Dreams

A researcher claims, based on information obtained from the *Harper's Index,* that 23% of Americans say that they dream in black and white. To test the claim, the researcher randomly selected 100 Americans and found that 28 said that they dreamed in black and white. At $\alpha = 0.05$, is there enough evidence to reject the claim?

SOLUTION

Step 1   State the hypotheses and identify the claim.

$$H_0: p = 0.23 \text{ (claim)} \qquad \text{and} \qquad H_1: p \neq 0.23$$

Step 2   Find the critical values. Since $\alpha = 0.05$ and the test is two-tailed, the critical values are ± 1.96.

Step 3   Compute the test statistic. First, it is necessary to find $\hat{p}$.

$$\hat{p} = \frac{X}{n} = \frac{28}{100} = 0.28 \qquad p = 0.23; \qquad q = 1 - 0.23 = 0.77$$

Substitute in the formula.

$$z = \frac{\hat{p} - p}{\sqrt{pq/n}} = \frac{0.28 - 0.23}{\sqrt{(0.23)(0.77)/100}} = 1.19$$

Step 4   Make the decision. Do not reject the null hypothesis since the test statistic falls in the noncritical region. See Figure 8–24.

FIGURE 8–24

Critical Value and Test Statistic for Example 8–17

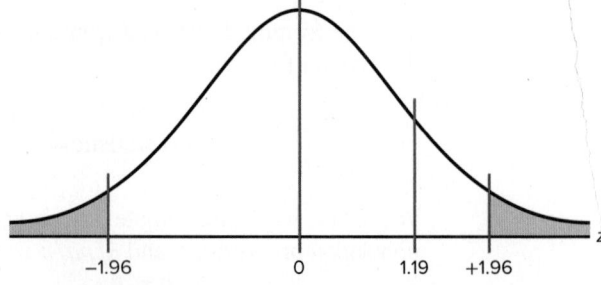

Step 5   Summarize the results. There is not enough evidence to reject the claim that 23% of Americans dream in black and white.

EXAMPLE 8–18   Caesarean Babies

A report stated that 31.9% of babies are delivered by Caesarean section. A researcher believes that the percentage is less than 31.9% in a large hospital. The researcher randomly selected 50 newborn infants and found that 13 were born by Caesarean section. At $\alpha = 0.01$, is there enough evidence to support the claim?

SOLUTION

Step 1 State the hypotheses and identify the claim.

$$H_0: p = 0.319 \quad \text{and} \quad H_1: p < 0.319 \text{ (claim)}$$

Step 2 Find the critical value. Since $\alpha = 0.01$ and the test is one-tailed, the critical value is -2.33.

Step 3 Compute the test statistic.

$$\hat{p} = \frac{13}{50} = 0.26, \quad q = 1 - p = 1 - 0.319 = 0.681$$

Substitute in the formula.

$$z = \frac{\hat{p} - p}{\sqrt{pq/n}} = \frac{0.26 - 0.319}{\sqrt{\dfrac{(0.319)(0.681)}{50}}} = -0.895$$

Step 4 Make the decision. Do not reject the null hypothesis since the test statistic does not fall in the critical region. See Figure 8–25.

FIGURE 8–25
Critical Value and Test
Statistic for Example 8–18

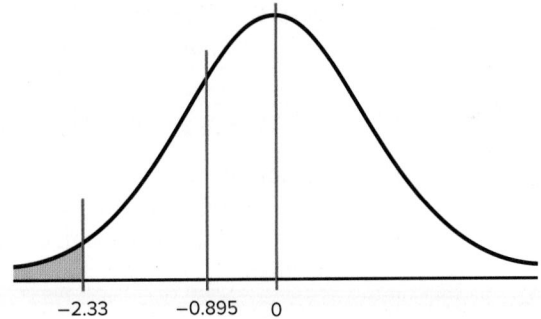

$-2.33 \quad -0.895 \quad 0$

Step 5 Summarize the results. There is not enough evidence to support the claim that the proportion of Caesarian births is less than 31.9%. The test statistic does not fall in the rejection region.

EXAMPLE 8–19   Replacing $1 Bills with $1 Coins

A statistician read that at least 77% of the population oppose replacing $1 bills with $1 coins. To see if this claim is valid, the statistician selected a random sample of 80 people and found that 55 were opposed to replacing the $1 bills. At $\alpha = 0.01$, test the claim that at least 77% of the population are opposed to the change.

Source: USA TODAY.

SOLUTION

Step 1 State the hypotheses and identify the claim.

$$H_0: p = 0.77 \text{ (claim)} \quad \text{and} \quad H_1: p < 0.77$$

Step 2   Find the critical value(s). Since $\alpha = 0.01$ and the test is left-tailed, the critical value is -2.33.

Step 3   Compute the test statistic.

$$\hat{p} = \frac{X}{n} = \frac{55}{80} = 0.6875$$

$$p = 0.77 \qquad \text{and} \qquad q = 1 - 0.77 = 0.23$$

$$z = \frac{\hat{p} - p}{\sqrt{pq/n}} = \frac{0.6875 - 0.77}{\sqrt{(0.77)(0.23)/80}} = -1.75$$

Step 4   Do not reject the null hypothesis, since the test statistic does not fall in the critical region, as shown in Figure 8–26.

FIGURE 8–26
Critical Values and Test
Statistic for Example 8–19

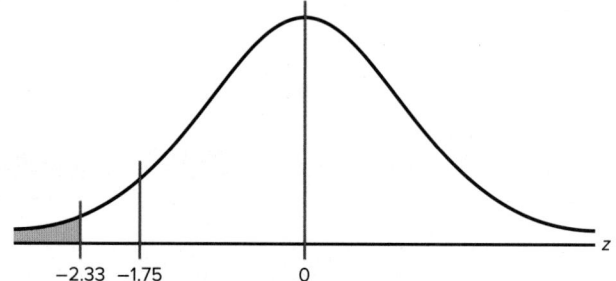

-2.33 -1.75 0

Step 5   There is not enough evidence to reject the claim that at least 77% of the population oppose replacing \$1 bills with \$1 coins.

EXAMPLE 8–20   Attorney Advertisements

An attorney claims that more than 25% of all lawyers advertise. A random sample of 200 lawyers in a certain city showed that 63 had used some form of advertising. At $\alpha = 0.05$, is there enough evidence to support the attorney's claim? Use the P-value method.

SOLUTION

Step 1   State the hypotheses and identify the claim.

$$H_0\colon p = 0.25 \qquad \text{and} \qquad H_1\colon p > 0.25 \text{ (claim)}$$

Step 2   Compute the test statistic.

$$\hat{p} = \frac{X}{n} = \frac{63}{200} = 0.315$$

$$p = 0.25 \qquad \text{and} \qquad q = 1 - 0.25 = 0.75$$

$$z = \frac{\hat{p} - p}{\sqrt{pq/n}} = \frac{0.315 - 0.25}{\sqrt{(0.25)(0.75)/200}} = 2.12$$

Step 3   Find the P-value. The area under the curve in Table A–4 for $z = 2.12$ is 0.9830. Subtracting the area from 1.0000, you get $1.0000 - 0.9830 = 0.0170$. The P-value is 0.0170.

Step 4   Reject the null hypothesis, since $0.0170 < 0.05$ (that is, P-value $< \alpha$). See Figure 8–27.

FIGURE 8–27
P-Value and α Value for Example 8–20

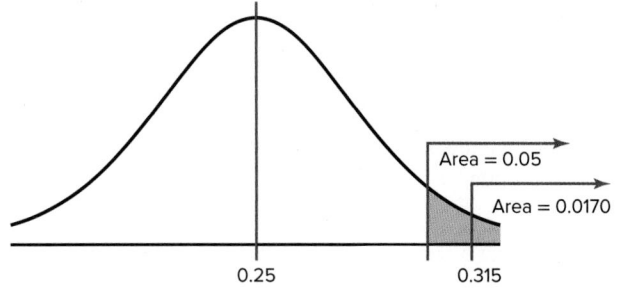

Step 5   There is enough evidence to support the attorney's claim that more than 25% of the lawyers use some form of advertising.

Applying the Concepts 8–4

Quitting Smoking

Assume you are part of a research team that compares products designed to help people quit smoking. Condor Consumer Products Company would like more specific details about the study to be made available to the scientific community. Review the following and then answer the questions about how you would have conducted the study.

New StopSmoke

No method has been proved more effective. StopSmoke provides significant advantages over all other methods. StopSmoke is simpler to use, and it requires no weaning. StopSmoke is also significantly less expensive than the leading brands. StopSmoke's superiority has been proved in two independent studies.

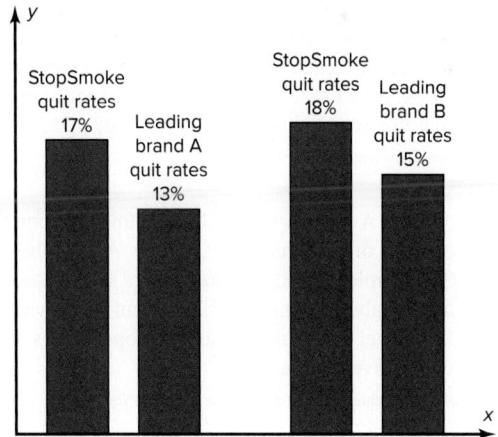

1. What were the statistical hypotheses?

2. What were the null hypotheses?

3. What were the alternative hypotheses?

4. Were any statistical tests run?

5. Were one- or two-tailed tests run?

6. What were the levels of significance?

7. If a type I error was committed, explain what it would have been.

8. If a type II error was committed, explain what it would have been.

9. What did the studies prove?

10. Two statements are made about significance. One states that StopSmoke provides significant advantages, and the other states that StopSmoke is significantly less expensive than other leading brands. Are they referring to statistical significance? What other type of significance is there?

See pages 487–488 for the answers.

⬒ Exercises 8–4

1. Give three examples of proportions. Answers will vary.

2. Why is a proportion considered a binomial variable?

3. When you are testing hypotheses by using proportions, what are the necessary requirements? $np \geq 5$ and $nq \geq 5$

4. What are the mean and the standard deviation of a proportion? $\mu = p$; $\sigma = \sqrt{pq/n}$

For Exercises 5 through 20, perform each of the following steps.

    a. State the hypotheses and identify the claim.

    b. Find the critical value(s) or use the *P*-value method.

    c. Compute the test statistic.

    d. Make the decision.

    e. Summarize the results.

Use the traditional method of hypothesis testing unless the P-value method is specified by your instructor.

5. **Exercise** A survey by Louis Harris and Associates found the 25% of adults never exercise at all. A researcher selected a random sample of 120 adults and found that 33 adults said that they do not exercise at all. At $\alpha = 0.10$, is there sufficient evidence that more than 25% of adults do not exercise at all?

6. **Stocks and Mutual Fund Ownership** It has been found that 50.3% of U.S. households own stocks and mutual funds. A random sample of 300 heads of households indicated that 171 owned some type of stock. At what level of significance would you conclude that this was a significant difference?
Source: www.census.gov

7. **Money Arguments** A survey found that one in five couples often argue about money. A random sample of 200 couples found that 36 couples said that they often argued about money. Is there significant evidence at the 0.05 level to conclude that the proportion is less than one in five couples?
Source: Center for the New Middle Class Survey

8. **Female Physicians** The percentage of physicians who are women is 35.2%. In a survey of physicians employed by a large university health system, 56 of 120 randomly selected physicians were women. Is there sufficient evidence at the 0.05 level of significance to conclude that the proportion of women physicians at the university health system exceeds 35.2%?
Source: AAMC Association of American Medical Colleges

9. **Returned Money** A *Reader's Digest* survey found that 73% of the subjects said that their family doctor would be most likely to return $100 that they lost. A random sample of 80 college students found that 62 said that they believed that their family doctor would return $100 if they lost it in the physician's office. At $\alpha = 0.01$, can it be concluded that more than 73% of them would say that their family doctor would return $100 if they lost it in the physician's office?

10. **Undergraduate Enrollment** It has been found that 85.6% of all enrolled college and university students in the United States are undergraduates. A random sample of 500 enrolled college students in a particular state revealed that 420 of them were undergraduates. Is there sufficient evidence to conclude that the proportion differs from the national percentage? Use $\alpha = 0.05$.
Source: Time Almanac.

11. **Automobiles Purchased** An automobile owner found that 20 years ago, 76% of Americans said that they would prefer to purchase an American automobile. He believes that the number is much less than 76% today. He selected a random sample of 56 Americans and found that 38 said that they would prefer an American automobile. Can it be concluded that the percentage today is less than 76%? At $\alpha = 0.01$, is he correct?
Source: Opinion Research Corporation.

12. **Television Set Ownership** According to Nielsen Media Research, of all the U.S. households that owned at least one television set, 83% had two or more sets. A local cable company canvassing the town to promote a new cable service found that of the 300 randomly selected households visited, 240 had two or more television sets. At $\alpha = 0.05$, is there sufficient evidence to conclude that the proportion is less than the one in the report?
Source: World Almanac.

13. **Legalized Marijuana** A survey found that 56% of voters believe that marijuana should be legalized for recreational use. A random sample of 60 nineteen-year-old students showed that 43 said that marijuana should be legalized for recreational use. Can it be concluded at $\alpha = 0.05$ that the proportion of nineteen-year-old students who believe that marijuana should be legalized for recreational use is the same as the proportion of voters?
Source: Civis Analytics Survey

14. **Natural Gas Heat** The Energy Information Administration reported that 51.7% of homes in the United States were heated by natural gas. A random sample of 200 homes found that 115 were heated by natural gas. Does the evidence support the claim, or has the percentage changed? Use $\alpha = 0.05$ and the *P*-value method. What could be different if the sample were taken in a different geographic area?

15. Youth Smoking Researchers suspect that 37.3% of all high school students vape. At Wilson High School, a randomly selected sample of 300 students found that 105 students vape. At $\alpha = 0.05$, test the claim that less than 37.3% of all high school students vape. Use the *P*-value method.

16. Exercise to Reduce Stress A survey by *Men's Health* magazine stated that 14% of men said they used exercise to reduce stress. Use $\alpha = 0.10$. A random sample of 100 men was selected, and 10 said that they used exercise to relieve stress. Use the *P*-value method to test the claim. Could the results be generalized to all adult Americans?

17. Borrowing Library Books For Americans using library services, the American Library Association (ALA) claims that 67% borrow books. A library director feels that this is not true so he randomly selects 100 borrowers and finds that 82 borrowed books. Can he show that the ALA claim is incorrect? Use $\alpha = 0.05$.

Source: American Library Association; *USA TODAY.*

18. Doctoral Students' Salaries Nationally, at least 60% of Ph.D. students have paid assistantships. A college dean feels that this is not true in his state, so he randomly selects 50 Ph.D. students and finds that 26 have assistantships. At $\alpha = 0.05$, is the dean correct?

Source: U.S. Department of Education, *Chronicle of Higher Education.*

19. Football Injuries A report by the NCAA states that 57.6% of football injuries occur during practices. A head trainer claims that this is too high for his conference, so he randomly selects 36 injuries and finds that 17 occurred during practices. Is his claim correct, at $\alpha = 0.05$?

Source: NCAA Sports Medicine Handbook.

20. Life Satisfaction A survey reported by RH Bruskin Associates found that 77% of adult Americans are satisfied with their lives. A researcher selects a random sample of 250 adults and found that 202 stated that they were satisfied with their lives. At $\alpha = 0.01$, is there sufficient evidence to conclude that the proportion of adults who are satisfied with their lives is more than 77%?

Extending the Concepts

When np *or* nq *is not 5 or more, the binomial table (Table A–2 in Appendix A) must be used to find critical values in hypothesis tests involving proportions.*

21. Coin Tossing A coin is tossed 9 times and 3 heads appear. Can you conclude that the coin is not balanced? Use $\alpha = 0.10$. [*Hint:* Use the binomial table and find $2P(X \le 3)$ with $p = 0.5$ and $n = 9$.] No, since $p = 0.508$.

22. First-Class Airline Passengers In the past, 20% of all airline passengers flew first class. In a sample of 15 passengers, 5 flew first class. At $\alpha = 0.10$, can you conclude that the proportions have changed?

23. Show that $z = \dfrac{\hat{p} - p}{\sqrt{pq/n}}$ can be derived from $z = \dfrac{X - \mu}{\sigma}$ by substituting $\mu = np$ and $\sigma = \sqrt{npq}$ and dividing both numerator and denominator by *n*.

Technology   Step by Step

TI-84 Plus
Step by Step

Hypothesis Test for the Proportion

1. Press **STAT** and move the cursor to TESTS.
2. Press **5** for 1-PropZTest.
3. Type in the appropriate values.
4. Move the cursor to the appropriate alternative hypothesis and press **ENTER.**
5. Move the cursor to Calculate and press **ENTER.**

Example

Test the claim that 40% of all cell phone customers have games on their phones, when $n = 100$ and $\hat{p} = 37\%$. Use $\alpha = 0.01$. First, you will need to calculate *x* by taking 0.37*200 = 74.

  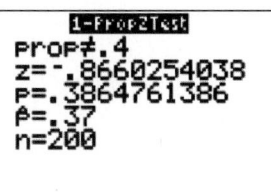

The test statistic is $z = -0.866$, and the *P*-value is 0.3865. Do not reject the null hypothesis.

EXCEL
Step by Step

Hypothesis Test for the Proportion: *z* Test

Excel does not have a procedure to conduct a hypothesis test for a single population proportion. However, you may conduct the test of the proportion, using the MegaStat Add-in available in your online resources. If you have not installed this add-in, do so, following the instructions from the Chapter 1 Excel Step by Step.

Example XL8–2

This example relates to the previous example. At the 1% significance level, test the claim that $p = 0.40$. The MegaStat test of the population proportion uses the *P*-value method. Therefore, it is not necessary to enter a significance level.

1. From the toolbar, select Add-Ins, **MegaStat>Hypothesis Tests>Proportion vs. Hypothesized Value.** *Note:* You may need to open MegaStat from the MegaStat.xls file on your computer's hard drive.

2. Type **0.37** for the Observed proportion, *p*.

3. Type **0.40** for the Hypothesized proportion, *p*.

4. Type **200** for the sample size, *n*.

5. Select the "not equal" Alternative.

6. Click [OK].

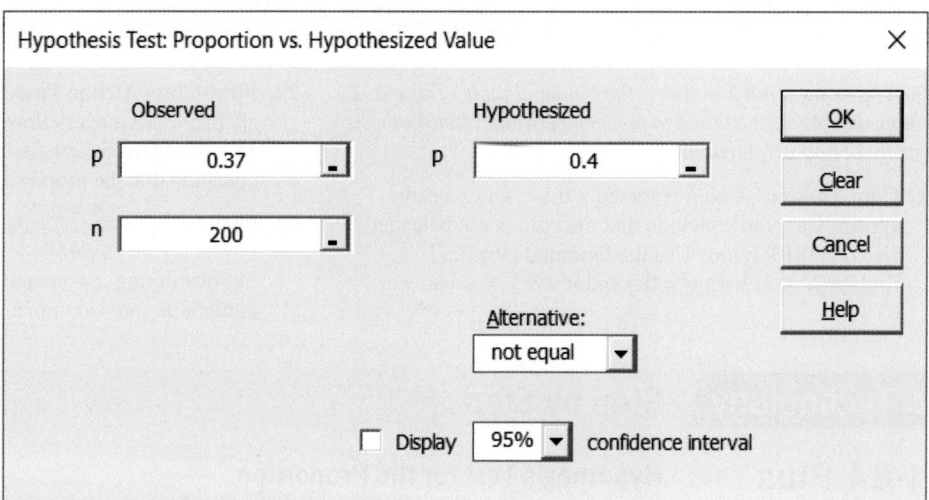

The result of the procedure is shown next.

Hypothesis test for proportion vs hypothesized value

Observed	Hypothesized	
0.37	0.4	p (as decimal)
74/200	80/200	p (as fraction)
74.	80.	X
200	200	n
	0.0346	std. error
	-0.87	z
	.3865	p-value (two-tailed)

MINITAB
Step by Step

Hypothesis Test for One Proportion and the *z* Distribution

MINITAB can be used to find a critical value of chi-square.

Example 8–17

Test the claim that 17% of young people between the ages of 2 and 19 are obese.
MINITAB will calculate the test statistic and *P*-value based on the normal distribution. There are no data for this example.

Step 1   Select **Stat>Basic Statistics> 1-proportion.**

Step 2   Select **Summarized data** from the drop-down menu.

a) In the dialog box for Number of events, type in the number of successes in the sample, **42.**

b) In the dialog box for Number of trials, type in the sample size, **200.**

Step 3   Select the box for **Perform hypothesis test,** then type the decimal form of the Hypothesized proportion, **0.17.**

Step 4   Click the button for **[Options].**

a) Type in the confidence level, **95.**

b) Click the drop-down menu for the Alternative hypothesis, "Proportion ≠ hypothesized proportion."

c) Click the drop-down menu for Method, choose "Normal approximation."

d) Click [OK] twice.

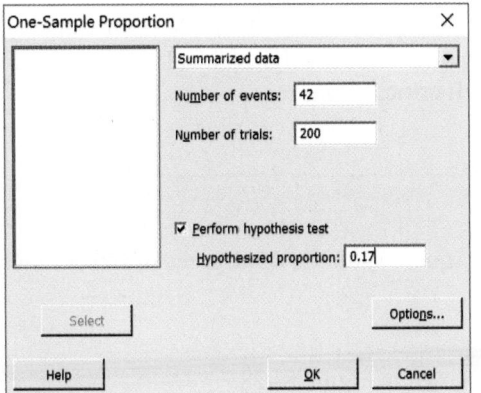
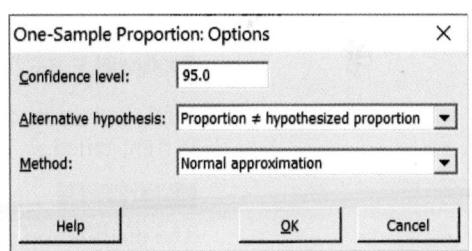

In the Session Window the output will include the test statistics, *t* = 1.51 and its *P*-value 0.132. The null hypothesis cannot be rejected.

Test and CI for One Proportion

```
Test of p = 0.17 vs p ≠ 0.17


Sample   X    N   Sample p          95% CI          Z-Value   P-Value
1       42  200   0.210000   (0.153551, 0.266449)     1.51      0.132

Using the normal approximation.
```

8–5 χ^2 Test for a Variance or Standard Deviation

OBJECTIVE

Test variances or standard
deviations, using the
chi-square test.

In Chapter 7, the chi-square distribution was used to construct a confidence interval for a single variance or standard deviation. This distribution is also used to test a claim about a single variance or standard deviation.

Recall from Chapter 7 the characteristics of the chi-square distribution:

1. All chi-square values are greater than or equal to 0.

2. The chi-square distribution is a family of curves based on the degrees of freedom.

3. The area under each chi-square distribution is equal to 1.

4. The chi-square distributions are positively skewed.

To find the area under the chi-square distribution, use Table A–6 in Appendix A. There are three cases to consider:

1. Finding the chi-square critical value for a specific α when the hypothesis test is right-tailed

2. Finding the chi-square critical value for a specific α when the hypothesis test is left-tailed

3. Finding the chi-square critical values for a specific α when the hypothesis test is two-tailed

Table A–6 is set up so it gives the areas to the right of the critical value; so if the test is right-tailed, just use the area under the α value for the specific degrees of freedom. If the test is left-tailed, subtract the α value from 1; then use the area in the table for that value for a specific d.f. If the test is two-tailed, divide the α value by 2; then use the area under that value for a specific d.f. for the right critical value and the area for the $1 - \alpha/2$ value for the d.f. for the left critical value.

EXAMPLE 8–21

Find the critical chi-square value for 15 degrees of freedom when $\alpha = 0.05$ and the test is right-tailed.

SOLUTION

The distribution is shown in Figure 8–28.

FIGURE 8–28
Chi-Square Distribution for
Example 8–21

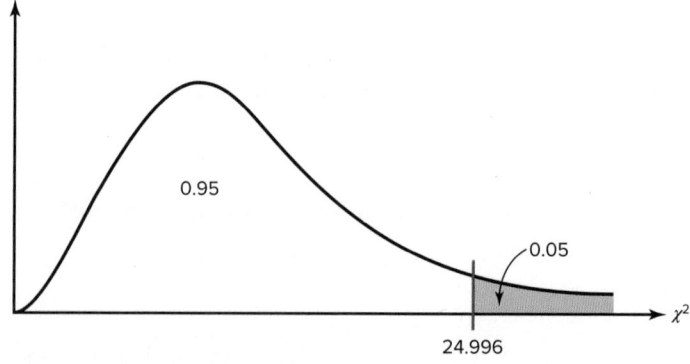

Find the α value at the top of Table A–6, and find the corresponding degrees of freedom in the left column. The critical value is located where the two columns meet—in this case, 24.996. See Figure 8–29.

FIGURE 8–29

Locating the Critical Value in Table A–6 for Example 8–21

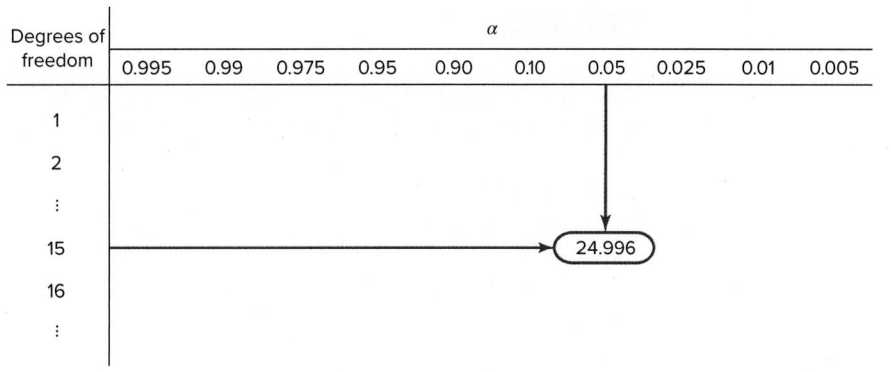

EXAMPLE 8–22

Find the critical chi-square value for 10 degrees of freedom when $\alpha = 0.05$ and the test is left-tailed.

SOLUTION

This distribution is shown in Figure 8–30.

FIGURE 8–30

Chi-Square Distribution for Example 8–22

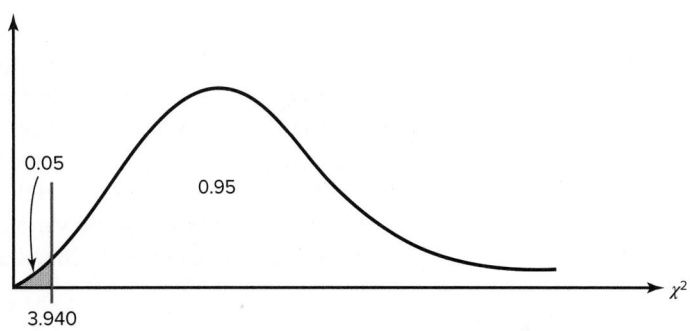

When the test is left-tailed, the α value must be subtracted from 1, that is, $1 - 0.05 = 0.95$. The left side of the table is used, because the chi-square table gives the area to the right of the critical value, and the chi-square statistic cannot be negative. The table is set up so that it gives the values for the area to the right of the critical value. In this case, 95% of the area will be to the right of the value.

For 0.95 and 10 degrees of freedom, the critical value is 3.940. See Figure 8–31.

FIGURE 8–31

Locating the Critical Value in Table A–6 for Example 8–22

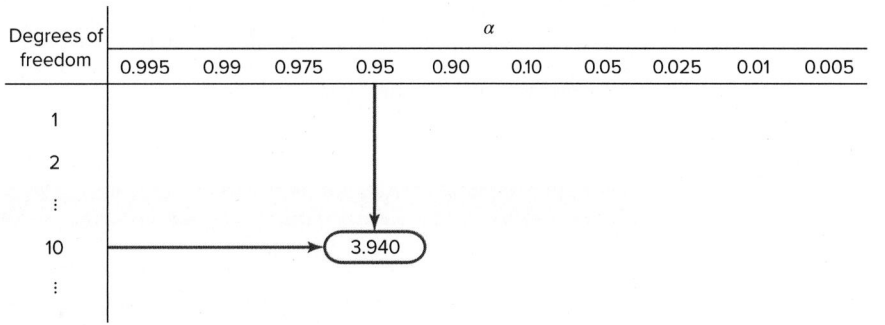

EXAMPLE 8–23

Find the critical chi-square values for 22 degrees of freedom when $\alpha = 0.05$ and a two-tailed test is conducted.

SOLUTION

When a two-tailed test is conducted, the area must be split, as shown in Figure 8–32. Note that the area to the right of the larger value is 0.025 (0.05/2 or $\alpha/2$), and the area to the right of the smaller value is 0.975 (1.00 − 0.05/2 or 1 − $\alpha/2$).

FIGURE 8–32
Chi-Square Distribution for Example 8–23

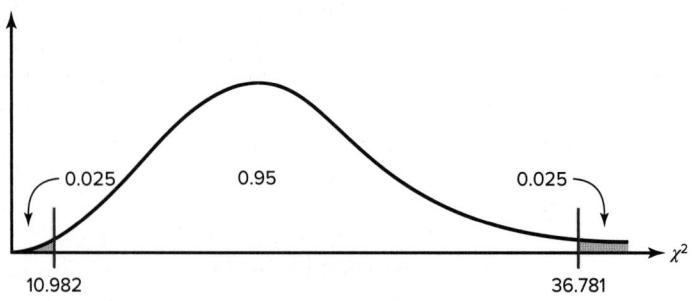

Remember that chi-square values cannot be negative. Hence, you must use α values in the table of 0.025 and 0.975. With 22 degrees of freedom, the critical values are 36.781 and 10.982, respectively.

Table A–6 gives values only up to 30 degrees of freedom. When the degrees of freedom exceed those specified in the table, use the table value for 30 degrees of freedom. This guideline keeps the type 1 error equal to or below the α value.

When you are testing a claim about a single variance using the **chi-square test,** there are three possible test situations: right-tailed test, left-tailed test, and two-tailed test.

If a researcher believes the variance of a population to be greater than some specific value, say, 225, then the researcher states the hypotheses as

$$H_0: \sigma^2 = 225 \qquad \text{and} \qquad H_1: \sigma^2 > 225$$

and conducts a right-tailed test.

If the researcher believes the variance of a population to be less than 225, then the researcher states the hypotheses as

$$H_0: \sigma^2 = 225 \qquad \text{and} \qquad H_1: \sigma^2 < 225$$

and conducts a left-tailed test.

Finally, if a researcher does not wish to specify a direction, a researcher states the hypotheses as

$$H_0: \sigma^2 = 225 \qquad \text{and} \qquad H_1: \sigma^2 \neq 225$$

and conducts a two-tailed test.

Formula for the Chi-Square Test for a Single Variance

$$\chi^2 = \frac{(n-1)s^2}{\sigma^2}$$

with degrees of freedom equal to $n - 1$ and where
n = sample size
s^2 = sample variance
σ^2 = population variance

Unusual Stat

About 55% of cats owned in the United States are overweight.

Three assumptions are made for the chi-square test, as outlined here.

Assumptions for the Chi-Square Test for a Single Variance

1. The sample must be randomly selected from the population.
2. The population must be normally distributed for the variable under study.
3. The observations must be independent of one another.

In this book, the assumptions will be stated in the exercises; however, when encountering statistics in other situations, you must check to see that these assumptions have been met before proceeding.

The methods used to test a hypothesis about a population variance or population standard deviation are not robust. So if the data come from a population that is not normally distributed, these methods cannot be used.

The traditional method for hypothesis testing follows the same five steps listed earlier. They are repeated here.

Step 1 State the hypotheses and identify the claim.

Step 2 Find the critical value(s).

Step 3 Compute the test statistic.

Step 4 Make the decision.

Step 5 Summarize the results.

Examples 8–24 through 8–26 illustrate the traditional hypothesis-testing procedure for variances.

You might ask, Why is it important to test variances? There are several reasons. First, in any situation where consistency is required, such as in manufacturing, you would like to have the smallest variation possible in the products. For example, when bolts are manufactured, the variation in diameters due to the process must be kept to a minimum, or else the nuts will not fit them properly. In education, consistency is required on a test. That is, if the same students take the same test several times, they should get approximately the same grades, and the variance of each of the student's grades should be small. On the other hand, if the test is to be used to judge learning, the overall standard deviation of all the grades should be large so that you can differentiate those who have learned the subject from those who have not learned it.

EXAMPLE 8–24   IQ Test

A psychologist wishes to see if the variance in IQ of 10 counseling patients is less than the variance of the population, which is 225. The variance of the IQs of the 10 patients was 206. Test her claim at $\alpha = 0.05$.

SOLUTION

Step 1 State the hypotheses.

$$H_0: \sigma^2 = 225 \quad \text{and} \quad H_1: \sigma^2 < 225 \text{ (claim)}$$

Step 2 Find the critical value. Since this is a left-tailed test and $\alpha = 0.05$, the value $1 - 0.05 = 0.95$ should be used. The degrees of freedom are $n - 1 = 10 - 1 = 9$. Hence, the critical value is 3.325.

Step 3 Compute the test statistic.

$$\chi^2 = \frac{(n-1)s^2}{\sigma^2} = \frac{(10-1)(206)}{225} = 8.24$$

Step 4   Make the decision. Since 8.24 falls in the noncritical region, do not reject the null hypothesis. See Figure 8–33.

FIGURE 8–33
Critical Value and Test
Statistic for Example 8–33

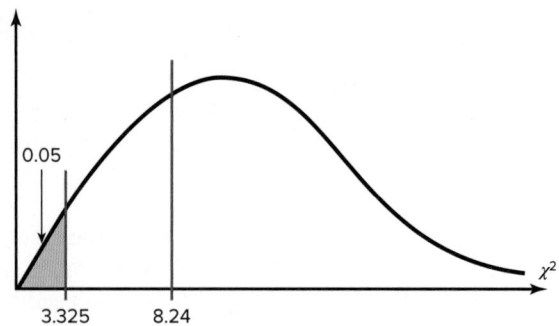

Step 5   Summarize the results. There is not enough evidence to support the claim that the variance of her 10 patients is less than 225.

EXAMPLE 8–25   Outpatient Surgery

A hospital administrator believes that the standard deviation of the number of people using outpatient surgery per day is greater than 8. A random sample of 15 days is selected. The data are shown. At $\alpha = 0.10$, is there enough evidence to support the administrator's claim? Assume the variable is normally distributed.

25	30	5	15	18
42	16	9	10	12
12	38	8	14	27

SOLUTION

Step 1   State the hypotheses and identify the claim.

$$H_0: \sigma = 8 \qquad \text{and} \qquad H_1: \sigma > 8 \text{ (claim)}$$

Since the standard deviation is given, it should be squared to get the variance.

Step 2   Find the critical value. Since this test is right-tailed with d.f. of $15 - 1 = 14$ and $\alpha = 0.10$, the critical value is 21.064.

Step 3   Compute the test statistic. Since raw data are given, the standard deviation of the sample must be found by using the formula in Chapter 3 or your calculator. It is $s = 11.2$.

$$\chi^2 = \frac{(n-1)s^2}{\sigma^2} = \frac{(15-1)(11.2)^2}{64} = 27.44$$

Step 4   Make the decision. The decision is to reject the null hypothesis since the test statistic, 27.44, is greater than the critical value, 21.064, and falls in the critical region. See Figure 8–34.

FIGURE 8–34
Critical Value and Test
Statistic for Example 8–25

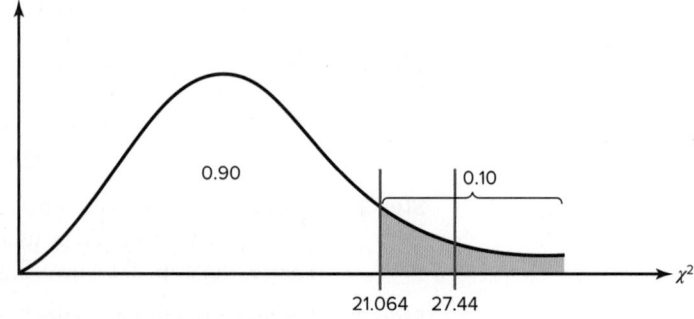

Step 5   Summarize the results. There is enough evidence to support the claim that the standard deviation is greater than 8.

EXAMPLE 8–26   Nicotine Content of Cigarettes

A cigarette manufacturer wishes to test the claim that the variance of the nicotine content of its cigarettes is 0.644. Nicotine content is measured in milligrams, and assume that it is normally distributed. A random sample of 20 cigarettes has a standard deviation of 1.00 milligram. At $\alpha = 0.05$, is there enough evidence to reject the manufacturer's claim?

SOLUTION

Step 1   State the hypotheses and identify the claim.

$$H_0\colon \sigma^2 = 0.644 \text{ (claim)} \qquad \text{and} \qquad H_1\colon \sigma^2 \neq 0.644$$

Step 2   Find the critical values. Since this test is a two-tailed test at $\alpha = 0.05$, the critical values for 0.025 and 0.975 must be found. The degrees of freedom are 19; hence, the critical values are 32.852 and 8.907, respectively. The critical or rejection regions are shown in Figure 8–35.

FIGURE 8–35
Critical Values for
Example 8–26

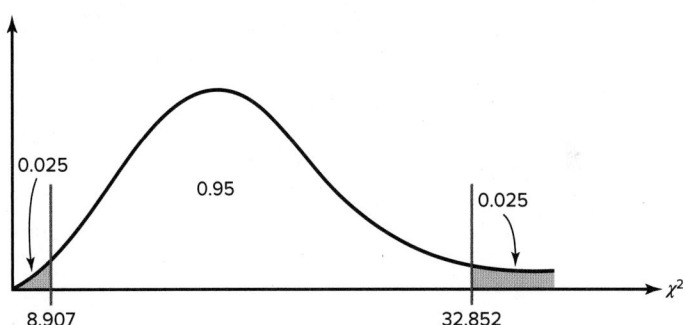

Step 3   Compute the test statistic.

$$\chi^2 = \frac{(n-1)s^2}{\sigma^2} = \frac{(20-1)(1.0)^2}{0.644} = 29.5$$

Since the sample standard deviation s is given in the problem, it must be squared for the formula.

Step 4   Make the decision. Do not reject the null hypothesis, since the test statistic falls between the critical values ($8.907 < 29.5 < 32.852$) and in the noncritical region, as shown in Figure 8–36.

FIGURE 8–36
Critical Values and Test
Statistic for Example 8–26

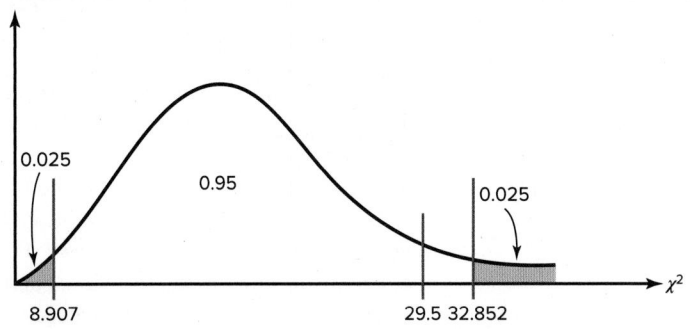

Step 5   Summarize the results. There is not enough evidence to reject the manufacturer's claim that the variance of the nicotine content of the cigarettes is equal to 0.644.

Approximate P-values for the chi-square test can be found by using Table A–6 in Appendix A. The procedure is somewhat more complicated than the previous procedures for finding *P*-values for the z and t tests since the chi-square distribution is not exactly symmetric and χ^2 values cannot be negative. As we did for the t test, we will determine an *interval* for the *P*-value based on the table. Examples 8–27 through 8–29 show the procedure.

EXAMPLE 8–27

Find the *P*-value when $\chi^2 = 19.274$, $n = 8$, and the test is right-tailed.

SOLUTION

To get the *P*-value, look across the row with d.f. = 7 in Table A–6 and find the two values that 19.274 falls between. They are 18.475 and 20.278. Look up to the top row and find the α values corresponding to 18.475 and 20.278. They are 0.01 and 0.005, respectively. See Figure 8–37. Hence, the *P*-value is contained in the interval $0.005 < P\text{-value} < 0.01$. (The *P*-value obtained from a calculator is 0.007.)

FIGURE 8–37 *P*-Value Interval for Example 8–27

Degrees of freedom	0.995	0.99	0.975	0.95	0.90	0.10	0.05	0.025	0.01	0.005
1	—	—	0.001	0.004	0.016	2.706	3.841	5.024	6.635	7.879
2	0.010	0.020	0.051	0.103	0.211	4.605	5.991	7.378	9.210	10.597
3	0.072	0.115	0.216	0.352	0.584	6.251	7.815	9.348	11.345	12.838
4	0.207	0.297	0.484	0.711	1.064	7.779	9.488	11.143	13.277	14.860
5	0.412	0.554	0.831	1.145	1.610	9.236	11.071	12.833	15.086	16.750
6	0.676	0.872	1.237	1.635	2.204	10.645	12.592	14.449	16.812	18.548
7	0.989	1.239	1.690	2.167	2.833	12.017	14.067	16.013	18.475	20.278
8	1.344	1.646	2.180	2.733	3.490	13.362	15.507	17.535	20.090	21.955
9	1.735	2.088	2.700	3.325	4.168	14.684	16.919	19.023	21.666	23.589
10	2.156	2.558	3.247	3.940	4.865	15.987	18.307	20.483	23.209	25.188
⋮	⋮	⋮	⋮	⋮	⋮	⋮	⋮	⋮	⋮	⋮
30	13.787	14.954	16.791	18.493	20.599	40.256	43.773	46.979	50.892	53.672

*19.274 falls between 18.475 and 20.278

EXAMPLE 8–28

Find the *P*-value when $\chi^2 = 3.823$, $n = 13$, and the test is left-tailed.

SOLUTION

To get the *P*-value, look across the row with d.f. = 12 and find the two values that 3.823 falls between. They are 3.571 and 4.404. Look up to the top row and find the values corresponding to 3.571 and 4.404. They are 0.99 and 0.975, respectively. When the χ^2 test statistic falls on the left side, each of the values must be subtracted from 1 to get the interval that *P*-value falls between.

$$1 - 0.99 = 0.01 \quad \text{and} \quad 1 - 0.975 = 0.025$$

Hence, the *P*-value falls in the interval

$$0.01 < P\text{-value} < 0.025$$

(The *P*-value obtained from a calculator is 0.014.)

When the χ^2 test is two-tailed, both interval values must be doubled. If a two-tailed test were being used in Example 8–28, then the interval would be $2(0.01) < P$-value $< 2(0.025)$, or $0.02 < P$-value < 0.05.

The P-value method for hypothesis testing for a variance or standard deviation follows the same steps shown in the preceding sections.

Step 1   State the hypotheses and identify the claim.

Step 2   Compute the test statistic.

Step 3   Find the P-value.

Step 4   Make the decision.

Step 5   Summarize the results.

Example 8–29 shows the P-value method for variances or standard deviations.

EXAMPLE 8–29   Car Inspection Times

A researcher knows from past studies that the standard deviation of the time it takes to inspect a car is 16.8 minutes. A random sample of 24 cars is selected and inspected. The standard deviation is 12.5 minutes. At $\alpha = 0.05$, can it be concluded that the standard deviation has changed? Use the P-value method. Assume the variable is normally distributed.

SOLUTION

Step 1   State the hypotheses and identify the claim.

$$H_0: \sigma = 16.8 \qquad \text{and} \qquad H_1: \sigma \neq 16.8 \text{ (claim)}$$

Step 2   Compute the test statistic.

$$\chi^2 = \frac{(n-1)s^2}{\sigma^2} = \frac{(24-1)(12.5)^2}{(16.8)^2} = 12.733$$

Step 3   Find the P-value. Using Table A–6 with d.f. = 23, the value 12.733 falls between 11.689 and 13.091, corresponding to 0.975 and 0.95, respectively. Since these values are found on the left side of the distribution, each value must be subtracted from 1. Hence, $1 - 0.975 = 0.025$ and $1 - 0.95 = 0.05$. Since this is a two-tailed test, the area must be doubled to obtain the P-value interval. Hence, $0.05 < P$-value < 0.10, or somewhere between 0.05 and 0.10. (The P-value obtained from a calculator is 0.085.)

Step 4   Make the decision. Since $\alpha = 0.05$ and the P-value is between 0.05 and 0.10, the decision is to not reject the null hypothesis since P-value $> \alpha$.

Step 5   Summarize the results. There is not enough evidence to support the claim that the standard deviation of the time it takes to inspect a car has changed.

Applying the Concepts 8–5

Testing Gas Mileage Claims

Assume that you are working for the Consumer Protection Agency and have recently been getting complaints about the highway gas mileage of the new Dodge Caravans. Chrysler Corporation agrees to allow you to randomly select 40 of its new Dodge Caravans to test the highway mileage.

Chrysler claims that the Caravans get 28 mpg on the highway. Your results show a mean of 26.7 and a standard deviation of 4.2. You support Chrysler's claim.

1. Show whether or not you support Chrysler's claim by listing the *P*-value from your output. After more complaints, you decide to test the variability of the miles per gallon on the highway. From further questioning of Chrysler's quality control engineers, you find they are claiming a standard deviation of no more than 2.1. Use a one-tailed test.

2. Test the claim about the standard deviation.

3. Write a short summary of your results and any necessary action that Chrysler must take to remedy customer complaints.

4. State your position about the necessity to perform tests of variability along with tests of the means.

See page 488 for the answers.

Exercises 8–5

1. Using Table A–6, find the critical value(s) for each. Indicate the noncritical region or regions, and state the null and alternative hypotheses. Use $\sigma^2 = 225$.

    a. $\alpha = 0.05$, $n = 22$, two-tailed

    b. $\alpha = 0.10$, $n = 14$, left-tailed

    c. $\alpha = 0.05$, $n = 9$, right-tailed

    d. $\alpha = 0.01$, $n = 11$, right-tailed

2. Using Table A–6, find the critical value(s) for each. Show the critical and noncritical regions, and state the appropriate null and alternative hypotheses. Use $\sigma^2 = 225$.

    a. $\alpha = 0.01$, $n = 12$, right-tailed

    b. $\alpha = 0.05$, $n = 7$, left-tailed

    c. $\alpha = 0.10$, $n = 23$, right-tailed

    d. $\alpha = 0.05$, $n = 28$, two-tailed

3. Using Table A–6, find the *P*-value interval for each χ^2 test statistic.

    a. $\chi^2 = 29.321$, $n = 16$, right-tailed

    b. $\chi^2 = 10.215$, $n = 25$, left-tailed

    c. $\chi^2 = 24.672$, $n = 11$, two-tailed

    d. $\chi^2 = 23.722$, $n = 9$, right-tailed

4. Using Table A–6, find the *P*-value interval for each χ^2 test statistic.

    a. $\chi^2 = 13.974$, $n = 28$, two-tailed

    b. $\chi^2 = 10.571$, $n = 19$, left-tailed

    c. $\chi^2 = 12.144$, $n = 6$, two-tailed

    d. $\chi^2 = 8.201$, $n = 23$, two-tailed

For Exercises 5 through 20, assume that the variables are normally or approximately normally distributed. Use the traditional method of hypothesis testing unless the P-value method is specified by your instructor.

5. **Calories in Cheeseburgers** The number of calories in a random selection of cheeseburgers from 10 fast food restaurants is listed.

447	523	496	481	452
515	498	519	476	503

    Is there sufficient evidence to conclude that the variance is greater than 700? Use the 0.05 level of significance.

6. **Carbohydrates in Fast Foods** The number of carbohydrates found in a random sample of fast-food entrees is listed. Is there sufficient evidence to conclude that the variance differs from 100? Use the 0.05 level of significance.

53	46	39	39	30
47	38	73	43	41

    Source: Fast Food Explorer (www.fatcalories.com).

7. **Transferring Phone Calls** The manager of a large company claims that the standard deviation of the time (in minutes) that it takes a telephone call to be transferred to the correct office in her company is 1.2 minutes or less. A random sample of 15 calls is selected, and the calls are timed. The standard deviation of the sample is 1.8 minutes. At $\alpha = 0.01$, test the claim that the standard deviation is less than or equal to 1.2 minutes. Use the *P*-value method.

8. **Soda Bottle Content** A machine fills 12-ounce bottles with soda. For the machine to function properly, the standard deviation of the population must be less than or equal to 0.03 ounce. A random sample of 8 bottles is selected, and the number of ounces of soda in each bottle is given. At $\alpha = 0.05$, can we reject the claim that the machine is functioning properly? Use the *P*-value method.

12.03	12.10	12.02	11.98
12.00	12.05	11.97	11.99

9. **Length of Songs** A random sample of eight new songs had lengths in seconds as shown. Test the claim at $\alpha = 0.10$ that the standard deviation of the songs is less than 15 seconds.

227	241	238	244
233	225	262	222

10. **Exam Grades** A statistics professor is used to having a variance in his class grades of no more than 100. He feels that his current group of students is different, and so he examines a random sample of midterm grades as shown. At $\alpha = 0.05$, can it be concluded that the variance in grades exceeds 100?

92.3	89.4	76.9	65.2	49.1
96.7	69.5	72.8	67.5	52.8
88.5	79.2	72.9	68.7	75.8

11. **Tornado Deaths** A researcher claims that the standard deviation of the number of deaths annually from tornadoes in the United States is less than 35. If a random sample of 11 years had a standard deviation of 32, is the claim believable? Use $\alpha = 0.05$.

Source: National Oceanic and Atmospheric Administration.

12. **Interstate Speeds** It has been reported that the standard deviation of the speeds of drivers on Interstate 75 near Findlay, Ohio, is 8 miles per hour for all vehicles. A driver feels from experience that this is very low. A survey is conducted, and for 50 randomly selected drivers the standard deviation is 10.5 miles per hour. At $\alpha = 0.05$, is the driver correct?

13. **Car Payments** A random sample of 16 people who had new car payments found the standard deviation of the data was $52. Test the claim at $\alpha = 0.05$ that the standard deviation is greater than $50.

14. **Vitamin C in Fruits and Vegetables** The amounts of vitamin C (in milligrams) for 100 g (3.57 ounces) of various randomly selected fruits and vegetables are listed. Is there sufficient evidence to conclude that the standard deviation differs from 12 mg? Use $\alpha = 0.10$.

7.9	16.3	12.8	13.0	32.2	28.1	34.4
46.4	53.0	15.4	18.2	25.0	5.2	

Source: Time Almanac 2012.

15. **eBooks** The standard deviation for the cost of a sample of 23 eBooks is $0.46. Test the claim at $\alpha = 0.10$ that the standard deviation is not equal to $0.50.

16. **Golf Scores** A random sample of second-round golf scores from a major tournament is

listed below. At $\alpha = 0.10$, is there sufficient evidence to conclude that the population variance exceeds 9?

75	67	69	72	70
66	74	69	74	71

17. **Calories in Pancake Syrup** A nutritionist claims that the standard deviation of the number of calories in 1 tablespoon of the major brands of pancake syrup is 60. A random sample of major brands of syrup is selected, and the number of calories is shown. At $\alpha = 0.10$, can the claim be rejected?

53	210	100	200	100	220
210	100	240	200	100	210
100	210	100	210	100	60

Source: Based on information from Netzer, Corinne T., *The Complete Book of Food Counts.* New York: Dell Publishers, 2011.

18. **High Temperatures in January** Daily weather observations for southwestern Pennsylvania for the first three weeks of January for randomly selected years show daily high temperatures as follows: 55, 44, 51, 59, 62, 60, 46, 51, 37, 30, 46, 51, 53, 57, 57, 39, 28, 37, 35, and 28 degrees Fahrenheit. The normal standard deviation in high temperatures for this time period is usually no more than 8 degrees. A meteorologist believes that with the unusual trend in temperatures the standard deviation is greater. At $\alpha = 0.05$, can we conclude that the standard deviation is greater than 8 degrees?

Source: www.wunderground.com

19. **College Room and Board Costs** Room and board fees for a random sample of independent religious colleges are shown.

7460	7959	7650	8120	7220
8768	7650	8400	7860	6782
8754	7443	9500	9100	

Estimate the standard deviation in costs based on $s \approx R/4$. Is there sufficient evidence to conclude that the sample standard deviation differs from this estimated amount? Use $\alpha = 0.05$.

Source: World Almanac.

20. **Heights of Volcanoes** A random sample of heights (in feet) of active volcanoes in North America, outside of Alaska, is shown. Is there sufficient evidence that the standard deviation in heights of volcanoes outside Alaska is less than the standard deviation in heights of Alaskan volcanoes, which is 2385.9 feet? Use $\alpha = 0.05$.

10,777	8159	11,240	10,456
14,163	8363		

Source: Time Almanac.

≡ Technology | Step by Step

TI-84 Plus
Step by Step

The TI-84 Plus does not have a built-in hypothesis test for the variance or standard deviation. However, the downloadable program named SDHYP is available in your online resources. Follow the instructions online for downloading the program.

Performing a Hypothesis Test for the Variance and Standard Deviation (Data)

1. Enter the values into L_1.
2. Press **PRGM,** move the cursor to the program named SDHYP, and press **ENTER** twice.
3. Press **1** for Data.
4. Type L_1 (Press [2nd] [1]) for the list and press **ENTER.**
5. Type the number corresponding to the symbol of the alternative hypothesis.
6. Type the value of the hypothesized variance and press **ENTER.**
7. Press **ENTER** to clear the screen.

Example TI8–3

This pertains to Example 8–25 in the text. Test the claim that $\sigma > 8$ for these data.

$$25 \quad 30 \quad 5 \quad 15 \quad 18 \quad 42 \quad 16 \quad 9 \quad 10 \quad 12 \quad 12 \quad 38 \quad 8 \quad 14 \quad 27$$

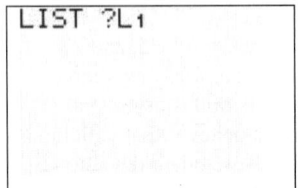 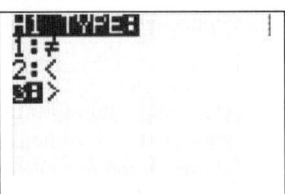 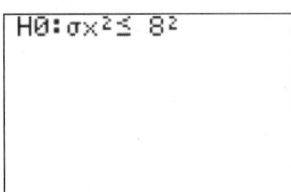 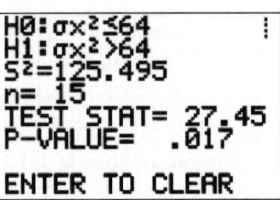

Since P-value $= 0.017 < 0.1$, we reject H_0 and conclude H_1. Therefore, there is enough evidence to support the claim that the standard deviation of the number of people using outpatient surgery is greater than 8.

Performing a Hypothesis Test for the Variance and Standard Deviation (Statistics)

1. Press **PRGM,** move the cursor to the program named SDHYP, and press **ENTER** twice.
2. Press **2** for Stats.
3. Type the sample standard deviation and press **ENTER.**
4. Type the sample size and press **ENTER.**
5. Type the number corresponding to the symbol of the alternative hypothesis.
6. Type the value of the hypothesized variance and press **ENTER.**
7. Press **ENTER** to clear the screen.

Example TI8–4

This pertains to Example 8–26 in the text. Test the claim that $\sigma^2 = 0.644$, given $n = 20$ and $s = 1$.

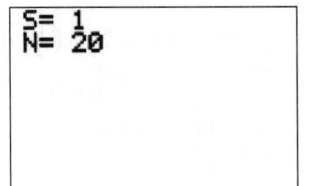 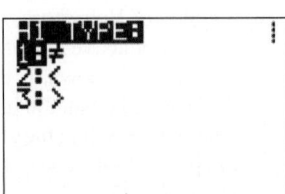 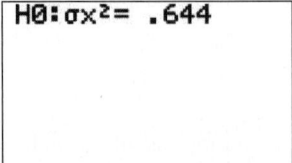 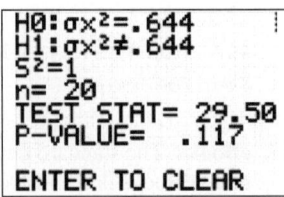

Since P-value $= 0.117 > 0.05$, we do not reject H_0 and do not conclude H_1. Therefore, there is not enough evidence to reject the manufacturer's claim that the variance of the nicotine content of the cigarettes is equal to 0.644.

Hypothesis Test for the Variance: Chi-Square Test

Excel does not have a procedure to conduct a hypothesis test for a single population variance. However, you may conduct the test of the variance using the MegaStat Add-in available in your online resources. If you have not installed this add-in, do so, following the instructions from the Chapter 1 Excel Step by Step.

Example XL8–3

This example relates to Example 8–26 from the text. At the 5% significance level, test the claim that $\sigma^2 = 0.644$. The MegaStat chi-square test of the population variance uses the *P*-value method. Therefore, it is not necessary to enter a significance level.

1. Select summary input.
2. Type a label for the variable: Nicotine in cell A1.
3. Type the sample variance: **1** in cell A2.
4. Type the sample size: **20** in cell A3.
5. Type the hypothesized variance 0.644 in cell A4.
6. From the toolbar, select Add-Ins, **MegaStat>Hypothesis Tests>Chi-Square Variance Test**. *Note:* You may need to open MegaStat from the MegaStat.xls file on your computer's hard drive.
7. Select summary input.
8. Type **A1:A3** for the Input Range.
9. Type **A4** for the Hypothesized variance and select the Alternative not equal.
10. Click [OK].

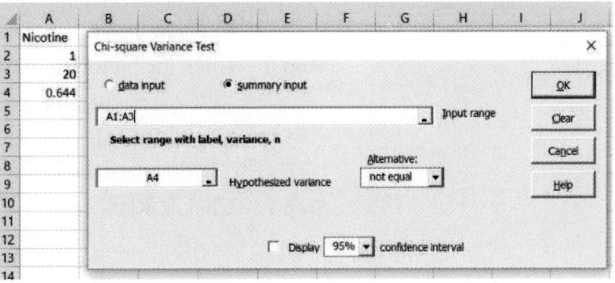

The result of the procedure is shown next.

Chi-square Variance Test

    0.64 hypothesized variance
    1.00 observed variance of Nicotine
      20 n
      19 df
  29.50 chi-square

   .1169 p-value (two-tailed)

MINITAB

Step by Step

Hypothesis Test for Standard Deviation or Variance

MINITAB can be used to find a critical value of chi-square. It can also calculate the test statistic and *P*-value for a chi-square test of variance.

Example 8–22

Find the critical χ^2 value for $\alpha = 0.05$ for a left-tailed test with d.f. = 10.

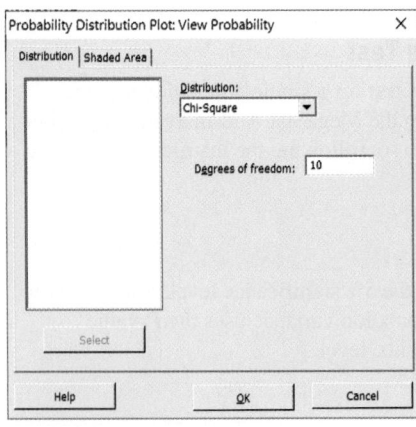

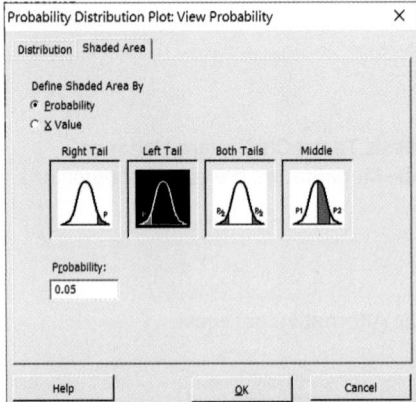

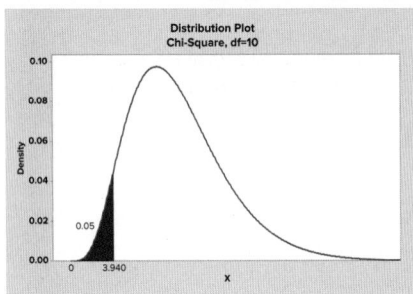

Step 1   To find the critical value of *t* for a right-tailed test, select **Graph>Probability Distribution Plot**, then **View Probability**, then click [**OK**].

Step 2   Change the Distribution to a Chi-square distribution and type in the degrees of freedom, **10.**

Step 3   Click the tab for **Shaded Area.**

   a) Select the radio button for **Probability.**

   b) Select **Left Tail.**

   c) Type in the value of alpha for probability, **0.05.**

   d) Click [**OK**].

You may click the Edit Last Dialog button and then change the settings for additional critical values.

Example 8–25 Outpatient Surgery

MINITAB will calculate the test statistic and *P*-value. There are data for this example.

Step 1   Type the data into column C1. Label the column Surgeries.

Step 2   Select **Stat>Basic Statistics> 1 Variance**

Step 3   Select **One or more samples, each in a column** from the drop-down menu, if not already selected.

Step 4   To select the data, click inside the next dialog box for Columns; then select C1 Surgeries from the list.

Step 5   Select the box for Perform hypothesis test.

   a) Select Hypothesized standard deviation from the drop-down list.

   b) Type in the hypothesized value of **8.**

Step 6   Click the button for [**Options**].

   a) Type the default confidence level, that is, **90.**

   b) Click the drop-down menu for the Alternative hypothesis, "Standard deviation > hypothesized standard deviation."

Step 7   Click [**OK**] twice.

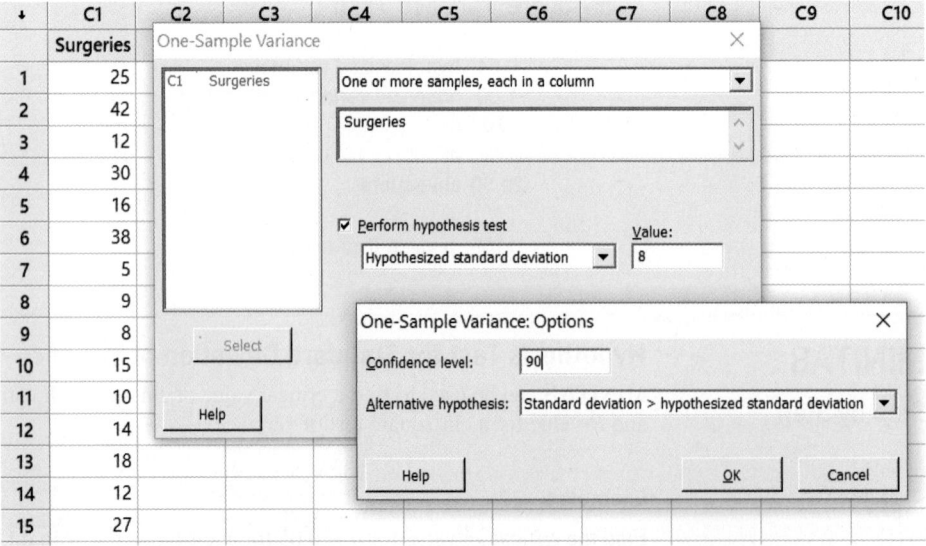

In the Session Window scroll down to the output labeled Statistics and further to the output labeled Tests. You should see the test statistic and P-value for the chi-square test. Since the P-value is less than 0.10, the null hypothesis will be rejected. The standard deviation, $s = 11.2$ is significantly greater than 8.

Test and CI for One Variance: Surgeries

```
Method

Null hypothesis        σ = 8
Alternative hypothesis σ > 8

The chi-square method is only for the normal distribution.
The Bonett method is for any continuous distribution.


Statistics

Variable    N  StDev  Variance
Surgeries  15   11.2       125


90% One-Sided Confidence Intervals

                       Lower
                       Bound
                        for   Lower Bound
Variable   Method     StDev   for Variance
Surgeries  Chi-Square   9.1             83
           Bonett       8.7             76


Tests

                        Test
Variable   Method     Statistic  DF  P-Value
Surgeries  Chi-Square     27.45  14    0.017
           Bonett             —   —    0.046
```

Although the text shows how to calculate a P-value, these are included in the MINITAB output of all hypothesis tests. The Alternative hypothesis in the Options dialog box must match your Alternative hypothesis.   ▬

8–6   Additional Topics Regarding Hypothesis Testing

In hypothesis testing, there are several other concepts that might be of interest to students in elementary statistics. These topics include the relationship between hypothesis testing and confidence intervals, and some additional information about the type II error.

OBJECTIVE

Test hypotheses, using confidence intervals.

Confidence Intervals and Hypothesis Testing

There is a relationship between confidence intervals and hypothesis testing. When the null hypothesis is rejected in a hypothesis-testing situation, the confidence interval for the mean using the same level of significance *will not* contain the hypothesized mean. Likewise, when the null hypothesis is not rejected, the confidence interval computed using the same level of significance *will* contain the hypothesized mean. Examples 8–30 and 8–31 show this concept for two-tailed tests.

EXAMPLE 8–30   Bank Robberies

A researcher read that the average amount of money stolen in a bank robbery is $4330. The researcher randomly selected 50 recent successful bank robberies and found that the average amount of money taken was $4186, and the standard deviation was $362. Is there enough evidence at $\alpha = 0.05$ to conclude that the average amount is not $4330? Assume the variable is normally distributed.

SOLUTION

Step 1   State the hypotheses and identify the claim.

$$H_0: \mu = 4330 \quad\text{and}\quad H_1: \mu \neq 4330 \text{ (claim)}$$

Step 2   At $\alpha = 0.05$ and d.f. $= 49$ (use d.f. $= 45$), the critical values are $+2.014$ and -2.014.

Step 3   Compute the test statistic.

$$t = \frac{\overline{X} - \mu}{s/\sqrt{n}} = \frac{4186 - 4330}{362/\sqrt{50}} = -2.81$$

Step 4   Make the decision. Since $-2.81 < -2.014$, the decision is to reject the null hypothesis. See Figure 8–38.

FIGURE 8–38

Critical Values and Test
Statistic for Example 8–30

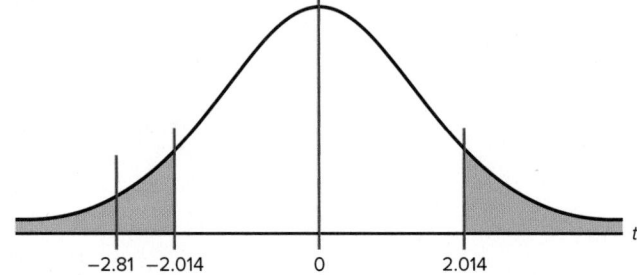

-2.81 -2.014 0 2.014 t

Step 5   Summarize the results. There is enough evidence to support the claim that the mean amount of money stolen is not $4330.
The 95% confidence for the mean is given by

$$\overline{X} - t_{\alpha/2}\frac{s}{\sqrt{n}} < \mu < \overline{X} + t_{\alpha/2}\frac{s}{\sqrt{n}}$$

$$4186 - (2.014)\left(\frac{362}{\sqrt{50}}\right) < \mu < 4186 + 2.014\left(\frac{362}{\sqrt{50}}\right)$$

$$4082.9 < \mu < 4289.1$$

Notice that the 95% confidence interval of μ does *not* contain the hypothesized value $\mu = \$4330$. Hence, there is agreement between the hypothesis test and the confidence interval.

EXAMPLE 8–31   Hog Weights

A researcher claims that adult hogs fed a special diet will have an average weight of 200 pounds. A random sample of 10 hogs has an average weight of 198.2 pounds and a standard deviation of 3.3 pounds. At $\alpha = 0.05$, can the claim be rejected? Also, find the 95% confidence interval of the true mean. Assume the variable is normally distributed.

SOLUTION

Step 1   State the hypotheses and identify the claim.

$$H_0: \mu = 200 \text{ lb (claim)} \quad\text{and}\quad H_1: \mu \neq 200 \text{ lb}$$

Step 2   Find the critical values. At $\alpha = 0.05$ and d.f. $= 9$, the critical values are $+2.262$ and -2.262.

Step 3   Compute the test statistic.

$$t = \frac{\overline{X} - \mu}{s/\sqrt{n}} = \frac{198.2 - 200}{3.3/\sqrt{10}} = \frac{-1.8}{1.0436} = -1.72$$

Step 4   Make the decision. Do not reject the null hypothesis. See Figure 8–39.

FIGURE 8–39
Critical Values and Test
Statistic for Example 8–31

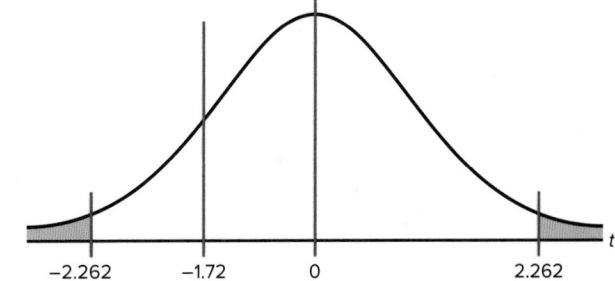

-2.262 -1.72 0 2.262 t

Step 5   Summarize the results. There is not enough evidence to reject the claim that
the mean weight of adult hogs is 200 lb.
The 95% confidence interval of the mean is

$$\overline{X} - t_{\alpha/2}\frac{s}{\sqrt{n}} < \mu < \overline{X} + t_{\alpha/2}\frac{s}{\sqrt{n}}$$

$$198.2 - (2.262)\left(\frac{3.3}{\sqrt{10}}\right) < \mu < 198.2 + (2.262)\left(\frac{3.3}{\sqrt{10}}\right)$$

$$198.2 - 2.361 < \mu < 198.2 + 2.361$$

$$195.8 < \mu < 200.6$$

The 95% confidence interval does contain the hypothesized mean $\mu = 200$.
Again there is agreement between the hypothesis test and the confidence
interval.

In summary, then, when the null hypothesis is rejected at a significance level of α, the
confidence interval computed at the $1 - \alpha$ level will not contain the value of the mean that
is stated in the null hypothesis. On the other hand, when the null hypothesis is not rejected, the confidence interval computed at the same significance level will contain the
value of the mean stated in the null hypothesis. These results are true for other hypothesis-
testing situations and are not limited to means tests.

The relationship between confidence intervals and hypothesis testing presented here
is valid for two-tailed tests. The relationship between one-tailed hypothesis tests and one-
sided or one-tailed confidence intervals is also valid; however, this technique is beyond
the scope of this text.

Type II Error and the Power of a Test

Recall that in hypothesis testing, there are two possibilities: Either the null hypothesis H_0
is true, or it is false. Furthermore, on the basis of the statistical test, the null hypothesis is
either rejected or not rejected. These results give rise to four possibilities, as shown in
Figure 8–40. This figure is similar to Figure 8–2.

As stated previously, there are two types of errors: type I and type II. A type I error
can occur only when the null hypothesis is rejected. By choosing a level of significance,
say, of 0.05 or 0.01, the researcher can determine the probability of committing a type I

OBJECTIVE

Explain the relationship
between type I and type II
errors and the power of
a test.

FIGURE 8–40
Possibilities in
Hypothesis Testing

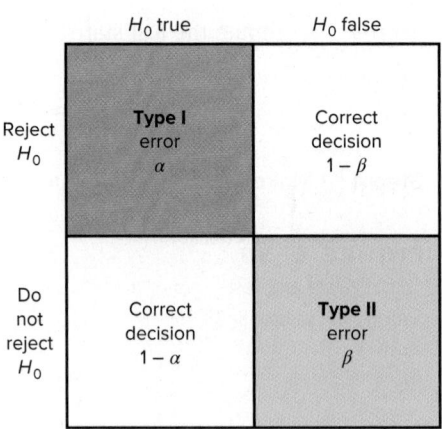

error. For example, suppose that the null hypothesis was H_0: $\mu = 50$, and it was rejected. At the 0.05 level (one tail), the researcher has only a 5% chance of being wrong, i.e., of rejecting a true null hypothesis.

On the other hand, if the null hypothesis is not rejected, then either it is true or a type II error has been committed. A type II error occurs when the null hypothesis is indeed false, but is not rejected. The probability of committing a type II error is denoted as β.

The value of β is not easy to compute. It depends on several things, including the value of α, the size of the sample, the population standard deviation, and the actual difference between the hypothesized value of the parameter being tested and the true parameter. The researcher has control over two of these factors, namely, the selection of α and the size of the sample. The standard deviation of the population is sometimes known or can be estimated. The major problem, then, lies in knowing the actual difference between the hypothesized parameter and the true parameter. If this difference were known, then the value of the parameter would be known; and if the parameter were known, then there would be no need to do any hypothesis testing. Hence, the value of β cannot be computed. But this does not mean that it should be ignored. What the researcher usually does is to try to minimize the size of β or to maximize the size of $1 - \beta$, which is called the **power of a test.**

The power of a statistical test measures the sensitivity of the test to detect a real difference in parameters if one actually exists. The power of a test is a probability and, like all probabilities, can have values ranging from 0 to 1. The higher the power, the more sensitive the test is to detecting a real difference between parameters if there is a difference. In other words, the closer the power of a test is to 1, the better the test is for rejecting the null hypothesis if the null hypothesis is, in fact, false.

The power of a test is equal to $1 - \beta$, that is, 1 minus the probability of committing a type II error. The power of the test is shown in the upper right-hand block of Figure 8–40. If somehow it were known that $\beta = 0.04$, then the power of a test would be $1 - 0.04 = 0.96$, or 96%. In this case, the probability of rejecting the null hypothesis when it is false is 96%.

As stated previously, the power of a test depends on the probability of committing a type II error, and since β is not easily computed, the power of a test cannot be easily computed. (See the Critical Thinking Challenges on page 486.)

However, there are some guidelines that can be used when you are conducting a statistical study concerning the power of a test. In that case, use the test that has the highest power for the data. There are times when the researcher has a choice of two or more statistical tests to test the hypotheses. The tests with the highest power should be used. It is important, however, to remember that statistical tests have assumptions that need to be considered.

If these assumptions cannot be met, then another test with lower power should be used. The power of a test can be increased by increasing the value of α. For example, instead of using $\alpha = 0.01$, use $\alpha = 0.05$. Recall that as α increases, β decreases. So if β is decreased, then $1 - \beta$ will increase, thus increasing the power of the test.

Another way to increase the power of a test is to select a larger sample size. A larger sample size would make the standard error of the mean smaller and consequently reduce β. (The derivation is omitted.)

These two methods should not be used at the whim of the researcher. Before α can be increased, the researcher must consider the consequences of committing a type I error. If these consequences are more serious than the consequences of committing a type II error, then α should not be increased.

Likewise, there are consequences to increasing the sample size. These consequences might include an increase in the amount of money required to do the study and an increase in the time needed to tabulate the data. When these consequences result, increasing the sample size may not be practical.

There are several other methods a researcher can use to increase the power of a statistical test, but these methods are beyond the scope of this text.

One final comment is necessary. When the researcher fails to reject the null hypothesis, this does not mean that there is not enough evidence to support alternative hypotheses. It may be that the null hypothesis is false, but the statistical test has too low a power to detect the real difference; hence, one can conclude only that in this study, there is not enough evidence to reject the null hypothesis.

The relationship among α, β, and the power of a test can be analyzed in greater detail than the explanation given here. However, it is hoped that this explanation will show you that there is no magic formula or statistical test that can guarantee foolproof results when a decision is made about the validity of H_0. Whether the decision is to reject H_0 or not to reject H_0, there is in either case a chance of being wrong. The goal, then, is to try to keep the probabilities of type I and type II errors as small as possible.

≡ Applying the Concepts 8–6

Consumer Protection Agency Complaints

Hypothesis testing and testing claims with confidence intervals are two different approaches that lead to the same conclusion. In the following activities, you will compare and contrast those two approaches.

Assume you are working for the Consumer Protection Agency and have recently been getting complaints about the highway gas mileage of the new Dodge Caravans. Chrysler Corporation agrees to allow you to randomly select 40 of its new Dodge Caravans to test the highway mileage. Chrysler claims that the vans get 28 mpg on the highway. Your results show a mean of 26.7 and a standard deviation of 4.2. You are not certain if you should create a confidence interval or run a hypothesis test. You decide to do both at the same time.

1. Draw a normal curve, labeling the critical values, critical regions, test statistic, and population mean. List the significance level and the null and alternative hypotheses.

2. Draw a confidence interval directly below the normal distribution, labeling the sample mean, error, and boundary values.

3. Explain which parts from each approach are the same and which parts are different.

4. Draw a picture of a normal curve and confidence interval where the sample and hypothesized means are equal.

5. Draw a picture of a normal curve and confidence interval where the lower boundary of the confidence interval is equal to the hypothesized mean.

6. Draw a picture of a normal curve and confidence interval where the sample mean falls in the left critical region of the normal curve.

See page 488 for the answers.

Exercises 8–6

1. **First-Time Births** According to the almanac, the mean age for a woman giving birth for the first time is 25.2 years. A random sample of ages of 35 professional women giving birth for the first time had a mean of 28.7 years and a standard deviation of 4.6 years. Use both a confidence interval and a hypothesis test at the 0.05 level of significance to test if the mean age of professional woman is different from 25.2 years at the time of their first birth.

2. **One-Way Airfares** The average one-way airfare from Pittsburgh to Washington, DC, is $236. A random sample of 20 one-way fares during a particular month had a mean of $210 with a standard deviation of $43. At $\alpha = 0.02$, is there sufficient evidence to conclude a difference from the stated mean? Use the sample statistics to construct a 98% confidence interval for the true mean one-way airfare from Pittsburgh to Washington, DC, and compare your interval to the results of the test. Do they support or contradict one another?

   Source: www.fedstats.gov

3. **IRS Audits** The IRS examined approximately 1% of individual tax returns for a specific year, and the average recommended additional tax per return was $19,150. Based on a random sample of 50 returns, the mean additional tax was $17,020. If the population standard deviation is $4080, is there sufficient evidence to conclude that the mean differs from $19,150 at $\alpha = 0.05$? Does a 95% confidence interval support this result?

   Source: New York Times Almanac.

4. **Prison Time** According to a public service website, 69.4% of white collar criminals get prison time. A randomly selected sample of 165 white collar criminals revealed that 120 were serving or had served prison time. Using $\alpha = 0.05$, test the conjecture that the proportion of white collar criminals serving prison time differs from 69.4% in two different ways.

5. **Working at Home** Workers with a formal arrangement with their employer to be paid for time worked at home worked an average of 19 hours per week. A random sample of 15 mortgage brokers indicated that they worked a mean of 21.3 hours per week at home with a standard deviation of 6.5 hours. At $\alpha = 0.05$, is there sufficient evidence to conclude a difference? Construct a 95% confidence interval for the true mean number of paid working hours at home. Compare the results of your confidence interval to the conclusion of your hypothesis test and discuss the implications.

   Source: www.bls.gov

6. **Newspaper Reading Times** A survey taken several years ago found that the average time a person spent reading the local daily newspaper was 10.8 minutes. The standard deviation of the population was 3 minutes. To see whether the average time had changed since the newspaper's format was revised, the newspaper editor surveyed 36 individuals. The average time that these 36 randomly selected people spent reading the paper was 12.2 minutes. At $\alpha = 0.02$, is there a change in the average time an individual spends reading the newspaper? Find the 98% confidence interval of the mean. Do the results agree? Explain.

7. What is meant by the power of a test?

8. How is the power of a test related to the type II error?

9. How can the power of a test be increased?

Summary

This chapter introduces the basic concepts of hypothesis testing. A statistical hypothesis is a conjecture about a population. There are two types of statistical hypotheses: the null and the alternative hypotheses. The null hypothesis states that there is no difference, and the alternative hypothesis specifies a difference. To test the null hypothesis, researchers use a statistical test. Many test statistics are computed by using

$$\text{Test statistic} = \frac{(\text{observed value}) - (\text{expected value})}{\text{standard error}}$$

- Researchers compute a test statistic from the sample data to decide whether the null hypothesis should be rejected. Statistical tests can be one-tailed or two-tailed, depending on the hypotheses.

The null hypothesis is rejected when the difference between the population parameter and the sample statistic is said to be significant. The difference is significant when the test statistic falls in the critical region of the distribution. The critical region is determined by α, the level of significance of the test. The level is the probability of committing a type I error. This error occurs when the null hypothesis is rejected when it is true. Three generally agreed upon significance levels are 0.10, 0.05, and 0.01. A second kind of error, the type II error, can occur when the null hypothesis is not rejected when it is false. (8–1)

- There are two common methods used to test hypotheses; they are the traditional method and the P-value method. (8–2)

- All hypothesis-testing situations using the traditional method should include the following steps:

  1. State the null and alternative hypotheses and identify the claim.
  2. State an alpha level and find the critical value(s).
  3. Compute the test statistic.
  4. Make the decision to reject or not reject the null hypothesis.
  5. Summarize the results.

- All hypothesis-testing situations using the P-value method should include the following steps:

  1. State the hypotheses and identify the claim.
  2. Compute the test statistic.
  3. Find the P-value.
  4. Make the decision.
  5. Summarize the results.

- The z test is used to test a mean when the population standard deviation is known. When the sample size is less than 30, the population values need to be normally distributed. (8–2)

- When the population standard deviation is not known, researchers use a t test to test a claim about a mean. If the sample size is less than 30, the population values need to be normally or approximately normally distributed. (8–3)

- The z test can be used to test a claim about a population when $np \geq 5$ and $nq \geq 5$. (8–4)

- A single variance can be tested by using the chi-square test. (8–5)

- There is a relationship between confidence intervals and hypothesis testing. When the null hypothesis is rejected, the confidence interval for the mean using the same level of significance will not contain the hypothesized mean. When the null hypothesis is not rejected, the confidence interval, using the same level of significance, will contain the hypothesized mean. (8–6)

- The power of a statistical test measures the sensitivity of the test to detect a real difference in parameters if one actually exists; $1 - \beta$ is called the power of a test. (8–6)

Important Terms

α (alpha) 420	hypothesis testing 414	power of a test 478	t test 442
alternative hypothesis 414	left-tailed test 420	P-value 425	two-tailed test 421
β (beta) 420	level of significance 420	research hypothesis 416	type I error 418
chi-square test 464	noncritical or nonrejection region 420	right-tailed test 420	type II error 418
critical or rejection region 420		statistical hypothesis 414	z test 428
critical value 420	null hypothesis 414	statistical test 418	
	one-tailed test 420	test statistic 418	

Important Formulas

Formula for the z test for means:

$$z = \frac{\overline{X} - \mu}{\sigma/\sqrt{n}} \quad \text{if } n < 30 \text{, variable must be normally distributed}$$

Formula for the t test for means:

$$t = \frac{\overline{X} - \mu}{s/\sqrt{n}} \quad \text{if } n < 30 \text{, variable must be normally distributed}$$

Formula for the z test for proportions:

$$z = \frac{\hat{p} - p}{\sqrt{pq/n}} \quad \text{if } np \geq 5 \text{ and } nq \geq 5$$

Formula for the chi-square test for variance or standard deviation:

$$\chi^2 = \frac{(n-1)s^2}{\sigma^2} \quad \text{if } n < 30 \text{, variable must be normally distributed}$$

≡ Review Exercises

For Exercises 1 through 20, perform each of the following steps.

a. State the hypotheses and identify the claim.

b. Find the critical value(s) or use the *P*-value method.

c. Compute the test statistic.

d. Make the decision.

e. Summarize the results.

Use the traditional method of hypothesis testing unless the P-value method is specified by your instructor.

Section 8–2

1. **Lifetime of $1 Bills** The average lifetime of circulated $1 bills is 18 months. A researcher believes that the average lifetime is not 18 months. He researched the lifetime of 50 $1 bills and found the average lifetime was 18.8 months. The population standard deviation is 2.8 months. At $\alpha = 0.02$, can it be concluded that the average lifetime of a circulated $1 bill differs from 18 months?

2. **Travel Times to Work** Based on information from the U.S. Census Bureau, the mean travel time to work in minutes for all workers 16 years old and older was 25.3 minutes. A large company with offices in several states randomly sampled 100 of its workers to ascertain their commuting times. The sample mean was 23.9 minutes, and the population standard deviation is 6.39 minutes. At the 0.01 level of significance, can it be concluded that the mean commuting time is less for this particular company?

   Source: factfinder.census.gov

3. **Debt of College Graduates** A random sample of the average debt (in dollars) at graduation from 30 of the top 100 public colleges and universities is listed below. Is there sufficient evidence at $\alpha = 0.01$ to conclude that the population mean debt at graduation is less than $18,000? Assume $\sigma = 2605.

16,012	15,784	16,597	18,105	12,665	14,734
17,225	16,953	15,309	15,297	14,437	14,835
13,607	13,374	19,410	18,385	22,312	16,656
20,142	17,821	12,701	22,400	15,730	17,673
18,978	13,661	12,580	14,392	16,000	15,176

   Source: www.Kiplinger.com

4. **Time Until Indigestion Relief** An advertisement claims that Fasto Stomach Calm will provide relief from indigestion in less than 10 minutes. For a test of the claim, 35 randomly selected individuals were given the product; the average time until relief was 9.25 minutes. From past studies, the standard deviation of the population is known to be 2 minutes. Can you conclude that the claim is justified? Find the *P*-value and let $\alpha = 0.05$.

5. **Shopper Purchases** A shopper in a grocery store purchases 22 items on average. A store manager believes that the mean is greater than 22. The manager surveyed a randomly selected group of 36 customers and found that the mean of the number of items purchased was 23.2. The population standard deviation is 3.7 items. At $\alpha = 0.05$, can it be concluded that the mean is greater than 22 items?

Section 8–3

6. **Trifecta Winnings** A random sample of $1 Trifecta tickets at a local racetrack paid the following amounts (in dollars and cents). Is there sufficient evidence to conclude that the average Trifecta winnings exceed $50? Use $\alpha = 0.10$. Assume the variable is normally distributed.

8.90	141.00	72.70	32.40
70.20	48.60	75.30	19.00
15.00	83.00	59.20	190.10
29.10			

7. **Weights of Men's Soccer Shoes** Is lighter better? A random sample of men's soccer shoes from an international catalog had the following weights (in ounces).

10.8	9.8	8.8	9.6	9.9
10	8.4	9.6	10	9.4
9.8	9.4	9.8		

   At $\alpha = 0.05$, can it be concluded that the average weight is less than 10 ounces? Assume the variable is normally distributed.

8. **Whooping Crane Eggs** Once down to about 15, the world's only wild flock of whooping cranes now numbers a record 506 birds in its Texas Coastal Bend wintering ground. The average whooping crane egg weighs 208 grams. A new batch of randomly selected eggs was recently weighed, and their weights are listed. At $\alpha = 0.01$, is there sufficient evidence to conclude that the weight is greater than 208 grams? Assume the variable is normally distributed.

210	208.5	211.6	212	210.3
210.2	209	206.4	209.7	

   Source: https://www.fws.gov/refuge/Aransas/wildlife/whooping_cranes.html

Section 8–4

9. **Medical School Choices** It has been reported that one in four medical doctors received their degrees from foreign schools. A hospital researcher believes that the percentage is less than 25%. A random survey of 100 medical doctors found that 19 received their degrees from a foreign school. At $\alpha = 0.05$, is there enough evidence to support the researcher's claim?

10. **Federal Prison Populations** Nationally 60.2% of federal prisoners are serving time for drug offenses. A warden feels that in his prison the percentage is even higher. He surveys 400 randomly selected inmates' records and finds that 260 of the inmates are drug offenders. At $\alpha = 0.05$, is he correct?

Source: New York Times Almanac.

11. **Free School Lunches** It has been reported that 59.3% of U.S. school lunches served are free or at a reduced price. A random sample of 300 children in a large metropolitan area indicated that 156 of them received lunch free or at a reduced price. At the 0.01 level of significance, is there sufficient evidence to conclude that the proportion is less than 59.3%?

Source: www.fns.usda.gov

12. **Cell Phone Ownership** A cell phone manufacturer claims that 65% of teenagers 13 to 16 years old have their own cell phones. A researcher wishes to test the claim and selects a random sample of 80 teenagers. The researcher finds that 57 have their own cell phones. At $\alpha = 0.05$, should the claim be rejected? Use the P-value method.

13. **Tobacco Use by High School Students** The use of tobacco by high school seniors has increased nationally in the last few years. The use of tobacco by high school seniors was recently reported at 37.3%. A random sample of 300 high school seniors from a large region indicated that 34% had used tobacco during the 30 days prior to the survey. At the 0.05 level of significance, does this differ from the national proportion?

14. **Men Aged 65 and Over in the Labor Force** Of men aged 65 and over 20.5% are still in the U.S. labor force. A random sample of 120 retired male teachers indicated that 38 were still working. Use both a confidence interval and a hypothesis test. Test the claim that the proportion is greater than 20.5% at $\alpha = 0.10$.

Section 8–5

15. **Fuel Consumption** The standard deviation of the fuel consumption of a certain automobile is hypothesized to be greater than or equal to 4.3 miles per gallon. A random sample of 20 automobiles produced a standard deviation of 2.6 miles per gallon. Is the standard deviation really less than previously thought? Use $\alpha = 0.05$ and the P-value method. Assume the variable is normally distributed.

16. **Movie Admission Prices** The average movie admission price for a recent year was $9.16. The population variance was 3.81. A random sample of 15 theater admission prices had a mean of $10.02 with a standard deviation of $2.08. At $\alpha = 0.05$, is there sufficient evidence to conclude a difference from the population variance? Assume the variable is normally distributed.

Source: statistic.com

17. **Games Played by NBA Scoring Leaders** A random sample of the number of games played by individual NBA scoring leaders is shown. Is there sufficient evidence to conclude that the variance in games played differs from 40? Use $\alpha = 0.05$. Assume the variable is normally distributed.

72	79	80	74	82
79	82	78	60	75

Source: Time Almanac.

18. **Fuel Consumption** The standard deviation of fuel consumption of a manufacturer's sport utility vehicle is hypothesized to be 3.3 miles per gallon. A random sample of 18 vehicles has a standard deviation of 2.8 miles per gallon. At $\alpha = 0.10$, is the claim believable?

Section 8–6

19. **Plant Leaf Lengths** A biologist knows that the average length of a leaf of a certain full-grown plant is 4 inches. The standard deviation of the population is 0.6 inch. A random sample of 20 leaves of that type of plant given a new type of plant food had an average length of 4.2 inches. Is there reason to believe that the new food is responsible for a change in the growth of the leaves? Use $\alpha = 0.01$. Find the 99% confidence interval of the mean. Do the results concur? Explain. Assume that the variable is approximately normally distributed.

20. **Tire Inflation** To see whether people are keeping their car tires inflated to the correct level of 35 pounds per square inch (psi), a tire company manager selects a random sample of 36 tires and checks the pressure. The mean of the sample is 33.5 psi, and the population standard deviation is 3 psi. Are the tires properly inflated? Use $\alpha = 0.10$. Find the 90% confidence interval of the mean. Do the results agree? Explain.

≡ STATISTICS TODAY

How Much Better Is Better? —Revisited

Now that you have learned the techniques of hypothesis testing presented in this chapter, you realize that the difference between the sample mean and the population mean must be *significant* before you can conclude that the students really scored above average. The superintendent should follow the steps in the hypothesis-testing procedure and be able to reject the null hypothesis before announcing that students scored higher than average.

Data Analysis

The Data Bank is found in Appendix B.

1. From the Data Bank, select a random sample of at least 30 individuals, and test one or more of the following hypotheses by using the z test. Use $\alpha = 0.05$.

   a. For serum cholesterol, H_0: $\mu = 220$ milligram percent (mg%). Use $\sigma = 5$.

   b. For systolic pressure, H_0: $\mu = 120$ millimeters of mercury (mm Hg). Use $\sigma = 13$.

   c. For IQ, H_0: $\mu = 100$. Use $\sigma = 15$.

   d. For sodium level, H_0: $\mu = 140$ milliequivalents per liter (mEq/l). Use $\sigma = 6$.

2. Select a random sample of 15 individuals and test one or more of the hypotheses in Exercise 1 by using the t test. Use $\alpha = 0.05$.

3. Select a random sample of at least 30 individuals, and using the z test for proportions, test one or more of the following hypotheses. Use $\alpha = 0.05$.

   a. For educational level, H_0: $p = 0.50$ for level 2.

   b. For smoking status, H_0: $p = 0.20$ for level 1.

   c. For exercise level, H_0: $p = 0.10$ for level 1.

   d. For gender, H_0: $p = 0.50$ for males.

4. Select a sample of 20 individuals and test the hypothesis H_0: $\sigma^2 = 225$ for IQ level. Use $\alpha = 0.05$. Assume the variable is normally distributed.

5. Using the data from Data Set XIII, select a sample of 10 hospitals, and test H_0: $\mu = 250$ and H_1: $\mu < 250$ for the number of beds. Use $\alpha = 0.05$. Assume the variable is normally distributed.

6. Using the sample of 10 hospitals obtained in Exercise 5, test the hypothesis H_0: $\sigma \geq 150$. Use $\alpha = 0.05$. Assume the variable is normally distributed.

Chapter Quiz

Determine whether each statement is true or false. If the statement is false, explain why.

1. No error is committed when the null hypothesis is rejected when it is false. True

2. When you are conducting the t test for n < 30, the population must be approximately normally distributed. True

3. The test statistic separates the critical region from the noncritical region. False

4. The values of a chi-square test cannot be negative. True

5. The chi-square test for variances is always one-tailed. False

Select the best answer.

6. When the value of α is increased, the probability of committing a type I error is

   a. Decreased

   b. Increased

   c. The same

   d. None of the above

7. If you wish to test the claim that the mean of the population is 100, the appropriate null hypothesis is

   a. $\overline{X} = 100$

   b. $\mu \geq 100$

   c. $\mu \leq 100$

   d. $\mu = 100$

8. The degrees of freedom for the chi-square test for variances or standard deviations are

   a. 1

   b. n

   c. n − 1

   d. None of the above

9. For the t test, one uses _____ instead of σ.

   a. n

   b. s

   c. χ^2

   d. t

Complete the following statements with the best answer.

10. Rejecting the null hypothesis when it is true is called a(n) _____ error. Type I

11. The probability of a type II error is referred to as _____. β

12. A conjecture about a population parameter is called a(n) _____. Statistical hypothesis

13. To test the claim that the mean is greater than 87, you would use a(n) _____-tailed test. Right

14. The degrees of freedom for the t test are ____$n - 1$____.

For the following exercises where applicable:

   a. State the hypotheses and identify the claim.

   b. Find the critical value(s) or use the *P*-value method.

   c. Compute the test statistic.

   d. Make the decision.

   e. Summarize the results.

Use the traditional method of hypothesis testing unless the *P*-value method is specified by your instructor. Assume all variables are normally distributed.

15. **Ages of Professional Women** A sociologist wishes to see if it is true that for a certain group of professional women, the average age at which they have their first child is 28.6 years. A random sample of 36 women is selected, and their ages at the birth of their first child are recorded. At $\alpha = 0.05$, does the evidence refute the sociologist's assertion? Assume $\sigma = 4.18$.

32	28	26	33	35	34
29	24	22	25	26	28
28	34	33	32	30	29
30	27	33	34	28	25
24	33	25	37	35	33
34	36	38	27	29	26

16. **Home Closing Costs** A real estate agent believes that the average closing cost of purchasing a new home is $6500 over the purchase price. She selects 40 new home sales at random and finds that the average closing costs are $6600. The standard deviation of the population is $120. Test her belief at $\alpha = 0.05$.

17. **Chewing Gum Use** A recent study stated that if a person chewed gum, the average number of sticks of gum the person chewed daily was 8. To test the claim, a researcher selected a random sample of 36 gum chewers and found the mean number of sticks of gum chewed per day was 9. The standard deviation of the population is 1. At $\alpha = 0.05$, is the number of sticks of gum a person chews per day actually greater than 8?

18. **Hotel Rooms** A travel agent claims that the average of the number of rooms in hotels in a large city is 500. At $\alpha = 0.01$, is the claim realistic? The data for a random sample of seven hotels are shown.

713   300   292   311   598   401   618

Give a reason why the claim might be deceptive.

19. **Heights of Models** In a New York modeling agency, a researcher wishes to see if the average height of female models is really less than 67 inches, as the chief claims. A random sample of 20 models has an average height of 65.8 inches. The standard deviation of the sample is 1.7 inches. At $\alpha = 0.05$, is the average height of the models really less than 67 inches? Use the *P*-value method.

20. **Experience of Taxi Drivers** A taxi company claims that its drivers have an average of at least 12.4 years experience. In a study of 15 randomly selected taxi drivers, the average experience was 11.2 years. The sample standard deviation was 2. At $\alpha = 0.10$, is the number of years experience of the taxi drivers really less than the taxi company claimed?

21. **Ages of Robbery Victims** A recent study in a small city stated that the average age of robbery victims was 63.5 years. A random sample of 20 recent victims had a mean of 63.7 years and a standard deviation of 1.9 years. At $\alpha = 0.05$, is the average age higher than originally believed? Use the *P*-value method.

22. **First-Time Marriages** A magazine article stated that the average age of women who are getting married for the first time is 26 years. A researcher decided to test this hypothesis at $\alpha = 0.02$. The researcher selected a random sample of 25 women who were recently married for the first time and found the average was 25.1 years. The sample standard deviation was 3 years. Should the null hypothesis be rejected on the basis of the sample?

23. **Survey on Vitamin Usage** A survey in *Men's Health* magazine reported that 39% of cardiologists said that they took vitamin E supplements. To see if this is still true, a researcher randomly selected 100 cardiologists and found that 36 said that they took vitamin E supplements. At $\alpha = 0.05$, test the claim that 39% of the cardiologists took vitamin E supplements.

24. **Breakfast Survey** A dietitian read in a survey that at least 55% of adults do not eat breakfast at least 3 days a week. To verify this, she selected a random sample of 80 adults and asked them how many days a week they skipped breakfast. A total of 50% responded that they skipped breakfast at least 3 days a week. At $\alpha = 0.10$, test the claim.

25. **Caffeinated Beverage Survey** A Harris Poll found that 35% of people said that they drink a caffeinated beverage to combat midday drowsiness. A recent survey found that 19 out of 48 randomly selected people stated that they drank a caffeinated beverage to combat midday drowsiness. At $\alpha = 0.02$, is the claim of the percentage found in the Harris Poll believable?

26. **Smartphone Ownership** A magazine claims that 75% of all teenage boys have their own smartphones. A researcher wished to test the claim and selected a random sample of 60 teenage boys. The researcher found that 54 had their own smartphones. At $\alpha = 0.01$, should the claim be rejected?

27. Find the *P*-value for the *z* test in Exercise 15.
   P-value = 0.0366

28. Find the *P*-value for the *z* test in Exercise 16.
   P-value < 0.0001

29. **Pages in Romance Novels** A copyeditor thinks the standard deviation for the number of pages in a romance novel is greater than 6. A random sample of 25 novels has a standard deviation of 9 pages. At $\alpha = 0.05$, is it higher, as the editor hypothesized?

30. **Seed Germination Times** It has been hypothesized that the standard deviation of the germination time of radish seeds is 8 days. The standard deviation of a random sample of 60 radish plants' germination times was 6 days. At $\alpha = 0.01$, test the claim.

31. **Pollution By-products** The standard deviation of the pollution by-products released in the burning of 1 gallon of gas is 2.3 ounces. A random sample of 20 automobiles tested produced a standard deviation of 1.9 ounces. Is the standard deviation really less than previously thought? Use $\alpha = 0.05$.

32. **Strength of Wrapping Cord** A manufacturer claims that the standard deviation of the strength of wrapping cord is 9 pounds. A random sample of 10 wrapping cords produced a standard deviation of 11 pounds. At $\alpha = 0.05$, test the claim. Use the *P*-value method.

33. Find the 90% confidence interval of the mean in Exercise 15. Is μ contained in the interval?
    $28.9 < \mu < 31.2$; no

34. Find the 95% confidence interval for the mean in Exercise 16. Is μ contained in the interval?
    $\$6562.81 < \mu < \$6637.19$; no

≡ Critical Thinking Challenges

The power of a test $(1 - \beta)$ can be calculated when a specific value of the mean is hypothesized in the alternative hypothesis; for example, let H_0: $\mu = 50$ and let H_1: $\mu = 52$. To find the power of a test, it is necessary to find the value of β. This can be done by the following steps:

Step 1 For a specific value of α find the corresponding value of $\overline{X}$, using $z = \dfrac{\overline{X} - \mu}{\sigma/\sqrt{n}}$, where μ is the hypothesized value given in H_0. Use a right-tailed test.

Step 2 Using the value of $\overline{X}$ found in step 1 and the value of μ in the alternative hypothesis, find the area corresponding to z in the formula $z = \dfrac{\overline{X} - \mu}{\sigma/\sqrt{n}}$.

Step 3 Subtract this area from 0.5000. This is the value of β.

Step 4 Subtract the value of β from 1. This will give you the power of a test. See Figure 8–41.

1. Find the power of a test, using the hypotheses given previously and $\alpha = 0.05$, $\sigma = 3$, and $n = 30$.

2. Select several other values for μ in H_1 and compute the power of the test. Generalize the results.

FIGURE 8–41
Relationship Among α, β, and the Power of a Test

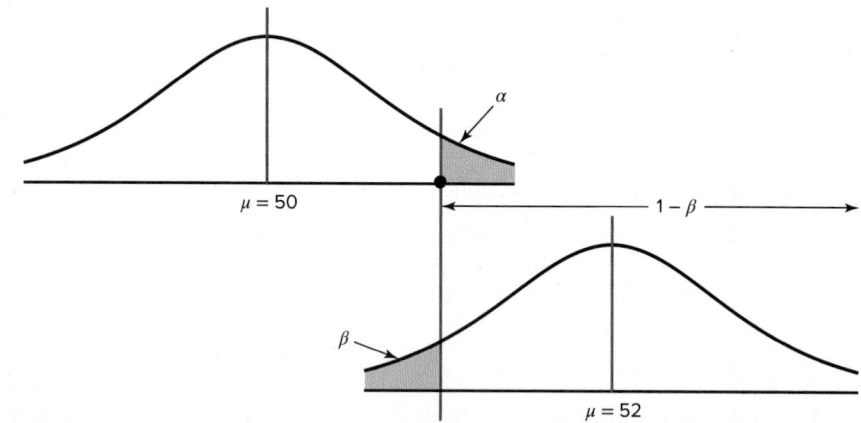

≡ Data Projects

Use a significance level of 0.05 for all tests below.

1. **Business and Finance** Use the Dow Jones Industrial stocks in data project 1 of Chapter 7 as your data set. Find the gain or loss for each stock over the last quarter. Test the claim that the mean is that the stocks broke even (no gain or loss indicates a mean of 0).

2. **Sports and Leisure** Use the most recent NFL season for your data. For each team, find the quarterback rating for the number one quarterback. Test the claim that the mean quarterback rating for a number one quarterback is more than 80.

3. **Technology** Use your last month's itemized cell phone bill for your data. Determine the percentage of your text messages that were outgoing. Test the claim that a majority of your text messages were outgoing. Determine the mean, median, and standard deviation for the length of a call. Test the claim that the mean length of a call is longer than the value you found for the median length.

4. **Health and Wellness** Use the data collected in data project 4 of Chapter 7 for this exercise. Test the claim that the mean body temperature is less than 98.6 degrees Fahrenheit.

5. **Politics and Economics** Use the most recent results of the Presidential primary elections for both parties. Determine what percentage of voters in your state voted for the eventual Democratic nominee for President and what percentage voted for the eventual Republican nominee. Test the claim that a majority of your state favored the candidate who won the nomination for each party.

6. **Your Class** Use the data collected in data project 6 of Chapter 7 for this exercise. Test the claim that the mean BMI for a student is more than 25.

Answers to Applying the Concepts

Section 8–1   Eggs and Your Health

1. The study was prompted by claims that linked eating eggs to high blood serum cholesterol.

2. The population under study is people in general.

3. A sample of 500 subjects was collected.

4. The hypothesis was that eating eggs did not increase blood serum cholesterol.

5. Blood serum cholesterol levels were collected.

6. Most likely, but we are not told which test.

7. The conclusion was that eating a moderate amount of eggs will not significantly increase blood serum cholesterol level.

Section 8–2   Car Thefts

1. The hypotheses are H_0: $\mu = 44$ and H_1: $\mu \neq 44$.

2. This sample can be considered large for our purposes.

3. The variable needs to be normally distributed.

4. We will use a z distribution.

5. Since we are interested in whether the car theft rate has changed, we use a two-tailed test.

6. Answers may vary. At the $\alpha = 0.05$ significance level, the critical values are $z = \pm 1.96$.

7. The sample mean is $\overline{X} = 55.97$ and the population standard deviation is 30.30. Our test statistic is
$$z = \frac{55.97 - 44}{30.30/\sqrt{36}} = 2.37.$$

8. Since $2.37 > 1.96$, we reject the null hypothesis.

9. There is enough evidence to conclude that the car theft rate has changed.

10. Answers will vary. Based on our sample data, it appears that the car theft rate has changed from 44 vehicles per 10,000 people. In fact, the data indicate that the car theft rate has increased.

11. Based on our sample, we would expect 55.97 car thefts per 10,000 people, so we would expect $(55.97)(5) = 279.85$, or about 280, car thefts in the city.

Section 8–3   How Much Nicotine Is in Those Cigarettes?

1. We have $15 - 1 = 14$ degrees of freedom.

2. This is a t test.

3. We are only testing one sample.

4. This is a right-tailed test, since the hypotheses of the tobacco company are H_0: $\mu = 40$ and H_1: $\mu > 40$.

5. The P-value is 0.008, which is less than the significance level of 0.01. We reject the tobacco company's claim.

6. Since the test statistic (2.72) is greater than the critical value (2.62), we reject the tobacco company's claim.

7. There is no conflict in this output, since the results based on the P-value and the test statistic value agree.

8. Answers will vary. It appears that the company's claim is false and that there is more than 40 mg of nicotine in its cigarettes.

Section 8–4   Quitting Smoking

1. The statistical hypotheses were that StopSmoke helps more people quit smoking than the other leading brands.

2. The null hypotheses were that StopSmoke has the same effectiveness as or is not as effective as the other leading brands.

3. The alternative hypotheses were that StopSmoke helps more people quit smoking than the other leading brands. (The alternative hypotheses are the statistical hypotheses.)

4. No statistical tests were run that we know of.

5. Had tests been run, they would have been one-tailed tests.

6. Some possible significance levels are 0.01, 0.05, and 0.10.

7. A type I error would be to conclude that StopSmoke is better when it really is not.

8. A type II error would be to conclude that StopSmoke is not better when it really is.

9. These studies proved nothing. Had statistical tests been used, we could have tested the effectiveness of StopSmoke.

10. Answers will vary. One possible answer is that more than likely the statements are talking about practical significance and not statistical significance, since we have no indication that any statistical tests were conducted.

Section 8–5   Testing Gas Mileage Claims

1. The hypotheses are H_0: $\mu = 28$ and H_1: $\mu < 28$. The value of our test statistic is $t = -1.96$, and the associated P-value is 0.0287. We would reject Chrysler's claim at $\alpha = 0.05$ that the Dodge Caravans are getting 28 mpg.

2. The hypotheses are H_0: $\sigma = 2.1$ and H_1: $\sigma > 2.1$. The value of our test statistic is $\chi^2 = \dfrac{(n-1)s^2}{\sigma^2} = \dfrac{(39)4.2^2}{2.1^2} = 156$, and the associated P-value is approximately zero. We would reject Chrysler's claim that the standard deviation is no more than 2.1 mpg.

3. Answers will vary. It is recommended that Chrysler lower its claim about the highway miles per gallon of the Dodge Caravans. Chrysler should also try to reduce variability in miles per gallon and provide confidence intervals for the highway miles per gallon.

4. Answers will vary. There are cases when a mean may be fine, but if there is a lot of variability about the mean, there will be complaints (due to the lack of consistency).

Section 8–6   Consumer Protection Agency Complaints

1. Answers will vary.

2. Answers will vary.

3. Answers will vary.

4. Answers will vary.

5. Answers will vary.

6. Answers will vary.

9

Testing the Difference Between Two Means, Two Proportions, and Two Variances

Fuse/Corbis/Getty Images

▰ STATISTICS TODAY

To Vaccinate or Not to Vaccinate? Small versus Large Nursing Homes

Influenza is a serious disease among the elderly, especially those living in nursing homes. Those residents are more susceptible to influenza than elderly persons living in the community because the former are usually older and more debilitated, and they live in a closed environment where they are exposed more so than community residents to the virus if it is introduced into the home. Three researchers decided to investigate the use of vaccine and its value in determining outbreaks of influenza in small nursing homes.

These researchers surveyed 83 randomly selected licensed homes in seven counties in Michigan. Part of the study consisted of comparing the number of people being vaccinated in small nursing homes (100 or fewer beds) with the number in larger nursing homes (more than 100 beds). Unlike the statistical methods presented in Chapter 8, these researchers used the techniques explained in this chapter to compare two sample proportions to see if there was a significant difference in the vaccination rates of patients in small nursing homes compared to those in large nursing homes. See Statistics Today—Revisited at the end of the chapter.

Source: Nancy Arden, Arnold S. Monto, and Suzanne E. Ohmit, "Vaccine Use and the Risk of Outbreaks in a Sample of Nursing Homes During an Influenza Epidemic," *American Journal of Public Health* 85, no. 3, pp. 399–401. Copyright by the American Public Health Association.

OUTLINE

Introduction

9–1 Testing the Difference Between Two Parameters

9–2 Testing the Difference Between Two Means: Using the *z* Test

9–3 Testing the Difference Between Two Means of Independent Samples: Using the *t* Test

9–4 Testing the Difference Between Two Means: Dependent Samples

9–5 Testing the Difference Between Proportions

9–6 Testing the Difference Between Two Variances

Summary

OBJECTIVES

After completing this chapter, you should be able to:

1 Test the difference between two means, using the *z* test.

2 Test the difference between two means for independent samples, using the *t* test.

3 Test the difference between two means for dependent samples.

4 Test the difference between two proportions.

5 Test the difference between two variances or standard deviations.

Introduction

The basic concepts of hypothesis testing were explained in Chapter 8. With the z, t, and χ^2 tests, a sample mean, variance, or proportion can be compared to a specific population mean, variance, or proportion to determine whether the null hypothesis should be rejected.

There are, however, many instances when researchers wish to compare two sample means, using experimental and control groups. For example, the average lifetimes of two different brands of bus tires might be compared to see whether there is any difference in tread wear. Two different brands of fertilizer might be tested to see whether one is better than the other for growing plants. Or two brands of cough syrup might be tested to see whether one brand is more effective than the other.

In the comparison of two means, the same basic steps for hypothesis testing shown in Chapter 8 are used, and the z and t tests are also used. When comparing two means by using the t test, the researcher must decide if the two samples are *independent* or *dependent*. The concepts of independent and dependent samples will be explained in Sections 9–3 and 9–4.

The z test can be used to compare two proportions, as shown in Section 9–5. Finally, two variances can be compared by using an F test as shown in Section 9–6.

9–1   Testing the Difference Between Two Parameters

Suppose a researcher wishes to determine whether there is a difference in the average age of nursing students who enroll in a nursing program at a community college and those who enroll in a nursing program at a university. In this case, the researcher is not interested in the average age of all beginning nursing students; instead, the researcher is interested in *comparing* the means of the two groups. His research question is, Does the mean age of nursing students who enroll at a community college differ from the mean age of nursing students who enroll at a university? Here, the hypotheses are

$$H_0: \mu_1 = \mu_2$$
$$H_1: \mu_1 \neq \mu_2$$

where

μ_1 = mean age of all beginning nursing students at a community college
μ_2 = mean age of all beginning nursing students at a university

Another way of stating the hypotheses for this situation is

$$H_0: \mu_1 - \mu_2 = 0$$
$$H_1: \mu_1 - \mu_2 \neq 0$$

If there is no difference in population means, subtracting them will give a difference of zero. If they are different, subtracting will give a number other than zero. Both methods of stating hypotheses are correct; however, the first method will be used in this text when the difference is zero.

When testing the difference between two proportions, the same reasoning applies as testing the difference between two means.

For example, suppose a researcher feels that the percentage of male workers who work more than 5 days a week is different from the percentage of female workers who work more than 5 days a week. The researcher would select two samples of workers; one sample would consist of all male workers and the other sample would consist of all female workers. Then the researcher would find the percentage of people in each group who would work more than 5 days a week. The researcher would then compare the two percentages.

The hypotheses would be

$$H_0: p_1 = p_2$$
$$H_1: p_1 \neq p_2$$

where p_1 is the percentage of male workers who work more than 5 days a week and p_2 would be the percentage of female workers who work more than 5 days a week.

Again, these hypotheses could be written as

$$H_0: p_1 - p_2 = 0$$
$$H_1: p_1 - p_2 \neq 0$$

The previous two examples show the hypotheses for two-tailed tests. If you were using a right-tailed test, the hypotheses would be

$$H_0: \mu_1 = \mu_2$$
$$H_1: \mu_1 > \mu_2$$

For two proportions, the hypotheses would be

$$H_0: p_1 = p_2$$
$$H_1: p_1 > p_2$$

If you are using a left-tailed test for means, the hypotheses would be

$$H_0: \mu_1 = \mu_2$$
$$H_1: \mu_1 < \mu_2$$

If you were using a left-tailed test for proportions, the hypotheses would be

$$H_0: p_1 = p_2$$
$$H_1: p_1 < p_2$$

If two samples are *independent* of each other, the subjects selected for the first sample in no way influence the way the subjects are selected in the second sample. For example, if a group of 50 people were randomly divided into two groups of 25 people each in order to test the effectiveness of a new drug, where one group gets the drug and the other group gets a placebo, the samples would be independent of each other.

On the other hand, two samples would be *dependent* if the selection of subjects for the first group in some way influenced the selection of subjects for the other group. For example, suppose you wanted to determine if a person's right foot was slightly larger than the left foot. In this case, the samples are dependent because once you selected a person's right foot for sample 1, you must select the left foot for sample 2 because you are using the same person for both feet.

The theory behind testing the difference between two means is based on selecting pairs of samples and comparing the means of the pairs. The population means need not be known.

All possible pairs of samples are taken from populations. The means for each pair of samples are computed and then subtracted, and the differences are plotted. If both populations have the same mean, then most of the differences will be zero or close to zero. Occasionally, there will be a few large differences due to chance alone, some positive and others negative. If the differences are plotted, the curve will be shaped like a normal distribution and have a mean of zero, as shown in Figure 9–1.

In the comparison of two sample means, the difference may be due to chance, in which case the null hypothesis will not be rejected and the researcher can assume that the means of the populations are basically the same. The difference in this case is not significant. See Figure 9–2(a). On the other hand, if the difference is significant, the null

FIGURE 9–1

Differences of Means of Pairs
of Samples

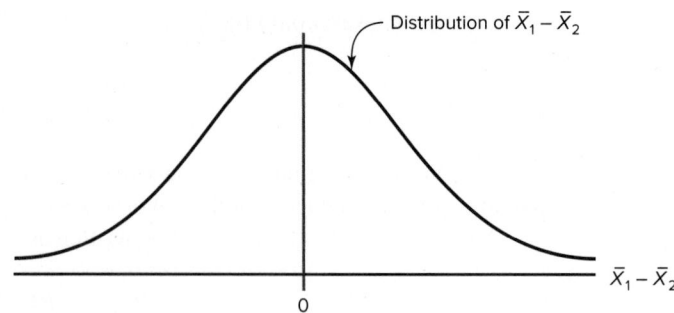

FIGURE 9–2 Differences of Means of Two Samples

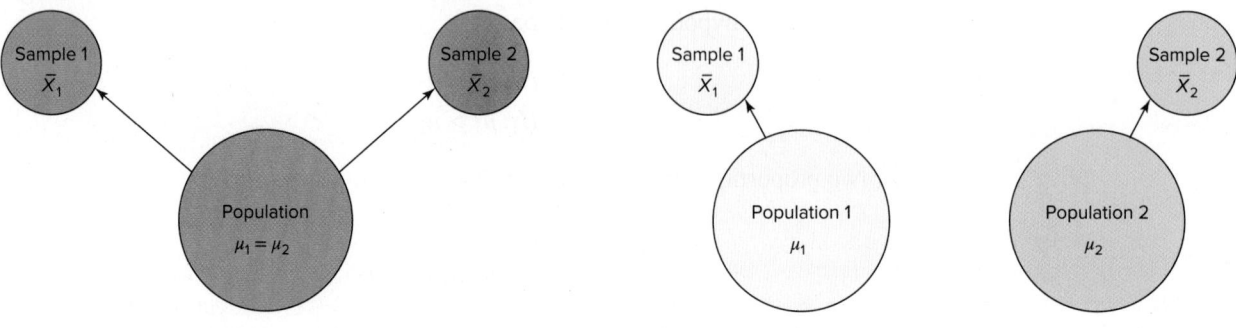

(a) Difference is not significant. The means of the populations are the same.

Do not reject H_0: $\mu_1 = \mu_2$ since $\bar{X}_1 - \bar{X}_2$ is not significant.

(b) Difference is significant. The means of the populations are different.

Reject H_0: $\mu_1 = \mu_2$ since $\bar{X}_1 - \bar{X}_2$ is significant.

hypothesis is rejected and the researcher can conclude that the population means are different. See Figure 9–2(b).

The same reasoning goes for the difference between two proportions. The general formula for testing the difference between two means or testing the difference between two proportions is

$$\text{Test statistic} = \frac{(\text{observed value}) - (\text{expected value})}{\text{standard error}}$$

The values for this formula are shown in the following sections.

Applying the Concepts 9–1

Highway Safety

A highway engineer wishes to compare the convenience and safety of two interstate highways in a large city. Two variables to consider are the time it takes to get to a destination and the number of accidents on the roads.

1. Define the populations.

2. What type of samples can be used?

3. Are the samples independent or dependent?

4. State the hypotheses for each:

    a. The time it takes to get from point A to point B.

    b. The proportions of accidents on the highways.

5. What significance level would you use?

See page 549 for the answers.

≡ Exercises 9–1

1. Explain the difference between testing a single mean and testing the difference between two means.

2. Explain the difference between testing a single proportion and testing the difference between two proportions.

3. What does it mean to say the two samples are independent? Give an example of independent samples.

4. What does it mean to say that two samples are dependent? Give an example of dependent samples.

For Exercises 5–10, state the null and alternative hypothesis for each conjecture.

5. A researcher believes that the mean number of cups of coffee that male college students drink per day is greater than the mean number of cups of coffee that female college students drink per day.

6. A nutritionist believes that the mean fiber content of wheat-type cereals is higher than the mean fiber of rice-type cereals.

7. Researchers believe that children ages 8 to 11 who get an hour of daily exercise perform better on a thinking skills test than those who do not get an hour of daily exercise.

8. An automobile engineer believes that the mean number of miles per gallon that a four-wheel drive vehicle gets is less than the mean number of miles per gallon that an all-wheel drive vehicle gets.

9. A researcher believes that women who stick to the Mediterranean diet for a year will have fewer strokes than those who are not on the diet.

10. A medical researcher believes that the mean time in minutes that ibuprofen relieves pain is less than the mean time in minutes that aspirin relieves pain.

For Exercises 11–16, write the null and alternate hypotheses for each claim.

11. A researcher believes that the percentage of emails that are junk and not read by males is greater than the percentage of junk emails that are not read by women.

12. An environmentalist believes that the percentage of air pollution produced by trucks is less than the percentage of air pollution produced by automobiles.

13. The percentage of college graduates who believe that chewing gum improves their memory is not equal to the percentage of high school students who believe that chewing gum improves their memory.

14. A media consultant thinks that the percentage of college-educated adults who watch the early news on television is greater than the percentage of adults who do not have a college degree who watch the early news on television.

15. An attorney states that the percentage of criminal trial lawyers who think that the bar exam does not measure their ability to practice law is not the same as the percentage of civil trial lawyers who feel that way.

16. A researcher believes that the percentage of people who forget their toothbrushes when they go on vacation is greater than the percentage of people who forget their deodorants.

9–2   Testing the Difference Between Two Means: Using the *z* Test

OBJECTIVE

Test the difference between two means, using the *z* test.

Before you can use the *z* test to test the difference between two independent sample means, you must make sure that the following assumptions are met.

> **Assumptions for the *z* Test to Determine the Difference Between Two Means**
>
> 1. Both samples are random samples.
> 2. The samples must be independent of each other. That is, there can be no relationship between the subjects in each sample.
> 3. The standard deviations of both populations must be known; and if the sample sizes are less than 30, the populations must be normally or approximately normally distributed.

In this book, the assumptions will be stated in the exercises; however, when encountering statistics in other situations, you must check to see that these assumptions have been met before proceeding.

The denominator of the *z* test formula is the standard deviation of the differences of the means. The reasoning is shown next.

Formula for the z Test for Comparing Two Means from Independent Populations

$$z = \frac{(\overline{X}_1 - \overline{X}_2) - (\mu_1 - \mu_2)}{\sqrt{\dfrac{\sigma_1^2}{n_1} + \dfrac{\sigma_2^2}{n_2}}}$$

Unusual Stats

Adult children who live with their parents spend more than 2 hours a day doing household chores. According to a study, daughters contribute about 17 hours a week and sons about 14.4 hours.

The variance of the difference $\overline{X}_1 - \overline{X}_2$ is equal to the sum of the individual variances of $\overline{X}_1$ and $\overline{X}_2$. That is,

$$\sigma_{\overline{X}_1 - \overline{X}_2}^2 = \sigma_{\overline{X}_1}^2 + \sigma_{\overline{X}_2}^2$$

where

$$\sigma_{\overline{X}_1}^2 = \frac{\sigma_1^2}{n_1} \quad \text{and} \quad \sigma_{\overline{X}_2}^2 = \frac{\sigma_2^2}{n_2}$$

So the standard deviation of $\overline{X}_1 - \overline{X}_2$ is

$$\sqrt{\frac{\sigma_1^2}{n_1} + \frac{\sigma_2^2}{n_2}}$$

This formula is based on the general format of

$$\text{Test statistic} = \frac{(\text{observed value}) - (\text{expected value})}{\text{standard error}}$$

where $\overline{X}_1 - \overline{X}_2$ is the observed difference, and the expected difference $\mu_1 - \mu_2$ is zero when the null hypothesis is $\mu_1 = \mu_2$, since that is equivalent to $\mu_1 - \mu_2 = 0$. Finally, the standard error of the difference is

$$\sqrt{\frac{\sigma_1^2}{n_1} + \frac{\sigma_2^2}{n_2}}$$

These tests can also be one-tailed, using the following hypotheses:

Two-tailed		Right-tailed		Left-tailed	
$H_0: \mu_1 = \mu_2$ $H_0: \mu_1 \neq \mu_2$	or	$H_0: \mu_1 = \mu_2$ $H_1: \mu_1 > \mu_2$	or	$H_0: \mu_1 = \mu_2$ $H_1: \mu_1 < \mu_2$	or
$H_1: \mu_1 - \mu_2 = 0$ $H_1: \mu_1 - \mu_2 \neq 0$		$H_0: \mu_1 - \mu_2 = 0$ $H_1: \mu_1 - \mu_2 > 0$		$H_0: \mu_1 - \mu_2 = 0$ $H_1: \mu_1 - \mu_2 < 0$	

The same critical values used in Section 8–2 are used here. They can be obtained from Table A–4 in Appendix A.

The basic format for hypothesis testing using the traditional method is reviewed here.

Step 1 State the hypotheses and identify the claim.

Step 2 Find the critical value(s).

Step 3 Compute the test statistic.

Step 4 Make the decision.

Step 5 Summarize the results.

EXAMPLE 9–1   Sodium Intake

A study using two random groups of 40 men and 40 women found that the average daily intake of sodium for men was 3653 milligrams and 3482 milligrams for women. Assume that the population standard deviation from previous studies is 324 milligrams for men and 287 milligrams for women. At $\alpha = 0.05$, can it be concluded that there is a significant difference in the average sodium intake between the groups?

SOLUTION

Step 1   State the hypotheses and identify the claim. H_0: $\mu_1 = \mu_2$ and H_1: $\mu_1 \neq \mu_2$ (claim)

Step 2   Find the critical values. Since $\alpha = 0.05$, the critical values are -1.96 and $+1.96$.

Step 3   Compute the test statistic:

$$z = \frac{(\overline{X}_1 - \overline{X}_2) - (\mu_1 - \mu_2)}{\sqrt{\dfrac{\sigma_1^2}{n_1} + \dfrac{\sigma_2^2}{n_2}}} = \frac{(3653 - 3482) - 0}{\sqrt{\dfrac{324^2}{40} + \dfrac{287^2}{40}}} = \frac{171}{68.44} = 2.50$$

Step 4   Make the decision. Reject the null hypothesis since $2.50 > 1.96$. See Figure 9–3.

FIGURE 9–3   Critical Values and Test Statistic for Example 9–1

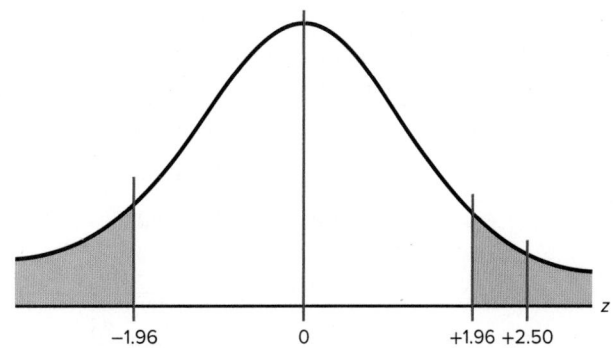

Step 5   Summarize the results. There is enough evidence to say that there is a difference in the mean amount of sodium consumed by men and women at the 0.05 significance level.

The P-values for this test can be determined by using the same procedure shown in Section 8–2. For example, if the test statistic for a two-tailed test is 2.90, then the P-value obtained from Table A–4 is 0.0038. This value is obtained by looking up the area for $z = 2.90$, which is 0.9981. Then 0.9981 is subtracted from 1.0000 to get 0.0019. Finally, this value is doubled to get 0.0038 since the test is two-tailed. If $\alpha = 0.05$, the decision would be to reject the null hypothesis, since P-value $< \alpha$ (that is, $0.0038 < 0.05$). *Note:* The P-value obtained on the TI-84 is 0.0037.

The P-value method for hypothesis testing for this chapter also follows the same format as stated in Chapter 8. The steps are reviewed here.

Step 1   State the hypotheses and identify the claim.

Step 2   Compute the test statistic.

Step 3   Find the P-value.

Step 4   Make the decision.

Step 5   Summarize the results.

Example 9–2 illustrates these steps.

EXAMPLE 9–2　College Sports Offerings

A researcher hypothesizes that the average number of sports that colleges offer for males is greater than the average number of sports that colleges offer for females. A random sample of the number of sports offered by colleges for males and females is shown. At $\alpha = 0.10$, is there enough evidence to support the claim? Assume σ_1 and $\sigma_2 = 3.3$.

Males					Females				
6	11	11	8	15	6	8	11	13	8
6	14	8	12	18	7	5	13	14	6
6	9	5	6	9	6	5	5	7	6
6	9	18	7	6	10	7	6	5	5
15	6	11	5	5	16	10	7	8	5
9	9	5	5	8	7	5	5	6	5
8	9	6	11	6	9	18	13	7	10
9	5	11	5	8	7	8	5	7	6
7	7	5	10	7	11	4	6	8	7
10	7	10	8	11	14	12	5	8	5

Source: USA TODAY.

SOLUTION

Step 1　State the hypotheses and identify the claim.

$$H_0: \mu_1 = \mu_2 \quad \text{and} \quad H_1: \mu_1 > \mu_2 \text{ (claim)}$$

Step 2　Compute the test statistic. Using a calculator or the formula in Chapter 3, find the mean for each data set.

For the males　　$\overline{X}_1 = 8.6$　　and　　$\sigma_1 = 3.3$

For the females　$\overline{X}_2 = 7.9$　　and　　$\sigma_2 = 3.3$

Substitute in the formula.

$$z = \frac{(\overline{X}_1 - \overline{X}_2) - (\mu_1 - \mu_2)}{\sqrt{\dfrac{\sigma_1^2}{n_1} + \dfrac{\sigma_2^2}{n_2}}} = \frac{(8.6 - 7.9) - 0}{\sqrt{\dfrac{3.3^2}{50} + \dfrac{3.3^2}{50}}} = 1.06*$$

Step 3　Find the *P*-value from Table A–4. For $z = 1.06$, the area is 0.8554, and $1.0000 - 0.8554 = 0.1446$, or a *P*-value of 0.1446.

Step 4　Make the decision. Since the *P*-value is larger than α (that is, $0.1446 > 0.10$), the decision is to not reject the null hypothesis. See Figure 9–4.

Step 5　Summarize the results. There is not enough evidence to support the claim that colleges offer more sports for males than they do for females at the 0.10 level of significance.

FIGURE 9–4　*P*-Value and α Value for Example 9–2

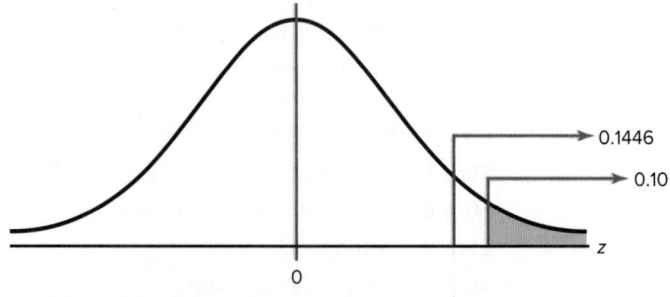

0.1446

0.10

0

z

Note: Calculator results may differ due to rounding.

Sometimes, the researcher is interested in testing a specific difference in means other than zero. For example, the researcher might hypothesize that the nursing students at a community college are, on average, 3.2 years older than those at a university. In this case, the hypotheses are

$$H_0: \mu_1 - \mu_2 = 3.2 \qquad \text{and} \qquad H_1: \mu_1 - \mu_2 > 3.2$$

The formula for the z test is still

$$z = \frac{(\overline{X}_1 - \overline{X}_2) - (\mu_1 - \mu_2)}{\sqrt{\dfrac{\sigma_1^2}{n_1} + \dfrac{\sigma_2^2}{n_2}}}$$

where $\mu_1 - \mu_2$ is the hypothesized difference or expected value. In this case, $\mu_1 - \mu_2 = 3.2$.

Confidence intervals for the difference between two means can also be found. When you are hypothesizing a difference of zero, if the confidence interval contains zero, the null hypothesis is not rejected. If the confidence interval does not contain zero, the null hypothesis is rejected.

Confidence intervals for the difference between two means can be found by using this formula:

Formula for the z Confidence Interval for Difference Between Two Means

$$(\overline{X}_1 - \overline{X}_2) - z_{\alpha/2}\sqrt{\frac{\sigma_1^2}{n_1} + \frac{\sigma_2^2}{n_2}} < \mu_1 - \mu_2 < (\overline{X}_1 - \overline{X}_2) + z_{\alpha/2}\sqrt{\frac{\sigma_1^2}{n_1} + \frac{\sigma_2^2}{n_2}}$$

EXAMPLE 9–3   Sodium Intake

Find the 95% confidence interval for the difference between the means in Example 9–1.

SOLUTION

Substitute in the formula, using $z_{\alpha/2} = 1.96$.

$$(\overline{X}_1 - \overline{X}_2) - z_{\alpha/2}\sqrt{\frac{\sigma_1^2}{n_1} + \frac{\sigma_2^2}{n_2}} < \mu_1 - \mu_2 < (\overline{X}_1 - \overline{X}_2) + z_{\alpha/2}\sqrt{\frac{\sigma_1^2}{n_1} + \frac{\sigma_2^2}{n_2}}$$

$$(3653 - 3482) - 1.96\sqrt{\frac{324^2}{40} + \frac{287^2}{40}} < \mu_1 - \mu_2 < (3653 - 3482) + 1.96\sqrt{\frac{324^2}{40} + \frac{287^2}{40}}$$

$$171 - 134.14 < \mu_1 - \mu_2 < 171 + 134.14$$

$$36.86 < \mu_1 - \mu_2 < 305.14$$

The confidence interval obtained from the TI-84 is $36.866 < \mu_1 - \mu_2 < 305.13$.

Since the confidence interval does not contain zero, the decision is to reject the null hypothesis, which agrees with the previous result.

Applying the Concepts 9–2

Home Runs

For a sports podcast, you are asked to research the question whether more home runs are hit by players in the National League or by players in the American League. You decide to use the home run leaders from each league for a 40-year period as your data. The numbers are shown.

National League									
47	49	73	50	65	70	49	47	40	43
46	35	38	40	47	39	49	37	37	36
40	37	31	48	48	45	52	38	38	36
44	40	48	45	45	36	39	44	52	47

American League									
47	57	52	47	48	56	56	52	50	40
46	43	44	51	36	42	49	49	40	43
39	39	22	41	45	46	39	32	36	32
32	32	37	33	44	49	44	44	49	32

Using the data given, answer the following questions.

1. Define a population.

2. What kind of sample was used?

3. Do you feel that the samples are representative?

4. What are your hypotheses?

5. What significance level will you use?

6. What statistical test will you use?

7. What are the test results? (Assume $\sigma_1 = 8.8$ and $\sigma_2 = 7.8$.)

8. What is your decision?

9. What can you conclude?

10. Do you feel that using the data given really answers the original question asked?

11. What other data might be used to answer the question?

See page 549 for the answers.

Exercises 9–2

1. What are the assumptions for testing the difference between two means?

2. When a researcher selects all possible pairs of samples from a population in order to find the difference between the means of each pair, what will be the shape of the distribution of the differences when the original distributions are normally distributed? What will be the mean of the distribution? What will be the standard deviation of the distribution?

3. What three assumptions must be met when you are using the z test to test differences between two means when σ_1 and σ_2 are known?

4. Show two different ways to state that the means of two populations are equal. H_0: $\mu_1 = \mu_2$ or H_0: $\mu_1 - \mu_2 = 0$

For Exercises 5 through 16, perform each of the following steps.

a. State the hypotheses and identify the claim.

b. Find the critical value(s) or use the *P*-value method.

c. Compute the test statistic.

d. Make the decision.

e. Summarize the results.

Use the traditional method of hypothesis testing unless the P-value method is specified by your instructor.

5. **Sodium Content of Popcorn** The mean sodium content of movie popcorn is 980 mg of sodium per container. A researcher randomly selects two samples of 30 containers of popcorn from two different movie theaters and finds that the mean sodium content from theater A was 973 mg and the mean sodium content from theater B was 968 mg. If the population standard deviation of the sodium content is 9 mg, test the claim that there is a difference in the sodium content of the popcorn containers from the two theaters at $\alpha = 0.05$.

6. **Teachers' Salaries** New York and Massachusetts lead the list of average teacher's salaries. The New York

average is $76,409 while teachers in Massachusetts make an average annual salary of $73,195. Random samples of 45 teachers from each state yielded the following.

	Massachusetts	New York
Sample means	$73,195	$76,409
Population standard deviation	8,200	7,800

At $\alpha = 0.10$, is there a difference in means of the salaries?

Source: World Almanac.

7. **Commuting Times** The U.S. Census Bureau reports that the average commuting time for citizens of both Baltimore, Maryland, and Miami, Florida, is approximately 29 minutes. To see if their commuting times appear to be any different in the winter, random samples of 40 drivers were surveyed in each city and the average commuting time for the month of January was calculated for both cities. The results are shown. At the 0.05 level of significance, can it be concluded that the commuting times are different in the winter?

	Miami	Baltimore
Sample size	40	40
Sample mean	28.5 min	35.2 min
Population standard deviation	7.2 min	9.1 min

Source: www.census.gov

8. **Heights of 9-Year-Olds** At age 9 the average weight (21.3 kg) and the average height (124.5 cm) for both boys and girls are exactly the same. A random sample of 9-year-olds yielded these results. At $\alpha = 0.05$, do the data support the given claim that there is a difference in heights?

	Boys	Girls
Sample size	60	50
Mean height, cm	123.5	126.2
Population variance	98	120

Source: www.healthepic.com

9. **Length of Hospital Stays** The average length of "short hospital stays" for men is slightly longer than that for women, 5.2 days versus 4.5 days. A random sample of recent hospital stays for both men and women revealed the following. At $\alpha = 0.01$, is there sufficient evidence to conclude that the average hospital stay for men is longer than the average hospital stay for women?

	Men	Women
Sample size	32	30
Sample mean	5.5 days	4.2 days
Population standard deviation	1.2 days	1.5 days

Source: www.cdc.gov/nchs

10. **Years Married before Divorce** *Divorce Magazine* found that the mean time for first-time divorced couples is 7.8 years. A researcher took two random samples of 36 divorced couples and found that the mean time for the males was 7.6 years and for females it was 7.9 years. If the population standard deviations were 2.3 years for males and 2.6 years for females, is there a

difference in the mean years for the males and the mean years for females? Use $\alpha = 0.10$.

11. **Prices of a Used Car** For a specific year the *Kelly Bluebook* stated that the average price of a used car was $15,900. A researcher wanted to see if the mean amount of money spent by college students for a used car was less than the mean amount of money spent for a used car in general. She randomly selected 50 college students who purchased a used car for college and found that the sample had a mean of $15,236. For the general population who were not attending college at that time, the mean amount of money spent by 50 non-college students for a used car was $15,307 and the population standard deviation was $289. At $\alpha = 0.01$, can it be concluded that college student spent less for a used car than those in the general population?

12. **Number of Cars a Person Owns** In a survey, Experian Automotive found that people owned on average 12 cars in their lifetimes. A researcher wished to see if the average number of cars for male car owners was greater than the average number of cars for female car owners. The researcher selected two random samples of 40 individual car owners and found that the average number of cars owned by the males was 14.2 and the average number of cars owned by the females was 13.6. If the population standard deviation was 2.1 for both samples, can it be concluded that males owned more automobiles than females in their lifetimes? Use $\alpha = 0.05$.

13. **Per Capita Income** The average per capita income for Wisconsin is reported to be $59,209, and for Pennsylvania it is $59,445—almost the same thing. A random sample of 50 workers from each state indicated the following sample statistics.

	Wisconsin	Pennsylvania
Size	50	50
Mean	$40,275	$38,750
Population standard deviation	$10,500	$12,500

At $\alpha = 0.05$, can we conclude a difference in means of the personal incomes?

Source: New York Times Almanac.

14. **Monthly Social Security Benefits** The average monthly Social Security benefit for a specific year for retired workers was $1514 and for disabled workers was $1259. Researchers used data from the Social Security records to test the claim that the difference in monthly benefits between the two groups was greater than $30. Based on the following information, can the researchers' claim be supported at the 0.05 level of significance?

	Retired	Disabled
Sample size	60	60
Mean benefit	$1,460.50	$1,402.69
Population standard deviation	$98	$101

Source: New York Times Almanac.

15. **Self-Esteem Scores** In a study of a group of women science majors who remained in their profession and a group who left their profession within a few months of graduation, the researchers collected the data shown here on a self-esteem questionnaire. At $\alpha = 0.05$, can it be concluded that there is a difference in the self-esteem scores of the two groups? Use the P-value method.

Leavers	Stayers
$\overline{X}_1 = 3.05$	$\overline{X}_2 = 2.96$
$\sigma_1 = 0.75$	$\sigma_2 = 0.75$
$n_1 = 103$	$n_2 = 225$

Source: Rayman, Paula and Brett, Belle, "Women Science Majors: What Makes a Difference in Persistence after Graduation?" The Journal of Higher Education, 66, 4, July–August 1995, 388–414.

16. **Ages of College Students** The dean of students wants to see whether there is a significant difference in ages of resident students and commuting students. She selects a random sample of 50 students from each group. The ages are shown here. At $\alpha = 0.05$, decide if there is enough evidence to reject the claim of no difference in the ages of the two groups. Use the P-value method. Assume $\sigma_1 = 3.68$ and $\sigma_2 = 4.7$.

Resident students

22	25	27	23	26	28	26	24
25	20	26	24	27	26	18	19
18	30	26	18	18	19	32	23
19	19	18	29	19	22	18	22
26	19	19	21	23	18	20	18
22	21	19	21	21	22	18	20
19	23						

Commuter students

18	20	19	18	22	25	24	35
23	18	23	22	28	25	20	24
26	30	22	22	22	21	18	20
19	26	35	19	19	18	19	32
29	23	21	19	36	27	27	20
20	21	18	19	23	20	19	19
20	25						

17. **Working Breath Rate** Two random samples of 32 individuals were selected. One sample participated in an activity which simulates hard work. The average breath rate of these individuals was 21 breaths per minute. The other sample did some normal walking. The mean breath rate of these individuals was 14. Find the 90% confidence interval of the difference in the breath rates if the population standard deviation was 4.2 for breath rate per minute.

18. **Traveling Distances** Find the 95% confidence interval of the difference in the distance that day students travel to school and the distance evening students travel to

school. Two random samples of 40 students are taken, and the data are shown. Find the 95% confidence interval of the difference in the means.

	$\overline{X}$	σ	n
Day students	4.7	1.5	40
Evening Students	6.2	1.7	40

19. **Literacy Scores** Adults aged 16 or older were assessed in three types of literacy: prose, document, and quantitative. The scores in document literacy were the same for 19- to 24-year-olds and for 40- to 49-year-olds. A random sample of scores from a later year showed the following statistics.

Age group	Mean score	Population standard deviation	Sample size
19–24	280	56.2	40
40–49	315	52.1	35

Construct a 95% confidence interval for the true difference in mean scores for these two groups. What does your interval say about the claim that there is no difference in mean scores?

Source: www.nces.ed.gov

20. **Hospital Chief Executives** A survey of 30 random selected large hospitals found that the average salary of the Chief Executive Officers was $368,720, while in 30 randomly selected smaller hospitals, the salary was $359,806. The population standard deviation from past studies was $14,336. At $\alpha = 0.01$, is there a difference in the mean salaries? Find the 99% confidence interval of the difference in the means.

21. **Battery Voltage** Two brands of batteries are tested, and their voltages are compared. The summary statistics follow. Find the 95% confidence interval of the true difference in the means. Assume that both variables are normally distributed.

Brand X	Brand Y
$\overline{X}_1 = 9.2$ volts	$\overline{X}_2 = 8.8$ volts
$\sigma_1 = 0.3$ volt	$\sigma_2 = 0.1$ volt
$n_1 = 27$	$n_2 = 30$

22. **Commuting Times for College Students** The mean travel time to work for Americans is 25.3 minutes. An employment agency wanted to test the mean commuting times for college graduates and those with only some college. Thirty-five college graduates spent a mean time of 40.5 minutes commuting to work with a population variance of 67.24. Thirty workers who had completed some college had a mean commuting time of 34.8 minutes with a population variance of 39.69. At the 0.05 level of significance, can a difference in means be concluded?

Source: World Almanac 2012.

23. **Store Sales** A company owned two small Bath and Body Goods stores in different cities. It was desired to see if there was a difference in their mean daily sales. The following results were obtained from a random sample of daily sales over a six-week period. At $\alpha = 0.01$, can a difference in sales be concluded? Use the *P*-value method.

Store	Mean	Population standard deviation	Sample size
A	$995	$120	30
B	1120	250	30

24. **Home Prices** The average sales price of a single-family home in the metropolitan Dallas, Texas, area is $238,156. The average home price in Pittsburgh, Pennsylvania, is $190,589. The mean of a random sample of 45 homes in Dallas was $216,000 with a population standard deviation of $30,000. In Pittsburgh, a sample of 40 homes had a mean price of $203,000 with a population standard deviation of $32,500. At the 0.05 level of significance, can it be concluded that the mean price in Dallas exceeds the mean price in Pittsburgh? Use the *P*-value method.

Source: Zillow

Extending the Concepts

25. **Exam Scores at Private and Public Schools** A researcher claims that students in a private school have exam scores that are at most 8 points higher than those of students in public schools. Random samples of 60 students from each type of school are selected and given an exam. The results are shown. At $\alpha = 0.05$, test the claim.

Private school	Public school
$\overline{X}_1 = 110$	$\overline{X}_2 = 104$
$\sigma_1 = 15$	$\sigma_2 = 15$
$n_1 = 60$	$n_2 = 60$

26. **Sale Prices for Houses** The average sales price of new one-family houses in the Midwest is $250,000 and in the South is $253,400. A random sample of 40 houses in each region was examined with the following results. At the 0.05 level of significance, can it be concluded that the difference in mean sales price for the two regions is greater than $3400?

	South	Midwest
Sample size	40	40
Sample mean	$261,500	$248,200
Population standard deviation	$10,500	$12,000

Source: New York Times Almanac.

27. **Average Earnings for College Graduates** The average earnings of year-round full-time workers with bachelor's degrees or more is $88,641 for men and $58,000 for women—a difference of slightly over $30,000 a year. One hundred of each were randomly sampled, resulting in a sample mean of $90,200 for men, and the population standard deviation is $15,000; and a mean of $57,800 for women, and the population standard deviation is $12,800. At the 0.01 level of significance, can it be concluded that the difference in means is not $30,000?

Source: New York Times Almanac.

Technology Step by Step

TI-84 Plus

Step by Step

Hypothesis Test for the Difference Between Two Means and *z* Distribution (Data)

Example TI9–1

1. Enter the data values into L_1 and L_2.

2. Press **STAT** and move the cursor to TESTS.

3. Press **3** for 2-SampZTest.

4. Move the cursor to Data and press **ENTER**.

5. Type in the appropriate values.

6. Move the cursor to the appropriate alternative hypothesis and press **ENTER**.

7. Move the cursor to Calculate and press **ENTER**.

This refers to Example 9–2 in the text.

Hypothesis Test for the Difference Between Two Means and *z* Distribution (Statistics)

This refers to Example 9–1 in the text.

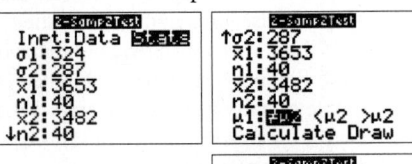

Example TI9–2

1. Press **STAT** and move the cursor to TESTS.
2. Press **3** for 2-SampZTest.
3. Move the cursor to Stats and press **ENTER**.
4. Type in the appropriate values.
5. Move the cursor to the appropriate alternative hypothesis and press **ENTER**.
6. Move the cursor to Calculate and press **ENTER**.

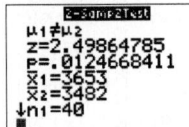

Confidence Interval for the Difference Between Two Means and *z* Distribution (Data)

1. Enter the data values into L_1 and L_2.
2. Press **STAT** and move the cursor to TESTS.
3. Press **9** for 2-SampZInt.
4. Move the cursor to Data and press **ENTER**.
5. Type in the appropriate values.
6. Move the cursor to Calculate and press **ENTER**.

Confidence Interval for the Difference Between Two Means and *z* Distribution (Statistics)

This refers to Example 9–3 in the text.

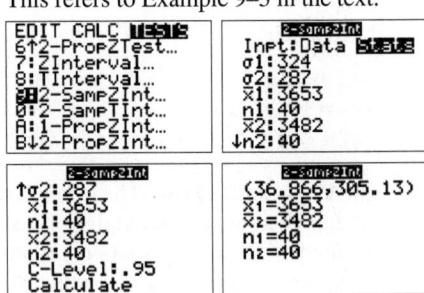

Example TI9–3

1. Press **STAT** and move the cursor to TESTS.
2. Press **9** for 2-SampZInt.
3. Move the cursor to Stats and press **ENTER**.
4. Type in the appropriate values.
5. Move the cursor to Calculate and press **ENTER**.

EXCEL
Step by Step

z Test for the Difference Between Two Means

Excel has a two-sample *z* test included in the Data Analysis Add-in.

Example XL9–1

Test the claim that the two population means are equal, using the sample data provided here, at $\alpha = 0.05$. Assume the population variances are $\sigma_A^2 = 10.067$ and $\sigma_B^2 = 7.067$.

Set A	10	2	15	18	13	15	16	14	18	12	15	15	14	18	16
Set B	5	8	10	9	9	11	12	16	8	8	9	10	11	7	6

1. Enter the first sample data set into column A.
2. Enter the second sample data set into column B.
3. Select the Data tab from the toolbar. Then select Data Analysis.
4. In the Analysis Tools box, select *z* test: Two Sample for Means.
5. Type the ranges for the data in columns A and B and type a value (usually 0) for the Hypothesized Mean Difference.

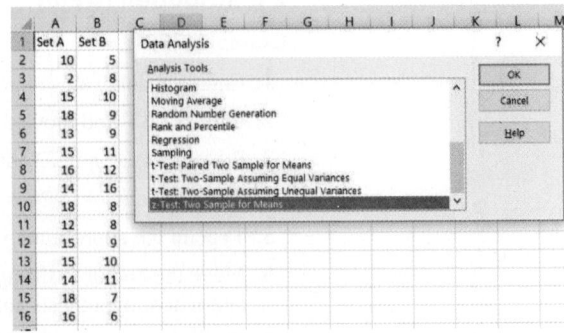

6. Type the known population variances in for Variable 1 Variance (known) and Variable 2 Variance (known).

7. Check the box for labels if you selected the labels in the input ranges.

8. Specify the confidence level Alpha.

9. Specify a location for the output, and click [OK].

The two-sample *z* test dialog box is shown; the results appear in the table that Excel generates.

Note that the *P*-value and critical *z* score are provided for both the one-tailed test and the two-tailed test. The *P*-values here are expressed in scientific notation: $7.084\text{E-}06 = 7.084 \times 10^{-6} = 0.000007084$. Because this value is less than 0.05, we reject the null hypothesis and conclude that the population means are not equal.

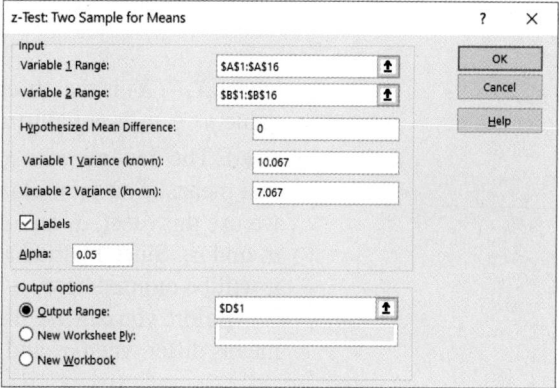

z-Test: Two Sample for Means		
	Set A	*Set B*
Mean	14.06666667	9.2666667
Known Variance	10.067	7.067
Observations	15	15
Hypothesized Mean Difference	0	
z	4.491149228	
P(Z<=z) one-tail	3.54199E-06	
z Critical one-tail	1.644853627	
P(Z<=z) two-tail	7.08399E-06	
z Critical two-tail	1.959963985	

9–3 Testing the Difference Between Two Means of Independent Samples: Using the *t* Test

OBJECTIVE ❷

Test the difference between two means for independent samples, using the *t* test.

In Section 9–2, the *z* test was used to test the difference between two means when the population standard deviations were known and the variables were normally or approximately normally distributed, or when both sample sizes were greater than or equal to 30. In many situations, however, these conditions cannot be met—that is, the population standard deviations are not known. In these cases, a *t* test is used to test the difference between means when the two samples are independent and when the samples are taken from two normally or approximately normally distributed populations. Samples are **independent samples** when they are not related. Also it will be assumed that the variances are not equal.

> **Formula for the *t* Test for Testing the Difference Between Two Means, Independent Samples**
>
> Variances are assumed to be unequal:
>
> $$t = \frac{(\overline{X}_1 - \overline{X}_2) - (\mu_1 - \mu_2)}{\sqrt{\dfrac{s_1^2}{n_1} + \dfrac{s_2^2}{n_2}}}$$
>
> where the degrees of freedom are equal to the smaller of $n_1 - 1$ or $n_2 - 1$.

The formula

$$t = \frac{(\overline{X}_1 - \overline{X}_2) - (\mu_1 - \mu_2)}{\sqrt{\dfrac{s_1^2}{n_1} + \dfrac{s_2^2}{n_2}}}$$

follows the format of

$$\text{Test statistic} = \frac{(\text{observed value}) - (\text{expected value})}{\text{standard error}}$$

where $\overline{X}_1 - \overline{X}_2$ is the observed difference between sample means and where the expected value $\mu_1 - \mu_2$ is equal to zero when no difference between population means is hypothesized. The denominator $\sqrt{s_1^2/n_1 + s_2^2/n_2}$ is the standard error of the difference between two means. This formula is similar to the one used when σ_1 and σ_2 are known; but when we use this t test, σ_1 and σ_2 are unknown, so s_1 and s_2 are used in the formula in place of σ_1 and σ_2. Since mathematical derivation of the standard error is somewhat complicated, it will be omitted here.

Before you can use the testing methods to determine whether two independent sample means differ when σ_1 and σ_2 are unknown, the following assumptions must be met.

Assumptions for the t Test for Two Independent Means When σ_1 and σ_2 Are Unknown

1. The samples are random samples.
2. The sample data are independent of one another.
3. When the sample sizes are less than 30, the populations must be normally or approximately normally distributed.

In this book, the assumptions will be stated in the exercises; however, when encountering statistics in other situations, you must check to see that these assumptions have been met before proceeding.

Again the hypothesis test here follows the same steps as those in Section 9–2; however, the formula uses s_1 and s_2 and Table A–5 to get the critical values.

EXAMPLE 9–4 Non-mortgage Debt

A study was done to see if there is a difference between the non-mortgage debts of Generation X individuals and Millennials. Random samples of 10 individuals of each group were selected. The average debt of Generation X individuals was $28,436, and the average debt of Millennials was $27,164. The standard deviations of the samples were $1647 and $1853, respectfully. At $\alpha = 0.05$, can it be concluded that there is a difference in the means of the two samples? Assume the variables are normally distributed.

SOLUTION

Step 1 State the hypotheses and identify the claim. $H_0: \mu_1 = \mu_2$ and $H_1: \mu_1 \neq \mu_2$ (claim)

Step 2 Find the critical values. Since the test is two-tailed and $\alpha = 0.05$, the degrees of freedom are the smaller of $n_1 - 1$ and $n_2 - 1$. In this case, $n_1 - 1$ and $n_2 - 1$ are both equal to $10 - 1 = 9$. From Table A–5, the critical values are $+2.262$ and -2.262.

Step 3 Find the test statistic.

$$t = \frac{(\overline{X}_1 - \overline{X}_2) - (\mu_1 - \mu_2)}{\sqrt{\dfrac{s_1^2}{n_1} + \dfrac{s_2^2}{n_2}}} = \frac{(28436 - 27164) - 0}{\sqrt{\dfrac{1647^2}{10} + \dfrac{1853^2}{10}}} = \frac{1272}{783.98} = 1.622$$

Step 4   Make the decision. Do not reject the null hypothesis since 1.622 < 2.262. See Figure 9–5.

FIGURE 9–5   Critical Values and Test Statistic for Example 9–4

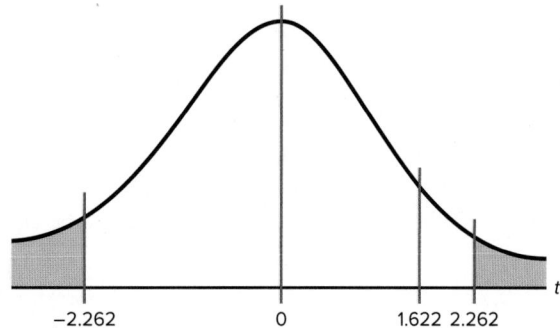

Step 5   Summarize the results. There is not enough evidence to support the claim that the means are different.

Note: The *P*-value for the test from the TI-84 is 0.1393, which is larger than 0.05.

When raw data are given in the exercises, use your calculator or the formulas in Chapter 3 to find the means and variances for the data sets. Then follow the procedures shown in this section to test the hypotheses.

Confidence intervals can also be found for the difference of two means with this formula:

Confidence Intervals for the Difference of Two Means: Independent Samples

Variances assumed to be unequal:

$$(\overline{X}_1 - \overline{X}_2) - t_{\alpha/2}\sqrt{\frac{s_1^2}{n_1} + \frac{s_2^2}{n_2}} < \mu_1 - \mu_2 < (\overline{X}_1 - \overline{X}_2) + t_{\alpha/2}\sqrt{\frac{s_1^2}{n_1} + \frac{s_2^2}{n_2}}$$

d.f. = smaller value of $n_1 - 1$ or $n_2 - 1$

EXAMPLE 9–5

Find the 95% confidence interval for the data in Example 9–4.

SOLUTION

Substitute in the formula.

$$(\overline{X}_1 - \overline{X}_2) - t_{\alpha/2}\sqrt{\frac{s_1^2}{n_1} + \frac{s_2^2}{n_2}} < \mu_1 - \mu_2 < (\overline{X}_1 - \overline{X}_2) + t_{\alpha/2}\sqrt{\frac{s_1^2}{n_1} + \frac{s_2^2}{n_2}}$$

$$(28436 - 27164) - 2.262\sqrt{\frac{1647^2}{10} + \frac{1853^2}{10}} < \mu_1 - \mu_2 < (28436 - 27164)$$
$$+ 2.262\sqrt{\frac{1647^2}{10} + \frac{1853^2}{10}}$$

$$1272 - 1773.36 < \mu_1 - \mu_2 < 1272 + 1773.36$$
$$-501.36 < \mu_1 - \mu_2 < 3045.36$$

Since 0 is contained in the interval, there is not enough evidence to support the claim that the means are different.

In many statistical software packages, a different method is used to compute the degrees of freedom for this t test. They are determined by the formula

$$\text{d.f.} = \frac{(s_1^2/n_1 + s_2^2/n_2)^2}{(s_1^2/n_1)^2/(n_1 - 1) + (s_2^2/n_2)^2/(n_2 - 1)}$$

This formula will not be used in this textbook.

There are actually two different options for the use of t tests. *One option is used when the variances of the populations are not equal, and the other option is used when the variances are equal.* To determine whether two sample variances are equal, the researcher can use an F test, as shown in Section 9–6.

When the variances are assumed to be equal, this formula is used and

$$t = \frac{(\overline{X}_1 - \overline{X}_2) - (\mu_1 - \mu_2)}{\sqrt{\dfrac{(n_1 - 1)s_1^2 + (n_2 - 1)s_2^2}{n_1 + n_2 - 2}} \sqrt{\dfrac{1}{n_1} + \dfrac{1}{n_2}}}$$

follows the format of

$$\text{Test statistic} = \frac{(\text{observed value}) - (\text{expected value})}{\text{standard error}}$$

For the numerator, the terms are the same as in the previously given formula. However, a note of explanation is needed for the denominator of the second test statistic. Since both populations are assumed to have the same variance, the standard error is computed with what is called a pooled estimate of the variance. A **pooled estimate of the variance** is a weighted average of the variance using the two sample variances and the *degrees of freedom* of each variance as the weights. Again, since the algebraic derivation of the standard error is somewhat complicated, it is omitted.

Note, however, that not all statisticians are in agreement about using the F test before using the t test. Some believe that conducting the F and t tests at the same level of significance will change the overall level of significance of the t test. Their reasons are beyond the scope of this text. Because of this, we will assume that $\sigma_1 \neq \sigma_2$ in this text.

Applying the Concepts 9–3

Too Long on the Telephone

A company collects data on the lengths of telephone calls made by employees in two different divisions. The sample mean and the sample standard deviation for the sales division are 10.26 and 8.56, respectively. The sample mean and sample standard deviation for the shipping and receiving division are 6.93 and 4.93, respectively. A hypothesis test was run, and the computer output follows.

> Degrees of freedom = 56
> Confidence interval limits = −0.18979, 6.84979
> Test statistic $t = 1.89566$
> Critical value $t = -2.0037, 2.0037$
> P-value = 0.06317
> Significance level = 0.05

1. Are the samples independent or dependent?
2. Which number from the output is compared to the significance level to check if the null hypothesis should be rejected?
3. Which number from the output gives the probability of a type I error?
4. Was a right-, left-, or two-tailed test done? Why?
5. What are your conclusions?
6. What would your conclusions be if the level of significance were initially set at 0.10?

See page 549 for the answers.

≡ Exercises 9–3

For these exercises, perform each of these steps. Assume that all variables are normally or approximately normally distributed.

    a. State the hypotheses and identify the claim.

    b. Find the critical value(s) or use the *P*-value method.

    c. Compute the test statistic.

    d. Make the decision.

    e. Summarize the results.

Use the traditional method of hypothesis testing unless the P-value method is specified by your instructor. Assume the variances are unequal.

1. **Waterfall Heights** Is there a significant difference at $\alpha = 0.10$ in the mean heights in feet of waterfalls in Europe and the ones in Asia? The data are shown.

Europe			Asia		
487	1246	1385	614	722	964
470	1312	984	1137	320	830
900	345	820	350	722	1904

Source: World Almanac and Book of Facts.

2. **Tax-Exempt Properties** A tax collector wishes to see if the mean values of the tax-exempt properties are different for two cities. The values of the tax-exempt properties for the two random samples are shown. The data are given in millions of dollars. At $\alpha = 0.05$, is there enough evidence to support the tax collector's claim that the means are different?

City A				City B			
113	22	14	8	82	11	5	15
25	23	23	30	295	50	12	9
44	11	19	7	12	68	81	2
31	19	5	2	20	16	4	5

3. **Urban Auto Traffic** A researcher wishes to see if there is a difference between the number of peak hours of auto traffic in the United States compared to other areas of the world. Using a *t* test, compare the means of the two data sets at $\alpha = 0.10$.

United States

79	102	91	70	64	85	101	72	80	92

Other countries

75	86	74	69	91	68	79	81	77	89	75	66	84

4. **Ages of Gamblers** The mean age of a random sample of 25 people who were playing the slot machines is 48.7 years, and the standard deviation is 6.8 years. The mean age of a random sample of 35 people who were playing roulette is 55.3 with a standard deviation of 3.2 years. Can it be concluded at $\alpha = 0.05$ that the mean age of those playing the slot machines is less than those playing roulette?

5. **Carbohydrates in Candies** The number of grams of carbohydrates contained in 1-ounce servings of randomly selected chocolate and nonchocolate candy is listed here. Is there sufficient evidence to conclude that the difference in the means is statistically significant? Use $\alpha = 0.10$.

Chocolate:	29	25	17	36	41	25	32	29
	38	34	24	27	29			

Nonchocolate:	41	41	37	29	30	38	39	10
	29	55	29					

Source: The Doctor's Pocket Calorie, Fat, and Carbohydrate Counter.

6. **Essays** A professor wishes to see if two groups of students' essays differ in lengths, that is, the number of words in each essay. The professor randomly selects 12 essays from a group of students who are science majors and 10 essays from a group of humanities majors to compare. The data are shown. At $\alpha = 0.05$, can it be concluded that there is a difference in the lengths of the essays between the two groups?

Science majors

1730	3637	3968	2427	1592	2735	3192	2561
3048	2192	2841	1830				

Humanities majors

2666	700	2218	2561	2071	1974	2315	2919
2246	1672						

7. **Weights of Running Shoes** The weights in ounces of a sample of running shoes for men and women are shown. Test the claim that the means are different. Use the *P*-value method with $\alpha = 0.05$.

Men		Women		
10.4	12.6	10.6	10.2	8.8
11.1	14.7	9.6	9.5	9.5
10.8	12.9	10.1	11.2	9.3
11.7	13.3	9.4	10.3	9.5
12.8	14.5	9.8	10.3	11.0

8. **Presidential Addresses** A researcher wishes to see if the lengths of the inaugural addresses in words of Presidents differ according to political parties. The researcher randomly selects nine inaugural addresses from Democrats and nine inaugural addresses from Republicans to compare. Can it be concluded at $\alpha = 0.10$ that there is a difference in the lengths of the inaugural addresses?

Republicans

1459	2427	1803	2459	2124	2320	1592
1457	2572					

Democrats

1366	1229	2155	2096	2372	2550	2460
1598	2103					

Source: The American Presidency Project

9. Find the 90% confidence for the difference of the means in Exercise 1 of this section. $-338.3 < \mu_1 - \mu_2 < 424.1$

10. Find the 95% confidence interval for the difference of the means in Exercise 6 of this section. $-94.3 < \mu_1 - \mu_2 < 1118.1; -145.481 < \mu_1 - \mu_2 < 1169.247$

11. **Hours Spent Watching Television** According to Nielsen Media Research, children (ages 2–11) spend an average of 21 hours 30 minutes watching television per week while teens (ages 12–17) spend an average of 20 hours 40 minutes. Based on the sample statistics shown, is there sufficient evidence to conclude a difference in average television watching times between the two groups? Use $\alpha = 0.01$.

	Children	Teens
Sample mean	22.45	18.50
Sample variance	16.4	18.2
Sample size	15	15

Source: Time Almanac.

12. **Professional Golfers' Earnings** Two random samples of earnings of professional golfers were selected. One sample was taken from the Professional Golfers Association, and the other was taken from the Ladies Professional Golfers Association. At $\alpha = 0.05$, is there a difference in the means? The data are in thousands of dollars.

PGA

446	1147	1344	9188	5687
10,508	4910	8553	7573	375

LPGA

48	76	122	466	863
100	1876	2029	4364	2921

13. **Patient Times with Medical Practitioners** A study of 10 randomly selected doctors found that they spent an average time of 11.6 minutes with their patients. The standard deviation of the sample was 3.6 minutes. A random sample of 12 physician's assistants found that they spent an average of 14.3 minutes with their patients. The sample standard deviation for this sample was 3.22 minutes. At $\alpha = 0.10$, do the physician's assistants spend more time with patients?

14. **Hockey's Highest Scorers** The number of points held by random samples of the NHL's highest scorers for both the Eastern Conference and the Western Conference is shown. At $\alpha = 0.05$, can it be concluded that there is a difference in means based on these data?

Eastern Conference				Western Conference			
83	60	75	58	77	59	72	58
78	59	70	58	37	57	66	55
62	61	59		61			

Source: www.foxsports.com

15. **Hospital Stays for Maternity Patients** Health Care Knowledge Systems reported that an insured woman spends on average 2.3 days in the hospital for a routine childbirth, while an uninsured woman spends on average 1.9 days. Assume two random samples of 16 women each were used in both samples. The standard deviation of the first sample is equal to 0.6 day, and the standard deviation of the second sample is 0.3 day. At $\alpha = 0.01$, test the claim that the means are equal using the P-value method. Find the 99% confidence interval for the differences of the means.

Source: Michael D. Shook and Robert L. Shook, The Book of Odds.

16. **Ages of Homes** Whiting, Indiana, leads the "Top 100 Cities with the Oldest Houses" list with the average age of houses being 66.4 years. Farther down the list resides Franklin, Pennsylvania, with an average house age of 59.4 years. Researchers selected a random sample of 20 houses in each city and obtained the following statistics. At $\alpha = 0.05$, can it be concluded that the houses in Whiting are older? Use the P-value method.

	Whiting	Franklin
Mean age	62.1 years	55.6 years
Standard deviation	5.4 years	3.9 years

Source: www.city-data.com

17. **Medical School Enrollments** A random sample of enrollments from medical schools that specialize in research and from those that are noted for primary care is listed. Find the 90% confidence interval for the difference in the means. $9.9 < \mu_1 - \mu_2 < 219.6$

Research				Primary care			
474	577	605	663	783	605	427	728
783	467	670	414	546	474	371	107
813	443	565	696	442	587	293	277
692	694	277	419	662	555	527	320
884							

Source: U.S. News & World Report Best Graduate Schools.

18. **Out-of-State Tuitions** The out-of-state tuitions (in dollars) for random samples of both public and private 4-year colleges in a New England state are listed. Find the 95% confidence interval for the difference in the means.

Private		Public	
13,600	13,495	7,050	9,000
16,590	17,300	6,450	9,758
23,400	12,500	7,050	7,871
		16,100	

Source: New York Times Almanac. $\$1789.70 < \mu_1 - \mu_2 < \$12,425.41$

19. **Gasoline Prices** A random sample of monthly gasoline prices was taken from 2011 and from 2015. The samples are shown. Using $\alpha = 0.01$, can it be concluded that gasoline cost more in 2015? Use the P-value method.

2011	2.02	2.47	2.50	2.70	3.13	2.56	
2015	2.36	2.46	2.63	2.76	3.00	2.85	2.77

20. Miniature Golf Scores A large group of friends went miniature golfing together at a par 54 course and decided to play on two teams. A random sample of scores from each of the two teams is shown. At $\alpha = 0.05$, is there a difference in mean scores between the two teams? Use the *P*-value method.

Team 1	61	44	52	47	56	63	62	55
Team 2	56	40	42	58	48	52	51	

21. Home Runs Two random samples of professional baseball players were selected and the number of home runs hit were recorded. One sample was obtained from the National League, and the other sample was obtained from the American League. At $\alpha = 0.10$, is there a difference in the means?

National League				American League			
18	4	8	2	6	11	18	11
9	2	6	5	3	12	25	4
6	8	29	25	24	9	12	5

22. Batting Averages Random samples of batting averages from the leaders in both leagues prior to the All-Star break are shown. At the 0.05 level of significance, can a difference be concluded?

National	.360	.654	.652	.338	.313	.309
American	.340	.332	.317	.316	.314	.306

≡ Technology   Step by Step

TI-84 Plus
Step by Step

Hypothesis Test for the Difference Between Two Means and *t* Distribution (Statistics)

Example TI9–4

This refers to Example 9–4 in the text.

1. Press **STAT** and move the cursor to TESTS.
2. Press **4** for 2-SampTTest.
3. Move the cursor to Stats and press **ENTER**.
4. Type in the appropriate values.
5. Move the cursor to the appropriate alternative hypothesis and press **ENTER**.
6. On the line for Pooled, move the cursor to No (standard deviations are assumed not equal) and press **ENTER**.
7. Move the cursor to Calculate and press **ENTER**.

Confidence Interval for the Difference Between Two Means and *t* Distribution (Data)

1. Enter the data values into L$_1$ and L$_2$.
2. Press **STAT** and move the cursor to TESTS.
3. Press **0** for 2-SampTInt.
4. Move the cursor to Data and press **ENTER**.
5. Type in the appropriate values.
6. On the line for Pooled, move the cursor to No (standard deviations are assumed not equal) and press **ENTER**.
7. Move the cursor to Calculate and press **ENTER**.

Confidence Interval for the Difference Between Two Means and *t* Distribution (Statistics)

Example TI9–5

This refers to Example 9–5 in the text. Answers may be different if using the smaller of $n_1 - 1$ or $n_2 - 1$.

1. Press **STAT** and move the cursor to TESTS.
2. Press **0** for 2-SampTInt.
3. Move the cursor to Stats and press **ENTER**.
4. Type in the appropriate values.
5. On the line for Pooled, move the cursor to No (standard deviations are assumed not equal) and press **ENTER**.
6. Move the cursor to Calculate and press **ENTER**.

EXCEL
Step by Step

Testing the Difference Between Two Means: Independent Samples

Excel has a two-sample t test included in the Data Analysis Add-in. The following example shows how to perform a t test for the difference between two means.

Example XL9–2

The following represent the delivery time in minutes for two different food delivery companies. Test the claim that there is a difference between population means based on these sample data. Assume the population variances are not equal. Use $\alpha = 0.05$. Assume that the variable is approximately normally distributed.

Company A	32	38	37	36	36	34	39	36	37	42
Company B	30	36	35	36	31	34	37	33	32	

1. Enter the Company A data into column A.
2. Enter the Company B data into column B.
3. Select the Data tab from the toolbar. Then select Data Analysis.
4. In the Data Analysis box, under Analysis Tools select t-test: Two-Sample Assuming Unequal Variances, and click [OK].
5. In Input, type in the Variable 1 Range: **A1:A11** and the Variable 2 Range: **B1:B10**.
6. Type **0** for the Hypothesized Mean Difference.

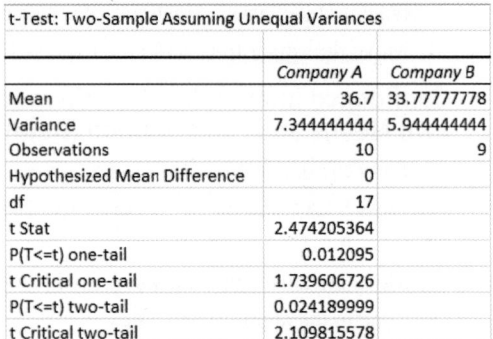

7. Check the box for labels if you selected the labels in the input ranges.
8. Type **0.05** for Alpha.
9. In Output options, type D1 for the Output Range, then click [OK].

t-Test: Two-Sample Assuming Unequal Variances		
	Company A	*Company B*
Mean	36.7	33.77777778
Variance	7.344444444	5.944444444
Observations	10	9
Hypothesized Mean Difference	0	
df	17	
t Stat	2.474205364	
P(T<=t) one-tail	0.012095	
t Critical one-tail	1.739606726	
P(T<=t) two-tail	0.024189999	
t Critical two-tail	2.109815578	

Note: You may need to increase the column width to see all the results. To do this:

1. Highlight the columns D, E, and F.
2. Select **Format>AutoFit** Column Width.

Note that the P-value and critical t value are provided for both the one-tailed test and the two-tailed test. Because the P-value of 0.024189999 is less than 0.05, we reject the null hypothesis and conclude that there is a significant difference in the population mean delivery times.

MINITAB
Step by Step

Test the Difference Between Two Means: Independent Samples*

MINITAB will calculate the test statistic and P-value for differences between the means for two populations when the population standard deviations are unknown.

Example MT9–1

The following represent the delivery time in minutes for two different food delivery companies. Test the claim that there is a difference between population means based on these sample data.

*MINITAB does not calculate a z test statistic. This statistic can be used instead.

Assume the population variances are not equal. Use $\alpha = 0.05$. Assume that the variable is approximately normally distributed.

Company A	32	38	37	36	36	34	39	36	37	42
Company B	30	36	35	36	31	34	37	33	32	

1. Enter the data into columns C1 and C2. Label the columns **Company A** and **Company B.**

2. Select **Stat>Basic Statistics>2-Sample t.**

3. Select Each sample is in its own column from the drop-down menu.

4. Click in the box for Sample 1. Double-click C1 Company A in the list.

5. Click in the box for Sample 2, then double-click C2 Company B in the list. Do not check the box for Assume equal variances. MINITAB will use the large sample formula. The completed dialog box is shown.

6. Click [Options].

   a) Type in **95** for the Confidence level.

   b) Type **0** for the Hypothesized difference.

   c) Select Difference $\neq$ hypothesized difference for the Alternative hypothesis.

   d) Make sure that Assume equal variances is not checked.

7. Click [OK] twice.

Since the P-value is less than the significance level, $0.025 < 0.05$, reject the null hypothesis.

Two-Sample T-Test and CI: Company A, Company B

```
Two-sample T for Company A vs Company B

            N   Mean   StDev   SE Mean
Company A   10  36.70  2.71    0.86
Company B   9   33.78  2.44    0.81


Difference = μ (Company A) - μ (Company B)
Estimate for difference:  2.92
95% CI for difference:  (0.42, 5.43)
T-Test of difference = 0 (vs ≠): T-Value = 2.46  P-Value = 0.025  DF = 17
Both use Pooled StDev = 2.5857
```

9–4   Testing the Difference Between Two Means: Dependent Samples

OBJECTIVE ③

Test the difference between two means for dependent samples.

In Section 9–2, the z test was used to compare two sample means when the samples were independent and σ_1 and σ_2 were known. In Section 9–3, the t test was used to compare two sample means when the samples were independent. In this section, a different version of the t test is explained. This version is used when the samples are dependent. Samples are considered to be **dependent samples** when the subjects are paired or matched in some way. Dependent samples are sometimes called matched-pair samples.

For example, suppose a medical researcher wants to see whether a drug will affect the reaction time of its users. To test this hypothesis, the researcher must pretest the subjects in the sample. That is, they are given a test to ascertain their normal reaction times. Then after taking the drug, the subjects are tested again, using a posttest. Finally, the means of the two tests are compared to see whether there is a difference. Since the same subjects are used in both cases, the samples are *related;* subjects scoring high on the pretest will generally score high on the posttest, even after consuming the drug. Likewise, those scoring lower on the pretest will tend to score lower on the posttest. To take this effect into account, the researcher employs a t test, using the differences between the pretest values and the posttest values. Thus, only the gain or loss in values is compared.

Here are some other examples of dependent samples. A researcher may want to design an SAT preparation course to help students raise their test scores the second time they take the SAT. Hence, the differences between the two exams are compared. A medical specialist may want to see whether a new counseling program will help subjects lose weight. Therefore, the preweights of the subjects will be compared with the postweights.

Besides samples in which the same subjects are used in a pre-post situation, there are other cases where the samples are considered dependent. For example, students might be matched or paired according to some variable that is pertinent to the study; then one student is assigned to one group, and the other student is assigned to a second group. For instance, in a study involving learning, students can be selected and paired according to their IQs. That is, two students with the same IQ will be paired. Then one will be assigned to one sample group (which might receive instruction by computers), and the other student will be assigned to another sample group (which might receive instruction by the lecture discussion method). These assignments will be done randomly. Since a student's IQ is important to learning, it is a variable that should be controlled. By matching subjects on IQ, the researcher can eliminate the variable's influence, for the most part. Matching, then, helps to reduce type II error by eliminating extraneous variables.

Two notes of caution should be mentioned. First, when subjects are matched according to one variable, the matching process does not eliminate the influence of other variables. Matching students according to IQ does not account for their mathematical ability or their familiarity with computers. Since not all variables influencing a study can be controlled, it is up to the researcher to determine which variables should be used in matching. Second, when the same subjects are used for a pre-post study, sometimes the knowledge that they are participating in a study can influence the results. For example, if people are placed in a special program, they may be more highly motivated to succeed simply because they have been selected to participate; the program itself may have little effect on their success.

When the samples are dependent, a special t test for dependent means is used. This test employs the difference in values of the matched pairs. The hypotheses are as follows:

Two-tailed	Left-tailed	Right-tailed
$H_0: \mu_D = 0$	$H_0: \mu_D = 0$	$H_0: \mu_D = 0$
$H_1: \mu_D \neq 0$	$H_1: \mu_D < 0$	$H_1: \mu_D > 0$

Here, μ_D is the symbol for the expected mean of the difference of the matched pairs. The general procedure for finding the test statistic involves several steps.

First, find the differences of the values of the pairs of data.

$$D = X_1 - X_2$$

Second, find the mean $\overline{D}$ of the differences, using the formula

$$\overline{D} = \frac{\Sigma D}{n}$$

where n is the number of data pairs. Third, find the standard deviation s_D of the differences, using the formula

$$s_D = \sqrt{\frac{n\Sigma D^2 - (\Sigma D)^2}{n(n-1)}}$$

Fourth, find the estimated standard error $s_{\overline{D}}$ of the differences, which is

$$s_{\overline{D}} = \frac{s_D}{\sqrt{n}}$$

Finally, find the test statistic, using the formula

$$t = \frac{\overline{D} - \mu_D}{s_D/\sqrt{n}} \quad \text{with d.f.} = n - 1$$

The formula in the final step follows the basic format of

$$\text{Test statistic} = \frac{\text{(observed value)} - \text{(expected value)}}{\text{standard error}}$$

where the observed value is the mean of the differences. The expected value μ_D is zero if the hypothesis is $\mu_D = 0$. The standard error of the difference is the standard deviation of the difference, divided by the square root of the sample size. Both populations must be normally or approximately normally distributed.

Before you can use the testing method presented in this section, the following assumptions must be met.

Assumptions for the *t* Test for Two Means When the Samples Are Dependent

1. The sample or samples are random.
2. The sample data are dependent.
3. When the sample size or sample sizes are less than 30, the population or populations must be normally or approximately normally distributed.

In this book, the assumptions will be stated in the exercises; however, when encountering statistics in other situations, you must check to see that these assumptions have been met before proceeding.

The formulas for this *t* test are given next.

Formulas for the *t* Test for Dependent Samples

$$t = \frac{\overline{D} - \mu_D}{s_D/\sqrt{n}}$$

with d.f. $= n - 1$ and where

$$\overline{D} = \frac{\Sigma D}{n} \quad \text{and} \quad s_D = \sqrt{\frac{n\Sigma D^2 - (\Sigma D)^2}{n(n-1)}}$$

The steps for this *t* test are summarized in the Procedure Table.

Procedure Table

Testing the Difference Between Means for Dependent Samples

Step 1   State the hypotheses and identify the claim.

Step 2   Find the critical value(s).

Step 3   Compute the test statistic.

a. Make a table, as shown.

X_1	X_2	A $D = X_1 - X_2$	B $D^2 = (X_1 - X_2)^2$
⋮	⋮	$\Sigma D =$ _____	$\Sigma D^2 =$ _____

b. Find the differences and place the results in column A.
$$D = X_1 - X_2$$

c. Find the mean of the differences.
$$\overline{D} = \frac{\Sigma D}{n}$$

d. Square the differences and place the results in column B. Complete the table.
$$D^2 = (X_1 - X_2)^2$$

e. Find the standard deviation of the differences.
$$s_D = \sqrt{\frac{n\Sigma D^2 - (\Sigma D)^2}{n(n-1)}}$$

f. Find the test statistic.
$$t = \frac{\overline{D} - \mu_D}{s_D/\sqrt{n}} \quad \text{with d.f.} = n - 1$$

Step 4   Make the decision.

Step 5   Summarize the results.

Unusual Stat

About 4% of Americans spend at least one night in jail each year.

EXAMPLE 9–6   Bank Deposits

A random sample of nine local banks shows their deposits (in billions of dollars) 3 years ago and their deposits (in billions of dollars) today. At $\alpha = 0.05$, can it be concluded that the average in deposits for the banks is greater today than it was 3 years ago? Use $\alpha = 0.05$. Assume the variable is normally distributed.

Source: SNL Financial.

Bank	1	2	3	4	5	6	7	8	9
3 years ago	11.42	8.41	3.98	7.37	2.28	1.10	1.00	0.9	1.35
Today	16.69	9.44	6.53	5.58	2.92	1.88	1.78	1.5	1.22

SOLUTION

Step 1 State the hypothesis and identify the claim. Since we are interested to see if there has been an increase in deposits, the deposits 3 years ago must be less than the deposits today; hence, the deposits must be significantly less 3 years ago than they are today. Hence, the mean of the differences must be less than zero.

$$H_0: \mu_D = 0 \qquad \text{and} \qquad H_1: \mu_D < 0 \text{ (claim)}$$

Step 2 Find the critical value. The degrees of freedom are $n - 1$, or $9 - 1 = 8$. Using Table A–5, the critical value for a left-tailed test with $\alpha = 0.05$ is -1.860.

Step 3 Compute the test statistic.

a. Make a table.

3 years ago (X_1)	Today (X_2)	A $D = X_1 - X_2$	B $D^2 = (X_1 - X_2)^2$
11.42	16.69		
8.41	9.44		
3.98	6.53		
7.37	5.58		
2.28	2.92		
1.10	1.88		
1.00	1.78		
0.90	1.50		
1.35	1.22		

b. Find the differences and place the results in column A.

$$11.42 - 16.69 = -5.27$$
$$8.41 - 9.44 = -1.03$$
$$3.98 - 6.53 = -2.55$$
$$7.37 - 5.58 = +1.79$$
$$2.28 - 2.92 = -0.64$$
$$1.10 - 1.88 = -0.78$$
$$1.00 - 1.78 = -0.78$$
$$0.9 - 1.50 = -0.60$$
$$1.35 - 1.22 = +0.13$$
$$\Sigma D = -9.73$$

c. Find the means of the differences.

$$\bar{D} = \frac{\Sigma D}{n} = \frac{-9.73}{9} = -1.081$$

d. Square the differences and place the results in column B.

$$(-5.27)^2 = 27.7729$$
$$(-1.03)^2 = 1.0609$$
$$(-2.55)^2 = 6.5025$$
$$(+1.79)^2 = 3.2041$$
$$(-0.64)^2 = 0.4096$$
$$(-0.78)^2 = 0.6084$$
$$(-0.78)^2 = 0.6084$$
$$(-0.60)^2 = 0.3600$$
$$(+0.13)^2 = \underline{0.0169}$$
$$\Sigma D^2 = 40.5437$$

The completed table is shown next.

3 years ago (X_1)	Today (X_2)	A $D = X_1 - X_2$	B $D^2 = (X_1 - X_2)^2$
11.42	16.69	−5.27	27.7729
8.41	9.44	−1.03	1.0609
3.98	6.53	−2.55	6.5025
7.37	5.58	+1.79	3.2041
2.28	2.92	−0.64	0.4096
1.10	1.88	−0.78	0.6084
1.00	1.78	−0.78	0.6084
0.90	1.50	−0.60	0.3600
1.35	1.22	+0.13	0.0169
		$\Sigma D = -9.73$	$\Sigma D^2 = 40.5437$

e. Find the standard deviation of the differences.

$$s_D = \sqrt{\frac{n\Sigma D^2 - (\Sigma D)^2}{n(n-1)}}$$

$$= \sqrt{\frac{9(40.5437) - (-9.73)^2}{9(9-1)}}$$

$$= \sqrt{\frac{270.2204}{72}}$$

$$= 1.937$$

f. Find the test statistic.

$$t = \frac{\overline{D} - \mu_D}{s_D/\sqrt{n}} = \frac{-1.081 - 0}{1.937/\sqrt{9}} = -1.674$$

Step 4   Make the decision. Do not reject the null hypothesis since the test statistic, −1.674, is greater than the critical value, −1.860. See Figure 9–6.

FIGURE 9–6   Critical Value and Test Statistic for Example 9–6

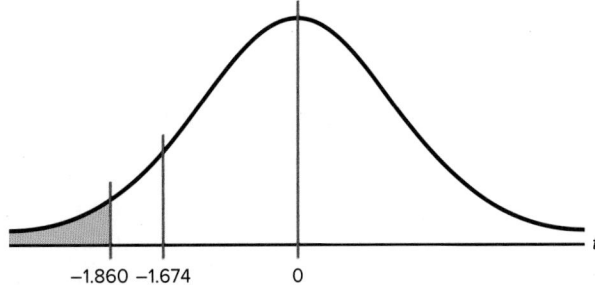

Step 5   Summarize the results. There is not enough evidence to show that the deposits have increased over the last 3 years.

EXAMPLE 9–7   Cholesterol Levels

A dietitian wishes to see if a person's cholesterol level will change if the diet is supplemented by a certain mineral. Six randomly selected subjects were pretested, and then they took the mineral supplement for a 6-week period. The results are shown in the table. (Cholesterol level is measured in milligrams per deciliter.) Can it be concluded that the cholesterol level has been changed at $\alpha = 0.10$? Assume the variable is approximately normally distributed.

Subject	1	2	3	4	5	6
Before (X_1)	210	235	208	190	172	244
After (X_2)	190	170	210	188	173	228

SOLUTION

Step 1 State the hypotheses and identify the claim. If the diet is effective, the before cholesterol levels should be different from the after levels.

$$H_0: \mu_D = 0 \quad \text{and} \quad H_1: \mu_D \neq 0 \text{ (claim)}$$

Step 2 Find the critical value. The degrees of freedom are $6 - 1 = 5$. At $\alpha = 0.10$, the critical values are ± 2.015.

Step 3 Compute the test statistic.

  a. Make a table.

Before (X_1)	After (X_2)	A $D = X_1 - X_2$	B $D^2 = (X_1 - X_2)^2$
210	190		
235	170		
208	210		
190	188		
172	173		
244	228		

  b. Find the differences and place the results in column A.

$$
\begin{aligned}
210 - 190 &= 20 \\
235 - 170 &= 65 \\
208 - 210 &= -2 \\
190 - 188 &= 2 \\
172 - 173 &= -1 \\
244 - 228 &= \underline{16} \\
\Sigma D &= 100
\end{aligned}
$$

  c. Find the mean of the differences.

$$\overline{D} = \frac{\Sigma D}{n} = \frac{100}{6} = 16.7$$

  d. Square the differences and place the results in column B.

$$
\begin{aligned}
(20)^2 &= 400 \\
(65)^2 &= 4225 \\
(-2)^2 &= 4 \\
(2)^2 &= 4 \\
(-1)^2 &= 1 \\
(16)^2 &= \underline{256} \\
\Sigma D^2 &= 4890
\end{aligned}
$$

Then complete the table as shown.

Before (X_1)	After (X_2)	A $D = X_1 - X_2$	B $D^2 = (X_1 - X_2)^2$
210	190	20	400
235	170	65	4225
208	210	−2	4
190	188	2	4
172	173	−1	1
244	228	16	256
		$\Sigma D = 100$	$\Sigma D^2 = 4890$

e. Find the standard deviation of the differences.

$$s_D = \sqrt{\frac{n\Sigma D^2 - (\Sigma D)^2}{n(n-1)}}$$

$$= \sqrt{\frac{6 \cdot 4890 - 100^2}{6(6-1)}}$$

$$= \sqrt{\frac{29{,}340 - 10{,}000}{30}}$$

$$= 25.4$$

f. Find the test statistic.

$$t = \frac{\overline{D} - \mu_D}{s_D/\sqrt{n}} = \frac{16.7 - 0}{25.4/\sqrt{6}} = 1.610$$

Step 4   Make the decision. The decision is to not reject the null hypothesis, since the test statistic 1.610 is in the noncritical region, as shown in Figure 9–7.

FIGURE 9–7   Critical Value and Test Statistic for Example 9–7

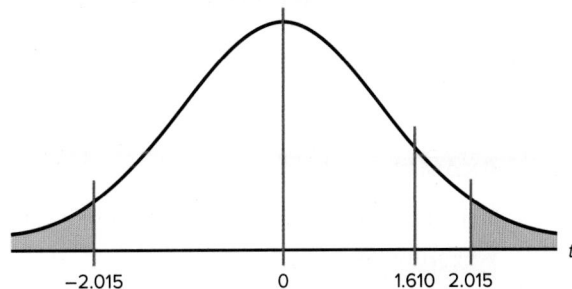

Step 5   Summarize the results. There is not enough evidence to support the claim that the mineral changes a person's cholesterol level.

The *P*-values for the *t* test are found in Table A–5. For a two-tailed test with d.f. = 5 and *t* = 1.610, the *P*-value is found between 1.476 and 2.015; hence, 0.10 < *P*-value < 0.20. Thus, the null hypothesis cannot be rejected at $\alpha = 0.10$.

If a specific difference is hypothesized, this formula should be used

$$t = \frac{\overline{D} - \mu_D}{s_D/\sqrt{n}}$$

where μ_D is the hypothesized difference.

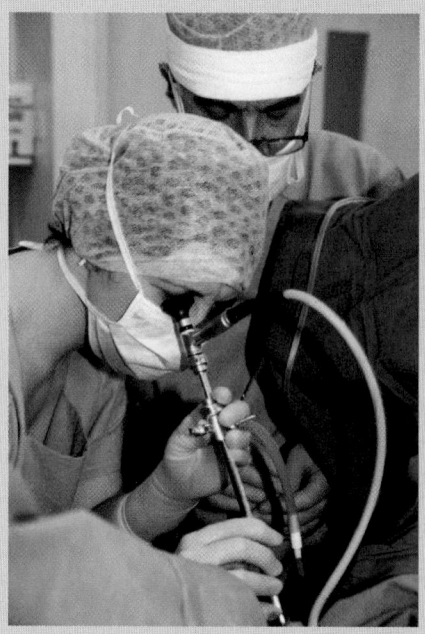
For example, if a dietitian claims that people on a specific diet will lose an average of 3 pounds in a week, the hypotheses are

$$H_0: \mu_D = 3 \quad \text{and} \quad H_1: \mu_D \neq 3$$

The value 3 will be substituted in the test statistic formula for μ_D.

Confidence intervals can be found for the mean differences with this formula.

Confidence Interval for the Mean Difference

$$\overline{D} - t_{\alpha/2}\frac{s_D}{\sqrt{n}} < \mu_D < \overline{D} + t_{\alpha/2}\frac{s_D}{\sqrt{n}}$$

$$\text{d.f.} = n - 1$$

EXAMPLE 9–8

Find the 90% confidence interval for the data in Example 9–7.

SOLUTION

Substitute in the formula.

$$\overline{D} - t_{\alpha/2}\frac{s_D}{\sqrt{n}} < \mu_D < \overline{D} + t_{\alpha/2}\frac{s_D}{\sqrt{n}}$$

$$16.7 - 2.015 \cdot \frac{25.4}{\sqrt{6}} < \mu_D < 16.7 + 2.015 \cdot \frac{25.4}{\sqrt{6}}$$

$$16.7 - 20.89 < \mu_D < 16.7 + 20.89$$

$$-4.19 < \mu_D < 37.59$$

$$-4.2 < \mu_D < 37.6$$

Since 0 is contained in the interval, the decision is to not reject the null hypothesis $H_0: \mu_D = 0$. Hence, there is not enough evidence to support the claim that the mineral changes a person's cholesterol, as previously shown.

Applying the Concepts 9–4

Air Quality

As a researcher for the EPA, you have been asked to determine if the air quality in the United States has changed over the past 2 years. You select a random sample of 10 metropolitan areas and find the number of days each year that the areas failed to meet acceptable air quality standards. The data are shown.

Year 1	18	125	9	22	138	29	1	19	17	31
Year 2	24	152	13	21	152	23	6	31	34	20

Source: The World Almanac and Book of Facts.

Based on the data, answer the following questions.

1. What is the purpose of the study?
2. Are the samples independent or dependent?
3. What hypotheses would you use?
4. What is (are) the critical value(s) that you would use?
5. What statistical test would you use?
6. How many degrees of freedom are there?
7. What is your conclusion?
8. Could an independent means test have been used?
9. Do you think this was a good way to answer the original question?

See page 549 for the answers.

Exercises 9–4

1. Classify each as independent or dependent samples.
   a. Heights of identical twins Dependent
   b. Test scores of the same students in English and psychology Dependent
   c. The effectiveness of two different brands of aspirin on two different groups of people Independent
   d. Effects of a drug on reaction time of two different groups of people, measured by a before-and-after test Dependent
   e. The effectiveness of two different diets on two different groups of individuals Independent

For Exercises 2 through 12, perform each of these steps. Assume that all variables are normally or approximately normally distributed.

   a. State the hypotheses and identify the claim.
   b. Find the critical value(s) or use the P-value method.
   c. Compute the test statistic.
   d. Make the decision.
   e. Summarize the results.

Use the traditional method of hypothesis testing unless the P-value method is specified by your instructor.

2. **Retention Test Scores** A random sample of non-English majors at a selected college was used in a study to see if the student retained more from reading a 19th-century novel or by watching it in DVD form. Each student was assigned one novel to read and a different one to watch, and then they were given a 100-point written quiz on each novel. The test results are shown. At $\alpha = 0.05$, can it be concluded that the book scores are higher than the DVD scores?

Book	90	80	90	75	80	90	84
DVD	85	72	80	80	70	75	80

3. **Improving Study Habits** As an aid for improving students' study habits, nine students were randomly selected to attend a seminar on the importance of education in life. The table shows the number of hours each student studied per week before and after the

seminar. At $\alpha = 0.10$, did attending the seminar increase the number of hours the students studied per week?

Before	9	12	6	15	3	18	10	13	7
After	9	17	9	20	2	21	15	22	6

4. **Obstacle Course Times** An obstacle course was set up on a campus, and 8 randomly selected volunteers were given a chance to complete it while they were being timed. They then sampled a new energy drink and were given the opportunity to run the course again. The "before" and "after" times in seconds are shown. Is there sufficient evidence at $\alpha = 0.05$ to conclude that the students did better the second time? Discuss possible reasons for your results.

Student	1	2	3	4	5	6	7	8
Before	67	72	80	70	78	82	69	75
After	68	70	76	65	75	78	65	68

5. **Physical Therapy** A random sample of 10 physical therapy patients who had knee surgery shows the angle of knee bend before physical therapy and after 6 weeks of physical therapy. At $\alpha = 0.05$, has there been an increase in the angle range after the therapy?

Patient	1	2	3	4	5	6	7	8	9	10
Degrees before	62	80	76	92	72	96	85	91	79	92
Degrees after	140	142	127	115	131	105	110	132	125	102

6. **PGA Golf Scores** At a recent PGA tournament (the Honda Classic at Palm Beach Gardens, Florida) the following scores were posted for eight randomly selected golfers for two consecutive days. At $\alpha = 0.05$, is there evidence of a difference in mean scores for the 2 days?

Golfer	1	2	3	4	5	6	7	8
Thursday	67	65	68	68	68	70	69	70
Friday	68	70	69	71	72	69	70	70

Source: Washington Observer-Reporter.

7. **Self-esteem** A psychologist has a 3-week program to raise the self-esteem of elementary school students. A questionnaire was given to the students before and after the program. At $\alpha = 0.10$, based on the scores of a random sample of twelve students, can it be concluded that the program increases the self-esteem scores of the students?

Student	1	2	3	4	5	6	7	8	9	10	11	12
Before score	62	57	76	48	41	59	71	64	49	77	63	55
After score	72	65	93	60	55	52	72	64	52	70	68	56

8. **Overweight Dogs** A veterinary nutritionist developed a diet for overweight dogs. The total volume of food

consumed remains the same, but one-half of the dog food is replaced with a low-calorie "filler" such as canned green beans. Six overweight dogs were randomly selected from her practice and were put on this program. Their initial weights were recorded, and they were weighed again after 4 weeks. At the 0.05 level of significance, can it be concluded that the dogs lost weight?

Before	42	53	48	65	40	52
After	39	45	40	58	42	47

9. **Pulse Rates of Identical Twins** A researcher wanted to compare the pulse rates of identical twins to see whether there was any difference between two blood pressure medications. Eight sets of twins were randomly selected. One twin was given medication A and the other twin medication B for 4 weeks and then their pulses were taken after a walk. The rates are given in the table as number of beats per minute. At $\alpha = 0.01$, is there a significant difference in the average pulse rates of twins? Use the P-value method. Find the 99% confidence interval for the difference of the two.

Twin A	87	92	78	83	88	90	84	93
Twin B	83	95	79	83	86	93	80	86

10. **Toy Assembly Test** An educational researcher devised a wooden toy assembly project to test learning in 6-year-olds. The time in seconds to assemble the project was noted, and the toy was disassembled out of the child's sight. Then the child was given the task to repeat. The researcher would conclude that learning occurred if the mean of the second assembly times was less than the mean of the first assembly times. At $\alpha = 0.01$, can it be concluded that learning took place? Use the P-value method, and find the 99% confidence interval of the difference in means.

Child	1	2	3	4	5	6	7
Trial 1	100	150	150	110	130	120	118
Trial 2	90	130	150	90	105	110	120

11. **Recharging Batteries** An engineer wants to see if rechargeable batteries last as long as new batteries. The engineer selects a random sample of 14 batteries and times them to see how long they last. Then the engineer recharges the same batteries to see how long they last. The times are given in minutes. Can it be concluded at $\alpha = 0.10$ that the new batteries last longer than the same batteries that were recharged?

Battery	1	2	3	4	5	6	7
Newly charged	345	374	250	356	272	387	291
Recharged	296	395	247	412	256	333	305

Battery	8	9	10	11	12	13	14
Newly charged	371	293	447	398	275	298	304
Recharged	394	295	420	390	274	275	301

12. **Sales Training** An automotive dealer wishes to try out a new customer relations sales program. The dealer randomly selects 11 salespeople and has them complete the program. The dealer then compares the number of automobiles sold over a 1-month period before the program and after the program. At $\alpha = 0.05$, has the program been successful?

Salesperson	1	2	3	4	5	6	7	8	9	10	11
Before	16	22	14	31	25	15	22	10	20	28	21
After	18	20	21	36	33	17	20	12	20	25	27

≡ Extending the Concepts

13. Instead of finding the mean of the differences between X_1 and X_2 by subtracting $X_1 - X_2$, you can find it by finding the means of X_1 and X_2 and then subtracting the means. Show that these two procedures will yield the same results.

≡ Technology   Step by Step

TI-84 Plus
Step by Step

Hypothesis Test for the Difference Between Two Means: Dependent Samples

This refers to Example 9–7 in the text.

Example TI9–6

1. Enter the data values into L_1 and L_2.
2. Move the cursor to the top of the L_3 column so that L_3 is highlighted.
3. Type $L_1 - L_2$, then press **ENTER**.
4. Press **STAT** and move the cursor to TESTS.
5. Press **2** for TTest.
6. Move the cursor to Data and press **ENTER**.
7. Type in the appropriate values, using **0** for μ_0 and L_3 for the list.
8. Move the cursor to the appropriate alternative hypothesis and press **ENTER**.
9. Move the cursor to Calculate and press **ENTER**.

Confidence Interval for the Difference Between Two Means: Dependent Samples

This refers to Example 9–8 in the text.

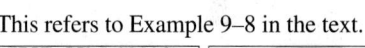
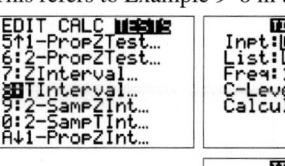

Example TI9–7

1. Enter the data values into L_1 and L_2.
2. Move the cursor to the top of the L_3 column so that L_3 is highlighted.
3. Type $L_1 - L_2$, then press **ENTER**.
4. Press **STAT** and move the cursor to TESTS.
5. Press **8** for TInterval.
6. Move the cursor to Data and press **ENTER**.
7. Type in the appropriate values, using L_3 for the list.
8. Move the cursor to Calculate and press **ENTER**.

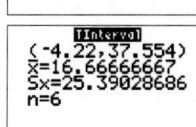

EXCEL
Step by Step

Testing the Difference Between Two Means: Dependent Samples

Example XL9–3

Use the data from Example 9–7.

1. Enter the Before data into column A.
2. Enter the After data into column B.

3. Select the Data tab from the toolbar. Then select Data Analysis.

4. In the Data Analysis box, under Analysis Tools select *t*-test: Paired Two Sample for Means, and click [OK].

5. In Input, type in the Variable 1 Range: **A1:A7** and the Variable 2 Range: **B1:B7**.

6. Type **0** for the Hypothesized Mean Difference.

7. Check the box for labels if you selected the labels in the input ranges.

8. Type **0.10** for Alpha.

9. In Output options, type **D1** for the Output Range, then click [OK].

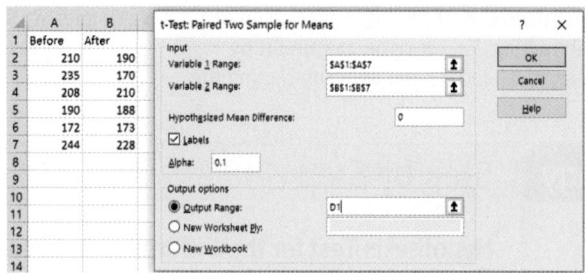

t-Test: Paired Two Sample for Means		
	Before	*After*
Mean	209.8333	193.1667
Variance	725.7667	495.3667
Observations	6	6
Pearson Correlation	0.480709	
Hypothesized Mean Difference	0	
df	5	
t Stat	1.607892	
P(T<=t) one-tail	0.084385	
t Critical one-tail	1.475884	
P(T<=t) two-tail	0.168771	
t Critical two-tail	2.015048	

Note: You may need to increase the column width to see all the results. To do this:

1. Highlight the columns D, E, and F.

2. Under the Home tab, select **Format>AutoFit** Column Width.

The output shows a *P*-value of 0.168771 for the two-tailed case. This value is greater than the alpha level of 0.10, so we fail to reject the null hypothesis.

MINITAB

Step by Step

Test the Difference Between Two Means: Dependent Samples

A sports fitness trainer claims by taking a special vitamin, a weight lifter can increase their strength. Eight athletes are selected and given a test of strength, using the standard bench press. After 2 weeks of regular training, supplemented with the vitamin, they are tested again. Test the effectiveness of the vitamin regimen at $\alpha = 0.05$. Each value in these data represents the maximum number of pounds the athlete can bench-press. Assume that the variable is approximately normally distributed.

Athlete	1	2	3	4	5	6	7	8
Before (X_1)	210	230	182	205	262	253	219	216
After (X_2)	219	236	179	204	270	250	222	216

1. Enter the data into C1 and C2. Name the columns **Before** and **After.**

2. Select **Stat>Basic Statistics>Paired t.**

3. Select Each sample is in a column from the drop-down menu.

4. Double-click C1 Before for Sample 1.

5. Double-click C2 After for Sample 2. The second sample will be subtracted from the first. The differences are not stored or displayed.

6. Click [Options].

   a) Type in **95** for the Confidence level.

   b) Type **0** for the Hypothesized difference.

   c) Change Alternative hypothesis to Difference < hypothesized difference.

7. Click [OK] twice.

	C1	C2	C3	C4	C5	C6	C7	C8
	Before	After						
1	210	219						
2	230	236						
3	182	179						
4	205	204						
5	262	270						
6	253	250						
7	219	222						
8	216	216						
9								
10								
11								
12								
13								
14								

Paired t for the Mean

C1 Before Each sample is in a column
C2 After

Sample 1: Before

Sample 2: After

Paired t Options

Difference = mean of (sample 1 - sample 2)

Confidence level: 95.0

Hypothesized difference: 0.0

Alternative hypothesis: Difference < hypothesized difference

Help   OK   Cancel

Paired T-Test and CI: Before, After

```
Paired T for Before - After

            N    Mean   StDev   SE Mean
Before      8  222.13   25.92      9.16
After       8  224.50   27.91      9.87
Difference  8   -2.38    4.84      1.71


95% upper bound for mean difference: 0.87
T-Test of mean difference = 0 (vs < 0): T-Value = -1.39  P-Value = 0.104
```

Since the *P*-value of 0.104 is greater than $\alpha = 0.05$, do not reject the null hypothesis. There is not enough evidence to conclude that the vitamin supplement significantly increased the athlete's strength.

9–5 Testing the Difference Between Proportions

OBJECTIVE

Test the difference between two proportions.

In Chapter 8, an inference about a single proportion was explained. In this section, testing the difference between two sample proportions will be explained.

The *z* test with some modifications can be used to test the equality of two proportions. For example, a researcher might ask, Is the proportion of men who exercise regularly less than the proportion of women who exercise regularly? Is there a difference in the percentage of students who own a mobile device and the percentage of nonstudents who own one? Is there a difference in the proportion of college graduates who pay cash for purchases and the proportion of noncollege graduates who pay cash?

Recall from Chapter 7 that the symbol $\hat{p}$ ("*p* hat") is the sample proportion used to estimate the population proportion, denoted by *p*. For example, if in a sample of 300 college students, 9 are on probation, then the sample proportion is $\hat{p} = \frac{9}{300}$, or 0.03. The population proportion *p* is the number of all students who are on probation, divided by the number of students who attend the college. The formula for the sample proportion $\hat{p}$ is

$$\hat{p} = \frac{X}{n}$$

where

   X = number of units that possess the characteristic of interest
   n = sample size

When you are testing the difference between two population proportions p_1 and p_2, the hypotheses can be stated thus, if no specific difference between the proportions is hypothesized.

$H_0: p_1 = p_2$ $H_0: p_1 - p_2 = 0$
        or
$H_1: p_1 \neq p_2$ $H_1: p_1 - p_2 \neq 0$

Similar statements using < or > in the alternate hypothesis can be formed for one-tailed tests.

For two proportions, $\hat{p}_1 = X_1/n_1$ is used to estimate p_1 and $\hat{p}_2 = X_2/n_2$ is used to estimate p_2. The standard error of the difference is

$$\sigma_{\hat{p}_1 - \hat{p}_2} = \sqrt{\sigma_{\hat{p}_1}^2 + \sigma_{\hat{p}_2}^2} = \sqrt{\frac{p_1 q_1}{n_1} + \frac{p_2 q_2}{n_2}}$$

where $\sigma_{\hat{p}_1}^2$ and $\sigma_{\hat{p}_2}^2$ are the variances of the proportions, $q_1 = 1 - p_1$, $q_2 = 1 - p_2$, and n_1 and n_2 are the respective sample sizes.

Since p_1 and p_2 are unknown, a weighted estimate of p can be computed by using the formula

$$\bar{p} = \frac{n_1 \hat{p}_1 + n_2 \hat{p}_2}{n_1 + n_2}$$

and $\bar{q} = 1 - \bar{p}$. This weighted estimate is based on the hypothesis that $p_1 = p_2$. Hence, $\bar{p}$ is a better estimate than either $\hat{p}_1$ or $\hat{p}_2$, since it is a combined average using both $\hat{p}_1$ and $\hat{p}_2$.

Since $\hat{p}_1 = X_1/n_1$ and $\hat{p}_2 = X_2/n_2$, $\bar{p}$ can be simplified to

$$\bar{p} = \frac{X_1 + X_2}{n_1 + n_2}$$

Finally, the standard error of the difference in terms of the weighted estimate is

$$\sigma_{\hat{p}_1 - \hat{p}_2} = \sqrt{\bar{p}\,\bar{q} \left(\frac{1}{n_1} + \frac{1}{n_2} \right)}$$

The formula for the test statistic is shown next.

Formula for the z Test Statistic for Comparing Two Proportions

$$z = \frac{(\hat{p}_1 - \hat{p}_2) - (p_1 - p_2)}{\sqrt{\bar{p}\,\bar{q} \left(\frac{1}{n_1} + \frac{1}{n_2} \right)}}$$

where

$$\bar{p} = \frac{X_1 + X_2}{n_1 + n_2} \qquad \hat{p}_1 = \frac{X_1}{n_1}$$

$$\bar{q} = 1 - \bar{p} \qquad \hat{p}_2 = \frac{X_2}{n_2}$$

This formula follows the format

$$\text{Test statistic} = \frac{(\text{observed value}) - (\text{expected value})}{\text{standard error}}$$

Before you can test the difference between two sample proportions, the following assumptions must be met.

Assumptions for the z Test for Two Proportions

1. The samples must be random samples.
2. The sample data are independent of one another.
3. For both samples $np \geq 5$ and $nq \geq 5$.

In this book, the assumptions will be stated in the exercises; however, when encountering statistics in other situations, you must check to see that these assumptions have been met before proceeding.

The hypothesis-testing procedure used here follows the five-step procedure presented previously except that $\hat{p}_1$, $\hat{p}_2$, $\bar{p}$, and $\bar{q}$ must be computed.

EXAMPLE 9–9   Vaccination Rates in Nursing Homes

In the nursing home study mentioned in the chapter-opening Statistics Today, the researchers found that 12 out of 34 randomly selected small nursing homes had a resident vaccination rate of less than 80%, while 17 out of 24 randomly selected large nursing homes had a vaccination rate of less than 80%. At $\alpha = 0.05$, test the claim that there is no difference in the proportions of the small and large nursing homes with a resident vaccination rate of less than 80%.

Source: Nancy Arden, Arnold S. Monto, and Suzanne E. Ohmit, "Vaccine Use and the Risk of Outbreaks in a Sample of Nursing Homes During an Influenza Epidemic," *American Journal of Public Health.* v 85 (3):399–401

SOLUTION

Step 1   State the hypotheses and identify the claim.

$$H_0: p_1 = p_2 \text{ (claim)} \qquad \text{and} \qquad H_1: p_1 \neq p_2$$

Step 2   Find the critical values. Since $\alpha = 0.05$, the critical values are $+1.96$ and -1.96.

Step 3   Compute the test statistic. First compute $\hat{p}_1$, $\hat{p}_2$, $\bar{p}$, and $\bar{q}$. Then substitute in the formula.

Let $\hat{p}_1$ be the proportion of the small nursing homes with a vaccination rate of less than 80% and $\hat{p}_2$ be the proportion of the large nursing homes with a vaccination rate of less than 80%. Then

$$\hat{p}_1 = \frac{X_1}{n_1} = \frac{12}{34} = 0.35 \quad \text{and} \quad \hat{p}_2 = \frac{X_2}{n_2} = \frac{17}{24} = 0.71$$

$$\bar{p} = \frac{X_1 + X_2}{n_1 + n_2} = \frac{12 + 17}{34 + 24} = \frac{29}{58} = 0.5$$

$$\bar{q} = 1 - \bar{p} = 1 - 0.5 = 0.5$$

$$z = \frac{(\hat{p}_1 - \hat{p}_2) - (p_1 - p_2)}{\sqrt{\bar{p}\bar{q}\left(\frac{1}{n_1} + \frac{1}{n_2}\right)}}$$

$$= \frac{(0.35 - 0.71) - 0}{\sqrt{(0.5)(0.5)\left(\frac{1}{34} + \frac{1}{24}\right)}} = \frac{-0.36}{0.1333} = -2.70$$

Step 4   Make the decision. Reject the null hypothesis, since $-2.70 < -1.96$. See Figure 9–8.

FIGURE 9–8   Critical Values and Test Statistic for Example 9–9

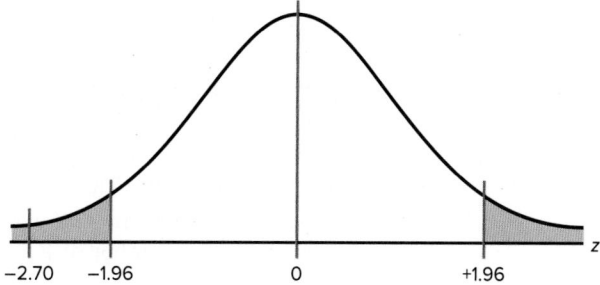

Step 5   Summarize the results. There is enough evidence to reject the claim that there is no difference in the proportions of small and large nursing homes with a resident vaccination rate of less than 80%.

EXAMPLE 9–10   Census

A study of 200 Democrats found that 68% believe that the U.S. Census is important for the American economy, while for a random sample of 100 Republicans, 54% state that the census is important for the American economy. At $\alpha = 0.10$, can it be concluded that the percentage of Democrats who believe that the U.S. Census is important for the American economy is greater than the percentage of Republicans who believe so?

SOLUTION

Step 1   State the hypotheses and identify the claim.

$$H_0: p_1 = p_2 \qquad \text{and} \qquad H_1: p_1 > p_2 \text{ (claim)}$$

Step 2   Find the critical value, using Table A–4. At $\alpha = 0.10$, the critical value is 1.28.

Step 3   Compute the test statistic. Since percentages are given, you need to find $\bar{p}$ and $\bar{q}$.

$$X_1 = \hat{p}_1 n_1 = 0.68(200) = 136$$

$$X_2 = \hat{p}_2 n_2 = 0.54(100) = 54$$

$$\bar{p} = \frac{X_1 + X_2}{n_1 + n_2} = \frac{136 + 54}{200 + 100} = \frac{190}{300} = 0.633$$

$$\bar{q} = 1 - \bar{p} = 1 - 0.63 = 0.367$$

$$z = \frac{(\hat{p}_1 - \hat{p}_2) - (p_1 - p_2)}{\sqrt{\bar{p}\bar{q}\left(\frac{1}{n_1} + \frac{1}{n_2}\right)}} = \frac{(0.68 - 0.54) - 0}{\sqrt{(0.633)(0.367)\left(\frac{1}{200} + \frac{1}{100}\right)}} = \frac{0.14}{0.059} = 2.37$$

Step 4   Make the decision. Reject the null hypothesis since 2.37 > 1.28. See Figure 9–9.

FIGURE 9–9   Critical Value and Test Statistic for Example 9–10

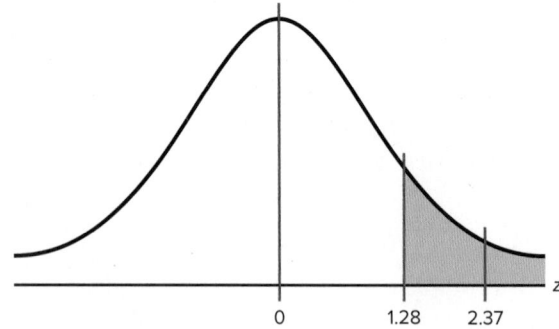

Step 5   Summarize the results. There is enough evidence that the proportion of Democrats who think the U.S. Census is important to the U.S. economy is greater than the number of Republicans who think that way.

The *P*-value for the differences of proportions can be found in Table A–4, as shown in Section 9–2. The table value for 2.37 is 0.9911 and the complement is $1 - 0.9911 = 0.0089$. Hence, the *P*-value is $0.0899 < 0.10$. The decision is to reject the null hypothesis.

SPEAKING OF STATISTICS   Is More Expensive Better?

An article in the *Journal of the American Medical Association* explained a study done on placebo pain pills. Researchers randomly assigned 82 healthy people to two groups. The individuals in the first group were given sugar pills, but they were told that the pills were a new, fast-acting opioid pain reliever similar to codeine and that they were listed at $2.50 each. The individuals in the other group received the same sugar pills but were told that the pills had been marked down to 10¢ each.

Each group received electrical shocks before and after taking the pills. They were then asked if the pills reduced the pain. Eighty-five percent of the group who were told that the pain pills cost $2.50 said that they were effective, while 61% of the group who received the supposedly discounted pills said that they were effective.

State possible null and alternative hypotheses for this study. What statistical test could be used

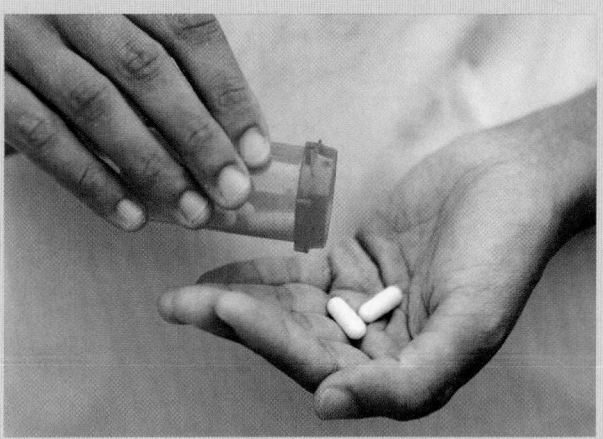

Amphotora/iStock/Getty Images

in this study? What might be the conclusion of the study?

The sampling distribution of the difference of two proportions can be used to construct a confidence interval for the difference of two proportions. The formula for the confidence interval for the difference between two proportions is shown next.

Confidence Interval for the Difference Between Two Proportions

$$(\hat{p}_1 - \hat{p}_2) - z_{\alpha/2}\sqrt{\frac{\hat{p}_1\hat{q}_1}{n_1} + \frac{\hat{p}_2\hat{q}_2}{n_2}} < p_1 - p_2 < (\hat{p}_1 - \hat{p}_2) + z_{\alpha/2}\sqrt{\frac{\hat{p}_1\hat{q}_1}{n_1} + \frac{\hat{p}_2\hat{q}_2}{n_2}}$$

Here, the confidence interval uses a standard deviation based on estimated values of the population proportions, but the hypothesis test uses a standard deviation based on the assumption that the two population proportions are equal. As a result, you may obtain different conclusions when using a confidence interval or a hypothesis test. So when testing for a difference of two proportions, you use the *z* test rather than the confidence interval.

EXAMPLE 9–11

Find the 95% confidence interval for the difference of proportions for the data in Example 9–9.

SOLUTION

$$\hat{p}_1 = \frac{12}{34} = 0.35 \qquad \hat{q}_1 = 0.65$$

$$\hat{p}_2 = \frac{17}{24} = 0.71 \qquad \hat{q}_2 = 0.29$$

Substitute in the formula.

$$(\hat{p}_1 - \hat{p}_2) - z_{\alpha/2}\sqrt{\frac{\hat{p}_1\hat{q}_1}{n_1} + \frac{\hat{p}_2\hat{q}_2}{n_2}} < p_1 - p_2$$

$$< (\hat{p}_1 - \hat{p}_2) + z_{\alpha/2}\sqrt{\frac{\hat{p}_1\hat{q}_1}{n_1} + \frac{\hat{p}_2\hat{q}_2}{n_2}}$$

$$(0.35 - 0.71) - 1.96\sqrt{\frac{(0.35)(0.65)}{34} + \frac{(0.71)(0.29)}{24}}$$

$$< p_1 - p_2 < (0.35 - 0.71) + 1.96\sqrt{\frac{(0.35)(0.65)}{34} + \frac{(0.71)(0.29)}{24}}$$

$$-0.36 - 0.242 < p_1 - p_2 < -0.36 + 0.242$$

$$-0.602 < p_1 - p_2 < -0.118$$

Applying the Concepts 9–5

Smoking and Education

You are researching the hypothesis that there is no difference in the percent of public school students who vape and the percent of private school students who vape. You find these results from a recent survey.

School	Percent who vape
Public	32.3
Private	14.5

Based on these figures, answer the following questions.

1. What hypotheses would you use if you wanted to compare percentages of the public school students who vape with the private school students who vape?
2. What critical value(s) would you use?
3. What statistical test would you use to compare the two percentages?
4. What information would you need to complete the statistical test?
5. Suppose you found that 1000 randomly selected individuals in each group were surveyed. Could you perform the statistical test?
6. If so, complete the test and summarize the results.

See pages 549–550 for the answers.

Exercises 9–5

1. Find the proportions $\hat{p}$ and $\hat{q}$ for each.

 a. $n = 54, X = 46$ $\hat{p} = 0.852, \hat{q} = 0.148$
 b. $n = 80, X = 32$ $\hat{p} = 0.4, \hat{q} = 0.6$
 c. $n = 120, X = 60$ $\hat{p} = 0.5, \hat{q} = 0.5$
 d. $n = 32, X = 12$ $\hat{p} = 0.375, \hat{q} = 0.625$
 e. $n = 154, X = 24$ $\hat{p} = 0.156, \hat{q} = 0.844$

2. Find $\hat{p}$ and $\hat{q}$ for each.

 a. $n = 100, X = 36$ $\hat{p} = 0.36, \hat{q} = 0.64$
 b. $n = 48, X = 24$ $\hat{p} = 0.5, \hat{q} = 0.5$
 c. $n = 36, X = 9$ $\hat{p} = 0.25, \hat{q} = 0.75$
 d. $n = 150, X = 60$ $\hat{p} = 0.4, \hat{q} = 0.6$
 e. $n = 72, X = 8$ $\hat{p} = 0.111, \hat{q} = 0.889$

3. Find each X, given $\hat{p}$.
   a. $\hat{p} = 0.20$, $n = 175$ 35
   b. $\hat{p} = 0.09$, $n = 60$ 5.4
   c. $\hat{p} = 12\%$, $n = 600$ 72
   d. $\hat{p} = 48\%$, $n = 300$ 144
   e. $\hat{p} = 15\%$, $n = 180$ 27

4. Find each X, given $\hat{p}$.
   a. $\hat{p} = 0.36$, $n = 400$ 144
   b. $\hat{p} = 0.05$, $n = 650$ 32.5
   c. $\hat{p} = 75\%$, $n = 300$ 225
   d. $\hat{p} = 50\%$, $n = 180$ 90
   e. $\hat{p} = 35\%$, $n = 500$ 175

5. Find $\bar{p}$ and $\bar{q}$ for each.
   a. $X_1 = 70$, $n_1 = 100$, $X_2 = 30$, $n_2 = 100$ $\bar{p} = 0.5$; $\bar{q} = 0.5$
   b. $X_1 = 36$, $n_1 = 50$, $X_2 = 18$, $n_2 = 60$ $\bar{p} = 0.491$; $\bar{q} = 0.509$
   c. $X_1 = 24$, $n_1 = 40$, $X_2 = 16$, $n_2 = 48$ $\bar{p} = 0.455$; $\bar{q} = 0.545$
   d. $X_1 = 20$, $n_1 = 36$, $X_2 = 24$, $n_2 = 30$ $\bar{p} = 0.667$; $\bar{q} = 0.333$
   e. $X_1 = 12$, $n_1 = 20$, $X_2 = 18$, $n_2 = 27$ $\bar{p} = 0.638$; $\bar{q} = 0.362$

6. Find $\bar{p}$ and $\bar{q}$.
   a. $X_1 = 5$, $n_1 = 25$, $X_2 = 12$, $n_2 = 20$ $\bar{p} = 0.378$; $\bar{q} = 0.622$
   b. $X_1 = 18$, $n_1 = 30$, $X_2 = 15$, $n_2 = 36$ $\bar{p} = 0.5$; $\bar{q} = 0.5$
   c. $X_1 = 21$, $n_1 = 42$, $X_2 = 19$, $n_2 = 25$ $\bar{p} = 0.597$; $\bar{q} = 0.403$
   d. $X_1 = 16$, $n_1 = 50$, $X_2 = 18$, $n_2 = 50$ $\bar{p} = 0.34$; $\bar{q} = 0.66$
   e. $X_1 = 8$, $n_1 = 32$, $X_2 = 6$, $n_2 = 35$ $\bar{p} = 0.209$; $\bar{q} = 0.791$

For Exercises 7 through 27, perform these steps.

   a. State the hypotheses and identify the claim.
   b. Find the critical value(s) or use the P-value method.
   c. Compute the test statistic.
   d. Make the decision.
   e. Summarize the results.

Use the traditional method of hypothesis testing unless the P-value method is specified by your instructor.

7. **Workers with College Degrees** A recent study of 50 randomly selected workers ages 25 to 29 years old found that 40% have a college degree, whereas another study of 50 randomly selected workers ages 35 to 39 years old found that 32% had a college degree. At $\alpha = 0.05$, test the claim that there is no difference in the proportions. Find the 95% confidence interval for the difference of the two proportions.

8. **Leisure Time** In a sample of 150 men, 132 said that they had less leisure time today than they had 10 years ago. In a random sample of 250 women, 240 women said that they had less leisure time than they had 10 years ago. At $\alpha = 0.10$, is there a difference in the proportions? Find the 90% confidence interval for the difference of the two proportions. Does the confidence interval

contain 0? Give a reason why this information would be of interest to a researcher.
Source: Based on statistics from Market Directory.

9. **Marriage Difficulties** A random sample of 60 men found that 42 said that they never thought about leaving their wives, while for a random sample of 40 women, 25 said that they never thought about leaving their husbands. At $\alpha = 0.10$, is there a difference in the proportions?

10. **Animal Bites of Postal Workers** In Cleveland, a random sample of 73 mail carriers showed that 10 had been bitten by an animal during one week. In Philadelphia, in a random sample of 80 mail carriers, 16 had received animal bites. Is there a significant difference in the proportions? Use $\alpha = 0.05$. Find the 95% confidence interval for the difference of the two proportions.

11. **Bedroom Sanctuary** A randomly selected survey of 80 recently hired college graduates found that 60% considered their bedrooms as a sanctuary for peace and relaxation, whereas a randomly selected group of 60 workers who had a college degree and had been working for at least 5 years found the 70% considered their bedrooms a sanctuary for peace and relaxation. At $\alpha = 0.05$, is there a difference in the proportions? Find the 95% confidence interval of the difference in the proportions.

12. **Love at First Sight** In a random sample of 80 college graduates, 44 said that they would not marry a person based only on love-at-first-sight criteria. For a random sample of 120 high school graduates, 42 said that they would not marry a person based only on love-at-first-sight criteria. At $\alpha = 0.02$, would you say that here is a difference in the two proportions? Use the P-value method.

13. **Victims of Violence** A random survey of 80 women who were victims of violence found that 24 were attacked by relatives. A random survey of 50 men found that 6 were attacked by relatives. At $\alpha = 0.10$, can it be shown that the percentage of women who were attacked by relatives is greater than the percentage of men who were attacked by relatives?

14. **Hypertension** It has been found that 26% of men and 31.5% of women suffer from hypertension. A random sample of 150 of each gender was selected from recent hospital records, and the following results were obtained. Can you conclude that a higher percentage of women have high blood pressure? Use $\alpha = 0.05$.

   Men   43 patients had high blood pressure
   Women   52 patients had high blood pressure
   Source: www.nchs.gov

15. **Hours of Television Watching** In a random sample of 50 children ages 3 to 5, 34 have limits on the television shows they watch, while a random selection of

60 children ages 6 to 10 found that 45 have no limits on the television programs that they can watch. At $\alpha = 0.05$, is there a difference in the two proportions?

16. **Smoking Survey** National statistics show that 15.6% of men smoke and 12% of women smoke. A random sample of 250 men indicated that 48 were smokers, and a random sample of 300 women surveyed indicated that 39 smoked. Construct a 98% confidence interval for the true difference in proportions of male and female smokers. Comment on your interval—does it support the claim that there is a difference? $-0.0115 < p_1 - p_2 < 0.1355$

    Source: www.cdc.gov

17. **Success of Parenting** In a random sample of 80 parents who were college graduates, 50% stated that their success in raising their children was determined by the success of their children. A random sample of 60 parents who were not college graduates found that 40% considered their parenting success was based on the success of their children. Is there a difference in the proportions at $\alpha = 0.01$?

18. **Airlines On-Time Arrivals** The percentages of on-time arrivals for major U.S. airlines range from 73.8 to 87.4. Two regional airlines were surveyed with the following results. At $\alpha = 0.01$, is there a difference in proportions?

	Airline A	Airline B
No. of flights	300	250
No. of on-time flights	213	185

    Source: New York Times Almanac.

19. **College Education** The percentages of women who have completed 4 or more years of college has been rising steadily over the last 80 years. A random sample of women and men were surveyed with these results. Estimate the true difference in proportions with 95% confidence. $-0.053 < p_1 - p_2 < 0.0836$

	Women	Men
Sample size	350	400
No. who completed 4 or more years	126	138

    Source: New York Times Almanac.

20. **Valentine's Day** In a random sample of 70 single men, 30 gave their sweethearts candy for Valentine's Day, while in another random sample of 80 single men, 20 gave their sweethearts perfume for Valentine's Day. At $\alpha = 0.10$, can it be concluded that more single men gave their sweethearts candy than those who gave their sweethearts perfume for Valentine's Day?

21. **Undergraduate Financial Aid** A study is conducted to determine if the percent of women who receive financial aid in undergraduate school is different from the percent of men who receive financial aid in undergraduate school.

A random sample of undergraduates revealed these results. At $\alpha = 0.01$, is there significant evidence to reject the null hypothesis?

	Women	Men
Sample size	250	300
Number receiving aid	200	180

Source: U.S. Department of Education, National Center for Education Statistics.

22. **High School Graduation Rates** The overall U.S. public high school graduation rate is 85%. For Pennsylvania it is 86% and for Idaho 81%—a difference of 5%. Random samples of 1200 students from each state indicated that 980 graduated in Pennsylvania and 940 graduated in Idaho. At the 0.05 level of significance, can it be concluded that there is a difference in the proportions of graduating students between the states?

23. **Interview Errors** It has been found that many first-time interviewees commit errors that could very well affect the outcome of the interview. An astounding 77% are guilty of using their cell phones or texting during the interview! A researcher wanted to see if the proportion of male offenders differed from the proportion of female ones. Out of 120 males, 72 used their cell phone and 80 of 150 females did so. At the 0.01 level of significance, is there a difference?

    Source: Careerbuilder.com

24. **Medical Supply Sales** According to the U.S. Bureau of Labor Statistics, approximately equal numbers of men and women are engaged in sales and related occupations. Although that may be true for total numbers, perhaps the proportions differ by industry. A random sample of 200 salespersons from the industrial sector indicated that 114 were men, and in the medical supply sector, 80 of 200 were men. At the 0.05 level of significance, can we conclude that the proportion of men in industrial sales differs from the proportion of men in medical supply sales?

25. **Movies** A survey of 50 randomly selected adults ages 21 to 30 found that 30% never went to movies shown at a theater, while a survey of 50 adults ages 31 to 40 found that 48% never went to movies at a theater. At $\alpha = 0.10$, can it be concluded that the percentages are different? Use the *P*-value method.

26. **Never Married People** The percentage of males 18 years and older who have never married is 30.4. For females the percentage is 23.6. Looking at the records in a particular populous county, a random sample of 250 men showed that 78 had never married and 58 of 200 women had never married. At the 0.05 level of significance, is the proportion of men greater than the proportion of women? Use the *P*-value method.

27. Bullying Bullying is a problem at any age but especially for students aged 12 to 18. A study showed that 7.2% of all students in this age bracket reported being bullied at school during the past six months with 6th grade having the highest incidence at 13.9% and 12th grade the lowest at 2.2%. To see if there is a difference between public and private schools, 200 students were randomly selected from each. At the 0.05 level of significance, can a difference be concluded?

	Private	Public
Sample size	200	200
No. bullied	13	16

Source: www.nces.ed.gov

Extending the Concepts

28. If there is a significant difference between p_1 and p_2 and between p_2 and p_3, can you conclude that there is a significant difference between p_1 and p_3? No, p_1 could equal p_3.

Technology Step by Step

TI-84 Plus
Step by Step

Hypothesis Test for the Difference Between Two Proportions

Example TI9–8

1. Press **STAT** and move the cursor to TESTS.
2. Press **6** for 2-PropZTEST.
3. Type in the appropriate values.
4. Move the cursor to the appropriate alternative hypothesis and press **ENTER.**
5. Move the cursor to Calculate and press **ENTER.**

This refers to Example 9–9 in the text.

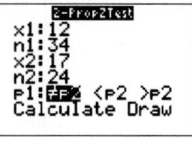 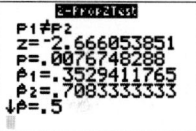

Confidence Interval for the Difference Between Two Proportions

Example TI9–9

1. Press **STAT** and move the cursor to TESTS.
2. Press **B (ALPHA APPS)** for 2-PropZInt.
3. Type in the appropriate values.
4. Move the cursor to Calculate and press **ENTER.**

This refers to Example 9–11 in the text.

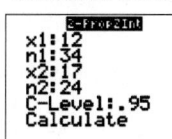 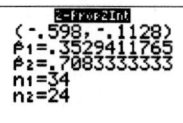

EXCEL
Step by Step

Testing the Difference Between Two Proportions

Excel does not have a procedure to test the difference between two population proportions. However, you may conduct this test using the MegaStat Add-in available in your online resources. If you have not installed this add-in, do so, following the instructions from the Chapter 1 Excel Step by Step.

We will use the summary information from Example 9–9.

1. From the toolbar, select Add-Ins, **MegaStat>Hypothesis Tests>Compare Two Independent Proportions**. *Note:* You may need to open MegaStat from the MegaStat.xls file on your computer's hard drive.
2. Under Group 1, type **12** for p and **34** for n. Under Group 2, type **17** for p and **24** for n. MegaStat automatically changes p to X unless a decimal value less than 1 is typed in for these.
3. Type **0** for the Hypothesized difference, select the not equal Alternative, and click [OK].

Hypothesis Test for Two Independent Proportions

p_1	p_2		p_c	
0.3529	0.7083		0.5	p (as decimal)
12/34	17/24		29/58	p (as fraction)
12.	17.		29.	X
34	24		58	n
	−0.3554	Difference		
	0.	Hypothesized difference		
	0.1333	Standard error		
	−2.67	z		
	0.0077	P-value (two-tailed)		

MINITAB

Step by Step

Test the Difference Between Two Proportions

For Example 9–9, test for a difference in the resident vaccination rates between small and large nursing homes.

This test does not require data.

1. Select **Stat>Basic Statistics> 2 Proportions**.

2. Select Summarized data from the drop-down menu.

3. Move the cursor to the Sample 1 box for Number of events.

   a) Enter **12, TAB,** then enter **34** in the Number of trials box.

   b) Press **TAB** or click in the Sample 2 text box for Number of events.

   c) Enter **17, TAB,** then enter **24** in the Number of trials box.

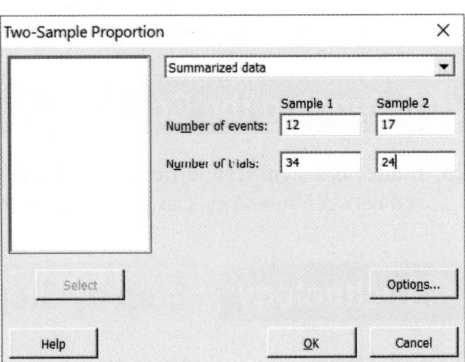

4. Click on [Options]. The Confidence level should be 95%, and the Hypothesized difference should be 0.

   a) For the Alternative hypothesis, select Difference ≠ hypothesized difference.

   b) For the Test method, select Use the pooled estimate of the proportion.

5. Click [OK] twice. The results are shown in the session window.

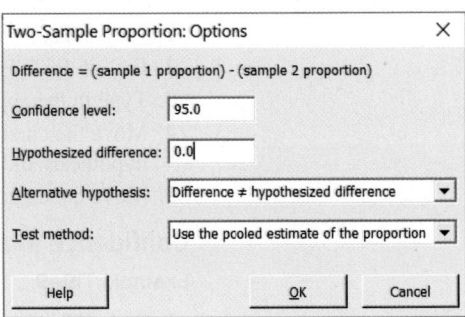

Test and CI for Two Proportions

```
Sample   X    N   Sample p
1        12   34  0.352941
2        17   24  0.708333


Difference = p (1) - p (2)
Estimate for difference:  -0.355392
95% CI for difference:  (-0.598025, -0.112759)
Test for difference = 0 (vs ≠ 0):  Z = -2.67  P-Value = 0.008

Fisher's exact test: P-Value = 0.016
```

The *P*-value of the test is 0.008. Reject the null hypothesis, since the *P*-value $< \alpha = 0.05$. The difference is statistically significant. Of all small nursing homes 35%, compared to 71% of all large nursing homes, have an immunization rate of less than 80%. We can't tell why, only that there is a difference. ∎

9–6   Testing the Difference Between Two Variances

OBJECTIVE

Test the difference between two variances or standard deviations.

In addition to comparing two means, statisticians are interested in comparing two variances or standard deviations. For example, is the variation in the temperatures for a certain month for two cities different?

In another situation, a researcher may be interested in comparing the variance of the cholesterol of men with the variance of the cholesterol of women. For the comparison of two variances or standard deviations, an *F* **test** is used. The *F* test should not be confused with the chi-square test, which compares a single sample variance to a specific population variance, as shown in Chapter 8.

Figure 9–10 shows the shapes of several curves for the *F* distribution.

FIGURE 9–10
The *F* Family of Curves

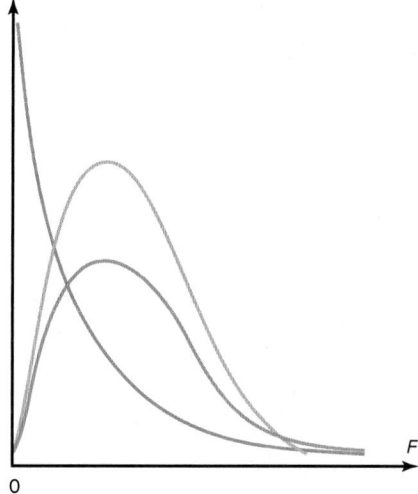

If two independent samples are selected from two normally distributed populations in which the population variances are equal ($\sigma_1^2 = \sigma_2^2$) and if the sample variances s_1^2 and s_2^2 are compared as $\frac{s_1^2}{s_2^2}$, the sampling distribution of the variances is called the ***F* distribution.**

Characteristics of the *F* Distribution

1. The values of *F* cannot be negative, because variances are always positive or zero.
2. The distribution is positively skewed.
3. The mean value of *F* is equal to 1.
4. The *F* distribution is a family of curves based on the degrees of freedom of the variance of the numerator and the degrees of freedom of the variance of the denominator.

Formula for the *F* Test

$$F = \frac{s_1^2}{s_2^2}$$

where the larger of the two variances is placed in the numerator regardless of the subscripts. (See note on page 538.)

The *F* test has two values for the degrees of freedom: that of the numerator, $n_1 - 1$, and that of the denominator, $n_2 - 1$, where n_1 is the sample size from which the larger variance was obtained.

When you are finding the *F* test statistic, *the larger of the variances is placed in the numerator of the F formula;* this is not necessarily the variance of the larger of the two sample sizes.

Table A–7 in Appendix A gives the *F* critical values for $\alpha = 0.005, 0.01, 0.025, 0.05,$ and 0.10 (each α value involves a separate table in Table A–7). These are one-tailed values; if a two-tailed test is being conducted, then the $\alpha/2$ value must be used. For example, if a two-tailed test with $\alpha = 0.05$ is being conducted, then the $0.05/2 = 0.025$ table of Table A–7 should be used.

EXAMPLE 9–12

Find the critical value for a right-tailed *F* test when $\alpha = 0.05$, the degrees of freedom for the numerator (abbreviated d.f.N.) are 15, and the degrees of freedom for the denominator (d.f.D.) are 21.

SOLUTION

Since this test is right-tailed with $\alpha = 0.05$, use the 0.05 table. The d.f.N. is listed across the top, and the d.f.D. is listed in the left column. The critical value is found where the row and column intersect in the table. In this case, it is 2.18. See Figure 9–11.

FIGURE 9–11 Finding the Critical Value in Table A–7 for Example 9–12

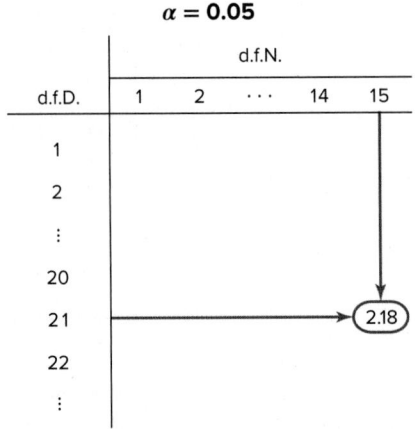

As noted previously, when the F test is used, the larger variance is always placed in the numerator of the formula. When you are conducting a two-tailed test, α is split; and even though there are two values, only the right tail is used. The reason is that the F test statistic is always greater than or equal to 1.

EXAMPLE 9–13

Find the critical value for a two-tailed F test with $\alpha = 0.05$ when the sample size from which the variance for the numerator was obtained was 21 and the sample size from which the variance for the denominator was obtained was 12.

SOLUTION

Since this is a two-tailed test with $\alpha = 0.05$, the $0.05/2 = 0.025$ table must be used. Here, d.f.N. $= 21 - 1 = 20$, and d.f.D. $= 12 - 1 = 11$; hence, the critical value is 3.23. See Figure 9–12.

FIGURE 9–12 Finding the Critical Value in Table A–7 for Example 9–13

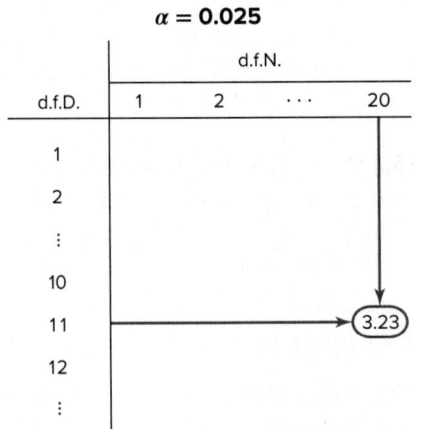

If the exact degrees of freedom are not specified in Table A–7, the closest smaller value should be used. For example, if $\alpha = 0.05$ (right-tailed test), d.f.N. = 18, and d.f.D. = 20, use the column d.f.N. = 15 and the row d.f.D. = 20 to get $F = 2.20$. Using the smaller value is the more conservative approach.

When you are testing the equality of two variances, these hypotheses are used:

Right-tailed	Left-tailed	Two-tailed
$H_0: \sigma_1^2 = \sigma_2^2$	$H_0: \sigma_1^2 = \sigma_2^2$	$H_0: \sigma_1^2 = \sigma_2^2$
$H_1: \sigma_1^2 > \sigma_2^2$	$H_1: \sigma_1^2 < \sigma_2^2$	$H_1: \sigma_1^2 \neq \sigma_2^2$

There are four key points to keep in mind when you are using the F test.

Unusual Stat

Of all U.S. births, 2% are twins.

Notes for the Use of the F Test

1. The larger variance should always be placed in the numerator of the formula regardless of the subscripts. (See note on page 538.)

$$F = \frac{s_1^2}{s_2^2}$$

2. For a two-tailed test, the α value must be divided by 2 and the critical value placed on the right side of the F curve.
3. If the standard deviations instead of the variances are given in the problem, they must be squared for the formula for the F test.
4. When the degrees of freedom cannot be found in Table A–7, the closest value on the smaller side should be used.

Before you can use the testing method to determine the difference between two variances, the following assumptions must be met.

Assumptions for Testing the Difference Between Two Variances

1. The samples must be random samples.
2. The populations from which the samples were obtained must be normally distributed. (*Note:* The test should not be used when the distributions depart from normality.)
3. The samples must be independent of one another.

In this book, the assumptions will be stated in the exercises; however, when encountering statistics in other situations, you must check to see that these assumptions have been met before proceeding.

Remember also that in tests of hypotheses using the traditional method, these five steps should be taken:

Step 1   State the hypotheses and identify the claim.

Step 2   Find the critical value.

Step 3   Compute the test statistic.

Step 4   Make the decision.

Step 5   Summarize the results.

This procedure is not robust, so minor departures from normality will affect the results of the test. So this test should not be used when the distributions depart from normality because standard deviations are not a good measure of the spread in nonsymmetrical distributions. The reason is that the standard deviation is not resistant to outliers or extreme values. These values increase the value of the standard deviation when the distribution is skewed.

EXAMPLE 9–14 Fast-food Restaurants

A fast-food manager wishes to see if the variance of the times it takes adult men to eat lunch is different from the variance of the times it takes adult women to eat lunch. The manager selects random samples of men and women and compares the variances of each. At $\alpha = 0.05$, is there enough evidence to support the claim that the variances are not equal? Assume the variable is normally distributed.

Men	Women
$n_1 = 31$	$n_2 = 22$
$s_1^2 = 32$	$s_2^2 = 15$

SOLUTION

Step 1   State the hypothesis and identify the claim.

$$H_0: \sigma_1^2 = \sigma_2^2 \qquad \text{and} \qquad H_1: \sigma_1^2 \neq \sigma_2^2 \text{ (claim)}$$

Step 2   Find the critical value. Use Table A–7 with 0.025 since $\alpha = 0.05$ and this is a two-tailed test. Here d.f.N. = 31 − 1 = 30 and d.f.D. = 22 − 1 = 21. The critical value is 2.31. See Figure 9–13.

Step 3   Compute the test statistic.

$$F = \frac{s_1^2}{s_2^2} = \frac{32}{15} = 2.13$$

FIGURE 9–13   Critical Value and Test Statistic for Example 9–14

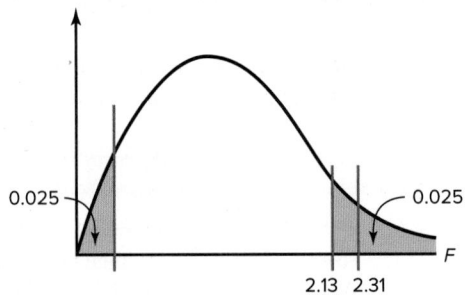

Step 4   Make the decision. Do not reject the null hypothesis since 2.13 < 2.31. (*Note:* The *P*-value is 0.0749.)

Step 5   Summarize the results. There is not enough evidence to support the claim that the variances are not equal.

EXAMPLE 9–15 Grade Point Averages

A researcher selected a random sample of 10 psychology graduates and found the standard deviation of their grade point average was 0.72. Then the researcher selected a random sample of 14 engineering students and found that the standard deviation of their grade point average was 0.51. At $\alpha = 0.01$, can we conclude that the variance of the grade point averages of the psychology graduates is greater than the variance of the grade point averages of the engineering graduates?

SOLUTION

Step 1   State the hypotheses and identify the claim.

$$H_0: \sigma_1^2 = \sigma_2^2 \qquad \text{and} \qquad H_1: \sigma_1^2 > \sigma_2^2 \text{ (claim)}$$

Step 2   Find the critical value. Hence, d.f.N. = 10 − 1 = 9 and d.f.D. = 14 − 1 = 13. From Table A–7 at $\alpha = 0.01$ the critical value is 4.19.

Step 3   Compute the test statistic.

$$F = \frac{s_1^2}{s_2^2} = \frac{0.72^2}{0.51^2} = 1.99$$

Step 4   Make the decision. Do not reject the null hypothesis since $1.99 < 4.19$. That is, 1.99 does not fall in the critical region. See Figure 9–14.

FIGURE 9–14   Critical Value and Test Statistic for Example 9–15

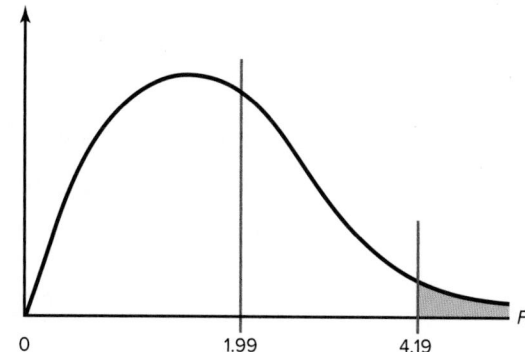

Step 5   Summarize the results. There is not enough evidence to support the claim that the variance in the grade point average of psychology graduates is greater than the variance in the grade point average of the engineering graduates.

Finding P-values for the F test statistic is somewhat more complicated since it requires looking through all the F tables (Table A–7 in Appendix A) using the specific d.f.N. and d.f.D. values. For example, suppose that a certain test has $F = 3.58$, d.f.N. = 5, and d.f.D. = 10. To find the P-value interval for $F = 3.58$, you must first find the corresponding F values for d.f.N. = 5 and d.f.D. = 10 for α equal to 0.005, 0.01, 0.025, 0.05, and 0.10 in Table A–7. Then make a table as shown.

α	0.10	0.05	0.025	0.01	0.005
F	2.52	3.33	4.24	5.64	6.87

Now locate the two F values that the test statistic 3.58 falls between. In this case, 3.58 falls between 3.33 and 4.24, corresponding to 0.05 and 0.025. Hence, the P-value for a right-tailed test for $F = 3.58$ falls between 0.025 and 0.05 (that is, $0.025 < P\text{-value} < 0.05$). For a right-tailed test, then, you would reject the null hypothesis at $\alpha = 0.05$, but not at $\alpha = 0.01$. The P-value obtained from a calculator is 0.0408. Remember that for a two-tailed test the values found in Table A–7 for α must be doubled. In this case, $0.05 < P\text{-value} < 0.10$ for $F = 3.58$. Once again, if the P-value is less than α, we reject the null hypothesis.

Once you understand the concept, you can dispense with making a table as shown and find the P-value directly from Table A–7.

Recall the P-value method for hypothesis testing. The steps are reviewed here.

Step 1   State the hypothesis and identify the claim.

Step 2   Compute the test statistic.

Step 3   Find the P-value.

Step 4   Make the decision.

Step 5   Summarize the results.

EXAMPLE 9–16   Airport Passengers

The CEO of an airport hypothesizes that the variance in the number of passengers for American airports is greater than the variance in the number of passengers for foreign airports. At $\alpha = 0.10$, is there enough evidence to support the hypothesis? The data in millions of passengers per year are shown for selected airports. Use the P-value method. Assume the variable is normally distributed and the samples are random and independent.

American airports		Foreign airports	
36.8	73.5	60.7	51.2
72.4	61.2	42.7	38.6
60.5	40.1		

Source: Airports Council International.

SOLUTION

Step 1   State the hypotheses and identify the claim.

$$H_0: \sigma_1^2 = \sigma_2^2 \qquad \text{and} \qquad H_1: \sigma_1^2 > \sigma_2^2 \text{ (claim)}$$

Step 2   Compute the test statistic. Using the formula in Chapter 3 or a calculator, find the variance for each group.

$$s_1^2 = 246.38 \qquad \text{and} \qquad s_2^2 = 95.87$$

Substitute in the formula and solve.

$$F = \frac{s_1^2}{s_2^2} = \frac{246.38}{95.87} = 2.57$$

Step 3   Find the *P*-value in Table A–7, using d.f.N. $= 6 - 1 = 5$ and d.f.D. $= 4 - 1 = 3$.

α	0.10	0.05	0.025	0.01	0.005
F	5.31	9.01	14.88	28.24	45.39

Since 2.57 is less than 5.31, the *P*-value is greater than 0.10. (The *P*-value obtained from a calculator is 0.234.)

Step 4   Make the decision. The decision is to not reject the null hypothesis since *P*-value > 0.10.

Step 5   Summarize the results. There is not enough evidence to support the claim that the variance in the number of passengers for American airports is greater than the variance in the number of passengers for foreign airports.

Note: It is not absolutely necessary to place the larger variance in the numerator when you are performing the *F* test. Critical values for left-tailed hypotheses tests can be found by interchanging the degrees of freedom and taking the reciprocal of the value found in Table A–7.

Also, you should use caution when performing the *F* test since the data can run contrary to the hypotheses on rare occasions. For example, if the hypotheses are $H_0: \sigma_1^2 \leq \sigma_2^2$ (written $H_0: \sigma_1^2 = \sigma_2^2$) and $H_1: \sigma_1^2 > \sigma_2^2$, but if $s_1^2 < s_2^2$, then the *F* test should not be performed and you would not reject the null hypothesis.

≡ Applying the Concepts 9–6

Automatic Transmissions

Assume the following data values are from a 2016 Auto Guide. The guide compared various parameters of U.S.- and foreign-made cars. This report centers on the price of an optional automatic transmission. Which country has the greater variability in the price of automatic transmissions? Answer the following questions.

Germany (2016)		U.S. Cars (2016)	
BMW 6 Series	$77,300	Ford Mustang	$47,795
Audi TT	$46,400	Chevrolet Corvette	$55,400
Porsche Boxster	$82,100	Dodge Challenger	$62,495
BMW 2 Series	$50,750	Dodge Viper	$87,895

1. What is the null hypothesis?

2. What test statistic is used to test for any significant differences in the variances?

3. Is there a significant difference in the variability in the prices between the German cars and the U.S. cars?

4. What effect does a small sample size have on the standard deviations?

5. What degrees of freedom are used for the statistical test?

6. Could two sets of data have significantly different variances without having significantly different means?

See page 550 for the answers.

Exercises 9–6

1. When one is computing the F test statistic, what condition is placed on the variance that is in the numerator? The variance in the numerator should be the larger of the two variances.

2. Why is the critical region always on the right side in the use of the F test? The larger variance is placed in the numerator of the formula; hence, $F \geq 1$.

3. What are the two different degrees of freedom associated with the F distribution?

4. What are the characteristics of the F distribution?

5. Using Table A–7, find the critical value for each:
   a. Sample 1: $s_1^2 = 164$, $n_1 = 31$
      Sample 2: $s_2^2 = 118$, $n_2 = 24$
      Two-tailed, $\alpha = 0.05$
   b. Sample 1: $s_1^2 = 35$, $n_1 = 10$
      Sample 2: $s_2^2 = 62$, $n_2 = 8$
      Right-tailed, $\alpha = 0.10$
   c. Sample 1: $s_1^2 = 432$, $n_1 = 9$
      Sample 2: $s_2^2 = 206$, $n_2 = 17$
      Right-tailed, $\alpha = 0.01$

6. Using Table A–7, find the critical value for each:
   a. Sample 1: $s_1^2 = 213$, $n_1 = 7$
      Sample 2: $s_2^2 = 574$, $n_2 = 11$
      Right-tailed, $\alpha = 0.01$
   b. Sample 1: $s_1^2 = 162$, $n_1 = 41$
      Sample 2: $s_2^2 = 48$, $n_2 = 29$
      Two-tailed, $\alpha = 0.10$
   c. Sample 1: $s_1^2 = 95.6$, $n_1 = 13$
      Sample 2: $s_2^2 = 55.2$, $n_2 = 13$
      Right-tailed, $\alpha = 0.025$

7. Using Table A–7, find the P-value interval for each F test statistic.
   a. $F = 2.97$, d.f.N. = 9, d.f.D. = 14, right-tailed
   b. $F = 3.32$, d.f.N. = 6, d.f.D. = 12, two-tailed
   c. $F = 2.28$, d.f.N. = 12, d.f.D. = 20, right-tailed
   d. $F = 3.51$, d.f.N. = 12, d.f.D. = 21, right-tailed

8. Using Table A–7, find the P-value interval for each F test statistic.
   a. $F = 4.07$, d.f.N. = 6, d.f.D. = 10, two-tailed
   b. $F = 1.65$, d.f.N. = 19, d.f.D. = 28, right-tailed
   c. $F = 1.77$, d.f.N. = 28, d.f.D. = 28, right-tailed
   d. $F = 7.29$, d.f.N. = 5, d.f.D. = 8, two-tailed

For Exercises 9 through 24, perform the following steps. Assume that all variables are normally distributed.

   a. State the hypotheses and identify the claim.
   b. Find the critical value or use the P-value method.
   c. Compute the test statistic.
   d. Make the decision.
   e. Summarize the results.

Use the traditional method of hypothesis testing unless the P-value method is specified by your instructor.

9. Wolf Pack Pups Does the variance in the number of pups per pack differ between Montana and Idaho wolf packs? Random samples of packs were selected for each area, and the numbers of pups per pack were recorded. At the 0.05 level of significance, can a difference in variances be concluded?

Montana wolf packs	4	3	5	6	1	2	8	2
	3	1	7	6	5			
Idaho wolf packs	2	4	5	4	2	4	6	3
	1	4	2	1				

Source: www.fws.gov

10. Noise Levels in Hospitals In a hospital study, it was found that the standard deviation of the sound levels from 20 randomly selected areas designated as "casualty doors" was 4.1 dBA and the standard deviation of 24 randomly selected areas designated as operating theaters was 7.5 dBA. At $\alpha = 0.05$, can you substantiate the claim that there is a difference in the standard deviations?

Source: M. Bayo, A. Garcia, and A. Garcia, "Noise Levels in an Urban Hospital and Workers' Subjective Responses," *Archives of Environmental Health.*

11. **Calories in Ice Cream** The numbers of calories contained in $\frac{1}{2}$-cup servings of randomly selected flavors of ice cream from two national brands are listed. At the 0.05 level of significance, is there sufficient evidence to conclude that the variance in the number of calories differs between the two brands?

Brand A		Brand B	
330	300	280	310
310	350	300	370
270	380	250	300
310	300	290	310

Source: The Doctor's Pocket Calorie, Fat and Carbohydrate Counter.

12. **Winter Temperatures** A random sample of daily high temperatures in January and February is listed. At $\alpha = 0.05$, can it be concluded that there is a difference in variances in high temperature between the two months?

Jan.	31	31	38	24	24	42	22	43	35	42
Feb.	31	29	24	30	28	24	27	34	27	

13. **Population and Area** Cities were randomly selected from the list of the 50 largest cities in the United States (based on population). The areas of each in square miles are shown. Is there sufficient evidence to conclude that the variance in area is greater for eastern cities than for western cities at $\alpha = 0.05$? At $\alpha = 0.01$?

Eastern		Western	
Atlanta, GA	132	Albuquerque, NM	181
Columbus, OH	210	Denver, CO	155
Louisville, KY	385	Fresno, CA	104
New York, NY	303	Las Vegas, NV	113
Philadelphia, PA	135	Portland, OR	134
Washington, DC	61	Seattle, WA	84
Charlotte, NC	242		

Source: New York Times Almanac.

14. **Carbohydrates in Candy** The number of grams of carbohydrates contained in 1-ounce servings of randomly selected chocolate and nonchocolate candy is shown. Is there sufficient evidence to conclude that there is a difference between the variation in carbohydrate content for chocolate and nonchocolate candy? Use $\alpha = 0.10$.

Chocolate	29	25	17	36	41	25	32	29
	38	34	24	27	29			
Nonchocolate	41	41	37	29	30	38	39	10
	29	55	29					

Source: The Doctor's Pocket Calorie, Fat and Carbohydrate Counter.

15. **Treadmills** The time people spent on a treadmill during their exercise periods are shown. At $\alpha = 0.05$, can it be concluded that the variance for people under 30 years

of age is greater than the variance for people 30 and over?

Under 30	56	43	28	36	42	60	29	66	30	45
30 or over	42	47	35	21	28	31	37	41	45	25	60	38

16. **County Size in Indiana and Iowa** A researcher wishes to see if the variance of the areas in square miles for counties in Indiana is less than the variance of the areas for counties in Iowa. A random sample of counties is selected, and the data are shown. At $\alpha = 0.01$, can it be concluded that the variance of the areas for counties in Indiana is less than the variance of the areas for counties in Iowa?

Indiana				Iowa			
406	393	396	485	640	580	431	416
431	430	369	408	443	569	779	381
305	215	489	293	717	568	714	731
373	148	306	509	571	577	503	501
560	384	320	407	568	434	615	402

Source: The World Almanac and Book of Facts.

17. **Heights of Tall Buildings** Test the claim that the variance of heights of randomly selected tall buildings in Denver is equal to the variance in heights of randomly selected tall buildings in Nashville at $\alpha = 0.10$. The data are given in feet.

Denver			Nashville		
714	698	544	617	524	489
504	438	408	459	453	417
404			410	404	

Source: SkyscraperCenter.com

18. **Attention Spans** The attention span in minutes of students in science classes and the attention spans of students in English classes are shown. Can it be concluded at $\alpha = 0.01$ that the variances of the attention spans of the students for the subjects are different? Assume the variable is normally distributed and the students were randomly selected.

Science	32	18	24	28	26	25	25	30	35
English	36	41	20	32	27	25	42	33	

19. **Weights of Running Shoes** The weights in ounces of a random sample of running shoes for men and women are shown. Calculate the variances for each sample, and test the claim that the variances are equal at $\alpha = 0.05$. Use the *P*-value method.

Men			Women		
11.9	10.4	12.6	10.6	10.2	8.8
12.3	11.1	14.7	9.6	9.5	9.5
9.2	10.8	12.9	10.1	11.2	9.3
11.2	11.7	13.3	9.4	10.3	9.5
13.8	12.8	14.5	9.8	10.3	11.0

20. **School Teachers' Salaries** A researcher claims that the variation in the salaries of elementary school teachers is greater than the variation in the salaries of secondary

school teachers. A random sample of the salaries of 30 elementary school teachers has a variance of 8324, and a random sample of the salaries of 30 secondary school teachers has a variance of 2862. At $\alpha = 0.05$, can the researcher conclude that the variation in the elementary school teachers' salaries is greater than the variation in the secondary school teachers' salaries? Use the *P*-value method.

21. **Shopping Times** The average time it takes a person to buy groceries is 47 minutes. Two random samples of shoppers are selected. A random sample of 13 married shoppers had a standard deviation of time spent of 5.6 minutes. A random sample of 27 unmarried shoppers had a standard deviation of time spent of 3.7 minutes. At $\alpha = 0.05$, is there a difference in the variances of the times it takes the two groups of shoppers to complete their shopping? Assume shopping times are normally distributed.

Source: South Florida Sun-Sentinel

22. **Daily Stock Prices** Two portfolios were randomly assembled from the New York Stock Exchange, and the daily stock prices are shown. At the 0.05, level of significance, can it be concluded that a difference in variance in price exists between the two portfolios?

Portfolio A	36.44	44.21	12.21	59.60	55.44	39.42	51.29	48.68	41.59	19.49
Portfolio B	32.69	47.25	49.35	36.17	63.04	17.74	4.23	34.98	37.02	31.48

Source: Washington Observer-Reporter.

23. **Test Scores** An instructor who taught an online statistics course and a classroom course feels that the variance of the final exam scores for the students who took the online course is greater than the variance of the final exam scores of the students who took the classroom final exam. The following data were obtained. At $\alpha = 0.05$, is there enough evidence to support the claim?

Online Course	Classroom Course
$s_1 = 3.2$	$s_2 = 2.8$
$n_1 = 11$	$n_2 = 16$

24. **Museum Attendance** A metropolitan children's museum open year-round wants to see if the variance in daily attendance differs between the summer and winter months. Random samples of 30 days each were selected and showed that in the winter months, the sample mean daily attendance was 300 with a standard deviation of 52, and the sample mean daily attendance for the summer months was 280 with a standard deviation of 65. At $\alpha = 0.05$, can we conclude a difference in variances?

Technology   Step by Step

TI-84 Plus
Step by Step

Hypothesis Test for the Difference Between Two Variances (Data)

This refers to Example 9–16 in the text.

1. Enter the data values into L_1 and L_2.
2. Press **STAT** and move the cursor to TESTS.
3. Press **E (ALPHA SIN)** for 2-SampFTest.
4. Move the cursor to Data and press **ENTER**.
5. Type in the appropriate values.
6. Move the cursor to the appropriate Alternative hypothesis and press **ENTER**.
7. Move the cursor to Calculate and press **ENTER**.

 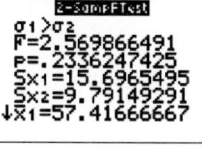

Hypothesis Test for the Difference Between Two Variances (Statistics)

Example TI9–10

1. Press **STAT** and move the cursor to TESTS.
2. Press **E (ALPHA SIN)** for 2-SampFTest.
3. Move the cursor to Stats and press **ENTER**.
4. Type in the appropriate values.
5. Move the cursor to the appropriate Alternative hypothesis and press **ENTER**.
6. Move the cursor to Calculate and press **ENTER**.

This refers to Example 9–14 in the text.

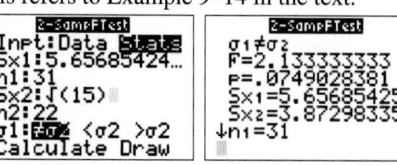

EXCEL

Step by Step

F Test for the Difference Between Two Variances

Excel has a two-sample *F* test included in the Data Analysis Add-in. Calculate the sample variance and choose group one to have the larger variance.

Example XL9–4

An instructor believes that there is a difference in the variance of test scores between their early morning class compared to their evening class. At $\alpha = 0.05$, test the hypothesis that there is a difference in the two population variances.

Morning	63	73	80	60	86	83	70	72	82
Evening	86	93	64	82	81	75	88	63	63

1. Enter the Evening data into column A.
2. Enter the Morning data into column B.
3. Select the Data tab from the toolbar. Then select Data Analysis.
4. In the Data Analysis box, under Analysis Tools select F-test Two-sample for Variances, and click [OK].

5. In Input, type in the Variable 1 Range: **A1:A10** and the Variable 2 Range: **B1:B10.**
6. Specify the confidence level Alpha. Excel only does a right-tailed *F*-test, so if you have a two-tailed test, use $\alpha/2 = 0.05/2 = 0.025$. (If you are doing a left-tailed test, use $1 - \alpha$.)
7. Check the box for labels if you selected the labels in the input ranges.
8. Specify a location for the output, and click [OK].

The results appear in the table that Excel generates, shown here. For this example, the output shows the *P*-value for only one tail. For a two-tailed test, multiply this by 2. The *P*-value = 2*0.258814 = 0.517628. Do not reject the null hypothesis at an α level of 0.05.

F-Test Two-Sample for Variances		
	Evening	*Morning*
Mean	77.22222	74.33333
Variance	132.9444	82.75
Observations	9	9
df	8	8
F	1.606579	
P(F<=f) one-tail	0.258814	
F Critical one-tail	4.43326	

MINITAB

Step by Step

Test for the Difference Between Two Variances

For Example 9–16, test the hypothesis that the variance in the number of passengers for American and foreign airports is different. Use the *P*-value approach.

American airports	Foreign airports
36.8	60.7
72.4	42.7
60.5	51.2
73.5	38.6
61.2	
40.1	

1. Enter the data into two columns of MINITAB.

2. Label the columns American and Foreign.

3. Select **Stat>Basic Statistics>2-Variances.**

4. Select Each sample is in its own column from the drop-down menu.

5. Click in the text box for Sample 1, then double-click C1 American.

6. Double-click C2 Foreign.

7. Click on [Options]. The dialog box is shown.

   a) For ratio, select (sample 1 variance) / (sample 2 variance)

   b) Change the confidence level to **90**.

   c) The hypothesized ratio should be 1.

   d) For the Alternative hypothesis, select Ratio > hypothesized ratio.

   e) Check the box for Use test and confidence intervals based on normal distribution.

8. Click [OK] twice.

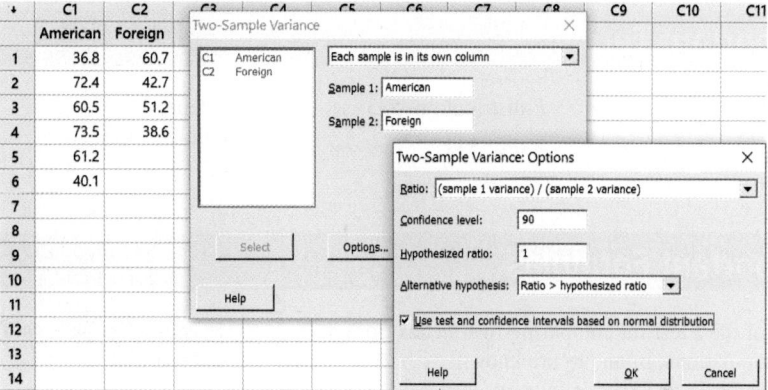

A graph window will open that includes a small window that says the *P*-value is 0.234. In the session window, the *F*-test statistic is shown as the Ratio of variances = 2.570. You can view the session window by closing the graph or clicking and dragging it to the right hand part of your screen.

```
Test and CI for Two Variances: American, Foreign

Method
Null hypothesis          Variance(American) / Variance(Foreign) = 1
Alternative hypothesis   Variance(American) / Variance(Foreign) > 1
Significance level       α = 0.1

F method was used. This method is accurate for normal data only.

Statistics
                                 90% Lower
                                 Bound for
Variable   N   StDev   Variance  Variances
American   6  15.697   246.382    133.376
Foreign    4   9.791    95.873     46.009

Ratio of standard deviations = 1.603
Ratio of variances = 2.570

90% One-Sided Confidence Intervals
            Lower Bound   Lower Bound
            for StDev     for Variance
Method         Ratio         Ratio
F              0.696         0.484

Tests
                         Test
Method  DF1  DF2  Statistic  P-Value
F        5    3      2.57      0.234
```

There is not enough evidence in the sample to conclude there is greater variance in the number of passengers in American airports compared to foreign airports.

⛃ Summary

Many times researchers are interested in comparing two parameters such as two means, two proportions, or two variances. These measures are obtained from two samples, then compared using a z test, t test, or an F test.

- If two sample means are compared, when the samples are independent and the population standard deviations are known, a z test is used. If the sample sizes are less than 30, the populations should be normally distributed. (9–2)
- If two means are compared when the samples are independent and the sample standard deviations are used, then a t test is used. The two variances are assumed to be unequal. (9–3)

- When the two samples are dependent or related, such as using the same subjects and comparing the means of before-and-after tests, then the t test for dependent samples is used. (9–4)
- Two proportions can be compared by using the z test for proportions. In this case, each of $n_1 p_1$, $n_1 q_1$, $n_2 p_2$, and $n_2 q_2$ must all be 5 or more. (9–5)
- Confidence intervals for differences between two parameters can also be found.
- Two variances can be compared by using an F test. The critical values for the F test are obtained from the F distribution. (9–6)

⛃ Important Terms

dependent samples 511	F distribution 533 F test 532	independent samples 503	pooled estimate of the variance 506

⛃ Important Formulas

Formula for the z test for comparing two means from independent populations; σ_1 and σ_2 are known:

$$z = \frac{(\overline{X}_1 - \overline{X}_2) - (\mu_1 - \mu_2)}{\sqrt{\dfrac{\sigma_1^2}{n_1} + \dfrac{\sigma_2^2}{n_2}}}$$

Formula for the confidence interval for difference of two means when σ_1 and σ_2 are known:

$$(\overline{X}_1 - \overline{X}_2) - z_{\alpha/2}\sqrt{\frac{\sigma_1^2}{n_1} + \frac{\sigma_2^2}{n_2}} < \mu_1 - \mu_2$$
$$< (\overline{X}_1 - \overline{X}_2) + z_{\alpha/2}\sqrt{\frac{\sigma_1^2}{n_1} + \frac{\sigma_2^2}{n_2}}$$

Formula for the t test for comparing two means (independent samples, variances not equal), σ_1 and σ_2 unknown:

$$t = \frac{(\overline{X}_1 - \overline{X}_2) - (\mu_1 - \mu_2)}{\sqrt{\dfrac{s_1^2}{n_1} + \dfrac{s_2^2}{n_2}}}$$

and d.f. = the smaller of $n_1 - 1$ or $n_2 - 1$.

Formula for the confidence interval for the difference of two means (independent samples, variances unequal), σ_1 and σ_2 unknown:

$$(\overline{X}_1 - \overline{X}_2) - t_{\alpha/2}\sqrt{\frac{s_1^2}{n_1} + \frac{s_2^2}{n_2}} < \mu_1 - \mu_2$$
$$< (\overline{X}_1 - \overline{X}_2) + t_{\alpha/2}\sqrt{\frac{s_1^2}{n_1} + \frac{s_2^2}{n_2}}$$

and d.f. = smaller of $n_1 - 1$ and $n_2 - 1$.

Formula for the t test for comparing two means from dependent samples:

$$t = \frac{\overline{D} - \mu_D}{s_D/\sqrt{n}}$$

d.f. $= n - 1$

where $\overline{D}$ is the mean of the differences

$$\overline{D} = \frac{\Sigma D}{n}$$

and s_D is the standard deviation of the differences

$$s_D = \sqrt{\frac{n\Sigma D^2 - (\Sigma D)^2}{n(n-1)}}$$

Formula for confidence interval for the mean of the difference for dependent samples:

$$\overline{D} - t_{\alpha/2}\frac{s_D}{\sqrt{n}} < \mu_D < \overline{D} + t_{\alpha/2}\frac{s_D}{\sqrt{n}}$$

and d.f. $= n - 1$.

Formula for the z test for comparing two proportions:

$$z = \frac{(\hat{p}_1 - \hat{p}_2) - (p_1 - p_2)}{\sqrt{\overline{p}\,\overline{q}\left(\dfrac{1}{n_1} + \dfrac{1}{n_2}\right)}}$$

where

$$\overline{p} = \frac{X_1 + X_2}{n_1 + n_2} \qquad \hat{p}_1 = \frac{X_1}{n_1}$$

$$\overline{q} = 1 - \overline{p} \qquad \hat{p}_2 = \frac{X_2}{n_2}$$

Formula for confidence interval for the difference of two proportions:

$$(\hat{p}_1 - \hat{p}_2) - z_{\alpha/2} \sqrt{\frac{\hat{p}_1\,\hat{q}_1}{n_1} + \frac{\hat{p}_2\,\hat{q}_2}{n_2}} < p_1 - p_2$$

$$< (\hat{p}_1 - \hat{p}_2) + z_{\alpha/2} \sqrt{\frac{\hat{p}_1\,\hat{q}_1}{n_1} + \frac{\hat{p}_2\,\hat{q}_2}{n_2}}$$

Formula for the F test for comparing two variances:

$$F = \frac{s_1^2}{s_2^2} \quad \begin{array}{l} \text{d.f.N.} = n_1 - 1 \\ \text{d.f.D.} = n_2 - 1 \end{array}$$

The larger variance is placed in the numerator.

Review Exercises

For each exercise, perform these steps. Assume that all variables are normally or approximately normally distributed.

    a. State the hypotheses and identify the claim.

    b. Find the critical value(s) or use the *P*-value method.

    c. Compute the test statistic.

    d. Make the decision.

    e. Summarize the results.

Use the traditional method of hypothesis testing unless the P-value method is specified by your instructor.

Section 9–2

1. Driving for Pleasure Two groups of randomly selected drivers are surveyed to see how many miles per week they drive for pleasure trips. The data are shown. At $\alpha = 0.01$, can it be concluded that single drivers do more driving for pleasure trips on average than married drivers? Assume $\sigma_1 = 16.7$ and $\sigma_2 = 16.1$.

Single drivers					Married drivers				
106	110	115	121	132	97	104	138	102	115
119	97	118	122	135	133	120	119	136	96
110	117	116	138	142	139	108	117	145	114
115	114	103	98	99	140	136	113	113	150
108	117	152	147	117	101	114	116	113	135
154	86	115	116	104	115	109	147	106	88
107	133	138	142	140	113	119	99	108	105

2. Average Earnings of College Graduates The average yearly earnings of male college graduates (with at least a bachelor's degree) are $81,354 for men. The average yearly earnings of female college graduates with the same qualifications are $60,069. A sample of college graduates aged 25 to 29 was taken. Based on the results below, can it be concluded that there is a difference in mean earnings between male and female college graduates aged 25 to 29? Use the 0.01 level of significance.

	Male	Female
Sample mean	$59,235	$52,487
Population standard deviation	$8,945	$10,125
Sample size	40	35

Section 9–3

3. Physical Therapy A recent study of 20 individuals found that the average number of therapy sessions a person takes for a shoulder problem is 9.6. The standard deviation of the sample was 2.8. A study of 25 individuals with a hip problem found that they had a mean of 10.3 sessions. The standard deviation for this sample was 2.3. At $\alpha = 0.01$, is there a significant difference in the means?

4. Average Temperatures The average temperatures for a 25-day period for Birmingham, Alabama, and Chicago, Illinois, are shown. Based on the samples, at $\alpha = 0.10$, can it be concluded that it is warmer in Birmingham?

Birmingham					Chicago				
78	82	68	67	68	70	74	73	60	77
75	73	75	64	68	71	72	71	74	76
62	73	77	78	79	71	80	65	70	83
74	72	73	78	68	67	76	75	62	65
73	79	82	71	66	66	65	77	66	64

5. Receptionists' Salaries A random sample of 15 receptionists from Rhode Island has an average salary of $35,270, with a standard deviation of $3256. A random sample of 30 receptionists from Pennsylvania has an average salary of $29,512, with a standard deviation of $1432. Is there a significant difference in receptionists' salaries between the two states? Use $\alpha = 0.02$. Find the 98% confidence interval for the difference of the two means.

6. Soft Drinks in School The data show the amounts (in thousands of dollars) of the contracts for soft drinks in randomly selected local school districts. At $\alpha = 0.10$, can it be concluded that there is a difference in the averages? Use the *P*-value method. Give a reason why the result would be of concern to a cafeteria manager.

Pepsi						Coca-Cola		
46	120	80	500	100	59	420	285	57

Source: Local school districts.

Section 9–4

7. High and Low Temperatures March is a month of variable weather in the Northeast. The table shows records of the actual high and low temperatures for a selection of days in March from the weather report for Pittsburgh, Pennsylvania. At the 0.01 level of significance, is there sufficient evidence to conclude that there is more than a 10° difference between average highs and lows?

Maximum	44	46	46	36	34	36	57	62	73	53
Minimum	27	34	24	19	19	26	33	57	46	26

Source: www.wunderground.com

8. **Testing After Review** A statistics class was given a pretest on probability (since many had previous experience in some other class). Then the class was given a six-page review handout to study for 2 days. At the next class they were given another test. Is there sufficient evidence that the scores improved? Use $\alpha = 0.05$.

Student	1	2	3	4	5	6
Pretest	52	50	40	58	60	52
Posttest	62	65	50	65	68	63

Section 9–5

9. **Lay Teachers in Religious Schools** A study found a slightly lower percentage of lay teachers in religious secondary schools than in elementary schools. A random sample of 200 elementary school and 200 secondary school teachers from religious schools in a large diocese found the following. At the 0.05 level of significance, is there sufficient evidence to conclude a difference in proportions?

	Elementary	Secondary
Sample size	200	200
Lay teachers	49	62

Source: New York Times Almanac.

10. **Gambling** A survey of 60 men found that 36 gamble. Another survey of 50 women found that 28 gamble. At $\alpha = 0.01$, is there a difference in the proportions?

Section 9–6

11. **Noise Levels in Hospitals** In the hospital study cited previously, the standard deviation of the noise levels of the 11 intensive care units was 4.1 dBA, and the standard deviation of the noise levels of 24 nonmedical care areas, such as kitchens and machine rooms, was 13.2 dBA. At $\alpha = 0.10$, is there a significant difference between the standard deviations of these two areas?

Source: Bayo, M., Garcia, A. and Garcia, A., "Noise Levels in an Urban Hospital and Workers' Subjective Responses," Archives of Environmental Health, 50, 3, May–June 1995, 247–51.

12. **Heights of World Famous Cathedrals** The heights (in feet) for a random sample of world famous cathedrals are listed. In addition, the heights for a random sample of the tallest buildings in the world are listed. Is there sufficient evidence at $\alpha = 0.05$ to conclude that there is a difference in the variances in height between the two groups?

Cathedrals	72 114 157 56 83 108 90 151
Tallest buildings	452 442 415 391 355 344 310 302 209

Source: www.infoplease.com

13. **Sodium Content of Cereals** The sodium content of brands of cereal produced by two major manufacturers is shown. At $\alpha = 0.01$, is there a significant difference in the variances?

Manufacturer 1			Manufacturer 2		
87	92	96	87	92	93
100	94	94	91	100	94
101	103	98	103	96	98
91	92	96	87	92	91

STATISTICS TODAY

To Vaccinate or Not to Vaccinate? Small or Large? —Revisited

Using a z test to compare two proportions, the researchers found that the proportion of residents in smaller nursing homes who were vaccinated (80.8%) was statistically greater than that of residents in large nursing homes who were vaccinated (68.7%). Using statistical methods presented in later chapters, they also found that the larger size of the nursing home and the lower frequency of vaccination were significant predictions of influenza outbreaks in nursing homes.

Data Analysis

The Data Bank is found in Appendix B.

1. From the Data Bank, select a variable and compare the mean of the variable for a random sample of at least 30 men with the mean of the variable for the random sample of at least 30 women. Use a z test.

2. Repeat the experiment in Exercise 1, using a different variable and two samples of size 15. Compare the means by using a t test.

3. Compare the proportion of men who are smokers with the proportion of women who are smokers. Use the data in the Data Bank. Choose random samples of size 30 or more. Use the z test for proportions.

4. Select two samples of 20 values from the data in Data Set IV in Appendix B. Test the hypothesis that the mean heights of the buildings are equal.

5. Using the same data obtained in Exercise 4, test the hypothesis that the variances are equal.

Chapter Quiz

Determine whether each statement is true or false. If the statement is false, explain why.

1. When you are testing the difference between two means, it is not important to distinguish whether the samples are independent of each other. False

2. If the same diet is given to two groups of randomly selected individuals, the samples are considered to be dependent. False

3. When computing the F test statistic, you should place the larger variance in the numerator of the fraction. True

4. Tests for variances are always two-tailed. False

Select the best answer.

5. To test the equality of two variances, you would use a(n) _____ test.
   - *a.* z
   - *b.* t
   - *c.* Chi-square
   - *d.* F ✓

6. To test the equality of two proportions, you would use a(n) _____ test.
   - *a.* z ✓
   - *b.* t
   - *c.* Chi-square
   - *d.* F

7. The mean value of F is equal to
   - *a.* 0
   - *b.* 0.5
   - *c.* 1 ✓
   - *d.* It cannot be determined.

8. What test can be used to test the difference between two sample means when the population variances are known?
   - *a.* z ✓
   - *b.* t
   - *c.* Chi-square
   - *d.* F

Complete these statements with the best answer.

9. If you hypothesize that there is no difference between means, this is represented as H_0: _____. $\mu_1 = \mu_2$

10. When you are testing the difference between two means, the _____ test is used when the population variances are not known. t

11. When the t test is used for testing the equality of two means, the populations must be _____. Normal

12. The values of F cannot be _____. Negative

13. The formula for the F test for variances is _____. $F = \dfrac{s_1^2}{s_2^2}$

For each of these problems, perform the following steps.

- *a.* State the hypotheses and identify the claim.
- *b.* Find the critical value(s) or use the P-value method.
- *c.* Compute the test statistic.
- *d.* Make the decision.
- *e.* Summarize the results.

Use the traditional method of hypothesis testing unless the P-value method is specified by your instructor.

14. **Cholesterol Levels** A researcher wishes to see if there is a difference in the cholesterol levels of two groups of men. A random sample of 30 men between the ages of 25 and 40 is selected and tested. The average level is 223. A second random sample of 25 men between the ages of 41 and 56 is selected and tested. The average of this group is 229. The population standard deviation for both groups is 6. At $\alpha = 0.01$, is there a difference in the cholesterol levels between the two groups? Find the 99% confidence interval for the difference of the two means.

15. **Room Rental Fees** The data shown are the rental fees (in dollars) for two random samples of rooms in a large city. At $\alpha = 0.10$, can it be concluded that the average rental fee for rooms in the east is greater than the average rental fee in the west? Assume $\sigma_1 = 119$ and $\sigma_2 = 103$.

East					West				
495	390	540	445	420	525	400	310	375	750
410	550	499	500	550	390	795	554	450	370
389	350	450	530	350	385	395	425	500	550
375	690	325	350	799	380	400	450	365	425
475	295	350	485	625	375	360	425	400	475
275	450	440	425	675	400	475	430	410	450
625	390	485	550	650	425	450	620	500	400
685	385	450	550	425	295	350	300	360	400

Source: Pittsburgh Post-Gazette.

16. **Prices of Salad Dressings** The average price of a random sample of 12 bottles of diet salad dressing taken from different stores is $4.43. The sample standard deviation is $0.09. The average price of a random sample of 16 bottles of regular salad dressings taken from different stores is $4.03. The sample standard deviation is $0.10. At $\alpha = 0.01$, is there a significant difference in price? Find the 99% confidence interval of the difference in the means.

17. **Jet Ski Accidents** The data shown represent the number of accidents people had when using jet skis and other types of wet bikes. At $\alpha = 0.05$, can it be concluded that the average number of accidents per year has increased from one period to the next?

Earlier period			Later period		
376	650	844	1650	2236	3002
1162	1513		4028	4010	

Source: USA TODAY.

18. **Salaries of Salespeople** A random sample of 12 salespeople from Washington state shows an average salary of $39,420 with a standard deviation of $1659, while a random sample of 26 salespeople from New Mexico has an average salary of $30,215 with a standard deviation of $4116. Is there a significant difference between the two states in salespeople's salaries at $\alpha = 0.02$? Find the 98% confidence interval of the difference in the means.

19. Family Incomes The average income of 15 randomly selected people who reside in a large metropolitan East Coast city is $62,456. The standard deviation is $9652. The average income of 11 randomly selected people who reside in a rural area of the Midwest is $60,213, with a standard deviation of $2009. At $\alpha = 0.05$, can it be concluded that the people who live in the cities have a higher income than those who live in the rural areas? Use the *P*-value method.

20. Mathematical Skills In an effort to improve the mathematical skills of 10 students, a teacher provides a weekly 1-hour tutoring session for the students. A pretest is given before the sessions, and a posttest is given after. The results are shown here. At $\alpha = 0.01$, can it be concluded that the sessions help to improve the students' mathematical skills?

Student	1	2	3	4	5	6	7	8	9	10
Pretest	82	76	91	62	81	67	71	69	80	85
Posttest	88	80	98	80	80	73	74	78	85	93

21. Egg Production To increase egg production, a farmer decided to increase the amount of time the lights in his hen house were on. Ten hens were randomly selected, and the number of eggs each produced was recorded. After one week of lengthened light time, the same hens were monitored again. The data are given here. At $\alpha = 0.05$, can it be concluded that the increased light time increased egg production?

Hen	1	2	3	4	5	6	7	8	9	10
Before	4	3	8	7	6	4	9	7	6	5
After	6	5	9	7	4	5	10	6	9	6

22. Factory Worker Literacy Rates In a random sample of 80 workers from a factory in city A, it was found that 5% were unable to read, while in a random sample of

50 workers in city B, 8% were unable to read. Can it be concluded that there is a difference in the proportions of nonreaders in the two cities? Use $\alpha = 0.10$. Find the 90% confidence interval for the difference of the two proportions.

23. Male Head of Household A recent survey of 200 randomly selected households showed that 8 had a single male as the head of household. Forty years ago, a survey of 200 randomly selected households showed that 6 had a single male as the head of household. At $\alpha = 0.05$, can it be concluded that the proportion has changed? Find the 95% confidence interval of the difference of the two proportions. Does the confidence interval contain 0? Why is this important to know?

Source: Based on data from the U.S. Census Bureau.

24. Money Spent on Road Repair A politician wishes to compare the variances of the amount of money spent for road repair in two different counties. The data are given here. At $\alpha = 0.05$, is there a significant difference in the variances of the amounts spent in the two counties? Use the *P*-value method.

County A	County B
$s_1 = \$11,596$	$s_2 = \$14,837$
$n_1 = 15$	$n_2 = 18$

25. Heights of Basketball Players A researcher wants to compare the variances of the heights (in inches) of 4-year college basketball players with those of players in junior colleges. A random sample of 30 players from each type of school is selected, and the variances of the heights for each type are 2.43 and 3.15, respectively. At $\alpha = 0.10$, is there a significant difference between the variances of the heights in the two types of schools?

Data Projects

Use a significance level of 0.05 for all tests below.

1. Business and Finance Use the data collected in data project 1 of Chapter 2 to complete this problem. Test the claim that the mean earnings per share for Dow Jones stocks are greater than for NASDAQ stocks.

2. Sports and Leisure Use the data collected in data project 2 of Chapter 7 regarding home runs for this problem. Test the claim that the mean number of home runs hit by the American League sluggers is the same as the mean for the National League.

3. Technology Use the cell phone data collected for data project 2 in Chapter 8 to complete this problem. Test the claim that the mean length for outgoing calls is the same as that for incoming calls. Test the claim that the standard deviation for outgoing calls is more than that for incoming calls.

4. Health and Wellness Use the data regarding BMI that were collected in data project 6 of Chapter 7 to complete this problem. Test the claim that the mean BMI for males is the same as that for females. Test the claim that the standard deviation for males is the same as that for females.

5. Politics and Economics Using data from the Internet for the last Presidential election to categorize the 50 states as "red" or "blue" based on who was supported for President in that state, the Democratic or Republican candidate, test the claim that the mean incomes for red states and blue states are equal.

6. Your Class Use the data collected in data project 6 of Chapter 2 regarding heart rates. Test the claim that the heart rates after exercise are more variable than the heart rates before exercise.

Answers to Applying the Concepts

Section 9–1   Highway Safety

1. The populations would be traffic on the two interstate highways.

2. Cluster samples would probably be best.

3. The sample for the most part would be independent since there would be a small probability that the same vehicles would use both highways during the sampling time period.

4. a. H_0: $\mu_1 = \mu_2$ and H_1: $\mu_1 \neq \mu_2$ where μ_1 is the mean time it takes vehicles to travel from Point A to Point B on highway number one and μ_2 would be the mean time it takes vehicles to travel from Point A to Point B on highway number two.

   b. H_0: $p_1 = p_2$ and H_1: $p_1 \neq p_2$ where p_1 is the proportion of accidents that occur on highway one during the given time period and p_2 is the proportion of accidents that occur on highway two during the given time period.

5. Answer will vary. The most common α value would be 0.05.

Section 9–2   Home Runs

1. The population of all home runs hit by major league baseball players.

2. A cluster sample was used.

3. Answers will vary. While this sample is not representative of all major league baseball players per se, it does allow us to compare the leaders in each league.

4. H_0: $\mu_1 = \mu_2$ and H_1: $\mu_1 \neq \mu_2$

5. Answers will vary. Possible answers include the 0.05 and 0.01 significance levels.

6. We will use the z test for the difference in means.

7. Our test statistic is $z = \dfrac{44.75 - 42.88}{\sqrt{\dfrac{8.8^2}{40} + \dfrac{7.8^2}{40}}} = 1.01$, and our P-value is 0.3124.

8. We fail to reject the null hypothesis.

9. There is not enough evidence to conclude that there is a difference in the number of home runs hit by National League versus American League baseball players.

10. Answers will vary. One possible answer is that since we do not have a random sample of data from each league, we cannot answer the original question asked.

11. Answers will vary. One possible answer is that we could get a random sample of data from each league from a recent season.

Section 9–3   Too Long on the Telephone

1. These samples are independent.

2. We compare the P-value of 0.06317 to the significance level to check if the null hypothesis should be rejected.

3. The P-value is 0.06317. The significance value of 0.05 gives the probability of a type I error. The probability of a type I error is set when we choose the significance level.

4. Since two critical values are shown, we know that a two-tailed test was done.

5. Since the P-value of 0.06317 is greater than the significance value of 0.05, we fail to reject the null hypothesis and find that we do not have enough evidence to conclude that there is a difference in the lengths of telephone calls made by employees in the two divisions of the company.

6. If the significance level had been 0.10, we would have rejected the null hypothesis, since the P-value would have been less than the significance level.

Section 9–4   Air Quality

1. The purpose of the study is to determine if the air quality in the United States has changed over the past 2 years.

2. These are dependent samples, since we have two readings from each of 10 metropolitan areas.

3. The hypotheses we will test are H_0: $\mu_D = 0$ and H_1: $\mu_D \neq 0$.

4. We will use the 0.05 significance level and critical values of $t = \pm 2.262$.

5. We will use the t test for dependent samples.

6. There are $10 - 1 = 9$ degrees of freedom.

7. Our test statistic is $t = \dfrac{-6.7 - 0}{11.27/\sqrt{10}} = -1.879$. We fail to reject the null hypothesis and find that there is not enough evidence to conclude that the air quality in the United States has changed over the past 2 years.

8. No, we could not use an independent means test since we have two readings from each metropolitan area.

9. Answers will vary. One possible answer is that there are other measures of air quality that we could have examined to answer the question.

Section 9–5   Vaping and Education

1. Our hypotheses are H_0: $p_1 = p_2$ and H_1: $p_1 \neq p_2$.

2. At the 0.05 significance level, our critical values are $z = \pm 1.96$.

3. We will use the z test for the difference between proportions.

4. To complete the statistical test, we would need the sample sizes.

5. Knowing the sample sizes were 1000, we can now complete the test.

6. Our test statistic is

$$z = \frac{0.323 - 0.145}{\sqrt{(0.234)(0.766)\left(\frac{1}{1000} + \frac{1}{1000}\right)}} = 9.40,$$

and our *P*-value is very close to zero. We reject the null hypothesis and find that there is enough evidence to conclude that there is a difference in the proportions of public school students and private school students who smoke.

Section 9–6   Variability and Automatic Transmissions

1. The null hypothesis is that the variances are the same: $H_0: \sigma_1^2 = \sigma_2^2$ ($H_1: \sigma_1^2 \neq \sigma_2^2$).

2. We will use an *F* test.

3. The value of the test statistic is $F = \dfrac{s_1^2}{s_2^2} = \dfrac{18{,}163.58^2}{17{,}400.57^2} =$ 1.090 and the *P*-value > 0.05. There is not a significant difference in the variability of the prices between the two countries.

4. Small sample sizes are highly impacted by outliers.

5. The degrees of freedom for the numerator and denominator are both 3.

6. Yes, two sets of data can center on the same mean but have very different standard deviations.

Hypothesis-Testing Summary 1

1. Comparison of a sample mean with a specific population mean.

Example: $H_0: \mu = 100$

a. Use the *z* test when σ is known:

$$z = \frac{\overline{X} - \mu}{\sigma/\sqrt{n}}$$

b. Use the *t* test when σ is unknown:

$$t = \frac{\overline{X} - \mu}{s/\sqrt{n}} \text{ with d.f.} = n - 1$$

2. Comparison of a sample variance or standard deviation with a specific population variance or standard deviation.

Example: $H_0: \sigma^2 = 225$

Use the chi-square test:

$$\chi^2 = \frac{(n-1)s^2}{\sigma^2} \text{ with d.f.} = n - 1$$

3. Comparison of two sample means.

Example: $H_0: \mu_1 = \mu_2$

a. Use the *z* test when the population variances are known:

$$z = \frac{(\overline{X}_1 - \overline{X}_2) - (\mu_1 - \mu_2)}{\sqrt{\dfrac{\sigma_1^2}{n_1} + \dfrac{\sigma_2^2}{n_2}}}$$

b. Use the *t* test for independent samples when the population variances are unknown and assume the sample variances are unequal:

$$t = \frac{(\overline{X}_1 - \overline{X}_2) - (\mu_1 - \mu_2)}{\sqrt{\dfrac{s_1^2}{n_1} + \dfrac{s_2^2}{n_2}}}$$

with d.f. = the smaller of $n_1 - 1$ or $n_2 - 1$.

c. Use the *t* test for means for dependent samples:

Example: $H_0: \mu_D = 0$

$$t = \frac{\overline{D} - \mu_D}{s_D/\sqrt{n}} \text{ with d.f.} = n - 1$$

where n = number of pairs.

4. Comparison of a sample proportion with a specific population proportion.

Example: $H_0: p = 0.32$

Use the *z* test:

$$z = \frac{X - \mu}{\sigma} \quad \text{or} \quad z = \frac{\hat{p} - p}{\sqrt{pq/n}}$$

5. Comparison of two sample proportions.

Example: $H_0: p_1 = p_2$

Use the *z* test:

$$z = \frac{(\hat{p}_1 - \hat{p}_2) - (p_1 - p_2)}{\sqrt{\overline{p}\,\overline{q}\left(\dfrac{1}{n_1} + \dfrac{1}{n_2}\right)}}$$

where

$$\overline{p} = \frac{X_1 + X_2}{n_1 + n_2} \qquad \hat{p}_1 = \frac{X_1}{n_1}$$

$$\overline{q} = 1 - \overline{p} \qquad \hat{p}_2 = \frac{X_2}{n_2}$$

6. Comparison of two sample variances or standard deviations.

Example: $H_0: \sigma_1^2 = \sigma_2^2$

Use the *F* test:

$$F = \frac{s_1^2}{s_2^2}$$

where

s_1^2 = larger variance   d.f.N. = $n_1 - 1$

s_2^2 = smaller variance   d.f.D. = $n_2 - 1$

Correlation and Regression

Design Pics Inc./Alamy Stock Photo

≛ STATISTICS TODAY

Can Temperature Predict Homicides?

Over the last years, researchers have been interested in the relationship between increasing temperatures and increasing homicide rates. To test this relationship, the author selected a city in the Midwest and obtained the average monthly temperatures for that city as well as the number of homicides committed each month for a recent year. The data are shown.

Month	Average High Temperature	Homicides
January	32	32
February	38	20
March	47	35
April	59	35
May	70	49
June	80	49
July	84	53
August	83	56
September	76	62
October	64	29
November	49	36
December	37	32

Source: Chicago Tribune

Using the statistical methods described in this chapter, you will be able to answer these questions:

1. Is there a linear relationship between the monthly average temperatures and the number of homicides committed during the month?
2. If so, how strong is the relationship between the average monthly temperature and the number of homicides committed?
3. If a relationship exists, can it be said that an increase in temperatures will cause an increase in the number of homicides occurring in that city?

See Statistics Today—Revisited at the end of the chapter for the answers to these questions.

OUTLINE

OBJECTIVES

After completing this chapter, you should be able to:

1. Draw a scatter plot for a set of ordered pairs.

2. Compute the correlation coefficient.

3. Test the hypothesis H_0: $\rho = 0$.

4. Compute the equation of the regression line.

5. Compute the coefficient of determination.

6. Compute the standard error of the estimate.

7. Find a prediction interval.

8. Be familiar with the concept of multiple regression.

Introduction

In Chapters 7 and 8, two areas of inferential statistics—confidence intervals and hypothesis testing—were explained. Another area of inferential statistics involves determining whether a relationship exists between two or more numerical or quantitative variables. For example, a businessperson may want to know whether the volume of sales for a given month is related to the amount of advertising the firm does that month. Educators are interested in determining whether the number of hours a student studies is related to the student's score on a particular exam. Medical researchers are interested in questions such as, Is caffeine related to heart damage? or Is there a relationship between age and blood pressure? A zoologist may want to know whether the birth weight of a certain animal is related to its life span. These are only some of the many questions that can be answered by using the techniques of correlation and regression analysis.

The purpose of this chapter then is to answer these questions statistically:

1. Are two or more variables linearly related?
2. If so, what is the strength of the relationship?
3. What type of relationship exists?
4. What kind of predictions can be made from the relationship?

10–1 Scatter Plots and Correlation

OBJECTIVE

Draw a scatter plot for a set of ordered pairs.

In simple correlation and regression studies, the researcher collects data on two numerical or quantitative variables to see whether a relationship exists between the variables. For example, if a researcher wishes to see whether there is a relationship between number of hours of study and test scores on an exam, she must select a random sample of students, determine the number of hours each studied, and obtain their grades on the exam. A table can be made for the data, as shown here.

Student	Hours of study x	Grade y (%)
A	6	82
B	2	63
C	1	57
D	5	88
E	2	68
F	3	75

The two variables for this study are called the **independent variable** and the **dependent variable.** The independent variable is the variable in regression that can be controlled or manipulated. In this case, the number of hours of study is the independent variable and is designated as the x variable. The dependent variable is the variable in regression that cannot be controlled or manipulated. The grade the student received on the exam is the dependent variable, designated as the y variable. The reason for this distinction between the variables is that you assume that the grade the student earns *depends* on the number of hours the student studied. Also, you assume that, to some extent, the student can regulate or *control* the number of hours spent studying for an exam. The independent variable is also known as the *explanatory variable,* and the dependent variable is also called the *response variable.*

The determination of the x and y variables is not always clear-cut and is sometimes an arbitrary decision. For example, if a researcher studies the effects of age on a person's blood pressure, the researcher can generally assume that age affects blood pressure. Hence, the variable *age* can be called the *independent variable,* and the variable *blood pressure* can be called the *dependent variable.* On the other hand, if a researcher is studying the attitudes of husbands on a certain issue and the attitudes of their wives on the same issue, it is difficult to say which variable is the independent variable and which is the dependent variable. In this study, the researcher can arbitrarily designate the variables as independent and dependent.

FIGURE 10–1

Types of Relationships

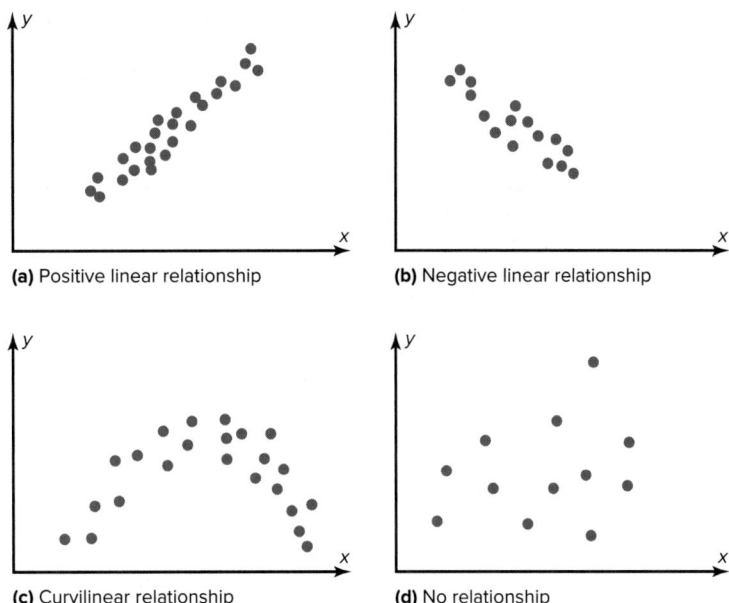

(a) Positive linear relationship

(b) Negative linear relationship

(c) Curvilinear relationship

(d) No relationship

The independent and dependent variables can be plotted on a graph called a *scatter plot*. The independent variable x is plotted on the horizontal axis, and the dependent variable y is plotted on the vertical axis.

> A **scatter plot** is a graph of the ordered pairs (x, y) of numbers consisting of the independent variable x and the dependent variable y.

The scatter plot is a visual way to describe the nature of the relationship between the independent and dependent variables. The scales of the variables can be different, and the coordinates of the axes are determined by the smallest and largest data values of the variables.

Researchers look for various types of patterns in scatter plots. For example, in Figure 10–1(a), the pattern in the points of the scatter plot shows a **positive linear relationship.** Here, as the values of the independent variable (x variable) increase, the values of the dependent variable (y variable) increase. Also, the points form somewhat of a straight line going in an upward direction from left to right.

The pattern of the points of the scatter plot shown in Figure 10–1(b) shows a **negative linear relationship.** In this case, as the values of the independent variable increase, the values of the dependent variable decrease. Also, the points show a somewhat straight line going in a downward direction from left to right.

The pattern of the points of the scatter plot shown in Figure 10–1(c) shows some type of a nonlinear relationship or a curvilinear relationship.

Finally, the scatter plot shown in Figure 10–1(d) shows basically no relationship between the independent variable and the dependent variable since no pattern (line or curve) can be seen.

The procedure table for drawing a scatter plot is given next.

Procedure Table

Drawing a Scatter Plot

Step 1   Draw and label the x and y axes.

Step 2   Plot each point on the graph.

Step 3   Determine the type of relationship (if any) that exists for the variables.

The procedure for drawing a scatter plot is shown in Examples 10–1 through 10–3.

EXAMPLE 10–1 Heights of Buildings

The data show the heights in feet and the number of stories of a random selection of six buildings in Chicago, Illinois. Construct a scatter plot for the data.

Height	1136	887	756	668	595	501
Stories	83	76	50	49	54	39

Source: The World Almanac and Book of Facts

SOLUTION

Step 1 Draw and label the *x* and *y* axes.

Step 2 Plot each point on the graph, as shown in Figure 10–2.

FIGURE 10–2 Scatter Plot for Example 10–2

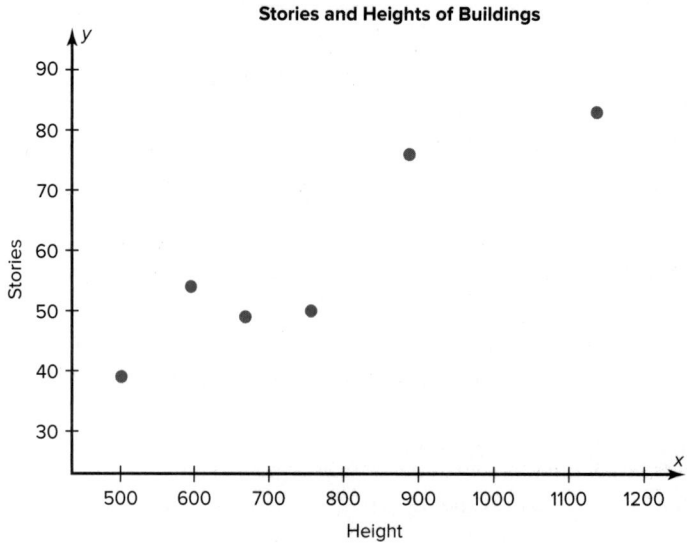

Step 3 Determine the type of relationship (if any) that exists.

In this example, it looks like there is a positive relationship between the heights of the buildings and the number of stories in the building.

EXAMPLE 10–2 Absences and Final Grades

Construct a scatter plot for the data obtained in a study on the number of absences and the final grades of seven randomly selected students from a statistics class. The data are shown here.

Student	Number of absences *x*	Final grade *y* (%)
A	6	82
B	2	86
C	15	43
D	9	74
E	12	58
F	5	90
G	8	78

SOLUTION

Step 1   Draw and label the *x* and *y* axes.

Step 2   Plot each point on the graph, as shown in Figure 10–3.

FIGURE 10–3   Scatter Plot for Example 10–2

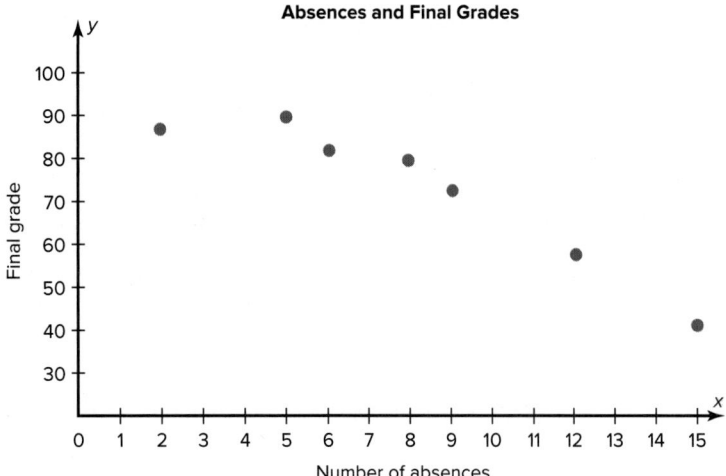

Step 3   Determine the type of relationship (if any) that exists.

In this example, it looks as if a negative linear relationship exists between the number of student absences and the final grade of the students.

EXAMPLE 10–3   Wind Speeds

A meteorologist wishes to see if there is a relationship between the average wind speeds in miles per hour and the maximum wind speeds in miles per hour for seven randomly selected areas. Construct a scatter plot for the data.

Area	Average wind speeds	Maximum wind speeds
A	8.2	83
B	6.2	72
C	11.5	76
D	9.6	68
E	10	74
F	7.4	70
G	6.1	72

SOLUTION

Step 1   Draw and label the *x* and *y* axes.

Step 2   Plot each point on the graph as shown in Figure 10–4.

FIGURE 10–4 Scatter Plot for Example 10–3

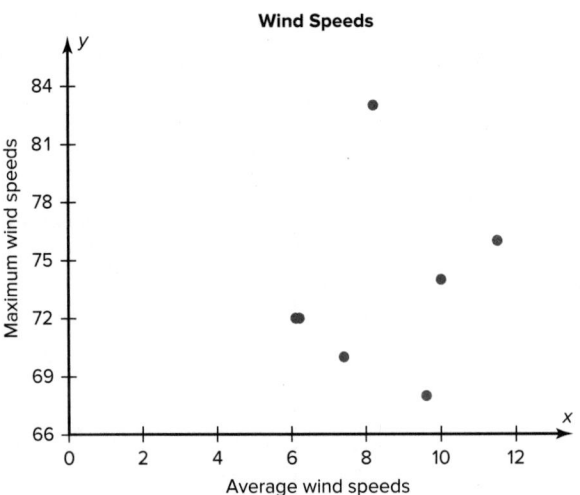

Step 3 Determine the type of relationship (if any) that exists.

In this case, there is no strong positive or negative linear relationship between the average wind speeds and the maximum wind speeds for the seven areas.

Correlation

Correlation Coefficient Statisticians use a measure called the *correlation coefficient* to determine the strength of the linear relationship between two variables. There are several types of correlation coefficients.

> The **population correlation coefficient** denoted by the Greek letter ρ is the correlation computed by using all possible pairs of data values (x, y) taken from a population.

> The linear **correlation coefficient** computed from the sample data measures the strength and direction of a linear relationship between two quantitative variables. The symbol for the sample correlation coefficient is r.

The linear correlation coefficient explained in this section is called the **Pearson product moment correlation coefficient (PPMC),** named after statistician Karl Pearson, who pioneered the research in this area.

The *range of the linear correlation coefficient* is from -1 to $+1$. If there is a *strong positive linear relationship* between the variables, the value of r will be close to $+1$. If there is a *strong negative linear relationship* between the variables, the value of r will be close to -1. When there is no linear relationship between the variables or only a weak relationship, the value of r will be close to 0. See Figure 10–5. When the value of r is 0 or close to zero, it implies only that there is no linear relationship between the variables. The data may be related in some other nonlinear way.

FIGURE 10–5

Range of Values for the Correlation Coefficient

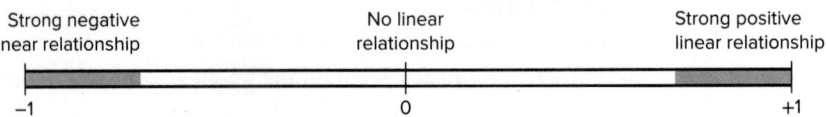

FIGURE 10–6

Relationship Between the
Correlation Coefficient and
the Scatter Plot

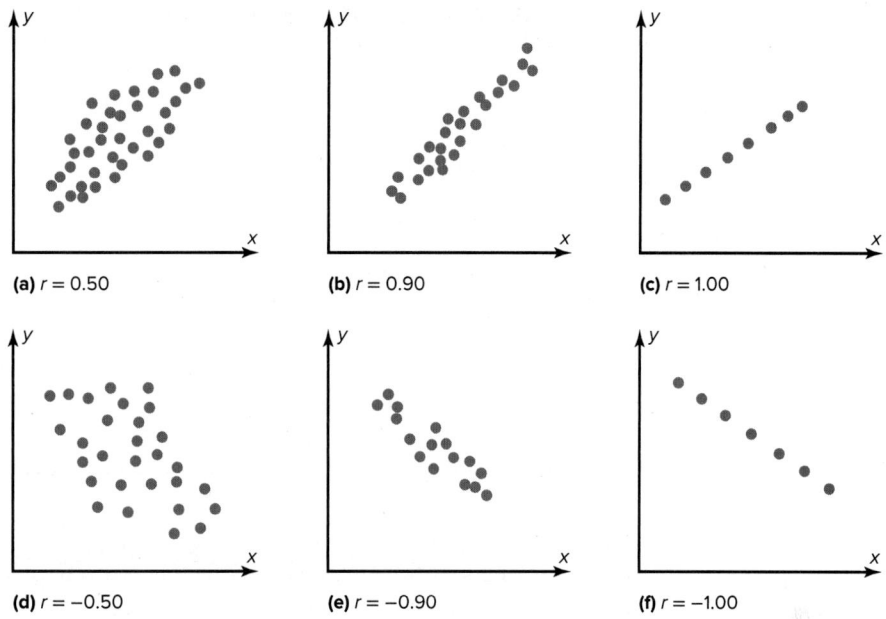

(a) $r = 0.50$ **(b)** $r = 0.90$ **(c)** $r = 1.00$

(d) $r = -0.50$ **(e)** $r = -0.90$ **(f)** $r = -1.00$

Properties of the Linear Correlation Coefficient

1. The correlation coefficient is a unitless measure.
2. The value of r will always be between -1 and $+1$ inclusively. That is, $-1 \leq r \leq 1$.
3. If the values of x and y are interchanged, the value of r will be unchanged.
4. If the values of x and/or y are converted to a different scale, the value of r will be unchanged.
5. The value of r is sensitive to outliers and can change dramatically if they are present in the data.

The graphs in Figure 10–6 show the relationship between the correlation coefficients and their corresponding scatter plots. Notice that as the value of the correlation coefficient increases from 0 to $+1$ (parts a, b, and c), data values become closer to a straight line and to an increasingly strong relationship. As the value of the correlation coefficient decreases from 0 to -1 (parts d, e, and f), the data values also become closer to a straight line. Again this suggests a stronger relationship.

Assumptions for the Correlation Coefficient

1. The sample is a random sample.
2. The data pairs fall approximately on a straight line and are measured at the interval or ratio level.
3. The variables have a bivariate normal distribution. (This means that given any specific value of x, the y values are normally distributed; and given any specific value of y, the x values are normally distributed.)

In this book, the assumptions will be assumed to be met in the exercises; however, when encountering statistics in other situations, you must check to see that these assumptions have been met before proceeding.

There are several ways to compute the value of the correlation coefficient. One method is to use the formula shown here.

Formula for the Linear Correlation Coefficient r

$$r = \frac{n(\Sigma xy) - (\Sigma x)(\Sigma y)}{\sqrt{[n(\Sigma x^2) - (\Sigma x)^2][n(\Sigma y^2) - (\Sigma y)^2]}}$$

where n is the number of data pairs.

Rounding Rule for the Correlation Coefficient Round the value of r to three decimal places.

The formula looks somewhat complicated, but using a table to compute the values, as shown in Example 10–4, makes it somewhat easier to determine the value of r.

There are no units associated with r, and the value of r will remain unchanged if the x and y values are switched.

The procedure for finding the value of the linear correlation coefficient is given next.

Procedure Table

Finding the Value of the Linear Correlation Coefficient

Step 1 Make a table as shown.

x	y	xy	x^2	y^2

Step 2 Place the values of x in the x column and the values of y in the y column. Multiply each x value by the corresponding y value, and place the products in the xy column.

Square each x value and place the squares in the x^2 column.

Square each y value and place the squares in the y^2 column.

Find the sum of each column.

Step 3 Substitute in the formula and find the value for r.

$$r = \frac{n(\Sigma xy) - (\Sigma x)(\Sigma y)}{\sqrt{[n(\Sigma x^2) - (\Sigma x)^2][n(\Sigma y^2) - (\Sigma y)^2]}}$$

where n is the number of data pairs.

EXAMPLE 10–4 Heights of Buildings

Compute the linear correlation coefficient for the data in Example 10–1.

SOLUTION

Step 1 Make a table as shown here.

Heights, x	Stories, y	xy	x^2	y^2
1136	83			
887	76			
756	50			
668	49			
595	54			
501	39			

Step 2 Find the values of xy, x^2, and y^2, and place these values in the corresponding columns of the table.

Heights, x	Stories, y	xy	x^2	y^2
1136	83	94288	1290496	6889
887	76	67412	786769	5776
756	50	37800	571536	2500
668	49	32732	446224	2401
595	54	32130	354025	2916
501	39	19539	251001	1521
$\Sigma x = 4543$	$\Sigma y = 351$	$\Sigma xy = 283901$	$\Sigma x^2 = 3700051$	$\Sigma y^2 = 22003$

Step 3   Substitute in the formula and solve for r.

$$r = \frac{n(\Sigma xy) - (\Sigma x)(\Sigma y)}{\sqrt{[n(\Sigma x^2) - (\Sigma x)^2][n(\Sigma y^2) - (\Sigma y)^2]}}$$

$$r = \frac{6(283901) - (4543)(351)}{\sqrt{[6(3700051) - (4543)^2][6(22003) - (351)^2]}}$$

$$= \frac{1703406 - 1594593}{\sqrt{(1561457)(8817)}} = \frac{108813}{117334.4211} = 0.927$$

The linear correlation coefficient suggests a positive linear relationship between the heights of buildings and the number of stories in the building. That is, the taller the building is, the more stories the building has.

EXAMPLE 10–5   Absences and Final Grades

Compute the value of the linear correlation coefficient for the data obtained in the study of the number of absences and the final grade of the seven students in the statistics class given in Example 10–2.

SOLUTION

Step 1   Make a table.

Step 2   Find the values of xy, x^2, and y^2; place these values in the corresponding columns of the table.

Student	Number of absences, x	Final grade, y (%)	xy	x^2	y^2
A	6	82	492	36	6,724
B	2	86	172	4	7,396
C	15	43	645	225	1,849
D	9	74	666	81	5,476
E	12	58	696	144	3,364
F	5	90	450	25	8,100
G	8	78	624	64	6,084
	$\Sigma x = 57$	$\Sigma y = 511$	$\Sigma xy = 3745$	$\Sigma x^2 = 579$	$\Sigma y^2 = 38,993$

Step 3   Substitute in the formula and solve for r.

$$r = \frac{n(\Sigma xy) - (\Sigma x)(\Sigma y)}{\sqrt{[n(\Sigma x^2) - (\Sigma x)^2][n(\Sigma y^2) - (\Sigma y)^2]}}$$

$$= \frac{(7)(3745) - (57)(511)}{\sqrt{[(7)(579) - (57)^2][(7)(38,993) - (511)^2]}} = -0.944$$

The value of r suggests a strong negative linear relationship between a student's final grade and the number of absences a student has. That is, the more absences a student has, the lower their grade.

EXAMPLE 10–6   Wind Speeds

Compute the value of the correlation coefficient for the data given in Example 10–3 for the average wind speeds and the maximum wind speeds.

SOLUTION

Step 1   Make a table.

Step 2   Find the values of xy, x^2, and y^2; place these values in the corresponding columns of the tables.

Area	Average wind speeds, x	Maximum wind speeds, y	xy	x^2	y^2
A	8.2	83	680.6	67.24	6889
B	6.2	72	446.4	38.44	5184
C	11.5	76	874	132.25	5776
D	9.6	68	652.8	92.16	4624
E	10	74	740	100	5476
F	7.4	70	518	54.76	4900
G	6.1	72	439.2	37.21	5184
	$\Sigma x = 59$	$\Sigma y = 515$	$\Sigma xy = 4351$	$\Sigma x^2 = 522.06$	$\Sigma y^2 = 38033$

Step 3   Substitute in the formula and solve for r.

$$r = \frac{n(\Sigma xy) - (\Sigma x)(\Sigma y)}{\sqrt{[n(\Sigma x^2) - (\Sigma x)^2][n(\Sigma y^2) - (\Sigma y)^2]}}$$

$$= \frac{7(4351) - (59)(515)}{\sqrt{[7(522.06) - (59)^2][7(38033) - (515)^2]}}$$

$$= \frac{72}{\sqrt{(173.42)(1006)}}$$

$$= \frac{72}{417.68} = 0.172$$

The value of r indicates a weak positive linear relationship between average wind speeds and maximum wind speeds.

In Example 10–4, the value of r was high (close to 1.00); in Example 10–6, the value of r was much lower (close to 0). This question then arises, When is the value of r due to chance, and when does it suggest a significant linear relationship between the variables? This question will be answered next.

OBJECTIVE ❸

Test the hypothesis $H_0: \rho = 0$.

The Significance of the Correlation Coefficient   As stated before, the range of the correlation coefficient is between -1 and $+1$. When the value of r is near $+1$ or -1, there is a strong linear relationship. When the value of r is near 0, the linear relationship is weak or nonexistent. Since the value of r is computed from data obtained from samples, there are two possibilities when r is not equal to zero: either the value of r is high enough to conclude that there is a significant linear relationship between the variables, or the value of r is due to chance.

To make this decision, you use a hypothesis-testing procedure. The traditional method is similar to the one used in previous chapters.

Step 1 State the hypotheses.

Step 2 Find the critical values.

Step 3 Compute the test statistic.

Step 4 Make the decision.

Step 5 Summarize the results.

The sample correlation coefficient can then be used as an estimator of ρ if the following assumptions are valid.

Assumptions for Testing the Significance of the Linear Correlation Coefficient

1. The data are quantitative and are obtained from a simple random sample.
2. The scatter plot shows that the data are approximately linearly related.
3. There are no outliers in the data.
4. The variables x and y must come from normally distributed populations.

In this book, the assumptions will be assumed to be met in the exercises; however, when encountering statistics in other situations, you must check to see that these assumptions have been met before proceeding.

In hypothesis testing, one of these is true:

H_0: $\rho = 0$ This null hypothesis means that there is no correlation between the x and y variables in the population.

H_1: $\rho \neq 0$ This alternative hypothesis means that there is a significant correlation between the variables in the population.

When the null hypothesis is rejected at a specific level, it means that there is a significant difference between the value of r and 0. When the null hypothesis is not rejected, it means that the value of r is not significantly different from 0 (zero) and is probably due to chance.

Several methods can be used to test the significance of the correlation coefficient. Three methods will be shown in this section. The first uses the t test.

Formula for the t Test for the Correlation Coefficient

$$t = r\sqrt{\frac{n-2}{1-r^2}}$$

with degrees of freedom equal to $n - 2$, where n is the number of ordered pairs (x, y).

You do not have to identify the claim here, since the question will always be whether there is a significant linear relationship between the variables.

The two-tailed critical values are used. These values are found in Table A–5 in Appendix A. Also, when you are testing the significance of a correlation coefficient, both variables x and y must come from normally distributed populations.

EXAMPLE 10–7

Test the significance of the correlation coefficient found in Example 10–4. Use $\alpha = 0.05$ and $r = 0.927$.

SOLUTION

Step 1 State the hypotheses.

$$H_0\text{: } \rho = 0 \qquad \text{and} \qquad H_1\text{: } \rho \neq 0$$

Interesting Fact

Scientists think that a person is never more than 3 feet away from a spider at any given time!

Historical Notes

A mathematician named Karl Pearson (1857–1936) became interested in Francis Galton's work and saw that his correlation and regression theory could be applied to other areas besides heredity. Pearson developed the correlation coefficient that bears his name.

Step 2   Find the critical values. Since $\alpha = 0.05$ and there are $6 - 2 = 4$ degrees of freedom, the critical values obtained from Table A–5 are ± 2.776, as shown in Figure 10–7.

FIGURE 10–7
Critical Values for
Example 10–7

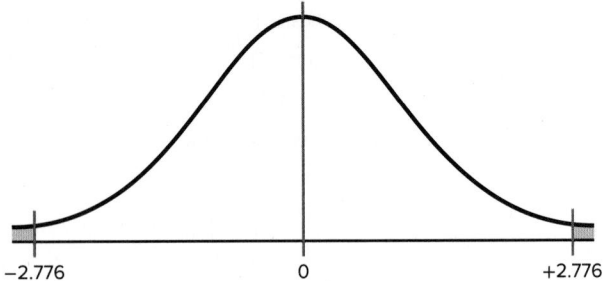

Step 3   Compute the test statistic.

$$t = r\sqrt{\frac{n-2}{1-r^2}} = 0.927\sqrt{\frac{6-2}{1-(0.927)^2}} = 4.943$$

Step 4   Make the decision. Reject the null hypothesis, since the test statistic falls in the critical region, as shown in Figure 10–8.

FIGURE 10–8
Critical Values and Test
Statistic for Example 10–7

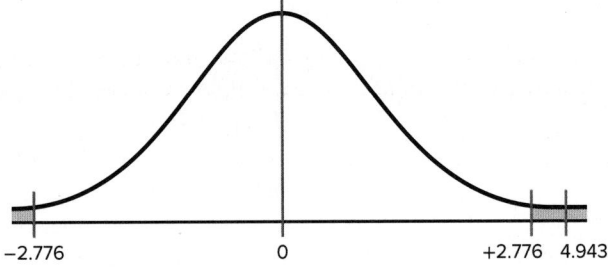

Step 5   Summarize the results. There is a significant relationship between the heights of the buildings and the number of stories in the buildings.

The second method that can be used to test the significance of r is the P-value method. The method is the same as that shown in Chapters 8 and 9. It uses the following steps.

Step 1   State the hypotheses.

Step 2   Find the test statistic. (In this case, use the t test.)

Step 3   Find the P-value. (In this case, use Table A–5.)

Step 4   Make the decision.

Step 5   Summarize the results.

Consider an example where $t = 4.059$, d.f. $= 4$, and $\alpha = 0.05$. Using Table A–5 with d.f. $= 4$ and the row Two tails, the test statistic 4.059 falls between 3.747 and 4.604; hence, $0.01 < P\text{-value} < 0.02$. (The P-value obtained from a calculator is 0.015.) That is, the P-value falls between 0.01 and 0.02. The decision, then, is to reject the null hypothesis since $P\text{-value} < 0.05$.

The third method of testing the significance of r is to use Table A–8 in Appendix A. This table shows the values of the correlation coefficient that are significant for a specific α level and a specific number of degrees of freedom. For example, for 7 degrees of freedom and $\alpha = 0.05$, the table gives a critical value of 0.666. Any value of r greater than $+0.666$ or less than -0.666 will be significant, and the null hypothesis will be rejected. See Figure 10–9. When Table A–8 is used, you need not compute the t test statistic. Table A–8 is for two-tailed tests only.

FIGURE 10–9

Finding the Critical Value from Table A–8

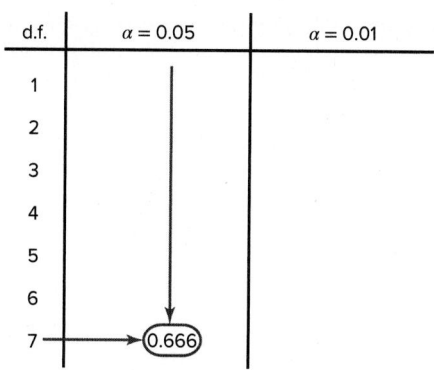

EXAMPLE 10–8

Using Table A–8, test the significance at $\alpha = 0.01$ of the correlation coefficient $r = 0.172$ obtained in Example 10–6.

SOLUTION

$$H_0: \rho = 0 \quad \text{and} \quad \rho \neq 0$$

The critical values from Table A–8 at $\alpha = 0.05$ with 5 degrees of freedom are ± 0.754. Since $0.172 < 0.754$, the decision is do not reject the null hypothesis. See Figure 10–10. Hence, there is not enough evidence to say that there is a significant relationship between the average wind speeds and the maximum wind speeds. (*Note:* The *P*-value is 0.7117.)

FIGURE 10–10

Rejection and Nonrejection Regions and the *r* Value for Example 10–8

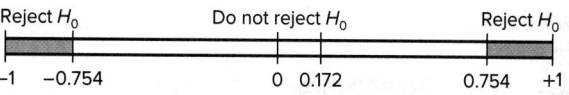

Generally, significance tests for correlation coefficients are two-tailed; however, they can be one-tailed. For example, if a researcher hypothesized a positive linear relationship between two variables, the hypotheses would be

$$H_0: \rho = 0$$
$$H_1: \rho > 0$$

If the researcher hypothesized a negative linear relationship between two variables, the hypotheses would be

$$H_0: \rho = 0$$
$$H_1: \rho < 0$$

In these cases, the *t* tests and the *P*-value tests would be one-tailed. Also, tables such as Table A–8 are available for one-tailed tests. In this book, the examples and exercises will involve two-tailed tests.

Correlation and Causation   Researchers must understand the nature of the linear relationship between the independent variable *x* and the dependent variable *y*. When a hypothesis test indicates that a significant linear relationship exists between the variables, researchers must consider the possibilities outlined next.

When two variables are highly correlated, item 3 in the box states that there exists a possibility that the correlation is due to a third variable. If this is the case and the third

---

Possible Relationships Between Variables

When the null hypothesis has been rejected for a specific α value, any of the following five possibilities can exist.

1. *There is a direct cause-and-effect relationship between the variables.* That is, x causes y. For example, water causes plants to grow, poison causes death, and heat causes ice to melt.

2. *There is a reverse cause-and-effect relationship between the variables.* That is, y causes x. For example, suppose a researcher believes excessive coffee consumption causes nervousness, but the researcher fails to consider that the reverse situation may occur. That is, it may be that an extremely nervous person craves coffee to calm the person's nerves.

3. *The relationship between the variables may be caused by a third variable.* For example, if a statistician correlated the number of deaths due to drowning and the number of cans of soft drink consumed daily during the summer, the statistician would probably find a significant relationship. However, the soft drink is not necessarily responsible for the deaths, since both variables may be related to heat and humidity.

4. *There may be a complexity of interrelationships among many variables.* For example, a researcher may find a significant relationship between students' high school grades and college grades. But there probably are many other variables involved, such as IQ, hours of study, influence of parents, motivation, age, and instructors.

5. *The relationship may be coincidental.* For example, a researcher may be able to find a significant relationship between the increase in the number of people who are exercising and the increase in the number of people who are committing crimes. But common sense dictates that any relationship between these two values must be due to coincidence.

---

variable is unknown to the researcher or not accounted for in the study, it is called a **lurking variable.** An attempt should be made by the researcher to identify such variables and to use methods to control their influence.

It is important to restate the fact that even if the correlation between two variables is high, it does not necessarily mean causation. There are other possibilities, such as lurking variables or just a coincidental relationship.

Also, you should be cautious when the data for one or both of the variables involve averages rather than individual data. It is not wrong to use averages, but the results cannot be generalized to individuals since averaging tends to smooth out the variability among individual data values. The result could be a higher correlation than actually exists.

Thus, when the null hypothesis is rejected, the researcher must consider all possibilities and select the appropriate one as determined by the study. Remember, correlation does not necessarily imply causation.

≡ Applying the Concepts 10–1

Stopping Distances

In a study on speed control, it was found that the main reasons for regulations were to make traffic flow more efficient and to minimize the risk of danger. An area that was focused on in the study was the distance required to completely stop a vehicle at various speeds. Use the following table to answer the questions.

MPH	Braking distance (feet)
20	20
30	45
40	81
50	133
60	205
80	411

Assume MPH is going to be used to predict stopping distance.

1. Which of the two variables is the independent variable?
2. Which is the dependent variable?
3. What type of variable is the independent variable?
4. What type of variable is the dependent variable?
5. Construct a scatter plot for the data.
6. Is there a linear relationship between the two variables?
7. Redraw the scatter plot, and change the distances between the independent-variable numbers. Does the relationship look different?
8. Is the relationship positive or negative?
9. Can braking distance be accurately predicted from MPH?
10. List some other variables that affect braking distance.
11. Compute the value of r.
12. Is r significant at $\alpha = 0.05$?

See pages 611–612 for the answers.

Exercises 10–1

1. What is meant by the statement that two variables are related? Two variables are related when a discernible pattern exists between them.

2. How is a linear relationship between two variables measured in statistics? Explain.

3. What is the symbol for the sample correlation coefficient? The population correlation coefficient? r, ρ (rho)

4. What is the range of values for the correlation coefficient? The range of r is from -1 to $+1$.

5. What is meant when the relationship between the two variables is called positive? Negative?

6. Give examples of two variables that are positively correlated and two that are negatively correlated. Answers will vary.

7. What is the diagram of the independent and dependent variables called? Why is drawing this diagram important? The diagram is called a scatter plot. It shows the nature of the relationship.

8. What is the name of the correlation coefficient used in this section? Pearson product moment correlation coefficient

9. What statistical test is used to test the significance of the correlation coefficient? *t* test

10. When two variables are correlated, can the researcher be sure that one variable causes the other? Why or why not? No, there are many other possibilities, such as chance or relationship to a third variable.

For Exercises 11 through 27, perform the following steps.

a. Draw the scatter plot for the variables.
b. Compute the value of the correlation coefficient.
c. State the hypotheses.
d. Test the significance of the correlation coefficient at $\alpha = 0.05$, using Table A–8 or the *P*-value method.
e. Give a brief explanation of the type of relationship. Assume all assumptions have been met.

11. **Accidents and Drivers' Ages** For a random selection of drivers, their ages and the number of automobile accidents that they had over a 3-year period are shown.

Age	21	22	40	35	41	50	28	25
Accidents	5	6	1	2	3	0	4	4

(The information in this exercise will be used for Exercise 11 in Section 10–2.)

12. **Final Exam Grades** The data show the final exam grades for 16 randomly selected students taking both College Algebra and Statistics. Use the College Algebra scores for the independent variable and Statistics scores for the dependent variable.

Student	1	2	3	4	5	6	7	8
College Algebra	88	97	73	92	81	79	71	90
Statistics	86	95	78	97	87	81	75	85

Student	9	10	11	12	13	14	15	16
College Algebra	86	58	87	68	74	86	62	95
Statistics	90	70	85	77	76	81	65	89

(The information in this exercise will be used for Exercise 12 in Section 10–2.)

13. **Commercial Movie Releases** The yearly data have been published showing the number of releases for each of the commercial movie studios and the gross receipts for those studios thus far. Based on these data, can it be concluded that there is a linear relationship between the number of releases and the gross receipts?

No. of releases, x	361	270	306	22	35	10	8	12	21
Gross receipts, y (million $)	3844	1962	1371	1064	334	241	188	154	125

(The information in this exercise will be used for Exercises 13 and 36 in Section 10–2 and Exercises 15 and 19 in Section 10–3.)

Source: www.showbizdata.com

14. **Forest Fires and Acres Burned** An environmentalist wants to determine the relationships between the numbers (in thousands) of forest fires over the year and the number (in hundred thousands) of acres burned. The data for 8 recent years are shown. Describe the relationship.

Number of fires, x	72	69	58	47	84	62	57	45
Number of acres burned, y	62	42	19	26	51	15	30	15

Source: National Interagency Fire Center.

(The information in this exercise will be used for Exercise 14 in Section 10–2 and Exercises 16 and 20 in Section 10–3.)

15. **Alumni Contributions** The director of an alumni association for a small college wants to determine whether there is any type of relationship between the amount of an alumnus's contribution (in dollars) and the number of years the alumnus has been out of school. The data follow.

Years, x	1	5	3	10	7	6
Contribution, y	500	100	300	50	75	80

(The information is used for Exercises 15, 36, and 37 in Section 10–2 and Exercises 17 and 21 in Section 10–3.)

16. **State Debt and Per Capita Tax** An economics student wishes to see if there is a relationship between the amount of state debt per capita and the amount of tax per capita at the state level. Based on the following data, can the person conclude that per capita state debt and per capita state taxes are related? Both amounts are in dollars and represent five randomly selected states.

Per capita debt, x	8,567	9,606	10,227	10,584	7,782
Per capita tax, y	4,713	5,201	4,161	6,665	3,522

Source: World Almanac.

(The information in this exercise will be used for Exercises 16 and 37 in Section 10–2 and Exercises 18 and 22 in Section 10–3.)

17. **Blood Pressure and Sodium Content** The data show the blood levels of sodium in mEq/L and the systolic blood pressure of 7 randomly selected subjects.

Sodium	125	136	141	144	148	152	155
Blood pressure	118	122	128	132	141	136	146

(The information in this exercise will be used for Exercise 17 in Section 10–2.)

18. **Hours Watching Videos and GPA** The data show a random selection of students' GPAs and the number of hours per week that they spend watching videos.

Student	1	2	3	4	5	6	7	8	9	10	11	12
Hours	15	18	23	30	9	12	10	21	12	5	7	14
GPA	2.6	3	2.3	2.1	3.5	3.1	3.27	2.9	3.3	3.75	3.8	2.86

(The information in this exercise will be used for Exercise 18 in Section 10–2.)

19. **Imports and Exports** A random sample of countries in the world shows the number of U.S. exports and the U.S. imports to each country for a recent year. The data are in hundreds of millions of dollars. Assume the independent variable is exports.

Country	1	2	3	4	5	6	7	8	9	10	11
Exports	55	16	10	26	13	22	5	72	12	21	64
Imports	54	45	42	17	22	9	17	50	6	22	33

Source: The World Almanac and Book of Facts

(The information in this exercise will be used for Exercise 19 in Section 10–2.)

20. **Water and Carbohydrates** Here are the number of grams of water and the number of grams of carbohydrates for a random selection of raw foods (100 g each). Is there a linear relationship between the variables?

Water	83.93	80.76	87.66	85.20	72.85	84.61	83.81
Carbs	15.25	16.55	11.10	13.01	24.27	14.13	15.11

Source: Time Almanac.

(The information in this exercise will be used for Exercises 20 and 38 in Section 10–2.)

21. **Faculty and Students** The number of faculty and the number of students are shown for a random selection of small colleges. Is there a significant relationship between the two variables? Switch x and y and repeat the process. Which do you think is really the independent variable?

Faculty	99	110	113	116	138	174	220
Students	1353	1290	1091	1213	1384	1283	2075

Source: World Almanac.

(The information in this exercise will be used for Exercises 21 and 36 in Section 10–2.)

22. **Automobiles and Light Commercial Vehicles** The data show the number of automobiles and the number of light commercial vehicles produced for a random sample of top motor-vehicle-producing countries. The data are in millions of vehicles produced.

Automobiles	7.8	4.2	1.2	0.2	1.6
Light commercial vehicles	1.3	3.8	6.1	0.2	1.4

Source: The World Almanac and Book of Facts

(The information in this exercise will be used for Exercise 22 in Section 10–2.)

23. **Nuclear Reactors** Is there a significant relationship between the number of nuclear reactors a country has and the number of megawatts (in thousands) that a country has?

Numbers	19	36	58	22	25	10	15
Megawatts	13	31	63	6	23	9	13

Source: Nuclear Power Reactors in the World

(The information in this exercise will be used for Exercise 23 in Section 10–2.)

24. **American Concert Tours** Is there a significant relationship between the number of cities visited and the number of shows a random sample of musical groups completed?

Cities visited	41	30	38	43	41	21	42	43	30	56
Shows	62	32	42	76	54	31	48	60	47	80

Source: World Almanac and Book of Facts

(The information in this exercise will be used for Exercise 24 in Section 10–2.)

25. **Air Pollution and Memory** A researcher is studying the relationship between air pollution and memory. A random sample of people with similar demographics from different cities were asked to take a memory recall test and the corresponding day's AQI was recorded. Higher AQI score means a higher air pollution, and memory scores measure the number of items a person remembered during the memory test.

Person	1	2	3	4	5	6	7	8	9	10
AQI	24	51	37	20	54	61	49	27	21	35
Memory	20	12	12	19	11	9	10	16	18	14

(The information in this exercise will be used in Exercise 25 in Section 10–2.)

26. **Shipping** The data show the number of ships (in hundreds) a country has and the number of tons (in millions) of cargo that the country ships.

Number of ships	36	11	25	78	40	16	53
Cargo	127	33	8	18	76	16	32

Source: The World Almanac and Books of Facts

(The information in this exercise will be used for Exercise 26 in Section 10–2.)

27. **Class Size and Grades** School administrators wondered whether class size and grade achievement (in percent) were related. A random sample of classes revealed the following data. Are the variables linearly related?

No. of students	15	10	8	20	18	6
Avg. grade (%)	85	90	82	80	84	92

(The information in this exercise will be used for Exercise 28 of this section and Exercise 27 in Section 10–2.)

Extending the Concepts

28. One of the formulas for computing r is
$$r = \frac{\Sigma(x - \bar{x})(y - \bar{y})}{(n - 1)(s_x)(s_y)}$$
Using the data in Exercise 27, compute r with this formula. Compare the results.

29. Compute r for the data set shown. Explain the reason for the value of r. Interchange the values of x and y. Compute r for this data set. Explain the results of the comparison.

x	1	2	3	4	5
y	4	7	10	13	16

30. Compute r for the following data and test the hypothesis H_0: $\rho = 0$. Draw the scatter plot; then explain the results.

x	−3	−2	−1	0	1	2	3
y	9	4	1	0	1	4	9

31. **NHL Wins and Points** The data show the number of wins and the total number of points scored by select teams in the Eastern and Western Conferences of NHL Hockey.

Eastern Conference

Wins	42	40	42	33	50	39	28
Total points	103	95	94	79	111	88	70

Western Conference

Wins	49	41	34	47	39	30	46
Total points	106	94	79	103	88	70	105

Compare the correlation coefficients of the two data sets.

10–2 Regression

OBJECTIVE **4**

Compute the equation of the regression line.

In studying relationships between two variables, collect the data and then construct a scatter plot. The purpose of the scatter plot, as indicated previously, is to determine the nature of the relationship between the variables. The possibilities include a positive linear relationship, a negative linear relationship, a curvilinear relationship, or no discernible relationship. After the scatter plot is drawn and a linear relationship is determined, the next steps are to compute the value of the correlation coefficient and to test the significance of the relationship. If the value of the correlation coefficient is significant, the next step is to determine the equation of the **regression line,** which is the data's line of best fit. (*Note:* Determining the regression line when r is not significant and then making predictions using the regression line are meaningless.) The purpose of the regression line is to enable the researcher to see the trend and make predictions on the basis of the data.

Line of Best Fit

Historical Notes

Francis Galton drew the line of best fit visually. An assistant of Karl Pearson's named G. Yule devised the mathematical solution using the least-squares method, employing a mathematical technique developed by Adrien-Marie Legendre about 100 years earlier.

Figure 10–11 shows a scatter plot for the data of two variables. It shows that several lines can be drawn on the graph near the points. Given a scatter plot, you must be able to draw the *line of best fit. Best fit* means that the sum of the squares of the vertical distances from each point to the line is at a minimum.

The difference between the actual value y and the predicted value y' (that is, the vertical distance) is called a **residual** or a predicted error. Residuals are used to determine the line that best describes the relationship between the two variables.

The method used for making the residuals as small as possible is called the *method of least squares.* As a result of this method, the regression line is also called the *least squares regression line.*

The reason you need a line of best fit is that the values of y will be predicted from the values of x; hence, the closer the points are to the line, the better the fit and the prediction will be. See Figure 10–12. When r is positive, the line slopes upward and to the right. When r is negative, the line slopes downward from left to right.

Determination of the Regression Line Equation

In algebra, the equation of a line is usually given as $y = mx + b$, where m is the slope of the line and b is the y intercept. (Students who need an algebraic review of the properties

FIGURE 10–11

Scatter Plot with Three Lines Fit to the Data

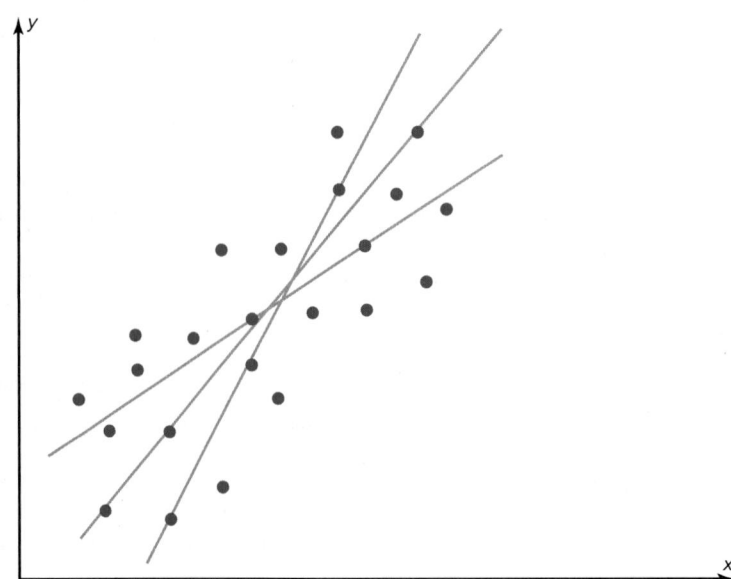

FIGURE 10–12 Line of Best Fit for a Set of Data Points

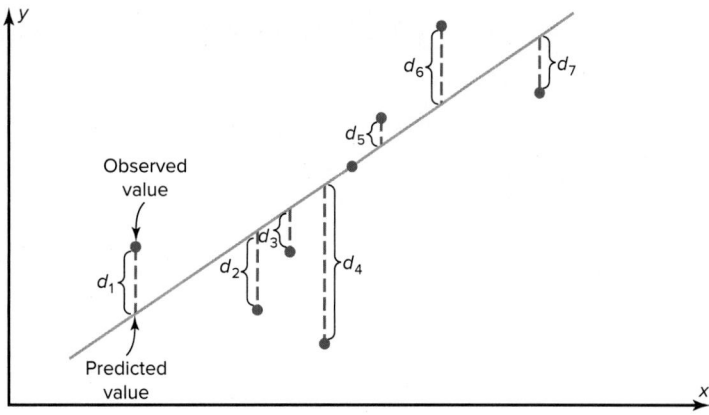

FIGURE 10–13 A Line as Represented in Algebra and in Statistics

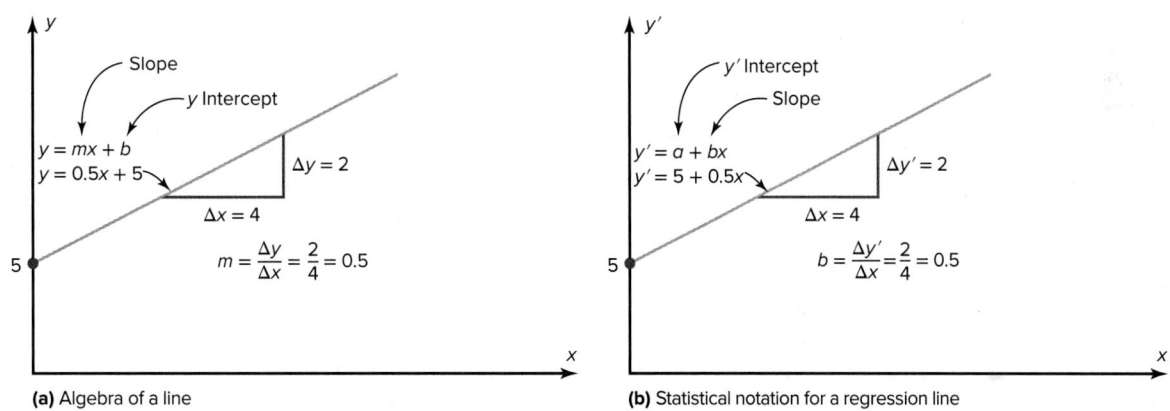

(a) Algebra of a line   **(b)** Statistical notation for a regression line

of a line should refer to the online resources, before studying this section.) In statistics, the equation of the regression line is written as $y' = a + bx$, where a is the y' intercept and b is the slope of the line. See Figure 10–13.

There are several methods for finding the equation of the regression line. Two formulas are given here. *These formulas use the same values that are used in computing the value of the correlation coefficient.* The mathematical development of these formulas is beyond the scope of this book.

Formulas for the Regression Line $y' = a + bx$

$$a = \frac{(\Sigma y)(\Sigma x^2) - (\Sigma x)(\Sigma xy)}{n(\Sigma x^2) - (\Sigma x)^2}$$

$$b = \frac{n(\Sigma xy) - (\Sigma x)(\Sigma y)}{n(\Sigma x^2) - (\Sigma x)^2}$$

where a is the y' intercept and b is the slope of the line.

Rounding Rule for the Intercept and Slope   Round the values of a and b to three decimal places.

The steps for finding the regression line equation are summarized in this Procedure Table.

> **Procedure Table**
>
> **Finding the Regression Line Equation**
>
> **Step 1** Make a table, as shown in step 2.
>
> **Step 2** Find the values of xy, x^2, and y^2. Place them in the appropriate columns and sum each column.
>
> | x | y | xy | x^2 | y^2 |
> |---|---|---|---|---|
> | . | . | . | . | . |
> | . | . | . | . | . |
> | . | . | . | . | . |
> | $\Sigma x =$ | $\Sigma y =$ | $\Sigma xy =$ | $\Sigma x^2 =$ | $\Sigma y^2 =$ |
>
> **Step 3** When r is significant, substitute in the formulas to find the values of a and b for the regression line equation $y' = a + bx$.
>
> $$a = \frac{(\Sigma y)(\Sigma x^2) - (\Sigma x)(\Sigma xy)}{n(\Sigma x^2) - (\Sigma x)^2} \qquad b = \frac{n(\Sigma xy) - (\Sigma x)(\Sigma y)}{n(\Sigma x^2) - (\Sigma x)^2}$$

EXAMPLE 10–9   Heights of Buildings

Find the equation of the regression line for the data in Example 10–4, and graph the line on the scatter plot of the data.

SOLUTION

The values needed for the equation obtained from the table in Example 10–4 are $n = 6$, $\Sigma x = 4543$, $\Sigma y = 351$, $\Sigma xy = 283,901$, and $\Sigma x^2 = 3,700,051$, $\Sigma y^2 = 22,003$.

$$a = \frac{(\Sigma y)(\Sigma x^2) - (\Sigma x)(\Sigma xy)}{n(\Sigma x^2) - (\Sigma x)^2} = \frac{(351)(3,700,051) - (4543)(283,901)}{6(3,700,051) - (4543)^2}$$

$$= \frac{8,955,658}{1,561,457} = 5.735$$

$$b = \frac{n(\Sigma xy) - (\Sigma x)(\Sigma y)}{n(\Sigma x^2) - (\Sigma x)^2} = \frac{6(283,901) - (4543)(351)}{6(3,700,051) - (4543)^2}$$

$$= \frac{108,813}{1,561,457} = 0.0697$$

Hence, the equation of the regression line $y' = a + bx$ is

$$y' = 5.735 + 0.0697x$$

To graph the line, use any two x values between 501 and 1136 and find the corresponding y values.

For example, use $x = 600$:

$$y' = 5.735 + 0.0697(600)$$

$$y' = 47.555$$

Let $x = 900$:

$$y' = 5.735 + 0.0697(900)$$

$$y' = 68.465$$

Then plot the two points (600, 47.615) and (900, 68.555) and draw a line connecting these two points on the scatter plot. See Figure 10–14.

FIGURE 10–14 Regression Line for Example 10–9

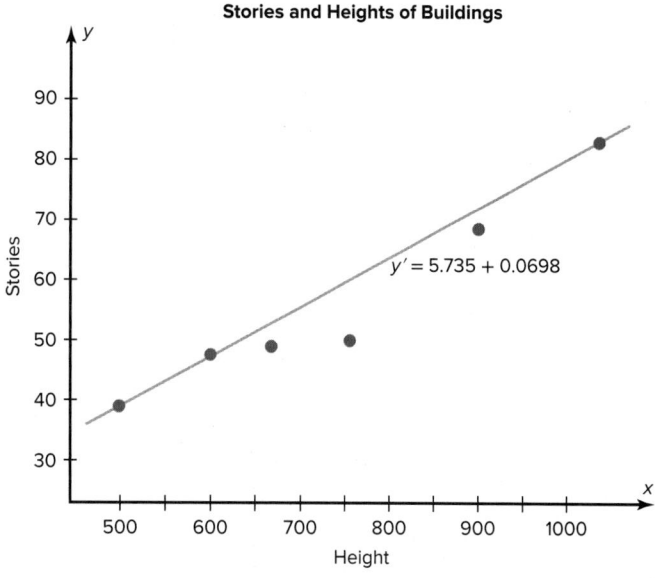

Note: When you draw the regression line, it is sometimes necessary to *truncate* the graph (see Chapter 2). This is done when the distance between the origin and the first labeled coordinate on the *x* axis is not the same as the distance between the rest of the labeled *x* coordinates or the distance between the origin and the first labeled *y'* coordinate is not the same as the distance between the other labeled *y'* coordinates. When the *x* axis or the *y* axis has been truncated, do not use the *y'* intercept value to graph the line. When you graph the regression line, always select *x* values between the smallest *x* data value and the largest *x* data value.

Historical Note

In 1795, Adrien-Marie Legendre (1752–1833) measured the meridian arc on the earth's surface from Barcelona, Spain, to Dunkirk, England. This measure was used as the basis for the measure of the meter. Legendre developed the least-squares method around the year 1805.

EXAMPLE 10–10   Absences and Final Grades

Find the equation of the regression line for the data in Example 10–5, and graph the line on the scatter plot.

SOLUTION

The values needed for the equation are $n = 7$, $\Sigma x = 57$, $\Sigma y = 511$, $\Sigma xy = 3745$, and $\Sigma x^2 = 579$. Substituting in the formulas, you get

$$a = \frac{(\Sigma y)(\Sigma x^2) - (\Sigma x)(\Sigma xy)}{n(\Sigma x^2) - (\Sigma x)^2} = \frac{(511)(579) - (57)(3745)}{(7)(579) - (57)^2} = 102.493$$

$$b = \frac{n(\Sigma xy) - (\Sigma x)(\Sigma y)}{n(\Sigma x^2) - (\Sigma x)^2} = \frac{(7)(3745) - (57)(511)}{(7)(579) - (57)^2} = -3.622$$

Hence, the equation of the regression line $y' = a + bx$ is

$$y' = 102.493 - 3.622x$$

The graph of the line is shown in Figure 10–15.

FIGURE 10–15

Regression Line for
Example 10–10

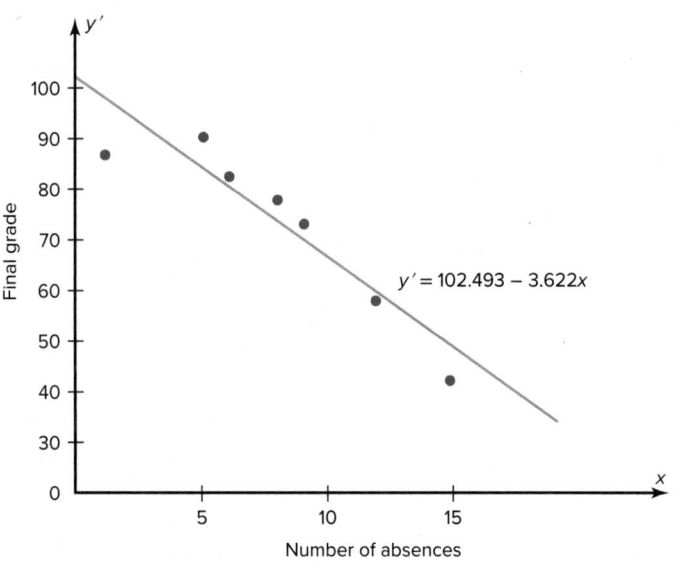

$$y' = 102.493 - 3.622x$$

The sign of the correlation coefficient and the sign of the slope of the regression line will always be the same. That is, if r is positive, then b will be positive; if r is negative, then b will be negative. The reason is that the numerators of the formulas are the same and determine the signs of r and b, and the denominators are always positive. The regression line will always pass through the point whose x coordinate is the mean of the x values and whose y coordinate is the mean of the y values, that is, $(\bar{x}, \bar{y})$.

The regression line can be used to make predictions for the dependent variable. You should use these guidelines when you are making predictions.

1. The points of the scatter plot fit the linear regression line reasonably well.

2. The value of r is significant.

3. The value of a specific x is not much beyond the observed values (x values) in the original data.

4. If r is not significant, then the best predicted value for a specific x value is the mean of the y value in the original data.

Assumptions for Valid Predictions in Regression

1. The sample is a random sample.
2. For any specific value of the independent variable x, the value of the dependent variable y must be normally distributed about the regression line. See Figure 10–16(a).
3. The standard deviation of each of the dependent variables must be the same for each value of the independent variable. See Figure 10–16(b).

FIGURE 10–16 Assumptions for Predictions

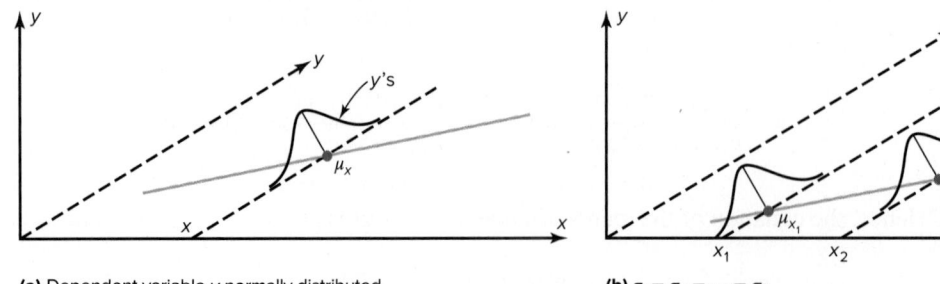

(a) Dependent variable y normally distributed

(b) $\sigma_1 = \sigma_2 = \cdots = \sigma_n$

In this book, the assumptions will be stated in the exercises; however, when encountering statistics in other situations, you must check to see that these assumptions have been met before proceeding.

The method for making predictions is shown in Example 10–11.

EXAMPLE 10–11   Absences and Final Grades

Use the equation of the regression line in Example 10–10 to predict the final grade for a student who missed 4 classes.

SOLUTION

Substitute 4 for x in the regression line equation $y' = 102.493 - 3.622x$.

$$y' = 102.493 - 3.622x$$
$$= 102.493 - 3.622(4)$$
$$= 88.005$$
$$= 88 \text{ (rounded)}$$

Hence, when a student misses 4 classes, the student's grade on the final exam is predicted to be about 88.

The value obtained in Example 10–11 is a point prediction, and with point predictions, no degree of accuracy or confidence can be determined. More information on prediction is given in Section 10–3.

The magnitude of the change in one variable when the other variable changes exactly 1 unit is called a **marginal change.** The value of slope b of the regression line equation represents the marginal change. For example, in Example 10–9 the slope of the regression line is 0.106, which means for each additional increase of 10,000 cars, the value of y changes 0.106 unit ($106 million) on average.

Extrapolation, or making predictions beyond the bounds of the data, must be interpreted cautiously. For example, in 1979, some experts predicted that the United States would run out of oil by the year 2003. This prediction was based on the current consumption and on known oil reserves at that time. However, since then, the automobile industry has produced many new fuel-efficient vehicles. Also, there are many as yet undiscovered oil fields. Finally, science may someday discover a way to run a car on something as unlikely but as common as peanut oil. In addition, the price of a gallon of gasoline was predicted to reach $10 a few years later. Fortunately this has not come to pass. *Remember that when predictions are made, they are based on present conditions or on the premise that present trends will continue.* This assumption may or may not prove true in the future.

A scatter plot should be checked for outliers. An outlier is a point that seems out of place when compared with the other points (see Chapter 3). Some of these points can affect the equation of the regression line. When this happens, the points are called **influential points** or **influential observations.**

When a point on the scatter plot appears to be an outlier, it should be checked to see if it is an influential point. An influential point tends to "pull" the regression line toward the point itself. To check for an influential point, the regression line should be graphed with the point included in the data set. Then a second regression line should be graphed that excludes the point from the data set. If the position of the second line is changed considerably, the point is said to be an influential point. Points that are outliers in the x direction tend to be influential points.

Researchers should use their judgment as to whether to include influential observations in the final analysis of the data. If the researcher feels that the observation is not necessary, then it should be excluded so that it

Interesting Fact

It is estimated that wearing a motorcycle helmet reduces the risk of a fatal accident by 30%.

Malcolm Fife/Pixtal/age fotostock

does not influence the results of the study. However, if the researcher feels that it is necessary, then the researcher may want to obtain additional data values whose x values are near the x value of the influential point and then include them in the study.

Applying the Concepts 10–2

Stopping Distances Revisited

In a study on speed and braking distance, researchers looked for a method to estimate how fast a person was traveling before an accident by measuring the length of the skid marks. An area that was focused on in the study was the distance required to completely stop a vehicle at various speeds. Use the following table to answer the questions.

MPH	Braking distance (feet)
20	20
30	45
40	81
50	133
60	205
80	411

Assume MPH is going to be used to predict stopping distance.

1. Find the linear regression equation.
2. What does the slope tell you about MPH and the braking distance? How about the y' intercept?
3. Find the braking distance when MPH = 45.
4. Find the braking distance when MPH = 100.
5. Comment on predicting beyond the given data values.

See page 612 for the answers.

Exercises 10–2

1. What two things should be done before one performs a regression analysis?

2. What are the assumptions for regression analysis?

3. What is the general form for the regression line used in statistics? $y' = a + bx$

4. What is the symbol for the slope? For the y' intercept? b, a

5. What is meant by the *line of best fit?*

6. When all the points fall on the regression line, what is the value of the correlation coefficient? r would equal +1 or −1.

7. What is the relationship between the sign of the correlation coefficient and the sign of the slope of the regression line? When r is positive, b will be positive. When r is negative, b will be negative.

8. As the value of the correlation coefficient increases from 0 to 1, or decreases from 0 to −1, how do the points of the scatter plot fit the regression line? They would be clustered closer to the line.

9. How is the value of the correlation coefficient related to the accuracy of the predicted value for a specific value of x? The closer r is to +1 or −1, the more accurate the predicted value will be.

10. When the value of r is not significant, what value should be used to predict y? When r is not significant, the mean of the y values should be used to predict y.

For Exercises 11 through 27, use the same data as for the corresponding exercises in Section 10–1. For each exercise, find the equation of the regression line and find the y' value for the specified x value. Remember that no regression should be done when r is not significant.

11. **Accidents and Drivers' Ages** For a random selection of drivers, their ages and the number of automobile accidents that they had over a 3-year period are shown.

Age	21	22	40	35	41	50	28	25
Accidents	5	6	1	2	3	0	4	4

Find y' when $x = 30$ years old. $y' = 9.022 - 0.180x$; $y' = 3.62$ or 4 accidents

12. **Final Exam Grades** The data show the final exam grades for 16 randomly selected students taking both College Algebra and Statistics. Use the College Algebra scores for the independent variable and Statistics scores for the dependent variable.

Student	1	2	3	4	5	6	7	8
College Algebra	88	97	73	92	81	79	71	90
Statistics	86	95	78	97	87	81	75	85
Student	9	10	11	12	13	14	15	16
College Algebra	86	58	87	68	74	86	62	95
Statistics	90	70	85	77	76	81	65	89

Find y' when $x = 80$. $y' = 27.964 + 0.676x$; $y' = 82.017$

13. **Commercial Movie Releases** New movie releases per studio and gross receipts are as follows:

No. of releases	361	270	306	22	35	10	8	12	21
Gross receipts (million $)	3844	1962	1371	1064	334	241	188	154	125

Find y' when $x = 200$ new releases. $y' = 181.661 + 7.319x$; $y' = 1645.4$ (million $)

14. **Forest Fires and Acres Burned** Number of fires and number of acres burned are as follows:

Fires, x	72	69	58	47	84	62	57	45
Acres, y	62	42	19	26	51	15	30	15

Find y' when $x = 60$ fires. $y' = -31.460 + 1.036x$; 30.7 acres

15. **Alumni Contributions** Years and contribution data are as follows:

Years, x	1	5	3	10	7	6
Contribution, y ($)	500	100	300	50	75	80

Find y' when $x = 4$ years. $y' = 453.176 - 50.439x$; $251.42

16. **State Debt and Per Capita Taxes** Data for per capita state debt and per capita state tax are as follows:

Per capita debt	8,567	9,606	10,227	1,058	7,782
Per capita tax	473	5,201	4,161	6,665	3,522

Find y' when $x = \$9000$ in per capita debt.
Since r is not significant, no regression should be done.

17. **Blood Pressure and Sodium Content** The data show the blood levels of sodium in mEq/L and the systolic blood pressure of 7 randomly selected subjects.

Sodium	125	136	141	144	148	152	155
Blood pressure	118	122	128	132	141	136	146

Find y' when $x = 143$. $y' = 0.015 + 0.922x$; $y' = 131.9$

18. **Hours Watching Videos and GPA** The data show a random selection of students' GPAs and the number of hours per week that they spend watching videos.

Student	1	2	3	4	5	6
Hours	15	18	23	30	9	12
GPA	2.6	3	2.3	2.1	3.5	3.1
Student	7	8	9	10	11	12
Hours	10	21	12	5	7	14
GPA	3.27	2.9	3.3	3.75	3.8	2.86

Find y' when $x = 20$ hours. $y' = 4.028 - 0.067x$; $y' = 2.681$

19. **Imports and Exports** A random sample of countries in the world shows the number of U.S. exports and the U.S. imports to each country for a recent year. The data are in hundreds of millions of dollars. Assume the independent variable is exports.

Country	1	2	3	4	5	6
Exports	55	16	10	26	13	22
Imports	54	45	42	17	22	9
Country	7	8	9	10	11	
Exports	5	72	12	21	64	
Imports	17	50	6	22	33	

Source: The World Almanac and Book of Facts

Find y' when $x = 18$ hundred million dollars. Since r is not significant, no regression should be done.

20. **Water and Carbohydrates** Here are the number of grams of water and the number of grams of carbohydrates for a random selection of raw foods (100 g each).

Water	83.93	80.76	87.66	85.20	72.85	84.61	83.81
Carbs	15.25	16.55	11.10	13.01	24.27	14.13	15.11

Find y' for $x = 75$. $y' = 87.409 - 0.868x$; $y' = 22.309$ grams of carbohydrates

21. **Faculty and Students** The number of faculty and the number of students in a random selection of small colleges are shown.

Faculty	99	110	113	116	138	174	220
Students	1353	1290	1091	1213	1384	1283	2075

Now find the equation of the regression line when x is the variable of the number of students. $y' = -14.974 + 0.111x$

22. **Automobiles and Light Commercial Vehicles** The data show the number of automobiles and the number of light commercial vehicles produced for a random sample of top motor-vehicle-producing countries. The data are in millions of vehicles produced.

Automobiles	7.8	4.2	1.2	0.2	1.6
Light commercial vehicles	1.3	3.8	6.1	0.2	1.4

Source: The World Almanac and Book of Facts

Find y' when $x = 2.0$ automobiles. Since r is not significant, no regression should be done.

23. Nuclear Reactors Is there a significant relationship between the number of nuclear reactors a country has and the number of megawatts (in thousands) that a country has?

Numbers	19	36	58	22	25	10	15
Megawatts	13	31	63	6	23	9	13

Source: Nuclear Power Reactors in the World

Find y' when $x = 40$. $y' = -8.374 + 1.171x$; 38.466 thousand megawatts

24. American Concert Tours Is there a significant relationship between the number of cities visited and the number of shows a random sample of musical groups completed?

Cities visited	41	30	38	43	41	21	42	43	30	56
Shows	62	32	42	76	54	31	48	60	47	80

Source: World Almanac and Book of Facts

Find y' when $x = 35$. $y' = -4.609 + 1.502x$; 47.961

25. Air Pollution and Memory A researcher is studying the relationship between air pollution and memory. A random sample of people with similar demographics from different cities were asked to take a memory recall test and the corresponding day's AQI was recorded. Higher AQI score means a higher air pollution, and memory scores measure the number of items a person remembered during the memory test.

Person	1	2	3	4	5	6	7	8	9	10
AQI	24	51	37	20	54	61	49	27	21	35
Memory	20	12	12	19	11	9	10	16	18	14

Source: The World Almanac and Book of Facts

Find y' when $x = 40$ AQI. $y' = 23.409 - 0.246x$; $y' = 13.584$

26. Shipping The data show the number of ships (in hundreds) a country has and the number of tons (in millions) of cargo that the country ships.

Number of ships	36	11	25	78	40	16	53
Cargo	127	33	8	18	76	16	32

Source: The World Almanac and Books of Facts

Find y' when $x = 40$ ships. Since r is not significant, no regression should be done.

27. Class Size and Grades School administrators wondered whether class size and grade achievement (in percent) were related. A random sample of classes revealed the following data.

No. of students	15	10	8	20	18	6
Avg. grade (%)	85	90	82	80	84	92

Find y' when $x = 12$. Since r is not significant, no regression should be done.

For Exercises 28 through 33, do a complete regression analysis by performing these steps.
 a. Draw a scatter plot.
 b. Compute the correlation coefficient.
 c. State the hypotheses.
 d. Test the hypotheses at $\alpha = 0.05$. Use Table A–8.
 e. Determine the regression line equation if r is significant.
 f. Plot the regression line on the scatter plot, if appropriate.
 g. Summarize the results.

28. Fireworks and Injuries These data were obtained for the years 2009 through 2014 and indicate the number of fireworks (in millions) used and the related injuries. Predict the number of injuries if 100 million fireworks are used during a given year.

Fireworks in use, x	213.9	205.9	234.1	207.5	186.4	225.3
Related injuries, y	8800	8600	9600	8600	11,400	10,500

Source: National Council of Fireworks Safety, American Pyrotechnic Assoc.

29. Farm Acreage Is there a relationship between the number of farms in a state and the acreage per farm? A random selection of states across the country, both eastern and western, produced the following results. Can a relationship between these two variables be concluded?

No. of farms (thousands), x	77	52	20.8	49	28	58.2
Acreage per farm, y	347	173	173	218	246	132

Source: World Almanac.

30. SAT Scores Educational researchers desired to find out if a relationship exists between the average SAT verbal score and the average SAT mathematical score. Several states were randomly selected, and their SAT average scores are recorded below. Is there sufficient evidence to conclude a relationship between the two scores?

Verbal, x	526	504	594	585	503	589
Math, y	530	522	606	588	517	589

Source: World Almanac.

31. Coal Production These data were obtained from a sample of counties in southwestern Pennsylvania and indicate the number (in thousands) of tons of bituminous coal produced in each county and the number of employees working in coal production in each county. Predict the amount of coal produced for a county that has 500 employees.

No. of employees, x	110	731	1031	20	118	1162	103	752
Tons, y	227	5410	5328	147	729	8095	635	6157

32. Television Viewers A television executive selects 10 television shows and compares the average number of viewers the show had last year with the average number of viewers this year. The data (in millions) are shown. Describe the relationship.

Viewers last year, x	26.6	17.85	20.3	16.8	20.8
Viewers this year, y	28.9	19.2	26.4	13.7	20.2

Viewers last year, x	16.7	19.1	18.9	16.0	15.8
Viewers this year, y	18.8	25.0	21.0	16.8	15.3

Source: Nielsen Media Research.

33. Absences and Final Grades An educator wants to see how the number of absences for a student in her class affects the student's final grade. The data obtained from a sample are shown.

No. of absences, x	10	12	2	0	8	5
Final grade, y	70	65	96	94	75	82

For Exercises 34 and 35, do a complete regression analysis and test the significance of r at α = 0.05, using the P-value method.

34. Soccer The data show the number of wins a soccer team has and the total number of points the team scored.

Wins	15	11	9	17	12	10	8
Points	54	45	41	60	52	39	38

Source: The World Almanac and Book of Facts

Find y' when $x = 13$ wins.

35. Children The data show the number of births of twins (in thousands) and quadruplets for a random sample of 8 recent years.

Twins	133	135	132	131	131	137	138	138
Quadruplets	228	246	270	276	239	313	355	345

Source: The World Almanac and Book of Facts

Find y' when $x = 134$.

Extending the Concepts

36. For Exercises 13, 15, and 21 in Section 10-1, find the mean of the x and y variables. Then substitute the mean of the x variable into the corresponding regression line equations found in Exercises 13, 15, and 21 in this section and find y'. Compare the value of y' with $\bar{y}$ for each exercise. Generalize the results.

37. The y intercept value a can also be found by using the equation

$$a = \bar{y} - b\bar{x}$$

Verify this result by using the data in Exercises 15 and 16 of Sections 10-1 and 10-2. 453.173; regression should not be done.

38. The value of the correlation coefficient can also be found by using the formula

$$r = \frac{bs_x}{s_y}$$

where s_x is the standard deviation of the x values and s_y is the standard deviation of the y values. Verify this result for Exercises 18 and 20 of Section 10-1. $r = 0.968$; $r = -0.993$

≡ Technology | Step by Step

TI-84 Plus

Step by Step

Correlation and Regression

To graph a scatter plot:

1. Enter the x values in L₁ and the y values in L₂.
2. Press **2nd [STAT PLOT] 1** for Plot 1. The other y functions should be turned off.
3. Move the cursor to On and press **ENTER** on the Plot 1 menu.
4. Move the cursor to the graphic that looks like a scatter plot next to Type (first graph), and press **ENTER**. Make sure the X list is L₁ and the Y list is L₂.
5. Press **ZOOM**. Press **9** for **ZoomStat** then **ENTER**.

Example TI10-1

Draw a scatter plot for the following data.

X	43	48	56	61	67	70
Y	128	120	135	143	141	152

The input and output screens are shown.

To find the equation of the regression line:

1. Press **STAT** and move the cursor to Tests.
2. Press **8 F (ALPHA COS)** for LinRegTTest then **ENTER**.
3. Make sure the X list is L_1 and the Y list is L_2, Freq is 1, and the $\neq 0$ is selected. Leave the RegEQ blank.
4. Move the cursor to Calculate and press **ENTER**.
5. Scroll down to locate the values a and b.

Example TI10–2

Find the equation of the regression line for the data in Example TI10–1. The input and output screens are shown.

 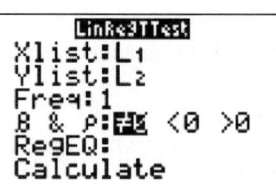 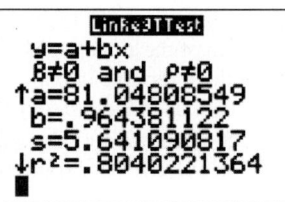

The equation of the regression line is $y' = 81.04808549 + 0.964381122x$.

To plot the regression line on the scatter plot:

1. Press **Y=** and **CLEAR** to clear any previous equations.
2. Press **VARS** and then **5** for Statistics.
3. Move the cursor to EQ and press **1** for RegEQ. The line will be in the Y= screen.
4. Press **ZOOM**. Press **9** for **ZoomStat** then **ENTER**.

Example TI10–3

Draw the regression line found in Example TI10–2 on the scatter plot.
The output screens are shown.

  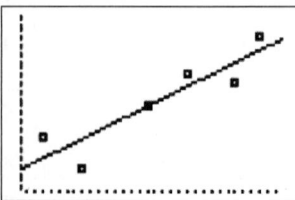

To test the significance of b and ρ:

1. Press **STAT** and move the cursor to TESTS.
2. Press **F (ALPHA COS)** for LinRegTTest. Make sure the Xlist is L_1, the Ylist is L_2, and the Freq is 1.
3. Select the appropriate Alternative hypothesis.
4. Move the cursor to Calculate and press **ENTER.**

Example TI10–4

Test the hypothesis H_0: $\rho = 0$ for the data in Example TI 10–1. Use $\alpha = 0.05$.

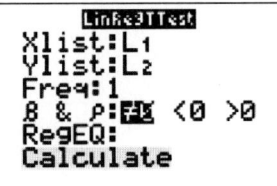 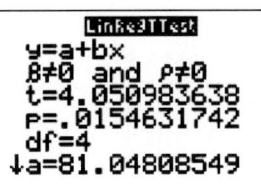 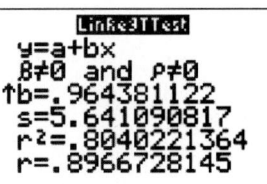

In this case, the t statistic is 4.050983638. The P-value is 0.0154631742, which is significant. The decision is to reject the null hypothesis at $\alpha = 0.05$, since $0.0154631742 < 0.05$; $r = 0.8966728145$, $r^2 = 0.8040221364$.

To store the equation for the regression line in Y_1 for graphing:

1. In the LinRegTTest menu, move the cursor down to the RegEQ line.
2. Press **VARS** for variables, move cursor to Y-VARS, press **1** for Function, and press **1** for Y_1.

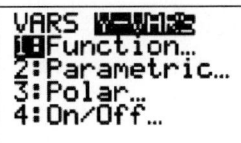 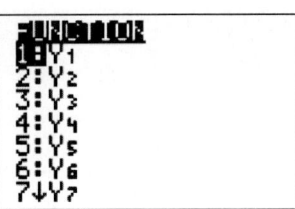 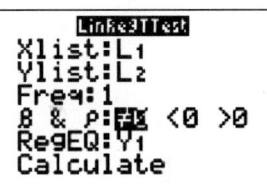

EXCEL
Step by Step

Example XL10–1

Use the following data to create a **Scatter Plot,** calculate a **Correlation Coefficient,** and perform a simple linear **Regression Analysis.**

X	43	48	56	61	67	70
Y	128	120	135	143	141	152

Enter the data from the example above in a new worksheet. Enter the six values for the x variable in column A and the corresponding y variable in column B.

Scatter Plot

1. Select the Insert tab from the toolbar.
2. Highlight the cells containing the data by holding the left mouse key over the first cell and dragging over the other cells.

3. Select the Scatter Chart type and choose the Scatter plot type in the upper left-hand corner.

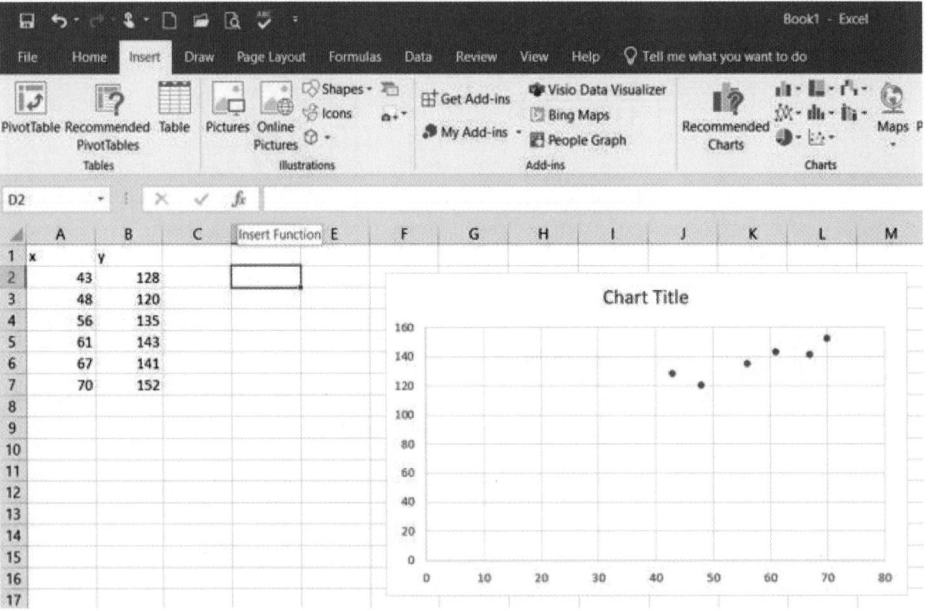

Correlation Coefficient

1. Select any blank cell in the worksheet and then select the insert Function tab from the toolbar.

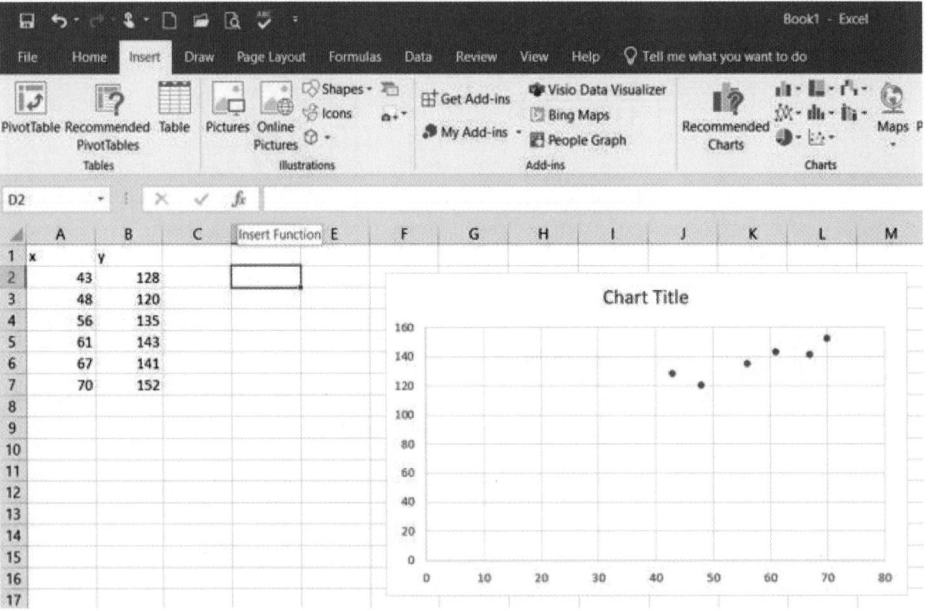

2. From the Insert Function dialog box, select the Statistical category and scroll to the CORREL function (this function will produce the Pearson-Product Moment Correlation Coefficient for the data).

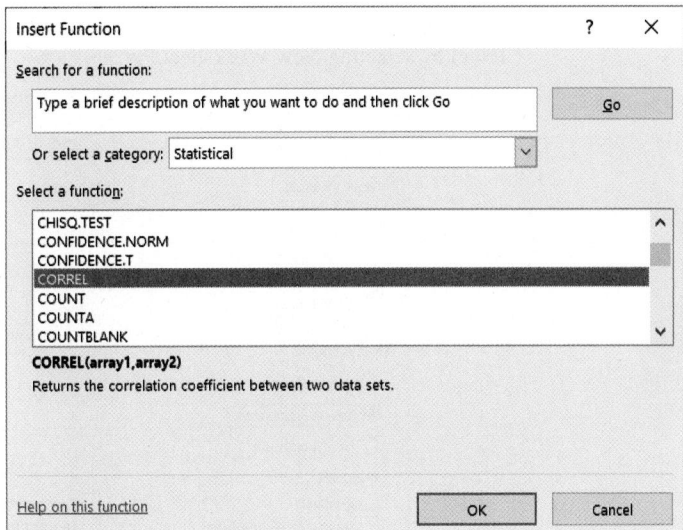

3. Enter the data range A2:A7 for the *x* variable in Array 1 and B2:B7 for the *y* variable in Array 2.

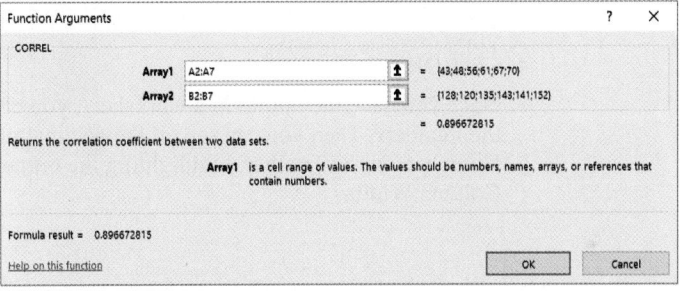

4. Click OK.

Correlation and Regression

1. Select the Data tab from the toolbar, then select the Data Analysis add-in.

2. From Analysis Tools, choose Regression and then click OK.

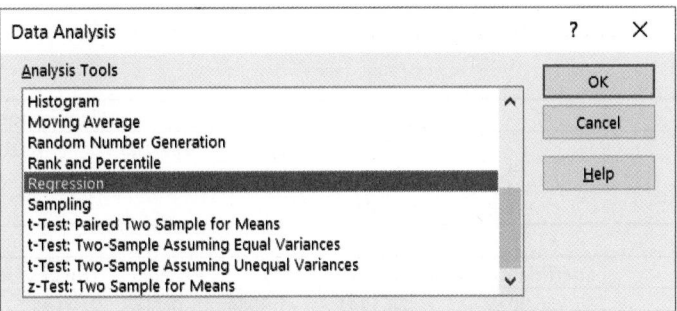

3. In the Regression dialog box, type B1:B7 in the Input Y Range and A1:A7 in the Input X Range. Check the box for Labels (make sure you selected the labels in your input range or the first number will be selected as your label). Under Output Options, you can choose to insert the regression analysis in the current worksheet by selecting Output Range and typing in a blank cell name. Or you can choose to have the analysis inserted into a new worksheet in Excel by selecting New Worksheet Ply.

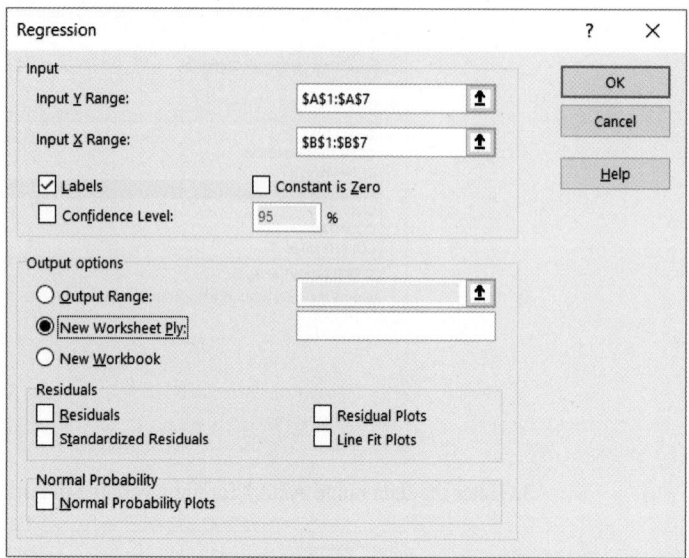

4. Click OK.

5. Once you have the output in a worksheet, you can adjust the cell widths to accommodate the numbers. Then you can see all the decimal places in the output by choosing the Home tab on the Toolbar, highlighting the output, then selecting Format>AutoFit Column Width.

	A	B	C	D	E	F	G	H	I
1	SUMMARY OUTPUT								
2									
3	*Regression Statistics*								
4	Multiple R	0.8967							
5	R Square	0.8040							
6	Adjusted R Square	0.7550							
7	Standard Error	5.2450							
8	Observations	6							
9									
10	ANOVA								
11		*df*	*SS*	*MS*	*F*	*Significance F*			
12	Regression	1	451.4584	451.4584	16.4105	0.0155			
13	Residual	4	110.0416	27.5104					
14	Total	5	561.5						
15									
16		*Coefficients*	*Standard Error*	*t Stat*	*P-value*	*Lower 95%*	*Upper 95%*	*Lower 95.0%*	*Upper 95.0%*
17	Intercept	-56.3025	28.1741	-1.9984	0.1163	-134.5263	21.9212	-134.5263	21.9212
18	y	0.8337	0.2058	4.0510	0.0155	0.2623	1.4051	0.2623	1.4051

MINITAB
Step by Step

Use these data from Examples 10–2, 10–5, and 10–10 concerning final grades versus absences.

C1 Subject	C2 Absences	C3 Final Grade
A	6	82
B	2	86
C	15	43
D	9	74
E	12	58
F	5	90
G	8	78

Create a Scatter Plot

1. Enter these data into the first three columns of a MINITAB worksheet.

2. Select **Graph>Scatterplot,** then choose **Simple with Regression** and click [OK].

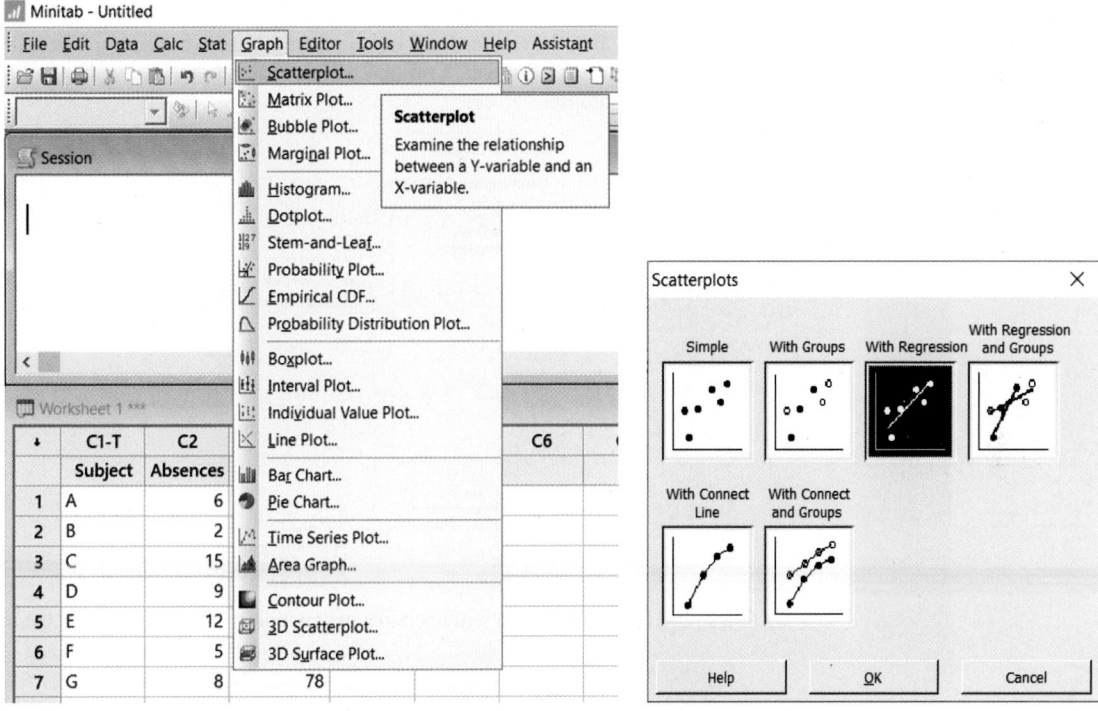

a) Double-click C3 Final grade for the Y variable.

b) Double-click C2 Absences for the X variable.

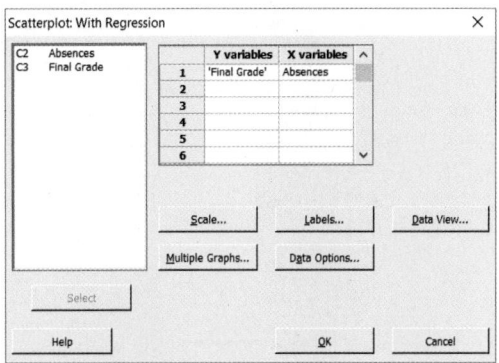

c) Click the button for [Labels].

   i) Type in a title for the graph such as Final Grade vs. Number of Absences.

   ii) Type your name in the box for Footnote 1.

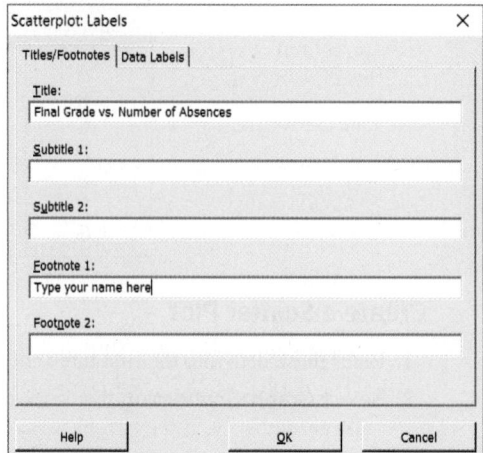

   iii) Optional: Click the tab for Data Labels then the radio button for Use labels from column; select C1 Subject. You may need to click in the dialog box before you see the list of columns.

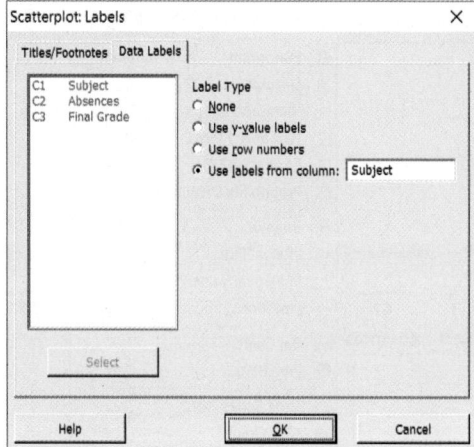

d) Click [**OK**] twice. The graph will open in a new window. MINITAB shows the regression line.

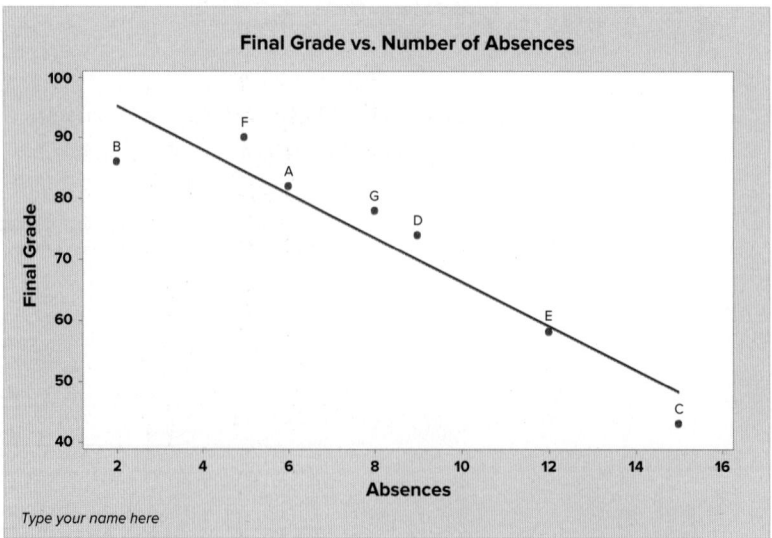

Calculate the Correlation Coefficient, *r*

Select **Stat>Basic Statistics>Correlation.**

    a) Double-click C3 Final Grade then C2 Absences. Put Y, the dependent variable, first.

    b) Click [OK].

The correlation coefficient $r = -0.944$ and the *P*-value = 0.001 for the test will be displayed in the Session Window.

Determine the Line of Best Fit

  3. Select **Stat>Regression>Regression>Fit Regression Model.**

    a) Double-click C3 Final Grade for the Response variable Y.

    b) Double-click C2 Absences for the Continuous Predictor variable.

    c) Click the button for [Storage], then select Residuals and Fits, and click [OK] twice.

  4. Select **Data>Data Display.**

    a) Drag your mouse over all five columns; then click the [Select] button and [OK].

    b) The data in the worksheet will be copied into the Session Window.

    c) Right-click over the highlighted items, then select **Send to Microsoft Word®**. Alternately you may send it to a presentation instead of a document.

      Caution: If a Word document is open, the content will be inserted into the open document.

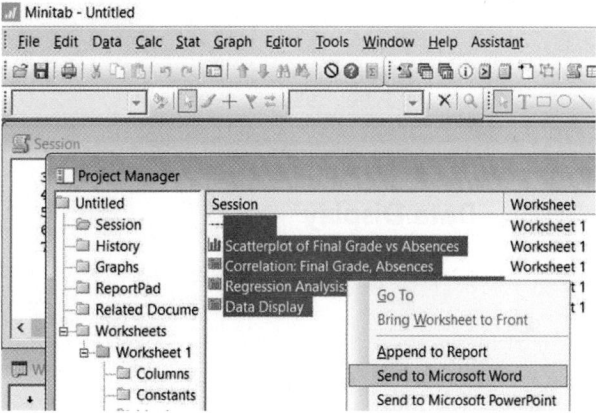

Here is a copy of the report.

─────────────────────────────── **Date & Time** ───────────────────────────────

Correlation: Final Grade, Absences

Final Grade vs. Number of Absences

Type your name here

```
Pearson correlation of Final Grade and Absences = -0.944
P-Value = 0.001
```

Regression Analysis: Final Grade versus Absences

```
Analysis of Variance
Source      DF  Adj SS   Adj MS  F-Value  P-Value
Regression   1  1506.7  1506.71    41.10    0.001
  Absences   1  1506.7  1506.71    41.10    0.001
Error        5   183.3    36.66
Total        6  1690.0

Model Summary
      S    R-sq  R-sq(adj)  R-sq(pred)
6.05464  89.15%     86.99%      67.62%

Coefficients
Term         Coef  SE Coef  T-Value  P-Value   VIF
Constant   102.49     5.14    19.95    0.000
Absences   -3.622    0.565    -6.41    0.001  1.00

Regression Equation
Final Grade = 102.49 - 3.622 Absences

Fits and Diagnostics for Unusual Observations

     Final
Obs  Grade    Fit  Resid  Std Resid
  2  86.00  95.25  -9.25      -2.10  R

R  Large residual
```

Data Display

```
                      Final
Row  Subject  Absences  Grade    FITS1     RESI1
  1  A              6      82  80.7612   1.23881
  2  B              2      86  95.2488  -9.24876
  3  C             15      43  48.1642  -5.16418
  4  D              9      74  69.8955   4.10448
  5  E             12      58  59.0299  -1.02985
  6  F              5      90  84.3831   5.61692
  7  G              8      78  73.5174   4.48259
```

10–3 Coefficient of Determination and Standard Error of the Estimate

The previous sections stated that if the correlation coefficient is significant, the equation of the regression line can be determined. Also, for various values of the independent variable x, the corresponding values of the dependent variable y can be predicted. Several other measures are associated with the correlation and regression techniques. They include the coefficient of determination, the standard error of the estimate, and the prediction interval. But before these concepts can be explained, the different types of variation associated with the regression model must be defined.

Types of Variation for the Regression Model

Consider the following hypothetical regression model.

x	1	2	3	4	5
y	10	8	12	16	20

The equation of the regression line is $y' = 4.8 + 2.8x$, and $r = 0.919$. The sample y values are 10, 8, 12, 16, and 20. The predicted values, designated by y', for each x can be found by substituting each x value into the regression equation and finding y'. For example, when $x = 1$,

$$y' = 4.8 + 2.8x = 4.8 + (2.8)(1) = 7.6$$

Now, for each x, there is an observed y value and a predicted y' value; for example, when $x = 1$, $y = 10$ and $y' = 7.6$. Recall that the closer the observed values are to the predicted values, the better the fit is and the closer r is to $+1$ or -1.

The *total variation* $\Sigma(y - \bar{y})^2$ is the sum of the squares of the vertical distances each point is from the mean. The total variation can be divided into two parts: that which is attributed to the relationship of x and y and that which is due to chance. The variation obtained from the relationship (i.e., from the predicted y' values) is $\Sigma(y' - \bar{y})^2$ and is called the *explained variation.*

In other words, the explained variation is the vertical distance $y' - \bar{y}$, which is the distance between the predicted value y' and the mean value $\bar{y}$. Most of the variation can be explained by the relationship. The closer the value r is to $+1$ or -1, the better the points fit the line and the closer $\Sigma(y' - \bar{y})^2$ is to $\Sigma(y - \bar{y})^2$. In fact, if all points fall on the regression line, $\Sigma(y' - \bar{y})^2$ will equal $\Sigma(y - \bar{y})^2$, since y' is equal to y in each case.

On the other hand, the variation due to chance, found by $\Sigma(y - y')^2$, is called the *unexplained variation.* In other words, the unexplained variation is the vertical distance $y - y'$, which is the distance between the observed value, y, and the predicted value y'. This variation cannot be attributed to the relationship. When the unexplained variation is small, the value of r is close to $+1$ or -1. If all points fall on the regression line, the unexplained variation $\Sigma(y - y')^2$ will be 0. Hence, the *total variation* is equal to the sum of the explained variation and the unexplained variation. That is,

$$\Sigma(y - \bar{y})^2 = \Sigma(y' - \bar{y})^2 + \Sigma(y - y')^2$$

These values are shown in Figure 10–17. For a single point, the differences are called *deviations.* For the hypothetical regression model given earlier, for $x = 1$ and $y = 10$, you get $y' = 7.6$ and $\bar{y} = 13.2$.

FIGURE 10–17

Deviations for the Regression Equation

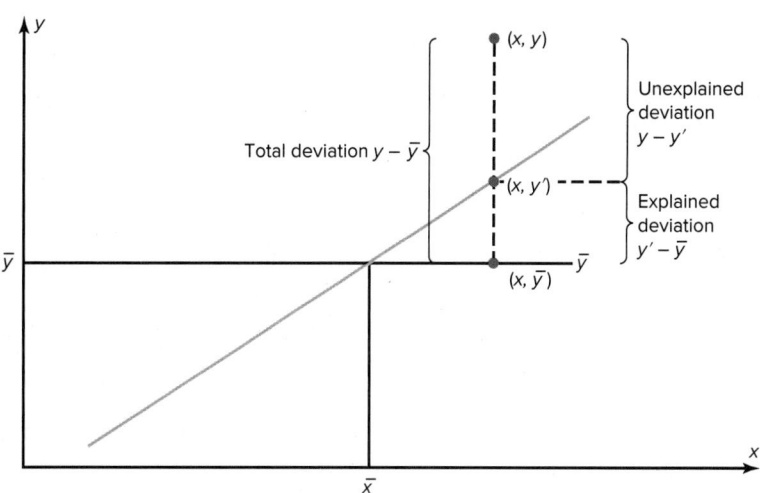

The procedure for finding the three types of variation is illustrated next.

Step 1   Find the predicted y' values.

For $x = 1$ $y' = 4.8 + 2.8x = 4.8 + (2.8)(1) = 7.6$

For $x = 2$ $y' = 4.8 + (2.8)(2) = 10.4$

For $x = 3$ $y' = 4.8 + (2.8)(3) = 13.2$

For $x = 4$ $y' = 4.8 + (2.8)(4) = 16.0$

For $x = 5$ $y' = 4.8 + (2.8)(5) = 18.8$

Hence, the values for this example are as follows:

x	y	y'
1	10	7.6
2	8	10.4
3	12	13.2
4	16	16.0
5	20	18.8

Step 2   Find the mean of the y values.

$$\bar{y} = \frac{10 + 8 + 12 + 16 + 20}{5} = 13.2$$

Step 3   Find the total variation $\Sigma(y - \bar{y})^2$.

$(10 - 13.2)^2 = 10.24$

$(8 - 13.2)^2 = 27.04$

$(12 - 13.2)^2 = 1.44$

$(16 - 13.2)^2 = 7.84$

$(20 - 13.2)^2 = \underline{46.24}$

$\Sigma(y - \bar{y})^2 = 92.8$

Step 4   Find the explained variation $\Sigma(y' - \bar{y})^2$.

$(7.6 - 13.2)^2 = 31.36$

$(10.4 - 13.2)^2 = 7.84$

$(13.2 - 13.2)^2 = 0.00$

$(16 - 13.2)^2 = 7.84$

$(18.8 - 13.2)^2 = \underline{31.36}$

$\Sigma(y' - \bar{y})^2 = 78.4$

Step 5   Find the unexplained variation $\Sigma(y - y')^2$.

$(10 - 7.6)^2 = 5.76$

$(8 - 10.4)^2 = 5.76$

$(12 - 13.2)^2 = 1.44$

$(16 - 16)^2 = 0.00$

$(20 - 18.8)^2 = \underline{1.44}$

$\Sigma(y - y')^2 = 14.4$

Notice that

Total variation = explained variation + unexplained variation

$92.8 =$ 78.4 $+$ 14.4

Residual Plots

As previously stated, the values $y - y'$ are called *residuals* (sometimes called the *prediction errors*). These values can be plotted with the x values, and the plot, called a **residual plot,** can be used to determine how well the regression line can be used to make predictions.

The residuals for the previous example are calculated as shown.

x	y	y'	$y - y'$ = residual
1	10	7.6	$10 - 7.6 = 2.4$
2	8	10.4	$8 - 10.4 = -2.4$
3	12	13.2	$12 - 13.2 = -1.2$
4	16	16	$16 - 16 = 0$
5	20	18.8	$20 - 18.8 = 1.2$

The x values are plotted using the horizontal axis, and the residuals are plotted using the vertical axis. Since the mean of the residuals is always zero, a horizontal line with a y coordinate of zero is placed on the y axis as shown in Figure 10–18.

Plot the x and residual values as shown in Figure 10–18.

x	1	2	3	4	5
$y - y'$	2.4	−2.4	−1.2	0	1.2

To interpret a residual plot, you need to determine if the residuals form a pattern. Figure 10–19 shows four examples of residual plots. If the residual values are more or less evenly distributed about the line, as shown in Figure 10–19(a), then the relationship between x and y is linear and the regression line can be used to make predictions. This means that the standard deviations of each of the dependent variables must be the same for each value of the independent variable. This is called the *homoscedasticity assumption.* See assumption 3 on page 572.

Figure 10–19(b) shows that the variance of the residuals increases as the values of x increase. This means that the regression line is not suitable for predictions.

Figure 10–19(c) shows a curvilinear relationship between the x values and the residual values; hence, the regression line is not suitable for making predictions.

Figure 10–19(d) shows that as the x values increase, the residuals increase and become more dispersed. This means that the regression line is not suitable for making predictions.

FIGURE 10–18

Residual Plot

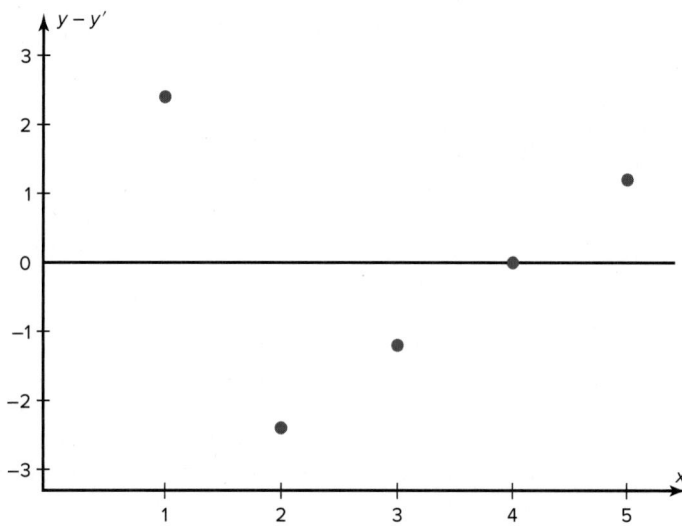

FIGURE 10–19

Examples of
Residual Plots

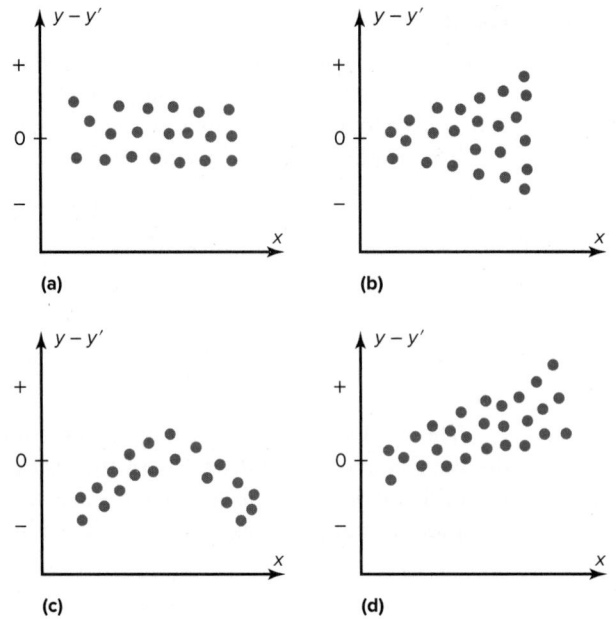

The residual plot in Figure 10–18 shows that the regression line $y' = 4.8 + 2.8x$ is somewhat questionable for making predictions due to a small sample size.

OBJECTIVE

Compute the coefficient of determination.

Coefficient of Determination

The *coefficient of determination* is the ratio of the explained variation to the total variation and is denoted by r^2. That is,

$$r^2 = \frac{\text{explained variation}}{\text{total variation}}$$

> The **coefficient of determination** is a measure of the variation of the dependent variable that is explained by the regression line and the independent variable. The symbol for the coefficient of determination is r^2.

The coefficient of determination is a number between 0 and 1 inclusive, or $0 \leq r^2 \leq 1$. If $r^2 = 0$, then the least squares regression line cannot explain any of the variation. If $r^2 = 1$, the least squares regression line explains 100% of the variation in the dependent variable.

For the example, $r^2 = 78.4/92.8 = 0.845$. The term r^2 is usually expressed as a percentage. So in this case, 84.5% of the total variation is explained by the regression line using the independent variable.

Another way to arrive at the value for r^2 is to square the correlation coefficient. In this case, $r = 0.919$ and $r^2 = 0.845$, which is the same value found by using the variation ratio.

Of course, it is usually easier to find the coefficient of determination by squaring r and converting it to a percentage. Therefore, if $r = 0.90$, then $r^2 = 0.81$, which is equivalent to 81%. This result means that 81% of the variation in the dependent variable is accounted for by the variation in the independent variable. The rest of the variation, 0.19, or 19%, is unexplained. This value is called the *coefficient of nondetermination* and is found by subtracting the coefficient of determination from 1. As the value of r approaches 0, r^2 decreases more rapidly. For example, if $r = 0.6$, then $r^2 = 0.36$, which means that only 36% of the variation in the dependent variable can be attributed to the variation in the independent variable.

Historical Note

Karl Pearson recommended in 1897 that the French government close all its casinos and turn the gambling devices over to the academic community to use in the study of probability.

Coefficient of Nondetermination

$$1.00 - r^2$$

In Example 10–5 using absences and final grades, the correlation coefficient is $r = -0.944$. Then $r^2 = (-0.944)^2 = 0.891$. Hence, about 0.891, or 89.1%, of the variation in the final grades can be explained by the linear relationship between the number of absences and the final grades. About $1 - 0.891$ or 0.109 or 10.9% of the variation of the final grades cannot be explained by the variation of the absences.

Standard Error of the Estimate

OBJECTIVE

Compute the standard error of the estimate.

When a y' value is predicted for a specific x value, the prediction is a point prediction. The disadvantage of a point prediction is that it doesn't give us any information about how accurate the point prediction is. In previous chapters, we developed confidence interval estimates to overcome this disadvantage. In this section, we will use what is called a **prediction interval,** which is an interval estimate of a variable.

Recall in previous chapters an interval estimate of a parameter, such as the mean or standard deviation, is called a confidence interval.

A **prediction interval** is an interval estimate of a predicted value of y when the regression equation is used and a specific value of x is given.

A prediction interval about the y' value can be constructed, just as a confidence interval was constructed for an estimate of the population mean. The prediction interval uses a statistic called the *standard error of the estimate*.

The **standard error of the estimate,** denoted by s_{est}, is the standard deviation of the observed y values about the predicted y' values. The formula for the standard error of the estimate is

$$s_{est} = \sqrt{\frac{\Sigma(y - y')^2}{n - 2}}$$

The standard error of the estimate is similar to the standard deviation, but the mean is not used. Recall that the standard deviation measures how the values deviate from the mean. The standard error of the estimate measures how the data points deviate from the regression line.

As can be seen from the formula, the standard error of the estimate is the square root of the unexplained variation—that is, the variation due to the difference of the observed values and the expected values—divided by $n - 2$. So the closer the observed values are to the predicted values, the smaller the standard error of the estimate will be.

A Procedure Table for finding the standard error of the estimate is shown here.

Procedure Table

Finding the Standard Error of the Estimate

Step 1   Make a table using the column headings shown.

x	y	y'	$y-y'$	$(y-y')^2$

Step 2   Find the predicted values y' for each x value, and place these values under y' in the table.

Step 3   Subtract each y' value from each y value, and place these answers in the $y - y'$ column in the table.

Step 4   Square each of the values in step 3, and place these values in the column $(y - y')^2$.

Step 5   Find the sum of the values in the $(y - y')^2$ column.

Step 6   Substitute in the formula and find s_{est}.

$$s_{est} = \sqrt{\frac{\Sigma(y - y')^2}{n - 2}}$$

Example 10–12 shows how to compute the standard error of the estimate.

EXAMPLE 10–12   Copy Machine Maintenance Costs

A researcher collects the following data and determines that there is a significant relationship between the age of a copy machine and its monthly maintenance cost. The regression equation is $y' = 55.57 + 8.13x$. Find the standard error of the estimate.

Machine	Age x (years)	Monthly cost, y
A	1	$ 62
B	2	78
C	3	70
D	4	90
E	4	93
F	6	103

SOLUTION

Step 1   Make a table, as shown.

x	y	y'	$y - y'$	$(y - y')^2$
1	62			
2	78			
3	70			
4	90			
4	93			
6	103			

Step 2   Using the regression line equation $y' = 55.57 + 8.13x$, compute the predicted values y' for each x, and place the results in the column labeled y'.

$$x = 1 \quad y' = 55.57 + (8.13)(1) = 63.70$$
$$x = 2 \quad y' = 55.57 + (8.13)(2) = 71.83$$
$$x = 3 \quad y' = 55.57 + (8.13)(3) = 79.96$$
$$x = 4 \quad y' = 55.57 + (8.13)(4) = 88.09$$
$$x = 6 \quad y' = 55.57 + (8.13)(6) = 104.35$$

Step 3   For each y, subtract y' and place the answer in the column labeled $y - y'$.

$$62 - 63.70 = -1.70 \qquad 90 - 88.09 = 1.91$$
$$78 - 71.83 = 6.17 \qquad 93 - 88.09 = 4.91$$
$$70 - 79.96 = -9.96 \qquad 103 - 104.35 = -1.35$$

Step 4   Square the numbers found in step 3 and place the squares in the column labeled $(y - y')^2$.

Step 5   Find the sum of the numbers in the last column. The completed table is shown.

x	y	y′	y − y′	(y − y′)²
1	62	63.70	−1.70	2.89
2	78	71.83	6.17	38.0689
3	70	79.96	−9.96	99.2016
4	90	88.09	1.91	3.6481
4	93	88.09	4.91	24.1081
6	103	104.35	−1.35	1.8225

$$\Sigma(y - y')^2 = 169.7392$$

Step 6   Substitute in the formula and find s_{est}.

$$s_{est} = \sqrt{\frac{\Sigma(y - y')^2}{n - 2}} = \sqrt{\frac{169.7392}{6 - 2}} = 6.514$$

In this case, the standard deviation of observed values about the predicted values is 6.514.

The standard error of the estimate can also be found by using the formula

$$s_{est} = \sqrt{\frac{\Sigma y^2 - a\,\Sigma y - b\,\Sigma xy}{n - 2}}$$

This Procedure Table shows the alternate method for finding the standard error of the estimate.

Procedure Table

Alternative Method for Finding the Standard Error of Estimate

Step 1   Make a table using the column headings shown.

x	y	xy	y²

Step 2   Place the x values in the first column (the x column), and place the y values in the second column (the y column). Find the products of the x and y values and place them in the third column (the xy column). Square the y values and place them in the fourth column (the y² column).

Step 3   Find the sum of the values in the y, xy, and y² columns.

Step 4   Identify a and b from the regression equation, substitute in the formula, and evaluate.

$$s_{est} = \sqrt{\frac{\Sigma y^2 - a\,\Sigma y - b\,\Sigma xy}{n - 2}}$$

EXAMPLE 10–13

Find the standard error of the estimate for the data for Example 10–12 by using the preceding formula. The equation of the regression line is $y' = 55.57 + 8.13x$.

SOLUTION

Step 1   Make a table as shown in the Procedure Table.

Step 2   Place the x values in the first column (the x column), and place the y values in the second column (the y column). Find the product of x and y values, and place the results in the third column. Square the y values, and place the results in the y² column.

Step 3   Find the sums of the y, xy, and y^2 columns. The completed table is shown here.

x	y	xy	y^2
1	62	62	3,844
2	78	156	6,084
3	70	210	4,900
4	90	360	8,100
4	93	372	8,649
6	103	618	10,609
	$\Sigma y = 496$	$\Sigma xy = 1778$	$\Sigma y^2 = 42,186$

Step 4   From the regression equation $y' = 55.57 + 8.13x$, $a = 55.57$, and $b = 8.13$. Substitute in the formula and solve for s_{est}.

$$s_{est} = \sqrt{\frac{\Sigma y^2 - a\,\Sigma y - b\,\Sigma xy}{n - 2}}$$

$$= \sqrt{\frac{42,186 - (55.57)(496) - (8.13)(1778)}{6 - 2}} = 6.483$$

This value is close to the value found in Example 10–12. The difference is due to rounding.

OBJECTIVE **7**

Find a prediction interval.

Prediction Interval

The standard error of the estimate can be used for constructing a prediction interval (similar to a confidence interval) about a y' value.

Recall that when a specific value x is substituted into the regression equation, the predicted value y' that you get is a point estimate for y. For example, if the regression line equation for the age of a machine and the monthly maintenance cost is $y' = 55.57 + 8.13x$ (Example 10–12), then the predicted maintenance cost for a 3-year-old machine would be $y' = 55.57 + 8.13(3)$, or $79.96. Since this is a point estimate obtained from the regression equation, you have no idea how accurate it is because there are possible sources of prediction errors in finding the regression line equation. One source occurs when finding the standard error of the estimate s_{est}. Two others are errors made in estimating the slope and the y' intercept, since the equation of the regression line will change somewhat if different random samples are used when calculating the equation. However, you can construct a prediction interval about the estimate. By selecting an α value, you can achieve $(1 - \alpha) \cdot 100\%$ confidence that the interval contains the actual mean of the y values that correspond to the given value of x.

Formula for the Prediction Interval about a Value y'

$$y' - t_{\alpha/2}s_{est}\sqrt{1 + \frac{1}{n} + \frac{n(x - \overline{X})^2}{n\,\Sigma x^2 - (\Sigma x)^2}} < y < y' + t_{\alpha/2}s_{est}\sqrt{1 + \frac{1}{n} + \frac{n(x - \overline{X})^2}{n\,\Sigma x^2 - (\Sigma x)^2}}$$

with d.f. $= n - 2$.

The next Procedure Table can be used to find the prediction.

Procedure Table

Finding a Prediction Interval for a Specific Independent Data Value

Step 1   Find Σx, Σx^2, and $\bar{x}$.

Step 2   Find y' for the specific x value.

Step 3   Find s_{est}.

Step 4   Substitute in the formula and evaluate.

$$y' - t_{\alpha/2}s_{\text{est}}\sqrt{1 + \frac{1}{n} + \frac{n(x - \bar{X})^2}{n\,\Sigma x^2 - (\Sigma x)^2}} < y < y' + t_{\alpha/2}s_{\text{est}}\sqrt{1 + \frac{1}{n} + \frac{n(x - \bar{X})^2}{n\,\Sigma x^2 - (\Sigma x)^2}}$$

with d.f. $= n - 2$.

EXAMPLE 10–14

For the data in Example 10–12, find the 95% prediction interval for the monthly maintenance cost of a machine that is 3 years old.

SOLUTION

Step 1   Find Σx, Σx^2, and $\bar{X}$.

$$\Sigma x = 20 \qquad \Sigma x^2 = 82 \qquad \bar{X} = \frac{20}{6} = 3.3$$

Step 2   Find y' for $x = 3$.

$$y' = 55.57 + 8.13x$$
$$= 55.57 + 8.13(3) = 79.96$$

Step 3   Find s_{est}.

$$s_{\text{est}} = 6.48$$

as shown in Example 10–13.

Step 4   Substitute in the formula and solve: $t_{\alpha/2} = 2.776$, d.f. $= 6 - 2 = 4$ for 95%.

$$y' - t_{\alpha/2}s_{\text{est}}\sqrt{1 + \frac{1}{n} + \frac{n(x - \bar{X})^2}{n\,\Sigma x^2 - (\Sigma x)^2}} < y < y' + t_{\alpha/2}s_{\text{est}}\sqrt{1 + \frac{1}{n} + \frac{n(x - \bar{X})^2}{n\,\Sigma x^2 - (\Sigma x)^2}}$$

$$79.96 - (2.776)(6.48)\sqrt{1 + \frac{1}{6} + \frac{6(3 - 3.3)^2}{6(82) - (20)^2}} < y < 79.96$$

$$+ (2.776)(6.48)\sqrt{1 + \frac{1}{6} + \frac{6(3 - 3.3)^2}{6(82) - (20)^2}}$$

$$79.96 - (2.776)(6.48)(1.08) < y < 79.96 + (2.776)(6.48)(1.08)$$
$$79.96 - 19.43 < y < 79.96 + 19.43$$
$$60.53 < y < 99.39$$

Hence, you can be 95% confident that the interval $60.53 < y < 99.39$ contains the actual value of y.

That is, if a copy machine is 3 years old, we can be 95% confident that the maintenance cost would be between \$60.53 and \$99.39. This range is large because the sample size is small, $n = 6$, and the standard error of estimate is 6.48.

▤ Applying the Concepts **10–3**

Interpreting Simple Linear Regression

Answer the questions about the following computer-generated information.

Linear correlation coefficient $r = 0.794556$
Coefficient of determination $= 0.631319$
Standard error of estimate $= 12.9668$
Explained variation $= 5182.41$
Unexplained variation $= 3026.49$
Total variation $= 8208.90$
Equation of regression line $\quad y' = 0.725983x + 16.5523$
Level of significance $= 0.1$
Test statistic $= 0.794556$
Critical value $= 0.378419$

1. Are both variables moving in the same direction?

2. Which number measures the distances from the prediction line to the actual values?

3. Which number is the slope of the regression line?

4. Which number is the y intercept of the regression line?

5. Which number can be found in a table?

6. Which number is the allowable risk of making a type I error?

7. Which number measures the variation explained by the regression?

8. Which number measures the scatter of points about the regression line?

9. What is the null hypothesis?

10. Which number is compared to the critical value to see if the null hypothesis should be rejected?

11. Should the null hypothesis be rejected?

See page 612 for the answers.

▤ Exercises **10–3**

1. What is meant by the *explained variation?* How is it computed? Explained variation is the variation due to the relationship. It is computed by $\Sigma(y' - \bar{y})^2$.

2. What is meant by the *unexplained variation?* How is it computed? Unexplained variation is the variation due to chance. It is computed by $\Sigma(y - y')^2$.

3. What is meant by the *total variation?* How is it computed?

4. Define the coefficient of determination.

5. How is the coefficient of determination found?

6. Define the coefficient of nondetermination. It is the percent of the variation in y that is not due to the variation in x.

7. How is the coefficient of nondetermination found? The coefficient of nondetermination is found by subtracting r^2 from 1.

For Exercises 8 through 13, find the coefficients of determination and nondetermination and explain the meaning of each.

8. $r = 0.62$ 0.3844

9. $r = 0.44$ 0.1936

10. $r = 0.51$ 0.2601

11. $r = 0.97$ 0.9409

12. $r = 0.12$ 0.0144

13. $r = 0.15$ 0.0225

14. Define the standard error of the estimate for regression. When can the standard error of the estimate be used to construct a prediction interval about a value y'?

15. Compute the standard error of the estimate for Exercise 13 in Section 10–1. The regression line equation was found in Exercise 13 in Section 10–2. 629.49

16. Compute the standard error of the estimate for Exercise 14 in Section 10–1. The regression line equation was found in Exercise 14 in Section 10–2. 12.03* (TI value 12.06)

17. Compute the standard error of the estimate for Exercise 15 in Section 10–1. The regression line equation was found in Exercise 15 in Section 10–2. 94.22*

18. Compute the standard error of the estimate for Exercise 16 in Section 10–1. The regression line equation was found in Exercise 16 in Section 10–2. The standard error should not be calculated.

19. For the data in Exercises 13 in Sections 10–1 and 10–2 and 15 in Section 10–3, find the 90% prediction interval when $x = 200$ new releases. $365.82 < y < 2924.98$

20. For the data in Exercises 14 in Sections 10–1 and 10–2 and 16 in Section 10–3, find the 95% prediction interval when $x = 60$. $-0.64 < y < 62.04$ or $0 < y < 62$

21. For the data in Exercises 15 in Sections 10–1 and 10–2 and 17 in Section 10–3, find the 90% prediction interval when $x = 4$ years. $\$31.12 < y < \$471.72$

22. For the data in Exercises 16 in Sections 10–1 and 10–2 and 18 in Section 10–3, find the 98% prediction interval when $x = 47$ years. The prediction interval should not be calculated.

*Answers may vary due to rounding.

10–4 Multiple Regression (Optional)

OBJECTIVE

Be familiar with the concept of multiple regression.

The previous sections explained the concepts of simple linear regression and correlation. In simple linear regression, the regression equation contains one independent variable x and one dependent variable y' and is written as

$$y' = a + bx$$

where a is the y' intercept and b is the slope of the regression line.

In **multiple regression,** there are several independent variables and one dependent variable, and the equation is

$$y' = a + b_1x_1 + b_2x_2 + \cdots + b_kx_k$$

where $x_1, x_2, \ldots, x_k$ are the independent variables.

For example, suppose a nursing instructor wishes to see whether there is a relationship between a student's grade point average, age, and score on the state board nursing examination. The two independent variables are GPA (denoted by x_1) and age (denoted by x_2). The instructor will collect the data for all three variables for a sample of nursing students. Rather than conduct two separate simple regression studies, one using the GPA and state board scores and another using ages and state board scores, the instructor can conduct one study using multiple regression analysis with two independent variables—GPA and ages—and one dependent variable—state board scores.

A multiple regression correlation R can also be computed to determine if a significant relationship exists between the independent variables and the dependent variable. Multiple regression analysis is used when a statistician thinks there are several independent

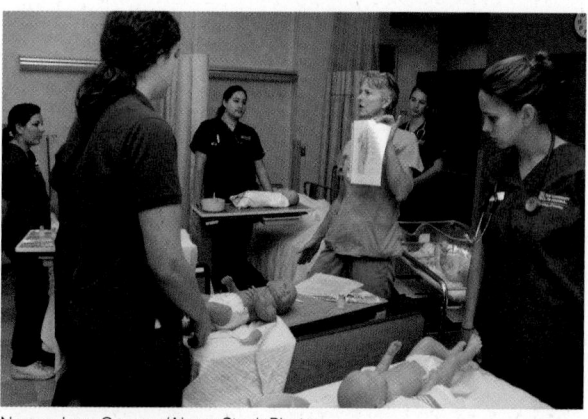

Norma Jean Gargasz/Alamy Stock Photo

variables contributing to the variation of the dependent variable. This analysis then can be used to increase the accuracy of predictions for the dependent variable over one independent variable alone.

Two other examples for multiple regression analysis are when a store manager wants to see whether the amount spent on advertising and the amount of floor space used for a display affect the amount of sales of a product, and when a sociologist wants to see whether the amount of time children spend watching television and playing video games is related to their weight. Multiple regression analysis can also be conducted by using more than two independent variables, denoted by $x_1, x_2, x_3, \ldots, x_k$. Since these computations are quite complicated and for the most part would be done on a computer, this chapter will show the computations for two independent variables only.

If a multiple regression equation fits the data well, it can be used to make predictions. For example, the nursing instructor wishes to see whether a student's grade point average and age are related to the student's score on the state board nursing examination. The instructor selects five students and obtains the following data.

Student	GPA, x_1	Age, x_2	State board score, y
A	3.2	22	550
B	2.7	27	570
C	2.5	24	525
D	3.4	28	670
E	2.2	23	490

The multiple regression equation obtained from the data using technology is

$$y' = -44.81 + 87.64x_1 + 14.533x_2$$

If a student has a GPA of 3.0 and is 25 years old, her predicted state board score can be computed by substituting these values in the equation for x_1 and x_2, respectively, as shown.

$$y' = -44.81 + 87.64(3.0) + 14.533(25)$$

$$= 581.44 \text{ or } 581$$

Hence, if a student has a GPA of 3.0 and is 25 years old, the student's predicted state board score is 581.

The Multiple Regression Equation

A multiple regression equation with two independent variables (x_1 and x_2) and one dependent variable has the form

$$y' = a + b_1x_1 + b_2x_2$$

A multiple regression equation with three independent variables (x_1, x_2, and x_3) and one dependent variable has the form

$$y' = a + b_1x_1 + b_2x_2 + b_3x_3$$

General Form of the Multiple Regression Equation

The general form of the multiple regression equation with k independent variables is

$$y' = a + b_1x_1 + b_2x_2 + \cdots + b_kx_k$$

The x's are the independent variables. The value for a is more or less an intercept, although a multiple regression equation with two independent variables constitutes a plane rather than a line. The b's are called *partial regression coefficients*. Each b represents the amount of change in y' for one unit of change in the corresponding x value when the other x values are held constant. In the example just shown, the regression equation was $y' = -44.81 + 87.64x_1 + 14.533x_2$. In this case, for each unit of change in the student's GPA, there is a change of 87.64 units in the state board score with the student's age x_2 being held constant. And for each unit of change in x_2 (the student's age), there is a change of 14.533 units in the state board score with the GPA held constant.

The assumptions for multiple regression are as follows.

Assumptions for Multiple Regression

The assumptions for multiple regression are similar to those for simple regression.

1. For any specific value of the independent variable, the values of the y variable are normally distributed. (This is called the *normality* assumption.)
2. The variances (or standard deviations) for the y variables are the same for each value of the independent variable. (This is called the *equal-variance* assumption.)
3. There is a linear relationship between the dependent variable and the independent variables. (This is called the *linearity* assumption.)
4. The independent variables are not correlated. (This is called the *nonmulticollinearity* assumption.)
5. The values for the y variables are independent. (This is called the *independence* assumption.)

Since these assumptions are somewhat difficult to verify, we will assume throughout this section that they are satisfied.

In multiple regression, as in simple regression, the strength of the relationship between the independent variables and the dependent variable is measured by a correlation coefficient. This **multiple correlation coefficient** is symbolized by R. The value of R can range from 0 to $+1$; R can never be negative. The closer to $+1$, the stronger the relationship; the closer to 0, the weaker the relationship. The value of R takes into account all the independent variables and can be computed by using the values of the individual correlation coefficients. The multiple correlation coefficient is always higher than the individual correlation coefficients. The formula for the multiple correlation coefficient when there are two independent variables is shown next.

Formula for the Multiple Correlation Coefficient

The formula for R is

$$R = \sqrt{\frac{r_{yx_1}^2 + r_{yx_2}^2 - 2r_{yx_1} \cdot r_{yx_2} \cdot r_{x_1x_2}}{1 - r_{x_1x_2}^2}}$$

where r_{yx_1} is the value of the correlation coefficient for variables y and x_1; r_{yx_2} is the value of the correlation coefficient for variables y and x_2; and $r_{x_1x_2}$ is the value of the correlation coefficient for variables x_1 and x_2.

In this case regarding the state board nursing examination scores, R is 0.989, as shown in Example 10–15. The multiple correlation coefficient is always higher than the individual correlation coefficients. For this specific example, the multiple correlation coefficient is higher than the two individual correlation coefficients computed by using grade point average and state board scores ($r_{yx_1} = 0.845$) or age and state board scores ($r_{yx_2} = 0.791$). *Note:* $r_{x_1x_1} = 0.371$.

EXAMPLE 10–15   State Board Scores

For the data regarding nursing state board scores, find the value of R.

SOLUTION

The values of the correlation coefficients are

$$r_{yx_1} = 0.845$$

$$r_{yx_2} = 0.791$$

$$r_{x_1x_2} = 0.371$$

Substituting in the formula, you get

$$R = \sqrt{\frac{r_{yx_1}^2 + r_{yx_2}^2 - 2r_{yx_1} \cdot r_{yx_2} \cdot r_{x_1x_2}}{1 - r_{x_1x_2}^2}}$$

$$= \sqrt{\frac{(0.845)^2 + (0.791)^2 - 2(0.845)(0.791)(0.371)}{1 - 0.371^2}}$$

$$= \sqrt{\frac{0.8437569}{0.862359}} = \sqrt{0.9784288} = 0.989$$

Hence, the correlation between a student's grade point average and age with the student's score on the nursing state board examination is 0.989. In this case, there is a strong relationship among the variables; the value of R is close to 1.00.

As with simple regression, R^2 is the **coefficient of multiple determination,** and it is the amount of variation explained by the regression model. The expression $1 - R^2$ represents the amount of unexplained variation, called the *error* or *residual variation.* In Example 10–15, since $R = 0.989$, $R^2 = 0.978$ and $1 - R^2 = 1 - 0.978 = 0.022$.

Testing the Significance of R

An F test is used to test the significance of R. The hypotheses are

$$H_0: \rho = 0 \qquad \text{and} \qquad H_1: \rho \neq 0$$

where ρ represents the population correlation coefficient for multiple correlation.

F Test for Significance of R

The formula for the F test is

$$F = \frac{R^2/k}{(1 - R^2)/(n - k - 1)}$$

where n is the number of data groups ($x_1, x_2, \ldots, y$) and k is the number of independent variables.

The degrees of freedom are d.f.N. $= n - k$ and d.f.D. $= n - k - 1$.

EXAMPLE 10-16   State Board Scores

Test the significance of the R obtained in Example 10-15 at $\alpha = 0.05$.

SOLUTION

$$F = \frac{R^2/k}{(1 - R^2)/(n - k - 1)}$$

$$= \frac{0.978/2}{(1 - 0.978)/(5 - 2 - 1)} = \frac{0.489}{0.011} = 44.45$$

The critical value obtained from Table A-7 with $\alpha = 0.05$, d.f.N. = 3, and d.f.D. = $5 - 2 - 1 = 2$ is 19.16. Hence, the decision is to reject the null hypothesis and conclude that there is a significant relationship among the student's GPA, age, and score on the nursing state board examination.

Adjusted R^2

Since the value of R^2 is dependent on n (the number of data pairs) and k (the number of variables), statisticians also calculate what is called an **adjusted R^2,** denoted by R^2_{adj}. This is based on the number of degrees of freedom.

Formula for the Adjusted R^2

The formula for the adjusted R^2 is

$$R^2_{adj} = 1 - \frac{(1 - R^2)(n - 1)}{n - k - 1}$$

The adjusted R^2 is smaller than R^2 and takes into account the fact that when n and k are approximately equal, the value of R may be artificially high, due to sampling error rather than a true relationship among the variables. This occurs because the chance variations of all the variables are used in conjunction with one another to derive the regression equation. Even if the individual correlation coefficients for each independent variable and the dependent variable were all zero, the multiple correlation coefficient due to sampling error could be higher than zero.

Hence, both R^2 and R^2_{adj} are usually reported in a multiple regression analysis.

EXAMPLE 10-17   State Board Scores

Calculate the adjusted R^2 for the data in Example 10-15. The value for R is 0.989.

SOLUTION

$$R^2_{adj} = 1 - \frac{(1 - R^2)(n - 1)}{n - k - 1}$$

$$= 1 - \frac{(1 - 0.989^2)(5 - 1)}{5 - 2 - 1}$$

$$= 1 - 0.043758$$

$$= 0.956$$

In this case, when the number of data pairs and the number of independent variables are accounted for, the adjusted multiple coefficient of determination is 0.956.

☰ Applying the Concepts **10–4**

More Math Means More Money

In a study to determine a person's yearly income 10 years after high school, it was found that the two biggest predictors are number of math and science courses taken and number of hours worked per week during a person's senior year of high school. The multiple regression equation generated from a sample of 20 individuals is

$$y' = 6000 + 4540x_1 + 1290x_2$$

Let x_1 represent the number of math and science courses taken and x_2 represent hours worked during senior year. The correlation between income and math and science courses is 0.63. The correlation between income and hours worked is 0.84, and the correlation between math and science courses and hours worked is 0.31. Use this information to answer the following questions.

1. What is the dependent variable?
2. What are the independent variables?
3. What are the multiple regression assumptions?
4. Explain what 4540 and 1290 in the equation tell us.
5. What is the predicted income if a person took 8 math and science classes and worked 20 hours per week during their senior year in high school?
6. What does a multiple correlation coefficient of 0.926 mean?
7. Compute R^2.
8. Compute the adjusted R^2.
9. Would the equation be considered a good predictor of income?
10. What are your conclusions about the relationship among courses taken, hours worked, and yearly income?

See page 612 for the answers.

☰ Exercises **10–4**

1. Explain the similarities and differences between simple linear regression and multiple regression.

2. What is the general form of the multiple regression equation? What does a represent? What do the b's represent? $y' = a + b_1x_1 + b_2x_2 + \cdots + b_kx_k$; a is the y-intercept and the b's are the partial regression coefficients.

3. Why would a researcher prefer to conduct a multiple regression study rather than separate regression studies using one independent variable and the dependent variable? The relationship would include all variables in one equation.

4. What are the assumptions for multiple regression? Normality, equal variance, linearity, nonmulticollinearity, and independence

5. How do the values of the individual correlation coefficients compare to the value of the multiple correlation coefficient? They will all be smaller.

6. **Age, GPA, and Income** A researcher has determined that a significant relationship exists among an employee's age x_1, grade point average x_2, and income y. The multiple regression equation is

$y' = -34,127 + 132x_1 + 20,805x_2$. Predict the income of a person who is 32 years old and has a GPA of 3.4. $40,834

7. **Nursing Home Satisfaction** A researcher found that there are relationships between nursing home satisfaction and the age of the patient and their physical health. Nursing home satisfaction is measured on a scale of 1 to 10, with 10 being the highest satisfaction. Physical health is measured in a scale of 1 to 10 and is based on the patient's own evaluation of their physical health. The multiple regression equation is $y' = 0.217 + 0.0654x_1 + 0.32x_2$, where x_1 is the patient's age and x_2 is the person's physical health. Find a person's satisfaction if their age is 72 and their physical health is 8. 7.5

8. **Special Occasion Cakes** A pastry chef who specializes in special occasion cakes uses the following equation to help calculate the price of a cake: $y = -26.279 + 14.855x_1 + 3.1035x_2 + 0.73079x_3$, where x_1 is the number of layers desired, x_2 the number of servings needed, and x_3 the amount of filling mix used. Calculate the price of a three-layer cake using 40 ounces of filling to serve 48 people. $196.49

9. **Aspects of Students' Academic Behavior** A college statistics professor is interested in the relationship among various aspects of students' academic behavior and their final grade in the class. The professor found a significant relationship between the number of hours spent studying statistics per week, the number of classes attended per semester, the number of assignments turned in during the semester, and the student's final grade. This relationship is described by the multiple regression equation $y' = -14.9 + 0.93359x_1 + 0.99847x_2 + 5.3844x_3$. Predict the final grade for a student who studies statistics 8 hours per week (x_1), attends 34 classes (x_2), and turns in 11 assignments (x_3). 85.75 (grade) or 86

10. **Age, Cholesterol, and Sodium** A medical researcher found a significant relationship among a person's age x_1, cholesterol level x_2, sodium level of the blood x_3, and systolic blood pressure y. The regression equation is $y' = 97.7 + 0.691x_1 + 219x_2 - 299x_3$. Predict the systolic blood pressure of a person who is 35 years old and has a cholesterol level of 194 milligrams per deciliter (mg/dl) and a sodium blood level of 142 milliequivalents per liter (mEq/l). 149.885 or 150

11. Explain the meaning of the multiple correlation coefficient R.

12. What is the range of values R can assume? 0 to 1

13. Define R^2 and R^2_{adj}. R^2 is the coefficient of multiple determination. R^2_{adj} is adjusted for sample size and number of predictors.

14. What are the hypotheses used to test the significance of R? $H_0: \rho = 0$ and $H_1: \rho \neq 0$

15. What test is used to test the significance of R? F test

16. What is the meaning of the adjusted R^2? Why is it computed?

≡ Technology | Step by Step

TI-84 Plus
Step by Step

The TI-84 Plus does not have a built-in function for multiple regression. However, the downloadable program named MULREG is available in your online resources. Follow the instructions online for downloading the program.

Finding a Multiple Regression Equation

1. Press **2nd [X$_{-1}$]** for **MATRIX** and move the cursor to Edit; then press **ENTER**.

2. Enter the number of rows and columns. The number of rows would be the sample size and then number of columns is the number of variables including the dependent variable. Then press **ENTER**.

3. Enter the data into matrix [A]. Make sure the dependent variable is in the last column.

4. Press **PRGM,** move the cursor to the program named MULREG, and press **ENTER** twice.

5. Type the number of variables and press **ENTER**.

6. Type the sample size and press **ENTER**.

7. The program will store the regression coefficients in matrix [D] and display the adjusted R^2, the F test statistic, P-value, and standard error of estimate.

8. To see the coefficients, press **2nd [X$_{-1}$]** for **MATRIX** and move the cursor to Edit; then press 4: [D].

Find the multiple regression equation for these data used in this section:

Student	GPA, x_1	Age, x_2	State board score, y
A	3.2	22	550
B	2.7	27	570
C	2.5	24	525
D	3.4	28	670
E	2.2	23	490

```
MATRIX[A]  5 ×3
[ 3.2   22   550 ]
[ 2.7   27   570 ]
[ 2.5   24   525 ]
[ 3.4   28   670 ]
[ 2.2   23   490 ]
```

```
PrgmMULREG
How many
columns?
?3
What is the
sample size?
How many rows?
?5
```

```
Coef. stored
in matrix [D].
          Done

adjR^2=.9574
F-test=45.9289
p-value=.0213
s=14.0091
```

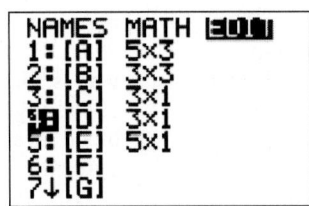 

EXCEL

Step by Step

Multiple Regression

These instructions use data from the nursing examination example discussed at the beginning of Section 10–4.

1. Enter the data from the example into four separate columns of a new worksheet—student in cells A2:A6, GPA in cells B2:B6, age in cells C2:C6, and score in cells D2:D6. Labels can be typed into the first cells of each column.

	A	B	C	D
1	Student	GPA	Age	y
2	A	3.2	22	550
3	B	2.7	27	570
4	C	2.5	24	525
5	D	3.4	28	670
6	E	2.2	23	490

2. Select the Data tab on the toolbar, then **Data Analysis>Regression.**

3. In the Regression dialog box, type D1:D6 for the input Y Range and type B1:C6 for the Input X Range. Check the Labels option if you include labels in the worksheet.

4. Select the Output Range and type in F1, click OK.

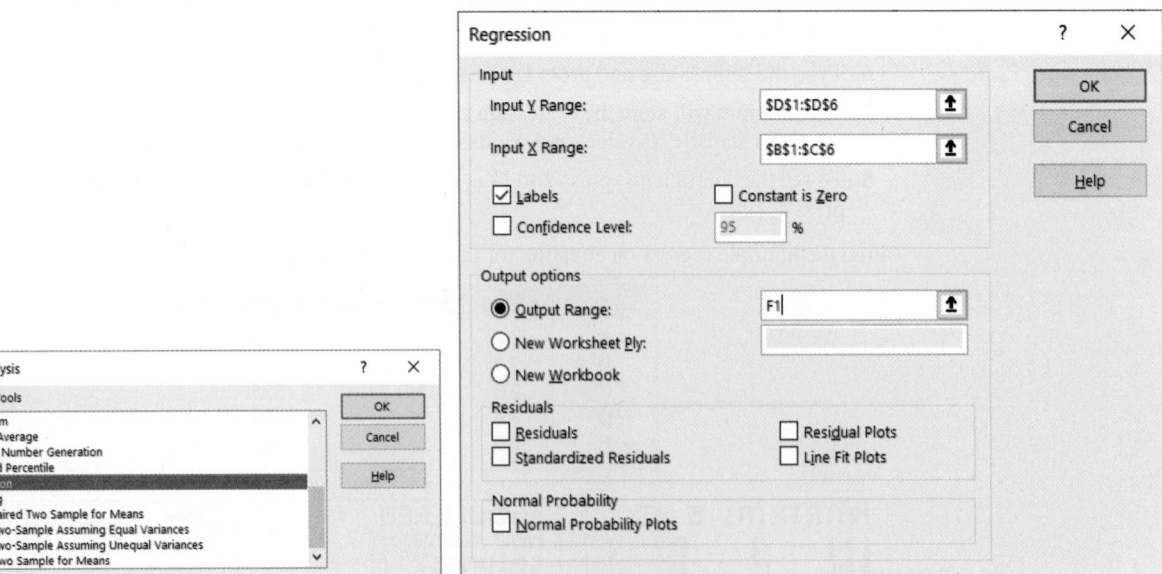

5. To expand the Regression Output to accommodate the decimal places, highlight the output, then select the Home tab, and choose Format>AutoFit Column Width.

	F	G	H	I	J	K	L	M	N
	SUMMARY OUTPUT								
	Regression Statistics								
	Multiple R	0.989288203							
	R Square	0.978691148							
	Adjusted R Square	0.957382297							
	Standard Error	14.00908721							
	Observations	5							
	ANOVA								
		df	*SS*	*MS*	*F*	*Significance F*			
	Regression	2	18027.49095	9013.745475	45.92885435	0.021308852			
	Residual	2	392.5090492	196.2545246					
	Total	4	18420						
		Coefficients	*Standard Error*	*t Stat*	*P-value*	*Lower 95%*	*Upper 95%*	*Lower 95.0%*	*Upper 95.0%*
	Intercept	-44.81018805	69.24686663	-0.647107808	0.583915745	-342.7554078	253.1350317	-342.7554078	253.1350317
	GPA	87.64015185	15.23718666	5.751727913	0.028922601	22.07982905	153.2004746	22.07982905	153.2004746
	Age	14.53297431	2.913737536	4.987743106	0.037924877	1.996173545	27.06977507	1.996173545	27.06977507

MINITAB
Step by Step

Multiple Regression

In Example 10–15, is there a correlation between a student's score and their age and grade point average?

1. Enter the data for the example into three columns of MINITAB. Do not enter the student's letter. Name the columns **GPA, AGE,** and **SCORE.**

2. Select **Stat>Regression>Regression>Fit Regression Model.**

3. Move the cursor into the Responses box. Double-click on C3 SCORE, the response variable.

4. Move the cursor into the Continuous predictors box. Double-click C1 GPA, then C2 AGE.

5. Click on [Storage].

   a) Check the box for Fits.

   b) Check the box for Residuals.

6. Click [OK] twice.

↓	C1	C2	C3
	GPA	Age	Score
1	3.2	22	550
2	2.7	27	570
3	2.5	24	525
4	3.4	28	670
5	2.2	23	490

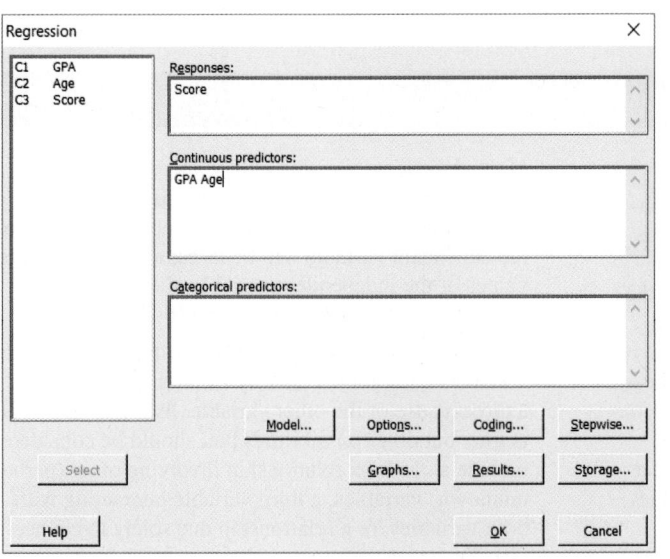

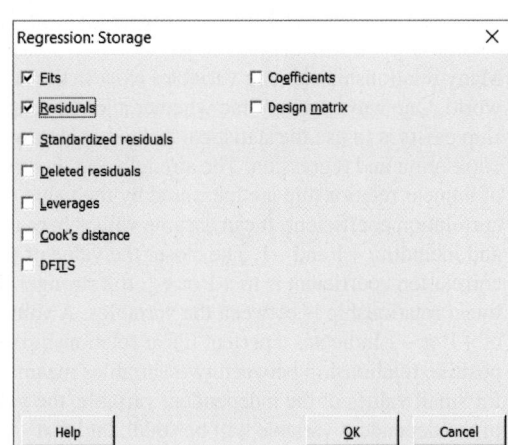

The output for the regression appears in the Session window and the residuals are stored in the Worksheet window.

Regression Analysis: Score versus GPA, Age

Analysis of Variance

Source	DF	Adj SS	Adj MS	F-Value	P-Value
Regression	2	18027.5	9013.7	45.93	0.021
GPA	1	6492.6	6492.6	33.08	0.029
Age	1	4882.3	4882.3	24.88	0.038
Error	2	392.5	196.3		
Total	4	18420.0			

Model Summary

S	R-sq	R-sq(adj)	R-sq(pred)
14.0091	97.87%	95.74%	63.72%

Coefficients

Term	Coef	SE Coef	T-Value	P-Value	VIF
Constant	-44.8	69.2	-0.65	0.584	
GPA	87.6	15.2	5.75	0.029	1.16
Age	14.53	2.91	4.99	0.038	1.16

Regression Equation

Score = -44.8 + 87.6 GPA + 14.53 Age

+	C1	C2	C3	C4	C5
	GPA	Age	Score	FITS1	RESI1
1	3.2	22	550	555.364	-5.3637
2	2.7	27	570	584.209	-14.2085
3	2.5	24	525	523.082	1.9184
4	3.4	28	670	660.090	9.9104
5	2.2	23	490	482.257	7.7434

The test statistic and P-value are 45.93 and 0.021, respectively. Since the P-value is less than α, reject the null hypothesis. There is enough evidence in the sample to conclude the scores are related to age and grade point average.

Summary

- Many relationships among variables exist in the real world. One way to determine whether a linear relationship exists is to use the statistical techniques known as correlation and regression. The strength and direction of a linear relationship are measured by the value of the correlation coefficient. It can assume values between and including +1 and −1. The closer the value of the correlation coefficient is to +1 or −1, the stronger the linear relationship is between the variables. A value of +1 or −1 indicates a perfect linear relationship. A positive relationship between two variables means that for small values of the independent variable, the values of the dependent variable will be small; and that for large values of the independent variable, the values of the dependent variable will be large. A negative relationship between two variables means that for small values of the independent variable, the values of the dependent variable will be large; and that for large values of the independent variable, the values of the dependent variable will be small. (10–1)

- Remember that a significant relationship between two variables does not necessarily mean that one variable is a direct cause of the other variable. In some cases this is true, but other possibilities that should be considered include a complex relationship involving other (perhaps unknown) variables, a third variable interacting with both variables, or a relationship due solely to chance. (10–1)

- Relationships can be linear or curvilinear. To determine the shape, you draw a scatter plot of the variables. If the relationship is linear, the data can be approximated by a straight line, called the *least-squares regression line,* or the *line of best fit.* The closer the value of r is to +1 or −1, the more closely the points will fit the line. (10–2)

- A residual plot can be used to determine if the regression line equation can be used for predictions. (10–3)

- The coefficient of determination is a better indicator of the strength of a linear relationship than the correlation coefficient. It is better because it identifies the percentage of variation of the dependent variable that is directly attributable to the variation of the independent variable. The coefficient of determination is obtained by squaring the correlation coefficient and converting the result to a percentage. (10–3)

- Another statistic used in correlation and regression is the standard error of the estimate, which is an estimate of the standard deviation of the y values about the predicted y′ values. The standard error of the estimate can be used to construct a prediction interval about a specific value point estimate y′ of the mean of the y values for a given value of x. (10–3)

- In addition, relationships can be multiple. That is, there can be two or more independent variables and one dependent variable. A coefficient of correlation and a regression equation can be found for multiple relationships, just as they can be found for simple relationships. (10–4)

Important Terms

Important Formulas

Formula for the correlation coefficient:

$$r = \frac{n(\Sigma xy) - (\Sigma x)(\Sigma y)}{\sqrt{[n(\Sigma x^2) - (\Sigma x)^2][n(\Sigma y^2) - (\Sigma y)^2]}}$$

Formula for the t test for the correlation coefficient:

$$t = r\sqrt{\frac{n-2}{1-r^2}} \qquad \text{d.f.} = n - 2$$

The regression line equation:

$$y' = a + bx$$

where

$$a = \frac{(\Sigma y)(\Sigma x^2) - (\Sigma x)(\Sigma xy)}{n(\Sigma x^2) - (\Sigma x)^2}$$

$$b = \frac{n(\Sigma xy) - (\Sigma x)(\Sigma y)}{n(\Sigma x^2) - (\Sigma x)^2}$$

Formula for the standard error of the estimate:

$$s_{est} = \sqrt{\frac{\Sigma(y - y')^2}{n-2}}$$

or

$$s_{est} = \sqrt{\frac{\Sigma y^2 - a\Sigma y - b\Sigma xy}{n-2}}$$

Formula for the prediction interval for a value y′:

$$y' - t_{\alpha/2}s_{est}\sqrt{1 + \frac{1}{n} + \frac{n(x - \overline{X})^2}{n\Sigma x^2 - (\Sigma x)^2}} < y$$

$$< y' + t_{\alpha/2}s_{est}\sqrt{1 + \frac{1}{n} + \frac{n(x - \overline{X})^2}{n\Sigma x^2 - (\Sigma x)^2}}$$

$$\text{d.f.} = n - 2$$

Formula for the multiple correlation coefficient:

$$R = \sqrt{\frac{r_{yx_1}^2 + r_{yx_2}^2 - 2r_{yx_1} \cdot r_{yx_2} \cdot r_{x_1x_2}}{1 - r_{x_1x_2}^2}}$$

Formula for the F test for the multiple correlation coefficient:

$$F = \frac{R^2/k}{(1 - R^2)/(n - k - 1)}$$

with d.f.N. = n − k and d.f.D. = n − k − 1.

Formula for the adjusted R^2:

$$R_{adj}^2 = 1 - \frac{(1 - R^2)(n - 1)}{n - k - 1}$$

Review Exercises

For Exercises 1 through 7, do a complete regression analysis by performing the following steps.

    a. Draw the scatter plot.

    b. Compute the value of the correlation coefficient.

    c. Test the significance of the correlation coefficient at $\alpha = 0.01$, using Table A–8 or the *P*-value method.

    d. Determine the regression line equation if *r* is significant.

    e. Plot the regression line on the scatter plot, if appropriate.

    f. Predict *y'* for a specific value of *x*, if appropriate.

Sections 10–1 and 10–2

1. **Customer Satisfaction and Purchases** At a large department store customers were asked to rate the service and the materials purchased on a scale from 1 to 10, with 10 being the highest rating. Then the amount that they spent was recorded. Is there evidence of a relationship between the rating and the amount that they spent?

Rating, *x*	6	8	2	9	1	5
Amount spent, *y*	\$90	\$83	\$42	\$110	\$27	\$31

2. **Deaths from Lightning** NOAA keeps track of not only deaths from lightning each year but also the circumstances under which those deaths occur. Listed below are the number of deaths from lightning other than when standing under a tree and the number that occurred when the victim was under a tree, for a random selection of years. Is there a linear relationship between the variables?

Death under a tree	8	5	13	6	11	9	6
Other types of deaths	21	29	34	36	40	37	26

Find *y'* when *x* = 10.

Source: Noaa.gov

3. **Puppy Cuteness and Cost** A researcher feels that a pet store bases the cost of puppies on the cuteness of the animals. Eight puppies were rated on their cuteness. The ratings were from 1 to 6, with 6 being the highest rating. The ratings and the cost in dollars of the puppies are shown. Is there a significant relationship between the variables?

Rating	6	2	1	4	5	2	3	4
Cost	\$80	\$42	\$27	\$64	\$50	\$39	\$18	\$44

4. **Driver's Age and Accidents** A study is conducted to determine the relationship between a driver's age and the number of accidents the driver had over a 1-year period. The data are shown here. (This information will be used for Exercise 8.) If there is a significant relationship, predict the number of accidents of a driver who is 28.

Driver's age, *x*	16	24	18	17	23	27	32
No. of accidents, *y*	3	2	5	2	0	1	1

5. **Typing Speed and Word Processing** A researcher desires to know whether the typing speed of a secretary (in words per minute) is related to the time (in hours) that it takes the secretary to learn to use a new word processing program. The data are shown.

Speed, *x*	48	74	52	79	83	56	85	63	88	74	90	92
Time, *y*	7	4	8	3.5	2	6	2.3	5	2.1	4.5	1.9	1.5

If there is a significant relationship, predict the time it will take the average secretary who has a typing speed of 72 words per minute to learn the word processing program. (This information will be used for Exercises 9 and 11.)

6. **Protein and Diastolic Blood Pressure** A study was conducted with vegetarians to see whether the number of grams of protein each ate per day was related to diastolic blood pressure. The data are given here. If there is a significant relationship, predict the diastolic pressure of a vegetarian who consumes 8 grams of protein per day. (This information will be used for Exercises 10 and 12.)

Grams, *x*	4	6.5	5	5.5	8	10	9	8.2	10.5
Pressure, *y*	73	79	83	82	84	92	88	86	95

7. **Internet Use and Isolation** A researcher wishes to see if there is a relationship between Internet use by high school students and isolation of the students. Internet use is measured by the number of hours per week that the students spend on the computer. Isolation is measured by having the students complete a questionnaire. The questionnaire score ranges from 20 to 50, with 50 being the most isolated students. The data are shown. Is there a significant relationship between the variables?

Internet use	32	15	23	8	12
Isolation score	45	37	22	15	39

Section 10–3

8. For Exercise 4, find the standard error of the estimate. 1.417* For calculation purposes only. No regression should be done.

9. For Exercise 5, find the standard error of the estimate. 0.513*

10. For Exercise 6, find the standard error of the estimate. 2.845*

11. For Exercise 5, find the 90% prediction interval for time when the speed is 72 words per minute. $3.24 < y < 5.18$

12. For Exercise 6, find the 95% prediction interval for pressure when the number of grams is 8. $79.11 < y < 93.35$

Section 10–4

13. **(Opt.)** A study found a significant relationship among a person's years of experience on a particular job x_1,

the number of workdays missed per month x_2, and the person's age y. The regression equation is $y' = 12.8 + 2.09x_1 + 0.423x_2$. Predict a person's age if they have been employed for 4 years and have missed 2 workdays a month. 22.01*

14. **(Opt.)** Find R when $r_{yx_1} = 0.681$ and $r_{yx_2} = 0.872$ and $r_{x_1x_2} = 0.746$. $R = 0.873$

15. **(Opt.)** Find R^2_{adj} when $R = 0.873$, $n = 10$, and $k = 3$. $R^2_{adj} = 0.643*$

*Answers may vary due to rounding.

▤ STATISTICS TODAY

Can Temperature Predict Homicides? —Revisited

In this situation, the average temperature for each month was correlated with the total homicides for that month. It was found that $r = 0.836$, which is significant at $\alpha = 0.05$. The critical values are ±0.576 for 10 degrees of freedom. This means that there is a significant relationship between the average monthly temperatures and the total monthly homicides in the city. Since $r^2 = 0.698$, approximately 69.8% of the variation in the number of homicides is explained by the variation in the monthly temperatures.

Can we conclude that an increase in temperature causes an increase in the number of homicides? No. There are other factors to consider. First, the sample was not random; however, it seems to be, for the most part, representative. Second, even though other studies have found similar results, researchers believe that when the weather warms (up to a certain temperature), more people are outside and there are more personal interactions among the groups of people, thus contributing to an increased homicide rate. Finally, the city selected has a large number of warm-weather tourists, and this means more people, which could also influence the homicide rates. Other similar studies have been done over the last 30 years, and similar results were obtained.

▤ Data Analysis

The Data Bank is found in Appendix B.

1. From the Data Bank, choose two variables that might be related: for example, IQ and educational level; age and cholesterol level; exercise and weight; or weight and systolic pressure. Do a complete correlation and regression analysis by performing the following steps. Select a random sample of at least 10 subjects.

   a. Draw a scatter plot.
   b. Compute the correlation coefficient.
   c. Test the hypothesis H_0: $\rho = 0$.

   d. Find the regression line equation if r is significant.
   e. Summarize the results.

2. Repeat Exercise 1, using samples of values of 10 or more obtained from Data Set V in Appendix B. Let $x =$ the number of suspensions and $y =$ the enrollment size.

3. Repeat Exercise 1, using samples of 10 or more values obtained from Data Set XIII. Let $x =$ the number of beds and $y =$ the number of personnel employed.

▤ Chapter Quiz

Determine whether each statement is true or false. If the statement is false, explain why.

1. A negative relationship between two variables means that for the most part, as the x variable increases, the y variable increases. False

2. A correlation coefficient of −1 implies a perfect linear relationship between the variables. True

3. Even if the correlation coefficient is high (near +1) or low (near −1), it may not be significant. True

4. When the correlation coefficient is significant, you can assume x causes y. False

5. It is not possible to have a significant correlation by chance alone. False

6. In multiple regression, there are several dependent variables and one independent variable. False

Select the best answer.

7. The strength of the linear relationship between two quantitative variables is determined by the value of

    a. r *c.* x

    b. a *d.* s_{est}

8. To test the significance of r, a(n) _____ test is used.

    a. t *c.* χ^2

    b. F *d.* None of the above

9. The test of significance for r has _____ degrees of freedom.

    a. 1   *c.* $n-1$

    b. n *d.* $n-2$

10. The equation of the regression line used in statistics is

    a. $x = a + by$ *c.* $y' = a + bx$

    b. $y = bx + a$ *d.* $x = ay + b$

11. The coefficient of determination is

    a. r *c.* a

    b. r^2 *d.* b

Complete the following statements with the best answer.

12. A statistical graph of two quantitative variables is called a(n) _____. Scatter plot

13. The x variable is called the _____ variable. Independent

14. The range of r is from _____ to _____. $-1, +1$

15. The sign of r and _____ will always be the same. b (slope)

16. The regression line is called the _____. Line of best fit

17. If all the points fall on a straight line, the value of r will be _____ or _____. $+1, -1$

For Exercises 18 through 21, do a complete regression analysis.

    a. Draw the scatter plot.

    b. Compute the value of the correlation coefficient.

    c. Test the significance of the correlation coefficient at $\alpha = 0.05$.

    d. Determine the regression line equation if r is significant.

    e. Plot the regression line on the scatter plot if appropriate.

    f. Predict y' for a specific value of x if appropriate.

18. Prescription Drug Prices A medical researcher wants to determine the relationship between the price per dose of prescription drugs in the United States and the price of the same dose in Australia. The data are shown. Describe the relationship.

U.S. price, x	3.31	3.16	2.27	3.13	2.54	1.98	2.22
Australian price, y	1.29	1.75	0.82	0.83	1.32	0.84	0.82

19. Age and Driving Accidents A study is conducted to determine the relationship between a driver's age and the number of accidents the driver has over a 1-year period. The data are shown here. If there is a significant relationship, predict the number of accidents of a driver who is 64.

Driver's age, x	63	65	60	62	66	67	59
No. of accidents, y	2	3	1	0	3	1	4

20. Age and Cavities A researcher desires to know if the age of a child is related to the number of cavities the child has. The data are shown here. If there is a significant relationship, predict the number of cavities for a child of 11.

Age of child, x	6	8	9	10	12	14
No. of cavities, y	2	1	3	4	6	5

21. Fat and Cholesterol A study is conducted with a group of dieters to see if the number of grams of fat each consumes per day is related to cholesterol level. The data are shown here. If there is a significant relationship, predict the cholesterol level of a dieter who consumes 8.5 grams of fat per day.

Fat grams, x	6.8	5.5	8.2	10	8.6	9.1	8.6	10.4
Cholesterol level, y	183	201	193	283	222	250	190	218

22. For Exercise 20, find the standard error of the estimate. 1.129*

23. For Exercise 21, find the standard error of the estimate. 29.5* For calculation purposes only. No regression should be done.

24. For Exercise 20, find the 90% prediction interval of the number of cavities for a 7-year-old. $0 < y < 5$

25. For Exercise 21, find the 95% prediction interval of the cholesterol level of a person who consumes 10 grams of fat. 217.5 (average of y values is used since there is no significant relationship)

26. (Opt.) A study was conducted, and a significant relationship was found among the number of hours a teenager watches television per day x_1, the number of hours the teenager talks on the telephone per day x_2, and the teenager's weight y. The regression equation is $y' = 98.7 + 3.82x_1 + 6.51x_2$. Predict a teenager's weight if she averages 3 hours of TV and 1.5 hours on the phone per day. 119.9*

27. (Opt.) Find R when $r_{yx_1} = 0.561$ and $r_{yx_2} = 0.714$ and $r_{x_1x_2} = 0.625$. $R = 0.729$*

28. (Opt.) Find R^2_{adj} when $R = 0.774$, $n = 8$, and $k = 2$. $R^2_{adj} = 0.439$*

*These answers may vary due to the method of calculation or rounding.

Critical Thinking Challenges

Product Sales When the points in a scatter plot show a curvilinear trend rather than a linear trend, statisticians have methods of fitting curves rather than straight lines to the data, thus obtaining a better fit and a better prediction model. One type of curve that can be used is the logarithmic regression curve. The data shown are the number of items of a new product sold over a period of 15 months at a certain store. Notice that sales rise during the beginning months and then level off later on.

Month, x	1	3	6	8	10	12	15
No. of items sold, y	10	12	15	19	20	21	21

1. Draw the scatter plot for the data.
2. Find the equation of the regression line.
3. Describe how the line fits the data.
4. Using the log key on your calculator, transform the x values into log x values.
5. Using the log x values instead of the x values, find the equation of a and b for the regression line.
6. Next, plot the curve $y = a + b \log x$ on the graph.
7. Compare the line $y = a + bx$ with the curve $y = a + b \log x$ and decide which one fits the data better.
8. Compute r, using the x and y values; then compute r, using the log x and y values. Which is higher?
9. In your opinion, which (the line or the logarithmic curve) would be a better predictor for the data? Why?

Data Projects

Use a significance level of 0.05 for all tests below.

1. **Business and Finance** Use the stocks in data project 1 of Chapter 2 identified as the Dow Jones Industrials as the sample. For each, note the current price and the amount of the last year's dividends. Are the two variables linearly related? How much variability in amount of dividend is explained by the price?

2. **Sports and Leisure** For each team in major league baseball note the number of wins the team had last year and the number of home runs by its best home run hitter. Is the number of wins linearly related to the number of home runs hit? How much variability in total wins is explained by home runs hit? Write a regression equation to determine how many wins you would expect a team to have, knowing its top home run output.

3. **Technology** Use the data collected in data project 3 of Chapter 2 for this problem. For the data set note the length of the song and the year it was released. Is there a linear relationship between the length of a song and the year it was released? Is the sign on the correlation coefficient positive or negative? What does the sign on the coefficient indicate about the relationship?

4. **Health and Wellness** Use a fast-food restaurant to compile your data. For each menu item note its fat grams and its total calories. Is there a linear relationship between the two variables? How much variance in total calories is explained by fat grams? Write a regression equation to determine how many total calories you would expect in an item, knowing its fat grams.

5. **Politics and Economics** For each state find its average SAT Math score, SAT English score, and average household income. Which has the strongest linear relationship, SAT Math and SAT English, SAT Math and income, or SAT English and income?

6. **Your Class** Use the data collected in data project 6 of Chapter 2 regarding heart rates. Is there a linear relationship between the heart rates before and after exercise? How much of the variability in heart rate after exercise is explained by heart rate before exercise? Write a regression equation to determine what heart rate after exercise you would expect for a person, given the person's heart rate before exercise.

Answers to Applying the Concepts

Section 10–1   Stopping Distances

1. The independent variable is miles per hour (mph).

2. The dependent variable is braking distance (feet).

3. Miles per hour is a continuous quantitative variable.

4. Braking distance is a continuous quantitative variable.

5. A scatter plot of the data is shown.

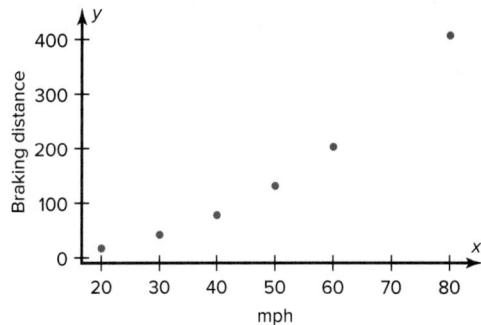

Scatter plot of braking distance vs. mph

6. There might be a linear relationship between the two variables, but there is a bit of a curve in the plot.

7. Changing the distances between the mph increments will change the appearance of the relationship.

8. There is a positive relationship between the two variables—higher speeds are associated with longer braking distances.

9. The strong relationship between the two variables suggests that braking distance can be accurately predicted from mph. We might still have some concern about the curve in the plot.

10. Answers will vary. Some other variables that might affect braking distance include road conditions, driver response time, and condition of the brakes.

11. The correlation coefficient is $r = 0.966$.

12. The value for $r = 0.966$ is significant at $\alpha = 0.05$. This confirms the strong positive relationship between the variables.

Section 10–2   Stopping Distances Revisited

1. The linear regression equation is
$y' = -151.900 + 6.451x$

2. The slope says that for each additional mile per hour a car is traveling, we expect the stopping distance to increase by 6.45 feet, on average. The y intercept is the braking distance we would expect for a car traveling 0 mph—this is meaningless in this context, but is an important part of the model.

3. $y' = -151.900 + 6.451(45) = 138.4$ The braking distance for a car traveling 45 mph is approximately 138 feet.

4. $y' = -151.900 + 6.451(100) = 493.2$ The braking distance for a car traveling 100 mph is approximately 493 feet.

5. It is not appropriate to make predictions of braking distance for speeds outside of the given data values (for example, the 100 mph in the previous problem) because we know nothing about the relationship between the two variables outside of the range of the data.

Section 10–3   Interpreting Simple Linear Regression

1. Both variables are moving in the same direction. In other words, the two variables are positively associated. This is so because the correlation coefficient is positive.

2. The unexplained variation of 3026.49 measures the distances from the prediction line to the actual values.

3. The slope of the regression line is 0.725983.

4. The y intercept is 16.5523.

5. The critical value of 0.378419 can be found in a table.

6. The allowable risk of making a type I error is 0.10, the level of significance.

7. The variation explained by the regression is 0.631319, or about 63.1%.

8. The average scatter of points about the regression line is 12.9668, the standard error of the estimate.

9. The null hypothesis is that there is no correlation, $H_0: \rho = 0$.

10. We compare the test statistic of 0.794556 to the critical value to see if the null hypothesis should be rejected.

11. Since $0.794556 > 0.378419$, we reject the null hypothesis and find that there is enough evidence to conclude that the correlation is not equal to zero.

Section 10–4   More Math Means More Money

1. The dependent variable is yearly income 10 years after high school.

2. The independent variables are number of math and science courses taken and number of hours worked per week during the senior year of high school.

3. Multiple regression assumes that the independent variables are not highly correlated, and also assumes normality, equal variances, and nonmulticollinearity.

4. We expect a person's yearly income 10 years after high school to be $4540 more, on average, for each additional math or science course taken, all other variables held constant. We expect a person's yearly income 10 years after high school to be $1290 more, on average, for each additional hour worked per week during the senior year of high school, all other variables held constant.

5. $y' = 6000 + 4540(8) + 1290(20) = 68,120$. The predicted yearly income 10 years after high school is $68,120.

6. The multiple correlation coefficient of 0.926 means that there is a fairly strong positive relationship between the independent variables (number of math and science courses and hours worked during senior year of high school) and the dependent variable (yearly income 10 years after high school).

7. $R^2 = (0.926)^2 = 0.857$

8. $R_{adj}^2 = 1 - \dfrac{(1 - R^2)(n - 1)}{n - k - 1}$

$= 1 - \dfrac{(1 - 0.857)(20 - 1)}{20 - 2 - 1}$

$= 1 - \dfrac{(0.143)(19)}{17} = 0.840$

9. The equation appears to be a fairly good predictor of income, since 84% of the variation in yearly income 10 years after high school is explained by the regression model.

10. Answers will vary. One possible answer is that yearly income 10 years after high school increases with more math and science classes and more hours of work during the senior year of high school. The number of math and science classes has a higher coefficient, so more math and science does mean more money!

Other Chi-Square Tests

Mitch Hrdlicka/Photodisc/Getty Images

≜ STATISTICS TODAY

Statistics and Heredity

An Austrian monk, Gregor Mendel (1822–1884), studied genetics, and his principles are the foundation for modern genetics. Mendel used his spare time to grow a variety of peas at the monastery. One of his many experiments involved crossbreeding peas that had smooth yellow seeds with peas that had wrinkled green seeds. He noticed that the results occurred with regularity. That is, some of the offspring had smooth yellow seeds, some had smooth green seeds, some had wrinkled yellow seeds, and some had wrinkled green seeds. Furthermore, after several experiments, the percentages of each type seemed to remain approximately the same. Mendel formulated his theory based on the assumption of dominant and recessive traits and tried to predict the results. He then crossbred his peas and examined 556 seeds over the next generation.

Finally, he compared the actual results with the theoretical results to see if his theory was correct. To do this, he used a "simple" chi-square test, which is explained in this chapter. See Statistics Today—Revisited at the end of this chapter.

OUTLINE

OBJECTIVES

After completing this chapter, you should be able to:

1 Test a distribution for goodness of fit, using chi-square.

2 Test two variables for independence, using chi-square.

3 Test proportions for homogeneity, using chi-square.

Introduction

The chi-square distribution was used in Chapters 7 and 8 to find a confidence interval for a variance or standard deviation and to test a hypothesis about a single variance or standard deviation.

It can also be used for tests concerning *frequency distributions,* such as "If a sample of buyers is given a choice of automobile colors, will each color be selected with the same frequency?" The chi-square distribution can be used to test the *independence* of two variables, for example, "Are senators' opinions on gun control independent of party affiliations?" That is, do the Republicans feel one way and the Democrats feel differently, or do they have the same opinion?

Finally, the chi-square distribution can be used to test the *homogeneity of proportions.* For example, is the proportion of high school seniors who attend college immediately after graduating the same for the northern, southern, eastern, and western parts of the United States?

This chapter explains the chi-square distribution and its applications. In addition to the applications mentioned here, chi-square has many other uses in statistics.

11–1   Test for Goodness of Fit

OBJECTIVE

Test a distribution for goodness of fit, using chi-square.

In addition to being used to test a single variance, the chi-square statistic can be used to see whether a frequency distribution fits a specific pattern. For example, to meet customer demands, a manufacturer of running shoes may wish to see whether buyers show a preference for a specific style. A traffic engineer may wish to see whether accidents occur more often on some days than on others, so that she can increase police patrols accordingly. An emergency service may want to see whether it receives more calls at certain times of the day than at others, so that it can provide adequate staffing.

Recall the characteristics of the chi-square distribution:

1. The chi-square distribution is a family of curves based on the degrees of freedom.

2. The chi-square distributions are positively skewed.

3. All chi-square values are greater than or equal to zero.

4. The total area under each chi-square distribution is equal to 1.

When you are testing to see whether a frequency distribution fits a specific pattern, you can use the chi-square *goodness-of-fit test.*

> The **chi-square goodness-of-fit test** is used to test the claim that an observed frequency distribution fits some given expected frequency distribution.

For example, suppose you wanted to see if there was a difference in the number of arrests in a certain city for four types of crimes. A random sample of 160 arrests showed the following distribution.

Larceny thefts	Property crimes	Drug use	Driving under the influence
38	50	28	44

Since the frequencies for each crime were obtained from a sample, these actual frequencies are called the **observed frequencies.** The frequencies obtained by calculation (as if there were no preference) are called the **expected frequencies.**

To calculate the expected frequencies, there are two rules to follow.

1. If all the expected frequencies are equal, the expected frequency E can be calculated by using $E = n/k$, where n is the total number of observations and k is the number of categories.

Historical Note

Karl Pearson (1857–1936) first used the chi-square distribution as a goodness-of-fit test for data. He developed many types of descriptive graphs and gave them unusual names such as stigmograms, topograms, stereograms, and radiograms.

2. If all the expected frequencies are not equal, then the expected frequency E can be calculated by $E = n \cdot p$, where n is the total number of observations and p is the probability for that category.

Looking at the number of arrests example, if there were no difference, you would expect $160 \div 4 = 40$ arrests for each category. That is, *approximately* 40 people would be arrested for each type of crime. A completed table is shown.

	Larceny thefts	Property crimes	Drug use	Driving under the influence
Observed	38	50	28	44
Expected	40	40	40	40

The observed frequencies will almost always differ from the expected frequencies due to sampling error; that is, the values differ from sample to sample. But the question is: Are these differences significant (there is a difference in the number of arrests for these types of crimes) or are they due to chance? The chi-square goodness-of-fit test will enable the researcher to determine the answer.

Before computing the test statistic, you must state the hypotheses. The null hypothesis should be a statement indicating that there is no difference or no change. For this example, the hypotheses are as follows:

H_0: There is no difference in the number of arrests for each type of crime.

H_1: There is a difference in the number of arrests for each type of crime.

Next, we need a measure of discrepancy between the observed values O and the expected values E, so we use the test statistic for the chi-square goodness-of-fit test.

Formula for the Chi-Square Goodness-of-Fit Test

$$\chi^2 = \sum \frac{(O - E)^2}{E}$$

with degrees of freedom equal to the number of categories minus 1, and where
O = observed frequency
E = expected frequency

Notice that the value of the test statistic is based on the difference between the observed values and the expected values. If the observed values are significantly different from the expected values, then there is enough evidence to reject the null hypothesis.

When there is perfect agreement between the observed and the expected values, $\chi^2 = 0$. Also, χ^2 can never be negative. Finally, the test is right-tailed because "H_0: Good fit" and "H_1: Not a good fit" mean that χ^2 will be small in the first case and large in the second case.

In the goodness-of-fit test, the degrees of freedom are equal to the number of categories minus 1. In this example, there are four categories; hence, the degrees of freedom are $4 - 1 = 3$. This is so because the number of subjects in each of the first three categories is free to vary. But in order for the sum to be 160, the total number of subjects in the last category is fixed.

Two assumptions are needed for the goodness-of-fit test. These assumptions are given next.

Assumptions for the Chi-Square Goodness-of-Fit Test

1. The data are obtained from a random sample.
2. The expected frequency for each category must be 5 or more.

In this book, the assumptions will be stated in the exercises; however, when encountering statistics in other situations, you must check to see that these assumptions have been met before proceeding.

For use of the chi-square goodness-of-fit test, statisticians have determined that the expected frequencies should be at least 5, as stated in the assumptions. The reasoning is as follows: The chi-square distribution is continuous, whereas the goodness-of-fit test is discrete. However, the continuous distribution is a good approximation and can be used when the expected value for each class is at least 5. If an expected frequency of a class is less than 5, then that class can be combined with another class so that the expected frequency is 5 or more.

The steps for the chi-square goodness-of-fit test are summarized in this Procedure Table.

Procedure Table

The Chi-Square Goodness-of-Fit Test

Step 1   State the hypotheses and identify the claim.

Step 2   Find the critical value from Table A–6. The test is always right-tailed.

Step 3   Compute the test statistic.

Find the sum of the $\dfrac{(O - E)^2}{E}$ values.

Step 4   Make the decision.

Step 5   Summarize the results.

Example 11–1 demonstrates the situation when the expected values of the categories are equal.

EXAMPLE 11–1   Arrests for Crimes

Is there enough evidence to reject the claim that the number of arrests for each category of crimes is the same? Use $\alpha = 0.05$.

SOLUTION

Step 1   State the hypotheses and identify the claim.

H_0: There is no difference in the number of arrests for each type of crime. (claim)
H_1: There is a difference in the number of arrests for each type of crime.

Step 2   Find the critical value. The degrees of freedom are $4 - 1 = 3$, and at $\alpha = 0.05$ the critical value from Table A–6 in Appendix A is 7.815.

Step 3   Compute the test statistic. Note the expected values are found by $E = n/k = 160/4 = 40$.

The table looks like this.

	Larceny thefts	Property crimes	Drug use	Driving under the influence
Observed	38	50	28	44
Expected	40	40	40	40

The test statistic is computed by subtracting the expected value corresponding to the observed value, squaring the result, and dividing by the expected value. Then find the sum of these values.

$$\chi^2 = \sum \frac{(O - E)^2}{E} = \frac{(38 - 40)^2}{40} + \frac{(50 - 40)^2}{40} + \frac{(28 - 40)^2}{40} + \frac{(44 - 40)^2}{40}$$

$$= 0.1 + 2.5 + 3.6 + 0.4$$

$$= 6.6$$

Step 4   Make the decision. The decision is to not reject the null hypothesis since $6.6 < 7.815$, as shown in Figure 11–1.

FIGURE 11–1

Critical Value and Test
Statistic for Example 11–1

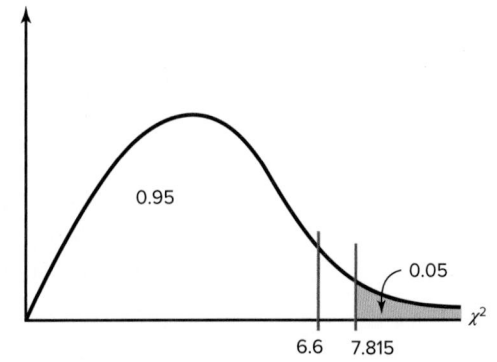

Step 5   Summarize the results. There is not enough evidence to reject the claim that there is no difference in the number of arrests for each type of crime.

Also the *P*-values can be found for this test. In Example 11–1, the test statistic was 6.6. If you look across the row with d.f. = 3 of Table A–6, you will find that 6.6 is between 6.251 and 7.815, that is, between 0.10 and 0.05 at the top of the table. This corresponds to $0.05 < p < 0.10$. Since the *P*-value is greater than 0.05, the decision is to not reject the null hypothesis.

To get some idea of why this test is called the goodness-of-fit test, examine graphs of the observed values and expected values from Example 11–1. See Figure 11–2. From the graphs, you can see whether the observed values and expected values are close together or far apart. In this case, the observed values and the expected values are far apart, so this is not a good fit. As a result, we reject the null hypothesis.

FIGURE 11–2

Graphs of the Observed and
Expected Values for Arrests

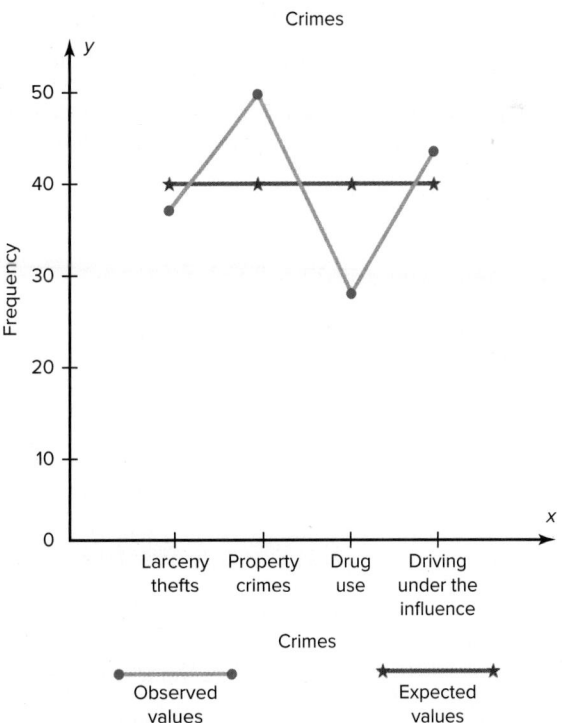

When the observed values and expected values are close together, the chi-square test statistic will be small. Then the decision will be to not reject the null hypothesis—hence, this is "a good fit." See Figure 11–3(a). When the observed values and the expected values are far apart, the chi-square test statistic will be large. Then the null hypothesis will be rejected—hence, there is "not a good fit." See Figure 11–3(b).

FIGURE 11–3

Results of the
Goodness-of-Fit Test

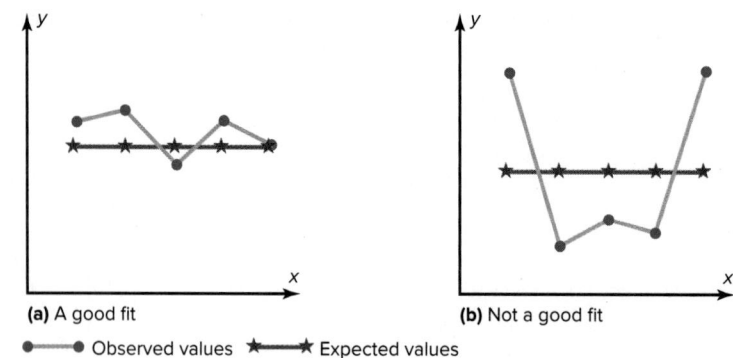

(a) A good fit   **(b)** Not a good fit

●————● Observed values   ★————★ Expected values

EXAMPLE 11–2   Home Heating

A researcher hypothesizes that 50% of American homes are heated by natural gas, 30% are heated by electricity, 10% are heated by fuel oil, and 10% are heated by other methods. A random survey of 300 homes in a specific area found that 163 were heated by natural gas, 92 were heated by electricity, 34 were heated by fuel oil, and 11 were heated by other methods. At $\alpha = 0.10$, test the claim that the proportions are the same as the researcher hypothesized.

SOLUTION

Step 1   State the hypotheses and identify the claim.

H_0: The proportion of homes heated by gas is 50%, by electricity is 30%, by fuel oil is 10%, and by other methods is 10% (claim).

H_1: The distribution is not the same as stated in the null hypothesis.

Step 2   Find the critical value. Since $\alpha = 0.10$ and the degrees of freedom are $4 - 1 = 3$, the critical value is 6.251.

Step 3   Compute the test statistic. First, we must calculate the expected values. Multiply the total number of homes surveyed (300) by the percentages of homes in each category.

$$0.50 \times 300 = 150$$
$$0.30 \times 300 = 90$$
$$0.10 \times 300 = 30$$
$$0.10 \times 300 = 30$$

The table looks like this:

Frequency	Natural gas	Electricity	Fuel oil	Other
Observed	163	92	34	11
Expected	150	90	30	30

Next calculate the test statistic.

$$\chi^2 = \sum \frac{(O - E)^2}{E} = \frac{(163 - 150)^2}{150} + \frac{(92 - 90)^2}{90} + \frac{(34 - 30)^2}{30} + \frac{(11 - 30)^2}{30}$$

$$= 1.127 + 0.044 + 0.533 + 12.033$$

$$= 13.737$$

Step 4   Make the decision. Since 13.737 > 6.251, the decision is to reject the null hypothesis. See Figure 11–4.

FIGURE 11–4
Critical Value and Test
Statistic for Example 11–2

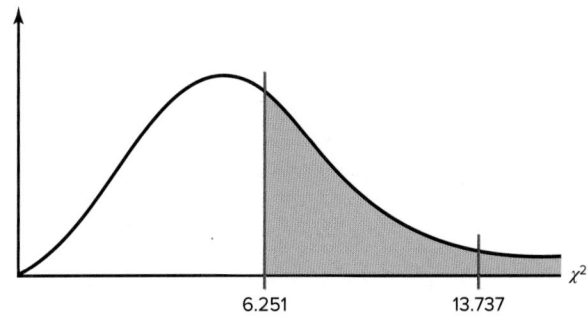

Step 5   Summarize the results. There is enough evidence to reject the null hypothesis. It can be concluded that the proportions are significantly different than those stated by the researcher.

EXAMPLE 11–3   Firearm Deaths

A researcher read that firearm-related deaths for people aged 1 to 18 years were distributed as follows: 74% were accidental, 16% were homicides, and 10% were suicides. In her district, there were 68 accidental deaths, 27 homicides, and 5 suicides during the past year. At $\alpha = 0.10$, test the claim that the percentages are equal.

Source: Centers for Disease Control and Prevention.

SOLUTION

Step 1   State the hypotheses and identify the claim:

H_0: The deaths due to firearms for people aged 1 through 18 years are distributed as follows: 74% accidental, 16% homicides, and 10% suicides (claim).

H_1: The distribution is not the same as stated in the null hypothesis.

Step 2   Find the critical value. Since $\alpha = 0.10$ and the degrees of freedom are $3 - 1 = 2$, the critical value is 4.605.

Step 3   Compute the test statistic.

First calculate the expected values, using the formula $E = n \cdot p$ as shown.

$$100 \times 0.74 = 74$$
$$100 \times 0.16 = 16$$
$$100 \times 0.10 = 10$$

The table looks like this.

Frequency	Accidental	Homicides	Suicides
Observed	68	27	5
Expected	74	16	10

$$\chi^2 = \sum \frac{(O - E)^2}{E}$$
$$= \frac{(68 - 74)^2}{74} + \frac{(27 - 16)^2}{16} + \frac{(5 - 10)^2}{10}$$
$$= 10.549$$

Step 4 Reject the null hypothesis, since $10.549 > 4.605$, as shown in Figure 11–5.

FIGURE 11–5
Critical Value and Test
Statistic for Example 11–3

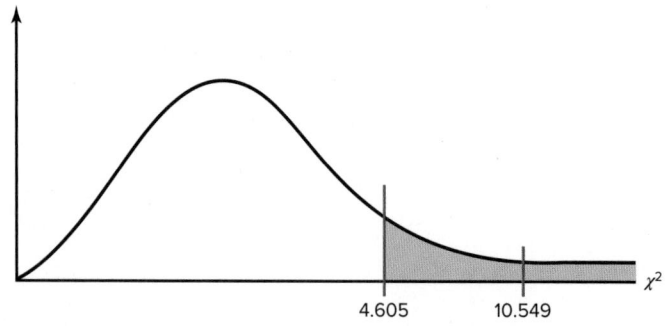

4.605   10.549 χ^2

Step 5 Summarize the results. There is enough evidence to reject the claim that the distribution is 74% accidental, 16% homicides, and 10% suicides.

Test of Normality (Optional)

The chi-square goodness-of-fit test can be used to test a variable to see if it is normally distributed. The null hypotheses are

H_0: The variable is normally distributed.

H_1: The variable is not normally distributed.

The procedure is somewhat complicated. It involves finding the expected frequencies for each class of a frequency distribution by using the standard normal distribution. Then the actual frequencies (i.e., observed frequencies) are compared to the expected frequencies, using the chi-square goodness-of-fit test. If the observed frequencies are close in value to the expected frequencies, then the chi-square test statistic will be small and the null hypothesis cannot be rejected. In this case, it can be concluded that the variable is approximately normally distributed.

On the other hand, if there is a large difference between the observed frequencies and the expected frequencies, then the chi-square test statistic will be larger and the null hypothesis can be rejected. In this case, it can be concluded that the variable is not normally distributed. Example 11–4 illustrates the procedure for the chi-square test of normality. To find the areas in the examples, you might want to review Section 6–2.

Example 11–4 shows how to do the calculations.

EXAMPLE 11–4   Test of Normality

Use chi-square to determine if the variable shown in the frequency distribution is normally distributed. Use $\alpha = 0.05$.

Boundaries	Frequency
89.5–104.5	24
104.5–119.5	62
119.5–134.5	72
134.5–149.5	26
149.5–164.5	12
164.5–179.5	4
	Total = 200

SOLUTION

H_0: The variable is normally distributed.
H_1: The variable is not normally distributed.

First find the mean and standard deviation of the variable. (*Note:* s is used to approximate σ.)

Unusual Stat

Drinking milk may lower your risk of stroke. A 22-year study of men over 55 found that only 4% of men who drank 16 ounces of milk every day suffered a stroke, compared with 8% of the nonmilk drinkers.

Boundaries	f	X_m	$f \cdot X_m$	$f \cdot X_m^2$
89.5–104.5	24	97	2,328	225,816
104.5–119.5	62	112	6,944	777,728
119.5–134.5	72	127	9,144	1,161,288
134.5–149.5	26	142	3,692	524,264
149.5–164.5	12	157	1,884	295,788
164.5–179.5	4	172	688	118,336
	200		24,680	3,103,220

$$\overline{X} = \frac{24{,}680}{200} = 123.4$$

$$s = \sqrt{\frac{200(3{,}103{,}220) - 24{,}680^2}{200(199)}} = \sqrt{290} = 17.03$$

Next find the area under the standard normal distribution, using z scores and Table A–4 for each class.

The z score for $x = 104.5$ is found as

$$z = \frac{104.5 - 123.4}{17.03} = -1.11$$

The area for $z < -1.11$ is 0.1335.

The z score for 119.5 is found as

$$z = \frac{119.5 - 123.4}{17.03} = -0.23$$

The area for $-1.11 < z < -0.23$ is $0.4090 - 0.1335 = 0.2755$.

The z score for 134.5 is found as

$$z = \frac{134.5 - 123.4}{17.03} = 0.65$$

The area for $-0.23 < z < 0.65$ is $0.7422 - 0.4090 = 0.3332$.

The z score for 149.5 is found as

$$z = \frac{149.5 - 123.4}{17.03} = 1.53$$

The area for $0.65 < z < 1.53$ is $0.9370 - 0.7422 = 0.1948$.

The z score for 164.5 is found as

$$z = \frac{164.5 - 123.4}{17.03} = 2.41$$

The area for $1.53 < z < 2.41$ is $0.9920 - 0.9370 = 0.0550$.
The area for $z > 2.41$ is $1.0000 - 0.9920 = 0.0080$.

Find the expected frequencies for each class by multiplying the area by 200. The expected frequencies are found by

$$0.1335 \cdot 200 = 26.7$$
$$0.2755 \cdot 200 = 55.1$$
$$0.3332 \cdot 200 = 66.64$$
$$0.1948 \cdot 200 = 38.96$$
$$0.0550 \cdot 200 = 11.0$$
$$0.0080 \cdot 200 = 1.6$$

Note: Since the expected frequency for the last category is less than 5, it can be combined with the previous category.

The table looks like this.

O	24	62	72	26	16
E	26.7	55.1	66.64	38.96	12.6

Finally, find the chi-square test statistic using the formula $\chi^2 = \sum \dfrac{(O - E)^2}{E}$.

$$\chi^2 = \frac{(24 - 26.7)^2}{26.7} + \frac{(62 - 55.1)^2}{55.1} + \frac{(72 - 66.64)^2}{66.64} + \frac{(26 - 38.96)^2}{38.96}$$
$$+ \frac{(16 - 12.6)^2}{12.6}$$
$$= 6.797$$

The critical value in this test has the degrees of freedom equal to the number of categories minus 3 since 1 degree of freedom is lost for each parameter that is estimated. In this case, the mean and standard deviation have been estimated, so 2 additional degrees of freedom are needed.

The C.V. with d.f. $= 5 - 3 = 2$ and $\alpha = 0.05$ is 5.991, so the null hypothesis is rejected. Hence, the distribution can be considered not normally distributed.

Note: At $\alpha = 0.01$, the C.V. $= 9.210$ and the null hypothesis would not be rejected. Hence, we could consider that the variable is normally distributed at $\alpha = 0.01$. So it is important to decide which level of significance you want to use prior to conducting the test.

≡ Applying the Concepts **11–1**

Skittles Color Distribution

M&M/Mars, the makers of Skittles candies, states that the flavor blend is 20% for each flavor. Skittles is a combination of lemon, lime, orange, strawberry, and grape flavored candies. The following data list the results of four randomly selected bags of Skittles and their flavor blends. Use the data to answer the questions.

	Flavor				
Bag	Yellow	Green	Orange	Red	Purple
1	14	7	20	10	7
2	17	20	5	5	13
3	4	4	16	13	21
4	17	12	9	16	3
Total	52	43	50	44	44

1. Are the variables quantitative or qualitative?

2. What type of test can be used to compare the observed values to the expected values?

3. Compute a chi-square test on the total values.

4. What hypotheses should you use?

5. What are the degrees of freedom for the test? What is the critical value?

6. What is your conclusion?

See page 650 for the answers.

Exercises 11–1

1. How does the goodness-of-fit test differ from the chi-square variance test?

2. How are the degrees of freedom computed for the goodness-of-fit test? The degrees of freedom are the number of categories minus 1.

3. How are the expected values computed for the goodness-of-fit test?

4. When the expected frequency is less than 5 for a specific class, what should be done so that you can use the goodness-of-fit test? The classes should be combined with another class.

For Exercises 5 through 18, perform these steps.

   a. State the hypotheses and identify the claim.
   b. Find the critical value or use the *P*-value method.
   c. Compute the test statistic.
   d. Make the decision.
   e. Summarize the results.

Use the traditional method or the P-value method. Assume all assumptions are met.

5. **Fast Food** A deli manager wishes to see if there is a preference for the four types of hoagies it sells. The manager selects a week at random and records the number of hoagies of each type that the store sold. At $\alpha = 0.01$, is there a preference in the type of hoagies sold?

Italian	Steak	Meatball	Vegetable
108	97	52	43

6. **Blood Types** A medical researcher wishes to see if hospital patients in a large hospital have the same blood type distribution as those in the general population. The distribution for the general population is as follows: type A, 20%; type B, 28%; type O, 36%; and type AB = 16%. The researcher selects a random sample of 50 patients and finds the following: 12 have type A blood, 8 have type B, 24 have type O, and 6 have type AB blood.

At $\alpha = 0.10$, can it be concluded that the distribution is the same as that of the general population?

7. **Kids and Guns** A researcher hypothesizes that 40% of kids get guns from their friends, 30% get them from family members, 20% get them from the street, and 10% get them from other sources. Statistics collected from a random sample of police departments obtained the following data.

Friends	Family members	Street	Other
46	24	17	13

At $\alpha = 0.05$, is there enough evidence to support the researcher's claim?

8. **Old Tires** An environmentalist hypothesizes that 45% of used tires are illegally dumped, 26% are recycled, 17% are exported, and 12% are burned. The environmentalist randomly selects a municipality and records the number of tires that they found in each category. The data are shown.

Illegally dumped	Recycled	Exported	Burned
237	120	88	55

At $\alpha = 0.05$, is there enough evidence to reject the researcher's claim?

9. **Genetically Modified Food** An ABC News poll asked adults whether they felt genetically modified food was safe to eat. Thirty-five percent felt it was safe, 52% felt it was not safe, and 13% had no opinion. A random sample of 120 adults was asked the same question at a local county fair. Forty people felt that genetically modified food was safe, 60 felt that it was not safe, and 20 had no opinion. At the 0.01 level of significance, is there sufficient evidence to conclude that the proportions differ from those reported in the poll?

Source: ABCNews.com Poll, www.pollingreport.com

10. **Truck Colors** In a recent year, the most popular colors for light trucks were white, 31%; black, 19%; silver 11%; red 11%; gray 10%; blue 8%; and other 10%. A survey of randomly selected light truck owners in a particular area revealed the following. At $\alpha = 0.05$, do the proportions differ from those stated?

White	Black	Silver	Red	Gray	Blue	Other
45	32	30	30	22	15	6

Source: World Almanac.

11. Voter Issues A random survey of 64 voters showed the number of each who said the subject shown was the most important issue in the upcoming election. At $\alpha = 0.025$, can it be concluded that the proportion of votes is equally distributed over the categories?

Economy	Deficit	Taxes	Medical care
20	16	18	10

12. Crime Weapons A researcher randomly selected a large city and counted the types of weapons used in 100 homicides. The count is shown.

Firearms	65
Knives	14
Hands (strangulation)	12
Blunt objects	9

At the 0.05 level of significance, is the distribution different from the national distribution, which is firearms, 75%; knives, 15%; hands, 6%; and blunt objects, 4%?

13. Firearms Deaths According to the National Safety Council, 10% of the annual deaths from firearms were victims from birth through 19 years of age. Half of the deaths from firearms were victims aged 20 through 44 years, and 40% of victims were aged 45 years and over. A random sample of 100 deaths by firearms in a particular state indicated the following: 13 were victims from birth through 19 years, 62 were aged 20 through 44 years, and the rest were 45 years old and older. At the 0.05 level of significance, are the results different from those cited by the National Safety Council?

Source: World Almanac.

14. Ages of Crime Victims A random sample of 60 crime victims showed the ages of the victims when the crimes occurred. At $\alpha = 0.10$, is there a difference in the numbers for the age groups of the victims?

Under 20 years	20–39	40–59	60 and over
7	22	18	13

15. Coffee Flavors A researcher randomly selects 100 coffee drinkers, asking them what was their favorite coffee flavor for the holiday season. At $\alpha = 0.025$, are the flavor choices by the drinkers equally distributed?

Mint mocha	White chocolate	Eggnog	Gingerbread
32	26	23	19

16. Reasons for Workplace Violence A researcher selected a random sample of 120 workplace violence situations and found the reasons given for the attacks were as follows.

	Number
Dissatisfied with management	27
Interpersonal conflict	34
Being disciplined	18
Personal problems	13
Being fired or laid off	16
Other	12

At $\alpha = 0.05$, can it be concluded that the reasons given are equally distributed?

17. Merchandise Returns A large department store wants to see if the number of returned items is equally distributed during the week. A week is selected at random and the number of returns is shown. At $\alpha = 0.10$, test the claim that the number of items returned is equally distributed during each day of the week.

Mon	Tue	Wed	Thurs	Fri	Sat	Sun
62	57	43	66	56	71	44

18. Puzzle Books A bookstore manager wishes to see if there is a difference in the proportion of sales for three types of puzzle books. The manager selects a week at random and records the number of each type of book sold. At $\alpha = 0.10$, can it be concluded that there is a difference in the proportion of sales for three types of puzzle books?

Crossword	Sudoku	Word search
28	17	24

≣ Extending the Concepts

19. Tossing Coins Three coins are tossed 72 times, and the number of heads is shown. At $\alpha = 0.05$, test the null hypothesis that the coins are balanced and randomly tossed. (*Hint:* Use the binomial distribution.)

No. of heads	0	1	2	3
Frequency	3	10	17	42

20. State Lottery Numbers Select a three-digit state lottery number over a period of 50 days. Count the number of times each digit, 0 through 9, occurs. Test the claim, at $\alpha = 0.05$, that the digits occur at random.

Answers will vary.

Technology Step by Step

TI-84 Plus
Step by Step

Goodness-of-Fit Test

Example TI11–1

At the 5% significance level, test the claim that there is no preference in the selection of fruit soda flavors for the data.

Frequency	Cherry	Strawberry	Orange	Lime	Grape
Observed	32	28	16	14	10
Expected	20	20	20	20	20

To calculate the test statistic:

1. Enter the observed frequencies in L_1 and the expected frequencies in L_2.
2. Move the cursor to the top header of L_3.
3. Type $(L_1 - L_2)_2/L_2)$, then press **ENTER**.
4. Press **2nd [QUIT]** to return to the home screen.
5. Press **2nd [LIST]**, move the cursor to MATH, and press **5** for sum(.
6. Type L_3, then press **ENTER**.

To calculate the *P*-value:

Press **2nd [DISTR]**, then press **8** to get χ^2cdf(.
For this *P*-value, the χ^2cdf(command has the form χ^2cdf(test statistic, ∞, degrees of freedom).
Use E99 for ∞. Type **2nd [EE]** to get the small E.

Note: On newer TI84s, the χ^2cdf will come up as a menu. **Enter** the test statistic as the lower values, E99 as the upper, and 4 as df. After highlighting **PASTE** and pressing **ENTER** twice, the result will be the same as that shown.

For this example use χ^2cdf(18, E99,4):

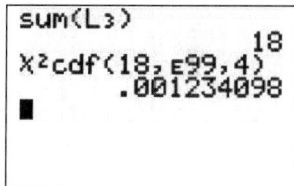

Since *P*-value = 0.001234098 < 0.05 = significance level, reject H_0 and conclude H_1. Therefore, there is enough evidence to reject the claim that consumers show no preference for soda flavors.

Note: On the newer TI-84 calculator, there is a goodness-of-fit test. Put the observed values in L1 and the expected values in L2 and then in TESTS-ALPHA D, enter df, and calculate.

EXCEL
Step by Step

Chi-Square Goodness-of-Fit Test

Excel does not have a procedure to conduct the goodness-of-fit test. However, you may conduct this test using the MegaStat Add-in available in your online resources. If you have not installed this add-in, do so, following the instructions from the Chapter 1 Excel Step by Step.

Example XL11–1

Test the claim that there is no preference for soda flavor. Use a significance level of $\alpha = 0.05$. The table of frequencies is shown below.

Frequency	Cherry	Strawberry	Orange	Lime	Grape
Observed	32	28	16	14	10
Expected	20	20	20	20	20

1. Enter the observed frequencies in row 1 (cells: A1 to E1) of a new worksheet.

2. Enter the expected frequencies in row 2 (cells: A2 to E2).

3. From the toolbar, select Data (or Add-ins on a Mac), **MegaStat>Chi-Square/Crosstab>Goodness of Fit Test.** *Note:* You may need to open MegaStat from the MegaStat.xls file on your computer's hard drive.

4. In the dialog box, type **A1:E1** for the Observed values and **A2:E2** for the Expected values. Then click [OK].

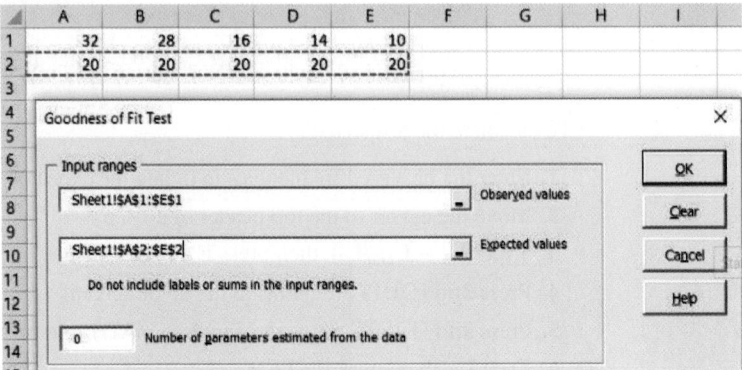

Goodness of Fit Test

observed	expected	O - E	(O - E)² / E	% of chisq
32	20.000	12.000	7.200	40.00
28	20.000	8.000	3.200	17.78
16	20.000	-4.000	0.800	4.44
14	20.000	-6.000	1.800	10.00
10	20.000	-10.000	5.000	27.78
100	100.000	0.000	18.000	100.00

18.00 chi-square
4 df
.0012 p-value

Since the *P*-value is less than the significance level, the null hypothesis is rejected and thus the claim of no preference is rejected.

Chi-Square Test for Normality

Example XL11–2

This example refers to Example 11–4. At the 5% significance level, determine if the variable is normally distributed.

Start with the table of observed and expected values:

Observed	24	62	72	26	16
Expected	26.7	55.1	66.64	38.96	12.6

1. Enter the Observed values in row 1 of a new worksheet.

2. Enter the Expected values in row 2.

Note: You may include labels for the observed and expected values in cells A1 and A2, respectively.

3. Select the Insert Function Icon from the Toolbar.

4. In the Insert Function dialog box, select the Statistical category and the CHISQ.TEST function.

5. Type **B1:F1** for the Actual Range and **B2:F2** for the Expected Range, then click [OK].

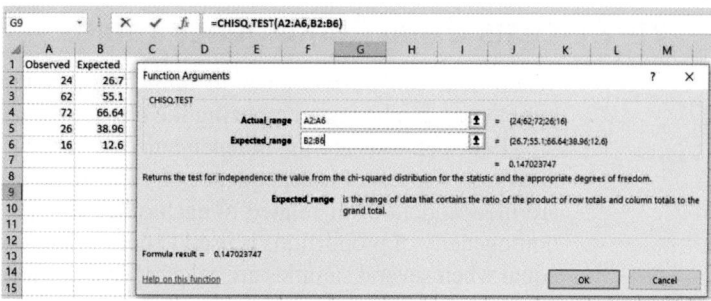

The *P*-value of 0.1470 is greater than the significance level of 0.05. So we do not reject the null hypothesis. Thus, the distribution of the variable is approximately normal.

MINITAB

Step by Step

Chi-Square Goodness of Fit

Is there a preference for flavor of soda?

Frequency	Cherry	Strawberry	Orange	Lime	Grape
Observed	32	28	16	14	10
Expected	20	20	20	20	20

1. Enter the Observed Frequencies.
   a) Optional: type in the flavors in C1. Name the column Flavors.
   b) Type in the Observed counts in C2. Name the column Observed.
2. Select **Stat>Tables>Chi-Square Square Goodness-of-Fit Test (One Variable)**.
   a) Check the radio button for Observed Counts then select C2 Observed.
   b) In the dialog box for Categorical names, select C1 Flavors (optional).
   c) Select the option for Equal proportions, then click [OK].

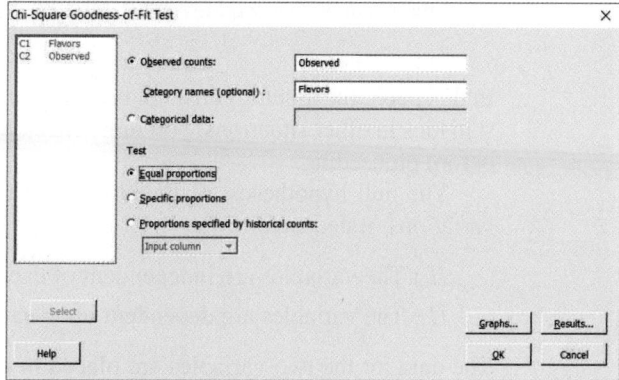

The session window will contain the results as shown:

Chi-Square Goodness-of-Fit Test for Observed Counts in Variable: Observed

```
Using category names in Flavors
                            Test                 Contribution
Category     Observed  Proportion    Expected      to Chi-Sq
Cherry             32         0.2          20            7.2
Strawberry         28         0.2          20            3.2
Orange             16         0.2          20            0.8
Lime               14         0.2          20            1.8
Grape              10         0.2          20            5.0

  N  DF  Chi-Sq  P-Value
100   4      18    0.001
```

11–2   Tests Using Contingency Tables

When data can be tabulated in table form in terms of frequencies, several types of hypotheses can be tested by using the chi-square test.

Two such tests are the independence of variables test and the homogeneity of proportions test. The test of independence of variables is used to determine whether two variables are independent of or related to each other when a single sample is selected. The test of homogeneity of proportions is used to determine whether the proportions for a variable are equal when several samples are selected from different populations. Both tests use the chi-square distribution and a contingency table, and the test statistic is found in the same way. The independence test will be explained first.

OBJECTIVE

Test two variables for independence, using chi-square.

Test for Independence

The chi-square **independence test** is used to test whether two variables are independent of each other.

Formula for the Chi-Square Independence Test

$$\chi^2 = \sum \frac{(O - E)^2}{E}$$

with degrees of freedom equal to the (number of rows minus 1)(number of columns minus 1) and where
O = observed frequency
E = expected frequency

Assumptions for Chi-Square Independence Test

1. The data are obtained from a random sample.
2. The expected value in each cell must be 5 or more. If the expected values are not 5 or more, combine categories.

In this book, the assumptions will be stated in the exercises; however, when encountering statistics in other situations, you must check to see that these assumptions have been met before proceeding.

The null hypotheses for the chi-square independence test are generally, with some variations, stated as follows:

H_0: The variables are independent of each other.

H_1: The variables are dependent upon each other.

The data for the two variables are placed in a **contingency table.** One variable is called the *row variable,* and the other variable is called the *column variable.* The table is called an $R \times C$ *table,* where R is the number of rows and C is the number of columns. (Remember, rows go across or horizontally, and columns go up and down or vertically.) For example, a 2×3 contingency table would look like this.

	Column 1	Column 2	Column 3
Row 1	$C_{1,2}$	$C_{1,2}$	$C_{1,3}$
Row 2	$C_{2,1}$	$C_{2,2}$	$C_{2,3}$

Each value in the table is called a **cell value.** For example, the cell value $C_{2,3}$ means that it is in the second row (2) and third column (3).

The observed values are obtained from the sample data. (That is, they are given in the problem.) The expected values are computed from the observed values, and they are based on the assumption that the two variables are independent.

> The formula for computing the expected values for each cell is
>
> $$\text{Expected value} = \frac{(\text{row sum})(\text{column sum})}{\text{grand total}}$$

As with the chi-square goodness-of-fit test, if there is little difference between the observed values and the expected values, then the value of the test statistic will be small and the null hypothesis will not be rejected. Hence, the variables are independent of each other.

However, if there are large differences in the observed values and the expected values, then the test statistic will be large and the null hypothesis will be rejected. In this case, there is enough evidence to say that the variables are dependent on or related to each other. This test is always right-tailed.

The degrees of freedom for the chi-square test of independence are based on the size of the contingency table. The formula for the degrees of freedom is $(R - 1)(C - 1)$, that is, (rows $-$ 1)(columns $-$ 1). For a 2×3 table, the degrees of freedom would be $(2 - 1)(3 - 1) = 1(2) = 2$.

As an example, suppose a new postoperative procedure is administered to a number of patients in a large hospital. The researcher can ask the question, Do the doctors feel differently about this procedure from the nurses, or do they feel basically the same way? Note that the question is not whether they prefer the procedure but whether there is a difference of opinion between the two groups.

To answer this question, a researcher selects a sample of nurses and doctors and tabulates the data in table form, as shown.

Group	Prefer new procedure	Prefer old procedure	No preference
Nurses	100	80	20
Doctors	50	120	30

As the survey indicates, 100 nurses prefer the new procedure, 80 prefer the old procedure, and 20 have no preference; 50 doctors prefer the new procedure, 120 like the old procedure, and 30 have no preference. Since the main question is whether there is a difference in opinion, the null hypothesis is stated as follows:

H_0: The opinion about the procedure is *independent* of the profession.

The alternative hypothesis is stated as follows:

H_1: The opinion about the procedure is *dependent* on the profession.

If the null hypothesis is not rejected, the test means that both professions feel basically the same way about the procedure and that the differences are due to chance. If the null hypothesis is rejected, the test means that one group feels differently about the procedure from the other. Remember that rejection does *not* mean that one group favors the procedure and the other does not. Perhaps both groups favor it or both dislike it, but in different proportions.

Recall that the degrees of freedom for any contingency table are (rows $-$ 1) times (columns $-$ 1); that is, d.f. $= (R - 1)(C - 1)$. In this case, $(2 - 1)(3 - 1) = (1)(2) = 2$. The reason for this formula for d.f. is that all the expected values except one are free to vary in each row and in each column. The critical value for $\alpha = 0.05$ from Table A–6 is 5.991.

To test the null hypothesis by using the chi-square independence test, you must compute the expected frequencies, assuming that the null hypothesis is true. These frequencies are computed by using the observed frequencies given in the table.

Using the previous table, you can compute the expected frequencies for each block (or cell), as shown next.

1. Find the sum of each row and each column, and find the grand total, as shown.

Group	Prefer new procedure	Prefer old procedure	No preference	Total
Nurses	100	80	20	Row 1 sum ⟶ 200
Doctors	+50	+120	+30	Row 2 sum ⟶ 200
Total	150	200	50	400
	Column 1 sum	Column 2 sum	Column 3 sum	Grand total

2. For each cell, multiply the corresponding row sum by the column sum and divide by the grand total, to get the expected value:

$$\text{Expected value} = \frac{\text{row sum} \times \text{column sum}}{\text{grand total}}$$

For example, for $C_{1,2}$, the expected value, denoted by $E_{1,2}$, is (refer to the previous tables)

$$E_{1,2} = \frac{(200)(200)}{400} = 100$$

For each cell, the expected values are computed as follows:

$$E_{1,1} = \frac{(200)(150)}{400} = 75 \qquad E_{1,2} = \frac{(200)(200)}{400} = 100 \qquad E_{1,3} = \frac{(200)(50)}{400} = 25$$

$$E_{2,1} = \frac{(200)(150)}{400} = 75 \qquad E_{2,2} = \frac{(200)(200)}{400} = 100 \qquad E_{2,3} = \frac{(200)(50)}{400} = 25$$

The expected values can now be placed in the corresponding cells along with the observed values, as shown.

Group	Prefer new procedure	Prefer old procedure	No preference	Total
Nurses	100 (75)	80 (100)	20 (25)	200
Doctors	50 (75)	120 (100)	30 (25)	200
Total	150	200	50	400

The rationale for the computation of the expected frequencies for a contingency table uses proportions. For $C_{1,1}$ a total of 150 out of 400 people prefer the new procedure. And since there are 200 nurses, you would expect, if the null hypothesis were true, (150/400)(200), or 75, of the nurses to be in favor of the new procedure.

The test statistic can now be computed by using the formula

$$\chi^2 = \sum \frac{(O - E)^2}{E}$$

$$= \frac{(100 - 75)^2}{75} + \frac{(80 - 100)^2}{100} + \frac{(20 - 25)^2}{25} + \frac{(50 - 75)^2}{75}$$

$$+ \frac{(120 - 100)^2}{100} + \frac{(30 - 25)^2}{25}$$

$$= 26.667$$

FIGURE 11–6

Critical Value and Test
Statistic for the Postoperative
Procedures Example

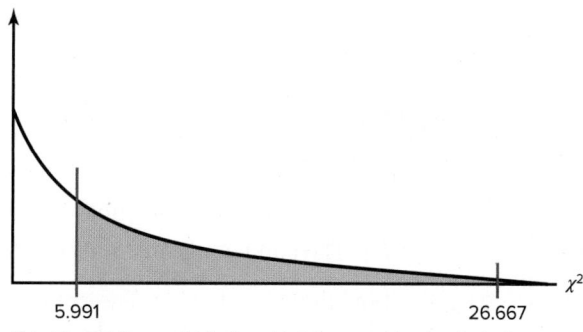

Note: The Chi-Square distribution with 2 degrees of freedom looks like
the one shown here.

Next make the decision. Since the test statistic 26.667 is larger than the critical value 5.991, the decision is to reject the null hypothesis. See Figure 11–6.

The conclusion is that there is enough evidence to support the claim that opinion is related to (dependent on) profession, that is, that the doctors and nurses differ in their opinions about the procedure.

The P-values can be found as previously shown. In this case, if we look across row 2 (d.f. = 2), we see that the chi-square value of 10.597 corresponds to the α value of 0.005. Since our test statistic is 26.667 and is larger than 10.597, the P-value < 0.005, and the null hypothesis can be rejected.

The Procedure Table for performing the chi-square independence test is given next.

Procedure Table

The Chi-Square Independence Test

Step 1   State the hypotheses and identify the claim.

Step 2   Find the critical value for the right tail. Use Table A–6.

Step 3   Compute the test statistic. To compute the test statistic, first find the expected values. For each cell of the contingency table, use the formula

$$E = \frac{(\text{row sum})(\text{column sum})}{\text{grand total}}$$

to get the expected value. To find the test statistic, use the formula

$$\chi^2 = \sum \frac{(O - E)^2}{E}$$

Step 4   Make the decision.

Step 5   Summarize the results.

Examples 11–5 and 11–6 illustrate the procedure for the chi-square test of independence.

EXAMPLE 11–5   Hospitals and Infections

A researcher wishes to see if there is a relationship between the hospital and the number of patient infections. A random sample of 3 hospitals was selected, and the number of infections for a specific year has been reported. The data are shown next.

Hospital	Surgical site infections	Pneumonia infections	Bloodstream infections	Total
A	41	27	51	119
B	36	3	40	79
C	169	106	109	384
Total	246	136	200	582

Source: Pennsylvania Health Care Cost Containment Council.

At $\alpha = 0.05$, can it be concluded that the number of infections is related to the hospital where they occurred?

SOLUTION

Step 1   State the hypothesis and identify the claim.

H_0: The number of infections is independent of the hospital.

H_1: The number of infections is dependent on the hospital (claim).

Step 2   Find the critical value. The critical value using Table A–6 at $\alpha = 0.05$ with $(3 - 1)(3 - 1) = (2)(2) = 4$ degrees of freedom is 9.488.

Step 3   Compute the test statistic. First find the expected values.

$$E_{1,1} = \frac{(119)(246)}{582} = 50.30 \quad E_{1,2} = \frac{(119)(136)}{582} = 27.81 \quad E_{1,3} = \frac{(119)(200)}{582} = 40.89$$

$$E_{2,1} = \frac{(79)(246)}{582} = 33.39 \quad E_{2,2} = \frac{(79)(136)}{582} = 18.46 \quad E_{2,3} = \frac{(79)(200)}{582} = 27.15$$

$$E_{3,1} = \frac{(384)(246)}{582} = 162.31 \quad E_{3,2} = \frac{(384)(136)}{582} = 89.73 \quad E_{3,3} = \frac{(384)(200)}{582} = 131.96$$

The completed table is shown.

Hospital	Surgical site infections	Pneumonia infections	Bloodstream infections	Total
A	41 (50.30)	27 (27.81)	51 (40.89)	119
B	36 (33.39)	3 (18.46)	40 (27.15)	79
C	169 (162.31)	106 (89.73)	109 (131.96)	384
Total	246	136	200	582

Then substitute in the formula and evaluate to find the test statistic.

$$\chi^2 = \sum \frac{(O - E)^2}{E}$$

$$= \frac{(41 - 50.30)^2}{50.30} + \frac{(27 - 27.81)^2}{27.81} + \frac{(51 - 40.89)^2}{40.89}$$

$$+ \frac{(36 - 33.39)^2}{33.39} + \frac{(3 - 18.46)^2}{18.46} + \frac{(40 - 27.15)^2}{27.15}$$

$$+ \frac{(169 - 162.31)^2}{162.31} + \frac{(106 - 89.73)^2}{89.73} + \frac{(109 - 131.96)^2}{131.96}$$

$$= 1.719 + 0.024 + 2.500 + 0.204 + 12.948 + 6.082$$

$$+ 0.276 + 2.950 + 3.995$$

$$= 30.698$$

Step 4   Make the decision. The decision is to reject the null hypothesis since $30.698 > 9.488$. That is, the test statistic lies in the critical region, as shown in Figure 11–7.

FIGURE 11–7

Critical Value and Test
Statistic for Example 11–5

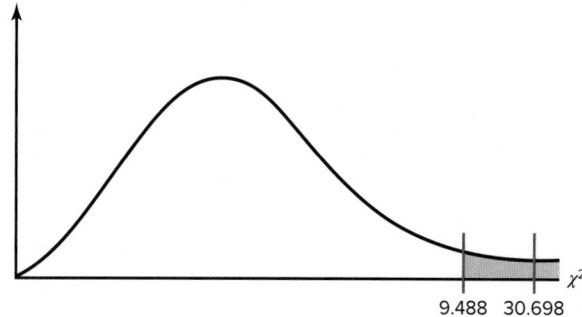

9.488 30.698

Step 5   Summarize the results. There is enough evidence to support the claim that the number of infections is related to the hospital where they occurred.

EXAMPLE 11–6   Vehicle Leasing

A researcher wishes to see if there is a difference between men and women in the type of vehicles they lease. The researcher randomly selects 36 males and 32 females and lists the type of vehicles they lease. The results are shown. At $\alpha = 0.10$, is there a difference in the type of vehicles listed?

Gender	SUV	Midsize	Small	Total
Male	18	14	4	36
Female	14	11	7	32
Total	32	25	11	68

SOLUTION

Step 1   State the hypotheses and identify the claim.

H_0: The type of vehicle leased is independent of the gender of the person who leases the vehicle.

H_1: The type of vehicle leased is related to the gender of the person who leases the car (claim).

Step 2   Find the critical value. The critical value is 4.605 since the degrees of freedom are $(2 - 1)(3 - 1) = 2$.

Step 3   Compute the test statistic. First compute the expected values.

$$E_{1,1} = \frac{(36)(32)}{68} = 16.94 \quad E_{1,2} = \frac{(36)(25)}{68} = 13.24 \quad E_{1,3} = \frac{(36)(11)}{68} = 5.82$$

$$E_{2,1} = \frac{(32)(32)}{68} = 15.06 \quad E_{2,2} = \frac{(32)(25)}{68} = 11.76 \quad E_{2,3} = \frac{(32)(11)}{68} = 5.18$$

The completed table is shown.

Gender	SUV	Midsize	Small	Total
Male	18 (16.94)	14 (13.24)	4 (5.82)	36
Female	14 (15.06)	11 (11.76)	7 (5.18)	32
Total	32	25	11	68

The test statistic is

$$\chi^2 = \Sum \frac{(O - E)^2}{E}$$

$$= \frac{(18 - 16.94)^2}{16.94} + \frac{(14 - 13.24)^2}{13.24} + \frac{(4 - 5.82)^2}{5.82}$$

$$+ \frac{(14 - 15.06)^2}{15.06} + \frac{(11 - 11.76)^2}{11.76} + \frac{(7 - 5.18)^2}{5.18}$$

$$= 0.066 + 0.044 + 0.569 + 0.075 + 0.049 + 0.639 = 1.442$$

Step 4   Make the decision. The decision is not to reject the null hypothesis since 1.442 < 4.605. See Figure 11–8.

FIGURE 11–8
Critical Value and Test
Statistic for Example 11–6

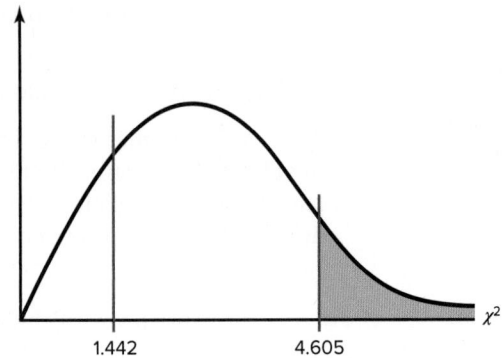

Step 5   Summarize the results. There is not enough evidence to support the claim that the type of vehicle leased is related to the gender of the person leasing the vehicle. (*Note:* The *P*-value is 0.4863.)

Test for Homogeneity of Proportions

OBJECTIVE ❸

Test proportions for homogeneity, using chi-square.

The second chi-square test that uses a contingency table is called the **homogeneity of proportions test.**

The *test of* **homogeneity of proportions** is used to test the claim that different populations have the same proportion of subjects who have a certain attitude or characteristic.

 Interesting Facts

Water is the most critical nutrient in your body. It is needed for just about everything that happens. Water is lost fast: 2 cups daily are lost just exhaling, 10 cups through normal waste and body cooling, and 1 to 2 quarts per hour running, biking, or working out.

In this situation, samples are selected from several different populations, and the researcher is interested in determining whether the proportions of elements that have a common characteristic are the same for each population. The sample sizes are specified in advance, making either the row totals or column totals in the contingency table known before the samples are selected. For example, a researcher may select a sample of 50 first-year students, 50 sophomores, 50 juniors, and 50 seniors and then find the proportion of students who are smokers in each level. The researcher will then compare the proportions for each group to see if they are equal. The hypotheses in this case would be

H_0: $p_1 = p_2 = p_3 = p_4$

H_1: At least one proportion is different from the others.

If the researcher does not reject the null hypothesis, it can be assumed that the proportions are equal and the differences in them are due to chance. Hence, the proportion of students who smoke is the same for grade levels first-year student through senior. When the null hypothesis is rejected, it can be assumed that the proportions are not all equal.

The assumptions for the test of homogeneity of proportions are the same as the assumptions for the chi-square test of independence. The procedure for this test is the same as the procedure for the chi-square test of independence.

EXAMPLE 11–7   Happiness and Income

A psychologist randomly selected 100 people from each of four income groups and asked them if they were "very happy." For people who made less than \$30,000, 24% responded yes. For people who made \$30,000 to \$74,999, 33% responded yes. For people who made \$75,000 to \$90,999, 38% responded yes, and for people who made \$100,000 or more, 49% responded yes. At $\alpha = 0.05$, test the claim that there is no difference in the proportion of people in each economic group who were very happy.

SOLUTION

It is necessary to make a table showing the number of people in each group who responded yes and the number of people in each group who responded no.

For group 1, 24% of the people responded yes, so 24% of 100 = 0.24(100) = 24 responded yes and 100 − 24 = 76 responded no.

For group 2, 33% of the people responded yes, so 33% of 100 = 0.33(100) = 33 responded yes and 100 − 33 = 67 responded no.

For group 3, 38% of the people responded yes, so 38% of 100 = 0.38(100) = 38 people responded yes and 100 − 38 = 62 people responded no.

For group 4, 49% of the people responded yes, so 49% of 100 = 0.49(100) = 49 responded yes, and 100 − 49 = 51 people responded no.

Tabulate the data in a table, and find the sums of the rows and columns as shown.

Household income	Less than $30,000	$30,000–$74,999	$75,000–$99,999	$100,000 or more	Total
Yes	24	33	38	49	144
No	76	67	62	51	256
	100	100	100	100	400

Source: Based on information from Princeton Survey Research Associates International.

Step 1   State the hypotheses and identify the claim.

H_0: $p_1 = p_2 = p_3 = p_4$ (claim)

H_1: At least one proportion differs from the others.

Step 2   Find the critical value. The formula for the degrees of freedom is the same as before: $(R - 1)(C - 1) = (2 - 1)(4 - 1) = 1(3) = 3$. The critical value is 7.815.

Step 3   Compute the test statistic. Since we want to test the claim that the proportions are equal, we use the expected value as $\frac{1}{4} \cdot 400 = 100$. First compute the expected values as shown previously.

$$E_{1,1} = \frac{(144)(100)}{400} = 36 \qquad E_{1,2} = \frac{(144)(100)}{400} = 36 \qquad E_{1,3} = \frac{(144)(100)}{400} = 36 \qquad E_{1,4} = \frac{(144)(100)}{400} = 36$$

$$E_{2,1} = \frac{(256)(100)}{400} = 64 \qquad E_{2,2} = \frac{(256)(100)}{400} = 64 \qquad E_{2,3} = \frac{(256)(100)}{400} = 64 \qquad E_{2,4} = \frac{(256)(100)}{400} = 64$$

The completed table is shown.

Household income	Less than $30,000	$30,000–$74,999	$75,000–$99,999	$100,000 or more	Total
Yes	24 (36)	33 (36)	38 (36)	49 (36)	144
No	76 (64)	67 (64)	62 (64)	51 (64)	256
	100	100	100	100	400

Next calculate the test statistic.

$$\chi^2 = \sum \frac{(O - E)^2}{E}$$

$$= \frac{(24 - 36)^2}{36} + \frac{(33 - 36)^2}{36} + \frac{(38 - 36)^2}{36} + \frac{(49 - 36)^2}{36}$$

$$+ \frac{(76 - 64)^2}{64} + \frac{(67 - 64)^2}{64} + \frac{(62 - 64)^2}{64} + \frac{(51 - 64)^2}{64}$$

$$= 4.000 + 0.250 + 0.111 + 4.694 + 2.250 + 0.141 + 0.063 + 2.641$$

$$= 14.150$$

Step 4 Make the decision. Reject the null hypothesis since $14.150 > 7.815$. See Figure 11–9.

FIGURE 11–9

Critical Value and Test Statistic for Example 11–7

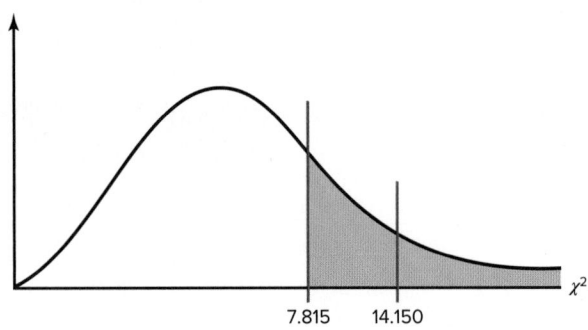

Step 5 Summarize the results. There is enough evidence to reject the claim that there is no difference in the proportions. Hence, the incomes seem to make a difference in the proportions.

When the degrees of freedom for a contingency table are equal to 1—that is, the table is a 2×2 table—some statisticians suggest using the *Yates correction for continuity*. The formula for the test statistic is then

$$\chi^2 = \sum \frac{(|O - E| - 0.5)^2}{E}$$

Since the chi-square test is already conservative, most statisticians agree that the Yates correction is not necessary. (See Exercise 33 in Extending the Concepts.)

Applying the Concepts 11–2

Satellite Dishes in Restricted Areas

The Senate is expected to vote on a bill to allow the installation of satellite dishes of any size in deed-restricted areas. The House had passed a similar bill. An opinion poll was taken to see whether how a person felt about satellite dish restrictions was related to the person's age. A chi-square test was run, creating the following computer-generated information.

Degrees of freedom d.f. = 6
Test statistic $\chi^2 = 61.25$
Critical value C.V. = 12.6
P-value = 0.00
Significance level = 0.05

	18–29	30–49	50–64	65 and up
For	96 (79.5)	96 (79.5)	90 (79.5)	36 (79.5)
Against	201 (204.75)	189 (204.75)	195 (204.75)	234 (204.75)
Don't know	3 (15.75)	15 (15.75)	15 (15.75)	30 (15.75)

1. Which number from the output is compared to the significance level to check if the null hypothesis should be rejected?

2. Which number from the output gives the probability of a type I error that is calculated from your sample data?

3. Was a right-, left-, or two-tailed test run? Why?

4. Can you tell how many rows and columns there were by looking at the degrees of freedom?

5. Does increasing the sample size change the degrees of freedom?

6. What are your conclusions? Look at the observed and expected frequencies in the table to draw some of your own specific conclusions about response and age.

7. What would your conclusions be if the level of significance were initially set at 0.10?

8. Does chi-square tell you which cell's observed and expected frequencies are significantly different?

See page 650 for the answers.

Exercises 11–2

1. How is the chi-square independence test similar to the goodness-of-fit test? How is it different?

2. How are the degrees of freedom computed for the independence test? d.f. = (rows − 1)(columns − 1)

3. Generally, how would the null and alternative hypotheses be stated for the chi-square independence test?

4. What is the name of the table used in the independence test? Contingency table

5. How are the expected values computed for each cell in the table? The expected values are computed as (row total × column total) ÷ grand total.

6. How are the null and alternative hypotheses stated for the test of homogeneity of proportions?

For Exercises 7 through 31, perform the following steps.

   a.   State the hypotheses and identify the claim.
   b.   Find the critical value or use the P-value method.
   c.   Compute the test statistic.
   d.   Make the decision.
   e.   Summarize the results.

Use the traditional method or the P-value method. Assume all assumptions are met.

7. **Living Arrangements** A recent study of 100 individuals found the following living arrangement for men and

women. The results are shown. Check the data for a dependent relationship at $\alpha = 0.05$.

	Spouse	Relative	Nonrelative	Alone
Men	57	8	25	10
Women	53	5	28	14

Source: Based on information from U.S. Census Bureau.

8. **Accidents and Gender** Are the types of accidents related to the gender of the individual at $\alpha = 0.05$?

Type	Motor vehicle	Falls	Poisoning	Drowning
Male	26	12	6	2
Female	22	8	3	1

Source: Based on the National Safety Council

9. **Pet Owners** A study of pet owners showed the following information concerning the ownership of the dogs and cats. At $\alpha = 0.10$, is there a relationship between the number of people in a family and dog or cat ownership?

	1 person	2 people	3 people	4 or more people
Dog	7	16	11	16
Cat	9	14	16	11

10. **Disabling Injuries** Is the type of injury related to the age of the individual at $\alpha = 0.10$?

Type	Motor vehicle	Home	Work	Public
Under 35	24	19	24	22
35 and over	16	22	35	29

Source: Based on the National Safety Council

11. **Violent Crimes** A record of violent crimes for a random sample of cities from the list of U.S. cities with the fewest crimes is shown below. At $\alpha = 0.05$, is there sufficient evidence to indicate a relationship between the city and the type of crime committed?

	Forcible rape	Robbery	Aggravated assault
Cary, NC	14	35	70
Amherst, NY	10	33	76
Simi Valley, CA	14	37	77
Norman, OK	47	36	53

Source: Time Almanac.

12. **Out of Work** Are the reasons for people being out of work based on the gender of the individual? Use $\alpha = 0.10$.

Reason	Company closing	Position abolished	Insufficient work
Men	153	87	32
Women	122	64	56

Source: Based on Department of Labor Statistics

13. **Unemployment Time and Type of Industry** Is the length of unemployment related to the type of industry? A random sample of unemployed workers from three different sectors yielded the following data. At the 0.05 level of significance, are the two categories dependent?

	Less than 5 weeks	5–14 weeks	15–26 weeks
Transportation/ utilities	85	110	80
Information	48	57	45
Financial activities	83	111	114

Source: World Almanac.

14. **Mall Crimes** Are the types of crimes that occur at a shopping mall related to the gender of the criminal? Use $\alpha = 0.05$.

Type	Shoplifting	Auto break-ins	Customer robberies
Male	48	27	23
Female	55	21	14

15. **Student Majors at Colleges** The table shows the number of students (in thousands) participating in various programs at both two-year and four-year institutions. At $\alpha = 0.05$, can it be concluded that there is a relationship between program of study and type of institution?

	Two-year	Four-year
Agriculture and related sciences	36	52
Criminal justice	210	231
Foreign languages and literature	28	59
Mathematics and statistics	28	63

Source: Time Almanac.

16. **Organ Transplantation** Listed is information regarding organ transplantation for three different years. Based on these data, is there sufficient evidence at $\alpha = 0.01$ to conclude that a relationship exists between year and type of transplant?

Year	Heart	Kidney/pancreas	Lung
2003	2056	870	1085
2004	2016	880	1173
2005	2127	903	1408

Source: www.infoplease.com

17. **Automobile Ownership** A study was done on the type of automobiles owned by women and men. The data are shown. At $\alpha = 0.10$, is there a relationship between the type of automobile owned and the gender of the individual?

	Luxury	Large	Midsize	Small
Men	15	9	49	27
Women	9	6	62	14

18. Advertisements Is the type of commercial advertisement based on the type of products or services that are advertised? Amounts are in millions of dollars. Use $\alpha = 0.05$.

Type	TV	Direct mail	Radio	Newspapers
Products	18	13	4	12
Services	6	7	3	10

19. Type of Medicine A medical researcher wishes to determine if the type of vitamin pills taken is related to the age of the person. The data are shown. At $\alpha = 0.10$, is the type of vitamin related to the age of the person taking the vitamin?

	Type		
Age	Liquid	Tablet	Gummy
20–39	5	16	6
40–59	10	25	12
60–over	19	6	5

20. Effectiveness of New Drug To test the effectiveness of a new drug, a researcher gives one group of randomly selected individuals the new drug and another group of randomly selected individuals a placebo. The results of the study are shown here. At $\alpha = 0.10$, can the researcher conclude that the drug results differ from those of the placebo? Use the P-value method.

Medication	Effective	Not effective
Drug	32	9
Placebo	12	18

21. Hospitals and Cesarean Delivery Rates The national Cesarean delivery rate for a recent year was 32.2% (number of live births performed by Cesarean section). A random sample of 100 birth records from three large hospitals showed the following results for type of birth. Test for homogeneity of proportions using $\alpha = 0.10$.

	Hospital A	Hospital B	Hospital C
Cesarean	44	28	39
Non-Cesarean	56	72	61

Source: World Almanac.

22. Foreign Language Speaking Dorms A local college recently made the news by offering foreign language–speaking dorm rooms to its students. When questioned at another school, 50 randomly selected students from each class responded as shown. At $\alpha = 0.05$, is there sufficient evidence to conclude that the proportions of students favoring foreign language–speaking dorms are not the same for each class?

	First-year students	Sophomores	Juniors	Seniors
Yes (favor)	10	15	20	22
No	40	35	30	28

23. Youth Physical Fitness According to a recent survey, 64% of Americans between the ages of 6 and 17 years cannot pass a basic fitness test. A physical education instructor wishes to determine if the percentages of such students in different schools in his school district are the same. He administers a basic fitness test to 120 randomly selected students in each of four schools. The results are shown here. At $\alpha = 0.05$, test the claim that the proportions who pass the test are equal.

	Southside	West End	East Hills	Jefferson
Passed	49	38	46	34
Failed	71	82	74	86
Total	120	120	120	120

Source: The Harper's Index Book.

24. Participation in Gambling The mall manager wanted to see how many of its mall shoppers will use the new mini-casino being established in its malls. A random survey of 75 shoppers of three malls wishing to establish casinos was taken. They were asked if they would use the casino in their mall. The results are shown. At $\alpha = 0.025$, test the claim that the proportions of those willing to use the casinos are equal.

	Mall A	Mall B	Mall C
Yes	38	31	35
No	37	44	40
	75	75	75

25. Athletic Status and Sports A study was done using a random sample of 60 athletes and 60 non-athletes. They were asked what was their favorite sport to watch on television. The data are shown. As $\alpha = 0.05$ test the claim that the proportions are the same.

	Baseball	Football	Hockey	Basketball
Athletes	7	32	16	5
Non-athletes	12	27	12	9

26. TikTok Visitors A psychology professor wishes to see if the proportions of men and women who visit TikTok daily are the same. The professor randomly selects 50 people from each group to see how many are men and how many are women who used TikTok. The data are shown. At $\alpha = 0.025$, are the proportions equal?

	Several times a day	Once a day	Less often
Men	25	18	22
Women	25	32	28

27. **Media and News** A media researcher wishes to see if the type of media that people use to get the news is related to the area that they live in. Random surveys of 100 people were taken in four geographical area of the United States. The data are shown. At $\alpha = 0.05$, test the claim that the proportions are equal.

	NE	SE	NW	SW
Television	44	48	39	51
Other	56	52	61	49

Source: Based on a Pew Research Center Survey

28. **Fathers in the Delivery Room** On average, 79% of American fathers are in the delivery room when their children are born. A physician's assistant surveyed 300 randomly selected first-time fathers to determine if they had been in the delivery room when their children were born. The results are shown here. At $\alpha = 0.05$, is there enough evidence to reject the claim that the proportions of those who were in the delivery room at the time of birth are the same?

	Hospital A	Hospital B	Hospital C	Hospital D
Present	66	60	57	56
Not present	9	15	18	19
Total	75	75	75	75

Source: Daniel Weiss, *100% American.*

29. **Influenza and Age** A medical researcher surveyed the type of emergency visits to four randomly selected hospitals to see if the proportions of influenza cases are the same at each hospital. The data are shown. At $\alpha = 0.10$, are the proportions equal?

	Hospital A	Hospital B	Hospital C	Hospital D
Influenza	26	30	23	28
Other injuries	104	100	107	102

30. **Thanksgiving Travel** According to the American Automobile Association, 31 million Americans travel over the Thanksgiving holiday. To determine whether to stay open or not, a national restaurant chain surveyed 125 customers at each of four locations to see if they would be traveling over the holiday. The results are shown here. At $\alpha = 0.10$, test the claim that the proportions of Americans who will travel over the Thanksgiving holiday are equal. Use the *P*-value method.

	Location A	Location B	Location C	Location D
Will travel	37	52	46	49
Will not travel	88	73	79	76
Total	125	125	125	125

Source: Michael D. Shook and Robert L. Shook, *The Book of Odds.*

31. **Overweight Dogs** A veterinarian wishes to see if the proportion of overweight dogs is related to the breed of dog. The veterinarian selects random samples of four breeds and weighs each, then classifies them as healthy or overweight. The data are shown.

	Labrador retriever	Dachshund	English bulldog	Basset hound
Healthy weight	38	43	52	46
Overweight	62	57	48	54

At $\alpha = 0.10$, are the proportions of the healthy weight dogs related to the breed of the dog?

Extending the Concepts

32. For a 2×2 table, *a*, *b*, *c*, and *d* are the observed values for each cell, as shown.

a	b
c	d

The chi-square test statistic can be computed as

$$\chi^2 = \frac{n(ad - bc)^2}{(a + b)(a + c)(c + d)(b + d)}$$

where $n = a + b + c + d$. Using this formula, compute the χ^2 test statistic and then the formula $\Sigma(O - E)^2/E$, and compare the results. Use the following table.

Both answers are the same. $\chi^2 = 1.70$

12	15
9	23

33. For the contingency table shown in Exercise 32, compute the chi-square test statistic by using the Yates correction (page 636) for continuity. $\chi^2 = 1.064$

34. When the chi-square test statistic is significant and there is a relationship between the variables, the strength of this relationship can be measured by using the *contingency coefficient*. The formula for the contingency coefficient is

$$C = \sqrt{\frac{\chi^2}{\chi^2 + n}}$$

where χ^2 is the test statistic and *n* is the sum of frequencies of the cells. The contingency coefficient will always be less than 1. Compute the contingency coefficient for Exercises 8 and 20. 0.0919; 0.3610

SPEAKING OF STATISTICS Does Color Affect Your Appetite?

It has been suggested that color is related to appetite in humans. For example, if the walls in a restaurant are painted certain colors, it is thought that the customer will eat more food. A study was done at the University of Illinois and the University of Pennsylvania. When people were given six varieties of jellybeans mixed in a bowl or separated by color, they ate about twice as many from the bowl with the mixed jellybeans as from the bowls that were separated by color.

It is thought that when the jellybeans were mixed, people felt that it offered a greater variety of choices, and the variety of choices increased their appetites.

In this case one variable—color—is categorical, and the other variable—amount of jellybeans eaten—is numerical. Could a chi-square goodness-of-fit test be used here? If so, suggest how it could be set up.

Siede Preis/Getty Images

Technology

TI-84 Plus
Step by Step

Step by Step

Chi-Square Test for Independence

1. Press **2nd** $[X^{-1}]$ for **MATRIX** and move the cursor to Edit; then press **ENTER**.
2. Enter the number of rows and columns. Then press **ENTER**.
3. Enter the values in the matrix as they appear in the contingency table.
4. Press **STAT** and move the cursor to TESTS. Press **C (ALPHA PRGM)** for χ^2-Test. Make sure the observed matrix is [A] and the expected matrix is [B].
5. Move the cursor to Calculate and press **ENTER**.

Example TI11–2

Test the claim of independence at $\alpha = 0.10$.

	Football	Baseball	Hockey
Male	18	10	4
Female	20	16	12

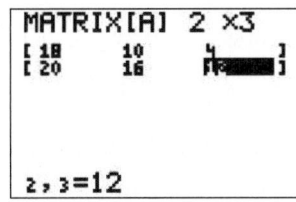

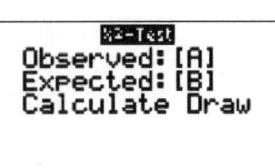

The test statistic is 2.385290148. The P-value is 0.3034176395. The decision is to not reject the null hypothesis, since the P-value is greater than 0.10. You can find the expected values by pressing **MATRIX,** moving the cursor to [B], and pressing **ENTER** twice.

EXCEL

Step by Step

Tests Using Contingency Tables

Excel does not have a procedure to conduct tests using contingency tables without including the expected values. However, you may conduct such tests using the MegaStat Add-in available in your online resources. If you have not installed this add-in, do so, following the instructions from the Chapter 1 Excel Step by Step.

Example XL11–3

The table below shows the number of years of college a person has completed and the residence of the person.

Using a significance level $\alpha = 0.05$, determine whether the number of years of college a person has completed is related to residence.

◢	A	B	C	D
1		None	4-Year	Advanced
2	Urban	15	12	8
3	Suburban	8	15	9
4	Rural	6	8	7

1. Enter the location variable labels in column A, beginning at cell A2.
2. Enter the categories for the number of years of college in cells B1, C1, and D1, respectively.
3. Enter the observed values in the appropriate block (cell).
4. From the toolbar, select Add-Ins, **MegaStat>Chi-Square/Crosstab>Contingency Table.** *Note:* You may need to open MegaStat from the MegaStat.xls file on your computer's hard drive.
5. In the dialog box, type **A1:D4** for the Input range.
6. Check chi-square, Expected values, and $(O - E)_2/E$ from the Output Options.
7. Click [OK].

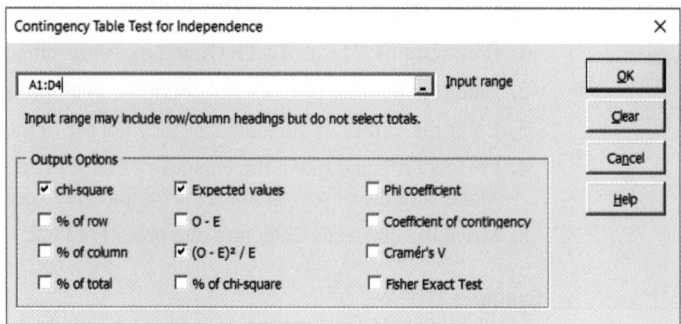

Chi-square Contingency Table Test for Independence

		None	4-Year	Advanced	Total
Urban	Observed	15	12	8	35
	Expected	11.53	13.92	9.55	35.00
	$(O - E)^2 / E$	1.04	0.26	0.25	1.56
Suburban	Observed	8	15	9	32
	Expected	10.55	12.73	8.73	32.00
	$(O - E)^2 / E$	0.61	0.41	0.01	1.03
Rural	Observed	6	8	7	21
	Expected	6.92	8.35	5.73	21.00
	$(O - E)^2 / E$	0.12	0.01	0.28	0.42
Total	Observed	29	35	24	88
	Expected	29.00	35.00	24.00	88.00
	$(O - E)^2 / E$	1.78	0.69	0.54	3.01

3.01 chi-square
4 df
.5569 p-value

The results of the test indicate that at the 5% level of significance, there is not enough evidence to conclude that a person's location is dependent on number of years of college.

MINITAB

Step by Step

Chi-Square Test of Independence from Contingency Table

Example 11–5

Is there a relationship between the type of infection and the hospital?

1. Enter the Observed Frequencies for the type of infection in C1 Surgical Site, C2 Pneumonia, and C3 Bloodstream. Do not include row labels or totals.

2. Select **Stat>Tables>Chi-Square Test for Association.**

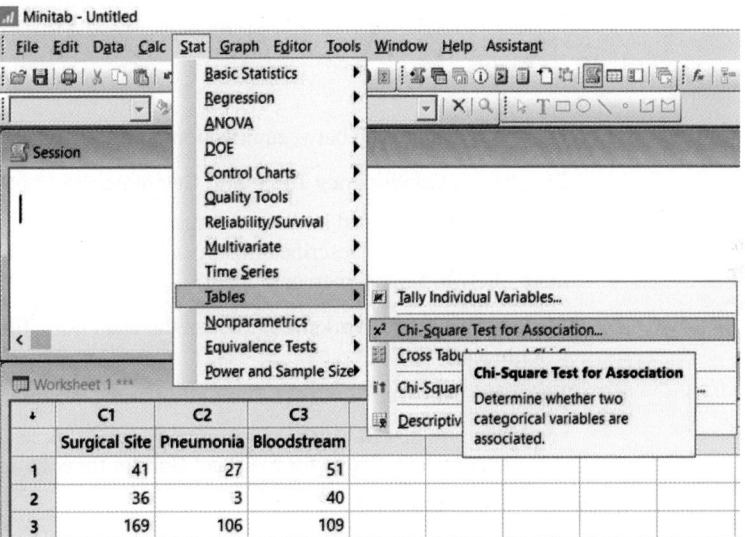

a) In the drop-down menu select Summarized data in a two-way table.
b) Click the text box for Columns containing the table and then double click each column name to include it in the list.
c) Click on Statistics. Select Each cells contribution to chi-square, then [OK] twice.

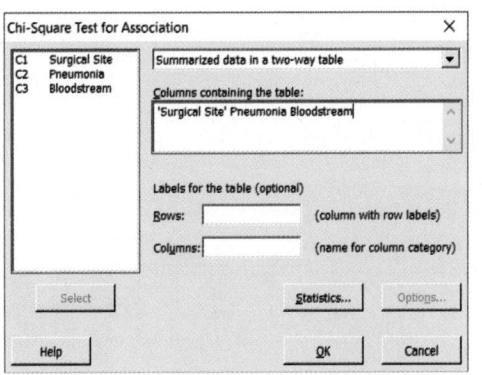

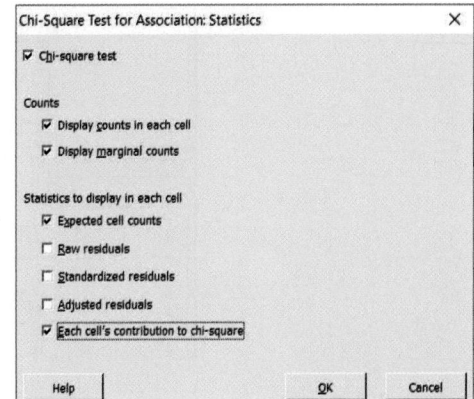

The results are displayed in the session window.

Chi-Square Test for Association: Worksheet rows, Worksheet columns

```
    Surgical Site  Pneumonia  Bloodstream      All
1             41         27           51      119
           50.30      27.81        40.89
           1.719      0.023        2.498

2             36          3           40       79
           33.39      18.46        27.15
           0.204     12.948        6.084

3            169        106          109      384
          162.31      89.73       131.96
           0.276      2.949        3.994

All          246        136          200      582

Cell Contents:        Count
                      Expected count
                      Contribution to Chi-square

Pearson Chi-Square = 30.696, DF = 4, P-Value = 0.000
Likelihood Ratio Chi-Square = 37.000, DF = 4, P-Value = 0.000
```

There is a relationship between infection type and hospital.

Construct a Contingency Table and Calculate the Chi-Square Test Statistic

In Chapter 4 we learned how to construct a contingency table by using gender and smoking status in the Data Bank file described in Appendix B. Are smoking status and gender related? Who is more likely to smoke, men or women?

1. Use **File>Open Worksheet** to open the Data Bank file. Remember, do *not* click the file icon.

2. Select **Stat>Tables>Cross Tabulation and Chi-Square.**

3. Make sure that Raw data (categorical variables) is selected in the drop-down menu. Double-click Smoking Status for rows and Gender for columns.

4. Click on Statistics.

5. Click [Chi-Square].

    a) Check Chi-Square test.
    b) Check Display counts in each cell.
    c) Display Marginal Counts
    d) Check Expected cell counts.
    e) Check Each cell's contribution to chi-square.

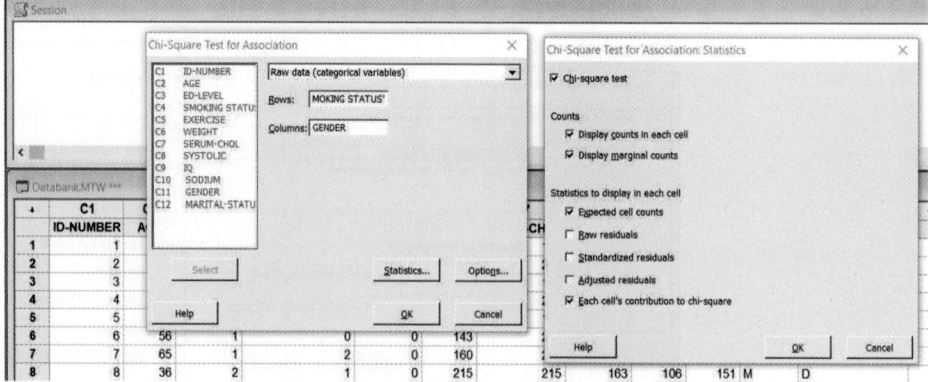

6. Click [OK] twice.

In the session window the contingency table and the chi-square analysis will be displayed.

Chi-Square Test for Association: SMOKING STATUS, GENDER

```
Rows: SMOKING STATUS   Columns: GENDER
               F         M       All
0             25        22        47
           23.50     23.50
          0.09574   0.09574

1             18        19        37
           18.50     18.50
          0.01351   0.01351

2              7         9        16
            8.00      8.00
          0.12500   0.12500

All           50        50       100

Cell Contents:        Count
                      Expected count
                      Contribution to Chi-square

Pearson Chi-Square = 0.469, DF = 2, P-Value = 0.791
Likelihood Ratio Chi-Square = 0.469, DF = 2, P-Value = 0.791
```

There is not enough evidence to conclude that smoking is related to gender.

Summary

- Three uses of the chi-square distribution were explained in this chapter. It can be used as a goodness-of-fit test to determine whether the frequencies of a distribution are the same as the hypothesized frequencies. For example, is the number of defective parts produced by a factory the same each day? This test is always a right-tailed test. (11–1)

- The test of independence is used to determine whether two variables are related or are independent. This test uses a contingency table and is always a right-tailed test.

An example of its use is a test to determine if attitudes about trash recycling are dependent on whether residents live in urban or rural areas. (11–2)

- Finally, the homogeneity of proportions test is used to determine if several proportions are all equal when samples are selected from different populations. (11–2)

The chi-square distribution is also used for other types of statistical hypothesis tests, such as the Kruskal-Wallis test, which is explained in Chapter 13.

Important Terms

cell value 628

chi-square goodness-of-fit test 614

contingency table 628

expected frequency 614

homogeneity of proportions test 634

independence test 628

observed frequency 614

Important Formulas

Formula for the chi-square test for goodness of fit:

$$\chi^2 = \sum \frac{(O-E)^2}{E}$$

with degrees of freedom equal to the (number of rows minus 1)(number of columns minus 1) and where

O = observed frequency

E = expected frequency

Formula for the chi-square independence and homogeneity of proportions tests:

$$\chi^2 = \sum \frac{(O-E)^2}{E}$$

with degrees of freedom equal to (rows − 1) times (columns − 1). Formula for the expected value for each cell:

$$E = \frac{(\text{row sum})(\text{column sum})}{\text{grand total}}$$

Review Exercises

For Exercises 1 through 10, follow these steps.

   a. State the hypotheses and identify the claim.

   b. Find the critical value(s) or use the *P*-value method.

   c. Compute the test statistic.

   d. Make the decision.

   e. Summarize the results.

Use the traditional method or the P-value method. Assume all assumptions are met.

Section 11–1

1. **Traffic Accident Fatalities** A traffic safety report indicated that for the 21–24 year age group, 31.58% of traffic fatalities were victims who had used a seat belt. Victims who were not wearing a seat belt accounted for 59.83% of the deaths, and the status of the rest was unknown. A study of 120 randomly selected traffic fatalities in a particular region showed that for this age group, 35 of the victims had used a seat belt, 78 had not, and the status of the rest was unknown. At $\alpha = 0.05$, is there sufficient evidence that the proportions differ from those in the report?

   Source: New York Times Almanac.

2. **Displaced Workers** The reasons that workers in the 25–54 year old category were displaced are listed.

Plant closed/moved	44.8%
Insufficient work	25.2%
Position eliminated	30%

   A random sample of 180 displaced workers (in this age category) found that 40 lost their jobs due to their position being eliminated, 53 due to insufficient work, and the rest due to the company being closed or moving. At the 0.01 level of significance, are these proportions different from those from the U.S. Department of Labor?

   Source: BLS-World Almanac.

3. **Gun Sale Denials** A police investigator read that the reasons why gun sales to applicants were denied were distributed as follows: criminal history of felonies, 75%; domestic violence conviction, 11%; and drug abuse, fugitive, etc., 14%. A random sample of applicants in a large study who were refused sales is obtained and is distributed as follows. At $\alpha = 0.10$, can it be concluded that the distribution is as stated? Do you think the results might be different in a rural area?

Reason	Criminal history	Domestic violence	Drug abuse, etc.
Number	120	42	38

   Source: Based on FBI statistics.

4. **Type of Music Preferred** A store manager wishes to see if the employees of the store had a preference in the types of music played on the speaker system. A survey of 60 employees stated the type of music they preferred. The data are shown. At $\alpha = 0.05$, is there a preference?

Type	Classical	Country	Pop	Rock
Number	9	18	22	11

Section 11–2

5. **Pension Investments** A survey was conducted on how a lump-sum pension would be invested by randomly selected 45-year-olds and randomly selected 65-year-olds. The data are shown here. At $\alpha = 0.05$, is there a relationship between the age of the investor and the way the money would be invested?

	Large company stock funds	Small company stock funds	International stock funds	CDs or money market funds	Bonds
Age 45	20	10	10	15	45
Age 65	42	24	24	6	24

   Source: USA TODAY.

6. **Tornadoes** According to records from the Storm Prediction Center, the following numbers of tornadoes occurred in the first quarter of each of years 2012–2015. Is there sufficient evidence to conclude that a relationship exists between the month and year in which the tornadoes occurred? Use $\alpha = 0.05$.

	2015	2014	2013	2012
January	26	4	87	97
February	2	41	46	63
March	13	25	18	225

   Source: National Weather Service Storm Prediction Center.

7. **Employment of High School Females** A guidance counselor wishes to determine if the proportions of female high school students in his school district who have jobs are equal to the national average of 36%. He randomly surveys 80 female students, ages 16 through 18 years, to determine if they work. The results are shown. At $\alpha = 0.01$, test the claim that the proportions of female students who work are equal. Use the *P*-value method.

	16-year-olds	17-year-olds	18-year-olds
Work	45	31	38
Don't work	35	49	42
Total	80	80	80

   Source: Michael D. Shook and Robert L. Shook, The Book of Odds.

8. **Risk of Injury** The risk of injury is higher for males compared to females (57% versus 43%). A hospital emergency room supervisor wishes to determine if the proportions of injuries to males in his hospital are the

≡ STATISTICS TODAY

Statistics and Heredity— **Revisited**

Using probability, Mendel predicted the following:

	Smooth		Wrinkled	
	Yellow	Green	Yellow	Green
Expected	0.5625	0.1875	0.1875	0.0625

The observed results were these:

	Smooth		Wrinkled	
	Yellow	Green	Yellow	Green
Observed	0.5666	0.1942	0.1816	0.0556

Using chi-square tests on the data, Mendel found that his predictions were accurate in most cases (i.e., a good fit), thus supporting his theory. He reported many highly successful experiments. Mendel's genetic theory is simple but useful in predicting the results of hybridization.

A Fly in the Ointment

Although Mendel's theory is basically correct, an English statistician named R. A. Fisher examined Mendel's data some 50 years later. He found that the observed (actual) results agreed too closely with the expected (theoretical) results and concluded that the data had been falsified in some way. The results were too good to be true. Several explanations have been proposed, ranging from deliberate misinterpretation to an assistant's error, but no one can be sure how this happened.

same for each of 4 months. He randomly surveys 100 injuries treated in his ER for each month. The results are shown. At $\alpha = 0.05$, can he reject the claim that the proportions of injuries for males are equal for each of the four months?

	May	June	July	August
Male	51	47	58	63
Female	49	53	42	37
Total	100	100	100	100

Source: Michael D. Shook and Robert L. Shook, *The Book of Odds.*

9. Living Arrangements A study was done on the living arrangement of individuals aged 18 to 24 years to see if the proportions of people are different today than those of 10 years ago. The data are shown. At $\alpha = 0.05$, test the claim.

	Parents	Spouse	Non–family member	Other
10 years ago	47	38	5	10
Today	57	20	9	14

10. Cardiovascular Procedures Is the frequency of cardiovascular procedure related to gender? The following data were obtained for selected procedures for a recent year. At $\alpha = 0.10$, is there sufficient evidence to conclude a dependent relationship between gender and procedure?

	Coronary artery stent	Coronary artery bypass	Pacemaker
Men	425	320	198
Women	227	123	219

Source: New York Times Almanac.

≡ Data Analysis

The Data Bank is located in Appendix B.

1. Select a random sample of 40 individuals from the Data Bank. Use the chi-square goodness-of-fit test to see if the marital status of individuals is equally distributed.

2. Use the chi-square test of independence to test the hypothesis that smoking is independent of gender. Use a random sample of at least 75 people.

3. Using the data from Data Set X in Appendix B, classify the data as 1–3, 4–6, 7–9, etc. Use the chi-square goodness-of-fit test to see if the number of times each ball is drawn is equally distributed.

⬛ Chapter Quiz

Determine whether each statement is true or false. If the statement is false, explain why.

1. The chi-square test of independence is always two-tailed. False

2. The test statistics for the chi-square goodness-of-fit test and the independence test are computed by using the same formula. True

3. When the null hypothesis is rejected in the goodness-of-fit test, it means there is close agreement between the observed and expected frequencies. False

Select the best answer.

4. The values of the chi-square variable cannot be
   a. Positive   c. Negative
   b. 0   d. None of the above

5. The null hypothesis for the chi-square test of independence is that the variables are
   a. Dependent   c. Related
   b. Independent   d. Always 0

6. The degrees of freedom for the goodness-of-fit test are
   a. 0   c. Sample size − 1
   b. 1   d. Number of categories − 1

Complete the following statements with the best answer.

7. The degrees of freedom for a 4 × 3 contingency table are _____. 6

8. An important assumption for the chi-square test is that the observations must be _____. Independent

9. The chi-square goodness-of-fit test is always _____-tailed. Right

10. In the chi-square independence test, the expected frequency for each class must always be _____. At least 5

For Exercises 11 through 19, follow these steps.
   a. State the hypotheses and identify the claim.
   b. Find the critical value or use the *P*-value method.
   c. Compute the test statistic.
   d. Make the decision.
   e. Summarize the results.

Use the traditional method or the P-value method. Assume all assumptions are met.

11. **Job Loss Reasons** A survey of why randomly selected people lost their jobs produced the following results. At α = 0.05, test the claim that the number of responses is equally distributed. Do you think the results might be different if the study were done 10 years ago?

Reason	Company closing	Position abolished	Insufficient work
Number	26	18	28

Source: Based on information from U.S. Department of Labor.

12. **Consumption of Takeout Foods** A food service manager read that the place where people consumed takeout food is distributed as follows: home, 53%; car, 19%; work, 14%; other, 14%. A survey of 300 randomly selected individuals showed the following results. At α = 0.01, can it be concluded that the distribution is as stated? Where would a fast-food restaurant want to target its advertisements?

Place	Home	Car	Work	Other
Number	142	57	51	50

Source: Beef Industry Council.

13. **Television Viewing** A survey of randomly selected people found that 62% of the respondents stated that they never watched the home shopping channels on cable television, 23% stated that they watched the channels rarely, 11% stated that they watched them occasionally, and 4% stated that they watched them frequently. A group of 200 randomly selected college students was surveyed; 105 stated that they never watched the home shopping channels, 72 stated that they watched them rarely, 13 stated that they watched them occasionally, and 10 stated that they watched them frequently. At α = 0.05, can it be concluded that the college students differ in their preference for the home shopping channels?

Source: Based on information obtained from *USA TODAY* Snapshots.

14. **Ways to Get to Work** The 2010 Census indicated the following percentages for means of commuting to work for workers over 15 years of age.

Alone	76.6
Carpooling	9.7
Public	4.7
Walked	2.8
Other	1.7
Worked at home	4.3

A random sample of workers found that 320 drove alone, 100 carpooled, 30 used public transportation, 20 walked, 10 used other forms of transportation, and 20 worked at home. Is there sufficient evidence to conclude that the proportions of workers using each type of transportation differ from those in the Census report? Use α = 0.05.

Source: U.S. Census Bureau, *Washington Observer-Reporter.*

15. **Favorite Ice Cream Flavor** A survey of randomly selected women and randomly selected men asked what their favorite ice cream flavor was. The results are shown. At α = 0.05, can it be concluded that the favorite flavor is independent of gender?

	Flavor			
	Vanilla	**Chocolate**	**Strawberry**	**Other**
Women	62	36	10	2
Men	49	37	5	9

16. Types of Pizzas Purchased A pizza shop owner wishes to determine if the type of pizza a person selects is related to the age of the individual. The data obtained from a sample are shown. At $\alpha = 0.10$, is the age of the purchaser related to the type of pizza ordered? Use the P-value method.

Type of pizza

Age	Plain	Pepperoni	Mushroom	Double cheese
10–19	12	21	39	71
20–29	18	76	52	87
30–39	24	50	40	47
40–49	52	30	12	28

17. Pennant Colors Purchased A survey at a ballpark shows the following selection of pennants sold to randomly selected fans. The data are presented here. At $\alpha = 0.10$, is the color of the pennant purchased independent of the gender of the individual?

	Blue	Yellow	Red
Men	519	659	876
Women	487	702	787

18. Tax Credit Refunds In a survey of randomly selected children ages 8 through 11 years, data were obtained as to what they think their parents should do with the money from a $400 tax credit.

	Keep it for themselves	Give it to their children	Don't know
Girls	162	132	6
Boys	147	147	6

At $\alpha = 0.10$, is there a relationship between the feelings of the children and the gender of the children?

Source: Based on information from *USA TODAY* Snapshot.

19. Employment Satisfaction A survey of 60 randomly selected men and 60 randomly selected women asked if they would be happy spending the rest of their careers with their present employers. The results are shown. At $\alpha = 0.10$, can it be concluded that the proportions are equal? If they are not equal, give a possible reason for the difference.

	Yes	No	Undecided
Men	40	15	5
Women	36	9	15

Source: Based on information from a Maritz Poll.

Critical Thinking Challenges

1. **Random Digits** Use your calculator or the MINITAB random number generator to generate 100 two-digit random numbers. Make a grouped frequency distribution, using the chi-square goodness-of-fit test to see if the distribution is random. To do this, use an expected frequency of 10 for each class. Can it be concluded that the distribution is random? Explain.

2. **Lottery Numbers** Simulate the state lottery by using your calculator or MINITAB to generate 100 three-digit random numbers. Group these numbers 000–099, 100–199, etc. Use the chi-square goodness-of-fit test to see if the numbers are random. The expected frequency for each class should be 10. Explain why.

3. **M&M's Colors** Purchase a bag of M&M's candy and count the number of pieces of each color. Using the information as your sample, state a hypothesis for the distribution of colors, and compare your hypothesis to H_0: The distribution of colors of M&M's candy is 13% brown, 13% red, 14% yellow, 16% green, 20% orange, and 24% blue.

Data Projects

Use a significance level of 0.05 for all tests below.

1. **Business and Finance** Many of the companies that produce multicolored candy will include on their website information about the production percentages for the various colors. Select a favorite multicolored candy. Find out what percentage of each color is produced. Open up a bag of the candy, noting how many of each color are in the bag (be careful to count them before you eat them). Is the bag distributed as expected based on the production percentages? If no production percentages can be found, test to see if the colors are uniformly distributed.

2. **Sports and Leisure** Use a local (or favorite) basketball, football, baseball, or hockey team as the data set. For the most recently completed season, note the team's home record for wins and losses. Test to see whether home field advantage is independent of sport.

3. **Technology** Use the data collected in data project 3 of Chapter 2 regarding song genres. Do the data indicate that songs are uniformly distributed among the genres?

4. **Health and Wellness** Research the percentages of each blood type that the Red Cross states are in the population. Now use your class as a sample. For each student note the blood type. Is the distribution of blood types in your class as expected based on the Red Cross percentages?

5. **Politics and Economics** Research the distribution (by percent) of registered Republicans, Democrats, and Independents in your state. Use your class as a sample.

For each student, note the party affiliation. Is the distribution as expected based on the percentages for your state? What might be problematic about using your class as a sample for this exercise?

6. **Your Class** Conduct a classroom poll to determine which of the following sports each student likes best: baseball, football, basketball, hockey, or NASCAR. Also, note the gender of the individual. Is preference for sport independent of gender?

Answers to Applying the Concepts

Section 11–1   Skittles Color Distribution

1. The variables are qualitative, and we have the counts for each category.

2. We can use a chi-square goodness-of-fit test.

3. There are a total of 233 candies, so we would expect 46.6 of each color. Our test statistic is $\chi^2 = 1.442$.

4. H_0: The colors are equally distributed.
   H_1: The colors are not equally distributed.

5. There are $5 - 1 = 4$ degrees of freedom for the test. The critical value depends on the choice of significance level. At the 0.05 significance level, the critical value is 9.488.

6. Since $1.442 < 9.488$, we fail to reject the null hypothesis. There is not enough evidence to conclude that the colors are not equally distributed.

Section 11–2   Satellite Dishes in Restricted Areas

1. We compare the P-value to the significance level of 0.05 to check if the null hypothesis should be rejected.

2. The significance level gives the probability of a type I error.

3. This is a right-tailed test, since chi-square tests of independence are always right-tailed.

4. You cannot tell how many rows and columns there were just by looking at the degrees of freedom.

5. Increasing the sample size does not increase the degrees of freedom, since the degrees of freedom are based on the number of rows and columns.

6. We will reject the null hypothesis. There are a number of cells where the observed and expected frequencies are quite different.

7. If the significance level were initially set at 0.10, we would still reject the null hypothesis.

8. No, the chi-square value does not tell us which cells have observed and expected frequencies that are very different.

12

Analysis of Variance

Caiaimage/Glow Images

STATISTICS TODAY

Can Bringing Your Dog to Work Reduce Stress?

A study done by Virginia Commonwealth University researchers found that employees who brought their dogs to work had reduced job-related stress. The researchers selected a business that allowed employees to bring their dogs to work. Then they divided the employees into three groups: those who brought their dogs to work, those who owned dogs but did not bring them to work, and those who did not own any pets. For one week, the researchers measured the levels of the stress hormone cortisol in the workers' saliva and used surveys to gauge the stress levels of the three groups of employees.

After the week was up, the researchers compared the average levels of cortisol and the stress survey results of the three groups. Since there were three groups, the statistical methods that have been presented so far cannot be used to compare means of three groups. This chapter will show how to compare three or more means. See Statistics Today—Revisited at the end of the chapter to see how this might be done.

OBJECTIVES

After completing this chapter, you should be able to

1 Use the one-way ANOVA technique to determine if there is a significant difference among three or more means.

2 Determine which means differ, using the Scheffé, Tukey, or Bonferroni tests if the null hypothesis is rejected in the ANOVA.

3 Use the two-way ANOVA technique to determine if there is a significant difference in the main effects or interaction.

Introduction

The *F* test, used to compare two variances as shown in Chapter 9, can also be used to compare three or more means. This technique is called *analysis of variance,* or *ANOVA.* It is used to test claims involving three or more means. (*Note:* The *F* test can also be used to test the equality of two means. But since it is equivalent to the *t* test in this case, the *t* test is usually used instead of the *F* test when there are only two means.) For example, suppose a researcher wishes to see whether the means of the time it takes three groups of students to solve a computer problem using HTML, Java, and PHP are different. The researcher will use the ANOVA technique for this test. The *z* and *t* tests should not be used when three or more means are compared, for reasons given later in this chapter.

For three groups, the *F* test can show only whether a difference exists among the three means. It cannot reveal where the difference lies—that is, between $\overline{X}_1$ and $\overline{X}_2$, or $\overline{X}_1$ and $\overline{X}_3$, or $\overline{X}_2$ and $\overline{X}_3$. If the *F* test indicates that there is a difference among the means, other statistical tests are used to find where the difference exists. The most commonly used tests are the Scheffé test and the Tukey test, which are also explained in this chapter.

The analysis of variance that is used to compare three or more means is called a *one-way analysis of variance* since it contains only one variable. In the previous example, the variable is the type of computer language used. The analysis of variance can be extended to studies involving two variables, such as type of computer language used and mathematical background of the students. These studies involve a *two-way analysis of variance.* Section 12–3 explains the two-way analysis of variance.

12–1   One-Way Analysis of Variance

OBJECTIVE

Use the one-way ANOVA technique to determine if there is a significant difference among three or more means.

When an *F* test is used to test a hypothesis concerning the means of three or more populations, the technique is called **analysis of variance** (commonly abbreviated as **ANOVA**).

> The **one-way analysis of variance** test is used to test the equality of three or more means using sample variances.

The procedure used in this section is called the one-way analysis of variance because there is only one independent variable that distinguishes between the different populations in the study. The independent variable is also called a *factor.*

At first glance, you might think that to compare the means of three or more samples, you can use multiple *t* tests comparing two means at a time. But there are several reasons why the *t* test should not be done.

First, when you are comparing two means at a time, the rest of the means under study are ignored. With the *F* test, all the means are compared simultaneously. Second, when you are comparing two means at a time and making all pairwise comparisons, the probability of rejecting the null hypothesis when it is true is increased, since the more *t* tests that are conducted, the greater is the likelihood of getting significant differences by chance alone. Third, the more means there are to compare, the more *t* tests are needed. For example, for the comparison of 3 means two at a time, 3 *t* tests are required. For the comparison of 5 means two at a time, 10 tests are required. And for the comparison of 10 means two at a time, 45 tests are required.

As the number of populations to be compared increases, the probability of making a type I error using multiple *t* tests for a given level of significance α also increases. To address this problem, the technique of analysis of variance is used. This technique involves a comparison of two estimates of the same population variance.

Recall that the characteristics of the *F* distribution are as follows:

1. The values of *F* cannot be negative, because variances are always positive or zero.

2. The distribution is positively skewed.

3. The mean value of *F* is approximately equal to 1.

4. The *F* distribution is a family of curves based on the degrees of freedom of the variance of the numerator and the degrees of freedom of the variance of the denominator.

Even though you are comparing three or more means in this use of the F test, *variances* are used in the test instead of means.

With the F test, two different estimates of the population variance are made. The first estimate is called the **between-group variance,** and it involves finding the variance of the means. The second estimate, the **within-group variance,** is made by computing the variance using all the data and is not affected by differences in the means. If there is no difference in the means, the between-group variance estimate will be approximately equal to the within-group variance estimate, and the F test statistic will be approximately equal to one. The null hypothesis will not be rejected. However, when the means differ significantly, the between-group variance will be much larger than the within-group variance; the F test statistic will be significantly greater than one; and the null hypothesis will be rejected. Since variances are compared, this procedure is called *analysis of variance* (ANOVA).

The formula for the F test is

$$F = \frac{\text{variance between groups}}{\text{variance within groups}}$$

The variance between groups measures the differences in the means that result from the different treatments given to each group. To calculate this value, it is necessary to find the *grand mean* $\overline{X}_{\text{GM}}$, which is the mean of all the values in all of the samples. The formula for the grand mean is

$$\overline{X}_{\text{GM}} = \frac{\Sigma X}{N}$$

This value is used to find the between-group variance s_B^2. This is the variance among the means using the sample sizes as weights.

The formula for the between-group variance, denoted by s_B^2, is

$$s_B^2 = \frac{\Sigma n_i(\overline{X}_i - \overline{X}_{\text{GM}})^2}{k - 1}$$

where k = number of groups

    n_i = sample size

    $\overline{X}_i$ = sample mean

This formula can be written out as

$$s_B^2 = \frac{n_1(\overline{X}_1 - \overline{X}_{\text{GM}})^2 + n_2(\overline{X}_2 - \overline{X}_{\text{GM}})^2 + \cdots + n_k(\overline{X}_k - \overline{X}_{\text{GM}})^2}{k - 1}$$

Next find the within group variance, denoted by s_W^2. The formula finds the overall variance by calculating a weighted average of the individual variances. It does not involve using differences of means. The formula for the within-group variance is

$$s_W^2 = \frac{\Sigma(n_i - 1)s_i^2}{\Sigma(n_i - 1)}$$

where n_i = sample size

    s_i^2 = variance of sample

This formula can be written out as

$$s_W^2 = \frac{(n_1 - 1)s_1^2 + (n_2 - 1)s_2^2 + \cdots + (n_k - 1)s_k^2}{(n_1 - 1) + (n_2 - 1) + \cdots + (n_k - 1)}$$

Finally, the F test statistic is computed. The formula can now be written using the symbols s_B^2 and s_W^2.

The formula for the F test for one-way analysis of variance is

$$F = \frac{s_B^2}{s_W^2}$$

where s_B^2 = between-group variance

    s_W^2 = within-group variance

For a test of the difference among three or more means, the following hypotheses can be used.

$$H_0: \mu_1 = \mu_2 = \cdots = \mu_n$$
$$H_1: \text{At least one mean is different from the others}$$

The alternative hypothesis means that at least one mean differs from one or more of the other means and as previously stated, a significant test statistic means that there is a high probability that this difference in means is not due to chance, but it does not indicate where the difference lies.

The degrees of freedom for this F test are d.f.N. $= k - 1$, where k is the number of groups, and d.f.D. $= N - k$, where N is the sum of the sample sizes of the groups $N = n_1 + n_2 + \cdots + n_k$. The sample sizes need not be equal. The F test to compare means is always right-tailed.

The results of the one-way analysis of variance can be summarized by placing them in an **ANOVA summary table.** The numerator of the fraction of the s_B^2 term is called the **sum of squares between groups,** denoted by SS_B. The numerator of the s_W^2 term is called the **sum of squares within groups,** denoted by SS_W. This statistic is also called the *sum of squares for the error.* SS_B is divided by d.f.N. to obtain the between-group variance. SS_W is divided by $N - k$ to obtain the within-group or error variance. These two variances are sometimes called **mean squares,** denoted by MS_B and MS_W. These terms are used to summarize the analysis of variance and are placed in a summary table, as shown in Table 12–1.

TABLE 12–1 Analysis of Variance Summary Table

Source	Sum of squares	d.f.	Mean square	F
Between groups	SS_B	$k - 1$	MS_B	
Within groups (error)	SS_W	$N - k$	MS_W	
Total				

In the table,

$$SS_B = \text{sum of squares between groups} = \Sigma n_i (\overline{X}_i - \overline{X}_{GM})^2$$
$$SS_W = \text{sum of squares within groups} = \Sigma (n_i - 1)s_i^2$$
$$k = \text{number of groups}$$
$$N = n_1 + n_2 + \cdots + n_k = \text{sum of sample sizes for groups}$$
$$MS_B = s_B^2 = \frac{SS_B}{k - 1}$$
$$MS_W = s_W^2 = \frac{SS_W}{N - k}$$
$$F = \frac{s_B^2}{s_W^2} = \frac{MS_B}{MS_W}$$

To use the F test to compare two or more means, the following assumptions must be met.

Assumptions for the F Test for Comparing Three or More Means

1. The populations from which the samples were obtained must be normally or approximately normally distributed.
2. The samples must be independent of one another.
3. The variances of the populations must be equal.
4. The samples must be simple random samples, one from each of the populations.

In this book, the assumptions will be stated in the exercises; however, when encountering statistics in other situations, you must check to see that these assumptions have been met before proceeding.

The steps for computing the F test statistic for the ANOVA are summarized in this Procedure Table.

Procedure Table

Finding the *F* Test Statistic for the Analysis of Variance

Step 1   Find the mean and variance of each sample.

$$(\overline{X}_1, s_1^2), (\overline{X}_2, s_2^2), \ldots, (\overline{X}_k, s_k^2)$$

Step 2   Find the grand mean.

$$\overline{X}_{GM} = \frac{\Sigma X}{N}$$

Step 3   Find the between-group variance.

$$s_B^2 = \frac{\Sigma n_i(\overline{X}_i - \overline{X}_{GM})^2}{k - 1}$$

Step 4   Find the within-group variance.

$$s_W^2 = \frac{\Sigma(n_i - 1)s_i^2}{\Sigma(n_i - 1)}$$

Step 5   Find the *F* test statistic.

$$F = \frac{s_B^2}{s_W^2}$$

The degrees of freedom are

$$\text{d.f.N.} = k - 1$$

where *k* is the number of groups, and

$$\text{d.f.D.} = N - k$$

where *N* is the sum of the sample sizes of the groups

$$N = n_1 + n_2 + \cdots + n_k$$

The one-way analysis of variance follows the regular five-step hypothesis-testing procedure.

Step 1   State the hypotheses.

Step 2   Find the critical values.

Step 3   Compute the test statistic.

Step 4   Make the decision.

Step 5   Summarize the results.

Examples 12–1 and 12–2 illustrate the computational procedure for the ANOVA technique for comparing three or more means, and the steps are summarized in the Procedure Table.

EXAMPLE 12–1   Miles per Gallon

A researcher wishes to see if there is a difference in the fuel economy for city driving for three different types of automobiles: small automobiles, sedans, and luxury automobiles. He randomly samples four small automobiles, five sedans, and three luxury automobiles. The miles per gallon for each is shown. At $\alpha = 0.05$, test the claim that there is no difference among the means. The data are shown.

Small	Sedans	Luxury
36	43	29
44	35	25
34	30	24
35	29	
	40	

Source: U.S. Environmental Protection Agency.

Step 1   State the hypotheses and identify the claim.

H_0: $\mu_1 = \mu_2 = \mu_3$ (claim)
H_1: At least one mean is different from the others

Step 2   Find the critical value.

$$N = 12 \qquad k = 3$$
$$\text{d.f.N.} = k - 1 = 3 - 1 = 2$$
$$\text{d.f.D.} = N - k = 12 - 3 = 9$$

The critical value from Table A–7 in Appendix A with $\alpha = 0.05$ is 4.26.

Step 3   Compute the test statistic.

a. Find the mean and variance for each sample. (Use the formulas in Chapter 3.)

For the small cars: $\quad \overline{X} = 37.25 \qquad s^2 = 20.917$
For the sedans: $\qquad\;\; \overline{X} = 35.4 \qquad\;\; s^2 = 37.3$
For the luxury cars: $\;\;\; \overline{X} = 26 \qquad\quad\;\; s^2 = 7$

b. Find the grand mean.

$$\overline{X}_{GM} = \frac{\Sigma X}{N} = \frac{36 + 44 + 34 + \cdots + 24}{12} = \frac{404}{12} = 33.667$$

c. Find the between-group variance.

$$s_B^2 = \frac{\Sigma n_i(\overline{X}_i - \overline{X}_{GM})^2}{k - 1}$$

$$= \frac{4(37.25 - 33.667)^2 + 5(35.4 - 33.667)^2 + 3(26 - 33.667)^2}{3 - 1}$$

$$= \frac{242.717}{2} = 121.359$$

d. Find the within-group variance.

$$s_W^2 = \frac{\Sigma(n_i - 1)s_i^2}{\Sigma(n_i - 1)} = \frac{(4 - 1)(20.917) + (5 - 1)(37.3) + (3 - 1)7}{(4 - 1) + (5 - 1) + (3 - 1)}$$

$$= \frac{225.951}{9} = 25.106$$

e. Find the F test statistic.

$$F = \frac{s_B^2}{s_W^2} = \frac{121.359}{25.106} = 4.83$$

Step 4   Make the decision. The test statistic 4.83 > 4.26, so the decision is to reject the null hypothesis. See Figure 12–1.

FIGURE 12–1   Critical Value and Test Statistic for Example 12–1

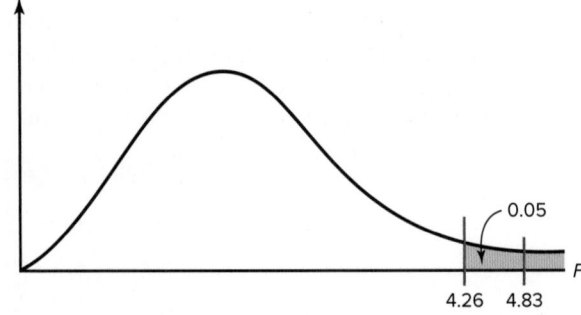

Step 5   Summarize the results. There is enough evidence to conclude that at least one mean is different from the others.

The ANOVA summary table is shown in Table 12–2.

TABLE 12–2	Analysis of Variance Summary Table for Example 12–1			
Source	Sum of squares	d.f.	Mean square	F
Between groups	242.717	2	121.359	4.83
Within groups (error)	225.954	9	25.106	
Total	468.671	11		

The *P*-values for ANOVA are found by using the same procedure shown in Section 9–5. For Example 12–1, the *F* test statistic is 4.83. In Table A–7 with d.f.N. = 2 and d.f.D. = 9, the *F* test statistic falls between $\alpha = 0.025$ with an *F* value of 5.71 and $\alpha = 0.05$ with an *F* value of 4.26. Hence, $0.025 < P\text{-value} < 0.05$. In this case, the null hypothesis is rejected at $\alpha = 0.05$ since the *P*-value < 0.05. The TI-84 *P*-value is 0.0375.

EXAMPLE 12–2   Tall Buildings

A researcher wishes to see if there is a difference in the number of stories in the tall buildings of Chicago, Houston, and New York City. The researcher randomly selects five buildings in each city and records the number of stories in each building. The data are shown. At $\alpha = 0.05$, can it be concluded that there is a significant difference in the mean number of stories in the tall buildings in each city?

Chicago	Houston	New York City
98	53	85
54	52	67
60	45	75
57	41	52
83	36	94
49	34	42

Source: The World Almanac and Book of Facts

SOLUTION

Step 1   State the hypotheses and identify the claim.

$H_0: \mu_1 = \mu_2 = \mu_3$

H_1: At least one mean is different from the others (claim).

Step 2   Find the critical value. Since $k = 3$, $N = 18$, and $\alpha = 0.05$,

d.f.N. $= k - 1 = 3 - 1 = 2$

d.f.D. $= N - k = 18 - 3 = 15$

The critical value is 3.68.

Step 3   Compute the test statistic.

a. Find the mean and variance of each sample. The mean and variance for each sample are

Chicago $\overline{X}_1 = 66.8$ $s_1^2 = 371.8$

Houston $\overline{X}_2 = 43.5$ $s_2^2 = 63.5$

New York $\overline{X}_3 = 69.2$ $s_3^2 = 387.7$

b. Find the grand mean.

$$\overline{X}_{GM} = \frac{\Sigma X}{N} = \frac{98 + 54 + 60 + \cdots + 42}{18} = \frac{1077}{18} = 59.8$$

c. Find the between-group variance.

$$s_B^2 = \frac{\Sigma n_i(\overline{X}_i - \overline{X}_{GM})^2}{k-1}$$

$$= \frac{6(66.8 - 59.8)^2 + 6(43.5 - 59.8)^2 + 6(69.2 - 59.8)^2}{3-1}$$

$$= \frac{2418.3}{2} = 1209.15$$

d. Find the within-group variance.

$$s_W^2 = \frac{\Sigma(n_i - 1)s_i^2}{\Sigma(n_i - 1)}$$

$$= \frac{(6-1)(371.8) + (6-1)(63.5) + (6-1)(387.7)}{(6-1) + (6-1) + (6-1)} = \frac{4115}{15}$$

$$= 274.33$$

e. Find the *F* test statistic.

$$F = \frac{s_B^2}{s_W^2} = \frac{1209.15}{274.33} = 4.41$$

Step 4   Make the decision. Since 4.41 > 3.68, the decision is to reject the null hypothesis. See Figure 12–2.

FIGURE 12–2   Critical Value and Test Statistic for Example 12–2

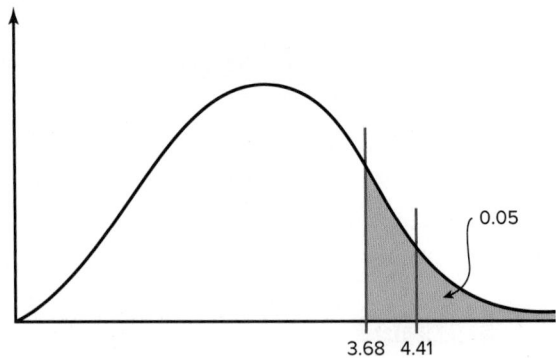

3.68 4.41

Step 5   Summarize the results. There is enough evidence to support the claim that at least one mean is different from the others. The ANOVA summary table for this example is shown in Table 12–3.

TABLE 12–3 Analysis of Variance Summary Table for Example 12–2				
Source	Sum of squares	d.f.	Mean square	F
Between groups	2418.3	2	1209.15	4.41
Within groups (error)	4115	15	274.33	
Total	6533.3	17		

In this case, 4.41 falls between 4.77 and 3.68, which corresponds to 0.025 at the 0.05 level. Hence, $0.025 < P$-value < 0.05. Since the P-value is less than 0.05, the decision is to reject the null hypothesis. The P-value obtained from the calculator is 0.031.

When the null hypothesis is rejected in ANOVA, it only means that at least one mean is different from the others. To locate the difference or differences among the means, it is necessary to use other tests such as the Tukey or the Scheffé test.

≜ Applying the Concepts 12–1

Colors That Make You Smarter

The following set of data values was obtained from a study of people's perceptions on whether the color of a person's clothing is related to how intelligent the person looks. The subjects rated the person's intelligence on a scale of 1 to 10. Randomly selected group 1 subjects were shown people with clothing in shades of blue and gray. Randomly selected group 2 subjects were shown people with clothing in shades of brown and yellow. Randomly selected group 3 subjects were shown people with clothing in shades of pink and orange. The results follow.

Group 1	Group 2	Group 3
8	7	4
7	8	9
7	7	6
7	7	7
8	5	9
8	8	8
6	5	5
8	8	8
8	7	7
7	6	5
7	6	4
8	6	5
8	6	4

1. Use ANOVA to test for any significant differences between the means.
2. What is the purpose of this study?
3. Explain why separate t tests are not accepted in this situation.

See page 694 for the answers.

≜ Exercises 12–1

1. What test is used to compare three or more means?

2. State three reasons why multiple t tests cannot be used to compare three or more means.

3. What are the assumptions for ANOVA?

4. Define between-group variance and within-group variance.

5. State the hypotheses used in the ANOVA test.

6. When there is no significant difference among three or more means, the value of F will be close to what number?

For Exercises 7 through 20, assume that all variables are normally distributed, that the samples are independent, that the population variances are equal, and that the samples are simple random samples, one from each of the populations. Also, for each exercise, perform the following steps.

   a. State the hypotheses and identify the claim.

   b. Find the critical value or the *P*-value method.

   c. Compute the test statistic.

   d. Make the decision.

   e. Summarize the results, and explain where the differences in the means are.

Use the traditional method of hypothesis testing unless otherwise specified.

7. **Leading Businesses** The following data show the yearly budgets for leading business sectors in the United States. At $\alpha = 0.05$, is there a significant difference in the mean budgets of the business sectors? The data are in thousands of dollars.

Beverages	Electronics	Food producers	Supportive services
170	46	59	56
128	24	58	37
19	18	33	19
16	14	31	19
12	13	28	17
11	12	22	15
10	10	16	15

Source: Financial Times 500.

8. Sodium Contents of Foods The amount of sodium (in milligrams) in one serving for a random sample of three different kinds of foods is listed. At the 0.05 level of significance, is there sufficient evidence to conclude that a difference in mean sodium amounts exists among condiments, cereals, and desserts?

Condiments	Cereals	Desserts
270	260	100
130	220	180
230	290	250
180	290	250
80	200	300
70	320	360
200	140	300
		160

Source: The Doctor's Pocket Calorie, Fat, and Carbohydrate Counter.

9. Hybrid Vehicles A study was done before the recent surge in gasoline prices to compare the cost to drive 25 miles for different types of hybrid vehicles. The cost of a gallon of gas at the time of the study was approximately $2.50. Based on the information given for different models of hybrid cars, trucks, and SUVs, is there sufficient evidence to conclude a difference in the mean cost to drive 25 miles? Use $\alpha = 0.05$. (The information in this exercise will be used in Exercise 3 in Section 12–2.)

Hybrid cars	Hybrid SUVs	Hybrid trucks
2.10	2.10	3.62
2.70	2.42	3.43
1.67	2.25	
1.67	2.10	
1.30	2.25	

Source: www.fueleconomy.com

10. Phone Scams A researcher asked randomly selected people to record the number of phone scams that they received over a 6-month period for each type of phone scam. At $\alpha = 0.05$, is there a significant difference in the mean number of each type of scam phone calls that were received?

Credit calls	Travel	IRS	Medical
10	4	5	2
8	7	9	3
12	15	15	8
6	3	18	9
7	9	7	5
8	11	5	10
4	5	6	6
9		10	8
10			9

11. Hours Spent in Traffic A researcher wishes to see if there is a difference in the mean number of hours people spent in traffic over a year in four selected large cities. At $\alpha = 0.10$, is there a significant difference in the means?

New York	San Francisco	Atlanta	Miami
87	80	70	64
92	79	62	59
95	71	68	62
74	86	54	68
86	91	60	65
71	75	71	71
91	89	53	82
86	90	72	61
93	68	59	63
75	71	61	75

Source: Based on INRIX

12. Weight Gain of Athletes A researcher wishes to see whether there is any difference in the weight gains of athletes following one of three special diets. Athletes are randomly assigned to three groups and placed on the diet for 6 weeks. The weight gains (in pounds) are shown here. At $\alpha = 0.05$, can the researcher conclude that there is a difference in the diets?

Diet A	Diet B	Diet C
3	10	8
6	12	3
7	11	2
4	14	5
	8	
	6	

A computer printout for this problem is shown. Use the *P*-value method and the information in this printout to test the claim. (The information in this exercise will be used in Exercise 4 of Section 12–2.)

Computer Printout for Exercise 12

ANALYSIS OF VARIANCE SOURCE TABLE

Source	df	Sum of Squares	Mean Square	F	P-value
Bet Groups	2	101.095	50.548	7.740	0.00797
W/I Groups	11	71.833	6.530		
Total	13	172.929			

DESCRIPTIVE STATISTICS

Condit	N	Means	St Dev
diet A	4	5.000	1.826
diet B	6	10.167	2.858
diet C	4	4.500	2.646

13. Expenditures per Pupil The per-pupil costs (in thousands of dollars) for cyber charter school tuition for school districts in three areas of southwestern Pennsylvania are shown. At $\alpha = 0.05$, is there a difference in the means? If so, give a possible reason for the difference. (The information in this exercise will be used in Exercise 5 of Section 12–2.)

Area I	Area II	Area III
6.2	7.5	5.8
9.3	8.2	6.4
6.8	8.5	5.6
6.1	8.2	7.1
6.7	7.0	3.0
6.9	9.3	3.5

Source: Tribune-Review.

14. Matrimonial Rings A survey was conducted with couples who looked at engagement and wedding rings. Each couple was asked how many rings they looked at before they purchased one and the best age bracket that best described their ages. At $\alpha = 0.05$, is there a difference in the number of rings looked at before purchasing one for each of the age groups?

Under 26	26–40	41–56	Over 56
3	22	14	8
16	18	19	12
12	12	23	14
8	16	21	13
5	9	15	21
10	12	8	12
8	10	11	11
9	15	14	20
15	19	12	8
16	18	10	12
8	14	7	12

Source: Based on Knots Jewelry & Engagement Study

15. Lengths of Presidential Speeches A random sample of the lengths of presidential speeches (in the number of words) is shown for 3 centuries. At $\alpha = 0.05$, is there a significant difference in the mean lengths of the speeches?

1800s	1900s	2000s
1176	2218	2273
4809	1526	1366
1127	1339	2561
8460	3329	2096
4472	5434	1433
4392	1366	2395
1128	559	1592
2166	1229	2071
700	4055	
3968	1658	
	1598	

16. Lifetime of Federal Reserve Bills A study was done on the lifetimes (in months) of Federal Reserve paper bills. At $\alpha = 0.05$, is there a difference in the means of the lifetimes of the bills?

1$ bills	5$ bills	10$ bills	20$ bills
22	24	32	42
28	26	36	48
19	21	25	36
16	15	28	39
24	25	24	36
20	20	35	42
17	18	30	35
30	20	29	38
19	21	35	44
17	24	41	
22	17		
18			

Source: Based on information from the Federal Reserve

17. Microwave Oven Prices A research organization tested microwave ovens. At $\alpha = 0.10$, is there a significant difference in the average prices of the three types of oven?

	Watts	
1000	**900**	**800**
270	240	180
245	135	155
190	160	200
215	230	120
250	250	140
230	200	180
	200	140
	210	130

A computer printout for this exercise is shown. Use the *P*-value method and the information in this printout to test the claim. (The information in this exercise will be used in Exercise 6 of Section 12–2.)

Computer Printout for Exercise 17

ANALYSIS OF VARIANCE SOURCE TABLE

Source	df	Sum of Squares	Mean Square	F	P-value
Bet Groups	2	21729.735	10864.867	10.118	0.00102
W/I Groups	19	20402.083	1073.794		
Total	21	42131.818			

DESCRIPTIVE STATISTICS

Condit	N	Means	St Dev
1000	6	233.333	28.23
900	8	203.125	39.36
800	8	155.625	28.21

18. Calories in Fast-Food Sandwiches Three popular fast-food restaurant franchises specializing in burgers were surveyed to find out the number of calories in their frequently ordered sandwiches. At the 0.05 level of significance, can it be concluded that a difference in mean number of calories per burger exists? (The information in this exercise will be used for Exercise 7 in Section 12–2.)

FF#1	FF#2	FF#3
970	1010	740
880	970	540
840	920	510
710	850	510
	820	

Source: www.fatcalories.com

19. Sleeping and Medical Costs A researcher asked randomly selected subjects classified as good sleepers, people who had insomnia, and people who suffered from sleep apnea what their yearly medical costs were. At $\alpha = 0.10$, is there a difference in the mean amount of money that they spent for medical costs?

Healthy sleepers	Insomnia	Apnea
1432	1807	1960
1657	1932	2005
1298	1656	1872
1561	1732	1715
1392	1933	2573
2210	1825	1427
960	1692	2315
1529	1735	1956

20. Average Debt of College Graduates Kiplinger's listed the top 100 public colleges based on many

factors. From that list, here is the average debt at graduation for various schools in four selected states. At $\alpha = 0.05$, can it be concluded that the average debt at graduation differs for these four states?

New York	Virginia	California	Pennsylvania
14,734	14,524	13,171	18,105
16,000	15,176	14,431	17,051
14,347	12,665	14,689	16,103
14,392	12,591	13,788	22,400
12,500	18,385	15,297	17,976

Source: www.Kiplinger.com

☰ Technology   Step by Step

TI-84 Plus
Step by Step

One-Way Analysis of Variance (ANOVA)

1. Enter the data into L_1, L_2, L_3, etc.
2. Press **STAT** and move the cursor to TESTS.
3. Press **H (ALPHA∧)** for ANOVA(.
4. Type each list followed by a comma. End with) and press **ENTER.**

Example TI12–1

Test the claim H_0: $\mu_1 = \mu_2 = \mu_3$ at $\alpha = 0.05$ for these data from Example 12–1.

Small	Sedans	Luxury
36	43	29
44	35	25
34	30	24
35	29	
	40	

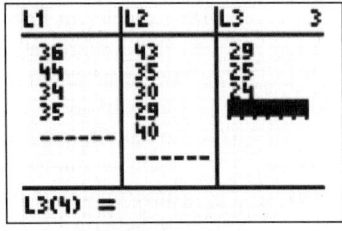

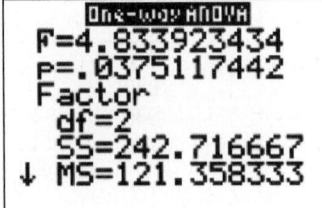
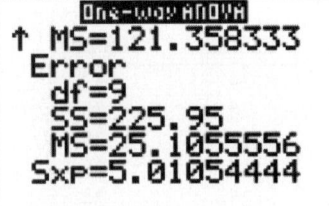

The *F* test statistic is 4.833923434. The *P*-value is 0.0375117442, which is significant at $\alpha = 0.05$. The factor variable has

$$\text{d.f.} = 2$$
$$\text{SS} = 242.716667$$
$$\text{MS} = 121.358333$$

The error has

$$\text{d.f.} = 9$$
$$\text{SS} = 225.95$$
$$\text{MS} = 25.1055556$$

EXCEL
Step by Step

One-Way Analysis of Variance (ANOVA)

Example XL12–1

1. Enter the data below in columns A, B, and C of an Excel worksheet.

Small	Sedans	Luxury
36	43	29
44	35	25
34	30	24
35	29	
	40	

2. From the toolbar, select **Data,** then **Data Analysis.**

3. Select **Anova: Single Factor.**

4. Type in **A1:C6** in the **Input Range** box.

5. Check **Grouped By: Columns.**

6. Check Labels in first row. Note, do not check this box unless your labels are selected in the input range.

7. Type **0.05** for the **Alpha level.**

8. Under the **Output options,** check the **Output Range** and type **E2.**

9. Click [OK].

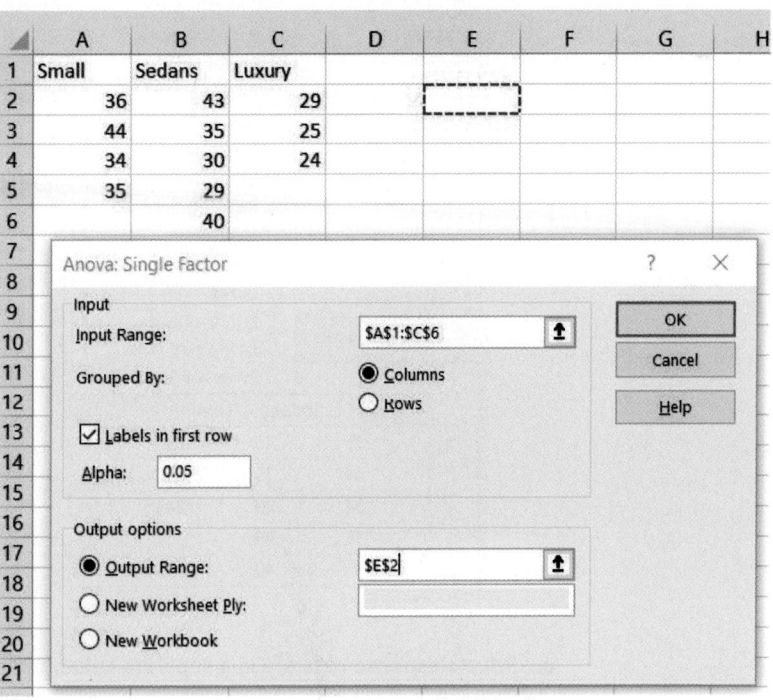

The results of the ANOVA are shown below.

Anova: Single Factor

SUMMARY

Groups	Count	Sum	Average	Variance
Small	4	149	37.25	20.9167
Sedans	5	177	35.4	37.3
Luxury	3	78	26	7

ANOVA

Source of Variation	SS	df	MS	F	P-value	F crit
Between Groups	242.7167	2	121.3583	4.83392	0.0375	4.2565
Within Groups	225.95	9	25.10556			
Total	468.6667	11				

MINITAB

Step by Step

One-Way Analysis of Variance (ANOVA)

Example 12–1

Is there a difference in the average city MPG rating by type of vehicle?

1. Enter the MPG ratings in C1 Small, C2 Sedan, and C3 Luxury.

2. Select **Stat>ANOVA>One-way**.

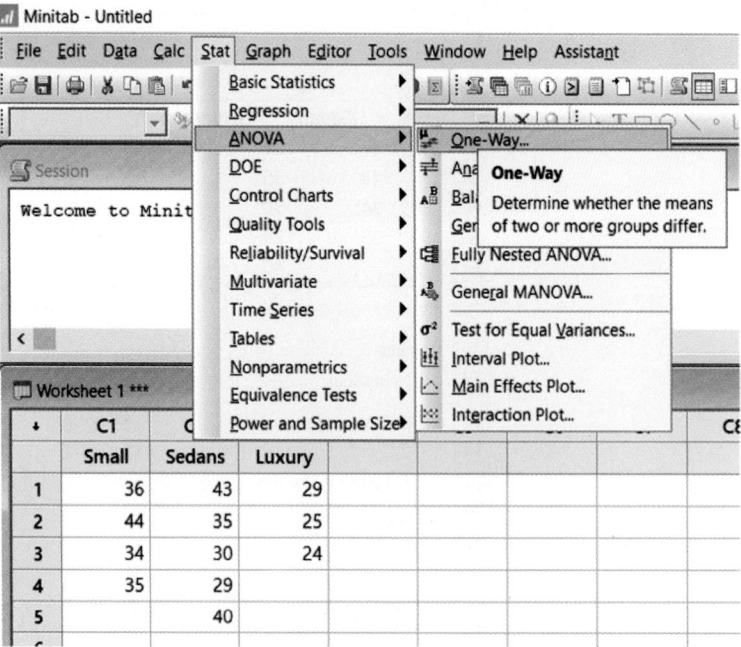

a. Select **Response data are in a separate column for each factor level** in the drop-down menu.

b. Click in the Responses: dialog box.

c. Drag the mouse over the three columns of Observed counts.

   d. Click on [Select].

   e. Click [OK].

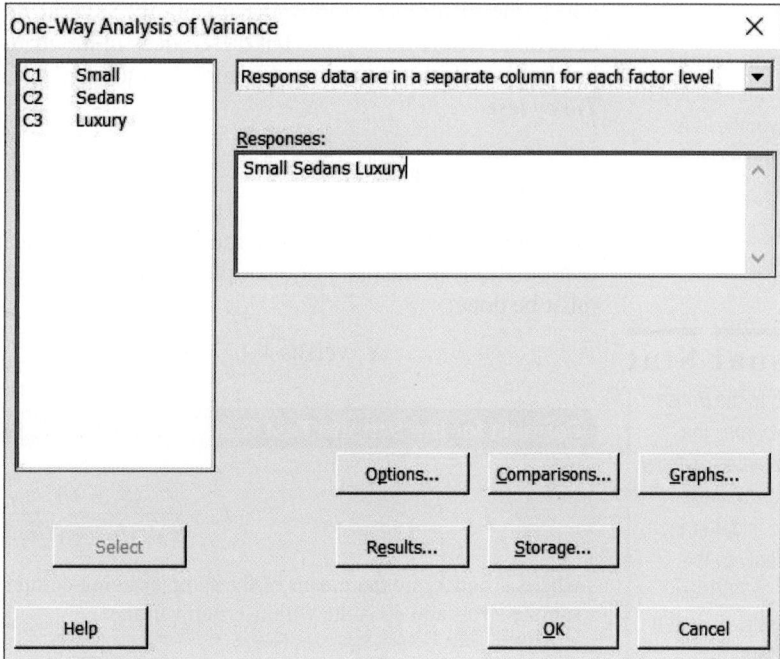

The results are displayed in the session window.

One-way ANOVA: Small, Sedans, Luxury

```
Method
Null hypothesis          All means are equal
Alternative hypothesis   At least one mean is different
Significance level       α = 0.05

Equal variances were assumed for the analysis.

Factor Information
Factor   Levels   Values
Factor       3    Small, Sedans, Luxury

Analysis of Variance
Source  DF  Adj SS  Adj MS  F-Value  P-Value
Factor   2   242.7  121.36     4.83    0.038
Error    9   225.9   25.11
Total   11   468.7


Model Summary
      S    R-sq  R-sq(adj)  R-sq(pred)
5.01054  51.79%     41.08%      19.73%


Means
Factor   N   Mean  StDev       95% CI
Small    4  37.25   4.57  (31.58, 42.92)
Sedans   5  35.40   6.11  (30.33, 40.47)
Luxury   3  26.00   2.65  (19.46, 32.54)

Pooled StDev = 5.01054
```

12–2   The Scheffé Test, Tukey Test, and Bonferroni Test

OBJECTIVE

Determine which means differ, using the Scheffé, Tukey, or Bonferroni tests if the null hypothesis is rejected in the ANOVA.

When the null hypothesis is rejected using the F test, the researcher may want to know where the difference among the means is. Several procedures have been developed to determine where the significant differences in the means lie after the ANOVA procedure has been performed. Among the most commonly used tests are the *Scheffé test* and the *Tukey test.*

Scheffé Test

To conduct the **Scheffé test,** you must compare the means two at a time, using all possible combinations of means. For example, if there are three means, the following comparisons must be done:

$$\overline{X}_1 \text{ versus } \overline{X}_2 \qquad \overline{X}_1 \text{ versus } \overline{X}_3 \qquad \overline{X}_2 \text{ versus } \overline{X}_3$$

Unusual Stat

According to the *British Medical Journal,* the body's circadian rhythms produce drowsiness during the midafternoon, matched only by the 2:00 A.M. to 7:00 A.M. period for sleep-related traffic accidents.

Formula for the Scheffé Test Statistic

$$F_s = \frac{(\overline{X}_i - \overline{X}_j)^2}{s_W^2[(1/n_i) + (1/n_j)]}$$

where $\overline{X}_i$ and $\overline{X}_j$ are the means of the samples being compared, n_i and n_j are the respective sample sizes, and s_W^2 is the within-group variance.

To find the critical value F' for the Scheffé test, multiply the critical value for the F test by $k - 1$:

$$F' = (k - 1)(\text{C.V.})$$

There is a significant difference between the two means being compared when the F test statistic, F_S, is greater than the critical value, F'. Example 12–3 illustrates the use of the Scheffé test.

EXAMPLE 12–3

Use the Scheffé test to test each pair of means in Example 12–1 to see if a significant difference exists between each pair of means. Use $\alpha = 0.05$.

SOLUTION

The F critical value for Example 12–1 is 4.26. Then the critical value for the individual tests with d.f.N. = 2 and d.f.D. = 9 is

$$F' = (k - 1)(\text{C.V.}) = (3 - 1)(4.26) = 8.52$$

a. For $\overline{X}_1$ versus $\overline{X}_2$,

$$F_S = \frac{(\overline{X}_1 - \overline{X}_2)^2}{s_W^2[(1/n_1) + (1/n_2)]} = \frac{(37.25 - 35.4)^2}{25.106\left(\frac{1}{4} + \frac{1}{5}\right)} = 0.30$$

Since $0.30 < 8.52$, the decision is that μ_1 is not significantly different from μ_2.

b. For $\overline{X}_1$ versus $\overline{X}_3$,

$$F_S = \frac{(\overline{X}_1 - \overline{X}_3)^2}{s_W^2[(1/n_1) + (1/n_3)]} = \frac{(37.25 - 26)^2}{25.106\left(\frac{1}{4} + \frac{1}{3}\right)} = 8.64$$

Since $8.64 > 8.52$, the decision is that μ_1 is significantly different from μ_3.

c. For $\overline{X}_2$ versus $\overline{X}_3$,

$$F_S = \frac{(\overline{X}_2 - \overline{X}_3)^2}{s_W^2[(1/n_2) + (1/n_3)]} = \frac{(35.4 - 26)^2}{25.106\left(\frac{1}{5} + \frac{1}{3}\right)} = 6.60$$

Since $6.60 < 8.52$, the decision is that μ_2 is not significantly different from μ_3. Hence, only the mean of the small cars is not equal to the mean of luxury cars.

On occasion, when the F test statistic is greater than the critical value, the Scheffé test may not show any significant differences in the pairs of means. This result occurs because the difference may actually lie in the average of two or more means when compared with the other mean. The Scheffé test can be used to make these types of comparisons, but the technique is beyond the scope of this book.

Tukey Test

The **Tukey test** can also be used after the analysis of variance has been completed to make pairwise comparisons between means when the groups have the same sample size. The symbol for the test statistic in the Tukey test is q.

Formula for the Tukey Test

$$q = \frac{\overline{X}_i - \overline{X}_j}{\sqrt{s_W^2/n}}$$

where $\overline{X}_i$ and $\overline{X}_j$ are the means of the samples being compared, n is the common sample size, and s_W^2 is the within-group variance.

When the absolute value of q is greater than the critical value for the Tukey test, there is a significant difference between the two means being compared.

The critical value for the Tukey test is found using Table A–9 in Appendix A, where k is the number of means in the original problem and v is the degrees of freedom for s_W^2, which is $N - k$. The value of k is found across the top row, and v is found in the left column.

EXAMPLE 12–4

Using the Tukey test, test each pair of means in Example 12–2 to see whether a specific difference exists, at $\alpha = 0.05$.

SOLUTION

a. For $\overline{X}_1$ versus $\overline{X}_2$,

$$q = \frac{\overline{X}_1 - \overline{X}_2}{\sqrt{s_W^2/n}} = \frac{66.8 - 43.5}{\sqrt{274.33/6}} = 3.446$$

b. For $\overline{X}_1$ versus $\overline{X}_3$,

$$q = \frac{\overline{X}_1 - \overline{X}_3}{\sqrt{s_W^2/n}} = \frac{66.8 - 69.2}{\sqrt{274.33/6}} = -0.355$$

c. For $\overline{X}_2$ versus $\overline{X}_3$,

$$q = \frac{\overline{X}_2 - \overline{X}_3}{\sqrt{s_W^2/n}} = \frac{43.5 - 69.2}{\sqrt{274.33/6}} = -3.801$$

To find the critical value for the Tukey test, use Table A–9 in Appendix A. The number of means k is found in the row at the top, and the degrees of freedom for s_W^2 are found in the left column (denoted by v). Since $k = 3$, d.f. $= 18 - 3 = 15$, and $\alpha = 0.05$, the critical value is 3.67. See Figure 12–3. Hence, the only q value that is greater in absolute value than the critical value is the one for the difference between $\overline{X}_2$ and $\overline{X}_3$. The conclusion, then, is that there is a significant difference in means for the Houston buildings and the New York City buildings.

FIGURE 12–3   Finding the Critical Value in Table A–9 for the Tukey Test (Example 12–4)

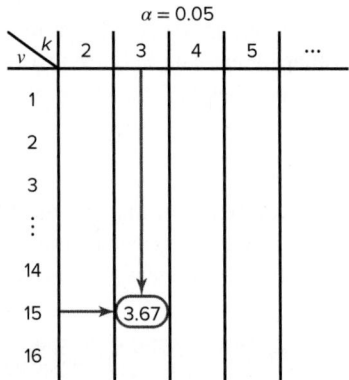

Bonferroni Test

The **Bonferroni test** uses t tests, but the critical value and P-value are adjusted to overcome the problem of the increase in the significance level due to the increase in the number of tests that are being done.

Formula for the Bonferroni Test Statistic

$$t = \frac{\overline{X}_i - \overline{X}_j}{\sqrt{s_W^2\left(\frac{1}{n_i} + \frac{1}{n_j}\right)}} \quad \text{with d.f.} = N - k$$

where $\overline{X}_i$ and $\overline{X}_j$ are the means of the samples being compared, and n_i and n_j are the respective sample sizes. N is the total number of subjects in the study, and k is the number of groups.

The critical value is adjusted by dividing the α value by the number of different combinations of pairings $_kC_2$ of two sample means. For example, if there are 3 means (i.e., $k = 3$) there would be $_3C_2 = 3$ comparisons; hence, α would be divided by 3. If there are 4 means there would be $_4C_2 = 6$ comparisons; hence, α would be divided by 6.

For the P-value multiply the P-value for a single comparison of two means by the number of combinations of pairings $_kC_2$. For example, if there are 4 means, multiply the P-value by $_4C_2 = 6$.

EXAMPLE 12–5

Use the Bonferroni test and $\alpha = 0.05$ to compare each pair of means in Example 12–1.

H_0: $\mu_1 = \mu_2$

a. For $\overline{X}_1$ and $\overline{X}_2$

$$t = \frac{\overline{X}_1 - \overline{X}_2}{\sqrt{s_W^2\left(\frac{1}{n_1} + \frac{1}{n_2}\right)}}$$

$$= \frac{37.25 - 35.4}{\sqrt{25.106\left(\frac{1}{4} + \frac{1}{5}\right)}} = \frac{1.85}{3.3612} = 0.550$$

The P-value for $t = 0.550$ with d.f. $= 12 - 3 = 9$ is 0.5957. This needs to be adjusted by multiplying it by 3. $0.5957 \times 3 = 1.787$ or 1 since the P-value cannot be greater than 1. Hence, do not reject H_0.

b. For $\overline{X}_1$ versus $\overline{X}_3$

$$H_0: \mu_1 = \mu_3$$

$$t = \frac{37.25 - 26}{\sqrt{25.106\left(\frac{1}{4} + \frac{1}{3}\right)}} = \frac{11.25}{3.8269} = 2.940$$

The P-value for $t = 2.940$ is 0.0165.

The adjustment is $0.0165 \times 3 = 0.0495$.

The decision is to reject H_0 since $0.0495 < 0.05$.

c. For $\overline{X}_2$ versus $\overline{X}_3$

$$H_0: \mu_2 = \mu_3$$

$$t = \frac{35.4 - 26}{\sqrt{25.106\left(\frac{1}{5} + \frac{1}{3}\right)}} = \frac{9.4}{3.659} = 2.569$$

The P-value for 2.569 is 0.0302.

The adjustment $0.0302 \times 3 = 0.0907$ which is not less than $\alpha = 0.05$.

The decision is do not reject H_0.

Here the P-values are used since the adjusted α value would be $0.05 \div 3 = 0.017$. A critical value for the t test with 9 d.f. would be needed. Since $\alpha = 0.017$, the critical value cannot be obtained from Table A–5.

In this case, there is a difference between μ_1 and μ_3. The results here agree with those obtained from the Scheffé test results, since the Scheffé test shows a difference between μ_1 and μ_3. Sometimes the results will differ because of the adjustments made to the critical values and when the test statistics are close to the critical values. The question arises, then, which test should be used. Unfortunately, there is no common agreement among statisticians as to which test to use. One should use the test that is used in the academic discipline of the research study.

You might wonder why there are three different tests that can be used after the ANOVA. Actually, there are several other tests that can be used in addition to the Scheffé, Tukey, and Bonferroni tests. It is up to the researcher to select the most appropriate test. The Scheffé test is the most general, and it can be used when the samples are of different sizes. Furthermore, the Scheffé test can be used to make comparisons such as the average of $\overline{X}_1$ and $\overline{X}_2$ compared with $\overline{X}_3$. However, the Tukey test is more powerful than the Scheffé test for making pairwise comparisons for the means. A rule of thumb for pairwise comparisons is to use the Tukey test when the samples are equal in size and the Scheffé test when the samples differ in size. This rule will be followed in this textbook.

Applying the Concepts 12–2

Colors That Make You Smarter

The following set of data values was obtained from a study of people's perceptions on whether the color of a person's clothing is related to how intelligent the person looks. The subjects rated the person's intelligence on a scale of 1 to 10. Randomly selected group 1 subjects were shown people with clothing in shades of blue and gray. Randomly selected group 2 subjects were shown people with clothing in shades of brown and yellow. Randomly selected group 3 subjects were shown people with clothing in shades of pink and orange. The results follow.

Group 1	Group 2	Group 3
8	7	4
7	8	9
7	7	6
7	7	7
8	5	9
8	8	8
6	5	5
8	8	8
8	7	7
7	6	5
7	6	4
8	6	5
8	6	4

1. Use the Tukey test to test all possible pairwise comparisons.
2. Are there any contradictions in the results?
3. Explain why separate t tests are not accepted in this situation.
4. When would Tukey's test be preferred over the Scheffé method? Explain.

See page 694 for the answers.

Exercises 12–2

1. What three tests can be used to compare two means when the null hypothesis is rejected using the one-way ANOVA F test? The Scheffé, Tukey, and Bonferroni tests are used.

2. Explain the difference between the two tests used to compare two means when the null hypothesis is rejected using the one-way ANOVA F test.

For Exercises 3 through 8, the null hypothesis was rejected. Use the Scheffé test when sample sizes are unequal or the Tukey test when sample sizes are equal, to test the differences between the pairs of means. Assume all variables are normally distributed, samples are independent, and the population variances are equal.

3. Exercise 9 in Section 12–1.

4. Exercise 12 in Section 12–1.

5. Exercise 13 in Section 12–1.

6. Exercise 17 in Section 12–1.

7. Exercise 18 in Section 12–1.

8. Exercise 20 in Section 12–1.

For Exercises 9 through 13, do a complete one-way ANOVA. If the null hypothesis is rejected, use either the Scheffé or Tukey test to see if there is a significant difference in the pairs of means. Assume all assumptions are met.

9. **Emergency Room Visits** Fractures accounted for 2.4% of all U.S. emergency room visits for a total of 389,000 visits for a recent year. A random sample of weekly ER visits is recorded for three hospitals in a large metropolitan area during the summer months. At

$\alpha = 0.05$, is there sufficient evidence to conclude a difference in means?

Hospital X	Hospital Y	Hospital Z
28	30	25
27	18	20
40	34	30
45	28	22
29	26	18
25	31	20

Source: World Almanac.

10. **Sales for Leading Companies** The sales in millions of dollars for a year of a sample of leading companies are shown. At $\alpha = 0.01$, is there a significant difference in the means?

Cereal	Chocolate Candy	Coffee
578	311	261
320	106	185
264	109	302
249	125	689
237	173	

Source: Information Resources, Inc.

11. **Fiber Content of Foods** The number of grams of fiber per serving for a random sample of three different kinds of foods is listed. Is there sufficient evidence at the 0.05 level of significance to conclude that there is a difference in mean fiber content among breakfast cereals, fruits, and vegetables?

Breakfast cereals	Fruits	Vegetables
3	5.5	10
4	2	1.5
6	4.4	3.5
4	1.6	2.7
10	3.8	2.5
5	4.5	6.5
6	2.8	4
8		3
5		

Source: The Doctor's Pocket Calorie, Fat, and Carbohydrate Counter.

12. **Per-Pupil Expenditures** The expenditures (in dollars) per pupil for states in three sections of the country are listed. Using $\alpha = 0.05$, can you conclude that there is a difference in means?

Eastern third	Middle third	Western third
4946	6149	5282
5953	7451	8605
6202	6000	6528
7243	6479	6911
6113		

Source: New York Times Almanac.

13. **Weekly Unemployment Benefits** The average weekly unemployment benefit for the entire United States is $314.74. Three states are randomly selected, and a sample of weekly unemployment benefits is recorded for each. At $\alpha = 0.05$, is there sufficient evidence to conclude a difference in means? If so, perform the appropriate test to find out where the difference exists.

Florida	Pennsylvania	Maine
200	300	250
187	350	195
192	295	275
235	362	260
260	280	220
175	340	290

Source: World Almanac.

For exercises 14–18, use the Bonferroni test to find the significant difference between each pair of means.

14. **Number of Pupils in a Class** A large school district has several middle schools. Three schools were randomly selected and four classes were selected from each of these schools. The number of pupils in each class are shown here. At $\alpha = 0.05$, is there sufficient evidence that the mean number of students per class differs among the schools?

MS1	MS2	MS3
21	28	25
25	22	20
19	25	23
17	30	22

15. **Days Called in Sick** A large factory owner randomly selected subjects and asked them how many sick days they used in a year. At $\alpha = 0.10$, is there a difference in the mean number of days each age group used?

Boomers	Gen X	Millennials
3	11	2
2	6	4
5	10	1
6	8	5
10	5	8
4	3	2
3	8	4
	7	5
	6	

16. **Parking Prices** Random samples of working subjects were asked what it cost them to park in large cities daily. The data are shown. At $\alpha = 0.05$, is there a difference in the means?

Detroit	Los Angeles	Washington, DC
16.60	20.50	22.45
15.40	26.10	24.30
18.20	19.70	21.60
15.00	17.75	19.70
16.00	22.50	20.00
17.50	20.00	21.50
15.25	25.75	24.50
17.75		25.00
		21.25

Source: Based on information from INRIX

17. Maternity Leaves A researcher randomly selected samples of working women in various countries and asked them how many weeks of work they missed when they used paid maternity leaves. At $\alpha = 0.10$, is there a difference in the mean times of the countries?

Chile	Japan	Mexico	United States
16	9	12	6
18	10	15	10
14	12	13	5
20	7	10	9
10	6	14	3
16	11	16	6
12	12	10	12
18		9	9
		15	8
		12	

18. Debts of U.S. Citizens Random samples of non-mortgage debts (in thousands of dollars) of various subjects are shown. At $\alpha = 0.10$, is there a difference in the means of the samples?

Millennials	Gen X	Boomers
23	30	27
24	32	26
21	29	29
15	14	30
16	35	24
21	24	21
	32	34
	28	33
	31	26
	32	20
	21	

Source: Based on information from Experian

12–3   Two-Way Analysis of Variance

OBJECTIVE

Use the two-way ANOVA technique to determine if there is a significant difference in the main effects or interaction.

The analysis of variance technique shown previously is called a one-way ANOVA since there is only *one independent variable*. The **two-way ANOVA** is an extension of the one-way analysis of variance; it involves *two independent variables*. The independent variables are also called **factors.**

The two-way analysis of variance is quite complicated, and many aspects of the subject should be considered when you are using a research design involving a two-way ANOVA. For the purposes of this textbook, only a brief introduction to the subject will be given.

In doing a study that involves a two-way analysis of variance, the researcher is able to test the effects of two independent variables or factors on one *dependent variable*. In addition, the interaction effect of the two variables can be tested.

Photo by Jeff Vanuga, U.S. Department of Agriculture
Natural Resources Conservation Service

For example, suppose a researcher wishes to test the effects of two different types of plant food and two different types of soil on the growth of certain plants. The two independent variables are the type of plant food and the type of soil, while the dependent variable is the plant growth. Other factors, such as water, temperature, and sunlight, are held constant.

To conduct this experiment, the researcher sets up four groups of plants. See Figure 12–4. Assume that the plant food type is designated by the letters A_1 and A_2 and

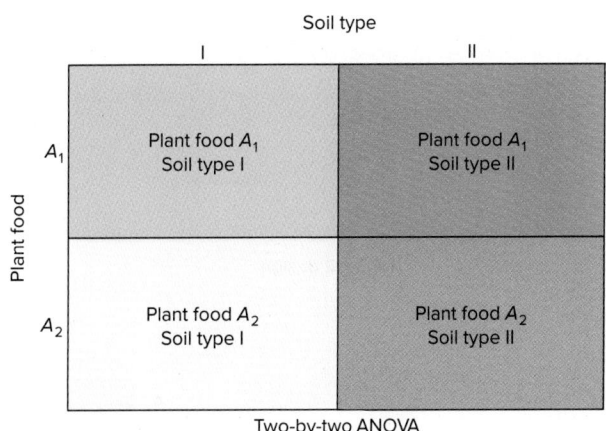

Soil type

FIGURE 12–4

Treatment Groups for the
Plant Food–Soil Type
Experiment

the soil type by the Roman numerals I and II. The groups for such a two-way ANOVA are sometimes called **treatment groups.** The four groups are

Group 1   Plant food A_1, soil type I

Group 2   Plant food A_1, soil type II

Group 3   Plant food A_2, soil type I

Group 4   Plant food A_2, soil type II

The plants are assigned to the groups at random. This design is called a 2×2 (read "two-by-two") design, since each variable consists of two **levels,** that is, two different treatments.

The two-way ANOVA enables the researcher to test the effects of the plant food and the soil type in a single experiment rather than in separate experiments involving the plant food alone and the soil type alone.

In this case, the effect of the plant food is the change in the response variable that results from changing the level or the type of food. The effect of soil type is the change in the response variable that results from changing the level or type of soil. These two effects of the independent variable are called the **main effects.** Furthermore, the researcher can test an additional hypothesis about the effect of the *interaction* of the two variables—plant food and soil type—on plant growth. For example, is there a difference between the growth of plants using plant food A_1 and soil type II and the growth of plants using plant food A_2 and soil type I? When a difference of this type occurs, the experiment is said to have a significant **interaction effect.** The interaction effect represents the joint effect of the two factors over and above the effects of each factor considered separately. That is, the types of plant food affect the plant growth differently in different soil types. When the interaction effect is statistically significant, the researcher should not consider the effects of the individual factors without considering the interaction effect.

There are many different kinds of two-way ANOVA designs, depending on the number of levels of each variable. Figure 12–5 shows a few of these designs. As stated previously, the plant food–soil type experiment uses a 2×2 ANOVA.

The design in Figure 12–5(a) is called a 3×2 design, since the factor in the rows has three levels and the factor in the columns has two levels. Figure 12–5(b) is a 3×3 design, since each factor has three levels. Figure 12–5(c) is a 4×3 design, since the factor in the rows has four levels and the factor in the columns has three levels.

The two-way ANOVA design has several null hypotheses. There is one for each independent variable and one for the interaction. In the plant food–soil type problem, the hypotheses are as follows:

1. The hypotheses regarding plant food are stated as follows.

H_0: There is no difference in means of heights of plants grown using different foods.

H_1: There is a difference in means of heights of plants grown using different foods.

FIGURE 12–5

Some Types of Two-Way
ANOVA Designs

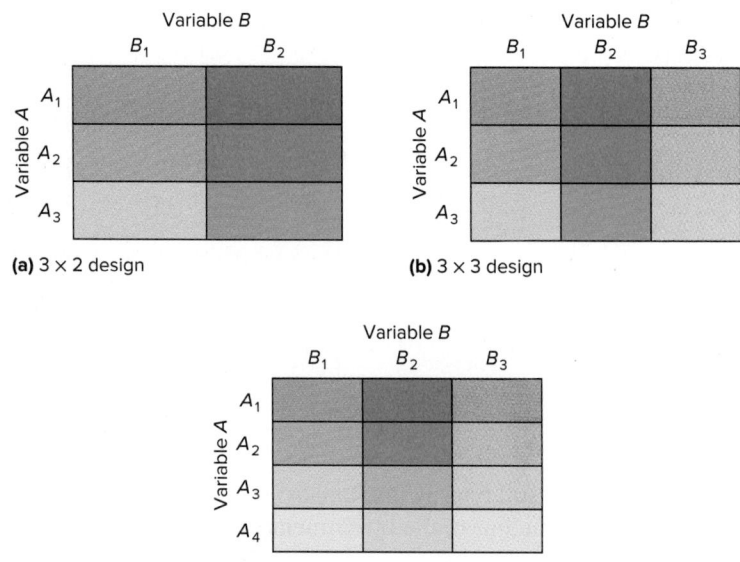

(a) 3 × 2 design

(b) 3 × 3 design

(c) 4 × 3 design

2. The hypotheses regarding soil type are stated as follows.

H_0: There is no difference in means of heights of plants grown in different soil types.

H_1: There is a difference in means of heights of plants grown in different soil types.

3. The hypotheses regarding the plant food–soil type interaction effect are stated as follows.

H_0: There is no interaction effect between type of plant food used and type of soil used on plant growth.

H_1: There is an interaction effect between food type and soil type on plant growth.

As with the one-way ANOVA, a between-group variance estimate is calculated, and a within-group variance estimate is calculated. An F test is then performed for each of the independent variables and the interaction. The results of the two-way ANOVA are summarized in a two-way table, as shown in Table 12–4 for the plant experiment.

TABLE 12–4 ANOVA Summary Table for Plant Food and Soil Type

Source	Sum of squares	d.f.	Mean square	F
Plant food				
Soil type				
Interaction				
Within (error)				
Total				

In general, the two-way ANOVA summary table is set up as shown in Table 12–5.

TABLE 12–5 ANOVA Summary Table

Source	Sum of squares	d.f.	Mean square	F
Row factor A	SS_A	$a - 1$	MS_A	F_A
Column factor B	SS_B	$b - 1$	MS_B	F_B
Interaction $A \times B$	$SS_{A \times B}$	$(a - 1)(b - 1)$	$MS_{A \times B}$	$F_{A \times B}$
Within (error)	SS_W	$ab(n - 1)$	MS_W	
Total	SS_{Total}	$N - 1$		

In the table,

$$SS_A = \text{sum of squares for factor } A$$

$$SS_B = \text{sum of squares for factor } B$$

$$SS_{A \times B} = \text{sum of squares for interaction}$$

$$SS_W = \text{sum of squares for within-group term or error term}$$

$$a = \text{number of levels of factor } A$$

$$b = \text{number of levels of factor } B$$

$$n = \text{number of subjects in each group}$$

$$MS_A = \frac{SS_A}{a-1}$$

$$MS_B = \frac{SS_B}{b-1}$$

$$MS_{A \times B} = \frac{SS_{A \times B}}{(a-1)(b-1)}$$

$$MS_W = \frac{SS_W}{ab(n-1)}$$

$$F_A = \frac{MS_A}{MS_W} \qquad \text{with d.f.N.} = a-1, \text{d.f.D.} = ab(n-1)$$

$$F_B = \frac{MS_B}{MS_W} \qquad \text{with d.f.N.} = b-1, \text{d.f.D.} = ab(n-1)$$

$$F_{A \times B} = \frac{MS_{A \times B}}{MS_W} \qquad \text{with d.f.N.} = (a-1)(b-1), \text{d.f.D.} = ab(n-1)$$

The assumptions for the two-way analysis of variance are basically the same as those for the one-way ANOVA, except for sample size.

Assumptions for the Two-Way ANOVA

1. The populations from which the samples were obtained must be normally or approximately normally distributed.
2. The samples must be independent.
3. The variances of the populations from which the samples were selected must be equal.
4. The groups must be equal in sample size.

In this book, the assumptions will be stated in the exercises; however, when encountering statistics in other situations, you must check to see that these assumptions have been met before proceeding.

The two-way analysis of variance follows the regular five-step hypothesis-testing procedure.

Step 1   State the hypotheses.
Step 2   Find the critical values.
Step 3   Compute the test statistic.
Step 4   Make the decision.
Step 5   Summarize the results.

The computational procedure for the sum of squares is quite lengthy. For this reason, it will be omitted in Example 12–6, and only the two-way ANOVA summary table will be shown. The table used in Example 12–6 is similar to the one generated by most computer programs. You should be able to interpret the table and summarize the results.

EXAMPLE 12–6 Gasoline Consumption

A researcher wishes to see whether the type of gasoline used and the type of automobile driven have any effect on gasoline consumption. Two types of gasoline, regular and high-octane, will be used, and two types of automobiles, two-wheel- and all-wheel-drive, will be used in each group. There will be two automobiles in each group, for a total of eight automobiles used. Using a two-way analysis of variance, determine if there is an interactive effect, an effect due to the type of gasoline used, and an effect due to the type of vehicle driven.

The data (in miles per gallon) are shown here, and the summary table is given in Table 12–6.

Gas	Type of automobile	
	Two-wheel-drive	All-wheel-drive
Regular	26.7	28.6
	25.2	29.3
High-octane	32.3	26.1
	32.8	24.2

TABLE 12–6 ANOVA Summary Table for Example 12–6

Source	Sum of squares	d.f.	Mean square	F
Gasoline (A)	3.920			
Automobile (B)	9.680			
Interaction ($A \times B$)	54.080			
Within (error)	3.300			
Total	70.980			

SOLUTION

Step 1 State the hypotheses. The hypotheses for the gasoline types are

H_0: There is no difference between the means of gasoline consumption for two types of gasoline.

H_1: There is a difference between the means of gasoline consumption for two types of gasoline.

The hypotheses for the types of automobile driven are

H_0: There is no difference between the means of gasoline consumption for two-wheel-drive and all-wheel-drive automobiles.

H_1: There is a difference between the means of gasoline consumption for two-wheel-drive and all-wheel-drive automobiles.

State the hypotheses. The hypotheses for the interaction are

H_0: There is no interaction effect between type of gasoline used and type of automobile a person drives on gasoline consumption.

H_1: There is an interaction effect between type of gasoline used and type of automobile a person drives on gasoline consumption.

Step 2 Find the critical values for each F test. In this case, each independent variable, or factor, has two levels. Hence, a 2×2 ANOVA table is used. Factor A is designated as the gasoline type. It has two levels, regular and high-octane; therefore, $a = 2$. Factor B is designated as the automobile type. It also has two levels; therefore, $b = 2$. The degrees of freedom for each factor are as follows:

$$\text{Factor } A: \quad \text{d.f.N.} = a - 1 = 2 - 1 = 1$$

$$\text{Factor } B: \quad \text{d.f.N.} = b - 1 = 2 - 1 = 1$$

$$\text{Interaction } (A \times B): \quad \text{d.f.N.} = (a - 1)(b - 1)$$

$$= (2 - 1)(2 - 1) = 1 \cdot 1 = 1$$

$$\text{Within (error):} \quad \text{d.f.D.} = ab(n - 1)$$

$$= 2 \cdot 2(2 - 1) = 4$$

where n is the number of data values in each group. In this case, $n = 2$.

The critical value for the F_A test is found by using $\alpha = 0.05$, d.f.N. = 1, and d.f.D. = 4. In this case, $F_A = 7.71$. The critical value for the F_B test is found by using $\alpha = 0.05$, d.f.N. = 1, and d.f.D. = 4; also F_B is 7.71. Finally, the critical value for the $F_{A \times B}$ test is found by using d.f.N. = 1 and d.f.D. = 4; it is also 7.71.

Note: If there are different levels of the factors, the critical values will not all be the same. For example, if factor A has three levels and factor b has four levels, and if there are two subjects in each group, then the degrees of freedom are as follows:

$$\text{d.f.N.} = a - 1 = 3 - 1 = 2 \qquad \text{factor } A$$

$$\text{d.f.N.} = b - 1 = 4 - 1 = 3 \qquad \text{factor } B$$

$$\text{d.f.N.} = (a - 1)(b - 1) = (3 - 1)(4 - 1)$$

$$= 2 \cdot 3 = 6 \qquad \text{factor } A \times B$$

$$\text{d.f.D.} = ab(n - 1) = 3 \cdot 4(2 - 1) = 12 \qquad \text{within (error) factor}$$

Step 3   Complete the ANOVA summary table to get the test statistics. The mean squares are computed first.

$$\text{MS}_A = \frac{\text{SS}_A}{a - 1} = \frac{3.920}{2 - 1} = 3.920$$

$$\text{MS}_B = \frac{\text{SS}_B}{b - 1} = \frac{9.680}{2 - 1} = 9.680$$

$$\text{MS}_{A \times B} = \frac{\text{SS}_{A \times B}}{(a - 1)(b - 1)} = \frac{54.080}{(2 - 1)(2 - 1)} = 54.080$$

$$\text{MS}_W = \frac{\text{SS}_W}{ab(n - 1)} = \frac{3.300}{4} = 0.825$$

The F statistics are computed next.

$$F_A = \frac{\text{MS}_A}{\text{MS}_W} = \frac{3.920}{0.825} = 4.752 \qquad \text{d.f.N.} = a - 1 = 1 \qquad \text{d.f.D.} = ab(n - 1) = 4$$

$$F_B = \frac{\text{MS}_B}{\text{MS}_W} = \frac{9.680}{0.825} = 11.733 \qquad \text{d.f.N.} = b - 1 = 1 \qquad \text{d.f.D.} = ab(n - 1) = 4$$

$$F_{A \times B} = \frac{\text{MS}_{A \times B}}{\text{MS}_W} = \frac{54.080}{0.825} = 65.552 \quad \text{d.f.N.} = (a - 1)(b - 1) = 1 \quad \text{d.f.D.} = ab(n - 1) = 4$$

The completed ANOVA table is shown in Table 12–7.

TABLE 12–7 ANOVA Summary Table for Example 12–6

Source	Sum of squares	d.f.	Mean square	F
Gasoline (A)	3.920	1	3.920	4.752
Automobile (B)	9.680	1	9.680	11.733
Interaction (A × B)	54.080	1	54.080	65.552
Within (error)	3.300	4	0.825	
Total	70.980	7		

Step 4 Make the decision. Since $F_B = 11.733$ and $F_{A \times B} = 65.552$ are greater than the critical value 7.71, the null hypotheses concerning the type of automobile driven and the interaction effect should be rejected. Since the interaction effect is statistically significant, no decision should be made about the automobile type without further investigation.

Step 5 Summarize the results. Since the null hypothesis for the interaction effect was rejected, it can be concluded that the combination of type of gasoline and type of automobile does affect gasoline consumption.

In the preceding analysis, the effect of the type of gasoline used and the effect of the type of automobile driven are called the *main effects*. If there is no significant interaction effect, the main effects can be interpreted independently. However, if there is a significant interaction effect, the main effects must be interpreted cautiously, if at all.

To interpret the results of a two-way analysis of variance, researchers suggest drawing a graph, plotting the means of each group, analyzing the graph, and interpreting the results. In Example 12–6, find the means for each group or cell by adding the data values in each cell and dividing by n. The means for each cell are shown in the chart here.

Gas	Type of automobile	
	Two-wheel-drive	**All-wheel-drive**
Regular	$\overline{X} = \dfrac{26.7 + 25.2}{2} = 25.95$	$\overline{X} = \dfrac{28.6 + 29.3}{2} = 28.95$
High-octane	$\overline{X} = \dfrac{32.3 + 32.8}{2} = 32.55$	$\overline{X} = \dfrac{26.1 + 24.2}{2} = 25.15$

The graph of the means for each of the variables is shown in Figure 12–6. In this graph, the lines cross each other. When such an intersection occurs and the interaction is significant, the interaction is said to be a **disordinal interaction.** When there is a disordinal interaction, you should not interpret the main effects without considering the interaction effect.

The other type of interaction that can occur is an *ordinal interaction*. Figure 12–7 shows a graph of means in which an ordinal interaction occurs between two variables. The lines do not cross each other, nor are they parallel. If the F test statistic for the interaction is significant and the lines do not cross each other, then the interaction is said to be an **ordinal interaction** and the main effects can be interpreted independently of each other.

Finally, when there is no significant interaction effect, the lines in the graph will be parallel or approximately parallel. When this situation occurs, the main effects can be interpreted

FIGURE 12–6

Graph of the Means of the Variables in Example 12–6

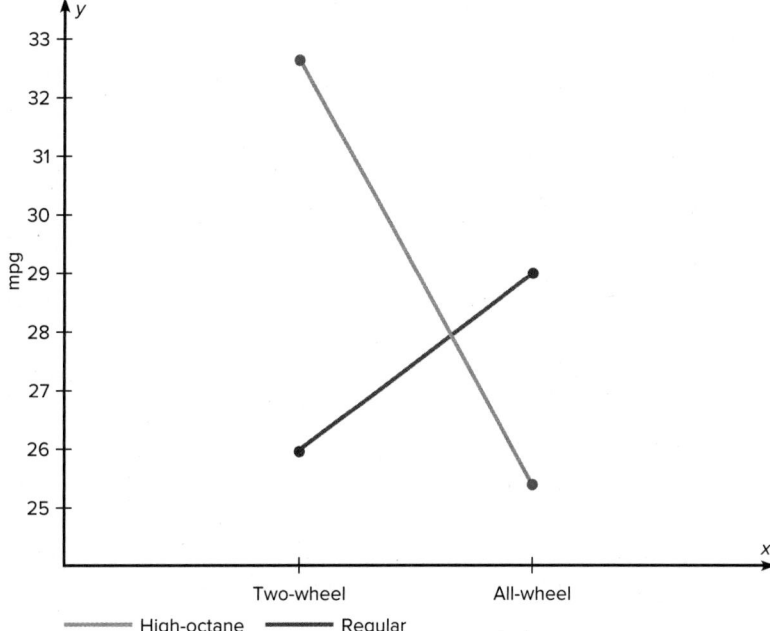

FIGURE 12–7

Graph of Two Variables Indicating an Ordinal Interaction

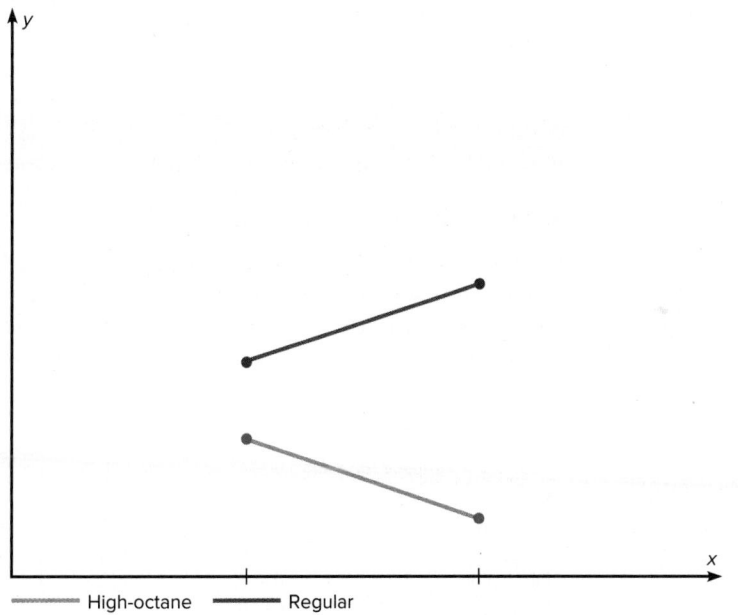

independently of each other because there is no significant interaction. Figure 12–8 shows the graph of two variables when the interaction effect is not significant; the lines are parallel.

Example 12–6 was an example of a 2×2 two-way analysis of variance, since each independent variable had two levels. For other types of variance problems, such as a 3×2 or a 4×3 ANOVA, interpretation of the results can be quite complicated. Procedures using tests such as the Tukey and Scheffé tests for analyzing the cell means exist and are similar to the tests shown for the one-way ANOVA, but they are beyond the scope of this textbook. Many other designs for analysis of variance are available to researchers, such as three-factor designs and repeated-measure designs; they are also beyond the scope of this book.

FIGURE 12–8

Graph of Two Variables Indicating No Interaction

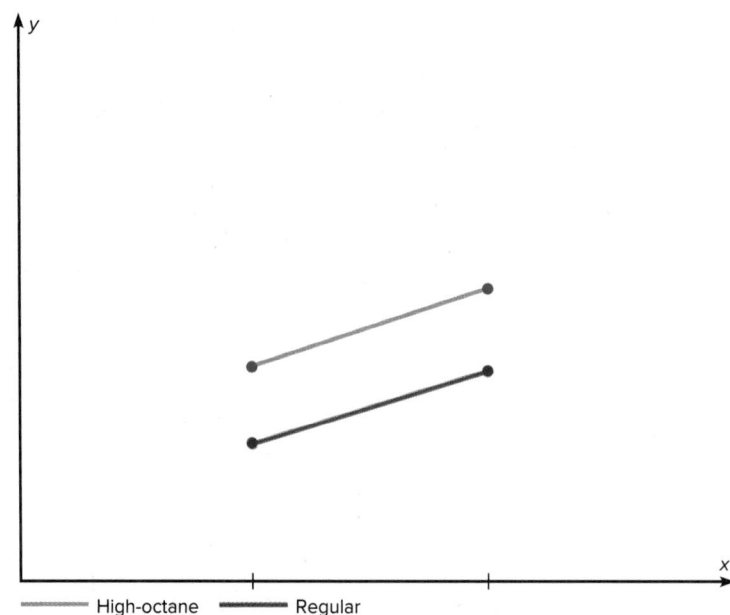

In summary, the two-way ANOVA is an extension of the one-way ANOVA. The former can be used to test the effects of two independent variables and a possible interaction effect on a dependent variable.

Applying the Concepts 12–3

Automobile Sales Techniques

The following outputs are from the result of an analysis of how car sales are affected by the experience of the salesperson and the type of sales technique used. Experience was broken up into four levels, and two different sales techniques were used. Analyze the results and draw conclusions about level of experience with respect to the two different sales techniques and how they affect car sales.

Two-Way Analysis of Variance

Analysis of Variance for Sales

Source	DF	SS	MS
Experience	3	3414.0	1138.0
Presentation	1	6.0	6.0
Interaction	3	414.0	138.0
Error	16	838.0	52.4
Total	23	4672.0	

```
                              Individual 95% CI
Experience    Mean      ------------+------------+------------+------------+------------
1             62.0       (----------*----------)
2             63.0         (----------*----------)
3             78.0                         (----------*----------)
4             91.0                                   (----------*----------)
                        ------------+------------+------------+------------+------------
                              60.0      70.0      80.0      90.0

                              Individual 95% CI
Presentation  Mean      -----------+-----------+-----------+-----------+-----------
1             74.0          (--------------------*--------------------)
2             73.0       (--------------------*--------------------)
                        -----------+-----------+-----------+-----------+-----------
```

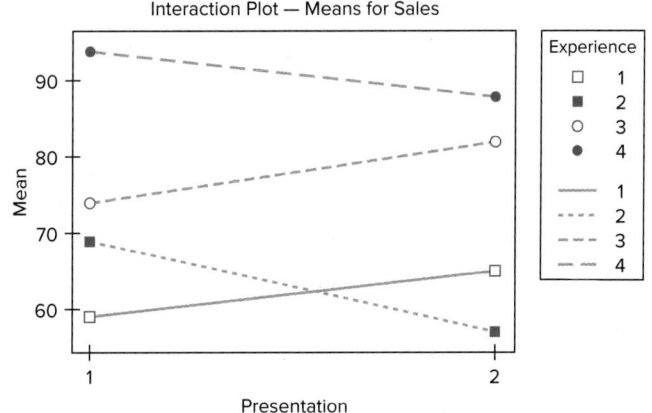

See page 694 for the answers.

☰ Exercises 12–3

1. How does the two-way ANOVA differ from the one-way ANOVA?

2. Explain what is meant by *main effects* and *interaction effect.*

3. How are the values for the mean squares computed?

4. How are the *F* test statistics computed?

5. In a two-way ANOVA, variable *A* has three levels and variable *B* has two levels. There are five data values in each cell. Find each degrees-of-freedom value.
   a. d.f.N. for factor *A*   For factor *A*, d.f.$_A$ = 2
   b. d.f.N. for factor *B*   For factor *B*, d.f.$_B$ = 1
   c. d.f.N. for factor $A \times B$ d.f.$_{A\times B}$ = 2
   d. d.f.D. for the within (error) factor   d.f.$_{within}$ = 24

6. In a two-way ANOVA, variable *A* has six levels and variable *B* has five levels. There are seven data values in each cell. Find each degrees-of-freedom value.
   a. d.f.N. for factor *A*   5
   b. d.f.N. for factor *B*   4
   c. d.f.N. for factor $A \times B$ 20
   d. d.f.D. for the within (error) factor   180

7. What are the two types of interactions that can occur in the two-way ANOVA?   The two types of interactions that can occur are ordinal and disordinal.

8. When can the main effects for the two-way ANOVA be interpreted independently?

For Exercises 9 through 15, perform these steps. Assume that all variables are normally or approximately normally distributed, that the samples are independent, and that the population variances are equal.
   a. State the hypotheses.
   b. Find the critical value for each *F* test.

c. Complete the summary table and find the test statistic.
d. Make the decision.
e. Summarize the results. (Draw a graph of the cell means if necessary.)

9. **Soap Bubble Experiments** Hands-on soap bubble experiments are a great way to teach mathematics. In an effort to find the best possible bubble solution, two different soap concentrations were used along with two different amounts of glycerin additive. Students were then given a flat glass plate and a straw and were asked to blow their best bubble. The diameters of the resulting bubbles (in millimeters) are listed below. Can an interaction be concluded between the soap solution and the glycerin? Is there a difference in mean length of bubble diameter with respect to the concentration of soap to water? With respect to amount of glycerin additive? Use $\alpha = 0.05$.

	+1 Unit glycerin	+2 Units glycerin
Soap:water 13:25	115, 113, 105, 110	98, 100, 90, 95
Soap:water 1:2	90, 102, 100, 98	99, 100, 102, 95

10. **Increasing Plant Growth** A gardening company is testing new ways to improve plant growth. Twelve plants are randomly selected and exposed to a combination of two factors, a "Grow-light" in two different strengths and a plant food supplement with different mineral supplements. After a number of days, the plants are measured for growth, and the results (in inches) are put into the appropriate boxes.

	Grow-light 1	Grow-light 2
Plant food A	9.2, 9.4, 8.9	8.5, 9.2, 8.9
Plant food B	7.1, 7.2, 8.5	5.5, 5.8, 7.6

Can an interaction between the two factors be concluded? Is there a difference in mean growth with respect to light? With respect to plant food? Use $\alpha = 0.05$.

11. **Environmentally Friendly Air Freshener** As a new type of environmentally friendly, natural air freshener is being developed, it is tested to see whether the effects of temperature and humidity affect the length of time that the scent is effective. The numbers of days that the air freshener had a significant level of scent are listed below for two temperature and humidity levels. Can an interaction between the two factors be concluded? Is there a difference in mean length of effectiveness with

respect to humidity? With respect to temperature? Use $\alpha = 0.05$.

	Temperature 1	Temperature 2
Humidity 1	35, 25, 26	35, 31, 37
Humidity 2	28, 22, 21	23, 19, 18

12. **Home-Building Times** A contractor wishes to see whether there is a difference in the time (in days) it takes two subcontractors to build three different types of homes. At $\alpha = 0.05$, analyze the data shown here, using a two-way ANOVA. See below for raw data.

Data for Exercise 12

	Home type		
Subcontractor	**I**	**II**	**III**
A	25, 28, 26, 30, 31	30, 32, 35, 29, 31	43, 40, 42, 49, 48
B	15, 18, 22, 21, 17	21, 27, 18, 15, 19	23, 25, 24, 17, 13

ANOVA Summary Table for Exercise 12

Source	SS	d.f.	MS	F
Subcontractor	162.553			
Home type	444.867			
Interaction	313.267			
Within	328.800			
Total	2759.487			

13. **Durability of Paint** A pigment laboratory is testing both dry additives and solution-based additives to see their effect on the durability rating (a number from 1 to 10) of a finished paint product. The paint to be tested is divided into four equal quantities, and a different combination of the two additives is added to one-fourth of each quantity. After a prescribed number of hours, the durability rating is obtained for each of the 16 samples, and the results are recorded below in the appropriate space.

	Dry additive 1	Dry additive 2
Solution additive A	9, 8, 5, 6	4, 5, 8, 9
Solution additive B	7, 7, 6, 8	10, 8, 6, 7

Can an interaction be concluded between the dry and solution additives? Is there a difference in mean durability rating with respect to dry additive used? With respect to solution additive? Use $\alpha = 0.05$.

14. **Types of Outdoor Paint** Two types of outdoor paint, enamel and latex, were tested to see how long (in months) each lasted before it began to crack, flake, and peel. They were tested in four geographic locations in the United States to study the effects of climate on the paint. At $\alpha = 0.01$, analyze the data shown, using a two-way ANOVA shown below. Each group contained five test panels. See below for raw data.

Data for Exercise 14

	Geographic location			
Type of paint	**North**	**East**	**South**	**West**
Enamel	60, 53, 58, 62, 57	54, 63, 62, 71, 76	80, 82, 62, 88, 71	62, 76, 55, 48, 61
Latex	36, 41, 54, 65, 53	62, 61, 77, 53, 64	68, 72, 71, 82, 86	63, 65, 72, 71, 63

ANOVA Summary Table for Exercise 14

Source	SS	d.f.	MS	F
Paint type	12.1			
Location	2501.0			
Interaction	268.1			
Within	2326.8			
Total	5108.0			

15. **Age and Sales** A company sells three items: swimming pools, spas, and saunas. The owner decides to see whether the age of the sales representative and the type of item affect monthly sales. At $\alpha = 0.05$, analyze the data shown, using a two-way ANOVA. Sales are given in hundreds of dollars for a randomly selected month, and five salespeople were selected for each group.

ANOVA Summary Table for Exercise 15

Source	SS	d.f.	MS	F
Age	168.033			
Product	1,762.067			
Interaction	7,955.267			
Within	2,574.000			
Total	12,459.367			

Data for Exercise 15

Age of salesperson	Product		
	Pool	**Spa**	**Sauna**
Over 30	56, 23, 52, 28, 35	43, 25, 16, 27, 32	47, 43, 52, 61, 74
30 or under	16, 14, 18, 27, 31	58, 62, 68, 72, 83	15, 14, 22, 16, 27

☰ Technology | Step by Step

TI-84 Plus
Step by Step

The TI-84 Plus does not have a built-in function for two-way analysis of variance. However, the downloadable program named TWOWAY is available in the online resources. Follow the instructions for downloading the program.

Performing a Two-Way Analysis of Variance

1. Enter the data values of the dependent variable into L_1 and the coded values for the levels of the factors into L_2 and L_3.
2. Press **PRGM,** move the cursor to the program named TWOWAY, and press **ENTER** twice.
3. Type L_1 (Press [2nd] [1]) for the list that contains the dependent variable and press **ENTER.**
4. Type L_2 (Press [2nd] [2]) for the list that contains the coded values for the first factor and press **ENTER.**
5. Type L_3 (Press [2nd] [3]) for the list that contains the coded values for the second factor and press **ENTER.**
6. The program will show the statistics for the first factor.
7. Press **ENTER** to see the statistics for the second factor.
8. Press **ENTER** to see the statistics for the interaction.
9. Press **ENTER** to see the statistics for the error.
10. Press **ENTER** to clear the screen.

Example TI12–2

Perform a two-way analysis of variance for the gasoline data (Example 12–6 in the text). The gas mileages are the data values for the dependent variable. Factor A is the type of gasoline (1 for regular, 2 for high-octane). Factor B is the type of automobile (1 for two-wheel-drive, 2 for all-wheel-drive).

Gas mileages (L_1)	Type of gasoline (L_2)	Type of automobile (L_3)
26.7	1	1
25.2	1	1
32.3	2	1
32.8	2	1
28.6	1	2
29.3	1	2
26.1	2	2
24.2	2	2

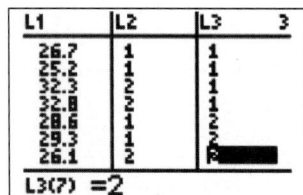
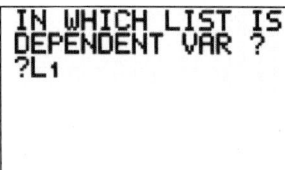
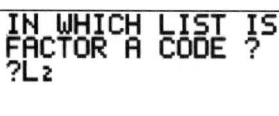
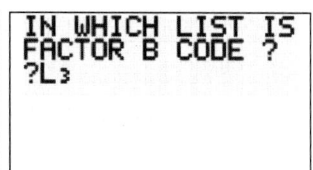

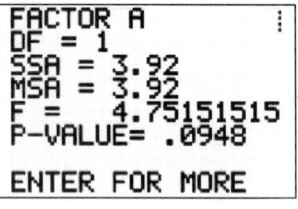

```
FACTOR A              ¦
DF = 1
SSA = 3.92
MSA = 3.92
F =     4.75151515
P-VALUE= .0948

ENTER FOR MORE
```

```
FACTOR B             |
DF = 1
SSB = 9.68
MSB = 9.68
F =     11.7333333
P-VALUE= .0266

ENTER FOR MORE
```

```
INTERACTION          |
DF = 1
SS(A*B) =54.08
MS(A*B) =54.08
F =     65.5515151
P-VALUE= .0013

ENTER FOR MORE
```

```
ERROR                ¦
DF = 4
SSE = 3.3
MSE = .825



ENTER TO END
```

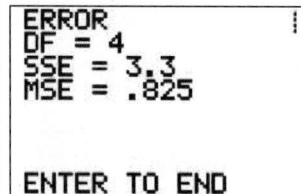

EXCEL
Step by Step

Two-Way Analysis of Variance (ANOVA)

This example pertains to Example 12–6 from the text.

Example XL12–3

A researcher wishes to see if type of gasoline used and type of automobile driven have any effect on gasoline consumption. Use $\alpha = 0.05$.

1. Enter the data exactly as shown in the figure below in an Excel worksheet.

◢	A	B	C
1		Two-wheel-drive	All-wheel-drive
2	Regular	26.7	28.6
3		25.2	29.3
4	Hi-octane	32.3	26.1
5		32.8	24.2
6			

2. From the toolbar, select **Data**, then **Data Analysis**.
3. Select **Anova: Two-Factor With Replication** under **Analysis tools**, then [OK].
4. In the **Anova: Single Factor dialog box**, type **A1:C5** for the **Input Range**.
5. Type **2** for the Rows per sample.
6. Type **0.05** for the **Alpha level**.
7. Under **Output options**, check **Output Range** and type **E2**.
8. Click [OK].

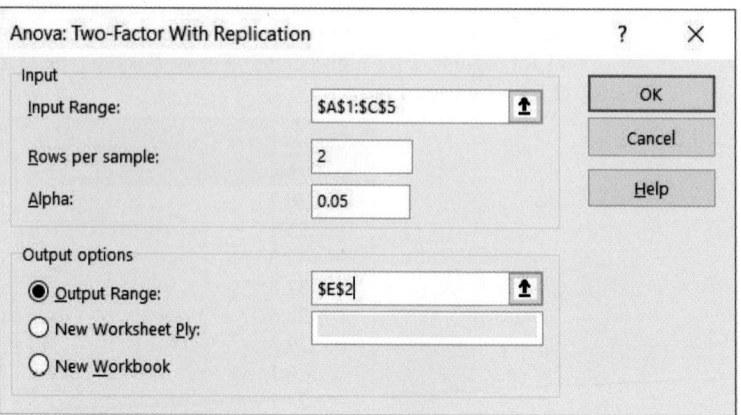

The two-way ANOVA table is shown below.

ANOVA						
Source of Variation	SS	df	MS	F	P-value	F crit
Sample	3.92	1	3.92	4.7515	0.0948	7.7086
Columns	9.68	1	9.68	11.7333	0.0266	7.7086
Interaction	54.08	1	54.08	65.5515	0.0013	7.7086
Within	3.3	4	0.825			
Total	70.98	7				

MINITAB
Step by Step

Two-Way Analysis of Variance

For Example 12–6, how do gasoline type and vehicle type affect gasoline mileage?

1. Enter the data into three columns of a worksheet. The data for this analysis have to be "stacked" as shown.

   a) All the gas mileage data are entered in a single column named MPG.

   b) The second column contains codes identifying the gasoline type, a 1 for regular or a 2 for high-octane.

   c) The third column will contain codes identifying the type of automobile, 1 for two-wheel-drive or 2 for all-wheel-drive.

↓	C1	C2	C3	
	MPG	GasCode	TypeCode	
1	26.7	1	1	
2	25.2	1	1	
3	32.3	2	1	
4	32.8	2	1	
5	28.6	1	2	
6	29.3	1	2	
7	26.1	2	2	
8	24.2	2	2	
9				

2. Select **Stat>ANOVA>General Linear Model>Fit General Linear Model.**

   a) Click into the Responses box. Double-click MPG in the list box and this will bring MPG over.

   b) Click into the Factors box. Double-click GasCode and TypeCode as factors.

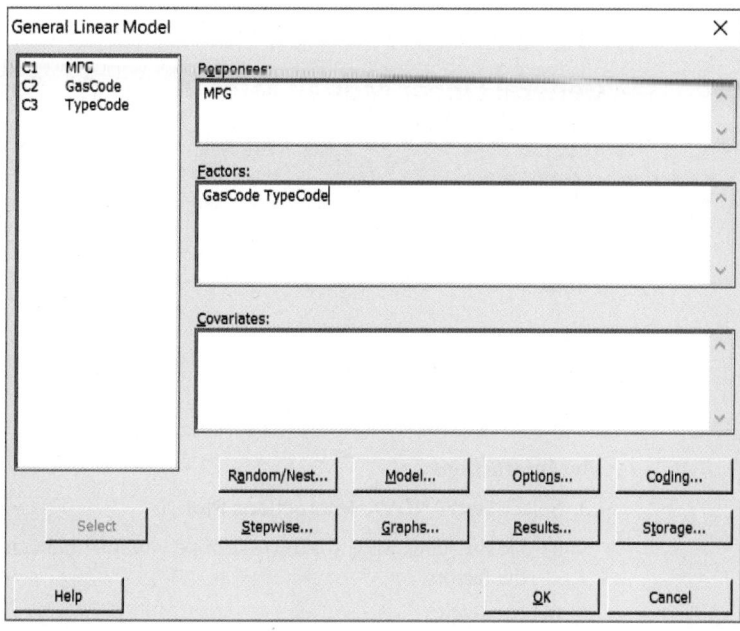

c) Click the Model button.

d) Drag the mouse over GasCode and TypeCode in the upper left, then click the Add button.

e) Click [OK]. This will add the interaction effect.

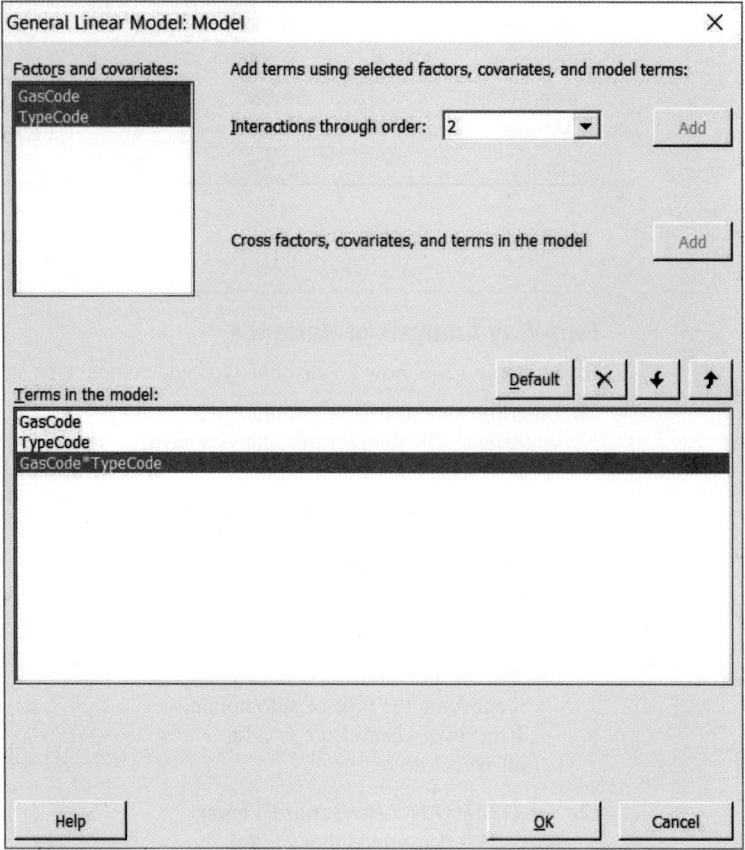

f) Click the Results button.

g) Check the boxes for Analysis of variance, Model summary, and Means. Deselect any other checked boxes.

h) Click [OK] twice.

The session window will contain the results.

General Linear Model: MPG versus GasCode, TypeCode

```
Analysis of Variance
Source            DF   Adj SS    Adj MS   F-Value   P-Value
  GasCode          1    3.920    3.9200      4.75     0.095
  TypeCode         1    9.680    9.6800     11.73     0.027
  GasCode*TypeCode 1   54.080   54.0800     65.55     0.001
Error              4    3.300    0.8250
Total              7   70.980
```

```
Model Summary
       S    R-sq   R-sq(adj)   R-sq(pred)
0.908295   95.35%     91.86%       81.40%
```

Plot Interactions

3. Select **Stat>ANOVA>Interactions Plot.**

a) Double-click MPG for the response variable and GasCodes and TypeCodes for the factors.

b) Click [OK].

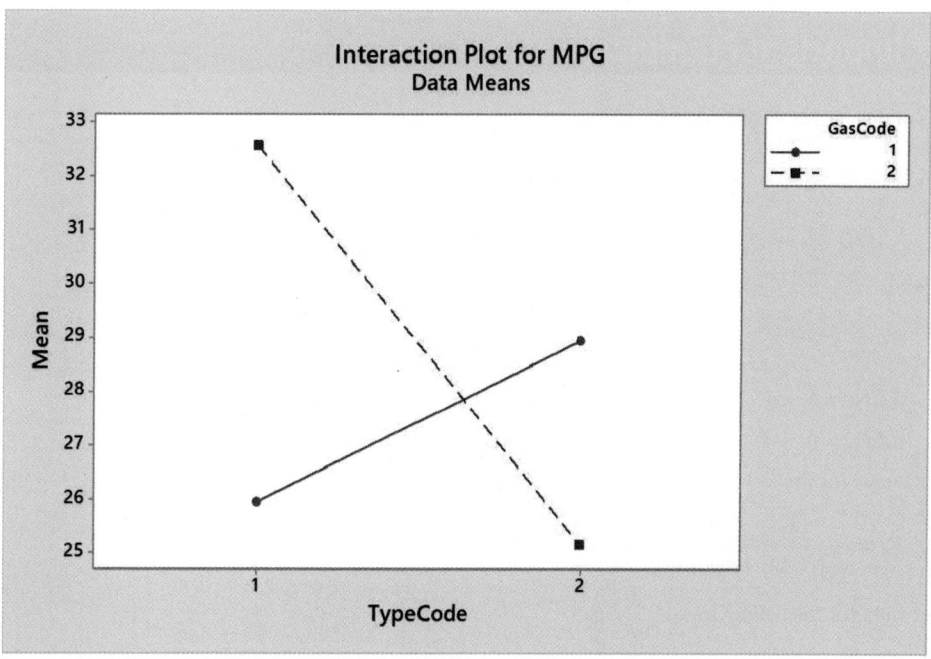

Intersecting lines indicate a significant interaction of the two independent variables.

Summary

- The F test, as shown in Chapter 9, can be used to compare two sample variances to determine whether they are equal. It can also be used to compare three or more means. When three or more means are compared, the technique is called analysis of variance (ANOVA). The ANOVA technique uses two estimates of the population variance. The between-group variance is the variance of the sample means; the within-group variance is the overall variance of all the values. When there is no significant difference among the means, the two estimates will be approximately equal and the F test statistic will be close to 1. If there is a significant difference among the means, the between-group variance estimate will be larger than the within-group variance estimate and a significant test statistic will result. (12–1)

- If there is a significant difference among means, the researcher may wish to see where this difference

lies. Several statistical tests can be used to compare the sample means after the ANOVA technique has been done. The most common are the Scheffé test and the Tukey test. When the sample sizes are the same, the Tukey test can be used. The Scheffé test is more general and can be used when the sample sizes are equal or not equal. (12–2)

- When there is one independent variable, the analysis of variance is called a one-way ANOVA. When there are two independent variables, the analysis of variance is called a two-way ANOVA. The two-way ANOVA enables the researcher to test the effects of two independent variables and a possible interaction effect on one dependent variable. If an interaction effect is found to be statistically significant, the researcher must investigate further to find out if the main effects can be examined. (12–3)

Important Terms

analysis of variance (ANOVA) 652

ANOVA summary table 654

between-group variance 653

Bonferroni test 668

disordinal interaction 678

factors 672

interaction effect 673

level 673

main effects 673

mean square 654

one-way ANOVA 652

ordinal interaction 678

Scheffé test 666

sum of squares between groups 654

sum of squares within groups 654

treatment groups 673

Tukey test 667

two-way ANOVA 672

within-group variance 653

⬛ Important Formulas

Formulas for the ANOVA test:

$$\overline{X}_{GM} = \frac{\Sigma X}{N}$$

$$F = \frac{s_B^2}{s_W^2}$$

where

$$s_B^2 = \frac{\Sigma n_i(\overline{X}_i - \overline{X}_{GM})^2}{k - 1} \qquad s_W^2 = \frac{\Sigma(n_i - 1)s_i^2}{\Sigma(n_i - 1)}$$

d.f.N. $= k - 1$ **$N = n_1 + n_2 + \cdots + n_k$**

d.f.D. $= N - k$ **k = number of groups**

Formulas for the Scheffé test:

$$F_s = \frac{(\overline{X}_i - \overline{X}_j)^2}{s_W^2[(1/n_i) + (1/n_j)]} \quad \text{and} \quad F' = (k - 1)(\text{C.V.})$$

Formula for the Tukey test:

$$q = \frac{\overline{X}_i - \overline{X}_j}{\sqrt{s_W^2/n}}$$

d.f.N. $= k$ and   **d.f.D. = degrees of freedom for s_W^2**

Formula for the Bonferroni test:

$$t = \frac{\overline{X}_i - \overline{X}_j}{\sqrt{s_W^2\left(\frac{1}{n_i} + \frac{1}{n_j}\right)}} \quad \text{with d.f.} = N - k$$

Formulas for the two-way ANOVA:

$$MS_A = \frac{SS_A}{a - 1} \qquad\qquad F_A = \frac{MS_A}{MS_W} \qquad \begin{array}{l}\textbf{d.f.N.} = a - 1 \\ \textbf{d.f.D.} = ab(n - 1)\end{array}$$

$$MS_B = \frac{SS_B}{b - 1} \qquad\qquad F_B = \frac{MS_B}{MS_W} \qquad \begin{array}{l}\textbf{d.f.N.} = b - 1 \\ \textbf{d.f.D.} = ab(n - 1)\end{array}$$

$$MS_{A\times B} = \frac{SS_{A\times B}}{(a - 1)(b - 1)} \qquad F_{A\times B} = \frac{MS_{A\times B}}{MS_W} \qquad \begin{array}{l}\textbf{d.f.N.} = (a - 1)(b - 1) \\ \textbf{d.f.D.} = ab(n - 1)\end{array}$$

$$MS_W = \frac{SS_W}{ab(n - 1)}$$

⬛ Review Exercises

If the null hypothesis is rejected in Exercises 1 through 8, use the Scheffé test when the sample sizes are unequal to test the differences between the means, and use the Tukey test when the sample sizes are equal. For these exercises, perform these steps. Assume the assumptions have been met.

   a. State the hypotheses and identify the claim.

   b. Find the critical value(s) or the *P*-value method.

   c. Compute the test statistics.

   d. Make the decision.

   e. Summarize the results.

Sections 12–1 and 12–2

Use the traditional method of hypothesis testing unless otherwise specified.

1. **Lengths of Various Types of Bridges** The data represent the lengths in feet of three types of bridges in the United States. At $\alpha = 0.01$, test the claim that there is no significant difference in the means of the lengths of the types of bridges.

Simple truss	Segmented concrete	Continuous plate
745	820	630
716	750	573
700	790	525
650	674	510
647	660	480
625	640	460
608	636	451
598	620	450
550	520	450
545	450	425
534	392	420
528	370	360

Source: World Almanac and Book of Facts.

2. **Number of State Parks** The numbers of state parks found in selected states in three different regions of the country are listed. At $\alpha = 0.05$, can it be concluded that the average number of state parks differs by region?

South	West	New England
51	28	94
64	44	72
35	24	14
24	31	52
47	40	

Source: Time Almanac.

3. **Carbohydrates in Cereals** The number of carbohydrates per serving in randomly selected cereals from three manufacturers is shown. At the 0.05 level of significance, is there sufficient evidence to conclude a difference in the average number of carbohydrates?

Manufacturer 1	Manufacturer 2	Manufacturer 3
25	23	24
26	44	39
24	24	28
26	24	25
26	36	23
41	27	32
26	25	
43		

Source: The Doctor's Pocket Calorie, Fat, and Carbohydrate Counter.

4. **Grams of Fat per Serving of Pizza** The number of grams of fat per serving for three different kinds of pizza from several manufacturers is listed. At the 0.01 level of significance, is there sufficient evidence that a difference exists in mean fat content?

Cheese	Pepperoni	Supreme/Deluxe
18	20	16
11	17	27
19	15	17
20	18	17
16	23	12
21	23	27
16	21	20

Source: The Doctor's Pocket Calorie, Fat, and Carbohydrate Counter.

5. **Iron Content of Foods and Drinks** The iron content in three different types of food is shown. At the 0.10 level of significance, is there sufficient evidence to conclude that a difference in mean iron content exists for meats and fish, breakfast cereals, and nutritional high-protein drinks?

Meats and fish	Breakfast cereals	Nutritional drinks
3.4	8	3.6
2.5	2	3.6
5.5	1.5	4.5
5.3	3.8	5.5
2.5	3.8	2.7
1.3	6.8	3.6
2.7	1.5	6.3
	4.5	

Source: The Doctor's Pocket Calorie, Fat, and Carbohydrate Counter.

6. **Temperatures in January** The average January high temperatures (in degrees Fahrenheit) for selected tourist cities on different continents are listed. Is there sufficient evidence to conclude a difference in mean temperatures for the three areas? Use the 0.05 level of significance.

Europe	Central and South America	Asia
41	87	89
38	75	35
36	66	83
56	84	67
50	75	48

Source: Time Almanac.

7. **School Incidents Involving Police Calls** A researcher wishes to see if there is a difference in the average number of times local police were called in school incidents. Random samples of school districts were selected, and the numbers of incidents for a specific year were reported. At $\alpha = 0.05$, is there a difference in the means? If so, suggest a reason for the difference.

County A	County B	County C	County D
13	16	15	11
11	33	12	31
2	12	19	3
	2	2	
	2		

Source: U.S. Department of Education.

8. **CO$_2$ Emissions** The CO$_2$ emissions in metric tons for selected countries are shown for selected years. At $\alpha = 0.10$, is there a difference in the means for the selected years?

1980	1990	2000	2010
291.2	578.6	991.0	564.6
131.7	202.1	321.5	468.7
613.6	470.6	290.5	451.0
235.0	302.2	560.3	414.5
198.8	415.4	266.2	388.7

Source: U.S. Department of Energy.

Section 12–3

9. **Review Preparation for Statistics** A statistics instructor wanted to see if student participation in review preparation methods led to higher examination scores. Five students were randomly selected and placed in each test group for a three-week unit on statistical inference. Everyone took the same examination at the end of the unit, and the resulting scores are shown. Is there sufficient evidence at $\alpha = 0.05$ to conclude an interaction between the two factors? Is there sufficient evidence to conclude a difference in mean scores based on formula delivery system? Is there sufficient evidence to conclude a difference in mean scores based on the review organization technique?

	Formulas provided	Student-made formula cards
Student-led review	89, 76, 80, 90, 75	94, 86, 80, 79, 82
Instructor-led review	75, 80, 68, 65, 79	88, 78, 85, 65, 72

10. **Effects of Different Types of Diets** A medical researcher wishes to test the effects of two different diets and two different exercise programs on the glucose level in a person's blood. The glucose level is measured in milligrams per deciliter (mg/dl). Three subjects are randomly assigned to each group. Analyze the data shown here, using a two-way ANOVA with $\alpha = 0.05$.

Exercise program	Diet	
	A	**B**
I	62, 64, 66	58, 62, 53
II	65, 68, 72	83, 85, 91

ANOVA Summary Table for Exercise 10

Source	SS	d.f.	MS	F
Exercise	816.750			
Diet	102.083			
Interaction	444.083			
Within	108.000			
Total	1470.916			

≡ STATISTICS TODAY

Can Bringing Your Dog to Work Reduce Stress? —Revisited

In this study the researchers found no difference in the cortisol levels of the three groups. They could have used an analysis of variance test if the assumptions were met to determine this. There are also other possible statistical methods that can be used to compare means.

The researchers did find that, on the survey, the stress levels during the day fell by 11% among the people who had brought their dogs to work, but rose as much as 70% for the workers in other groups. The surveys were given four times a day during the week.

≡ Data Analysis

The Data Bank is found in Appendix B.

1. From the Data Bank, select a random sample of subjects, and test the hypothesis that the mean cholesterol levels of the nonsmokers, less-than-one-pack-a-day smokers, and one-pack-plus smokers are equal. Use an ANOVA test. If the null hypothesis is rejected, conduct the Scheffé test to find where the difference is. Summarize the results.

2. Repeat Exercise 1 for the mean IQs of the various educational levels of the subjects.

3. Using the Data Bank, randomly select 12 subjects and randomly assign them to one of the four groups in the following classifications.

	Smoker	Nonsmoker
Male		
Female		

Use one of these variables—weight, cholesterol, or systolic pressure—as the dependent variable, and perform a two-way ANOVA on the data. Use a computer program to generate the ANOVA table.

≡ Chapter Quiz

Determine whether each statement is true or false. If the statement is false, explain why.

1. In analysis of variance, the null hypothesis should be rejected only when there is a significant difference among all pairs of means. False

2. The F test does not use the concept of degrees of freedom. False

3. When the F test statistic is close to 1, the null hypothesis should be rejected. False

4. The Tukey test is generally more powerful than the Scheffé test for pairwise comparisons. True

Select the best answer.

5. Analysis of variance uses the _____ test.
   a. z c. χ^2
   b. t d. F

6. The null hypothesis in ANOVA is that all the means are _____.
   a. Equal   c. Variable
   b. Unequal   d. None of the above

7. When you conduct an F test, _____ estimates of the population variance are compared.
   a. Two   c. Any number of
   b. Three   d. No

8. If the null hypothesis is rejected in ANOVA, you can use the _____ test to see where the difference in the means is found.
   a. z or t c. Scheffé or Tukey
   b. F or χ^2 d. Any of the above

Complete the following statements with the best answer.

9. When three or more means are compared, you use the _____ technique. ANOVA

10. If the null hypothesis is rejected in ANOVA, the _____ test should be used when sample sizes are equal. Tukey

For Exercises 11 through 17, use the traditional method of hypothesis testing unless otherwise specified. Assume the assumptions have been met.

11. **Gasoline Prices** Random samples of summer gasoline prices per gallon are listed for three different states. Is there sufficient evidence of a difference in mean prices? Use $\alpha = 0.01$.

State 1	State 2	State 3
3.20	3.68	3.70
3.25	3.50	3.65
3.18	3.70	3.75
3.15	3.65	3.72

12. **Voters in Presidential Elections** In a recent Presidential election, a random sample of the percentage of voters who voted is shown. At $\alpha = 0.05$, is there a difference in the mean percentage of voters who voted?

Northeast	Southeast	Northwest	Southwest
65.3	54.8	60.5	42.3
59.9	61.8	61.0	61.2
66.9	49.6	74.0	54.7
64.2	58.6	61.4	56.7

Source: Committee for the Study of the American Electorate.

13. **Ages of Late-Night TV Talk Show Viewers** A media researcher wanted to see if there was a difference in the ages of viewers of three late-night television talk shows. Three random samples of viewers were selected, and the ages of the viewers are shown. At $\alpha = 0.01$, is there a difference in the means of the ages of the viewers? Why is the average age of a viewer important to a television show writer?

Jimmy Kimmel	Jimmy Fallon	Steven Colbert
53	48	40
46	51	36
48	57	35
42	46	42
35	38	39

14. **Prices of Body Soap** A consumer group desired to compare the mean price for 12-ounce bottles of liquid body soap from two nationwide brands and one store brand. Four different bottles of each were randomly selected at a large discount drug store, and the prices are noted. At the 0.05 level of significance, is there sufficient evidence to conclude a difference in mean prices? If so, perform the appropriate test to find out where.

Brand X	Brand Y	Store brand
5.99	8.99	4.99
6.99	7.99	3.99
8.59	6.29	5.29
6.49	7.29	4.49

15. **Air Pollution** A lot of different factors contribute to air pollution. One particular factor, particulate matter, was measured for prominent cities of three continents. Particulate matter includes smoke, soot, dust, and liquid droplets from combustion such that the particle is less than 10 microns in diameter and thus capable of reaching deep into the respiratory system. The measurements are listed here. At the 0.05 level of significance, is there sufficient evidence to conclude a difference in means? If so, perform the appropriate test to find out where the differences in means are.

Asia	Europe	Africa
79	34	33
104	35	16
40	30	43
73	43	

Source: World Almanac.

16. Alumni Gift Solicitation Several students volunteered for an alumni phone-a-thon to solicit alumni gifts. The number of calls made by randomly selected students from each class is listed. At $\alpha = 0.05$, is there sufficient evidence to conclude a difference in means?

First-year students	Sophomores	Juniors	Seniors
25	17	20	20
29	25	24	25
32	20	25	26
15	26	30	32
18	30	15	19
26	28	18	20
35			

17. Diets and Exercise Programs A researcher conducted a study of two different diets and two different exercise programs. Three randomly selected subjects were assigned to each group for one month. The values indicate the amount of weight each lost.

Exercise program \ Diet	A	B
I	5, 6, 4	8, 10, 15
II	3, 4, 8	12, 16, 11

Answer the following questions for the information in the printout shown.

a. What procedure is being used? Two-way ANOVA
b. What are the names of the two variables? Diet and exercise program
c. How many levels does each variable contain? 2
d. What are the hypotheses for the study?
e. What are the F test statistics for the hypotheses? State which are significant, using the P-values.
f. Based on the answers to part e, which hypotheses can be rejected? Reject the null hypothesis for the diets.

Computer Printout for Problem 17

Datafile: NONAME.SST   Procedure: Two-way ANOVA

General Linear Model: Weight Loss versus Ex Program, Diet

```
Analysis of Variance
Source            DF    Adj SS    Adj MS   F-Value   P-Value
  Ex Program       1     3.000     3.000      0.43     0.531
  Diet             1   147.000   147.000     21.00     0.002
  Ex Program*Diet  1     3.000     3.000      0.43     0.531
Error              8    56.000     7.000
Total             11   209.000

Model Summary
      S    R-sq   R-sq(adj)   R-sq(pred)
2.64575  73.21%     63.16%       39.71%
```

≡ Critical Thinking Challenges

Adult Children of Alcoholics

Shown here are the abstract and two tables from a research study entitled "Adult Children of Alcoholics: Are They at Greater Risk for Negative Health Behaviors?" by Arlene E. Hall. Based on the abstract and the tables, answer these questions.

1. What was the purpose of the study?

2. How many groups were used in the study?

3. By what means were the data collected?

4. What was the sample size?

5. What type of sampling method was used?

6. How might the population be defined?

7. What may have been the hypothesis for the ANOVA part of the study?

8. Why was the one-way ANOVA procedure used, as opposed to another test, such as the t test?

9. What part of the ANOVA table did the conclusion "ACOAs had significantly lower wellness scores (WS) than non-ACOAs" come from?

10. What level of significance was used?

11. In the following excerpts from the article, the researcher states that

> . . . using the Tukey-HSD procedure revealed a significant difference between ACOAs and non-ACOAs, p = 0.05, but no significant difference was found between ACOAs and Unsures or between non-ACOAs and Unsures.

Using Tables 12–8 and 12–9 and the means, explain why the Tukey test would have enabled the researcher to draw this conclusion.

Abstract The purpose of the study was to examine and compare the health behaviors of adult children of alcoholics (ACOAs) and their non-ACOA peers within a university population. Subjects were 980 undergraduate students from a major university in the East. Three groups (ACOA, non-ACOA, and Unsure) were identified from subjects' responses to three direct questions regarding parental drinking behaviors. A questionnaire was used to collect data for the study. Included were questions related to demographics, parental drinking behaviors, and the College Wellness Check (WS), a health risk appraisal designed especially for college students (Dewey & Cabral, 1986). Analysis of variance procedures revealed that ACOAs had significantly lower wellness scores (WS) than non-ACOAs. Chi-square analyses of the individual variables revealed that ACOAs and non-ACOAs were significantly different on 15 of the 50 variables of the WS. A discriminant analysis procedure revealed the similarities between Unsure subjects and ACOA subjects. The results provide valuable information regarding ACOAs in a nonclinical setting and contribute to our understanding of the influences related to their health risk behaviors.

TABLE 12–8   Means and Standard Deviations for the Wellness Scores (WS) Group by (N = 945)

Group	N	$\bar{X}$	S.D.
ACOAs	143	69.0	13.6
Non-ACOAs	746	73.2	14.5
Unsure	56	70.1	14.0

TABLE 12–9   ANOVA of Group Means for the Wellness Scores (WS)

Source	Sum of squares	d.f.	Mean square	F
Between groups	2,403.5	2	1201.7	5.9
Within groups	193,237.4	942	205.1	
Total	195,640.9	944		

Data Projects

Use a significance level of 0.05 for all tests.

1. **Business and Finance** Select 10 stocks at random from the Dow Jones Industrials, the NASDAQ, and the S&P 500. For each, note the gain or loss in the last quarter. Use analysis of variance to test the claim that stocks from all three groups have had equal performance.

2. **Sports and Leisure** Use total earnings data for movies that were released in the previous year. Sort them by rating (G, PG, PG13, and R). Is the mean revenue for movies the same regardless of rating?

3. **Technology** Use the data collected in data project 3 of Chapter 2 regarding song lengths. Consider only three genres. For example, use rock, alternative, and hip hop/ rap. Conduct an analysis of variance to determine if the mean song lengths for the genres are the same.

4. **Health and Wellness** Select 10 cereals from each of the following categories: cereal targeted at children, cereal targeted at dieters, and cereal that fits neither of the previous categories. For each cereal note its calories per cup (this may require some computation since serving sizes vary for cereals). Use analysis of variance to test the claim that the calorie content of these different types of cereals is the same.

5. **Politics and Economics** Conduct an anonymous survey and ask the participants to identify which of the following categories describes them best: registered Republican, Democrat, or Independent, or not registered to vote. Also ask them to give their age to obtain your data. Use an analysis of variance to determine whether there is a difference in mean age between the different political designations.

6. **Your Class** Split the class into four groups, those whose favorite type of music is rock, whose favorite is country, whose favorite is rap or hip hop, and those whose favorite is another type of music. Make a list of the ages of students for each of the four groups. Use analysis of variance to test the claim that the means for all four groups are equal.

⬛ Answers to Applying the Concepts

Section 12–1   Colors That Make You Smarter

1. The ANOVA produces a test statistic of $F = 3.06$, with a P-value of 0.059. We would fail to reject the null hypothesis and find that there is not enough evidence to conclude at $\alpha = 0.05$ that the color of a person's clothing is related to people's perceptions of how intelligent the person looks.

2. The purpose of the study was to determine if the color of a person's clothing is related to people's perceptions of how intelligent the person looks.

3. We would have to perform three separate t tests, which would inflate the error rate.

Section 12–2   Colors That Make You Smarter

1. Tukey's pairwise comparisons show no significant difference in the three pairwise comparisons of the means.

2. This agrees with the nonsignificant results of the general ANOVA test conducted in Applying the Concepts 12–1.

3. The t tests should not be used since they would inflate the error rate.

4. We prefer the Tukey test over the Scheffé test when the samples are all the same size.

Section 12–3   Automobile Sales Techniques

There is no significant difference between levels 1 and 2 of experience. Level 3 and level 4 salespersons did significantly better than those at levels 1 and 2, with level 4 showing the best results, on average, than those at levels 1 and 2. Levels 3 and 4 are not significantly different in terms of experience. If interaction between experience and type of presentation is taken into consideration, the interaction plot shows a significant difference. The best combination seems to be level 4 experience with presentation style 1.

⬛ Hypothesis-Testing Summary 2*

7. Test of the significance of the correlation coefficient.

   Example: $H_0: \rho = 0$

   Use a t test:

   $$t = r\sqrt{\frac{n-2}{1-r^2}} \qquad \text{with d.f.} = n - 2$$

8. Formula for the F test for the multiple correlation coefficient.

   Example: $H_0: \rho = 0$

   $$F = \frac{R^2/k}{(1-R^2)/(n-k-1)}$$

   $$\text{d.f.N.} = n - k \qquad \text{d.f.D.} = n - k - 1$$

9. Comparison of a sample distribution with a specific population.

   Example: H_0: There is no difference between the two distributions.

   Use the chi-square goodness-of-fit test:

   $$\chi^2 = \sum \frac{(O-E)^2}{E}$$

   d.f. = no. of categories − 1

10. Comparison of the independence of two variables.

    Example: H_0: Variable A is independent of variable B.

    Use the chi-square independence test:

    $$\chi^2 = \sum \frac{(O-E)^2}{E}$$

    $$\text{d.f.} = (R-1)(C-1)$$

11. Test for homogeneity of proportions.

    Example: $H_0: p_1 = p_2 = p_3$

    Use the chi-square test:

    $$\chi^2 = \sum \frac{(O-E)^2}{E}$$

    $$\text{d.f.} = (R-1)(C-1)$$

12. Comparison of three or more sample means.

    Example: $H_0: \mu_1 = \mu_2 = \mu_3$

    Use the analysis of variance test:

    $$F = \frac{s_B^2}{s_W^2}$$

    where

    $$s_B^2 = \frac{\sum n_i(\overline{X}_i - \overline{X}_{\text{GM}})^2}{k-1}$$

    $$s_W^2 = \frac{\sum(n_i - 1)s_i^2}{\sum(n_i - 1)}$$

d.f.N. = $k - 1$	$N = n_1 + n_2 + \cdots + n_k$
d.f.D. = $N - k$	k = number of groups

*This summary is a continuation of Hypothesis-Testing Summary 1, at the end of Chapter 9.

13. Test when the *F* value for the ANOVA is significant. Use the Scheffé test to find what pairs of means are significantly different.

$$F_s = \frac{(\overline{X}_i - \overline{X}_j)^2}{s_W^2[(1/n_i) + (1/n_j)]}$$

$$F' = (k - 1)(\text{C.V.})$$

Use the Tukey test to find which pairs of means are significantly different.

$$q = \frac{\overline{X}_i - \overline{X}_j}{\sqrt{s_W^2/n}} \qquad \begin{array}{l} \text{d.f.N.} = k \\ \text{d.f.D.} = \text{degrees of freedom for } s_W^2 \end{array}$$

Use the Bonferroni test to find what pairs of means are significantly different.

$$t = \frac{\overline{X}_1 - \overline{X}_2}{\sqrt{s_W^2\left(\frac{1}{n_1} + \frac{1}{n_2}\right)}} \quad \text{with d.f.} = N - k$$

14. Test for the two-way ANOVA.

Example:

H_0: There is no significant difference between the variables.

H_0: There is no interaction effect between the variables.

$$\text{MS}_A = \frac{\text{SS}_A}{a - 1}$$

$$\text{MS}_B = \frac{\text{SS}_B}{b - 1}$$

$$\text{MS}_{A \times B} = \frac{\text{SS}_{A \times B}}{(a - 1)(b - 1)}$$

$$\text{MS}_W = \frac{\text{SS}_W}{ab(n - 1)}$$

$$F_A = \frac{\text{MS}_A}{\text{MS}_W} \qquad \begin{array}{l} \text{d.f.N.} = a - 1 \\ \text{d.f.D.} = ab(n - 1) \end{array}$$

$$F_B = \frac{\text{MS}_B}{\text{MS}_W} \qquad \begin{array}{l} \text{d.f.N.} = (b - 1) \\ \text{d.f.D.} = ab(n - 1) \end{array}$$

$$F_{A \times B} = \frac{\text{MS}_{A \times B}}{\text{MS}_W} \qquad \begin{array}{l} \text{d.f.N.} = (a - 1)(b - 1) \\ \text{d.f.D.} = ab(n - 1) \end{array}$$

13

Nonparametric Statistics

Andrew Resek/McGraw Hill

⬛ STATISTICS TODAY

Too Much or Too Little?

Suppose a manufacturer of ketchup wishes to check the bottling machines to see if they are functioning properly. That is, are they dispensing the right amount of ketchup per bottle? A 40-ounce bottle is currently used. Because of the natural variation in the manufacturing process, the amount of ketchup in a bottle will not always be exactly 40 ounces. Some bottles will contain less than 40 ounces, and others will contain more than 40 ounces. To see if the variation is due to chance or to a malfunction in the manufacturing process, a runs test can be used. The runs test is a nonparametric statistical technique. See Statistics Today—Revisited at the end of this chapter. This chapter explains such techniques, which can be used to help the manufacturer determine the answer to the question.

OUTLINE

OBJECTIVES

After completing this chapter, you should be able to:

1 State the advantages and disadvantages of nonparametric methods.

2 Test hypotheses, using the sign test.

3 Test hypotheses, using the Wilcoxon rank sum test.

4 Test hypotheses, using the signed-rank test.

5 Test hypotheses, using the Kruskal-Wallis test.

6 Compute the Spearman rank correlation coefficient.

7 Test hypotheses, using the runs test.

Introduction

Statistical tests, such as the z, t, and F tests, are called parametric tests. **Parametric tests** are statistical tests for population parameters such as means, variances, and proportions that involve assumptions about the populations from which the samples were selected. One assumption is that these populations are normally distributed. But what if the population in a particular hypothesis-testing situation is *not* normally distributed? Statisticians have developed a branch of statistics known as **nonparametric statistics** or **distribution-free statistics** to use when the population from which the samples are selected is not normally distributed or is distributed in any other particular way. Nonparametric statistics can also be used to test hypotheses that do not involve specific population parameters, such as μ, σ, or p.

> **Nonparametric statistical tests** are used to test hypotheses about population parameters when the assumption about normality cannot be met.

For example, a sportswriter may wish to know whether there is a relationship between the rankings of two judges on the diving abilities of 10 Olympic swimmers. In another situation, a sociologist may wish to determine whether men and women enroll at random for a specific drug rehabilitation program. The statistical tests used in these situations are nonparametric or distribution-free tests. The term *nonparametric* is used for both situations.

The nonparametric tests explained in this chapter are the sign test, the Wilcoxon rank sum test, the Wilcoxon signed-rank test, the Kruskal-Wallis test, and the runs test. In addition, the Spearman rank correlation coefficient, a statistic for determining the relationship between ranks, is explained.

13–1   Advantages and Disadvantages of Nonparametric Methods

OBJECTIVE

State the advantages and disadvantages of nonparametric methods.

As stated previously, nonparametric tests and statistics can be used in place of their parametric counterparts (z, t, and F) when the assumption of normality cannot be met. However, you should not assume that these statistics are a better alternative than the parametric statistics. There are both advantages and disadvantages in the use of nonparametric methods.

Advantages

There are six advantages that nonparametric methods have over parametric methods:

1. They can be used to test population parameters when the variable is not normally distributed.
2. They can be used when the data are nominal or ordinal.
3. They can be used to test hypotheses that do not involve population parameters.
4. In some cases, the computations are easier than those for the parametric counterparts.
5. They are easy to understand.
6. There are fewer assumptions that have to be met, and the assumptions are easier to verify.

Disadvantages

There are three disadvantages of nonparametric methods:

1. They are *less sensitive* than their parametric counterparts when the assumptions of the parametric methods are met. Therefore, larger differences are needed before the null hypothesis can be rejected.

Interesting Fact

Older men have the biggest ears. James Heathcote, M.D., says, "On average, our ears seem to grow 0.22 millimeter a year. This is roughly a centimeter during the course of 50 years."

2. They tend to use *less information* than the parametric tests. For example, the sign test requires the researcher to determine only whether the data values are above or below the median, not how much above or below the median each value is.

3. They are *less efficient* than their parametric counterparts when the assumptions of the parametric methods are met. That is, larger sample sizes are needed to overcome the loss of information. For example, the nonparametric sign test is about 60% as efficient as its parametric counterpart, the z test. Thus, a sample size of 100 is needed for use of the sign test, compared with a sample size of 60 for use of the z test to obtain the same results.

Since there are both advantages and disadvantages to the nonparametric methods, the researcher should use caution in selecting these methods. If the parametric assumptions can be met, the parametric methods are preferred. However, when parametric assumptions cannot be met, the nonparametric methods are a valuable tool for analyzing the data.

The basic assumption for nonparametric statistics are as follows:

Assumptions for Nonparametric Statistics

1. The sample or samples are randomly selected.
2. If two or more samples are used, they must be independent of each other unless otherwise stated.

In this book, the assumptions will be stated in the exercises; however, when encountering statistics in other situations, you must check to see that these assumptions have been met before proceeding.

Ranking

Many nonparametric tests involve the **ranking** of data, that is, the positioning of a data value in a data array according to some rating scale. Ranking is an ordinal variable. For example, suppose a judge decides to rate five speakers on an ascending scale of 1 to 10, with 1 being the best and 10 being the worst, for categories such as voice, gestures, logical presentation, and platform personality. The ratings are shown in the chart.

Speaker	A	B	C	D	E
Rating	8	6	10	3	1

The rankings are shown next.

Speaker	E	D	B	A	C
Rating	1	3	6	8	10
Ranking	1	2	3	4	5

Since speaker E received the lowest score, 1 point, this speaker is ranked first. Speaker D received the next-lower score, 3 points; speaker D is ranked second; and so on.

What happens if two or more speakers receive the same number of points? Suppose the judge awards points as follows:

Speaker	A	B	C	D	E
Rating	8	6	10	6	3

The speakers are then ranked as follows:

Speaker	E	D	B	A	C
Rating	3	6	6	8	10
Ranking	1	Tie for 2nd and 3rd		4	5

When there is a tie for two or more places, the average of the ranks must be used. In this case, each would be ranked as

$$\frac{2+3}{2} = \frac{5}{2} = 2.5$$

Hence, the rankings are as follows:

Speaker	E	D	B	A	C
Rating	3	6	6	8	10
Ranking	1	2.5	2.5	4	5

Many times, the data are already ranked, so no additional computations must be done. For example, if the judge does not have to award points but can simply select the speakers who are best, second-best, third-best, and so on, then these ranks can be used directly.

Also *P*-values can be found for nonparametric statistical tests, and the *P*-value method can be used to test hypotheses that use nonparametric tests. For this chapter, the *P*-value method will be limited to some of the nonparametric tests that use the standard normal distribution or the chi-square distribution.

Applying the Concepts 13–1

Ranking Data

The following table lists the percentages of patients who experienced side effects from a drug used to lower a person's cholesterol level.

Side effect	Percent
Chest pain	4.0
Rash	4.0
Nausea	7.0
Heartburn	5.4
Fatigue	3.8
Headache	7.3
Dizziness	10.0
Chills	7.0
Cough	2.6

Rank each value in the table.

See page 752 for the answer.

Exercises 13–1

1. What is meant by *nonparametric statistics?*

2. When should nonparametric statistics be used?

3. List the advantages of nonparametric statistics.

4. List the disadvantages of nonparametric statistics.

5. Why does the term *distribution-free* describe nonparametric procedures?

6. Explain what is meant by the efficiency of a nonparametric test.

For Exercises 7 through 12, rank each set of data.

7. 14, 34, 18, 27, 32, 36, 42

8. 97, 382, 115, 192, 115, 360

9. 19.2, 14.8, 32.3, 6.5, 14.8, 17.1, 32.3

10. 15.62, 18.43, 27.25, 33.09, 22.16

11. 27, 34, 21, 16, 34, 19, 27, 42, 45

12. 97.3, 122.2, 135.2, 89.3, 86.8, 115.6, 128.9, 122.2

13–2   The Sign Test

 OBJECTIVE ❷

Test hypotheses, using the sign test.

Single-Sample Sign Test

The simplest nonparametric test, the **sign test** for single samples, is used to test the value of a median for a specific sample.

> The **sign test** for a single sample is a nonparametric test used to test the value of a population median.

When using the sign test, the researcher hypothesizes the specific value for the median of a population; then the researcher selects a random sample of data and compares each value with the conjectured median. If the data value is above the conjectured median, it is assigned a plus sign. If the data value is below the conjectured median, it is assigned a minus sign. And if it is exactly the same as the conjectured median, it is assigned a 0. Then the numbers of plus and minus signs are compared to determine if they are significantly different. If the null hypothesis is true, the number of plus signs should be approximately equal to the number of minus signs. If the null hypothesis is not true, there will be a disproportionate number of plus or minus signs.

There are two cases for using the sign test. The first case is when the sample size n is less than or equal to 25. The other case is when the sample size n is greater than 25.

Test Statistic for the Sign Test

If $n \leq 25$, the test statistic is the smaller number of plus or minus signs. When $n > 25$, the test statistic is

$$z = \frac{(X + 0.5) - 0.5n}{\frac{\sqrt{n}}{2}}$$

where X is the smaller number of plus or minus signs and n is the total number of plus or minus signs.

For example, when $n \leq 25$, if there are 8 positive signs and 3 negative signs, the test statistic is 3. When the sample size is 25 or less, Table A–10 in Appendix A is used to determine the critical value. For a specific α, if the test statistic is less than or equal to the critical value obtained from the table, the null hypothesis should be rejected. The values in Table A–10 are obtained from the binomial distribution when $p = 0.5$. The derivation is omitted here. When $n > 25$, the normal approximation with Table A–4 can be used for the critical values. In this case, $\mu = np$ or $0.5n$ since $p = 0.5$ and $\sigma = \sqrt{npq}$ or $\sqrt{n}/2$ since p and $q = 0.5$ and $\sqrt{npq} = \sqrt{n(0.5)(0.5)}$ or $0.5\sqrt{n}$ which is the same as $\sqrt{n}/2$.

The Procedure Table for the sign test is given next.

Procedure Table

Performing the Sign Test

Step 1   State the hypotheses and identify the claim.

Step 2   Find the critical value. Use Table A–10 in Appendix A when $n \leq 25$ and Table A–4 when $n > 25$.

Step 3   Compute the test statistic.

Step 4   Make the decision.

Step 5   Summarize the result.

EXAMPLE 13–1   Flu Shots

A nurse at a medical center claims that the median number of flu shots they give per day is 30. To test the claim, the nurse randomly selects 20 days during the months of September, October, and November and determines how many flu shots were given each day. The data are shown. At $\alpha = 0.05$, test the claim that the median number of shots given is 30.

37	31	36	35	55
33	24	38	45	22
12	31	39	34	36
30	31	43	30	32

SOLUTION

Step 1   State the hypotheses and identify the claim.

H_0: Median = 30 (claim)

H_1: Median $\neq$ 30

Step 2   Find the critical value.

Subtract the hypothesized median, 30, from each data value. If the data value falls above the hypothesized median, assign the value a + sign. If the data value falls below the hypothesized median, assign the data value a − sign. If the data value is equal to the median, assign it a 0.

$37 - 30 = +7$, so 37 is assigned a + sign.
$33 - 30 = +3$, so 33 is assigned a + sign.
$12 - 30 = -18$, so 12 is assigned a − sign.
$30 - 30 = 0$, so 30 is assigned 0.
etc.

The completed table is shown.

+	+	+	+	+
+	−	+	+	−
−	+	+	+	+
0	+	+	0	+

Since $n \leq 25$, refer to Table A–10 in Appendix A. In this case, $n = 20 - 2 = 18$ (There are two zeros) and $\alpha = 0.05$. The critical value for a two-tailed test is 4. See Figure 13–1.

FIGURE 13–1

Finding the Critical
Value in Table A–10 for
Example 13–1

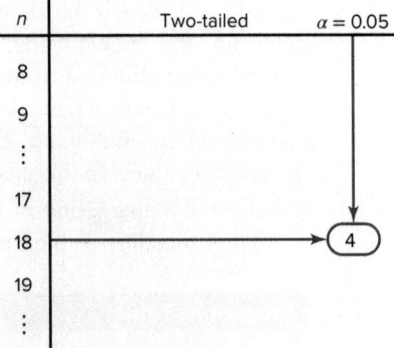

Step 3   Compute the test statistic. Count the number of + and − signs in step 2, and use the smaller value as the test statistic. In this case, there are 15 plus signs and 3 minus signs, so the test statistic is 3.

Step 4   Make the decision. Compare the test statistic 3 with the critical value 4. If the test statistic is less than or equal to the critical value, the null hypothesis is rejected. In this case, the null hypothesis is rejected since $3 < 4$.

Step 5   Summarize the results. There is enough evidence to reject the null hypothesis that the median of the number of patients seen per day is 30.

EXAMPLE 13–2   Easy Pass Users

The Pennsylvania Turnpike Commission allows travelers to use a purchased Easy Pass for tolls on the Pennsylvania Turnpike. A researcher hypothesizes that the median of the number of Easy Pass users at a small interchange on the turnpike is 900. A random sample of 40 days is selected and on 15 days there were fewer than 900 Easy Pass users at the interchange. At $\alpha = 0.05$, test the claim that the median number of Easy Pass users at the interchange is 900.

SOLUTION

Step 1   State the hypotheses and identify the claim.

$$H_0: \text{Median} = 900 \text{ (claim) and } H_1: \text{median} \neq 900$$

Step 2   Find the critical values. Since $\alpha = 0.05$ and $n = 40$ and the test is two-tailed, the critical values are $+1.96$ and -1.96.

Step 3   Compute the test statistic.

$$z = \frac{(X + 0.5) - 0.5n}{\sqrt{n}/2} = \frac{(15 + 0.5) - 0.5(40)}{\sqrt{40}/2} = -1.42$$

Step 4   Make the decision. Since the test statistic -1.42 is greater than -1.96, the decision is do not reject the null hypothesis. See Figure 13–2.

FIGURE 13–2
Critical Values and Test
Statistic for Example 13–2

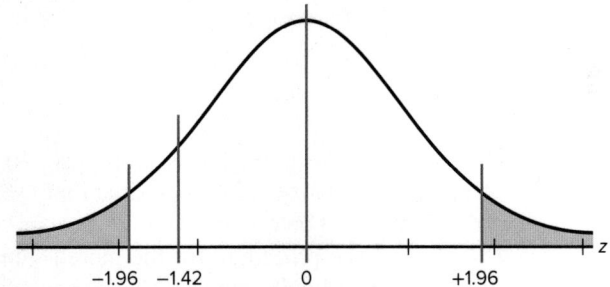

-1.96 -1.42 0 $+1.96$

Step 5   Summarize the results. There is not enough evidence to reject the claim that the median number of Easy Pass users is 900.

In Example 13–2, the sample size is 40, and on 15 days the number of Easy Pass users is less than 900. So, on $40 - 15 = 25$ days, the number of Easy Pass users were greater than or equal to 900. The value of X that is used is the smaller of the two numbers, 15 and 25. So, in this case, 15 is used for X.

Suppose a researcher hypothesized that the median age of houses in a certain municipality was 40 years. In a random sample of 100 houses, 68 were older than 40 years. Then the value used for X in the formula would be $100 - 68$, or 32, since it is the smaller of the two numbers 68 and 32. When 40 is subtracted from the age of a house older than 40 years, the answer is positive. When 40 is subtracted from the age of a house that is less than 40 years old, the result is negative. There would be 68 positive signs and 32 negative signs (assuming that no house was exactly 40 years old). Hence, 32 would be used for X, since it is the smaller of the two values.

Because the sign test uses the smaller number of plus or minus signs, the test is either a two-tailed test or a left-tailed test. When the test is two-tailed, the critical value is found on the left side of the standard normal distribution. When the sign test is a right-tailed test, the formula is

$$z = \frac{(X - 0.5) - 0.5n}{\sqrt{n}/2}$$

and the larger number of plus or minus signs is used for X. In this case, the hypotheses would be

$$H_0: \text{median} = k$$
$$H_1: \text{median} > k$$

The right side of the z distribution would be used for the critical value.

Paired-Sample Sign Test

The sign test can also be used to test sample means in a comparison of two dependent samples, such as a before-and-after test. Recall that when dependent samples are taken from normally distributed populations, the t test is used (Section 9–4). When the condition of normality cannot be met, the nonparametric sign test can be used.

> The **paired-sample sign test** is a nonparametric test that is used to test the difference between two population medians when the samples are dependent.

In a before-and-after test, the variable X_B represents the values before a treatment is given to the subjects while the variable X_A represents the value of the variables after the treatment is given. This test can be left-tailed, right-tailed, or two-tailed. Here the variables X_B and X_A are subtracted ($X_B - X_A$) from each other, and a plus or minus sign is given to each answer. Zeros are ignored. If the number of plus signs is approximately equal to the number of minus signs, then the null hypothesis is not rejected. If the difference in the number of $+$ and $-$ signs is significant, then the null hypothesis is rejected.

Two Assumptions for the Paired-Sign Test

1. The sample is random.
2. The variables are dependent or paired.

In this book, the assumptions will be stated in the exercises; however, when encountering statistics in other situations, you must check to see that these assumptions have been met before proceeding.

The procedure for the paired-sample sign test is the same as the procedure for the single-sample sign test shown previously.

EXAMPLE 13–3   Ear Infections in Swimmers

A medical researcher believed the number of ear infections in swimmers can be reduced if the swimmers use earplugs. A sample of 10 people was selected, and the number of infections for a four-month period was recorded. During the first two months, the swimmers did not use the earplugs; during the second two months, they did. At the beginning of the second two-month period, each swimmer was examined to make sure that no infection was present. The data are shown here. At $\alpha = 0.05$, can the researcher conclude that using earplugs reduced the number of ear infections?

| | Number of ear infections | |
Swimmer	Before, X_B	After, X_A
A	3	2
B	0	1
C	5	4
D	4	0
E	2	1
F	4	3
G	3	1
H	5	3
I	2	2
J	1	3

SOLUTION

Step 1 State the hypotheses and identify the claim.

H_0: The number of ear infections will not be reduced.

H_1: The number of ear infections will be reduced (claim).

Step 2 Find the critical value. Subtract the after values X_A from the before values X_B, and indicate the difference by a positive or negative sign or 0, according to the value, as shown in the table.

Swimmer	Before, X_B	After, X_A	Sign of difference
A	3	2	+
B	0	1	−
C	5	4	+
D	4	0	+
E	2	1	+
F	4	3	+
G	3	1	+
H	5	3	+
I	2	2	0
J	1	3	−

From Table A–10, with $n = 9$ (the total number of positive and negative signs; the 0 is not counted) and $\alpha = 0.05$ (one-tailed), at most 1 negative sign is needed to reject the null hypothesis because 1 is the smallest entry in the $\alpha = 0.05$ column of Table A–10.

Step 3 Compute the test statistic. Since $n \leq 25$, we will count the number of positive and negative signs found in step 2 and use the smaller value as the test statistic. There are 7 positive signs and 2 negative signs, so the test statistic is 2.

Step 4 Make the decision. Compare the test statistic 2 with the critical value 1. If the test statistic is less than or equal to the critical value, the null hypothesis is rejected. In this case, $2 > 1$, so the decision is not to reject the null hypothesis.

Step 5 Summarize the results. There is not enough evidence to support the claim that the use of earplugs reduced the number of ear infections.

When conducting a one-tailed sign test, the researcher must scrutinize the data to determine whether they support the null hypothesis. If the data support the null hypothesis, there is no need to conduct the test. In Example 13–3, the null hypothesis states that the number of ear infections will not be reduced. The data would support the null hypothesis if there were more negative signs than positive signs. The reason is that the before values X_B in most cases would be smaller than the after values X_A, and the $X_B - X_A$ values would be negative more often than positive. This would indicate that there is not enough evidence to reject the null hypothesis. The researcher would stop here, since there is no need to continue the procedure.

On the other hand, if the number of ear infections were reduced, the X_B values, for the most part, would be larger than the X_A values, and the $X_B - X_A$ values would most often be positive, as in Example 13–3. Hence, the researcher would continue the procedure. A word of caution is in order, and a little reasoning is required.

When the sample size is 26 or more, the normal approximation can be used in the same manner as in Example 13–2.

≡ Applying the Concepts 13–2

Clean Air

An environmentalist suggests that the median of the number of days per month that a large city failed to meet the EPA acceptable standards for clean air is 11 days per month. A random sample of 20 months shows the number of days per month that the air quality was below the EPA's standards.

15	14	1	9	0	3	3	1	10	8
6	16	21	22	3	19	16	5	23	13

1. What is the claim?
2. What test would you use to test the claim? Why?
3. State the hypotheses.
4. Select a value for α and find the corresponding critical value.
5. What is the test statistic?
6. What is your decision?
7. Summarize the results.
8. Could a parametric test be used?

See page 752 for the answers.

≡ Exercises 13–2

1. Why is the sign test the simplest nonparametric test to use? The sign test uses only positive or negative signs.

2. What population parameter can be tested with the sign test? The median

3. In the sign test, what is used as the test statistic when $n \le 25$? The smaller number of positive or negative signs

4. When $n > 25$, what is used in place of Table A–10 for the sign test? The normal approximation

For Exercises 5 through 20, perform these steps.

   a. State the hypotheses and identify the claim.
   b. Find the critical value(s).
   c. Compute the test statistic.
   d. Make the decision.
   e. Summarize the results.

Use the traditional method of hypothesis testing unless otherwise specified.

5. **Ages at First Marriage for Women** The median age at first marriage in 2014 for women was 27 years—the highest it has ever been. A random sample of women's ages (in years) from recently applied for marriage licenses resulted in the following set of ages. At $\alpha = 0.05$, is there sufficient evidence that the median is not 27 years?

34.6	31.2	28.9	28.4	24.3
29.8	25.9	21.4	25.1	26.2
28.3	30.6	35.6	34.2	34.1

Source: World Almanac

6. **Total Debt for School Districts** A sample of school districts in two Pennsylvania counties shows the total debt in thousands of dollars for each district. At $\alpha = 0.10$, is the median of the data equal to 11?

20	17.4	9.4	5.0	3.5	8.0
14.6	11.2	5.2	1.9	2.4	6.6

Source: Tribune Review

7. **Personal Tax Rates** A government research employee has suggested that the median personal income tax rate of countries of the world is 17%. The tax rates for a random sample of 20 countries are shown. Is the median tax rate at $\alpha = 0.05$ of the countries 17%?

36.2	19.7	14.0	17.9
15.0	12.3	9.8	10.7
21.6	18.6	15.4	9.5
16.9	7.2	15.2	12.6
14.8	17.9	16.7	18.5

Source: The World Almanac and Book of Facts

8. **Weekly Earnings of Women** According to the Women's Bureau of the U.S. Department of Labor, the occupation with the highest median weekly earnings among women is pharmacist with median weekly earnings of $1603. Based on the weekly earnings listed from a random sample of female pharmacists, can it

be concluded that the median is less than $1603? Use $\alpha = 0.05$.

1550	1355	1777
1430	1570	1701
2465	1655	1484
1429	1829	1812
1217	1501	1449

9. **Hidden Chemicals in Beer** A study was done for a selection of beers to determine the amounts in parts per billion of a chemical called glyphosate (a weed killer) that was in the beers. The data are shown. At $\alpha = 0.10$, is the median of the sample equal to 14?

49.7	31.1	27	11.8
20.9	18.7	20.3	11.2
14.5	29.8	25.1	9.1
5.7			

Source: U.S. Public Interest Research

10. **Lottery Ticket Sales** A lottery outlet owner hypothesizes that she sells 200 lottery tickets a day. She randomly sampled 40 days and found that on 15 days she sold fewer than 200 tickets. At $\alpha = 0.05$, is there sufficient evidence to conclude that the median is below 200 tickets?

11. **Number of Faculty for Proprietary Schools** An educational researcher believes that the median number of faculty for proprietary (for-profit) colleges and universities is 150. The data provided list the number of faculty at a randomly selected number of proprietary colleges and universities. At the 0.05 level of significance, is there sufficient evidence to reject his claim?

372	111	165	95	191	83	136	149	37	119
142	136	137	171	122	133	133	342	126	64
61	100	225	127	92	140	140	75	108	96
138	318	179	243	109					

Source: World Almanac

12. **Gold Reserves** The gold reserves in millions of fine Troy ounces for a recent year for a selection of countries are shown. At $\alpha = 0.05$, is the median equal to 100? The numbers are given in millions of fine Troy ounces.

0.0	59.2	78.3	108.6	17.9	78.8
24.6	19.7	51.9	33.4	10.0	261.5

13. **Students' Opinions on Lengthening the School Year** One hundred randomly selected students are asked if they favor increasing the school year by 20 days. The responses are 62 no, 36 yes, and 2 undecided. At $\alpha = 0.10$, test the hypothesis that 50% of the students are against extending the school year. Use the P-value method.

14. **Television Viewers** A researcher read that the median age for viewers of the Jimmy Fallon show is 52.7 years. To test the claim, 75 randomly selected viewers were surveyed, and 27 were under the age of 52.7. At $\alpha = 0.05$, test the claim. Give one reason why an advertiser might like to know the results of this study. Use the P-value method.

Source: Nielsen Media Research.

15. **Swimming Pool Violations** In order to cut down on the number of swimming pool violations, a health department employee instructed the pool managers on several ways to reduce on the number of violations. At $\alpha = 0.05$, can it be concluded that the number of pool violations was reduced the next year?

Pool	A	B	C	D	E	F	G	H
Last year	9	16	20	6	7	5	10	12
This year	10	12	14	8	4	2	9	8

16. **Exam Scores** A statistics professor wants to investigate the relationship between a student's midterm examination score and the score on the final. Eight students were randomly selected, and their scores on the two examinations are noted. At the 0.10 level of significance, is there sufficient evidence to conclude that there is a difference in scores?

Student	1	2	3	4	5	6	7	8
Midterm	75	92	68	85	65	80	75	80
Final	82	90	79	95	70	83	72	79

17. **Soft Drinks** Ten college students were selected and asked how many soft drinks they drink over a two-week period. These students were asked to replace some of the soft drinks with water in order to cut down on the amount of soft drinks that they consumed. At $\alpha = 0.10$, was there a decrease in the amount of soft drinks consumed over a two-week period? The results are shown.

Student	A	B	C	D	E	F	G	H	I	J
Before	6	12	15	20	18	24	9	7	26	21
After	8	10	12	17	14	21	11	8	23	17

18. **Effects of a Pill on Appetite** A researcher wishes to test the effects of a pill on a person's appetite. Twelve randomly selected subjects are allowed to eat a meal of their choice, and their caloric intake is measured. The next day, the same subjects take the pill and eat a meal of their choice. The caloric intake of the second meal is measured. The data are shown here. At $\alpha = 0.02$, can the researcher conclude that the pill had an effect on a person's appetite?

Subject	1	2	3	4	5	6	7
Meal 1	856	732	900	1321	843	642	738
Meal 2	843	721	872	1341	805	531	740

Subject	8	9	10	11	12
Meal 1	1005	888	756	911	998
Meal 2	900	805	695	878	914

19. Internet Activities A sixth grade class was given a brief course on various types of Internet activities that they can use. They were asked to keep track of the number of times that they used the Internet for one week before the class and then after completing the class. Then nine students were randomly selected, and the number of times that they used the Internet before and after the class were compared. At $\alpha = 0.01$, can it be concluded that attending the class increased the use of the Internet for one week?

Student	1	2	3	4	5	6	7	8	9
Visits before	14	18	9	22	17	17	20	16	10
Visits after	16	19	8	21	25	23	27	15	13

20. Routine Maintenance and Defective Parts A manufacturer believes that if routine maintenance (cleaning and oiling of machines) is increased to once a day rather than once a week, the number of defective parts produced by the machines will decrease. Nine machines are randomly selected, and the number of defective parts produced over a 24-hour operating period is counted. Maintenance is then increased to once a day for a week, and the number of defective parts each machine produces is again counted over a 24-hour operating period. The data are shown. At $\alpha = 0.01$, can the manufacturer conclude that increased maintenance reduces the number of defective parts manufactured by the machines?

Machine	1	2	3	4	5	6	7	8	9
Before	6	18	5	4	16	13	20	9	3
After	5	16	7	4	18	12	14	7	1

Extending the Concepts

Confidence Interval for the Median

The confidence interval for the median of a set of values less than or equal to 25 in number can be found by ordering the data from smallest to largest, finding the median, and using Table A–10. For example, to find the 95% confidence interval of the true median for 17, 19, 3, 8, 10, 15, 1, 23, 2, 12, order the data:

  1, 2, 3, 8, 10, 12, 15, 17, 19, 23

From Table A–10, select $n = 10$ and $\alpha = 0.05$, and find the critical value. Use the two-tailed row. In this case, the critical value is 1. Add 1 to this value to get 2. In the ordered list, count from the left two numbers and from the right two numbers, and use these numbers to get the confidence interval, as shown:

  1, 2, 3, 8, 10, 12, 15, 17, 19, 23

  $2 \leq$ Median ≤ 19

Always add 1 to the number obtained from the table before counting. For example, if the critical value is 3, then count 4 values from the left and right.

For Exercises 21 through 25, find the confidence interval of the median, indicated in parentheses, for each set of data.

21. 5, 16, 23, 14, 3, 18, 15, 30, 28, 11 (95%)

22. 106, 114, 125, 96, 101, 97, 99, 104, 116, 118, 112, 103 (90%)

23. 6.7, 8.5, 7.3, 12.5, 14.2, 6.2, 14.3, 15.6, 16.5, 12.7, 13.3, 15.6, 19.2, 23.1, 5.2 (98%)

24. 3, 2, 17, 15, 19, 8, 10, 19, 6, 12, 14, 16, 12, 22, 9, 20, 7, 14 (99%)

25. 162, 149, 111, 106, 195, 143, 151, 123, 156, 144, 165, 147, 108, 117 (95%)

Technology Step by Step

EXCEL

Step by Step

The Sign Test

Excel does not have a procedure to conduct the sign test. However, you may conduct this test by using the MegaStat Add-in available online. If you have not installed this add-in, do so, following the instructions from the Chapter 1 Excel Step by Step.

  1. Enter the data from Example 13–1 into column A of a new worksheet.

  2. From the toolbar, select Add-Ins, **MegaStat>Nonparametric Tests>Sign Test**. *Note:* You may need to open MegaStat from the MegaStat.xls file on your computer's hard drive.

  3. Type **A1:A20** for the Input range.

  4. Type **30** for the Hypothesized value, and select the "not equal" Alternative.

5. Click [OK].

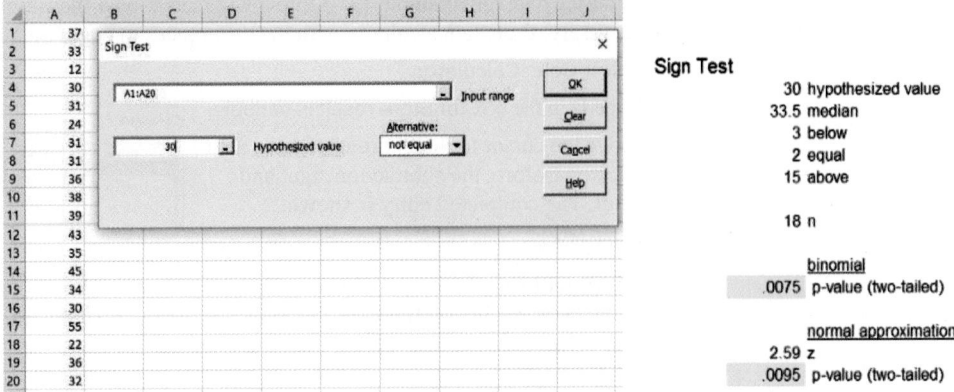

Use the binomial *P*-value of 0.0075. Reject the null hypothesis.

MINITAB
Step by Step

The Sign Test

Example 13–1

Is the median number of flu shots given by the medical clinic 30 per day?

1. Enter the data into C1 of a MINITAB worksheet. Name the column FluShots.

2. Select **Stat>Nonparametrics>1-Sample Sign.**

  a) Double-click C1 FluShots for the variable.
  b) Click on the radio button for Test Median, then type 30 in the dialog box.
  c) Click [OK].

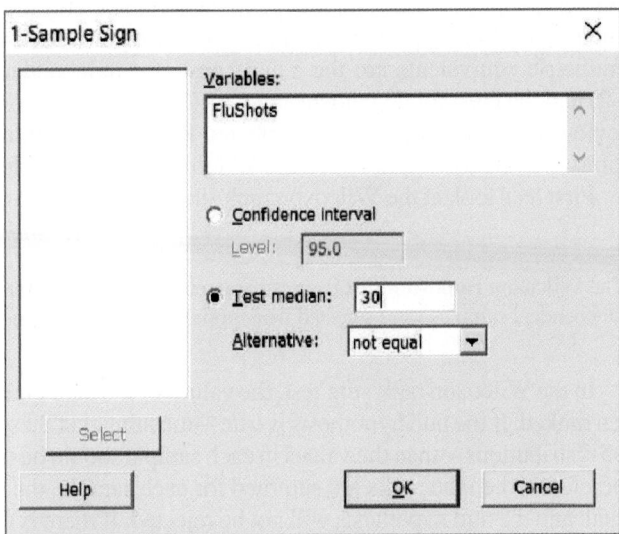

Sign Test for Median: FluShots

```
Sign test of median =  30.00 versus ≠ 30.00

            N  Below  Equal  Above       P  Median
FluShots   20      3      2     15  0.0075   33.50
```

The results are displayed in the session window. The sample median is 33.5. Since the *P*-value of 0.0075 is less than alpha, the null hypothesis is rejected.

The Paired-Sample Sign Test

1. Enter the data for Example 13–3 into a worksheet; only the Before and After columns are necessary. Calculate a column with the differences to begin the process.

2. Select **Calc>Calculator**.

3. Type **D** in the box for Store result in variable.

4. Move the cursor to the Expression box, then click on Before, the subtraction sign, and After. The completed entry is shown.

5. Click [OK].

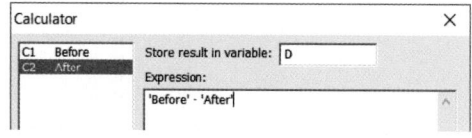

MINITAB will calculate the differences and store them in the first available column with the name "D." Use the instructions for the Sign Test on the differences *D* with a hypothesized value of zero.

Sign Test for Median: D
```
Sign test of median = 0.00000 versus ≠ 0.00000

     N  Below  Equal  Above       P  Median
D   10      2      1      7  0.1797   1.000
```

The *P*-value is 0.1797. Do not reject the null hypothesis.

13–3   The Wilcoxon Rank Sum Test

OBJECTIVE

Test hypotheses, using the Wilcoxon rank sum test.

Interesting Fact

One in two married women now earns more than her husband.

The sign test does not consider the magnitude of the data. For example, whether a value is 1 point or 100 points below the median, it will receive a negative sign. And when you compare values in the pretest/posttest situation, the magnitude of the differences is not considered. The Wilcoxon tests consider differences in magnitudes by using ranks.

The two tests considered in this section and in Section 13–4 are the **Wilcoxon rank sum test,** which is used for independent samples, and the **Wilcoxon signed-rank test,** which is used for dependent samples. Both tests are used to compare distributions. The parametric equivalents are the *z* and *t* tests for independent samples (Sections 9–1 and 9–2) and the *t* test for dependent samples (Section 9–3). For the parametric tests, as stated previously, the samples must be selected from approximately normally distributed populations, but the assumptions for the Wilcoxon tests are different.

First let's look at the Wilcoxon rank sum test, sometimes called the Mann-Whitney test.

> The **Wilcoxon rank sum test** is a nonparametric test that uses ranks to determine if two independent samples were selected from populations that have the same distributions.

In the Wilcoxon rank sum test, the values of the data for both samples are combined and then ranked. If the null hypothesis is true—meaning that there is no difference in the population distributions—then the values in each sample should be ranked approximately the same. Therefore, when the ranks are summed for each sample, the sums should be approximately equal, and the null hypothesis will not be rejected. If there is a large difference in the sums of the ranks, then the distributions are not identical and the null hypothesis will be rejected.

There are two assumptions for this test.

Assumptions for the Wilcoxon Rank Sum Test

1. The samples are random and independent of one another.
2. The size of each sample must be greater than or equal to 10.

In this book, the assumptions will be stated in the exercises; however, when encountering statistics in other situations, you must check to see that these assumptions have been met before proceeding.

For the Wilcoxon rank sum test for independent samples, both sample sizes must be greater than or equal to 10. The formulas needed for the test are given next.

Formula for the Wilcoxon Rank Sum Test When Samples Are Independent

$$z = \frac{R - \mu_R}{\sigma_R}$$

where

$$\mu_R = \frac{n_1(n_1 + n_2 + 1)}{2}$$

$$\sigma_R = \sqrt{\frac{n_1 n_2 (n_1 + n_2 + 1)}{12}}$$

R = sum of ranks for smaller sample size (n_1)
n_1 = smaller of sample sizes
n_2 = larger of sample sizes
$n_1 \geq 10$ and $n_2 \geq 10$

Note that if both samples are the same size, either size can be used as n_1.

Table A–4 is used for the critical values.

The steps for the Wilcoxon rank sum test are given in the Procedure Table.

Procedure Table

Wilcoxon Rank Sum Test

Step 1   State the hypotheses and identify the claim.

Step 2   Find the critical value(s). Use Table A–4.

Step 3   Compute the test statistic.
   a. Combine the data from the two samples, arrange the combined data in order, and rank each value.
   b. Sum the ranks of the group with the smaller sample size. (*Note:* If both groups have the same sample size, either one can be used.)
   c. Use these formulas to find the test statistic.

$$\mu_R = \frac{n_1(n_1 + n_2 + 1)}{2}$$

$$\sigma_R = \sqrt{\frac{n_1 n_2 (n_1 + n_2 + 1)}{12}}$$

$$z = \frac{R - \mu_R}{\sigma_R}$$

where R is the sum of the ranks of the data in the smaller sample and n_1 and n_2 are each greater than or equal to 10.

Step 4   Make the decision.

Step 5   Summarize the results.

Example 13–4 illustrates the Wilcoxon rank sum test for independent samples.

EXAMPLE 13–4   Times to Complete an Obstacle Course

Two independent random samples of army and marine recruits are selected, and the time in minutes it takes each recruit to complete an obstacle course is recorded, as shown in the table. At $\alpha = 0.05$, is there a difference in the times it takes the recruits to complete the course?

Army	15	18	16	17	13	22	24	17	19	21	26	28
Marines	14	9	16	19	10	12	11	8	15	18	25	

SOLUTION

Step 1 State the hypotheses and identify the claim.

H_0: There is no difference in the times it takes the recruits to complete the obstacle course.

H_1: There is a difference in the times it takes the recruits to complete the obstacle course (claim).

Step 2 Find the critical value. Since $\alpha = 0.05$ and this test is a two-tailed test, use the critical values of $+1.96$ and -1.96 from Table A–4.

Step 3 Compute the test statistic.

a. Combine the data from the two samples, arrange the combined data in ascending order, and rank each value. Be sure to indicate the group.

Time	8	9	10	11	12	13	14	15	15	16	16	17
Group	M	M	M	M	M	A	M	A	M	A	M	A
Rank	1	2	3	4	5	6	7	8.5	8.5	10.5	10.5	12.5

Time	17	18	18	19	19	21	22	24	25	26	28
Group	A	M	A	A	M	A	A	A	M	A	A
Rank	12.5	14.5	14.5	16.5	16.5	18	19	20	21	22	23

b. Sum the ranks of the group with the smaller sample size. (*Note:* If both groups have the same sample size, either one can be used.) In this case, the sample size for the marines is smaller.

$$R = 1 + 2 + 3 + 4 + 5 + 7 + 8.5 + 10.5 + 14.5 + 16.5 + 21$$
$$= 93$$

c. Substitute in the formulas to find the test statistic.

$$\mu_R = \frac{n_1(n_1 + n_2 + 1)}{2} = \frac{(11)(11 + 12 + 1)}{2} = 132$$

$$\sigma_R = \sqrt{\frac{n_1 n_2 (n_1 + n_2 + 1)}{12}} = \sqrt{\frac{(11)(12)(11 + 12 + 1)}{12}}$$

$$= \sqrt{264} = 16.2$$

$$z = \frac{R - \mu_R}{\sigma_R} = \frac{93 - 132}{16.2} = -2.41$$

Step 4   Make the decision. The decision is to reject the null hypothesis, since $-2.41 < -1.96$. See Figure 13–3.

FIGURE 13–3
Critical Values and Test
Statistic for Example 13–4

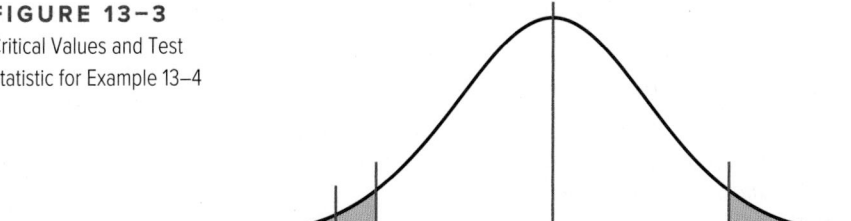

Step 5   Summarize the results. There is enough evidence to support the claim that there is a difference in the times it takes the recruits to complete the course.

The *P*-values can be used for Example 13–4. The *P*-value for $z = -2.41$ is 0.0080, and since this is a two-tailed test, $2(0.0080) = 0.016$. Hence, the null hypothesis is rejected at $\alpha = 0.05$.

Applying the Concepts **13–3**

School Lunch

A nutritionist decided to see if there was a difference in the number of calories served for lunch in elementary and secondary schools. She selected a random sample of eight elementary schools and another random sample of eight secondary schools in Pennsylvania. The data are shown.

Elementary	Secondary
648	694
589	730
625	750
595	810
789	860
727	702
703	657
564	761
501	650
568	704

1. Are the samples independent or dependent?
2. What are the hypotheses?
3. What nonparametric test would you use to test the claim?
4. What critical value would you use?
5. What is the test statistic?
6. What is your decision?
7. What is the corresponding parametric test?
8. What assumption would you need to meet to use the parametric test?
9. If this assumption were not met, would the parametric test yield the same results?

See page 752 for the answers.

≡ Exercises 13–3

1. What are the minimum sample sizes for the Wilcoxon rank sum test? n_1 and n_2 are each greater than or equal to 10.

2. What is the parametric equivalent test for the Wilcoxon rank sum test? The t test for independent samples

For Exercises 3 through 12, use the Wilcoxon rank sum test. Assume that the samples are independent. Also perform each of these steps.

    a. State the hypotheses and identify the claim.

    b. Find the critical value(s).

    c. Compute the test statistic.

    d. Make the decision.

    e. Summarize the results.

Use the traditional method of hypothesis testing unless otherwise specified.

3. Speed Skating Times The 2014 women's 1000-meter speed skating winning time was 1:14:02, posted by Zhang Hong of China. In preparation for the 2018 Winter Olympics in Pyeongchang, South Korea several randomly selected students from two different universities posted the following times (rounded to the nearest second). Test the claim that there is no difference in times between universities at $\alpha = 0.05$.

UA	2:05	2:15	1:58	1:42	2:01	1:40	1:39	2:20	1:51	2:03
UB	2:10	2:06	1:35	1:48	1:38	2:00	2:15	2:14	2:27	1:48

4. Lengths of Prison Sentences A random sample of men and women in prison was asked to give the length of sentence each received for a certain type of crime. At $\alpha = 0.05$, test the claim that there is no difference in the sentence received by each gender. The data (in months) are shown here.

Males	8	12	6	14	22	27	32	24	26
Females	7	5	2	3	21	26	30	9	4

Males	19	15	13
Females	17	23	12	11	16

5. Transfer Credits A university dean wishes to see if there is a difference in the number of credits community college students transfer as opposed to students who attend a 4-year college and transfer after 2 years. The data are shown. Use the Wilcoxon rank sum test to test this claim at $\alpha = 0.05$.

Community College	61	63	42	35	48	62	64	60	59	65
Four-Year Schools	58	64	37	46	45	63	71	58	68	66

6. Lifetimes of Handheld Video Games To test the claim that there is no difference in the lifetimes of two brands of handheld video games, a researcher selects a random sample of 11 video games of each brand. The lifetimes (in months) of each brand are shown. At $\alpha = 0.01$, can the researcher conclude that there is a difference in the distributions of lifetimes for the two brands?

Brand A	42	34	39	42	22	47	51	34	41	39	28
Brand B	29	39	38	43	45	49	53	38	44	43	32

7. Stopping Distances of Automobiles A researcher wishes to see if the stopping distance for midsize automobiles is different from the stopping distance for compact automobiles at a speed of 70 miles per hour. The data are shown for two random samples. At $\alpha = 0.10$, test the claim that the stopping distances are the same. If one of your safety concerns is stopping distance, will it make a difference which type of automobile you purchase?

Automobile	1	2	3	4	5	6	7	8	9	10
Midsize	188	190	195	192	186	194	188	187	214	203
Compact	200	211	206	297	198	204	218	212	196	193

Source: Based on information from the National Highway Traffic Safety Administration.

8. Winning Baseball Games For the years 1970–1993 the National League (NL) and the American League (AL) (major league baseball) were each divided into two divisions: East and West. Below are random samples of the number of games won by each league's Eastern Division. At $\alpha = 0.05$, is there sufficient evidence to conclude a difference in the number of wins?

NL	89	96	88	101	90	91	92	96	108	100	95
AL	108	86	91	97	100	102	95	104	95	89	88	101

Source: World Almanac.

9. Hunting Accidents A game commissioner wishes to see if the number of hunting accidents in counties in western Pennsylvania is different from the number of hunting accidents in counties in eastern Pennsylvania. Random samples of counties from the two regions are selected, and the numbers of hunting accidents are shown. At $\alpha = 0.05$, is there a difference in the number of accidents in the two areas? If so, give a possible reason for the difference.

Western Pa.	10	21	11	11	9	17	13	8	15	17
Eastern Pa.	14	3	7	13	11	2	8	5	5	6

Source: Pennsylvania Game Commission.

10. Medical School Enrollments Random samples of enrollments from medical schools that specialize in research and in primary care are listed. At $\alpha = 0.05$, can it be concluded that there is a difference?

Research	474	577	605	663	813	443	565	696	692	217
Primary care	783	546	442	662	605	474	587	555	427	320	293

Source: U.S. News & World Report Best Graduate Schools.

11. Job Satisfaction Two groups of employees were given a questionnaire to assess their degree of satisfaction with their jobs. The questionnaire scores range from 0 to 100. The groups are divided according to years of service. The data are shown. At $\alpha = 0.10$, can you conclude that there is a difference in job satisfaction between the groups?

Under 5 years of service	79 99 84 85 76 78 73 69 57 94 98 68 87
5 or more years of service	95 80 83 86 71 65 63 59 51 57 62 96 92

12. Student Participation in a Blood Drive Students in Greek organizations at schools throughout the country sent volunteers to a yearly blood drive. The numbers from each randomly selected participating school are listed. Test the claim that there is no difference in the number of students participating from fraternities and sororities at $\alpha = 0.10$.

Fraternities	4, 5, 10, 7, 7, 15, 12, 11, 13, 15, 12, 12
Sororities	3, 5, 6, 7, 4, 7, 10, 9, 9, 14

13. Bed Falls in Hospitals Hospitals are concerned with the number of patients who fall out of bed at night. One sample of hospitals (B) had a medical staff person check on the patients every half hour at night to see if they can prevent patients from falling out of bed at night. The other hospital (A) did not check on their patients every half hour at night. At $\alpha = 0.05$, can it be concluded that there was a decrease in the number of patient falls at night?

Hospital A	6	8	3	10	4	8	11	12	2	5	7
Hospital B	4	5	5	8	6	7	9	10	3	4	3

14. Traffic Accidents On a large parkway, state police decided to reduce the speed from 65 miles per hour to 55 miles per hour to see if the number of accidents would be reduced. The data are shown. At $\alpha = 0.10$, test the claim that the number of accidents was reduced at the lower speed for two randomly selected weeks.

65 mph	10	14	8	16	12	15	8	9	13	10
55 mph	6	3	10	14	15	11	9	7	12	8

15. Number of Libraries A researcher wished to know if there are more libraries in the Eastern United States or in the Western United States. Ten states in each area are randomly selected and the number of libraries in each state is listed. At $\alpha = 0.05$, can it be concluded that there is a difference in the number of libraries per state in the East and West?

East	80	182	21	80	24	368	219	80	72	455
West	247	87	72	62	23	184	62	131	112	22

Source: The World Almanac and Book of Facts

16. Bus Passengers A manager in a transportation center wishes to compare the number of passengers that use the buses on two routes within the city. The manager randomly selects 12 weekdays in both systems to compare. At $\alpha = 0.10$, can it be concluded that there is a difference in the number of passengers that use the systems?

East system	320 283 256 432 372 512 295 354 318 432 462 378
West system	487 503 762 532 312 243 660 832 416 681 476 536

17. Cell Phone Sales The manager of two cell phone stores wishes to compare the number of phones two stores sell per week. The manager randomly selects 11 weeks to compare. At $\alpha = 0.10$, is there a difference in the number of phone sales in the stores?

Store A	33	46	18	27	29	37	34	25	29	15	42
Store B	19	23	35	22	28	39	44	42	51	29	45

18. Subway Passengers New York City has several subway systems. Compare the number of passengers in the two systems at $\alpha = 0.10$. Is there a difference in the number of passengers who ride each system? The data are in thousands and are for a random selection of stops in each system.

Source: MTA

The Bronx	Brooklyn
944	1909
8392	981
2562	1571
1502	2378
1026	650
3596	3998
668	3572
2531	1746
844	652
1867	310

Technology   Step by Step

EXCEL
Step by Step

The Wilcoxon Mann-Whitney Test

Excel does not have a procedure to conduct the Mann-Whitney rank sum test. However, you may conduct this test by using the MegaStat Add-in available online. If you have not installed this add-in, do so, following the instructions from the Chapter 1 Excel Step by Step.

1. Enter the data from Example 13–4 into columns A and B of a new worksheet.

2. From the toolbar, select Add-Ins, **MegaStat>Nonparametric Tests>Wilcoxon-Mann/ Whitney Test**. *Note:* You may need to open MegaStat from the MegaStat.xls file on your computer's hard drive.

3. Type **A1:A12** in the box for Group 1.

4. Type **B1:B11** in the box for Group 2.

5. Check the option labeled Correct for ties, and select the "not equal" Alternative. Note: Check the box for continuity correction.

6. Click [OK].

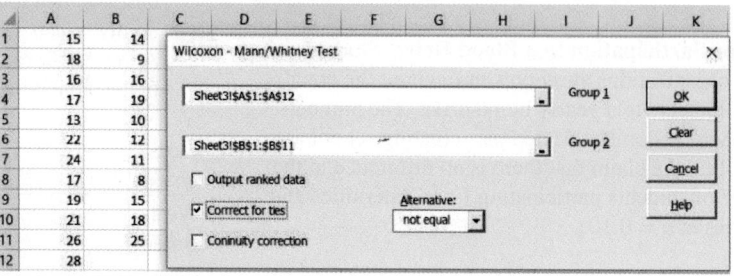

Wilcoxon Mann-Whitney Test

n	Sum of ranks	
12	183	Group 1
11	93	Group 2
23	276	Total

144.00	Expected value
16.23	Standard deviation
2.37	z, corrected for ties
0.0177	P-value (two-tailed)

The *P*-value is 0.0177. Reject the null hypothesis.

MINITAB
Step by Step

Wilcoxon Rank Sum Test (Mann-Whitney)

1. Enter the data for Example 13–4 into two columns of a worksheet.

2. Name the columns **Army** and **Marines**.

3. Select **Stat>Nonparametrics>Mann-Whitney**.

4. Double-click Army for the First Sample.

5. Double-click Marines for the Second Sample.

6. Click [OK].

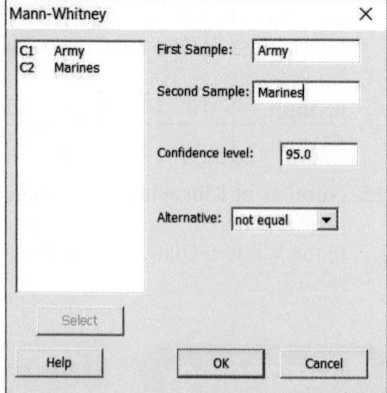

Mann-Whitney Test and CI: Army, Marines

```
           N  Median
Army      12  18.500
Marines   11  14.000

Point estimate for η1 - η2 is 6.000
95.5 Percent CI for η1 - η2 is (1.003,9.998)
W = 183.0
Test of η1 = η2 vs η1 ≠ η2 is significant at 0.0178
The test is significant at 0.0177 (adjusted for ties)
```

The *P*-value for the test is 0.0177. Reject the null hypothesis. There is a significant difference in the times it takes the recruits to complete the course.

13–4   The Wilcoxon Signed-Rank Test

When the samples are dependent, as they would be in a before-and-after test using the same subjects, the Wilcoxon signed-rank test can be used in place of the *t* test for dependent samples. Again, this test does not require the condition of normality.

> The **Wilcoxon signed-rank test** is a nonparametric test used to test whether two dependent samples have been selected from two populations having the same distributions.

However, the following assumptions for the Wilcoxon signed-rank test must be met before it can be used.

Assumptions for the Wilcoxon Signed-Rank Test

1. The paired data have been obtained from a random sample.
2. The population of differences has a distribution that is approximately symmetric.

In this book, the assumptions will be stated in the exercises; however, when encountering statistics in other situations, you must check to see that these assumptions have been met before proceeding.

Table A–11 in Appendix A is used for the critical values when $n \leq 30$. Use the column for the critical value along with the row for the value of *n*. See Example 13–5.

To find the test statistic for the Wilcoxon signed-rank test, denoted by w_s, when $n \leq 30$, rank the absolute values of the differences of each pair of data values. Assign either a + or a − sign to each rank according to the original value of the difference. Then sum the positive ranks and the negative ranks separately. Finally, when $n \leq 30$, select the smaller of the absolute value of the sums as the test statistic w_s.

When $n > 30$, the normal distribution can be used to approximate the Wilcoxon distribution. The same critical values from Table A–4 used for the *z* test for specific α values are used. The formula is

$$z = \frac{w_s - \frac{n(n+1)}{4}}{\sqrt{\frac{n(n+1)(2n+1)}{24}}}$$

where
  n = number of pairs where difference is not 0
  w_s = smaller sum in absolute value of signed ranks

The steps for the Wilcoxon signed-rank test are given in the Procedure Table.

Procedure Table

Wilcoxon Signed-Rank Test

Step 1   State the hypotheses and identify the claim.

Step 2   Find the critical value from Table A–11 when $n \leq 30$ and from Table A–4 when $n > 30$.

Step 3   Compute the test statistic.

When $n \leq 30$:

a. Make a table, as shown.

Before, X_B	After, X_A	Difference $D = X_B - X_A$	Absolute value $|D|$	Rank	Signed rank

b. Find the differences (before − after), denoted by $X_B − X_A$, and place the values in the Difference column.

c. Find the absolute value of each difference, and place the results in the Absolute value column.

d. Rank each absolute value from lowest to highest, and place the rankings in the Rank column.

e. Give each rank a positive or negative sign, according to the sign in the Difference column.

f. Find the sum of the positive ranks and the sum of the negative ranks separately.

g. Select the smaller of the absolute values of the sums, and use this absolute value as the test statistic w_s.

When $n > 30$, use Table A–4 and the test statistic

$$z = \frac{w_s - \dfrac{n(n+1)}{4}}{\sqrt{\dfrac{n(n+1)(2n+1)}{24}}}$$

where
n = number of pairs where difference is not 0
w_s = smaller sum in absolute value of signed ranks

Step 4   Make the decision. Reject the null hypothesis if the test statistic is less than or equal to the critical value.

Step 5   Summarize the results.

The procedure for this test is shown in Example 13–5.

EXAMPLE 13–5   Shoplifting Incidents

In a large department store, the owner wishes to see whether the number of shoplifting incidents per day will change if the number of uniformed security officers is doubled. A random sample of 7 days before security is increased and 7 days after the increase shows the number of shoplifting incidents.

Day	Number of shoplifting incidents	
	Before	**After**
Monday	7	5
Tuesday	2	3
Wednesday	3	4
Thursday	6	3
Friday	5	1
Saturday	8	6
Sunday	12	4

Is there enough evidence to support the claim, at $\alpha = 0.05$, that there is a difference in the number of shoplifting incidents before and after the increase in security?

SOLUTION

Step 1   State the hypotheses and identify the claim.

H_0: There is no difference in the number of shoplifting incidents before and after the increase in security.

H_1: There is a difference in the number of shoplifting incidents before and after the increase in security (claim).

Step 2   Find the critical value from Table A–11 because $n \leq 30$. Since $n = 7$ and $\alpha = 0.05$ for this two-tailed test, the critical value is 2. See Figure 13–4.

FIGURE 13–4

Finding the Critical Value in Table A–11 for Example 13–5

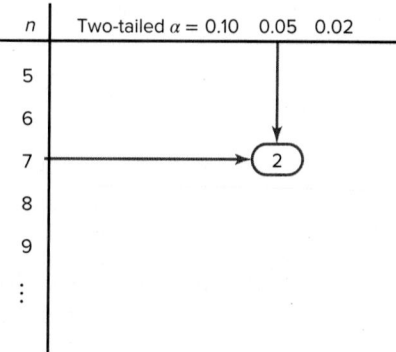

Step 3   Find the test statistic.

a. Make a table as shown.

Day	Before, X_B	After, X_A	Difference $D = X_B - X_A$	Absolute value $|D|$	Rank	Signed rank
Mon.	7	5				
Tues.	2	3				
Wed.	3	4				
Thurs.	6	3				
Fri.	5	1				
Sat.	8	6				
Sun.	12	4				

b. Find the differences (before minus after), and place the values in the Difference column.

$$7 - 5 = 2 \qquad 6 - 3 = 3 \qquad 8 - 6 = 2$$
$$2 - 3 = -1 \qquad 5 - 1 = 4 \qquad 12 - 4 = 8$$
$$3 - 4 = -1$$

c. Find the absolute value of each difference, and place the results in the Absolute value column. (*Note:* The absolute value of any number except 0 is the positive value of the number. Any differences of 0 should be ignored.)

$$|2| = 2 \qquad |3| = 3 \qquad |2| = 2$$
$$|-1| = 1 \qquad |4| = 4 \qquad |8| = 8$$
$$|-1| = 1$$

d. Rank each absolute value from lowest to highest, and place the rankings in the Rank column. In the case of a tie, assign the values that rank plus 0.5.

Value	2	1	1	3	4	2	8
Rank	3.5	1.5	1.5	5	6	3.5	7

e. Give each rank a plus or minus sign, according to the sign in the Difference column. The completed table is shown here.

Day	Before, X_B	After, X_A	Difference $D = X_B - X_A$	Absolute value $|D|$	Rank	Signed rank
Mon.	7	5	2	2	3.5	+3.5
Tues.	2	3	−1	1	1.5	−1.5
Wed.	3	4	−1	1	1.5	−1.5
Thurs.	6	3	3	3	5	+5
Fri.	5	1	4	4	6	+6
Sat.	8	6	2	2	3.5	+3.5
Sun.	12	4	8	8	7	+7

f. Find the sum of the positive ranks and the sum of the negative ranks separately.

Positive rank sum	$(+3.5) + (+5) + (+6) + (+3.5) + (+7) = +25$
Negative rank sum	$(-1.5) + (-1.5)$ $\qquad\qquad\qquad = -3$

g. Select the smaller of the absolute values of the sums ($|-3|$), and use this absolute value as the test statistic w_s. In this case, $w_s = |-3| = 3$.

Step 4   Make the decision. Reject the null hypothesis if the test statistic is less than or equal to the critical value. In this case, $3 > 2$; hence, the decision is to not reject the null hypothesis.

Step 5   Summarize the results. There is not enough evidence at $\alpha = 0.05$ to support the claim that there is a difference in the number of shoplifting incidents before and after the increase in security. Hence, the security increase probably made no difference in the number of shoplifting incidents.

The rationale behind the signed-rank test can be explained by a diet example. If the diet is working, then the majority of the postweights will be smaller than the preweights. When the postweights are subtracted from the preweights, the majority of the signs will be positive, and the absolute value of the sum of the negative ranks will be small. This sum will probably be smaller than the critical value obtained from Table A–11, and the null hypothesis will be rejected. On the other hand, if the diet does not work, some people will gain weight, other people will lose weight, and still other people will remain about the same weight. In this case, the sum of the positive ranks and the absolute value of the sum of the negative ranks will be approximately equal and will be about one-half of the sum of the absolute value of all the ranks. In this case, the smaller of the absolute values of the two sums will still be larger than the critical value obtained from Table A–11, and the null hypothesis will not be rejected.

Applying the Concepts 13–4

Pain Medication

A researcher decides to see how effective a pain medication is. Eight randomly selected subjects were asked to determine the severity of their pain by using a scale of 1 to 10, with 1 being very minor and 10 being very severe. Then each was given the medication, and after 1 hour, they were asked to rate the severity of their pain, using the same scale.

Subject	1	2	3	4	5	6	7	8
Before	8	6	2	3	4	6	2	7
After	6	5	3	1	2	6	1	6

1. What is the purpose of the study?

2. Are the samples independent or dependent?

3. What are the hypotheses?

4. What nonparametric test could be used to test the claim?

5. What significance level would you use?

6. What is your decision?

7. What parametric test could you use?

8. Would the results be the same?

See page 752 for the answers.

≡ Exercises 13–4

1. What is the parametric equivalent test for the Wilcoxon signed-rank test? The *t* test for dependent samples

2. What is the difference between the Wilcoxon rank sum test and the Wilcoxon signed-rank test?

For Exercises 3 and 4, find the sum of the signed ranks. Assume that the samples are dependent. State which sum is used as the test statistic.

3.
Pretest	108	67	119	157	103	156
Posttest	116	63	109	162	118	149

4.
Before	17	35	63	46	65	27	66	85
After	26	56	55	46	73	33	67	92

For Exercises 5 through 8, use Table A–11 to determine whether the null hypothesis should be rejected.

5. $w_s = 15$, $n = 10$, $\alpha = 0.01$, two-tailed

6. $w_s = 18$, $n = 17$, $\alpha = 0.05$, one-tailed

7. $w_s = 45$, $n = 20$, $\alpha = 0.025$, one-tailed

8. $w_s = 63$, $n = 24$, $\alpha = 0.05$, two-tailed

For Exercises 9–14, use the Wilcoxon signed-rank test to test each hypothesis.

9. **Drug Prices** Eight drugs were randomly selected, and the prices for the human doses and the animal doses for the same amounts were compared. At $\alpha = 0.05$, can it be concluded that the prices for the animal doses are significantly less than the prices for the human doses? If the null hypothesis is rejected, give one reason why animal doses might cost less than human doses.

Human dose	0.67	0.64	1.20	0.51	0.87	0.74	0.50	1.22
Animal dose	0.13	0.18	0.42	0.25	0.57	0.57	0.49	1.28

Source: House Committee on Government Reform.

10. **Classroom Absences** In order to cut down on student absences in statistics class, the instructor decides to count attendance as extra credit. After the midterm exam, the instructor announces that attendance will count as a 10-point quiz. If a student attends 95% or more of classes, the student gets an extra 10 points. If a student attends 94–90% of classes, the student will get an extra 9 points. If the student attends 80–89% of the classes, the student will get an extra 8 points, 70–79%, 7 points, 60–69%, 6 points. The instructor then selects 10 students at random and sees if their attendance improves for the second half of the semester. The classes each student missed are shown. At $\alpha = 0.05$, can it be shown that attendance has improved?

Student	A	B	C	D	E	F	G	H	I	J
First half of semester	6	8	5	9	2	7	6	4	3	8
Second half of semester	3	4	6	5	4	3	3	2	3	6

11. **Compulsive Gamblers** A group of compulsive gamblers was selected. The amounts (in dollars) they spent on lottery tickets for one week are shown. Then they were required to complete a workshop showing that the chances of winning were not in their favor. After they complete the workshop, test the claim that, at $\alpha = 0.05$, the workshop was effective in reducing the weekly amount spent on lottery tickets.

Subject	A	B	C	D	E	F	G	H
Before	86	150	161	197	98	56	122	76
After	72	143	123	186	102	53	125	72

12. **Legal Costs for School Districts** A random sample of legal costs (in thousands of dollars) for school districts for two recent consecutive years is shown. At $\alpha = 0.05$, is there a difference in the costs?

Year 1	108	36	65	108	87	94	10	40
Year 2	138	28	67	181	97	126	18	67

Source: Pittsburgh Tribune-Review.

13. **Drug Prices** A researcher wishes to compare the prices for randomly selected prescription drugs in the United States with those in Canada. The same drugs and dosages were compared in each country. At $\alpha = 0.05$, can it be concluded that the drugs in Canada are cheaper?

Drug	1	2	3	4	5	6
United States	3.31	2.27	2.54	3.13	23.40	3.16
Canada	1.47	1.07	1.34	1.34	21.44	1.47

Drug	7	8	9	10
United States	1.98	5.27	1.96	1.11
Canada	1.07	3.39	2.22	1.13

Source: IMS Health and other sources.

14. **Traffic Accidents** In order to reduce the number of traffic accidents at eight intersections in a large city, the traffic commissioner decided to make the intersections four-way stop signs instead of two-way stop signs. The traffic commissioner then keeps a record of the accidents before the extra stop signs were added and then after the stop signs were added. At $\alpha = 0.01$, can it be concluded that the addition of two stop signs reduced the number of accidents at the intersections?

Intersection	1	2	3	4	5	6	7	8
Before stop signs	6	3	14	7	4	9	7	5
After stop signs	5	4	10	1	6	5	3	2

15. **Mall Walkers** A researcher decided to test a new brand of walking shoes to see if it helped the walkers decrease their walking times (in minutes) around a mall. The data show the before and after times it took nine walkers to

complete the course. At $\alpha = 0.05$, did the new shoes help to increase the walking speeds of the walkers?

Before	10	8	12	14	15	12	7	15	13
After	7	9	10	14	9	11	8	13	9

16. **More Sleep** A medical researcher wanted to know if people who took a special herb containing chamomile would help increase the number of hours that they slept at night. The data show the average hours subjects slept in one week. At $\alpha = 0.05$, is there sufficient evidence to show that the subjects increased their sleep times?

Before	6.3	7.2	5.4	8.2	5.8	7.4	5.5	6.1
After	7.1	8.3	5.9	7.3	6.8	6.2	5.3	6.4

≣ Technology Step by Step

MINITAB
Step by Step

Wilcoxon Signed-Rank Test

Test the median value for the differences of two dependent samples. Use Example 13–5.

1. Enter the data into two columns of a worksheet. Name the columns **Before** and **After.**

2. Calculate the differences, using **Calc>Calculator.**

3. Type **D** in the box for Store result in variable.

4. In the expression box, type **Before − After.**

5. Click [OK].

6. Select **Stat>Nonparametrics> 1-Sample Wilcoxon.**

7. Select D for the Variable.

8. Click on Test median. The value should be 0.

9. Click [OK].

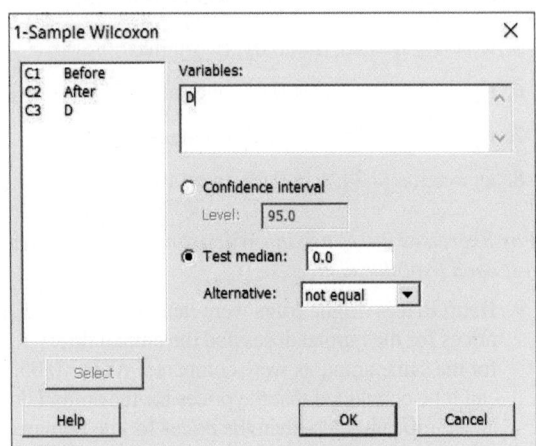

Wilcoxon Signed Rank Test: D
Test of median = 0.000000 versus median ≠ 0.000000

	N	N for Test	Wilcoxon Statistic	P	Estimated Median
D	7	7	25.0	0.076	2.250

The *P*-value of the test is 0.076. Do not reject the null hypothesis.

13–5 The Kruskal-Wallis Test

OBJECTIVE **5**

Test hypotheses, using the Kruskal-Wallis test.

The analysis of variance uses the *F* test to compare the means of three or more populations. The assumptions for the ANOVA test are that the populations are normally distributed and that the population variances are equal. When these assumptions cannot be met, the nonparametric **Kruskal-Wallis test,** sometimes called the *H test,* can be used to compare three or more means.

> The **Kruskal-Wallis test** is a nonparametric test that is used to determine whether three or more samples came from populations with the same distributions.

The following assumptions must be met to use the Kruskal-Wallis test.

Assumptions for the Kruskal-Wallis Test

1. There are at least three random samples.
2. The size of each sample must be at least 5.

In this book, the assumptions will be stated in the exercises; however, when encountering statistics in other situations, you must check to see that these assumptions have been met before proceeding.

In this test, each sample size must be 5 or more. In these situations, the distribution can be approximated by the chi-square distribution with $k - 1$ degrees of freedom, where k = number of groups. This test also uses ranks. The formula for the test is given next.

In the Kruskal-Wallis test, you consider all the data values as a group and then rank them. Next, the ranks are separated and the H formula is computed. This formula approximates the variance of the ranks. If the samples are from different populations, the sums of the ranks will be different and the H value will be large; hence, the null hypothesis will be rejected if the H value is large enough. If the samples are from the same population, the sums of the ranks will be approximately the same and the H value will be small; therefore, the null hypothesis will not be rejected. This test is always a right-tailed test. The chi-square table, Table A–6, with d.f. = $k - 1$, should be used for critical values.

Since the test is right-tailed, the null hypothesis will be rejected if the test statistic is greater than or equal to the critical value.

Formula for the Kruskal-Wallis Test

$$H = \frac{12}{N(N + 1)}\left(\frac{R_1^2}{n_1} + \frac{R_2^2}{n_2} + \cdots + \frac{R_k^2}{n_k}\right) - 3(N + 1)$$

where
R_1 = sum of ranks of sample 1
n_1 = size of sample 1
R_2 = sum of ranks of sample 2
n_2 = size of sample 2
.
.
.
R_k = sum of ranks of sample k
n_k = size of sample k
$N = n_1 + n_2 + \cdots + n_k$
k = number of samples

Procedure Table

Kruskal-Wallis Test

Step 1 State the hypotheses and identify the claim.

Step 2 Find the critical value. Use the chi-square table, Table A–6, with d.f. = $k - 1$ (k = number of groups).

Step 3 Compute the test statistic.

a. Arrange the data from lowest to highest and rank each value.

b. Find the sum of the ranks of each group.

c. Substitute in the formula.

$$H = \frac{12}{N(N + 1)}\left(\frac{R_1^2}{n_1} + \frac{R_2^2}{n_2} + \cdots + \frac{R_k^2}{n_k}\right) - 3(N + 1)$$

where

$$N = n_1 + n_2 + \cdots + n_k$$
$$R_k = \text{sum of ranks for } k\text{th group}$$
$$k = \text{number of groups}$$

Step 4 Make the decision.

Step 5 Summarize the results.

Example 13–6 illustrates the procedure for conducting the Kruskal-Wallis test.

EXAMPLE 13–6 Hidden Chemicals in Beers

A study was done to detect hidden chemicals in various types of beers. Three beers were tested for glyphosate (a weed killer). The following amounts (in parts per billion) were found. The data are shown. At $\alpha = 0.05$, is there enough evidence to claim that the amount of the chemical glyphosate differs in the beers?

Beer A	Beer B	Beer C
29.8	25.4	19.6
27.6	26.2	20.2
30.1	28.2	23.1
29.2	22.7	22.9
28.3	22.9	25.4

Source: Based on U.S. Public Interest Research

SOLUTION

Step 1 State the hypotheses and identify the claim.

H_0: There is no difference in the amounts of the chemical glyphosate in three groups of beers.

H_1: There is a difference in the amounts of the chemical glyphosate in three groups of beers (claim).

Step 2 Find the critical value. Use the chi-square table (Table A–6) with d.f. $= k - 1$, where $k =$ the number of groups. With $\alpha = 0.05$ and d.f. $= 3 - 1 = 2$, the critical value is 5.991.

Step 3 Compute the test statistic.

a. Arrange all the data from the lowest value to the highest value and rank each value.

Amount	Group	Rank
19.6	C	1
20.2	C	2
22.7	B	3
22.9	C	4.5
22.9	B	4.5
23.1	C	6
25.4	B	7.5
25.4	C	7.5
26.2	B	9
27.6	A	10
28.2	B	11
28.3	A	12
29.2	A	13
29.8	A	14
30.1	A	15

  b. Find the sum of the ranks for each group.

Group A $10 + 12 + 13 + 14 + 15 = 64$
Group B $3 + 4.5 + 7.5 + 9 + 11 = 35$
Group C $1 + 2 + 4.5 + 6 + 7.5 = 21$

  c. Substitute in the formula.

$$H = \frac{12}{N(N+1)}\left(\frac{R_1^2}{n_1} + \frac{R_2^2}{n_2} + \frac{R_3^2}{n_3}\right) - 3(N+1)$$

where

$$N = 15 \quad R_1 = 64 \quad R_2 = 35 \quad R_3 = 21$$
$$n_1 = n_2 = n_3 = 5$$

$$H = \frac{12}{15(15+1)}\left(\frac{64^2}{5} + \frac{35^2}{5} + \frac{21^2}{5}\right) - 3(15+1) = 9.654$$

Step 4   Make the decision. Since the test statistic of 24.025 is greater than 5.991, reject the null hypothesis. See Figure 13–5.

FIGURE 13–5
Critical Value and Test
Statistic for Example 13–6

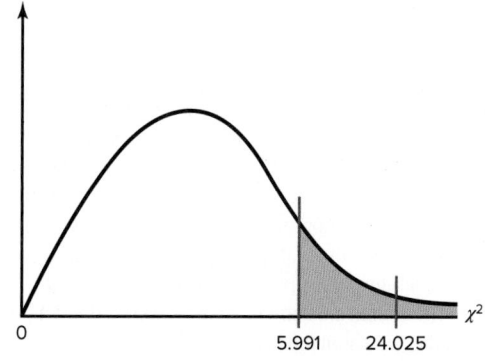

Step 5   Summarize the results. There is enough evidence to support the claim that there is a difference in the amount of the chemical glyphosate in the three groups of beer.

The *P*-value for 24.025 is 0.00006. Hence, the null hypothesis is still rejected.

Applying the Concepts 13–5

Heights of Waterfalls

You are doing research for an article on the waterfalls on our planet. You want to make a statement about the heights of waterfalls on three continents. Three random samples of waterfall heights (in feet) are shown.

North America	Africa	Asia
600	406	330
1200	508	830
182	630	614
620	726	1100
1170	480	885
442	2014	330

1. What questions are you trying to answer?
2. What nonparametric test would you use to find the answer?
3. What are the hypotheses?

4. Select a significance level and run the test. What is the *H* value?

5. What is your conclusion?

6. What is the corresponding parametric test?

7. What assumptions would need to be made to conduct the corresponding parametric test?

See page 752 for the answers.

Exercises 13–5

For Exercises 1 through 12, use the Kruskal-Wallis test and perform these steps.

   a. State the hypotheses and identify the claim.

   b. Find the critical value.

   c. Compute the test statistic.

   d. Make the decision.

   e. Summarize the results.

Use the traditional method of hypothesis testing unless otherwise specified.

1. **Speaking Confidence** Fear of public speaking is a common problem for many individuals. A researcher wishes to see if educating individuals on the aspects of public speaking will help people be more confident when they speak in public. She designs three programs for individuals to complete. Group A studies the aspects of writing a good speech. Group B is given instruction on delivering a speech. Group C is given practice and evaluation sessions on presenting a speech. Then each group is given a questionnaire on self-confidence. The scores are shown. At $\alpha = 0.05$, is there a difference in the scores on the tests?

Group A	Group B	Group C
22	18	16
25	24	17
27	25	19
26	27	23
33	29	18
35	31	31
30	17	15
36	15	36

2. **Mathematics Literacy Scores** Through the Organization for Economic Cooperation and Development (OECD), 15-year-olds are tested in member countries in mathematics, reading, and science literacy. Listed are randomly selected total mathematics literacy scores (i.e., both genders) for selected countries in different parts of the world. Test, using the Kruskal-Wallis test, to see if there is a difference in means at $\alpha = 0.05$.

Western Hemisphere	Europe	Eastern Asia
527	520	523
406	510	547
474	513	547
381	548	391
411	496	549

Source: www.nces.ed.gov

3. **Depression Levels** A psychologist designed a questionnaire to measure the level of depression among her patients. She divided the patients into three groups: never married, married, and divorced. Then she randomly selected subjects from each group and administered a questionnaire to measure their level of depression. The scale ranges from 0 to 50. The higher the score, the more severe the patient's depression. The scores are shown. At $\alpha = 0.10$, is there a difference in the means?

Never married	Married	Divorced
37	40	38
39	36	35
32	32	21
31	33	19
37	39	31
32	33	24
	30	

4. **Sodium Content of Microwave Dinners** Three brands of microwave dinners were advertised as low in sodium. Random samples of the three different brands show the following milligrams of sodium. At $\alpha = 0.05$, is there a difference in the amount of sodium among the brands?

Brand A	Brand B	Brand C
810	917	893
702	912	790
853	952	603
703	958	744
892	893	623
732		743
713		609
613		

5. **Sugar Content** The sugar content in grams of three different brands of candy bars is shown. At $\alpha = 0.05$, is there a difference in the number of calories in each type?

Brand A	Brand B	Brand C
7.6	9.2	18.6
9.3	11.1	16.2
8.4	12.3	15.4
11.3	10.1	18.0
10.2	10.2	17.3
9.8		

6. **Job Offers for Chemical Engineers** A recent study recorded the number of job offers received by randomly selected, newly graduated chemical engineers at three colleges. The data are shown here. At $\alpha = 0.05$, is there a difference in the average number of job offers received by the graduates at the three colleges?

College A	College B	College C
6	2	10
8	1	12
7	0	9
5	3	13
6	6	4

7. **Expenditures for Pupils** The expenditures in dollars per pupil for randomly selected states in three sections of the country are listed below. At $\alpha = 0.05$, can it be concluded that there is a difference in spending between regions?

Eastern third	Middle third	Western third
6701	9854	7584
6708	8414	5474
9186	7279	6622
6786	7311	9673
9261	6947	7353

Source: New York Times Almanac.

8. **Printer Costs** An electronics store manager wishes to compare the costs (in dollars) of three types of computer printers. The randomly selected data are shown. At $\alpha = 0.05$, can it be concluded that there is a difference in the prices? Based on your answer, do you think that a certain type of printer generally costs more than the other types?

Inkjet printers	Multifunction printers	Laser printers
149	98	192
199	119	159
249	149	198
239	249	198
99	99	229
79	199	

9. **Number of Crimes per Week** In a large city, the number of crimes per week in five precincts is recorded for five randomly selected weeks. The data are shown here. At $\alpha = 0.01$, is there a difference in the number of crimes?

Precinct 1	Precinct 2	Precinct 3	Precinct 4	Precinct 5
105	87	74	56	103
108	86	83	43	98
99	91	78	52	94
97	93	74	58	89
92	82	60	62	88

10. **Amounts of Caffeine in Beverages** The amounts of caffeine in randomly selected regular (small) servings of assorted beverages are listed. If someone wants to limit caffeine intake, does it really matter which beverage is chosen? Is there a difference in caffeine content at $\alpha = 0.05$?

Teas	Coffees	Colas
70	120	35
40	80	48
30	160	55
25	90	43
40	140	42

Source: Doctor's Pocket Calorie, Fat & Carbohydrate Counter.

11. **Maximum Speeds of Animals** A human is said to be able to reach a maximum speed of 27.89 miles per hour. The maximum speeds of various randomly selected types of other animals are listed below. Based on these particular groupings, is there evidence of a difference in speeds? Use the 0.05 level of significance.

Predatory mammals	Deerlike animals	Domestic animals
70	50	47.5
50	35	39.35
43	32	35
42	30	30
40	61	11

12. **Prices of Vitamin/Mineral Supplements** The prices for 30-count packages of randomly selected store-brand vitamin/mineral supplements are listed from three different sources. At the 0.01 level of significance, can a difference in prices be concluded?

Grocery store	Drugstore	Discount store
6.79	7.69	7.49
6.09	8.19	6.89
5.49	6.19	7.69
7.99	5.15	7.29
6.10	6.14	4.95

13. **Bridge Spans** The following data consist of the main spans (in feet) of a selection of bridges in North America. At $\alpha = 0.05$, is there a difference in the main spans of the three types of bridges?

Suspension	Cantilever	Truss
2800	1575	1200
2150	1182	902
1750	1070	845
1549	1212	810
1447	1644	780
1380		

Source: The World Almanac and Book of Facts

14. Tall Buildings A sample of the number of stories in three selected cities is shown. At $\alpha = 0.10$, is there a difference in the number of stories in the buildings among the cities?

Houston	Boston	Las Vegas
71	62	53
49	54	63
50	41	60
44	35	47
64	32	36
52		

Source: The World Almanac and Book of Facts

15. Areas of Natural Lakes of the World The data show the areas (in square miles) of three samples of lakes in the world. At $\alpha = 0.10$, is there a difference among the areas of the lakes in three continents?

North America	Africa	Asia
31,700	26,828	2,355
22,300	12,700	4,040
9,910	11,150	7,115
3,100	2,473	12,162
2,568	2,075	888

Source: The World Almanac and Book of Facts

16. Lengths of Major Rivers At $\alpha = 0.10$, can it be concluded that there is a difference in the lengths (in miles) of the major rivers shown?

Africa	Europe	South America
2720	500	1750
1100	1420	2100
4160	635	1584
700	325	1640
1000	850	1400

Source: The World Almanac and Book of Facts

17. Lengths of Sentences for Crimes At $\alpha = 0.025$, can it be concluded that the lengths (in months) of sentences for various crimes are different for the types of crimes committed?

Assaults	Arson	Fraud
32	72	35
44	68	46
41	74	52
36	63	31
39	59	38
37	70	40

Source: Based on U.S. Sentencing Commission Statistics

18. Lengths of Songs At $\alpha = 0.10$, is there a difference in the length of songs (in seconds) on three types of music?

Romantic guitar songs	Elvis songs	Polkas
200	103	142
165	192	125
188	128	104
193	140	129
215	262	120
195	147	130
179	180	
	187	

Technology Step by Step

EXCEL
Step by Step

The Kruskal-Wallis Test

Excel does not have a procedure to conduct the Kruskal-Wallis test. However, you may conduct this test by using the MegaStat Add-in available online. If you have not installed this add-in, do so, following the instructions from the Chapter 1 Excel Step by Step.

Example: Milliequivalents of Potassium in Breakfast Drinks

A researcher tests three different brands of breakfast drinks to see how many milliequivalents of potassium per quart each contains. These data are obtained.

Brand A	Brand B	Brand C
4.7	5.3	6.3
3.2	6.4	8.2
5.1	7.3	6.2
5.2	6.8	7.1
5.0	7.2	6.6

At $\alpha = 0.05$, is there enough evidence to reject the hypothesis that all brands contain the same amount of potassium?

1. Enter the data from the example into columns A, B, and C of a new worksheet.

2. From the toolbar, select Add-Ins, **MegaStat>Nonparametric Tests>Kruskal-Wallis Test.** *Note:* You may need to open MegaStat from the MegaStat.xls file on your computer's hard drive.

3. Type **A1:C6** in the box for Input range.

4. Click [OK].

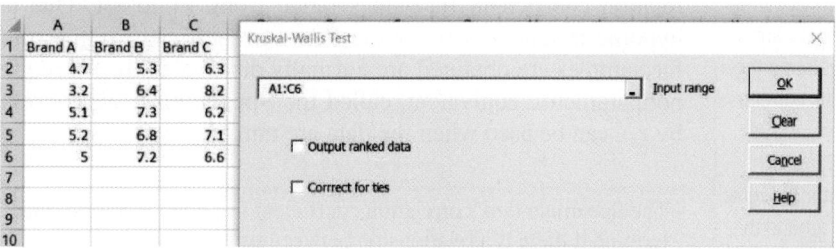

Kruskal-Wallis Test

Median	n	Avg. Rank	
5.00	5	3.00	Brand A
6.80	5	10.60	Brand B
6.60	5	10.40	Brand C
6.30	15		Total

9.380	H
2	d.f.
.0092	p-value

The *P*-value is 0.0092. Reject the null hypothesis. There is enough evidence to reject the claim that the three brands of breakfast drinks contain the same amount of potassium.

MINITAB
Step by Step

Kruskal-Wallis Test

Hidden Chemical in Beer—Example 13–6

Is the number of infections that occurred in three groups of hospitals the same?

Enter all of the glyphosate data into C1 of a MINITAB worksheet. Name the column Glyphosate.

Enter the group identifiers A, B, or C into C2. Name the column **Beer.** The data must be entered in this stacked format.

Select **Stat>Nonparametrics>Kruskal-Wallis.**

a) Double-click C1 **Glyphosate** for the response variable.

b) Double-click C2 **Beer** for the factor variable.

c) Click [OK].

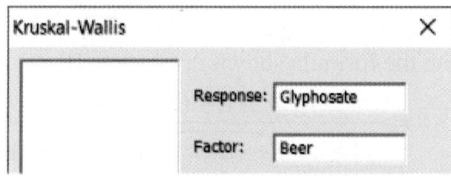

↓	C1	C2-T
	Glyphosate	Beer
3	30.1	A
4	29.2	A
5	28.3	A
6	25.4	B
7	26.2	B
8	28.2	B
9	22.7	B
10	22.9	B
11	19.6	C
12	20.2	C
13	23.1	C
14	22.9	C
15	25.4	C

Kruskal-Wallis Test: Glyphosate versus Beer

```
Kruskal-Wallis Test on Glyphosate

Beer      N    Median   Ave Rank     Z
A         5     29.20     12.8     2.94
B         5     25.40      7.0    -0.61
C         5     22.90      4.2    -2.33
Overall  15                8.0

H = 9.62  DF = 2  P = 0.008
H = 9.65  DF = 2  P = 0.008  (adjusted for ties)
```

The null hypothesis is rejected since the *P*-value of 0.0081 is less than alpha.

13–6 The Spearman Rank Correlation Coefficient and the Runs Test

The techniques of regression and correlation were explained in Chapter 10. To determine whether two variables are linearly related, you use the Pearson product moment correlation coefficient. Its values range from $+1$ to -1. One assumption for testing the hypothesis that $\rho = 0$ for the Pearson coefficient is that the populations from which the samples are obtained are normally distributed. If this requirement cannot be met, the nonparametric equivalent, called the **Spearman rank correlation coefficient** (denoted by r_s), can be used when the data are ranked.

> The Spearman rank correlation coefficient is a nonparametric statistic that uses ranks to determine if there is a relationship between two variables.

Rank Correlation Coefficient

The computations for the rank correlation coefficient are simpler than those for the Pearson coefficient and involve ranking each set of data. The difference in ranks is found, and r_s is computed by using these differences. If both sets of data have the same ranks, r_s will be $+1$. If the sets of data are ranked in exactly the opposite way, r_s will be -1. If there is no relationship between the rankings, r_s will be near 0.

The assumptions for the Spearman rank correlation coefficients are given next.

Assumptions for Spearman's Rank Correlation Coefficient

1. The sample is a random sample.
2. The data consist of two measurements or observations taken on the same individual.

In this book, the assumptions will be stated in the exercises; however, when encountering statistics in other situations, you must check to see that these assumptions have been met before proceeding.

OBJECTIVE

Compute the Spearman rank correlation coefficient.

Formula for Computing the Spearman Rank Correlation Coefficient

$$r_s = 1 - \frac{6\,\Sigma d^2}{n(n^2 - 1)}$$

where
d = difference in ranks
n = number of data pairs

The preceding formula uses ranks and is used if there are no ties in the ranks. If there are ties in the ranks, you use the formula shown in Chapter 10.

$$r = \frac{n\Sigma xy - (\Sigma x)(\Sigma y)}{\sqrt{[n(\Sigma x^2) - (\Sigma x)^2][n(\Sigma y^2) - (\Sigma y)^2]}}$$

The computational procedure is shown in Example 13–7. For a test of the significance of r_s, Table A–12 is used for values of n up to 30. For larger values, the normal distribution can be used.

This test can be left-tailed, right-tailed, or two-tailed. However, in this book, all tests will be two-tailed. The hypotheses are

$$H_0: \rho = 0$$
$$H_1: \rho \neq 0$$

where ρ is the population correlation coefficient.

Procedure Table

Finding and Testing the Value of Spearman's Rank Correlation Coefficient

Step 1 State the hypotheses.

Step 2 Find the critical values.

Step 3 Find the test statistic.

    a. Rank the values in each data set.

    b. Subtract the rankings for each pair of data values $(X_1 - X_2)$.

    c. Square the differences.

    d. Find the sum of the squares.

    e. Substitute in the formula.

$$r_s = 1 - \frac{6\Sigma d^2}{n(n^2 - 1)}$$

    where

        d = difference in ranks

        n = number of pairs of data

Step 4 Make the decision.

Step 5 Summarize the results.

EXAMPLE 13–7 School Enrollment and Debt

A researcher wishes to see if the total debt a school district has is related to the number of students enrolled in the school. Eight school districts are selected and the debt and number of students in the districts are shown. At $\alpha = 0.05$, is there a significant linear relationship between the number of students enrolled and the current debt of the school district?

District	Enrollment	Debt
A	2,107	$ 6,562
B	3,719	$ 3,500
C	3,481	$ 1,951
D	2,482	$20,000
E	2,100	$ 5,160
F	2,915	$ 5,000
G	5,744	$17,421
H	5,229	$ 2,350

Source: Tribune Review

SOLUTION

Step 1 State the hypotheses.

    $H_0: \rho = 0$ and $H_1: \rho \neq 0$

Step 2 Find the critical value. Use Table A–12 to find the value for $n = 8$ and $\alpha = 0.05$. It is ± 0.738. See Figure 13–6.

FIGURE 13–6
Finding the Critical Value in
Table A–12 for Example 13–7

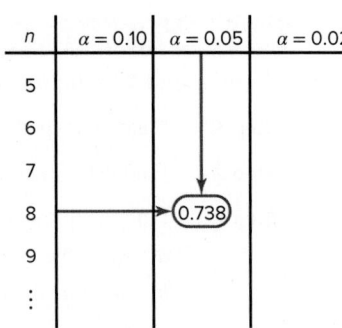

n	$\alpha = 0.10$	$\alpha = 0.05$	$\alpha = 0.02$
5			
6			
7			
8		0.738	
9			
⋮			

Step 3 Find the test statistic.

a. Rank each data set as shown in the table.

District	Enrollment	Rank	Debt	Rank
A	2,107	2	$ 6,562	6
B	3,719	6	$ 3,500	3
C	3,481	5	$ 1,951	1
D	2,482	3	$20,000	8
E	2,100	1	$ 5,160	5
F	2,915	4	$ 5,000	4
G	5,744	8	$17,421	7
H	5,229	7	$ 2,350	2

Let X_1 be the rank of the enrollments and X_2 be the rank of the debts.

b. Subtract the ranking $(X_1 - X_2)$.

$2 - 6 = -4$ $1 - 5 = -4$
$6 - 3 = 3$ $4 - 4 = 0$
$5 - 1 = 4$ $8 - 7 = 1$
$3 - 8 = -5$ $7 - 2 = 5$

c. Square the differences.

$(-4)^2 = 16$ $(-4)^2 = 16$
$3^2 = 9$ $0^2 = 0$
$4^2 = 16$ $1^1 = 1$
$(-5)^2 = 25$ $5^2 = 25$

d. Find the sum of the squares.

$$16 + 9 + 16 + 25 + 16 + 0 + 1 + 25 = 108$$

The results can be summarized in a table as shown.

X_1	X_2	$d = X_1 - X_2$	d^2
2	6	−4	16
6	3	3	9
5	1	4	16
3	8	−5	25
1	5	−4	16
4	4	0	0
8	7	1	1
7	2	5	25
			$\Sigma d^2 = 108$

e. Substitute in the formula for r_s.

$$r_s = 1 - \frac{6\Sigma d^2}{n(n^2 - 1)} \quad \text{where } n = \text{number of pairs}$$

$$r_s = 1 - \frac{6(108)}{8(8^2 - 1)} = 1 - \frac{648}{504} = -0.286$$

Step 4   Make the decision. Do not reject the null hypothesis since $-0.286 > -0.738$.
See Figure 13-7.

FIGURE 13-7
Critical Values and Test Statistic for
Example 13-7

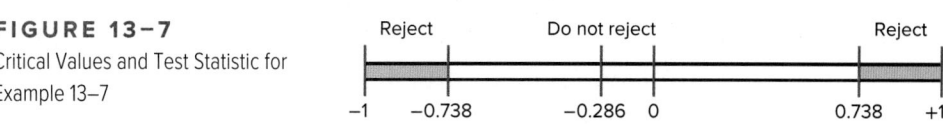

Step 5   Summarize the results. There is not enough evidence to say there is a linear
relationship between the school enrollment and the school debt.

OBJECTIVE

Test hypotheses, using
the runs test.

The Runs Test

When samples are selected, you assume that they are selected at random. How do you
know if the data obtained from a sample are truly random?

One way to answer this question is to use the *runs test*. Before you can use the runs
test, you must be able to determine the number of runs in a sequence of events.

> A **run** is a succession of identical letters preceded or followed by a different letter or
> no letter at all, such as the beginning or end of the succession.

Consider the following situations for a researcher interviewing 20 people for a survey.
Let their gender be denoted by M for male and F for female. Suppose the participants were
chosen as follows:

Situation 1   M M M M M M M M M M F F F F F F F F F F

It does not look as if the people in this sample were selected at random, since 10 males
were selected first, followed by 10 females.

Consider a different selection:

Situation 2   F M F M F M F M F M F M F M F M F M F M

In this case, it seems as if the researcher selected a female, then a male, etc. This selection
is probably not random either.

Finally, consider the following selection:

Situation 3   F F F M M F M F M M F F M M F F M M M F

This selection of data looks as if it may be random, since there is a mix of males and
females and no apparent pattern to their selection.

Let's examine each of the three situations to determine the number of runs. The first
situation presented has two runs:

Run 1   M M M M M M M M M M
Run 2   F F F F F F F F F F

The second situation has 20 runs. (Each letter constitutes one run.)
The third situation has 11 runs.

Run 1	F F F	Run 5	F	Run 9	F F
Run 2	M M	Run 6	M M	Run 10	M M M
Run 3	F	Run 7	F F	Run 11	F
Run 4	M	Run 8	M M		

The number of runs is used to determine the value of the test statistic. Here, n_1 represents
the number of items in category 1 and n_2 represents the number of items in category 2.

In the preceding situation, there were 10 males and 10 females; hence, $n_1 = 10$ and $n_2 = 10$. Also, G is used to denote the number of runs. In situation 1, $G = 2$; in situation 2, $G = 20$; and in situation 3, $G = 11$.

EXAMPLE 13–8   Number of Runs

Determine the number of runs and the values of n_1 and n_2 in each sequence.

a. MMMFFMMF

b. OOEOEEEEOO

c. TTHHTHHHTTH

SOLUTION

a. There are four runs.

MMM	FF	MM	F
1	2	3	4

There are five M's and three F's, so $n_1 = 5$ and $n_2 = 3$.

b. There are five runs.

OO	E	O	EEEE	OO
1	2	3	4	5

There are five O's and five E's, so $n_1 = 5$ and $n_2 = 5$.

c. There are six runs.

TT	HH	T	HHH	TT	H
1	2	3	4	5	6

There are five T's and six H's, so $n_1 = 5$ and $n_2 = 6$.

Rather than try to guess whether the numbers of runs occur at random, statisticians have devised a nonparametric test to determine this. As previously mentioned, it is called the runs test.

> The **runs test for randomness** is a nonparametric test that is used to determine if a sequence of data values occurs at random.

The test for randomness considers the number of runs rather than the frequency of the letters. For example, for data to be selected at random, there should not be too few or too many runs, as in situations 1 and 2. The runs test does not consider the questions of how many males or females were selected or how many of each are in a specific run.

When the data are numerical, you can use the median of the data to determine the number of runs. First find the median for the data, and then subtract the median from each value. If the data value is above the median, assign it the letter A. If the data value falls below the median, assign it the letter B. Ignore any data values that are equal to the median.

The runs test can be used provided that the following assumptions are met.

Assumptions for the Runs Test for Randomness

1. The data from the sample are arranged in the order in which they were selected.
2. Each letter, number, or event can be classified into one or two mutually exclusive categories.

In this book, the assumptions will be stated in the exercises; however, when encountering statistics in other situations, you must check to see that these assumptions have been met before proceeding.

Formulas for the Test Statistic Value for the Runs Test

When $n_1 \leq 20$ and $n_2 \leq 20$, use the number of runs denoted by G, as the test statistic value. When $n_1 > 20$ or $n_2 > 20$—or when $n_1 > 20$ *and* $n_2 \geq 20$—use

$$z = \frac{G - \mu_G}{\sigma_G}$$

where

$$\mu_G = \frac{2n_1 n_2}{n_1 + n_2} + 1$$

$$\sigma_G = \sqrt{\frac{2n_1 n_2 (2n_1 n_2 - n_1 - n_2)}{(n_1 + n_2)^2 (n_1 + n_2 - 1)}}$$

Procedure Table

The Runs Test

Step 1 State the hypotheses and identify the claim.

Step 2 Find the critical values.

  a. Use Table A–13 when $n_1 \leq 20$ and $n_2 \leq 20$.

  b. Use Table A–4 when $n_1 > 20$ or $n_2 > 20$ or when $n_1 > 20$ *and* $n_2 > 20$.

Step 3 Find the test statistic.

  a. Use the number of runs if $n_1 \leq 20$ and $n_2 \leq 20$.

  b. Use the formula when $n_1 > 20$ or $n_2 > 20$ or when $n_1 > 20$ *and* $n_2 > 20$.

$$z = \frac{G - \mu_G}{\sigma_G}$$

Step 4 Make the decision.

Step 5 Summarize the results.

To determine whether the number of runs is within the random range, use Table A–13 in Appendix A when $n_1 \leq 20$ and $n_2 \leq 20$. The values are for a two-tailed test with $\alpha = 0.05$. For a sample of 12 males and 8 females, the table values shown in Figure 13–8 mean that any number of runs from 7 to 15 would be considered random. If the number of runs is 6 or less or is 16 or more, then the sample is probably not random and the null hypothesis should be rejected. Hence, the critical values are 6 and 16.

FIGURE 13–8

Finding the Critical Value in Table A–13

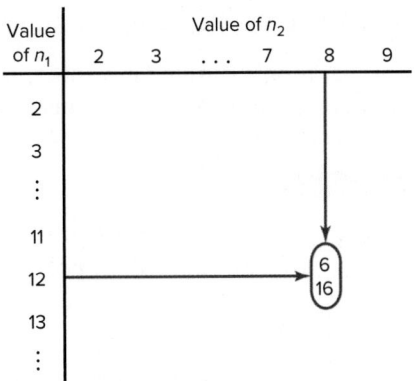

Example 13–9 shows the procedure for conducting the runs test by using letters as data. Example 13–10 shows how the runs test can be used for numerical data. Example 13–11 shows how to use the runs test when $n_1 > 20$ and $n_2 > 20$.

EXAMPLE 13–9   Gender of Train Passengers

On a commuter train, the conductor wishes to see whether the passengers enter the train at random. He observes the first 25 people, with the following sequence of males (M) and females (F).

F F F M M F F F F M F M M M M F F F F M M F F F M M

Test for randomness at $\alpha = 0.05$.

SOLUTION

Step 1   State the hypotheses and identify the claim.

H_0: The passengers board the train at random, according to gender (claim).

H_1: The passengers do not board the train at random, according to gender.

Step 2   Determine the critical value. There are 10 M's and 15 F's, so $n_1 = 10$ and $n_2 = 15$. Using Table A–13 and $\alpha = 0.05$, the critical value is $\frac{7}{18}$ which means reject H_0 if the number of runs (G) is $G \leq 7$ or $G \geq 18$. The critical values are 7 and 18.

Step 3   Find the test statistic. Determine the number of runs. Arrange the letters according to runs of males and females, as shown.

Run	Gender
1	F F F
2	M M
3	F F F F
4	M
5	F
6	M M M
7	F F F F
8	M M
9	F F F
10	M M

There are 10 runs.

Step 4   Make the decision. Compare these critical values with the number of runs. Since the number of runs is 10 and 10 is not less than or equal to 7 or greater than or equal to 18; hence, do not reject the null hypothesis.

Step 5   Summarize the results. There is not enough evidence to reject the hypothesis that the passengers board the train at random according to gender.

EXAMPLE 13–10   Ages of Substance Abuse Program Participants

Twenty people enrolled in a substance abuse program. Test the claim that the ages of the people, according to the order in which they enroll, occur at random, at $\alpha = 0.05$. The data are 18, 36, 19, 22, 25, 44, 23, 27, 27, 35, 19, 43, 37, 32, 28, 43, 46, 19, 20, 22.

SOLUTION

Step 1   State the hypotheses and identify the claim.

H_0: The ages of the people, according to the order in which they enroll in a substance abuse program, occur at random (claim).

H_1: The ages of the people, according to the order in which they enroll in a substance abuse program, do not occur at random.

Step 2   Find the critical value.

Find the median of the data. Arrange the data in ascending order.

18 19 19 19 20 22 22 23 25 27 27

28 32 35 36 37 43 43 44 46

The median is 27.

Replace each number in the original sequence as written in the example with an A if it is above the median and with a B if it is below the median. Eliminate any numbers that are equal to the median.

Recall the original sequence is 18, 36, 19, 22, . . . , 22. Then

18 is below the median, so it is B;

36 is above the median, so it is A;

19 is below the median, so it is B;

etc.

The sequence of letters, then, is

B A B B B A B A B A A A A A A B B B

There are 9 A's and 9 B's. Table A–13 shows that with $n_1 = 9$, $n_2 = 9$, and $\alpha = 0.05$, the number of runs should be 5 or less or 15 or greater to reject H_0.

Step 3   Find the test statistic. Determine the number of runs from the sequence of letters.

Run	Letters
1	B
2	A
3	B B B
4	A
5	B
6	A
7	B
8	A A A A A A
9	B B B

The number of runs $G = 9$.

Step 4   Make the decision. Since there are 9 runs and 9 falls between the critical values 5 and 15, the null hypothesis is not rejected.

Step 5   Summarize the results. There is not enough evidence to reject the hypothesis that the ages of the people who enroll occur at random.

EXAMPLE 13–11   NBA Most Valuable Players

The data show the Conference (E = Eastern, W = Western) where the most valuable players came from for a 45-year time frame. At $\alpha = 0.05$, can it be concluded that the sequence of winners is random?

W W W W E E E E E W W W W W E W W W W E W E W W W E E W W E W E W E E E E W E W W W W W E E E E

n_1 (Eastern) = 20 n_2 (Western) = 25

SOLUTION

Step 1   State the hypotheses and identify the claim.

H_0: The winners occur at random (claim).

H_1: The winners do not occur at random.

Step 2   Determine the actual values.

Since $n_1 > 20$ and $n_2 > 20$, Table A–4 is used. At $\alpha = 0.05$, the critical values are ± 1.96.

Step 3   Find the test statistic.

The number of runs is

1. W W W W
2. E E E E
3. W W W W W
4. E
5. W W W
6. E
7. W
8. E
9. W W W
10. E E

11. W W
12. E
13. W
14. E E E E
15. W
16. E
17. W W W W W
18. E E E E

There are $G = 18$ runs.

$$\mu_G = \frac{2n_1n_2}{n_1 + n_2} + 1$$

$$= \frac{2(20)(25)}{20 + 25} + 1 = 23.2$$

$$\sigma_G = \sqrt{\frac{2n_1n_2(2n_1n_2 - n_1 - n_2)}{(n_1 + n_2)^2(n_1 + n_2 - 1)}}$$

$$= \sqrt{\frac{2(20)(25)[2(20)(25) - 20 - 25]}{(21 + 24)^2(21 + 24 - 1)}} = \sqrt{\frac{955000}{89100}} = \sqrt{10.718}$$

$$= 3.27$$

$$z = \frac{G - \mu_G}{\sigma_G}$$

$$= \frac{18 - 23.2}{3.27} = -1.59$$

Step 4   Make the decision. Since $-1.96 < -1.59$, the decision is do not reject the null hypothesis. See Figure 13–9.

FIGURE 13–9

Critical Values and Test Statistic for Example 13–11

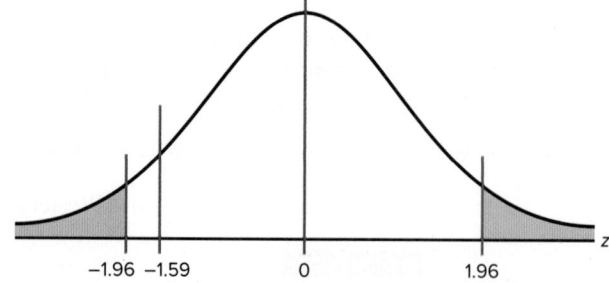

Step 5   Summarize the results. There is not enough evidence to reject the claim that the sequence of winners occurs at random.

≡ Applying the Concepts 13–6

Tall Trees

As a biologist, you wish to see if there is a relationship between the heights of tall trees and their diameters. You find the following data for the diameter (in inches) of the tree at 4.5 feet from the ground and the corresponding heights (in feet).

Diameter (in.)	Height (ft)
1024	261
950	321
451	219
505	281
761	159
644	83
707	191
586	141
442	232
546	108

Source: The World Almanac and Book of Facts.

1. What question are you trying to answer?

2. What type of nonparametric analysis could be used to answer the question?

3. What would be the corresponding parametric test that could be used?

4. Which test do you think would be better?

5. Perform both tests and write a short statement comparing the results.

See page 752 for the answer.

≡ Exercises 13–6

For Exercises 1 through 4, find the critical value from Table A–12 for the rank correlation coefficient, given sample size n and α. Assume that the test is two-tailed.

1. $n = 28$, $\alpha = 0.05$

2. $n = 16$, $\alpha = 0.01$

3. $n = 8$, $\alpha = 0.02$

4. $n = 21$, $\alpha = 0.05$

For Exercises 5 through 14, perform these steps.

   a. Find the Spearman rank correlation coefficient.

   b. State the hypotheses.

   c. Find the critical value. Use $\alpha = 0.05$.

   d. Make the decision.

   e. Summarize the results.

Use the traditional method of hypothesis testing unless otherwise specified.

5. Mathematics Achievement Test Scores The National Assessment of Educational Progress (U.S. Department of Education) tests mathematics, reading, and science achievement in grades 4 and 8. A random sample of states is selected, and their mathematics achievement scores are noted for fourth- and eighth-graders. At $\alpha = 0.05$, can a linear relationship be concluded between the data?

Grade 4	90	84	80	87	88	77	79
Grade 8	81	75	66	76	80	59	74

Source: World Almanac.

6. Subway and Commuter Rail Passengers Six cities are randomly selected, and the number of daily passenger trips (in thousands) for subways and commuter rail service is obtained. At $\alpha = 0.05$, is there a relationship between the variables? Suggest one reason why the transportation authority might use the results of this study.

City	1	2	3	4	5	6
Subway	845	494	425	313	108	41
Rail	39	291	142	103	33	38

Source: American Public Transportation Association.

7. NFL Coaching Victories A random selection of years an NFL coach worked and the number of victories the coaches had are shown. Is there a linear relationship between the two at $\alpha = 0.10$?

Years	17	20	19	21	23	33	22
Victories	161	170	172	200	193	226	237

Source: The World Almanac and Book of Facts

8. Hospitals and Nursing Homes Find the Spearman rank correlation coefficient for the following data, which represent the number of hospitals and nursing homes in each of seven randomly selected states. At the 0.05 level of significance, is there enough evidence to conclude that there is a correlation between the two?

Hospitals	107	61	202	133	145	117	108
Nursing homes	230	134	704	376	431	538	373

Source: World Almanac.

9. Calories and Cholesterol in Fast-Food Sandwiches Use the Spearman rank correlation coefficient to see if there is a linear relationship between these two sets of data, representing the number of calories and the amount of cholesterol in randomly selected fast-food sandwiches. Use $\alpha = 0.05$.

Calories	580	580	270	470	420	415	330	430
Cholesterol (mg)	205	225	285	270	185	215	185	220

Source: www.fatcalories.com

10. Tall Buildings in Denver The data show the heights (in feet) of eight tall buildings in Denver, Colorado, and the number of stories in each building. At $\alpha = 0.05$, is there a significant linear relationship between the data?

Height	714	709	698	639	617	544	522	507
Stories	56	52	50	45	40	43	42	40

11. Age and Blood Pressure It is generally agreed that a person's blood pressure increases with a person's age. Persons' ages and their systolic blood pressure are shown. At $\alpha = 0.05$, is there a significant linear relationship between the two measures?

Age	18	48	64	24	56	33	28
Pressure	118	142	138	123	133	129	120

12. Snowfall and Ski Patrons A ski lodge wishes to see if there is a relationship between the number of inches it snows and the number of patrons that use the ski slopes. The data are shown. At $\alpha = 0.05$, is there a significant linear relationship between the data?

Amt. of snow	1.6	2.2	2.8	3.6	4.2	3.3	5.1
No. of patrons	328	316	432	440	395	406	451

13. Online School Enrollments Shown are the numbers of students enrolled in online school for five randomly selected school districts and the per-pupil costs for the online school education. At $\alpha = 0.10$, is there a relationship between the two variables? How might this information be useful to school administrators?

Number of students	10	6	17	8	11
Per-pupil cost	7200	9393	7385	4500	8203

Source: Pittsburgh Tribune-Review.

14. Drug Prices Shown are the price for a human dose of several randomly selected prescription drugs and the price for an equivalent dose for animals. At $\alpha = 0.10$, is there a relationship between the variables?

Humans	0.67	0.64	1.20	0.51	0.87	0.74	0.50	1.22
Animals	0.13	0.18	0.42	0.25	0.57	0.58	0.49	1.28

Source: House Committee on Government Reform.

15. Determine the number of runs in each sequence:

   a. H T T T H H T H H T T H

   b. 21, 31, 15, 18, 19, 16, 15, 14, 27, 17

   c. F F F M M F F F F M M M M F F

   d. O E E E E E O O O E E E

   e. 86, 93, 101, 106, 88, 97, 100, 89, 92, 105

16. Using Table A–13, determine when the null hypothesis would be rejected. Use two-tailed hypotheses with $\alpha = 0.05$.

   a. $n_1 = 7, n_2 = 9$

   b. $n_1 = 11, n_2 = 8$

   c. $n_1 = 4, n_2 = 15$

   d. $n_1 = 17, n_2 = 6$

   e. $n_1 = 19, n_2 = 19$

For Exercises 17 through 28, use the Runs test and perform these steps.

   a. State the hypotheses and identify the claim.

   b. Find the critical values.

   c. Compute the test statistic.

   d. Make the decision.

   e. Summarize the results.

17. Amusement Park Admission Price A popular amusement park charges a daily admission price that includes all rides. At the end of summer they sponsor a series of nightly parades featuring high school bands from the tristate area. A spectator admission, substantially less than the standard one, is available for people who just want to eat and watch the parade, but not ride. Denoting full admission by F and spectator admission by S, the following 40 admissions were sold on a given day. At $\alpha = 0.05$, test for randomness.

S S F S F S F F S F S S F F F S F F S S
S F F F F S F F F S F S S F S S F F S S

18. **Random Numbers** Random? A calculator generated these integers randomly. Apply the runs test to see if you can reject the hypothesis that the numbers are truly random. Use $\alpha = 0.05$.

1	1	1	1	1	1	2	1	1	1	1
2	2	1	2	1	2	2	1	2	1	1
2	1	1								

19. **Stock Market** A stockbroker observes whether the market goes up (U) or down (D) over a 20-day period. The sequence is shown. At $\alpha = 0.05$, test for randomness.

U U U U D D U U U D U U U U U D D D U D

20. **Ground Hog's Shadow** In Pennsylvania, February 2 is called Ground Hog Day. In the town of Punxsutawney at Gobler's Knob, a ground hog named "Punxsutawney Phil" is taken from his borrow, and if he sees his shadow, there will be six more weeks of winter. If he does not see his shadow, spring will come early. (We will not discuss the believability of this claim here.) The question, though, is this: Is seeing his shadow a random happening? The data are shown for 20 years. S = Sees shadow; N = does not see shadow. Test the claim at $\alpha = 0.05$ that seeing his shadow occurs at random.

S N S S N S N S S S N S S S S S S S N S

21. **Nightmares** A psychologist wishes to see if a patient's nightmares occur at random. The psychologist asks the patient to keep a record for 25 days using Y if the patient has a nightmare or N if the patient does not have a nightmare on that night. The data are shown. At $\alpha = 0.05$, can it be concluded that the nightmares occur at random?

N N N N Y Y N N N N N Y N Y Y Y N N Y N Y N N N N Y

22. **Skiing Conditions** A ski lodge manager observes the weather for 27 days. If his customers are able to ski, he records S; if weather conditions do not permit skiing, he records N. Test for randomness, at $\alpha = 0.05$.

S S S S S N N N N N N N
N S S S N N S S S S S S S

23. **On-Demand Movie Rentals** Listed are the numbers of on-demand movies rented per month for 20 customers of a particular cable service. Test the data for randomness at the 0.05 level of significance. What would have

to occur to effect the opposite result? Discuss how the data would have to change.

0	2	14	20	13	6	1	20	4	8
2	5	17	7	12	12	1	0	0	14

24. **Tossing a Coin** Toss a coin 30 times and record the outcomes (H or T). Test the results for randomness at $\alpha = 0.05$. Repeat the experiment a few times and compare your results. Answers will vary.

25. **Sock Sales** An online store that sells socks wishes to see if the number of pairs of socks that they sell per day occurs at random. The number of pairs sold for 30 days are shown. Use $\alpha = 0.05$ to test the claim that the sales occur at random.

50	42	36	62	77	89	43	55	56	32
67	64	51	48	45	49	51	44	56	54
52	47	56	59	54	60	63	68	61	67

26. **Speeding Tickets** A police chief records the gender of the drivers who receive speeding tickets. Test the claim at $\alpha = 0.05$ that the gender of the ticketed drivers is random.

M	M	M	F	F	M	F	M	F	M
M	F	M	M	M	F	M	M	F	F
F	M	M	F	M	M	F	M	M	M
M	M	F	M	F	F	F	M	M	M
F	F	M	F	F	F	M	M	M	M

27. **Accidents or Illnesses** The people who went to the emergency room at a local hospital were treated for an accident (A) or illness (I). Test the claim $\alpha = 0.10$ that the reason given occurred at random.

I	A	I	A	A	A	A	A	A	I
A	I	I	A	A	I	I	A	A	A
A	I	A	I	A	A	A	I	I	A
A	I	I	A	A	I	A	I	A	I
A	I	A	A	I	I	A	A	A	I
I	A	I	A	A	I	I	A	A	A

28. **True or False Exam** An instructor wishes to see if the answers to a true/false final exam are random. The answers are shown. Test the claim at $\alpha = 0.05$.

F F T T T F F F T F T T F F F
F T T F F T T F F F T F T T T

Extending the Concepts

When $n \geq 30$, the formula $r = \dfrac{\pm z}{\sqrt{n-1}}$ can be used to find the critical values for the rank correlation coefficient. For example, if $n = 40$ and $\alpha = 0.05$ for a two-tailed test,

$$r = \frac{\pm 1.96}{\sqrt{40-1}} = \pm 0.314$$

Hence, any r_s greater than or equal to $+0.314$ or less than or equal to -0.314 is significant.

For Exercises 29 through 33, find the critical r value for each (assume that the test is two-tailed).

29. $n = 35, \alpha = 0.10$

30. $n = 44, \alpha = 0.05$

31. $n = 55, \alpha = 0.02$

32. $n = 39, \alpha = 0.05$

33. $n = 49, \alpha = 0.01$

≜Technology | **Step by Step**

EXCEL
Step by Step

Spearman Rank Correlation Coefficient

Example: Textbook Ratings

Two students were asked to rate eight different textbooks for a specific course on an ascending scale from 0 to 20 points. Points were assigned for each of several categories, such as reading level, use of illustrations, and use of color. At $\alpha = 0.05$, test the hypothesis that there is a significant linear correlation between the two students' ratings. The data are shown in the following table.

Textbook	Student 1's rating	Student 2's rating
A	4	4
B	10	6
C	18	20
D	20	14
E	12	16
F	2	8
G	5	11
H	9	7

Excel does not have a procedure to compute the Spearman rank correlation coefficient. However, you may compute this statistic by using the MegaStat Add-in available online. If you have not installed this add-in, do so, following the instructions from the Chapter 1 Excel Step by Step.

1. Enter the rating scores from the example into columns A and B of a new worksheet.
2. From the toolbar, select Add-Ins, **MegaStat>Nonparametric Tests>Spearman Coefficient of Rank Correlation**. *Note:* You may need to open MegaStat from the MegaStat.xls file on your computer's hard drive.
3. Type **A1:B9** in the box for Input range.
4. Click [OK].

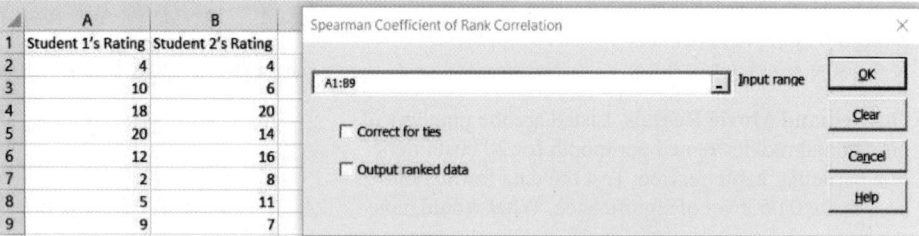

Spearman Coefficient of Rank Correlation

	Student 1's Rating	Student 2's Rating
Student 1's Rating	1.000	
Student 2's Rating	.643	1.000

8 sample size

± .707 critical value of r .05 (two-tail)
± .834 critical value of r .01 (two-tail)

Since the correlation coefficient 0.643 is less than the critical value, there is not enough evidence to reject the null hypothesis of a nonzero correlation between the variables.

MINITAB

Step by Step

Spearman Rank Correlation

Example 13–7 School Enrollment and Debt

Is there a correlation between the total debt a school district has and the number of students enrolled in the school? Use the calculator to determine the ranks; then use Pearson's correlation to calculate r_s.

1. Enter the data into C1 and C2 of a new MINITAB worksheet.

2. Name the columns Enrollment and Debt.

3. Calculate the ranks and store them.

   a) Select **Data>Rank**.

   b) Choose Enrollment for **Rank data in:** and then name the column RankEnrollment.

   c) Repeat the rank process for Deposits. Choose Debt for **Rank data in.** Name this column RankDebt.

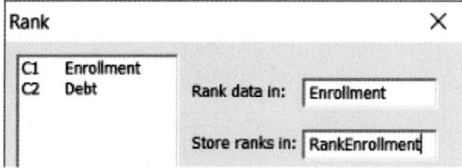

The worksheet is shown. The Pearson correlation on these ranks will produce Spearman's rank correlation.

4. **Stat>Basic Statistics>Correlation.**

   a) Select the two columns of Ranks, C3 and C4.

   b) Deselect the *P*-value as this will not be correct for Spearman's test.

   c) Click [OK].

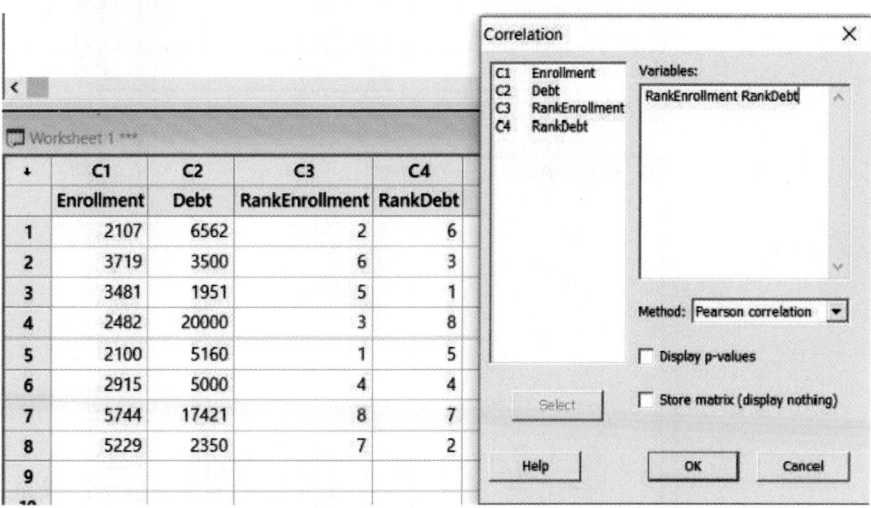

The results are displayed in the session window. Compare the correlation coefficient to the critical value.

Correlation: RankEnrollment, RankDebt

```
Pearson correlation of RankEnrollment and RankDebt = -0.286
```

Do not reject the null hypothesis since $r_s = -0.286$ is less than the critical value of -0.738.

Runs Test for Randomness

1. Sequence is important! Enter the data down C1 in the same order they were collected. Do not sort them! Use the data from Example 13–10.

2. Calculate the median and store it as a constant.

   a) Select **Calc>Column Statistics**.

   b) Check the option for Median.

c) Use C1 Age for the Input Variable.

d) Type the name of the constant MedianAge in the Store result in text box.

e) Click [OK].

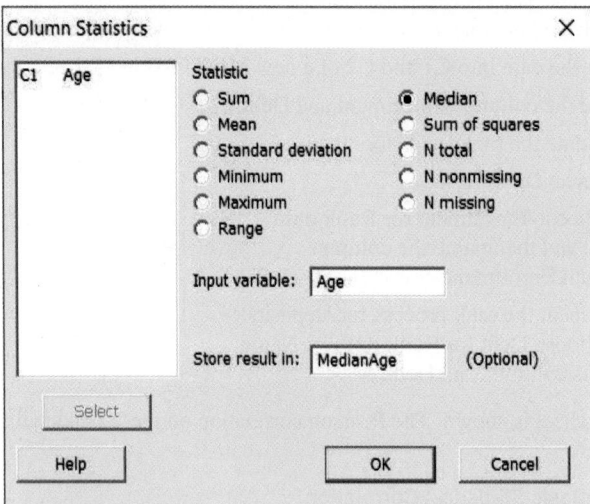

3. Select **Stat>Nonparametrics>Runs Test**.

4. Select C1 Age as the variable.

5. Click the button for Above and below, then select MedianAge in the text box.

6. Click [OK]. The results will be displayed in the session window.

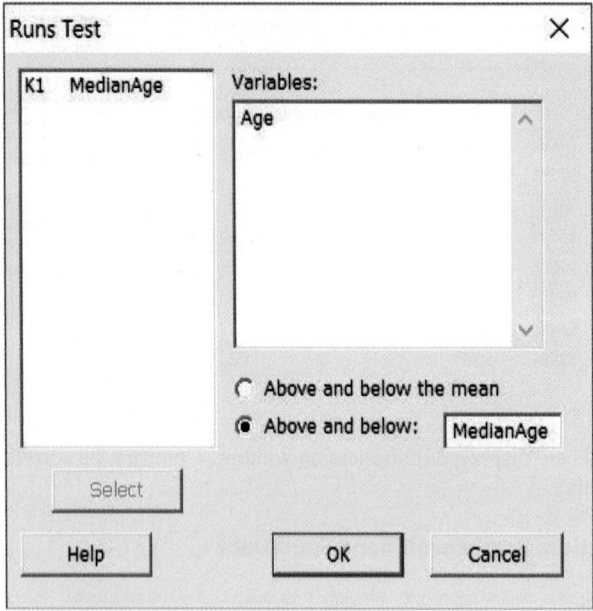

Runs Test: Age
Runs test for Age

Runs above and below K = 27

The observed number of runs = 9
The expected number of runs = 10.9
9 observations above K, 11 below
* N is small, so the following approximation may be invalid.
P-value = 0.378

The *P*-value is 0.378. Do not reject the null hypothesis.

Summary

- In many research situations, the assumptions (particularly the assumption of normality) for the use of parametric statistics cannot be met. Also, some statistical studies do not involve parameters such as means, variances, and proportions. For both situations, statisticians have developed nonparametric statistical methods, also called *distribution-free methods*. (13–1)

- There are several advantages to the use of nonparametric methods. The most important one is that no knowledge of the population distributions is required.

Other advantages include ease of computation and understanding. The major disadvantage is that they are less efficient than their parametric counterparts when the assumptions for the parametric methods are met. In other words, larger sample sizes are needed to get results as accurate as those given by their parametric counterparts. (13–1)

- This list gives the nonparametric statistical tests presented in this chapter, along with their parametric counterparts.

Nonparametric test	Parametric test	Condition
Single-sample sign test (13–2)	z or t test	One sample
Paired-sample sign test (13–2)	z or t test	Two dependent samples
Wilcoxon rank sum test (13–3)	z or t test	Two independent samples
Wilcoxon signed-rank test (13–4)	t test	Two dependent samples
Kruskal-Wallis test (13–5)	ANOVA	Three or more independent samples
Spearman rank correlation coefficient (13–6)	Pearson's correlation coefficient	Relationships between variables
Runs test (13–6)	None	Randomness

- When the assumptions of the parametric tests can be met, the parametric tests should be used instead of their nonparametric counterparts.

Important Terms

distribution-free statistics 698

Kruskal-Wallis test 722

nonparametric statistics 698

paired-sample sign test 704

parametric tests 698

ranking 699

run 733

runs test for randomness 734

sign test 701

Spearman rank correlation coefficient 730

Wilcoxon rank sum test 710

Wilcoxon signed-rank test 710

Important Formulas

Formula for the z test statistic in the sign test:

$$z = \frac{(X + 0.5) - 0.5n}{\sqrt{n}/2}$$

where

n = sample size (greater than or equal to 26)

X = smaller number of positive or negative signs

Formula for the Wilcoxon rank sum test:

$$z = \frac{R - \mu_R}{\sigma_R}$$

where

$$\mu_R = \frac{n_1(n_1 + n_2 + 1)}{2}$$

$$\sigma_R = \sqrt{\frac{n_1 n_2(n_1 + n_2 + 1)}{12}}$$

R = sum of ranks for smaller sample size (n_1)

n_1 = smaller of sample sizes

n_2 = larger of sample sizes

$n_1 \geq 10$ and $n_2 \geq 10$

Formula for the Wilcoxon signed-rank test:

$$z = \frac{w_s - \frac{n(n+1)}{4}}{\sqrt{\frac{n(n+1)(2n+1)}{24}}}$$

where

n = number of pairs where difference is not 0 and
  $n \geq 30$

w_s = smaller sum in absolute value of signed ranks

Formula for the Kruskal-Wallis test:

$$H = \frac{12}{N(N+1)}\left(\frac{R_1^2}{n_1} + \frac{R_2^2}{n_2} + \cdots + \frac{R_k^2}{n_k}\right) - 3(N+1)$$

where

R_1 = sum of ranks of sample 1
n_1 = size of sample 1
R_2 = sum of ranks of sample 2
n_2 = size of sample 2
  .
  .
  .
R_k = sum of ranks of sample k
n_k = size of sample k

$N = n_1 + n_2 + \cdots + n_k$
k = number of samples

Formula for the Spearman rank correlation coefficient:

$$r_s = 1 - \frac{6\Sigma d^2}{n(n^2-1)}$$

where

d = difference in ranks
n = number of data pairs

Formulas for the test statistic value for the runs test:

When $n_1 \leq 20$ and $n_2 \leq 20$, use the number of runs, denoted by G, as the test statistic value.

When $n_1 > 20$ or $n_2 > 20$ or when $n_1 > 20$ *and* $n_2 > 20$, use

$$z = \frac{G - \mu_G}{\sigma_G}$$

where

$$\mu_G = \frac{2n_1 n_2}{n_1 + n_2} + 1$$

$$\sigma_G = \sqrt{\frac{2n_1 n_2(2n_1 n_2 - n_1 - n_2)}{(n_1 + n_2)^2(n_1 + n_2 - 1)}}$$

Review Exercises

For Exercises 1 through 13, follow this procedure:
  a. State the hypotheses and identify the claim.
  b. Find the critical value(s).
  c. Compute the test statistic.
  d. Make the decision.
  e. Summarize the results.

Use the traditional method of hypothesis testing unless otherwise specified.

Section 13–2

1. **Price of Pizza** A marketing student hypothesized that the median price for a 12-inch pepperoni pizza is $9.00. A random selection of 30 restaurants within a 30-mile radius indicated the following prices for a 12-inch pepperoni pizza. Test the claim that the median price is not over 9.00 at $\alpha = 0.05$.

10.00	6.99	12.00	10.99	11.99	9.50	9.85	10.00	12.00	12.00
8.75	12.00	11.99	6.99	9.99	10.50	10.00	9.50	9.99	8.99
12.00	9.95	8.99	9.50	7.99	8.99	10.95	7.99	8.75	10.00

2. **Rechargeable Batteries** A manufacturer suggests that the median time a rechargeable battery on an electric grass trimmer will last is 420 minutes. A random sample of 30 newly charged batteries shows that 11 lasted longer than 420 minutes. Is there enough evidence to reject the claim at $\alpha = 0.02$?

3. **Grocery Store Repricing** A grocery store chain has decided to help customers save money by instituting "temporary repricing" to help cut costs. Nine randomly selected products from the sale flyer are featured below with their regular price and their "temporary" new price. Using the paired-sample sign test and $\alpha = 0.05$, is there evidence of a difference in price? Comment on your results.

Old	2.59	0.69	1.29	3.10	1.89	2.05	1.58	2.75	1.99
New	2.09	0.70	1.18	2.95	1.59	1.75	1.32	2.19	1.99

Section 13–3

4. **Record High Temperatures** Shown here are the record high temperatures (in degrees Fahrenheit) for Dawson Creek in British Columbia, Canada, and for

Whitehorse in Yukon, Canada, for a randomly selected 12-month period. Using the Wilcoxon rank sum test at $\alpha = 0.05$, do you find a difference in the record high temperatures? Use the P-value method.

Dawson Creek	52	60	57	71	86	89	94	93	88	80	66	52
White-horse	47	50	51	69	86	89	91	86	80	66	51	47

Source: The USA TODAY Weather Almanac.

5. **Hours Worked by Student Employees** Student employees are a major part of most college campus employment venues. Two major randomly selected departments that participate in student hiring are listed with the number of hours worked by students for a month. At the 0.10 level of significance, is there sufficient evidence to conclude a difference? Is the conclusion the same for the 0.05 level of significance?

Athletics	20	24	17	12	18	22	25	30	15	19
Library	35	28	24	20	25	18	22	26	31	21	19

Section 13–4

6. **Fuel Efficiency of Automobiles** Twelve randomly selected automobiles were tested to see how many miles per gallon each one obtained. Under similar driving conditions, they were tested again, using a special additive. The data are shown. At $\alpha = 0.05$, did the additive improve gas mileage? Use the Wilcoxon signed-rank test.

Before		After	
13.6	18.3	22.6	23.7
18.2	19.5	21.9	20.8
16.1	18.2	25.3	25.3
15.3	16.7	28.6	27.2
19.2	21.3	15.2	17.2
18.8	17.2	16.3	18.5

7. **Lunch Costs** Randomly selected full-time employees in a large city were asked how much they spent on a typical weekday lunch and how much they spent on the weekend. The amounts are listed. At $\alpha = 0.05$, is there sufficient evidence to conclude a difference in the amounts spent?

Weekday	7.00	5.50	4.50	10.00	6.75	5.00	6.00
Weekend	6.00	10.00	7.00	12.00	8.50	7.00	8.00

Section 13–5

8. **Breaking Strength of Cable** A random sample of cable from three different manufacturers is tested for breaking strength. The data (in pounds) are shown. At $\alpha = 0.05$ is there a difference in the breaking strength of the cables? Use the Kruskal-Wallis test.

Manufacturer A	Manufacturer B	Manufacturer C
602	416	372
587	404	431
433	483	552
551	504	508
552	516	416

9. **Beach Temperatures for July** The National Oceanographic Data Center provides useful data for vacation planning. Below are listed beach temperatures in the month of July for various randomly selected U.S. coastal areas. Using the 0.05 level of significance, can it be concluded that there is a difference in temperatures? Omit the Southern Pacific temperatures and repeat the procedure. Is the conclusion the same?

Southern Pacific	Western Gulf	Eastern Gulf	Southern Atlantic
67	86	87	76
68	86	87	81
66	84	86	82
69	85	86	84
63	79	85	80
62	85	84	86
		85	87

Source: www.nodc.noaa.gov

Section 13–6

10. **Homework Exercises and Exam Scores** A statistics instructor wishes to see whether there is a relationship between the number of homework exercises a student completes and the exam score. The randomly selected data are shown. Using the Spearman rank correlation coefficient, test the hypothesis that there is no relationship at $\alpha = 0.05$.

Homework problems	63	55	58	87	89	52	46	75	105
Exam score	85	71	75	98	93	63	72	89	100

11. **Manuscript Pages and References** A professor examined a random selection of mathematics research papers to see if there was a relationship between the number of pages in the paper and the number of resources cited in the bibliography. Using the Spearman rank coefficient of correlation, test for a relationship at $\alpha = 0.05$.

Pages	15	25	23	30	18	28	35
Sources	10	18	18	15	13	23	20

12. **NBA Scoring Leaders** The scoring leaders for the last 28 years of the NBA are shown below, where E is the Eastern Conference and W is the Western Conference. Test for randomness at $\alpha = 0.05$.

```
W  E  W  W  W  E  E  W  W  E  E  E  E
W  E  E  E  E  E  E  W  E  E  E  E  E
```

Source: The World Almanac and Book of Facts.

13. Exam Scores An instructor wishes to see whether grades of students who finish an exam occur at random. Shown here are the grades of 30 students in the order that they finished an exam. (Read from left to right across each row, and then proceed to the next row.) Test for randomness, at $\alpha = 0.05$.

87	93	82	77	64	98
100	93	88	65	72	73
56	63	85	92	95	91
88	63	72	79	55	53
65	68	54	71	73	72

14. Fiction or Nonfiction Books A bookstore owner records the 48 books purchased by customers. He classifies them as either fiction (F) or nonfiction (N). (Read from left to right across each row, and then proceed to the next row.) At $\alpha = 0.10$, does the typical book purchased occur at random?

F	F	F	F	F	F	N	N
F	N	N	N	N	F	F	F
F	F	F	F	N	N	N	F
N	N	N	N	N	F	F	F
N	N	N	F	F	F	F	F
F	F	F	F	N	N	F	F

═ STATISTICS TODAY

Too Much or Too Little? —Revisited

In this case, the manufacturer would select a sequence of bottles and see how many bottles contained more than 40 ounces, denoted by plus, and how many bottles contained less than 40 ounces, denoted by minus. The sequence could then be analyzed according to the number of runs, as explained in Section 13–6. If the sequence were not random, then the machine would need to be checked to see if it was malfunctioning. Another method that can be used to see if machines are functioning properly is *statistical quality control*. This method is beyond the scope of this book.

═ Data Analysis

The Data Bank is found in Appendix B.

1. From the Data Bank, choose a sample and use the sign test to test one of the following hypotheses.

   a. For serum cholesterol, test H_0: median = 220 milligram percent (mg%).

   b. For systolic pressure, test H_0: median = 120 millimeters of mercury (mm Hg).

   c. For IQ, test H_0: median = 100.

   d. For sodium level, test H_0: median = 140 mEq/l.

2. From the Data Bank, select a sample of subjects. Use the Kruskal-Wallis test to see if the sodium levels of smokers and nonsmokers are equal.

3. From the Data Bank select a sample of 50 subjects. Use the Wilcoxon rank sum test to see if the means of the sodium levels of the males differ from those of the females.

═ Chapter Quiz

Determine whether each statement is true or false. If the statement is false, explain why.

1. Nonparametric statistics cannot be used to test the difference between two means. False

2. Nonparametric statistics are more sensitive than their parametric counterparts. False

3. Nonparametric statistics can be used to test hypotheses about parameters other than means, proportions, and standard deviations. True

4. Parametric tests are preferred over their nonparametric counterparts, if the assumptions can be met. True

Select the best answer.

5. The _____ test is used to test means when samples are dependent and the normality assumption cannot be met.

   ⓐ Wilcoxon signed-rank   c. Sign

   b. Wilcoxon rank sum   d. Kruskal-Wallis

6. The Kruskal-Wallis test uses the _____ distribution.

   a. z

   b. t

   c. Chi-square ⟵ *(circled)*

   d. F

7. The nonparametric counterpart of ANOVA is the _____.

   a. Wilcoxon signed-rank test

   b. Sign test

   c. Runs test

   d. None of the above ⟵ *(circled)*

8. To see if two rankings are related, you can use the _____.

   a. Runs test

   b. Spearman correlation coefficient ⟵ *(circled)*

   c. Sign test

   d. Kruskal-Wallis test

Complete the following statements with the best answer.

9. When the assumption of normality cannot be met, you can use _____ tests. Nonparametric, distribution-free

10. When data are _____ or _____ in nature, nonparametric methods are used. Nominal, ordinal

11. To test to see whether a median was equal to a specific value, you would use the _____ test. Sign

12. Nonparametric tests are less _____ than their parametric counterparts. Sensitive

For the following exercises, use the traditional method of hypothesis testing unless otherwise specified.

13. Home Prices The median price for an existing home in 2015 was $230,500. A random sample of homes for sale listed by a local realtor indicated homes available for the following prices. Test the claim that the median is not $230,500. Use $\alpha = 0.05$.

184,500	174,900	155,000	210,000	235,500	399,900
355,900	182,500	229,900	199,900	169,900	219,900

Source: World Almanac.

14. Lifetimes of Batteries A battery manufacturer claims that the median lifetime of a certain brand of heavy-duty battery is 1200 minutes. A sample of 25 batteries shows that 15 lasted longer than 1200 minutes. Test the claim at $\alpha = 0.05$. Use the sign test.

15. Weights of Turkeys A special diet is fed to adult turkeys to see if they will gain weight. The before-and-after weights (in pounds) are given here. Use the paired-sample sign test at $\alpha = 0.05$ to see if there is weight gain.

Before	28	24	29	30	32	33	25	26	28
After	30	29	31	32	32	35	29	25	31

16. Charity Donations Two teams of 10 members each solicited donations for their participation in a charity walk for blood cancer research. The teams received the following amounts. At $\alpha = 0.05$, can it be concluded that there is a difference in amounts?

Team A	100	50	65	50	60	75	100	150	108	120
Team B	135	90	80	140	155	60	200	58	70	72

17. Textbook Costs Samples of students majoring in law and nursing are randomly selected, and the amount each spent on textbooks for the spring semester is recorded here, in dollars. Using the Wilcoxon rank sum test at $\alpha = 0.10$, is there a difference in the amount spent by each group?

Law	167	158	162	106	98	206	112	121
Nursing	98	198	209	168	157	126	104	122

Law	133	145	151	199
Nursing	111	138	116	201

18. Student Grade Point Averages The grade point average of a group of students was recorded for one month. During the next nine-week grading period, the students attended a workshop on study skills. Their GPAs were recorded at the end of the grading period, and the data are shown. Using the Wilcoxon signed-rank test at $\alpha = 0.05$, can it be concluded that the GPA increased?

Before	3.0	2.9	2.7	2.5	2.1	2.6	1.9	2.0
After	3.2	3.4	2.9	2.5	3.0	3.1	2.4	2.8

19. Sodium Content of Fast-Food Sandwiches Sometimes calories and cholesterol are not the only considerations in healthy eating. The sodium contents (in mg) are shown for randomly selected sandwiches from three popular fast-food restaurants. Use $\alpha = 0.05$. Is there a difference in the sodium content?

No. 1	No. 2	No. 3
2940	2010	1130
3720	1850	1190
3180	1980	1220
2260	1640	1640
2780	1440	1240

Source: www.fatcalories.com

20. Medication and Reaction Times Three different groups of monkeys were fed three different medications for one month to see if the medication has any effect on reaction time. Each monkey was then taught to repeat a series of steps to receive a reward. The number of trials it took each to receive the reward is shown. At $\alpha = 0.05$, does the medication have an effect on reaction time? Use the Kruskal-Wallis test. Use the *P*-value method.

Med. 1	8	7	11	14	8	6	5
Med. 2	3	4	6	7	9	3	4
Med. 3	8	14	13	7	5	9	12

21. Drug Prices Is there a relationship between the prescription drug prices in Canada and Great Britain? Use $\alpha = 0.10$.

Canada	1.47	1.07	1.34	1.36	1.49	1.09	3.39	1.11	1.13
Great Britain	1.67	1.08	1.68	0.82	1.73	0.95	2.86	0.41	1.70

Source: USA TODAY.

22. Funding and Enrollment for Head Start Students Is there a relationship between the amount of money (in millions of dollars) spent on the Head Start Program by the states and the number of students enrolled (in thousands)? Use $\alpha = 0.10$.

Funding	100	50	22	88	49	219
Enrollment	16	7	3	14	8	31

Source: Gannet News Service.

23. Birth Registry At the state registry of vital statistics, the birth certificates issued for females (F) and males (M) were tallied. At $\alpha = 0.05$, test for randomness. The data are shown.

M M F F F F F F F F M M M M F F
M F M F M M M F F F

24. Output of Motors The output in revolutions per minute (rpm) of 10 motors was obtained. The motors

were tested again under similar conditions after they had been reconditioned. The data are shown. At $\alpha = 0.05$, did the reconditioning improve the motors' performance? Use the Wilcoxon signed-rank test.

Before	413	701	397	602	405	512	450	487	388	351
After	433	712	406	650	450	550	450	500	402	415

25. State Lottery Numbers A statistician wishes to determine if a state's lottery numbers are selected at random. The winning numbers selected for the month of February are shown. Test for randomness at $\alpha = 0.05$.

321 909 715 700 487 808 509 606 943 761
200 123 367 012 444 576 409 128 567 908
103 407 890 193 672 867 003 578

26. Type of Movies The Old-Time movie channel shows movies 24 hours a day. The movies are either black and white (B) or color (C). A movie buff records 48 movies shown in a row. Test the claim at $\alpha = 0.05$ that the movies are shown in random order.

B B B B B C C C
C C C C C B B B
B B B B B B C C
C C C C C C C C
C C B B B B B B
B B B B B C C C

Critical Thinking Challenges

1. **Tolls for Bridge** Two commuters ride to work together in one car. To decide who pays the toll for a bridge on the way to work, they flip a coin and the loser pays. Explain why over a period of one year, one person might have to pay the toll 5 days in a row. There is no toll on the return trip. (*Hint:* You may want to use random numbers.)

2. **Olympic Medals** Shown in the table are the type and number of medals each country won in the 2012 Summer Olympic Games. You are to rank the countries from highest to lowest. Gold medals are highest, followed by silver, followed by bronze. There are many different ways to rank objects and events. Here are several suggestions.

   a. Rank the countries according to the total medals won.
   b. List some advantages and disadvantages of this method.
   c. Rank each country separately for the number of gold medals won, then for the number of silver medals won, and finally for the number of bronze medals won. Next rank the countries according to the sum of the *ranks* for the categories.
   d. Are the rankings of the countries the same as those in step *a*? Explain any differences.
   e. List some advantages and disadvantages of this method of ranking.
   f. A third way to rank the countries is to assign a weight to each medal. In this case, assign 3 points

for each gold medal, 2 points for each silver medal, and 1 point for each bronze medal the country won. Multiply the number of medals by the weights for each medal, and find the sum. For example, since Argentina won 1 gold medal, 1 silver medal, and 2 bronze medals, its rank sum is $(1 \times 3) + (1 \times 2) + (2 \times 1) = 7$. Rank the countries according to this method.

   g. Compare the ranks using this method with those using the other two methods. Are the rankings the same or different? Explain.
   h. List some advantages and disadvantages of this method.
   i. Select two of the rankings, and run the Spearman rank correlation test to see if they differ significantly.

Summer Olympic Games 2012 Final Medal Standings

Country	Gold	Silver	Bronze
Argentina	1	1	2
Canada	1	5	12
Germany	11	19	14
Italy	8	9	11
Norway	2	1	1
Russia	24	26	32
Switzerland	2	2	0
United States	46	29	29

Source: http://www.london2012.com/medals-count/

Data Projects

Use a significance level of 0.05 for all tests below.

1. **Business and Finance** Monitor the price of a stock over a five-week period. Note the amount of gain or loss per day. Test the claim that the median is 0. Perform a runs test to see if the distribution of gains and losses is random.

2. **Sports and Leisure** Watch a basketball game, baseball game, or football game. For baseball, monitor an inning's pitches for balls and strikes (all fouls and balls in play also count as strikes). For football, monitor a series of plays for runs versus passing plays. For basketball, monitor one team's shots for misses versus made shots. For the collected data, conduct a runs test to see if the distribution is random.

3. **Technology** Use the data collected in data project 3 of Chapter 2 regarding song lengths. Consider only three genres. For example, use rock, alternative, and hip hop/rap.

Conduct a Kruskal-Wallis test to determine if the mean song lengths for the genres are the same.

4. **Health and Wellness** Have the students in class take their own pulse rates during the first minute of class. Have everyone take their pulse rates again 30 minutes into class. Conduct a paired-sample sign test to determine if there is a difference in pulse rates.

5. **Politics and Economics** Find the ranking for each state for its mean SAT Mathematics scores, its mean SAT English score, and its mean for income. Conduct a rank correlation analysis using Math and English, Math and income, and English and income. Which pair has the strongest relationship?

6. **Your Class** Have the students in class take their temperatures on a healthy day. Test the claim that the median body temperature is 98.6°F.

Hypothesis-Testing Summary 3*

15. Test to see whether the median of a sample is a specific value when $n > 25$.

    Example: H_0: median $= 100$

    Use the sign test:

    $$z = \frac{(X + 0.5) - 0.5n}{\sqrt{n}/2}$$

16. Test to see whether two independent samples are obtained from populations that have identical distributions.

    Example: H_0: There is no difference in the ages of the subjects.

    Use the Wilcoxon rank sum test:

    $$z = \frac{R - \mu_R}{\sigma_R}$$

    where

    $$\mu_R = \frac{n_1(n_1 + n_2 + 1)}{2}$$

    $$\sigma_R = \sqrt{\frac{n_1 n_2(n_1 + n_2 + 1)}{12}}$$

17. Test to see whether two dependent samples have identical distributions.

    Example: H_0: There is no difference in the effects of a tranquilizer on the number of hours a person sleeps at night.

    Use the Wilcoxon signed-rank test:

    $$z = \frac{w_s - \frac{n(n + 1)}{4}}{\sqrt{\frac{n(n + 1)(2n + 1)}{24}}}$$

    when $n \geq 30$.

18. Test to see whether three or more samples come from identical populations.

    Example: H_0: There is no difference in the weights of the three groups.

    Use the Kruskal-Wallis test:

    $$H = \frac{12}{N(N + 1)}\left(\frac{R_1^2}{n_1} + \frac{R_2^2}{n_2} + \cdots + \frac{R_k^2}{n_k}\right) - 3(N + 1)$$

19. Rank correlation coefficient.

    $$r_s = 1 - \frac{6\Sigma d^2}{n(n^2 - 1)}$$

20. Test for randomness: Use the runs test.

Formulas for the Test Statistic Value for the Runs Test

When and $n_1 \leq 20$ and $n_2 \leq 20$, use the number of runs, denoted by G, as the test statistic. When $n_1 > 20$ or $n_2 > 20$ or when $n_1 > 20$ *and* $n_2 > 20$, use

$$z = \frac{G - \mu_G}{\sigma_G}$$

where

$$\mu_G = \frac{2n_1 n_2}{n_1 + n_2} + 1$$

$$\sigma_G = \sqrt{\frac{2n_1 n_2(2n_1 n_2 - n_1 - n_2)}{(n_1 + n_2)^2(n_1 + n_2 - 1)}}$$

*This summary is a continuation of Hypothesis-Testing Summary 2 at the end of Chapter 12.

Answers to Applying the Concepts

Section 13–1   Ranking Data

Percent	2.6	3.8	4.0	4.0	5.4	7.0	7.0	7.3	10.0
Rank	1	2	3.5	3.5	5	6.5	6.5	8	9

Section 13–2   Clean Air

1. The claim is that the median number of days that a large city failed to meet EPA standards is 11 days per month.

2. We will use the sign test, since we do not know anything about the distribution of the variable and we are testing the median.

3. H_0: median $= 11$ and H_1: median $\neq 11$.

4. If $\alpha = 0.05$, then the critical value is 5.

5. The test statistic is 9.

6. Since $9 > 5$, do not reject the null hypothesis.

7. There is not enough evidence to conclude that the median is not 11 days per month.

8. We cannot use a parametric test in this situation.

Section 13–3   School Lunch

1. The samples are independent since two different random samples were selected.

2. H_0: There is no difference in the number of calories served for lunch in elementary and secondary schools.

   H_1: There is a difference in the number of calories served for lunch in elementary and secondary schools.

3. We will use the Wilcoxon rank sum test.

4. The critical value is ± 1.96 if we use $\alpha = 0.05$.

5. The test statistic is $z = 2.49$.

6. Since $2.49 > 1.96$, we reject the null hypothesis and conclude that there is a difference in the number of calories served for lunch in elementary and secondary schools.

7. The corresponding parametric test is the two-sample t test.

8. We would need to know that the samples were normally distributed to use the parametric test.

9. Since t tests are robust against variations from normality, the parametric test would yield the same results.

Section 13–4   Pain Medication

1. The purpose of the study is to see how effective a pain medication is.

2. These are dependent samples, since we have before-and-after readings on the same subjects.

3. H_0: The severity of pain after is the same as the severity of pain before the medication was administered.

   H_1: The severity of pain after is less than the severity of pain before the medication was administered.

4. We will use the Wilcoxon signed-rank test.

5. We will choose to use a significance level of 0.05.

6. The test statistic is $w_s = 2.5$. The critical value is 4. Since $2.5 < 4$, we reject the null hypothesis. There is enough evidence to conclude that the severity of pain after is less than the severity of pain before the medication was administered.

7. The parametric test that could be used is the t test for small dependent samples.

8. The results for the parametric test would be the same.

Section 13–5   Heights of Waterfalls

1. We are investigating the heights of waterfalls on three continents.

2. We will use the Kruskal-Wallis test.

3. H_0: There is no difference in the heights of waterfalls on the three continents.

   H_1: There is a difference in the heights of waterfalls on the three continents.

4. We will use the 0.05 significance level. The critical value is 5.991. Our test statistic is $H = 0.01$.

5. Since $0.01 < 5.991$, we fail to reject the null hypothesis. There is not enough evidence to conclude that there is a difference in the heights of waterfalls on the three continents.

6. The corresponding parametric test is analysis of variance (ANOVA).

7. To perform an ANOVA, the population must be normally distributed, the samples must be independent of each other, and the variances of the samples must be equal.

Section 13–6   Tall Trees

1. The biologist is trying to see if there is a relationship between the heights and diameters of tall trees.

2. We will use a Spearman rank correlation analysis.

3. The corresponding parametric test is the Pearson product moment correlation analysis.

4. Answers will vary.

5. The Pearson correlation coefficient is $r = 0.329$. The associated P-value is 0.353. We would fail to reject the null hypothesis that the correlation is zero. The Spearman's rank correlation coefficient is $r_s = 0.115$. We would reject the null hypothesis, at the 0.05 significance level, if $r_s > 0.648$. Since $0.115 < 0.648$, we fail to reject the null hypothesis that the correlation is zero. Both the parametric and nonparametric tests find that the correlation is not statistically significantly different from zero—it appears that no linear relationship exists between the heights and diameters of tall trees.

Sampling and Simulation

Sonja Flemming/CBS via Getty Images

OBJECTIVES

After completing this chapter, you should be able to:

1 Demonstrate a knowledge of the four basic sampling methods.

2 Recognize faulty questions on a survey and other factors that can bias responses.

3 Solve problems, using simulation techniques.

4 Explain the basic concepts of big data.

STATISTICS TODAY

Let's Make A Deal

On a game show, the host gives a contestant a choice of three doors. A valuable prize is behind one door and nothing is behind the other two doors. While a contestant selects one door, the host opens one of the other doors that the contestant didn't select and that has no prize behind it. (The host knows in advance which door has the prize.) Then the host asks the contestant if the contestant wants to change doors or keep the one that the contestant originally selected. Now the question is, Should the contestant switch doors, or does it really matter? This chapter will show you how you can solve this problem by simulation. For the answer, see Statistics Today—Revisited at the end of the chapter.

Introduction

Most people have heard of Gallup and Nielsen. These and other pollsters gather information about the habits and opinions of the U.S. people. Such survey firms, and the U.S. Census Bureau, gather information by selecting samples from well-defined populations. Recall from Chapter 1 that the subjects in the sample should be a subgroup of the subjects in the population. Sampling methods often use what are called *random numbers* to select samples.

Since many statistical studies use surveys and questionnaires, some information about these is presented in Section 14–2.

Random numbers are also used in *simulation techniques*. Instead of studying a real-life situation, which may be costly or dangerous, researchers create a similar situation in a laboratory or with a computer. Then, by studying the simulated situation, researchers can gain the necessary information about the real-life situation in a less expensive or safer manner. This chapter will explain some common methods used to obtain samples as well as the techniques used in simulations.

14–1   Common Sampling Techniques

OBJECTIVE

Demonstrate a knowledge of the four basic sampling methods.

In Chapter 1, a *population* was defined as all subjects (human or otherwise) under study. Since some populations can be very large, researchers cannot use every single subject, so a sample must be selected. A *sample* is a subgroup of the population. In other words, the number of individuals in the sample is less than the number of individuals in the population. Any subgroup of the population, technically speaking, can be called a sample. However, for researchers to make valid inferences about population characteristics, the sample must be random.

> For a sample to be a **random sample**, every member of the population must have an equal chance of being selected.

When a sample is chosen at random from a population, it is said to be an **unbiased sample.** That is, the sample, for the most part, is representative of the population. Conversely, if a sample is selected incorrectly, it may be a biased sample. Samples are said to be **biased samples** when some type of systematic error has been made in the selection of the subjects.

There are several types of biased samples. *Sampling* or *selection bias* occurs when some subjects are more likely to be included in a statistical survey or study than others. *Nonresponse bias* occurs when subjects who do not respond to a survey question would answer it differently than those who do respond to it. *Response* or *interviewer bias* occurs when the subject gives a different response than the respondent truly believes. *Volunteer bias* occurs when volunteers are used since they might be more interested in the survey or study and answer questions or participate differently than randomly selected subjects.

A sample is used to get information about a population for several reasons:

1. *It saves the researcher time and money.*

2. *It enables the researchers to get information that they might not be able to obtain otherwise.* For example, if a person's blood is to be analyzed for cholesterol, a researcher cannot analyze every single drop of blood without killing the person. Or if the breaking strength of cables is to be determined, a researcher cannot test to destruction every cable manufactured, since the company would not have any cables left to sell.

3. *It enables the researcher to get more detailed information about a particular subject.* If only a few people are surveyed, the researcher can conduct in-depth

interviews by spending more time with each person, thus getting more information about the subject. This is not to say that the smaller the sample, the better; in fact, the opposite is true. In general, larger samples—if correct sampling techniques are used—give more reliable information about the population.

It would be ideal if the sample were a perfect miniature of the population in all characteristics. This ideal, however, is impossible to achieve, because there are so many human traits (height, weight, IQ, etc.). The best that can be done is to select a sample that will be representative with respect to *some* characteristics, preferably those pertaining to the study. For example, if one-half of the population subjects are female, then approximately one-half of the sample subjects should be female. Likewise, other characteristics, such as age, socioeconomic status, and IQ, should be represented proportionately. To obtain unbiased samples, statisticians have developed several basic sampling methods. The most common methods are *random, systematic, stratified,* and *cluster sampling.* Each method will be explained in detail in this section.

In addition to the basic methods, there are other methods used to obtain samples. Some of these methods are also explained in this section.

Random Sampling

A random sample is obtained by using methods such as random numbers, which can be generated from calculators, computers, or tables. In *random sampling,* the basic requirement is that, for a sample of size *n,* all possible samples of this size have an equal chance of being selected from the population. But before the correct method of obtaining a random sample is explained, several incorrect methods commonly used by various researchers and agencies to gain information are discussed.

One incorrect method commonly used is to ask "the person on the street." News reporters use this technique quite often. Selecting people haphazardly on the street does not meet the requirement for simple random sampling, since not all possible samples of a specific size have an equal chance of being selected. Many people will be at home or at work when the interview is being conducted and therefore do not have a chance of being selected.

Another incorrect technique is to ask a question by either radio or television and have the listeners or viewers call the station to give their responses or opinions. Again, this sample is not random, since only those who feel strongly for or against the issue may respond and people may not have heard or seen the program. A third erroneous method is to ask people to respond by mail or email. Again, only those who are concerned and who have the time are likely to respond.

These methods do not meet the requirement of random sampling, since not all possible samples of a specific size have an equal chance of being selected. To meet this requirement, researchers can use one of two methods. The first method is to number each element of the population and then place the numbers on cards. Place the cards in a hat or fishbowl, mix them, and then select the sample by drawing the cards. When using this procedure, researchers must ensure that the numbers are well mixed. On occasion, when this procedure is used, the numbers are not mixed well, and the numbers chosen for the sample are those that were placed in the bowl last.

The second and preferred way of selecting a random sample is to use random numbers. Figure 14–1 shows a table of random numbers generated by a computer. A more detailed table of random numbers is found in Table A–1 of Appendix A.

The theory behind random numbers is that each digit, 0 through 9, has an equal probability of occurring. That is, in every sequence of 10 digits, each digit has a probability of $\frac{1}{10}$ of occurring. This does not mean that in every sequence of 10 digits, you will find each digit. Rather, it means that on the average, each digit will occur once. For example, the digit 2 may occur 3 times in a sequence of 10 digits, but in later sequences, it may not occur at all, thus averaging to a probability of $\frac{1}{10}$.

FIGURE 14–1 Part of Table A–1, the Table of Random Numbers

60035	97320	62543	61404	94367	07080	66112	56180	15813	15978	63578	13365	60115	99411
64072	76075	91393	88948	99244	60809	10784	36380	5721	24481	86978	74102	49979	28572
14914	85608	96871	74743	73692	53664	67727	21440	13326	98590	93405	63839	65974	05294
93723	60571	17559	96844	88678	89256	75120	62384	77414	24023	82121	01796	03907	35061
86656	43736	62752	53819	81674	43490	07850	61439	52300	55063	50728	54652	63307	83597
31286	27544	44129	51107	53727	65479	09688	57355	20426	44527	36896	09654	63066	92393
95519	78485	20269	64027	53229	59060	99269	12140	97864	31064	73933	37369	94656	57645
78019	75498	79017	22157	22893	88109	57998	02582	34259	11405	97788	37718	64071	66345
45487	22433	62809	98924	96769	24955	60283	16837	02070	22051	91191	40000	36480	07822
64769	25684	33490	25168	34405	58272	90124	92954	43663	39556	40269	69189	68272	60753
00464	62924	83514	97860	98982	84484	18856	35260	22370	22751	89716	33377	97720	78982
73714	36622	04866	00885	34845	26118	47003	28924	98813	45981	82469	84867	50443	00641
84032	71228	72682	40618	69303	58466	03438	67873	87487	33285	19463	02872	36786	28418
70609	51795	47988	49658	29651	93852	27921	16258	28666	41922	33353	38131	64115	39541
37209	94421	49043	11876	43528	93624	55263	29863	67709	39952	50512	93074	66938	09515

To obtain a sample by using random numbers, number the elements of the population sequentially and then select each person by using random numbers. This process is shown in Example 14–1.

Random samples can be selected with or without replacement. If the same member of the population cannot be used more than once in the study, then the sample is selected without replacement. That is, once a random number is selected, it cannot be used later.

Note: In the explanations and examples of the sampling procedures, a small population will be used, and small samples will be selected from this population. Small populations are used for illustrative purposes only, because the entire population could be included with little difficulty. In real life, however, researchers must usually sample from very large populations, using the procedures shown in this chapter.

EXAMPLE 14–1   State Governors on Capital Punishment

Suppose a researcher wants to produce a television show featuring in-depth interviews with state governors on the subject of capital punishment. Because of time constraints, the 60-minute program will have room for only 10 governors. The researcher wishes to select the governors at random. Select a random sample of 10 states from 50.

Note: This answer is not unique.

SOLUTION

Step 1   Number each state from 1 to 50, as shown. In this case, they are numbered alphabetically.

01. Alabama	14. Indiana	27. Nebraska	40. South Carolina
02. Alaska	15. Iowa	28. Nevada	41. South Dakota
03. Arizona	16. Kansas	29. New Hampshire	42. Tennessee
04. Arkansas	17. Kentucky	30. New Jersey	43. Texas
05. California	18. Louisiana	31. New Mexico	44. Utah
06. Colorado	19. Maine	32. New York	45. Vermont
07. Connecticut	20. Maryland	33. North Carolina	46. Virginia
08. Delaware	21. Massachusetts	34. North Dakota	47. Washington
09. Florida	22. Michigan	35. Ohio	48. West Virginia
10. Georgia	23. Minnesota	36. Oklahoma	49. Wisconsin
11. Hawaii	24. Mississippi	37. Oregon	50. Wyoming
12. Idaho	25. Missouri	38. Pennsylvania	
13. Illinois	26. Montana	39. Rhode Island	

Step 2 Using the random numbers shown in Figure 14–1, find a starting point. To find a starting point, you generally close your eyes and place your finger anywhere on the table. In this case, the first number is 98924 (see Figure 14–2). It is the ninth number in the fourth column. Use the last two digits of the number. They are 2 and 4. So, the first random number is 24. Continue down the column. The next number is 25168, but 68 is beyond the numbers 1 through 50, so skip this number. Continue down the column until you get to 40618. Hence the next number is 18. When you reach the bottom, start at the top of the next column. Hence, the third random number is 99244. Use 44.

Continue until you get 10 random numbers. They are 24, 18, 44, 27, 29, 05, 45, 03, 28, and 09. (*Note:* If you get the same number twice, just skip it.) Therefore, the ten random numbers are 24, 18, 44, 27, 29, 05, 45, 03, 28, and 09.

FIGURE 14–2 Selecting 10 Random Numbers

60035	97320	62543	61404	94367	07080	66112	56180	15813	15978	63578	13365	60115	99411
64072	76075	91393	88948	99244	60809	10784	36380	5721	24481	86978	74102	49979	28572
14914	85608	96871	74743	73692	53664	67727	21440	13326	98590	93405	63839	65974	05294
93723	60571	17559	96844	88678	89256	75120	62384	77414	24023	82121	01796	03907	35061
86656	43736	62752	53819	81674	43490	07850	61439	52300	55063	50728	54652	63307	83597
31286	27544	44129	51107	53727	65479	09688	57355	20426	44527	36896	09654	63066	92393
95519	78485	20269	64027	53229	59060	99269	12140	97864	31064	73933	37369	94656	57645
78019	75498	79017	22157	22893	88109	57998	02582	34259	11405	97788	37718	64071	66345
45487	22433	62809	98924	96769	24955	60283	16837	02070	22051	91191	40000	36480	07822
64769	25684	33490	25168	34405	58272	90124	92954	43663	39556	40269	69189	68272	60753
00464	62924	83514	97860	98982	84484	18856	35260	22370	22751	89716	33377	97720	78982
73714	36622	04866	00885	34845	26118	47003	28924	98813	45981	82469	84867	50443	00641
84032	71228	72682	40618	69303	58466	03438	67873	87487	33285	19463	02872	36786	28418
70609	51795	47988	49658	29651	93852	27921	16258	28666	41922	33353	38131	64115	39541
37209	94421	49043	11876	43528	93624	55263	29863	67709	39952	50512	93074	66938	09515

These correspond to the following states:

24	Mississippi	18	Louisiana
44	Utah	27	Nebraska
29	New Hampshire	5	California
45	Vermont	3	Arizona
28	Nevada	9	Florida

Thus, the governors of these ten states will constitute the sample.

Random sampling has one limitation. If the population is extremely large, it is time-consuming to number and select the sample elements.

Systematic Sampling

A **systematic sample** is a sample obtained by numbering each element in the population selecting some random starting point, and then selecting every kth element (third or fifth or tenth, etc.) from the population to be included in the sample.

The National Weather Service collects various types of data about the weather. For example, each year in the United States about 400 million lightning strikes occur. On average, 400 people are struck by lightning, and 85% of those struck are men. About 100 of these people die. The cause of most of these deaths is not burns, even though temperatures as high as 54,000°F are reached, but heart attacks. The lightning strike short-circuits the body's autonomic nervous system, causing the heart to stop beating. In some instances, the heart will restart on its own. In other cases, the heart victim will need emergency resuscitation.

The most dangerous places to be during a thunderstorm are open fields, golf courses, under trees, and near water, such as a lake or swimming pool. It's best to be inside a building during a thunderstorm although there's no guarantee that the building won't be struck by lightning. Are these statistics descriptive or inferential? Why do you think more men are struck by lightning than women? Should you be afraid of lightning?

Marc Rossmann/Shutterstock

The procedure of systematic sampling is illustrated in Example 14–2.

EXAMPLE 14–2   Television Show Interviews

Using the population of 50 states in Example 14–1, select a systematic sample of 10 states.

SOLUTION

Step 1   Number the population units as shown in Example 14–1.

Step 2   Since there are 50 states and 10 are to be selected, the rule is to select every fifth state. This rule was determined by dividing 50 by 10, which yields 5.

Step 3   Using the table of random numbers, select the first digit (from 1 to 5) at random. In this case, 3 was selected.

Step 4   Select every fifth number starting with 3.

1 2 **3** 4 5 6 7 **8** 9 10 11 12 **13** 14 15 . . .

The states selected are

3	Arizona	28	Nevada
8	Delaware	33	North Carolina
13	Illinois	38	Pennsylvania
18	Louisiana	43	Texas
23	Minnesota	48	West Virginia

The advantage of systematic sampling is the ease of selecting the sample elements. Also, in many cases, a numbered list of the population units may already exist. For example, the manager of a factory may have a list of employees who work for the company, or there may be an in-house telephone directory.

When doing systematic sampling, you must be careful how the items are arranged on the list. For example, if each unit were arranged, say, as

1. Husband

2. Wife

3. Husband

4. Wife

then the selection of the starting number could produce a sample of all males or all females, depending on whether the starting number is even or odd and whether the number to be added is even or odd. As another example, if the list were arranged in order of heights of individuals, you would get a different average from two samples if the first were selected by using a small starting number and the second by using a large starting number.

Stratified Sampling

> A **stratified sample** is a sample obtained by dividing the population into subgroups, called *strata*, according to various homogeneous (similar) characteristics and then randomly selecting members from each stratum for the sample.

For example, a population may consist of males and females who are smokers or nonsmokers. The researcher will want to include in the sample people from each group—that is, males who smoke, males who do not smoke, females who smoke, and females who do not smoke. To accomplish this selection, the researcher divides the population into four subgroups and then selects a random sample from each subgroup. This method ensures that the sample is representative on the basis of the characteristics of gender and smoking, although it may not be representative on the basis of other characteristics.

EXAMPLE 14–3   Selecting Students

Using the population of 20 students listed in the following table, select a sample of eight students on the basis of gender (male/female) and grade level (first-year/sophomore) by stratification.

1.	Ald, Peter	M	FY	11.	Martin, Janice	F	FY
2.	Brown, Danny	M	So	12.	Meloski, Gary	M	FY
3.	Bear, Theresa	F	FY	13.	Oeler, George	M	So
4.	Selman, Natalia	F	FY	14.	Jackson, Latisha	F	So
5.	Collins, Carolyn	F	FY	15.	Alzubaidi, Hasan	M	FY
6.	Veshgah, Amir	M	FY	16.	Nguyen, Sophia	F	FY
7.	Hogan, Michael	M	FY	17.	Mendoza, Clexious	M	So
8.	Jones, Lois	F	So	18.	Kinoshita, Yoko	F	So
9.	Lutz, Harry	M	So	19.	Unger, Roberta	F	So
10.	Acosta, Hugo	M	So	20.	Zibert, Mary	F	So

SOLUTION

Step 1   Divide the population into two subgroups, consisting of males and females, as shown in the following table.

Males			Females		
1. Ald, Peter	M	FY	1. Bear, Theresa	F	FY
2. Brown, Danny	M	So	2. Selman, Natalia	F	FY
3. Veshgah, Amir	M	FY	3. Collins, Carolyn	F	FY
4. Hogan, Michael	M	FY	4. Jones, Lois	F	So
5. Lutz, Harry	M	So	5. Martin, Janice	F	FY
6. Acosta, Hugo	M	So	6. Jackson, Latisha	F	So
7. Meloski, Gary	M	FY	7. Nguyen, Sophia	F	FY
8. Oeler, George	M	So	8. Kinoshita, Yoko	F	So
9. Alzubaidi, Hasan	M	FY	9. Unger, Roberta	F	So
10. Mendoza, Clexious	M	So	10. Zibert, Mary	F	So

Step 2   Divide each subgroup further into two groups of first-year students and sophomores, as shown in the following table.

Group 1			Group 2		
1. Ald, Peter	M	FY	1. Bear, Theresa	F	FY
2. Veshgah, Amir	M	FY	2. Selman, Natalia	F	FY
3. Hogan, Michael	M	FY	3. Collins, Carolyn	F	FY
4. Meloski, Gary	M	FY	4. Martin, Janice	F	FY
5. Alzubaidi, Hasan	M	FY	5. Nguyen, Sophia	F	FY

Group 3			Group 4		
1. Brown, Danny	M	So	1. Jones, Lois	F	So
2. Lutz, Harry	M	So	2. Jackson, Latisha	F	So
3. Acosta, Hugo	M	So	3. Kinoshita, Yoko	F	So
4. Oeler, George	M	So	4. Unger, Roberta	F	So
5. Mendoza, Clexious	M	So	5. Zibert, Mary	F	So

Step 3   Determine how many students need to be selected from each subgroup to have a proportional representation of each subgroup in the sample. There are four groups, and since a total of eight students is needed for the sample, two students must be selected from each subgroup.

Step 4   Select two students from each group by using random numbers. In this case, the random numbers are as follows:

     Group 1:   Students 4 and 2   Group 3:   Students 5 and 1

     Group 2:   Students 2 and 3   Group 4:   Students 2 and 5

The stratified sample then consists of the following people:

         Gary Meloski   Clexious Mendoza

         Amir Veshgah   Danny Brown

         Natalia Selman   Latisha Jackson

         Carolyn Collins   Mary Zibert

     The major advantage of stratification is that it ensures representation of all population subgroups that are important to the study. There are two major drawbacks to stratification, however. First, if there are many variables of interest, dividing a large population into representative subgroups requires a great deal of effort. Second, if the variables are somewhat complex or ambiguous (such as beliefs, attitudes, or prejudices), it is difficult to separate individuals into the subgroups according to these variables.

Cluster Sampling

> A **cluster sample** is a sample obtained by selecting a preexisting or natural group, called a *cluster*, and using the members in the cluster for the sample.

For example, many studies in education use already existing classes, such as the seventh grade in Wilson Junior High School. The voters of a certain electoral district might be surveyed to determine their preferences for a mayoral candidate in the upcoming election. Or the residents of an entire city block might be polled to ascertain the percentage of households that have two or more incomes. In cluster sampling, researchers may use all units of a cluster if that is feasible, or they may select only part of a cluster to use as a sample. This selection is done by random methods.

There are three advantages to using a cluster sample instead of other types of samples: (1) A cluster sample can reduce costs, (2) it can simplify fieldwork, and (3) it is convenient. For example, in a dental study involving X-raying fourth-grade students' teeth to see how many cavities each child had, it would be a simple matter to select a single classroom and bring the X-ray equipment to the school to conduct the study. If other sampling methods were used, researchers might have to transport the machine to several different schools or transport the pupils to the dental office.

The major disadvantage of cluster sampling is that the elements in a cluster may not have the same variations in characteristics as elements selected individually from a population. The reason is that groups of people may be more homogeneous (alike) in specific clusters such as neighborhoods or clubs. For example, the people who live in a certain neighborhood tend to have similar incomes, drive similar cars, live in similar houses, and, for the most part, have similar habits.

Interesting Fact

Folks in extra-large aerobics classes—those with 70 to 90 participants—show up more often and are more fond of their classmates than exercisers in sessions of 18 to 26 people, report researchers at the University of Arizona.

Other Types of Sampling Techniques

In addition to the four basic sampling methods, other methods are sometimes used. In **sequence sampling,** which is used in quality control, successive units taken from production lines are sampled to ensure that the products meet certain standards set by the manufacturing company.

In **double sampling,** a very large population is given a questionnaire to determine those who meet the qualifications for a study. After the questionnaires are reviewed, a second, smaller population is defined. Then a sample is selected from this group.

In **multistage sampling,** the researcher uses a combination of sampling methods. For example, suppose a research organization wants to conduct a nationwide survey for a new product being manufactured. A sample can be obtained by using the following combination of methods. First the researchers divide the 50 states into four or five regions (or clusters). Then several states from each region are selected at random. Next the states are divided into various areas by using large cities and small towns. Samples of these areas are then selected. Next, each city and each town are divided into districts or wards. Finally, streets in these wards are selected at random, and the families living on these streets are given samples of the product to test and are asked to report the results. This hypothetical example illustrates a typical multistage sampling method.

In **convenience sampling,** the researcher selects subjects from the population who are available to use. These samples are usually not representative of the population, and their use can lead to biased conclusions.

The steps for conducting a sample survey are given in the Procedure Table.

Procedure Table

Conducting a Sample Survey

Step 1 Decide what information is needed.

Step 2 Determine how the data will be collected (phone interview, mail survey, etc.).

Step 3 Select the information-gathering instrument or design the questionnaire if one is not available.

Step 4 Set up a sampling list, if possible.

Step 5 Select the best method for obtaining the sample (random, systematic, stratified, cluster, or other).

Step 6 Conduct the survey and collect the data.

Step 7 Tabulate the data.

Step 8 Conduct the statistical analysis.

Step 9 Report the results.

A question often asked about sampling is, "How large of a sample do I need?" The answer to this question is based on several things. Two important considerations are time and money. The more time and money a researcher has, the larger the sample can be. When random samples are used, larger samples can result in more reliable conclusions. Also as shown in Chapter 7, actual sample size numbers can be obtained if the researcher knows the confidence level and the degree of accuracy or the margin of error desired.

Applying the Concepts 14–1

The White or Wheat Bread Debate

Read the following study and answer the questions.

> *A baking company selected 36 women weighing different amounts and randomly assigned them to four different groups. The four groups were white bread only, brown bread only, low-fat white bread only, and low-fat brown bread only. Each group could eat only the type of bread assigned to the group. The study lasted for eight weeks. No other changes in any of the women's diets were allowed. A trained evaluator was used to check for any differences in the women's diets. The results showed that there were no differences in weight gain between the groups over the eight-week period.*

1. Did the researchers use a population or a sample for their study?
2. Based on who conducted this study, would you consider the study to be biased?
3. Which sampling method do you think was used to obtain the original 36 women for the study (random, systematic, stratified, or clustered)?
4. Which sampling method would you use? Why?
5. How would you collect a random sample for this study?
6. Does random assignment help representativeness the same as random selection does? Explain.

See page 785 for the answers.

Exercises 14–1

1. Name the four basic sampling techniques. Random, systematic, stratified, cluster

2. Why are samples used in statistics?

3. What is the basic requirement for a sample? A sample must be randomly selected.

4. Why should random numbers be used when you are selecting a random sample?

5. List three incorrect methods that are often used to obtain a sample.

6. What is the principle behind random numbers? Over the long run each digit, 0 through 9, will occur with the same probability.

7. List the advantages and disadvantages of random sampling.

8. List the advantages and disadvantages of systematic sampling.

9. List the advantages and disadvantages of stratified sampling.

10. List the advantages and disadvantages of cluster sampling.

Use the Overview of U.S. Public Schools data to answer Exercises 11 through 14.

Overview of U.S. Public Schools

State	Pupils per teacher	Enrollment
AL	17.5	732,900
AK	17.0	134,100
AZ	23.3	1,113,200
AR	13.8	496,600
CA	23.3	6,251,900
CO	17.4	917,600
CT	12.6	511,900
DE	14.8	138,000
FL	15.1	2,887,200
GA	15.4	1,765,900
HI	15.4	179,500
ID	18.3	308,100
IL	15.7	1,984,800
IN	17.4	1,050,200
IA	14.2	513,800
KS	13.7	492,400
KY	16.3	676,000
LA	14.8	703,900
ME	12.2	177,300
MD	14.8	908,300

State	Pupils per teacher	Enrollment
MA	13.3	958,400
MI	18.3	1,473,200
MN	15.4	903,300
MS	15.1	460,600
MO	13.5	911,700
MT	13.9	152,400
NE	13.5	330,400
NV	20.0	506,200
NH	12.3	174,600
NJ	12.2	1,392,000
NM	15.8	323,700
NY	13.1	2,710,800
NC	15.5	1,550,200
ND	11.8	115,100
OH	16.7	1,671,100
OK	16.9	699,900
OR	20.4	616,200
PA	14.1	1,713,800
RI	13.3	142,100
SC	15.2	787,900
SD	13.9	142,000
TN	15.6	1,000,200
TX	15.2	5,468,800
UT	22.9	687,800
VT	10.8	85,900
VA	14.0	1,295,600
WA	18.7	1,139,700
WV	14.1	262,500
WI	14.6	849,500
WY	12.5	93,200

11. **Teacher Data** Using the table of random numbers, select 10 states and find the mean of the average population and the mean of the pupils per teacher. How do your results compare with the U.S. figures? Answers will vary.

12. **Teacher Data** Select a systematic sample of 10 states, and find the mean of the average population and the mean of the pupils per teacher. How do your results compare with the U.S. figures? Answers will vary.

13. **Teacher Data** Select a cluster sample of 10 states, and find the mean of the average population and the mean of the pupils per teacher. How do your results compare with the U.S. figures? Answers will vary.

14. **Teacher Data** Are there any characteristics of these data that might create problems in sampling? Answers will vary.

Use the following data for Exercises 15 and 16.

Record high temperatures

AL	112	MT	117
AK	100	NE	118
AZ	128	NV	125
AR	120	NH	106
CA	134	NJ	110
CO	115	NM	122
CT	106	NY	109
DE	110	NC	110
FL	109	ND	122
GA	112	OH	113
HI	98	OK	122
ID	118	OR	119
IL	117	PA	111
IN	116	RI	104
IA	118	SC	113
KS	121	SD	120
KY	114	TN	113
LA	114	TX	120
ME	105	UT	117
MD	109	VT	105
MA	107	VA	110
MI	112	WA	118
MN	115	WV	112
MS	115	WI	114
MO	118	WY	115

15. Record High Temperatures Which method of sampling might be good for this set of data? Choose one to select 10 states and calculate the sample mean. Compare with the population mean. Answers will vary.

16. Record High Temperatures Choose a different method to select 10 states and compute the sample mean high temperature. Compare with your answer in Exercise 15 and with the population mean. Do you see any features of this data set that might affect the results of obtaining a sample mean? Answers will vary.

Use the following data for Exercises 17 through 19.

States and number of electoral votes for each

AL	9	GA	16
AK	3	HI	4
AZ	11	ID	4
AR	6	IL	20
CA	55	IN	11
CO	9	IA	6
CT	7	KS	6
DE	3	KY	8
DC	3	LA	8
FL	29	ME	4

MD	10	OK	7
MA	11	OR	7
MI	16	PA	20
MN	10	RI	4
MS	6	SC	9
MO	10	SD	3
MT	3	TN	11
NE	5	TX	38
NV	6	UT	6
NH	4	VT	3
NJ	14	VA	13
NM	5	WA	12
NY	29	WV	5
NC	15	WI	10
ND	3	WY	3
OH	18		

17. Electoral Votes Select a systematic sample of 10 states, and compute the mean number of electoral votes for the sample. Compare this mean with the population mean. Answers will vary.

18. Electoral Votes Divide the 50 states into five subgroups by geographic location, using a map of the United States. Each subgroup should include 10 states. The subgroups should be northeast, southeast, central, northwest, and southwest. Select two states from each subgroup, and find the mean number of electoral votes for the sample. Compare these means with the population mean. Answers will vary.

19. Electoral Votes Select a cluster of 10 states, and compute the mean number of electoral votes for the sample. Compare this mean with the population mean. Answers will vary.

20. Many research studies described in the news and social media do not report the sample size or the sampling method used. Try to find a research article that gives this information; state the sampling method that was used and the sample size. Answers will vary.

21. Define sampling or selection bias.

22. Give an example of how sampling or selection bias might occur.

23. Define nonresponsive bias.

24. Give an example of how nonresponsive bias might occur.

25. Define response or interview bias.

26. Give an example of how response bias might occur.

27. Define volunteer bias.

28. Give an example of how volunteer bias might occur.

📚 Technology | Step by Step

TI-84 Plus
Step by Step

Generate Random Numbers

To generate random numbers from 0 to 1 by using the TI-84 Plus:

1. Press **MATH** and move the cursor to PRB and press **1** for rand, then press **ENTER.** The calculator will generate a random decimal from 0 to 1.
2. To generate additional random numbers press **ENTER.**

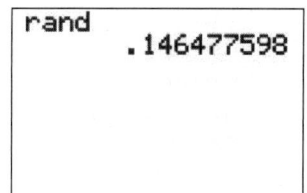

To generate a list of random integers between two specific values:

1. Press **MATH** and move the cursor to PRB.
2. Press **5** for randInt(.
3. Enter the lowest value followed by a comma, then the largest value followed by a comma, then the number of random numbers desired followed by). Press **ENTER.**

Example: Generate five three-digit random numbers.

Enter **0, 999, 5**) at the randInt(as shown.

```
randInt(0,999,5)
{194 538 405 45…
```

The calculator will generate five three-digit random numbers. Use the arrow keys to view the entire list.

EXCEL
Step by Step

Generate Random Numbers

The Data Analysis Add-In in Excel has a feature to generate random numbers from a specified probability distribution. For this example, a list of 50 random real numbers will be generated from a uniform distribution. The real numbers will then be rounded to integers between 1 and 50.

1. Open a new worksheet and select the Data tab, then **Data Analysis>Random Number Generation** from Analysis Tools. Click [OK].
2. In the dialog box, type **1** for the Number of Variables. Leave the Number of Random Numbers box empty.
3. For Distribution, select Uniform.
4. In the Parameters box, type **1** for the lower bound and **51** for the upper bound.
5. You may type in an integer value between **1** and **51** for the Random Seed. For this example, type **3** for the Random Seed.
6. Select Output Range and type in **A1:A50.**
7. Click [OK].

The first 10 output numbers are shown.

To convert the random numbers to a list of integers:

8. Select cell B1 and select the Formulas tab, and then the Insert Function icon.

9. Select the Math & Trig Function category and scroll to the Function name INT to convert the data in column A to integer values.

Note: The INT function rounds the argument (input) down to the nearest integer.

10. Type **A1** for the Number in the INT dialog box. Click [OK].

11. Copy and paste cell B1 down to cells **B2** through **B50**.

12. The numbers from column A should have been rounded to integers in column B.

Here is a sample of the data produced from the preceding procedure.

	A	B
1	1.073244	1
2	11.98056	11
3	15.18195	15
4	14.87219	14
5	11.72878	11
6	36.97674	36
7	28.01193	28
8	36.86383	36
9	42.53111	42
10	19.56746	19

MINITAB

Step by Step

Select a Random Sample with Replacement

A simple random sample selected with replacement allows some values to be used more than once, duplicates. In the first example, a random sample of integers will be selected with replacement.

1. Select **Calc>Random Data>Integer**.

2. Type **10** for rows of data.

3. Type the name of a column, Random1, in the box for Store in column(s).

4. Type **1** for Minimum and **50** for Maximum, then click [OK].

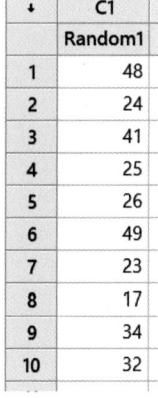

A sample of 10 integers between 1 and 50 will be displayed in the first column of the worksheet. Every list will be different.

Select a Random Sample Without Replacement

To sample without replacement, make a list of integers and sample from the columns.

1. Select **Calc>Make Patterned Data>Simple Set of Numbers.**

2. Type **Integers** in the text box for Store patterned data in.

3. Type **1** for From first value and **50** for To last value. Leave 1 for both number of times, and click [OK]. A list of the integers from 1 to 50 will be created in the worksheet.

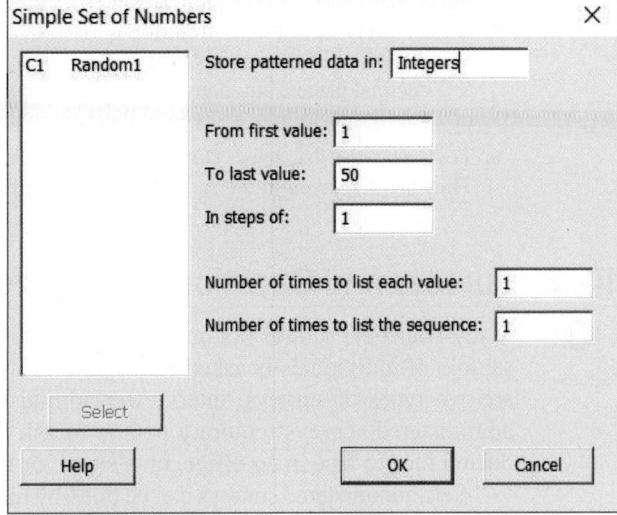

4. Select **Calc>Random Data>Sample from columns.**

5. Sample **10** for the number of rows to sample and Integers for the name of the column.

6. Type Random2 as the name of the new column. Be sure to leave the option for Sample with replacement unchecked.

7. Click [OK]. The new sample will be in the worksheet. There will be no duplicates.

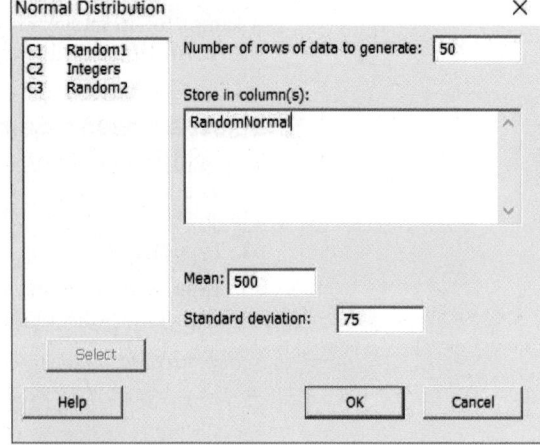

Random2
50
40
36
34
43
33
2
4
28
10

Select a Random Sample from a Normal Distribution

No data are required in the worksheet.

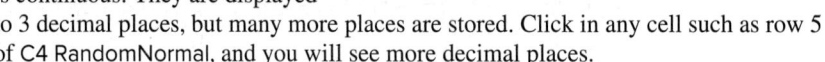

1. Select **Calc>Random Data>Normal . . .**

2. Type **50** for the number of rows.

3. Press TAB or click in the box for Store in column(s). Type in RandomNormal.

4. Type in **500** for the Mean and **75** for the Standard deviation.

5. Click [OK]. The random numbers are in a column of the worksheet. The distribution is sampled "with replacement." However, duplicates are not likely since this distribution is continuous. They are displayed to 3 decimal places, but many more places are stored. Click in any cell such as row 5 of C4 RandomNormal, and you will see more decimal places.

6. To display the list, select **Data>Display data,** then select RandomNormal and click [OK]. They are displayed in the same order they were selected, but going across not down.

14–2   Surveys and Questionnaire Design

OBJECTIVE ❷

Recognize faulty questions on a survey and other factors that can bias responses.

Many statistical studies obtain information from *surveys.* A survey is conducted when a sample of individuals is asked to respond to questions about a particular subject. There are two types of surveys: interviewer-administered and self-administered. Interviewer-administered surveys require a person to ask the questions. The interview can be conducted face to face in an office, on a street, or in the mall, or via telephone.

Self-administered surveys can be done by mail, email, the Internet; or in a group setting such as a classroom.

When analyzing the results of surveys, you should be very careful about the interpretations. The way a question is phrased can influence the way people respond. For example, when a group of people were asked if they favored a waiting period and background check before guns could be sold, 91% of the respondents were in favor of it and 7% were against it. However, when asked if there should be a national gun registration program costing about 20% of all dollars spent on crime control, only 33% of the respondents were in favor of it and 61% were against it.

As you can see, by phrasing questions in different ways, different responses can be obtained, since the purpose of a national gun registry would include a waiting period and a background check.

When you are writing questions for a questionnaire, it is important to avoid these common mistakes.

1. *Asking biased questions.* By asking questions in a certain way, the researcher can lead the respondents to answer in the way they want them to. For example, asking a question such as "Are you going to vote for candidate Jones even though the latest survey indicates that he will lose the election?" instead of "Are you going to vote for candidate Jones?" may dissuade some people from answering in the affirmative.

2. *Using confusing words.* In this case, the participant misinterprets the meaning of the words and answers the questions in a biased way. For example, the question "Do you think people would live longer if they were on a diet?" could be misinterpreted since there are many different types of diets—weight loss diets, low-salt diets, medically prescribed diets, etc.

3. *Asking double-barreled questions.* Sometimes questions contain compound sentences that require the participant to respond to two questions at the same time. For example, the question "Are you in favor of a special tax to provide national health care for the citizens of the United States?" asks two questions: "Are you in favor of a national health care program?" and "Do you favor a tax to support it?"

4. *Using double negatives in questions.* Questions with double negatives can be confusing to the respondents. For example, the question "Do you feel that it is not appropriate to have areas where people cannot smoke?" is very confusing since *not* is used twice in the sentence.

5. *Ordering questions improperly.* By arranging the questions in a certain order, the researcher can lead the participant to respond in a way that the researcher may otherwise not have done. For example, a question might ask the respondent, "At what age should an elderly person not be permitted to drive?" A later question might ask the respondent to list some problems of elderly people. The respondent may indicate that transportation is a problem based on reading the previous question.

Other factors can also bias a survey. For example, the participant may not know anything about the subject of the question but will answer the question anyway to avoid being considered uninformed. For example, many people might respond yes or no to the following question: "Would you be in favor of giving pensions to the widows of unknown soldiers?" In this case, the question makes no sense since if the soldiers were unknown, their widows would also be unknown.

Many people will make responses on the basis of what they think the person asking the questions wants to hear. For example, if a question states, "How often do you lie?" people may *understate* the incidences of their lying.

Participants will, in some cases, respond differently to questions depending on whether their identity is known. This is especially true if the questions concern sensitive issues such as income, sexuality, and abortion. Researchers try to ensure confidentiality (i.e., keeping the respondent's identity secret) rather than anonymity (soliciting unsigned responses); however, many people will be suspicious in either case.

Still other factors that could bias a survey include the time and place of the survey and whether the questions are open-ended or closed-ended. The time and place where a survey is conducted can influence the results. For example, if a survey on airline safety is conducted immediately after a major airline crash, the results may differ from those obtained in a year in which no major airline disasters occurred.

Finally, the type of questions asked influences the responses. In this case, the concern is whether the question is open-ended or closed-ended.

An *open-ended question* would be one such as "List three activities that you plan to spend more time on when you retire." A *closed-ended question* would be one such as "Which one of these activities do you plan to spend more time on after you retire: traveling; eating out; fishing and hunting; exercising; visiting relatives?"

One problem with a closed-ended question is that the respondents are forced to choose the answers that the researcher gives and cannot supply their own. But there is also a problem with open-ended questions in that the results may be so varied that attempting to summarize them might be difficult, if not impossible. Hence, you should be aware of what types of questions are being asked before you draw any conclusions from the survey.

There are several other things to consider when you are conducting a study that uses questionnaires. For example, a pilot study should be done to test the design and usage of the questionnaire (i.e., the *validity* of the questionnaire). The pilot study helps the researcher to pretest the questionnaire to determine if it meets the objectives of the study. It also helps the researcher to rewrite any questions that may be misleading, ambiguous, etc.

If the questions are being asked by an interviewer, some training should be given to that person. If the survey is being done by mail or online, background information and clear directions should accompany the questionnaire.

Questionnaires help researchers to gather needed statistical information for their studies; however, much care must be given to proper questionnaire design and usage; otherwise, the results will be unreliable.

Applying the Concepts 14–2

Plastic Bag Bans and Profits

Assume you are a store owner and are concerned about the recent bans on single-use plastic bags. Will your business lose money if you do not allow single-use plastic bags in your store? You decide to research this question and find two related articles in the regional news. The first article states that randomly selected stores in Derry, Pennsylvania, that have completely banned single-use plastic bags have lost 25% of their business. In that study, a survey was used and the owners were asked how much business they thought they lost. The survey was conducted by an anonymous group. It was reported in the second article that there had been a modest increase in business among stores that banned single-use plastic bags in that same area. Sales receipts were collected and analyzed against last year's profits. The second survey was conducted by the Pennsylvania Food Merchants Association.

1. How has the single-use plastic bag ban affected the store's business in Derry, Pennsylvania?
2. Why do you think the surveys reported conflicting results?
3. Should surveys based on anecdotal responses be allowed to be published?
4. Can the results of a sample be representative of a population and still offer misleading information?
5. How critical is measurement error in survey sampling?

See page 785 for the answers.

Exercises 14–2

Exercises 1 through 9 present survey questions. Determine if the question has a flaw. If there is a flaw, identify the flaw and rewrite the question following the guidelines presented in this section.

1. Which type of artificial sweetener do you think is the least unhealthy? Flaw—biased; it's confusing.

2. Do you like the mayor? Flaw—the purpose of the question is unclear. You could like him personally but not politically.

3. Do you approve of the mayor's political agenda? Flaw—the question is too broad.

4. Do you approve of the mayor's position on the new soft drink tax? Flaw—none. The question is good if the respondent knows the mayor's position; otherwise his position needs to be stated.

5. How long have you studied for this examination? Flaw— confusing words. How many hours did you study for this exam?

6. Which artificial sweetener do you prefer? Possible order problem—ask first, "Do you use artificial sweetener regularly?"

7. If a plane were to crash on the border of New York and New Jersey, where should the survivors be buried? Flaw—confusing words. If a plane were to crash on the border of New York and New Jersey, where should the victims be buried?

8. Are you in favor of imposing a tax on tobacco to pay for health care related to diseases caused by smoking? Flaw—none.

9. The following "Poll Question of the Day" appeared in social media. "With the passing of Neil Armstrong (first man to walk on the moon), many remembered the historical first walk on the moon. Do you remember the first time you watched the television coverage?" Answers included "Yes," "No," and "Vaguely." Flaw—The word *vaguely* is too general.

For Exercises 10–20 determine if the following questions are well written survey questions. If the question is not well written explain the mistake that was made.

10. What improvements would you like to see in the gun control laws?

11. How many members are in your family?

12. What do you dislike about Presidential debates?

13. Do you regularly use alcohol?

14. What is your income?

15. Four years ago there was a teachers' strike. Do you feel that the issues have been resolved?

16. What is your opinion of Thomas Jefferson owning slaves?

17. Why is it not good to text while driving?

18. Do you feel that health care copays are too high?

19. Are you in favor of repeated tours of duty for our military in war zones?

20. Do you feel that playing football causes too many concussions? (Yes or No)

21. Find a study that uses a questionnaire. Select any questions that you feel are improperly written. Answers will vary.

22. Many television and radio stations have a phone vote poll. If there is one in your area, select a specific day and write a brief paragraph stating the question of the day and state if it could be misleading in any way. Answers will vary.

14–3   Simulation Techniques and the Monte Carlo Method

Many real-life problems can be solved by employing simulation techniques.

> A **simulation technique** uses a probability experiment to mimic a real-life situation.

Instead of studying the actual situation, which might be too costly, too dangerous, or too time-consuming, scientists and researchers create a similar situation but one that is less expensive, less dangerous, or less time-consuming. For example, NASA uses space shuttle flight simulators so that its astronauts can practice flying the shuttle. Most video games use the computer to simulate real-life sports such as boxing, wrestling, baseball, and hockey.

Simulation techniques go back to ancient times when the game of chess was invented to simulate warfare. Modern techniques date to the mid-1940s when two physicists, John Von Neumann and Stanislaw Ulam, developed simulation techniques to study the behavior of neutrons in the design of atomic reactors.

Mathematical simulation techniques use probability and random numbers to create conditions similar to those of real-life problems. Computers have played an important role in simulation techniques, since they can generate random numbers, perform experiments, tally the outcomes, and compute the probabilities much faster than human beings. The basic simulation technique is called the *Monte Carlo method*. This topic is discussed next.

OBJECTIVE

Solve problems, using simulation techniques.

The Monte Carlo Method

The **Monte Carlo method** is a simulation technique using random numbers. Monte Carlo simulation techniques are used in business and industry to solve problems that are extremely difficult or involve a large number of variables. The steps for simulating real-life experiments in the Monte Carlo method are as follows:

Procedure Table

Simulating Experiments Using the Monte Carlo Method

Step 1 List all possible outcomes of the experiment.

Step 2 Determine the probability of each outcome.

Step 3 Set up a correspondence between the outcomes of the experiment and the random numbers.

Step 4 Select random numbers from a table and conduct the experiment.

Step 5 Compute any statistics and state the conclusions.

Before examples of the complete simulation technique are given, an illustration is needed for step 3 (set up a correspondence between the outcomes of the experiment and the random numbers). Tossing a coin, for instance, can be simulated by using random numbers as follows: Since there are only two outcomes, heads and tails, and since each outcome has a probability of $\frac{1}{2}$, the odd digits (1, 3, 5, 7, and 9) can be used to represent a head, and the even digits (0, 2, 4, 6, and 8) can represent a tail.

Suppose a random number 8631 is selected. This number represents four tosses of a single coin and the results T, T, H, H. Or this number could represent one toss of four coins with the same results.

An experiment of rolling a single die can also be simulated by using random numbers. In this case, the digits 1, 2, 3, 4, 5, and 6 can represent the number of spots that appear on the face of the die. The digits 7, 8, 9, and 0 are ignored, since they cannot be rolled.

When two dice are rolled, two random digits are needed. For example, the number 26 represents a 2 on the first die and a 6 on the second die. The random number 37 represents a 3 on the first die, but the 7 cannot be used, so another digit must be selected. As another example, a three-digit daily lotto number can be simulated by using three-digit random numbers. Finally, a spinner with four numbers, as shown in Figure 14–3, can be simulated by letting the random numbers 1 and 2 represent 1 on the spinner, 3 and 4 represent 2 on the spinner, 5 and 6 represent 3 on the spinner, and 7 and 8 represent 4 on the spinner, since each number has a probability of $\frac{1}{4}$ of being selected. The random numbers 9 and 0 are ignored in this situation.

Many real-life games, such as bowling and baseball, can be simulated by using random numbers, as shown in Figure 14–4.

FIGURE 14–3

Spinner with Four Numbers

EXAMPLE 14–4   Assault Victims

According to the U.S. Department of Justice, 30% of Americans who were assaulted took no protective actions against the person who assaulted them. Using random numbers, simulate a sample of 20 people who were assaulted and took no protective actions.

SOLUTION

Now 30% is $\frac{30}{100} = \frac{3}{10}$, so out of every 10 people, 3 were assaulted and took no protective actions. Using the table of random numbers, assign 1, 2, and 3 to those who took no protective actions and 4 through 9 and 0 as those who took protective actions.

FIGURE 14–4

Example of Simulation of a Game

Source: Based on Albert Shuylte, "Simulated Bowling Game," Student Math Notes, March 1986. Published by the National Council of Teachers of Mathematics.

Simulated Bowling Game

Let's use the random digit table to simulate a bowling game. Our game is much simpler than commercial simulation games.

First Ball		Second Ball			
		2-Pin Split		No split	
Digit	Results	Digit	Results	Digit	Results
1–3	Strike	1	Spare	1–3	Spare
4–5	2-pin split	2–8	Leave one pin	4–6	Leave 1 pin
6–7	9 pins down	9–0	Miss both pins	7–8	*Leave 2 pins
8	8 pins down			9	+Leave 3 pins
9	7 pins down			0	Leave all pins
0	6 pins down				

*If there are fewer than 2 pins, result is a spare.
+If there are fewer than 3 pins, those pins are left.

How to score bowling:
1. There are 10 frames to a **game**.
2. Each player rolls two balls for each frame per turn, unless all the pins are knocked down by a player with the first ball (a **strike**).
3. The score for a frame is the sum of the pins knocked down by the two balls, if all 10 are not knocked down.
4. If a player knocks all 10 pins down with two balls (a **spare**, shown as ▧), the score is 10 pins plus the number knocked down with the next ball.
5. If a player knocks all 10 pins down with the first ball (a **strike**, shown as ▨), the score is 10 pins plus the number knocked down by the next **two** balls.
6. A **split** (shown as 0) is when there is a big space between the remaining pins. Place in the circle the number of pins remaining after the second ball.
7. A **miss** is shown as —.

Here is how one person simulated a bowling game using the random digits 7 2 7 4 8 2 2 3 6 1 6 0 4 6 1 5 5, chosen in that order from the table.

Frame

	1	2	3	4	5	6	7	8	9	10
Digit(s)	7/2	7/4	8/2	2	3	6/1	6/0	4/6	1	5/5
Bowling result	8 ▧ 19	9 ▧ 38	9 ⓪ 47	▨ 66	9 ⓪ 75	9 ▧ 95	▨ 123	▨ 142	8 ① 151	8 ① 160	160

Now you try several.

Frame

	1	2	3	4	5	6	7	8	9	10
Digit(s)										
Bowling result										

	1	2	3	4	5	6	7	8	9	10
Digit(s)										
Bowling result										

If you wish to, you can change the probabilities in the simulation to better reflect *your* actual bowling ability.

EXAMPLE 14–5   Outcomes of a Basketball Shot

Using random numbers, simulate the outcomes of shooting a basketball from the foul line between Bennett and Aiden. Assume Bennett is twice as good as Aiden.

SOLUTION

Since Bennett is twice as good at making basketball shots from the foul line as Aiden, the probability the Bennett will make a shot is $\frac{2}{3}$ and the probability that Aiden will make his shot is $\frac{1}{3}$. Use random digits 1 through 6 to represent Bennett's shooting and 7, 8, and 9 to represent Aiden's shooting. Disregard 0. Then select a random digit, say 45396, for a five-shot series. In this case, Bennett will make four shots, 4, 5, 3, and 6, and Aiden will make one shot, 9.

More complex problems can be solved by using random numbers, as shown in Examples 14–6 to 14–8.

EXAMPLE 14–6   Rolling a Die

A die is rolled until a 6 appears. Using simulation, find the average number of rolls needed to obtain a 6. Try the experiment 20 times.

SOLUTION

Step 1   List all possible outcomes. They are 1, 2, 3, 4, 5, 6.

Step 2   Determine the probabilities. Each outcome has a probability of $\frac{1}{6}$.

Step 3   Set up a correspondence between the random numbers and the outcome. Use random numbers 1 through 6. Omit the numbers 7, 8, 9, and 0.

Step 4   Select a block of random numbers, and count each digit 1 through 6 until the first 6 is obtained. For example, the block 857236 means that it takes 4 rolls to get a 6.

$$
\begin{array}{cccccc}
8 & 5 & 7 & 2 & 3 & 6 \\
 & \uparrow & & \uparrow & \uparrow & \uparrow \\
 & 5 & & 2 & 3 & 6 \\
\end{array}
$$

Trial	Random number	Number of rolls
1	8 5 7 2 3 6	4
2	2 1 0 4 8 0 1 5 1 1 0 1 5 3 6	11
3	2 3 3 6	4
4	2 4 1 3 0 4 8 3 6	7
5	4 2 1 6	4
6	3 7 5 2 0 3 9 8 7 5 8 1 8 3 7 1 6	9
7	7 7 9 2 1 0 6	3
8	9 9 5 6	2
9	9 6	1
10	8 9 5 7 9 1 4 3 4 2 6	7
11	8 5 4 7 5 3 6	5
12	2 8 9 1 8 6	3
13	6	1
14	0 9 4 2 9 9 3 9 6	4
15	1 0 3 6	3
16	0 7 1 1 9 9 7 3 3 6	5
17	5 1 0 8 5 1 2 7 6	6
18	0 2 3 6	3
19	0 1 0 1 1 5 4 0 9 2 3 3 3 6	10
20	5 2 1 6	4
		Total 96

Step 5   Compute the results and draw a conclusion. In this case, you must find the average.

$$\bar{X} = \frac{\Sigma X}{n} = \frac{96}{20} = 4.8$$

Hence, the average is about 5 rolls.

   Note: The theoretical average obtained from the expected value formula is 6. If this experiment is done many times, say 1000 times, the results should be closer to the theoretical results.

EXAMPLE 14–7 Selecting a Key

A person selects a key at random from four keys to open a lock. Only one key opens the lock. If the first key does not open the lock, she tries other keys until one opens the lock. Find the average of the number of keys a person will have to try to open the lock. Try the experiment 25 times.

SOLUTION

Step 1 List all possible outcomes of the experiment. They are key 1, key 2, key 3, and key 4.

Step 2 Determine the probability of each outcome. Since a key is selected at random and there are four keys, the probability of selecting each key is $\frac{1}{4}$.

Step 3 Set up a correspondence between the random numbers and the outcomes. Assume that each key is numbered from 1 through 4 and that key 2 opens the lock. Naturally, the person doesn't know this, so she selects the keys at random. For the simulation, select a sequence of random digits, using only 1 through 4, until the digit 2 is reached. The trials are shown here.

Step 4 Select random numbers from the table and repeat the experiment 24 times.

Trial	Random digit (key)	Number	Trial	Random digit (key)	Number
1	2	1	14	2	1
2	2	1	15	4 2	2
3	1 2	2	16	1 3 2	3
4	1 4 3 2	4	17	1 2	2
5	3 2	2	18	2	1
6	3 1 4 2	4	19	3 4 2	3
7	4 2	2	20	2	1
8	4 3 2	3	21	2	1
9	4 2	2	22	2	1
10	2	1	23	4 2	2
11	4 2	2	24	4 3 1 2	4
12	3 1 2	3	25	3 1 2	3
13	3 1 2	3		Total	54

Step 5 Compute any statistics and state the conclusions.

Find the average:

$$\overline{X} = \frac{\Sigma X}{n} = \frac{1+1+\cdots+3}{25} = \frac{54}{25} = 2.16$$

The theoretical average is 2.5. Again, only 25 repetitions were used; more repetitions should give a result closer to the theoretical average.

EXAMPLE 14–8 Selecting a Monetary Bill

A box contains five \$1 bills, three \$5 bills, and two \$10 bills. A person selects a bill at random. What is the expected value of the bill? Perform the experiment 25 times.

SOLUTION

Step 1 List all possible outcomes. They are \$1, \$5, and \$10.

Step 2 Assign the probabilities to each outcome:

$$P(\$1) = \frac{5}{10} \qquad P(\$5) = \frac{3}{10} \qquad P(\$10) = \frac{2}{10}$$

Step 3   Set up a correspondence between the random numbers and the outcomes. Use random numbers 1 through 5 to represent a $1 bill being selected, 6 through 8 to represent a $5 bill being selected, and 9 and 0 to represent a $10 bill being selected.

Step 4   Select 25 random numbers and tally the results.

Number	Results ($)
4 5 8 2 9	1, 1, 5, 1, 10
2 5 6 4 6	1, 1, 5, 1, 5
9 1 8 0 3	10, 1, 5, 10, 1
8 4 0 6 0	5, 1, 10, 5, 10
9 6 9 4 3	10, 5, 10, 1, 1

Step 5   Compute the average:

$$\overline{X} = \frac{\Sigma X}{n} = \frac{\$1 + \$1 + \$5 + \cdots + \$1}{25} = \frac{\$116}{25} = \$4.64$$

Hence, the average (expected value) is $4.64.

Recall that using the expected value formula $E(X) = \Sigma[X \cdot P(X)]$ gives a theoretical average of

$$E(X) = \Sigma[X \cdot P(X)] = (0.5)(\$1) + (0.3)(\$5) + (0.2)(\$10) = \$4.00$$

Remember that simulation techniques do not give exact results. The more times the experiment is performed, however, the closer the actual results should be to the theoretical results. (Recall the law of large numbers.)

▤ Applying the Concepts 14–3

Simulations

Answer the following questions:

1. What is the definition of a simulation technique?
2. Have simulation techniques been used for very many years?
3. Is it cost-effective to do simulation testing on some things such as airplanes or automobiles?
4. Why might simulation testing be better than real-life testing? Give examples.
5. When did physicists develop computer simulation techniques to study neutrons?
6. When could simulations be misleading or harmful? Give examples.
7. Could simulations have prevented previous disasters such as the Hindenburg or the 1986 Space Shuttle disaster?
8. What discipline is simulation theory based on?

See page 785 for the answers.

▤ Exercises 14–3

1. Define simulation techniques.

2. Give three examples of simulation techniques.
    Answers will vary.

3. Who is responsible for the development of modern simulation techniques? John Von Neumann and Stanislaw Ulam

4. What role does the computer play in simulation?

5. What are the steps in the simulation of an experiment?

6. What purpose do random numbers play in simulation? Random numbers can be used to ensure the outcomes occur with appropriate probability.

7. What happens when the number of repetitions is increased? When the repetitions increase, there is a higher probability that the simulation will yield more precise answers.

8. Besides random numbers, what other items can be used to perform simulation experiments? Coins, dice, and cards can be used to perform simulation experiments.

For Exercises 9 through 14, explain how each experiment can be simulated by using random numbers.

9. Stay-at-Home Parents Fewer than one-half of all mothers are stay-at-home parents. Recent statistics indicate that 68.1% of all mothers with children under age 18 are in the labor force. Explain how to create a simulation to represent this situation.

Source: *New York Times Almanac.*

10. Playing Basketball Two basketball players have a free-throw contest—one is a 70% shooter and the other is a 75% shooter. They each shoot 20 shots in groups of 5 shots each. Use technology to simulate the contest and find out who wins. (Repeat a number of times and compare your answers.)

11. Television Set Ownership Thirty-five percent of U.S. households with at least one television set have premium cable service. Explain how to simulate this with random numbers. Use your method to select a random sample of 100 households, and test the hypothesis that *p* does not equal 35%.

12. Matching Pennies Two players match pennies. Use the odd digits to represent a match and the even digits to represent a nonmatch.

13. Odd Man Out Three players play odd man out. (Three coins are tossed; if all three match, the game is repeated and no one wins. If two players match, the third person wins all three coins.) Let an odd number represent heads and an even number represent tails. Then each person selects a digit at random.

14. Foreign-Born Residents Almost 16% of Texas residents are foreign-born. Explain how to select a sample of 40 based on this scenario.

Source: factfinder.census.gov

For Exercises 15 through 23, use random numbers to simulate the experiments. The number in parentheses is the number of times the experiment should be repeated.

15. Rolling a Die A die is rolled until all faces appear at least once. Find the average number of tosses. (30) Answers will vary.

16. Prizes in Caramel Corn Boxes A caramel corn company gives four different prizes, one in each box. They are placed in the boxes at random. Find the average number of boxes a person needs to buy to get all four prizes. (40) Answers will vary.

17. Keys to a Door The probability that a door is locked is 0.6, and there are five keys, one of which will unlock the door. The experiment consists of choosing one key at random and seeing if you can unlock the door. Repeat the experiment 50 times and calculate the empirical probability of unlocking the door. Compare your result to the theoretical probability for this experiment. Answers will vary.

18. Lottery Winner To win a certain lotto, a person must spell the word *big*. Sixty percent of the tickets contain the letter *b*, 30% contain the letter *i*, and 10% contain the letter *g*. Find the average number of tickets a person must buy to win the prize. (30) Answers will vary.

19. Clay Pigeon Shooting Two shooters shoot clay pigeons. Gail has an 80% accuracy rate and Paul has a 60% accuracy rate. Paul shoots first. The first person who hits the target wins. Find the probability that each wins. (30). Answers will vary.

20. Clay Pigeon Shooting In Exercise 19, find the average number of shots fired. (30) Answers will vary.

21. Basketball Foul Shots A basketball player has a 60% success rate for shooting foul shots. If she gets two shots, find the probability that she will make one or both shots. (50). Answers will vary.

22. Boxing Boxer A is favored to win over boxer B with odds 4:3. Simulate nine rounds between the two and declare a winner. (9) Answers will vary.

23. Beanbag Game A children's beanbag game is set up as follows: Two children toss beanbags at the board as shown. They hit the board with a probability of $\frac{1}{2}$ and score a 0 for a miss. When they hit the board, they receive the number of points indicated, with all squares equally likely. If a beanbag falls on a line, they receive the lower score.

Simulate a game between two players for six turns each. (6) Answers will vary.

2	3	2
3	5	3
2	3	2

24. Which would be easier to simulate with random numbers, baseball or soccer? Explain. Answers will vary.

25. Explain how cards can be used to generate random numbers. Answers will vary.

26. Explain how a pair of dice can be used to generate random numbers. Answers will vary.

14–4 Big Data

With the advent of computers and their expanding capacity, companies can secure large amounts of data every day. Hence a relatively new field of applications of data called **big data** is emerging.

Any kind of data which has these three characteristic is defined as big data:

1. There is an extremely large *volume* of data.

2. There is an extremely high *velocity* of data. (This means that the size of the data set is increasing very rapidly.)

3. There is an extremely wide *variety* of data in the data set.

These characteristics are known as the 3 V's of big data, first developed by industrial analyst Doug Laney. Another V that can be included in big data is *variability*. Hence, the data can be collected at various times, such as monthly, seasonally, or per event.

In addition, there are two kinds of data that can be collected, called structured data and unstructured data. **Structured data** are data that can be displayed in the form of tables using rows and columns. Numbers, names, dates, genders, income, and groups of words are examples of structured data. **Unstructured data** are data in which words and images are used. Text messages, comments about a business, emails, photographs, and data that includes various profiles of situations where words and images are used are some examples. It has been suggested that 20% of the data collected today is structured data, while 80% is unstructured data.

Big data sets are obtained from a variety of sources, such as web-connected devices. Every time you conduct a web search, the sites you visit are recorded. Big data can also come from marketing and sales sites. Finally, the U.S. government collects vast amounts of big data, and these data are available to the public through various sources.

There are three aspects of big data that need to be considered. They are:

1. How the data can be collected.

2. How the data can be stored so that it can be retrieved.

3. How the data can be analyzed or used easily.

Data can be collected on a day-to-day basis. For example, in manufacturing processes, the information about the use of a credit card is recorded. In health care, records of illnesses, treatments, and successes of patient treatments are recorded.

Data can be *machine-generated, computer-generated,* or *human-generated.* Sometimes data are obtained by a combination of human- and machine-generated processes. Machine-generated data can be obtained at the point of sale of items. Human-generated data can be obtained when a human collects the data and inputs it into a computer for storage.

The second aspect of big data is how and where it is stored. It is necessary to structure the data so that it can be retrieved to be analyzed. This is a complicated process since a large variety of data is collected. For example, a credit card transaction could include the customer's name, address, phone number, type of card used, credit card number, the items purchased, the amount of the purchase, and the time and date of purchase. Some companies that collect and store big data are IBM, Amazon, Google, HP, and Microsoft. In order to analyze big data, it is necessary to get the appropriate data from a large data set, and new technologies such as MapReduce and Hadoop have been created to do this job.

Big data sets are analyzed to give information to help business owners make better decisions and to help with more efficient ways to run their businesses. For example, UPS uses sensors in their delivery trucks to record information on the delivery of packages and to analyze the daily performance of their drivers. The company wanted to design a delivery system which resulted in the shortest routes, thus saving time, fuel, and wear and tear on the delivery trucks. They used a system called ORION (on road integration, optimization, and navigation) to analyze the pickup and drop-off of their packages. After the analyses were completed, UPS saved 85 million gallons of fuel and cut 85 million miles off the daily routes its drivers drove. Quite a savings!

Big data can be used in other areas, such as banking, education, health care, manufacturing, and retail sales. Big data analysis is used in banking to boost customer satisfaction with the banks' services. It is also used to minimize fraud and to keep up with the services of other banks. In education, big data analysis can identify students who are potential dropouts before they leave and provide appropriate services to keep them in school. It is also used to track the progress of students compared to students in other schools and to find better methods of student evaluations. Finally, big data analysis can help teachers and principals to provide better services for their students.

Government agencies use big data analysis to manage utilities and to help with managing their agencies. It can help to reduce traffic congestion and reduce crime in various areas.

In health care, big data analysis can improve patient care by keeping records of each patient's illnesses, prescriptions, treatments, and recoveries. Doctors can now access patient health records quickly and accurately.

In manufacturing, companies can use big data analysis to boost their output, to minimize waste, and to make sound decisions about their products and services.

In retail situations, businesses can use big data to find the most effective way to handle customer complaints and bring back customers who no longer use their business.

As you can see, big data is here to stay. Many of the statistical techniques in this book, along with other techniques, such as optimization, affinity analysis, and forecasting, can be used to make our lives easier and more exciting.

Applying the Concepts 14–4

Explain how big data can be used in the field that you plan on working in when you graduate.

1. What type of data would you collect?
2. Would your data be structured or unstructured?
3. What would be the purpose of the data?
4. Would you use machine-generated or human-generated data?
5. What statistics would you use?
6. What results would you be looking for?

See page 785 for the answers.

Exercises 14–4

1. What are three characteristics of big data?
2. Explain the differences between structured data and unstructured data.
3. Explain three concerns that need to be addressed when using big data.
4. Name four businesses that collect and use big data.
5. Name three situations where big data analysis can be used.
6. What is the difference between machine-generated data and human-generated data?
7. What are some uses of big data?

8. If you hold the position indicated here, what type of big data can you use to improve your company's growth?

    School superintendent
    College administrator
    CEO of a cable-provider company
    Manager of a nationwide car rental agency
    Life insurance company salesperson

9. What has prompted the development of big data?
10. Give an example of how big data can be used in the banking industry.

11. Is your school using big data?

12. Provide an example of big data that you might experience or have experienced.

13. Can you give an example of how human-generated data can be combined with machine-generated data?

14. Describe how errors can occur with human-generated data.

Summary

- To obtain information and make inferences about a large population, researchers select a sample. A sample is a subgroup of the population. Using a sample rather than a population, researchers can save time and money, get more detailed information, and get information that otherwise would be impossible to obtain. (14–1)

- The four most common methods researchers use to obtain samples are random, systematic, stratified, and cluster sampling methods. In random sampling, some type of random method (usually random numbers) is used to obtain the sample. In systematic sampling, the researcher selects every kth person or item after selecting the first one at random. In stratified sampling, the population is divided into subgroups according to various characteristics, and elements are then selected at random from the subgroups. In cluster sampling, the researcher selects an intact group to use as a sample. When the population is large, multistage sampling (a combination of methods) is used to obtain a subgroup of the population. (14–1)

- Researchers must use caution when conducting surveys and designing questionnaires; otherwise, conclusions obtained from these will be inaccurate. Guidelines were presented in Section 14–2. (14–2)

- Most sampling methods use random numbers, which can also be used to simulate many real-life problems or situations. The basic method of simulation is known as the Monte Carlo method. The purpose of simulation is to duplicate situations that are too dangerous, too costly, or too time-consuming to study in real life. Most simulation techniques can be done on the computer or calculator, since they can rapidly generate random numbers, count the outcomes, and perform the necessary computations. (14–3)

  Sampling and simulation are two techniques that enable researchers to gain information that might otherwise be unobtainable.

- Today a new area of statistics called big data is being used. With the advent of computer storing programs, people can keep track of large volumes of data which can be analyzed easily. The three aspects of big data are volume, velocity, and variety. (14–4)

Important Terms

biased sample 754	double sampling 761	sequence sampling 761	systematic sample 757
big data 778	Monte Carlo method 771	simulation technique 771	unbiased sample 754
cluster sample 761	multistage sampling 761	stratified sample 759	unstructured data 778
convenience sample 761	random sample 754	structured data 778	

Review Exercises

Section 14–1

Wind Speed of Hurricanes

The following table is for the 2015 hurricane season. The table lists named storms, the maximum wind speed (in miles per hour), classification (S = storm, H = hurricane), and where the storm originated from (A = Atlantic Ocean, P = Pacific Ocean). Use the data shown to answer questions 1 through 4.

Named Storms 2015

Name	Max. wind	Classification	Atlantic or Pacific
Ana	60	S	A
Bill	60	S	A
Claudette	50	S	A
Danny	115	H	A
Ela	45	S	P
Erika	50	S	A
Fred	85	H	A
Grace	50	S	A
Guillermo	105	H	P
Halola	65	S	P
Henri	50	S	A
Hilda	140	H	P
Ida	50	S	A
Ignacio	145	H	P
Iune	40	S	P
Jimena	120	H	P
Joaquin	155	H	A
Kate	75	H	A
Kilo	140	H	P
Loke	75	H	P
Malia	40	S	P
Niala	65	S	P
Oho	95	H	P

S = Storm, H = Hurricane, A = Atlantic, and P = Pacific

1. **Hurricanes** Select a random sample of eight storms by using random numbers, and find the average maximum wind speed. Compare with the population mean. Answers will vary.

2. **Hurricanes** Select a systematic sample of eight storms and calculate the average maximum wind speed. Compare with the population mean. Answers will vary.

3. **Hurricanes** Select a cluster of 10 storms. Compute the sample means wind speeds. Compare these sample means with the population means. Answers will vary.

4. **Hurricanes** Divide the 23 storms into 4 subgroups. (The fourth group will only have 5 storms.) Then select a sample of three storms from each group. Compute the means for wind speeds. Compare these means to the population mean. Answers will vary.

Use the data shown for Exercises 5 through 8.

Unemployment 2013
U.S. Department of Labor

State	Unemployment rate (%)	Average weekly benefit ($)
AL	6.5	207
AK	6.5	250
AZ	8.0	221
AR	7.5	289
CA	8.9	301
CO	6.8	356
CT	7.8	345
DE	6.7	245
FL	7.2	231
GA	8.2	267
HI	4.8	424
ID	6.2	264
IL	9.2	324
IN	7.5	243
IA	4.6	337
KS	5.4	341
KY	8.3	292
LA	6.2	207
ME	6.7	285
MD	6.6	329
MA	7.1	424
MI	8.8	293
MN	5.1	367
MS	8.6	194
MO	6.5	242
MT	5.6	290
NE	3.9	276
NV	9.8	308
NH	5.3	287
NJ	8.2	398
NM	6.9	303
NY	7.7	308
NC	8.0	290
ND	2.9	396
OH	7.4	318
OK	5.4	293
OR	7.7	316
PA	7.4	360
RI	9.5	351
SC	7.6	248
SD	3.8	276
TN	8.2	235
TX	6.3	341
UT	4.4	345
VT	4.4	313
VA	5.5	295
WA	7.0	387
WV	6.5	275
WI	6.7	276
WY	4.6	359

5. **Unemployment Benefits** Select a random sample of 10 states, and find the mean of the unemployment rates and the mean of average weekly benefits. How do your results compare with the U.S. figures? Answers will vary.

6. Unemployment Benefits Select a systematic sample of 10 states, and find the mean of the unemployment rates and the mean of the average weekly benefits. How do your results compare with the U.S. figures? Answers will vary.

7. Unemployment Benefits Find the mean of the unemployment rates and the mean of the average weekly benefits. How do your results compare with the U.S. figures? Answers will vary.

8. Unemployment Benefits Select a cluster sample of 10 states, and find the mean of the unemployment rates and the mean of the average weekly benefits. How do your results compare with the U.S. figures? Answers will vary.

Section 14–2

For Exercises 9 through 12, explain what is wrong with each question. Rewrite each one, following the guidelines in this chapter.

9. How often do you run red lights? Flaw—asking a biased question. Have you ever driven through a red light?

10. Do you think students who are not failing should not be tutored? Flaw—using a double negative. Do you think students who are not failing should be given tutoring if they request it?

11. Do you think all automobiles should have heavy-duty bumpers, even though it will raise the price of the cars by $500? Flaw—asking a double-barreled question. Do you think all automobiles should have heavy-duty bumpers?

12. When answering questions in a survey, do you prefer open-ended questions or closed-ended questions? Flaw—people might not know the meaning of open-ended or closed-ended questions.

Section 14–3

For Exercises 13 through 16, explain how to simulate each experiment by using random numbers.

13. A baseball player strikes out 40% of the time.

14. An airline overbooks 15% of the time.

15. Player 1 rolls two dice. Player 2 rolls one die. If the number on the single die matches one number of the player who rolled the two dice, player 2 wins. Otherwise, player 1 wins.

16. Rock, Paper, Scissors Two players play rock, paper, scissors. The rules are as follows: Since paper covers rock, paper wins. Since rock breaks scissors, rock wins. Since scissors cut paper, scissors win. Each person selects rock, paper, or scissors by random numbers and then compares results.

For Exercises 17 through 21, use random numbers to simulate the experiments. The number in parentheses is the number of times the experiment should be repeated.

17. Football A football is placed on the 10-yard line, and a team has four downs to score a touchdown. The team can move the ball only 0 to 5 yards per play. Find the average number of times the team will score a touchdown. (30) Answers will vary.

18. Football In Exercise 17, find the average number of plays it will take to score a touchdown. Ignore the four-downs rule and keep playing until a touchdown is scored. (30) Answers will vary.

19. Rolling a Die Four dice are rolled 50 times. Find the average of the sum of the number of spots that will appear. (50) Answers will vary.

20. Field Goals A field goal kicker is successful in 60% of his kicks inside the 35-yard line. Find the probability of kicking three field goals in a row. (50) Answers will vary.

21. Making a Sale A sales representative finds that there is a 30% probability of making a sale by visiting the potential customer personally. For every 20 calls, find the probability of making three sales in a row. (50) Answers will vary.

Data Analysis

The Data Bank is found in Appendix B.

1. From the Data Bank, choose a variable. Select a random sample of 20 individuals, and find the mean of the data.

2. Select a systematic sample of 20 individuals, and using the same variable as in Exercise 1, find the mean.

3. Select a cluster sample of 20 individuals, and using the same variable as in Exercise 1, find the mean.

4. Stratify the data according to marital status and gender, and sample 20 individuals. Compute the mean of the sample variable selected in Exercise 1 (use four groups of five individuals).

5. Compare all four means and decide which one is most appropriate. (*Hint:* Find the population mean.)

≡ STATISTICS TODAY

Let's Make A Deal —Revisited

It appears that it does not matter whether the contestant switches doors because he is given a choice of two doors, and the chance of winning the prize is 1 out of 2, or $\frac{1}{2}$. This reasoning, however, is incorrect. Consider the three possibilities for the prize. It could be behind door A, B, or C. Suppose that the contestant selected door A. Now the three situations look like this:

	Door		
Case	A	B	C
1	Prize	Empty	Empty
2	Empty	Prize	Empty
3	Empty	Empty	Prize

In case 1, the contestant selected door A, and if the contestant switched after being shown that there was no prize behind either door B or door C, the contestant loses. In case 2, the contestant selected door A, and the host will open door C, so if the contestant switched, the contestant would win the prize. In case 3, the contestant selected door A, and the host will open door B, so if the contestant switched, the contestant would win the prize. Hence, by switching, the probability of winning is $\frac{2}{3}$ and the probability of losing is $\frac{1}{3}$. The same reasoning can be used no matter which door is selected.

You can simulate this problem by using three cards, say, an ace (the prize), and two other cards. Have a person arrange the cards in a row and let you select a card. After the person turns over one of the cards (a non-ace), switch. Keep track of the number of times you win and compute the probability of winning.

This problem was supposedly used on the television show *Let's Make A Deal,* and the host of the show at that time was Monty Hall. Hence, the problem is known as the **Monty Hall Problem** or the **Monty Hall Paradox.** However, in an online interview, Monty Hall stated that he never used the door changing method but only offered the contestant money to give up the original door selected.

≡ Chapter Quiz

Determine whether each statement is true or false. If the statement is false, explain why.

1. When researchers are sampling from large populations, such as adult citizens living in the United States, they may use a combination of sampling techniques to ensure representativeness. True

2. Simulation techniques using random numbers are a substitute for performing the actual statistical experiment. True

3. When researchers perform simulation experiments, they do not need to use random numbers since they can make up random numbers. False

4. Random samples are said to be unbiased. True

Select the best answer.

5. When all subjects under study are used, the group is called a _____.
   a. Population
   b. Large group
   c. Sample
   d. Study group

6. When a population is divided into subgroups with similar characteristics and then a sample is obtained, this method is called _____ sampling.
   a. Random
   b. Systematic
   c. Stratified
   d. Cluster

7. Interviewing selected people at a local supermarket can be considered an example of _____ sampling.
   a. Random
   b. Systematic
   c. Convenience
   d. Stratified

Complete the following statements with the best answer.

8. In general, when you conduct sampling, the _____ the sample, the more representative it will be. Larger

9. When samples are not representative, they are said to be _____. Biased

10. When all residents of a street are interviewed for a survey, the sampling method used is _____. Cluster

Use the table in Appendix B Data Bank for Exercises 11 through 14.

11. **Blood Pressure** Select a random sample of 12 people, and find the mean of the blood pressures of the individuals. Compare this with the population mean. Answers will vary.

12. **Blood Pressure** Select a systematic sample of 12 people, and compute the mean of their blood pressures. Compare this with the population mean. Answers will vary.

13. **Blood Pressure** Divide the individuals into subgroups of six males and six females. Find the means of their blood pressures. Compare these means with the population mean. Answers will vary.

14. **Blood Pressure** Select a cluster sample of 12 people, and find the mean of their blood pressures. Compare this with the population mean. Answers will vary.

For Exercises 15 through 19, explain how each could be simulated by using random numbers.

15. **Chess** A chess player wins 45% of his games.

16. **Cancellation Rate** A travel agency has a 5% cancellation rate.

17. **Card Game** Two players select a card from a deck with no face cards. The player who gets the higher card wins.

18. **Dice/Card Game** One player rolls two dice. The other player selects a card from a deck. Face cards count as 11 for a jack, 12 for a queen, and 13 for a king. The player with the higher total points wins.

19. **Coin Toss** Two players each toss two coins. If they match, player 1 wins; otherwise, player 2 wins.

For Exercises 20 through 24, use random numbers to simulate the experiments. The number in
parentheses is the number of times the experiment should be done.

20. **Phone Sales** A telephone solicitor finds that there is a 15% probability of selling her product over the phone. For every 20 calls, find the probability of making two sales in a row. (100) Answers will vary.

21. **Field Goals** A field goal kicker is successful in 65% of his kicks inside the 40-yard line. Find the probability of his kicking four field goals in a row. (40) Answers will vary.

22. **Tossing Coins** Two coins are tossed. Find the average number of times two tails will appear. (40) Answers will vary.

23. **Selecting Cards** A single card is drawn from a deck. Find the average number of times it takes to draw an ace. (30) Answers will vary.

24. **Bowling** A bowler finds that there is a 30% probability that he will make a strike. For every 15 frames he bowls, find the probability of making two strikes. (30) Answers will vary.

For Exercises 25–30, explain why the survey question might be biased.

25. Do you attend class regularly? (Yes or No)

26. Do you think classes should be canceled when bad weather occurs? (Yes or No)

27. Is your textbook readable? (Yes or No)

28. Do you smoke a lot? (Yes or No)

29. Would you prefer to take herbal medicine rather than prescribed medicine for an illness?

30. Should your professor require additional written reports?

Critical Thinking Challenges

1. Explain why two different opinion polls might yield different results on a survey. Also, give an example of an opinion poll and explain how the data may have been collected.

2. Use a computer to generate random numbers to simulate the following real-life problem.

In a certain geographic region, 40% of the people have type O blood. On a certain day, the blood center needs 4 pints of type O blood. On average, how many donors are needed to obtain 4 pints of type O blood?

Data Projects

1. **Business and Finance** A car salesperson has six automobiles on the car lot. Roll a die, using the numbers 1 through 6 to represent each car. If only one car can be sold on each day, how long will it take him to sell all the automobiles? In other words, see how many tosses of the die it will take to get the numbers 1 through 6.

2. **Sports and Leisure** Using the rules given in Figure 14–4 on page 773, play the simulated bowling game. Each game consists of 10 frames.

3. **Technology** In a case of 12 smartphones, three are defective. If four are sold on Saturday, find the probability that at least one will be defective. Use random numbers to simulate this exercise 50 times.

4. Health and Wellness Of people who go on a special diet, 25% will lose at least 10 pounds in 10 weeks. A drug manufacturer says that if people take its special herbal pill, that will increase the number of people who lose at least 10 pounds in 10 weeks. The company conducts an experiment, giving its pills to 20 people. Seven people lost at least 10 pounds in 10 weeks. The drug manufacturer claims that the study "proves" the success of the herbal pills. Using random numbers, simulate the experiment 30 times, assuming the pills are ineffective. What can you conclude about the result that 7 out of 20 people lost at least 10 pounds?

5. Politics and Economics Find the number of signers of the Declaration of Independence that are from each

state. A student decides to write a paper on two of the signers, who are selected at random. What is the probability that both signers will be from the same state? Use random numbers to simulate the experiment, and perform the experiment 50 times.

6. Your Class Simulate the classical birthday problem given in the Critical Thinking Challenge 3 in Chapter 4. Select a sample size of 25 and generate random numbers between 1 and 365. Are there any two random numbers that are the same? Select a sample of 50. Are there any two random numbers that are the same? Repeat the experiments 10 times and explain your answers.

Answers to Applying the Concepts

Section 14–1   The White or Wheat Bread Debate

1. The researchers used a sample for their study.

2. Answers will vary. One possible answer is that we might have doubts about the validity of the study, since the baking company that conducted the experiment has an interest in the outcome of the experiment.

3. The sample was probably a convenience sample.

4. Answers will vary. One possible answer would be to use a simple random sample.

5. Answers will vary. One possible answer is that a list of women's names could be obtained from the city in which the women live. Then a simple random sample could be selected from this list.

6. The random assignment helps to spread variation among the groups. The random selection helps to generalize from the sample back to the population. These are two different issues.

Section 14–2   Plastic Bag Bans and Profits

1. It is uncertain how single-use plastic bag bans affected stores in Derry, Pennsylvania, since the survey results were conflicting.

2. Since the data were collected in different ways, the survey results were bound to have different answers. Perceptions of the owners will definitely be different from an analysis of actual sales receipts, particularly if the owners assumed that the single-use plastic bag bans would hurt business.

3. Answers will vary. One possible answer is that it would be difficult to not allow surveys based on anecdotal responses to be published. At the same time, it would

be good for those publishing such survey results to comment on the limitations of these surveys.

4. We can get results from a representative sample that offer misleading information about the population.

5. Answers will vary. One possible answer is that measurement error is important in survey sampling in order to give ranges for the population parameters that are being investigated.

Section 14–3   Simulations

1. A simulation uses a probability experiment to mimic a real-life situation.

2. Simulation techniques date back to ancient times.

3. It is definitely cost-effective to run simulations for expensive items such as airplanes and automobiles.

4. Simulation testing is safer, faster, and less expensive than many real-life testing situations.

5. Computer simulation techniques were developed in the mid-1940s.

6. Answers will vary. One possible answer is that some simulations are far less harmful than conducting an actual study on the real-life situation of interest.

7. Answers will vary. Simulations could have possibly prevented disasters such as the Hindenburg or the 1986 Space Shuttle disaster. For example, data analysis after the Space Shuttle disaster showed that there was a decent chance that something would go wrong on that flight.

8. Simulation theory is based in probability theory.

Section 14–4   Big Data

Answers will vary.

APPENDIX A

Tables

TABLE A-1 Random Numbers

51455	02154	06955	88858	02158	76904	28864	95504	68047	41196	88582	99062	21984	67932
06512	07836	88456	36313	30879	51323	76451	25578	15986	50845	57015	53684	57054	93261
71308	35028	28065	74995	03251	27050	31692	12910	14886	85820	42664	68830	57939	34421
60035	97320	62543	61404	94367	07080	66112	56180	15813	15978	63578	13365	60115	99411
64072	76075	91393	88948	99244	60809	10784	36380	5721	24481	86978	74102	49979	28572
14914	85608	96871	74743	73692	53664	67727	21440	13326	98590	93405	63839	65974	05294
93723	60571	17559	96844	88678	89256	75120	62384	77414	24023	82121	01796	03907	35061
86656	43736	62752	53819	81674	43490	07850	61439	52300	55063	50728	54652	63307	83597
31286	27544	44129	51107	53727	65479	09688	57355	20426	44527	36896	09654	63066	92393
95519	78485	20269	64027	53229	59060	99269	12140	97864	31064	73933	37369	94656	57645
78019	75498	79017	22157	22893	88109	57998	02582	34259	11405	97788	37718	64071	66345
45487	22433	62809	98924	96769	24955	60283	16837	02070	22051	91191	40000	36480	07822
64769	25684	33490	25168	34405	58272	90124	92954	43663	39556	40269	69189	68272	60753
00464	62924	83514	97860	98982	84484	18856	35260	22370	22751	89716	33377	97720	78982
73714	36622	04866	00885	34845	26118	47003	28924	98813	45981	82469	84867	50443	00641
84032	71228	72682	40618	69303	58466	03438	67873	87487	33285	19463	02872	36786	28418
70609	51795	47988	49658	29651	93852	27921	16258	28666	41922	33353	38131	64115	39541
37209	94421	49043	11876	43528	93624	55263	29863	67709	39952	50512	93074	66938	09515
80632	65999	34771	06797	02318	74725	10841	96571	12052	41478	50020	59066	30860	96357
37965	41203	81699	32569	65582	20487	41762	73416	07567	99716	22772	17688	07270	42332
58717	38359	32478	53525	11033	07972	05846	84437	65927	13209	21182	76513	42438	07292
79767	44901	65717	64152	65758	89418	21747	02369	12186	38207	05289	69216	23392	42084
69654	80921	52234	04390	74767	60103	07587	04278	43995	57763	07314	27938	82686	96248
17824	80806	62390	74895	12218	55960	13042	86515	32400	49230	67115	76469	37619	93038
04162	96245	11453	67464	50136	70913	62106	60151	69146	18271	69283	68753	71403	61534
48436	77893	67622	63267	25483	81669	28693	10244	65425	78743	79141	90187	43332	13488
06215	95516	43868	65471	15938	66017	89875	52044	69103	92506	14402	82113	47206	21052
56929	30317	39912	29571	78448	78358	34574	86688	40258	28535	35468	40844	62625	60849
66739	06645	08528	64618	99019	91898	32418	86791	92218	01583	58681	03546	45937	79368
43131	09326	24003	65181	22698	76051	53397	90819	70369	98376	31038	34103	89190	25975
95739	69155	62674	32165	57233	91798	25755	28065	66830	77934	44302	26613	65751	78320
49084	09215	15548	50323	83834	67699	65228	25187	02181	94262	14150	58755	69927	80574
23884	14902	59260	25429	52322	35716	73092	50749	32962	60721	24132	84922	18624	25856
17444	05860	77765	29271	48493	89725	96525	81458	43277	40681	92836	05850	54035	08666
83927	85817	21275	41603	98529	46724	96647	50577	36237	56190	15069	87856	87964	30220
29143	07127	98765	44027	98843	52316	65202	36857	33658	03221	04379	16378	80481	56242
21110	47917	36961	19251	44439	93324	03978	76357	43972	01172	39019	32757	84947	72214
69677	97071	93657	10555	49551	01886	38073	84767	35886	09302	54892	77664	45938	66375
10002	01789	69217	24461	89424	88608	63072	51783	36231	45758	44181	22001	86627	51948
85521	86852	02897	26202	92147	80981	49996	91161	58778	45395	53840	45500	87642	40266
69102	58778	45912	46884	27471	99334	44042	54375	97159	85928	94611	69345	95677	88067
33844	34428	10601	78504	28801	00880	39018	43329	43891	41871	71238	52190	90776	81368
57435	31213	55455	19010	30629	58110	48872	63863	89235	00257	85400	86329	75551	46450
58135	51679	87735	64352	39493	60192	42230	98750	49102	20346	77833	26210	15008	76733
27613	98443	36463	93096	31035	83653	39266	14249	31597	49581	78257	71723	67533	94050
12384	42026	48075	25731	01067	19498	42392	05569	26153	20178	38811	85663	23620	94531
43602	42950	94446	16192	93840	17992	65039	36718	09906	68635	93842	92696	99376	64857
82503	75172	68109	73859	78407	00933	77416	03080	24003	67863	08932	78888	70473	33734
74983	02581	74590	37440	41619	25672	91137	91920	94154	88743	08683	66045	53158	79852
39021	19176	19302	17698	77961	86850	47267	69571	82103	26958	48318	33175	93240	49019

TABLE A–2 The Binomial Distribution

n	x	0.05	0.1	0.2	0.25	0.3	0.4	0.5	0.6	0.7	0.75	0.8	0.9	0.95
								p						
2	0	0.902	0.810	0.640	0.563	0.490	0.360	0.250	0.160	0.090	0.063	0.040	0.010	0.002
	1	0.095	0.180	0.320	0.375	0.420	0.480	0.500	0.480	0.420	0.375	0.320	0.180	0.095
	2	0.002	0.010	0.040	0.063	0.090	0.160	0.250	0.360	0.490	0.563	0.640	0.810	0.902
3	0	0.857	0.729	0.512	0.422	0.343	0.216	0.125	0.064	0.027	0.016	0.008	0.001	
	1	0.135	0.243	0.384	0.422	0.441	0.432	0.375	0.288	0.189	0.141	0.096	0.027	0.007
	2	0.007	0.027	0.096	0.141	0.189	0.288	0.375	0.432	0.441	0.422	0.384	0.243	0.135
	3		0.001	0.008	0.016	0.027	0.064	0.125	0.216	0.343	0.422	0.512	0.729	0.857
4	0	0.815	0.656	0.410	0.316	0.240	0.130	0.062	0.026	0.008	0.004	0.002		
	1	0.171	0.292	0.410	0.422	0.412	0.346	0.250	0.154	0.076	0.047	0.026	0.004	
	2	0.014	0.049	0.154	0.211	0.265	0.346	0.375	0.346	0.265	0.211	0.154	0.049	0.014
	3		0.004	0.026	0.047	0.076	0.154	0.250	0.346	0.412	0.422	0.410	0.292	0.171
	4			0.002	0.004	0.008	0.026	0.062	0.130	0.240	0.316	0.410	0.656	0.815
5	0	0.774	0.590	0.328	0.237	0.168	0.078	0.031	0.010	0.002	0.001			
	1	0.204	0.328	0.410	0.396	0.360	0.259	0.156	0.077	0.028	0.015	0.006		
	2	0.021	0.073	0.205	0.264	0.309	0.346	0.312	0.230	0.132	0.088	0.051	0.008	0.001
	3	0.001	0.008	0.051	0.088	0.132	0.230	0.312	0.346	0.309	0.264	0.205	0.073	0.021
	4			0.006	0.015	0.028	0.077	0.156	0.259	0.360	0.396	0.410	0.328	0.204
	5				0.001	0.002	0.010	0.031	0.078	0.168	0.237	0.328	0.590	0.774
6	0	0.735	0.531	0.262	0.178	0.118	0.047	0.016	0.004	0.001				
	1	0.232	0.354	0.393	0.356	0.303	0.187	0.094	0.037	0.010	0.004	0.002		
	2	0.031	0.098	0.246	0.297	0.324	0.311	0.234	0.138	0.060	0.033	0.015	0.001	
	3	0.002	0.015	0.082	0.132	0.185	0.276	0.312	0.276	0.185	0.132	0.082	0.015	0.002
	4		0.001	0.015	0.033	0.060	0.138	0.234	0.311	0.324	0.297	0.246	0.098	0.031
	5			0.002	0.004	0.010	0.037	0.094	0.187	0.303	0.356	0.393	0.354	0.232
	6					0.001	0.004	0.016	0.047	0.118	0.178	0.262	0.531	0.735
7	0	0.698	0.478	0.210	0.133	0.082	0.028	0.008	0.002					
	1	0.257	0.372	0.367	0.311	0.247	0.131	0.055	0.017	0.004	0.001			
	2	0.041	0.124	0.275	0.311	0.318	0.261	0.164	0.077	0.025	0.012	0.004		
	3	0.004	0.023	0.115	0.173	0.227	0.290	0.273	0.194	0.097	0.058	0.029	0.003	
	4		0.003	0.029	0.058	0.097	0.194	0.273	0.290	0.227	0.173	0.115	0.023	0.004
	5			0.004	0.012	0.025	0.077	0.164	0.261	0.318	0.311	0.275	0.124	0.041
	6				0.001	0.004	0.017	0.055	0.131	0.247	0.311	0.367	0.372	0.257
	7						0.002	0.008	0.028	0.082	0.133	0.210	0.478	0.698
8	0	0.663	0.430	0.168	0.100	0.058	0.017	0.004	0.001					
	1	0.279	0.383	0.336	0.267	0.198	0.090	0.031	0.008	0.001				
	2	0.051	0.149	0.294	0.311	0.296	0.209	0.109	0.041	0.010	0.004	0.001		
	3	0.005	0.033	0.147	0.208	0.254	0.279	0.219	0.124	0.047	0.023	0.009		
	4		0.005	0.046	0.087	0.136	0.232	0.273	0.232	0.136	0.087	0.046	0.005	
	5			0.009	0.023	0.047	0.124	0.219	0.279	0.254	0.208	0.147	0.033	0.005
	6			0.001	0.004	0.010	0.041	0.109	0.209	0.296	0.311	0.294	0.149	0.051
	7					0.001	0.008	0.031	0.090	0.198	0.267	0.336	0.383	0.279
	8						0.001	0.004	0.017	0.058	0.100	0.168	0.430	0.663

TABLE A–2 *(continued)*

								p						
n	x	0.05	0.1	0.2	0.25	0.3	0.4	0.5	0.6	0.7	0.75	0.8	0.9	0.95
9	0	0.630	0.387	0.134	0.075	0.040	0.010	0.002						
	1	0.299	0.387	0.302	0.225	0.156	0.060	0.018	0.004					
	2	0.063	0.172	0.302	0.300	0.267	0.161	0.070	0.021	0.004	0.001			
	3	0.008	0.045	0.176	0.234	0.267	0.251	0.164	0.074	0.021	0.009	0.003		
	4	0.001	0.007	0.066	0.117	0.172	0.251	0.246	0.167	0.074	0.039	0.017	0.001	
	5		0.001	0.017	0.039	0.074	0.167	0.246	0.251	0.172	0.117	0.066	0.007	0.001
	6			0.003	0.009	0.021	0.074	0.164	0.251	0.267	0.234	0.176	0.045	0.008
	7				0.001	0.004	0.021	0.070	0.161	0.267	0.300	0.302	0.172	0.063
	8						0.004	0.018	0.060	0.156	0.225	0.302	0.387	0.299
	9							0.002	0.010	0.040	0.075	0.134	0.387	0.630
10	0	0.599	0.349	0.107	0.056	0.028	0.006	0.001						
	1	0.315	0.387	0.268	0.188	0.121	0.040	0.010	0.002					
	2	0.075	0.194	0.302	0.282	0.233	0.121	0.044	0.011	0.001				
	3	0.010	0.057	0.201	0.250	0.267	0.215	0.117	0.042	0.009	0.003	0.001		
	4	0.001	0.011	0.088	0.146	0.200	0.251	0.205	0.111	0.037	0.016	0.006		
	5		0.001	0.026	0.058	0.103	0.201	0.246	0.201	0.103	0.058	0.026	0.001	
	6			0.006	0.016	0.037	0.111	0.205	0.251	0.200	0.146	0.088	0.011	0.001
	7			0.001	0.003	0.009	0.042	0.117	0.215	0.267	0.250	0.201	0.057	0.010
	8					0.001	0.011	0.044	0.121	0.233	0.282	0.302	0.194	0.075
	9						0.002	0.010	0.040	0.121	0.188	0.268	0.387	0.315
	10							0.001	0.006	0.028	0.056	0.107	0.349	0.599
11	0	0.569	0.314	0.086	0.042	0.020	0.004							
	1	0.329	0.384	0.236	0.155	0.093	0.027	0.005	0.001					
	2	0.087	0.213	0.295	0.258	0.200	0.089	0.027	0.005	0.001				
	3	0.014	0.071	0.221	0.258	0.257	0.177	0.081	0.023	0.004	0.001			
	4	0.001	0.016	0.111	0.172	0.220	0.236	0.161	0.070	0.017	0.006	0.002		
	5		0.002	0.039	0.080	0.132	0.221	0.226	0.147	0.057	0.027	0.010		
	6			0.010	0.027	0.057	0.147	0.226	0.221	0.132	0.080	0.039	0.002	
	7			0.002	0.006	0.017	0.070	0.161	0.236	0.220	0.172	0.111	0.016	0.001
	8				0.001	0.004	0.023	0.081	0.177	0.257	0.258	0.221	0.071	0.014
	9					0.001	0.005	0.027	0.089	0.200	0.258	0.295	0.213	0.087
	10						0.001	0.005	0.027	0.093	0.155	0.236	0.384	0.329
	11								0.004	0.020	0.042	0.086	0.314	0.569
12	0	0.540	0.282	0.069	0.032	0.014	0.002							
	1	0.341	0.377	0.206	0.127	0.071	0.017	0.003						
	2	0.099	0.230	0.283	0.232	0.168	0.064	0.016	0.002					
	3	0.017	0.085	0.236	0.258	0.240	0.142	0.054	0.012	0.001				
	4	0.002	0.021	0.133	0.194	0.231	0.213	0.121	0.042	0.008	0.002	0.001		
	5		0.004	0.053	0.103	0.158	0.227	0.193	0.101	0.029	0.011	0.003		
	6			0.016	0.040	0.079	0.177	0.226	0.177	0.079	0.040	0.016		
	7			0.003	0.011	0.029	0.101	0.193	0.227	0.158	0.103	0.053	0.004	
	8			0.001	0.002	0.008	0.042	0.121	0.213	0.231	0.194	0.133	0.021	0.002
	9					0.001	0.012	0.054	0.142	0.240	0.258	0.236	0.085	0.017
	10						0.002	0.016	0.064	0.168	0.232	0.283	0.230	0.099
	11							0.003	0.017	0.071	0.127	0.206	0.377	0.341
	12								0.002	0.014	0.032	0.069	0.282	0.540

TABLE A-2 *(continued)*

								p						
n	x	0.05	0.1	0.2	0.25	0.3	0.4	0.5	0.6	0.7	0.75	0.8	0.9	0.95
13	0	0.513	0.254	0.055	0.024	0.010	0.001							
	1	0.351	0.367	0.179	0.103	0.054	0.011	0.002						
	2	0.111	0.245	0.268	0.206	0.139	0.045	0.010	0.001					
	3	0.021	0.100	0.246	0.252	0.218	0.111	0.035	0.006	0.001				
	4	0.003	0.028	0.154	0.210	0.234	0.184	0.087	0.024	0.003	0.001			
	5		0.006	0.069	0.126	0.180	0.221	0.157	0.066	0.014	0.005	0.001		
	6		0.001	0.023	0.056	0.103	0.197	0.209	0.131	0.044	0.019	0.006		
	7			0.006	0.019	0.044	0.131	0.209	0.197	0.103	0.056	0.023	0.001	
	8			0.001	0.005	0.014	0.066	0.157	0.221	0.180	0.126	0.069	0.006	
	9				0.001	0.003	0.024	0.087	0.184	0.234	0.210	0.154	0.028	0.003
	10					0.001	0.006	0.035	0.111	0.218	0.252	0.246	0.100	0.021
	11						0.001	0.010	0.045	0.139	0.206	0.268	0.245	0.111
	12							0.002	0.011	0.054	0.103	0.179	0.367	0.351
	13							0.001	0.010	0.024	0.055	0.254	0.513
14	0	0.488	0.229	0.044	0.018	0.007	0.001							
	1	0.359	0.356	0.154	0.083	0.041	0.007	0.001						
	2	0.123	0.257	0.250	0.180	0.113	0.032	0.006	0.001					
	3	0.026	0.114	0.250	0.240	0.194	0.085	0.022	0.003					
	4	0.004	0.035	0.172	0.220	0.229	0.155	0.061	0.014	0.001				
	5		0.008	0.086	0.147	0.196	0.207	0.122	0.041	0.007	0.002			
	6		0.001	0.032	0.073	0.126	0.207	0.183	0.092	0.023	0.008	0.002		
	7			0.009	0.028	0.062	0.157	0.209	0.157	0.062	0.028	0.009		
	8			0.002	0.008	0.023	0.092	0.183	0.207	0.126	0.073	0.032	0.001	
	9				0.002	0.007	0.041	0.122	0.207	0.196	0.147	0.086	0.008	
	10					0.001	0.014	0.061	0.155	0.229	0.220	0.172	0.035	0.004
	11						0.003	0.022	0.085	0.194	0.240	0.250	0.114	0.026
	12						0.001	0.006	0.032	0.113	0.180	0.250	0.257	0.123
	13							0.001	0.007	0.041	0.083	0.154	0.356	0.359
	14								0.001	0.007	0.018	0.044	0.229	0.488
15	0	0.463	0.206	0.035	0.013	0.005								
	1	0.366	0.343	0.132	0.067	0.031	0.005							
	2	0.135	0.267	0.231	0.156	0.092	0.022	0.003						
	3	0.031	0.129	0.250	0.225	0.170	0.063	0.014	0.002					
	4	0.005	0.043	0.188	0.225	0.219	0.127	0.042	0.007	0.001				
	5	0.001	0.010	0.103	0.165	0.206	0.186	0.092	0.024	0.003	0.001			
	6		0.002	0.043	0.092	0.147	0.207	0.153	0.061	0.012	0.003	0.001		
	7			0.014	0.039	0.081	0.177	0.196	0.118	0.035	0.013	0.003		
	8			0.003	0.013	0.035	0.118	0.196	0.177	0.081	0.039	0.014		
	9			0.001	0.003	0.012	0.061	0.153	0.207	0.147	0.092	0.043	0.002	
	10				0.001	0.003	0.024	0.092	0.186	0.206	0.165	0.103	0.010	0.001
	11					0.001	0.007	0.042	0.127	0.219	0.225	0.188	0.043	0.005
	12						0.002	0.014	0.063	0.170	0.225	0.250	0.129	0.031
	13							0.003	0.022	0.092	0.156	0.231	0.267	0.135
	14								0.005	0.031	0.067	0.132	0.343	0.366
	15									0.005	0.013	0.035	0.206	0.463

TABLE A–2 *(continued)*

								p						
n	x	0.05	0.1	0.2	0.25	0.3	0.4	0.5	0.6	0.7	0.75	0.8	0.9	0.95
16	0	0.440	0.185	0.028	0.010	0.003								
	1	0.371	0.329	0.113	0.053	0.023	0.003							
	2	0.146	0.275	0.211	0.134	0.073	0.015	0.002						
	3	0.036	0.142	0.246	0.208	0.146	0.047	0.009	0.001					
	4	0.006	0.051	0.200	0.225	0.204	0.101	0.028	0.004					
	5	0.001	0.014	0.120	0.180	0.210	0.162	0.067	0.014	0.001				
	6		0.003	0.055	0.110	0.165	0.198	0.122	0.039	0.006	0.001			
	7			0.020	0.052	0.101	0.189	0.175	0.084	0.019	0.006	0.001		
	8			0.006	0.020	0.049	0.142	0.196	0.142	0.049	0.020	0.006		
	9			0.001	0.006	0.019	0.084	0.175	0.189	0.101	0.052	0.020		
	10				0.001	0.006	0.039	0.122	0.198	0.165	0.110	0.055	0.003	
	11					0.001	0.014	0.067	0.162	0.210	0.180	0.120	0.014	0.001
	12						0.004	0.028	0.101	0.204	0.225	0.200	0.051	0.006
	13						0.001	0.009	0.047	0.146	0.208	0.246	0.142	0.036
	14							0.002	0.015	0.073	0.134	0.211	0.275	0.146
	15								0.003	0.023	0.053	0.113	0.329	0.371
	16									0.003	0.010	0.028	0.185	0.440
17	0	0.418	0.167	0.023	0.008	0.002								
	1	0.374	0.315	0.096	0.043	0.017	0.002							
	2	0.158	0.280	0.191	0.114	0.058	0.010	0.001						
	3	0.041	0.156	0.239	0.189	0.125	0.034	0.005						
	4	0.008	0.060	0.209	0.221	0.187	0.080	0.018	0.002					
	5	0.001	0.017	0.136	0.191	0.208	0.138	0.047	0.008	0.001				
	6		0.004	0.068	0.128	0.178	0.184	0.094	0.024	0.003	0.001			
	7		0.001	0.027	0.067	0.120	0.193	0.148	0.057	0.009	0.002			
	8			0.008	0.028	0.064	0.161	0.185	0.107	0.028	0.009	0.002		
	9			0.002	0.009	0.028	0.107	0.185	0.161	0.064	0.028	0.008		
	10				0.002	0.009	0.057	0.148	0.193	0.120	0.067	0.027	0.001	
	11					0.001	0.003	0.024	0.094	0.184	0.178	0.128	0.068	0.004
	12						0.001	0.008	0.047	0.138	0.208	0.191	0.136	0.017	0.001
	13							0.002	0.018	0.080	0.187	0.221	0.209	0.060	0.008
	14								0.005	0.034	0.125	0.189	0.239	0.156	0.041
	15								0.001	0.010	0.058	0.114	0.191	0.280	0.158
	16									0.002	0.017	0.043	0.096	0.315	0.374
	17										0.002	0.008	0.023	0.167	0.418

TABLE A-2 *(continued)*

n	x	0.05	0.1	0.2	0.25	0.3	0.4	0.5	0.6	0.7	0.75	0.8	0.9	0.95
								p						
18	0	0.397	0.150	0.018	0.006	0.002								
	1	0.376	0.300	0.081	0.034	0.013	0.001							
	2	0.168	0.284	0.172	0.096	0.046	0.007	0.001						
	3	0.047	0.168	0.230	0.170	0.105	0.025	0.003						
	4	0.009	0.070	0.215	0.213	0.168	0.061	0.012	0.001					
	5	0.001	0.022	0.151	0.199	0.202	0.115	0.033	0.004					
	6		0.005	0.082	0.144	0.187	0.166	0.071	0.015	0.001				
	7		0.001	0.035	0.082	0.138	0.189	0.121	0.037	0.005	0.001			
	8			0.012	0.038	0.081	0.173	0.167	0.077	0.015	0.004	0.001		
	9			0.003	0.014	0.039	0.128	0.185	0.128	0.039	0.014	0.003		
	10			0.001	0.004	0.015	0.077	0.167	0.173	0.081	0.038	0.012		
	11				0.001	0.005	0.037	0.121	0.189	0.138	0.082	0.035	0.001	
	12					0.001	0.015	0.071	0.166	0.187	0.144	0.082	0.005	
	13						0.004	0.033	0.115	0.202	0.199	0.151	0.022	0.001
	14						0.001	0.012	0.061	0.168	0.213	0.215	0.070	0.009
	15							0.003	0.025	0.105	0.170	0.230	0.168	0.047
	16							0.001	0.007	0.046	0.096	0.172	0.284	0.168
	17								0.001	0.013	0.034	0.081	0.300	0.376
	18									0.002	0.006	0.018	0.150	0.397
19	0	0.377	0.135	0.014	0.004	0.001								
	1	0.377	0.285	0.068	0.027	0.009	0.001							
	2	0.179	0.285	0.154	0.080	0.036	0.005							
	3	0.053	0.180	0.218	0.152	0.087	0.017	0.002						
	4	0.011	0.080	0.218	0.202	0.149	0.047	0.007	0.001					
	5	0.002	0.027	0.164	0.202	0.192	0.093	0.022	0.002					
	6		0.007	0.095	0.157	0.192	0.145	0.052	0.008	0.001				
	7		0.001	0.044	0.097	0.153	0.180	0.096	0.024	0.002				
	8			0.017	0.049	0.098	0.180	0.144	0.053	0.008	0.002			
	9			0.005	0.020	0.051	0.146	0.176	0.098	0.022	0.007	0.001		
	10			0.001	0.007	0.022	0.098	0.176	0.146	0.051	0.020	0.005		
	11				0.002	0.008	0.053	0.144	0.180	0.098	0.049	0.071		
	12					0.002	0.024	0.096	0.180	0.153	0.097	0.044	0.001	
	13					0.001	0.008	0.052	0.145	0.192	0.157	0.095	0.007	
	14						0.002	0.022	0.093	0.192	0.202	0.164	0.027	0.002
	15						0.001	0.007	0.047	0.149	0.202	0.218	0.080	0.011
	16							0.002	0.017	0.087	0.152	0.218	0.180	0.053
	17								0.005	0.036	0.080	0.154	0.285	0.179
	18								0.001	0.009	0.027	0.068	0.285	0.377
	19									0.001	0.004	0.014	0.135	0.377

TABLE A–2 *(concluded)*

n	x	0.05	0.1	0.2	0.25	0.3	0.4	0.5	0.6	0.7	0.75	0.8	0.9	0.95
20	0	0.358	0.122	0.012	0.003	0.001								
	1	0.377	0.270	0.058	0.021	0.007								
	2	0.189	0.285	0.137	0.067	0.028	0.003							
	3	0.060	0.190	0.205	0.134	0.072	0.012	0.001						
	4	0.013	0.090	0.218	0.190	0.130	0.035	0.005						
	5	0.002	0.032	0.175	0.202	0.179	0.075	0.015	0.001					
	6		0.009	0.109	0.169	0.192	0.124	0.037	0.005					
	7		0.002	0.055	0.112	0.164	0.166	0.074	0.015	0.001				
	8			0.022	0.061	0.114	0.180	0.120	0.035	0.004	0.001			
	9			0.007	0.027	0.065	0.160	0.160	0.071	0.012	0.003			
	10			0.002	0.010	0.031	0.117	0.176	0.117	0.031	0.010	0.002		
	11				0.003	0.012	0.071	0.160	0.160	0.065	0.027	0.007		
	12				0.001	0.004	0.035	0.120	0.180	0.114	0.061	0.022		
	13					0.001	0.015	0.074	0.166	0.164	0.112	0.055	0.002	
	14						0.005	0.037	0.124	0.192	0.169	0.109	0.009	
	15						0.001	0.015	0.075	0.179	0.202	0.175	0.032	0.002
	16							0.005	0.035	0.130	0.190	0.218	0.090	0.013
	17							0.001	0.012	0.072	0.134	0.205	0.190	0.060
	18								0.003	0.028	0.067	0.137	0.285	0.189
	19									0.007	0.021	0.058	0.270	0.377
	20									0.001	0.003	0.012	0.122	0.358

Note: All values of 0.0005 or less are omitted.

TABLE A–3 The Poisson Distribution

x	0.1	0.2	0.3	0.4	0.5	0.6	0.7	0.8	0.9
0	0.9048	0.8187	0.7408	0.6703	0.6065	0.5488	0.4966	0.4493	0.4066
1	0.0905	0.1637	0.2222	0.2681	0.3033	0.3293	0.3476	0.3595	0.3659
2	0.0045	0.0164	0.0333	0.0536	0.0758	0.0988	0.1217	0.1438	0.1647
3	0.0002	0.0011	0.0033	0.0072	0.0126	0.0198	0.0284	0.0383	0.0494
4	0.0000	0.0001	0.0003	0.0007	0.0016	0.0030	0.0050	0.0077	0.0111
5	0.0000	0.0000	0.0000	0.0001	0.0002	0.0004	0.0007	0.0012	0.0020
6	0.0000	0.0000	0.0000	0.0000	0.0000	0.0000	0.0001	0.0002	0.0003
7	0.0000	0.0000	0.0000	0.0000	0.0000	0.0000	0.0000	0.0000	0.0000

x	1	2	3	4	5	6	7	8	9	10
0	0.3679	0.1353	0.0498	0.0183	0.0067	0.0025	0.0009	0.0003	0.0001	0.0000
1	0.3679	0.2707	0.1494	0.0733	0.0337	0.0149	0.0064	0.0027	0.0011	0.0005
2	0.1839	0.2707	0.2240	0.1465	0.0842	0.0446	0.0223	0.0107	0.0050	0.0023
3	0.0613	0.1804	0.2240	0.1954	0.1404	0.0892	0.0521	0.0286	0.0150	0.0076
4	0.0153	0.0902	0.1680	0.1954	0.1755	0.1339	0.0912	0.0573	0.0337	0.0189
5	0.0031	0.0361	0.1008	0.1563	0.1755	0.1606	0.1277	0.0916	0.0607	0.0378
6	0.0005	0.0120	0.0504	0.1042	0.1462	0.1606	0.1490	0.1221	0.0911	0.0631
7	0.0001	0.0034	0.0216	0.0595	0.1044	0.1377	0.1490	0.1396	0.1171	0.0901
8	0.0000	0.0009	0.0081	0.0298	0.0653	0.1033	0.1304	0.1396	0.1318	0.1126
9	0.0000	0.0002	0.0027	0.0132	0.0363	0.0688	0.1014	0.1241	0.1318	0.1251
10	0.0000	0.0000	0.0008	0.0053	0.0181	0.0413	0.0710	0.0993	0.1186	0.1251
11	0.0000	0.0000	0.0002	0.0019	0.0082	0.0225	0.0452	0.0722	0.0970	0.1137
12	0.0000	0.0000	0.0001	0.0006	0.0034	0.0113	0.0263	0.0481	0.0728	0.0948
13	0.0000	0.0000	0.0000	0.0002	0.0013	0.0052	0.0142	0.0296	0.0504	0.0729
14	0.0000	0.0000	0.0000	0.0001	0.0005	0.0022	0.0071	0.0169	0.0324	0.0521
15	0.0000	0.0000	0.0000	0.0000	0.0002	0.0009	0.0033	0.0090	0.0194	0.0347
16	0.0000	0.0000	0.0000	0.0000	0.0000	0.0003	0.0014	0.0045	0.0109	0.0217
17	0.0000	0.0000	0.0000	0.0000	0.0000	0.0001	0.0006	0.0021	0.0058	0.0128
18	0.0000	0.0000	0.0000	0.0000	0.0000	0.0000	0.0002	0.0009	0.0029	0.0071

TABLE A-3 *(continued)*

					λ					
x	**11**	**12**	**13**	**14**	**15**	**16**	**17**	**18**	**19**	**20**
0	0.0000	0.0000	0.0000	0.0000	0.0000	0.0000	0.0000	0.0000	0.0000	0.0000
1	0.0002	0.0001	0.0000	0.0000	0.0000	0.0000	0.0000	0.0000	0.0000	0.0000
2	0.0010	0.0004	0.0002	0.0001	0.0000	0.0000	0.0000	0.0000	0.0000	0.0000
3	0.0037	0.0018	0.0008	0.0004	0.0002	0.0001	0.0000	0.0000	0.0000	0.0000
4	0.0102	0.0053	0.0027	0.0013	0.0006	0.0003	0.0001	0.0001	0.0000	0.0000
5	0.0224	0.0127	0.0070	0.0037	0.0019	0.0010	0.0005	0.0002	0.0001	0.0001
6	0.0411	0.0255	0.0152	0.0087	0.0048	0.0026	0.0014	0.0007	0.0004	0.0002
7	0.0646	0.0437	0.0281	0.0174	0.0104	0.0060	0.0034	0.0019	0.0010	0.0005
8	0.0888	0.0655	0.0457	0.0304	0.0194	0.0120	0.0072	0.0042	0.0024	0.0013
9	0.1085	0.0874	0.0661	0.0473	0.0324	0.0213	0.0135	0.0083	0.0050	0.0029
10	0.1194	0.1048	0.0859	0.0663	0.0486	0.0341	0.0230	0.0150	0.0095	0.0058
11	0.1194	0.1144	0.1015	0.0844	0.0663	0.0496	0.0355	0.0245	0.0164	0.0106
12	0.1094	0.1144	0.1099	0.0984	0.0829	0.0661	0.0504	0.0368	0.0259	0.0176
13	0.0926	0.1056	0.1099	0.1060	0.0956	0.0814	0.0658	0.0509	0.0378	0.0271
14	0.0728	0.0905	0.1021	0.1060	0.1024	0.0930	0.0800	0.0655	0.0514	0.0387
15	0.0534	0.0724	0.0885	0.0989	0.1024	0.0992	0.0906	0.0786	0.0650	0.0516
16	0.0367	0.0543	0.0719	0.0866	0.0960	0.0992	0.0963	0.0884	0.0772	0.0646
17	0.0237	0.0383	0.0550	0.0713	0.0847	0.0934	0.0963	0.0936	0.0863	0.0760
18	0.0145	0.0255	0.0397	0.0554	0.0706	0.0830	0.0909	0.0936	0.0911	0.0844
19	0.0084	0.0161	0.0272	0.0409	0.0557	0.0699	0.0814	0.0887	0.0911	0.0888
20	0.0046	0.0097	0.0177	0.0286	0.0418	0.0559	0.0692	0.0798	0.0866	0.0888
21	0.0024	0.0055	0.0109	0.0191	0.0299	0.0426	0.0560	0.0684	0.0783	0.0846
22	0.0012	0.0030	0.0065	0.0121	0.0204	0.0310	0.0433	0.0560	0.0676	0.0769
23	0.0006	0.0016	0.0037	0.0074	0.0133	0.0216	0.0320	0.0438	0.0559	0.0669
24	0.0003	0.0008	0.0020	0.0043	0.0083	0.0144	0.0226	0.0328	0.0442	0.0557
25	0.0001	0.0004	0.0010	0.0024	0.0050	0.0092	0.0154	0.0237	0.0336	0.0446
26	0.0000	0.0002	0.0005	0.0013	0.0029	0.0057	0.0101	0.0164	0.0246	0.0343
27	0.0000	0.0001	0.0002	0.0007	0.0016	0.0034	0.0063	0.0109	0.0173	0.0254
28	0.0000	0.0000	0.0001	0.0003	0.0009	0.0019	0.0038	0.0070	0.0117	0.0181
29	0.0000	0.0000	0.0001	0.0002	0.0004	0.0011	0.0023	0.0044	0.0077	0.0125
30	0.0000	0.0000	0.0000	0.0001	0.0002	0.0006	0.0013	0.0026	0.0049	0.0083
31	0.0000	0.0000	0.0000	0.0000	0.0001	0.0003	0.0007	0.0015	0.0030	0.0054
32	0.0000	0.0000	0.0000	0.0000	0.0001	0.0001	0.0004	0.0009	0.0018	0.0034
33	0.0000	0.0000	0.0000	0.0000	0.0000	0.0001	0.0002	0.0005	0.0010	0.0020
34	0.0000	0.0000	0.0000	0.0000	0.0000	0.0000	0.0001	0.0002	0.0006	0.0012
35	0.0000	0.0000	0.0000	0.0000	0.0000	0.0000	0.0000	0.0001	0.0003	0.0007

TABLE A–4 The Standard Normal Distribution

Cumulative Standard Normal Distribution

z	.00	.01	.02	.03	.04	.05	.06	.07	.08	.09
−3.4	.0003	.0003	.0003	.0003	.0003	.0003	.0003	.0003	.0003	.0002
−3.3	.0005	.0005	.0005	.0004	.0004	.0004	.0004	.0004	.0004	.0003
−3.2	.0007	.0007	.0006	.0006	.0006	.0006	.0006	.0005	.0005	.0005
−3.1	.0010	.0009	.0009	.0009	.0008	.0008	.0008	.0008	.0007	.0007
−3.0	.0013	.0013	.0013	.0012	.0012	.0011	.0011	.0011	.0010	.0010
−2.9	.0019	.0018	.0018	.0017	.0016	.0016	.0015	.0015	.0014	.0014
−2.8	.0026	.0025	.0024	.0023	.0023	.0022	.0021	.0021	.0020	.0019
−2.7	.0035	.0034	.0033	.0032	.0031	.0030	.0029	.0028	.0027	.0026
−2.6	.0047	.0045	.0044	.0043	.0041	.0040	.0039	.0038	.0037	.0036
−2.5	.0062	.0060	.0059	.0057	.0055	.0054	.0052	.0051	.0049	.0048
−2.4	.0082	.0080	.0078	.0075	.0073	.0071	.0069	.0068	.0066	.0064
−2.3	.0107	.0104	.0102	.0099	.0096	.0094	.0091	.0089	.0087	.0084
−2.2	.0139	.0136	.0132	.0129	.0125	.0122	.0119	.0116	.0113	.0110
−2.1	.0179	.0174	.0170	.0166	.0162	.0158	.0154	.0150	.0146	.0143
−2.0	.0228	.0222	.0217	.0212	.0207	.0202	.0197	.0192	.0188	.0183
−1.9	.0287	.0281	.0274	.0268	.0262	.0256	.0250	.0244	.0239	.0233
−1.8	.0359	.0351	.0344	.0336	.0329	.0322	.0314	.0307	.0301	.0294
−1.7	.0446	.0436	.0427	.0418	.0409	.0401	.0392	.0384	.0375	.0367
−1.6	.0548	.0537	.0526	.0516	.0505	.0495	.0485	.0475	.0465	.0455
−1.5	.0668	.0655	.0643	.0630	.0618	.0606	.0594	.0582	.0571	.0559
−1.4	.0808	.0793	.0778	.0764	.0749	.0735	.0721	.0708	.0694	.0681
−1.3	.0968	.0951	.0934	.0918	.0901	.0885	.0869	.0853	.0838	.0823
−1.2	.1151	.1131	.1112	.1093	.1075	.1056	.1038	.1020	.1003	.0985
−1.1	.1357	.1335	.1314	.1292	.1271	.1251	.1230	.1210	.1190	.1170
−1.0	.1587	.1562	.1539	.1515	.1492	.1469	.1446	.1423	.1401	.1379
−0.9	.1841	.1814	.1788	.1762	.1736	.1711	.1685	.1660	.1635	.1611
−0.8	.2119	.2090	.2061	.2033	.2005	.1977	.1949	.1922	.1894	.1867
−0.7	.2420	.2389	.2358	.2327	.2296	.2266	.2236	.2206	.2177	.2148
−0.6	.2743	.2709	.2676	.2643	.2611	.2578	.2546	.2514	.2483	.2451
−0.5	.3085	.3050	.3015	.2981	.2946	.2912	.2877	.2843	.2810	.2776
−0.4	.3446	.3409	.3372	.3336	.3300	.3264	.3228	.3192	.3156	.3121
−0.3	.3821	.3783	.3745	.3707	.3669	.3632	.3594	.3557	.3520	.3483
−0.2	.4207	.4168	.4129	.4090	.4052	.4013	.3974	.3936	.3897	.3859
−0.1	.4602	.4562	.4522	.4483	.4443	.4404	.4364	.4325	.4286	.4247
−0.0	.5000	.4960	.4920	.4880	.4840	.4801	.4761	.4721	.4681	.4641

For z scores less than −3.49, use 0.0001.

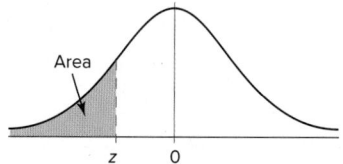

Area

z   0

TABLE A–4 *(continued)*

Cumulative Standard Normal Distribution

z	.00	.01	.02	.03	.04	.05	.06	.07	.08	.09
0.0	.5000	.5040	.5080	.5120	.5160	.5199	.5239	.5279	.5319	.5359
0.1	.5398	.5438	.5478	.5517	.5557	.5596	.5636	.5675	.5714	.5753
0.2	.5793	.5832	.5871	.5910	.5948	.5987	.6026	.6064	.6103	.6141
0.3	.6179	.6217	.6255	.6293	.6331	.6368	.6406	.6443	.6480	.6517
0.4	.6554	.6591	.6628	.6664	.6700	.6736	.6772	.6808	.6844	.6879
0.5	.6915	.6950	.6985	.7019	.7054	.7088	.7123	.7157	.7190	.7224
0.6	.7257	.7291	.7324	.7357	.7389	.7422	.7454	.7486	.7517	.7549
0.7	.7580	.7611	.7642	.7673	.7704	.7734	.7764	.7794	.7823	.7852
0.8	.7881	.7910	.7939	.7967	.7995	.8023	.8051	.8078	.8106	.8133
0.9	.8159	.8186	.8212	.8238	.8264	.8289	.8315	.8340	.8365	.8389
1.0	.8413	.8438	.8461	.8485	.8508	.8531	.8554	.8577	.8599	.8621
1.1	.8643	.8665	.8686	.8708	.8729	.8749	.8770	.8790	.8810	.8830
1.2	.8849	.8869	.8888	.8907	.8925	.8944	.8962	.8980	.8997	.9015
1.3	.9032	.9049	.9066	.9082	.9099	.9115	.9131	.9147	.9162	.9177
1.4	.9192	.9207	.9222	.9236	.9251	.9265	.9279	.9292	.9306	.9319
1.5	.9332	.9345	.9357	.9370	.9382	.9394	.9406	.9418	.9429	.9441
1.6	.9452	.9463	.9474	.9484	.9495	.9505	.9515	.9525	.9535	.9545
1.7	.9554	.9564	.9573	.9582	.9591	.9599	.9608	.9616	.9625	.9633
1.8	.9641	.9649	.9656	.9664	.9671	.9678	.9686	.9693	.9699	.9706
1.9	.9713	.9719	.9726	.9732	.9738	.9744	.9750	.9756	.9761	.9767
2.0	.9772	.9778	.9783	.9788	.9793	.9798	.9803	.9808	.9812	.9817
2.1	.9821	.9826	.9830	.9834	.9838	.9842	.9846	.9850	.9854	.9857
2.2	.9861	.9864	.9868	.9871	.9875	.9878	.9881	.9884	.9887	.9890
2.3	.9893	.9896	.9898	.9901	.9904	.9906	.9909	.9911	.9913	.9916
2.4	.9918	.9920	.9922	.9925	.9927	.9929	.9931	.9932	.9934	.9936
2.5	.9938	.9940	.9941	.9943	.9945	.9946	.9948	.9949	.9951	.9952
2.6	.9953	.9955	.9956	.9957	.9959	.9960	.9961	.9962	.9963	.9964
2.7	.9965	.9966	.9967	.9968	.9969	.9970	.9971	.9972	.9973	.9974
2.8	.9974	.9975	.9976	.9977	.9977	.9978	.9979	.9979	.9980	.9981
2.9	.9981	.9982	.9982	.9983	.9984	.9984	.9985	.9985	.9986	.9986
3.0	.9987	.9987	.9987	.9988	.9988	.9989	.9989	.9989	.9990	.9990
3.1	.9990	.9991	.9991	.9991	.9992	.9992	.9992	.9992	.9993	.9993
3.2	.9993	.9993	.9994	.9994	.9994	.9994	.9994	.9995	.9995	.9995
3.3	.9995	.9995	.9995	.9996	.9996	.9996	.9996	.9996	.9996	.9997
3.4	.9997	.9997	.9997	.9997	.9997	.9997	.9997	.9997	.9997	.9998

For *z* scores greater than 3.49, use 0.9999.

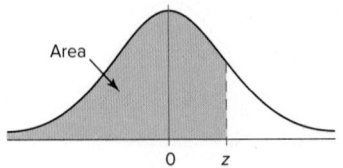

TABLE A–5 The *t* Distribution

d.f.	Confidence intervals	80%	90%	95%	98%	99%
	One tail, α	0.10	0.05	0.025	0.01	0.005
	Two tails, α	0.20	0.10	0.05	0.02	0.01
1		3.078	6.314	12.706	31.821	63.657
2		1.886	2.920	4.303	6.965	9.925
3		1.638	2.353	3.182	4.541	5.841
4		1.533	2.132	2.776	3.747	4.604
5		1.476	2.015	2.571	3.365	4.032
6		1.440	1.943	2.447	3.143	3.707
7		1.415	1.895	2.365	2.998	3.499
8		1.397	1.860	2.306	2.896	3.355
9		1.383	1.833	2.262	2.821	3.250
10		1.372	1.812	2.228	2.764	3.169
11		1.363	1.796	2.201	2.718	3.106
12		1.356	1.782	2.179	2.681	3.055
13		1.350	1.771	2.160	2.650	3.012
14		1.345	1.761	2.145	2.624	2.977
15		1.341	1.753	2.131	2.602	2.947
16		1.337	1.746	2.120	2.583	2.921
17		1.333	1.740	2.110	2.567	2.898
18		1.330	1.734	2.101	2.552	2.878
19		1.328	1.729	2.093	2.539	2.861
20		1.325	1.725	2.086	2.528	2.845
21		1.323	1.721	2.080	2.518	2.831
22		1.321	1.717	2.074	2.508	2.819
23		1.319	1.714	2.069	2.500	2.807
24		1.318	1.711	2.064	2.492	2.797
25		1.316	1.708	2.060	2.485	2.787
26		1.315	1.706	2.056	2.479	2.779
27		1.314	1.703	2.052	2.473	2.771
28		1.313	1.701	2.048	2.467	2.763
29		1.311	1.699	2.045	2.462	2.756
30		1.310	1.697	2.042	2.457	2.750
32		1.309	1.694	2.037	2.449	2.738
34		1.307	1.691	2.032	2.441	2.728
36		1.306	1.688	2.028	2.434	2.719
38		1.304	1.686	2.024	2.429	2.712
40		1.303	1.684	2.021	2.423	2.704
45		1.301	1.679	2.014	2.412	2.690
50		1.299	1.676	2.009	2.403	2.678
55		1.297	1.673	2.004	2.396	2.668
60		1.296	1.671	2.000	2.390	2.660
65		1.295	1.669	1.997	2.385	2.654
70		1.294	1.667	1.994	2.381	2.648
75		1.293	1.665	1.992	2.377	2.643
80		1.292	1.664	1.990	2.374	2.639
85		1.292	1.663	1.988	2.371	2.635
90		1.291	1.662	1.987	2.368	2.632
95		1.291	1.661	1.985	2.366	2.629
100		1.290	1.660	1.984	2.364	2.626
200		1.286	1.653	1.972	2.345	2.601
300		1.284	1.650	1.968	2.339	2.592
400		1.284	1.649	1.966	2.336	2.588
500		1.283	1.648	1.965	2.334	2.586
$(z)\infty$		1.282^a	1.645^b	1.960	2.326^c	2.576^d

[a]This value has been rounded to 1.28 in the textbook.
[b]This value has been rounded to 1.65 in the textbook.
[c]This value has been rounded to 2.33 in the textbook.
[d]This value has been rounded to 2.58 in the textbook.

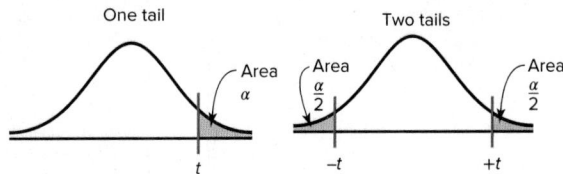

TABLE A–6 The Chi-Square Distribution

Degrees of freedom	α									
	0.995	0.99	0.975	0.95	0.90	0.10	0.05	0.025	0.01	0.005
1	—	—	0.001	0.004	0.016	2.706	3.841	5.024	6.635	7.879
2	0.010	0.020	0.051	0.103	0.211	4.605	5.991	7.378	9.210	10.597
3	0.072	0.115	0.216	0.352	0.584	6.251	7.815	9.348	11.345	12.838
4	0.207	0.297	0.484	0.711	1.064	7.779	9.488	11.143	13.277	14.860
5	0.412	0.554	0.831	1.145	1.610	9.236	11.071	12.833	15.086	16.750
6	0.676	0.872	1.237	1.635	2.204	10.645	12.592	14.449	16.812	18.548
7	0.989	1.239	1.690	2.167	2.833	12.017	14.067	16.013	18.475	20.278
8	1.344	1.646	2.180	2.733	3.490	13.362	15.507	17.535	20.090	21.955
9	1.735	2.088	2.700	3.325	4.168	14.684	16.919	19.023	21.666	23.589
10	2.156	2.558	3.247	3.940	4.865	15.987	18.307	20.483	23.209	25.188
11	2.603	3.053	3.816	4.575	5.578	17.275	19.675	21.920	24.725	26.757
12	3.074	3.571	4.404	5.226	6.304	18.549	21.026	23.337	26.217	28.300
13	3.565	4.107	5.009	5.892	7.042	19.812	22.362	24.736	27.688	29.819
14	4.075	4.660	5.629	6.571	7.790	21.064	23.685	26.119	29.141	31.319
15	4.601	5.229	6.262	7.261	8.547	22.307	24.996	27.488	30.578	32.801
16	5.142	5.812	6.908	7.962	9.312	23.542	26.296	28.845	32.000	34.267
17	5.697	6.408	7.564	8.672	10.085	24.769	27.587	30.191	33.409	35.718
18	6.265	7.015	8.231	9.390	10.865	25.989	28.869	31.526	34.805	37.156
19	6.844	7.633	8.907	10.117	11.651	27.204	30.144	32.852	36.191	38.582
20	7.434	8.260	9.591	10.851	12.443	28.412	31.410	34.170	37.566	39.997
21	8.034	8.897	10.283	11.591	13.240	29.615	32.671	35.479	38.932	41.401
22	8.643	9.542	10.982	12.338	14.042	30.813	33.924	36.781	40.289	42.796
23	9.262	10.196	11.689	13.091	14.848	32.007	35.172	38.076	41.638	44.181
24	9.886	10.856	12.401	13.848	15.659	33.196	36.415	39.364	42.980	45.559
25	10.520	11.524	13.120	14.611	16.473	34.382	37.652	40.646	44.314	46.928
26	11.160	12.198	13.844	15.379	17.292	35.563	38.885	41.923	45.642	48.290
27	11.808	12.879	14.573	16.151	18.114	36.741	40.113	43.194	46.963	49.645
28	12.461	13.565	15.308	16.928	18.939	37.916	41.337	44.461	48.278	50.993
29	13.121	14.257	16.047	17.708	19.768	39.087	42.557	45.722	49.588	52.336
30	13.787	14.954	16.791	18.493	20.599	40.256	43.773	46.979	50.892	53.672
40	20.707	22.164	24.433	26.509	29.051	51.805	55.758	59.342	63.691	66.766
50	27.991	29.707	32.357	34.764	37.689	63.167	67.505	71.420	76.154	79.490

Source: Values were calculated with Excel.

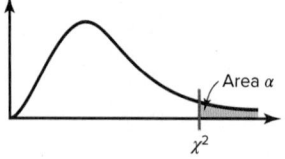

TABLE A–7 The F Distribution

$\alpha = 0.005$

d.f.D.: degrees of freedom, denominator	\multicolumn{17}{c}{d.f.N.: degrees of freedom, numerator}																
	1	2	3	4	5	6	7	8	9	10	12	15	20	24	30	40	60
1	16,211	20,000	21,615	22,500	23,056	23,437	23,715	23,925	24,091	24,224	24,426	24,630	24,836	24,940	25,044	25,148	25,253
2	198.5	199.0	199.2	199.2	199.3	199.3	199.4	199.4	199.4	199.4	199.4	199.4	199.4	199.5	199.5	199.5	199.5
3	55.55	49.80	47.47	46.19	45.39	44.84	44.43	44.13	43.88	43.69	43.39	43.08	42.78	42.62	42.47	42.31	42.15
4	31.33	26.28	24.26	23.15	22.46	21.97	21.62	21.35	21.14	20.97	20.70	20.44	20.17	20.03	19.89	19.75	19.61
5	22.78	18.31	16.53	15.56	14.94	14.51	14.20	13.96	13.77	13.62	13.38	13.15	12.90	12.78	12.66	12.53	12.40
6	18.63	14.54	12.92	12.03	11.46	11.07	10.79	10.57	10.39	10.25	10.03	9.81	9.59	9.47	9.36	9.24	9.12
7	16.24	12.40	10.88	10.05	9.52	9.16	8.89	8.68	8.51	8.38	8.18	7.97	7.75	7.65	7.53	7.42	7.31
8	14.69	11.04	9.60	8.81	8.30	7.95	7.69	7.50	7.34	7.21	7.01	6.81	6.61	6.50	6.40	6.29	6.18
9	13.61	10.11	8.72	7.96	7.47	7.13	6.88	6.69	6.54	6.42	6.23	6.03	5.83	5.73	5.62	5.52	5.41
10	12.83	9.43	8.08	7.34	6.87	6.54	6.30	6.12	5.97	5.85	5.66	5.47	5.27	5.17	5.07	4.97	4.86
11	12.23	8.91	7.60	6.88	6.42	6.10	5.86	5.68	5.54	5.42	5.24	5.05	4.86	4.76	4.65	4.55	4.44
12	11.75	8.51	7.23	6.52	6.07	5.76	5.52	5.35	5.20	5.09	4.91	4.72	4.53	4.43	4.33	4.23	4.12
13	11.37	8.19	6.93	6.23	5.79	5.48	5.25	5.08	4.94	4.82	4.64	4.46	4.27	4.17	4.07	3.97	3.87
14	11.06	7.92	6.68	6.00	5.56	5.26	5.03	4.86	4.72	4.60	4.43	4.25	4.06	3.96	3.86	3.76	3.66
15	10.80	7.70	6.48	5.80	5.37	5.07	4.85	4.67	4.54	4.42	4.25	4.07	3.88	3.79	3.69	3.58	3.48
16	10.58	7.51	6.30	5.64	5.21	4.91	4.69	4.52	4.38	4.27	4.10	3.92	3.73	3.64	3.54	3.44	3.33
17	10.38	7.35	6.16	5.50	5.07	4.78	4.56	4.39	4.25	4.14	3.97	3.79	3.61	3.51	3.41	3.31	3.21
18	10.22	7.21	6.03	5.37	4.96	4.66	4.44	4.28	4.14	4.03	3.86	3.68	3.50	3.40	3.30	3.20	3.10
19	10.07	7.09	5.92	5.27	4.85	4.56	4.34	4.18	4.04	3.93	3.76	3.59	3.40	3.31	3.21	3.11	3.00
20	9.94	6.99	5.82	5.17	4.76	4.47	4.26	4.09	3.96	3.85	3.68	3.50	3.32	3.22	3.12	3.02	2.92
21	9.83	6.89	5.73	5.09	4.68	4.39	4.18	4.01	3.88	3.77	3.60	3.43	3.24	3.15	3.05	2.95	2.84
22	9.73	6.81	5.65	5.02	4.61	4.32	4.11	3.94	3.81	3.70	3.54	3.36	3.18	3.08	2.98	2.88	2.77
23	9.63	6.73	5.58	4.95	4.54	4.26	4.05	3.88	3.75	3.64	3.47	3.30	3.12	3.02	2.92	2.82	2.71
24	9.55	6.66	5.52	4.89	4.49	4.20	3.99	3.83	3.69	3.59	3.42	3.25	3.06	2.97	2.87	2.77	2.66
25	9.48	6.60	5.46	4.84	4.43	4.15	3.94	3.78	3.64	3.54	3.37	3.20	3.01	2.92	2.82	2.72	2.61
26	9.41	6.54	5.41	4.79	4.38	4.10	3.89	3.73	3.60	3.49	3.33	3.15	2.97	2.87	2.77	2.67	2.56
27	9.34	6.49	5.36	4.74	4.34	4.06	3.85	3.69	3.56	3.45	3.28	3.11	2.93	2.83	2.73	2.63	2.52
28	9.28	6.44	5.32	4.70	4.30	4.02	3.81	3.65	3.52	3.41	3.25	3.07	2.89	2.79	2.69	2.59	2.48
29	9.23	6.40	5.28	4.66	4.26	3.98	3.77	3.61	3.48	3.38	3.21	3.04	2.86	2.76	2.66	2.56	2.45
30	9.18	6.35	5.24	4.62	4.23	3.95	3.74	3.58	3.45	3.34	3.18	3.01	2.82	2.73	2.63	2.52	2.42
40	8.83	6.07	4.98	4.37	3.99	3.71	3.51	3.35	3.22	3.12	2.95	2.78	2.60	2.50	2.40	2.30	2.18
60	8.49	5.79	4.73	4.14	3.76	3.49	3.29	3.13	3.01	2.90	2.74	2.57	2.39	2.29	2.19	2.08	1.96

TABLE A–7 (continued)

$\alpha = 0.01$

d.f.D.: degrees of freedom, denominator	d.f.N.: degrees of freedom, numerator																	
	1	2	3	4	5	6	7	8	9	10	12	15	20	24	30	40	60
1	4052	4999.5	5403	5625	5764	5859	5928	5982	6022	6056	6106	6157	6209	6235	6261	6287	6313
2	98.50	99.00	99.17	99.25	99.30	99.33	99.36	99.37	99.39	99.40	99.42	99.43	99.45	99.46	99.47	99.47	99.48
3	34.12	30.82	29.46	28.71	28.24	27.91	27.67	27.49	27.35	27.23	27.05	26.87	26.69	26.60	26.50	26.41	26.32
4	21.20	18.00	16.69	15.98	15.52	15.21	14.98	14.80	14.66	14.55	14.37	14.20	14.02	13.93	13.84	13.75	13.65
5	16.26	13.27	12.06	11.39	10.97	10.67	10.46	10.29	10.16	10.05	9.89	9.72	9.55	9.47	9.38	9.29	9.20
6	13.75	10.92	9.78	9.15	8.75	8.47	8.26	8.10	7.98	7.87	7.72	7.56	7.40	7.31	7.23	7.14	7.06
7	12.25	9.55	8.45	7.85	7.46	7.19	6.99	6.84	6.72	6.62	6.47	6.31	6.16	6.07	5.99	5.91	5.82
8	11.26	8.65	7.59	7.01	6.63	6.37	6.18	6.03	5.91	5.81	5.67	5.52	5.36	5.28	5.20	5.12	5.03
9	10.56	8.02	6.99	6.42	6.06	5.80	5.61	5.47	5.35	5.26	5.11	4.96	4.81	4.73	4.65	4.57	4.48
10	10.04	7.56	6.55	5.99	5.64	5.39	5.20	5.06	4.94	4.85	4.71	4.56	4.41	4.33	4.25	4.17	4.08
11	9.65	7.21	6.22	5.67	5.32	5.07	4.89	4.74	4.63	4.54	4.40	4.25	4.10	4.02	3.94	3.86	3.78
12	9.33	6.93	5.95	5.41	5.06	4.82	4.64	4.50	4.39	4.30	4.16	4.01	3.86	3.78	3.70	3.62	3.54
13	9.07	6.70	5.74	5.21	4.86	4.62	4.44	4.30	4.19	4.10	3.96	3.82	3.66	3.59	3.51	3.43	3.34
14	8.86	6.51	5.56	5.04	4.69	4.46	4.28	4.14	4.03	3.94	3.80	3.66	3.51	3.43	3.35	3.27	3.18
15	8.68	6.36	5.42	4.89	4.56	4.32	4.14	4.00	3.89	3.80	3.67	3.52	3.37	3.29	3.21	3.13	3.05
16	8.53	6.23	5.29	4.77	4.44	4.20	4.03	3.89	3.78	3.69	3.55	3.41	3.26	3.18	3.10	3.02	2.93
17	8.40	6.11	5.18	4.67	4.34	4.10	3.93	3.79	3.68	3.59	3.46	3.31	3.16	3.08	3.00	2.92	2.83
18	8.29	6.01	5.09	4.58	4.25	4.01	3.84	3.71	3.60	3.51	3.37	3.23	3.08	3.00	2.92	2.84	2.75
19	8.18	5.93	5.01	4.50	4.17	3.94	3.77	3.63	3.52	3.43	3.30	3.15	3.00	2.92	2.84	2.76	2.67
20	8.10	5.85	4.94	4.43	4.10	3.87	3.70	3.56	3.46	3.37	3.23	3.09	2.94	2.86	2.78	2.69	2.61
21	8.02	5.78	4.87	4.37	4.04	3.81	3.64	3.51	3.40	3.31	3.17	3.03	2.88	2.80	2.72	2.64	2.55
22	7.95	5.72	4.82	4.31	3.99	3.76	3.59	3.45	3.35	3.26	3.12	2.98	2.83	2.75	2.67	2.58	2.50
23	7.88	5.66	4.76	4.26	3.94	3.71	3.54	3.41	3.30	3.21	3.07	2.93	2.78	2.70	2.62	2.54	2.45
24	7.82	5.61	4.72	4.22	3.90	3.67	3.50	3.36	3.26	3.17	3.03	2.89	2.74	2.66	2.58	2.49	2.40
25	7.77	5.57	4.68	4.18	3.85	3.63	3.46	3.32	3.22	3.13	2.99	2.85	2.70	2.62	2.54	2.45	2.36
26	7.72	5.53	4.64	4.14	3.82	3.59	3.42	3.29	3.18	3.09	2.96	2.81	2.66	2.58	2.50	2.42	2.33
27	7.68	5.49	4.60	4.11	3.78	3.56	3.39	3.26	3.15	3.06	2.93	2.78	2.63	2.55	2.47	2.38	2.29
28	7.64	5.45	4.57	4.07	3.75	3.53	3.36	3.23	3.12	3.03	2.90	2.75	2.60	2.52	2.44	2.35	2.26
29	7.60	5.42	4.54	4.04	3.73	3.50	3.33	3.20	3.09	3.00	2.87	2.73	2.57	2.49	2.41	2.33	2.23
30	7.56	5.39	4.51	4.02	3.70	3.47	3.30	3.17	3.07	2.98	2.84	2.70	2.55	2.47	2.39	2.30	2.21
40	7.31	5.18	4.31	3.83	3.51	3.29	3.12	2.99	2.89	2.80	2.66	2.52	2.37	2.29	2.20	2.11	2.02
60	7.08	4.98	4.13	3.65	3.34	3.12	2.95	2.82	2.72	2.63	2.50	2.35	2.20	2.12	2.03	1.94	1.84

TABLE A–7 (continued)

$\alpha = 0.025$

d.f.D.: degrees of freedom, denominator	d.f.N.: degrees of freedom, numerator																
	1	2	3	4	5	6	7	8	9	10	12	15	20	24	30	40	60
1	647.8	799.5	864.2	899.6	921.8	937.1	948.2	956.7	963.3	968.6	976.7	984.9	993.1	997.2	1001	1006	1010
2	38.51	39.00	39.17	39.25	39.30	39.33	39.36	39.37	39.39	39.40	39.41	39.43	39.45	39.46	39.46	39.47	39.48
3	17.44	16.04	15.44	15.10	14.88	14.73	14.62	14.54	14.47	14.42	14.34	14.25	14.17	14.12	14.08	14.04	13.99
4	12.22	10.65	9.98	9.60	9.36	9.20	9.07	8.98	8.90	8.84	8.75	8.66	8.56	8.51	8.46	8.41	8.36
5	10.01	8.43	7.76	7.39	7.15	6.98	6.85	6.76	6.68	6.62	6.52	6.43	6.33	6.28	6.23	6.18	6.12
6	8.81	7.26	6.60	6.23	5.99	5.82	5.70	5.60	5.52	5.46	5.37	5.27	5.17	5.12	5.07	5.01	4.96
7	8.07	6.54	5.89	5.52	5.29	5.12	4.99	4.90	4.82	4.76	4.67	4.57	4.47	4.42	4.36	4.31	4.25
8	7.57	6.06	5.42	5.05	4.82	4.65	4.53	4.43	4.36	4.30	4.20	4.10	4.00	3.95	3.89	3.84	3.78
9	7.21	5.71	5.08	4.72	4.48	4.32	4.20	4.10	4.03	3.96	3.87	3.77	3.67	3.61	3.56	3.51	3.45
10	6.94	5.46	4.83	4.47	4.24	4.07	3.95	3.85	3.78	3.72	3.62	3.52	3.42	3.37	3.31	3.26	3.20
11	6.72	5.26	4.63	4.28	4.04	3.88	3.76	3.66	3.59	3.53	3.43	3.33	3.23	3.17	3.12	3.06	3.00
12	6.55	5.10	4.47	4.12	3.89	3.73	3.61	3.51	3.44	3.37	3.28	3.18	3.07	3.02	2.96	2.91	2.85
13	6.41	4.97	4.35	4.00	3.77	3.60	3.48	3.39	3.31	3.25	3.15	3.05	2.95	2.89	2.84	2.78	2.72
14	6.30	4.86	4.24	3.89	3.66	3.50	3.38	3.29	3.21	3.15	3.05	2.95	2.84	2.79	2.73	2.67	2.61
15	6.20	4.77	4.15	3.80	3.58	3.41	3.29	3.20	3.12	3.06	2.96	2.86	2.76	2.70	2.64	2.59	2.52
16	6.12	4.69	4.08	3.73	3.50	3.34	3.22	3.12	3.05	2.99	2.89	2.79	2.68	2.63	2.57	2.51	2.45
17	6.04	4.62	4.01	3.66	3.44	3.28	3.16	3.06	2.98	2.92	2.82	2.72	2.62	2.56	2.50	2.44	2.38
18	5.98	4.56	3.95	3.61	3.38	3.22	3.10	3.01	2.93	2.87	2.77	2.67	2.56	2.50	2.44	2.38	2.32
19	5.92	4.51	3.90	3.56	3.33	3.17	3.05	2.96	2.88	2.82	2.72	2.62	2.51	2.45	2.39	2.33	2.27
20	5.87	4.46	3.86	3.51	3.29	3.13	3.01	2.91	2.84	2.77	2.68	2.57	2.46	2.41	2.35	2.29	2.22
21	5.83	4.42	3.82	3.48	3.25	3.09	2.97	2.87	2.80	2.73	2.64	2.53	2.42	2.37	2.31	2.25	2.18
22	5.79	4.38	3.78	3.44	3.22	3.05	2.93	2.84	2.76	2.70	2.60	2.50	2.39	2.33	2.27	2.21	2.14
23	5.75	4.35	3.75	3.41	3.18	3.02	2.90	2.81	2.73	2.67	2.57	2.47	2.36	2.30	2.24	2.18	2.11
24	5.72	4.32	3.72	3.38	3.15	2.99	2.87	2.78	2.70	2.64	2.54	2.44	2.33	2.27	2.21	2.15	2.08
25	5.69	4.29	3.69	3.35	3.13	2.97	2.85	2.75	2.68	2.61	2.51	2.41	2.30	2.24	2.18	2.12	2.05
26	5.66	4.27	3.67	3.33	3.10	2.94	2.82	2.73	2.65	2.59	2.49	2.39	2.28	2.22	2.16	2.09	2.03
27	5.63	4.24	3.65	3.31	3.08	2.92	2.80	2.71	2.63	2.57	2.47	2.36	2.25	2.19	2.13	2.07	2.00
28	5.61	4.22	3.63	3.29	3.06	2.90	2.78	2.69	2.61	2.55	2.45	2.34	2.23	2.17	2.11	2.05	1.98
29	5.59	4.20	3.61	3.27	3.04	2.88	2.76	2.67	2.59	2.53	2.43	2.32	2.21	2.15	2.09	2.03	1.96
30	5.57	4.18	3.59	3.25	3.03	2.87	2.75	2.65	2.57	2.51	2.41	2.31	2.20	2.14	2.07	2.01	1.94
40	5.42	4.05	3.46	3.13	2.90	2.74	2.62	2.53	2.45	2.39	2.29	2.18	2.07	2.01	1.94	1.88	1.80
60	5.29	3.93	3.34	3.01	2.79	2.63	2.51	2.41	2.33	2.27	2.17	2.06	1.94	1.88	1.82	1.74	1.67

TABLE A–7 *(continued)*

$\alpha = 0.05$

d.f.D.: degrees of freedom, denominator	\multicolumn{17}{c	}{d.f.N.: degrees of freedom, numerator}
	1	2	3	4	5	6	7	8	9	10	12	15	20	24	30	40	60
1	161.4	199.5	215.7	224.6	230.2	234.0	236.8	238.9	240.5	241.9	243.9	245.9	248.0	249.1	250.1	251.1	252.2
2	18.51	19.00	19.16	19.25	19.30	19.33	19.35	19.37	19.38	19.40	19.41	19.43	19.45	19.45	19.46	19.47	19.48
3	10.13	9.55	9.28	9.12	9.01	8.94	8.89	8.85	8.81	8.79	8.74	8.70	8.66	8.64	8.62	8.59	8.57
4	7.71	6.94	6.59	6.39	6.26	6.16	6.09	6.04	6.00	5.96	5.91	5.86	5.80	5.77	5.75	5.72	5.69
5	6.61	5.79	5.41	5.19	5.05	4.95	4.88	4.82	4.77	4.74	4.68	4.62	4.56	4.53	4.50	4.46	4.43
6	5.99	5.14	4.76	4.53	4.39	4.28	4.21	4.15	4.10	4.06	4.00	3.94	3.87	3.84	3.81	3.77	3.74
7	5.59	4.74	4.35	4.12	3.97	3.87	3.79	3.73	3.68	3.64	3.57	3.51	3.44	3.41	3.38	3.34	3.30
8	5.32	4.46	4.07	3.84	3.69	3.58	3.50	3.44	3.39	3.35	3.28	3.22	3.15	3.12	3.08	3.04	3.01
9	5.12	4.26	3.86	3.63	3.48	3.37	3.29	3.23	3.18	3.14	3.07	3.01	2.94	2.90	2.86	2.83	2.79
10	4.96	4.10	3.71	3.48	3.33	3.22	3.14	3.07	3.02	2.98	2.91	2.85	2.77	2.74	2.70	2.66	2.62
11	4.84	3.98	3.59	3.36	3.20	3.09	3.01	2.95	2.90	2.85	2.79	2.72	2.65	2.61	2.57	2.53	2.49
12	4.75	3.89	3.49	3.26	3.11	3.00	2.91	2.85	2.80	2.75	2.69	2.62	2.54	2.51	2.47	2.43	2.38
13	4.67	3.81	3.41	3.18	3.03	2.92	2.83	2.77	2.71	2.67	2.60	2.53	2.46	2.42	2.38	2.34	2.30
14	4.60	3.74	3.34	3.11	2.96	2.85	2.76	2.70	2.65	2.60	2.53	2.46	2.39	2.35	2.31	2.27	2.22
15	4.54	3.68	3.29	3.06	2.90	2.79	2.71	2.64	2.59	2.54	2.48	2.40	2.33	2.29	2.25	2.20	2.16
16	4.49	3.63	3.24	3.01	2.85	2.74	2.66	2.59	2.54	2.49	2.42	2.35	2.28	2.24	2.19	2.15	2.11
17	4.45	3.59	3.20	2.96	2.81	2.70	2.61	2.55	2.49	2.45	2.38	2.31	2.23	2.19	2.15	2.10	2.06
18	4.41	3.55	3.16	2.93	2.77	2.66	2.58	2.51	2.46	2.41	2.34	2.27	2.19	2.15	2.11	2.06	2.02
19	4.38	3.52	3.13	2.90	2.74	2.63	2.54	2.48	2.42	2.38	2.31	2.23	2.16	2.11	2.07	2.03	1.98
20	4.35	3.49	3.10	2.87	2.71	2.60	2.51	2.45	2.39	2.35	2.28	2.20	2.12	2.08	2.04	1.99	1.95
21	4.32	3.47	3.07	2.84	2.68	2.57	2.49	2.42	2.37	2.32	2.25	2.18	2.10	2.05	2.01	1.96	1.92
22	4.30	3.44	3.05	2.82	2.66	2.55	2.46	2.40	2.34	2.30	2.23	2.15	2.07	2.03	1.98	1.94	1.89
23	4.28	3.42	3.03	2.80	2.64	2.53	2.44	2.37	2.32	2.27	2.20	2.13	2.05	2.01	1.96	1.91	1.86
24	4.26	3.40	3.01	2.78	2.62	2.51	2.42	2.36	2.30	2.25	2.18	2.11	2.03	1.98	1.94	1.89	1.84
25	4.24	3.39	2.99	2.76	2.60	2.49	2.40	2.34	2.28	2.24	2.16	2.09	2.01	1.96	1.92	1.87	1.82
26	4.23	3.37	2.98	2.74	2.59	2.47	2.39	2.32	2.27	2.22	2.15	2.07	1.99	1.95	1.90	1.85	1.80
27	4.21	3.35	2.96	2.73	2.57	2.46	2.37	2.31	2.25	2.20	2.13	2.06	1.97	1.93	1.88	1.84	1.79
28	4.20	3.34	2.95	2.71	2.56	2.45	2.36	2.29	2.24	2.19	2.12	2.04	1.96	1.91	1.87	1.82	1.77
29	4.18	3.33	2.93	2.70	2.55	2.43	2.35	2.28	2.22	2.18	2.10	2.03	1.94	1.90	1.85	1.81	1.75
30	4.17	3.32	2.92	2.69	2.53	2.42	2.33	2.27	2.21	2.16	2.09	2.01	1.93	1.89	1.84	1.79	1.74
40	4.08	3.23	2.84	2.61	2.45	2.34	2.25	2.18	2.12	2.08	2.00	1.92	1.84	1.79	1.74	1.69	1.64
60	4.00	3.15	2.76	2.53	2.37	2.25	2.17	2.10	2.04	1.99	1.92	1.84	1.75	1.70	1.65	1.59	1.53

TABLE A–7 (concluded)

$\alpha = 0.10$

d.f.D.: degrees of freedom, denominator	d.f.N.: degrees of freedom, numerator																
	1	2	3	4	5	6	7	8	9	10	12	15	20	24	30	40	60
1	39.86	49.50	53.59	55.83	57.24	58.20	58.91	59.44	59.86	60.19	60.71	61.22	61.74	62.00	62.26	62.53	62.79
2	8.53	9.00	9.16	9.24	9.29	9.33	9.35	9.37	9.38	9.39	9.41	9.42	9.44	9.45	9.46	9.47	9.47
3	5.54	5.46	5.39	5.34	5.31	5.28	5.27	5.25	5.24	5.23	5.22	5.20	5.18	5.18	5.17	5.16	5.15
4	4.54	4.32	4.19	4.11	4.05	4.01	3.98	3.95	3.94	3.92	3.90	3.87	3.84	3.83	3.82	3.80	3.79
5	4.06	3.78	3.62	3.52	3.45	3.40	3.37	3.34	3.32	3.30	3.27	3.24	3.21	3.19	3.17	3.16	3.14
6	3.78	3.46	3.29	3.18	3.11	3.05	3.01	2.98	2.96	2.94	2.90	2.87	2.84	2.82	2.80	2.78	2.76
7	3.59	3.26	3.07	2.96	2.88	2.83	2.78	2.75	2.72	2.70	2.67	2.63	2.59	2.58	2.56	2.54	2.51
8	3.46	3.11	2.92	2.81	2.73	2.67	2.62	2.59	2.56	2.54	2.50	2.46	2.42	2.40	2.38	2.36	2.34
9	3.36	3.01	2.81	2.69	2.61	2.55	2.51	2.47	2.44	2.42	2.38	2.34	2.30	2.28	2.25	2.23	2.21
10	3.29	2.92	2.73	2.61	2.52	2.46	2.41	2.38	2.35	2.32	2.28	2.24	2.20	2.18	2.16	2.13	2.11
11	3.23	2.86	2.66	2.54	2.45	2.39	2.34	2.30	2.27	2.25	2.21	2.17	2.12	2.10	2.08	2.05	2.03
12	3.18	2.81	2.61	2.48	2.39	2.33	2.28	2.24	2.21	2.19	2.15	2.10	2.06	2.04	2.01	1.99	1.96
13	3.14	2.76	2.56	2.43	2.35	2.28	2.23	2.20	2.16	2.14	2.10	2.05	2.01	1.98	1.96	1.93	1.90
14	3.10	2.73	2.52	2.39	2.31	2.24	2.19	2.15	2.12	2.10	2.05	2.01	1.96	1.94	1.91	1.89	1.86
15	3.07	2.70	2.49	2.36	2.27	2.21	2.16	2.12	2.09	2.06	2.02	1.97	1.92	1.90	1.87	1.85	1.82
16	3.05	2.67	2.46	2.33	2.24	2.18	2.13	2.09	2.06	2.03	1.99	1.94	1.89	1.87	1.84	1.81	1.78
17	3.03	2.64	2.44	2.31	2.22	2.15	2.10	2.06	2.03	2.00	1.96	1.91	1.86	1.84	1.81	1.78	1.75
18	3.01	2.62	2.42	2.29	2.20	2.13	2.08	2.04	2.00	1.98	1.93	1.89	1.84	1.81	1.78	1.75	1.72
19	2.99	2.61	2.40	2.27	2.18	2.11	2.06	2.02	1.98	1.96	1.91	1.86	1.81	1.79	1.76	1.73	1.70
20	2.97	2.59	2.38	2.25	2.16	2.09	2.04	2.00	1.96	1.94	1.89	1.84	1.79	1.77	1.74	1.71	1.68
21	2.96	2.57	2.36	2.23	2.14	2.08	2.02	1.98	1.95	1.92	1.87	1.83	1.78	1.75	1.72	1.69	1.66
22	2.95	2.56	2.35	2.22	2.13	2.06	2.01	1.97	1.93	1.90	1.86	1.81	1.76	1.73	1.70	1.67	1.64
23	2.94	2.55	2.34	2.21	2.11	2.05	1.99	1.95	1.92	1.89	1.84	1.80	1.74	1.72	1.69	1.66	1.62
24	2.93	2.54	2.33	2.19	2.10	2.04	1.98	1.94	1.91	1.88	1.83	1.78	1.73	1.70	1.67	1.64	1.61
25	2.92	2.53	2.32	2.18	2.09	2.02	1.97	1.93	1.89	1.87	1.82	1.77	1.72	1.69	1.66	1.63	1.59
26	2.91	2.52	2.31	2.17	2.08	2.01	1.96	1.92	1.88	1.86	1.81	1.76	1.71	1.68	1.65	1.61	1.58
27	2.90	2.51	2.30	2.17	2.07	2.00	1.95	1.91	1.87	1.85	1.80	1.75	1.70	1.67	1.64	1.60	1.57
28	2.89	2.50	2.29	2.16	2.06	2.00	1.94	1.90	1.87	1.84	1.79	1.74	1.69	1.66	1.63	1.59	1.56
29	2.89	2.50	2.28	2.15	2.06	1.99	1.93	1.89	1.86	1.83	1.78	1.73	1.68	1.65	1.62	1.58	1.55
30	2.88	2.49	2.28	2.14	2.05	1.98	1.93	1.88	1.85	1.82	1.77	1.72	1.67	1.64	1.61	1.57	1.54
40	2.84	2.44	2.23	2.09	2.00	1.93	1.87	1.83	1.79	1.76	1.71	1.66	1.61	1.57	1.54	1.51	1.47
60	2.79	2.39	2.18	2.04	1.95	1.87	1.82	1.77	1.74	1.71	1.66	1.60	1.54	1.51	1.48	1.44	1.40

From M. Merrington and C.M. Thompson (1943). Table of Percentage Points of the Inverted Beta (F) Distribution. Biometrika 33, pp. 74–87. Reprinted with permission from Biometrika.

TABLE A–8 Critical Values for the PPMC

Reject H_0: $\rho = 0$ if the absolute value of r is greater than the value given in the table. The values are for a two-tailed test; d.f. $= n - 2$.

d.f.	$\alpha = 0.05$	$\alpha = 0.01$
1	0.999	0.999
2	0.950	0.999
3	0.878	0.959
4	0.811	0.917
5	0.754	0.875
6	0.707	0.834
7	0.666	0.798
8	0.632	0.765
9	0.602	0.735
10	0.576	0.708
11	0.553	0.684
12	0.532	0.661
13	0.514	0.641
14	0.497	0.623
15	0.482	0.606
16	0.468	0.590
17	0.456	0.575
18	0.444	0.561
19	0.433	0.549
20	0.423	0.537
25	0.381	0.487
30	0.349	0.449
35	0.325	0.418
40	0.304	0.393
45	0.288	0.372
50	0.273	0.354

Source: From *Biometrika Tables for Statisticians*, vol. 1 (1962), p. 138. Reprinted with permission.

TABLE A–9 Critical Values for the Tukey Test

$\alpha = 0.01$

k \ v	2	3	4	5	6	7	8	9	10	11	12	13	14	15	16	17	18	19	20
1	90.03	135.0	164.3	185.6	202.2	215.8	227.2	237.0	245.6	253.2	260.0	266.2	271.8	277.0	281.8	286.3	290.4	294.3	298.0
2	14.04	19.02	22.29	24.72	26.63	28.20	29.53	30.68	31.69	32.59	33.40	34.13	34.81	35.43	36.00	36.53	37.03	37.50	37.95
3	8.26	10.62	12.17	13.33	14.24	15.00	15.64	16.20	16.69	17.13	17.53	17.89	18.22	18.52	18.81	19.07	19.32	19.55	19.77
4	6.51	8.12	9.17	9.96	10.58	11.10	11.55	11.93	12.27	12.57	12.84	13.09	13.32	13.53	13.73	13.91	14.08	14.24	14.40
5	5.70	6.98	7.80	8.42	8.91	9.32	9.67	9.97	10.24	10.48	10.70	10.89	11.08	11.24	11.40	11.55	11.68	11.81	11.93
6	5.24	6.33	7.03	7.56	7.97	8.32	8.61	8.87	9.10	9.30	9.48	9.65	9.81	9.95	10.08	10.21	10.32	10.43	10.54
7	4.95	5.92	6.54	7.01	7.37	7.68	7.94	8.17	8.37	8.55	8.71	8.86	9.00	9.12	9.24	9.35	9.46	9.55	9.65
8	4.75	5.64	6.20	6.62	6.96	7.24	7.47	7.68	7.86	8.03	8.18	8.31	8.44	8.55	8.66	8.76	8.85	8.94	9.03
9	4.60	5.43	5.96	6.35	6.66	6.91	7.13	7.33	7.49	7.65	7.78	7.91	8.03	8.13	8.23	8.33	8.41	8.49	8.57
10	4.48	5.27	5.77	6.14	6.43	6.67	6.87	7.05	7.21	7.36	7.49	7.60	7.71	7.81	7.91	7.99	8.08	8.15	8.23
11	4.39	5.15	5.62	5.97	6.25	6.48	6.67	6.84	6.99	7.13	7.25	7.36	7.46	7.56	7.65	7.73	7.81	7.88	7.95
12	4.32	5.05	5.50	5.84	6.10	6.32	6.51	6.67	6.81	6.94	7.06	7.17	7.26	7.36	7.44	7.52	7.59	7.66	7.73
13	4.26	4.96	5.40	5.73	5.98	6.19	6.37	6.53	6.67	6.79	6.90	7.01	7.10	7.19	7.27	7.35	7.42	7.48	7.55
14	4.21	4.89	5.32	5.63	5.88	6.08	6.26	6.41	6.54	6.66	6.77	6.87	6.96	7.05	7.13	7.20	7.27	7.33	7.39
15	4.17	4.84	5.25	5.56	5.80	5.99	6.16	6.31	6.44	6.55	6.66	6.76	6.84	6.93	7.00	7.07	7.14	7.20	7.26
16	4.13	4.79	5.19	5.49	5.72	5.92	6.08	6.22	6.35	6.46	6.56	6.66	6.74	6.82	6.90	6.97	7.03	7.09	7.15
17	4.10	4.74	5.14	5.43	5.66	5.85	6.01	6.15	6.27	6.38	6.48	6.57	6.66	6.73	6.81	6.87	6.94	7.00	7.05
18	4.07	4.70	5.09	5.38	5.60	5.79	5.94	6.08	6.20	6.31	6.41	6.50	6.58	6.65	6.73	6.79	6.85	6.91	6.97
19	4.05	4.67	5.05	5.33	5.55	5.73	5.89	6.02	6.14	6.25	6.34	6.43	6.51	6.58	6.65	6.72	6.78	6.84	6.89
20	4.02	4.64	5.02	5.29	5.51	5.69	5.84	5.97	6.09	6.19	6.28	6.37	6.45	6.52	6.59	6.65	6.71	6.77	6.82
24	3.96	4.55	4.91	5.17	5.37	5.54	5.69	5.81	5.92	6.02	6.11	6.19	6.26	6.33	6.39	6.45	6.51	6.56	6.61
30	3.89	4.45	4.80	5.05	5.24	5.40	5.54	5.65	5.76	5.85	5.93	6.01	6.08	6.14	6.20	6.26	6.31	6.36	6.41
40	3.82	4.37	4.70	4.93	5.11	5.26	5.39	5.50	5.60	5.69	5.76	5.83	5.90	5.96	6.02	6.07	6.12	6.16	6.21
60	3.76	4.28	4.59	4.82	4.99	5.13	5.25	5.36	5.45	5.53	5.60	5.67	5.73	5.78	5.84	5.89	5.93	5.97	6.01
120	3.70	4.20	4.50	4.71	4.87	5.01	5.12	5.21	5.30	5.37	5.44	5.50	5.56	5.61	5.66	5.71	5.75	5.79	5.83
∞	3.64	4.12	4.40	4.60	4.76	4.88	4.99	5.08	5.16	5.23	5.29	5.35	5.40	5.45	5.49	5.54	5.57	5.61	5.65

TABLE A-9 (continued)

$\alpha = 0.05$

k\v	2	3	4	5	6	7	8	9	10	11	12	13	14	15	16	17	18	19	20
1	17.97	26.98	32.82	37.08	40.41	43.12	45.40	47.36	49.07	50.59	51.96	53.20	54.33	55.36	56.32	57.22	58.04	58.83	59.56
2	6.08	8.33	9.80	10.88	11.74	12.44	13.03	13.54	13.99	14.39	14.75	15.08	15.38	15.65	15.91	16.14	16.37	16.57	16.77
3	4.50	5.91	6.82	7.50	8.04	8.48	8.85	9.18	9.46	9.72	9.95	10.15	10.35	10.53	10.69	10.84	10.98	11.11	11.24
4	3.93	5.04	5.76	6.29	6.71	7.05	7.35	7.60	7.83	8.03	8.21	8.37	8.52	8.66	8.79	8.91	9.03	9.13	9.23
5	3.64	4.60	5.22	5.67	6.03	6.33	6.58	6.80	6.99	7.17	7.32	7.47	7.60	7.72	7.83	7.93	8.03	8.12	8.21
6	3.46	4.34	4.90	5.30	5.63	5.90	6.12	6.32	6.49	6.65	6.79	6.92	7.03	7.14	7.24	7.34	7.43	7.51	7.59
7	3.34	4.16	4.68	5.06	5.36	5.61	5.82	6.00	6.16	6.30	6.43	6.55	6.66	6.76	6.85	6.94	7.02	7.10	7.17
8	3.26	4.04	4.53	4.89	5.17	5.40	5.60	5.77	5.92	6.05	6.18	6.29	6.39	6.48	6.57	6.65	6.73	6.80	6.87
9	3.20	3.95	4.41	4.76	5.02	5.24	5.43	5.59	5.74	5.87	5.98	6.09	6.19	6.28	6.36	6.44	6.51	6.58	6.64
10	3.15	3.88	4.33	4.65	4.91	5.12	5.30	5.46	5.60	5.72	5.83	5.93	6.03	6.11	6.19	6.27	6.34	6.40	6.47
11	3.11	3.82	4.26	4.57	4.82	5.03	5.20	5.35	5.49	5.61	5.71	5.81	5.90	5.98	6.06	6.13	6.20	6.27	6.33
12	3.08	3.77	4.20	4.51	4.75	4.95	5.12	5.27	5.39	5.51	5.61	5.71	5.80	5.88	5.95	6.02	6.09	6.15	6.21
13	3.06	3.73	4.15	4.45	4.69	4.88	5.05	5.19	5.32	5.43	5.53	5.63	5.71	5.79	5.86	5.93	5.99	6.05	6.11
14	3.03	3.70	4.11	4.41	4.64	4.83	4.99	5.13	5.25	5.36	5.46	5.55	5.64	5.71	5.79	5.85	5.91	5.97	6.03
15	3.01	3.67	4.08	4.37	4.59	4.78	4.94	5.08	5.20	5.31	5.40	5.49	5.57	5.65	5.72	5.78	5.85	5.90	5.96
16	3.00	3.65	4.05	4.33	4.56	4.74	4.90	5.03	5.15	5.26	5.35	5.44	5.52	5.59	5.66	5.73	5.79	5.84	5.90
17	2.98	3.63	4.02	4.30	4.52	4.70	4.86	4.99	5.11	5.21	5.31	5.39	5.47	5.54	5.61	5.67	5.73	5.79	5.84
18	2.97	3.61	4.00	4.28	4.49	4.67	4.82	4.96	5.07	5.17	5.27	5.35	5.43	5.50	5.57	5.63	5.69	5.74	5.79
19	2.96	3.59	3.98	4.25	4.47	4.65	4.79	4.92	5.04	5.14	5.23	5.31	5.39	5.46	5.53	5.59	5.65	5.70	5.75
20	2.95	3.58	3.96	4.23	4.45	4.62	4.77	4.90	5.01	5.11	5.20	5.28	5.36	5.43	5.49	5.55	5.61	5.66	5.71
24	2.92	3.53	3.90	4.17	4.37	4.54	4.68	4.81	4.92	5.01	5.10	5.18	5.25	5.32	5.38	5.44	5.49	5.55	5.59
30	2.89	3.49	3.85	4.10	4.30	4.46	4.60	4.72	4.82	4.92	5.00	5.08	5.15	5.21	5.27	5.33	5.38	5.43	5.47
40	2.86	3.44	3.79	4.04	4.23	4.39	4.52	4.63	4.73	4.82	4.90	4.98	5.04	5.11	5.16	5.22	5.27	5.31	5.36
60	2.83	3.40	3.74	3.98	4.16	4.31	4.44	4.55	4.65	4.73	4.81	4.88	4.94	5.00	5.06	5.11	5.15	5.20	5.24
120	2.80	3.36	3.68	3.92	4.10	4.24	4.36	4.47	4.56	4.64	4.71	4.78	4.84	4.90	4.95	5.00	5.04	5.09	5.13
∞	2.77	3.31	3.63	3.86	4.03	4.17	4.29	4.39	4.47	4.55	4.62	4.68	4.74	4.80	4.85	4.89	4.93	4.97	5.01

TABLE A–9 *(concluded)*

$\alpha = 0.10$

v \ k	2	3	4	5	6	7	8	9	10	11	12	13	14	15	16	17	18	19	20
1	8.93	13.44	16.36	18.49	20.15	21.51	22.64	23.62	24.48	25.24	25.92	26.54	27.10	27.62	28.10	28.54	28.96	29.35	29.71
2	4.13	5.73	6.77	7.54	8.14	8.63	9.05	9.41	9.72	10.01	10.26	10.49	10.70	10.89	11.07	11.24	11.39	11.54	11.68
3	3.33	4.47	5.20	5.74	6.16	6.51	6.81	7.06	7.29	7.49	7.67	7.83	7.98	8.12	8.25	8.37	8.48	8.58	8.68
4	3.01	3.98	4.59	5.03	5.39	5.68	5.93	6.14	6.33	6.49	6.65	6.78	6.91	7.02	7.13	7.23	7.33	7.41	7.50
5	2.85	3.72	4.26	4.66	4.98	5.24	5.46	5.65	5.82	5.97	6.10	6.22	6.34	6.44	6.54	6.63	6.71	6.79	6.86
6	2.75	3.56	4.07	4.44	4.73	4.97	5.17	5.34	5.50	5.64	5.76	5.87	5.98	6.07	6.16	6.25	6.32	6.40	6.47
7	2.68	3.45	3.93	4.28	4.55	4.78	4.97	5.14	5.28	5.41	5.53	5.64	5.74	5.83	5.91	5.99	6.06	6.13	6.19
8	2.63	3.37	3.83	4.17	4.43	4.65	4.83	4.99	5.13	5.25	5.36	5.46	5.56	5.64	5.72	5.80	5.87	5.93	6.00
9	2.59	3.32	3.76	4.08	4.34	4.54	4.72	4.87	5.01	5.13	5.23	5.33	5.42	5.51	5.58	5.66	5.72	5.79	5.85
10	2.56	3.27	3.70	4.02	4.26	4.47	4.64	4.78	4.91	5.03	5.13	5.23	5.32	5.40	5.47	5.54	5.61	5.67	5.73
11	2.54	3.23	3.66	3.96	4.20	4.40	4.57	4.71	4.84	4.95	5.05	5.15	5.23	5.31	5.38	5.45	5.51	5.57	5.63
12	2.52	3.20	3.62	3.92	4.16	4.35	4.51	4.65	4.78	4.89	4.99	5.08	5.16	5.24	5.31	5.37	5.44	5.49	5.55
13	2.50	3.18	3.59	3.88	4.12	4.30	4.46	4.60	4.72	4.83	4.93	5.02	5.10	5.18	5.25	5.31	5.37	5.43	5.48
14	2.49	3.16	3.56	3.85	4.08	4.27	4.42	4.56	4.68	4.79	4.88	4.97	5.05	5.12	5.19	5.26	5.32	5.37	5.43
15	2.48	3.14	3.54	3.83	4.05	4.23	4.39	4.52	4.64	4.75	4.84	4.93	5.01	5.08	5.15	5.21	5.27	5.32	5.38
16	2.47	3.12	3.52	3.80	4.03	4.21	4.36	4.49	4.61	4.71	4.81	4.89	4.97	5.04	5.11	5.17	5.23	5.28	5.33
17	2.46	3.11	3.50	3.78	4.00	4.18	4.33	4.46	4.58	4.68	4.77	4.86	4.93	5.01	5.07	5.13	5.19	5.24	5.30
18	2.45	3.10	3.49	3.77	3.98	4.16	4.31	4.44	4.55	4.65	4.75	4.83	4.90	4.98	5.04	5.10	5.16	5.21	5.26
19	2.45	3.09	3.47	3.75	3.97	4.14	4.29	4.42	4.53	4.63	4.72	4.80	4.88	4.95	5.01	5.07	5.13	5.18	5.23
20	2.44	3.08	3.46	3.74	3.95	4.12	4.27	4.40	4.51	4.61	4.70	4.78	4.85	4.92	4.99	5.05	5.10	5.16	5.20
24	2.42	3.05	3.42	3.69	3.90	4.07	4.21	4.34	4.44	4.54	4.63	4.71	4.78	4.85	4.91	4.97	5.02	5.07	5.12
30	2.40	3.02	3.39	3.65	3.85	4.02	4.16	4.28	4.38	4.47	4.56	4.64	4.71	4.77	4.83	4.89	4.94	4.99	5.03
40	2.38	2.99	3.35	3.60	3.80	3.96	4.10	4.21	4.32	4.41	4.49	4.56	4.63	4.69	4.75	4.81	4.86	4.90	4.95
60	2.36	2.96	3.31	3.56	3.75	3.91	4.04	4.16	4.25	4.34	4.42	4.49	4.56	4.62	4.67	4.73	4.78	4.82	4.86
120	2.34	2.93	3.28	3.52	3.71	3.86	3.99	4.10	4.19	4.28	4.35	4.42	4.48	4.54	4.60	4.65	4.69	4.74	4.78
∞	2.33	2.90	3.24	3.48	3.66	3.81	3.93	4.04	4.13	4.21	4.28	4.35	4.41	4.47	4.52	4.57	4.61	4.65	4.69

Source: "Tables of Range and Studentized Range," *Annals of Mathematical Statistics,* vol. 31, no. 4. Reprinted with permission of the Institute of Mathematical Sciences.

TABLE A–10 Critical Values for the Sign Test

Reject the null hypothesis if the smaller number of positive or negative signs is less than or equal to the value in the table.

n	One-tailed, $\alpha = 0.005$ Two-tailed, $\alpha = 0.01$	$\alpha = 0.01$ $\alpha = 0.02$	$\alpha = 0.025$ $\alpha = 0.05$	$\alpha = 0.05$ $\alpha = 0.10$
8	0	0	0	1
9	0	0	1	1
10	0	0	1	1
11	0	1	1	2
12	1	1	2	2
13	1	1	2	3
14	1	2	3	3
15	2	2	3	3
16	2	2	3	4
17	2	3	4	4
18	3	3	4	5
19	3	4	4	5
20	3	4	5	5
21	4	4	5	6
22	4	5	5	6
23	4	5	6	7
24	5	5	6	7
25	5	6	6	7

Note: Table A–10 is for one-tailed or two-tailed tests. The term n represents the total number of positive and negative signs. The test statistic is the number of less frequent signs.

TABLE A–11 Critical Values for the Wilcoxon Signed-Rank Test

Reject the null hypothesis if the test statistic is less than or equal to the value given in the table.

n	One-tailed, $\alpha = 0.05$ Two-tailed, $\alpha = 0.10$	$\alpha = 0.025$ $\alpha = 0.05$	$\alpha = 0.01$ $\alpha = 0.02$	$\alpha = 0.005$ $\alpha = 0.01$
5	1	–	–	–
6	2	1	–	–
7	4	2	0	–
8	6	4	2	0
9	8	6	3	2
10	11	8	5	3
11	14	11	7	5
12	17	14	10	7
13	21	17	13	10
14	26	21	16	13
15	30	25	20	16
16	36	30	24	19
17	41	35	28	23
18	47	40	33	28
19	54	46	38	32
20	60	52	43	37
21	68	59	49	43
22	75	66	56	49
23	83	73	62	55
24	92	81	69	61
25	101	90	77	68
26	110	98	85	76
27	120	107	93	84
28	130	117	102	92
29	141	127	111	100
30	152	137	120	109

Source: From Some Rapid Approximate Statistical Procedures, Copyright 1949, 1964 Lerderle Laboratories, American Cyanamid Co., Wayne, N.J. Reprinted with permission.

TABLE A–12 Critical Values for the Rank Correlation Coefficient

Reject H_0: $\rho = 0$ if the absolute value of r_S is greater than the value given in the table.

n	$\alpha = 0.10$	$\alpha = 0.05$	$\alpha = 0.02$	$\alpha = 0.01$
5	0.900	–	–	–
6	0.829	0.886	0.943	–
7	0.714	0.786	0.893	0.929
8	0.643	0.738	0.833	0.881
9	0.600	0.700	0.783	0.833
10	0.564	0.648	0.745	0.794
11	0.536	0.618	0.709	0.818
12	0.497	0.591	0.703	0.780
13	0.475	0.566	0.673	0.745
14	0.457	0.545	0.646	0.716
15	0.441	0.525	0.623	0.689
16	0.425	0.507	0.601	0.666
17	0.412	0.490	0.582	0.645
18	0.399	0.476	0.564	0.625
19	0.388	0.462	0.549	0.608
20	0.377	0.450	0.534	0.591
21	0.368	0.438	0.521	0.576
22	0.359	0.428	0.508	0.562
23	0.351	0.418	0.496	0.549
24	0.343	0.409	0.485	0.537
25	0.336	0.400	0.475	0.526
26	0.329	0.392	0.465	0.515
27	0.323	0.385	0.456	0.505
28	0.317	0.377	0.488	0.496
29	0.311	0.370	0.440	0.487
30	0.305	0.364	0.432	0.478

Source: From N.L. Johnson and F.C. Leone, *Statistical and Experimental Design*, vol. I (1964), p. 142. Reprinted with permission from the Institute of Mathematical Statistics.

TABLE A–13 Critical Values for the Number of Runs

This table gives the critical values at $\alpha = 0.05$ for a two-tailed test. Reject the null hypothesis if the number of runs is less than or equal to the smaller value or greater than or equal to the larger value.

Value of n_1	Value of n_2																		
	2	3	4	5	6	7	8	9	10	11	12	13	14	15	16	17	18	19	20
2	1	1	1	1	1	1	1	1	1	1	2	2	2	2	2	2	2	2	2
	6	6	6	6	6	6	6	6	6	6	6	6	6	6	6	6	6	6	6
3	1	1	1	1	2	2	2	2	2	2	2	2	2	3	3	3	3	3	3
	6	8	8	8	8	8	8	8	8	8	8	8	8	8	8	8	8	8	8
4	1	1	1	2	2	2	3	3	3	3	3	3	3	3	4	4	4	4	4
	6	8	9	9	9	10	10	10	10	10	10	10	10	10	10	10	10	10	10
5	1	1	2	2	3	3	3	3	3	4	4	4	4	4	4	4	5	5	5
	6	8	9	10	10	11	11	12	12	12	12	12	12	12	12	12	12	12	12
6	1	2	2	3	3	3	3	4	4	4	4	5	5	5	5	5	5	6	6
	6	8	9	10	11	12	12	13	13	13	13	14	14	14	14	14	14	14	14
7	1	2	2	3	3	3	4	4	5	5	5	5	5	6	6	6	6	6	6
	6	8	10	11	12	13	13	14	14	14	14	15	15	15	16	16	16	16	16
8	1	2	3	3	3	4	4	5	5	5	6	6	6	6	6	7	7	7	7
	6	8	10	11	12	13	14	14	15	15	16	16	16	16	17	17	17	17	17
9	1	2	3	3	4	4	5	5	5	6	6	6	7	7	7	7	8	8	8
	6	8	10	12	13	14	14	15	16	16	16	17	17	18	18	18	18	18	18
10	1	2	3	3	4	5	5	5	6	6	7	7	7	7	8	8	8	8	9
	6	8	10	12	13	14	15	16	16	17	17	18	18	18	19	19	19	20	20
11	1	2	3	4	4	5	5	6	6	7	7	7	8	8	8	9	9	9	9
	6	8	10	12	13	14	15	16	17	17	18	19	19	19	20	20	20	21	21
12	2	2	3	4	4	5	6	6	7	7	7	8	8	8	9	9	9	10	10
	6	8	10	12	13	14	16	16	17	18	19	19	20	20	21	21	21	22	22
13	2	2	3	4	5	5	6	6	7	7	8	8	9	9	9	10	10	10	10
	6	8	10	12	14	15	16	17	18	19	19	20	20	21	21	22	22	23	23
14	2	2	3	4	5	5	6	7	7	8	8	9	9	9	10	10	10	11	11
	6	8	10	12	14	15	16	17	18	19	20	20	21	22	22	23	23	23	24
15	2	3	3	4	5	6	6	7	7	8	8	9	9	10	10	11	11	11	12
	6	8	10	12	14	15	16	18	18	19	20	21	22	22	23	23	24	24	25
16	2	3	4	4	5	6	6	7	8	8	9	9	10	10	11	11	11	12	12
	6	8	10	12	14	16	17	18	19	20	21	21	22	23	23	24	25	25	25
17	2	3	4	4	5	6	7	7	8	9	9	10	10	11	11	11	12	12	13
	6	8	10	12	14	16	17	18	19	20	21	22	23	23	24	25	25	26	26
18	2	3	4	5	5	6	7	8	8	9	9	10	10	11	11	12	12	13	13
	6	8	10	12	14	16	17	18	19	20	21	22	23	24	25	25	26	26	27
19	2	3	4	5	6	6	7	8	8	9	10	10	11	11	12	12	13	13	13
	6	8	10	12	14	16	17	18	20	21	22	23	23	24	25	26	26	27	27
20	2	3	4	5	6	6	7	8	9	9	10	10	11	12	12	13	13	13	14
	6	8	10	12	14	16	17	18	20	21	22	23	24	25	25	26	27	27	28

Source: Adapted from C. Eisenhardt and F. Swed, "Tables for Testing Randomness of Grouping in a Sequence of Alternatives," The Annals of Statistics, vol. 14 (1943), pp. 83–86. Reprinted with permission of the Institute of Mathematical Statistics and of the Benjamin/Cummings Publishing Company, in whose publication, Elementary Statistics, 3rd ed. (1989), by Mario F. Triola, this table appears.

APPENDIX B

Data Bank

Data Bank Values

This list explains the values given for the categories in the Data Bank.

1. "Age" is given in years.
2. "Educational level" values are defined as follows:

   0 = no high school degree   2 = college graduate
   1 = high school graduate   3 = graduate degree

3. "Smoking status" values are defined as follows:

   0 = does not smoke
   1 = smokes less than one pack per day
   2 = smokes one or more than one pack per day

4. "Exercise" values are defined as follows:

   0 = none   2 = moderate
   1 = light   3 = heavy

5. "Weight" is given in pounds.
6. "Serum cholesterol" is given in milligram percent (mg%).
7. "Systolic pressure" is given in millimeters of mercury (mm Hg).
8. "IQ" is given in standard IQ test score values.
9. "Sodium" is given in milliequivalents per liter (mEq/1).
10. "Sex" is listed as male (M) or female (F).
11. "Marital status" values are defined as follows:

    M = married   S = single
    W = widowed   D = divorced

Data Bank

ID number	Age	Educational level	Smoking status	Exercise	Weight	Serum cholesterol	Systolic pressure	IQ	Sodium	Sex	Marital status
01	27	2	1	1	120	193	126	118	136	F	M
02	18	1	0	1	145	210	120	105	137	M	S
03	32	2	0	0	118	196	128	115	135	F	M
04	24	2	0	1	162	208	129	108	142	M	M
05	19	1	2	0	106	188	119	106	133	F	S
06	56	1	0	0	143	206	136	111	138	F	W
07	65	1	2	0	160	240	131	99	140	M	W
08	36	2	1	0	215	215	163	106	151	M	D
09	43	1	0	1	127	201	132	111	134	F	M
10	47	1	1	1	132	215	138	109	135	F	D
11	48	3	1	2	196	199	148	115	146	M	D
12	25	2	2	3	109	210	115	114	141	F	S
13	63	0	1	0	170	242	149	101	152	F	D
14	37	2	0	3	187	193	142	109	144	M	M

Data Bank *(continued)*

ID number	Age	Educational level	Smoking status	Exercise	Weight	Serum cholesterol	Systolic pressure	IQ	Sodium	Sex	Marital status
15	40	0	1	1	234	208	156	98	147	M	M
16	25	1	2	1	199	253	135	103	148	M	S
17	72	0	0	0	143	288	156	103	145	F	M
18	56	1	1	0	156	164	153	99	144	F	D
19	37	2	0	2	142	214	122	110	135	M	M
20	41	1	1	1	123	220	142	108	134	F	M
21	33	2	1	1	165	194	122	112	137	M	S
22	52	1	0	1	157	205	119	106	134	M	D
23	44	2	0	1	121	223	135	116	133	F	M
24	53	1	0	0	131	199	133	121	136	F	M
25	19	1	0	3	128	206	118	122	132	M	S
26	25	1	0	0	143	200	118	103	135	M	M
27	31	2	1	1	152	204	120	119	136	M	M
28	28	2	0	0	119	203	118	116	138	F	M
29	23	1	0	0	111	240	120	105	135	F	S
30	47	2	1	0	149	199	132	123	136	F	M
31	47	2	1	0	179	235	131	113	139	M	M
32	59	1	2	0	206	260	151	99	143	M	W
33	36	2	1	0	191	201	148	118	145	M	D
34	59	0	1	1	156	235	142	100	132	F	W
35	35	1	0	0	122	232	131	106	135	F	M
36	29	2	0	2	175	195	129	121	148	M	M
37	43	3	0	3	194	211	138	129	146	M	M
38	44	1	2	0	132	240	130	109	132	F	S
39	63	2	2	1	188	255	156	121	145	M	M
40	36	2	1	1	125	220	126	117	140	F	S
41	21	1	0	1	109	206	114	102	136	F	M
42	31	2	0	2	112	201	116	123	133	F	M
43	57	1	1	1	167	213	141	103	143	M	W
44	20	1	2	3	101	194	110	111	125	F	S
45	24	2	1	3	106	188	113	114	127	F	D
46	42	1	0	1	148	206	136	107	140	M	S
47	55	1	0	0	170	257	152	106	130	F	M
48	23	0	0	1	152	204	116	95	142	M	M
49	32	2	0	0	191	210	132	115	147	M	M
50	28	1	0	1	148	222	135	100	135	M	M
51	67	0	0	0	160	250	141	116	146	F	W
52	22	1	1	1	109	220	121	103	144	F	M
53	19	1	1	1	131	231	117	112	133	M	S
54	25	2	0	2	153	212	121	119	149	M	D
55	41	3	2	2	165	236	130	131	152	M	M
56	24	2	0	3	112	205	118	100	132	F	S
57	32	2	0	1	115	187	115	109	136	F	S

Data Bank *(concluded)*

ID number	Age	Educational level	Smoking status	Exercise	Weight	Serum cholesterol	Systolic pressure	IQ	Sodium	Sex	Marital status
58	50	3	0	1	173	203	136	126	146	M	M
59	32	2	1	0	186	248	119	122	149	M	M
60	26	2	0	1	181	207	123	121	142	M	S
61	36	1	1	0	112	188	117	98	135	F	D
62	40	1	1	0	130	201	121	105	136	F	D
63	19	1	1	1	132	237	115	111	137	M	S
64	37	2	0	2	179	228	141	127	141	F	M
65	65	3	2	1	212	220	158	129	148	M	M
66	21	1	2	2	99	191	117	103	131	F	S
67	25	2	2	1	128	195	120	121	131	F	S
68	68	0	0	0	167	210	142	98	140	M	W
69	18	1	1	2	121	198	123	113	136	F	S
70	26	0	1	1	163	235	128	99	140	M	M
71	45	1	1	1	185	229	125	101	143	M	M
72	44	3	0	0	130	215	128	128	137	F	M
73	50	1	0	0	142	232	135	104	138	F	M
74	63	0	0	0	166	271	143	103	147	F	W
75	48	1	0	3	163	203	131	103	144	M	M
76	27	2	0	3	147	186	118	114	134	M	M
77	31	3	1	1	152	228	116	126	138	M	D
78	28	2	0	2	112	197	120	123	133	F	M
79	36	2	1	2	190	226	123	121	147	M	M
80	43	3	2	0	179	252	127	131	145	M	D
81	21	1	0	1	117	185	116	105	137	F	S
82	32	2	1	0	125	193	123	119	135	F	M
83	29	2	1	0	123	192	131	116	131	F	D
84	49	2	2	1	185	190	129	127	144	M	M
85	24	1	1	1	133	237	121	114	129	M	M
86	36	2	0	2	163	195	115	119	139	M	M
87	34	1	2	0	135	199	133	117	135	F	M
88	36	0	0	1	142	216	138	88	137	F	M
89	29	1	1	1	155	214	120	98	135	M	S
90	42	0	0	2	169	201	123	96	137	M	D
91	41	1	1	1	136	214	133	102	141	F	D
92	29	1	1	0	112	205	120	102	130	F	M
93	43	1	1	0	185	208	127	100	143	M	M
94	61	1	2	0	173	248	142	101	141	M	M
95	21	1	1	3	106	210	111	105	131	F	S
96	56	0	0	0	149	232	142	103	141	F	M
97	63	0	1	0	192	193	163	95	147	M	M
98	74	1	0	0	162	247	151	99	151	F	W
99	35	2	0	1	151	251	147	113	145	F	M
100	28	2	0	3	161	199	129	116	138	M	M

Data Set I   Record Temperatures

Record high temperatures by state in degrees Fahrenheit

112	100	107	122	120
100	118	112	108	113
128	117	115	110	120
120	116	115	121	117
134	118	118	113	107
114	121	117	120	110
106	114	118	119	118
110	114	125	111	112
109	105	106	104	114
112	109	110	111	115

Record low temperatures by state in degrees Fahrenheit

−27	12	−35	−50	−58
−80	−60	−51	−52	−32
−40	−36	−60	−34	−23
−29	−36	−19	−60	−50
−45	−47	−40	−39	−50
−61	−40	−70	−27	−30
−32	−37	−47	−54	−48
−17	−16	−50	−42	−37
−2	−50	−46	−28	−55
−17	−40	−34	−19	−66

Source: Data from the *World Almanac and Book of Facts.*

Data Set II   Identity Theft Complaints

The data values show the number of complaints of identity theft for 50 selected cities.

2609	1202	2730	483	655
626	393	1268	279	663
817	1165	551	2654	592
128	189	424	585	78
1836	154	248	239	5888
574	75	226	28	205
176	372	84	229	15
148	117	22	211	31
77	41	200	35	30
88	20	84	465	136

Source: Federal Trade Commission.

Data Set III   Length of Major North American Rivers

729	610	325	392	524
1459	450	465	605	330
950	906	329	290	1000
600	1450	862	532	890
407	525	720	1243	850
649	730	352	390	420
710	340	693	306	250
470	724	332	259	2340
560	1060	774	332	3710

Data Set III   Length of Major North American Rivers *(continued)*

2315	2540	618	1171	460
431	800	605	410	1310
500	790	531	981	460
926	375	1290	1210	1310
383	380	300	310	411
1900	434	420	545	569
425	800	865	380	445
538	1038	424	350	377
540	659	652	314	360
301	512	500	313	610
360	430	682	886	447
338	485	625	722	525
800	309	435		

Source: Data from the *World Almanac and Book of Facts.*

Data Set IV   Heights (in Feet) of 80 Tallest Buildings in New York City

1250	861	1046	952	552
915	778	856	850	927
729	745	757	752	814
750	697	743	739	750
700	670	716	707	730
682	648	687	687	705
650	634	664	674	685
640	628	630	653	673
625	620	628	645	650
615	592	620	630	630
595	580	614	618	629
587	575	590	609	615
575	572	580	588	603
574	563	575	577	587
565	555	562	570	576
557	570	555	561	574

Heights (in Feet) of 25 Tallest Buildings in Calgary, Alberta

689	530	460	410
645	525	449	410
645	507	441	408
626	500	435	407
608	469	435	
580	468	432	
530	463	420	

Source: Data from the *World Almanac and Book of Facts.*

Data Set V School Suspensions

The data values show the number of suspensions and the number of students enrolled in 41 local school districts in southwestern Pennsylvania.

Suspensions	Enrollment	Suspensions	Enrollment
37	1316	63	1588
29	1337	500	6046
106	4904	5	3610
47	5301	117	4329
51	1380	13	1908
46	1670	8	1341
65	3446	71	5582
223	1010	57	1869
10	795	16	1697
60	2094	60	2269
15	926	51	2307
198	1950	48	1564
56	3005	20	4147
72	4575	80	3182
110	4329	43	2982
6	3238	15	3313
37	3064	187	6090
26	2638	182	4874
140	4949	76	8286
39	3354	37	539
42	3547		

Source: U.S. Department of Education, *Pittsburgh Tribune-Review.*

Data Set VI Acreage of U.S. National Parks, in Thousands of Acres

41	66	233	775	169
36	338	223	46	64
183	4724	61	1449	7075
1013	3225	1181	308	77
520	77	27	217	5
539	3575	650	462	1670
2574	106	52	52	236
505	913	94	75	265
402	196	70	13	132
28	7656	2220	760	143

Source: The Universal Almanac.

Data Set VII Acreage Owned by 35 Municipalities in Southwestern Pennsylvania

384	44	62	218	250
198	60	306	105	600
10	38	87	227	340
48	70	58	223	3700
22	78	165	150	160
130	120	100	234	1200
4200	402	180	200	200

Source: Pittsburgh Tribune-Review.

Data Set VIII Oceans of the World

Ocean	Area (thousands of square miles)	Maximum depth (feet)
Arctic	5,400	17,881
Caribbean Sea	1,063	25,197
Mediterranean Sea	967	16,470
Norwegian Sea	597	13,189
Gulf of Mexico	596	14,370
Hudson Bay	475	850
Greenland Sea	465	15,899
North Sea	222	2,170
Black Sea	178	7,360
Baltic Sea	163	1,440
Atlantic Ocean	31,830	30,246
South China Sea	1,331	18,241
Sea of Okhotsk	610	11,063
Bering Sea	876	13,750
Sea of Japan	389	12,280
East China Sea	290	9,126
Yellow Sea	161	300
Pacific Ocean	63,800	36,200
Arabian Sea	1,492	19,029
Bay of Bengal	839	17,251
Red Sea	169	7,370
Indian Ocean	28,360	24,442

Source: The Universal Almanac.

Data Set IX Commuter and Rapid Rail Systems in the United States

System	Stations	Miles	Vehicles operated
Long Island RR	134	638.2	947
N.Y. Metro North	108	535.9	702
New Jersey Transit	158	926.0	582
Chicago RTA	117	417.0	358
Chicago & NW Transit	62	309.4	277
Boston Amtrak/MBTA	101	529.8	291
Chicago, Burlington, Northern	27	75.0	139
NW Indiana CTD	18	134.8	39
New York City TA	469	492.9	4923
Washington Metro Area TA	70	162.1	534
Metro Boston TA	53	76.7	368
Chicago TA	137	191.0	924
Philadelphia SEPTA	76	75.8	300
San Francisco BART	34	142.0	415
Metro Atlantic RTA	29	67.0	136
New York PATH	13	28.6	282
Miami/Dade Co TA	21	42.2	82
Baltimore MTA	12	26.6	48
Philadelphia PATCO	13	31.5	102
Cleveland RTA	18	38.2	30
New York, Staten Island RT	22	28.6	36

Source: The Universal Almanac.

Data Set X   Keystone Jackpot Analysis*

Ball	Times drawn	Ball	Times drawn	Ball	Times drawn
1	11	12	10	23	7
2	5	13	11	24	8
3	10	14	5	25	13
4	11	15	8	26	11
5	7	16	14	27	7
6	13	17	8	28	10
7	8	18	11	29	11
8	10	19	10	30	5
9	16	20	7	31	7
10	12	21	11	32	8
11	10	22	6	33	11

*Times each number has been selected in the regular drawings of the Pennsylvania Lottery.

Source: Pittsburgh Post-Gazette.

Data Set XI   Pages in Statistics Books

The data values represent the number of pages found in statistics textbooks.

616	578	569	511	468
493	564	801	483	847
525	881	757	272	703
741	556	500	668	967
608	465	739	669	651
495	613	774	274	542
739	488	601	727	556
589	724	731	662	680
589	435	742	567	574
733	576	526	443	478
586	282			

Source: Allan G. Bluman.

Data Set XII   Fifty Top Grossing Movies—2000

The data values represent the gross income in millions of dollars for the 50 top movies for the year 2000.

253.4	123.3	90.2	61.3	57.3
215.4	122.8	90.0	61.3	57.2
186.7	117.6	89.1	60.9	56.9
182.6	115.8	77.1	60.8	56.0
161.3	113.7	73.2	60.6	53.3
157.3	113.3	71.2	60.1	53.3
157.0	109.7	70.3	60.0	51.9
155.4	106.8	69.7	59.1	50.9
137.7	101.6	68.5	58.3	50.8
126.6	90.6	68.4	58.1	50.2

Source: Data from the *World Almanac and Book of Facts.*

Data Set XIII   Hospital Data*

Number	Number of beds	Admissions	Payroll ($000)	Personnel
1	235	6,559	18,190	722
2	205	6,237	17,603	692
3	371	8,915	27,278	1,187
4	342	8,659	26,722	1,156
5	61	1,779	5,187	237
6	55	2,261	7,519	247
7	109	2,102	5,817	245
8	74	2,065	5,418	223
9	74	3,204	7,614	326
10	137	2,638	7,862	362
11	428	18,168	70,518	2,461
12	260	12,821	40,780	1,422
13	159	4,176	11,376	465
14	142	3,952	11,057	450
15	45	1,179	3,370	145
16	42	1,402	4,119	211
17	92	1,539	3,520	158
18	28	503	1,172	72
19	56	1,780	4,892	195
20	68	2,072	6,161	243
21	206	9,868	30,995	1,142
22	93	3,642	7,912	305
23	68	1,558	3,929	180
24	330	7,611	33,377	1,116
25	127	4,716	13,966	498
26	87	2,432	6,322	240
27	577	19,973	60,934	1,822
28	310	11,055	31,362	981
29	49	1,775	3,987	180
30	449	17,929	53,240	1,899
31	530	15,423	50,127	1,669
32	498	15,176	49,375	1,549
33	60	565	5,527	251
34	350	11,793	34,133	1,207
35	381	13,133	49,641	1,731
36	585	22,762	71,232	2,608
37	286	8,749	28,645	1,194
38	151	2,607	12,737	377
39	98	2,518	10,731	352
40	53	1,848	4,791	185
41	142	3,658	11,051	421
42	73	3,393	9,712	385
43	624	20,410	72,630	2,326
44	78	1,107	4,946	139
45	85	2,114	4,522	221

(continued)

Data Set XIII   Hospital Data* *(continued)*

Number	Number of beds	Admissions	Payroll ($000)	Personnel
46	120	3,435	11,479	417
47	84	1,768	4,360	184
48	667	22,375	74,810	2,461
49	36	1,008	2,311	131
50	598	21,259	113,972	4,010
51	1,021	40,879	165,917	6,264
52	233	4,467	22,572	558
53	205	4,162	21,766	527
54	80	469	8,254	280
55	350	7,676	58,341	1,525
56	290	7,499	57,298	1,502
57	890	31,812	134,752	3,933
58	880	31,703	133,836	3,914
59	67	2,020	8,533	280
60	317	14,595	68,264	2,772
61	123	4,225	12,161	504
62	285	7,562	25,930	952
63	51	1,932	6,412	472
64	34	1,591	4,393	205
65	194	5,111	19,367	753
66	191	6,729	21,889	946
67	227	5,862	18,285	731
68	172	5,509	17,222	680
69	285	9,855	27,848	1,180
70	230	7,619	29,147	1,216
71	206	7,368	28,592	1,185
72	102	3,255	9,214	359
73	76	1,409	3,302	198
74	540	396	22,327	788
75	110	3,170	9,756	409
76	142	4,984	13,550	552
77	380	335	11,675	543
78	256	8,749	23,132	907
79	235	8,676	22,849	883
80	580	1,967	33,004	1,059
81	86	2,477	7,507	309
82	102	2,200	6,894	225
83	190	6,375	17,283	618
84	85	3,506	8,854	380
85	42	1,516	3,525	166
86	60	1,573	15,608	236
87	485	16,676	51,348	1,559
88	455	16,285	50,786	1,537
89	266	9,134	26,145	939
90	107	3,497	10,255	431
91	122	5,013	17,092	589

Data Set XIII   Hospital Data* *(continued)*

Number	Number of beds	Admissions	Payroll ($000)	Personnel
92	36	519	1,526	80
93	34	615	1,342	74
94	37	1,123	2,712	123
95	100	2,478	6,448	265
96	65	2,252	5,955	237
97	58	1,649	4,144	203
98	55	2,049	3,515	152
99	109	1,816	4,163	194
100	64	1,719	3,696	167
101	73	1,682	5,581	240
102	52	1,644	5,291	222
103	326	10,207	29,031	1,074
104	268	10,182	28,108	1,030
105	49	1,365	4,461	215
106	52	763	2,615	125
107	106	4,629	10,549	456
108	73	2,579	6,533	240
109	163	201	5,015	260
110	32	34	2,880	124
111	385	14,553	52,572	1,724
112	95	3,267	9,928	366
113	339	12,021	54,163	1,607
114	50	1,548	3,278	156
115	55	1,274	2,822	162
116	278	6,323	15,697	722
117	298	11,736	40,610	1,606
118	136	2,099	7,136	255
119	97	1,831	6,448	222
120	369	12,378	35,879	1,312
121	288	10,807	29,972	1,263
122	262	10,394	29,408	1,237
123	94	2,143	7,593	323
124	98	3,465	9,376	371
125	136	2,768	7,412	390
126	70	824	4,741	208
127	35	883	2,505	142
128	52	1,279	3,212	158

*This information was obtained from a sample of hospitals in a selected state. The hospitals are identified by number instead of name.

APPENDIX C

Glossary

adjusted R^2 used in multiple regression when n and k are approximately equal, to provide a more realistic value of R^2

alpha the probability of a type I error, represented by the Greek letter α

alternative hypothesis a statistical hypothesis that states a difference between a parameter and a specific value or states that there is a difference between two parameters

analysis of variance (ANOVA) a statistical technique used to test a hypothesis concerning the means of three or more populations

ANOVA summary table the table used to summarize the results of an ANOVA test

Bayes' theorem a theorem that allows you to compute the revised probability of an event that occurred before another event when the events are dependent

beta the probability of a type II error, represented by the Greek letter β

between-group variance a variance estimate using the means of the groups or between the groups in an F test

biased sample a sample for which some type of systematic error has been made in the selection of subjects for the sample

big data a data set with an extremely large volume of data, an extremely high velocity of data, and an extremely wide variety of data

bimodal a data set with two modes

binomial distribution the outcomes of a binomial experiment and the corresponding probabilities of these outcomes

binomial experiment a probability experiment in which each trial has only two outcomes, there are a fixed number of trials, the outcomes of the trials are independent, and the probability of success remains the same for each trial

blinding subjects of the study do not know whether they are receiving a treatment or a placebo

blocks groups of subjects with similar characteristics in a statistical study that receive different treatments when these characteristics might make a difference in the outcomes of the experiment

Bonferroni test a test that can be used to compare pairs of means after a significant F test in ANOVA; P-values or adjusted critical values are used to determine significance

boundary a class of numbers in which a data value would be placed before the data value has been rounded

boxplot a graph used to represent a data set when the data set contains a small number of values

categorical frequency distribution a frequency distribution used when the data are categorical (nominal)

census a counting (usually done by government) of all members of the population

central limit theorem a theorem that states that as the sample size increases, the shape of the distribution of the sample means taken from the population with mean μ and standard deviation σ will approach a normal distribution; the distribution will have a mean μ and a standard deviation $\sigma/\sqrt{n}$

Chebyshev's theorem a theorem that states that the proportion of values from a data set that fall within k standard deviations of the mean will be at least $1 - 1/k^2$, where k is a number greater than 1

chi-square distribution a probability distribution obtained from the values of $(n-1)s^2/\sigma^2$ when random samples are selected from a normally distributed population whose variance is σ^2

class boundaries the upper and lower values of a class for a grouped frequency distribution whose values have one additional decimal place more than the data and end in the digit 5

class midpoint a value for a class in a frequency distribution obtained by adding the lower and upper class boundaries (or the lower and upper class limits) and dividing by 2

class width the difference between the upper class boundary and the lower class boundary for a class in a frequency distribution

classical probability the type of probability that uses sample spaces to determine the numerical probability that an event will happen

cluster sample a sample obtained by selecting a preexisting or natural group, called a cluster, and using the members in the cluster for the sample

coefficient of determination a measure of the variation of the dependent variable that is explained by the regression line and the independent variable; the ratio of the explained variation to the total variation

coefficient of variation the standard deviation divided by the mean with the result expressed as a percentage

combination a selection of objects without regard to order

complement of an event the set of outcomes in the sample space that are not among the outcomes of the event itself

completely randomized design a statistical study where the subjects are assigned to groups by randomization and treatments are assigned to groups by randomization

compound bar graph statistical bar graph which compares data from different groups using vertical or horizontal bars

compound event an event that consists of two or more outcomes or simple events

conditional probability the probability that an event *B* occurs after an event *A* has already occurred

confidence interval a specific interval estimate of a parameter determined by using data obtained from a sample and the specific confidence level of the estimate

confidence level the probability that a parameter lies within the specified interval estimate of the parameter

confounding variable a variable that influences the outcome variable but cannot be separated from the other variables that influence the outcome variable

consistent estimator an estimator whose value approaches the value of the parameter estimated as the sample size increases

contingency table data arranged in table form for the chi-square independence test, with *R* rows and *C* columns

continuous variable a variable that can assume all values between any two specific values; a variable obtained by measuring

control group a group in an experimental study that is not given any special treatment

convenience sample sample of subjects used because they are convenient and available

correction for continuity a correction employed when a continuous distribution is used to approximate a discrete distribution

correlation a statistical method used to determine whether a linear relationship exists between variables

correlation coefficient a statistic or parameter that measures the strength and direction of a linear relationship between two variables

critical or **rejection region** the range of values of the test value that indicates that there is a significant difference and the null hypothesis should be rejected in a hypothesis test

critical value (C.V.) a value that separates the critical region from the noncritical region in a hypothesis test

cross-sectional study a study in which data are collected at one point in time

cumulative frequency the sum of the frequencies accumulated up to the upper boundary of a class in a frequency distribution

data measurements or observations for a variable

data array a data set that has been ordered

data set a collection of data values

data transformation occurs when the researcher changes the form of the data to analyze it in a different way

data value or **datum** a value in a data set

decile a location measure of a data value; it divides the distribution into 10 groups

degrees of freedom the number of values that are free to vary after a sample statistic has been computed; used

when a distribution (such as the *t* distribution) consists of a family of curves

dependent events events for which the outcome or occurrence of the first event affects the outcome or occurrence of the second event in such a way that the probability is changed

dependent samples samples in which the subjects are paired or matched in some way; i.e., the samples are related

dependent variable a variable in correlation and regression analysis that cannot be controlled or manipulated

descriptive statistics a branch of statistics that consists of the collection, organization, summarization, and presentation of data

discrete variable a variable that assumes values that can be counted

disjoint sets two or more sets that have no items in common

disordinal interaction an interaction between variables in ANOVA, indicated when the graphs of the lines connecting the mean intersect

distribution-free statistics *see* nonparametric statistics

dotplot statistical graph in which each data value is plotted by using a dot above a horizontal axis

double blinding technique whereby subjects and researchers do not know whether the subjects are receiving a treatment or a placebo

double sampling a sampling method in which a very large population is given a questionnaire to determine those who meet the qualifications for a study; the questionnaire is reviewed, a second smaller population is defined, and a sample is selected from this group

empirical probability the type of probability that uses frequency distributions based on observations to determine numerical probabilities of events

empirical rule a rule that states that when a distribution is bell-shaped (normal), approximately 68% of the data values will fall within 1 standard deviation of the mean; approximately 95% of the data values will fall within 2 standard deviations of the mean; and approximately 99.7% of the data values will fall within 3 standard deviations of the mean

equally likely events the events in the sample space that have the same probability of occurring

estimation the process of estimating the value of a parameter from information obtained from a sample

estimator a statistic used to estimate a parameter

event the outcome of a probability experiment

expected frequency the frequency obtained by calculation (as if the two variables are independent) and used in the chi-square test

expected value the theoretical average of a variable that has a probability distribution

experimental study a study in which the researcher manipulates one of the variables and tries to determine how the manipulation influences other variables

explanatory variable a variable that is being manipulated by the researcher to see if it affects the outcome variable

exploratory data analysis the act of analyzing data to determine what information can be obtained by using stem and leaf plots, medians, interquartile ranges, and boxplots

extrapolation use of the equation for the regression line to predict y' for a value of x that is beyond the range of the data values of x

F distribution the sampling distribution of the variances when two independent samples are selected from two normally distributed populations in which the variances are equal and the variances s_1^2 and s_2^2 are compared as s_1^2/s_2^2

F test a statistical test used to compare two variances or three or more means

factors the independent variables in ANOVA tests

finite population correction factor a correction factor used to correct the standard error of the mean when the sample size is greater than 5% of the population size

five-number summary five specific values for a data set that consist of the lowest and highest values, Q_1 and Q_3, and the median

frequency the number of values in a specific class of a frequency distribution

frequency distribution an organization of raw data in table form, using classes and frequencies

frequency polygon a graph that displays the data by using lines that connect points plotted for the frequencies at the midpoints of the classes

geometric distribution the distribution of a probability experiment that has two outcomes and is repeated until a success outcome is obtained

goodness-of-fit test a chi-square test used to see whether a frequency distribution fits a specific pattern

grouped frequency distribution a distribution used when the range is large and classes of several units in width are needed

Hawthorne effect an effect on an outcome variable caused by the fact that subjects of the study know that they are participating in the study

histogram a graph that displays the data by using vertical bars of various heights to represent the frequencies of a distribution

homogeneity of proportions test a test used to determine the equality of three or more proportions

hypergeometric distribution the distribution of a variable that has two outcomes when sampling is done without replacement

hypothesis testing a decision-making process for evaluating claims about a population

independence test a chi-square test used to test the independence of two variables when data are tabulated in table form in terms of frequencies

independent events events for which the probability of the first occurring does not affect the probability of the second occurring

independent samples samples that are not related

independent variable a variable in correlation and regression analysis that can be controlled or manipulated

inferential statistics a branch of statistics that consists of generalizing from samples to populations, performing hypothesis testing, determining relationships among variables, and making predictions

influential observation an observation that when removed from the data values would markedly change the position of the regression line

interaction effect the effect of two or more variables on each other in a two-way ANOVA study

interquartile range $Q_3 - Q_1$ (i.e. the distance between the first and third quartiles)

interval estimate a range of values used to estimate a parameter

interval level of measurement a measurement level that ranks data and in which precise differences between units of measure exist. *See also* nominal, ordinal, and ratio levels of measurement

Kruskal-Wallis test a nonparametric test used to compare three or more means

law of large numbers a law that says that when a probability experiment is repeated a large number of times, the relative frequency probability of an outcome will approach its theoretical probability

least-squares line another name for the regression line

left-tailed test a test used on a hypothesis when the critical region is on the left side of the distribution

level a treatment in ANOVA for a variable

level of significance the maximum probability of committing a type I error in hypothesis testing

longitudinal study a study conducted over a period of time

lower class limit the lower value of a class in a frequency distribution that has the same decimal place value as the data

lurking variable a variable that influences the relationship between x and y, but was not considered in the study

main effect the effect of the factors or independent variables when there is a nonsignificant interaction effect in a two-way ANOVA study

marginal change the magnitude of the change in the dependent variable when the independent variable changes 1 unit

matched-pairs design a statistical study where subjects are matched and then one subject is assigned to a treatment group and the other subject is assigned to a control group

maximum error of estimate the maximum likely difference between the point estimate of a parameter and the actual value of the parameter

mean the sum of the values, divided by the total number of values

mean square the variance found by dividing the sum of the squares of a variable by the corresponding degrees of freedom; used in ANOVA

measurement scales a type of classification that tells how variables are categorized, counted, or measured; the four types of scales are nominal, ordinal, interval, and ratio

median the midpoint of a data array

midrange the sum of the lowest and highest data values, divided by 2

modal class the class with the largest frequency

mode the value that occurs most often in a data set

Monte Carlo method a simulation technique using random numbers

multimodal a data set with three or more modes

multinomial distribution a probability distribution for an experiment in which each trial has more than two outcomes

multiple correlation coefficient a measure of the strength of the relationship between the independent variables and the dependent variable in a multiple regression study

multiple regression a study that seeks to determine if several independent variables are related to a dependent variable

multiple relationship a relationship in which many variables are under study

multistage sampling a sampling technique that uses a combination of sampling methods

mutually exclusive events probability events that cannot occur at the same time

negative relationship a relationship between variables such that as one variable increases, the other variable decreases, and vice versa

negatively skewed or **left-skewed distribution** a distribution in which the majority of the data values fall to the right of the mean

nominal level of measurement a measurement level that classifies data into mutually exclusive (nonoverlapping) exhaustive categories in which no order or ranking can be imposed on them. *See also* interval, ordinal, and ratio levels of measurement

noncritical or **nonrejection region** the range of values of the test value that indicates that the difference was probably due to chance and the null hypothesis should not be rejected

nonparametric statistics a branch of statistics for use when the population from which the samples are selected is not normally distributed and for use in testing hypotheses that do not involve specific population parameters

nonrejection region *see* noncritical region

nonresistant statistic a statistic that is relatively less affected by outliers

non-response bias occurs when subjects do not respond to a survey question

nonsampling error an error that occurs erroneously or from a biased sample

normal distribution a continuous, symmetric, bell-shaped distribution of a variable

normal quantile plot graphical plot used to determine whether a variable is approximately normally distributed

null hypothesis a statistical hypothesis that states that there is no difference between a parameter and a specific value or that there is no difference between two parameters

observational study a study in which the researcher merely observes what is happening or what has happened in the past and draws conclusions based on these observations

observed frequency the actual frequency value obtained from a sample and used in the chi-square test

ogive a graph that represents the cumulative frequencies for the classes in a frequency distribution

one-tailed test a test that indicates that the null hypothesis should be rejected when the test statistic value is in the critical region on one side of the mean

one-way ANOVA a study used to test for differences among means for a single independent variable when there are three or more groups

open-ended distribution a frequency distribution that has no specific beginning value or no specific ending value

ordinal interaction an interaction between variables in ANOVA, indicated when the graphs of the lines connecting the means do not intersect

ordinal level of measurement a measurement level that classifies data into categories that can be ranked; however, precise differences between the ranks do not exist. *See also* interval, nominal, and ratio levels of measurement

outcome the result of a single trial of a probability experiment

outcome variable a variable that is studied to see if it has changed significantly due to the manipulation of the explanatory variable

outlier an extreme value in a data set; it is omitted from a boxplot

parameter a characteristic or measure obtained by using all the data values for a specific population

parametric tests statistical tests for population parameters such as means, variances, and proportions that involve assumptions about the populations from which the samples were selected

Pareto chart chart that uses vertical bars to represent frequencies for a categorical variable

Pearson product moment correlation coefficient (PPMCC) a statistic used to determine the strength of a relationship when the variables are normally distributed

Pearson's index of skewness value used to determine the degree of skewness of a variable

percentile a location measure of a data value; it divides the distribution into 100 groups

permutation an arrangement of n objects in a specific order

pie graph a circle that is divided into sections or wedges according to the percentage of frequencies in each category of the distribution

placebo effect results of a study obtained by subjects who improve but not due to the conditions of the study

point estimate a specific numerical value estimate of a parameter

Poisson distribution a probability distribution used when n is large and p is small and when the independent variables occur over a period of time

pooled estimate of the variance a weighted average of the variance using the two sample variances and their respective degrees of freedom as the weights

population the totality of all subjects possessing certain common characteristics that are being studied

population correlation coefficient the value of the correlation coefficient computed by using all possible pairs of data values (x, y) taken from a population

positive relationship a relationship between two variables such that as one variable increases, the other variable increases or as one variable decreases, the other decreases

positively skewed or **right-skewed distribution** a distribution in which the majority of the data values fall to the left of the mean

power of a test the probability of rejecting the null hypothesis when it is false

prediction interval a confidence interval for a predicted value y

probability the chance of an event occurring

probability distribution the values a random variable can assume and the corresponding probabilities of the values

probability experiment a chance process that leads to well-defined results called outcomes

proportion a part of a whole, represented by a fraction, a decimal, or a percentage

P-value the actual probability of getting the sample mean value if the null hypothesis is true

qualitative variable a variable that can be placed into distinct categories, according to some characteristic or attribute

quantiles values that separate the data set into approximately equal groups

quantitative variable a variable that is numerical in nature and that can be measured or counted

quartile a location measure of a data value; it divides the distribution into four groups

quasi-experimental study a study that uses intact groups rather than random assignment of subjects to groups

random sample a sample obtained by using random or chance methods; a sample for which every member of the population has an equal chance of being selected

random variable a variable whose values are determined by chance

range the highest data value minus the lowest data value

range rule of thumb dividing the range by 4, given an approximation of the standard deviation

ranking the positioning of a data value in a data array according to some rating scale

ratio level of measurement a measurement level that possesses all the characteristics of interval measurement and a true zero; it also has true ratios between different units of measure. *See also* interval, nominal, and ordinal levels of measurement

raw data data collected in original form

regression a statistical method used to describe the nature of the relationship between variables, that is, a positive or negative, linear or nonlinear relationship

regression line the line of best fit of the data

rejection region *see* critical region

relative frequency graph a graph using proportions instead of raw data as frequencies

relatively efficient estimator an estimator that has the smallest variance of all the statistics that can be used to estimate a parameter

replication repetition of the study using different subjects

residual the difference between the actual value of y and the predicted value y' for a specific value of x

residual plot plot of the x values and the residuals to determine how well the regression line can be used to make predictions

resistant statistic a statistic that is not affected by an extremely skewed distribution

response bias occurs when a subject gives a different response than he or she believes; also called interview bias

retrospective study a study in which data are collected from records obtained from the past

right-tailed test a test used on a hypothesis when the critical region is on the right side of the distribution

run a succession of identical letters preceded by or followed by a different letter or no letter at all, such as the beginning or end of the succession

runs test a nonparametric test used to determine whether data are random

sample a group of subjects selected from the population

sample space the set of all possible outcomes of a probability experiment

sampling distribution of sample means a distribution obtained by using the means computed from random samples taken from a population

sampling error the difference between the sample measure and the corresponding population measure due to the fact that the sample is not a perfect representation of the population

scatter plot a graph of the independent and dependent variables in regression and correlation analysis

Scheffé test a test used after ANOVA, if the null hypothesis is rejected, to locate significant differences in the means

selection bias occurs when some subjects are more likely to be included in a study than other subjects; also called sampling bias

sequence sampling a sampling technique used in quality control in which successive units are taken from production lines and tested to see whether they meet the standards set by the manufacturing company

sign test a nonparametric test used to test the value of the median for a specific sample or to test sample means in a comparison of two dependent samples

simple event an outcome that results from a single trial of a probability experiment

simple relationship a relationship in which only two variables are under study

simulation techniques techniques that use probability experiments to mimic real-life situations

Spearman rank correlation coefficient the nonparametric equivalent to the correlation coefficient, used when the data are ranked

standard deviation the square root of the variance

standard error of the estimate the standard deviation of the observed y values about the predicted y' values in regression and correlation analysis

standard error of the mean the standard deviation of the sample means for samples taken from the same population

standard normal distribution a normal distribution for which the mean is equal to 0 and the standard deviation is equal to 1

standard score the difference between a data value and the mean, divided by the standard deviation

statistic a characteristic or measure obtained by using the data values from a sample

statistical hypothesis a conjecture about a population parameter, which may or may not be true

statistical test a test that uses data obtained from a sample to make a decision about whether the null hypothesis should be rejected

statistics the science of conducting studies to collect, organize, summarize, analyze, and draw conclusions from data

stem and leaf plot a data plot that uses part of a data value as the stem and part of the data value as the leaf to form groups or classes

stratified sample a sample obtained by dividing the population into subgroups, called strata, according to various homogeneous characteristics and then selecting members from each stratum

structured data data that can be displayed in the form of tables, using rows and columns

subjective probability the type of probability that uses a probability value based on an educated guess or estimate, employing opinions and inexact information

sum of squares between groups a statistic computed in the numerator of the fraction used to find the between-group variance in ANOVA

sum of squares within groups a statistic computed in the numerator of the fraction used to find the within-group variance in ANOVA

symmetric distribution a distribution in which the data values are uniformly distributed about the mean

systematic sample a sample obtained by numbering each element in the population and then selecting every kth number from the population to be included in the sample

t **distribution** a family of bell-shaped curves based on degrees of freedom, similar to the standard normal distribution with the exception that the variance is greater than 1; used when you are testing small samples and when the population standard deviation is unknown

t **test** a statistical test for the mean of a population, used when the population is normally distributed and the population standard deviation is unknown

test statistic the numerical value obtained from a statistical test, computed from (observed value − expected value) ÷ standard error

time series graph a graph that represents data that occur over a specific time

treatment group a group in an experimental study that has received some type of treatment

treatment groups the groups used in an ANOVA study

tree diagram a device used to list all possibilities of a sequence of events in a systematic way

Tukey test a test used to make pairwise comparisons of means in an ANOVA study when samples are the same size

two-tailed test a test that indicates that the null hypothesis should be rejected when the test value is in either of the two critical regions

two-way ANOVA a study used to test the effects of two or more independent variables and the possible interaction between them

type I error the error that occurs if you reject the null hypothesis when it is true

type II error the error that occurs if you do not reject the null hypothesis when it is false

unbiased estimator an estimator whose value approximates the expected value of a population parameter, used for the variance or standard deviation when the sample size is less than 30; an estimator whose expected value or mean must be equal to the mean of the parameter being estimated

unbiased sample a sample chosen at random from the population that is, for the most part, representative of the population

ungrouped frequency distribution a distribution that uses individual data and has a small range of data

uniform distribution a distribution whose values are evenly distributed over its range

unstructured data data that are expressed in words and images, such as text messages, emails, photographs, etc.

upper class limit the upper value of a class in a frequency distribution that has the same decimal place value as the data

variable a characteristic or attribute that can assume different values

variance the average of the squares of the distance that each value is from the mean

Venn diagram a diagram used as a pictorial representative for a probability concept or rule

volunteer bias occurs when volunteers are used in a study rather than randomly selected subjects

volunteer sample subjects who decide for themselves to participate in a statistical study

weighted mean the mean found by multiplying each value by its corresponding weight and dividing by the sum of the weights

Wilcoxon rank sum test a nonparametric test used to test independent samples and compare distributions

Wilcoxon signed-rank test a nonparametric test used to test dependent samples and compare distributions

within-group variance a variance estimate using all the sample data for an F test; it is not affected by differences in the means

z **distribution** *see* standard normal distribution

z **score** *see* standard score

z **test** a statistical test for means and proportions of a population, used when the population is normally distributed and the population standard deviation is known

z **value** same as *z* score

Glossary of Symbols

a	y intercept of a line		$P(\overline{E})$	Probability of the complement of E
α	Probability of a type I error		$_nP_r$	Number of permutations of n objects taking r objects at a time
b	Slope of a line			
β	Probability of a type II error		π	Pi ≈ 3.14
C	Column frequency		Q	Quartile
cf	Cumulative frequency		q	$1 - p$; test value for Tukey test
$_nC_r$	Number of combinations of n objects taking r objects at a time		$\hat{q}$	$1 - \hat{p}$
			$\overline{q}$	$1 - \overline{p}$
C.V.	Critical value		R	Range; rank sum
CVar	Coefficient of variation		s_D	Standard deviation of the differences
D	Difference; decile		s_{est}	Standard error of estimate
$\overline{D}$	Mean of the differences		SS_B	Sum of squares between groups
d.f.	Degrees of freedom		SS_W	Sum of squares within groups
d.f.N.	Degrees of freedom, numerator		s_B^2	Between-group variance
d.f.D.	Degrees of freedom, denominator		s_W^2	Within-group variance
E	Event; expected frequency; maximum error of estimate		t	t test value
			$t_{\alpha/2}$	Two-tailed t critical value
$\overline{E}$	Complement of an event		μ	Population mean
e	Euler's constant ≈ 2.7183		μ_D	Mean of the population differences
$E(X)$	Expected value		$\mu_{\overline{X}}$	Mean of the sample means
f	Frequency		w	Class width; weight
F	F test value; failure		r	Sample correlation coefficient
F'	Critical value for the Scheffé test		R	Multiple correlation coefficient
F_S	Scheffé test value		r^2	Coefficient of determination
GM	Geometric mean		ρ	Population correlation coefficient
H	Kruskal-Wallis test value		r_S	Spearman rank correlation coefficient
H_0	Null hypothesis		S	Sample space; success
H_1	Alternative hypothesis		s	Sample standard deviation
HM	Harmonic mean		s^2	Sample variance
k	Number of samples		σ	Population standard deviation
λ	Number of occurrences for the Poisson distribution		σ^2	Population variance
			$\sigma_{\overline{X}}$	Standard error of the mean
MD	Median		Σ	Summation notation
MR	Midrange		w_s	Smaller sum of signed ranks, Wilcoxon signed-rank test
MS_B	Mean square between groups			
MS_W	Mean square within groups (error)		X	Data value; number of successes for a binomial distribution
n	Sample size			
N	Population size		$\overline{X}$	Sample mean
$n(E)$	Number of ways E can occur		x	Independent variable in regression
$n(S)$	Number of outcomes in the sample space		$\overline{X}_{GM}$	Grand mean
O	Observed frequency		X_m	Midpoint of a class
P	Percentile; probability		χ^2	Chi-square
p	Probability; population proportion		y	Dependent variable in regression
$\hat{p}$	Sample proportion		y'	Predicted y value
$\overline{p}$	Weighted estimate of p		z	z test value or z score
$P(B\|A)$	Conditional probability		$z_{\alpha/2}$	Two-tailed z critical value
$P(E)$	Probability of an event E		!	Factorial

APPENDIX D

Instructor's Teaching Tips and Selected Answers

Teaching Tips

Chapter 1

It is important to emphasize that statistical studies use *random variables* and the values of the variables are called *data.* Since data can be used in different ways, statistics can be divided into two main branches, *descriptive statistics* and *inferential statistics.* The two branches can be illustrated to the class with examples selected from newspapers and magazines.

A very important requirement of a statistical study is to define the population and select a random *sample.* These concepts should be introduced, and then, if desired, students can be referred to Chapter 14, which contains more information on the selection process. It should be pointed out that inferential statistics is based on *probability* theory.

Since statisticians use data, the various types of data and the measurement levels should be explained. Again, real-life examples can be selected from newspapers and magazine articles.

Two types of statistical studies are explained here. Students should be aware of the advantages and disadvantages of observational and experimental studies. Newspaper and magazine articles can be used to illustrate each type of study. A brief explanation of the uses and misuses of statistics is presented in Chapter 1.

Chapter 2

It is important to emphasize that the reason data are organized into a frequency distribution is to enable the researcher to make sense out of seemingly random occurrences. Once data are organized, they can be studied for various patterns and information. Also, a frequency distribution is used to draw various statistical graphs and is used in computing descriptive statistical measures, such as means and standard deviations.

When you are teaching the histogram, frequency polygon, and ogive, explain to students that the histogram and ogive use the class boundaries on the x axis and the frequency polygon uses class midpoints. Stress that the points for the ogive are

plotted at the *upper class* boundaries, except for the first point whose frequency is zero. Instructors wishing to teach scatter plots along with the other graphs in this chapter can teach Section 10–1 here.

Stem and leaf plots have been moved from Chapter 3 to Chapter 2.

Chapter 3

The purpose of Chapter 3 is to explain the basic descriptive measures that are used in statistics. They can be divided into three groups:

1. Measures of average (mean, median, and mode).
2. Measures of variation (range, variance, and standard deviation).
3. Measures of position (percentiles, deciles, and quartiles).

Before teaching this chapter, the instructor may wish to teach the summation notation section found in Appendix A: Algebra Review. In addition, students should be made aware that the measures of central tendency will usually be different for the same data, and that each measure has a specific purpose.

Students should know that there are differences between the population variance and the unbiased estimate of the variance. For those students who have statistical calculators, the two different keys should be explained.

Students sometimes have difficulty understanding what is meant by the standard deviation. It helps to explain that for many data sets, most of the values fall within 2 standard deviations on either side of the mean. A better approximation is given by Chebyshev's theorem.

Section 3–3 explains position measures. Note that there are several different ways to compute the percentile ranks for individual data. The method presented is consistent with the computation of the median. Procedures for finding percentiles for grouped data have been omitted in this textbook; instead, graphic methods are used. The relationship between the cumulative frequency graph and the percentile graph should be pointed out to students.

Finally, a graphic technique called the boxplot can be used to describe a data set that is too small to be represented by a histogram. Two boxplots drawn on the same axes can also be used to compare two data sets.

Chapter 4

Students should be made aware that probability is used as a basis for inferential statistics. It is important to emphasize the concept of a sample space and the basic probability rules and to distinguish among three types of probabilities. The addition, multiplication, and complementary rules build on the basic probability rules.

This chapter includes the counting rules. These rules are helpful in determining the number of outcomes in a sample space in order to compute probabilities. Section 4–5 shows how to use the counting rules along with the probability rules.

In teaching this chapter, most professors will want to review the factorial notation given in Appendix A unless students have covered it in a previous course. Also emphasize the difference between doing something when repetitions are allowed and when they are not allowed, and the difference between a permutation and a combination. Some students will have difficulty making this distinction at the end of the chapter. Explain that when order is important, such as in license plates, ID numbers, or street addresses, you should use the multiplication rule or the permutation rules.

Chapter 5

It is important to teach the binomial distribution (Sections 5–1 through 5–3). These sections are necessary prerequisites for later sections on hypothesis testing. Section 5–4, on the multinomial, geometric, Poisson, and hypergeometric distributions, can be omitted at the instructor's discretion.

Chapter 6

In Chapter 6, it is important to emphasize the characteristics of the theoretical normal distribution and to show that it can be used as a model for real-life variables that are approximately normally distributed. Using these properties and the Procedure Table, students can solve all problems involving finding areas under the normal distribution. Applications of the normal distribution to real-life variables involve transforming these variables to z values and using the Procedure Table.

Section 6–4 explains the central limit theorem, which will lead to hypothesis testing in Chapter 8.

Section 6–5 explains how the normal distribution can be used to approximate a variable that has the binomial distribution.

Since many applications of statistics require a distribution to be normal, several methods can be used to determine whether a distribution is normal. It should be emphasized that no real-world distribution is perfectly normal.

Chapter 7

Many statistical procedures involve making estimates. To reinforce this, the instructor can have students bring in examples of estimates from newspaper and magazine articles. In most cases, the estimate given will look like a point estimate; however, most editors omit the confidence interval. For example, if an estimate is 7 ± 2 years, it will be reported as 7 years.

Be sure to point out that the more confident you wish to be, the larger the interval should be. There are ways to reduce the size of the interval without changing the level of confidence, for example, by increasing sample size.

Chapter 8

The hypothesis-testing procedure is difficult for many students, since it involves many different concepts. It is important to explain that you can never be 100% sure of the correctness of the results when samples are used.

In teaching this chapter, it is helpful to explain generally what is happening, then follow this explanation by using specific examples. Be sure to emphasize that the claim could be either the null or alternative hypothesis and relate the level of significance to the central limit theorem.

The two methods of hypothesis testing are explained in this chapter. Both methods use five basic steps. With the advent of computers and calculators that can compute the P-value quickly, this method is being used more frequently than in the past. Explain that when one is finding P-values from Tables A–5, A–6, and A–7, only approximate interval values can be used. In the examples and exercises, the specific P-value obtained from a calculator has been given with the interval.

Since P-value intervals for the t and chi-square tests are somewhat difficult to find from the table, you may want to have students use technology for these exercises or use the traditional method for hypotheses testing.

It is important to show students how to use the chi-square table and to emphasize that the variance test can be one- or two-tailed. The one-tailed test can be either right or left. When testing a right-tailed hypothesis, students should use the right side of the table and the specific value, for example, 0.05. When testing a left-tailed hypothesis, the students should use the left side of the table and find the $1 - \alpha$ value. For example, if $\alpha = 0.05$, the $1 - 0.05$, or 0.95, column should be used.

For a two-tailed test, the area must be split. For example, if $\alpha = 0.05$, you should use the 0.025 and 0.975 columns.

Chapter 9

Once students have mastered Chapter 8, this chapter becomes a continuation of the concepts of hypothesis testing. One difficulty students encounter is that there are five different formulas for testing differences. It is important to emphasize the different situations and which test is appropriate in each case.

Section 9–2 explains the F test for comparing two variances. This section is somewhat difficult for students. This section can be taught with the ANOVA material in Chapter 12; however, the students would need to be told whether the variances are equal for the exercises in Section 9–3.

Chapter 10

It is important to stress that many real-life variables are related in some way. Using correlation and regression techniques, statisticians can determine the nature of the relationship. Examples of relationships found in newspapers and magazines can be used in a discussion of the topics involved, such as the strength and type of the relationship. Students should understand that if the graph is cut off, the y intercept value may not be appropriate when the regression line is plotted.

A brief explanation of extrapolation, lurking variables, marginal change, least-squares line, residuals, and influential observations has been added to this chapter.

Chapter 11

Emphasize that the variance test shown in Chapter 8 can be one- or two-tailed, but the goodness-of-fit test and the independence test are always right-tailed.

Chapter 12

It is important to make students aware that they should use the analysis of variance when testing the equality of three or more means. Also emphasize that the ANOVA will not specify where the difference lies. After a significant F, they can perform the Scheffé, Tukey, or Bonferroni test to determine where the difference lies. There are many other tests that can be conducted after the F test, but they are beyond the scope of this book.

Chapter 13

The important point to emphasize in this chapter is that the parametric statistics require the assumption of normality of the data. When this assumption cannot be met, the corresponding counterpart, nonparametric statistics, can be used to test similar hypotheses. In most cases, however, larger sample sizes are

needed to obtain the same results as with the parametric counterparts. Students should know that there is not complete agreement among statisticians as to the use of nonparametric statistics.

Chapter 14

There are two main topics in Chapter 14: sampling and simulation. Both topics use random numbers. For sampling, the instructor can explain the basic methods and have students actually select samples from a small population, then compute the mean of the variable being sampled. The instructor can have each student read the mean aloud to see how close it is to the actual population mean. This is an excellent introduction to the central limit theorem presented in Chapter 6. The mean of the sample means can be computed, and if the class is large, the students will see how close this mean is to the population mean.

The purpose of the second half of this chapter is to enable students to understand the nature of statistical simulation. Again using random numbers and sampling, the students will see how close the means found by simulation techniques are to the theoretical means computed mathematically.

In addition to the two main topics, a third topic on surveys and questionnaires has been added. This topic will help increase the statistical literacy of the students.

Finally, with the advent of computers, companies can quickly secure a large amount of and a large variety of data. A new area of statistics, "big data," has been created. This includes a variety of methods of sorting, retrieving, and analyzing this type of data. Students should be made aware of this new area of statistics since they may encounter it in their careers.

Selected Answers*

Chapter 1
Exercises 1–1

1. Statistics is the science of conducting studies to collect, organize, summarize, analyze, and draw conclusions from data.
2. A variable is a characteristic or attribute that can assume different values.
3. In a census, the researchers collect data from all subjects in the population.
4. A population consists of all subjects under study while a sample is a subgroup of the population.
5. Descriptive statistics consists of the collection, organization, summarization, and presentation of data while inferential statistics consists of generalizing from samples to populations, performing estimations and hypothesis testing, determining relationships among variables, and making predictions.
6. Probability is used in gambling, insurance, and weather forecasting.
7. Samples are used more than populations both because populations are usually large and because researchers are unable to use every subject in the population.
8. A biased sample is a sample that is not representative of the population.
9. This is inferential since it states what consumers think about small businesses staying open on holidays.
10. This is inferential since it makes a generalization about what Americans believe about their drinking water.
11. This is descriptive since it gives the number of patients treated at a specific hospital.
12. This is descriptive since it gives the specific statistics on the number of bridges that need repair.
13. This is a descriptive statistic since it is the result of a specific survey.
14. This is descriptive since it is the specific number of guns found at the U.S. airports.
15. This is descriptive since it is a specific number of people in the United States who were struck by lightning.
16. This is inferential since it is a generalization made about U.S. drivers.
17. This is inferential since it makes an inference to all Hispanics in the United States.
18. Answers will vary.
19. Answers will vary.

Exercises 1–2

1. Qualitative variables are variables that can be placed in distinct categories according to some characteristic or attribute and cannot be ranked, while quantitative variables are numerical in nature and can be ordered or counted.
2. Discrete variables assume values that can be counted while continuous variables are variables obtained by being measured. Theoretically, continuous variables can assume all values between any given two values.

*Answers may vary due to rounding or use of technology.

3. Continuous variables need to be rounded because of the limits of the measuring device.
4. There are four types of measurement levels used in statistics: nominal, ordinal, interval, and ratio levels of measurement. The nominal level of measurement classifies data into mutually exclusive categories which cannot be ordered or ranked. The ordinal level of measurement classifies data into categories that can be ranked; however, precise differences between the ranks do not exist. The interval level of measurement ranks data in such a way that precise differences between units of measure exist; however, there is no meaningful zero. Finally, the ratio level of measurement has all of the properties of the interval level of measurement, a true zero, and meaningful ratios when the same variable is measured for two different members of a population.
5. Quantitative
6. Quantitative
7. Qualitative
8. Quantitative
9. Quantitative
10. Qualitative
11. Continuous
12. Continuous
13. Continuous
14. Discrete
15. Discrete
16. Continuous
17. 17.5–18.5 inches
18. 2.25–2.35 kilometers
19. 75.5–76.5 miles
20. 9.665–9.675 tons
21. 33.15–33.25 feet
22. 44.5–45.5 pints
23. Nominal
24. Nominal
25. Interval
26. Ratio
27. Ratio
28. Ordinal
29. Ratio
30. Ratio

Exercises 1–3

1. Data can be collected by using telephone surveys, mail questionnaire surveys, personal interview surveys, by taking a look at records, or by direct observation methods.
2. Sampling error is the difference between a sample measure and a population measure. Nonsampling error is the result of collecting data incorrectly or selecting a biased sample.
3. Random numbers are used in sampling so that every subject in the population has an equal chance of being selected for a sample. Random numbers can be generated by computers or calculators; however, there are other ways of generating random numbers such as using a random number table or rolling dice.
4. The four basic sampling methods are random, systematic, stratified, and cluster. A random sample is a sample that is obtained in such a way that all members of the population have an equal chance of being selected. A systematic sample is a sample obtained by first deciding on a whole number k that is between 1 and the size of the population. Then, every kth member of the population is selected for the sample. A stratified sample is obtained by dividing the population into subgroups according to some characteristic that is relevant to the study. Then, some subjects from each subgroup are selected at random for the sample. A cluster sample is a sample obtained by first dividing the population into sections. Then, one or more of the sections is chosen at random and all members of these sections are selected for the sample.

5. The population could be all Americans who own a cell phone. A sample could be a random selection of cell phone customers from a specific phone company. Answers will vary.

6. The population could be all American families who have children in college. A sample could be a stratified one where the classes would be two-year colleges, four-year colleges, and universities. Answers will vary.

7. The population could be all people in the United States who use a credit card. A sample could be a systematic sample taken from a credit card company. Answers will vary.

8. The population could be all office workers who work with mobile devices. A sample could be a random sample taken from a specific city. Answers will vary.

9. The population is the pet owners in the United States. A sample could be the pet owners in a specific area.

10. The population could consist of all daily temperatures in Boston since records were kept, and a sample could be obtained by looking at weather report statistics.

11. Systematic
12. Stratified
13. Cluster
14. Random
15. Stratified
16. Random

Exercises 1–4

1. In an observational study, the researcher observes what is happening and tries to draw conclusions based on the observations. In an experimental study, the researcher manipulates one of the variables and tries to determine how this influences the other variables.

2. The three types of observational studies are
   a. Cross-sectional studies in which the data are collected at one point in time
   b. Retrospective studies in which the data are collected from past records
   c. Longitudinal studies in which the data are collected over a period of time

3. One advantage of an observational study is that it can occur in a natural setting. In addition, researchers can look at past instances of statistics and draw conclusions from these situations. Another advantage is that the researcher can use variables, such as drugs, that cannot be manipulated. One disadvantage is that since the variable cannot be manipulated, a definite cause-and-effect situation cannot be shown. Another disadvantage is that these studies can be expensive and time-consuming. These studies can also be influenced by confounding variables. Finally, in these studies, the researcher sometimes needs to rely on data collected by others.

4. One advantage of an experimental study is that the researcher can decide how to select the subjects and assign them to the specific groups. The researcher can also control the independent variable. One disadvantage of an experimental study is that it may not occur in a natural setting. Another one is called the Hawthorne effect, and which is when the subjects may change their natural behavior because they realize that they are participating in a research study.

5. In an experimental study, the researcher has control of the assignment of subjects to the groups, whereas in a quasi-experimental study, the researcher uses intact groups.

6. An independent variable is the one being manipulated by the researcher whereas the dependent variable is the one being studied to identify the effects of the independent variable.

7. In research studies, a treatment group subject receives a specific treatment and those in the control group do not receive a treatment or are given a placebo.

8. The Hawthorne effect was the effect discovered when researchers realized that the workers at the Hawthorne plant knew that they were participating in a research study and this fact actually changed workers' behavior.

9. A confounding variable is one that can influence the results of the research study when no precautions were taken to eliminate it from the study.

10. Sometimes subjects respond favorably when given a placebo rather than the real treatment.

11. Blinding is used to help eliminate the placebo effect. Here the subjects are given a sugar pill that looks like the real medical pill. The subjects do not know which pill they are getting. When double blinding occurs, neither the subjects nor the researchers are told who gets the real treatment or the placebo.

12. Randomization is used to help to eliminate confounding variables since randomly assigning subjects to groups tends to "balance out" the inconsistencies (such as age, social class, etc.) that each of the subjects brings to the study.

13. In a completely randomized design, the subjects are assigned to the groups randomly, whereas in a matched-pair design, subjects are matched on some variable. Then one subject is randomly assigned to one group, and the other subject is assigned to the other group. In both types of studies, the treatments can be randomly assigned to the groups.

14. Replication is done to determine if the results apply in different settings. For example, if the experiment was done with college students, the researchers might replicate the experiment with adults or in another part of the country.

15. Observational
16. Experimental
17. Observational
18. Experimental

19. Independent variable—exercise type
    Dependent variable—blood pressure

20. Independent variable—hugs and hand holding
    Dependent variable—heart rate and blood pressure

21. Independent variable—obsessive-compulsive measure
    Dependent variable—perfectionist measure

22. Independent variable—marital status
    Dependent variable—cause of death

23. Age, income, socioeconomic status. Answers will vary.

24. Age, socioeconomic status, family ties. Answers will vary.

25. Number of minutes run, running speed, and topography of running trail. Answers will vary.

26. Climate, diet, medicine. Answers will vary.

27. How is a perfect body defined statistically?

28. What is meant by the "whole truth"?

29. How are the number of thoughts measured? Answers will vary.

30. How can reading a book increase a person's IQ?

31. What is the definition of fast-food? What about the ages of the subjects? Answers will vary.

32. The steps in conducting a statistical study are as follows:

Step 1. Formulate the purpose of the study.

Step 2. Identify the variables for the study.

Step 3. Define the population.

Step 4. Decide what sampling method to use to collect the data.

Step 5. Collect the data.

Step 6. Summarize the data and perform any statistical calculations needed.

Step 7. Interpret the results.

33. Only 20 people were used in the study.

34. The only time claims can be proved is when the entire population is used.

35. It is meaningless since there is no definition of "the road less traveled." Also, there is no way to know that for *every* 100 women, 91 would say that they have taken "the road less traveled."

36. Since the results are not typical, the advertisers selected only a few people for whom the weight loss product worked extremely well.

37. There is no mention of how this conclusion was obtained.

38. "74% more calories" than what? No comparison group is stated.

39. Since the word *may* is used, there is no guarantee that the product will help fight cancer and heart disease.

40. What is meant by "24 hours of acid control"? Also *can provide* implies that it might or might not provide control.

41. No. There are many other factors that contribute to criminal behavior.

42. Possible answer: It could be the amount of caffeine in the coffee or tea. It could have been the brewing method.

43. Answers will vary.   **44.** Answers will vary.

45. Answers will vary.   **46.** Answers will vary.

Review Exercises

1. Inferential   **2.** Descriptive

3. Descriptive   **4.** Descriptive

5. Inferential   **6.** Inferential

7. Descriptive   **8.** Inferential

9. Ratio   **10.** Ordinal

11. Interval   **12.** Ratio

13. Ratio   **14.** Ratio

15. Ordinal   **16.** Ratio

17. Ratio   **18.** Nominal

19. Qualitative   **20.** Quantitative

21. Quantitative   **22.** Qualitative

23. Quantitative   **24.** Quantitative

25. Quantitative   **26.** Qualitative

27. Discrete   **28.** Continuous

29. Discrete   **30.** Continuous

31. Continuous   **32.** Discrete

33. Continuous   **34.** Continuous

35. 55.5–56.5 yards   **36.** 105.35–105.45 miles

37. 72.55–72.65 tons   **38.** 9.535–9.545 millimeters

39. Cluster   **40.** Cluster

41. Random   **42.** Systematic

43. Stratified   **44.** Volunteer or other

45. Experimental   **46.** Observational

47. Observational   **48.** Experimental

49. Independent variable—habitat of the animal
Dependent variable—weight of the animal

50. Independent variable—miles walked
Dependent variable—triglyceride level

51. Independent variable—thyme
Dependent variable—antioxidants

52. Independent variable—type of work schedule
Dependent variable—job satisfaction

53. A telephone survey won't contact all the types of people who shop online. Answers will vary.

54. It is impossible to count all the raccoons in a specific county.

55. It depends on where the survey was taken. Some places in the United States get very little or no snow at all during the winter.

56. Only 5% of men surveyed said that men may or may not want to say that they like romantic comedies. Answers will vary.

57. It depends on how the Internet is used. How can the Internet raise IQ? Answers will vary.

58. Since most people swim in shallow water, there would be more shark attacks in shallow water. Answers will vary.

Chapter Quiz

1. True   **2.** True

3. False. The difference between a sampling measure and a population measure is called a sampling error.

4. False. This sample is called a stratified sample.

5. True   **6.** True

7. False. The boundary is 5.5–6.5 inches.

8. *c*   **9.** *b*

10. *d*   **11.** *a*

12. *c*   **13.** *a*

14. Descriptive, inferential

15. Gambling, insurance. Answers can vary.

16. Population

17. Sample

18. *a.* Saves time
b. Saves money
c. Use when population is infinite

19. *a.* Random   *c.* Cluster
b. Systematic   *d.* Stratified

20. Quasi-experimental   **21.** Random

22. *a.* Descriptive *d.* Inferential
  b. Inferential *e.* Inferential
  c. Descriptive

23. *a.* Nominal *d.* Interval
  b. Ratio *e.* Ratio
  c. Ordinal

24. *a.* Continuous *d.* Continuous
  b. Discrete *e.* Discrete
  c. Continuous

25. *a.* 31.5–32.5 minutes
  b. 0.475–0.485 millimeters
  c. 6.15–6.25 inches
  d. 18.5–19.5 pounds
  e. 12.05–12.15 quarts

Chapter 2

Exercises 2–1

1. To organize data in a meaningful way, to determine the shape of the distribution, to facilitate computational procedures for statistics, to make it easier to draw charts and graphs, to make comparisons among different sets of data

2. The three types of frequency distributions are categorical, grouped, and ungrouped. Categorical frequency distributions should be used with qualitative data. Grouped frequency distributions should be used with quantitative data when the range is large and classes several units in width are need. Ungrouped frequency distributions should be used with quantitative data when the range is small.

3. 5–20; class width should be an odd number so that the midpoints of the classes are in the same place value as the data.

4. An open-ended frequency distribution has either a first class with no lower limit or a last class with no upper limit. They are necessary to accommodate all the data.

5. 57.5–62.5; 60; 5

6. 124.5–131.5, 128, 7

7. 17.405; 2.12

8. 16.25–18.55, 17.4, 2.3

9. Class width is not uniform.

10. Class limits overlap, and class width is not uniform.

11. A class has been omitted.

12. Class width is not uniform.

13.

Class	Tally	Frequency	Percent
F	𝒯𝒯𝒯𝒯 𝒯𝒯𝒯𝒯 //	12	24
D	𝒯𝒯𝒯𝒯 𝒯𝒯𝒯𝒯	10	20
B	𝒯𝒯𝒯𝒯 𝒯𝒯𝒯𝒯	10	20
C	𝒯𝒯𝒯𝒯 𝒯𝒯𝒯𝒯 ///	13	26
R	𝒯𝒯𝒯𝒯	5	10
		Total 100	

In this sample, most subjects own a cat followed by a fish. Actually 50% of the subjects own a cat or fish.

14.

Class	Tally	Frequency	Percent
A	////	4	10
M	𝒯𝒯𝒯𝒯 𝒯𝒯𝒯𝒯 𝒯𝒯𝒯𝒯 𝒯𝒯𝒯𝒯 𝒯𝒯𝒯𝒯 ///	28	70
H	𝒯𝒯𝒯𝒯 /	6	15
S	//	2	5
		40	100

15.

Limits	Boundaries	Tally	f
0	−0.5–0.5	//	2
1	0.5–1.5	𝒯𝒯𝒯𝒯	5
2	1.5–2.5	𝒯𝒯𝒯𝒯 𝒯𝒯𝒯𝒯 𝒯𝒯𝒯𝒯 𝒯𝒯𝒯𝒯 ////	24
3	2.5–3.5	𝒯𝒯𝒯𝒯 ///	8
4	3.5–4.5	𝒯𝒯𝒯𝒯 /	6
5	4.5–5.5	////	4
6	5.5–6.5		0
7	6.5–7.5	/	1
		Total	50

	cf
Less than −0.5	0
Less than 0.5	2
Less than 1.5	7
Less than 2.5	31
Less than 3.5	39
Less than 4.5	45
Less than 5.5	49
Less than 6.5	49
Less than 7.5	50

The category "twice a week" has more values than any other category.

16.

Limits	Boundaries	Tally	f
3	2.5–3.5	//	2
4	3.5–4.5	////	4
5	4.5–5.5	////	4
6	5.5–6.5	/	1
7	6.5–7.5	////	4
8	7.5–8.5	///	3
9	8.5–9.5	//	2
		Total	20

	cf
Less than 2.5	0
Less than 3.5	2
Less than 4.5	6
Less than 5.5	10
Less than 6.5	11
Less than 7.5	15
Less than 8.5	18
Less than 9.5	20

17.

Limits	Boundaries	Tally	f
48–54	47.5–54.5	//	2
55–61	54.5–61.5	/	1
62–68	61.5–68.5	ҭ⁄҃ ////	9
69–75	68.5–75.5	ҭ⁄҃ ҭ⁄҃ ҭ⁄҃ ////	19
76–82	75.5–82.5	ҭ⁄҃ ///	8
83–89	82.5–89.5	ҭ⁄҃ //	7
90–96	89.5–96.5	//	2
97–103	96.5–103.5	//	2
		Total	50

	cf
Less than 47.5	0
Less than 54.5	2
Less than 61.5	3
Less than 68.5	12
Less than 75.5	31
Less than 82.5	39
Less than 89.5	46
Less than 96.5	48
Less than 103.5	50

The distribution is peaked somewhat about the center.

18.

Limits	Boundaries	f
54–62	53.5–62.5	7
63–71	62.5–71.5	6
72–80	71.5–80.5	8
81–89	80.5–89.5	4
90–98	89.5–98.5	1
99–107	98.5–107.5	3
108–116	107.5–116.5	1
	Total	30

	cf
Less than 53.5	0
Less than 62.5	7
Less than 71.5	13
Less than 80.5	21
Less than 89.5	25
Less than 98.5	26
Less than 107.5	29
Less than 116.5	30

19.

Limits	Boundaries	Tally	f
16–28	15.5–28.5	ҭ⁄҃ /	6
29–41	28.5–41.5	//	2
42–54	41.5–54.5	ҭ⁄҃ /	6
55–67	54.5–67.5	ҭ⁄҃	5
68–80	67.5–80.5	///	3
		Total	22

	cf
Less than 15.5	0
Less than 28.5	6
Less than 41.5	8
Less than 54.5	14
Less than 67.5	19
Less than 80.5	22

The distribution has a peak at two classes 16–28, 42–54.

20.

Limits	Boundary	Tally	f
1–205	0.5–205.5	ҭ⁄҃ ҭ⁄҃ ҭ⁄҃ ҭ⁄҃ ҭ⁄҃ ///	28
206–410	205.5–410.5	ҭ⁄҃ ////	9
411–615	410.5–615.5	ҭ⁄҃ /	6
616–820	615.5–820.5	//	2
821–1025	820.5–1025.5	///	3
1026–1230	1025.5–1230.5	//	2
		Total	50

	cf
Less than 0.5	0
Less than 205	28
Less than 410.5	37
Less than 615.5	43
Less than 820.5	45
Less than 1025.5	48
Less than 1230.5	50

21.

Limits	Boundaries	Tally	f
61–69	60.5–69.5	///	3
70–78	69.5–78.5	ҭ⁄҃ ҭ⁄҃	10
79–87	78.5–87.5	ҭ⁄҃ /	6
88–96	87.5–96.5	//	2
97–105	96.5–105.5	/	1
		Total	22

	cf
Less than 60.5	0
Less than 69.5	3
Less than 78.5	13
Less than 87.5	19
Less than 96.5	21
Less than 105.5	22

22.

Limits	Boundaries	Tally	f
16–20	15.5–20.5	ҭ⁄҃ ///	8
21–25	20.5–25.5	ҭ⁄҃ ҭ⁄҃ ҭ⁄҃ ҭ⁄҃ ////	24
26–30	25.5–30.5	ҭ⁄҃ ҭ⁄҃ ///	13
31–35	30.5–35.5	//	2
36–40	35.5–40.5	///	3
		Total	50

	cf
Less than 15.5	0
Less than 20.5	8
Less than 25.5	32
Less than 30.5	45
Less than 35.5	47
Less than 40.5	50

This distribution is positively skewed with the class of 21–25 having almost one-half of the data values.

23.

Limits	Boundaries	Tally	f
206–218	205.5–218.5	ЖЖ /	6
219–231	218.5–231.5	ЖЖ /	6
232–244	231.5–244.5	////	4
245–257	244.5–257.5	ЖЖ /	6
258–270	257.5–270.5	ЖЖ /	6
271–283	270.5–283.5	////	4
		Total	32

	cf
Less than 205.5	0
Less than 218.5	6
Less than 231.5	12
Less than 244.5	16
Less than 257.5	22
Less than 270.5	28
Less than 283.5	32

This distribution is somewhat uniform with each class having between 4 and 6 data values.

24.

Limits	Boundaries	Tally	f
12–28	11.5–28.5	ЖЖ //	7
29–45	28.5–45.5	////	4
46–62	45.5–62.5	ЖЖ	5
63–79	62.5–79.5	//	2
80–96	79.5–96.5	//	2
97–113	96.5–113.5	////	4
		Total	24

	cf
Less than 11.5	0
Less than 28.5	7
Less than 45.5	11
Less than 62.5	16
Less than 79.5	18
Less than 96.5	20
Less than 113.5	24

The distribution is slightly positively skewed.

25.

Limits	Boundaries	f
6.2–7.0	6.15–7.05	1
7.1–7.9	7.05–7.95	7
8.0–8.8	7.95–8.85	9
8.9–9.7	8.85–9.75	7
9.8–10.6	9.75–10.65	8
10.7–11.5	10.65–11.55	4
11.6–12.4	11.55–12.45	4
	Total	40

	cf
Less than 6.15	0
Less than 7.05	1
Less than 7.95	8
Less than 8.85	17
Less than 9.75	24
Less than 10.65	32
Less than 11.55	36
Less than 12.45	40

26

Limits	Boundaries	f
17.3–20.2	17.25–20.25	4
20.3–23.2	20.25–23.25	6
23.3–26.2	23.25–26.25	18
26.3–29.2	26.25–29.25	8
29.3–32.2	29.25–32.25	6
32.3–35.2	32.25–35.25	7
35.3–38.2	35.25–38.25	1
	Total	50

	cf
Less than 17.25	0
Less than 20.25	4
Less than 23.25	10
Less than 26.25	28
Less than 29.25	36
Less than 32.25	42
Less than 35.25	49
Less than 38.25	50

27. The percents sum to 101. They should sum to 100% unless rounding was used.

28.

Class	f
0	1
1	4
2	5
3	6
4	4
5	4
6	3
7	3
8	5
9	5

No. Zero appears only once and 3 appears 6 times.

29. It is necessary to include the 16 people who didn't respond in order to get a total of 100 people surveyed. Also, we don't know why these people didn't respond or their feelings about the situation.

30. The total number of subjects should be shown at the bottom of the frequency column so that the reader can make comparisons for each category of the distribution and so that percents for each category can be computed.

31. Percents are easier to comprehend than just seeing the frequency numbers for each class. Also, the percents should total to 100%. If percents are used rather than the actual numbers, the total number of subjects in the sample should be given.

32. The "other" category gives almost no helpful information for interpreting the data since we don't know what information it contains—in this case, what type of mathematical books are in that category. Also, if the percent of the "other" category is relatively large, you should consider making more categories.

33. The sum of the frequencies is 51, so either a counting error was made or a person drives two different colored automobiles to school on different days and that person responded twice.

34. There are too many categories to make a reasonable interpretation of the data using a pie chart. Also, the sample size is very small for the number of categories.

35. Combining data in adjacent classes could change the shape of the distribution and this could change the interpretation of the data.

Exercises 2–2

1.

Limits	Boundaries	f	Midpoints
90–98	89.5–98.5	6	94
99–107	98.5–107.5	22	103
108–116	107.5–116.5	43	112
117–125	116.5–125.5	28	121
126–134	125.5–134.5	9	130
		Total 108	

	cf
Less than 89.5	0
Less than 98.5	6
Less than 107.5	28
Less than 116.5	71
Less than 125.5	99
Less than 134.5	108

Eighty applicants do not need to enroll in the developmental programs.

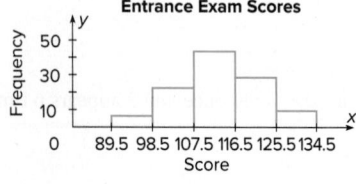

Entrance Exam Scores

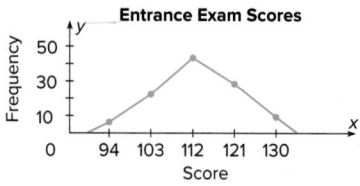

Entrance Exam Scores

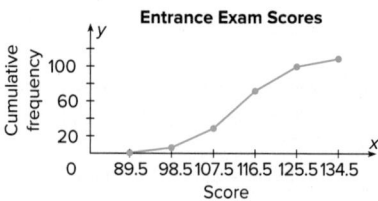

Entrance Exam Scores

2.

Limits	Boundaries	f	Midpoints
1–25	0.5–25.5	16	13
26–50	25.5–50.5	14	38
51–75	50.5–75.5	9	63
76–100	75.5–100.5	8	88
101–125	100.5–125.5	5	113
126–150	125.5–150.5	0	138
151–175	150.5–175.5	1	163
176–200	175.5–200.5	1	188
201–225	200.5–225.5	0	213
226–250	225.5–250.5	0	238
251–275	250.5–275.5	2	263
		Total 56	

	cf
Less than 0.5	0
Less than 25.5	16
Less than 50.5	30
Less than 75.5	39
Less than 100.5	47
Less than 125.5	52
Less than 150.5	52
Less than 175.5	53
Less than 200.5	54
Less than 225.5	54
Less than 250.5	54
Less than 275.5	56

The data are positively skewed or skewed to the right. There were 39 counties with 75 or fewer bears killed.

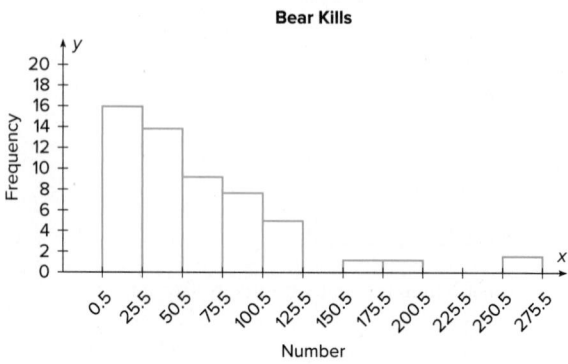

Bear Kills

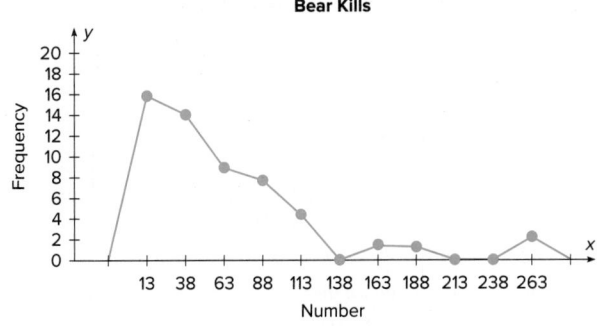

Bear Kills

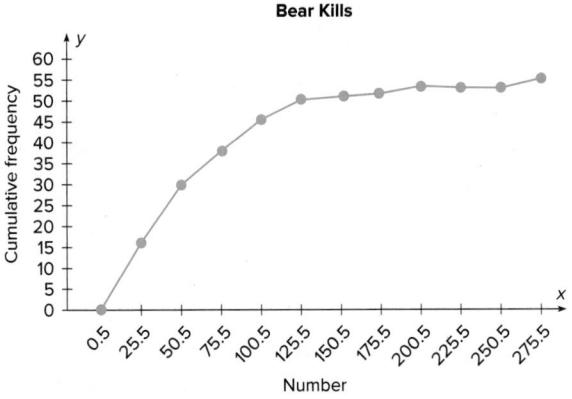

Bear Kills

3.

Limits	Boundaries	f	Midpoints
9–11	8.5–11.5	2	10
12–14	11.5–14.5	20	13
15–17	14.5–17.5	18	16
18–20	17.5–20.5	7	19
21–23	20.5–23.5	2	22
24–26	23.5–26.5	1	25
		Total 50	

	cf
Less than 8.5	0
Less than 11.5	2
Less than 14.5	22
Less than 17.5	40
Less than 20.5	47
Less than 23.5	49
Less than 26.5	50

The distribution is positively skewed with a peak at the class of 11.5–14.5.

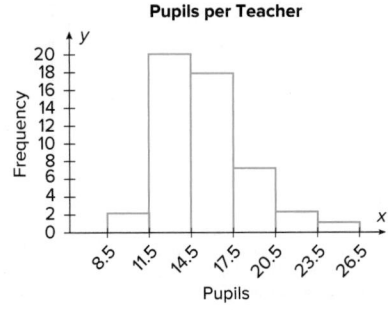

Pupils per Teacher

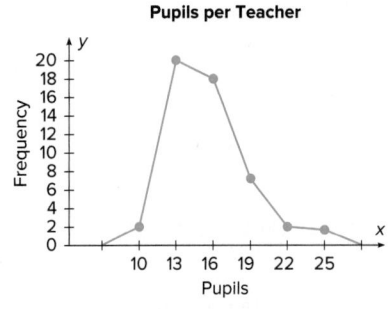

Pupils per Teacher

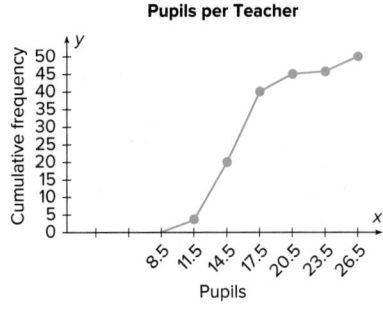

Pupils per Teacher

4.

Limits	Boundaries	f	Midpoints
70–116	69.5–116.5	5	93
117–163	116.5–163.5	9	140
164–210	163.5–210.5	6	187
211–257	210.5–257.5	6	234
258–304	257.5–304.5	0	281
305–351	304.5–351.5	1	328
352–398	351.5–398.5	1	375
		Total 28	

	cf
Less than 69.5	0
Less than 116.5	5
Less than 163.5	14
Less than 210.5	20
Less than 257.5	26
Less than 304.5	26
Less than 351.5	27
Less than 398.5	28

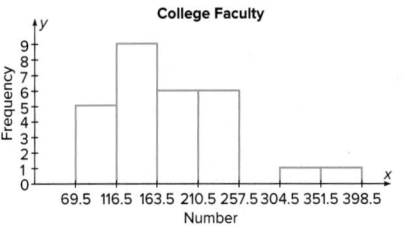

College Faculty

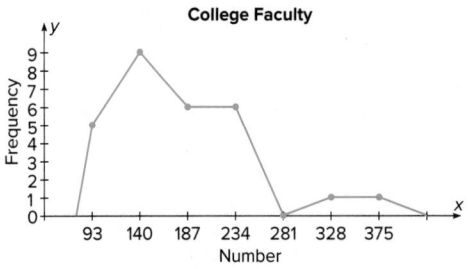

College Faculty

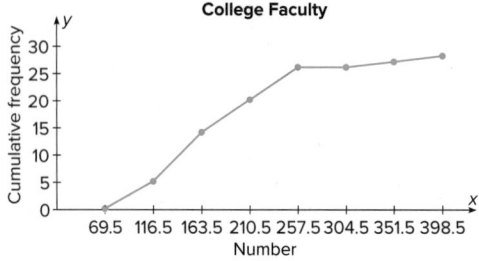

$\frac{12}{28} = 0.429$, or 42.9% have 180 or more. The histogram and frequency polygon are positively skewed.

5.

Limits	Boundaries	f	Midpoints
1–43	0.5–43.5	24	22
44–86	43.5–86.5	17	65
87–129	86.5–129.5	3	108
130–172	129.5–172.5	4	151
173–215	172.5–215.5	1	194
216–258	215.5–258.5	0	237
259–301	258.5–301.5	0	280
302–344	301.5–344.5	1	323
		Total 50	

	cf
Less than 0.5	0
Less than 43.5	24
Less than 86.5	41
Less than 129.5	44
Less than 172.5	48
Less than 215.5	49
Less than 258.5	49
Less than 301.5	49
Less than 344.5	50

The distribution is positively skewed.

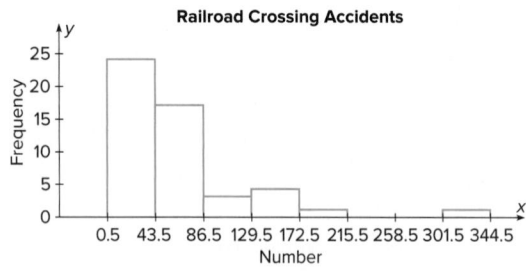

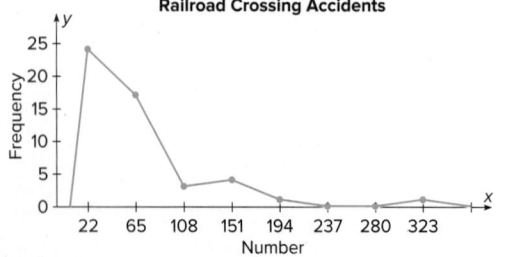

6.

Limits	Boundaries	f	Midpoints
39.9–42.8	39.85–42.85	2	41.35
42.9–45.8	42.85–45.85	2	44.35
45.9–48.8	45.85–48.85	5	47.35
48.9–51.8	48.85–51.85	5	50.35
51.9–54.8	51.85–54.85	12	53.35
54.9–57.8	54.85–57.85	5	56.35
		Total 31	

	cf
Less than 39.85	0
Less than 42.85	2
Less than 45.85	4
Less than 48.85	9
Less than 51.85	14
Less than 54.85	26
Less than 57.85	31

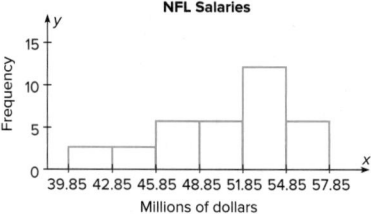

The distribution is negatively or left-skewed.

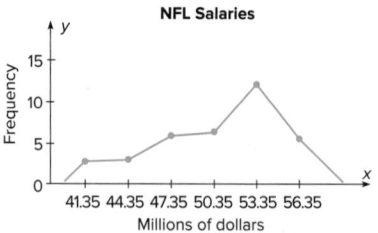

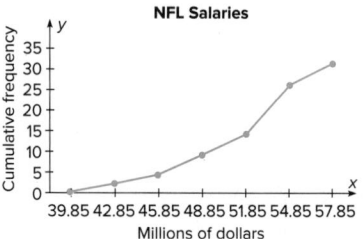

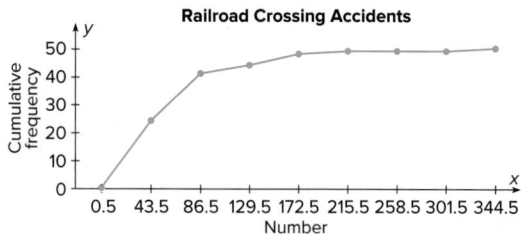

7.

Limits	Boundaries	f	Midpoints
1260–1734	1259.5–1734.5	12	1497
1735–2209	1734.5–2209.5	6	1972
2210–2684	2209.5–2684.5	3	2447
2685–3159	2684.5–3159.5	1	2922
3160–3634	3159.5–3634.5	1	3397
3635–4109	3634.5–4109.5	1	3872
4110–4584	4109.5–4584.5	2	4347

	cf
Less than 1259.5	0
Less than 1734.5	12
Less than 2209.5	18
Less than 2684.5	21
Less than 3159.5	22
Less than 3634.5	23
Less than 4109.5	24
Less than 4584.5	26

The distribution is positively skewed. The class with the most frequencies is 1259.5–1734.5.

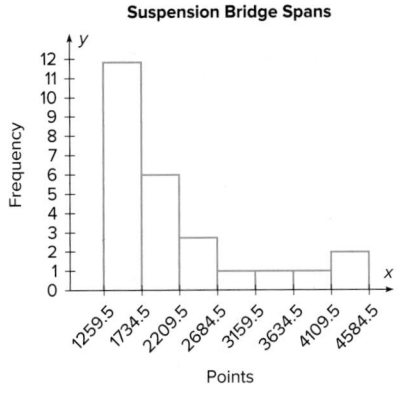

Suspension Bridge Spans

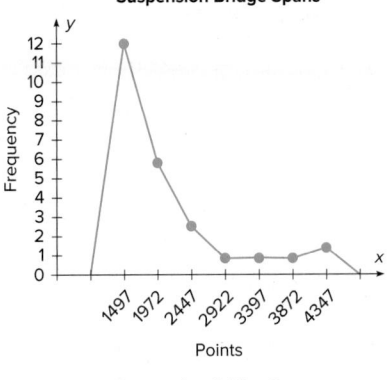

Suspension Bridge Spans

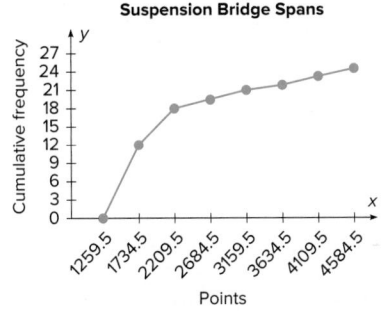

Suspension Bridge Spans

8.

Limits	Boundaries	f	Midpoints
27–31	26.5–31.5	23	29
32–36	31.5–36.5	28	34
37–41	36.5–41.5	19	39
42–46	41.5–46.5	15	44
47–51	46.5–51.5	11	49
52–56	51.5–56.5	4	54
	Total	100	

	cf
Less than 26.5	0
Less than 31.5	23
Less than 36.5	51
Less than 41.5	70
Less than 46.5	85
Less than 51.5	96
Less than 56.5	100

Yes. The distribution is positively skewed.

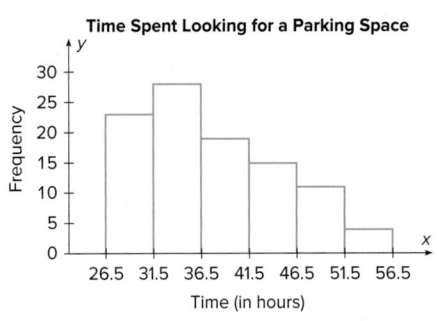

Time Spent Looking for a Parking Space

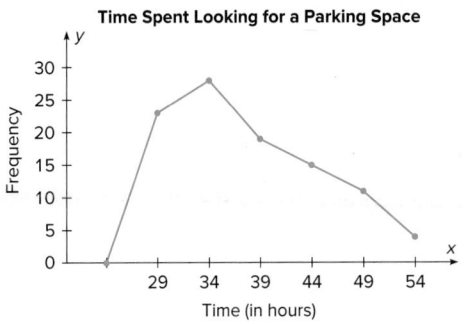

Time Spent Looking for a Parking Space

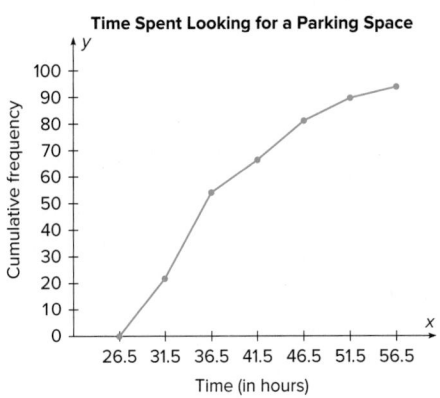

Time Spent Looking for a Parking Space

The distribution is positively skewed with a peak at 31.5–36.5.

9.

Limits	Boundaries	f	Midpoints
7–13	6.5–13.5	14	10
14–20	13.5–20.5	7	17
21–27	20.5–27.5	2	24
28–34	27.5–34.5	4	31
35–41	34.5–41.5	3	38
		Total 30	

	cf
Less than 6.5	0
Less than 13.5	14
Less than 20.5	21
Less than 27.5	23
Less than 34.5	27
Less than 41.5	30

The distributions are positively skewed.

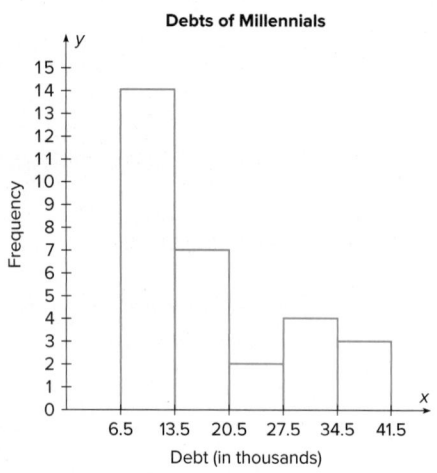

Debts of Millennials

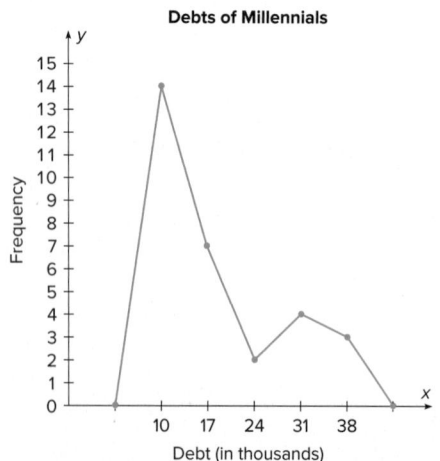

Debts of Millennials

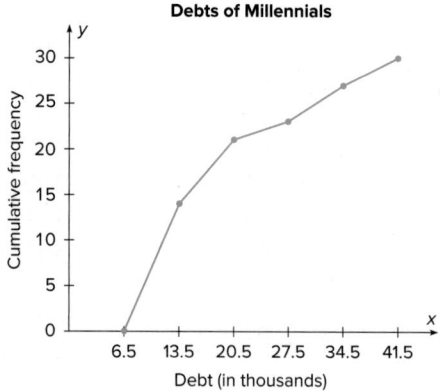

Debts of Millennials

The distribution is positively skewed with a peak at 6.5–13.5. There is a slight decrease for the category 20.5–27.5.

10. The distribution of math percentages is more bell-shaped than the distribution of reading percentages, and its peak in the class of 32.5–37.5 is not as high as the peak of the reading percentages.

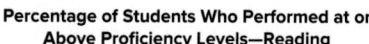
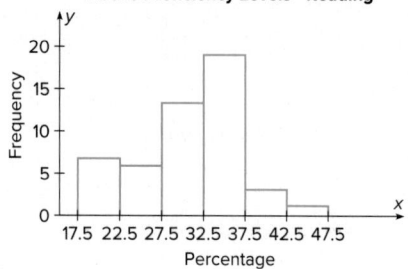

Percentage of Students Who Performed at or Above Proficiency Levels—Reading

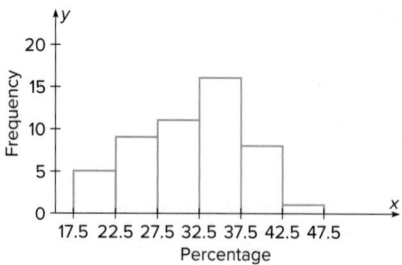

Percentage of Students Who Performed at or Above Proficiency Levels—Math

11.

Limits	Boundaries	f	Midpoints
1	0.5–1.5	10	1
2	1.5–2.5	12	2
3	2.5–3.5	8	3
4	3.5–4.5	7	4
5	4.5–5.5	6	5
6	5.5–6.5	5	6
7	6.5–7.5	2	7
		Total 50	

	cf
Less than 0.5	0
Less than 1.5	10
Less than 2.5	22
Less than 3.5	30
Less than 4.5	37
Less than 5.5	43
Less than 6.5	48
Less than 7.5	50

The distribution is positively skewed.

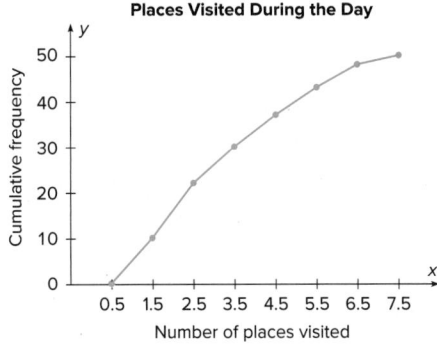

The distribution is positively skewed with a peak at 1.5–2.5.

12.

Limits	Boundaries	f	Midpoints
82–86	81.5–86.5	18	84
87–91	86.5–91.5	24	89
92–96	91.5–96.5	43	94
97–101	96.5–101.5	10	99
102–106	101.5–106.5	4	104
107–111	106.5–111.5	4	109
		Total 103	

	cf
Less than 81.5	0
Less than 86.5	18
Less than 91.5	42
Less than 96.5	85
Less than 101.5	95
Less than 106.5	99
Less than 111.5	103

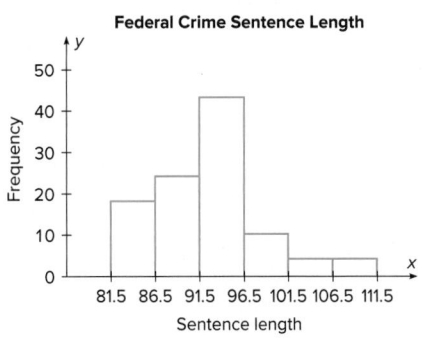

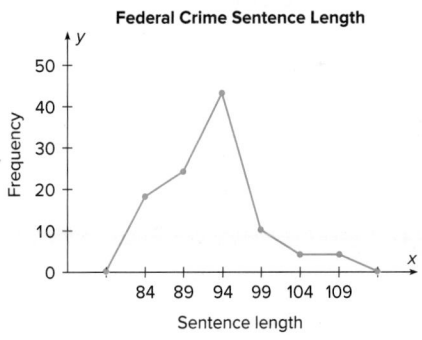

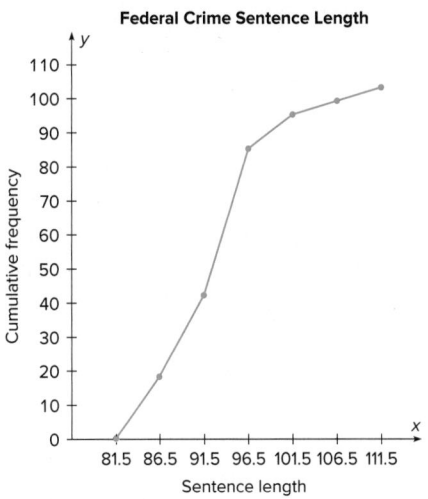

The distribution is slightly bell-shaped with a peak at 91.5–96.5. It drops sharply after the peak class.

13.

Boundaries	rf	Midpoints
89.5–98.5	0.06	94
98.5–107.5	0.20	103
107.5–116.5	0.40	112
116.5–125.5	0.26	121
125.5–134.5	0.08	130
Total	1.00	

	crf
Less than 89.5	0
Less than 98.5	0.06
Less than 107.5	0.26
Less than 116.5	0.66
Less than 125.5	0.92
Less than 134.5	1.00

The proportion of applicants who do not need to enroll in the developmental program is about 0.74.

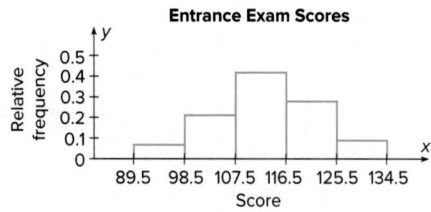

Entrance Exam Scores

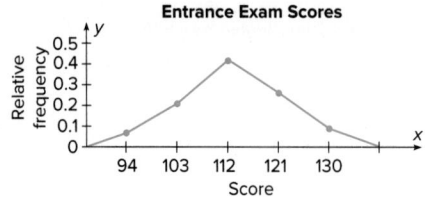

Entrance Exam Scores

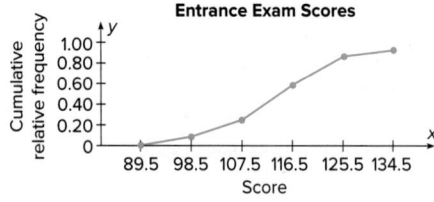

Entrance Exam Scores

14.

Boundaries	rf	Midpoints
0.5–25.5	0.29	13
25.5–50.5	0.25	38
50.5–75.5	0.16	63
75.5–100.5	0.14	88
100.5–125.5	0.09	113
125.5–150.5	0.00	138
150.5–175.5	0.02	163
175.5–200.5	0.02	188
200.5–225.5	0.00	213
225.5–250.5	0.00	238
250.5–275.5	0.04	263
	1.01 (due to rounding)	

	rcf
Less than 0.5	0.00
Less than 25.5	0.29
Less than 50.5	0.54
Less than 75.5	0.70
Less than 100.5	0.84
Less than 125.5	0.93
Less than 150.5	0.93
Less than 175.5	0.95
Less than 200.5	0.97
Less than 225.5	0.97
Less than 250.5	0.97
Less than 275.5	100.1 (due to rounding)

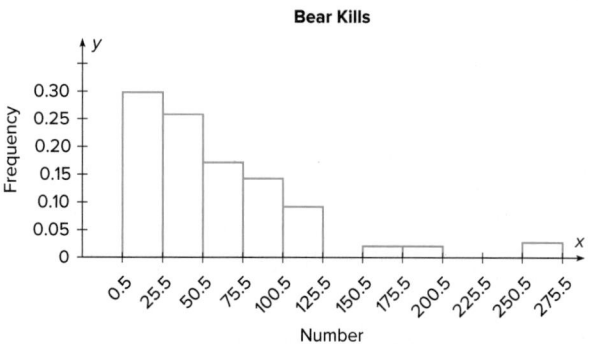

Bear Kills

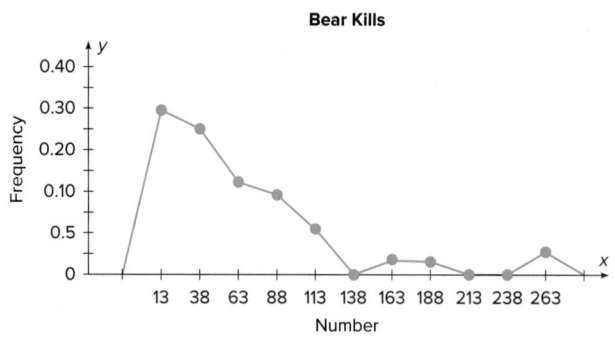

Bear Kills

Bear Kills

15.

Boundaries	rf	Midpoints
0.5–43.5	0.48	22
43.5–86.5	0.34	65
86.5–129.5	0.06	108
129.5–172.5	0.08	151
172.5–215.5	0.02	194
215.5–258.5	0.00	237
258.5–301.5	0.00	280
301.5–344.5	0.02	323
Total	1.00	

	rcf
Less than 0.5	0
Less than 43.5	0.48
Less than 86.5	0.82
Less than 129.5	0.88
Less than 172.5	0.96
Less than 215.5	0.98
Less than 258.5	0.98
Less than 301.5	0.98
Less than 344.5	1.00

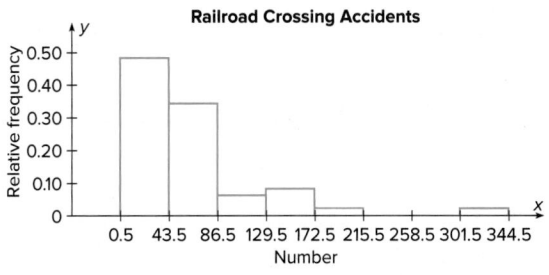

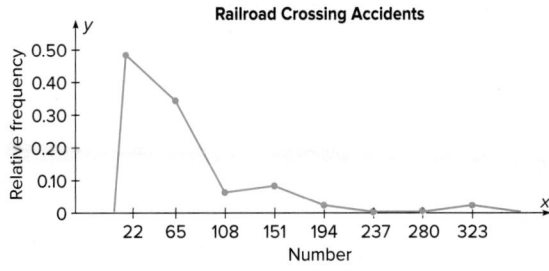

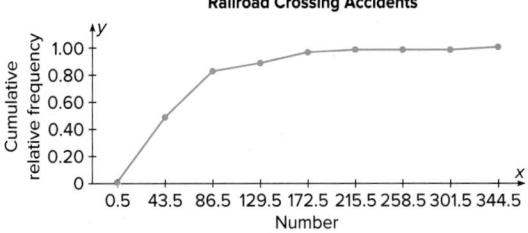

16.

Boundaries	rf	Midpoints
39.85–42.85	0.06	41.35
42.85–45.85	0.06	44.35
45.85–48.85	0.16	47.35
48.85–51.85	0.16	50.35
51.85–54.85	0.39	53.35
54.85–57.85	0.16	56.35
Total	0.99 (due to rounding)	

	crf
Less than 39.85	0
Less than 42.85	0.06
Less than 45.85	0.12
Less than 48.85	0.28
Less than 51.85	0.44
Less than 54.85	0.83
Less than 57.85	0.99

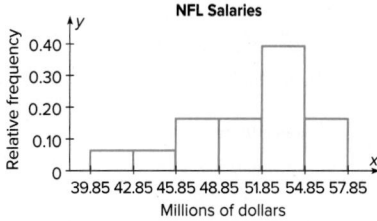

The distribution is negatively or left-skewed.

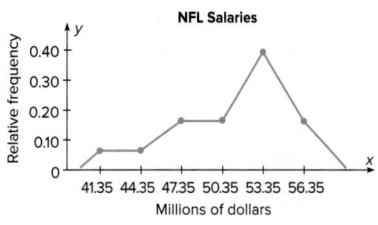

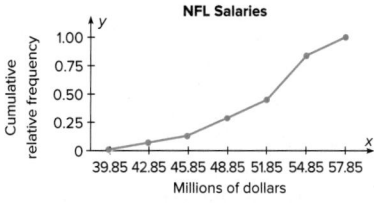

17.

Class boundaries	rf	Midpoints
35.5–40.5	0.23	38
40.5–45.5	0.20	43
45.5–50.5	0.23	48
50.5–55.5	0.23	53
55.5–60.5	0.10	58
	0.99	

	crf
Less than 35.5	0.00
Less than 40.5	0.23
Less than 45.5	0.43
Less than 50.5	0.66
Less than 55.5	0.89
Less than 60.5	0.99

The graph is fairly uniform except for the last class in which the relative frequency drops significantly.

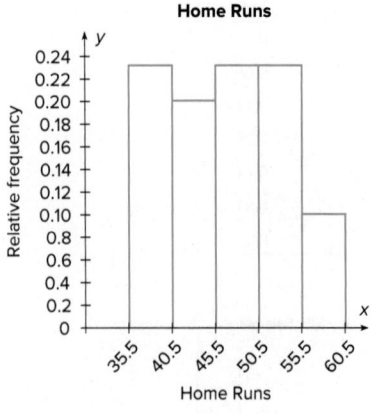

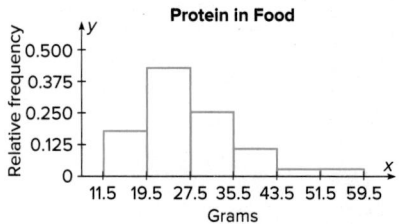

The histogram is positively skewed.

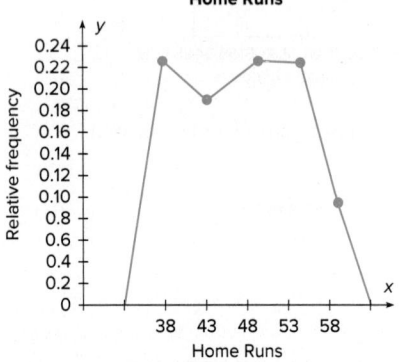

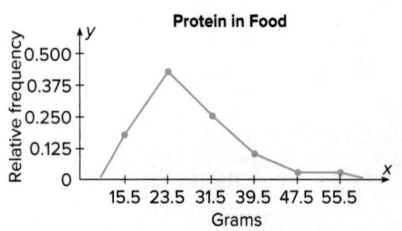

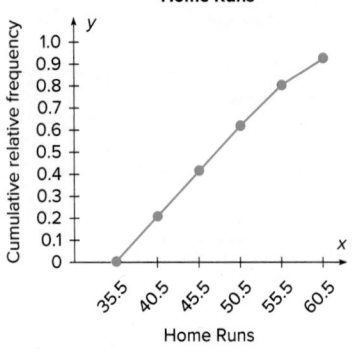

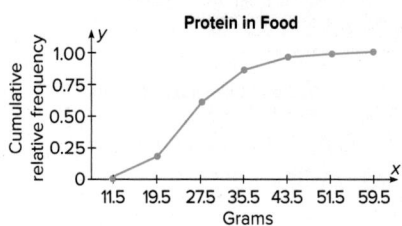

19. *a.*

Limits	Boundaries	Midpoints	f
22–24	21.5–24.5	23	1
25–27	24.5–27.5	26	3
28–30	27.5–30.5	29	0
31–33	30.5–33.5	32	6
34–36	33.5–36.5	35	5
37–39	36.5–39.5	38	3
40–42	39.5–42.5	41	2

	cf
Less than 21.5	0
Less than 24.5	1
Less than 27.5	4
Less than 30.5	4
Less than 33.5	10
Less than 36.5	15
Less than 39.5	18
Less than 42.5	20

18.

Class boundaries	rf	Midpoints
11.5–19.5	0.175	15.5
19.5–27.5	0.425	23.5
27.5–35.5	0.250	31.5
35.5–43.5	0.100	39.5
43.5–51.5	0.025	47.5
51.5–59.5	0.025	55.5
Total	1.000	

	cf
Less than 11.5	0
Less than 19.5	0.175
Less than 27.5	0.600
Less than 35.5	0.850
Less than 43.5	0.950
Less than 51.5	0.975
Less than 59.5	1.000

b.

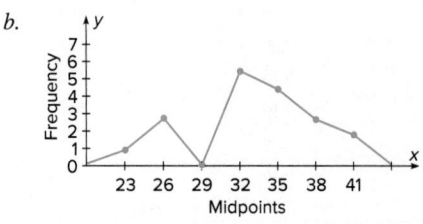

c.

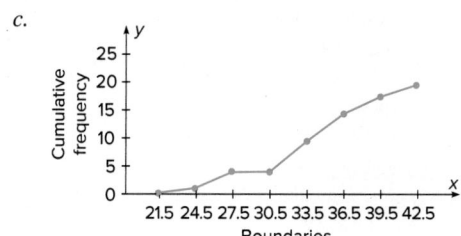

20. *a.* 0   *b.* 14   *c.* 10   *d.* 16

21.

Boundaries	f	Midpoints
468.5–495.5	6	482
495.5–522.5	15	509
522.5–549.5	10	536
549.5–576.5	7	563
576.5–603.5	6	590
603.5–630.5	6	617
Total	50	

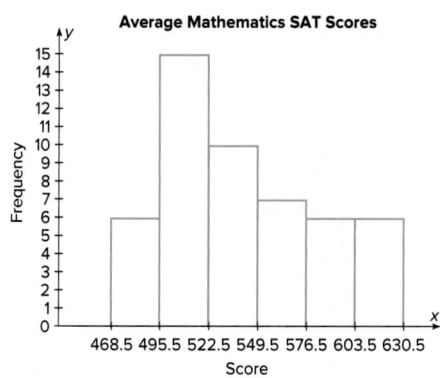

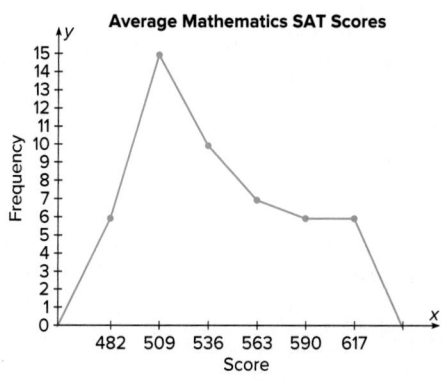

Exercises 2–3

1.

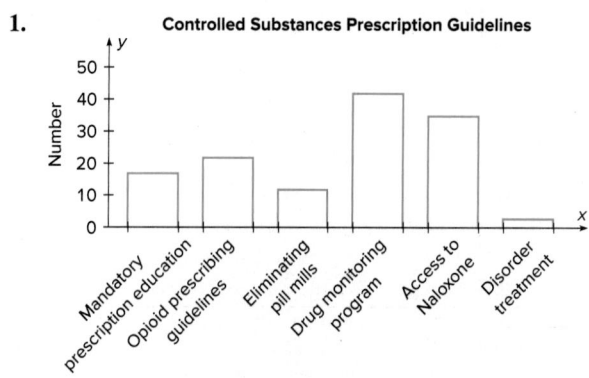

2.

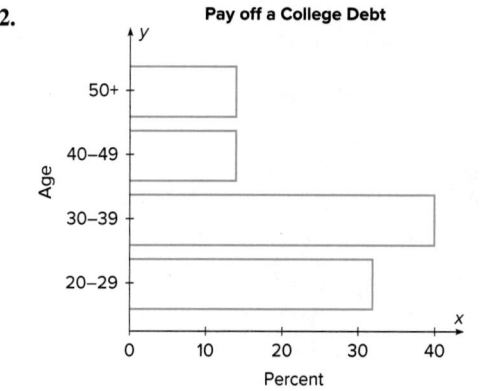

3.

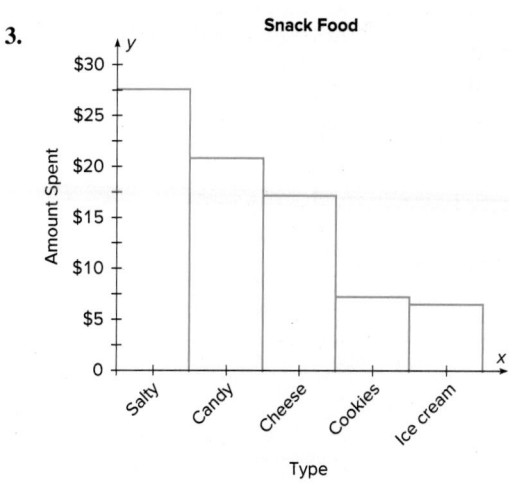

4.

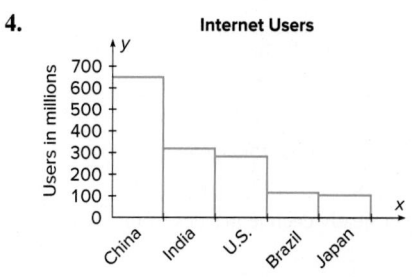

5.

Online Spending

(line graph: x-axis "Year" from 2014 to 2019; y-axis "Billions of dollars" from 0 to 80. Points approximately: 2014 ≈ 19, 2015 ≈ 32, 2016 ≈ 42, 2017 ≈ 53, 2018 ≈ 61, 2019 ≈ 69)

There is an increase over the years.

6.

Medical Prescriptions

(line graph: x-axis "Year" from 2015 to 2019; y-axis "Amount in millions of dollars" from 0 to 4500. Points approximately: 2015 ≈ 4365, 2016 ≈ 4455, 2017 ≈ 4235, 2018 ≈ 4210, 2019 ≈ 4220)

7.

World Population

(line graph: x-axis "Year" from 1995 to 2020; y-axis "Population in millions" from 5000 to 8000. Points approximately: 1995 ≈ 5300, 2000 ≈ 6150, 2005 ≈ 6550, 2010 ≈ 6950, 2015 ≈ 7400, 2020 ≈ 7800)

8.

Automobile Sales

(line graph: x-axis "Year" from 2014 to 2020; y-axis "Number" from 1000 to 4000. Points approximately: 2014 ≈ 3800, 2015 ≈ 3450, 2016 ≈ 2800, 2017 ≈ 2050, 2018 ≈ 1700, 2019 ≈ 1300, 2020 ≈ 1100)

There has been a steady decline in sales from 2014 to 2020.

9.

What's Cooking

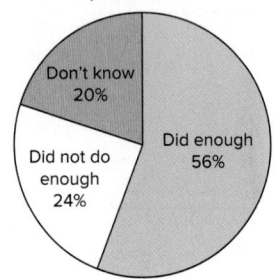

Most of the meal preparation is done on the stove-top followed by the oven and then the microwave.

10. **FEMA Help for Hurricane Victims**

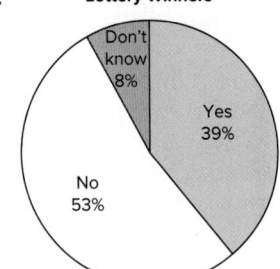

11. **Lottery Winners**

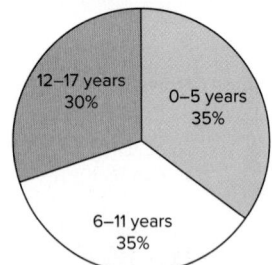

12. **Ages of Children Single Mothers**

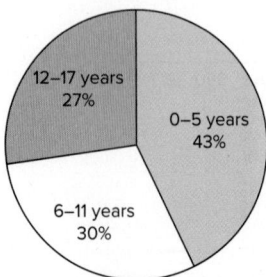

The percents for the single fathers are more variable than the percents for the single mothers.

13.

Prior Prison Sentences

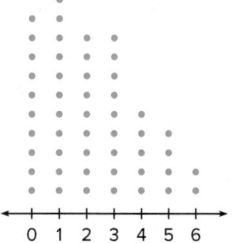

14.

Teacher Strikes

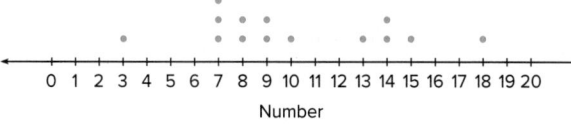

Number

The range of the number of strikes is 18 – 3, or 15. There are three gaps in the distribution and one peak at 7. There are two clusters. They are from 7 to 10 strikes and from 13 to 15 strikes.

15. The distribution is positively skewed. The class of 4 has more values than any other class, followed by the class with 3 years of experience.

Years of Experience

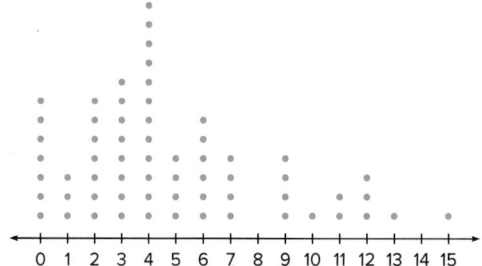

16.

Student Commuting Times

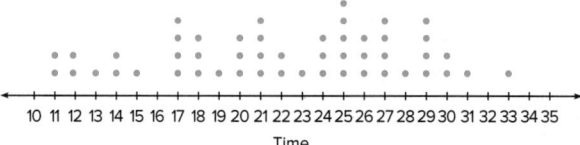

Time

The commuting times cluster from 17 to 31 minutes with a peak at 25 minutes and gaps at 16 and 32 minutes. The times range from 11 to 33 minutes.

17.

The 50-Home Run Club

5	0 0 0 0 0 0 1 1 1 1 1 2 2 2 2 2 2 3 3 4 4 4 4 4 4
5	6 6 6 7 7 8 8 8 8 9
6	0 1 3 4
6	5 6
7	0 3

Most players in the club have hit from 50 to 54 home runs in one season. The greatest number of home runs hit is 73.

18.

Terrorist Attacks

0	6 9 9
1	0 0 7 7 8 9
2	0 6
3	2 2 3 8
4	1

19.

Lengths of Major Rivers

South America		Europe
2	0	3 4 4 5 5 5 5 6 6 6 6 7 8 8 9
4 2 1 0 0 0 0 0 0 0	1	1 2 3 4
7 6 5 5	1	8
1	2	
5	2	
	3	
9	3	

The majority of rivers are longer in South America.

20. **Math and Reading Achievement Scores**

Math		Reading
9 9 9 7 5 5 2	5	
9 8 6 3 2 1	6	1 1 5 6 6 7 9
6 4 3 3 2	7	0 0 1 6 6 6 7 7 7 8
	8	0

The reading scores are somewhat higher than the math scores.

21. *a.* Pareto chart
    b. Pareto chart
    c. Pie graph
    d. Time series graph
    e. Pareto chart
    f. Time series graph

22. *a.* Time series graph
    b. Pie graph
    c. Pareto chart
    d. Pie graph
    e. Time series graph
    f. Pareto chart

23.

Credit Scores

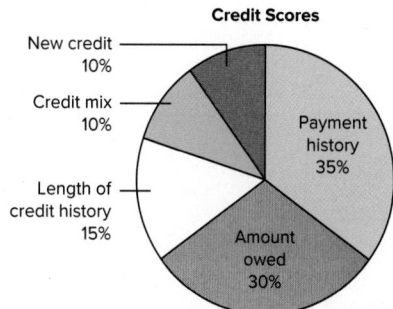

The pie chart is a better representation of the data since it shows the sizes of the sections compared to the whole. Answers may vary.

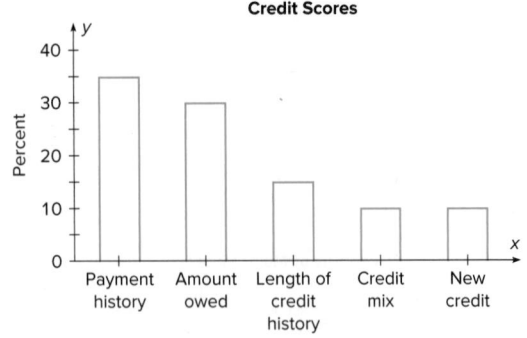

Credit Scores

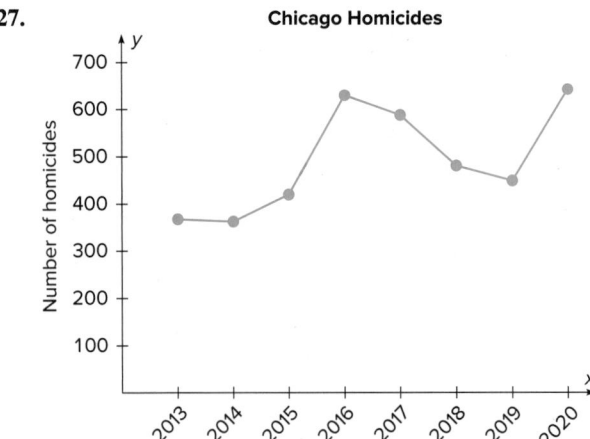

27.

Chicago Homicides

24.

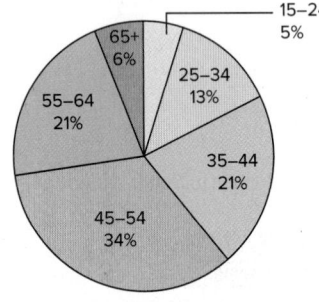

Alcohol Poisoning

The pie chart is a better representation of the data since it shows the sizes of the sections compared to the whole. Answers may vary.

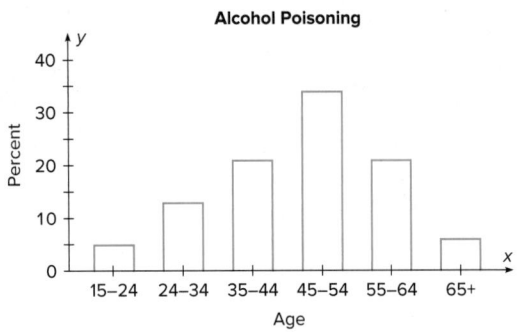

Alcohol Poisoning

28.

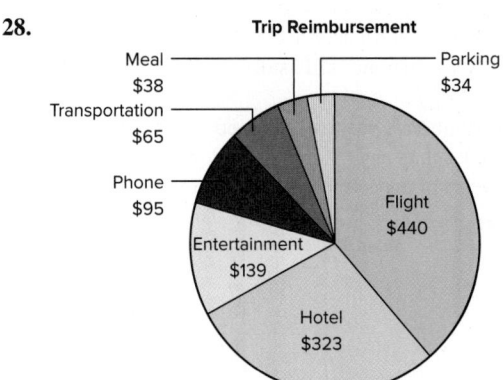

Trip Reimbursement

Note: Other graphs could be drawn.

Review Exercises

1.

Class	Tally	Frequency	Percents
B	THL THL THL THL THL /	26	50
W	THL ///	8	18
S	THL THL THL /	16	32
	Total	50	100

Half of the subjects consume beer, followed by spirits and then wine.

25. The bottle for 2020 is much bigger in area than the bottle for 1988. So your eyes compare areas rather than heights, making the difference appear to be much greater than it is.

26.

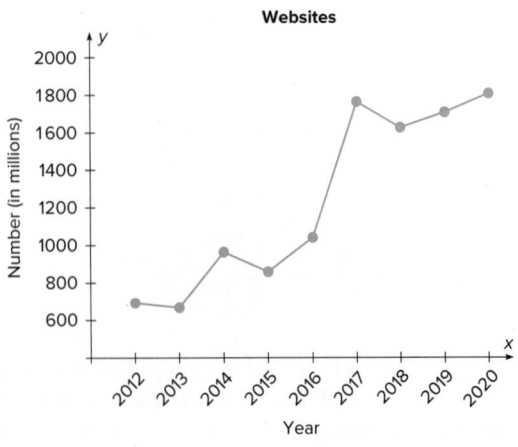

Websites

2.

Class	f	Percent
Hot dog	3	10
Hamburger	8	27
Pizza	7	23
Hoagie	5	17
Salad	7	23
	30	100

3.

Class	f
11	1
12	2
13	2
14	2
15	1
16	2
17	4
18	2
19	2
20	1
21	0
22	1
Total	20

	cf
Less than 10.5	0
Less than 11.5	1
Less than 12.5	3
Less than 13.5	5
Less than 14.5	7
Less than 15.5	8
Less than 16.5	10
Less than 17.5	14
Less than 18.5	16
Less than 19.5	18
Less than 20.5	19
Less than 21.5	19
Less than 22.5	20

4.

Limits	Boundaries	Frequency
8	7.5–8.5	11
9	8.5–9.5	10
10	9.5–10.5	4
11	10.5–11.5	2
12	11.5–12.5	2
13	12.5–13.5	4
14	13.5–14.5	2
15	14.5–15.5	1
	Total	36

	cf
7.5–8.5	11
8.5–9.5	21
9.5–10.5	25
10.5–11.5	27
11.5–12.5	29
12.5–13.5	33
13.5–14.5	35
14.5–15.5	36

5.

Class limits	Class boundaries	f
53–185	52.5–185.5	8
186–318	185.5–318.5	11
319–451	318.5–451.5	2
452–584	451.5–584.5	1
585–717	584.5–717.5	4
718–850	717.5–850.5	2
	Total	28

	cf
Less than 52.5	0
Less than 185.5	8
Less than 318.5	19
Less than 451.5	21
Less than 584.5	22
Less than 717.5	26
Less than 850.5	28

6.

Limits	Boundaries	f
51–59	50.5–59.5	5
60–68	59.5–68.5	12
69–77	68.5–77.5	11
78–86	77.5–86.5	8
87–95	86.5–95.5	3
96–104	95.5–104.5	2
	Total	41

	cf
Less than 50.5	0
Less than 59.5	5
Less than 68.5	17
Less than 77.5	28
Less than 86.5	36
Less than 95.5	39
Less than 104.5	41

7.

Class limits	Class boundaries	rf
53–185	52.5–185.5	0.29
186–318	185.5–318.5	0.39
319–451	318.5–451.5	0.07
452–584	451.5–584.5	0.04
585–717	584.5–717.5	0.14
718–850	717.5–850.5	0.07

	crf
Less than 52.5	0.00
Less than 185.5	0.29
Less than 318.5	0.68
Less than 451.5	0.75
Less than 584.5	0.79
Less than 717. 5	0.93
Less than 850.5	1.00

8.

Limits	Boundaries	rf
51–59	50.5–59.5	0.122
60–68	59.5–68.5	0.293
69–77	68.5–77.5	0.268
78–86	77.5–86.5	0.195
87–95	86.5–95.5	0.073
96–104	95.5–104.5	0.049
	Total	1.000

	crf
Less than 50.5	0
Less than 59.5	0.122
Less than 68.5	0.415
Less than 77.5	0.683
Less than 86.5	0.878
Less than 95.5	0.951
Less than 104.5	1.000

9.

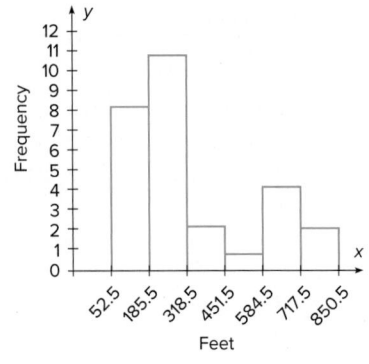

Waterfall Heights

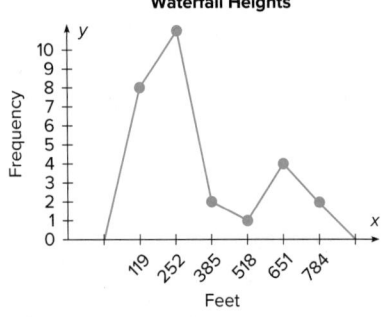

Waterfall Heights

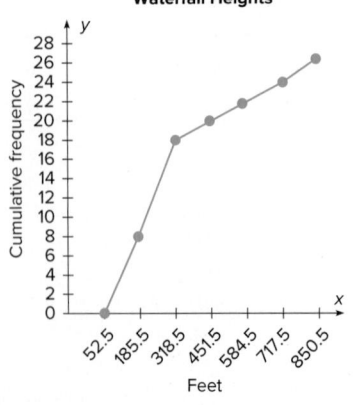

Waterfall Heights

10.

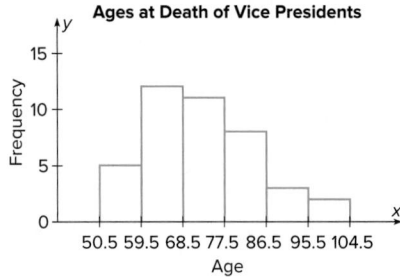

Ages at Death of Vice Presidents

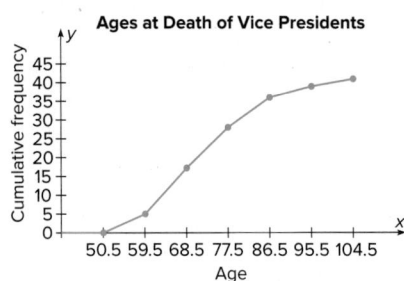

Ages at Death of Vice Presidents

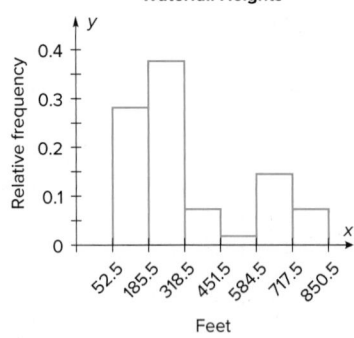

Ages at Death of Vice Presidents

11.

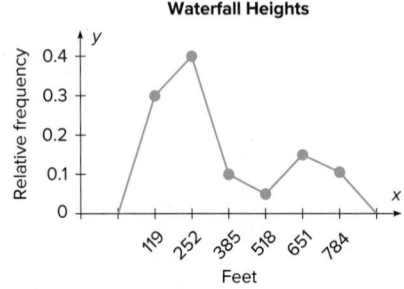

Waterfall Heights

Waterfall Heights

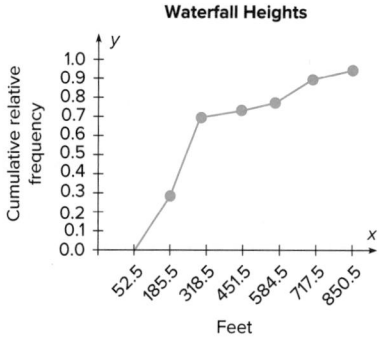

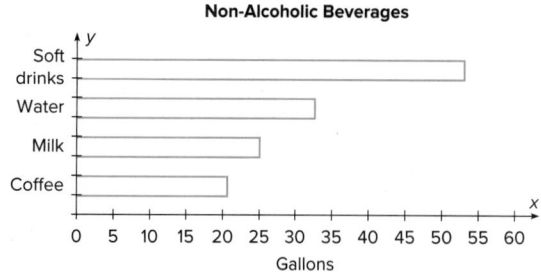

12.

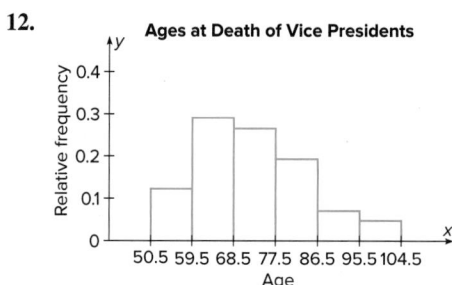

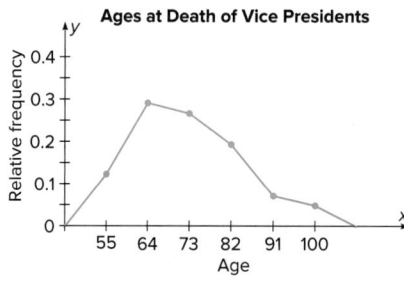

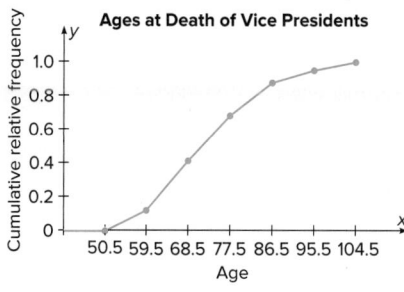

14.

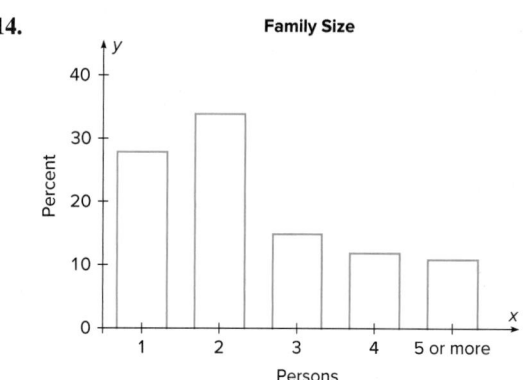

The most common family consists of two persons (34%), followed by one person (28%).

15.

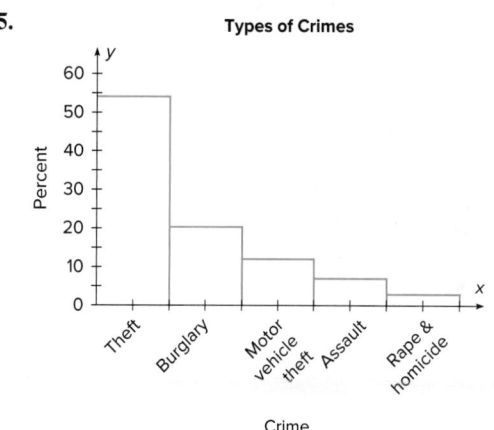

13.

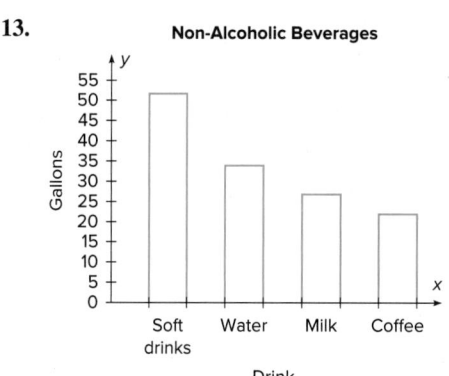

16.

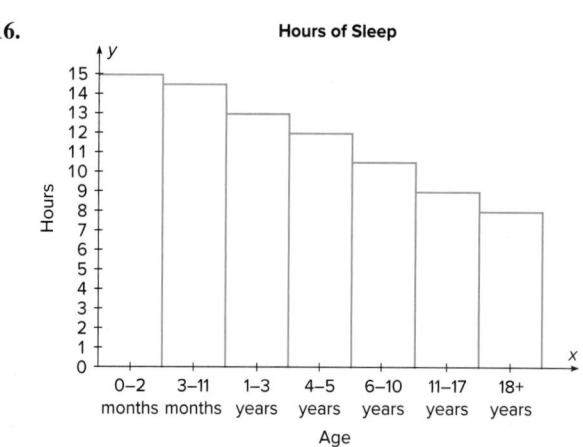

The older the children are, the less sleep they need. The range of the data is 8 to 15 hours.

17.

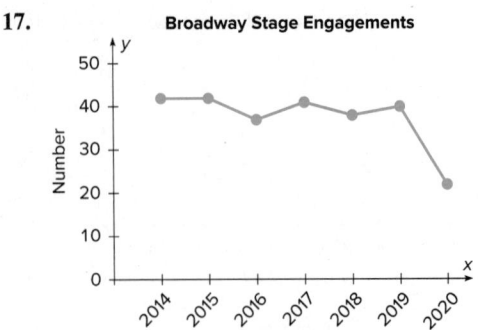

Broadway Stage Engagements

18.

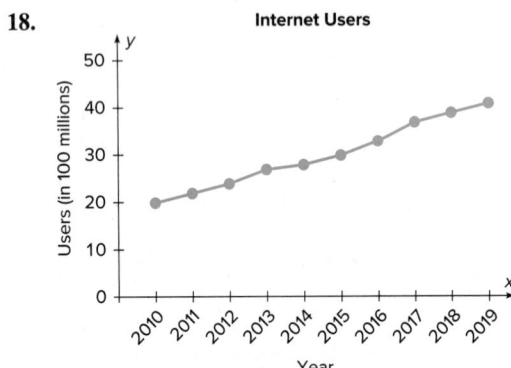

Internet Users

19. Spending of First-Year College Students

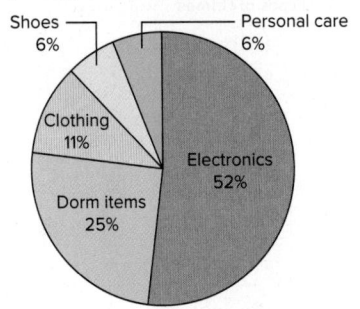

20.

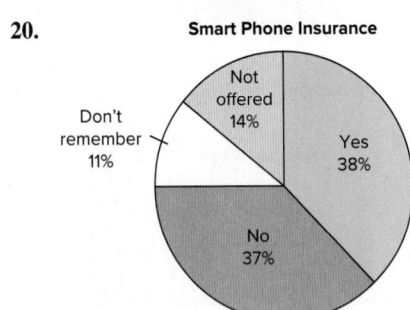

Smart Phone Insurance

The percentage of people who have insurance (38%) is almost the same as those who don't carry insurance (37%), but 14% of the people say that insurance is not offered and 11% don't remember whether or not they have insurance.

21.

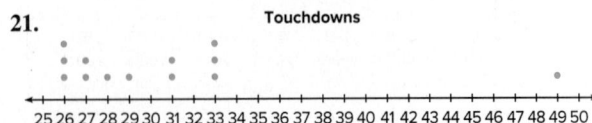

Touchdowns

The graph shows almost all but one of the touchdowns per season for Manning's career were between 26 and 33.

22.

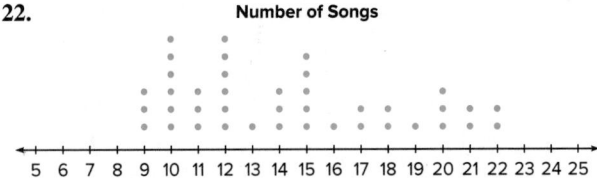

Number of Songs

The distribution is somewhat positively skewed, and the majority of the CDs (27) had between 9 and 15 songs on them.

23.
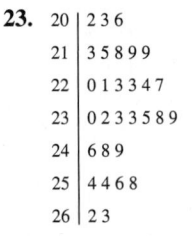

20	2 3 6
21	3 5 8 9 9
22	0 1 3 3 4 7
23	0 2 3 3 5 8 9
24	6 8 9
25	4 4 6 8
26	2 3

24.
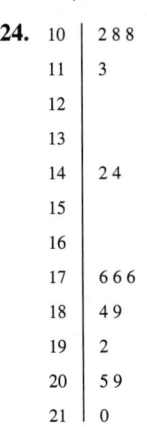

10	2 8 8
11	3
12	
13	
14	2 4
15	
16	
17	6 6 6
18	4 9
19	2
20	5 9
21	0

25. There are no numbers on the x and y axes. So it is impossible to tell the times of the pain relief.

26. The graph must have been truncated. There is a 3% difference, but it looks like a much larger difference.

Chapter Quiz

1. False. Classes should not be overlapping.

2. True

3. False. The class width should be the same for all classes.

4. True

5. True

6. False. Class midpoints should be used for the points on the x axis.

7. False. You should use the time series graph.

8. c

9. c   **10.** b

11. b   **12.** Categorical, ungrouped, grouped

13. 5, 20   **14.** Categorical

15. Time series   **16.** Stem and leaf plot

17. Vertical or y

18.

Class	f	Percent
H	6	24
A	5	20
M	6	24
C	8	32
Total	25	100

19.

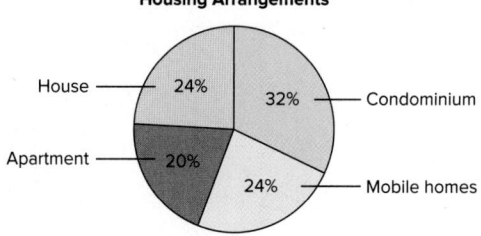

Housing Arrangements

House — 24%
Condominium — 32%
Apartment — 20%
Mobile homes — 24%

20.

Class limits	Class boundaries	f
1	0.5–1.5	1
2	1.5–2.5	5
3	2.5–3.5	3
4	3.5–4.5	4
5	4.5–5.5	2
6	5.5–6.5	6
7	6.5–7.5	2
8	7.5–8.5	3
9	8.5–9.5	4
	Total	30

	cf
Less than 0.5	0
Less than 1.5	1
Less than 2.5	6
Less than 3.5	9
Less than 4.5	13
Less than 5.5	15
Less than 6.5	21
Less than 7.5	23
Less than 8.5	26
Less than 9.5	30

21.

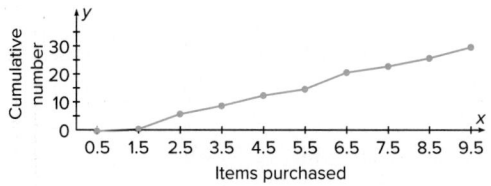

22.

Limits	Boundaries	f	rf	Midpoints
0–214	−0.5–214.5	20	0.39	107
215–429	214.5–429.5	15	0.29	322
430–644	429.5–644.5	5	0.10	537
645–859	644.5–859.5	5	0.10	752
860–1074	859.5–1074.5	2	0.04	967
1075–1289	1074.5–1289.5	2	0.04	1182
1290–1504	1289.5–1504.5	2	0.04	1397
	Total	51	1.00	

	cf	crf
Less than 0	0	0
Less than 214.5	20	0.39
Less than 429.5	35	0.69
Less than 644.5	40	0.78
Less than 859.5	45	0.88
Less than 1074.5	47	0.92
Less than 1289.5	49	0.96
Less than 1504.5	51	1.00

23.

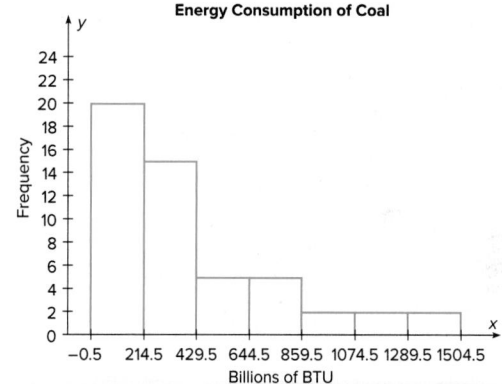

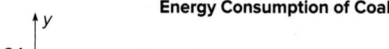

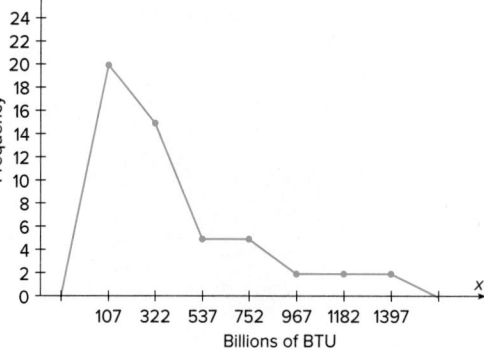

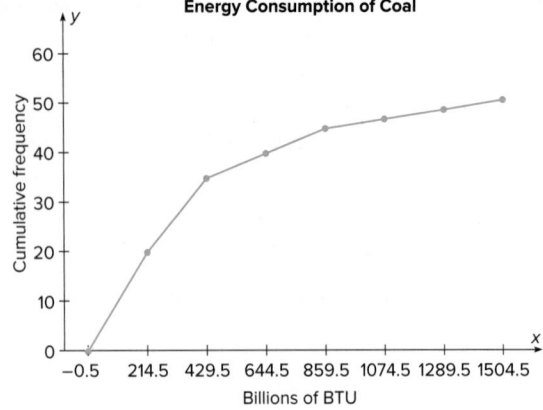

24.

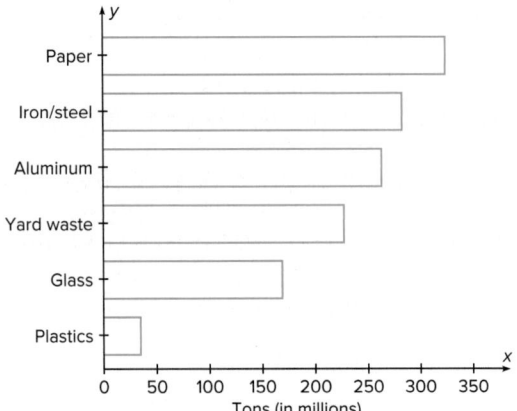

25.

Identity Thefts

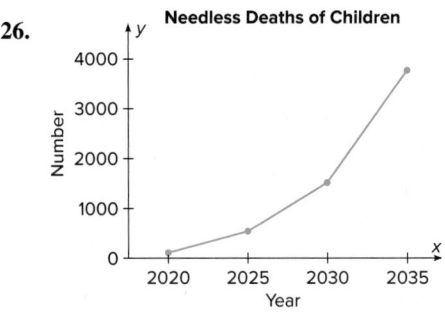

26.

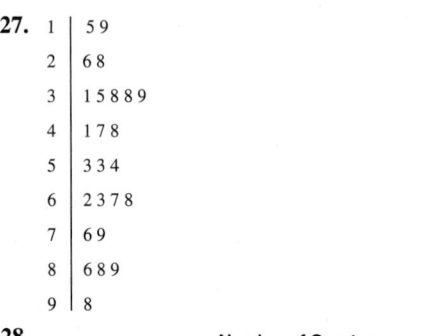

27.

1	5 9
2	6 8
3	1 5 8 8 9
4	1 7 8
5	3 3 4
6	2 3 7 8
7	6 9
8	6 8 9
9	8

28.

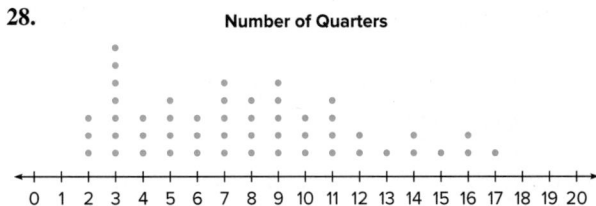

29. The bottles have different diameters, so your eyes will compare areas instead of heights.

Chapter 3

Exercises 3–1

1. 104.1, 102, 105, 50, 95, and 102
2. 9.5; 9.5; 10; 10.5
3. 162.9; 124; no mode; 270.5
4. 28.9; 18; no mode; 66.5; median seems to be the best measure of average.
5. 6,190,000; 5,600,000; no mode; 6,860,000
6. 19; 10; 7; 28.5; (Isn't it cool that Albert Einstein is on this list?) The data are positively skewed.
7. 89.2; 88; 84 and 92; 91
8. 24.42; 23.45; 16.9, 17.2, 18, 19.1, 24, 25.2, 31.7; 32.1. The mean and the median are close, and the midrange is higher than both. There are many modes. It appears that the mean and median are good measures of the average.
9. 365.1; 377.5; 440; 492.5
10. 25.3; 25; 25; 26.5
11. 37.4; 33.7; none; 46.15
12. 56.6; 47.5; 15 and 49; 116
13. 71.65; 68.5–75.5
14. 17.684; 2.48–7.48 and 17.51–22.51; Group mean is less.
15. 25.6; 25–27
16. 5.9; 3–5
17. 26.66; 24.2–28.6   18. 72; 71–79

19. 34.1; 0.5–19.5   **20.** 46.4; 46–54

21. 3.2 and 2

22. 1804.6; 1013–1345

Class limits	Frequency
1013–1345	11
1346–1678	4
1679–2011	7
2012–2344	3
2345–2677	5
2678–3010	3

23. $9866.67   **24.** 2.896

25. 35.4%   **26.** 4.8

27. 83.2   **28.** 82.7

29. *a.* Mode   *c.* Median   *e.* Mean
     b. Median   *d.* Mode   *f.* Median

30. *a.* Median   *c.* Mode   *e.* Mode
     b. Mean   *d.* Mode   *f.* Mean

31. Roman letters, $\overline{X}$; Greek letters, μ

32. Both could be true since one may be using the mean for the average salary and the other may be using the mode for the average.

33. Yes. It depends on the numbers in the data set. For example, if the data were 3, 4, and 5, the mean would be $(3 + 4 + 5)/3 = 12/3 = 4$.

34. If the data set contains an odd number of data values, the median would be one of the numbers in the data set.

35. If all the data values were the same, then the mean and median would be the largest (or smallest) data value.

36. The mean and median of the salaries will increase by $2500.

37. The mean and median will increase by 5%.

38. No. That value is called the midrange.

39. 320   **40.** 6

41. *a.* 40   *b.* 20   *c.* 300   *d.* 3
     e. The results will be the same as if you add, subtract, multiply, and divide the mean by 10.

42. *a.* 36 mph   *b.* 30.8 mph   *c.* $16.67

43. *a.* 25.5%   *b.* 5.7%   *c.* 8.4%   *d.* 3.2%

44. 5.5   **45.** 5.1

Exercises 3–2

1. The square root of the variance is the standard deviation.

2. One extremely high or one extremely low data value will influence the range.

3. σ^2; σ **4.** s^2; s

5. When the population is large and the sample is small (usually less than 30), dividing the sum of the squares of the deviations by n will underestimate the population variance. So we must divide by $n - 1$ instead, giving a slightly larger value and an unbiased estimate of the population variance.

6. No, the standard deviations are $s = 4.3$, $s = 5.1$, and $s = 6$. So *a* has the smallest variation and *c* has the biggest variation.

7. 90.7; 891.88; 29.86

8. 62; 332.4; 18.2; using the range rule of thumb, $s \approx 15.5$. This is close to the actual standard deviation of 18.2.

9. 35; 98.8; 9.9

10. The surface area for the Western states is more variable since the standard deviation is 16,178.4 as compared to 6440.2 for the Eastern states.

11. Triplets: 1233; 198,612.7; 445.7
     Quadruplets: 167; 3952.9; 62.9
     Quintuplets: 45; 180.8; 13.4
     The data for the triplets are the most variable.

12. 0.9; 0.111; 0.333

13. $s \approx R/4$ so $s \approx 5$ years.

14. Math 19, 30.6, 5.5
     Reading and Writing 108, 900, 30
     The reading and writing scores are more variable.

15. Russia 933; 159,120.8; 398.9
     U.S. 491; 30,218.2; 173.8
     The Russian launches are more variable.

16. 2721; 355,427.6; 596.2

17. 130; 1156.7; 34.0

18. Spending: $s = 29.9$, $R/4 = 22.7$
     Space launches:
     Russia $s = 398.9$; $R/4 = 233.25$
     U.S. $s = 173.8$; $R/4 = 122.75$
     Precip: Days: $s = 34.0$, $R/4 = 32.5$
     The closest estimate is for precipitation.

19. 74.4; 8.6   **20.** 98.8; 9.94

21. 11.3; 3.4   **22.** 88.9; 9.4

23. 8.8; 32.6; 5.7   **24.** 16.7; 29.2; 5.4

25. 29.1; 5.4   **26.** 12.7; 3.6

27. CVar = 20.9%; CVar = 22.5%. The factory workers' data are more variable.

28. United States: $\overline{X} = 3386.6$, $s = 693.9$, CVar = 20.49%.
     World: $\overline{X} = 4997.8$, $s = 803.2$, CVar = 16.07%.
     The United States is more variable.

29. CVar = 13.1%; CVar = 15.2%. The waiting time for people who are discharged is more variable.

30. CVar = 23.1%; CVar = 12.9%; age is more variable.

31. *a.* 75%   *b.* 56%

32. *a.* 96%   *b.* 93.75%

33. At least 93.75%

34. Between 164 and 316 calories

35. Between 84 and 276 minutes

36. Between 385 and 895 pounds

37. Between $161,100 and $355,100

38. At least 86%   **39.** At least 84%

40. About 16%   **41.** 490–586; About 2.5%

42. *a.* 25%   *b.* About 2.5%

43. $345; $52   **44.** 22.6; 3.2

45. $6.51; $1.65   **46.** $10,000; $1,625

47. $\overline{X} = 215.0$ and $s = 20.8$. All the data values fall within 2 standard deviations of the mean. This agrees with Chebyshev's theorem, which states that at least 75% of the data values will fall within 2 standard deviations of the mean.

48. $\overline{X} = 34.5$ and $s = 13.3$; 28 of the values (93.3%). This agrees with Chebyshev's theorem, which states that at least 75% of the data values will fall within 2 standard deviations of the mean.

49. 56%; 75%; 84%; 89%; 92%

50. *a.* 15.8 *b.* 15.8 *c.* 15.8 *d.* 79.1 *e.* 3.2

　f. The standard deviation is unchanged when a specific number is added to or subtracted from each data value. If each data value is multiplied by a number, the standard deviation increases by the number times the original standard deviation. For division, the standard deviation is divided by the number.

　g. When the same number is added to or subtracted from each data value, the mean will increase or decrease by that number, but the standard deviation will remain unchanged. When each data value is multiplied by the same number, the mean and standard deviation will be equal to that number times the original mean and standard deviation. When each data value is divided by the same number, the mean and standard deviation will be equal to the original mean and standard deviation divided by that number.

51. 4.36

52. *a.* 2, positively skewed *b.* −2.25, negatively skewed
　c. 0, symmetric *d.* 0.3, positively skewed

53. It must be an incorrect data value, since it is beyond the range using the formula $s\sqrt{n-1}$.

Exercises 3–3

1. A z score tells how many standard deviations a data value is above or below the mean.

2. A percentile rank indicates the percentage of data values that fall below the specific rank.

3. A percentile is a relative measurement of position; a percentage is an absolute measure of the part to the total.

4. A quartile is a relative measure of position obtained by dividing the data set into quarters.

5. $Q_1 = P_{25}$; $Q_2 = P_{50}$; $Q_3 = P_{75}$

6. A decile is a relative measure of position obtained by dividing the data set into tenths.

7. $D_1 = P_{10}$; $D_2 = P_{20}$; $D_3 = P_{30}$; etc.

8. P_{50}; Q_2; D_5

9. *a.* −1.6 *b.* 1.2 *c.* −0.86 *d.* 1.69 *e.* −0.48

10. *a.* −1.08 *b.* 1.75 *c.* 0.75 *d.* −0.58 *e.* 2.42

11. *a.* 0.5 *b.* −1.5 *c.* −2.25 *d.* −0.375 *e.* 1.5

12. *a.* −1 *b.* 2.67 *c.* −2 *d.* −1.33 *e.* 1.33

13. Geography test $z = 1.83$. Accounting test $z = 1.71$. The geography test score is relatively higher than the accounting test score.

14. 0.64; 0.95. The student from the university has a higher relative debt.

15. *a.* 0.55 *c.* 19,690; 12,340, 14,090
　b. −1.17

16. *a.* −0.93 *b.* −0.85
　c. −1.4; score in part *b* has the highest relative position.

17. *a.* 21 *e.* 57
　b. 43 *f.* 72
　c. 97 *g.* 80
　d. 19 *h.* 87

18. *a.* 437 *c.* 722 *e.* 69th
　b. 578 *d.* 27th *f.* 90th
　Answers are approximate.

19. *a.* 6 *c.* 68 *e.* 94 *g.* 251 *i.* 274
　b. 24 *d.* 76 *f.* 234 *h.* 263 *j.* 284

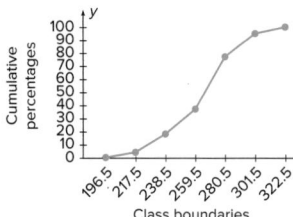

20. *a.* 375 *c.* 433 *e.* 504 *g.* 40th *i.* 76th
　b. 389 *d.* 477 *f.* 13th *h.* 54th *j.* 92nd

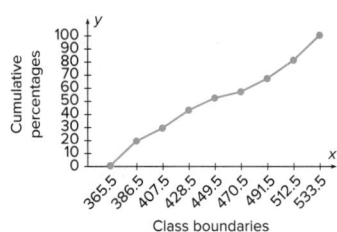

21. 94th; 72nd; 61st; 17th; 83rd; 50th; 39th; 28th; 6th; 597

22. 7th; 21st; 36th; 50th; 64th; 79th; 93rd; 47

23. 5th; 15th; 25th; 35th; 45th; 55th; 65th; 75th; 85th; 95th; 2.2

24. 8th; 25th; 42nd; 58th; 75th; 92nd; 12

25. $Q_1 = 11$; $Q_3 = 32$; IQR = 21

26. $Q_1 = 353,617$; $Q_3 = 512,838.5$

27. $Q_1 = 1.4$; $Q_3 = 2.7$; IQR = 1.3

28. $Q_1 = 4$; $Q_3 = 25$; IQR = 21

29. *a.* None *b.* 65 *c.* None

30. *a.* None *b.* 145 *c.* None

31. *a.* 12; 20.5; 32; 22; 20 *b.* 62; 94; 99; 80.5; 37

32. About 149.9

33. Tom, Harry, Dick. Find the z score for Tom, and it is less than Harry's z score; and both z scores are less than the 98th percentile.

34. The player with a z score of −1.5 is a better player since it indicates a regular score below the mean, and in golf the lower the score, the better it is.

35. A z score of zero means the data value is exactly at the mean.

36. The graphs have the same shapes.

Exercises 3–4

1. 3, 7, 9, 18, 20; 11

2. 7, 11.5, 19, 35, 48; 23.5

3. 21, 25, 32, 40.5, 43; 15.5

4. 391, 462, 536.5, 603, 625; 141

5. 10.6, 12, 15.2, 19.9, 22.2; 7.9

6. 2.2, 3.7, 4.6, 9.4, 9.7; 5.7

7. 27, 3, 18, 9, 21, 12

8. 7000, 2000, 5000, 3000, 6000, 3000

9. 145, 105, 120, 115, 140, 25

10. 625, 525, 575, 550, 600, 50

11.

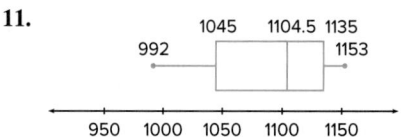

12.

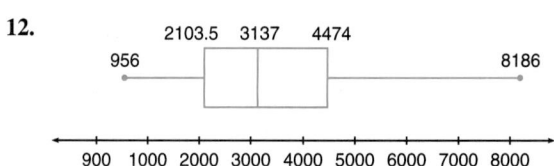

The distribution is positively skewed.

The five-number summary is

    Lowest value = 956

    $Q_1 = 2103.5$

    Median = 3137

    $Q_3 = 4474$

    Highest value = 8186

    IQR = 2370.5

13.

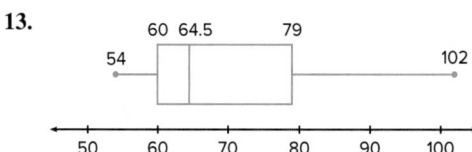

The five-number summary is

    Lowest value = 54

    $Q_1 = 60$ Median = 64.5 $Q_3 = 79$

    Highest value = 102

    IQR = 19

14.

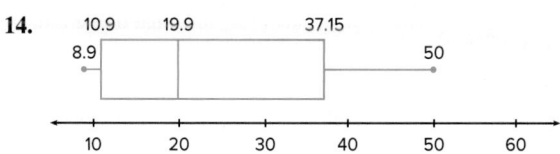

The distribution is slightly positively skewed.

15. The areas of the islands in the Baltic Sea are more variable than the ones in the Aleutian Islands. Also, they are in general larger in area.

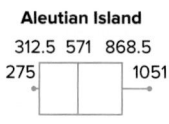

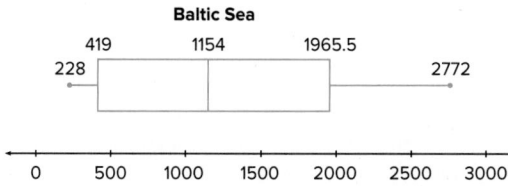

16. The range and variation of the capacity of the dams in South America are considerably larger than those of the United States.

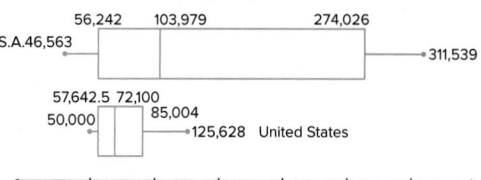

17.

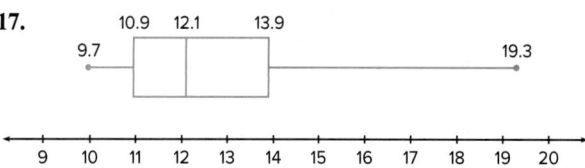

The distribution is positively skewed.

The five-number summary is

    Lowest value = 9.7

    $Q_1 = 10.9$ $Q_2 = 12.1$ $Q_3 = 13.9$

    Highest value = 19.3

    IQR = 3

18. *a.* May: 247.3.   *b.* 2015: 213

    c.

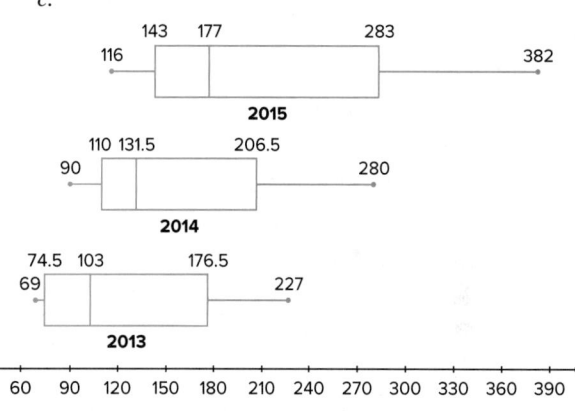

19.

            42 48   66

        39   97

       0   25   50   75   100

There are no outliers.

Review Exercises

1. 36.5; 11; 78.5; 0, 3, and 4.

2. Attacks:

    $\overline{X} = 63.6$; MD = 64; no mode; MR = 64

    Deaths:

    $\overline{X} = 4$; MD = 4; mode = 4; MR = 4

3. 120; 120–124; and 125–129

4. $\overline{X} = 531.5$; modal class 505–531

5. 1.43 viewers   **6.** $4700.00

7. 175; 2597.0; 51.0   **8.** 28; 78.9; 8.9

9. 7.1; 6–8; 12.7; 3.6   **10.** 19; 15–19; 52.0; 7.2

11. 6   **12.** 14

13. Books CVar = 31.25%; Ages CVar = 18.6%; the number of books is more variable

14. Magazine CVar = 21.4%; Years CVar = 41.7%; years are more variable

15. $0.26–$0.38

16. *a.* Nothing because $k = 1$
    b. At most ¼ or 25%   *c.* At most 7.3%

17. 56%   18. 83%

19. $17–$25   20. 26–62

21. *a.* −0.27   *b.* 0.77   *c* 1.53

22. *a.* −0.5   *b.* −0.8
    The grade in part a has better position.

23. *a.*

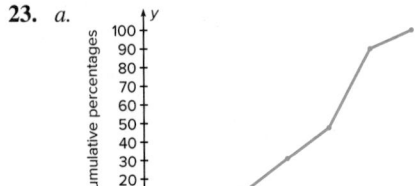

b. 50, 53, 55
c. 10th; 26th; 78th

24. *a.*

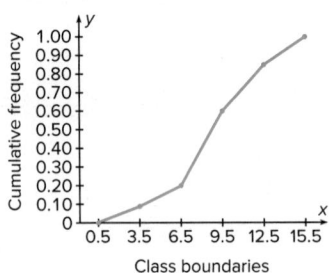

b. 6.5; 8.75; 10.7.
c. 14th; 64th; 93rd Answers are approximate.

25. *a.* 400   *b.* None

26. *a.* None   *b.* None

27. The variability for the named storms for the period 1941–1950 is about the same as for the period of 1851–1860. The range for the storms for 1941–1950 is larger.

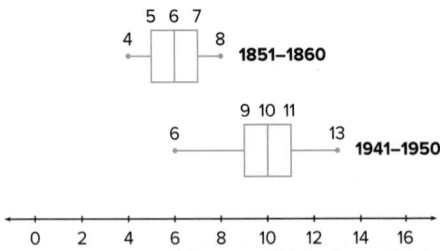

28. The employees worked more hours before Christmas than after Christmas. Also, the range and variability of the distribution of hours are greater before Christmas.

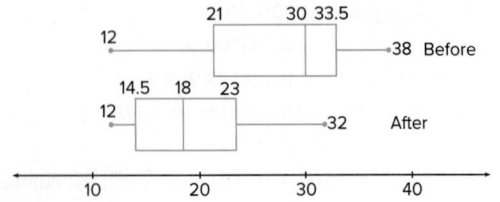

Chapter Quiz

1. True   2. True

3. False. It does not affect the median. It affects the mean.

4. False. One-half of the data values fall above the median, and one-half of the data values fall below the median.

5. False. The mode is not always unique.

6. False. Only the range is a measure of variation.

7. False. The median is unique.

8. False. The mode and midrange are measures of central tendency.

9. False. The score being the 75th percentile means that the score is above 75 percent of the scores on that exam.

10. *c*   11. *c*   12. *a* and *b*

13. *b*   14. *d*

15. *b*   16. Statistic

17. Parameters, statistics   18. Standard deviation

19. σ 20. Midrange

21. Positively   22. Outlier

23. *a.* 15.3   *c.* 15, 16, and 17   *e.* 6   *g.* 1.9
    b. 15.5   *d.* 15   *f.* 3.6

24. *a.* 6.4   *b.* 6–8   *c.* 11.6   *d.* 3.4

25. 4.5

26. The number of newspapers sold in a convenience store is more variable.

27. 88.89%   28. 16%; 97.5%

29. 4.5   30. −0.75; −1.67; science

31. *a.*

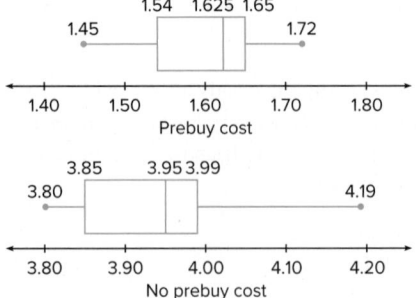

b. 47; 55; 64
c. 56th, 6th, 99th percentiles

32. The cost of prebuy gas is much less than that of the return without filling gas. The variability of the return without filling gas is larger than the variability of the prebuy gas.

Chapter 4

Exercises 4–1

1. A probability experiment is a chance process that leads to well-defined outcomes.

2. The set of all possible outcomes of a probability experiment is called a sample space.

3. An outcome is the result of a single trial of a probability experiment, but an event can consist of more than one outcome.

4. Equally likely events have the same probability of occurring.

5. The range of values is 0 to 1 inclusive.

6. 1

7. 0

8. 1

9. 0.80   Since the probability that it won't rain is 80%, you could leave your umbrella at home and be fairly safe.

10. *c, d, e, h*

11. *a.* Empirical   *c.* Empirical
    b. Classical   *d.* Classical

12. *a.* Empirical   *c.* Subjective
    b. Empirical   *d.* Subjective

13. *a.* 0   *b.* $\frac{2}{3}$ *c.* 1   *d.* $\frac{1}{2}$

14. *a.* 1   *b.* $\frac{2}{3}$ *c.* $\frac{1}{3}$ *d.* 0

15. *a.* $\frac{1}{9}$ *b.* $\frac{7}{36}$ *c.* $\frac{11}{36}$

16. *a.* $\frac{13}{18}$ *b.* $\frac{1}{6}$ *c.* $\frac{11}{36}$

17. *a.* $\frac{4}{13}$ *c.* $\frac{3}{26}$ *e.* $\frac{1}{2}$
    b. $\frac{1}{26}$ *d.* $\frac{1}{4}$

18. *a.* $\frac{1}{52}$ *c.* $\frac{1}{26}$ *e.* $\frac{1}{2}$
    b. $\frac{1}{26}$ *d.* $\frac{1}{2}$

19. *a.* 8.9%   *b.* 79.5%

20. *a.* $\frac{3}{52}$ *b.* $\frac{3}{25}$

21. *a.* 0.12   *b.* 0.48   *c.* 0.57

22. *a.* 24%   *b.* 86%   *c.* 72%

23. *a.* 3%   *b.* 81%   *c.* 92%

24. *a.* 0.32   *b.* 0.30   *c.* 0.94

25. *a.* $\frac{1}{16}$ *b.* $\frac{1}{4}$ *c.* $\frac{15}{16}$ *d.* $\frac{7}{8}$

26. *a.* 76%   *b.* 47%   *c.* 23%

27. $\frac{1}{3}$

28. *a.* 0.055   *b.* 0.907   *c.* 0.295

29. *a.* 27%   *c.* 67%
    b. 33%   *d.* 14%

30. 0.3227

31. 0.11; 0.92

32. 0.694; 0.925

33. 0.285, 0.725

34. 0.6

35.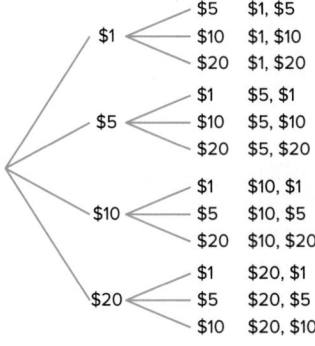

36.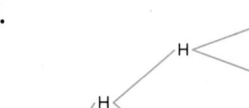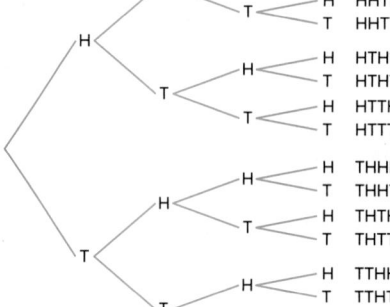

37.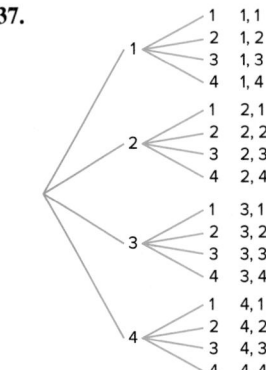

38.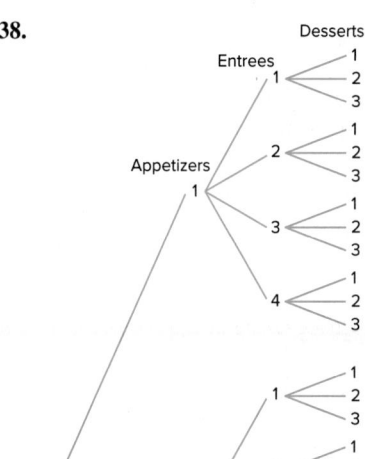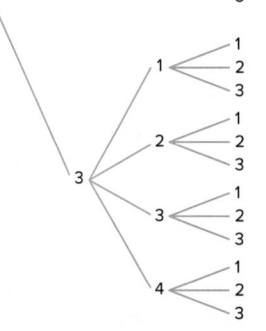

39.

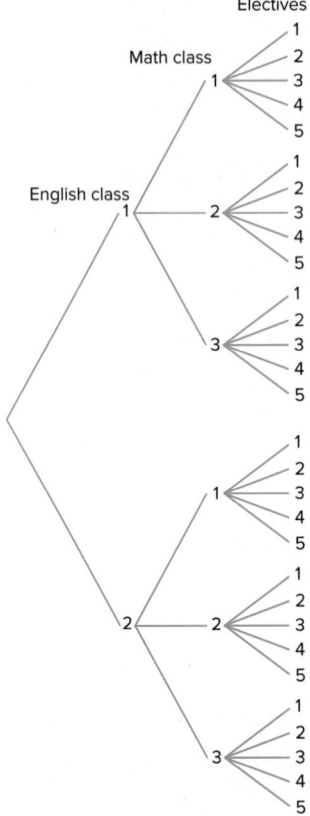

40.

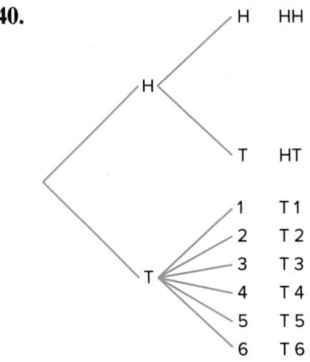

41. *a.* 0.08 *b.* 0.01 *c.* 0.35 *d.* 0.36

42. Probably

43. The statement is probably not based on empirical probability and is probably not true.

44. *a.* $\frac{6}{25}$ *b.* $\frac{2}{5}$ *c.* $\frac{9}{25}$ *d.* $\frac{12}{25}$ *e.* $\frac{1}{5}$

45. Answers will vary. However they should be approximately $\frac{1}{8}, \frac{3}{8}, \frac{3}{8}, \frac{1}{8}$.

46. Approximately $\frac{1}{4}, \frac{1}{2}$, and $\frac{1}{4}$, respectively

47. *a.* 1:5, 5:1 *d.* 1:1, 1:1 *g.* 1:1, 1:1
   b. 1:1, 1:1 *e.* 1:12, 12:1
   c. 1:3, 3:1 *f.* 1:3, 3:1

48. No. The probability of guessing the correct answer is $\frac{1}{5}$ since you have a total of 5 choices and only one choice is correct!

49. Both selections have the same probability of winning.

50. Either choice has the same probability of winning. Since the outcomes are independent, there is no such thing as a "run" when each outcome is independent.

51. No. In the long run, 5 heads will occur on average once in 32 times, but there is no guarantee that 5 heads will occur when you repeat the experiment 32 times.

52. The probability of getting 2 heads is $\frac{6}{16}$, while the probability of getting one or three heads is $\frac{8}{16}$. So, getting one or more heads is a better bet.

Exercises 4–2

1. Two events are mutually exclusive if they cannot occur at the same time (i.e., they have no outcomes in common). Examples will vary.

2. Addition rule 2 can be used because $P(A \text{ and } B) = 0$ when the events are mutually exclusive.

3. *a.* Not mutually exclusive since you can get the 6 of clubs
   b. Not mutually exclusive since 2 is both an even number and a prime number
   c. Mutually exclusive
   d. Not mutually exclusive, since a commuter student can also be a business major

4. *a.* Yes *b.* No *c.* Yes *d.* Yes

5. *a.* 0.707 *b.* 0.589 *c.* 0.011 *d.* 0.731

6. 0.63 **7.** *a.* $\frac{7}{38} = 0.184$ *b.* $\frac{35}{38} = 0.921$

8. *a.* 0.45 *b.* 0.183 *c.* 0.633 **9.** $\frac{5}{8}$

10. *a.* 0.53 *b.* 0.4 *c.* 0.86

11. *a.* $\frac{3}{10} = 0.3$ *b.* $\frac{6}{40} = 0.15$ *c.* $\frac{17}{20} = 0.85$

12. *a.* 0.5 *b.* 0.769 or $\frac{10}{13}$ *c.* 0.615 or $\frac{8}{13}$

13. *a.* 0.164 *b.* 0.168 *c.* 0.292

14. *a.* 0.072 *b.* 0.228 *c.* 0.486

15. *a.* 0.18 *b.* 0.93 *c.* 0.25 *d.* 0.82

16. *a.* 0.301 *b.* 0.592 *c.* 0.412

17. *a.* 0.789 *b.* 0.154 *c.* 0.057

18. *a.* $\frac{467}{1392}$ *b.* $\frac{47}{58}$ *c.* $\frac{833}{1392}$

19. *a.* $\frac{1}{15}$ *c.* $\frac{5}{6}$ *e.* $\frac{1}{3}$
   b. $\frac{1}{3}$ *d.* $\frac{5}{6}$

20. *a.* 0.479 *b.* 0.492 *c.* 0.21

21. *a.* $\frac{2}{15}$ *b.* $\frac{5}{6}$ *c.* $\frac{7}{15}$ *d.* $\frac{5}{6}$ *e.* $\frac{1}{6}$

22. *a.* $\frac{29}{100}$ *b.* $\frac{2}{3}$ *c.* $\frac{157}{300}$

23. *a.* $\frac{4}{13}$ *b.* $\frac{7}{26}$ *c.* $\frac{4}{13}$

24. *a.* $\frac{7}{36}$ *b.* $\frac{5}{18}$ *c.* $\frac{1}{6}$ *d.* c

25. 0.491 **26.** *a.* $\frac{5}{12}$ *b.* $\frac{1}{72}$

27. 0.06 **28.** 0.10

29. 0.30 **30.** No. $P(A \text{ and } B) \neq 0$

31. $(m + n)/(2m + n)$ **32.** *a.* 0.261 *b.* 0.608 *c.* 0

Exercises 4–3

1. *a.* Independent *c.* Dependent
   b. Dependent *d.* Dependent

2. *a.* Independent *c.* Dependent
   b. Dependent *d.* Independent

3. *a.* 0.500 *b.* 0.00066

4. 67.7% **5.** 0.25, unlikely

6. 2.8% **7.** *a.* 15% *b.* 36% *c.* 81%

8. 0.746, 0.0000249 **9.** 0.0041

10. *a.* 0.142 *b.* 0.312 *c.* 0.261

11. *a.* 0.0689 *b.* 0.205 *c.* 0.931

12. $\frac{1}{15}$ **13.** *a.* 0.00000369 *b.* 0.0552 *c.* 0.00264

14. $\frac{5}{28}$ **15.** *a.* $\frac{1}{17}$ *b.* $\frac{25}{102}$ *c.* $\frac{4}{17}$

16. $\frac{3}{29}$; unlikely **17.** $\frac{1}{66}$, highly unlikely

18. 0.116 **19.** *a.* 0.167 *b.* 0.406 *c.* 0.691

20. $\frac{19}{36}$ **21.** 0.03 **22.** 0.78; 0.018 **23.** 0.071

24. 0.116 **25.** 0.656; 0.438 **26.** 89% **27.** 0.2

28. *a.* $\frac{1}{4}$ *b.* $\frac{29}{40}$ *c.* $\frac{3}{4}$

29. 68.4% **30.** *a.* 0.714 *b.* 0.435 *c.* 0.156

31. *a.* 0.06 *b.* 0.435 *c.* 0.35 *d.* 0.167

32. *a.* 0.498 *b.* 0.109 *c.* No. P(path|female) $\neq P$(path)

33. *a.* $\frac{2}{3}$ *b.* $\frac{5}{12}$ *c.* $\frac{1}{4}$

34. *a.* $\frac{8}{21}$ *b.* $\frac{5}{8}$ *c.* $\frac{7}{100}$

35. *a.* 0.020 *b.* 0.611 **36.** 0.237

37. *a.* 0.172 *b.* 0.828

38. *a.* 0.157 *b.* 0.097 *c.* 0.903 **39.** 0.304

40. *a.* 0.324 *b.* 0.676 *c.* 0.999 *d.* *a* and *b*

41. 0.987 **42.** *a.* 0.216 *b.* 0.064 *c.* 0.936

43. $\frac{7411}{9520}$ **44.** *a.* 0.966 *b.* 0.034 *c.* 0.108

45. *a.* 0.139 *b.* 0.861 **46.** 96.8%

47. 0.875, likely

48. 0.111; the event is unlikely to occur since the probability is only about 11%.

49. 0.306

50. *a.* 0.0345 *b.* 0.028 *c.* 0.972 **51.** 0.319

52. 0.678; yes the event is more likely to occur than not since the probability is about 68%.

53. No, since $P(A \text{ and } B) = 0$ and does not equal $P(A) \cdot P(B)$.

54. No, since $P(C|D) \neq P(C)$.

55. Enrollment and meeting with DW and meeting with MH are dependent. Since meeting with MH has a low probability and meeting with LP has no effect, all students, if possible, should meet with DW.

56. *a.* The events are dependent, and the commercial hurts sales since the probability that a person buys the product after watching the commercial is less than 0.35.

b. The events are independent; hence, the commercial has no effect.

c. The events are dependent, and the commercial helps since the probability that a person buys the product after watching the commercial is higher than 0.35.

57. No; no; 0.072; 0.721; 0.02

58. $\frac{1}{9}$ **59.** 5

Exercises 4–4

1. 100,000; 30,240

2. MATH MAHT MTAH MTHA MHAT MHTA
ATHM ATMH AMTH AMHT AHMT AHTM
TAMH TAHM THMA THAM TMAH TMHA
HATM HAMT HTAM HTMA HMAT HMTA

3. 5040 **4.** 5040

5. 720 **6.** 362,880

7. 4096 **8.** 27,600; 35,152

9. 362,880; 40,320 **10.** 120

11. 7776 **12.** *a.* 720 *b.* 48

13. *a.* 1 *c.* 1 *e.* 210 *g.* 120 *i.* 15,120
b. 40,320 *d.* 120 *f.* 19,958,400 *h.* 1 *j.* 332,640

14. *a.* 24 *c.* 6 *e.* 3,628,800 *g.* 1 *i.* 8
b. 2 *d.* 5040 *f.* 2520 *h.* 5040 *j.* 24

15. 360 **16.** 210 **17.** 504

18. 30,240 **19.** 840 **20.** 120

21. 151,200 **22.** 286; 378 (count 0)

23. 5,527,200 **24.** 330

25. 495; 11,880 **26.** 2520

27. 210 **28.** 64,864,800

29. 1260 **30.** 27,720

31. 18,480 **32.** 50,400

33. *a.* 252 *b.* 1 *c.* 1 *d.* 10 *e.* 5

34. *a.* 35 *b.* 1 *c.* 5 *d.* 28 *e.* 84

35. 2,118,760 **36.** 30,240

37. 1024; 252 **38.** 1120

39. 1800 **40.** 1820; 496

41. 6400 **42.** 166,320

43. 495; 210; 420 **44.** 10,080

45. 475 **46.** 194,040

47. 106 **48.** 53,130

49. $_7C_2$ is 21 combinations + 7 double tiles = 28

50. 191,100 **51.** 27,720

52. 1287 **53.** 9000

54. 24,310 **55.** 125,970

56. 120 **57.** 126

58. 3080 **59.** 136

60. 6 **61.** 165

62. 300 **63.** 200

64. 126 **65.** 210

66. 11,880; 576 **67.** 15

68. 2; 6; $(n-1)!$

69. *a.* 48 *b.* 60 *c.* 72

70. *a.* 4 *b.* 36 *c.* 624 *d.* 3744

71. $(x+2)(x+1)/2$ **72.** 78

Exercises 4–5

1. $\frac{11}{221}$ **2.** 0.0000005

3. *a.* $\frac{1}{42}$ *b.* $\frac{10}{21}$ *c.* $\frac{1}{42}$ *d.* $\frac{5}{21}$

4. *a.* $\frac{1}{252}$ *b.* $\frac{5}{21}$

5. *a.* 0.192 *b.* 0.269 *c.* 0.538 *d.* 0.013

6. *a.* $\frac{14}{55}$ *b.* $\frac{28}{55}$ *c.* $\frac{1}{55}$

7. $\frac{1}{15}$ **8.** $\frac{18}{12,495} = \frac{6}{4165}$

9. *a.* $\frac{1}{21}$ *b.* $\frac{1}{14}$ *c.* $\frac{37}{42}$ *d.* $\frac{10}{84}$

10. *a.* 0.002 *b.* 0.246 *c.* 0.751 *d.* 0.249

11. *a.* 0.322 *b.* 0.164 *c.* 0.515

d. It probably got lost in the wash!

12. $\frac{882}{2431}$ **13.** $\frac{1}{72}$

14. *a.* 0.0003 *b.* 0.089 *c.* 0.053 *d.* 0.496

15. $\frac{1}{60}$

16. *a.* $\frac{4}{2,598,960}$ *b.* $\frac{36}{2,598,960}$ not including a Royal Flush

c. $\frac{624}{2,598,960}$ **17.** 0.727

Review Exercises

1. *a.* 0.125   *b.* 0.375   *c.* 0.50
2. *a.* $\frac{1}{4}$ *b.* $\frac{11}{26}$ *c.* $\frac{1}{52}$ *d.* $\frac{1}{13}$ *e.* $\frac{1}{2}$
3. *a.* 0.7   *b.* 0.5
4. *a.* 0.178   *b.* 0.311   *c.* 0.348   **5.** 0.33
6. *a.* $\frac{1}{4}$ *c.* $\frac{1}{4}$ *e.* 0
    b. $\frac{1}{6}$ *d.* $\frac{1}{4}$ *f.* 1
7. 0.2   **8.** $\frac{13}{60}$
9. 0.9   **10.** 0.176
11. *a.* 0.0001   *b.* 0.402   *c.* 0.598
12. *a.* $\frac{9}{35}$ *b.* $\frac{23}{35}$ *c.* $\frac{19}{35}$ *d.* $\frac{19}{35}$
13. *a.* $\frac{2}{17}$ *b.* $\frac{11}{850}$ *c.* $\frac{1}{5525}$
14. *a.* $\frac{1}{26}$ *b.* $\frac{1}{4}$ *c.* $\frac{1}{8}$
15. *a.* 0.603   *b.* 0.340   *c.* 0.324   *d.* 0.379
16. *a.* $\frac{57}{104}$ *b.* $\frac{10}{13}$ *c.* $\frac{3}{4}$
17. 0.4   **18.** 0.556
19. 0.507   **20.** 0.042; impossible; 0.25; 0.625
21. 57.3%   **22.** 0.058
23. *a.* $\frac{19}{44}$ *b.* $\frac{1}{4}$ **24.** 0.659; 0.341
25. 0.99999984   **26.** 55.6%
27. 676,000; 468,000; 650,000
28. 220   **29.** 350
30. 84   **31.** 252
32. 800
33. 100! (Answers may vary regarding calculator.)
34. 30   **35.** 495
36. 286   **37.** 60
38. Probability—4,989,600 more permutations
39. 8008   **40.** 60
41. 676,000; 0.2
42. 156,000,000; 0.022   **43.** 0.097
44. 0.0008; 0.0000006
45.

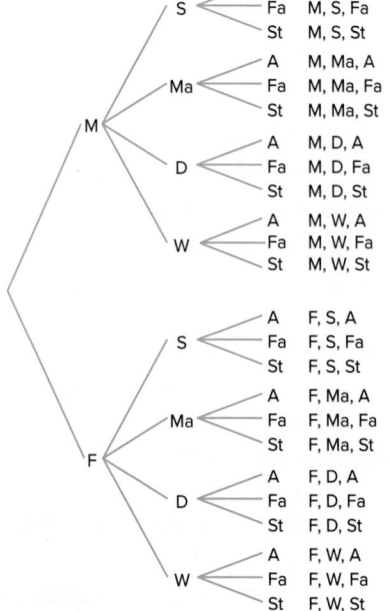

Chapter Quiz

1. False. Subjective probability is used in many real-life situations.
2. False. Empirical probability uses frequency distributions to compute probabilities.
3. True
4. False. When two events are mutually exclusive. $P(A \text{ or } B) = P(A) + P(B)$.
5. False. If two events are dependent, the occurrence of the first event affects the probability of the occurrence of the second event.
6. False. An event and its complement cannot occur at the same time.
7. True
8. False. When objects are arranged in a specific order, the arrangement is called a permutation of the objects.
9. *b*   **10.** *d*   **11.** *d*
12. *b*   **13.** *c*   **14.** *b*
15. *d*   **16.** *b*   **17.** *b*
18. Sample space   **19.** 0, 1   **20.** 0
21. 1   **22.** Mutually exclusive
23. *a.* $\frac{1}{13}$ *b.* $\frac{1}{13}$ *c.* $\frac{4}{13}$
24. *a.* $\frac{1}{4}$ *b.* $\frac{4}{13}$ *c.* $\frac{1}{52}$ *d.* $\frac{1}{13}$ *e.* $\frac{1}{2}$
25. *a.* $\frac{12}{31}$ *b.* $\frac{12}{31}$ *c.* $\frac{27}{31}$ *d.* $\frac{24}{31}$
26. *a.* $\frac{11}{36}$ *b.* $\frac{5}{18}$ *c.* $\frac{11}{36}$ *d.* $\frac{1}{3}$ *e.* 0   *f.* $\frac{11}{12}$
27. 0.68   **28.** 0.002
29. *a.* $\frac{253}{9996}$ *b.* $\frac{33}{66,640}$ *c.* 0
30. 0.538   **31.** 0.533
32. 0.814   **33.** 0.056
34. *a.* $\frac{1}{2}$ *b.* $\frac{3}{7}$ **35.** 0.992
36. 0.518   **37.** 0.9999886
38. 2646   **39.** 40,320
40. 1365   **41.** 1,188,137,600; 710,424,000
42. 720   **43.** 33,554,432
44. 56   **45.** $\frac{1}{4}$
46. $\frac{3}{14}$ **47.** $\frac{12}{55}$
48.

49. 120,120   **50.** 210

Chapter 5

Exercises 5–1

1. A random variable is a variable whose values are determined by chance. Examples will vary.

2. If the values that a random variable can assume are countable, then the variable is called discrete; otherwise, it is called a continuous random variable.

3. The number of commercials a radio station plays during each hour. The number of times a student uses a calculator during a mathematics exam. The number of leaves on a specific type of tree. (Answers will vary.)

4. The weights of strawberries grown in a specific plot; the heights of all seniors at a specific college; the times it takes students to complete a mathematics exam. (Answers will vary.)

5. Examples: Continuous variables: length of home run, length of game, temperature at game time, pitcher's ERA, batting average

   Discrete variables: number of hits, number of pitches, number of seats in each row, etc.

6. A probability distribution is a distribution that consists of the values a random variable can assume along with the corresponding probabilities of these values. Examples will vary.

7. No. Probabilities cannot be negative.

8. No. Probabilities cannot be negative.

9. Yes   10. Yes

11. No. The sum of the probabilities is greater than one.

12. Yes

13. Discrete   14. Discrete

15. Continuous   16. Continuous

17. Discrete   18. Continuous

19.

X	0	1	2	3
P(X)	$\frac{1}{8}$	$\frac{1}{2}$	$\frac{1}{4}$	$\frac{1}{8}$

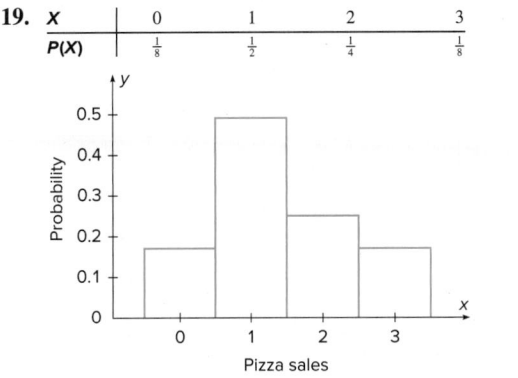

20.

X	0	1	2	3	4	5
P(X)	0.3	0.2	0.1	0.2	0.1	0.1

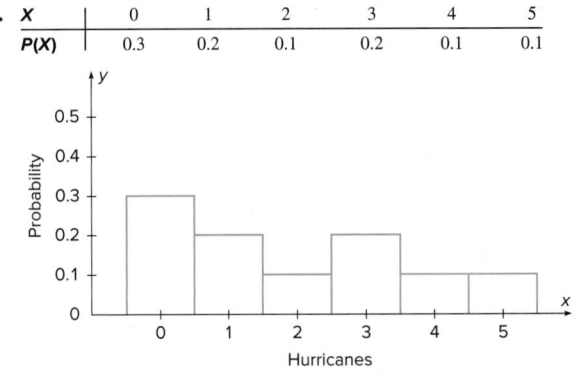

21.

X	1	2	3	4
P(X)	0.45	0.27	0.18	0.10

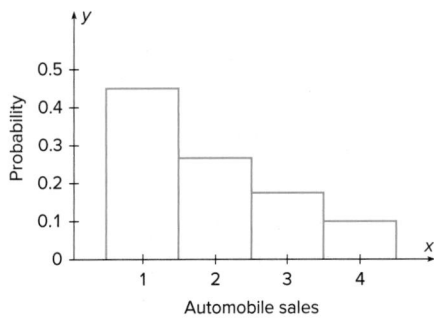

22.

X	0	1	2	3	4
P(X)	0.15	0.25	0.3	0.25	0.05

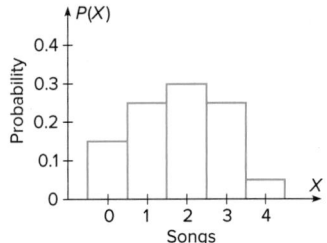

23.

X	1	2	3	4	5	6
P(X)	$\frac{1}{2}$	$\frac{1}{6}$	$\frac{1}{12}$	$\frac{1}{12}$	$\frac{1}{12}$	$\frac{1}{12}$

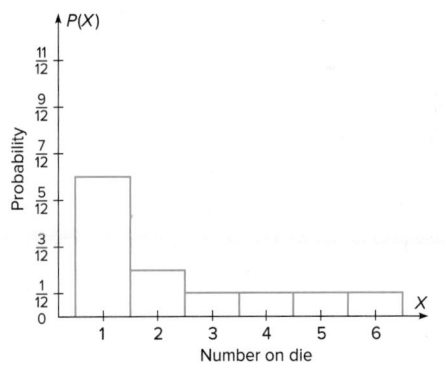

24.

X	1	2	3	4	5
P(X)	0.32	0.12	0.23	0.18	0.15

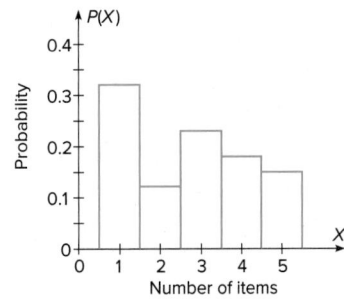

25.

X	2	3	4	5
P(X)	0.01	0.34	0.62	0.03

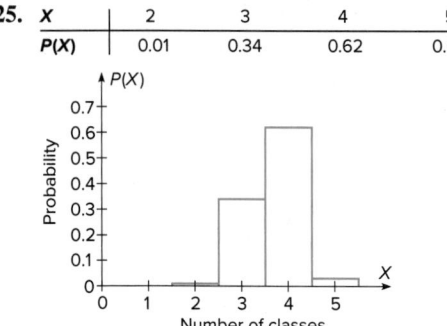

26.

X	0	1	2	3
P(X)	0.22	0.33	0.37	0.08

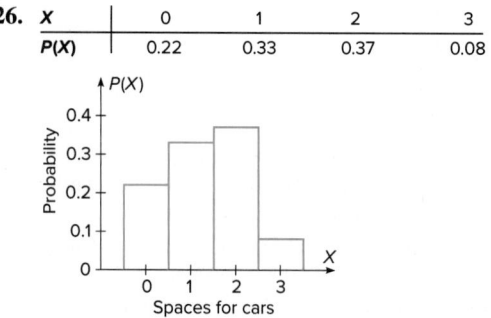

27.

X	4	7	9	11	13	16	18	21	22	24	25	27	31	36
P(X)	$\frac{1}{15}$	$\frac{1}{15}$	$\frac{1}{15}$	$\frac{1}{15}$	$\frac{1}{15}$	$\frac{2}{15}$	$\frac{1}{15}$	$\frac{1}{15}$	$\frac{1}{15}$	$\frac{1}{15}$	$\frac{1}{15}$	$\frac{1}{15}$	$\frac{1}{15}$	$\frac{1}{15}$

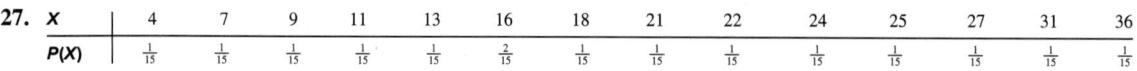

28.

X	Computer	Dress-up	Blocks	Paint
P(X)	0.45	0.27	0.18	0.1

29.

X	1	2	3	4	5
P(X)	0.124	0.297	0.402	0.094	0.083

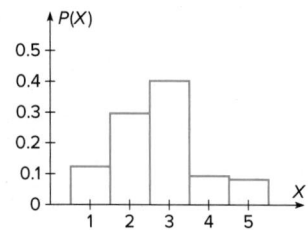

30. $P(8) = 0.137$

X	4	5	6	7	8
P(X)	0.117	0.123	0.295	0.328	0.137

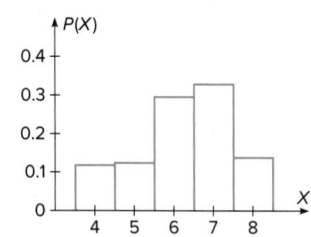

31.

X	1	2	3
P(X)	$\frac{1}{6}$	$\frac{1}{3}$	$\frac{1}{2}$

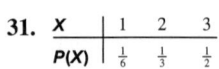

Yes

32.

X	6	4	2
P(X)	3	2	1

No. The sum of the probabilities is greater than 1.

33.

X	0.05	0.10	0.25
P(X)	0.25	0.30	0.45

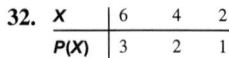

Yes

34.

X	0.1	0.02	0.04
P(X)	0.2	0.12	0.14

No, the sum of the probabilities is less than 1.

35.

X	1	2	4
P(X)	$\frac{1}{7}$	$\frac{2}{7}$	$\frac{4}{7}$

Yes

36.

X	0	1	2
P(X)	0	$\frac{1}{3}$	$\frac{1}{2}$

No, the sum of the probabilities is less than 1.

37.

X	1	2	3	4
P(X)	$\frac{3}{28}$	$\frac{6}{28}$	$\frac{12}{28}$	$\frac{7}{28}$

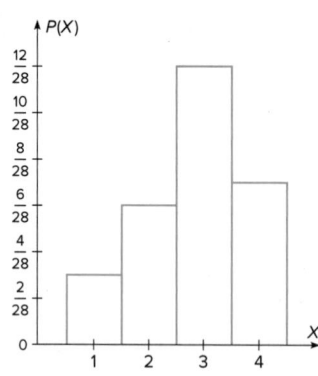

Exercises 5–2

1. 1.04, 0.858, 0.926
2. 1.36; 1.29; 1.14
3. 1.222; 0.8395; 0.916
4. 1.88; 0.986; 0.993
5. 2.1; 1.69; 1.3
6. 1.3; 1.8; 1.3
7. 1.175; 1.294; 1.138

8. $\mu = 3.441$

9. 1.125; 1.109; 1.053

10. 1.95; 3.25; 1.80

11. $5.00   **12.** 6.21

13. $0.83   **14.** −33.3 cents; no

15. −$1.00   **16.** −$2.00

17. −$0.50; −$0.52   **18.** $265.36

19. *a.* −5.26 cents   *c.* −5.26 cents   *e.* −5.26 cents
    b. −5.26 cents   *d.* −5.26 cents

20. 7; 5.8; 2.4

X	2	3	4	5	6	7	8	9	10	11	12
P(X)	$\frac{1}{36}$	$\frac{2}{36}$	$\frac{3}{36}$	$\frac{4}{36}$	$\frac{5}{36}$	$\frac{6}{36}$	$\frac{5}{36}$	$\frac{4}{36}$	$\frac{3}{36}$	$\frac{2}{36}$	$\frac{1}{36}$

21. 10.5

22. $\sigma^2 = \Sigma(X - \mu)^2 \times P(X)$
$\sigma^2 = \Sigma(X^2 - 2\mu X + \mu^2)P(X)$
$\sigma^2 = \Sigma X^2 \times P(X) - 2\mu\Sigma XP(X) + \mu^2\Sigma P(X)$
$\sigma^2 = \Sigma X^2 \times P(X) - 2\mu \times \mu + \mu^2(1)$
$\sigma^2 = \Sigma X^2 \times P(X) - 2\mu^2 + \mu^2$
$\sigma^2 = \Sigma X^2 \times P(X) - \mu^2$

23. $P(4) = 0.345$; $P(6) = 0.23$
$\overline{X} = 3.485$; $\sigma^2 = 3.820$; $\sigma = 1.954$

24. Answers will vary.

25. Answers will vary.

26. $2.00; $1.42 with a stamp price of $0.58.

27.

X	2	3	4	5	6	8	9	11	14
P(X)	0.1	0.1	0.1	0.1	0.1	0.2	0.1	0.1	0.1

$\mu = 7$; $\sigma^2 = 12.6$; $\sigma = 3.55$

Exercises 5–3

1. *a.* Yes   *b.* Yes   *c.* Yes   *d.* No   *e.* No

2. *a.* Yes   *b.* Yes   *c.* Yes   *d.* No   *e.* Yes

3. *a.* 0.064   *b.* 0.328   *c.* 0.138   *d.* 0.205   *e.* 0.071

4. *a.* 0.250   *b.* 0.418   *c.* 0.176   *d.* 0.246

5. *a.* 0.0768   *b.* 0.422   *c.* 0.0535

6. *a.* 0.007   *b.* 0.173

7. *a.* 0.93   *b.* 0.195   *c.* 0.205

8. 0.000; the probability is extremely small; this event is unlikely to occur.

9. *a.* 0.028   *b.* 0.006   *c.* 0.200

10. *a.* 0.526   *b.* 0.474   *c.* 0.188

11. 0.117

12. *a.* 0.000   *b.* 1.000   *c.* 0.002

13. *a.* 0.230   *c.* 0.317
    b. 0.990   *d.* 0.337

14. *a.* 0.198   *b.* 0.285   *c.* 0.065

15. *a.* 0.242   *b.* 0.547   *c.* 0.306

16. *a.* 0.001   *b.* 0.053   *c.* 0.225

17. *a.* 120; 48; 6.928   *c.* 9.6; 5.76; 2.4
    b. 8; 6.4; 2.53   *d.* 25; 12.5; 3.54

18. *a.* 18; 9; 3   *c.* 18; 12.6; 3.55
    b. 350; 105; 10.247   *d.* 8; 1.6; 1.265

19. 120; 91.2; 9.55   **20.** 10; 5; 2.236

21. 51.9; 8.1; 7.0; 2.6   **22.** 66.67; 44.444; 6.667

23. 210; 165.9; 12.9   **24.** 102; 15.3; 3.9

25. 0.199   **26.** 0.077

27. 0.559   **28.** 64; 43.5; 6.6

29. 0.104   **30.** 0.018

31. 0.42

32. Yes. $P(3) = 0.216$. This implies that $p = 0.6$ and then $q = 0.4$. $P(0)$, $P(1)$, and $P(2)$ all check out.

33.

X	0	1	2	3
P(X)	0.125	0.375	0.375	0.125

34.

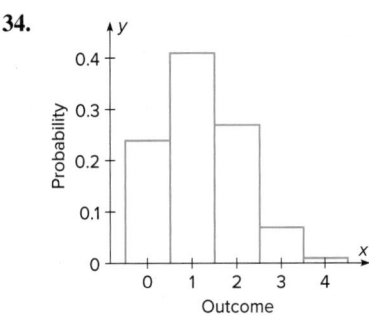

35. $\mu = 0q^3 + 3pq^2 + 6p^2q + 3p^3 = 3p(q^2 + 2pq + p^2)$
$= 3p(1) = 3p$

Exercises 5–4

1. *a.* 0.0896   *b.* 0.0348   *c.* 0.0788

2. *a.* 0.0523   *b.* 0.09216   *c.* 0.054

3. 0.0025   **4.** 0.0187

5. 0.0048   **6.** 0.002

7. *a.* 0.1042   *b.* 0.1404   *c.* 0.0902

8. *a.* 0.1014   *b.* 0.0413   *c.* 0.0842

9. *a.* 0.0183   *b.* 0.0733   *c.* 0.1465   *d.* 0.7619

10. 0.0888   **11.** 0.0178

12. 0.2642   **13.** 0.0498

14. 0.2205   **15.** 0.1563

16. 0.0004   **17.** 0.556

18. 0.252   **19.** 0.0909

20. 0.712   **21.** 0.597

22. $\frac{1}{12} \approx 0.083$ **23.** 0.099

24. $\frac{1}{6}$; $\frac{25}{216}$; $\left(\frac{5}{6}\right)^5 \approx 0.402$ **25.** 0.21

26. 0.032   **27.** 12

28. 16   **29.** 17.33 or 18

30. 25   **31.** 1.25; 0.559

32. 1.5; 0.866   **33.** 5; 4.472

34. 4; 3.464

Review Exercises

1. Yes
2. No. The sum of the probabilities does not equal 1.
3. No. The sum of the probabilities is greater than 1.
4.

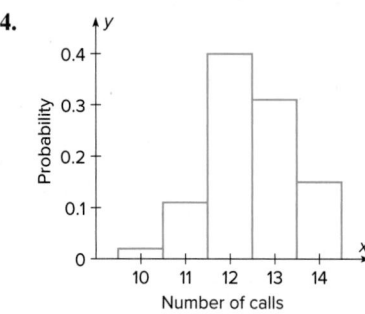

5. *a.* 0.35   *b.* 1.55; 1.808; 1.344

6.

X	$0.01	$0.10	$0.25	$0.50
P(X)	$\frac{1}{2}$	$\frac{3}{10}$	$\frac{1}{10}$	$\frac{1}{10}$

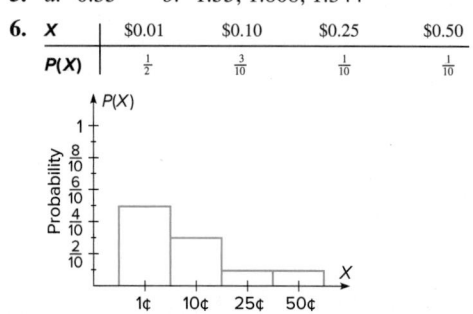

7.

Shoe Purchases

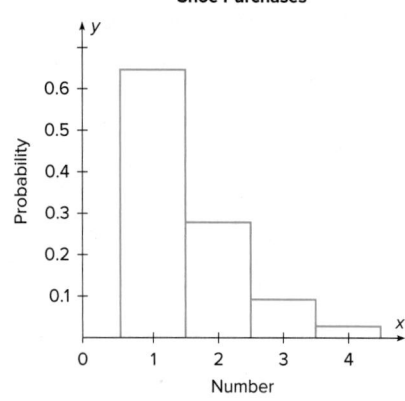

8. 2.1; 1.4; 1.2   9.   7.2; 2.2; 1.5
10. 2.1; 1.5; 1.2
11. 1.4; 0.9; 0.95. Two people at most should be employed.
12. $8100   13. $2.15   14. $4.92
15. *a.* 0.008   *b.* 0.724   *c.* 0.0002   *d.* 0.276
16. 0.264; 0.155   17.   145; 60.9; 7.8
18. 189; 69.9; 8.4   19.   0.886
20. 135; 98.6; 9.9   21.   0.190
22. 61.5; 46.4; 6.8   23.   0.026
24. 0.007   25.   0.012   26. 0.120
27. *a.* 0.5543   *b.* 0.8488   *c.* 0.4457
28. 0.0504   29.   0.274
30. 0.21   31.   0.4
32. $\frac{125}{1296}$ 33.   0.105

Chapter Quiz

1. True
2. False. The number of courses a student is taking this semester is an example of a discrete random variable.
3. False. When the binomial distribution is used, the outcomes must be independent.
4. True
5. Chance   6. $n \cdot p$
7. 1   8. *c*
9. *c*   10. *d*
11. No, since $\Sigma P(X) > 1$ 12. Yes
13. Yes   14. Yes

15.

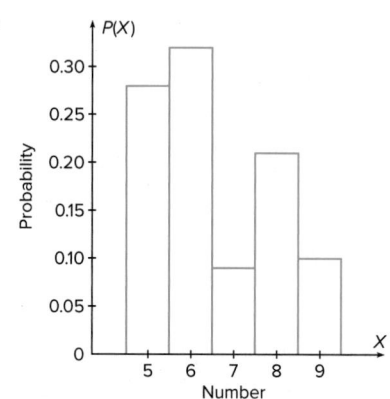

16.

X	0	1	2	3	4
P(X)	0.02	0.3	0.48	0.13	0.07

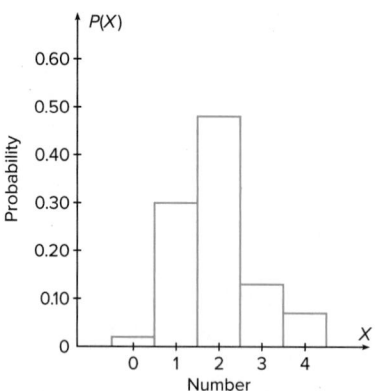

17. 2.0; 1.3; 1.1   18.   32.2; 1.1; 1.0
19. 5.2   20. $9.65
21. 0.124
22. *a.* 0.075   *b.* 0.872   *c.* 0.126
23. 240; 48; 6.9   24.   9; 7.9; 2.8
25. 0.008   26.   0.0003
27. 0.061   28.   0.122
29. *a.* 0.5470   *b.* 0.9862   *c.* 0.453
30. 0.128
31. *a.* 0.160   *b.* 0.42   *c.* 0.07
32. 0.033   33.   0.007

Chapter 6

Exercises 6–1

1. The characteristics of the normal distribution are as follows:
   a. It is bell-shaped.
   b. It is symmetric about the mean.
   c. Its mean, median, and mode are equal.
   d. It is continuous.
   e. It never touches the x axis.
   f. The area under the curve is equal to 1.
   g. It is unimodal.
   h. About 68% of the area lies within 1 standard deviation of the mean, about 95% within 2 standard deviations, and about 99.7% within 3 standard deviations of the mean.

2. Many variables are normally distributed, and the distribution can be used to describe these variables.

3. 1 or 100%

4. 50% of the area lies below the mean, and 50% of the area lies above the mean.

5. 68%; 95%; 99.7%

6. Gaussian distribution and bell curve

7. 0.0384

8. 0.2266

9. 0.4052

10. 0.0183

11. 0.3461

12. 0.3078

13. 0.4857

14. 0.1736

15. 0.8118

16. 0.0806

17. 0.0242

18. 0.1909

19. 0.0652

20. 0.4634

21. 0.9826

22. 0.9049

23. 0.5636

24. 0.9726

25. 0.3574

26. 0.0684

27. 0.2673

28. 0.4750

29. 0.4162

30. 0.3907

31. 0.0116

32. 0.2061

33. 0.0559

34. 0.0384

35. 0.9507

36. 0.5199

37. 0.0586

38. 0.0550

39. 0.9082

40. 0.9236

41. -1.39 (TI: -1.3885)

42. 1.32 (TI: 1.3201)

43. -2.08 (TI: -2.0792)

44. 1.98 (TI: 1.9791)

45. -1.26 (TI: -1.2602)

46. 1.84 (TI: 1.8398)

47. a. -2.28 (TI: -2.2801)
    b. -0.92 (TI: -0.91995)
    c. -0.27 (TI: -0.26995)

48. a. 0.12 (TI: 0.1201)   b. 0.52 (TI: 0.5201)   c. 1.18

49. a. $z = +1.96$ and $z = -1.96$ (TI: ± 1.95996)
    b. $z = +1.65$ and $z = -1.65$, approximately (TI: ± 1.64485)
    c. $z = +2.58$ and $z = -2.58$, approximately (TI: ± 2.57583)

50. $z = \pm 0.64$ (TI: ± 0.64335)

51. 0.6827; 0.9545; 0.9973; they are very close.

52. 0.6745; 0.8416; 1.41   53. 2.10

54. -0.75

55. -1.45 and 0.11

56. 1.175

57. $y = \dfrac{e^{-x^2/2}}{\sqrt{2\pi}}$

58.

x	−2	−1.5	−1	−0.5	0	0.5	1	1.5	2
y	0.05	0.13	0.24	0.35	0.4	0.35	0.24	0.13	0.05

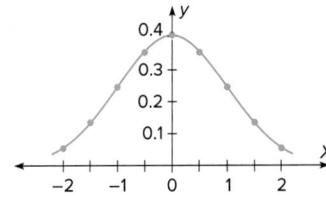

59. 1.00

60. 0

Exercises 6–2

1. 0.1014

2. a. 0.8490   b. 0.2119   c. 0.9772

3. a. 0.2005 (TI: 0.2007)   b. 0.4315 (TI: 0.4316)

4. 1146; 0.0307 (TI: 1146; 0.0308)

5. a. 0.3023   b. 0.0062

6. a. 0.4602   b. 0.0031
   c. 0.6676 (TI: 0.6687)

7. a. 0.0401   b. 0.1056

8. a. 0.1230 (TI: 0.1234)   b. 0.0549 (TI: 0.5042)
   c. 0.0418 (TI: 0.0419)

9. 0.0262; 0.0003; would want to know why it had only been driven less than 6000 miles (TI: 0.0260; 0.0002)

10. 0.2061; 0.1251 (TI: 0.1256)

11. a. 0.9803 (TI: 0.9801)
    b. 0.2514 (TI: 0.2511)
    c. 0.3434 (TI: 0.3430)

12. a. 0.9995   b. 0.3365 (TI: 0.3372)
    c. 0.9545 (TI: 0.9547)

13. a. 0.0082   b. 0.1587
    c. 0.5403 (TI: 0.5404)

14. Less than 0.0002

15. a. 0.6568 (TI: 0.6563)   b. 0.7475 (TI: 0.7486)
    c. 0.8413

16. Men: $104,053 (TI: men: $104,241)
    Women: $94,698 (TI: women: $94,706)

17. 0.4435   18. 6.129 and 7.871

19. a. 0.54   b. 22 people

20. 16 manatees

21. The maximum size is 1927.76 square feet; the minimum size is 1692.24 square feet.
    (TI: 1927.90 maximum, 1692.10 minimum)

22. $227,100 to $265,500 (TI: $227,077 to $265,523)

23. 0.006; $821   24. 92.99 or 93

25. 117.3–122.7

26. 4.05

27. 6.7; 4.05 (TI: for 10%, 6.657; for 30%, 4.040)

28. *a.* 588

  b. You would need a score of 184 to stay out of the group since a score of 183 is exactly 1.5%, and you would be included in the group with that score.

29. 118.22 **30.** 0.9996; 0.0562

31. 18.6 months **32.** 0.293

33. *a.* $\mu = 120, \sigma = 20$ *c.* $\mu = 30, \sigma = 5$

  b. $\mu = 15, \sigma = 2.5$

34. No. Any subgroup would not be a perfect representation of the seniors; therefore, the mean and standard deviation would be different.

35. 3.59

36. No. The shape of the distribution would be the same.

37. $1175.54 **38.** 95.68

39. 0.1075

40. 77 and up A

  69–76 B

  52–68 C

  44–51 D

  0–43 F

41. Somewhat positively skewed

42. Not significantly skewed

43. Not normal

44. Somewhat negatively skewed

45. Answers will vary.

Exercises 6–3

1. The distribution is called the sampling distribution of sample means.

2. A sample is not a perfect representation of the population. The difference is due to what is called sampling error.

3. The mean of the sample means is equal to the population mean.

4. The standard error of the mean: $\sigma_{\bar{x}} = \sigma / \sqrt{n}$.

5. The distribution will be approximately normal when the sample size is large.

6. $z = \dfrac{X - \mu}{\sigma}$ **7.** 0.8945 (TI: 0.8946)

8. 0.2047 (TI: 0.2038)

9. *a.* 0.9699 (TI: 0.9696) *b.* 0.0301 (TI: 0.0304)

  c. 0.4699 (TI: 0.4696)

10. 0.695 (TI: 0.6964) **11.** 0.092 (TI: 0.0926)

12. *a.* 0.0778 (TI: 0.0780) *b.* 0.3446 (TI: 0.3443)

13. 0.9990

14. Yes—the probability of such is less than 0.001.

15. 0.0301 (TI: 0.0304)

16. 0.9993 **17.** 0.4177 (TI: 0.4199)

18. *a.* 0.0051 *b.* 0.3632

19. 0.9037 (TI: 0.9044)

20. 0.9826 (TI: 0.9825); 0.0174

21. *a.* 0.3300 (TI: 0.3309) *b.* 0.0838 (TI: 0.0833)

  c. yes *d.* yes, but not as likely.

22. *a.* 0.5818 *b.* 0.785

  c. The answer to part *a* uses individual data, whereas the answer to part *b* uses a mean of sample size 30.

23. *a.* 0.3707 (TI: 0.3694) *b.* 0.0475 (TI: 0.04779)

24. *a.* 0.1567 (TI: 0.1589) *b.* 0.4963 (TI: 0.4961)

25. Approximately 60 **26.** 0.0025

27. 0.7454 (TI: 0.7462) **28.** 1963.10 pounds (TI: 1963.33)

29. $\sigma_{\bar{x}} = 1.5, n = 25$ **30.** 400

Exercises 6–4

1. When p is approximately 0.5, as n increases, the shape of the binomial distribution becomes similar to that of the normal distribution.

2. The conditions are that $n \cdot p$ and $n \cdot q$ are both ≥ 5.

3. The correction is necessary because the normal distribution is continuous and the binomial distribution is discrete.

4. When p is close to 0 or 1 and n is small, the normal distribution should not be used as an approximation to the binomial distribution. That is, when $np < 5$ and $nq < 5$, the normal distribution should not be used to approximate the binomial distribution.

5. *a.* 0.1156 *b.* 0.1176 *c.* 0.0332

6. *a.* 0.7517 *b.* 0.8289 *c.* 0.7910

7. *a.* Yes *b.* No *c.* No

8. *a.* Yes *b.* Yes *c.* No

9. 0.0166 **10.** 0.9965 (TI: 0.9970)

11. 0.9099 **12.** 0.1003

13. 0.4443 (TI: 0.4435) **14.** 0.1880 (TI: 0.1889)

15. 0.7054 (TI: 0.7066) **16.** 0.0985 (TI: 0.0988)

17. 0.7734 (TI: 0.7727); likely

18. 0.0793 (TI: 0.0791)

19. 0.0073 (TI: 0.0074) **20.** 0.0559 (TI: 0.0564)

21. 0.0118 (TI: 0.0114) **22.** 0.9951; yes (TI: 0.9950)

23. *a.* $n \geq 50$ *c.* $n \geq 10$ *e.* $n \geq 50$

  b. $n \geq 17$ *d.* $n \geq 25$

Review Exercises

1. *a.* 0.4803 *c.* 0.0629 *e.* 0.2158

  b. 0.2019 *d.* 0.7945

2. *a.* 0.8284 *c.* 0.9131 *e.* 0.9535

  b. 0.0233 *d.* 0.0183

3. *a.* 0.4871 *c.* 0.8841 *e.* 0.6151

  b. 0.4599 *d.* 0.0728

4. *a.* 0.0485 *c.* 0.8830 *e.* 0.9616

  b. 0.0212 *d.* 0.9732

5. 0.1131; $4872 and $5676

  (TI: $4869.31 minimum, $5678.69 maximum)

6. *a.* 0.1587 *b.* 0.0013

7. *a.* 0.3621 or 36.21% (TI: 0.3623 or 36.23%)

  b. 0.1190 or 11.9% (TI: 0.1186 or 11.86%)

  c. 0.0606 or 6.06% (TI: 0.0611 or 6.11%)

8. 0.0239; 0.1654 (TI: 0.1671) **9.** $130.92 (TI: 130.88)

10. $7220 (TI: 7222.67) **11.** Not normal

12. Not normal

13. *a.* 0.0143 (TI: 0.0142)   *b.* 0.9641

14. *a.* 0.7054 (TI: 0.7057)   *b.* 0.8869 (TI: 0.8868)

15. *a.* 0.3859 (TI: 0.3875)   *b.* 0.1841 (TI: 0.1831)

   c. Individual values are more variable than means.

16. 0.0023; yes, since the probability is less than 1%.

17. 0.5234 (TI: 0.5246)   18. 0.0496 (TI: 0.0484)

19. 0.7157; 0.9999 (TI: 0.7142)

20. 0.0668 (TI: 0.0662)   21. 0.2090 (TI: 0.2103)

22. 0.1251 (TI: 0.1257)

Chapter Quiz

1. False. The total area under a normal distribution is one.

2. True

3. True   4. True

5. False. All areas under a normal distributions curve are either zero or positive values.

6. False. The central limit theorem applies to the means of samples taken from the same population.

7. *a*   8. *a*

9. *b*   10. *b*

11. *c*   12. 0.5

13. sampling error

14. the population mean

15. standard error of the mean

16. 5   17. 5%

18. *a.* 0.4332   *d.* 0.1029   *g.* 0.0401   *j.* 0.9131
    b. 0.3944   *e.* 0.2912   *h.* 0.8997
    c. 0.0344   *f.* 0.8284   *i.* 0.017

19. *a.* 0.4846   *d.* 0.0188   *g.* 0.0089   *j.* 0.8461
    b. 0.4693   *e.* 0.7461   *h.* 0.9582
    c. 0.9334   *f.* 0.0384   *i.* 0.9788

20. *a.* 0.7734   *b.* 0.0516 (TI: 0.0521)
    c. 0.3837 (TI: 0.3802)
    d. Any rainfall above 65 inches could be considered an extremely wet year since this value is 2 standard deviations above the mean.

21. *a.* 0.0668   *b.* 0.0228   *c.* 0.4649   *d.* 0.0934

22. *a.* 0.4525 (TI: 0.4522)   *b.* 0.3707 (TI: 0.3694)
    c. 0.3707 (TI: 0.3694)   *d.* 0.019 (TI: 0.0189)

23. *a.* 0.0013   *b.* 0.5   *c.* 0.0082   *d.* 0.5511

24. *a.* 0.0038   *b.* 0.0228   *c.* 0.5
    d. 0.3232 (TI: 0.3217)

25. 8.804 centimeters (TI: 8.805)

26. 121.24 is the lowest acceptable score. (TI: 121.29)

27. 0.015 (TI: 0.0152)   28. 0.9738 (TI: 0.9736)

29. 0.0495 (TI: 0.0499); no

30. 0.0455 or 4.55% (TI: 0.0453 or 4.53%)

31. 0.618 (TI: 0.0614)   32. 0.0526 (TI: 0.530)

33. Approximately normal

34. Approximately normal

Chapter 7
Exercises 7–1

1. A point estimate of a parameter specifies a particular value, such as $\mu = 87$; an interval estimate specifies a range of values for the parameter, such as $84 < \mu < 90$. The advantage of an interval estimate is that a specific confidence level (say 95%) can be selected, and one can be 95% confident that the interval contains the parameter that is being estimated.

2. The standard deviation of the population must be known, or it must be estimated or specified in terms of E. Sample size must be specified, and the degree of confidence must be selected.

3. The margin of error is the likely range of values to the right or left of the statistic that may contain the parameter.

4. A 95% confidence interval means one can be 95% confident that the confidence interval will contain the parameter being estimated.

5. A good estimator should be unbiased, consistent, and relatively efficient.

6. A 99% confidence interval of a proportion means that you can be 99% confident that the interval will contain the population proportion.

7. 3.5   8. 0.026

9. 0.5   10. 0.004

11. 0.003   12. 5

13. No. It can only be concluded that there is a 95% probability that the population mean is between 13% and 17%.

14. No. In this case, you are saying that the probability is based on the population percentage rather than on the interval. The population percentage does not vary.

15. A narrow confidence interval with a high confidence level is the best choice.

Exercises 7–2

1. $\bar{X}$

2. The sample must be random and either $n \geq 30$ or the population is normally distributed if $n < 30$.

3. 2.58   4. 2.33

5. 1.96   6. 1.65

7. 1.88

8. For one to be able to determine sample size, the margin of error and the level of confidence must be specified and the population standard deviation must be known.

9. $53 < \mu < 55$ 10. $89 < \mu < 91$

11. *a.* 30 pounds
    b. $28.9 < \mu < 31.1$
    c. $28.6 < \mu < 31.4$
    d. The 99% confidence interval is larger because you can be more confident that it contains the mean.

12. *a.* 12.5 jobs
    b. $11.9 < \mu < 13.1$
    c. $11.7 < \mu < 13.3$
    d. The 95% confidence is smaller since there is less of a chance that the mean is contained in the interval as opposed to the 99% confidence interval.

13. $5.0 < \mu < 7.0$

14. $2.55 < \mu < 3.09$

15. $18.7 < \mu < 21.2$

16. $34.3 < \mu < 52.6$

17. $20.3 < \mu < 23.7$

$20.6 < \mu < 23.4$

Both confidence intervals are close in value.

18. $\$10,011 < \mu < \$10,305$; $\$10,011$

19. $59.5 < \mu < 62.9$ **20.** $172.7 < \mu < 208.7$

21. 55 people   **22.** $57.4 < \mu < 58.6$

23. 49 minutes   **24.** 12

25. 21 days   **26.** 154

27. It decreases.   **28.** It increases.

29. Increase the sample size, if possible.

30. No. You can only expect the interval to contain the population mean with the value of the confidence level.

31. No. It only involves errors due to the sampling process.

32. As you increase the sample size, the width of the interval gets smaller.

33. When you use the margin of error and compute the confidence intervals for both results, they overlap. Thus, you cannot say one candidate will win over the other candidate.

Exercises 7–3

1. The characteristics of the t distribution are as follows: It is bell-shaped, it is symmetric about the mean, and it approaches, but never touches the x axis. The mean, median, and mode are equal to 0 and are located at the center of the distribution. The variance is greater than 1. The t distribution is a family of curves based on degrees of freedom. As a sample size increases, the t distribution approaches the standard normal distribution.

2. The degrees of freedom are the number of values free to vary after a sample statistic has been computed.

3. *a.* 2.898   *c.* 2.624   *e.* 2.093

   b. 2.074   *d.* 1.833

4. The t distribution should be used when σ is unknown.

5. $96 < \mu < 101$

6. $4402 < \mu < 5698$

7. $\bar{X} = 184.4$; $s = 73.40$; $153.3 < \mu < 215.5$; the point estimate is 184.4. Also, the interval does indeed contain $\mu = 148$. The data value 424 is unusually large (an outlier). The mean may not be the best point estimate in this case since it is not in the interval.

8. $38.70 < \mu < 48.28$; yes

9. $226.3 < \mu < 260.1$

10. $25.8 < \mu < 33.9$

11. $16 < \mu < 18$

12. $13.6 < \mu < 16.4$; 16.4 miles per hour

13. $3488 < \mu < 3864$

14. 9.7 million $< \mu < 16.5$

15. $12.89 < \mu < 15.11$

16. $38.4 < \mu < 44.8$

17. $32.0 < \mu < 70.9$

18. $229.1229 < \mu < 230.9129$

19. $22.828 < \mu < 58.160$

20. $8.8 < \mu < 58.2$

21. $\bar{X} = 2.175$; $s = 0.585$; $\mu > \$1.95$ means one can be 95% confident that the mean revenue is greater than \$1.95; $\mu < \$2.40$ means one can be 95% confident that the mean revenue is less than \$2.40.

Exercises 7–4

1. *a.* 0.75, 0.25   *c.* 0.8, 0.2   *e.* 0.48, 0.52

   b. 0.92, 0.08   *d.* 0.35, 0.65

2. *a.* 0.7, 0.3   *d.* 0.28, 0.72

   b. 0.8, 0.2   *e.* 0.62, 0.38

   c. 0.58, 0.42

3. $0.302 < p < 0.578$; $0.145 < p < 0.255$

4. $0.027 < p < 0.098$

5. $0.832 < p < 0.928$

6. $0.233 < p < 0.401$ **7.** $0.324 < p < 0.576$

8. $0.400 < p < 0.462$ **9.** $0.596 < p < 0.704$

10. $0.574 < p < 0.692$ **11.** $0.151 < p < 0.249$

12. $0.128 < p < 0.272$

13. $0.812 < p < 0.908$

14. $0.831 < p < 0.913$

15. 385; 601

16. *a.* 225   *b.* 273

17. 574; 1068

18. 2124   **19.** 994

20. 1893   **21.** 95%

22. 96%

Exercises 7–5

1. Chi-square

2. The variable must be normally distributed.

3. *a.* 6.571, 23.685   *d.* 15.308, 44.461

   b. 10.283, 35.479   *e.* 4.575, 19.675

   c. 0.989, 20.278

4. $25.5 < \sigma^2 < 71.9$; $5.1 < \sigma < 8.5$

5. $56.6 < \sigma^2 < 236.3$; $7.5 < \sigma < 15.4$

6. $101.5 < \sigma^2 < 636.1$; $10.1 < \sigma < 25.2$

7. $9 < \sigma < 19$

8. $13.6 < \sigma^2 < 47.1$; $3.7 < \sigma < 6.9$

9. $46430.64 < \sigma^2 < 263446.76$; $215.48 < \sigma < 513.27$

10. $259.334 < \sigma^2 < 772.724$

$16.104 < \sigma < 27.798$

11. $4.0 < \sigma^2 < 13.5$; $2.0 < \sigma < 3.7$

12. $6.83 < \sigma^2 < 140.05$

$2.61 < \sigma < 11.83$

13. $17.3 < \sigma < 38.4$

14. $6410.7 < \sigma^2 < 65,897.9$

15. $31.5 < \sigma < 67.9$ **16.** $16.2 < \sigma < 19.8$

Review Exercises

1. $24 < \mu < 26$
2. 7.5; $7.46 < \mu < 7.54$
3. 16 female students
4. $23.45; $22.79 < \mu < $24.11
5. $76.9 < \mu < 88.3$
6. $25 < \mu < 31$
7. $0.311 < p < 0.369$
8. $0.395 < p < 0.445$ 9. $0.474 < p < 0.579$
10. $0.414 < p < 0.531$ 11. 754 (TI: 749)
12. 842 children; 1068 children
13. $0.22 < \sigma < 0.43$. Yes. It seems that there is a large standard deviation.
14. $1.5 < \sigma^2 < 5.3$ 15. $5.1 < \sigma^2 < 18.3$
16. $28.6 < \sigma^2 < 334.2$; $5.3 < \sigma < 18.3$

Chapter Quiz

1. True   2. True
3. False. An estimator is consistent if as sample size increases, the value of the estimator approaches the value of the parameter being estimated.
4. True   5. *b*
6. *a*   7. *b*
8. Unbiased, consistent, relatively efficient
9. Margin of error
10. Point   11. 90; 95; 99
12. $121.60; $119.85 < \mu < $123.35
13. $244.80; $243.15 < \mu < $246.45
14. 4150; $3954 < \mu < 4346$
15. $45.7 < \mu < 51.5$ 16. $418 < \mu < 458$
17. $26 < \mu < 36$ 18. 180
19. 25   20. $0.374 < p < 0.486$
21. $0.295 < p < 0.425$ 22. $0.342 < p < 0.547$
23. 545   24. $7 < \sigma < 13$
25. $30.9 < \sigma^2 < 78.2$ 26. $1.8 < \sigma < 3.2$
    $5.6 < \sigma < 8.8$

Chapter 8

Note: For Chapters 8–11, specific *P*-values are given in parentheses after the *P*-value intervals. When the specific *P*-value is extremely small, it is not given.

Exercises 8–1

1. The null hypothesis states that there is no difference between a parameter and a specific value or that there is no difference between two parameters. The alternative hypothesis states that there is a specific difference between a parameter and a specific value or that there is a difference between two parameters. Examples will vary.
2. A type I error occurs when the null hypothesis is rejected when it is true. A type II error occurs when the null hypothesis is not rejected when it is false. They are related in that decreasing the probability of one type of error increases the probability of the other type of error.

3. A statistical test uses the data obtained from a sample to make a decision about whether the null hypothesis should be rejected.
4. A one-tailed test indicates the null hypothesis should be rejected when the test statistic value is in the critical region on one side of the mean. A two-tailed test indicates the null hypothesis should be rejected when the test statistic value is in either critical region on either side of the mean.
5. The critical region is the range of values of the test statistic that indicates that there is a significant difference and the null hypothesis should be rejected. The noncritical region is the range of values of the test statistic that indicates that the difference was probably due to chance and the null hypothesis should not be rejected.
6. H_0 represents the null hypothesis; H_1 represents the alternative hypothesis.
7. α, β
8. When the difference between the sample mean and the hypothesized population mean is large, then the difference is said to be significant and probably not due to chance.
9. A one-tailed test should be used when a specific direction, such as greater than or less than, is being hypothesized; when no direction is specified, a two-tailed test should be used.
10. Hypotheses can be proved true only when the entire population is used to compute the test statistic. In most cases, this is impossible.
11. *a.* -2.33 *c.* ± 1.65 *e.* ± 2.58
    b. 2.58 *d.* 1.65
12. *a.* ± 1.96 *c.* -1.28 *e.* 1.75
    b. 2.05 *d.* ± 2.33
13. *a.* H_0: $\mu = 46.7$ and H_1: $\mu \neq 46.7$
    b. H_0: $\mu = 2.8$ and H_1: $\mu < 2.8$
    c. H_0: $\mu = 15.28 and H_1: $\mu > 15.28
    d. H_0: $\mu = 1.6$ and H_1: $\mu \neq 1.6$
    e. H_0: $\mu = 23.9$ and H_1: $\mu > 23.9$
14. *a.* H_0: $\mu = 88.98 and H_1: $\mu \neq 88.98
    b. H_0: $\mu = $27,923$ and H_1: $\mu \neq $27,923$
    c. H_0: $\mu = 4$ and H_1: $\mu < 4$
    d. H_0: $\mu = 54.8$ and H_1: $\mu > 54.8$
    e. H_0: $\mu = 2543 and H_1: $\mu > 2543
15. *a.* H_0: $p = 0.84$ and H_1: $p > 0.84$
    b. H_0: $p = 0.6$ and H_1: $p < 0.6$
    c. H_0: $p = 0.85$ and H_1: $p \neq 0.85$
16. *a.* H_0: $p = 0.90$ and H_1: $p \neq 0.90$
    b. H_0: $p = 0.45$ and H_1: $p > 0.45$
    c. H_0: $p = 0.25$, and H_1: $p < 0.25$
17. *a.* Reject H_0.
    b. Do not reject H_0.
    c. Do not reject H_0.
    d. Reject H_0.
18. *a.* Do not reject H_0.
    b. Reject H_0.
    c. Reject H_0.
    d. Do not reject H_0.

Exercises 8–2

1. H_0: $\mu = 305$; H_1: $\mu > 305$ (claim); C.V. $= 1.65$; $z = 2.47$; $P = 0.0068$; reject H_0. There is enough evidence to support the claim that the mean depth is greater than 305 feet. It might be due to warmer temperatures or more rainfall. $P < 0.0001$.

2. H_0: $\mu = 338$; H_1: $\mu > 338$ (claim); C.V. $= 1.65$; $z = 1.96$; reject H_0. There is enough evidence to support the claim that the mean number of Facebook friends is greater than 338. $P = 0.0248$.

3. H_0: $\mu = \$7521$; H_1: $\mu < \$7521$ (claim); C.V. $= 1.65$; $z = -1.84$; reject H_0. There is enough evidence to support the claim that the mean cost of Rolex watches is less than $7521. $P = 0.0330$.

4. H_0: $\mu = 8.5$; H_1: $\mu \neq 8.5$ (claim); C.V. $= \pm 1.96$; $z = 2.17$; reject H_0. There is enough evidence to support the claim that there is a difference. $P = 0.0297$.

5. H_0: $\mu = 26$; H_1: $\mu < 26$ (claim); C.V. $= -1.28$; $z = -2.26$; reject H_0. There is enough evidence to support the claim that the mean is less than 26 mg. $P = 0.0118$.

6. H_0: $\mu = \$117.91$; H_1: $\mu \neq \$117.91$ (claim); C.V. $= \pm 1.65$; $z = 1.40$; do not reject H_0. There is not enough evidence to support the claim that the mean cost of home building differs from \$117.91 per square foot. $P = 0.1621$.

7. H_0: $\mu = 29$ and H_1: $\mu \neq 29$ (claim); C.V. $= \pm 1.96$; $z = 0.944$; do not reject H_0. There is not enough evidence to say that the average height differs from 29 inches. $P = 0.3450$.

8. H_0: $\mu = 71.4$; H_1: $\mu < 71.4$ (claim); C.V. $= -2.33$; $z = -0.8015$; do not reject H_0. There is not enough evidence to reject the claim that the mean is less than 71.4 months. $P = 0.2114$.

9. H_0: $\mu = 2.8$; H_1: $\mu > 2.8$ (claim); C.V. $= 2.33$; $z = 2.05$; do not reject H_0. There is not enough evidence to support the claim that the mean number of cell phone calls a person makes is greater than 2.8. Yes, the null hypothesis could be rejected at $\alpha = 0.05$. $P = 0.0200$.

10. H_0: $\mu = 24$ H_1: $\mu < 24$ (claim); C.V. $= -1.65$; $z = -2.4$; reject H_0. There is enough evidence to support the claim that people over 60 drive less than 24 miles per day. $P = 0.0082$.

11. H_0: $\mu = \$655$; H_1: $\mu \neq \$655$ (claim); C.V. $= \pm 1.96$; $z = 2.82$; reject H_0. There is enough evidence to support the claim that the mean cost is not \$655. $P = 0.0047$.

12. H_0: $\mu = \$10{,}337$; H_1: $\mu \neq \$10{,}337$ (claim); C.V. $= \pm 1.65$ at 0.10, ± 1.96 at 0.05, and ± 2.58 at 0.01; $z = 3.62$; reject H_0 at 0.10, 0.05, and 0.01. There is enough evidence to support the claim that the mean expenditure has changed. $P = 0.0003$.

13. H_0: $\mu = \$10.50$; H_1: $\mu \neq \$10.50$ (claim); C.V. $= \pm 1.65$; $z = 1.42$; do not reject H_0. There is not enough evidence to support the claim that the average cost of a movie ticket is not \$10.50. $P = 0.1553$.

14. H_0: $\mu = 34.9$; H_1: $\mu \neq 34.9$ (claim); C.V. $= +/-2.05$; $z = -4.55$; reject H_0. There is enough evidence to support the claim that the mean term of prisoners is not equal to 34.9 months. $P < 0.0001$.

15. a. Do not reject H_0. d. Reject H_0.
    b. Reject H_0. e. Reject H_0.
    c. Do not reject H_0.

16. H_0: $\mu = 52$ (claim) and H_1: $\mu \neq 52$; $z = 8.69$; P-value < 0.01; reject H_0. There is enough evidence to reject the claim that the mean is 52. The researcher's claim is not valid. $P < 0.0001$.

17. H_0: $\mu = 264$ and H_1: $\mu < 264$ (claim); $z = -2.53$; P-value $= 0.0057$; reject H_0. There is enough evidence to support the claim that the average stopping distance is less than 264 ft. (TI: P-value $= 0.0056$)

18. H_0: $\mu = 40$ and H_1: $\mu < 40$ (claim); $z = -2.45$; P-value $= 0.0069$ (TI: P-value $= 0.0070$); reject H_0. There is enough evidence to support the claim that the average number of pages copied is less than 40.

19. H_0: $\mu = 14$; H_1: $\mu \neq 14$ (claim); C.V. $= \pm 1.96$; $z = -2.65$; reject H_0. There is enough evidence to support the claim that dogs do not sleep on average 14 hours per day. $P = 0.0081$.

20. H_0: $\mu = 800$ (claim) and H_1: $\mu \neq 800$; $z = -2.61$; P-value $= 0.0090$; reject H_0. There is enough evidence to reject the null hypothesis that the breaking strength is 800 pounds.

21. H_0: $\mu = 444$; H_1: $\mu \neq 444$; $z = -1.70$; P-value $= 0.0892$; do not reject H_0. There is insufficient evidence at $\alpha = 0.05$ to conclude that the average size differs from 444 acres. (TI: P-value $= 0.0886$)

22. H_0: $\mu = 65$ (claim) and H_1: $\mu \neq 65$; $z = -1.21$; P-value $= 0.2262$ (TI: P-value $= 0.2278$); do not reject H_0. There is not enough evidence to reject the hypothesis that the average acreage is 65 acres.

23. H_0: $\mu = 30{,}000$ (claim) and H_1: $\mu \neq 30{,}000$; $z = 1.71$; P-value $= 0.0872$; reject H_0. There is enough evidence to reject the claim that the customers are adhering to the recommendation. Yes, the 0.10 level is appropriate. (TI: P-value $= 0.0868$)

24. H_0: $\mu = 60$ (claim) and H_1: $\mu \neq 60$; $z = -0.03$; P-value $= 0.9783$; since P-value > 0.05, do not reject H_0. There is not enough evidence to reject the claim that the average number of tickets issued is 60.

25. H_0: $\mu = 10$ and H_1: $\mu < 10$ (claim); $z = -8.67$; P-value < 0.0001; since P-value < 0.05, reject H_0. Yes, there is enough evidence to support the claim that the average number of days missed per year is less than 10. (TI: P-value $= 0$)

26. Reject H_0 at $\alpha = 0.05$ but not at $\alpha = 0.01$. There is a contradiction. The level of significance should be chosen before the analysis.

27. H_0: $\mu = 8.65$ (claim) and H_1: $\mu \neq 8.65$; C.V. $= \pm 1.96$; $z = -1.27$; do not reject H_0. Yes; there is not enough evidence to reject the claim that the average hourly wage of the employees is \$8.65. $P = 0.2055$.

Exercises 8–3

1. It is bell-shaped, it is symmetric about the mean, and it approaches, but never touches the x axis. The mean, median, and mode are all equal to 0, and they are located at the center of the distribution. The t distribution differs from the standard normal distribution in that it is a family

of curves and the variance is greater than 1; and as the degrees of freedom increase, the t distribution approaches the standard normal distribution.

2. The degrees of freedom are the number of values that are free to vary after a sample statistic has been computed. They tell the researcher which specific curve to use when a distribution consists of a family of curves.

3. *a.* ±2.201   *c.* 2.306
   b. 2.518   *d.* −4.604

4. *a.* ±2.602   *c.* −2.807
   b. 2.479   *d.* ±2.365

5. Specific P-values are in parentheses.
   a. $0.01 < P\text{-value} < 0.025$ (0.018)
   b. $0.05 < P\text{-value} < 0.10$ (0.062)
   c. $0.10 < P\text{-value} < 0.25$ (0.123)
   d. $0.10 < P\text{-value} < 0.20$ (0.138)

6. *a.* $P\text{-value} < 0.005$ (0.003)
   b. $0.10 < P\text{-value} < 0.25$ (0.158)
   c. $P\text{-value} = 0.05$ (0.05)
   d. $P\text{-value} > 0.25$ (0.261)

7. $H_0: \mu = 31$, $H_1: \mu < 31$ (claim); C.V. $= -1.833$; d.f. $= 9$; $t = -3.514$; reject H_0. There is enough evidence to support the claim that the mean number of cigarettes that smokers smoke is less than 31 per day. $P = 0.0033$.

8. $H_0: \mu = \$5400$, $H_1: \mu < \$5400$ (claim); C.V. $= -2.052$; d.f. $= 27$; $t = -1.262$; do not reject H_0. There is not enough evidence to support the franchise's claim that its cost is lower than \$5400. $P = 0.1090$.

9. $H_0: \mu = 19$ and $H_1: \mu < 19$; C.V. $= -1.833$ (claim); d.f. $= 9$; $t = -2.115$; reject H_0. There is enough evidence to support the claim that the waiting time is less than 19 minutes. $P = 0.032$.

10. $H_0: \mu = 50{,}000$, $H_1: \mu > 50{,}000$ (claim); C.V. $= 1.440$; d.f. $= 6$; $t = 0.864$; do not reject H_0. There is not enough evidence to support the claim that the mean number of words in a novel is greater than 50,000 words. $P = 0.2104$.

11. $H_0: \mu = 58$; $H_1: \mu > 58$ (claim); C.V. $= 2.821$; d.f. $= 9$; $t = 5.27$; reject H_0. There is enough evidence to support the claim that the average is greater than the national average. $P > 0.0003$.

12. $H_0: \mu = 110$ and $H_1: \mu > 110$ (claim); C.V. $= 2.624$; d.f. $= 14$; $t = 4.389$; reject H_0. Yes. There is enough evidence to support the claim that the average calorie content is greater than 110 calories. $P = 0.0003$.

13. $H_0: \mu = 26.4$ and $H_1: \mu \neq 26.4$ (claim); C.V. $= \pm1.796$; $t = 1.404$; do not reject H_0. There is not enough evidence to support the claim that the mean is not 26.4 miles. $P = 0.1879$.

14. $H_0: \mu = 36$; $H_1: \mu \neq 36$ (claim); C.V. $= \pm2.807$; d.f. $= 23$; $t = 5.638$; reject H_0. There is enough evidence to support the claim that the mean is not 36 visits. $P < 0.0001$.

15. $H_0: \mu = \$50.07$; $H_1: \mu > \$50.07$ (claim); C.V. $= 1.833$; d.f. $= 9$; $t = 2.741$; reject H_0. There is enough evidence to support the claim that the average phone bill has increased. $P = 0.0114$.

16. $H_0: \mu = \$15{,}000$ and $H_1: \mu \neq \$15{,}000$; d.f. $= 11$; $t = -1.10$; C.V. $= \pm2.201$; do not reject H_0. There is

not enough evidence to conclude that the average stipend differs from \$15,000. $P = 0.2932$.

17. $H_0: \mu = 19.3$ and $H_1: \mu < 19.3$ (claim); C.V. $= -1.761$; $t = -1.3406$; do not reject H_0. There is not enough evidence to support the claim that the mean is less than 19.3 minutes. $P = 0.1007$.

18. $H_0: \mu = 2.27$; $H_1: \mu \neq 2.27$ (claim); C.V. $= \pm2.093$; d.f. $= 19$; $t = 3.240$; reject H_0. There is enough evidence to support the claim that the average time differs from 2.27. $P = 0.0043$.

19. $H_0: \mu = \$148.27$ and $H_1: \mu > \$148.27$ (claim); C.V. $= 1.341$; $t = 1.361$; reject H_0. There is enough evidence to support the claim that the mean amount is greater than \$148.27. $P = 0.0968$.

20. $H_0: \mu = 3.18$ and $H_1: \mu \neq 3.18$ (claim); C.V. $= \pm2.069$; d.f. $= 23$; $t = 2.231$; reject H_0. Yes. There is enough evidence to support the claim that the average family size is different from 3.18. $P = 0.0358$.

21. $H_0: \mu = 5.8$ and $H_1: \mu \neq 5.8$ (claim); d.f. $= 19$; $t = -3.462$; $P\text{-value} < 0.01$; reject H_0. There is enough evidence to support the claim that the mean number of times has changed. (TI: $P\text{-value} = 0.0026$)

22. $H_0: \mu = 9.2$ (claim) and $H_1: \mu \neq 9.2$; d.f. $= 7$; $t = -0.531$; $P\text{-value} > 0.05$ (0.6121); do not reject H_0. There is not enough evidence to reject the claim that the mean is 9.2. One reason why a person may not give the exact number of past jobs is that the person may have forgotten about a particular job.

23. $H_0: \mu = \$61{,}470$ and $H_1: \mu > \$61{,}470$ (claim); C.V. $= 1.314$; $t = 1.834$; reject H_0. There is enough evidence to support the claim that the mean is larger than \$61,470. $P = 0.0388$.

Exercises 8–4

1. Answers will vary.

2. The proportion of A items can be considered a success, whereas the proportion of items that are not included in A can be considered a failure. Hence, there are two outcomes.

3. $np \geq 5$ and $nq \geq 5$

4. $\mu = p$; $\sigma = \sqrt{pq/n}$

5. $H_0: p = 0.25$ and $H_1: p > 0.25$ (claim); C.V. $= 1.28$; $z = 0.63$; do not reject H_0. There is not enough evidence to support the claim that the proportion is greater than 0.25. $P = 0.2635$.

6. $H_0: p = 0.503$; $H_1: p \neq 0.503$ (claim); $z = 2.32$; therefore, reject H_0 at any $\alpha > 0.025$ (or any $P\text{-value} \leq 0.025$). $P = 0.0203$.

7. $H_0: p = 0.20$ and $H_1: p < 0.20$ (claim); C.V. $= -1.65$; $z = -0.71$; do not reject H_0. There is not enough evidence to support the claim that the proportion is less than 0.20. $P = 0.2397$.

8. $H_0: p = 0.352$ and $H_1: p > 0.352$ (claim); C.V. $= 1.65$; $z = 2.63$; reject H_0. Yes. There is enough evidence to conclude that the proportion of women physicians exceeds 35.2%. $P = 0.0043$.

9. $H_0: p = 0.73$ and $H_1: p > 0.73$ (claim); C.V. $= 2.33$; $z = 0.91$; do not reject H_0. There is not enough evidence to support the claim that the proportion is greater than 0.73. $P = 0.1823$.

10. H_0: $p = 0.856$; H_1: $p \neq 0.856$ (claim); C.V. $= \pm 1.96$; $z = -1.02$; do not reject H_0. There is insufficient evidence to conclude that the proportion differs from the national rate. $P = 0.3082$.

11. H_0: $p = 0.76$; H_1: $p < 0.76$ (claim); C.V. $= -2.33$; $z = -1.43$; do not reject H_0. There is not enough evidence to support the claim that the percentage of individuals who prefer American-made automobiles is less than 76%. $P = 0.0768$.

12. H_0: $p = 0.83$; H_1: $p < 0.83$ (claim); C.V. $= -1.65$; $z = -1.38$; do not reject H_0. There is not enough evidence to support the claim that the proportion is less than 83%. $P = 0.0833$.

13. H_0: $p = 0.56$ (claim) and H_1: $p \neq 0.56$; C.V. $= \pm 1.96$; C.V. $= 2.44$; reject H_0. There is enough evidence to reject the claim that the proportion is 0.56. $P = 0.0145$.

14. H_0: $p = 0.517$ (claim) and H_1: $p \neq 0.517$; $z = 1.64$; P-value $= 0.101$; do not reject H_0. There is not enough evidence to reject the claim that the proportion is 0.517. The evidence supports the claim. The percentage of homes heated by natural gas might be different. (TI: $P = 0.1007$)

15. H_0: $p = 0.373$ and H_1: $p < 0.373$ (claim); $z = -0.82$; P-value $= 0.2061$; since P-value > 0.05, do not reject H_0. There is not enough evidence to support the claim that less than 37.3% of all high school students smoke at least a pack of cigarettes a day. (TI: P-value $= 0.2050$)

16. H_0: $p = 0.14$ (claim) and H_1: $p \neq 0.14$; $z = -1.15$; P-value $= 0.250$; do not reject H_0. There is not enough evidence to reject the claim that 14% of men use exercise to relieve stress. No, the results cannot be generalized to all adult Americans since only men were surveyed. (TI: $P = 0.2490$)

17. H_0: $p = 0.67$ and H_1: $p \neq 0.67$ (claim); C.V. $= \pm 1.96$; $z = 3.19$; reject H_0. Yes. There is enough evidence to support the claim that the percentage is not 67%. $P = 0.0014$.

18. H_0: $p = 0.60$ and H_1: $p < 0.60$ (claim); C.V. $= -1.65$; $z = -1.15$; do not reject H_0. There is not enough evidence to support the claim that the proportion is less than 0.60. $P = 0.1241$.

19. H_0: $p = 0.576$ and H_1: $p < 0.576$ (claim); C.V. $= -1.65$; $z = -1.26$; do not reject H_0. There is not enough evidence to support the claim that the proportion is less than 0.576. $P = 0.1038$.

20. H_0: $p = 0.77$ and H_1: $p > 0.77$ (claim); C.V. $= 2.33$; $z = 1.43$; do not reject H_0. There is not enough evidence to support the claim that the proportion is more than 0.77. $P = 0.0769$.

21. No, since $p = 0.508$.

22. H_0: $p = 0.20$ and H_1: $p \neq 0.20$ (claim). We have a binomial with $p = 0.20$, $n = 15$. Our P-value is $2 \cdot P(X > = 5) = 2(0.164) = 0.328$. Do not reject H_0. There is not enough evidence to conclude that the proportions have changed.

23. $z = \dfrac{X - \mu}{\sigma}$

$z = \dfrac{X - np}{\sqrt{npq}}$ since $\mu = np$ and $\sigma = \sqrt{npq}$

$z = \dfrac{X/n - np/n}{\sqrt{npq}/n}$

$z = \dfrac{X/n - np/n}{\sqrt{npq/n^2}}$

$z = \dfrac{\hat{p} - p}{\sqrt{pq/n}}$ since $\hat{p} = X/n$

Exercises 8–5

1. a. H_0: $\sigma^2 = 225$ and H_1: $\sigma^2 \neq 225$; C.V. $= 10.283$, 35.479; d.f. $= 21$
   b. H_0: $\sigma^2 = 225$ and H_1: $\sigma^2 < 225$; C.V. $= 7.042$; d.f. $= 13$
   c. H_0: $\sigma^2 = 225$ and H_1: $\sigma^2 > 225$; C.V. $= 15.507$; d.f. $= 8$
   d. H_0: $\sigma^2 = 225$ and H_1: $\sigma^2 > 225$; C.V. $= 23.209$; d.f. $= 10$

2. a. H_0: $\sigma^2 = 225$ and H_1: $\sigma^2 > 225$; C.V. $= 24.725$; d.f. $= 11$
   b. H_0: $\sigma^2 = 225$ and H_1: $\sigma^2 < 225$; C.V. $= 1.635$; d.f. $= 6$
   c. H_0: $\sigma^2 = 225$ and H_1: $\sigma^2 > 225$; C.V. $= 40.289$; d.f. $= 22$
   d. H_0: $\sigma^2 = 225$ and H_1: $\sigma^2 \neq 225$; C.V. $= 14.573$, 43.194; d.f. $= 27$

3. a. $0.01 < P$-value < 0.025 (0.015)
   b. $0.005 < P$-value < 0.01 (0.006)
   c. $0.01 < P$-value < 0.02 (0.012)
   d. P-value < 0.005 (0.003)

4. a. $0.02 < P$-value < 0.05 (0.037)
   b. $0.05 < P$-value < 0.10 (0.088)
   c. $0.05 < P$-value < 0.10 (0.066)
   d. P-value < 0.01 (0.007)

5. H_0: $\sigma^2 = 700$ and H_1: $\sigma^2 > 700$ (claim); C.V. $= 16.919$; d.f. $= 9$; $\chi^2 = 9.120$; do not reject H_0. There is not enough evidence to support the claim that the variance is not equal to 700. $P = 0.4263$.

6. H_0: $\sigma^2 = 100$; H_1: $\sigma^2 \neq 100$ (claim); C.V. $= 2.700$, 19.023; d.f. $= 9$; $\chi^2 = 12.189$; do not reject H_0. There is not enough evidence to support the claim that the variance differs from 100. $P = 0.4057$.

7. H_0: $\sigma = 1.2$ (claim) and H_1: $\sigma > 1.2$; $\alpha = 0.01$; d.f. $= 14$; $\chi^2 = 31.5$; P-value < 0.005 (0.0047); since P-value < 0.01, reject H_0. There is enough evidence to reject the claim that the standard deviation is less than or equal to 1.2 minutes.

8. H_0: $\sigma = 0.03$ (claim) and H_1: $\sigma > 0.03$; $\alpha = 0.05$; d.f. $= 7$; $\chi^2 = 14.381$; $0.025 < P$-value < 0.05 (0.045); since P-value < 0.05, reject H_0. Yes, there is enough evidence to reject the claim that the standard deviation is less than or equal to 0.03 ounce.

9. H_0: $\sigma = 15$ and H_1: $\sigma < 15$ (claim); C.V. $= 2.833$; d.f. $= 7$; $\chi^2 = 5.2176$; do not reject H_0. There is not enough evidence to support the claim that the standard deviation is less than 15. $P = 0.3666$.

10. H_0: $\sigma^2 = 100$; H_1: $\sigma^2 > 100$ (claim); C.V. $= 23.685$; d.f. $= 14$; $\chi^2 = 25.729$; reject H_0. There is sufficient evidence to conclude that the variance in grades exceeds 100. $P = 0.0280$.

11. H_0: $\sigma = 35$ and H_1: $\sigma < 35$ (claim); C.V. $= 3.940$; d.f. $= 10$; $\chi^2 = 8.359$; do not reject H_0. There is not enough evidence to support the claim that the standard deviation is less than 35. $P = 0.4062$.

12. H_0: $\sigma = 8$ and H_1: $\sigma > 8$ (claim); C.V. $= 55.758$; d.f. $= 49$; $\chi^2 = 84.410$; reject H_0. Yes. There is enough evidence to

support the claim that the standard deviation is greater than 8. $P = 0.0012$.

13. H_0: $\sigma = \$50$ and H_1: $\sigma > \$50$ (claim); C.V. = 24.996; d.f. = 15; $\chi^2 = 16.244$; do not reject H_0. There is not enough evidence to support the claim that the standard deviation is greater than \$50. $P = 0.3660$.

14. H_0: $\sigma = 12$, H_1: $\sigma \neq 12$ (claim); C.V. = 5.226, 21.026; d.f. = 12; $\chi^2 = 17.783$; do not reject H_0. There is not enough evidence to support the claim that the standard deviation of the amounts of vitamin C in a random sample of various fruits and vegetables is different from 12 mg. $P = 0.2481$.

15. H_0: $\sigma = \$0.50$ and H_1: $\sigma \neq \$0.50$ (claim); C.V. = 12.338 and 36.781; d.f. = 22; $\chi^2 = 18.621$; do not reject H_0. There is not enough evidence to support the claim that the standard deviation is not \$0.50. $P = 0.3314$.

16. H_0: $\sigma^2 = 9$, H_1: $\sigma^2 > 9$ (claim); C.V. = 14.684; d.f. = 9; $\chi^2 = 9.344$; do not reject H_0. There is not enough evidence to support the claim that the variance for the golf scores is greater than 9. $P = 0.4061$.

17. H_0: $\sigma = 60$ (claim) and H_1: $\sigma \neq 60$; C.V. = 8.672; 27.587; d.f. = 17; $\chi^2 = 19.707$; do not reject H_0. There is not enough evidence to reject the claim that the standard deviation is 60. $P = 0.5790$.

18. H_0: $\sigma = 8$; H_1: $\sigma > 8$ (claim); C.V. = 30.144; d.f. = 19; $\chi^2 = 36.033$; reject H_0. There is sufficient evidence to conclude that the standard deviation is greater than 8 degrees. $P = 0.0105$.

19. H_0: $\sigma = 679.5$; H_1: $\sigma \neq 679.5$ (claim); C.V. = 5.009; 24.736; d.f. = 13; $\chi^2 = 16.723$; do not reject H_0. There is not enough evidence to support the claim that the sample standard deviation differs from the estimated standard deviation. $P = 0.4246$.

20. H_0: $\sigma = 2385.9$; H_1: $\sigma < 2385.9$ (claim); C.V. = 1.145; d.f. = 5; $\chi^2 = 4.231$; do not reject H_0. There is insufficient evidence to conclude that the standard deviation is less. $P = 0.4833$.

Exercises 8–6

1. H_0: $\mu = 25.2$; H_1: $\mu \neq 25.2$ (claim); C.V. = ±2.032; $t = 4.50$; $27.2 < \mu < 30.2$; reject H_0. There is enough evidence to support the claim that the average age is not 25.2 years. The confidence interval does not contain 25.2. $P < 0.0001$.

2. H_0: $\mu = \$236$; H_1: $\mu \neq \$236$ (claim); C.V. = ±2.539; d.f. = 19; $t = -2.704$; reject H_0. There is sufficient evidence to conclude that the mean cost differs from \$236. 98% C.I.: $185.59 < \mu < 234.41$. They support one another because \$236 is outside the interval, implying a difference. $P = 0.0141$.

3. H_0: $\mu = \$19,150$; H_1: $\mu \neq \$19,150$ (claim); C.V. = ±1.96; $z = -3.69$; $15,889 < \mu < 18,151$; reject H_0. There is enough evidence to support the claim that the mean differs from \$19,150. Yes, the interval supports the results because it does not contain the hypothesized mean \$19,150. $P < 0.0001$.

4. H_0: $p = 0.694$, H_1: $p \neq 0.694$ (claim); C.V. = ±1.96; $z = 0.920$; $0.659 < p < 0.795$; do not reject H_0. There is not enough evidence to support the claim that the proportion

of white collar criminals who serve time is not 69.4%. The confidence interval contains 0.694. $P = 0.3537$.

5. H_0: $\mu = 19$; H_1: $\mu \neq 19$ (claim); C.V. = ±2.145; d.f. = 14; $t = 1.37$; do not reject H_0. There is insufficient evidence to conclude that the mean number of hours differs from 19. 95% C.I.: $17.7 < \mu < 24.9$. Because the mean ($\mu = 19$) is in the interval, there is no evidence to support the idea that a difference exists. $P = 0.1921$.

6. H_0: $\mu = 10.8$ (claim) and H_1: $\mu \neq 10.8$; C.V. = ±2.33; $z = 2.80$; reject H_0; $11.0 < \mu < 13.4$. There is enough evidence to reject the claim that the average time a person spends reading a newspaper is 10.8 minutes. The confidence interval does not contain the hypothesized mean 10.8. $P = 0.0051$.

7. The power of a statistical test is the probability of rejecting the null hypothesis when it is false.

8. The power of a test is equal to $1 - \beta$, where β is the probability of a type II error.

9. The power of a test can be increased by increasing α or selecting a larger sample size.

Review Exercises

1. H_0: $\mu = 18$ and H_1: $\mu \neq 18$ (claim); C.V. = ±2.33; $z = 2.02$; do not reject H_0. There is not enough evidence to support the claim that the average lifetime of a \$1.00 bill is not 18 months. $P = 0.0434$.

2. H_0: $\mu = 25.3$; H_1: $\mu < 25.3$ (claim); C.V. = −2.33; $z = -2.19$; do not reject H_0. There is not enough evidence to support the claim that the average time is less than 25.3 minutes. $P = 0.0142$.

3. H_0: $\mu = 18,000$; H_1: $\mu < 18,000$ (claim); C.V. = −2.33; test statistic $z = -3.58$; reject H_0. There is sufficient evidence to conclude that the mean debt is less than \$18,000. $P = 0.0002$.

4. H_0: $\mu = 10$ and H_1: $\mu < 10$ (claim); $z = -2.22$; P-value = 0.0132; reject H_0. There is enough evidence to support the claim that the average time is less than 10 minutes.

5. H_0: $\mu = 22$ and H_1: $\mu > 22$ (claim); C.V. = 1.65; $z = 1.95$; reject H_0. There is enough evidence to support the claim that the average number of items purchased is greater than 22. $P = 0.0258$.

6. H_0: $\mu = \$50$, H_1: $\mu > \$50$ (claim); C.V. = 1.356; d.f. = 12; $t = 1.04$; do not reject H_0. There is not enough evidence to support the claim that the average winnings exceed \$50. $P = 0.1597$.

7. H_0: $\mu = 10$; H_1: $\mu < 10$ (claim); C.V. = −1.782; d.f. = 12; $t = -2.230$; reject H_0. There is enough evidence to support the claim that the mean weight is less than 10 ounces. $P = 0.0229$.

8. H_0: $\mu = 208$; H_1: $\mu > 208$ (claim); C.V. = 2.896; d.f. = 8; $t = 3.13$; reject H_0. There is sufficient evidence that the mean weight is greater than 208 g. $P = 0.0071$.

9. H_0: $p = 0.25$ and H_1: $p < 0.25$ (claim); C.V. = −1.65; $z = -1.39$; do not reject H_0. There is not enough evidence to support the claim that the percentage of doctors who received their medical degrees from a foreign school is less than 25%. $P = 0.0829$.

10. H_0: $p = 0.602$ and H_1: $p > 0.602$ (claim); C.V. = 1.65; $z = 1.96$; reject H_0. Yes. There is enough evidence to support the claim that the proportion is greater than 0.602. $P = 0.0249$.

11. H_0: $p = 0.593$; H_1: $p < 0.593$ (claim); C.V. = −2.33; $z = -2.57$; reject H_0. There is sufficient evidence to conclude that the proportion of free and reduced-cost lunches is less than 59.3%. $P = 0.0050$.

12. H_0: $p = 0.65$ (claim) and H_1: $p \neq 0.65$; $z = 1.17$; P-value = 0.242; since P-value > 0.05, do not reject H_0. There is not enough evidence to reject the claim that 65% of teenagers own their own cell phones. (TI: P-value = 0.2412)

13. H_0: $p = 0.373$; H_1: $p \neq 0.373$ (claim); C.V. = ±1.96; $z = -1.18$; do not reject H_0. There is not enough evidence to support the claim that the proportion is different from the national proportion. $P = 0.2372$.

14. H_0: $p = 0.205$; H_1: $p > 0.205$ (claim); C.V. = 1.28; $z = 3.03$; reject H_0. There is enough evidence to support the claim that the proportion of men over 65 still working is greater than 20.5%. $P = 0.0012$. The 90% confidence interval is (0.247, 0.387). Since 20.5% (0.205) is not in this interval, we reject the null hypothesis. The hypothesis test and the confidence interval test are in agreement.

15. H_0: $\sigma = 4.3$ (claim) and H_1: $\sigma < 4.3$; d.f. = 19; $\chi^2 = 6.95$; $0.005 < P$-value < 0.01 (0.006); since P-value < 0.05, reject H_0. Yes, there is enough evidence to reject the claim that the standard deviation is greater than or equal to 4.3 miles per gallon.

16. H_0: $\sigma^2 = 3.81$; H_1: $\sigma^2 \neq 3.81$ (claim); C.V. = 5.629, 26.119; d.f. = 14; $\chi^2 = 15.898$; do not reject H_0. There is not enough evidence to support the claim that the variance is different from 3.81. $P = 0.6393$.

17. H_0: $\sigma^2 = 40$; H_1: $\sigma^2 \neq 40$ (claim); C.V. = 2.700 and 19.023; test statistic $\chi^2 = 9.801$; do not reject H_0. There is insufficient evidence to conclude that the variance in the number of games played differs from 40.

18. H_0: $\sigma = 3.3$ and $\sigma \neq 3.3$; C.V. = 27.587 and 8.672; d.f. = 17; $\chi^2 = 12.239$; do not reject H_0. There is not enough evidence to reject the claim that the standard deviation is 3.3.

19. H_0: $\mu = 4$ and H_1: $\mu \neq 4$ (claim); C.V. = ±2.58; $z = 1.49$; $3.85 < \mu < 4.55$; do not reject H_0. There is not enough evidence to support the claim that the growth has changed. Yes, the results agree. The hypothesized mean is contained in the interval. $P = 0.1360$.

20. H_0: $\mu = 35$ (claim) and H_1: $\mu \neq 35$; C.V. = ±1.65; $z = -3.00$; reject H_0; $32.675 < \mu < 34.325$. No. There is enough evidence to reject the claim that the mean is 35 pounds. Yes, the results agree. The hypothesized mean is not contained in the interval. $P = 0.0027$.

Chapter Quiz

1. True   2. True

3. False. The critical value separates the critical region from the non-critical region.

4. True

5. False. The chi-square test for variances is either one-tailed or two-tailed.

6. b

7. d 8. c

9. b 10. Type I

11. β 12. Statistical hypothesis

13. Right   14. $n - 1$

15. H_0: $\mu = 28.6$ (claim) and H_1: $\mu \neq 28.6$; $z = 2.09$; C.V. = ±1.96; reject H_0. There is enough evidence to reject the claim that the average age of the mothers is 28.6 years. $P = 0.0367$.

16. H_0: $\mu = \$6500$ (claim) and H_1: $\mu \neq \$6500$; $z = 5.27$; C.V. = ±1.96; reject H_0. There is enough evidence to reject the agent's claim. $P < 0.0001$.

17. H_0: $\mu = 8$ and H_1: $\mu > 8$ (claim); $z = 6$; C.V. = 1.65; reject H_0. There is enough evidence to support the claim that the average is greater than 8. $P < 0.0001$.

18. H_0: $\mu = 500$ (claim) and H_1: $\mu \neq 500$; d.f. = 6; $t = -0.571$; C.V. = ±3.707; do not reject H_0. There is not enough evidence to reject the claim that the mean is 500. $P = 0.5888$.

19. H_0: $\mu = 67$ and H_1: $\mu < 67$ (claim); $t = -3.1568$; P-value < 0.005 (0.003); since P-value < 0.05, reject H_0. There is enough evidence to support the claim that the average height is less than 67 inches.

20. H_0: $\mu = 12.4$ and H_1: $\mu < 12.4$ (claim); $t = -2.324$; C.V. = −1.345; reject H_0. There is enough evidence to support the claim that the average is less than the company claimed. $P = 0.0179$.

21. H_0: $\mu = 63.5$ and H_1: $\mu > 63.5$ (claim); $t = 0.47075$; P-value > 0.25 (0.322); since P-value > 0.05, do not reject H_0. There is not enough evidence to support the claim that the average is greater than 63.5.

22. H_0: $\mu = 26$ (claim) and H_1: $\mu \neq 26$; $t = -1.5$; C.V. = ±2.492; do not reject H_0. There is not enough evidence to reject the claim that the average is 26. $P = 0.1467$.

23. H_0: $p = 0.39$ (claim) and H_1: $p \neq 0.39$; C.V. = ±1.96; $z = -0.62$; do not reject H_0. There is not enough evidence to reject the claim that 39% took supplements. $P = 0.5385$.

24. H_0: $p = 0.55$ (claim) and H_1: $p < 0.55$; $z = -0.8989$; C.V. = −1.28; do not reject H_0. There is not enough evidence to reject the survey's claim. $P = 0.1843$.

25. H_0: $p = 0.35$ (claim) and H_1: $p \neq 0.35$; C.V. = ±2.33; $z = 0.668$; do not reject H_0. There is not enough evidence to reject the claim that the proportion is 35%. $P = 0.5056$.

26. H_0: $p = 0.75$ (claim) and H_1: $p \neq 0.75$; $z = 2.6833$; C.V. = ±2.58; reject H_0. There is enough evidence to reject the claim that 75% of all teenage boys have their own cell phone. $P = 0.0073$.

27. P-value = 0.0366

28. P-value < 0.0001

29. H_0: $\sigma = 6$ and H_1: $\sigma > 6$ (claim); $\chi^2 = 54$; C.V. = 36.415; reject H_0. There is enough evidence to support the claim. $P < 0.0001$.

30. H_0: $\sigma = 8$ (claim) and H_1: $\sigma \neq 8$; $\chi^2 = 33.2$; C.V. = 34.770, 90.715; reject H_0. There is enough evidence to reject the claim that $\sigma = 8$. $P = 0.0053$.

31. $H_0: \sigma = 2.3$ and $H_1: \sigma < 2.3$ (claim); $\chi^2 = 13$; C.V. $= 10.117$; do not reject H_0. There is not enough evidence to support the claim that the standard deviation is less than 2.3.

32. $H_0: \sigma = 9$ (claim) and $H_1: \sigma \neq 9$; $\chi^2 = 13.4$;

P-value > 0.20 (0.2870); since P-value > 0.05, do not reject H_0. There is not enough evidence to reject the claim that $\sigma = 9$.

33. $28.9 < \mu < 31.2$; no.

34. $\$6562.81 < \mu < \$6637.19$

Chapter 9

Exercises 9–1

1. Testing a single mean involves comparing a population mean to a specific value such as $\mu = 100$; testing the difference between two means involves comparing the means of two populations, such as $\mu_1 = \mu_2$.

2. Testing a single proportion means comparing a proportion of a population proportion such as $p = 0.62$ whereas testing the difference between two proportions involves comparing the proportions of two samples, such as $p_1 = p_2$.

3. Two samples are independent when the way the subjects in the first sample are selected in no way influences the way the subjects in the second sample are selected. An example is selecting male subjects for one sample and the selecting female subjects for the other sample.

4. Two samples are dependent when the selection of the subjects in the first sample influences the way the subjects in the second sample are selected. An example would be using the same subjects in both samples and taking two measurements, such as a pretest and a posttest for the subjects.

5. $H_0: \mu_1 = \mu_2$ and $H_1: \mu_1 > \mu_2$ where μ_1 is the mean number of cups of coffee that male college students drink per day and μ_2 is the mean number of cups of coffee that female college students drink per day.

6. $H_0: \mu_1 = \mu_2$ and $H_1: \mu_1 > \mu_2$ where μ_1 is the mean fiber content of wheat cereal and μ_2 is the mean fiber content of rice cereals.

7. $H_0: \mu_1 = \mu_2$ and $H_1: \mu_1 > \mu_2$ where μ_1 is the mean score on the thinking skills test of children who get an hour of daily exercise, and μ_2 is the mean score on the thinking skills test of children who do not get an hour of daily exercise.

8. $H_0: \mu_1 = \mu_2$ and $H_1: \mu_1 < \mu_2$ where μ_1 is the mean number of miles per gallon a four-wheel drive vehicle gets and μ_2 is the mean number of miles per gallon an all-wheel drive vehicle gets.

9. $H_0: \mu_1 = \mu_2$ and $H_1: \mu_1 < \mu_2$ where μ_1 is the mean number of strokes women have who are on the Mediterranean diet and μ_2 is the mean number of strokes women have who are not on the Mediterranean diet.

10. $H_0: \mu_1 = \mu_2$ and $H_1: \mu_1 < \mu_2$ where μ_1 is the mean number of minutes that it takes ibuprofen to relieve pain and μ_2 is the mean number of minutes that it takes aspirin to relieve pain.

11. $H_0: p_1 = p_2$ and $H_1: p_1 > p_2$ where p_1 is the percentage of junk emails not read by males and p_2 is the percentage of junk emails not read by females.

12. $H_0: p_1 = p_2$ and $H_1: p_1 < p_2$ where p_1 is the percentage of air pollution produced by trucks and p_2 is the percentage of air pollution produced by automobiles.

13. $H_0: p_1 = p_2$ and $H_1: p_1 \neq p_2$ where p_1 is the percentage of college students who believe that chewing gum improves memory and p_2 is the percentage of high school students who believe that chewing gum improves memory.

14. $H_0: p_1 = p_2$ and $H_1: p_1 > p_2$ where p_1 is the percentage of college graduates who watch the early news on television and p_2 is the percentage of adults who do not have a college degree watch the early news on television.

15. $H_0: p_1 = p_2$ and $H_1: p_1 \neq p_2$ where p_1 is the percentage of criminal lawyers who think that the bar exam does not measure their ability to practice law and p_2 is the percentage of civil trial lawyers who feel that way.

16. $H_0: p_1 = p_2$ and $H_1: p_1 > p_2$ where p_1 is the percentage of people who forget their toothbrush and p_2 is the percentage of people who forget their deodorant when they go on vacation.

Exercises 9–2

1. Both samples must be random, independent, and the sample sizes must be 30 or more. The populations must be normally distributed if the sample sizes are less than 30.

2. When both samples are larger than or equal to 30, the distribution will be approximately normal. The mean of the differences will be equal to zero. The standard deviation of the differences will be

$$\sqrt{\frac{\sigma_1^2}{n_1} + \frac{\sigma_2^2}{n_2}}$$

3. Both samples are random samples. The populations must be independent of each other, and they must be normally or approximately normally distributed.

4. $H_0: \mu_1 = \mu_2$ or $H_0: \mu_1 - \mu_2 = 0$

5. $H_0: \mu_1 = \mu_2$; $H_1: \mu_1 \neq \mu_2$ (claim); C.V. $= \pm 1.96$, $z = 2.15$; reject H_0. There is enough evidence to support the claim that the mean sodium contents of the popcorns are different. $P = 0.0314$.

6. $H_0: \mu_1 = \mu_2$; $H_1: \mu_1 \neq \mu_2$ (claim); C.V. $= \pm 1.65$; $z = -1.91$; reject H_0. There is enough evidence to support the claim that the mean annual salaries for teachers in New York and Massachusetts are different. $P = 0.0568$.

7. $H_0: \mu_1 = \mu_2$; $H_1: \mu_1 \neq \mu_2$ (claim); C.V. $= \pm 1.96$; $z = -3.65$; reject H_0. There is sufficient evidence at $\alpha = 0.05$ to conclude that the commuting times differ in the winter. $P = 0.0003$.

8. $H_0: \mu_1 = \mu_2$, $H_1: \mu_1 \neq \mu_2$ (claim); C.V. $= \pm 1.96$; $z = -1.34$; do not reject H_0. There is not enough evidence to support the claim that the mean heights are different. $P = 0.1788$.

9. $H_0: \mu_1 = \mu_2$; $H_1: \mu_1 > \mu_2$ (claim); C.V. $= 2.33$; $z = 3.75$; reject H_0. There is sufficient evidence at $\alpha = 0.01$ to conclude that the average hospital stay for men is longer. $P < 0.0001$.

10. H_0: $\mu_1 = \mu_2$; H_1: $\mu_1 \neq \mu_2$ (claim); C.V. $= \pm 1.65$, $z = 0.51$; do not reject H_0. There is not enough evidence to support the claim that the means are not equal. $P = 0.6041$.

11. H_0: $\mu_1 = \mu_2$; H_1: $\mu_1 < \mu_2$ (claim); C.V. $= -2.33$; $z = -1.23$; do not reject H_0. There is not enough evidence to support the claim that college students spend less on used cars than those in the general population. $P = 0.1097$.

12. H_0: $\mu_1 = \mu_2$; H_1: $\mu_1 > \mu_2$ (claim); C.V. $= 1.65$; $z = 1.28$; do not reject H_0. There is not enough evidence to support the claim that males own more automobiles in their lifetimes than females do. $P = 0.1007$.

13. H_0: $\mu_1 = \mu_2$; H_1: $\mu_1 \neq \mu_2$ (claim); C.V. $= \pm 1.96$; $z = 0.66$; do not reject H_0. There is not enough evidence to support the claim that there is a difference in the means. $P = 0.5089$.

14. H_0: $\mu_1 - \mu_2 = 30$; H_1: $\mu_1 - \mu_2 > 30$ (claim); C.V. $= 1.65$; $z = 1.53$; do not reject H_0. There is insufficient evidence to conclude that the difference in benefits is greater than \$30. $P = 0.0643$.

15. H_0: $\mu_1 = \mu_2$ and H_1: $\mu_1 \neq \mu_2$ (claim); $z = 1.01$; P-value $= 0.3124$; do not reject H_0. There is not enough evidence to support the claim that there is a difference in self-esteem scores. (TI: P-value $= 0.3131$)

16. H_0: $\mu_1 = \mu_2$ (claim) and H_1: $\mu_1 \neq \mu_2$; $z = -0.76$; P-value $= 0.4472$; do not reject the null hypothesis. There is not enough evidence to reject the claim that there is no difference in the ages.

17. $5.3 < \mu_1 - \mu_2 < 8.7$

18. $-2.2 < \mu_1 - \mu_2 < -0.8$

19. $10.5 < \mu_1 - \mu_2 < 59.5$. The interval provides evidence to reject the null hypothesis. There is no evidence of a difference in mean scores because the interval for the difference is entirely positive. That is, 0 is not in the interval.

20. H_0: $\mu_1 = \mu_2$, H_1: $\mu_1 \neq \mu_2$ (claim); C.V. $= \pm 2.58$; $z = 2.41$; do not reject H_0. There is not enough evidence to support the claim that there is a difference in the means. $P = 0.0160$. $-620.5 < \mu_1 - \mu_2 < 18,449$

21. $0.281 < \mu_1 - \mu_2 < 0.519$

22. H_0: $\mu_1 = \mu_2$, H_1: $\mu_1 \neq \mu_2$ (claim); C.V. $= \pm 1.96$; $z = 3.16$; reject H_0. There is enough evidence to support the claim that the mean times are different. $P = 0.0016$.

23. H_0: $\mu_1 = \mu_2$, H_1: $\mu_1 \neq \mu_2$ (claim); $z = -2.47$; P-value $= 0.0136$; do not reject H_0. There is not enough evidence to support the claim that there is a significant difference in the mean daily sales of the two stores. $P = 0.0136$.

24. H_0: $\mu_1 = \mu_2$, H_1: $\mu_1 > \mu_2$ (claim); C.V. $= 1.65$; $z = 1.91$; reject H_0. There is enough evidence to support the claim that the mean price of homes in Dallas exceeds the mean price of homes in Pittsburgh. $P = 0.0282$.

25. H_0: $\mu_1 - \mu_2 = 8$ (claim) and H_1: $\mu_1 - \mu_2 > 8$; C.V. $= 1.65$; $z = -0.73$; do not reject H_0. There is not enough evidence to reject the claim that private school students have exam scores that are at most 8 points higher than those of students in public schools.

26. H_0: $\mu_1 - \mu_2 = \$3400$; H_1: $\mu_1 - \mu_2 > \$3400$ (claim); C.V. $= 1.65$; $z = 3.93$; reject H_0. There is enough evidence to support the claim that the difference in the means of the sale prices is greater than \$3400.

27. H_0: $\mu_1 - \mu_2 = \$30,000$; H_1: $\mu_1 - \mu_2 \neq \$30,000$ (claim); C.V. $= \pm 2.58$; $z = 1.22$; do not reject H_0. There is not enough evidence to support the claim that the difference in income is not \$30,000.

Exercises 9–3

1. H_0: $\mu_1 = \mu_2$; H_1: $\mu_1 \neq \mu_2$ (claim); C.V. $= \pm 1.860$; d.f. $= 8$; $t = 0.209$; do not reject H_0. There is not enough evidence to support the claim that the mean heights are different. $P = 0.8370$.

2. H_0: $\mu_1 = \mu_2$; H_1: $\mu_1 \neq \mu_2$ (claim); C.V. $= \pm 2.131$; d.f. $= 15$; $t = -0.942$; do not reject H_0. There is not enough evidence to support the claim that the means are different. (*Note:* In each data set there is a suspected outlier that may make the results suspect.) $P = 0.3582$.

3. H_0: $\mu_1 = \mu_2$; H_1: $\mu_1 \neq \mu_2$ (claim); C.V. $= \pm 1.833$; d.f. $= 9$; $t = 1.205$; do not reject H_0. There is not enough evidence to support the claim that the mean times are different. $P = 0.2482$.

4. H_0: $\mu_1 = \mu_2$; H_1: $\mu_1 < \mu_2$ (claim); C.V. $= -1.711$; d.f. $= 24$; $t = -4.509$; reject H_0. There is enough evidence to support the claim that the mean age of those playing the slot machines is less than that of those playing roulette. $P < 0.0001$.

5. H_0: $\mu_1 = \mu_2$; H_1: $\mu_1 \neq \mu_2$ (claim); C.V. $= \pm 1.812$; d.f. $= 10$; $t = -1.220$; do not reject H_0. There is not enough evidence to support the claim that the means are not equal. $P = 0.2408$.

6. H_0: $\mu_1 = \mu_2$; H_1: $\mu_1 \neq \mu_2$ (claim); C.V. $= \pm 2.262$; d.f. $= 9$; $t = 1.761$; do not reject H_0. There is not enough evidence to support the claim that the means are not equal. $P = 0.0935$.

7. H_0: $\mu_1 = \mu_2$; H_1: $\mu_1 \neq \mu_2$ (claim); d.f. $= 9$; $t = 5.103$; the P-value for the t test is P-value < 0.001; reject H_0. There is enough evidence to support the claim that the means are different. (TI: $P = 0.0003$)

8. H_0: $\mu_1 = \mu_2$; H_1: $\mu_1 \neq \mu_2$ (claim); C.V. $= \pm 1.860$; d.f. $= 8$; $t = 0.1435$; do not reject H_0. There is not enough evidence to support the claim that the mean times are different. $P = 0.8877$.

9. $-338.3 < \mu_1 - \mu_2 < 424.1$

10. $-94.3 < \mu_1 - \mu_2 < 1118.1$ (TI: $-145.481 < \mu_1 - \mu_2 < 1169.247$)

11. H_0: $\mu_1 = \mu_2$; H_1: $\mu_1 \neq \mu_2$ (claim); C.V. $= \pm 2.977$; d.f. $= 14$; $t = 2.601$; do not reject H_0. There is insufficient evidence to conclude a difference in viewing times. $P = 0.0147$.

12. H_0: $\mu_1 = \mu_2$; H_1: $\mu_1 \neq \mu_2$ (claim); C.V. $= \pm 2.262$; d.f. $= 9$; $t = 2.786$; reject H_0. There is enough evidence to support the claim that the mean earnings of professional golfers in the PGA and LPGA are different. $P = 0.0170$.

13. H_0: $\mu_1 = \mu_2$; H_1: $\mu_1 < \mu_2$ (claim); C.V. $= -1.383$; d.f. $= 9$; $t = -1.837$; reject H_0. There is enough evidence to support the claim that the assistants spend more time with patients than the medical doctors do. $P = 0.0412$.

14. H_0: $\mu_1 = \mu_2$; H_1: $\mu_1 \neq \mu_2$ (claim); C.V. $= \pm 2.306$; d.f. $= 8$; $t = 1.174$; do not reject H_0. There is insufficient evidence to conclude a difference in means. $P = 0.2583$.

15. H_0: $\mu_1 = \mu_2$ (claim) and H_1: $\mu_1 \neq \mu_2$; d.f. = 15; $t = 2.385$. The P-value for the t test is $0.02 < P\text{-value} < 0.05$ (0.026). Do not reject H_0 since P-value > 0.01. There is not enough evidence to reject the claim that the means are equal. $-0.1 < \mu_1 - \mu_2 < 0.9$ (TI: Interval $-0.07 < \mu_1 - \mu_2 < 0.87$)

16. H_0: $\mu_1 = \mu_2$; H_1: $\mu_1 > \mu_2$ (claim); d.f. = 19; $t = 4.364$; P-value < 0.005 (0.00005), reject H_0. There is sufficient evidence to conclude that the houses in Whiting are older.

17. $9.9 < \mu_1 - \mu_2 < 219.6$ (TI: Interval $13.23 < \mu_1 - \mu_2 < 216.24$)

18. $\$1789.70 < \mu_1 - \mu_2 < \$12,425.41$ (TI: Interval $\$2484.60 < \mu_1 - \mu_2 < \$11,731.00$)

19. H_0: $\mu_1 = \mu_2$, H_1: $\mu_1 < \mu_2$ (claim); $t = -0.7477$; P-value $= 0.238$; do not reject H_0. There is not enough evidence to say that the cost of gasoline in 2011 was less than in 2015.

20. H_0: $\mu_1 = \mu_2$, H_1: $\mu_1 \neq \mu_2$ (claim); $t = 1.529$; $0.10 < P\text{-value} < 0.20$; do not reject H_0. There is not enough evidence to support the claim that there is a significant difference between the mean scores of the two teams. $P = 0.1505$.

21. H_0: $\mu_1 = \mu_2$; H_1: $\mu_1 \neq \mu_2$ (claim); C.V. = ±1.796; d.f. = 11; $t = -0.451$; do not reject H_0. There is not enough evidence to support the claim that the mean number of home runs for the two leagues are different. $P = 0.6575$.

22. H_0: $\mu_1 = \mu_2$, H_1: $\mu_1 \neq \mu_2$ (claim); C.V. = ±2.571; $t = 1.701$; do not reject H_0. There is not enough evidence to support the claim that the means of the batting averages of the leaders are different. $P = 0.1490$.

Exercises 9–4

1. *a.* Dependent *d.* Dependent
b. Dependent *e.* Independent
c. Independent

2. H_0: $\mu_D = 0$; H_1: $\mu_D > 0$ (claim); C.V. = 1.943; d.f. = 6; $t = 2.812$; reject H_0. There is sufficient evidence to conclude that the book scores are higher than DVD scores. $P = 0.0153$.

3. H_0: $\mu_D = 0$ and H_1: $\mu_D < 0$ (claim); C.V. = −1.397; d.f. = 8; $t = -2.818$; reject H_0. There is enough evidence to support the claim that the seminar increased the number of hours students studied. $P = 0.0116$.

4. H_0: $\mu_D = 0$; H_1: $\mu_D > 0$ (claim); C.V. = 1.895; $t = 4.249$; reject H_0. There is sufficient evidence to conclude that students did better the second time. Possible reasons: familiar with course; warmed up, etc. $P = 0.0019$.

5. H_0: $\mu_D = 0$ and H_1: $\mu_D < 0$ (claim); C.V. = −1.833; d.f. = 9; $t = -5.52$; reject H_0. There is enough evidence to support the claim that physical therapy increased the range of motion of the knee. $P = 0.0002$.

6. H_0: $\mu_D = 0$; H_1: $\mu_D \neq 0$ (claim); C.V. = ±2.365; d.f. = 7; $t = -2.411$; reject H_0. There is sufficient evidence to conclude a difference in mean scores. $P = 0.0467$.

7. H_0: $\mu_D = 0$ and H_1: $\mu_D < 0$ (claim); C.V. = −1.363; d.f. = 11; $t = -2.13$; reject H_0. There is enough evidence to support the claim that the mean of the scores before the program are less than the mean of the scores after the program. $P = 0.0283$.

8. H_0: $\mu_D = 0$; H_1: $\mu_D > 0$ (claim); C.V. = 2.015; d.f. = 5; $t = 3.060$; reject H_0. There is enough evidence to support the claim that the dogs lost weight. $P = 0.0140$.

9. H_0: $\mu_D = 0$ and H_1: $\mu_D \neq 0$ (claim); d.f. = 7; $t = 0.978$; P-value > 0.20 (0.361). Do not reject H_0 since P-value > 0.01. There is not enough evidence to support the claim that there is a difference in the pulse rates. $-3.2 < \mu_D < 5.7$.

10. H_0: $\mu_D = 0$, H_1: $\mu_D > 0$ (claim); $t = 3.026$; $0.01 < P\text{-value} < 0.025$ (0.012); do not reject H_0. There is not enough evidence to support the claim that learning has occurred. $-2.7 < \mu_D < 26.4$.

11. H_0: $\mu_D = 0$ and H_1: $\mu_D > 0$ (claim); C.V. = +1.350; d.f. = 13; $t = 0.628$; do not reject H_0. There is not enough evidence to support the claim that the new batteries last longer than the recharged batteries. $P = 0.2705$.

12. H_0: $\mu_D = 0$ and H_1: $\mu_D < 0$ (claim); C.V. = −1.812; d.f. = 10; $t = -1.972$; reject H_0. There is enough evidence to support the claim that customer relations sales program works. $P = 0.0385$.

13. $\overline{X_1 - X_2} = \Sigma \dfrac{X_1 - X_2}{n} = \Sigma \left(\dfrac{X_1}{n} - \dfrac{X_2}{n} \right)$

$= \Sigma \dfrac{X_1}{n} - \Sigma \dfrac{X_2}{n} = \overline{X}_1 - \overline{X}_2$

Exercises 9–5

1. *a.* $\hat{p} = 0.852$, $\hat{q} = 0.148$ *d.* $\hat{p} = 0.375$, $\hat{q} = 0.625$
b. $\hat{p} = 0.4$, $\hat{q} = 0.6$ *e.* $\hat{p} = 0.156$, $\hat{q} = 0.844$
c. $\hat{p} = 0.5$, $\hat{q} = 0.5$

2. *a.* $\hat{p} = 0.36$, $\hat{q} = 0.64$ *d.* $\hat{p} = 0.4$, $\hat{q} = 0.6$
b. $\hat{p} = 0.5$, $\hat{q} = 0.5$ *e.* $\hat{p} = 0.111$, $\hat{q} = 0.889$
c. $\hat{p} = 0.25$, $\hat{q} = 0.75$

3. *a.* 35 *c.* 72 *e.* 27
b. 5.4 *d.* 144

4. *a.* 144 *c.* 225 *e.* 175
b. 32.5 *d.* 90

5. *a.* $\bar{p} = 0.5$; $\bar{q} = 0.5$
b. $\bar{p} = 0.491$; $\bar{q} = 0.509$
c. $\bar{p} = 0.455$; $\bar{q} = 0.545$
d. $\bar{p} = 0.667$; $\bar{q} = 0.333$
e. $\bar{p} = 0.638$; $\bar{q} = 0.362$

6. *a.* $\bar{p} = 0.378$; $\bar{q} = 0.622$
b. $\bar{p} = 0.5$; $\bar{q} = 0.5$
c. $\bar{p} = 0.597$; $\bar{q} = 0.403$
d. $\bar{p} = 0.34$; $\bar{q} = 0.66$
e. $\bar{p} = 0.209$; $\bar{q} = 0.791$

7. $\hat{p}_1 = 0.4$; $\hat{p}_2 = 0.32$; $\bar{p} = 0.36$; $\bar{q} = 0.64$; H_0: $p_1 = p_2$ and H_1: $p_1 \neq p_2$ (claim); C.V. = ±1.96; $z = 0.83$; do not reject H_0. There is not enough evidence to support the claim that the proportions are different. $-0.1075 < p_1 - p_2 < 0.2675$; $P = 0.4047$.

8. $\hat{p}_1 = 0.88$; $\hat{p}_2 = 0.96$; $\bar{p} = 0.93$; $\bar{q} = 0.07$; H_0: $p_1 = p_2$ and H_1: $p_1 \neq p_2$ (claim); C.V. = ±1.65; $z = -3.04$; reject H_0. (TI interval: $-0.128 < p_1 - p_2 < 0.032$) There is enough evidence to support the claim that there is a difference in the proportions. A researcher might want to find out why people feel that they have less leisure time now as opposed to 10 years ago. Are they working more? Raising a family? etc. $P = 0.0024$.

9. $\hat{p}_1 = 0.7$; $\hat{p}_2 = 0.625$; $\bar{p} = 0.67$; $\bar{q} = 0.33$; H_0: $p_1 = p_2$ and H_1: $p_1 \neq p_2$ (claim); C.V. $= \pm 1.65$; $z = 0.78$; do not reject H_0. There is not enough evidence to support the claim that the proportions are different. $P = 0.4346$.

10. $\hat{p}_1 = \frac{10}{73} = 0.14$; $\hat{p}_2 = \frac{16}{80} = 0.20$; $\bar{p} = 0.17$; $\bar{q} = 0.83$; H_0: $p_1 = p_2$ and H_1: $p_1 \neq p_2$ (claim); C.V. $= \pm 1.96$; $z = -0.99$ (TI: $z = -1.04$); do not reject H_0. No, there is not enough evidence to support the claim that there is a difference in the proportions. $-0.181 < p_1 - p_2 < 0.055$; $P = 0.3000$.

11. $\hat{p}_1 = 0.6$; $\hat{p}_2 = 0.7$; $\bar{p} = 0.643$; $\bar{q} = 0.357$; H_0: $p_1 = p_2$ and H_1: $p_1 \neq p_2$ (claim); C.V. $= \pm 1.96$; $z = -1.22$; do not reject H_0. There is not enough evidence to support the claim that the proportions are different. $-0.258 < p_1 - p_2 < 0.05802$; $P = 0.2217$.

12. $\hat{p}_1 = 0.55$; $\hat{p}_2 = 0.35$; $\bar{p} = 0.43$; $\bar{q} = 0.57$; H_0: $p_1 = p_2$ and H_1: $p_1 \neq p_2$ (claim); $z = 2.80$; P-value $= 0.0052$; reject H_0. There is enough evidence to support the claim that the proportions are different.

13. $\hat{p}_1 = 0.3$; $\hat{p}_2 = 0.12$; $\bar{p} = 0.231$; $\bar{q} = 0.769$; H_0: $p_1 = p_2$ and H_1: $p_1 > p_2$ (claim); C.V. $= 1.28$; $z = 2.37$; reject H_0. There is enough evidence to support the claim that the proportion of women who were attacked by relatives is greater than the proportion of men who were attacked by relatives. $P = 0.0089$.

14. $\hat{p}_1 = 0.287$; $\hat{p}_2 = 0.347$; $\bar{p} = 0.317$; $\bar{q} = 0.683$; H_0: $p_1 = p_2$; H_1: $p_1 < p_2$ (claim); C.V. $= -1.65$; $z = -1.12$; do not reject H_0. There is insufficient evidence to conclude that the proportion of women is higher. $P = 0.1320$.

15. $\hat{p}_1 = 0.68$; $\hat{p}_2 = 0.75$; $\bar{p} = 0.718$; $\bar{q} = 0.282$; H_0: $p_1 = p_2$ and H_1: $p_1 \neq p_2$ (claim); C.V. $= \pm 1.96$; $z = -0.81$; do not reject H_0. There is not enough evidence to support the claim that the proportions are different. $P = 0.4165$.

16. $\hat{p}_1 = 0.192$; $\hat{p}_2 = 0.13$; $-0.0115 < p_1 - p_2 < 0.1355$. The interval does not support the claim that there is a difference because 0 is contained in the interval and thus allows for the possibility that no difference exists.

17. $\hat{p}_1 = 0.5$; $\hat{p}_2 = 0.4$; $\bar{p} = 0.4571$; $\bar{q} = 0.5429$; H_0: $p_1 = p_2$ and H_1: $p_1 \neq p_2$ (claim); C.V. $= \pm 2.58$; $z = 1.18$; do not reject H_0. There is not enough evidence to support the claim that the proportions are different. $P = 0.2398$.

18. $\hat{p}_1 = 0.71$; $\hat{p}_2 = 0.74$; $\bar{p} = 0.724$; $\bar{q} = 0.276$; H_0: $p_1 = p_2$; H_1: $p_1 \neq p_2$ (claim); C.V. $= \pm 2.58$; $z = -0.78$; do not reject H_0. There is not enough evidence to support the claim that the proportions are different. $P = 0.4334$.

19. $-0.053 < p_1 - p_2 < 0.0836$.

20. $\hat{p}_1 = 0.429$; $\hat{p}_2 = 0.25$; $\bar{p} = 0.333$; $\bar{q} = 0.667$; H_0: $p_1 = p_2$ and H_1: $p_1 > p_2$ (claim); C.V. $= 1.28$; $z = 2.31$; reject H_0. There is enough evidence to support the claim that the proportion of single men who give their sweethearts candy is greater than the proportion who give their sweethearts perfume. $P = 0.0103$.

21. $\hat{p}_1 = 0.80$; $\hat{p}_2 = 0.60$; $\bar{p} = 0.69$; $\bar{q} = 0.31$; H_0: $p_1 = p_2$ and H_1: $p_1 \neq p_2$ (claim); C.V. $= \pm 2.58$; $z = 5.05$; reject H_0. There is enough evidence to support the claim that the proportions are different. $P < 0.0001$.

22. $\hat{p}_1 = 0.817$; $\hat{p}_2 = 0.783$; $\bar{p} = 0.8$; $\bar{q} = 0.2$; H_0: $p_1 = p_2$; H_1: $p_1 \neq p_2$ (claim); C.V. $= \pm 1.96$; $z = 2.04$; reject H_0. There is enough evidence to support the claim that the proportions are different. $P = 0.0412$.

23. $\hat{p}_1 = 0.6$, $\hat{p}_2 = 0.533$; $\bar{p} = 0.563$, $\bar{q} = 0.437$. H_0: $p_1 = p_2$ and H_1: $p_1 \neq p_2$ (claim); C.V. $= \pm 2.58$; $z = 1.10$; do not reject H_0. There is not enough evidence to support the claim that the proportion of males who commit interview errors is different from the proportion of females who commit interview errors. $P = 0.2725$.

24. $\hat{p}_1 = 0.57$, $\hat{p}_2 = 0.4$; $\bar{p} = 0.485$, $\bar{q} = 0.515$; H_0: $p_1 = p_2$ and H_1: $p_1 \neq p_2$ (claim); C.V. $= \pm 1.96$; $z = 3.40$; reject H_0. There is enough evidence to support the claim that the proportions are different. $P = 0.0007$.

25. $\hat{p}_1 = 0.30$; $\hat{p}_2 = 0.48$; $\bar{p} = 0.39$; $\bar{q} = 0.61$; H_0: $p_1 = p_2$ and H_1: $p_1 \neq p_2$ (claim); $z = -1.85$; P-value $= 0.0650$; reject H_0. There is enough evidence to support the claim that the proportions are different.

26. $\hat{p}_1 = 0.312$, $\hat{p}_2 = 0.290$; $\bar{p} = 0.302$, $\bar{q} = 0.698$; H_0: $p_1 = p_2$ and H_1: $p_1 > p_2$ (claim); $z = 0.51$; P-value $= 0.3050$; do not reject H_0. There is not enough evidence to support the claim that the proportion of men who never have been married is greater than the proportion of women who never have been married. $P = 0.3068$.

27. $\hat{p}_1 = 0.065$; $\hat{p}_2 = 0.08$; $\bar{p} = 0.0725$; $\bar{q} = 0.9275$; H_0: $p_1 = p_2$; H_1: $p_1 \neq p_2$ (claim); C.V. $= \pm 1.96$; $z = -0.58$; do not reject H_0. There is insufficient evidence to conclude a difference. $P = 0.5630$.

28. No, p_1 could equal p_3.

Exercises 9–6

1. The variance in the numerator should be the larger of the two variances.

2. The larger variance is placed in the numerator of the formula; hence, $F \geq 1$.

3. One degree of freedom is used for the variance associated with the numerator, and one is used for the variance associated with the denominator.

4. The characteristics of the F distribution are as follows:
   a. The values of F cannot be negative.
   b. The distribution is positively skewed.
   c. The mean value of the F distribution is approximately equal to 1.
   d. The F distribution is a family of curves based on the degrees of freedom.

5. a. d.f.N. $= 30$; d.f.D. $= 23$; C.V. $= 2.24$
   b. d.f.N. $= 7$; d.f.D. $= 9$; C.V. $= 2.51$
   c. d.f.N. $= 8$; d.f.D. $= 16$; C.V. $= 3.89$

6. a. d.f.N. $= 10$; d.f.D. $= 6$; C.V. $= 7.87$
   b. d.f.N. $= 40$; d.f.D. $= 28$; C.V. $= 1.82$
   c. d.f.N. $= 12$; d.f.D. $= 12$; C.V. $= 3.28$

7. Specific P-values are in parentheses.
   a. $0.025 < P$-value < 0.05 (0.033)
   b. $0.05 < P$-value < 0.10 (0.072)
   c. P-value $= 0.05$
   d. $0.005 < P$-value < 0.01 (0.006)

8. *a.* P-value = 0.05

   b. P-value > 0.10 (0.112)

   c. 0.05 < P-value < 0.10 (0.068)

   d. 0.01 < P-value < 0.02 (0.015)

9. H_0: $\sigma_1^2 = \sigma_2^2$; H_1: $\sigma_1^2 \neq \sigma_2^2$ (claim); C.V. = 3.43; d.f.N. = 12; d.f.D. = 11; $F = 2.08$; do not reject H_0. There is not enough evidence to support the claim that the variances are different. $P = 0.2340$.

10. H_0: $\sigma_1 = \sigma_2$ and H_1: $\sigma_1 \neq \sigma_2$ (claim); C.V. = 2.51; d.f.N. = 23; d.f.D. = 19; $F = 3.35$; reject H_0. There is enough evidence to support the claim that the standard deviations are different. $P = 0.0097$.

11. H_0: $\sigma_1^2 = \sigma_2^2$ and H_1: $\sigma_1^2 \neq \sigma_2^2$ (claim); C.V. = 4.99; d.f.N. = 7; d.f.D. = 7; $F = 1.00$; do not reject H_0. There is not enough evidence to support the claim that there is a difference in the variances. $P > 0.9999$.

12. H_0: $\sigma_1^2 = \sigma_2^2$; H_1: $\sigma_1^2 \neq \sigma_2^2$ (claim); C.V. = 4.36; d.f.N. = 9; d.f.D. = 8; $F = 6.19$; reject H_0. There is enough evidence to support the claim that the variances are not equal. $P = 0.0173$.

13. H_0: $\sigma_1^2 = \sigma_2^2$; H_1: $\sigma_1^2 > \sigma_2^2$ (claim); C.V. = 4.950; d.f.N. = 6; d.f.D. = 5; $F = 9.80$; reject H_0. There is sufficient evidence at $\alpha = 0.05$ to conclude that the variance in area is greater for Eastern cities. C.V. = 10.67; do not reject H_0. There is insufficient evidence to conclude the variance is greater at $\alpha = 0.01$. $P = 0.0121$.

14. H_0: $\sigma_1^2 = \sigma_2^2$ and H_1: $\sigma_1^2 \neq \sigma_2^2$ (claim); C.V. = 2.75; d.f.N. = 10; d.f.D. = 12; $F = 2.97$; reject H_0. There is enough evidence to support the claim that the variances are not equal. $P = 0.0778$.

15. H_0: $\sigma_1^2 = \sigma_2^2$; H_1: $\sigma_1^2 > \sigma_2^2$ (claim); C.V. = 2.90; d.f.N. = 9; d.f.D. = 11; $F = 1.588$; do not reject H_0. There is not enough evidence to support the claim that the variance of the scores of those under 30 is greater than the variances of those 30 and over. $P = 0.2315$.

16. H_0: $\sigma_1^2 = \sigma_2^2$ and H_1: $\sigma_1^2 < \sigma_2^2$ (claim); C.V. = 3.15; d.f.N. = 19; d.f.D. = 19; $F = 1.45$; do not reject H_0. There is not enough evidence to support the claim that the variance of the areas for the counties in Indiana is less than the variance of the areas for the counties in Iowa. $P = 0.2105$.

17. H_0: $\sigma_1^2 = \sigma_2^2$ (claim) and H_1: $\sigma_1^2 \neq \sigma_2^2$; C.V. = 3.87; d.f.N. = 6; d.f.D. = 7; $F = 3.31$; do not reject H_0. There is not enough evidence to reject the claim that the variance of the heights of the buildings in Denver is equal to the variance of the heights of the building in Nashville. $P = 0.1429$.

18. Let Group 1 = English, Group 2 = Science; H_0: $\sigma_1^2 = \sigma_2^2$; H_1: $\sigma_1^2 \neq \sigma_2^2$ (claim); C.V. = 7.69; d.f.N. = 7; d.f.D. = 8; $F = 2.401$; do not reject H_0. There is not enough evidence to say that there is a difference in the two variances. $P = 0.243$.

19. H_0: $\sigma_1^2 = \sigma_2^2$ (claim) and H_1: $\sigma_1^2 \neq \sigma_2^2$; $F = 5.32$; d.f.N. = 14; d.f.D. = 14; P-value < 0.01 (0.0035); reject H_0. There is enough evidence to reject the claim that the variances of the weights are equal. The variance for men is 2.363 and the variance for women is 0.444.

20. H_0: $\sigma_1^2 = \sigma_2^2$ and H_1: $\sigma_1^2 > \sigma_2^2$ (claim); $F = 2.91$; d.f.N. = 29; d.f.D. = 29; P-value < 0.005 (0.003); reject H_0. There is enough evidence to support the claim that the variation in the salaries of the elementary school teachers is greater than the variation in the salaries of the secondary school teachers.

21. H_0: $\sigma_1^2 = \sigma_2^2$ and H_1: $\sigma_1^2 \neq \sigma_2^2$ (claim); C.V. = 2.49; d.f.N. = 12; d.f.D. = 26; $F = 2.291$; do not reject H_0. There is not enough evidence to say that the variances are different. $P = 0.0748$.

22. H_0: $\sigma_1^2 = \sigma_2^2$; H_1: $\sigma_1^2 \neq \sigma_2^2$ (claim); C.V. = 4.03; d.f.N. = 9; d.f.D. = 9; $F = 1.18$; do not reject H_0. There is insufficient evidence to conclude a difference in variances. $P = 0.8112$.

23. H_0: $\sigma_1^2 = \sigma_2^2$; H_1: $\sigma_1^2 > \sigma_2^2$ (claim); C.V. = 2.54; d.f.N. = 10; d.f.D. = 15; $F = 1.31$; do not reject H_0. There is not enough evidence to support the claim that the students' exams who took the online course is greater than the variances of the students' exams who took the classroom course. $P = 0.3101$.

24. H_0: $\sigma_1^2 = \sigma_2^2$; H_1: $\sigma_1^2 \neq \sigma_2^2$ (claim); C.V. = 2.15; d.f.N. = 29; d.f.D. = 29; $F = 1.56$; do not reject H_0. There is not enough evidence to support the claim that the variances are different. $P = 0.2354$.

Review Exercises

1. H_0: $\mu_1 = \mu_2$ and H_1: $\mu_1 > \mu_2$ (claim); C.V. = 2.33; $z = 0.59$; do not reject H_0. There is not enough evidence to support the claim that single drivers do more pleasure driving than married drivers. $P = 0.2772$.

2. H_0: $\mu_1 = \mu_2$; H_1: $\mu_1 \neq \mu_2$ (claim); C.V. = ±2.58; $z = 3.04$; reject H_0. There is sufficient evidence to conclude a difference in mean earnings. $P = 0.0024$.

3. H_0: $\mu_1 = \mu_2$, H_1: $\mu_1 \neq \mu_2$ (claim); C.V. = ±2.861; $t = -0.901$; do not reject H_0. There is not enough evidence to support the claim that the means are different. $P = 0.3735$.

4. H_0: $\mu_1 = \mu_2$ and H_1: $\mu_1 > \mu_2$ (claim); C.V. = 1.318; $t = 1.324$; reject H_0. There is enough evidence to support the claim that it is warmer in Birmingham. $P = 0.0959$.

5. H_0: $\mu_1 = \mu_2$ and H_1: $\mu_1 \neq \mu_2$ (claim); C.V. = ±2.624; d.f. = 14; $t = 6.540$; reject H_0. Yes, there is enough evidence to support the claim that there is a difference in the receptionists' salaries. $\$3447.80 < \mu_1 - \mu_2 < \$8068.20$ $P < 0.0001$.

6. H_0: $\mu_1 = \mu_2$ and H_1: $\mu_1 \neq \mu_2$ (claim); d.f. = 2; $t = -0.810$; do not reject H_0. Since $P > 0.10$, there is not enough evidence to support the claim that the means are different. A cafeteria manager would want to choose the company that offered the best contract. $P = 0.4647$.

7. H_0: $\mu_D = 10$; H_1: $\mu_D > 10$ (claim); C.V. = 2.821; d.f. = 9; $t = 3.249$; reject H_0. There is sufficient evidence to conclude that the difference in temperature is greater than 10 degrees. $P = 0.005$.

8. H_0: $\mu_D = 0$, H_1: $\mu_D < 0$ (claim); C.V. = -2.015; d.f. = 5; $t = -8.94$; reject H_0. There is enough evidence to support the claim that the review improved the student's scores. $P = 0.0001$.

9. $\hat{p}_1 = 0.245$, $\hat{p}_2 = 0.31$, $\bar{p} = 0.2775$, $\bar{q} = 0.7225$;
H_0: $p_1 = p_2$; H_1: $p_1 \neq p_2$ (claim); C.V. = ± 1.96;
$z = -1.45$; do not reject H_0. There is not enough evidence
to support the claim that the proportions are different.
$P = 0.1466$.

10. $\hat{p}_1 = 0.60$; $\hat{p}_2 = 0.56$; $\bar{p} = 0.582$; $\bar{q} = 0.418$;
H_0: $p_1 = p_2$; H_1: $p_1 \neq p_2$ (claim); C.V. = ± 2.58;
$z = 0.42$; do not reject H_0. There is not enough evidence to
support the claim that the proportions of men and women
who gamble are different. $P = 0.6719$.

11. H_0: $\sigma_1 = \sigma_2$ and H_1: $\sigma_1 \neq \sigma_2$ (claim); C.V. = 2.77;
$\alpha = 0.10$; d.f.N. = 23; d.f.D. = 10; $F = 10.37$; reject H_0.
There is enough evidence to support the claim that there
is a difference in the standard deviations. $P = 0.0005$.

12. H_0: $\sigma_1^2 = \sigma_2^2$; H_1: $\sigma_1^2 \neq \sigma_2^2$ (claim); C.V. = 4.90;
d.f.N. = 8; d.f.D. = 7; $F = 4.62$; do not reject H_0. There is
insufficient evidence to conclude a difference in
variances. $P = 0.0582$.

13. H_0: $\sigma_1^2 = \sigma_2^2$; H_1: $\sigma_1^2 \neq \sigma_2^2$ (claim); C.V. = 5.42;
d.f.N. = 11; d.f.D. = 11; $F = 1.11$; do not reject H_0.
There is not enough evidence to support the claim that the
variances are not equal. $P = 0.8648$.

Chapter Quiz

1. False. When testing the difference between two means, it
is important to distinguish whether or not the samples are
independent.

2. False. The samples could be either independent or
dependent, depending on other factors.

3. True

4. False. Tests for variances can be either one- or two-tailed.

5. d 6. a

7. c 8. a

9. $\mu_1 = \mu_2$ 10. t

11. Normal   12. Negative

13. $F = \dfrac{s_1^2}{s_2^2}$

14. H_0: $\mu_1 = \mu_2$ and H_1: $\mu \neq \mu_2$ (claim); $z = -3.69$;
C.V. = ± 2.58; reject H_0. There is enough evidence
to support the claim that there is a difference in the
cholesterol levels of the two groups. $-10 < \mu_1 - \mu_2 < -2$
$P = 0.0002$.

15. H_0: $\mu_1 = \mu_2$ and H_1: $\mu_1 > \mu_2$ (claim); C.V. = 1.28; $z = 1.61$;
reject H_0. There is enough evidence to support the claim
that the average rental fees for a room in the East are
greater than the average rental fees for a room in the West.
$P = 0.0537$.

16. H_0: $\mu_1 = \mu_2$ and H_1: $\mu_1 \neq \mu_2$ (claim); $t = 11.094$;
d.f. = 11; C.V. = ± 3.106; reject H_0. There is enough
evidence to support the claim that the average prices
are different. $0.29 < \mu_1 - \mu_2 < 0.51$.
(TI: Interval $0.2995 < \mu_1 - \mu_2 < 0.50049$) $P < 0.0001$

17. H_0: $\mu_1 = \mu_2$ and H_1: $\mu_1 < \mu_2$ (claim); C.V. = -2.132;
d.f. = 4; $t = -4.046$; reject H_0. There is enough evidence
to support the claim that accidents have increased.
$P = 0.0043$.

18. H_0: $\mu_1 = \mu_2$ and H_1: $\mu_1 \neq \mu_2$ (claim); $t = 9.807$;
d.f. = 11; C.V. = ± 2.718; reject H_0. There is enough
evidence to support the claim that the salaries are different.
$\$6653 < \mu_1 - \mu_2 < \$11,757$ (TI: Interval $\$6619 < \mu_1 - \mu_2$
$< \$11,491$) $P < 0.0001$.

19. H_0: $\mu_1 = \mu_2$ and H_1: $\mu_1 > \mu_2$ (claim); d.f. = 10; $t = 0.874$;
$P = 0.198$; do not reject H_0 since P-value > 0.05. There is
not enough evidence to support the claim that the incomes
of city residents are greater than the incomes of rural
residents.

20. H_0: $\mu_D = 0$ and H_1: $\mu_D < 0$ (claim); $t = -4.172$; d.f. = 9;
C.V. = -2.821; reject H_0. There is enough evidence to
support the claim that the sessions improved math skills.
$P = 0.0012$.

21. H_0: $\mu_D = 0$ and H_1: $\mu_D < 0$ (claim); $t = -1.714$;
d.f. = 9; C.V. = -1.833; do not reject H_0. There is not
enough evidence to support the claim that egg production
was increased. $P = 0.0603$.

22. $\hat{p}_1 = 0.05$, $\hat{p}_2 = 0.08$, $\bar{p} = 0.0615$, $\bar{q} = 0.9385$;
H_0: $p_1 = p_2$ and H_1: $p_1 \neq p_2$ (claim); $z = -0.69$;
C.V. = ± 1.65; do not reject H_0. There is not enough
evidence to support the claim that the proportions are
different. $-0.105 < p_1 - p_2 < 0.045$; $P = 0.4886$.

23. $\hat{p}_1 = 0.04$, $\hat{p}_2 = 0.03$, $\bar{p} = 0.035$, $\bar{q} = 0.965$;
H_0: $p_1 = p_2$ and H_1: $p_1 \neq p_2$ (claim); C.V. = ± 1.96;
$z = 0.54$; do not reject H_0. There is not enough evidence
to support the claim that the proportions have changed.
$-0.026 < p_1 - p_2 < 0.046$. Yes, the confidence interval
contains 0; hence, the null hypothesis is not rejected.
$P = 0.5864$.

24. H_0: $\sigma_1^2 = \sigma_2^2$ and H_1: $\sigma_1^2 \neq \sigma_2^2$ (claim); $F = 1.64$; d.f.N. = 17;
d.f.D. = 14; P-value > 0.20 (0.357). Do not reject H_0 since
P-value > 0.05. There is not enough evidence to support
the claim that the variances are different.

25. H_0: $\sigma_1^2 = \sigma_2^2$ and H_1: $\sigma_1^2 \neq \sigma_2^2$ (claim); $F = 1.30$;
C.V. = 1.90; do not reject H_0. There is not enough
evidence to support the claim that the variances are
different. $P = 0.4891$.

Chapter 10
Exercises 10–1

1. Two variables are related when a discernible pattern exists
between them.

2. Relationships are measured by the correlation coefficient.
When r is near $+1$, there is a strong positive linear relationship between the variables. When r is near -1, there
is a strong negative linear relationship. When r is near 0,
there is no linear relationship between the variables.

3. r, ρ (rho)

4. The range of r is from -1 to $+1$.

5. A positive relationship means that as x increases,
y increases. A negative relationship means that as
x increases, y decreases.

6. Answers will vary.

7. The diagram is called a scatter plot. It shows the nature of
the relationship.

8. Pearson product moment correlation coefficient

9. *t* test

10. No, there are many other possibilities, such as chance or relationship to a third variable.

11. H_0: $\rho = 0$; H_1: $\rho \neq 0$; $r = -0.923$; C.V. $= \pm 0.707$; reject H_0. There is enough evidence to say that there is a significant negative linear relationship between the ages of the drivers and the number of accidents over a 3-year period. $P = 0.0011$.

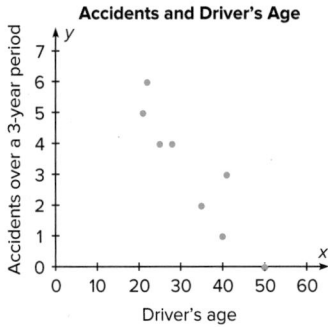

Accidents and Driver's Age

12. H_0: $\rho = 0$; H_1: $\rho \neq 0$; $r = 0.914$; C.V. $= \pm 0.497$; reject H_0. There is enough evidence to say that there is a significant positive linear relationship between the College Algebra final exam and the Statistics final exam grades. $P = 0.0000007$.

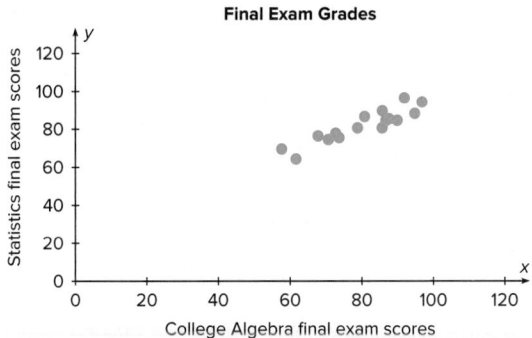

Final Exam Grades

13. H_0: $\rho = 0$; H_1: $\rho \neq 0$; $r = 0.880$; C.V. $= \pm 0.666$; reject H_0. There is sufficient evidence to conclude that a significant linear relationship exists between the number of releases and gross receipts. $P = 0.0017$.

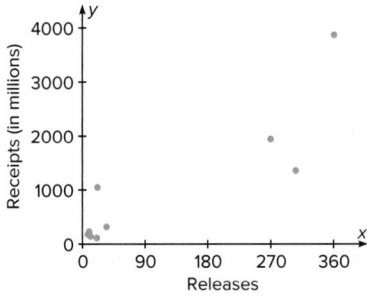

14. H_0: $\rho = 0$; H_1: $\rho \neq 0$; $r = 0.771$; C.V. $= \pm 0.707$; reject H_0. There is a significant linear relationship between the number of forest fires and the number of acres burned. $P = 0.0253$.

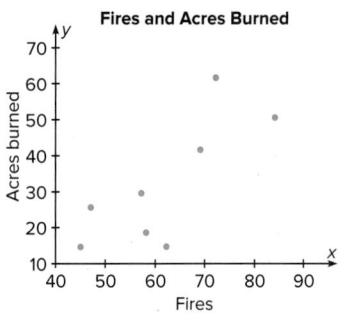

Fires and Acres Burned

15. H_0: $\rho = 0$; H_1: $\rho \neq 0$; $r = -0.883$; C.V. $= \pm 0.811$; reject H_0. There is a significant linear relationship between the number of years a person has been out of school and the person's contribution. $P = 0.0198$.

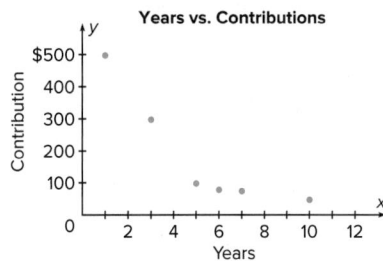

Years vs. Contributions

16. H_0: $\rho = 0$; H_1: $\rho \neq 0$; $r = 0.705$; C.V. $= \pm 0.878$; do not reject H_0. There is insufficient evidence to conclude a linear relationship exists between per capita debt and tax. $P = 0.1833$.

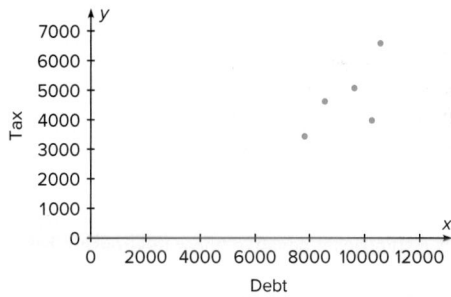

17. H_0: $\rho = 0$; H_1: $\rho \neq 0$; $r = 0.939$; C.V. $= \pm 0.754$; reject H_0. There is enough evidence to say that there is a significant linear relationship between sodium content and blood pressure. $P = 0.0017$.

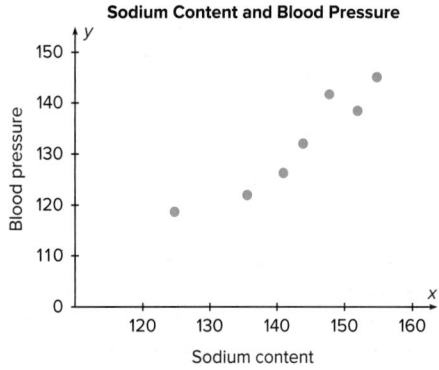

Sodium Content and Blood Pressure

18. $H_0: \rho = 0$; $H_1: \rho \neq 0$; $r = -0.920$; C.V. $= \pm 0.576$; reject H_0. There is enough evidence to say that there is a significant negative linear relationship between the number of hours students spend watching videos and their GPAs. $P = 0.00002$.

Hours Watching Videos and GPA

19. $H_0: \rho = 0$; $H_1: \rho \neq 0$; $r = 0.573$; C.V. $= \pm 0.602$; do not reject H_0. There is not enough evidence to conclude that there is a significant linear relationship between exports and imports. $P = 0.0656$.

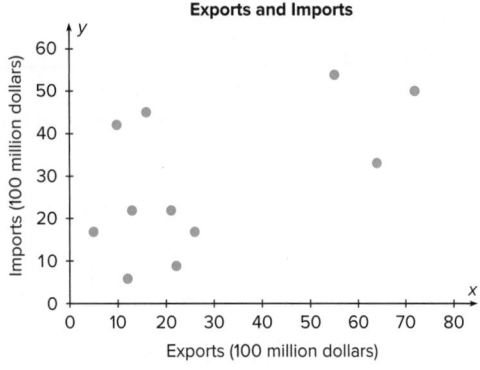

Exports and Imports

20. $H_0: \rho = 0$; $H_1: \rho \neq 0$; $r = -0.993$; C.V. $= \pm 0.754$; reject H_0. There is a significant negative linear relationship between the number of grams of water and the number of grams of carbohydrates in 100-gram servings of fruits and vegetables. $P < 0.0001$.

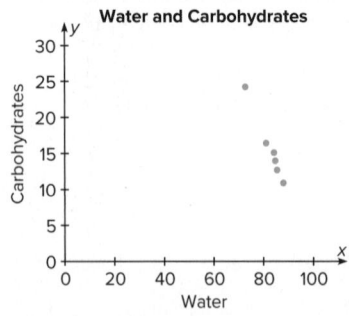

Water and Carbohydrates

21. $H_0: \rho = 0$; $H_1: \rho \neq 0$; $r = 0.812$; C.V. $= \pm 0.754$; reject H_0. There is a significant linear relationship between the number of faculty and the number of students at small colleges. When the values for x and y are switched, the

results are identical. The independent variable is most likely the number of students. $P = 0.0265$.

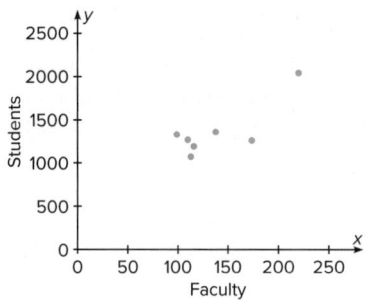

22. $H_0: \rho = 0$; $H_1: \rho \neq 0$; $r = -0.093$; C.V. $= \pm 0.878$; do not reject H_0. There is not enough evidence to say that there is a significant linear relationship between the number of automobiles and the number of light commercial vehicles produced. $P = 0.8820$.

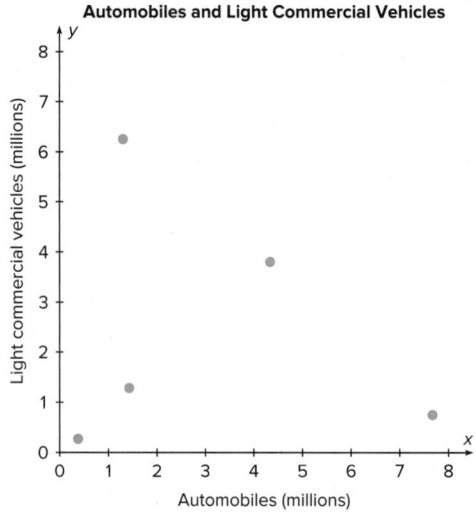

Automobiles and Light Commercial Vehicles

23. $H_0: \rho = 0$; $H_1: \rho \neq 0$; $r = 0.956$; C.V. $= \pm 0.754$; reject H_0. There is enough evidence to say that there is a significant linear relationship between the number of nuclear reactors a country has and the number of megawatts (in thousands) of energy generated. $P = 0.00075$.

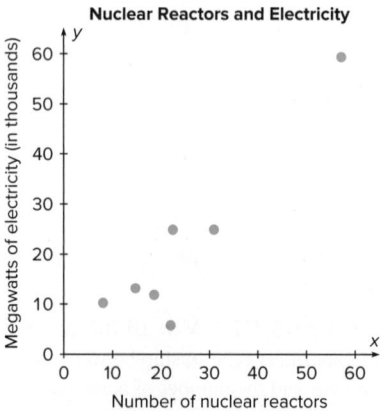

Nuclear Reactors and Electricity

24. $H_0: \rho = 0$; $H_1: \rho \neq 0$; $r = 0.862$; C.V. = ± 0.632; reject H_0. There is enough evidence to support the claim that there is a significant linear relationship between the number of cities visited and the number of shows. $P = 0.0013$.

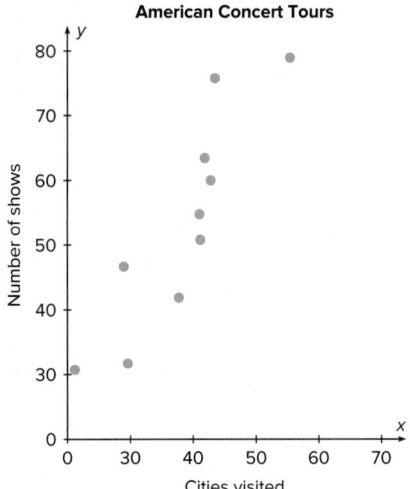

25. $H_0: \rho = 0$; $H_1: \rho \neq 0$; $r = -0.935$; C.V. = ± 0.632; reject H_0; there is enough evidence to say that there is a significant negative linear relationship between the AQI and the person's score on a memory test. $P = 0.00007$.

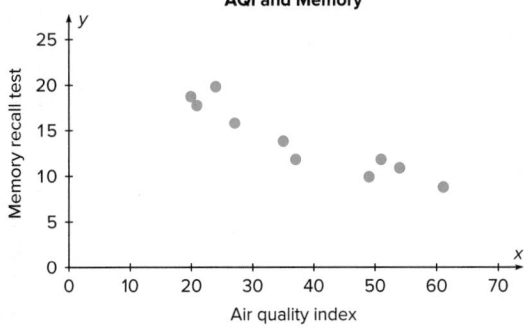

26. $H_0: \rho = 0$; $H_1: \rho \neq 0$; $r = 0.010$; C.V. = ± 0.754; do not reject H_0. There is not enough evidence to say there is a significant linear relationship between the number of ships and the amount of cargo transported. $P = 0.9825$.

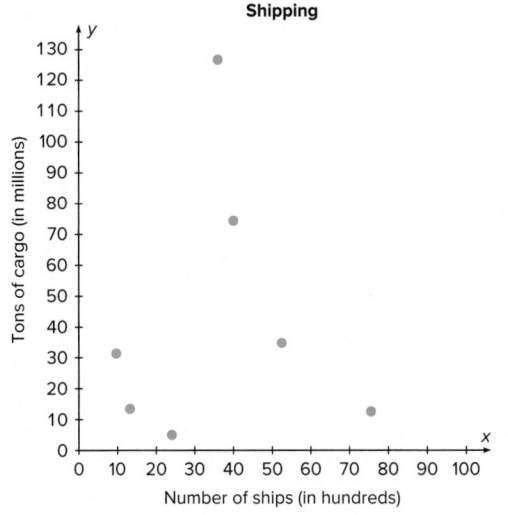

27. $H_0: \rho = 0$; $H_1: \rho \neq 0$; $r = -0.673$; C.V. = ± 0.811; do not reject H_0. There is not enough evidence to say that there is a significant linear relationship between class size and average grades for students. $P = 0.1429$.

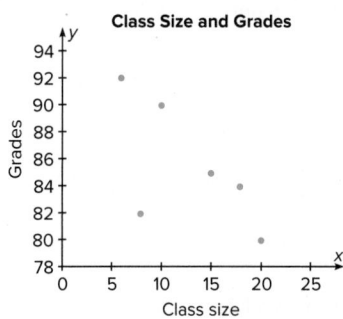

28. $r = -0.673$. The results are the same. (*Note:* There may be a slight difference due to rounding.)

29. $r = 1.00$: All points fall in a straight line. $r = 1.00$: The value of r between x and y is the same when x and y are interchanged.

30. $H_0: \rho = 0$; $H_1: \rho \neq 0$; C.V. = ± 0.754; d.f. = 5; do not reject. $r = 0$. The relationship is nonlinear as shown.

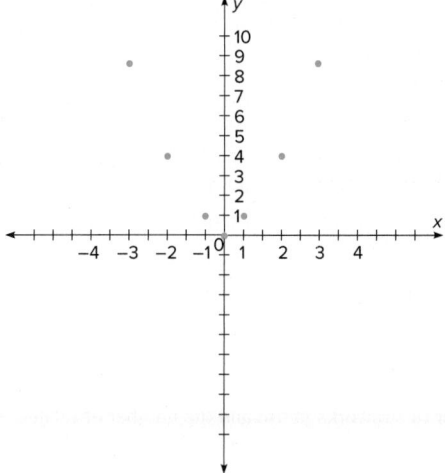

31. $H_0: \rho = 0$; $H_1: \rho \neq 0$ for both conferences; $r_1 = 0.973$; $r_2 = 0.993$; C.V. = ± 0.754. Both correlations are significant; however, the one for the Western Conference is slightly higher than the one for the Eastern Conference. $P = 0.0002$ and $P = 0.000009$.

Exercises 10–2

1. A scatter plot should be drawn, and the value of the correlation coefficient should be tested to see whether it is significant.

2. a. The sample is a random sample.

b. For any specific value of the independent variable x, the value of the dependent variable y must be normally distributed about the regression line.

c. The standard deviation of each of the dependent variables must be the same for each value of the independent variable.

3. $y' = a + bx$

4. b, a

5. It is the line that is drawn on a scatter plot such that the sum of the squares of the vertical distances from each point to the line is a minimum.

6. r would equal $+1$ or -1.

7. When r is positive, b will be positive. When r is negative, b will be negative.

8. They would be clustered closer to the line.

9. The closer r is to $+1$ or -1, the more accurate the predicted value will be.

10. When r is not significant, the mean of the y values should be used to predict y.

11. $y' = 9.022 - 0.180x$; $y' = 3.62$ or 4 accidents.

12. $y' = 27.964 + 0.676x$; $y' = 82.017$

13. $y' = 181.661 + 7.319x$; $y' = 1645.4$ (million $)

14. $y' = -31.460 + 1.036x$; 30.7 acres

15. $y' = 453.176 - 50.439x$; $251.42

16. Since r is not significant, no regression should be done.

17. $y' = 0.015 + 0.922x$; $y' = 131.9$

18. $y' = 4.028 - 0.067x$; $y' = 2.681$

19. Since r is not significant, no regression should be done.

20. $y' = 87.409 - 0.868x$; $y' = 22.309$ grams of carbohydrates

21. $y' = -14.974 + 0.111x$

22. Since r is not significant, no regression should be done.

23. $y' = -8.374 + 1.171x$; $y' = 38.466$ thousand megawatts

24. $y' = -4.609 + 1.502x$; $y' = 47.961$

25. $y' = 23.409 - 0.246x$; $y' = 13.584$

26. Since r is not significant, no regression should be done.

27. Since r is not significant, no regression should be done.

28. $H_0: \rho = 0$; $H_1: \rho \neq 0$; $r = -0.260$; C.V. $= \pm 0.811$; do not reject H_0. There is insufficient evidence to conclude there is a significant linear relationship between the number of fireworks in use and the number of related injuries. No regression should be done. $P = 0.6185$.

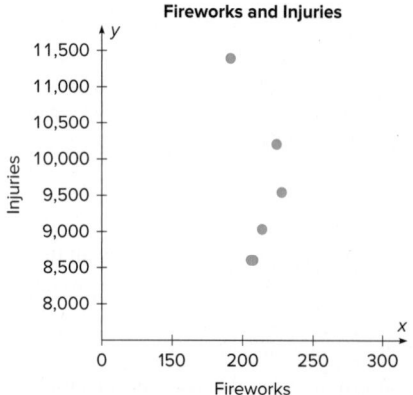

29. $H_0: \rho = 0$; $H_1: \rho \neq 0$; $r = 0.429$; C.V. $= \pm 0.811$; do not reject H_0. There is insufficient evidence to conclude a relationship exists between number of farms and acreage. $P = 0.3958$.

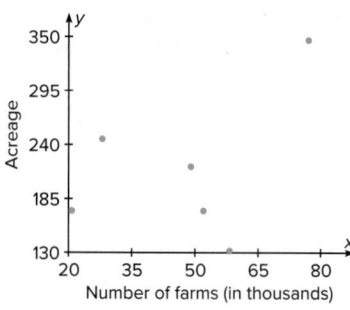

30. $H_0: \rho = 0$; $H_1: \rho \neq 0$; $r = 0.990$; C.V. $= \pm 0.811$; reject H_0. There is sufficient evidence to conclude a relationship exists between verbal and mathematical scores. $y' = 63.472 + 0.900x$; $P = 0.0002$.

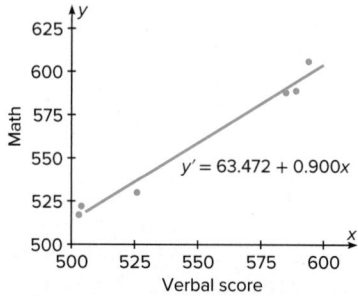

31. $H_0: \rho = 0$; $H_1: \rho \neq 0$; $r = 0.970$; C.V. $= \pm 0.707$; reject H_0; $y' = -33.358 + 6.703x$; when $x = 500$, $y' = 3318.142$, or about 3318 tons. There is a significant relationship between number of employees and tons of coal produced. $P < 0.0001$.

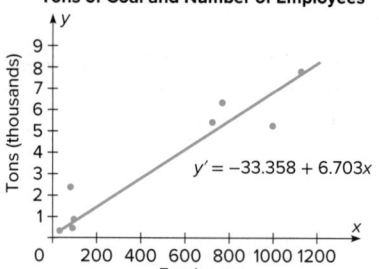

32. $H_0: \rho = 0$; $H_1: \rho \neq 0$; $r = 0.839$; C.V. $= \pm 0.632$; reject H_0. There is a significant linear relationship between the number of viewers of last year's show and the number of viewers of the same shows this year. $y' = -3.668 + 1.281x$; $P = 0.0024$.

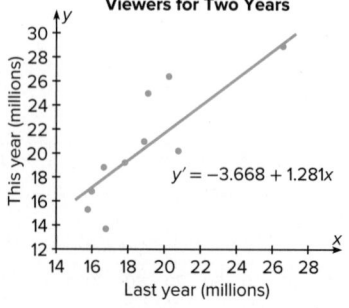

33. $H_0: \rho = 0$; $H_1: \rho \neq 0$; $r = -0.981$; C.V. $= \pm 0.811$; reject H_0. There is a significant linear relationship between the number of absences and the final grade. $y' = 96.784 - 2.668x$; $P = 0.0006$.

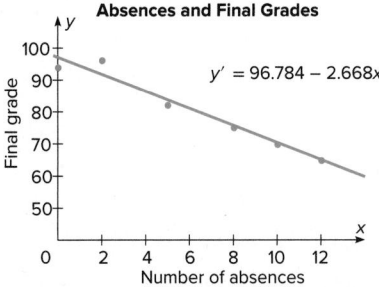

34. $H_0: \rho = 0$; $H_1: \rho \neq 0$; $r = 0.959$; $P = 0.0006$; reject H_0. There is a significant relationship between the number of wins and the total points scored. $y' = 16.901 + 2.545x$; $y' = 50$.

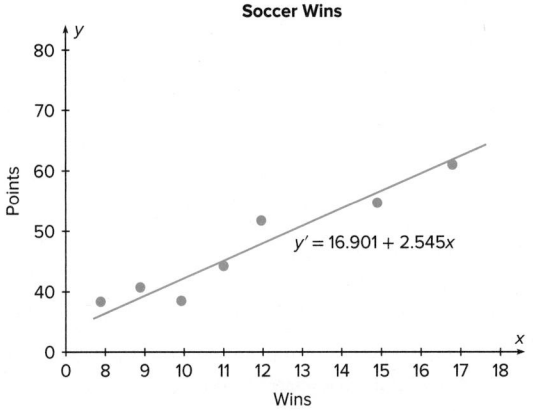

35. $H_0: \rho = 0$; $H_1: \rho \neq 0$; $r = 0.800$; $P = 0.0172$; reject H_0. There is a significant linear relationship between the number of twins born and the number of quadruplets born. $y' = -1441.049 + 12.838x$; $y' = 279$.

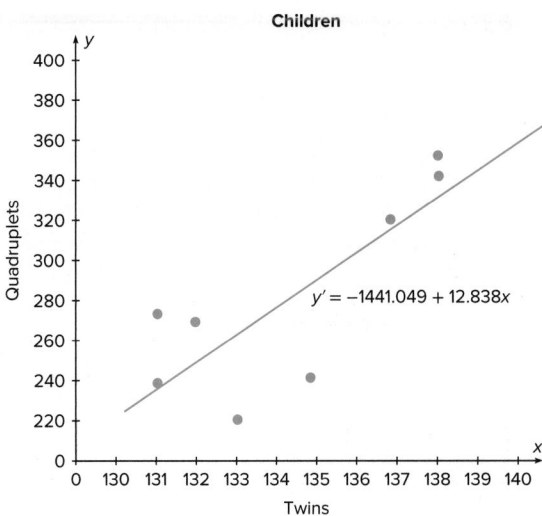

36. $\bar{y} = y' = 1031.44$; $\bar{y} = y' = 184$; $\bar{y} = y' = 136.6$; in all cases, $\bar{y} = y'$; hence, the regression line will always pass through the point $(\overline{X}, \overline{Y})$. Slight differences occur due to rounding.

37. 453.173; regression should not be done.

38. $r = 0.968$; $r = -0.993$

Exercises 10–3

1. Explained variation is the variation due to the relationship. It is computed by $\Sigma(y' - \bar{y})^2$.

2. Unexplained variation is the variation due to chance. It is computed by $\Sigma(y - y')^2$.

3. Total variation is the sum of the squares of the vertical distances of the points from the mean. It is computed by $\Sigma(y - \bar{y})^2$.

4. The coefficient of determination is a measure of variation of the dependent variable that is explained by the regression line and the independent variable.

5. The coefficient of determination is found by squaring the value of the correlation coefficient.

6. It is the percent of the variation in y that is not due to the variation in x.

7. The coefficient of nondetermination is found by subtracting r^2 from 1.

8. $r^2 = 0.3844$; 38.44% of the variation of y is due to the variation of x; 61.56% is due to chance.

9. $r^2 = 0.1936$; 19.36% of the variation of y is due to the variation of x; 80.64% is due to chance.

10. $r^2 = 0.2601$; 26.01% of the variation of y is due to the variation of x; 73.99% is due to chance.

11. $r^2 = 0.9409$; 94.09% of the variation of y is due to the variation of x; 5.91% is due to chance.

12. $r^2 = 0.0144$; 1.44% of the variation of y is due to the variation of x; 98.56% is due to chance.

13. $r^2 = 0.0225$; 2.25% of the variation of y is due to the variation of x; 97.75% is due to chance.

14. The standard error of the estimate is the standard deviation of the observed y values about the predicted y' values. It can be used when you are using the t distribution.

15. 629.49

16. 12.03* (TI value 12.06)

17. 94.22*

18. The standard error should not be calculated.

19. $365.82 < y < 2924.98$

20. $0 < y < 62$

21. $\$31.12 < y < \$471.72$

22. The prediction interval should not be calculated.

*Answers may vary due to rounding.

Exercises 10–4

1. Simple regression has one dependent variable and one independent variable. Multiple regression has one dependent variable and two or more independent variables.

2. $y' = a + b_1x_1 + b_2x_2 + \cdots + b_kx_k$; a is the y-intercept and the b's are the partial regression coefficients.

3. The relationship would include all variables in one equation.

4. Normality, equal variance, linearity, nonmulticollinearity, and independence

5. They will all be smaller.

6. $40,834

7. 7.5

8. $196.49

9. 85.75 (grade) or 86

10. 149.885 or 150

11. R is the strength of the relationship between the dependent variable and all the independent variables.

12. 0 to 1

13. R^2 is the coefficient of multiple determination. R^2_{adj} is adjusted for sample size and number of predictors.

14. $H_0: \rho = 0$ and $H_1: \rho \neq 0$

15. F test

16. It is the adjusted coefficient of multiple determination. It is computed when sample size is small and is a better estimate since R^2 is larger when sample size is small. ($n \approx k$)

Review Exercises

1. $H_0: \rho = 0$; $H_1: \rho \neq 0$; $r = 0.864$; C.V. = ± 0.917; d.f. = 4; do not reject H_0. There is not a significant linear relationship between the rating and the amount that they spent. No regression analysis should be done. $P = 0.0263$.

2. $H_0: \rho = 0$; $H_1: \rho \neq 0$; $r = 0.440$; d.f. = 5; C.V. = ± 0.875; do not reject H_0. There is not enough evidence to say that there is a significant linear relationship between the number of lightning deaths for people who were under a tree and the number of lightning deaths for people who were at other places. Since r is not significant, no regression should be done. $P = 0.3235$.

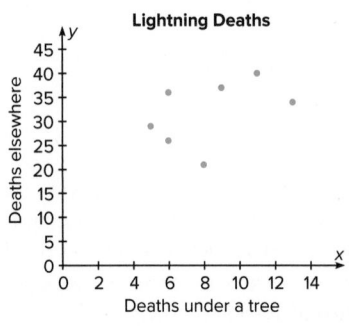

3. $H_0: \rho = 0$; $H_1: \rho \neq 0$; $r = 0.761$; C.V. = ± 0.834; d.f. = 6; do not reject H_0. There is not a significant linear relationship between the rating and the cost. No regression analysis should be done. $P = 0.0284$.

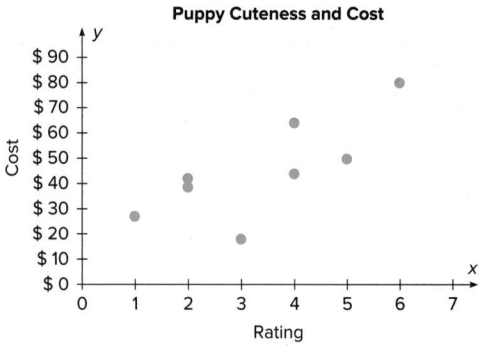

4. $H_0: \rho = 0$; $H_1: \rho \neq 0$; $r = -0.610$; C.V. = ± 0.875; d.f. = 5; do not reject H_0. There is not a significant linear relationship between age and the number of accidents a person has. No regression analysis should be done, since the null hypothesis has not been rejected. $P = 0.1458$.

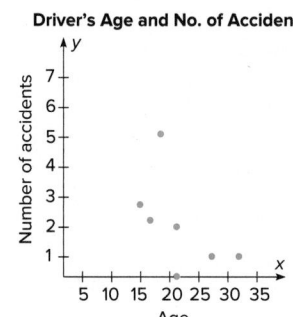

5. $H_0: \rho = 0$; $H_1: \rho \neq 0$; $r = -0.974$; C.V. = ± 0.708; d.f. = 10; reject H_0. There is a significant linear relationship between speed and time; $y' = 14.086 - 0.137x$; $y' = 4.2$ hours. $P < 0.0001$.

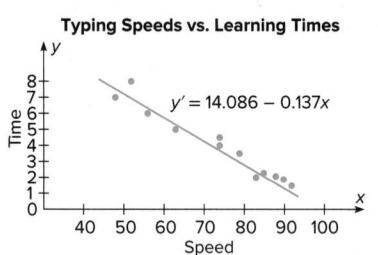

6. $H_0: \rho = 0$; $H_1: \rho \neq 0$; $r = 0.916$; C.V. = ± 0.798; d.f. = 7; reject H_0. There is a significant linear relationship between grams and pressure. $y' = 64.936 + 2.662x$; $y' = 86.23$ $P = 0.0005$.

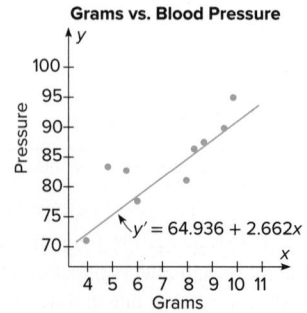

7. $H_0: \rho = 0$; $H_1: \rho \neq 0$; $r = 0.510$; C.V. $= \pm 0.959$; d.f. $= 3$ do not reject H_0. There is not a significant linear relationship between Internet use and isolation. No regression should be done since r is not significant. $P = 0.3808$.

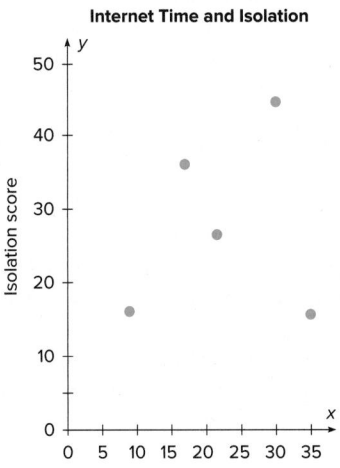

Internet Time and Isolation

8. 1.417* For calculation purposes only. No regression should be done.
9. 0.513*
10. 2.845*
11. $3.24 < y < 5.18$
12. $79.11 < y < 93.35$
13. 22.01*
14. $R = 0.873$
15. $R^2_{adj} = 0.643$*

*Answers may vary due to rounding.

Chapter Quiz

1. False. A negative relationship between two variables means that as one variable increases, the other variable decreases.
2. True
3. True
4. False. Even if the correlation coefficient is significant, you cannot assume that the variation of one variable causes the variation of the other variable.
5. False. Significant correlations can be attributed by chance alone.
6. False. In multiple regression, there are several independent variables and one dependent variable.
7. a
8. a
9. d
10. c
11. b
12. Scatter plot
13. Independent
14. $-1, +1$
15. b (slope)
16. Line of best fit
17. $+1, -1$
18. $H_0: \rho = 0$; $H_1: \rho \neq 0$; d.f. $= 5$; $r = 0.600$; C.V. $= \pm 0.754$; do not reject H_0. There is no significant linear relationship between the price of the same drugs in the United States and in Australia. No regression should be done. $P = 0.1547$.

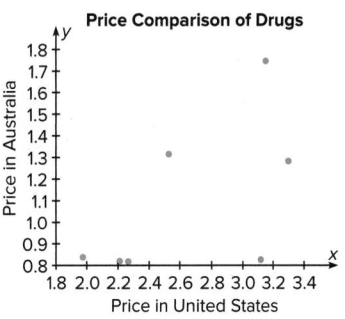

Price Comparison of Drugs

19. $H_0: \rho = 0$; $H_1: \rho \neq 0$; d.f. $= 5$; $r = -0.078$; C.V. $= \pm 0.754$; do not reject H_0. No regression should be done.

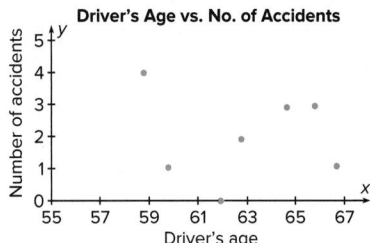

Driver's Age vs. No. of Accidents

20. $H_0: \rho = 0$; $H_1: \rho \neq 0$; $r = 0.842$; d.f. $= 4$; C.V. $= \pm 0.811$; reject H_0. $y' = -1.918 + 0.551x$; 4.14 or 4; $P = 0.0356$.

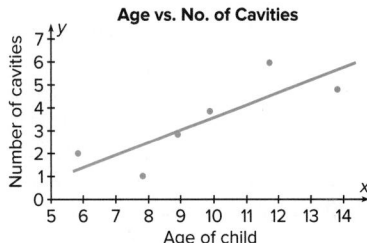

Age vs. No. of Cavities

21. $H_0: \rho = 0$; $H_1: \rho \neq 0$; $r = 0.602$; d.f. $= 6$; C.V. $= \pm 0.707$; do not reject H_0. No regression should be done. $P = 0.1145$.

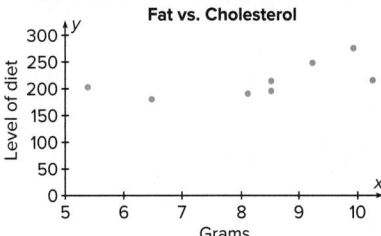

Fat vs. Cholesterol

22. 1.129*
23. 29.5* For calculation purposes only. No regression should be done.
24. $0 < y < 5$
25. 217.5 (average of y values is used since there is no significant relationship)
26. 119.9*
27. $R = 0.729$*
28. $R^2_{adj} = 0.439$*

*These answers may vary due to the method of calculation or rounding.

Chapter 11

Exercises 11–1

1. The variance test compares a sample variance with a hypothesized population variance; the goodness-of-fit test compares a distribution obtained from a sample with a hypothesized distribution.

2. The degrees of freedom are the number of categories minus 1.

3. The expected values are computed on the basis of what the null hypothesis states about the distribution.

4. The classes should be combined with another class.

5. H_0: The customers show no preference for the type of hoagies that they purchase. H_1: The customers show a preference for the type of hoagies that they purchase (claim). C.V. $= 11.345$; $\chi^2 = 41.68$; d.f. $= 3$; reject H_0. There is enough evidence to support the claim that there is a preference for the type of hoagies that customers prefer. $P < 0.01$.

6. H_0: The blood type of the patients is type A $= 20\%$, type B $= 28\%$, type O $= 36\%$, and type AB $= 16\%$ (claim). H_1: The distribution differs from those of the population. C.V. $= 6.251$; d.f. $= 3$; $\alpha = 0.10$; $\chi^2 = 5.471$; do not reject H_0. There is not enough evidence to reject the claim that the distribution is the same as the general population. $P = 0.1404$.

7. H_0: The distribution is as follows: 40% get guns from friends, 30% get guns from family members, 20% get guns from the street, and 10% get guns from other sources (claim). H_1: The distribution is not the same as stated in the null hypothesis. C.V. $= 7.815$; $\chi^2 = 3.45$; d.f. $= 3$; do not reject H_0. There is not enough evidence to reject the claim stated in the null hypothesis. $P = 0.3273$.

8. H_0: The distribution is as follows: 45% of used tires are dumped illegally, 26% are recycled, 17% are exported, and 12% are burned (claim). H_1: The distribution is different than stated in the null hypothesis. C.V. $= 7.815$; $\chi^2 = 1.932$; d.f. $= 3$; $\alpha = 0.05$; do not reject H_0. There is not enough evidence to reject the claim that the distribution is not the same as stated in the null hypothesis. $P = 0.5866$.

9. H_0: 35% feel that genetically modified food is safe to eat, 52% feel that genetically modified food is not safe to eat, and 13% have no opinion. H_1: The distribution is not the same as stated in the null hypothesis (claim). C.V. $= 9.210$; d.f. $= 2$; $\alpha = 0.01$; $\chi^2 = 1.429$; do not reject H_0. There is not enough evidence to support the claim that the proportions are different from those reported in the poll. $P = 0.4894$.

10. H_0: The distribution of truck colors is white, 31%; black, 19%; silver, 11%; red, 11%; gray, 10%; blue, 8%, and other, 10%. H_1: The distribution differs from that stated in the null hypothesis (claim). C.V. $= 12.592$; d.f. $= 6$; $\alpha = 0.05$; $\chi^2 = 21.655$; reject H_0. There is enough evidence to support the claim that the distribution differs from that stated in the null hypothesis. $P = 0.0014$.

11. H_0: The proportions of voters in each category are equal. (claim). H_1: The proportions of voters in each category are not equal. C.V. $= 9.348$; $\chi^2 = 3.5$; d.f. $= 3$; do not reject H_0. There is not enough evidence to reject the claim that the proportions are equal. $P = 0.3208$.

12. H_0: The distribution is as follows: firearms, 75%; knives, 15%; hands, 6%; and blunt objects, 4%. H_1: The distribution is different than that stated in the null hypothesis (claim). C.V. $= 7.815$; $\chi^2 = 13.65$; d.f. $= 3$; reject H_0. There is enough evidence to support the claim that the distribution is different than that stated in the null hypothesis. $P = 0.0034$.

13. H_0: 10% of the annual deaths from firearms occurred at birth to age 19 years, 50% were from ages 20–44, and 40% were ages 45 years and over. H_1: The distribution is not the same as stated in the null hypothesis (claim). C.V. $= 5.991$; d.f. $= 2$; $\alpha = 0.05$; $\chi^2 = 9.405$; reject H_0. There is enough evidence to support the claim that the proportions are different from those stated by the National Safety Council. $P = 0.0091$.

14. H_0: The ages of the crime victims are equally distributed over the four categories. H_1: The ages of the crime victims are not equally distributed over the four categories (claim). C.V. $= 6.251$; $\chi^2 = 8.4$; d.f. $= 3$; reject H_0. There is enough evidence to support the claim that the ages are not equally distributed over the four categories. $P = 0.0384$.

15. H_0: The proportions of the favorite flavor choices by the subjects are equally distributed over the categories (claim). H_1: The proportions of the favorite flavor choices by the subjects are not equally distributed over the categories. C.V. $= 9.348$; $\chi^2 = 3.6$; d.f. $= 3$; do not reject H_0. There is not enough evidence to reject the claim that the proportions of choices by the subjects are equally distributed over the categories. $P = 0.3080$.

16. H_0: The occurrences of work place violence are equally distributed over the six categories of reasons (claim). H_1: The occurrences of work place violence are not equally distributed over the six categories of reasons. C.V. $= 11.071$; $\chi^2 = 18.9$; d.f. $= 5$; reject H_0. There is enough evidence to reject the claim that the occurrences are equally distributed over the six categories. $P = 0.002$.

17. H_0: The number of returns is equally distributed over the seven-day week (claim). H_1: The number of returns is not equally distributed over the seven-day week. C.V. $= 10.645$; $\chi^2 = 11.702$; TI: 11.719; d.f. $= 6$; reject H_0. There is enough evidence to reject the claim that the number of returns is equally distributed over the seven days. $P = 0.0700$.

18. H_0: The number of magazines sold for the three types of magazines is equally distributed. H_1: The number of magazines sold for the three types of magazines is not equally distributed (claim). C.V. $= 4.605$; $\chi^2 = 2.70$; d.f. $= 2$; do not reject H_0. There is not enough evidence to say that the number of magazines sold is not equally distributed. $P = 0.2592$.

19. H_0: The coins are balanced and randomly tossed (claim). H_1: The coins are not balanced or are not randomly tossed. C.V. $= 7.815$; d.f. $= 3$; $\chi^2 = 139.407$; reject the null hypothesis. There is enough evidence to reject the claim that the coins are balanced and randomly tossed. $P < 0.0001$.

20. Answers will vary.

Exercises 11–2

1. The independence test and the goodness-of-fit test both use the same formula for computing the test statistic. However, the independence test uses a contingency table, whereas the goodness-of-fit test does not.

2. d.f. = (rows − 1)(columns − 1)

3. H_0: The variables are independent (or not related). H_1: The variables are dependent (or related).

4. Contingency table

5. The expected values are computed as (row total × column total) ÷ grand total.

6. H_0: $p_1 = p_2 = p_3 = p_4 = \cdots = p_n$. H_1: At least one proportion is different from the others.

7. H_0: The living arrangement of a person is independent of the gender of the person. H_1: The living arrangement of a person is dependent upon the gender of the person (claim). C.V. = 7.815; d.f. = 3; $\alpha = 0.05$; $\chi^2 = 1.674$; do not reject H_0. There is not enough evidence to support the claim that the living arrangement is dependent on the gender of the individual. $P = 0.6427$.

8. H_0: The types of accidents are independent of the gender of the individual. H_1: The types of accidents are related to the gender of the individual (claim). C.V. = 7.815; $\chi^2 = 0.682$; d.f. = 3; do not reject H_0. There is not enough evidence to say that the type of accident is related to the gender of the individual. $P = 0.8774$.

9. H_0: Pet ownership is independent of the number of persons living in the household. H_1: Pet ownership is dependent on the number of persons living in the household (claim). C.V. = 6.251; d.f. = 3; $\alpha = 0.10$; $\chi^2 = 2.235$; do not reject H_0. There is not enough evidence to support the claim that pet ownership is dependent on the number of persons living in the household. $P = 0.5251$.

10. H_0: The types of accidents are independent of the ages of the individual. H_1: The types of accidents are related to the ages of the individuals (claim). C.V. = 6.251; $\chi^2 = 3.965$; d.f. = 3; do not reject H_0. There is not enough evidence to support the claim that the types of accidents are related to the gender of the individuals. $P = 0.2653$.

11. H_0: The types of violent crimes committed are independent of the cities where they are committed. H_1: The types of violent crimes committed are dependent upon the cities where they are committed (claim). C.V. = 12.592; d.f. = 6; $\alpha = 0.05$; $\chi^2 = 43.890$; reject H_0. There is enough evidence to support the claim that the types of violent crimes are dependent upon the cities where they are committed. $P < 0.0001$.

12. H_0: The reasons that people are out of work is independent of the gender of the individuals. H_1: The reasons that people are out of work is related to the gender of the individuals (claim). C.V. = 4.605; $\chi^2 = 11.832$; d.f. = 2; reject H_0. There is enough evidence to support the claim that the reasons people are out of work is related to the gender of the individual. $P = 0.0027$.

13. H_0: The length of unemployment time is independent of the type of industry where the worker is employed. H_1: The length of unemployment time is dependent upon the type of industry where the worker is employed (claim). C.V. = 9.488; d.f. = 4; $\alpha = 0.05$; $\chi^2 = 4.974$; do not reject H_0. There is not enough evidence to support the claim that the length of unemployment time is dependent upon the type of industry where the worker is employed. $P = 0.2899$.

14. H_0: The types of mall crimes are independent of the gender of the criminals. H_1: The types of mall crimes are related to the gender of the criminals (claim). C.V. = 5.991; $\chi^2 = 3.080$; d.f. = 2; do not reject H_0. There is not enough evidence to support the claim that the types of mall crimes are related to the gender of the criminals. $P = 0.2144$.

15. H_0: The program of study of a student is independent of the type of institution. H_1: The program of study of a student is dependent upon the type of institution (claim). C.V. = 7.815; d.f. = 3; $\alpha = 0.05$; $\chi^2 = 13.702$; reject H_0. There is sufficient evidence to conclude that there is a relationship between program of study and type of institution. $P = 0.0033$.

16. H_0: The type of transplant is independent of the year in which the transplant was received. H_1: The type of transplant is dependent upon the year it was received (claim). C.V. = 13.277; d.f. = 4; $\alpha = 0.01$; $\chi^2 = 23.211$; reject H_0. There is sufficient evidence to conclude that a relationship exists between year and type of transplant. $P = 0.0001$.

17. H_0: The type of automobile owned by a person is independent of the gender of the individual. H_1: The type of automobile owned by a person is dependent on the gender of the individual (claim). C.V. = 6.251; d.f. = 3; $\alpha = 0.10$; $\chi^2 = 7.337$; reject H_0. There is enough evidence to support the claim that the type of automobile is related to the gender of the owner. $P = 0.0619$.

18. H_0: The types of commercial advertisements are independent of the products or services advertised. H_1: The types of commercial advertisement are related to the products or services advertised (claim). C.V. = 7.815; $\chi^2 = 2.272$; d.f. = 3; do not reject H_0. There is not enough evidence to support the claim that the types of advertisements are related to the products or services advertised. $P = 0.5180$.

19. H_0: The type of vitamin pill preferred by an individual is independent on the age of the person taking the pill. H_1: The type of vitamin pill preferred by the individual is dependent on the age of the individual (claim). C.V. = 7.779; d.f. = 4; $\alpha = 0.10$; $\chi^2 = 18.860$; reject H_0. There is enough evidence to support the claim that the type of vitamin pill preferred is dependent upon the age of the individual. $P = 0.0008$.

20. H_0: The drug results do not differ from the placebo results. H_1: The drug results differ from the placebo results. $\alpha = 0.10$; $\chi^2 = 10.642$; d.f. = 1; P-value = 0.001; reject H_0. There is enough evidence to support the claim that the drug results differ from the placebo.

21. H_0: $p_1 = p_2 = p_3$ (claim). H_1: At least one proportion is different from the others. C.V. = 4.605; d.f. = 2; $\alpha = 0.10$; $\chi^2 = 5.749$; reject H_0. There is enough evidence to reject the claim that the proportions are equal. $P = 0.0565$.

22. H_0: $p_1 = p_2 = p_3 = p_4$ (claim). H_1: At least one proportion is different (claim). C.V. = 7.815; d.f. = 3; $\alpha = 0.05$; $\chi^2 = 7.788$; do not reject H_0. There is insufficient evidence to conclude that the proportions differ. $P = 0.0506$.

23. H_0: $p_1 = p_2 = p_3 = p_4$ (claim). H_1: At least one proportion is different. C.V. = 7.815; d.f. = 3; $\alpha = 0.05$; $\chi^2 = 5.317$; do not reject H_0. There is not enough evidence to reject the claim that the proportions are equal. $P = 0.1500$.

24. H_0: $p_1 = p_2 = p_3$ (claim); H_1: At least one proportion is different. C.V. = 7.378; d.f. = 2; $\alpha = 0.025$; $\chi^2 = 1.323$; do not reject H_0. There is not enough evidence to reject the claim that the proportions are equal. $P = 0.5160$.

25. H_0: $p_1 = p_2 = p_3 = p_4$ (claim); H_1: At least one proportion is different. C.V. = 7.815; d.f. = 3; $\alpha = 0.05$; $\chi^2 = 3.454$; do not reject H_0. There is not enough evidence to reject the claim that the proportions are equal. $P = 0.3268$.

26. H_0: $p_1 = p_2 = p_3$ (claim); H_1: At least one proportion is different from the others. C.V. = 7.378; d.f. = 2; $\alpha = 0.025$; $\chi^2 = 2.009$; do not reject H_0. There is not enough evidence to reject the claim that the proportions are equal. $P = 0.3662$.

27. H_0: $p_1 = p_2 = p_3 = p_4$ (claim); H_1: At least one proportion is different. C.V. = 7.815; d.f. = 3; $\alpha = 0.05$; $\chi^2 = 3.266$; do not reject H_0. There is not enough evidence to reject the claim that the proportions are equal. $P = 0.3523$.

28. H_0: $p_1 = p_2 = p_3 = p_4$ (claim). H_1: At least one proportion is different. C.V. = 7.815; d.f. = 3; $\alpha = 0.05$; $\chi^2 = 5.000$; do not reject H_0. There is not enough evidence to reject the claim that the proportions are equal. $P = 0.1718$.

29. H_0: $p_1 = p_2 = p_3 = p_4$ (claim); H_1: At least one proportion is different than the others. C.V. = 6.251; d.f. = 3; $\alpha = 0.10$; $\chi^2 = 1.25$; do not reject H_0. There is not enough evidence to reject the claim that the proportions are equal. $P = 0.7389$.

30. H_0: $p_1 = p_2 = p_3 = p_4$ (claim). H_1: At least one proportion is different. $\alpha = 0.10$; $\chi^2 = 4.334$; d.f. = 3; P-value > 0.10 (0.228); do not reject H_0 since P-value > 0.10. There is not enough evidence to reject the claim that the proportions are equal.

31. H_0: $p_1 = p_2 = p_3 = p_4$; H_1: At least one proportion is different from the others (claim). C.V. = 6.251; d.f. = 3; $\alpha = 0.10$; $\chi^2 = 4.156$; do not reject H_0. There is not enough evidence to support the claim that at least one proportion is different from the others. $P = 0.2451$.

32. Both answers are the same. $\chi^2 = 1.70$.

33. $\chi^2 = 1.064$

34. 0.0919; 0.3610

Review Exercises

1. H_0: The distribution of traffic fatalities was as follows: used seat belt, 31.58%; did not use seat belt, 59.83%; status unknown, 8.59%. H_1: The distribution is not as stated in the null hypothesis (claim). C.V. = 5.991; d.f. = 2; $\alpha = 0.05$; $\chi^2 = 1.819$; do not reject H_0. There is not enough evidence to support the claim that the distribution differs from the one stated in the null hypothesis. $P = 0.4027$.

2. H_0: The distribution of the reasons why workers were displaced is as follows: plant closed or moved, 44.8%; insufficient work, 25.2%; and position eliminated, 30%. H_1: The distribution of reasons why workers were displaced is not the same as stated in the null hypothesis (claim). C.V. = 9.210; d.f. = 2; $\alpha = 0.01$; $\chi^2 = 5.418$; do not reject H_0. There is not enough evidence to support the claim that the distribution is different from that stated in the null hypothesis. $P = 0.0666$.

3. H_0: The distribution of denials for gun permits is as follows: 75% for criminal history, 11% for domestic violence, and 14% for other reasons (claim). H_1: The distribution is not the same as stated in the null hypothesis. C.V. = 4.605; d.f. = 2; $\alpha = 0.10$; $\chi^2 = 27.753$; reject H_0. There is enough evidence to reject the claim that the distribution is as stated in the null hypothesis. Yes, the distribution may vary in different geographic locations. $P < 0.001$.

4. H_0: The employees show no preference in the type of music played. H_1: The employees show a preference for the type of music played (claim). C.V. = 7.815; d.f. = 3; $\alpha = 0.05$; $\chi^2 = 7.333$; do not reject H_0. There is not enough evidence to support the claim that there is a preference for the type of music played. $P = 0.0620$.

5. H_0: The type of investment is independent of the age of the investor. H_1: The type of investment is dependent on the age of the investor (claim). C.V. = 9.488; d.f. = 4; $\alpha = 0.05$; $\chi^2 = 27.998$; reject H_0. There is enough evidence to support the claim that the type of investment is dependent on the age of the investor. $P < 0.001$.

6. H_0: The month in which tornadoes occurred is independent of the year in which they occurred. H_1: The month in which tornadoes occurred is dependent upon the year in which they occurred (claim). C.V. = 12.592; d.f. = 6; $\alpha = 0.05$; $\chi^2 = 172.89$; reject H_0. There is sufficient evidence to conclude that a relationship exists between the month and the year in which the tornadoes occurred. $P < 0.0001$.

7. H_0: $p_1 = p_2 = p_3$ (claim). H_1: At least one proportion is different. $\alpha = 0.01$; $\chi^2 = 4.912$; d.f. = 2; $0.05 < P$-value < 0.10 (0.086); do not reject H_0 since P-value > 0.01. There is not enough evidence to reject the claim that the proportions are equal. $P = 0.086$.

8. H_0: $p_1 = p_2 = p_3 = p_4$ (claim). H_1: At least one proportion is different. C.V. = 7.815; d.f. = 3; $\alpha = 0.05$; $\chi^2 = 6.166$; do not reject H_0. There is not enough evidence to reject the claim that the proportions are equal. $P = 0.1038$.

9. H_0: $p_1 = p_2$. H_1: At least one proportion is different from the others (claim). C.V. = 7.815; d.f. = 3; $\alpha = 0.05$; $\chi^2 = 8.357$; reject H_0. There is enough evidence to support the claim that at least one proportion is different from the others. $P = 0.0392$.

10. H_0: The incidence of the cardiovascular procedure is independent of the gender of the individual. H_1: The incidence of cardiovascular procedure is dependent on the gender of the individual (claim). C.V. = 4.605; d.f. = 2; $\alpha = 0.10$; $\chi^2 = 59.949$; reject H_0. There is enough evidence to support the claim that the procedure is dependent on the gender of the individual. $P = 0.0001$.

Chapter Quiz

1. False. The chi-square test of independence can be one-tailed or two-tailed.

2. True

3. False. When the null hypothesis is rejected in the goodness-of-fit test, it means that there is not a close agreement between the observed frequencies and the expected frequencies.

4. *c*

5. *b*   6. *d*

7. 6   8. Independent

9. Right   10. At least 5

11. H_0: The reasons why people lost their jobs are equally distributed (claim). H_1: The reasons why people lost their jobs are not equally distributed. C.V. = 5.991; d.f. = 2; $\chi^2 = 2.333$; do not reject H_0. There is not enough evidence to reject the claim that the reasons why people lost their jobs are equally distributed. The results could have been different 10 years ago since different factors of the economy existed then. $P = 0.3115$.

12. H_0: Takeout food is consumed according to the following distribution: 53% at home, 19% in the car, 14% at work, and 14% at other places (claim). H_1: The distribution is different from that stated in the null hypothesis. C.V. = 11.345; d.f. = 3; $\chi^2 = 5.27$; do not reject H_0. There is not enough evidence to reject the claim that the distribution is as stated. Fast-food restaurants may want to make their advertisements appeal to those who like to take their food home to eat. $P = 0.1530$.

13. H_0: College students show the same preference for shopping channels as those surveyed. H_1: College students show a different preference for shopping channels (claim). C.V. = 7.815; d.f. = 3; $\alpha = 0.05$; $\chi^2 = 21.789$; reject H_0. There is enough evidence to support the claim that college students show a different preference for shopping channels. $P < 0.0001$.

14. H_0: The number of commuters is distributed as follows: 76.6% alone, 9.7% carpooling, 4.7% public transportation, 2.8% walking, 1.7% other, and 4.3% working at home. H_1: The proportion of workers using each type of transportation differs from the stated proportions (claim). C.V. = 11.071; d.f. = 5; $\chi^2 = 69.222$; reject H_0. There is enough evidence to support the claim that the distribution is different from the one stated in the null hypothesis. $P < 0.0001$.

15. H_0: Ice cream flavor is independent of the gender of the purchaser (claim). H_1: Ice cream flavor is dependent upon the gender of the purchaser. C.V. = 7.815; d.f. = 3; $\chi^2 = 7.198$; do not reject H_0. There is not enough evidence to reject the claim that ice cream flavor is independent of the gender of the purchaser. $P = 0.0659$.

16. H_0: The type of pizza ordered is independent of the age of the individual who purchases it. H_1: The type of pizza ordered is dependent on the age of the individual who purchases it (claim). $\chi^2 = 107.3$; d.f. = 9; $\alpha = 0.10$; P-value < 0.005; reject H_0 since P-value < 0.10. There is enough evidence to support the claim that the pizza purchased is related to the age of the purchaser. $P = 0.0001$.

17. H_0: The color of the pennant purchased is independent of the gender of the purchaser (claim). H_1: The color of the pennant purchased is dependent on the gender of the purchaser. $\chi^2 = 5.632$; d.f. = 2; C.V. = 4.605; reject H_0. There is enough evidence to reject the claim that the color of the pennant purchased is independent of the gender of the purchaser. $P = 0.0598$.

18. H_0: The opinion of the children on the use of the tax credit is independent of the gender of the children. H_1: The opinion of the children on the use of the tax credit is dependent upon the gender of the children (claim). C.V. = 4.605; d.f. = 2; $\chi^2 = 1.534$; do not reject H_0. There is not enough evidence to support the claim that the opinion of the children on the use of the tax credit is dependent on their gender. $P = 0.4642$.

19. H_0: $p_1 = p_2 = p_3$ (claim). H_1: At least one proportion is different from the others. C.V. = 4.605; d.f. = 2; $\chi^2 = 6.711$; reject H_0. There is enough evidence to reject the claim that the proportions are equal. It seems that more women are undecided about their jobs. Perhaps they want better income or greater chances of advancement. $P = 0.0349$.

Chapter 12

Exercises 12–1

1. The analysis of variance using the F test can be employed to compare three or more means.

2. a. Comparing two means at a time ignores all other means.
   b. The probability of a type I error is larger than α when multiple t tests are used.
   c. The more sample means, the more t tests are needed.

3. The populations from which the samples were obtained must be normally or approximately normally distributed. The samples must be independent of one another. The variances of the populations must be equal, and the samples should be random.

4. The between-group variance estimates the population variance using the means of each group. The within-group variance estimates the population variance using all the data values.

5. H_0: $\mu_1 = \mu_2 = \cdots = \mu_n$. H_1: At least one mean is different from the others.

6. 1

7. H_0: $\mu_1 = \mu_2 = \mu_3 = \mu_4$. H_1: At least one mean is different from the others (claim); C.V. = 3.01; d.f.N. = 3; d.f.D. = 24; $\alpha = 0.05$; $F = 1.10$; do not reject H_0. There is not enough evidence to support the claim that at least one mean is different from the others. $P = 0.3670$.

8. H_0: $\mu_1 = \mu_2 = \mu_3$. H_1: At least one mean is different from the others (claim). C.V. = 3.52; $\alpha = 0.05$; d.f.N. = 2; d.f.D. = 19; $F = 2.40$; do not reject H_0. There is not enough evidence to support the claim that at least one mean is different from the others. $P = 0.1180$.

9. H_0: $\mu_1 = \mu_2 = \mu_3$. H_1: At least one of the means differs from the others. C.V. = 4.26; d.f.N. = 2; d.f.D. = 9; $\alpha = 0.05$; $F = 14.15$; reject H_0. There is sufficient evidence to conclude at least one mean is different from the others. $P = 0.0017$.

10. H_0: $\mu_1 = \mu_2 = \mu_3 = \mu_4$; H_1: At least one mean is different from the others. (claim). C.V. = 2.93; d.f.N. = 3; d.f.D. = 29; $F = 0.812$; do not reject H_0. There is not enough evidence to conclude that at least one mean is different from the others. $P = 0.4961$.

11. H_0: $\mu_1 = \mu_2 = \mu_3 = \mu_4$; H_1: At least one mean is different from the others (claim). C.V. = 2.28; d.f.N. = 3; d.f.D. = 36; $F = 17.57$; reject H_0. There is enough evidence to say that at least one mean is different from the others. $P = 0.0000003$.

12. H_0: $\mu_1 = \mu_2 = \mu_3$. H_1: At least one mean is different from the others (claim). d.f.N. = 2; d.f.D. = 11; $\alpha = 0.05$; $F = 7.74$; P-value = 0.00797; reject H_0. There is enough evidence to conclude that at least one mean is different from the others. $P = 0.00797$.

13. H_0: $\mu_1 = \mu_2 = \mu_3$. H_1: At least one mean is different from the others (claim). C.V. = 3.68; d.f.N. = 2; d.f.D. = 15; $\alpha = 0.05$; $F = 8.14$; reject H_0. There is enough evidence to support the claim that at least one mean is different from the others. $P = 0.0040$.

14. H_0: $\mu_1 = \mu_2 = \mu_3 = \mu_4$; H_1: At least one mean is different from the others (claim). C.V. = 2.84; d.f.N. = 3; d.f.D. = 40; $F = 2.59$; do not reject H_0. There is not enough evidence to say that at least one mean is different from the others. $P = 0.0665$.

15. H_0: $\mu_1 = \mu_2 = \mu_3$; H_1: At least one mean is different from the others (claim). C.V. = 3.37; d.f.N. = 2; d.f.D. = 26; $F = 1.46$; do not reject H_0. There is not enough evidence to say that at least one mean is different from the others. $P = 0.2505$.

16. H_0: $\mu_1 = \mu_2 = \mu_3 = \mu_4$; H_1: At least one mean is different from the others (claim). C.V. = 2.92; d.f.N. = 3; d.f.D. = 38; $F = 43.293$; reject H_0. There is enough evidence to say that at least one mean is different from the others. $P = 0.000000000002$.

17. H_0: $\mu_1 = \mu_2 = \mu_3$. H_1: At least one mean is different from the others (claim). d.f.N. = 2; d.f.D. = 19; $\alpha = 0.10$; $F = 10.12$; P-value = 0.00102; reject H_0. There is enough evidence to conclude that at least one mean is different from the others. $P = 0.0010$.

18. H_0: $\mu_1 = \mu_2 = \mu_3$. H_1: At least one mean is different from the others (claim). C.V. = 4.10; d.f.N. = 2; d.f.D. = 10; $\alpha = 0.05$; $F = 14.20$; reject H_0. There is enough evidence to conclude that at least one mean is different from the others. $P = 0.0012$.

19. H_0: $\mu_1 = \mu_2 = \mu_3$; H_1: At least one mean is different from the others (claim). C.V. = 2.57; d.f.N. = 2; d.f.D. = 21; $F = 5.26$; reject H_0. There is enough evidence to say that at least one mean is different from the others. $P = 0.0141$.

20. H_0: $\mu_1 = \mu_2 = \mu_3 = \mu_4$. H_1: At least one of the means differs from the others (claim). C.V. = 3.24; d.f.N. = 3; d.f.D. = 16; $\alpha = 0.05$; $F = 5.54$; reject H_0. There is sufficient evidence to conclude that at least one of the means differs from the others. $P = 0.0080$.

Exercises 12–2

1. The Scheffé, Tukey, and Bonferroni tests can be used.

2. The Scheffé test is usually used when sample sizes are not the same. The Tukey test is usually used when the sample sizes are equal.

3. $F_{1 \times 2} = 2.06$; $F_{2 \times 3} = 17.64$; $F_{1 \times 3} = 27.923$. Scheffé test: C.V. = 8.52. There is sufficient evidence to conclude a difference in mean cost to drive 25 miles between hybrid cars and hybrid trucks and between hybrid SUVs and hybrid trucks.

4. Scheffé test: C.V. = 7.96; $\overline{X}_1$ versus $\overline{X}_2$: $F_S = 9.81$; $\overline{X}_1$ versus $\overline{X}_3$: $F_S = 0.08$; $\overline{X}_2$ versus $\overline{X}_3$: $F_S = 11.80$. There is a significant difference between $\overline{X}_1$ and $\overline{X}_2$ and between $\overline{X}_2$ and $\overline{X}_3$.

5. Tukey test: C.V. = 3.67; $\overline{X}_1 = 7.0$; $\overline{X}_2 = 8.12$; $\overline{X}_3 = 5.23$; $\overline{X}_1$ versus $\overline{X}_2$, $q = -2.20$; $\overline{X}_1$ versus $\overline{X}_3$, $q = 3.47$; $\overline{X}_2$ versus $\overline{X}_3$, $q = 5.67$. There is a significant difference between $\overline{X}_2$ and $\overline{X}_3$. One reason for the difference might be that the students are enrolled in cyber schools with different fees.

6. Scheffé test: C.V. = 5.22; $\overline{X}_1$ versus $\overline{X}_2$, $F = 2.91$; $\overline{X}_1$ versus $\overline{X}_3$, $F = 19.30$; $\overline{X}_2$ versus $\overline{X}_3$, $F = 8.40$. There is a significant difference between $\overline{X}_1$ and $\overline{X}_3$ and between $\overline{X}_2$ and $\overline{X}_3$.

7. Scheffé test: C.V. = 8.20; $\overline{X}_1$ versus $\overline{X}_2$, $F_3 = 0.94$; $\overline{X}_1$ versus $\overline{X}_3$, $F = 15.56$; $\overline{X}_2$ versus $\overline{X}_3$, $F = 26.27$. There is a significant difference between $\overline{X}_1$ and $\overline{X}_3$ and between $\overline{X}_2$ and $\overline{X}_3$.

8. *Tukey Test:* C.V. = 4.05; $\overline{X}_1$ versus $\overline{X}_2$, $q = -0.331$; $\overline{X}_1$ versus $\overline{X}_3$, $q = 0.144$; $\overline{X}_1$ versus $\overline{X}_4$, $q = -4.75$; $\overline{X}_2$ versus $\overline{X}_3$, $q = 0.475$; $\overline{X}_2$ versus $\overline{X}_4$, $q = -4.42$; $\overline{X}_3$ versus $\overline{X}_4$, $q = -4.898$. There is a significant difference between $\overline{X}_1$ and $\overline{X}_4$, $\overline{X}_2$ and $\overline{X}_4$, $\overline{X}_3$ and $\overline{X}_4$.

9. H_0: $\mu_1 = \mu_2 = \mu_3$. H_1: At least one mean is different from the others (claim). C.V. = 3.68; d.f.N. = 2; d.f.D. = 15; $F = 3.76$; reject H_0. There is enough evidence to support the claim that at least one mean differs from the others. Tukey test: C.V. = 3.67; $\overline{X}_1 = 32.33$; $\overline{X}_2 = 27.83$; $\overline{X}_3 = 22.5$; $\overline{X}_1$ versus $\overline{X}_2$, $q = 1.77$; $\overline{X}_2$ versus $\overline{X}_3$, $q = 2.10$; $\overline{X}_1$ versus $\overline{X}_3$, $q = 3.87$. There is a significant difference between $\overline{X}_1$ and $\overline{X}_3$.

10. H_0: $\mu_1 = \mu_2 = \mu_3$. H_1: At least one mean is different from the others (claim); C.V. = 7.21; d.f.N. = 2; d.f.D. = 11; $F = 2.17$; do not reject H_0. There is not enough evidence to support the claim that at least one mean is different from the others.

11. H_0: $\mu_1 = \mu_2 = \mu_3$. H_1: At least one mean is different from the others (claim). C.V. = 3.47; $\alpha = 0.05$; d.f.N. = 2; d.f.D. = 21; $F = 1.99$; do not reject. There is not enough evidence to support the claim that at least one mean is different from the others.

12. H_0: $\mu_1 = \mu_2 = \mu_3$. H_1: At least one mean is different from the others (claim). C.V. = 4.10; $\alpha = 0.05$; d.f.N. = 2; d.f.D. = 10; $F = 0.65$; do not reject H_0. There is not enough evidence to support the claim that at least one mean is different from the others.

13. H_0: $\mu_1 = \mu_2 = \mu_3$. H_1: At least one mean differs from the others (claim). C.V. = 3.68; d.f.N. = 2; d.f.D. = 15; $F = 17.17$; reject H_0. There is enough evidence to support the claim that at least one mean differs from the others. Tukey test: C.V. = 3.67; $\overline{X}_1$ versus $\overline{X}_2$, $q = -8.17$; $\overline{X}_1$ versus $\overline{X}_3$, $q = -2.91$; $\overline{X}_2$ versus $\overline{X}_3$, $q = 5.27$. There is a significant difference between $\overline{X}_1$ and $\overline{X}_2$ and between $\overline{X}_2$ and $\overline{X}_3$.

14. H_0: $\mu_1 = \mu_2 = \mu_3$; H_1: At least one mean is different from the others (claim). $F = 3.62$; $P = 0.0702$; do not reject H_0. There is not enough evidence to support the claim that at least one mean is different from the other means. No further analysis should be done since there is no significant differences in the means at $\alpha = 0.05$.

15. H_0: $\mu_1 = \mu_2 = \mu_3$; H_1: At least one mean is different from the others (claim); C.V. = 2.575; d.f.N. = 2; d.f.D. = 21; $F = 3.974$; reject H_0. There is enough evidence to say that at least one mean is different from the others. $P = 0.0344$. Bonferroni test: $\overline{X}_1$ versus $\overline{X}_2$, $t = -1.933$, $P = 0.2007$; $\overline{X}_1$ versus $\overline{X}_3$, $t = 0.659$, $P = 1$; $\overline{X}_2$ versus $\overline{X}_3$, $t = 2.706$, $P = 0.0397$. There is a significant difference between μ_1 and μ_2 and μ_2 and μ_3.

16. H_0: $\mu_1 = \mu_2 = \mu_3$; H_1: At least one mean is different from the others (claim); C.V. = 3.467; d.f.N. = 2; d.f.D. = 21; $F = 17.257$; reject H_0. There is enough evidence to say that at least one mean is different from the others. $P = 0.00004$. Bonferroni test: $\overline{X}_1$ versus $\overline{X}_2$, $t = -4.654$, $P = 0.0004$; $\overline{X}_1$ versus $\overline{X}_3$, $t = -5.424$, $P = 0.00007$; $\overline{X}_2$ versus $\overline{X}_3$, $t = -0.45$, $P = 1$. There is a significant difference between μ_1 and μ_2 and between μ_1 and μ_3.

17. H_0: $\mu_1 = \mu_2 = \mu_3$; H_1: At least one mean is different from the others (claim); C.V. = 2.276; d.f.N. = 3; d.f.D. = 30; $F = 13.48$; reject H_0. There is enough evidence to support the claim that at least one mean is different from the others. $P = 0.000009$. Bonferroni test: $\overline{X}_1$ versus $\overline{X}_2$, $t = 4.17$, $P = 0.0014$; $\overline{X}_1$ versus $\overline{X}_3$, $t = 2.226$, $P = 0.2020$; $\overline{X}_1$ versus $\overline{X}_4$, $t = 5.952$, $P = 0.0000096$; $\overline{X}_2$ versus $\overline{X}_3$, $t = -2.237$, $P = 0.1970$; $\overline{X}_2$ versus $\overline{X}_4$, $t = 1.456$, $P = 1$; $\overline{X}_3$ versus $\overline{X}_4$, $t = 3.997$, $P = 0.0023$. There is a significant difference between μ_1 and μ_2, between μ_1 and μ_4, and between μ_3 and μ_4.

18. H_0: $\mu_1 = \mu_2 = \mu_3$; H_1: At least one mean is different from the others (claim); C.V. = 3.403; d.f.N. = 2; d.f.D. = 24; $F = 5.099$; reject H_0. There is enough evidence to support the claim that at least one mean is different from the others. $P = 0.0143$. Bonferroni test: $\overline{X}_1$ versus $\overline{X}_2$, $t = -3.067$, $P = 0.0160$; $\overline{X}_1$ versus $\overline{X}_3$, $t = -2.637$, $P = 0.0433$; $\overline{X}_2$ versus $\overline{X}_3$, $t = 1.074$, $P = 1$. There is a significant difference between μ_1 and μ_2, between μ_1 and μ_3, and between μ_2 and μ_3.

Exercises 12–3

1. The two-way ANOVA allows the researcher to test the effects of two independent variables and a possible interaction effect. The one-way ANOVA can test the effects of only one independent variable.

2. The main effects are the effects of the independent variables taken separately. The interaction effect occurs when one independent variable affects the dependent variable differently at different levels of the other independent variable.

3. The mean square values are computed by dividing the sum of squares by the corresponding degrees of freedom.

4. One computes the F test statistic by dividing the mean square for the variable or interaction by the mean square for the within (error) term.

5. *a.* For factor A, $\text{d.f.}_A = 2$ *c.* $\text{d.f.}_{A \times B} = 2$
   b. For factor B, $\text{d.f.}_B = 1$ *d.* $\text{d.f.}_{\text{within}} = 24$

6. *a.* 5   *b.* 4   *c.* 20   *d.* 180

7. The two types of interactions that can occur are ordinal and disordinal.

8. The main effects can be interpreted independently when the interaction effect is not significant or the interaction is ordinal.

9. *Glycerin additives:* H_0: There is no difference in the means of the glycerin additives. H_1: There is a difference in the means of the glycerin additives.

Soap concentrations: H_0: There is no difference in the means of the soap concentrations. H_1: There is a difference in the means of the soap concentrations.

Interaction: H_0: There is no interaction between the amount of glycerin additive and the soap concentration. H_1: There is an interaction between the amount of glycerin additives.

ANOVA Summary Table

Source of variation	SS	d.f.	MS	F	P-value
Soap additive	100.00	1	100.00	5.39	0.0387
Glycerin concentration	182.25	1	182.25	9.83	0.0086
Interaction	272.25	1	272.25	14.68	0.0022
Within	222.5	12	18.54		
Total	777.0	15			

The critical value at $\alpha = 0.05$ with d.f.N. = 1 and d.f.D. = 12 is 4.75. There is a significant difference at $\alpha = 0.05$ for the interaction and a significant difference for the soap additive and the glycerin concentration. However, since the interaction is significant, the main effects should not be examined individually.

10. *Plant food:* H_0: There is no difference in the mean growth with respect to the type of plant food supplement. H_1: There is a difference in the mean growth with respect to the type of plant food supplement. *Grow-light:* H_0: There is no difference in the mean growth with respect to the strength of the Grow-light. H_1: There is a difference in the mean growth with respect to the strength of the Grow-light. *Interaction:* H_0: There is no interaction effect between the Grow-light strength and the plant food supplement. H_1: There is an interaction effect between the Grow-light strength and the plant food supplement. C.V. = 5.32; d.f.N. = 1; d.f.D. = 8; $F = 24.56$ for plant food. There is sufficient evidence to conclude there is a difference in the mean growth for the plant food. Plant light strength and the interaction have no effect.

ANOVA Summary

Source	SS	d.f.	MS	F	P-value
Plant food	12.8133	1	12.8133	24.56	0.001
Grow-light	1.9200	1	1.9200	3.68	0.091
Interaction	0.7500	1	0.7500	1.44	0.265
Within	4.1733	8	0.5217		
Total	19.6567	11			

11. *Humidity:* H_0: There is no difference in mean length of effectiveness with respect to humidity. H_1: There is a difference in mean length of effectiveness with respect to humidity. *Temperature:* H_0: There is no difference in the mean length of effectiveness based on temperature. H_1: There is a difference in mean length of effectiveness based on temperature. *Interaction:* H_0: There is no interaction effect between the temperature and the level of humidity. H_1: There is an interactive effect between the temperature and the level of humidity.

C.V. = 5.32; d.f.N. = 1; d.f.D. = 8; F = 18.38 for humidity. There is sufficient evidence to conclude a difference in mean length of effectiveness based on the humidity level. The temperature and interaction effects are not significant.

ANOVA Summary Table for Exercise 11

Source of variation	SS	d.f.	MS	F	P-value
Humidity	280.3333	1	280.3333	18.383	0.003
Temperature	3	1	3	0.197	0.669
Interaction	65.33333	1	65.33333	4.284	0.0722
Within	122	8	15.25		
Total	470.6667	11			

12. H_0: There is no difference in the means of the times it takes the subcontractors to build the homes. H_1: There is a difference in the means of the times it takes the subcontractors to build the homes.

H_0: There is no difference among the means of the times for the types of homes built. H_1: There is a difference among the means of the times for the types of homes built.

H_0: There is no interaction effect between the subcontractors and the types of homes they build on the times it takes to build the homes. H_1: There is an interaction effect between the subcontractors and the types of homes they build on the times it takes to build the homes.

ANOVA Summary Table

Source	SS	d.f.	MS	F	P-value
Subcontractor	1672.553	1	1672.553	122.08	$P < 0.0001$
Home type	444.867	2	222.434	16.24	$P < 0.0001$
Interaction	313.267	2	156.634	11.43	$P = 0.0003$
Within	328.800	24	13.700		
Total	2759.487	29			

The critical values at $\alpha = 0.05$: for the subcontractor with d.f.N. = 1 and d.f.D. = 24, C.V. = 4.26; for the home type and interaction with d.f.N. = 2 and d.f.D. = 24, C.V. = 3.40. All F test statistics exceed the critical values, and all the null hypotheses are rejected. Since there is a significant interaction effect, the means of the cells must be computed and graphed to determine the type of interaction. Cell means:

Home type			
Subcontractor	I	II	III
A	28	31.4	44.4
B	18.6	20.0	20.4

Since all three means for the home types for subcontractor A are greater than the three means for subcontractor B and the differences are not equal, there is an ordinal interaction. Hence, it can be concluded that there is a difference in means for the subcontractors and home types. In addition, there is a significant interaction between subcontractors and home types.

13. *Solution-based additive:* H_0: There is no difference in the mean durability rating with respect to the solution-based additives. H_1: There is a difference in the mean durability rating with respect to the solution-based additives. *Dry additive:* H_0: There is no difference in the mean durability rating with respect to the dry additive. H_1: There is a difference in the mean durability rating with respect to the dry additive. *Interaction:* H_0: There is no interaction effect on the durability rating between the dry additives and the solution-based additives. H_1: There is an interaction effect on the durability rating between the dry additives and the solution-based additives. C.V. = 4.75; d.f.N. = 1; d.f.D. = 12. There is not a significant interaction effect. Neither the solution additive nor the dry additive has a significant effect on mean durability.

ANOVA Summary Table for Exercise 13

Source	SS	d.f.	MS	F	P-value
Solution additive	1.563	1	1.563	0.50	0.494
Dry additive	0.063	1	0.063	0.020	0.890
Interaction	1.563	1	1.563	0.50	0.494
Within	37.750	12	3.146		
Total	40.939	15			

14. H_0: There is no difference between the means of the lifetimes of the two types of paints. H_1: There is a difference between the means of the lifetimes of the two types of paints.

H_0: There is no difference among the means of the lifetimes of the paints used in different geographic locations.

H_1: There is a difference in the means of the lifetimes of the paints used in different geographic locations.

H_0: There is no interaction effect between the type of paint and the geographic location on the lifetimes of the paint. H_1: There is an interaction effect between the type of paint and the geographic location on the lifetimes of the paint.

ANOVA Summary Table

Source	SS	d.f.	MS	F	P-value
Paint type	12.1	1	12.1	0.17	$P = 0.6829$
Location	2501.0	3	833.667	11.47	$P = 0.0001$
Interaction	268.1	3	89.367	1.23	$P = 0.3149$
Within	2326.8	32	72.713		
Total	5108.0	39			

The critical values for $\alpha = 0.01$: for the paint type with d.f.N. = 1 and d.f.D. = 32 (use 30), C.V. = 7.56; for the location and interaction with d.f.N. = 3 and d.f.D. = 32 (use 30), C.V. = 4.51.

There is not a significant interaction effect, so the main effects can be interpreted. There is a significant difference in the means for the geographic location, but not for the type of paint.

15. H_0: There is no difference in the means of the monthly sales of the two age groups. H_1: There is a difference in the means of the monthly sales of the two age groups.

H_0: There is no difference among the means of the sales for the different products. H_1: There is a difference among the means of the sales for the different products.

H_0: There is no interaction effect between the ages of the salespeople and the products they sell on the monthly sales. H_1: There is an interaction effect between the ages of the salespeople and the products they sell on the monthly sales.

ANOVA Summary Table

Source	SS	d.f.	MS	F	P-value
Age	168.033	1	168.033	1.57	$P = 0.2223$
Product	1,762.067	2	881.034	8.22	$P = 0.0019$
Interaction	7,955.267	2	3,977.634	37.09	$P < 0.0001$
Within	2,574.000	24	107.250		
Total	12,459.367	29			

At $\alpha = 0.05$, the critical values are as follows: for age, d.f.N. = 1, d.f.D. = 24, C.V. = 4.26; for product and interaction, d.f.N. = 2, d.f.D. = 24, C.V. = 3.40. There is a significant interaction between the age of the salesperson and the type of product sold, so no main effects should be interpreted without further study.

Age \ Product	Pools	Spas	Saunas
Over 30	38.8	28.6	55.4
30 and under	21.2	68.6	18.8

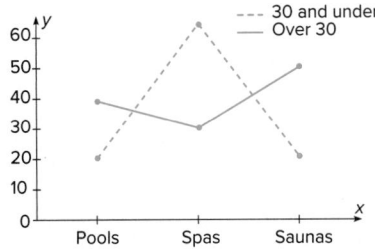

Since the lines cross, there is a disordinal interaction; hence, there is an interaction effect between the ages of salespeople and the type of products sold.

Review Exercises

1. H_0: $\mu_1 = \mu_2 = \mu_3$ (claim). H_1: At least one mean is different from the others. C.V. = 5.39; d.f.N. = 2; d.f.D. = 33; $\alpha = 0.01$; $F = 6.94$; reject H_0. Tukey test: C.V. = 4.45; $\overline{X}_1$ versus $\overline{X}_2$: $q = 0.34$; $\overline{X}_1$ versus $\overline{X}_3$: $q = 4.72$; $\overline{X}_2$ versus $\overline{X}_3$: $q = 4.38$. There is a significant difference between $\overline{X}_1$ and $\overline{X}_3$. $P = 0.0030$.

2. H_0: $\mu_1 = \mu_2 = \mu_3$. H_1: At least one of the means differs from the others. C.V. = 3.98; d.f.N. = 2; d.f.D. = 11; $F = 1.58$; do not reject H_0. There is insufficient evidence to conclude at least one mean differs from the others. $P = 0.2494$.

3. H_0: $\mu_1 = \mu_2 = \mu_3$. H_1: At least one mean is different from the others (claim). C.V. = 3.55; $\alpha = 0.05$; d.f.N. = 2; d.f.D. = 18; $F = 0.04$; do not reject H_0. There is not enough evidence to support the claim that at least one mean is different from the others. $P = 0.9602$.

4. H_0: $\mu_1 = \mu_2 = \mu_3$. H_1: At least one mean is different from the others (claim). C.V. = 6.01; $\alpha = 0.01$; d.f.N. = 2;

d.f.D. = 18; $F = 0.65$; do not reject H_0. There is not enough evidence to support the claim that at least one mean is different from the others. $P = 0.5330$.

5. H_0: $\mu_1 = \mu_2 = \mu_3$. H_1: At least one mean is different from the others (claim). C.V. = 2.61; $\alpha = 0.10$; d.f.N. = 2; d.f.D. = 19; $F = 0.49$; do not reject H_0. There is not enough evidence to support the claim that at least one mean is different from the others. $P = 0.6216$.

6. H_0: $\mu_1 = \mu_2 = \mu_3$. H_1: At least one of the means differs from the others. C.V. = 3.89; d.f.N. = 2; d.f.D. = 12; $F = 6.320$; reject H_0. There is sufficient evidence to conclude a difference in means. Tukey test: C.V. (from Table N) C.V. = 3.77; $F_{1 \times 2} = -5.0$; $F_{2 \times 3} = 2.00$; $F_{1 \times 3} = -3.04$. There is sufficient evidence to conclude a difference in mean January high temperatures between Europe and Central and South America. $P = 0.0133$.

7. H_0: $\mu_1 = \mu_2 = \mu_3 = \mu_4$. H_1: At least one mean is different from the others (claim). C.V. = 3.59; $\alpha = 0.05$; d.f.N. = 3; d.f.D. = 11; $F = 0.18$; do not reject H_0. There is not enough evidence to support the claim that at least one mean is different from the others. $P = 0.9077$.

8. H_0: $\mu_1 = \mu_2 = \mu_3 = \mu_4$. H_1: At least one mean is different from the others (claim); C.V. = 2.46; d.f.N. = 3; d.f.D. = 16; $F = 0.93$; do not reject H_0. There is not enough evidence to support the claim that at least one mean is different from the others. $P = 0.4467$.

9. *Review:* H_0: There is no difference in mean scores based on who leads the review. H_1: There is a difference in mean scores based on who leads the review. *Formulas:* H_0: There is no difference in mean scores based on who provides the formulas. H_1: There is a difference in mean scores based on who provides the formulas. *Interaction:* H_0: There is no interaction effect between type of formula delivery system and review organization. H_1: There is an interaction effect between type of formula delivery system and review organization.

C.V. = 4.49; d.f.N. = 1; d.f.D. = 16; $F = 5.244$ for review organization. There is sufficient evidence to conclude a difference in mean scores based on who leads the review. The formula and interaction effects are not significant.

ANOVA Summary Table for Exercise 9

Source of variation	SS	d.f.	MS	F	P-value
Sample	288.8	1	288.8	5.24	0.036
Columns	51.2	1	51.2	0.93	0.349
Interaction	5	1	5	0.09	0.767
Within	881.2	16	55.075		
Total	1226.2	19			

10. H_0: There is no difference in the means for the glucose levels of the people in the two exercise programs. H_1: There is a difference in the means for the glucose levels of the people in the two exercise programs.

H_0: There is no difference in the means for the glucose levels of the people in the two diet programs. H_1: There is a difference in the means for the glucose levels of the people in the two diet programs.

H_0: There is no interaction effect between the type of exercise program and the type of diet on a person's glucose level. H_1: There is an interaction effect between type of exercise program and type of diet on a person's glucose level.

ANOVA Summary Table

Source	SS	d.f.	MS	F	P-value
Exercise	816.750	1	816.750	60.50	$P < 0.0001$
Diet	102.083	1	102.083	7.56	$P = 0.0251$
Interaction	444.083	1	444.083	32.90	$P = 0.0004$
Within	108.000	8	13.500		
Total	1470.916	11			

At $\alpha = 0.05$, d.f.N. $= 1$, d.f.D. $= 8$, and the critical value is 5.32 for each F_A, F_B, and $F_{A \times B}$. Hence, all three null hypotheses are rejected. The cell means should be calculated.

Exercise \\ Diet	A	B
I	64.000	57.667
II	68.333	86.333

Since the means for exercise program I are both smaller than those for exercise program II and the vertical differences are not the same, the interaction is ordinal. Hence, you can say that there is a difference for exercise and diet, and that an interaction effect is present.

Chapter Quiz

1. False. The null hypothesis can be rejected if there is a significant difference between two means.
2. False. The F test uses degrees of freedom.
3. False. When the F test statistic is in the rejection region, the null hypothesis is rejected.
4. True
5. *d*   6. *a*
7. *a*   8. *c*
9. ANOVA   10. Tukey
11. H_0: $\mu_1 = \mu_2 = \mu_3$. H_1: At least one mean is different from the others (claim). C.V. $= 8.02$; d.f.N. $= 2$; d.f.D. $= 9$; $F = 77.69$; reject H_0. There is enough evidence to support the claim that at least one mean is different from the others. Tukey test: C.V. $= 5.43$; $\overline{X}_1 = 3.195$; $\overline{X}_2 = 3.633$; $\overline{X}_3 = 3.705$; $\overline{X}_1$ versus $\overline{X}_2$, $q = -13.99$; $\overline{X}_1$ versus $\overline{X}_3$, $q = -16.29$; $\overline{X}_2$ versus $\overline{X}_3$, $q = -2.30$. There is a significant difference between $\overline{X}_1$ and $\overline{X}_2$ and between $\overline{X}_1$ and $\overline{X}_3$. $P = 0.0100$.
12. H_0: $\mu_1 = \mu_2 = \mu_3 = \mu_4$. H_1: At least one mean is different from the others (claim). C.V. $= 3.49$; $\alpha = 0.05$; d.f.N. $= 3$; d.f.D. $= 12$; $F = 3.23$; do not reject H_0. There is not enough evidence to support the claim that there is a difference in the means. $P = 0.0609$.
13. H_0: $\mu_1 = \mu_2 = \mu_3$. H_1: At least one mean is different from the others (claim). C.V. $= 6.93$; $\alpha = 0.01$; d.f.N. $= 2$; d.f.D. $= 12$; $F = 3.49$; do not reject H_0. There is not enough evidence to support the claim that at least one mean is different from the others. Writers would want to target their material to the age group of the viewers. $P = 0.0639$.
14. H_0: $\mu_1 = \mu_2 = \mu_3$. H_1: At least one mean differs from the others (claim). C.V. $= 4.26$; d.f.N. $= 2$; d.f.D. $= 9$; $F = 10.03$; reject H_0. There is enough evidence to conclude that at least one mean differs from the others. Tukey test: C.V. $= 3.95$; $\overline{X}_1$ versus $\overline{X}_2$, $q = -1.28$; $\overline{X}_1$ versus $\overline{X}_3$, $q = 4.74$; $\overline{X}_2$ versus $\overline{X}_3$, $q = 6.02$. There is a significant difference between $\overline{X}_1$ and $\overline{X}_3$ and between $\overline{X}$ and $\overline{X}_3$. $P = 0.0051$.
15. H_0: $\mu_1 = \mu_2 = \mu_3$. H_1: At least one mean differs from the others (claim). C.V. $= 4.46$; d.f.N. $= 2$; d.f.D. $= 8$; $F = 6.65$; reject H_0. Scheffé test: C.V. $= 8.92$; $\overline{X}$ versus $\overline{X}_2$, $F_s = 9.32$; $\overline{X}_1$ versus $\overline{X}_3$, $F_s = 10.13$; $\overline{X}_2$ versus $\overline{X}_3$, $F_s = 0.13$. There is a significant difference between $\overline{X}_1$ and $\overline{X}_2$ and between $\overline{X}_1$ and $\overline{X}_3$. $P = 0.0199$.
16. H_0: $\mu_1 = \mu_2 = \mu_3 = \mu_4$. H_1: At least one mean is different from the others (claim). C.V. $= 3.07$; $\alpha = 0.05$; d.f.N. $= 3$; d.f.D. $= 21$; $F = 0.46$; do not reject H_0. There is not enough evidence to support the claim that at least one mean is different from the others. $P = 0.7131$.
17. *a.* Two-way ANOVA
   b. Diet and exercise program
   c. 2
   d. H_0: There is no difference in the means of the weight losses of people in the exercise programs. H_1: There is a difference in the means of the weight losses of people in the exercise programs.

   H_0: There is no difference in the means of the weight losses of people in the diet programs. H_1: There is a difference in the means of the weight losses of people in the diet programs.

   H_0: There is no interaction effect between the type of exercise program and the type of diet on a person's weight loss. H_1: There is an interaction effect between the type of exercise program and the type of diet on a person's weight loss.
   e. Diet: $F = 21.0$, significant; exercise program: $F = 0.429$, not significant; interaction: $F = 0.429$, not significant.
   f. Reject the null hypothesis for the diets.

Chapter 13

Exercises 13–1

1. *Nonparametric* means hypotheses other than those using population parameters can be tested; *distribution-free* means no assumptions about the population distributions have to be satisfied.
2. When the assumptions for the parametric methods cannot be met, statisticians use nonparametric methods.
3. Nonparametric methods have the following advantages:
   a. They can be used to test population parameters when the variable is not normally distributed.
   b. They can be used when data are nominal or ordinal.
   c. They can be used to test hypotheses other than those involving population parameters.

d. The computations are easier in some cases than the computations of the parametric counterparts.

e. They are easier to understand.

f. There are fewer assumptions that have to be met, and the assumptions are easier to verify.

4. The disadvantages are as follows:

   a. They are less sensitive than their parametric counterparts.

   b. They tend to use less information than their parametric counterparts.

   c. They are less efficient than their parametric counterparts.

5. Distribution-free means the samples can be selected from populations that are not normally distributed.

6. The efficiency of a nonparametric test means the percent rating of the nonparametric test compared to the corresponding parametric test to obtain the same results.

7.

Data	14	18	27	32	34	36	42
Rank	1	2	3	4	5	6	7

8.

Data	97	115	115	192	360	382
Rank	1	2.5	2.5	4	5	6

9.

Data	6.5	14.8	14.8	17.1	19.2	32.3	32.3
Rank	1	2.5	2.5	4	5	6.5	6.5

10.

Data	15.62	18.43	22.16	27.25	33.09
Rank	1	2	3	4	5

11.

Data	16	19	21	27	27	34	34	42	45
Rank	1	2	3	4.5	4.5	6.5	6.5	8	9

12.

Data	86.8	89.3	97.3	115.6	122.2	122.2	128.9	135.2
Rank	1	2	3	4	5.5	5.5	7	8

Exercises 13–2

1. The sign test uses only positive or negative signs.

2. The median

3. The smaller number of positive or negative signs

4. The normal approximation

5. H_0: median = 27 and H_1: median ≠ 27 (claim); test statistic = 5; C.V. = 3; do not reject H_0. There is not enough evidence to support the claim that the median age is not 27 years.

6. H_0: median = 11 (claim) and H_1: median ≠ 11; test statistic = 4; C.V. = 2; do not reject H_0. There is not enough evidence to reject the claim that the median debt is $11,000.

7. H_0: median = 17% (claim) and H_1: median ≠ 17%; test statistic = 7; C.V. = 5; do not reject H_0. There is not enough evidence to reject the claim that the median is 17%.

8. H_0: median = $1603 and H_1: median < $1603 (claim); test statistic = 6; C.V. = 3; do not reject H_0. There is not enough evidence to support the claim that the median is less than $1603.

9. H_0: median = 14 (claim) and H_1: median ≠ 14; test statistic = 4; C.V. = 3; do not reject H_0. There is not enough evidence to reject the claim that the median is 14.

10. H_0: median = 200 and H_1: median < 200 (claim); C.V. = −1.65; z = −1.42; do not reject H_0. There is not enough evidence to support the claim that she sells fewer than 200 tickets per day.

11. H_0: median number of faculty = 150 (claim) and H_1: median ≠ 150; C.V. = ±1.96; z = −2.70; reject H_0. There is sufficient evidence at the 0.05 level of significance to reject the claim that the median number of faculty is 150.

12. H_0: median = 100 (claim) and H_1: median ≠ 100; test statistic = 2; C.V. = 2; reject H_0. There is enough evidence to reject the claim that the median is 100 million fine Troy ounces.

13. H_0: median = 50% (claim) and H_1: median ≠ 50%; z = −2.53; P-value = 0.0114; reject H_0. There is enough evidence to reject the claim that 50% of the students are against extending the school year.

14. H_0: median = 52.7 (claim) and H_1: median ≠ 52.7; z = −2.31; P-value = 0.0209; reject H_0. There is enough evidence to reject the claim that the median is 52.7. One reason that this information would be valuable is that the sponsors of the show could target viewers based on median age.

15. H_0: The number of pool violations is reduced (claim) and H_1: The number of pool violations is not reduced; C.V. = 1; test statistic = 2; reject H_0. There is not enough evidence to say that the number of pool violations has been reduced.

16. H_0: There is no difference between scores and H_1: There is a difference between scores (claim); test statistic = 3; C.V. = 1; do not reject H_0. There is insufficient evidence to conclude a difference in scores.

17. H_0: The number of soft drinks will not change. H_1: The number of soft drinks will decrease (claim). C.V. = 1; test statistic = 3; do not reject H_0. There is not enough evidence to support the claim that the number of soft drinks was reduced.

18. H_0: The pill has no effect on the caloric intake of the person eating and H_1: The pill has an effect on the caloric intake of the person eating (claim); C.V. = 1; test statistic = 2; do not reject H_0. There is not enough evidence to support the claim that the pill has an effect on caloric intake.

19. H_0: The number of Internet visits will not change and H_1: The number of Internet visits will increase (claim); C.V. = 0; test statistic = 3; do not reject H_0. There is not enough evidence to support the claim that the number of visits increased.

20. H_0: Increased maintenance does not reduce the number of defective parts a machine produces and H_1: Increased maintenance reduces the number of defective parts a machine produces (claim); C.V. = 0; test statistic = 2; do not reject H_0. There is not enough evidence to support the claim that increased maintenance reduces the number of defective parts manufactured by the machines.

21. $5 \le$ median ≤ 28 **22.** $99 \le$ median ≤ 116

23. $6.7 \le$ median ≤ 16.5 **24.** $7 \le$ median ≤ 19

25. $117 \le$ median ≤ 156

Exercises 13–3

1. n_1 and n_2 are each greater than or equal to 10.

2. The z and t tests for independent samples

3. H_0: There is no difference in the speed skating times of the students at the two universities (claim) and H_1: There is a difference in the speed skating times of the students at the two universities; C.V. $= \pm 1.96$; $z = -0.26$; do not reject H_0. There is not enough evidence to reject the claim that there is no difference in the times.

4. H_0: There is no difference in the length of the sentences of the males and females (claim) and H_1: There is a difference in the length of the sentences of the males and females; C.V. $= \pm 1.96$; $z = 1.49$; do not reject H_0. There is not enough evidence to reject the claim that there are no differences in the sentences received by the males and females.

5. H_0: There is no difference in the number of credits transferred; H_1: There is a difference in the number of credits transferred (claim); C.V. $= \pm 1.96$; $z = -0.53$; do not reject H_0. There is not enough evidence to support the claim that there is a difference in the number of credits transferred.

6. H_0: There is no difference in the lifetimes of the two brands of video game (claim) and H_1: There is a difference in the lifetimes of the two brands of video game; C.V. $= \pm 2.58$; $z = -0.89$; do not reject H_0. There is not enough evidence to reject the claim that there is no difference in the lifetimes of the two brands of video game.

7. H_0: There is no difference between the stopping distances of the two types of automobiles (claim) and H_1: There is a difference between the stopping distances of the two types of automobiles; C.V. $= \pm 1.65$; $z = -2.72$; reject H_0. There is enough evidence to reject the claim that there is no difference in the stopping distances of the automobiles. In this case, midsize cars have a smaller stopping distance.

8. H_0: There is no difference in the number of wins and H_1: There is a difference in the number of wins (claim); C.V. $= \pm 1.96$; $z = -0.43$; do not reject H_0. There is insufficient evidence to conclude a difference in the number of wins.

9. H_0: There is no difference in the number of hunting accidents in the two geographic areas and H_1: There is a difference in the number of hunting accidents (claim); C.V. $= \pm 1.96$; $z = -2.58$; reject H_0. There is enough evidence to support the claim that there is a difference in the number of accidents in the two areas. The number of accidents may be related to the number of hunters in the areas.

10. H_0: There is no difference in the size of enrollments and H_1: There is a difference in the size of enrollments (claim); C.V. $= \pm 1.96$; $z = 1.20$; do not reject H_0. There is insufficient evidence to conclude a difference in enrollments.

11. H_0: There is no difference in job satisfaction; H_1: There is a difference in job satisfaction (claim); C.V. $= \pm 1.65$; $z = 1.13$; do not reject H_0. There is not enough evidence to support the claim that there is a difference in job satisfaction between the two groups.

12. H_0: There is no difference in the number of students at fraternities and sororities who participated in the student blood drive (claim); H_1: There is a difference in the number of students at fraternities and sororities who participated in the student blood drive; C.V. $= \pm 1.65$; $z = -1.81$; reject H_0. There is enough evidence to reject the claim that there is no difference in the number of students at fraternities and sororities who participated in the student blood drive.

13. H_0: There is no difference in the number of falls; H_1: the number of falls is reduced (claim); C.V. $= -1.65$; $z = 0.79$; do not reject H_0. There is not enough evidence to say that the number of falls had decreased.

14. H_0: There is no difference in the number of accidents; H_1: The number of accidents has been reduced (claim); C.V. $= -1.28$; $z = -1.21$; do not reject H_0. There is not enough evidence to support the claim that the number of accidents has been reduced.

15. H_0: There is no difference in the number of libraries in the East and the West; H_1: There is a difference in the number of libraries in the East and West (claim); C.V. $= \pm 1.96$; $z = 0.416$; do not reject H_0. There is not enough evidence to support the claim that there is a difference in the number of libraries in the states in the East and West.

16. H_0: There is no difference in the number of passengers per week in the East System and the West System; H_1: There is a difference in the number of passengers in the East System and the West System (claim); C.V. $= \pm 1.65$; $z = -2.54$; reject H_0. There is enough evidence to support the claim that there is a difference in the number of passengers per week in the East System and the West System.

17. H_0: There is no difference in the number of cell phones each store sells per week; H_1: There is a difference in the number of cell phones each store sells per week (claim); C.V. $= \pm 1.65$; $z = -0.79$; do not reject H_0. There is not enough evidence to support the claim that there is a difference in the number of cell phones each store sold each week.

18. H_0: There is no difference in the number of passengers in the two systems; H_1: There is a difference in the number of passengers in the two systems (claim); C.V. $= \pm 1.65$; $z = 0.60$; do not reject H_0. There is not enough evidence to support the claim that there is a difference in the two systems.

Exercises 13–4

1. The t test for dependent samples

2. The Wilcoxon rank sum test is used when the random samples are independent while the Wilcoxon signed-rank test is used when the random samples are dependent.

3. The sum of the minus ranks is 12. The sum of the plus ranks is 9. The test statistic is 9.

4. The sum of the minus ranks is -23.5. The sum of the plus ranks is 4.5. The test statistic is 4.5.

5. C.V. = 3; do not reject H_0.

6. C.V. = 41; reject H_0.

7. C.V. = 52; reject H_0.

8. C.V. = 81; reject H_0.

9. H_0: The human dose is equal to the animal dose and H_1: The human dose is more than the animal dose (claim); C.V. = 6; $w_s = 2$; reject H_0. There is enough evidence to support the claim that the human dose costs more than the equivalent animal dose. One reason is that some people might not be inclined to pay a lot of money for their pets' medication.

10. H_0: There is no difference in the number of absences and H_1: The number of absences decreased after the introduction of the new policy (claim); C.V. = 11; $w_s = 4$; reject H_0. There is enough evidence to support the claim that the number of absences decreased after the new policy was instituted.

11. H_0: The amount spent on lottery tickets does not change; H_1: The amount spent on lottery tickets is reduced (claim); C.V. = 6, $w_s = 5$; reject H_0. There is enough evidence to support the claim that the workshop reduced the amount the participants spent on lottery tickets.

12. H_0: There is no difference in legal costs and H_1: There is a difference in legal costs (claim); $w_s = 2.5$; C.V. = 4; reject H_0. There is sufficient evidence to conclude a difference in legal costs.

13. H_0: The prices of prescription drugs in the United States are equal to the prices in Canada and H_1: The drugs sold in Canada are cheaper (claim); C.V. = 11; $w_s = 3$; reject H_0. There is enough evidence to support the claim that the drugs are less expensive in Canada.

14. H_0: There is no difference in the number of accidents and H_1: The number of accidents was reduced after the two stop signs were added (claim); C.V. = 2; $w_s = 4.5$; do not reject H_0. There is not enough evidence to support the claim that the additional two stop signs reduced the number of accidents at the intersections.

15. H_0: There is no difference in the walking times of the walkers and H_1: The walking times decreased after the walkers were given new shoes (claim); C.V. = 8; $w_s = 4$; reject H_0. There is enough evidence to support the claim that the new shoes on the walkers reduced the walking times.

16. H_0: There is no difference in the number of hours of sleep before and after the drug and H_1: The number of hours of sleep increased after the drug (claim); C.V. = 6; $w_s = 14$; do not reject H_0. There is not enough evidence to support the claim that the drug increased the number of hours a person sleeps.

Exercises 13–5

1. H_0: There is no difference in the results of the questionnaires among the three groups; H_1: There is a difference in the results of the questionnaires among the three groups (claim); C.V. = 5.991; $H = 4.891$; do not reject H_0. There is not enough evidence to support

the claim that there is a difference in the results of the questionnaire.

2. H_0: There is no difference in the mathematical literacy scores of the individuals and H_1: There is a difference in the mathematical literacy of the individuals (claim); C.V. = 5.991; $H = 4.160$; do not reject H_0. There is not enough evidence to support the claim that there is a difference in the mathematical literacy scores of the individuals.

3. H_0: There is no difference in the scores on the questionnaire; H_1: There is a difference in the scores on the questionnaire (claim); C.V. = 4.605; $H = 3.254$; do not reject H_0. There is not enough evidence to support the claim that there is a difference in the results of the questionnaire.

4. H_0: There is no difference in the amounts of sodium in the different brands of microwave dinners and H_1: There is a difference in the amounts of sodium in the different brands of microwave dinners (claim); C.V. = 5.991; $H = 10.537$; reject H_0. There is enough evidence to support the claim that there is a difference in the amounts of sodium in the different brands of microwave dinner.

5. H_0: There is no difference in the sugar content of the three different types of candy bars and H_1: There is a difference in the sugar content of the three different types of candy bars (claim); C.V. = 5.991; $H = 10.389$; reject H_0. There is enough evidence to support the claim that the sugar content of the three of candy bars is different.

6. H_0: There is no difference in the number of job offers received by each group and H_1: There is a difference in the number of job offers received by each group (claim); C.V. = 5.991; $H = 8.540$; reject H_0. There is enough evidence to support the claim that the number of job offers is different.

7. H_0: There is no difference in spending between regions and H_1: There is a difference in spending between regions (claim); $H = 0.740$; C.V. = 5.991; do not reject H_0. There is insufficient evidence to conclude a difference in spending.

8. H_0: There is no difference in the prices of the three types of printer and H_1: There is a difference in the prices of the three types of printer (claim); C.V. = 5.991; $H = 0.809$; do not reject H_0. There is not enough evidence to support the claim that there is a difference in the prices of the printers. No, based on these samples, you cannot conclude that one type of printer generally costs more than another type.

9. H_0: There is no difference in the number of crimes in the five precincts and H_1: There is a difference in the number of crimes in the five precincts (claim); C.V. = 13.277; $H = 20.753$; reject H_0. There is enough evidence to support the claim that there is a difference in the number of crimes in the five precincts.

10. H_0: There is no difference in caffeine content and H_1: There is a difference in caffeine content (claim); $H = 9.980$; C.V. = 5.991; reject H_0. There is sufficient evidence to conclude a difference in caffeine content.

11. H_0: There is no difference in speeds and H_1: There is a difference in speeds (claim); $H = 3.815$; C.V. = 5.991; do not reject H_0. There is insufficient evidence to conclude a difference in speeds.

12. H_0: There is no difference in the prices of the supplements at the different stores and H_1: There is a difference in the prices of the supplements at the different stores (claim); C.V. = 9.210; $H = 0.55$; do not reject H_0. There is not enough evidence to support the claim that there is a difference in the prices of the supplements at the different stores.

13. H_0: There is no difference in the lengths of the main spans of the three different types of bridges and H_1: There is a difference in the lengths of the main spans of the three types of bridges (claim); C.V. = 5.991; $H = 9.993$; reject H_0. There is enough evidence to support the claim that the lengths of the main spans of the three different types of bridges are different.

14. H_0: There is no difference in the number of stories in the buildings in the three cities and H_1: There is a difference in the number of stories in the buildings in the three cities (claim); C.V. = 4.605; $H = 1.818$; do not reject H_0. There is not enough evidence to support the claim that the number of stories in the buildings in the three cities is different.

15. H_0: The areas of the natural lakes in the three continents are the same and H_1: The areas of the natural lakes in the three continents are different (claim); C.V. = 4.605; $H = 1.68$; do not reject H_0. There is not enough evidence to support the claim that the areas of the lakes on the three continents are different.

16. H_0: The lengths of the rivers in three continents are the same and H_1: The lengths of the rivers in the three continents are different (claim); C.V. = 4.605; $H = 6.32$; reject H_0. There is enough evidence to support the claim that the lengths of the rivers in the three continents are different.

17. H_0: The lengths of the sentences for the three types of crimes are the same and H_1: The lengths of the sentences for the three types of crimes are different (claim); C.V. = 7.378; $H = 11.415$; reject H_0. There is enough evidence to support the claim that the sentences are different.

18. H_0: The lengths of songs on the three different types of music are the same and H_1: The lengths of the songs on the three different types of music are different (claim); C.V. = 4.605; $H = 9.848$; reject H_0. There is enough evidence to support the claim that the lengths of songs for the three types of music are different.

Exercises 13–6

1. 0.377 **2.** 0.666
3. 0.833 **4.** 0.438
5. $r_s = 0.964$; H_0: $\rho = 0$ and H_1: $\rho \neq 0$; C.V. = ±0.786; reject H_0. There is a significant linear relationship between the scores of the 4th and 8th grade students.

6. $r_s = 0.6$; H_0: $\rho = 0$ and H_1: $\rho \neq 0$; C.V. = ±0.886; do not reject H_0. There is no significant linear relationship.

7. $r_s = 0.786$; H_0: $\rho = 0$; H_1: $\rho \neq 0$; C.V. = ±0.714; reject H_0. There is enough evidence to say that there is a significant linear relationship between the years and the victims.

8. $r_s = 0.893$; H_0: $\rho = 0$ and H_1: $\rho \neq 0$; C.V. = ±0.786; reject H_0. There is a significant relationship between the number of hospitals and the number of nursing homes in a state.

9. $r_s = 0.048$; H_0: $\rho = 0$ and H_1: $\rho \neq 0$; C.V. = ±0.738; do not reject H_0. There is not enough evidence to say that a significant correlation exists between calories and the cholesterol amounts in fast-food sandwiches.

10. $r_s = 0.899$; H_0: $\rho = 0$; H_1: $\rho \neq 0$; C.V. = ±7.38; reject H_0. There is enough evidence to say that there is a significant linear relationship between the heights and the number of stories in the buildings in Denver.

11. $r_s = 0.857$; H_0: $\rho = 0$; H_1: $\rho \neq 0$; C.V. = ±0.786; reject H_0. There is enough evidence to say that there is a significant linear relationship between a person's age and a person's systolic blood pressure.

12. $r_s = 0.714$; H_0: $\rho = 0$; H_1: $\rho \neq 0$; C.V. = ±0.786; do not reject H_0. There is not enough evidence to say that there is a significant linear relationship between the number of inches of snow and the number of patrons at the ski lodge.

13. $r_s = -0.100$; H_0: $\rho = 0$ and H_1: $\rho \neq 0$; C.V. = ±0.900; do not reject H_0. There is no significant relationship between the number of online school students and the cost per pupil. In this case, the cost per pupil is different in each district.

14. $r_s = 0.524$; H_0: $\rho = 0$ and H_1: $\rho \neq 0$; C.V. = ±0.643; do not reject H_0. There is no significant relationship between the costs of the drugs.

15. *a.* = 7   *c.* = 5   *e.* = 6
   b. = 6   *d.* = 4

16. *a.* Reject the null hypothesis when the number of runs is less than or equal to 4 or greater than or equal to 14.
   b. Reject the null hypothesis when the number of runs is less than or equal to 5 or greater than or equal to 15.
   c. Reject the null hypothesis when the number of runs is less than or equal to 3 or greater than or equal to 10.
   d. Reject the null hypothesis when the number of runs is less than or equal to 5 or greater than or equal to 14.
   e. Reject the null hypothesis when the number of runs is less than or equal to 13 or greater than or equal to 27.

17. H_0: The types of admissions occur at random (claim) and H_1: The types of admissions do not occur at random. C.V. = ±1.96; $z = 0.659$; do not reject. There is not enough evidence to reject the hypothesis that the types of admissions appear at random.

18. H_0: The integers generated by a calculator occur at random (claim) and H_1: The integers generated by a calculator do not occur at random. There are 13 runs, and C.V. = 7, 17, so the null hypothesis is not rejected. There is not enough evidence to reject. The integers occur at random.

19. H_0: The ups and downs in the stock market occur at random (claim) and H_1: The ups and downs in the stock market do not occur at random. There are eight runs. Since C.V. = 5, 15, do not reject H_0. There is not enough evidence to reject. The ups and downs in the stock market occur at random.

20. H_0: Seeing shadows occurs at random (claim) and H_1: Seeing shadows does not occur at random. There are 11 runs. Since C.V. = 4, 12, do not reject the null hypothesis. Seeing shadows occurs at random.

21. H_0: The nightmares occur at random (claim) and H_1: The nightmares do not occur at random. There are 12 runs and C.V. = 7, 17; therefore, nightmares occur at random.

22. H_0: The days customers are able to ski occur at random (claim) and H_1: The days the customers are able to ski do not occur at random. There are 5 runs. Since C.V. = 9, 20, the decision is to reject the null hypothesis. There is enough evidence to reject the claim that the days customers are able to ski occur at random.

23. H_0: The number of on-demand movie rentals occurs at random (claim) and H_1: The number of on-demand movie rentals does not occur at random. The number of runs is 10. Do not reject the null hypothesis since C.V. = 6, 16. It can be concluded that the number of rentals occurs at random.

24. Answers will vary.

25. H_0: Online sales of pairs of socks occur at random (claim) and H_1: Online sales of pairs of socks do not occur at random. The number of runs is 12 and since C.V. = 10, 22, do not reject the null hypothesis. The sales occur at random.

26. H_0: The gender of the speeders occurs at random (claim) and H_1: The gender of the speeders does not occur at random; C.V. = ±1.96; $z = 0$; do not reject H_0. There is not enough evidence to reject the claim that the sequence occurs at random.

27. H_0: The patients who were treated for an accident or illness occur at random (claim) and H_1: The patients who were treated for an accident or illness do not occur at random; C.V. = ±1.65; $z = 1.14$; do not reject H_0. There is not enough evidence to reject the claim that the sequence occurs at random.

28. H_0: The answers "true" and "false" occur at random (claim) and H_1: The answers do not occur at random. There are 14 runs. Since C.V. = 10, 22, the decision is to not reject the null hypothesis. Hence, the answers occur at random.

29. ±0.283

30. ±0.300

31. ±0.317

32. ±0.318

33. ±0.372

Review Exercises

1. H_0: median = $9.00 (claim) and H_1: median < $9.00; $z = -2.01$; C.V. = ±1.65; reject H_0. There is enough evidence to reject the claim that the median price is $9.00.

2. H_0 median = 420 (claim) and H_1: median ≠ 420; $z = -1.28$; C.V. = ±2.33; do not reject H_0. There is not enough evidence to reject the claim that the median is equal to 420 minutes.

3. H_0: There is no difference in prices and H_1: There is a difference in prices (claim); test statistic = 1; C.V. = 1; reject H_0. There is sufficient evidence to conclude a difference in prices.

4. H_0: There is no difference in the record high temperatures of the two cities and H_1: There is a difference in the record high temperatures of the two cities (claim); $z = -1.24$; P-value = 0.2150; do not reject H_0. There is not enough evidence to support the claim that there is a difference in the record high temperatures of the two cities.

5. H_0: There is no difference in the hours worked and H_1: There is a difference in the hours worked (claim); $z = -1.76$; C.V. = ±1.645; reject H_0. There is sufficient evidence to conclude a difference in the hours worked. C.V. = ±1.96; do not reject.

6. H_0: The additive did not improve the gas mileage and H_1: The additive did improve the gas mileage (claim); C.V. = 17; $w_s = 14$; reject H_0. There is enough evidence to support the claim that the additive improved the gas mileage.

7. H_0: There is no difference in the amount spent and H_1: There is a difference in the amount spent (claim); $w_s = 1$; C.V. = 2; reject H_0. There is sufficient evidence of a difference in amount spent at the 0.05 level of significance.

8. H_0: There is no difference in the breaking strengths of the cables and H_1: There is a difference in the breaking strengths of the cables (claim); C.V. = 5.991; $H = 5.135$; do not reject H_0. There is not enough evidence to support the claim that the mean breaking point strengths of the cables is different.

9. H_0: There is no difference in beach temperatures and H_1: There is a difference in temperatures (claim); $H = 15.524$; C.V. = 7.815; reject H_0. There is sufficient evidence to conclude a difference in beach temperatures. (Without the Southern Pacific: $H = 3.661$; C.V. = 5.991; do not reject.)

10. $r_s = 0.933$; H_0: $\rho = 0$ and H_1: $\rho \neq 0$; C.V. = ±0.700; reject H_0. There is a significant relationship between the rankings.

11. $r_s = 0.705$; H_0: $\rho = 0$ and H_1: $\rho \neq 0$; C.V. = ±0.786; do not reject H_0. There is not a significant relationship between the number of pages and the number of references.

12. H_0: The scoring leaders of the NBA occur at random (claim) and H_1: The scoring leaders of the NBA do not occur at random. There are 10 runs. C.V. = 7, 17. Do not reject H_0. There is not enough evidence to reject the claim. The number of scoring leaders occurs at random.

13. H_0: The grades of students who finish the exam occur at random (claim) and H_1: The grades do not occur at random. Since there are 8 runs and C.V. = 9, 21, the null hypothesis is rejected. The grades do not occur at random.

14. H_0: The choice of the book (fiction or nonfiction) occurs at random (claim) and H_1: The choice of book does not occur at random; C.V. = ±1.65; $z = -3.35$; reject H_0. There is enough evidence to reject the claim that the selection occurs at random.

Chapter Quiz

1. False. Nonparametric statistics are used to test the difference between two means.

2. False. Nonparametric statistics are less sensitive than their parametric counterparts.

3. True

4. True

5. a

6. c

7. d

8. b

9. Nonparametric, distribution-free

10. Nominal, ordinal

11. Sign   12. Sensitive

13. H_0: median = \$230,500; H_1: median ≠ \$230,500 (claim); C.V. = 2; test statistic = 3; do not reject H_0. There is not enough evidence to say that the median is not \$230,500.

14. H_0: median = 1200 and H_1: median ≠ 1200 (claim); C.V. = 6, test statistic = 10; do not reject H_0. Since 6 is less than the test statistic of 10, do not reject the null hypothesis. There is insufficient evidence to support the claim that the median is not 1200.

15. H_0: There will be no change in the weight of the turkeys after the special diet and H_1: The turkeys will weigh more after the special diet (claim). There is 1 plus sign; hence, the null hypothesis is rejected, since the critical value is zero. There is enough evidence to support the claim that the turkeys gained weight on the special diet.

16. H_0: There is no difference in the amounts of money received by the teams and H_1: There is a difference in the amounts of money each team received (claim); C.V. = ±1.96; $z = -0.79$; do not reject H_0. There is not enough evidence to say that the amounts differ.

17. H_0: The amounts are the same and H_1: The amounts are different (claim); $z = -0.14$; C.V. = ±1.65; do not reject the null hypothesis. There is not enough evidence to support the claim that the distributions are different.

18. H_0: There is no difference in the GPA of the students before and after the workshop and H_1: There is a difference in the GPA of the students before and after the workshop (claim); test statistic = 0; C.V. = 6; reject the null hypothesis. There is enough evidence to support the claim that there is a difference in the GPAs of the students.

19. H_0: There is no difference in the amounts of sodium in the three sandwiches and H_1: There is a difference in the amounts of sodium in the sandwiches (claim); C.V. = 5.991; $H = 11.795$; reject H_0. There is enough evidence to conclude that there is a difference in the amounts of sodium in the sandwiches.

20. H_0: There is no difference in the reaction times of the monkeys and H_1: There is a difference in the reaction times of the monkeys (claim); $H = 6.85$; $0.025 < P$-value < 0.05 (0.032); reject the null hypothesis. There is enough evidence to support the claim that there is a difference in the reaction times of the monkeys.

21. $r_s = 0.633$; H_0: $\rho = 0$ and H_1: $\rho \neq 0$; C.V. = ±0.600; reject H_0. There is enough evidence to say that there is a significant relationship between the drug prices.

22. $r_s = 0.943$; H_0: $\rho = 0$ and H_1: $\rho \neq 0$; C.V. = ±0.829; reject H_0. There is a significant relationship between the amount of money spent on Head Start and the number of students enrolled in the program.

23. H_0: The births of babies occur at random according to gender (claim) and H_1: The births according to gender do not occur at random. There are 10 runs, and since C.V. = 8, 19, the null hypothesis is not rejected. There is not enough evidence to reject the null hypothesis that gender occurs at random.

24. H_0: There is no difference in the rpm of the motors before and after the reconditioning and H_1: There is a difference in the rpm of the motors before and after the reconditioning (claim); test statistic = 0; C.V. = 8; reject the null hypothesis. There is enough evidence to support the claim that there is a difference in the rpm of the motors before and after reconditioning.

25. H_0: The numbers occur at random (claim) and H_1: The numbers do not occur at random. There are 16 runs, and since C.V. = 9, 21, the null hypothesis is not rejected. There is not enough evidence to reject the null hypothesis that the numbers occur at random.

26. H_0: The showing of the type of movie (black and white or color) occurs at random (claim). H_1: The showing of the type of movie does not occur at random. C.V. = ±1.96; $z = -5.54$; reject H_0. There is enough evidence to reject the claim that the showing of the type of movie occurs at random.

Chapter 14

Exercises 14–1

1. Random, systematic, stratified, cluster

2. Samples can save the researcher time and money. They are used when the population is large or infinite. They are used when the original units are to be destroyed, such as in testing the breaking strength of ropes.

3. A sample must be randomly selected.

4. Random numbers are used to ensure every element of the population has the same chance of being selected.

5. Talking to people on the street, calling people on the phone, and asking your friends are three incorrect ways of obtaining a sample.

6. Over the long run each digit, 0 through 9, will occur with the same probability.

7. Random sampling has the advantage that each unit of the population has an equal chance of being selected. One disadvantage is that the units of the population must be numbered; if the population is large, this could be somewhat time-consuming.

8. Systematic sampling has an advantage in that once the first unit is selected, each succeeding unit selected has been determined. This saves time. A disadvantage would be if the list of units were arranged in some manner so that a bias would occur, such as selecting all men when the population consists of both men and women.

9. An advantage of stratified sampling is that it ensures representation for the groups used in stratification; however, it is virtually impossible to stratify the population so that all groups are represented.

10. Clusters are easy to use since they already exist, but it is difficult to justify that the clusters actually represent the population.

11–20. Answers will vary.

21. Sampling or selection bias occurs when some subjects are more likely to be included in a study than others.

22. Answers will vary. One possible answer is that if there are many more males in the population than females, such

as football players, it is possible that some samples would be all male subjects.

23. Nonresponse bias occurs when subjects who do not respond to a survey question would answer the question differently than the subjects who responded to the survey question.

24. Answers will vary. Nonresponse bias can occur if people who are addicted to drugs might give different answers to questions on drug use than those who are not addicted to drugs.

25. Response or interview bias occurs when the subject does not give a true opinion and gives an opinion that they feel is politically correct.

26. Answers will vary. Response or interview bias could occur if the subject feels intimidated by the interviewer.

27. Volunteer bias occurs when people volunteer to participate in a study because they are interested in the study or survey.

28. Volunteer bias can occur in a call-in survey where only those who have a strong opinion will make the call.

Exercises 14–2

1. Flaw—biased; it's confusing.

2. Flaw—the purpose of the question is unclear. You could like him personally but not politically.

3. Flaw—the question is too broad.

4. Flaw—none. The question is good if the respondent knows the mayor's position; otherwise his position needs to be stated.

5. Flaw—confusing words. How many hours did you study for this exam?

6. Possible order problem—ask first, "Do you use artificial sweetener regularly?"

7. Flaw—confusing words. If a plane were to crash on the border of New York and New Jersey, where should the victims be buried?

8. Flaw—none.

9. Flaw—The word *vaguely* is too general.

10. A respondent might not know what the present gun control laws are.

11. The word *family* could mean different things to the respondent, for example, in cases of separated families.

12. A person might not even care about presidential debates.

13. The word *regularly* is vague.

14. People might not want others to know their incomes.

15. A person might not know of the situation four years ago.

16. Here people have varied opinions about slavery.

17. This question assumes the subject feels texting while driving is bad. Not all people will agree with this.

18. Almost all people will answer "Yes" to this question.

19. Here the question limits the response to "repeated" tours. Subjects might not be in favor of any tour.

20. The question can be answered in several ways besides "Yes" and "No."

21. Answers will vary.

22. Answers will vary.

Exercises 14–3

1. Simulation involves setting up probability experiments that mimic the behavior of real-life events.

2. Answers will vary.

3. John Von Neumann and Stanislaw Ulam

4. Using the computer to simulate real-life situations can save time, since the computer can generate random numbers and keep track of the outcomes very quickly and easily.

5. The steps are as follows:

    a. List all possible outcomes.

    b. Determine the probability of each outcome.

    c. Set up a correspondence between the outcomes and the random numbers.

    d. Conduct the experiment by using random numbers.

    e. Repeat the experiment and tally the outcomes.

    f. Compute any statistics and state the conclusions.

6. Random numbers can be used to ensure the outcomes occur with appropriate probability.

7. When the repetitions increase, there is a higher probability that the simulation will yield more precise answers.

8. Coins, dice, and cards can be used to perform simulation experiments.

9. Use three-digit random numbers; numbers 001 through 681 mean that the mother is in the labor force.

10. Select two-digit random numbers in groups of 5. For one person, 01 through 70 means a success. For the other person, 01 through 75 means a success.

11. Select 100 two-digit random numbers. Numbers 00 to 34 mean the household has at least one set with premium cable service. Numbers 35 to 99 mean the household does not have the service.

12. Use the odd digits to represent a match and the even digits to represent a nonmatch.

13. Let an odd number represent heads and an even number represent tails. Then each person selects a digit at random.

14. Use a table of random numbers. Select 40 random numbers. Numbers 01 through 16 mean the person is foreign-born.

15–26. Answers will vary.

Exercises 14–4

1. The characteristics of big data are volume, velocity, and variety.

2. Structured data are data values such as numbers, names, dates, etc. They can be put in table form. Unstructured data are data such as emails, photographs, and text messages.

3. Three concerns that need to be addressed when using big data are the methods to collect the data, the storage of the data, and the analysis of the data.

4. Four businesses that use big data are banks, credit card companies, health care, and delivery services.

5. Three situations where big data analysis can be used are identifying potential dropout students, boosting customer satisfaction, and improving manufacturing processes.

6. Machine-generated data use computers to record the data. Human-generated data are collected by humans.

7. Big data analysis can be used in reducing traffic, reducing crime, and generating new businesses. Other answers can be used.

8. Answers will vary.

9. Big data came about with the advent of computer record keeping.

10. Banks can use big data record keeping to keep track of customer deposits and withdrawals.

11. Answers will vary.

12. Answers will vary.

13. The human-generated data can be input into a computer.

14. Errors can occur in human-generated data by people making mistakes in recording the data.

Review Exercises

1–8. Answers will vary.

9. Flaw—asking a biased question. Have you ever driven through a red light?

10. Flaw—using a double negative. Do you think students who are not failing should be given tutoring if they request it?

11. Flaw—asking a double-barreled question. Do you think all automobiles should have heavy-duty bumpers?

12. Flaw—people might not know the meaning of open-ended or closed-ended questions.

13. Use one-digit random numbers 1 through 4 for a strikeout, and 5 through 9 and 0 represent anything other than a strikeout.

14. Use two-digit random numbers: 01 through 15 represent an overbooked plane, and 16 through 99 and 00 represent a plane that is not overbooked.

15. The first person selects a two-digit random number. Any two-digit random number that has a 7, 8, 9, or 0 is ignored, and another random number is selected. Player 1 selects a one-digit random number; any random number that is not 1 through 6 is ignored, and another one is selected.

16. Let the digits 1 through 3 represent rock, let 4 through 6 represent paper, let 7 through 9 represent scissors, and omit 0.

17–21. Answers will vary.

Chapter Quiz

1. True   2. True

3. False. Random numbers should be obtained from calculators or computers, not made up by researchers.

4. True

5. *a*   6. *c*

7. *c*   8. Larger

9. Biased   10. Cluster

11–14. Answers will vary.

15. Use two-digit random numbers: 01 through 45 means the player wins. Any other two-digit random number means the player loses.

16. Use two-digit random numbers: 01 through 05 means a cancellation. Any other two-digit random number means the person shows up.

17. The random numbers 01 through 10 represent the 10 cards in hearts. The random numbers 11 through 20 represent the 10 cards in diamonds. The random numbers 21 through 30 represent the 10 spades, and 31 through 40 represent the 10 clubs. Any number over 40 is ignored.

18. Use two-digit random numbers to represent the spots on the face of the dice. Ignore any two-digit random numbers with 7, 8, 9, or 0. For cards, use two-digit random numbers between 01 and 13.

19. Use two-digit random numbers. The first digit represents the first player, and the second digit represents the second player. If both numbers are odd or even, player 1 wins. If a digit is odd and the other digit is even, player 2 wins.

20–24. Answers will vary.

25. Here *regularly* is vague.

26. *Bad weather* means different things to different people.

27. What is meant by *readable*?

28. Smoking a lot means different things to different people.

29. Some respondents might not know much about herbal medicine.

30. Almost everybody would answer "No" to this question.

APPENDIX E

Important Formulas

Chapter 3 Data Description

Mean for individual data: $\overline{X} = \dfrac{\Sigma X}{n}$

Mean for grouped data: $\overline{X} = \dfrac{\Sigma f \cdot X_m}{n}$

Standard deviation for a sample:

$$s = \sqrt{\dfrac{\Sigma(X - \overline{X})^2}{n - 1}} \quad \text{or} \quad s = \sqrt{\dfrac{n(\Sigma X^2) - (\Sigma X)^2}{n(n - 1)}}$$

(Shortcut formula)

Standard deviation for grouped data:

$$s = \sqrt{\dfrac{n(\Sigma f \cdot X_m^2) - (\Sigma f \cdot X_m)^2}{n(n - 1)}}$$

Range rule of thumb: $s \approx \dfrac{\text{range}}{4}$

Chapter 4 Probability and Counting Rules

Addition rule 1 (mutually exclusive events):

$$P(A \text{ or } B) = P(A) + P(B)$$

Addition rule 2 (events not mutually exclusive):

$$P(A \text{ or } B) = P(A) + P(B) - P(A \text{ and } B)$$

Multiplication rule 1 (independent events):

$$P(A \text{ and } B) = P(A) \cdot P(B)$$

Multiplication rule 2 (dependent events):

$$P(A \text{ and } B) = P(A) \cdot P(B \mid A)$$

Conditional probability: $P(B \mid A) = \dfrac{P(A \text{ and } B)}{P(A)}$

Complementary events: $P(\overline{E}) = 1 - P(E)$

Fundamental counting rule: Total number of outcomes of a sequence when each event has a different number of possibilities: $k_1 \cdot k_2 \cdot k_3 \cdots k_n$

Permutation rule: Number of permutations of n objects taking r at a time is $_nP_r = \dfrac{n!}{(n - r)!}$

Permutation rule of n objects with r_1 objects identical, r_2 objects identical, etc.

$$\dfrac{n!}{r_1! \, r_2! \cdots r_p!}$$

Combination rule: Number of combinations of r objects selected from n objects is $_nC_r = \dfrac{n!}{(n - r)! \, r!}$

Chapter 5 Discrete Probability Distributions

Mean for a probability distribution: $\mu = \Sigma[X \cdot P(X)]$

Variance and standard deviation for a probability distribution:

$$\sigma^2 = \Sigma[X^2 \cdot P(X)] - \mu^2$$

$$\sigma = \sqrt{\Sigma[X^2 \cdot P(X)] - \mu^2}$$

Expectation: $E(X) = \Sigma[X \cdot P(X)]$

Binomial probability: $P(X) = \dfrac{n!}{(n - X)! \, X!} \cdot p^X \cdot q^{n - X}$

Mean for binomial distribution: $\mu = n \cdot p$

Variance and standard deviation for the binomial distribution:
$\sigma^2 = n \cdot p \cdot q \qquad \sigma = \sqrt{n \cdot p \cdot q}$

Multinomial probability:

$$P(X) = \dfrac{n!}{X_1! \, X_2! \, X_3! \cdots X_k!} \cdot p_1^{X_1} \cdot p_2^{X_2} \cdot p_3^{X_3} \cdots p_k^{X_k}$$

Poisson probability: $P(X; \lambda) = \dfrac{e^{-\lambda} \lambda^X}{X!}$ where

$X = 0, 1, 2, \ldots$

Hypergeometric probability: $P(X) = \dfrac{_aC_X \cdot {}_bC_{n - X}}{_{a+b}C_n}$

Geometric probability: $P(n) = p(1 - p)^{n - 1}$ where n is the number of the trial in which the first success occurs and p is the probability of a success

Chapter 6 The Normal Distribution

Standard score: Population: $z = \dfrac{X - \mu}{\sigma}$ or Sample: $z = \dfrac{X - \overline{X}}{s}$

Mean of sample means: $\mu_{\overline{X}} = \mu$

Standard error of the mean: $\sigma_{\overline{X}} = \dfrac{\sigma}{\sqrt{n}}$

Central limit theorem formula: $z = \dfrac{\overline{X} - \mu}{\sigma / \sqrt{n}}$

Chapter 7 Confidence Intervals and Sample Size

z confidence interval for means:

$$\overline{X} - z_{\alpha/2}\left(\dfrac{\sigma}{\sqrt{n}}\right) < \mu < \overline{X} + z_{\alpha/2}\left(\dfrac{\sigma}{\sqrt{n}}\right)$$

t confidence interval for means:

$$\overline{X} - t_{\alpha/2}\left(\dfrac{s}{\sqrt{n}}\right) < \mu < \overline{X} + t_{\alpha/2}\left(\dfrac{s}{\sqrt{n}}\right)$$

Sample size for means: $n = \left(\dfrac{z_{\alpha/2} \cdot \sigma}{E}\right)^2$ where E is the margin of error

Confidence interval for a proportion:

$$\hat{p} - (z_{\alpha/2}) \sqrt{\dfrac{\hat{p}\hat{q}}{n}} < p < \hat{p} + (z_{\alpha/2}) \sqrt{\dfrac{\hat{p}\hat{q}}{n}}$$

Sample size for a proportion: $n = \hat{p}\hat{q}\left(\dfrac{z_{\alpha/2}}{E}\right)^2$

where $\quad \hat{p} = \dfrac{X}{n} \quad$ and $\quad \hat{q} = 1 - \hat{p}$

Confidence interval for variance:

$$\frac{(n-1)s^2}{\chi^2_{\text{right}}} < \sigma^2 < \frac{(n-1)s^2}{\chi^2_{\text{left}}}$$

Confidence interval for standard deviation:

$$\sqrt{\frac{(n-1)s^2}{\chi^2_{\text{right}}}} < \sigma < \sqrt{\frac{(n-1)s^2}{\chi^2_{\text{left}}}}$$

Chapter 8 Hypothesis Testing

z test: $z = \dfrac{\overline{X} - \mu}{\sigma/\sqrt{n}}$ for any value n. If $n < 30$,
population must be normally distributed.

t test: $t = \dfrac{\overline{X} - \mu}{s/\sqrt{n}} \qquad$ (d.f. $= n - 1$)

z test for proportions: $z = \dfrac{\hat{p} - p}{\sqrt{pq/n}}$

Chi-square test for a single variance: $\chi^2 = \dfrac{(n-1)s^2}{\sigma^2}$
(d.f. $= n - 1$)

Chapter 9 Testing the Difference Between Two Means, Two Proportions, and Two Variances

z test for comparing two means (independent samples):

$$z = \frac{(\overline{X}_1 - \overline{X}_2) - (\mu_1 - \mu_2)}{\sqrt{\dfrac{\sigma_1^2}{n_1} + \dfrac{\sigma_2^2}{n_2}}}$$

Formula for the confidence interval for difference of two means (large samples):

$$(\overline{X}_1 - \overline{X}_2) - z_{\alpha/2}\sqrt{\frac{\sigma_1^2}{n_1} + \frac{\sigma_2^2}{n_2}} < \mu_1 - \mu_2$$
$$< (\overline{X}_1 - \overline{X}_2) + z_{\alpha/2}\sqrt{\frac{\sigma_1^2}{n_1} + \frac{\sigma_2^2}{n_2}}$$

t test for comparing two means (independent samples, variances not equal):

$$t = \frac{(\overline{X}_1 - \overline{X}_2) - (\mu_1 - \mu_2)}{\sqrt{\dfrac{s_1^2}{n_1} + \dfrac{s_2^2}{n_2}}}$$

(d.f. $=$ the smaller of $n_1 - 1$ or $n_2 - 1$)

Formula for the confidence interval for difference of two means (small independent samples, variances unequal):

$$(\overline{X}_1 - \overline{X}_2) - t_{\alpha/2}\sqrt{\frac{s_1^2}{n_1} + \frac{s_2^2}{n_2}} < \mu_1 - \mu_2$$
$$< (\overline{X}_1 - \overline{X}_2) + t_{\alpha/2}\sqrt{\frac{s_1^2}{n_1} + \frac{s_2^2}{n_2}}$$

(d.f. $=$ smaller of $n_1 - 1$ and $n_2 - 1$)

t test for comparing two means for dependent samples:

$$t = \frac{\overline{D} - \mu_D}{s_D/\sqrt{n}} \qquad \text{where} \qquad \overline{D} = \frac{\Sigma D}{n} \qquad \text{and}$$

$$s_D = \sqrt{\frac{n\Sigma D^2 - (\Sigma D)^2}{n(n-1)}} \qquad (\text{d.f.} = n - 1)$$

Formula for confidence interval for the mean of the difference for dependent samples:

$$\overline{D} - t_{\alpha/2}\frac{s_D}{\sqrt{n}} < \mu_D < \overline{D} + t_{\alpha/2}\frac{s_D}{\sqrt{n}}$$

(d.f. $= n - 1$)

z test for comparing two proportions:

$$z = \frac{(\hat{p}_1 - \hat{p}_2) - (p_1 - p_2)}{\sqrt{\overline{p}\,\overline{q}\left(\dfrac{1}{n_1} + \dfrac{1}{n_2}\right)}}$$

where $\quad \overline{p} = \dfrac{X_1 + X_2}{n_1 + n_2} \qquad \hat{p}_1 = \dfrac{X_1}{n_1}$

$\qquad\qquad \overline{q} = 1 - \overline{p} \qquad\quad \hat{p}_2 = \dfrac{X_2}{n_2}$

Formula for the confidence interval for the difference of two proportions:

$$(\hat{p}_1 - \hat{p}_2) - z_{\alpha/2}\sqrt{\frac{\hat{p}_1\hat{q}_1}{n_1} + \frac{\hat{p}_2\hat{q}_2}{n_2}} < p_1 - p_2$$
$$< (\hat{p}_1 - \hat{p}_2) + z_{\alpha/2}\sqrt{\frac{\hat{p}_1\hat{q}_1}{n_1} + \frac{\hat{p}_2\hat{q}_2}{n_2}}$$

F test for comparing two variances: $F = \dfrac{s_1^2}{s_2^2}$ where s_1^2 is the
larger variance and d.f.N. $= n_1 - 1$, d.f.D. $= n_2 - 1$

Chapter 10 Correlation and Regression

Correlation coefficient:

$$r = \frac{n(\Sigma xy) - (\Sigma x)(\Sigma y)}{\sqrt{[n(\Sigma x^2) - (\Sigma x)^2][n(\Sigma y^2) - (\Sigma y)^2]}}$$

t test for correlation coefficient: $t = r\sqrt{\dfrac{n-2}{1-r^2}}$
(d.f. $= n - 2$)

The regression line equation: $y' = a + bx$

where $\quad a = \dfrac{(\Sigma y)(\Sigma x^2) - (\Sigma x)(\Sigma xy)}{n(\Sigma x^2) - (\Sigma x)^2}$

$$b = \frac{n(\Sigma xy) - (\Sigma x)(\Sigma y)}{n(\Sigma x^2) - (\Sigma x)^2}$$

Coefficient of determination: $r^2 = \dfrac{\text{explained variation}}{\text{total variation}}$

Standard error of estimate:

$$s_{est} = \sqrt{\frac{\Sigma y^2 - a\,\Sigma y - b\,\Sigma xy}{n-2}}$$

Prediction interval for y:

$$y' - t_{\alpha/2} s_{est}\sqrt{1 + \frac{1}{n} + \frac{n(x - \overline{X})^2}{n\,\Sigma x^2 - (\Sigma x)^2}}$$

$$< y < y' + t_{\alpha/2} s_{est}\sqrt{1 + \frac{1}{n} + \frac{n(x - \overline{X})^2}{n\,\Sigma x^2 - (\Sigma x)^2}}$$

(d.f. $= n - 2$)

Formula for the multiple correlation coefficient:

$$R = \sqrt{\frac{r_{yx_1}^2 + r_{yx_2}^2 - 2r_{yx_1} \cdot r_{yx_2} \cdot r_{x_1 x_2}}{1 - r_{x_1 x_2}^2}}$$

Formula for the F test for the multiple correlation coefficient:

$$F = \frac{R^2/k}{(1 - R^2)/(n - k - 1)}$$

(d.f.N. $= n - k$ and d.f.D. $= n - k - 1$)

Formula for the adjusted R^2:

$$R_{adj}^2 = 1 - \left[\frac{(1 - R^2)(n - 1)}{n - k - 1}\right]$$

Chapter 11 Other Chi-Square Tests

Chi-square test for goodness-of-fit:

$$\chi^2 = \Sigma \frac{(O - E)^2}{E}$$

(d.f. $=$ no. of categories $- 1$)

Chi-square test for independence and homogeneity of proportions:

$$\chi^2 = \Sigma \frac{(O - E)^2}{E}$$

[d.f. $=$ (rows $- 1$)(columns $- 1$)]

Chapter 12 Analysis of Variance

ANOVA test: $F = \dfrac{s_B^2}{s_W^2}$ where $\overline{X}_{GM} = \dfrac{\Sigma X}{N}$

d.f.N. $= k - 1$ where $N = n_1 + n_2 + \cdots + n_k$
d.f.D. $= N - k$ where $k = $ number of groups

$$s_B^2 = \frac{\Sigma n_i(\overline{X}_i - \overline{X}_{GM})^2}{k - 1}$$

$$s_W^2 = \frac{\Sigma(n_i - 1)s_i^2}{\Sigma(n_i - 1)}$$

Scheffé test: $F_S = \dfrac{(\overline{X}_i - \overline{X}_j)^2}{s_w^2(1/n_i + 1/n_j)}$ and

$$F' = (k - 1)(C.V.)$$

Tukey test: $q = \dfrac{\overline{X}_i - \overline{X}_j}{\sqrt{s_W^2/n}}$

Bonferroni test: $t = \dfrac{\overline{X}_i - \overline{X}_j}{\sqrt{s_W^2\left(\frac{1}{n_i} + \frac{1}{n_j}\right)}}$ with d.f. $= N - k$

Formulas for two-way ANOVA:

$$MS_A = \frac{SS_A}{a - 1} \qquad F_A = \frac{MS_A}{MS_W}$$

$$MS_B = \frac{SS_B}{b - 1} \qquad F_B = \frac{MS_B}{MS_W}$$

$$MS_{A\times B} = \frac{SS_{A\times B}}{(a - 1)(b - 1)} \qquad F_{A\times B} = \frac{MS_{A\times B}}{MS_W}$$

$$MS_W = \frac{SS_W}{ab(n - 1)}$$

Chapter 13   Nonparametric Statistics

z test statistic in the sign test: $z = \dfrac{(X + 0.5) - 0.5n}{\sqrt{n}/2}$

where n = sample size (greater than or equal to 26)

X = smaller number of + or − signs

Wilcoxon rank sum test: $z = \dfrac{R - \mu_R}{\sigma_R}$

where

$\mu_R = \dfrac{n_1(n_1 + n_2 + 1)}{2}$

$\sigma_R = \sqrt{\dfrac{n_1 n_2 (n_1 + n_2 + 1)}{12}}$

R = sum of the ranks for the smaller sample size (n_1)
n_1 = smaller of the sample sizes
n_2 = larger of the sample sizes
$n_1 \geq 10$ and $n_2 \geq 10$

Wilcoxon signed-rank test: $z = \dfrac{w_s - \dfrac{n(n + 1)}{4}}{\sqrt{\dfrac{n(n + 1)(2n + 1)}{24}}}$

where

n = number of pairs where the difference is not 0
and $n \geq 30$
w_s = smaller sum in absolute value of the signed ranks

Kruskal-Wallis test:

$$H = \frac{12}{N(N + 1)}\left(\frac{R_1^2}{n_1} + \frac{R_2^2}{n_2} + \cdots + \frac{R_k^2}{n_k}\right) - 3(N + 1)$$

where
R_1 = sum of the ranks of sample 1
n_1 = size of sample 1
R_2 = sum of the ranks of sample 2
n_2 = size of sample 2
$\vdots$
R_k = sum of the ranks of sample k
n_k = size of sample k
$N = n_1 + n_2 + \cdots + n_k$
k = number of samples

Spearman rank correlation coefficient:

$$r_s = 1 - \frac{6\Sigma d^2}{n(n^2 - 1)}$$

where
d = difference in the ranks
n = number of data pairs

Procedure Table

Solving Hypothesis-Testing Problems (Traditional Method)

Step 1   State the hypotheses and identify the claim.

Step 2   Find the critical value(s) from the appropriate table in Appendix A.

Step 3   Compute the test statistic.

Step 4   Make the decision to reject or not reject the null hypothesis.

Step 5   Summarize the results.

Procedure Table

Solving Hypothesis-Testing Problems (*P*-Value Method)

Step 1   State the hypotheses and identify the claim.

Step 2   Compute the test statistic.

Step 3   Find the *P*-value.

Step 4   Make the decision.

Step 5   Summarize the results.

INDEX